# ENCYCLOPEDIA
# OF
# WORLD CRIME

# ENCYCLOPEDIA

# OF

# WORLD CRIME

Criminal Justice, Criminology, and Law Enforcement

## Volume VIII
## R-Z
## 1989-1999
## Chronology

# Jay Robert Nash

History, Inc.
Wilmette, IL 1999

History, Inc., 810 D. Skokie Blvd., Wilmette, IL 60091. Telephone:
847-256-2468. FAX: 847-256-2473.

Library of Congress Catalog Card Number: 88-92729
ISBN: 0-923582-00-2 ENCYCLOPEDIA OF WORLD CRIME
    (8 vols.)
    1-928831-08-7 ENCYCLOPEDIA OF WORLD CRIME
    (1989-1999, Vol. VIII, R-Z)

Printed in the United States of America

9 8 7 6 5 4 3 2 1

# HOW TO USE THIS ENCYCLOPEDIA

## ALPHABETICAL ORDER

Each entry name in the *Encyclopedia of World Crime* is bold-faced and listed alphabetically. Biographical entries are alphabetized by the subject's last name. Everything preceding the comma is treated as a unit when alphabetizing. Hyphens, diacritical marks, periods following initials, and spaces do not influence its alphabetization. For example, La **Pietra** follows **Lang,** and **Black Bart** follows **Black, Robert.** Names with prefixes such as **de, von,** or **le** are listed under the most common form of the name, such as **de Gaulle, Charles** and **Ribbentrop, Joachim von.** Names beginning in **Mc** or **M'** are treated as if spelled **Mac**; thus **McManus, Fred** appears before **MacMichael**, Sir **Harold.** Asian names, in which the family name comes first, are alphabetized by the family name, omitting the comma. Identical names are alphabetized chronologically. Monarchs commonly known by one name, such as **Elizabeth I** or **Louis XIV,** are usually listed under that name only and would precede an identically spelled surname in entry order. Entries with numbers or abbreviations in them are alphabetized as though spelled out. When an entry heading refers to an event rather than to a person, it is alphabetized according to the first key word in the commonly used title, as in **Popish Plot** or **King Ranch Murders.** When the names of two or more people head an entry, it is usually alphabetized according to the most prominent person's last name.

## ENTRY HEADINGS

Appearing in boldface type at the beginning of each *Encyclopedia of World Crime* entry is the name by which that entry is most commonly known. Entries are categorized alphabetically under the name of the offender, criminal event, or the professional in the field of crime. If a crime remains unsolved, the entry is found under the victim's name, and is denoted by the abbreviation **unsolv.** in parentheses immediately preceding the crime category. Other entries appearing under the victim's name include **assassinations**; thus, information concerning the assassination of President Abraham Lincoln would be found under Lincoln and not John Wilkes Booth. The royal or political title or military rank held by the assassination victim precedes the category abbreviation. Parenthetical remarks immediately following an entry name indicate an alternate spelling, that person's original or maiden name, or the entry's alias if preceded by **AKA:.** These names also appear in boldface.

Following the name are **date(s)** relevant to that entry. The letter b. preceding the date signifies that only the person's date of birth is known, while the letter d. signifies that only the person's date of death is known. The letter c. (circa) signifies that the date which immediately follows is approximate. In some cases **prom.** (prominent) is used to denote the year(s) in which that entry was noteworthy. All years B.C. are designated as such.

In a number of entries the phrase **Case of** follows the date, designating that the person named was tried for the crime which follows but found not guilty.

The country designation in each entry heading refers to the country in which the crime was committed or the country in which persons in the field of crime are known professionally. The country is named as it was known at the time the crime was committed; thus, Russia is referenced prior to the Russian Revolution, while U.S.S.R. is used for crimes committed since that time. Entries where crimes are committed in more than three countries or committed on the high seas are designated as Int'l (International).

The last piece of information contained in the Entry Heading is the **crime category**, designating the crime(s) the subject was convicted of, or the professional field of crime with which the subject is associated. For persons wrongly convicted of a crime, prior to the crime category is the designation (**wrong. convict.**). If however, the subject's conviction was overturned on a legal technicality or there is some doubt as to his actual innocence, then the designation (**wrong. convict.?**) is used. In some cases a question mark may follow the crime category. This denotes that there is uncertainty as to whether the crime in question actually occurred; e.g., mur.?, might denote that there is some doubt as to whether a person was killed, committed suicide, or died from other causes.

A number of entries may include more than one person if the criminals or professionals worked together. When the relevant dates of a **multiple name entry** coincide, one date will follow the last person named in the entry heading.

## REFERENCES

After each *Encyclopedia or World Crime* entry, the references used in compiling it are cited. The abbreviation **CBA** denotes **CrimeBooks Archives**. Other sources are cited in four categories; nonfiction, fiction, drama, and film. Nonfiction works are listed first, alphabetically by the author's last name. If two or more works by the same author are used, the second and all following citations are indicated by a blank line and are alphabetized by the first word (ignoring articles A, An, The). If a source is anonymous, this is indicated in parentheses after the title. Sources without a specific author (pamphlets, reports, tracts, trial transcripts, compilations, etc.) are listed alphabetically by the title. Plays based on a case appear after (**DRAMA**) and are listed alphabetically by author. Fictional accounts of a case appear alphabetically by author after (**FICHON**). Films based on the case appear after (**FILM**), and are listed chronologically, each title followed by the year of its U.S. release. Silent films are denoted by the letters preceding the year of release. Often alternate titles (**alt. title**) of films follow U.S. titles in parentheses.

Cross references immediately following an entry refer the reader to entries containing additional information relevant to the case person, place, or event being consulted. Direct references are also used frequently throughout the volumes to lead the readers from a well known name (alias, victim, event) to the name under which that entry appears (**Bonney, William H.,** See: **Billy the Kid**).

# KEY TO ABBREVIATIONS USED IN THE
## *ENCYCLOPEDIA OF WORLD CRIME*

| | |
|---|---|
| 2d lt. | = second lieutenant |
| abduc. | = abduction |
| abor. | = abortion |
| accom. | = accomplices |
| adm. | = admiral |
| adult. | = adultery |
| Afg. | = Afghanistan |
| Ala. | = Alabama |
| Alb. | = Albania |
| Alg. | = Algeria |
| Arg. | = Argentina |
| Ariz. | = Arizona |
| Ark. | = Arkansas |
| assass. | = assassination |
| asslt. | = assault |
| asslt.&bat. | = assault and battery |
| attempt. | = attempted |
| atty. gen. | = attorney general |
| Aus. | = Australia |
| Aust. | = Austria |
| banish. | = banishment |
| Bav. | = Bavaria |
| Belg. | = Belgium |
| Ber. | = Bermuda |
| big. | = bigamy |
| blk. | = blackmail |
| Bol. | = Bolivia |
| bomb. | = bombing |
| boot. | = bootlegging |
| Braz. | = Brazil |
| brib. | = bribery |
| Brit. | = Britain/England including Wales |
| Bul. | = Bulgaria |
| burg. | = burglary |
| Calif. | = California |
| can. | = cannibalism |
| Can. | = Canada |
| cap. pun. | = capital punishment |
| capt. | = captain |
| coin. | = coining |
| col. | = colonel |
| Col. | = Columbia |
| Cob. | = Colorado |
| comdr. | = commander |
| Conn. | = Connecticut |
| consp. | = conspiracy |
| cont./ct. | = contempt of court |
| corr. | = corruption |
| Cos. | = Costa Rica |
| count. | = counterfeiting |
| cpl. | = corporal |
| crim. insan. | = criminal insanity |
| crim. just. | = criminal justice |
| crim. law. | = criminal lawyer |
| crtm. neg. | = criminal negligence |
| crime preven. | = crime prevention |
| crime&punish. | = crime and punishment |
| criminol. | = criminologist or criminology |
| ct. mar. | = court-martial |
| Czech. | = Czechoslovakia |
| Del. | = Delaware |
| del. | = delinquency |
| Den. | = Denmark |
| det. | = detective |
| Dom. | = Dominican Republic |
| Dr. | = doctor |
| duel. | = dueling |
| Ecu. | = Ecuador |
| El Sal. | = El Salvador |
| embez. | = embezzlement |
| emp. | = emperor or empress |
| esc. | = escape |
| esp. | = espionage |
| Eth. | = Ethiopia |
| euth. | = euthanasia |
| execut. | = executioner |
| extor. | = extortion, extortionist |
| fenc. | = fencing |
| Fin. | = Finland |
| fing. ident. | = fingerprint identification |
| Fla. | = Florida |
| forg. | = forgery |
| Fr. | = France |
| Ga. | = Georgia |
| gamb. | = gambling, gambler |
| gen. | = general |
| geno. | = genocide |
| Ger. | = Germany |
| Gr. | = Greece |
| Guat. | = Guatemala |
| harass. | = harassment |
| her. | = heresy |
| hijack. | = hijacking |
| Hond. | = Honduras |
| host. | = hostage |
| Hung. | = Hungary |
| Ice. | = Iceland |
| Ill. | = Illinois |
| impris. | = imprisoned |
| Ind. | = Indiana |
| Indo. | = Indonesia |
| Int'l. | = International |
| Ire. | = Ireland |
| Isr. | = Israel |
| Jam. | = Jamaica |
| Jor. | = Jordan |
| jur. | = jurist |
| Kan. | = Kansas |
| kid. | = kidnapper, kidnapping |
| Kor. | = Korea |
| Ky. | = Kentucky |
| La. | = Louisiana |
| law enfor. off. | = law enforcement officer or official |
| Leb. | = Lebanon |

| | | | |
|---|---|---|---|
| loot. | = looting | pick. | = pickpocket |
| lt. | = lieutenant | pir. | = piracy |
| lt. col. | = lieutenant colonel | Pol. | = Poland |
| lt. comdr. | = lieutenant commander | pol. | = police |
| lt. gen. | = lieutenant general | pol. mal. | = police malpractice |
| lt. gov. | = lieutenant governor | polit. | = politician |
| Lux. | = Luxemburg | polit. corr. | = political corruption |
| lynch. | = lynching | poly. | = polygamy |
| Mac. | = Macedonia | porn. | = pornography |
| maj. | = major | Port. | = Portugal |
| mansl. | = manslaughter | pres. | = president |
| Mass. | = Massachusetts | pris. | = prison |
| Md. | = Maryland | prof. | = professor |
| med. mal. | = medical malpractice | prohib. | = prohibition |
| Mex. | = Mexico | pros. | = prostitution |
| Mich. | = Michigan | R.I. | = Rhode Island |
| Mid. East | = Middle East | rack. | = racketeering |
| milit. | = military | rebel. | = rebellion |
| milit. des. | = military desertion | rev. | = reverend |
| Minn. | = Minnesota | rob. | = robbery |
| Miss. | = Mississippi | Rom. | = Romania |
| miss. per. | = missing persons | Roman. | = Roman Empire |
| Mo. | = Missouri | Rus. | = Russia (prior to 1918) |
| mob vio. | = mob violence | S. Afri. | = South Africa |
| Mont. | = Montana | S.C. | = South Carolina |
| Mor. | = Morocco | S.D. | = South Dakota |
| mur. | = murder, murderer | sab. | = sabotage |
| mut. | = mutiny | Saud. | = Saudi Arabia |
| mutil. | = mutilation | Scot. | = Scotland |
| N. Zea. | = New Zealand | sec. firm | = security firm |
| N.C. | = North Carolina | secret cnm. soc. | = secret criminal societies |
| N.D. | = North Dakota | secret soc. | = secret society |
| N.H. | = New Hampshire | Sen. | = Senegal |
| NJ. | = New Jersey | sgt. | = sergeant |
| N.M. | = New Mexico | Si. | = Sicily |
| N.Y. | = New York | Sing. | = Singapore |
| Neb. | = Nebraska | skyjack. | = skyjacking |
| necro. | - necrophilia | sland. | = slander |
| Neth. | = Netherlands | smug. | = smuggling |
| Nev. | = Nevada | sod. | = sodomy |
| Nic. | = Nicaragua | Sri. | = Sri Lanka |
| Nig. | = Nigeria | Sudan | = Sudan |
| Nor. | = Norway | suic. | = suicide |
| obsc. | = obscenity | supt. | = superintendent |
| Okla. | = Oklahoma | Swed. | = Sweden |
| Ore. | = Oregon | Switz. | = Switzerland |
| org. crime | = organized crime | Tai. | = Taiwan |
| P.R. | = Puerto Rico | Tan. | = Tanzania |
| Pa. | = Pennsylvania | tax evas. | = tax evasion |
| Pak. | = Pakistan | Tenn. | = Tennessee |
| Pan. | = Panama | terr. | = terrorism, terrorist |
| Para. | = Paraguay | Thai. | = Thailand |
| path. | = pathologist | tort. | = torture |
| penal col. | = penal colonies | toxicol. | = toxicologist |
| penol. | = penology, penologist | treas. | = treason |
| Per. | = Persia | Tun. | = Tunisia |
| perj. | = perjury | Turk. | = Turkey |
| Phil. | = Philippines | U.A.E. | = United Arab Emirates |

| | |
|---|---|
| U.K. | = United Kingdom |
| U.S. | = United States of America |
| U.S.S.R. | = Union of Soviet Socialist Republics (after 1918) |
| unsolv. | = unsolved |
| Urug. | = Uruguay |
| Va. | = Virginia |
| vandal. | = vandalism |
| Venez. | = Venezuela |
| vice dist. | = vice district |
| vict. | = victim |
| Viet. | = Vietnam |
| vigil. | = vigilantism |
| Vt. | = Vermont |
| W.Va. | = West Virginia |
| Wash. | = Washington |
| west. gunman | = western gunman |
| west. lawman | = western lawman |
| west. outl. | = western outlaw |
| wh. slav. | = white slavery |
| Wis. | = Wisconsin |
| Wyo. | = Wyoming |
| Yug. | = Yugoslavia |

# TABLE OF CONTENTS

# R

**Rabin, Yitzhak,** 1922-1995, Israel, assass. A soldier-politician and one of the youthful founders of Israel, Yitzhak Rabin proved to be a masterful battlefield commander in the 1948 war for Israel's independence. He rose to chief of staff by the time of the Six Day War in 1967, a lightning conflict that saw East Jerusalem, Gaza, the Golan Heights, and the West Bank come under Israeli control. Rabin replaced Golda Meir in 1974 as Israel's prime minister, the first native-born Israeli to hold that high office. It was Rabin who gave the go-ahead for the daring raid on Entebbe, Uganda, in 1976, to free Jewish hostages taken in a terrorist airplane hijacking.

Israel's Prime Minister Yitzhak Rabin, assassinated in Tel Aviv on November 4, 1995.

Resigning in 1977 over a scandal involving his wife's finances, Rabin then served as ambassador to Washington and cemented U.S.-Israeli ties. He was again elected to the post of prime minister following a campaign that did not suggest the eventual and prolonged peace negotiations with Palestinian leader Yasir Arafat. Because of his role in the historic 1993 peace accords in Oslo between Israel and Palestine, Rabin, along with his political rival Shimon Peres and PLO chairman Arafat, received the Nobel Peace Prize.

Rabin was slow to move in the direction of peace. When Palestine declared its dedicated uprising, the Intifada, in 1987, Rabin initially cracked down on the protestors, but he came to realize that the persistent and bloody demonstrations on the part of the Palestinians constituted "a full-blown popular uprising that ... could not be quelled by force," according to one of his biographers.

The sustained month-after-month violence convinced Rabin that the Palestinian entity had to be recognized as an independent state, and toward that end he moved in the direction of peace. He recognized that the Palestinians were operating in the same pattern as had his own people during the Zionist movement that had led to the establishment of the Israeli state. Right-wing Zionists, however, resisted any peace settlement with the Palestinians, and among those ranks was a young ultranationalist, Yigal Amir, who, with his brother, Hagai Amir, and a friend, Dror Adani, conspired to assassinate the popular prime minister.

The conspirators considered several ways in which to murder Rabin. They thought they might rig the prime minister's car with explosives and blow him up. They considered poisoning him in a restaurant or even at home. The conspirators finally opted for the most direct method; someone would simply shoot down Rabin when he appeared at a public function. This was accomplished with more ease than expected, particularly since Rabin was a friendly, outgoing person who readily greeted his fellow Israelis wherever he went.

Grinning plotters—Yigal Amir, bottom, shot and killed Yitzhak Rabin in 1995, and went to prison for life. His friend Dror Adani, right, and his brother Hagai Amir, top, received lesser sentences for their roles in the assassination.

To that end, Yigal Amir waited in the crowds of a peace rally in Tel Aviv on November 4, 1995, and, when he got close enough to Rabin, shot and killed the prime minister. The young, gum-chewing assassin, a wide smile fixed to his face, was taken into custody. He was quickly tried and convicted, then sentenced to life in prison. Hagai Amir was sent to prison for twelve years and Adani was given a seven-year sentence.

One of Yigal Amir's friends, Margalit Har-Shefi, was later indicted for failing to inform authorities of the plot. She admitted that Amir had boasted to her that he planned to kill Rabin in order to stop the peace process and to prevent handing over any Israeli territory to the Palestinians. Convicted, Har-Shefi was given a two-year prison sentence.

In November 1998, Avishai Raviv, an informer for the Shin Bet intelligence service who operated under the code name "Champagne," was also indicted for failing to tell his superiors of the Amir plot. Raviv had been a friend of Amir's and reportedly learned of the assassin's plans long in advance of the murder. Raviv, who had founded the radical right-wing group Eyal, which had led some of the most virulent demonstrations against Rabin, faces a maximum two-year prison term if convicted. He awaits trial at this writing.

**Rado, Janice,** 1947- , U.S., fraud. U.S. District Court Judge Ferdinand F. Fernandez sentenced Janice Rado of Malibu, California, to eight years in prison on January 25, 1989, for operating a fraudulent telemarketing business. Rado defrauded thousands of people of an estimated $10 million by offering them "gift giveaways" that were never delivered. When she feared a government investigation would discover her operation, she offered to publish a book written by U.S. Postal Service Inspector Charles Yarton in exchange for Yarton's information about the investigation. She then tried to cover her fraud by destroying her firm's documents. Both Rado and Yarton pleaded guilty to conspiracy to cover the fraud.

---

**Ramey, Jonathan,** 1956- , U.S., sex. asslt. On May 15, 1989, Baptist minister Jonathan Ramey was sentenced to twelve years in prison for raping a 22-year-old woman in his Chicago, Illinois, apartment on July 19, 1988. Ramey was convicted of the crime even though his victim did not testify against him. Criminal Court Judge William Hibbler allowed as evidence Ramey's confession to police that he had sex with the woman against her wishes and tied her to a chair with his belt afterward. The woman died six months after the rape, of unrelated causes. Defense attorneys used three ministers as witnesses to Ramey's character, but prosecuting attorneys countered with testimony from Ramey's stepdaughter that he had sexually molested her when she was 10.

---

**Ramirez, Carlos Joseph,** 1976- , U.S., abduct.-suic.-mur. Wanted for murder, Carlos Ramirez broke into the Antioch, California, home of his ex-girlfriend, Cami Viramontes, on July 10, 1998. He drove Viramontes and her mother and father from the home after shooting and wounding the father. He held his two children with Viramontes, two daughters, ages 1 and 3, as hostages as he barricaded himself inside the Viramontes home.

Swarms of police including more than 100 SWAT team members poured into the area, while negotiators began to attempt to talk Ramirez into surrendering. Friends and relatives of the abductor appeared outside waving a sign that read, "Carlos, we love you!" Police evacuated sixty-six residents from nearby homes, including Antioch Mayor Mary Rocha, whose residence was only two doors away from the house occupied by Ramirez.

**Carlos Joseph Ramirez, who killed himself and his two children in Antioch, California in 1998, after a police standoff of forty-one hours.**

The negotiations dragged on for more than forty-one hours, but were suddenly and inexplicably broken off by Ramirez, who was heard to say, "What is wrong with me—Oh, my God, I love you." Police then heard the abductor counting down, "Five, four, three, two ..." and this was followed by the sound of one or more gunshots.

When black-garbed SWAT teams slowly entered the house they found Ramirez dead. He had fired a bullet into his own head, apparently after killing his youngest daughter and fatally wounding the 3-year-old, who died before reaching a hospital.

Ironically, an identical abduction had occurred in Antioch on July 11, 1993, five years to the day of Ramirez's suicide-murders, when 35-year-old Joel Souza, upset by the breakup of his marriage, barricaded himself and his two children inside his house while police surrounded the place. After nine hours, police grew impatient and told Souza that he had ten minutes to surrender. Souza killed his 8-year-old son and 5-year-old daughter, then killed himself.

Because the police in that case had been so aggressive, the city of Antioch wound up awarding a $175,000 settlement to Souza's widow. When Ramirez duplicated Souza's actions, city officials decided not to take the same kind of tough stance as they had in 1993. The prolonged negotiations in the Ramirez case, however, proved just as fruitless.

---

**Ramirez, Richard** (AKA: The Night Stalker), 1960- , U.S., burg.-tort.-rape-mur. After the trial of Richard Ramirez, Southern California's infamous "Night Stalker" serial killer, chief prosecutor P. Philip Halpin, a deputy district attorney, said that he regretted not learning more about how Ramirez's mind worked. Describing Ramirez as "a twisted man but an intelligent fellow," Halpin said, "It's a tragedy not to see how all this happened."

"All this" was a crime spree that terrorized Los Angeles County in summer 1985. In a five-month period, Ramirez committed a series of home invasions in which thirteen people were killed and several more beaten, raped, and robbed. Ramirez is also suspected of other murders in Los Angeles, San Francisco, and Orange County.

Ramirez was born in 1960 in El Paso, Texas. A petty thief in his adolescence, Ramirez became a drifter, ending up in California in the early 1980s. There he took up burglary but lacked finesse; convicted burglar Sandra Hotchkiss, testifying under immunity at Ramirez's trial, said she tried to teach him the ropes, but after more than thirty burglaries together, she found him too amateurish and sloppy to continue working with him.

The first "Night Stalker" killing occurred on June 27 or 28, 1984, when Ramirez entered the first-floor apartment of 79-year-old Jennie Vincow, ransacked the apartment, slashed the woman's throat, and stabbed her several times after she died. He left three identifiable fingerprints on a screen frame and a window pane while letting himself in.

Nine months later, the Night Stalker struck again. This time he committed two attacks in one night. On March 17, 1985, Ramirez shot Dale Okazaki, 34, of suburban Rosemead in the head with a .22 caliber bullet, killing her, and wounded her roommate, Maria Hernandez. Hernandez was one of the first to identify Ramirez when he was apprehended. Later that morning, using the same gun, Ramirez shot Veronica Tsai-Lian Yu to death in her car on a street in Monterey Park.

Eleven days later, Ramirez committed two murders, details of which were repeated in his later attacks. Breaking into

**California's deadly "Night Stalker," Richard Ramirez, holding up the palm of his hand to show the Satanic sign of the encircled pentagram; the arrogant serial killer was sentenced to death on November 7, 1989.**

the Whittier home of Vincent and Maxine Zazzara, he shot the husband to death as he slept, then handcuffed, beat, and raped the wife. In the course of robbing the house, Ramirez demanded Maxine's help in finding money. When she refused, he stabbed her repeatedly and gouged out her eyes. At the scene of this crime he left another essential clue, a distinctive footprint of an Avia-brand athletic shoe.

After the May 14 murder of William Doi of Monterey Park, police found the same Avia shoeprint and other procedural similarities to the previous burglary-killings, including severed telephone wires and the use of thumbcuffs as restraints. Despite some progress in the investigation, the series of gruesome assaults took their toll on the citizens of Los Angeles. Sales of home security systems and firearms boomed.

The level of terror increased two weeks later as the Night Stalker invaded the Monrovia home of Mabel Bell and Florence Lang on May 30 or 31. The Avia shoeprint was found at the scene and stolen property was later recovered. Lang survived to testify about the beating Ramirez gave her, and how he beat Bell to death with a hammer. But the most distinctive detail of this attack was the first appearance of a pentagon—a five-pointed star that, when drawn with two points up and one point down, is a symbol of devil-worship—drawn on a bedroom wall, and also carved into Mabel Bell's thigh.

Ramirez murdered Mary Louise Cannon of Arcadia on July 2. He beat, stabbed, and strangled her, then beat and strangled Joyce Nelson of Monterey Park five days later. In both attacks, Ramirez left several Avia shoeprints in the house, including one on the left side of Joyce Nelson's face. On July 20, he killed Maxon and Lela Kneiding, shooting and stabbing them both and cutting Maxon's throat so badly he was almost decapitated. Survivors and the crime scenes attested to the pentagrams, the cut telephone wires, the use of handcuffs and ligatures to restrain victims, the procedure of shooting the men in the head before raping their wives, and of macabre obsessions. According to survivors, Ramirez repeated many of the same

phrases when demanding money and used the same obscenities when assaulting the women. He also forced some of his victims to swear allegiance to Satan, sometimes just before killing them. Of his methods of killing, he seemed particularly drawn to cutting throats, and seemed attracted to yellow houses near freeways. (Veronica Yu was driving a yellow car when Ramirez attacked her, the only known non-home invasion killing during the rampage.)

On July 20, Chainarong Khovananth was killed in his Sun Valley home. On August 8, Elyas Abowath was killed in Diamond Bar. The wives of both men survived and identified Ramirez after his capture. He had raped each one near the bodies of their husbands.

After a final attack on August 25 in Mission Hills, Ramirez left a partial fingerprint on a stolen car used in the attack, allowing police to finally identify him. Reward money acted as an added inducement for terrified city dwellers to provide information for the Night Stalker's capture. One man led police to one of the four guns Ramirez used in his shootings, and a woman recognized Ramirez as the man she had seen outside a victim's house. The sister of a former roommate of Ramirez recognized his face from a police composite, and several other citizens came forward with other pieces of the puzzle. Police were handed the clue ultimately responsible for solving the puzzle when, as Ramirez left the scene of the August 8 attack, he ran a stoplight. His fingerprints were taken as a matter of course in the misdemeanor traffic offense, allowing police to link him to the Vincow killing.

Police published Ramirez' photograph on August 30. Detectives staked out the Greyhound bus depot, suspecting that he might try to leave the city. Ramirez, however, had been visiting a brother in Arizona that week, came in on one of the incoming buses, and unknowingly slipped past the waiting police. However, on August 31, twelve hours after his photo appeared in the newspaper, Ramirez was recognized by angry citizens in East Los Angeles. Attempting to escape them, Ramirez tried to hijack a car. The frightened woman driver screamed to bystanders as Ramirez tried to throw her from the car, *"Esta el matador!"* ("It's the killer!") Eight men threw themselves on Ramirez and beat him until police arrived.

Ramirez was charged with thirteen counts of murder and thirty additional felony counts, with nineteen "special circumstances" attached. (Under California law, a special circumstance must accompany the charge in order for it to qualify as a capital crime. Such circumstances include premeditation, commission of murder during a burglary, and torture, rape, or mutilation of a murder victim. Among the crimes police believe Ramirez committed for which they had insufficient evidence to charge him were the murder of Patti Higgins, whose throat was cut in Arcadia in June 1985, and the abduction and sodomization of up to twelve children, the youngest of them 6 years old.)

Impaneling a jury was an arduous task, because the case was so widely publicized that only one of 2,400 prospective jurors had not heard of Ramirez. As an extra measure against the possibility of a mistrial, Los Angeles Superior Court Judge Michael A. Tynan took the unusual step of swearing in twelve alternate jurors along with the original twelve. The controversial jury choice took over six months to complete, ending with twenty-four people. Due to the diverse ethnic makeup of Los Angeles County—Latinos, Asians, blacks, and Caucasians, with no one group in the majority—the prosecution and defense accused each other of ethnic bias. The crimes of which Ramirez, a Latino, was accused were committed against Asians and whites; none of his victims were black or Latino. The defense accused the prosecution of trying to exclude blacks and Latinos from the jury, and the prosecution accused the defense of trying to exclude whites and Asians. The original twelve jurors were six blacks and six Latinos. One of these twelve, a black man, was dismissed when two other jurors, both black women, told the judge they had overheard him say in the hall that if Ramirez was convicted he, the juror, would not send another minority person to Death Row unless the legal system started putting more whites there, too. These delays were costly; by the time counsel began presenting evidence in January 1989, the case of the Night Stalker had already cost Los Angeles County taxpayers $1.12 million.

The formal trial began with the defense under a cloud. Four days before presentation of evidence began, a state Court of Appeal ruled that defense attorney Daniel Hernandez was professionally inadequate in both preparation and legal research in a murder case he had tried in 1985, but that the representation he offered was not sufficiently inadequate to grant his client a new trial. Such criticism of Hernandez became a recurring motif in Ramirez's trial. The defense tried to stall by requesting a change of venue, asking Tynan to excuse himself, moving to suppress evidence, and pleading to have all charges dropped. The tactics annoyed the prosecution and antagonized the judge. Ramirez's defense was also hampered on several other fronts. Besides a strong case for the prosecution, perhaps the greatest impediment to Ramirez's case was Ramirez himself. He refused to present evidence in his own favor, and wore sunglasses in court throughout the trial. At one point he drew a pentagram on the palm of his hand, flashed it at the spectators and the jury, and shouted "Hail Satan!" as he was being led from court. He also called one of the witnesses a liar, used a mirror to flash light in the eyes of another witness, and once even screamed obscenities at the judge.

Once the trial got underway, the jurors heard numerous horror stories. A 63-year-old woman from Monterey Park told the court of how Ramirez bound her hands behind her before raping and sodomizing her. A woman from Burbank said that he robbed, beat, raped, and sodomized her, then said to her, "I don't know why I'm letting you live. I've killed people before." Whitney Bennett, 16 at the time of the attack, survived Ramirez beating her in the face with a tire iron.

Midway through the trial, Daniel Hernandez's request to be excused from the case due to "nervous exhaustion" was denied by Judge Tynan. However, on March 6, Judge Tynan appointed a new defense attorney to work with Hernandez's team. Ray Clark, while technically subordinate to Hernandez, was a far more experienced trial attorney and was regarded by courtroom observers as a valuable addition to a team clearly fighting an uphill battle.

Ramirez's counsel built their case around mistaken iden-

tity, arguing that it was not necessary to prove their client's innocence, but only to instill reasonable doubt in the jurors' minds. The closest they came to disproving one of the charges was when the defendant's father, Julian Ramirez Tapia, claimed Ramirez was visiting the family in El Paso when two of the attacks took place. The prosecution disproved his testimony by introducing Dr. Peter Leung, a Los Angeles dentist, whose records showed that Ramirez was in Los Angeles receiving dental treatment at the time his father claimed he was in Texas. Coincidentally, Dr. Leung figured prominently once again in solving the case. On June 15, 1989, a child was assaulted in Highland Park—an attack that police believe was committed by the Night Stalker. That same night, a police officer pulled a car over for running a stop sign. The driver, whom police deduced was Ramirez, jumped from the car and escaped. In the abandoned car, police found Dr. Leung's business card.

In all, more than 165 witnesses testified, thirty-eight of them for the defense. Six-hundred fifty-eight exhibits were introduced, including photographs of the crime scenes. The evidence—eyewitness identifications, fingerprints, footprints, pentagrams, 375 pieces of victims' jewelry recovered by police—was overwhelming. After fourteen months of preliminaries, testimony, and deliberations, on September 20, 1989, the jury returned a verdict of guilty on all charges of thirteen murders and thirty other felonies. Judge Tynan allowed Ramirez, at his own request, to hear the verdict alone in a holding cell over a sound system. Each count was read separately. The ritual took almost forty-five minutes, with the court clerk asking to be relieved of the duty of reading the verdicts after the first ten. Judge Tynan finished the task of reading the counts himself.

The punishment phase of the trial was as surprising as the rest of it, in that the defense called no witnesses to present mitigating evidence to forestall the death penalty. Clark, an opponent of the death penalty, made perhaps the most unconsciously revealing comment of the entire procedure when he said afterward, "I could not condone taking even Hitler's life." When asked if Ramirez was guilty, Clark said simply, "I didn't ask."

The jury agreed with all nineteen of the prosecution's "special circumstances." They recommended the death penalty, which prompted Ramirez to say, "Big deal. Death always went with the territory. See you in Disneyland." Judge Tynan, citing the "cruelty, callousness, and viciousness beyond any human understanding" of the Night Stalker's crimes, sentenced Ramirez on November 7, 1989, to death in the gas chamber.

Ramirez agreed with the judge. He told the court after sentencing, "You don't understand me. You are not expected to. You are not capable of it. I am beyond your experience." After chanting Satanic musings, he said, "I am beyond good and evil. I will be avenged. Lucifer dwells within us all. That's it."

---

**Ramirez Sanchez, Illich** (AKA: Carlos, the Jackal), 1949- , Aust.-Libya, terr.-kid.-bomb.-mur. The father of the man who came to be known as Carlos, or the Jackal, the world's most feared terrorist, was a wealthy Venezuelan attorney in Caracas. He and his wife were devout Communists and raised their son on communism, indoctrinating the boy at an early age with unswerving Marxist theory and philosophy, as had been the case with his brothers, Vladimir and Lenin Ramirez Sanchez. Illich Ramirez Sanchez—his parents gave him Lenin's middle name—joined the Communist student movement in Venezuela in 1964 and was then sent to Cuba, where, under the wing of Communist dictator Fidel Castro, he was trained to become a terrorist.

**International terrorist Illich Ramirez Sanchez, the infamous "Carlos," or "the Jackal," shown early in his murderous career.**

Castro saw to it that Ramirez-Sanchez, coming from an elitist Communist family in Venezuela, received special attention from experts in the Cuban Direccion General de Inteligencia (DGI). He was then known to his fellow trainees as "Pudgy" or "Fatty." So eager did the apprentice terrorist appear, however, that he was brought to the attention of KGB General Simenov, a Russian spymaster who was overseeing DGI training inside Cuba. Simenov arranged for the overweight youth to travel to Moscow, where his talent for murder and mayhem could be sharpened to razor-like effectiveness.

In 1968, Ramirez Sanchez received more intense training at Patrice Lumumba University in Moscow, an institution notorious for educating terrorists in the bloody techniques of their trade, as well as KGB agents who were used exclusively in covert operations. In 1970, he joined the most deadly terrorist organization in the Middle East, the Popular Front for the Liberation of Palestine, or the PFLP, which had, throughout the 1960s, been responsible for countless bombings, assassinations, kidnappings and mass murders.

A willing and eager PFLP disciple, Ramirez Sanchez soon became a group leader and then a PFLP strategist engineering terrorism against Israel and Western democracies. His code name of Carlos became widely known, as well as his sobriquet among his enemies, the Jackal, so much so that author Frederick Forsyth used him as a role model in his devastating portrait of the terrorist-assassin who stalks French President Charles de Gaulle in his 1971 novel, *The Day of the Jackal*. This book, and the 1973 film by the same name, more than any of his actual exploits to that time, elevated Ramirez Sanchez to the high and unenviable rank of international terrorist, a position he would soon occupy in reality.

In 1972, Carlos was linked to the massacre of eleven Israeli athletes at the Munich Olympics, and he was also connected to the takeover of the French Embassy in The Hague, Netherlands, in 1974, along with the bombing of a drugstore in Paris, France, that same year, an explosion that took the lives of two people and wounded another thirty.

In early 1975, Ramirez Sanchez had engineered attacks against Israel's El Al airlines at Paris' Orly Airport. Two French intelligence agents, members of the DST, France's version of

the FBI, got on to Carlos through one of his friends, a Lebanese informer, and were tracking down the terrorist in Paris when he turned the tables on them. Carlos lured the three to a Paris apartment and then shot and killed the two French agents, Raymond Dous and Jean Donatini, along with his former Lebanese colleague, Michel Moukharbal.

**A fat, balding Carlos (Illich Ramirez Sanchez), shown on a street in Khartoum, Sudan, in a snapshot taken by French agents, shortly before they seized the infamous terrorist in 1994 and returned him to France to face life imprisonment.**

This triple murder vaulted Carlos to the top of the terrorist heap in the estimation of his ruthless peers, but it also set upon his trail scores of dogged DST agents who would not give up the hunt for him. Defying capture, Ramirez Sanchez then performed his most spectacular terrorist coup on December 21, 1975, when he and six other heavily armed terrorists invaded an OPEC conference in Vienna, Austria, holding eighty-one members hostage.

Austrian negotiators were informed by Carlos, in the name of the "Arm of the Arab Revolution," that if his demands were not met, he would slaughter the entire OPEC membership, representing the richest men in the world who controlled the global flow of oil. Forty-one Austrian hostages were released through negotiations, but the other African, South American and Arab delegates were forced to accompany Carlos on a flight to Algiers and then on to Tripoli, where they were released unharmed, but only after the Shah of Iran and King Khaled paid Ramirez Sanchez an estimated $50 million in cash. (The terrorist had reportedly demanded $1 billion.)

Almost immediately after completing this terrorist coup, Carlos vanished, the most reliable reports having him in Libya, where he was protected by one of his employers and fellow terrorist, Muammar Qadaffi, the country's Islamic fundamentalist dictator, who reportedly received a goodly share of the loot from the OPEC kidnappings. Ramirez Sanchez did not remain inactive for long. On June 24, 1976, Carlos sent seven terrorists, five PFLP members and two German Communists, to skyjack an Air France airbus en route from Tel Aviv to Paris.

The plane was ordered to fly to Entebbe, Uganda, where it remained grounded with the collusion of Ugandan dictator Idi Amin, the mostly Jewish passengers held hostage in a nearby building complex. Israeli commandos, ordered to Entebbe by Israel's then-prime minister, Yitzhak Rabin, effected the release of the hostages by storming the complex and the plane. Thirty-one persons were killed, including two hostages, all seven of the terrorists and Colonel Netanyahu, leader of the Israeli commandos and the older brother of future Prime Minister Benjamin Netanyahu.

For almost five years Carlos appeared to be inactive, but

during 1982-1983 he resumed his terrorist campaigns with a vengeance. Carlos directed the March 29, 1982, bombing of a Paris-to-Toulouse express train that killed six persons and wounded another fifteen. He was thought to be behind the August 9, 1982, bombing of a Jewish restaurant in Paris and the machine-gunning of fleeing patrons, a massacre that killed six people and wounded another twenty-two. Carlos was also behind a Paris bombing of the Champs Elysees that killed a pregnant woman and injured another sixty-three persons.

In 1982, Ramirez Sanchez was himself almost killed when Palestinian guerrillas were driven out of Beirut by Israeli forces, but he managed to escape. Carlos renewed his attacks in 1983, directing the bombing of the main terminal in Marseille, France, an explosion that killed five people and wounded another fifty. He was also behind the bombing of the French cultural center in West Berlin, a blast that killed one person and injured another twenty-three.

Again, Carlos went underground. In 1992, a French court convicted Ramirez Sanchez *in absentia* of killing the two French counterintelligence agents and the Lebanese informer. He was sentenced to thirty-two years in prison, but this mattered little to the terrorist, who remained at large, becoming an arms merchant and hiding in Khartoum, Sudan. There he drank the best whiskey in the capital's nightclubs. Though married to a new Jordanian wife, Carlos was infamous throughout Khartoum as a woman-chaser.

To the strict Islamic Sudanese government, the high-living Carlos was an embarrassment, and through its tacit cooperation, Ramirez Sanchez was seized on a hospital operating table in August 1994 by French agents. He was reportedly injected with an incapacitating drug and stuffed into a sack before he was bundled aboard a plane and flown to France, where he sat in solitary confinement for two years, awaiting a retrial for the three murders for which he had already been convicted.

Carlos demanded that retrial, even though he condemned the right of any French court to try him because he had been illegally seized in the Sudan. He was finally brought before a French court in 1997, wearing an ascot and proudly stating, "My name is Illich Ramirez Sanchez. My profession is professional revolutionary."

To one observer, the fat, balding terrorist was a thing of the past: "He knows he's a has-been. His mental universe is the Palestinian guerrilla movement. He's nothing but a dinosaur of the Cold War stranded in the 1990s."

Ramirez Sanchez insisted that he was a "political prisoner" and that "there is no law for me." He could not refute the evidence brought forth that eventually convicted him of the 1975 killing of the two French agents and his former Lebanese friend. Carlos stood smug and smirking as the French tribunal announced his conviction on December 24, 1997. He shook his fist in the air four times and shouted, "Viva la revolución!" He was then sentenced to life in prison.

Before he was led away, Carlos stated, "They want to sentence me to life in prison. I'm 48 years old, so it could be another forty or fifty years. That doesn't horrify me." Also See: **Qadaffi, Muammar al- ; Rabin, Yitzhak.**

---

**Ramirez Talavera, Norman**, See: **Segarra Palmer, Juan.**

---

**Ramsey, JonBenet**, 1990-1996, U.S., unsolv. mur. On December 26, 1996, JonBenet, a pretty 6-year-old girl who had won several beauty contests—she was Little Miss Colorado for 1995—was found murdered in the basement of her parents' sprawling Boulder, Colorado, home. An autopsy revealed that the girl had been sexually attacked and then strangled to death. Her skull had also been crushed by a powerful blow to the head.

A ransom note, found on the stairwell leading to the basement of the Ramsey home, claimed that the girl had been kidnapped (even though her body was present) by a group representing "a small foreign faction" and demanded $118,000 for her release. Police and media speculated that the kidnappers—if,

**Child beauty queen, 6-year-old JonBenet Ramsey, mysteriously murdered in her Boulder, Colorado, home on December 26, 1996.**

indeed, that's who the killers had been—had attempted to abduct the girl, but that she put up a fight and they killed her, dropping the ransom note they had prepared in advance.

Much of the case remained enigmatic in that the Boulder police, even after a prolonged investigation, never charged anyone with the rape-killing. What evidence detectives collected was never made public. Shrouding the murder further was the fact that the child's parents, John and Patsy Ramsey, shielded themselves behind expensive lawyers and talked to authorities only in carefully screened interviews, as was the case when they faced the media.

Though no suspects in the killing were ever named, John and Patsy Ramsey remained under an "umbrella of suspicion." Theories abound. One investigator surmised that an intruder killed the child in her bedroom, then attempted to hide the body in the basement, and left the note so that he would not have to risk taking the body from the home in the hope that the parents would pay the ransom before the body was discovered. Another suspected that one of JonBenet's older siblings killed her.

A scream was heard by a Ramsey neighbor on the night of the murder, one report stated. Another said there was no scream. A writing expert said that the ransom note bore a striking resemblance to Patsy Ramsey's own handwriting. Another expert said no. Then a bevy of experts tried to figure out why the so-called kidnappers would demand the odd ransom amount of $118,000, instead of a million, which her tycoon father could reportedly afford to pay. The case drowned in questions and was starved for answers.

Criticism was rampant. Police in Boulder were lambasted for allowing John Ramsey to search his own house eight hours after he had called police in response to finding the ransom note, a search that led to his discovery of his daughter's body.

Moreover, police were blasted for allowing friends and relatives to roam through the house at that time. Then prosecutors and police fell out, accusing each other of bungling the case.

In fall 1997, Detective Steve Thomas of the Boulder force, who had investigated the murder, quit his position. He accused District Attorney Alex Hunter of botching the case in an extraordinary effort to protect the Ramseys. Lou Smit, a special investigator who looked into the case, also quit, but he stated that he thought the Ramseys, who later relocated to Atlanta, Georgia, were innocent. In the end, there was no solution, only silence and wonder.

---

**Ranaan, Schlomo**, 1935-1998, West Bank, mur. (vict.) On August 20, 1998, Schlomo Ranaan, a rabbi and part of a pioneering Israeli dynasty that colonized the West Bank, was reportedly attacked and stabbed to death by a Palestinian terrorist who invaded his trailer home in the heavily fortified Jewish enclave of Tel Romeida in the center of Hebron. The terrorist set fire to Ranaan's trailer by exploding a firebomb as he fled.

The murder prompted widespread demands from Israelis for revenge and retaliation. Prime Minister Benjamin Netanyahu vowed that he would replace the trailer community in Hebron with permanent structures and that Jewish settlers, instead of being moved back into Israel, would remain where they were. A Palestinian terrorist, Salem Sarsour, was later charged with Ranaan's murder. Also See: **Sarsour, Salem Rajahal**.

---

**Randall, Patrick**, See: **Smart, Pamela**.

---

**Randley, Loretta**, 1940- , U.S., manslgt. In 1981, in retaliation for sexual abuse, Loretta Randley shot and killed her boyfriend, Hartman Delano Poitier, in Tallahassee, Florida. She was convicted in 1982 and sentenced to eight years in prison. Randley filed an appeal and was released on bond pending the results of that appeal. When the appeal was denied, Randley did not turn herself in. She simply remained at home, waiting for someone to come and get her. No one came for sixteen years. She stayed at the same residence and raised her children, then her grandchildren.

In May 1997, someone unraveled the red tape of the Randley case, and officials came to her door and took the woman to prison. When a judge reviewed her case in June 1998, he decided that Randley had led an exemplary life while waiting to go to jail and that her time at home served as good probation time. He commuted her prison time to time served. Randley was freed on September 18, 1998. "Life is going to be good," she told reporters. "I'm going to find me a church and I'm going to get in that church and I'm going to serve God."

---

**Randy, Michael**, 1941- , U.S., fraud-money laund. A former Chicago cop, Michael Randy had a knack for convincing gullible elderly people to invest in his so-called money management business. He promised investors more than 14 per-

cent on their money, saying he could achieve these returns by buying special certificates of deposit from an offshore bank in the Caribbean.

Randy took in more than $14 million from gulled investors, but he had no investment to make with their money. He simply spent it as needed, eating up the life savings of elderly people. Convicted, Randy was sentenced to sixteen years in prison on April 28, 1995, by Judge Harry Leinenweber, who told Randy, "You probably would have been better off with some of your investments if you bought lottery tickets. You might have won."

---

**Rathbun, Charles**, 1957- , U.S., rape-mur. Linda Sobek, an attractive 27-year-old blonde who worked as a model and had been a cheerleader for the Los Angeles Raiders, vanished from her home in Hermosa Beach, California, on November 16, 1995. Police looked everywhere for a clue and finally learned that photographer Charles Rathbun, also of Hermosa Beach, had been the last person to see Sobek.

Photographer Charles Rathbun, the brutal sex slayer of model Linda Sobek of Hermosa Beach, California; he is shown impassively listening to the 1996 verdict that found him guilty of first-degree murder.

Police called the photographer and asked him to come to headquarters, but Rathbun stalled them time and again. Finally, he arrived almost dead drunk to spin off a strange story, one that involved him driving Sobek into the desert, where he began a photo session with her, using a Lexus sport utility vehicle as a prop. He said she suddenly was seized by a fit that compelled him to sit on her to calm her down. Inexplicably, he said, she suddenly died of asphyxiation.

Panic gripped him, Rathbun explained, so he hid the body. He would gladly take police to the site and he did. Nine days after Sobek's disappearance, the photographer took police to her shallow grave next to a lonely road in Angeles National Forest amidst the rugged San Gabriel Mountains.

The condition of Linda Sobek's body, according to a coroner's report, indicated that she had been raped, sodomized with a blunt instrument, and then strangled to death. All of this pointed to murder, and Rathbun was charged and tried. He attempted to mount a defense by placing into evidence an unclear photo of a naked woman touching herself sexually, the gesture, Rathbun insisted, which caused the model to go into spasms and die.

Stephen Kay, Los Angeles deputy district attorney, examined the photo carefully and realized that it showed the dashboard of a car, which was not that of the Lexus used in the fatal photo shoot. When he brought this to the attention of Rathbun on the witness stand, the defendant mumbled some sort of incoherent explanation. The photo was a blatant fake Rathbun had staged to mislead prosecutors. Kay, one of the best prosecutors in the business, would not be misled.

"He literally tortured Linda Sobek," Kay told the jury, "as he repeatedly assaulted her." The excruciating pain suffered by the victim, he said, "defies comprehension."

On November 1, 1996, a jury in Torrance, California, returned a guilty verdict of first-degree murder. Rathbun, a pale-faced, fish-mouthed killer with deep-set eyes glaring from behind large glasses, said nothing. He was just as impassive when he was sentenced to life in prison by Superior Court Judge Donald Pitts on December 16, 1996. He received an additional eight-year sentence for the felony of anal rape with a foreign object.

Judge Pitts concluded by stating, "Linda Sobek experienced a death of unspeakable horror and brutality. The physical torture and emotional torture she experienced prior to her death demonstrates the monster within Charles Rathbun."

---

**Ratliff, Clarence,** 1936- , U.S., mansl.-attempt. mur. On October 20, 1988, Grand Rapids, Michigan, police officer Clarence Ratliff entered the judicial chambers of his estranged wife, District Judge Carol S. Irons, 40, and shot her to death. Following a shootout with police who came to the judge's aid, Ratliff reportedly said, "I just couldn't take the bitch anymore." Originally charged with first-degree murder, Ratliff was convicted on May 11 of the lesser charge of voluntary manslaughter. The jury, which reportedly thought Judge Irons had provoked her husband by dating other men and not agreeing to a divorce settlement, took into account the fact that Ratliff was drunk when he shot his wife. "All of that provoked him into doing it," a juror said. Ratliff was also found guilty of two counts of assault with intent to commit murder for shooting at two police officers who were called to the crime scene. On June 12, 1989, Circuit Judge Dennis Kolenda sentenced Ratliff to ten to fifteen years in prison for killing his wife and gave him two life sentences for shooting at the two police officers. The terms are all concurrent.

Clarence Ratliff and some community leaders expressed disgust with Ratliff's conviction and sentence, pointing out he was punished more severely for shooting at and missing two officers than for the death of his wife.

---

**Ray, James Earl**, 1928-1998, U.S., mur. The death of James Earl Ray, the convicted assassin of civil rights leader Martin Luther King, of liver disease on April 23, 1998, only added more mystery to Ray's reported killing of King in Memphis, Tennessee, on April 4, 1968. At the time, King and his entourage had taken second-floor rooms 306 and 307 in the downtown Lorraine Motel. At about 6 p.m., King stepped from his room and leaned over a railing to speak to his driver just as he was about to leave for a dinner engagement with a local preacher. At that moment King was fatally shot, dying an hour later.

The rifle shot that killed King was apparently fired from the second-story bathroom window of a cheap boarding house that faced the back of the motel. Ray had taken a room in this boarding house under the alias John Willard. Within minutes of the assassination, a bundle containing a 30.06 Remington rifle and some of Ray's personal effects was discovered in the doorway of the Canipe Amusement Company, which was in the building next to the boarding house.

**James Earl Ray, shown in 1966, two years before he killed Martin Luther King.**

Ray insisted that at the time of the shooting he was on Main Street, a block from the Lorraine Motel on Mulberry Street, changing a tire on his car. He later told police that he had purchased the Remington rifle for a mysterious person named "Raul," who, according to Ray, was the real assassin. Following the killing, Ray, who had escaped a Missouri prison a year earlier, fled not only from Memphis but from the U.S. in an expensive and circuitous route that took him to Toronto, then to London, then to Portugal and then back to London, where, on June 8, 1968, he was arrested at Heathrow Airport while waiting for a plane to take him to Belgium. On March 10, 1969, Ray entered a guilty plea to avoid a possible death sentence and was given a 99-year prison term.

Ray never explained why he chose to fly to these cities or who paid for the expensive plane travel in what appeared to be a well-mapped-out and purposely confusing escape route, one that James Earl Ray, a minor hoodlum with limited intelligence and no funds, could not or would not have conceived and executed alone. Ray all but stated this when he recanted his confession three days after he made his plea. He asked for a trial, but state and federal courts denied his request and officially rejected such appeals seven times.

Imprisoned for thirty years, Ray never ceased to insist that he was innocent of murdering King, stating that he was a patsy in a large conspiracy to murder the civil rights leader and that the real killer, "Raul," had escaped punishment. Members of Martin Luther King's family, including his widow, Coretta Scott King, and her son, Dexter King, came to believe Ray and, in 1997, asked that he be given a trial. It was too late. Ray died at age 69 in prison of liver failure in April 1998.

The refusal of state officials to allow Ray to leave the state for a liver transplant became suspect, particularly after Ray's lawyers unsuccessfully argued that without the operation he would be dead within a few months. Tennessee hospitals refused to consider Ray as a transplant patient because of his age. Prison officials refused to let him travel out of state for such an operation. Moreover, Judge Cheryl Blackburn decreed in September 1997 that Ray's attorneys had failed to produce any convincing evidence that would cause Ray's plea to be set aside so that he could be granted a new trial.

Conspiracy theories abound to this day about the King assassination. One held that President Lyndon B. Johnson was behind the murder, another that FBI Director J. Edgar Hoover masterminded the killing. (Hoover, indeed, had little regard for King, secretly taping the civil rights leader in his travels and calling him "a womanizer.") Still another surmised that King was killed by the Joint Chiefs of Staff and that he had been killed with the precision of a military execution by specially trained army snipers.

**Civil rights leader Martin Luther King, assassinated in 1968.**

These wild notions aside, the FBI investigation into the shooting was accomplished on the side of expediency. Its files on the case are still, for the most part, sealed. A congressional subcommittee headed by Louis Stokes, a black Democrat from Ohio, did examine all of the evidence at hand and concluded that Ray was the actual killer of King, and that if he had been aided in his gruesome chore, that help stemmed from violent white supremacists, not from anyone in the U.S. government.

Yet, evidence of sorts surfaced over the years that caused many to ponder the dark heart of a King conspiracy. Former FBI agent Donald G. Wilson came forward in March 1998 to state that he had found some papers in Ray's abandoned car in Atlanta, Georgia, on April 11, 1968, which he kept to himself out of fear that he would be accused of disturbing a crime scene, since Ray had by that time been captured.

The papers showed the name "Raul," written in Ray's handwriting, and a phone number that reportedly, at one time, rang up the Vegas Club, a Dallas nightclub owned by none other than Jack Ruby, the man who killed Lee Harvey Oswald, the assassin of President John F. Kennedy. Wilson's evidence was labelled "a total fabrication" by the FBI. Yet Wilson's motive in coming forward, he said, was a sincere wish to shed more light on the case. He stated, "The King family wants to know the truth ... I thought I might be able to help."

At the time of his discovery, Wilson was a new 25-year-old FBI agent stationed in Atlanta, Georgia. He accompanied another, older agent to Atlanta's Capital Homes housing project on April 11, 1968, after local police informed the Atlanta field office of the Bureau that Ray's abandoned Mustang car had been found. When arriving at the scene, the other agent began talking with police officers. Wilson stated that he noticed the door to the passenger side of the Mustang was ajar and, using a handkerchief so as not to disturb any fingerprints, he opened it and out fell a small white envelope.

Wilson panicked, picked up the enveloped and placed it in his pocket. He felt that he had made a misstep in a major case that might have brought down the considerable wrath of J. Edgar Hoover on his head. Said Wilson in 1998, "Taking that split-second action had nothing to do with grand or noble reasons. This gets to the basic philosophy of the FBI: Everything was predicated on fear. Fear of Mr. Hoover."

The envelope retrieved by Wilson bears Ray's handwritten notes, including the name "Raul," which was written twice, the second time with the annotation "Canada," and notes on a torn-out page from a 1963 Dallas, Texas, phone book, one that bears the name of many persons named Hunt, including the Hunt Oil Corp., which was headed by right-wing billionaire H. L. Hunt, an avowed enemy of Kennedy, and later his son, Nelson Bunker Hunt, who paid for an anti-Kennedy newspaper ad that ran on the day President Kennedy was shot and killed in Dallas, Texas.

The envelope also contained cards from a Louisiana towing company and a Texas gun shop. All of this, of course, explained little, other than to support Ray's claim that a person named "Raul" existed, or, perhaps, existed as an intentional fabrication, a mythical person to whom Ray, if he were caught, could later point an accusatory finger.

Fueling the conspiracy theory was a Memphis native named Lloyd Jowers, who owned and operated Jim's Grill, on the ground level of the boarding house in Memphis where Ray roomed at the time of the King assassination. Jowers stated that he overheard customers in his bar plotting to kill King, and that Ray had nothing to do with the crime. He said that he was told to go to the rear entrance of his restaurant on the evening of April 4, 1968, the day of the shooting. He did so, he said, and was given a smoking rifle by a local police officer.

Jowers went on national TV in 1993 to state that he had actually hired the gunman who killed King and that it was not James Earl Ray. He said that he hired the professional killer as a favor to a then-deceased produce dealer who was reportedly tied to organized crime, but that he had no idea who the intended victim might be. In response to these 1993 statements and updated comments made by Jowers, the King family filed a suit on October 2, 1998, against Jowers, accusing him and "unknown co-conspirators" of being involved in the murder of Martin Luther King.

By that time, at the urging of President William Clinton, U.S. Attorney Janet Reno ordered a limited inquiry into the 1968 assassination, certainly at the urging of the King family. Dexter King, the son of the slain civil rights leader, had met with James Earl Ray in March 1997. Their emotional conversation was recorded on film. King asked Ray if he had killed his father.

Ray stuttered the reply, "No, no, no. I didn't."

"I want you to know that I believe you," said King, "and my family believes you."

They were in a decided minority. Most believed Ray was the lone killer responsible for King's death, including David Garrow, author of *The FBI and Martin Luther King, Jr.* Said Garrow, "People are unwilling to accept that something as historically huge as the death of Martin Luther King could have been brought about singlehandedly by someone as humanely insignificant as James Earl Ray. People would rather believe that huge forces bring about huge events. But that's just not the way the world works." Also See: **King, Martin Luther, Jr.,** Vol. III.

---

**Razo, Jose Luis, Jr.,** 1967- , U.S., rob. Jose Luis Razo, Jr. was a role model within the Hispanic community of La Habra, California. Named the Boy's Club "Boy of the Year," the former altar boy earned a scholarship to Harvard University in 1985, following his scholastic and athletic accomplishments at the Servite Roman Catholic High School in Anaheim. But Razo never completely acclimated to the Ivy League institution. He wrote a term paper about the hopelessness and despair in the inner-city Latino barrios and the number of young men who ended up in prison. In the end he was writing about himself.

Early signs of trouble were covered over. In 1983, Razo was arrested for theft in Fullerton, California, but the police, who did not want to ruin his apparently bright future, handled the matter informally. The following year Razo became the ward of a juvenile court when he stole a wallet from a parked car, and later was arrested for assault and battery following a fight at a party. Charges in both incidents were dropped. In 1986, Razo was charged with misdemeanor grand theft, but again the charges were dropped and he went back to Harvard with a clean record.

When Razo returned home during school breaks starting in December 1985, he began robbing stores and fast-food restaurants. In summer 1987, Razo was brought to a police station to testify about a murder in neighboring Santa Ana. Suddenly he confessed to twelve armed robberies. Although Razo later recanted, saying the robberies were committed and related to him by a close friend, he was arrested for ten counts of armed robbery and imprisoned for sixteen months before being released on $150,000 bond in November 1988. In June 1989, Razo was brought to trial before Judge Jean H. Rheinheimer at the Orange County Superior Court in Santa Ana.

Defense attorney John Barnett claimed that Razo had confessed in a drug-induced stupor and pleaded that he was a victim of the cultural differences between Harvard and the barrio. Prosecutor Ravi Mehta countered that Razo had abused an extremely rare opportunity. He also showed that the robberies were obviously premeditated and committed with precision over a two-year period. On June 11, 1989, the jury concurred and found Razo guilty on six of the ten counts of armed robbery. On August 25, the 22-year-old Razo was sentenced to ten years and four months in prison. He was also fined $500.

---

**"Recovered Memory,"** See: **Franklin, George**.

---

**Red Brigade, The**, prom. 1989, Case of, Italy, terr. More than 200 members of the Italian Red Brigade, a domestic terrorist group responsible for hundreds of bombings, kidnappings, and political murders in the late 1970s, were acquitted by a court in Rome on October 13, 1989, on charges that they had carried on an armed insurrection against the state. The eight-month trial ended when the judges ruled that the defendants had never actually carried out an armed insurrection against the nation. In essence, the ruling meant that the courts refused to recognize that coordinated acts of terrorism by extremist political groups constituted war against the state, an interpretation that intentionally discounted the Red Brigade's power. Among the 253 defendants who were freed by the court were Prospero Gallinari, convicted killer of Italian Prime Min-

ister Aldo Moro, and the founder of the movement, Renato Curcio. (Editor's Note: Additional information on this group can be found in Vol. III.)

---

**Reed, James Earl**, 1966- , U.S., mur. Ann Lafayette came from a good family in Charleston, South Carolina. Her parents, Joseph and Barbara Ann Lafayette, had worked hard to send her and her brother and sister through college. Lafayette joined the Army and was commissioned an officer. She married and had a small son from the marriage, which ended in divorce. While in the Army she met and began an affair with an enlisted man, James Earl Reed, who had unpredictable mood swings and was soon in trouble with superior officers. In May 1991, Reed received an honorable discharge, mostly through the help of Lafayette.

The relationship continued between Lafayette and Reed, but it became more and more volatile as Reed showed himself to be jealous to the point of violence. Lafayette broke off the relationship, but Reed persisted in following her from one military base to another. On February 14, 1992, Reed appeared at a military base where Lafayette was assigned and tried to renew the relationship. When she rebuffed him, he said that if she tried to leave him he would kill her. Lafayette attempted to flee with the help of another officer. Reed raced after her, jumping into his car and running down Lafayette's friend, breaking his leg. He was convicted of assault and sent to prison for thirty-seven months.

Upon his release from a federal prison on April 25, 1994, Reed was given $300 and a bus ticket to Fayetteville, North Carolina, where he was to report to a federal halfway house. He never appeared, going instead to the home of Ann Lafayette's parents in Charleston. Neighbors of the Lafayettes heard noises that sounded like gunshots on May 18, 1994, and gathered outside the Lafayette home. A young man emerged, and one of the neighbors asked what the shooting was about. "I don't know," he replied, and then got into the 1989 Chevrolet Cavalier owned by Mrs. Lafayette and drove away.

Police arrived a short time later to find 51-year-old Joseph Lafayette and 46-year-old Barbara Ann Lafayette dead, both of them sitting in their living room, each shot five times. From the placement of the wounds, detectives concluded that the killer had fired as if to inflict pain before executing the pair with bullets fired into their foreheads. One investigator thought the murderer might have fired the bullets as a form of torture in order to extract information from the couple.

On questioning neighbors, police learned that the young man who had taken Mrs. Lafayette's car was James Earl Reed, who had been to the Lafayette home many times when he was dating Ann Lafayette years earlier. An all-points bulletin was sent out for the arrest of Reed. Mrs. Lafayette's car was soon found abandoned and a manhunt, with bloodhounds leading the way, ensued, but Reed slipped through the dragnet.

Police then provided truckers throughout the area with Reed's description, asking that they call police over their CB radios if they spotted the fugitive. Just such a call led officers in Dorchester County to arrest Reed as he casually walked along a highway outside of Harleyville, South Carolina. Reed was arrested and charged with the murders of Joseph and Barbara Ann Lafayette.

From the beginning, Reed openly defied authorities to prove a murder case against him, telling reporters in Charleston that if prosecutor David Schwacke got a murder conviction and death sentence, he could personally shoot him. Arrogant and smug, Reed stated that the prosecution had no evidence by which to convict him—no fingerprints, no blood to be found on him when he was arrested, no physical evidence of any kind (he had even been careful to pick up the shell casings from the bullets he had fired into the Lafayettes before fleeing their home), and certainly not a murder weapon.

Reed's trial began in June 1996, and from the start, he proved to be a truculent defendant, firing Ashley Pennington, his court-appointed public defender, and insisting that he represent himself, which the court was obligated to permit. Though Reed attempted to make a shambles of the trial, prosecutor Schwacke was convincing in how he described Reed's double murder, inferring that Reed had shot the Lafayettes repeatedly in order to get them to tell him where he could find their daughter. The couple apparently died bravely without divulging their daughter's whereabouts.

Damning Reed were the statements of several witnesses who testified that they saw him leave the Lafayette house almost immediately after they heard the gunshots and watched him drive off in Mrs. Lafayette's car. This was enough for the jury of four men and eight women, who convicted Reed of first-degree murder on June 7, 1996. Reed demanded the jury be polled, and each juror had to voice a guilty verdict while the killer glared menacingly at them. Several of the women jurors began crying and one even fled the courtroom in tears, but all echoed the verdict of guilty. Judge William Howard sentenced Reed to death and he awaits execution at this writing.

---

**Reed, Thomas,** 1928- , U.S., brib. Thomas Reed, president of the Alabama chapter of the National Association for the Advancement of Colored People, began serving a four-year term in a federal prison in Pensacola, Florida, on December 6, 1989, for bribery. Reed, a 61-year-old former Alabama state legislator, was convicted in September 1988 of accepting a $10,000 bribe to help free a convicted murderer. He was fired from his legislative post following his conviction.

---

**Reggiani Martinelli, Patrizia** (AKA: The Black Widow), 1948- , Italy, mur. Milan is the chic capital of Italy's fashion industry, and no one's name in that dizzying designer world of glitz and glamour is more potent than that of Gucci. Three generations of Guccis have imprinted the founder's initials, "GG," on the most coveted leather goods and shoes to be found anywhere. Maurizio Gucci was the grandson and last of the direct descendants of Guccio Gucci to hold a stake in the company, and he sold out his interest in 1993 for $120 million following years of family discord and acrimony.

Much of that acrimony had to do with Maurizio Gucci's former wife, Patrizia Reggiani Martinelli Gucci, a social-climbing, money-loving ex-spouse who was so unsatisfied with her

$860,000-a-year alimony that she planned to obtain all of Gucci's millions through a murder-for-hire plan. Having been divorced years earlier by Gucci, the once glamorous Neapolitan, who had humble origins and who had given birth to two of Gucci's daughters, had threatened the fashion king with all sorts of terrible fates and even told him to his face that she would have him killed unless he turned over many millions to her.

Gucci waved her off. On March 27, 1995, as he was mounting the stairs to his elegant offices in Milan, Gucci was shot to death by an unknown assailant who fled in a fast car with another conspirator behind the wheel. Police doggedly worked on the killing until they identified the getaway driver, Orazio Cicala, an unemployed auto worker. Cicala led police to the

Italy's "black widow" killer, Patrizia Reggiani Martinelli, convicted and sentenced to prison in 1998 in the contract killing of her former husband, fashion tycoon Maurizio Gucci.

gunman, Benedetto Ceraulo, the owner of a pizzeria who was swimming in debt. Ceraulo told detectives that he had received his orders from Ivano Savioni, the doorman of a broken-down Milan hotel.

The doorman was picked up and, following grueling interrogations, said that he had followed the orders of Giuseppina Auriemma, a mysterious psychic, warning officers that her spiritual powers could overwhelm and destroy any law enforcement agencies probing into her dark doings. Police then learned that Auriemma had for years been the personal psychic "adviser" to Gucci's ex-wife, Reggiani Martinelli.

The one-time queen of Milan's social world bristled when investigators cautiously approached her, gently quizzing her about her husband's murder. She said she had nothing to do with it. She later admitted that she had for some time been seeking someone to kill her miserly ex-husband, but, she emphasized, she had never gone through with that plan. Of course, nodded the polite police inquisitors, but her personal psychic now stood accused of acting on her behalf.

Reggiani Martinelli then said that Auriemma had arranged for the murder without her approval and that the psychic had been blackmailing her ever since, taking more than $375,000. But, the ex-wife insisted, she was nevertheless innocent of having her former husband killed. "Never let even a friendly wolf into the chicken coop," she confided to police, a statement she would often repeat in months to come. "Sooner or later it will get hungry." She was, of course, referring to the scheming psychic, Auriemma, the real mastermind behind the murder of Maurizio Gucci, she said.

In June 1998, Reggiani Martinelli and her four co-conspirators were brought to trial in Milan, all charged with capital murder. The former queen bee denied having anything to do with the other four defendants, insisting that they had acted on their own under Auriemma's orders and that the psychic was an evil person who had seized upon Reggiani Martinelli's dislike of her former husband to initiate a murder and involve her in it, so that she could become the perfect blackmail victim.

"I have been naive to the point of stupidity," Reggiani Martinelli cried out to the court where her mother sat with a worried look on her face. "I found myself involved against my will. I deny categorically that I was an accomplice."

The costly trial dragged on for five months while the seamy side of Milan's social set was exposed. Tawdry tales of greed, intrigue, calculating social climbing and murderous betrayals were told and retold in detail, an army of reporters in the courtroom writing down every sensational word and photographing every move made by witnesses and defendants, especially the former grande dame, Reggiani Martinelli, who played the role of the discarded wife and blackmail victim.

On November 3, 1998, Reggiani Martinelli and her four co-defendants were all found guilty of capital murder. Instead of the life term expected for her, Reggiani Martinelli was sentenced to twenty-nine years in prison. Auriemma, the scheming psychic, received a 25-year sentence. Savioni, her stooge the doorman, got a 26-year sentence, while Cicala, the getaway driver, received a 29-year sentence and Ceraulo, the gunman who continued to shout out his innocence, was sent to prison for life.

Only Savioni, the go-between, seemed repentant, stating: "I know that I face many long years in prison for what I've done. I ask the pardon of Gucci's children. I am horrified that things went so much further than I intended."

At the announcement of the verdict and sentence, Reggiani Martinelli's two daughters, who had sat patiently through the trial, burst into tears. The defendant's mother sat stone-faced and silent. Reggiani Martinelli herself then turned to her lawyer, Giovanni Dedola, and, showing her best bewildered face, said in a soft and knowing tone: "Truth is the child of time. Evidently, they didn't believe me."

As Italy's most notorious "Black Widow" was being escorted from the courtroom and en route to prison, hordes of journalists began brawling with police. Reporters and photographers struggled, jostled, pushed, and shoved to get close to Reggiani Martinelli, to scribble down a final statement, to snap just one more photo.

---

**Regino, Angelo** (AKA: Cave Man), 1969- , U.S., rob.-mur. Angelo Regino, 20, wearing a dark fedora and claiming to be Freddy Krueger, a fictional killer portrayed in the film *Nightmare on Elm Street*, committed a series of attacks and robberies in January and February 1988 in San Pedro, California. Regino was convicted in January 1989 of murdering John Healey in one of the attacks and robbing three other men. Compton Superior Court Commissioner Anita Rae Shapiro sentenced Regino on April 12, 1989, to life in prison without a chance for parole.

---

**Reilly, Robert Michael**, 1928- , Case of, U.S., mur. A Dade County, Florida, murder case that lay dormant for twenty-two years finally reached its conclusion in August 1989. Bob Reilly, a one-time Miami Beach "beach boy" and convicted robber who went straight and ended up as the respected chief of orthopedic services at a Miami area hospital, was acquitted of charges that he murdered a 76-year-old widow more than twenty-two years earlier.

The case against Reilly, chief of orthopedic services at Kendall, Florida's Baptist Hospital, began when Dade County's renowned "Cold Case" squad found sufficient evidence after a twenty-year hiatus and arrested Robert W. Ball, Jr., 48, in relation to the March 29, 1967, death of Josephine Barnhill. Based on evidence gathered by this investigative unit, which specialized in solving old cases, Ball pleaded guilty to manslaughter. At Reilly's trial, he testified that he had driven Reilly and an ex-convict named Charles F. Gibson to the elderly woman's North Dade trailer and waited in the car as the two men went to rob Barnhill. Ball claimed that when the two men exited the trailer, Reilly said he had gagged Barnhill tightly and hoped she would not die. Barnhill did die and under Florida state law, committing a felony causing death counts as first-degree murder. As a result of Ball's accusations, Reilly was arrested and charged with the crime in 1987.

Reilly was brought to trial in August 1989 and pleaded innocent. His attorney, John Thornton, Jr., explained Ball's testimony against Reilly as the action of a desperate man—the authorities had evidence against Ball and he was forced to bargain to save his own neck. Thornton presented witnesses who testified that Ball was known to lie to get himself out of trouble. Dade Circuit Court Judge Richard Margolius refused to allow Thornton to bring forth evidence of Reilly's moral rehabilitation, saying that the good name he had built for himself since being released from jail in 1973 was irrelevant to his defense. Reilly himself testified that on the day that the murder was committed he was making and selling hats to Miami Beach tourists. Prosecutor Gene Rothenberg was permitted to introduce evidence that Reilly had participated in a similar robbery later that same day with Gibson and Ball's father, Robert W. Ball, Sr., for which he was convicted and served seven years of a life term before winning parole and eventually a pardon. On August 25, 1989, the jury found Reilly not guilty of the murder of Josephine Barnhill.

---

**Reinhart, Norbert**, 1949- , Col., kid. (vict.) On June 24, 1998, Ed Leonard, the drill foreman of a Canadian mining company operating in Colombia, was seized and held for ransom by a terrorist group, the Revolutionary Armed Forces of Colombia. One of the top executives of the Canadian firm, 49-year-old Norbert Reinhart, who had apparently been handling negotiations with the terrorists, decided to take Leonard's place when talks with the terrorists broke down.

Against the wishes of his family and the Canadian government, Reinhart, in a courageous display of employer responsibility, traveled to a remote mountain pass in Colombia and, on October 6, 1998, exchanged himself for Leonard, a man he had never met. Reinhart looked at Leonard and said: "Your shift is done. You can go home."

Three months later, in early January 1999, after an undisclosed ransom amount was paid to the terrorists, Reinhart was released and returned to his family. His wife Casey Reinhart, who had been opposed to her husband swapping himself for Leonard, stated, "My first reaction was 'don't do it,' but you can't help admire his nobility in doing it."

---

**Reno, Janet**, 1938- , U.S., law enforcement. As U.S. Attorney General since 1992, Janet Reno became one of the most controversial persons to ever hold that distinguished office. A native of Miami, Florida, where she worked as a lawyer and government attorney, Reno was appointed to her post by President Bill Clinton during his first term in office. From that point onward, Reno, a workaholic who worked from 5 a.m. to late at night, proved her independence and apolitical posture by appointing many independent counsels to probe the accusations of wrongdoing on the part of the White House, from Travelgate to Whitewater, irrespective of what President Clinton might have felt about such actions.

**The obstinate, unpredictable and error-plagued U.S. Attorney General Janet Reno.**

An opponent of capital punishment, Reno was nevertheless unyielding when it came to employing deadly force to maintain law and order. This was the case in her first great test when FBI and other federal agents confronted the arms-hoarding Branch Davidian cult outside of Waco, Texas, in 1993. After federal agents had been driven away from the Davidian compound in a bloody shootout on February 28, 1993, and subsequent but ineffective negotiations failed to persuade the cultists to leave their bastion, Reno ordered a frontal attack on the compound on April 19, 1993.

Reno's decision resulted in disaster—all inside the compound (seventy-two bodies were counted, but eighty persons in all were estimated to have perished), including the unschooled, egomaniacal leader, David Koresh, were killed, either perishing in the flames that consumed the building complex or dying from gunshot wounds administered by other members. Immediately following this botched mission, Reno held a press conference in which she took full responsibility for the shambles in Waco, saying that she had received reports that children inside the compound were in danger, and she felt it necessary to order the attack to save them. None of those children survived the attack and fire.

A cry for Reno's resignation went up from many quarters, but she refused to step down, even after publicly proving herself inept in a hostage-taking fiasco that most professional lawmen and criminologists felt could have been averted by denying the limelight-seeking Koresh any access to the media, the use of phones, electricity or the flow of foodstuffs. That tactic eventually worked in 1996, when FBI and other federal agents totally isolated the Montana Freemen and their families, who endured a three-month standoff before meekly vacating their remote farmhouse and surrendering without violence.

On the positive side, the U.S. Department of Justice under Reno has successfully prosecuted many high-profile criminals such as Ramzi Yousuf, the mastermind of the World Trade Center bombing, and billionaire Mexican drug cartel boss Juan Garcia Abrego. Also under the seemingly indefatigable Reno (who battles the debilitating Parkinson's disease), the Department's divisions addressing civil rights, anti-trust and environment were goaded into renewed and effective efforts. Accusations of illegal and massive financial contributions to the Democratic Party by foreign interests, notably China, and mounting allegations in the late 1990s that China had pilfered widespread U.S. military secrets again brought an unresponsive Reno under fire.

In the end, Janet Reno has withstood tremendous criticism and perhaps even undisclosed requests from President Clinton to stand down. As the top law enforcement officer in the country after the president, Reno has proved to be a fair-minded though sometimes belligerent occupant of one of the most demanding and exhausting offices in the federal government. Also See: **Clinton, William Jefferson**; **Garcia Brego, Juan**; **Koresh, David**; **Montana Freemen**; **Whitewater**; **World Trade Center bombing**.

---

**Rentas, Johnny**, 1975- , U.S., mur. Four days after he was released from prison, Johnny Rentas moved back into the Chicago home of his wife and 3-year-old daughter, Jahnie. On April 11, 1996, Rentas was playing with his daughter outside when she began crying. He told her to stop and when she didn't, Rentas dragged her into the home, where he punched her in the abdomen and slammed her head repeatedly on the hardwood floor. When the girl showed no signs of life, Rentas called 911.

Paramedics could not revive the 3-year-old, and doctors could find no sign of brain activity. She was pronounced dead the next day and Rentas was charged with murder. Convicted, Rentas was sentenced to life imprisonment by Cook County Circuit Court Judge Stanley Sacks on July 14, 1998.

---

**Reszcynski, Stanislaw,** 1939- , U.S., drunk driving. On April 23, 1989, Stanislaw Reszcynski ran his car over 6-year-old Bobby Havansek, causing the suburban Chicago boy to suffer partial paralysis and severe brain damage. Bobby had been riding his bicycle and fell off into the path of Reszcynski's vehicle. Reszcynski left the scene but was later arrested by police, who traced his abandoned car. At the time of his arrest, his blood alcohol level was two and a half times the legal intoxication limit. Cook County Criminal Court Judge Themis Karnezis sentenced Reszcynski, who had had his driver's license revoked for five other drunk driving offenses since 1982, to the maximum allowable term of six years in prison. Reszcynski maintained his innocence in the courtroom as Havansek family members watched. "Why am I here?" he asked, wanting to know why he was being prosecuted, since he had paid his previous tickets.

---

**Reynolds, Melvin J.**, 1952- , U.S., sexual asslt.-obstruct. of just. President Bill Clinton and Illinois Representative Mel Reynolds had many things in common. Both men grew up poor, Clinton in Arkansas and, just across the border, Reynolds in Mound Bayou, Mississippi. Both were Democrats, and both had been Rhodes scholars and had gone to Harvard. Both were also accused of sexual misconduct. That's where the similarities ended. Clinton, though impeached, managed to escape being voted out of office by the U.S. Senate. Reynolds, on the other hand, went to prison.

For years Reynolds' congressional district was represented by an angry little man who constantly hurled insults at whites and Jews. He was aptly named Gus Savage. In 1992 Reynolds ran against Savage in a campaign where Reynolds chastised Savage for his bigotry and his tendency to always play the race card when under pressure. Reynolds easily won the primary and went on to replace

**U.S. Congressman Mel Reynolds of Chicago, who went to prison for five years for having sex with an underage campaign volunteer.**

Savage in the U.S. House of Representatives. As a new 1993 congressman, he quickly rose in stature and took seats on important committees.

To many, Reynolds was the "great black hope," an intelligent moderate who promised to bring about many reforms. But before he could make his political mark, Reynolds' reputation began eroding at home in Illinois. On June 2, 1994, 18-year-old Beverly Heard, who had served as a campaign worker for Reynolds in 1992, told Chicago officials that she had had a sexual relationship with Reynolds at the time, having sex with the married Reynolds about twice each week in his office, in a south suburban apartment, or in a motel.

The problem was that Heard at the time was 16 years old when the legal age of consent was 17. Police began to tape Heard's phone conversations with Reynolds, which amounted to no more than sex talk. In one phone conversation, the congressman reportedly asked Heard to give him photos that showed her 15-year-old girlfriend naked and in lascivious poses.

Reynolds quickly learned of the police probe through police spokesman William Davis, who once worked for Reynolds, and who reportedly and illegally contacted his former employer to "tip him off." Police later stated that Reynolds immediately paid off Heard and had her sign statements that recanted her allegations, then had Heard's mother take her out of state so that she could not testify against him. Another teenager came forward, telling police that she, too, had had an illegal sexual relationship with Reynolds. She recanted her statements the next day, reportedly after Reynolds gave her money to keep quiet.

Reynolds was nevertheless indicted on August 19, 1994, charged with twenty counts, including witness tampering, solicitation of child pornography and having sex with a minor. He was convicted and sentenced to five years in prison, entering the East Moline (Illinois) Correctional Center in October 1995. While serving his sentence, Reynolds, along with his wife, Marisol, who was Reynolds' campaign treasurer, were both indicted on charges that they had illegally spent $85,000 in campaign funds during his elections, and that they had defrauded banks using forged documents in attempts to obtain loans.

---

**Rezaq, Omar Mohammaed Ali**, 1963- , Gr./U.S., terr.-skyjack.-mur. On November 23, 1985, three Palestinian terrorists commandeered EgyptAir flight 648 just after it took off from Athens airport. Omar Rezaq, leader of the trio, announced to startled passengers that he and his companions were taking over the plane in the name of the Egyptian Revolutionary Organization and that they were opposed to the recently signed Camp David Peace agreement between Egyptian President Anwar Sadat and Israeli Prime Minister Menachem Begin.

**Egyptian commandos are shown with survivors and bodies from the 1985 explosion of EgyptAir Flight 648 at Valletta, Malta, after an abortive skyjacking by Palestinian terrorist Omar Rezaq.**

Wearing a mask and jamming a gun to the head of the plane's pilot, Rezaq ordered him to fly to Malta. Once the plane landed there, Maltese officials refused to allow the plane to refuel and take off. Rezaq said that he would shoot a passenger every fifteen minutes until the officials complied. When officials did not respond, Rezaq shot five persons, killing two women, including an American, Scarlett Rogenkamp of Oceanside, California, and wounding another three persons.

**Terrorist Omar Rezaq, in custody in 1993; he was sent to prison for life in 1996.**

Egyptian commandos then stormed the plane and an explosion rocked the plane as it sat on the runway. Sixty persons were killed, including the two terrorists accompanying Rezaq. The surviving terrorist was imprisoned in Malta for seven years and then released. He fled, but FBI agents tracked him down and arrested him in Nigeria, returning him to the U.S. where, in July 1996, he was tried in Washington, D.C., under the anti-terrorism statutes, which permit prosecution when Americans are victimized.

Defense attorneys attempted to persuade a jury that Rezaq had been driven insane by the daily bloodshed and killing in the Middle East, along with terrorist indoctrination, and was not in his right mind when skyjacking the plane and shooting the helpless passengers. No, said prosecutors. Rezaq was in complete control throughout the skyjacking. A jury convicted him on July 19, 1996, and he was sentenced to life in prison by U.S. District Court Judge Royce Lamberth on October 7, 1996.

---

**Rice, Laura Lee,** 1951- , Case of, U.S., mur. Laura Lee Rice had been a troubled woman most of her life. When she was 10 her mother suffered a miscarriage, and Rice blamed her for the loss of a sibling. When she was 17, she lost her first child due to birth defects. Rice became a heavy drug user and during the next ten years had four children, each with a different father. During the early 1980s her behavior became markedly more eccentric. Rice told others that she had been born with paws and a tail, and that she had a bag containing a deed to a gold mine, as well as teeth, glasses, and a driver's license, sewn into her stomach. She began living with Daniel Runyon in a trailer park near Gillette, Wyoming, and bore two baby girls. Although diagnosed as a schizophrenic, Rice did not take her medication regularly, and by April 1989 her condition had worsened. She now believed that her two infant daughters were clones who had been taking bites out of her body with their eyes.

On April 24, 1989, Rice put 15-month-old Danielle Lee and 4-month-old Joan in bed for a midmorning nap. As they lay in their cribs, she slit their throats, mutilated the bodies and decapitated them, then placed the remains in plastic bags. The bodies were discovered later that day and Rice was arraigned on two murder charges. Her attorney entered a plea of not guilty by reason of insanity, and County Judge Michael Deegan ordered Rice to undergo a thirty-day psychiatric examination.

On October 13, Rice reiterated her plea of insanity at her trial before Judge Terrence O'Brien at the District Court in Gillette. Under cross-examination by deputy prosecutor Allan Massey, Rice, 38, claimed Runyon had committed the murders but later admitted her guilt under the guise of her schizophrenic delusions. At the conclusion of the bench trial on December 4, Judge O'Brien concurred with the insanity motion and, following the suggestion of prosecutor John Young, sentenced her to life in a mental institution without furlough privileges. Rice, who was diagnosed as having Capgras Syndrome, in which one believes family members have been replaced by doubles, now resides at the State Mental Hospital in Evanston, Wyoming.

---

**Richardson, Alvin,** 1968- , U.S., child abuse-sex. asslt.-mur. On August 15, 1989, Alvin Richardson was sentenced in Baltimore (Maryland) Circuit Court to life in prison without parole plus fifteen years for the brutal murder of his girlfriend's 2-year-old son, Michael Shaw. On the morning of December 15, 1988, Susan Davis, the child's mother, left him in Richardson's care when she went to work. Less than an hour later, Michael was rushed to Johns Hopkins Hospital, where he died from massive internal injuries. An autopsy showed that the child had suffered repeated blows by a blunt object, possibly a fist, and had also been sodomized. Throughout the trial Richardson, 21, maintained his innocence, testifying that the child's fatal injuries were caused when he fell in the bathtub. However, Richardson's testimony was contradicted by that of the surgeon who operated on the boy and the pathologist who performed the autopsy—both of whom testified that the boy's injuries could not have been the result of a fall.

---

**Richardson, Herbert Lee**, 1946-1989, U.S., mur. On August 18, 1989, convicted murderer Herbert Lee Richardson, 43, became 116th person to be executed since the Supreme Court's 1976 decision to allow individual states to reinstate the death penalty. Since 1976, Richardson was the sixth felon to be put to death in Alabama. "I have no ill feeling and hold nothing against anyone," he said in a statement to the press shortly before he died. An eleventh-hour plea for a stay of execution was turned down by Federal District Judge Robert Varneron on the grounds that it was "beyond ... reason to believe that a device that maimed and killed an 11-year-old child by exploding in her hands could be thought of as not presenting a serious risk of harm."

Richardson, a Vietnam veteran, left a pipe bomb on the porch of Rena Mae Calins of Dothan, Alabama, in 1977. The girl picked up the device and it exploded in her hands. Richardson had become angry with Rena Mae's aunt when she broke off a relationship with him. Lucia Penland, director of a group of citizens opposed to the death penalty, described Richardson as an "all-around American boy" who became a mental wreck as a result of his experiences in Vietnam. Just nine days before he was strapped into the electric chair, Richardson married a woman with whom he had corresponded through the mail.

---

**Richardson, Nathan Arnold**, 1955-1989, U.S., (unsolv.) mur. A 34-year-old criminal defense attorney charged with embezzling funds from his employer was shot and killed on October 9, 1989. Nathan Arnold Richardson was shot as he walked through the lobby of the Los Angeles office building in which he worked just nine days prior to his scheduled trial date. The attorney, a graduate of Stanford University and University of California at Berkeley, was charged with pocketing monies he collected from clients of the Jacoby and Meyers law firm, where he worked until he was fired in June 1986. The Los Angeles police, investigating the possibility that Richardson's attacker was an unhappy client, found no suspects.

---

**Richardson, Ralph** (AKA: Caprice), 1971-1989, Case of, U.S., suic.-mur. A 20-year-old Brooklyn man wanted in several homicides was found dead in his car, an apparent suicide, at the end of a dead-end Brooklyn street. Ralph Richardson, wanted for a 1988 murder in Pennsylvania and another in Brooklyn in early January 1989, shot and wounded two New York City police officers in a Brooklyn apartment building on January 20, 1989. The two men, Officer William Gunn and Detective Louis Rango, had gone to Richardson's last known address in Brooklyn with a warrant for his arrest. When they arrived, they were told that Richardson was in the building next door. As the officers waited for permission from the police department's legal department to arrest Richardson at the new address, one of them called out to Richardson to exit the apartment. The officers were taken by surprise when Richardson exited, firing a gun.

Richardson shot Rango in the shoulder, stole his gun, and pushed his way past Gunn, shooting him in the head as he fled. Richardson then allegedly broke into another Brooklyn apartment and killed its 67-year-old occupant, Linda Manning Walston, when she arrived home from work. Manning's body was found approximately three days after she had been stabbed to death with a kitchen knife.

Richardson next appeared on January 24 at a video store in the Flatbush section of Brooklyn. After entering the store, Richardson pulled two guns, announced that he was robbing the store, and forced the store's four occupants to lie on the floor. One of the store's two owners, Jannet Caban, an off-duty New York police officer, handed over the contents of the cash register, pulled her service revolver out and began shooting as he backed toward the door. The two fired a total of nine rounds, sometimes coming within six feet of each other. Caban wounded Richardson in the hip before he managed to escape. None of the store's occupants were injured. He was found dead on January 25.

Richardson, who had also been wounded in the thigh during the first shoot-out, apparently shot himself with the police revolver he stole from the injured officer. Despite the fact that Richardson, a right-hander, was shot in the left temple, police medical examiners remained certain the death was a suicide, stating that such a wound is unusual, but not unheard of.

---

**Richmond, Earl, Jr.**, 1961- , U.S., mur. On November 4, 1991, Helissa Hayes and her two small children were found strangled to death in their mobile home in Fayetteville, North Carolina. Hayes had been raped before being murdered. Police soon determined that the victim had dated several soldiers stationed at Fort Bragg, only ten miles distant. They interviewed these men, but none of them were likely suspects. On January 9, 1992, Philip Wilkinson, a soldier from Fort Bragg, admitted that he had killed a mother, her 19-year-old daughter and young son in a mobile home in July 1991, but he proved not to be the killer of Hayes and her children.

The Criminal Investigation Department then notified Fayetteville police that they were about to question a former soldier, 29-year-old Earl Richmond, Jr., who had been dishonorably discharged in 1990 for misconduct and who was suspected of having raped and strangled a female soldier in 1991, along with several other offenses, including rape, when he was

in the service. Fayetteville officers sat in on the interview and learned that Richmond had been a roommate of Helissa's Hayes' ex-husband and lived not too far from the murder site. In fact he had been a pallbearer at the funeral of Hayes' young son.

DNA samples were taken from Richmond, although he insisted that he had met Hayes only once and had never been in her mobile home. Some weeks later, the DNA analysis pinpointed Richmond as Hayes' attacker. Confronted with the evidence, Richmond admitted that he had strangled Hayes and her two children. He said that, after sex, she had argued with him and then slapped his face. Said Richmond: "If a woman hits me, I tell them I am going to kill them and then I do."

Confronted with more evidence in other murders, Richmond admitted killing 24-year-old Lisa Ann Nadeau, an Army specialist, in New Jersey, saying that he followed the murder depicted in the film *Presumed Innocent*. He was taken to Camden, New Jersey, and was convicted of the Nadeau murder in March 1993. On May 22, 1995, Richmond went to trial in the Hayes triple slaying case. He was found guilty on May 24, and on June 1, 1995, he was given three death sentences.

---

**Ridley, Alvin**, 1942- , U.S., mur. A TV repairman living in Ringgold, Georgia, Alvin Ridley complained for thirty years of how his wife, Virginia Ridley, had deserted him thirty years earlier, returning to the home of her parents or simply going north. On October 4, 1997, however, Ridley called police to his home to say that his wife had just died. Officers found the place with bars on the windows and a high fence surrounding the place, which appeared to be a home-made prison. That's exactly what it was—Ridley had kept his wife prisoner in the house for more than three decades.

When the woman's body was examined, it was determined that she had been suffocated. Virginia Ridley had last been seen in 1967, when relatives filed a complaint that her husband might be mistreating her. Ridley took his wife to court and there she stated that she was in good health and wished to go on living with her husband. Charges against Ridley were not pressed until July 1998, and he awaits trial at this writing.

---

**Riggans, Stephan,** See: **Ryan, James.**

---

**Riggs, Beth Michelle,** 1953- , U.S., mur. On February 14, 1989, Judge Kenneth Trabue of the Roanoke County (Virginia) Circuit Court sentenced Beth Michelle Riggs, 36, to twelve years in prison for the second-degree murder of her 4-year-old adopted daughter, Heather. Riggs had force-fed Heather a fatal dose of salt on May 16, 1988, as punishment for stealing sugar.

---

**Riina, Salvatore**, ? - , Italy, org. crime-mur. In the early 1990s, Italian officials worn out by the vampire-like Mafia, which had been sucking the lifeblood from the nation's economy for decades, decided to throw off the yoke of this oppressive criminal brotherhood. Leading the crusade to dismantle the Mafia's control of government and business in Italy and, particularly, in Sicily were two dedicated criminal prosecutors, Paolo Borsellino and Giovanni Falcone. So effective were these prosecutors in imprisoning scores of Mafiosi that Salvatore Riina, the Mafia "boss of bosses," ordered them killed in 1992.

Riina was an old-fashioned Mafia don who brazenly declared war on the Italian state and unleashed a terror campaign in 1993 against judges, prosecutors and other officials who opposed the murderous Mafia. Instead of retreating as in former times, the government stepped up its arrests and prosecutions of scores of Mafia figures, high and low.

Riina and twenty-one of his top lieutenants were arrested and jailed in 1993, most of them, including Riina, given life terms after being convicted of many murders. Further, Riina and his underbosses were all convicted for their role in the killing of Giovanni Falcone, and all were given additional life sentences on September 26, 1997. Also See: **Italy**; **Mafia**; **Mafia**, Vol. III.

---

**Rippo, Michael**, 1966- , U.S., rob.-mur. For all its ersatz glamour and glitz, Las Vegas teems with every kind of lowlife imaginable—sharpers, hustlers, male and female prostitutes, dope peddlers, and those who would kill a tourist for the cash in his pocket or the credit cards in his wallet. Pretty young girls flock from all points of America by the tens of thousands to Vegas each year, each hoping to get a job as a showgirl or a dancer in one of the many upscale casinos. Then, perhaps, she might meet some wealthy man who will sweep her into marital security. Almost always, this is not the case. The girls arrive to find jobs only as cocktail waitresses or hostesses in the small clubs along the sleazy main Strip and there they stay, until they move on or worsen their plight through drug peddling or prostitution.

Two such girls were Laurie Jacobson, a tall blonde from Missoula, Montana, who went to Las Vegas in 1991, and Denise Lizzi, a petite brunette, who also arrived in town about the same time and met Jacobson. The two women shared an apartment at the Katie Arms Apartments, both working as cocktail waitresses. When the manager of the apartment complex went to collect the rent on February 20, 1992, no one answered his knock. He used his master key to enter the apartment and recoiled in shock at the sight of two pairs of legs protruding from a closet. He ran to call police.

Investigators found the bodies of 27-year-old Jacobson and 25-year-old Lizzi; they had been dead for about two days. There were burn marks on their legs and buttocks. Both had been strangled, Jacobson by hand, Lizzi with a cord that had been ripped from an iron, which officers found discarded in a kitchen waste can. Since there was no evidence of a forced entry, it was assumed that the killer or killers had known the girls. Neither had been sexually molested, but a gold card that had been loaned to Lizzi had been taken.

Someone later used the card to charge rooms and room service, including meals and liquor, in a four-day stay at the Queens Hotel in downtown Las Vegas. A tall, attractive blonde woman was described as the user of the card, but she went

unidentified. Police then got a break when officers responded to a fight outside a Las Vegas home on March 1, 1992. A group of young persons were outside, and one of them explained that he had had a fight with a man named Michael Rippo after Rippo had bragged of burying two girls, including Denise Lizzi. The young man who swung at Rippo had once dated Lizzi, he said.

Rippo had, by the time police arrived, fled with his statuesque blonde girlfriend, 26-year-old Diana Hunt. They had run off on foot, apparently when hearing the police siren, and abandoned their 1986 Isuzu pickup. On the dashboard of this vehicle, detectives found two pairs of expensive sunglasses, identified as being purchased by Hunt with Lizzi's gold card, designer glasses that had cost $285.

A widespread hunt then ensued for Michael Rippo, but he was nowhere to be found. Diana Hunt was another matter. She was located in Yerington, Nevada, a tiny town with a single gas station, on March 15, 1992. Detectives immediately confronted her with the Jacobson-Lizzi killings, telling her that she would be identified as the person who used Lizzi's stolen gold card to buy the expensive sunglasses—one investigator dramatically threw the designer glasses down on a table before her—and used the same card to party at the Queens Hotel for four days.

Hunt quickly broke down and admitted that she had been present when the two girls were murdered, but she said Michael Rippo was the killer. She said she accompanied him to the girls' apartment but was in a drugged state. Hunt said that she had been using drugs for some time and Rippo had stepped her up to heroin, which she took by injection. She agreed to testify against Rippo once he was caught and brought to trial.

Rippo was soon located and arrested. He was charged with the double murders but immediately claimed that Hunt, not he, had murdered Jacobson and Lizzi, that he hardly knew the girls. Hunt had befriended them, he said, and he merely went along with her on the night of the murder to help her collect money due her from Lizzi.

Hunt, however, had already cut her deal with prosecutors, pleading guilty on August 15, 1992, to a single count of robbery—taking Lizzi's gold card—and received an automatic 15-year prison sentence. Rippo was brought to trial, charged with murdering Jacobson and Lizzi, in March 1996. Rippo's long criminal background was profiled, one that dated back into the 1970s and included shoplifting, burglary and assault. He stole cameras and rifles and was caught and sent to the Spring Mountain Youth Camp.

Shortly after his release from this juvenile detention camp, Rippo, on January 16, 1982, broke into the Las Vegas apartment of a 24-year-old woman who was then asleep in bed. She awoke to see Rippo sitting atop her. He held a knife to her throat as he tried to rape her but he was unable to perform. Frustrated, he assaulted her with a fountain pen and then beat her savagely before fleeing.

The woman had recognized Rippo as a teenager whom she had seen earlier inside the complex's hot tub and she reported him to police. As she later testified: "He choked me with a coat hanger and threatened to kill me if I told anyone." Rippo was convicted of the attempted rape and sent to prison for eight years. Released, Rippo was still on parole for this crime when he killed Jacobson and Lizzi.

Diana Hunt testified against Rippo at his trial, as did the victim of his 1982 sexual assault. Evidence against the defendant was strong. He was convicted of the murders after a six-week trial and, on March 14, 1996, he was sentenced to death by lethal injection.

---

**Risner, Joe**, See: **Cornett, Natasha**.

---

**Rivera, Juan A.**, 1972- , U.S., mur. On August 17, 1992, 11-year-old Holly Staker was baby-sitting a 5-year-old boy and an infant in an apartment in North Waukegan, Illinois. A neighbor, Juan Rivera, entered the apartment and stabbed Staker twenty-seven times, killing her before fleeing (the children she was baby-sitting remained unharmed). Waukegan police, who had reports that Rivera had been seen entering the apartment on the night of the killing, picked up Rivera. Ten weeks after the slaying, on October 30, 1992, following an extensive interrogation, Rivera confessed to killing Staker.

Rivera broke down crying and said Staker invited him into the apartment to have sex, which turned into a struggle. He said he grabbed a kitchen knife and stabbed her repeatedly. He said he then fled, returning home, where he showered and got rid of his bloodstained clothes. He said he was high on cocaine when he killed the girl.

Other than Rivera's confession, prosecutors had very little evidence, but they managed to get a conviction in 1993 and Rivera was sentenced to prison for life. In 1996, however, an Illinois Appellate Court ordered a retrial for Rivera, saying that the presiding judge in the 1993 trial had made four minor errors. A new trial in 1998 came to the same results. Rivera was again convicted and resentenced to life in prison. Holly Staker's twin sister, 17-year-old Heather Staker, was present at the last sentencing. As she left the courtroom she said of Rivera, "He is evil." She added, "I'm alone now ... he took half of me away."

---

**Rivera Leyva, Alvarez Oscar**, ? - , Mex., mur. Teacher and opposition politician Alvarez Oscar Rivera Leyva was giving a speech against the current Mexican regime in Caclutla, a small town in the province of Guerrero, on April 19, 1998. Immediately after he finished his speech, Rivera Leyva was shot to death by a young man who simply walked up to him and fired a bullet into his head. Although police later reported that several suspects had been taken into custody, the killer was not identified at this writing.

---

**Rizzitello, Michael Anthony**, 1927- , and **Grosso, Joseph Angelo**, 1943- , U.S., consp.-attempt. mur. An alleged underboss of the Milano crime family in Los Angeles, 62-year-old Michael Anthony Rizzitello, unsuccessfully attempted to take control of a topless Santa Ana, California, bar, the Mustang Club. When Rizzitello and Joseph Angelo Grosso later went to dinner with club owner William Carroll, 58, Rizzitello shot the proprietor three times in the head. Carroll, who survived the murder attempt, was left blinded. On November 15,

1989, Grosso, who held Carroll down during the shooting, was convicted of attempted murder, mayhem, and conspiracy to commit murder. Grosso, 46, was sentenced by a Santa Ana Superior Court judge to twenty-six years to life imprisonment. On February 7, 1990, Rizzitello was found guilty of conspiracy to commit first-degree murder. He was sentenced to thirty-three years to life in prison.

---

**Rizzo, Todd**, 1979- , U.S., mur. Obsessed with serial killers, 18-year-old Todd Rizzo of Waterbury, Connecticut, randomly picked out 13-year-old Stanley Edwards to murder as Edwards rode past Rizzo's home on the evening of September 30, 1997. Rizzo hailed the boy, who knew him slightly when Rizzo worked at a local video store. Rizzo had served in the Marine Corps but had been discharged after only one year.

Inviting Edwards to hunt for snakes, Rizzo went to his car and retrieved a flashlight. As he did so, he also grabbed a three-pound sledgehammer. Asking the boy to hold the light on the ground, Rizzo then repeatedly hit Edwards with the hammer until he was dead. He then took the body and dumped it in a rural area, but his car was identified and so was Rizzo by a woman living in the area.

When police arrested Rizzo, he stated, "I decided I wanted to try and kill him for no good reason and get away with it." Convicted of first-degree murder in 1998, Rizzo awaits sentencing at this writing.

---

**Roark, Dennis**, 1963- , U.S., mur. An unemployed Gary, Indiana, man with an I.Q. of seventy-two stabbed to death his live-in girlfriend, her two infant children, and their grandmother in a vicious early-morning attack on February 3, 1989, in Hammond. It was the worst multiple homicide in that city's history. Dennis Roark, described by court-appointed psychiatrists as a "borderline mental defective," was obsessed with his live-in girlfriend, 19-year-old Mary Waggoner, despite her fervent wish to break off their relationship. Hammond police were frequently summoned to the Waggoner residence to quell domestic quarrels between Waggoner and the hot-tempered Roark.

Police were called to the area at 6:15 a.m. on February 3, when a neighbor noticed a man in bloodstained clothing walking away from the home. By the time the police arrived on the scene, the house was in flames and Roark was gone. The bodies of 61-year-old Betty Waggoner, her daughter Mary, and the two children, Dennis and Elizabeth, twenty months and four months old, respectively, were pulled out of the smoldering house, which smelled of gasoline. Meanwhile, Roark hitchhiked to Gary, where police found him hiding at a friend's home.

The murder trial of Dennis Roark began at the Lake County Courthouse in Crown Point, Indiana, in September 1989. Prosecutor Jack Crawford announced he would seek the death penalty against Roark. Alex Woloshansky, the attorney assigned to defend Roark, argued that the man's actions were due to a weakness of mind. Roark was convicted of four counts of murder on September 28, and on October 17, the 26-year-old defendant was sentenced to die in the electric chair.

---

**Robards, Dorothy Marie**, 1977- , U.S., mur. A hard-working letter carrier in the Fort Worth, Texas, area, 38-year-old Steven Robards had won custody of his daughter, Dorothy Marie Robards, in a divorce. He proved to be a kind and loving father who provided well for his teenage daughter. On February 17, 1993, Robards and his 16-year-old daughter went to a Mexican fast-food restaurant and bought lunch. Robards ordered a burrito and a side order of refried beans. His daughter ordered a soft taco.

When Robards later left to buy some soft drinks, Dorothy Marie Robards took out some lethal barium and mixed this in with her father's refried beans. Following dinner, Robards began to complain of stomach pains. His daughter gave him an anti-acid tablet, and later some Imodium. He continued to grow worse, vomiting and suffering from diarrhea. Within hours he felt clammy and was in intense pain. Weak, trembling and nauseated, Robards found it difficult to breathe. He complained of not being able to swallow and was choking on his own saliva.

Robards' fiancee, who lived nearby and was summoned by Dorothy Robards, thought Robards was having a heart attack and called paramedics. He was rushed to a hospital and died that night. A medical examiner determined that Robards suffered from heart disease and that he had died of natural causes.

Dorothy Robards went to live with relatives. In February 1994, however, police were contacted by a school counselor who told them that a student had been told by Dorothy Robards that she had killed her father, poisoned him with barium, which she had taken from her chemistry class. Police had the Tarrant County Medical Examiner's Office re-examine Robards' blood samples which showed barium—twenty-eight times the amount it would take to kill a normal human being.

The chemical found was barium acetate, a silvery metallic chemical used as a standard ingredient in bleach, paint pigment, hydrogen peroxide and rat poison. An officer of the medical department explained that barium was rarely used in poison murders because it was so hard to obtain. Dorothy Robards had obtained barium acetate from her chemistry class, where small doses were being employed in experiments. She was fascinated when her teacher told the class how dangerous barium acetate could be.

Arrested and charged with her father's murder, Dorothy Robards admitted poisoning his food, saying that she was at the time a confused teenager who wanted to be with her mother, even though she admitted that she loved her father, who was kind to her and never abused her. "I just wanted to be with my mom so bad that I would do anything to be with her."

Even though she was 16 at the time of the murder, Robards was tried as an adult. At her 1996 trial, she stated that she did not really intend to kill her father with poison, only to make him sick. "I never thought anything through. I didn't realize what I was doing." Prosecutors pointed out that the killing was no mistake, but a long-planned, premeditated murder. They also stated that Robards had an abiding passion to become a pathologist and that she was abnormally fascinated with how people die. A jury of four women and eight men convicted Robards and she was sentenced to 28 years in prison.

**Robbins, Bryan J.**, See: **Sanders, Michael Martin.**

**Roberts, Angelo**, 1969-1995, U.S., weap. viol.-drugs. The ambitious leader of the Four Corner Hustlers street gang in Chicago, Angelo Roberts grew rich through peddling drugs, but his operations were regularly impeded by stepped-up police raids and arrests. So incensed was Roberts with the police that he set up a meeting in 1994 with an arms dealer and arranged to purchase machine guns and antitank rocket launchers. When asked by the arms dealer why he wanted these weapons, Roberts told him that he intended to get rid of several unruly members of his gang and then turn the weapons on the Chicago police. Roberts went on to state that as soon as he got his hands on the rocket launcher, he would blow up the Chicago police station at 3151 West Harrison Street, the very headquarters that had been causing his drug operations so many problems.

The gang leader never received the heavy weapons. The arms dealer was a government informant who took the tale to the police and soon an all-points bulletin was issued for Roberts' arrest, along with several other gang members. The search for Roberts ended, however, when his bullet-riddled body was found in the trunk of a car on January 16, 1995. Detectives theorized that he had been killed by fellow gang members who wanted no part in an all-out war with the Chicago Police Department.

**Roberts, John H. Jr.**, prom. 1989, U.S., fraud. Due to widespread fraud and corruption, the U.S. savings and loan industry came under intense scrutiny in the 1980s as one after another institution closed its doors. On July 5, 1989, as President George Bush requested extra funding from Congress for the Justice Department to investigate savings and loan fraud, John H. Roberts, Jr., former president and owner of the Summit Savings Association of Dallas, Texas, pleaded guilty to fraud charges.

In 1984, Roberts used a "nominee borrower" in order to borrow $4.5 million from his own institution. However, Summit was unable to provide more than $1 million, so Roberts sent his borrower to another Dallas savings and loan for the remaining $3 million. He eventually repaid the second savings and loan, but not Summit, and used the money to purchase an airplane for his own use.

Roberts agreed to cooperate with federal prosecutors in an investigation of former officers of another Texas savings and loan association, where he had been a borrower. In January 1990, Roberts pleaded guilty to two charges and was sentenced to five years in federal prison and fined $15,000.

**Robin, Lee**, 1958- , U.S., mur. Twenty-nine-year-old Dr. Lee Robin of Palatine, Illinois, tried to kill himself with sleeping pills in early August 1988. A week after his suicide attempt, he began thinking that he was the devil and that God was going to punish him, or that people were coming to beat him to death. On August 13, he hit his 28-year-old wife, Annette, with an ax more than twenty times, then drowned his infant daughter, Denise, in the bathtub. He was found unfit for trial later that month because he was suffering from severe depression and was ordered to undergo psychiatric treatment until he was well enough to aid his attorney in his defense.

At his trial in September 1989, Palatine police testified that Robin told them on the day of the murders that he had been miserable ever since he was born on Friday the 13th. (August 13 fell on a Saturday in 1988.) Robin admitted he did not know why he killed his wife, but murdered their daughter afterward because she should not have to grow up without a mother. Cook County Criminal Court Judge James Bailey found, based on the testimony of three mental health experts, that Robin was not guilty due to legal insanity at the time of the killings. Robin was involuntarily committed to the Elgin, Illinois, Mental Health Center.

---

**Robinson, Bearling**, 1976- , U.S., mur. Alderman Robert Shaw of Chicago's 9th Ward had fought violence and drugs in his streets all his life. Yet these very social evils claimed his own son, 27-year-old John Shaw, on the night of January 4, 1997. Shaw, a cable repairman, helped a friend who was attacked after winning in a dice game. One of those Shaw drove away with his fists was Bearling Robinson, a resident of DeKalb, Illinois. When both young men met later that night, Shaw drew a .38-caliber handgun from his waistband and brandished the weapon at Robinson, telling him that he could have shot him earlier if he had wanted. He then put the gun back into his waistband and began walking away.

Robinson, a college student, then pulled his own gun and shot Shaw three times. Shaw begged one of his friends to take him to a hospital, saying that he knew he was mortally wounded and did not want to die in the street. He died a short time later at a hospital. Robinson was charged with the killing and was convicted on July 23, 1998. Cook County Circuit Court Judge Bertina Lampkin sentenced Robinson to thirty-two years in prison on August 27, 1998. Alderman Shaw stood in the court listening to the sentence and said, "It brings closure to this part of it. The pain and suffering will never be closed."

---

**Robinson, Calvin**, 1942- , U.S., drugs. On June 9, 1989, Calvin Robinson, a 47-year-old San Francisco tugboat pilot, was fined $4 million and sentenced to life in prison without parole after being convicted of trying to smuggle fifty-six tons of hashish and marijuana through the Golden Gate bridge. Robinson acted as his own lawyer during the trial.

---

**Robinson, Carl,** 1959- , U.S., drugs. Carl Robinson, the first person convicted in Los Angeles under the nationwide Schoolyard Law Program, a law that mandates heavier sentences for those convicted of selling drugs within 1,000 feet of a school, was sentenced to fourteen years in prison on January 26,1989. Robinson, 30, alleged by prosecutors to be a member of the Los Angeles street gang known as the East Coast Crips, was convicted of selling a PCP-dipped cigarette to undercover police officers near the Bethune Junior High School in South Los Angeles. The Schoolyard Law Program went into effect in October 1986.

---

**Robinson, Harvey**, 1974- , U.S., burg.-rape-rob.-attempt. mur.-mur. The city of Allentown, Pennsylvania, underwent a reign of terror in 1992-1993 when a serial burglar-rapist-killer stalked its citizens. The first attack came on the night of August 9, 1992, when Joan Mary Burghardt, a 29-year-old woman with mental problems, was brutally attacked and bludgeoned to death with a heavy instrument, her killer striking her more than thirty times on the head.

Police could find no fingerprints inside the victim's first-floor apartment, but they did discover semen left at the scene and sent it off for DNA analysis. Ten months later in the pre-dawn hours of June 20, 1993, 13-year-old Charlotte Schmoyer, a bright and happy high school freshman who was delivering the town paper, the Allentown *Morning Call*, suddenly vanished.

Schmoyer's customers found the shopping cart Schmoyer used to deliver her papers on the sidewalk. It was half full of papers and other papers were scattered on the ground. So too was Schmoyer's Walkman and earphones, which had been crushed. Customers called the newspaper and the *Call* contacted police. Officers began searching for the missing girl and found her later that day in thick underbrush near the Allentown reservoir. The girl had been stabbed twenty-two times. Police would not confirm that she had been sexually attacked before being murdered.

The *Call* posted a reward of $10,000 for the arrest and conviction of the killer. A witness came forward to tell police that he had seen a medium blue four-door subcompact car with heavy damage to the passenger side about 6:30 a.m. on the morning of the murder, about an hour after Schmoyer disappeared, near Allentown's East Side reservoir, but he did not get a good look at the driver.

Police were still following this lead when, on June 30, 1993, a man entered an apartment on Maxwell Street that was occupied by a woman and her 5-year-old daughter. The woman was asleep on the couch in the living room. The intruder slipped into the little girl's room and raped her, then fled when he apparently heard a noise. Forensic specialists were able to capture some semen left by the attacker, but no fingerprints were in evidence.

A little more than a week later, the same rapist-killer struck again, attacking a woman on her front lawn, raping and beating her. The woman was unconscious when the attacker fled. Police guessed that the attacker believed he had killed his victim. A few nights later, the attacker returned to break into the home of the rape victim but she was not at home at the time. Police discovered that the intruder had taken a handgun along with other items in his burglary of the woman's home.

On July 14, 1993, the brazen rapist-killer raped and murdered 47-year-old Jessica Fortney. The woman had been beaten repeatedly and then strangled to death. Again no fingerprints were found, but semen was discovered, as in all the other attacks, and was sent on for DNA analysis.

Allentown police held all-night strategy meetings and concluded that they not only had a determined serial rapist-killer stalking citizens, but that he was so egotistical that he seemed to be challenging lawmen to catch him. He had proved this by returning to the home of his rape victim to steal the woman's gun. Detectives then concluded that the killer would return a second time to the same address, that he intended to kill the woman with her own gun to prevent her from ever identifying him.

Police decided to stake out the woman's home. On the night of July 31, 1993, Officer Brian Lewis was on duty inside the home when a man wearing a black hat and gloves broke into the house, entering through a window. Lewis shouted: "Halt—put up your hands." The burglar answered with gunfire. Lewis fired back. The wild shootout smashed glass items inside the house and bullets from the intruder's gun plowed into walls. The burglar then ran for a deadbolted door with a glass top and smashed through it to freedom. Lewis realized that the burglar had either been hit by one of his bullets or had been cut by the glass broken on the door, since the fugitive left a trail of blood leading from the house.

A short time later police received a call from a hospital saying that they had just received a patient with many cuts on his arms and legs. Officers went to the hospital and there met 19-year-old Harvey Robinson, a surly, glaring young man who was immediately confronted with the fact that the gun he had used to shoot at Officer Lewis was the same one stolen from the woman's house earlier. Robinson snorted and said that he was merely trying to return the gun.

A check of Robinson's address showed that he lived in east Allentown, close to where all the rapes and murders had occurred. Further, his old light blue Ford Tempo had considerable damage to its passenger side, just as described by the witness who saw a man speeding away from the site where Charlotte Schmoyer's body had been found.

Charged with the two rapes and three murders, Robinson pleaded not guilty. His defense attorney told a jury that prosecutors had no evidence to prove their charges, no fingerprints, no murder weapons, no eyewitnesses. Prosecutors did have evidence, however. The 5-year-old child attacked by Robinson identified him as the man who had invaded her home. So did the woman he raped and had left for dead. Worse for Robinson, the DNA evidence that was analyzed definitely put him at those sites. He was found guilty and was given three death sentences for the three murders he committed. Another 157 years was added to these sentences for the rapes. Robinson is currently on Pennsylvania's Death Row and awaits execution at this writing.

---

**Robinson, Johnny Ray,** 1959- , U.S., mur. New York City police officer Anthony McLean, while investigating reports of a lost child at the Tilden public housing project in the crime-ridden Brooklyn, New York, neighborhood of Brownsville on April 13, 1988, was accosted by crack dealer Johnny Ray Robinson. A four-year veteran of the force, McLean, 27, assigned to the housing police detail, was killed by shots to his chest and neck as he entered a stairwell inside the complex.

Robinson, arrested on the strength of eyewitness testimony given to police, was identified as a member of the Brooklyn drug gang led by Samuel "Baby Sam" Edmondson. While awaiting trial, Robinson killed a rival drug dealer at the Rikers Men's House of Detention on July 14, 1989. Christopher "Jughead" Williams was stabbed to death in what authorities labeled as a gang-related incident. Robinson was immediately transferred to the Brooklyn House of Detention.

The accused police killer was tried in September 1989 at the Brooklyn Supreme Court. Robinson was found guilty of murder and was sentenced to twenty-five years to life in prison by Justice Robert Kreindler on October 24, 1989. Prosecutor Kenneth Taub urged the judge to show no leniency toward the defendant after producing a list of witnesses and relatives targeted for death by Robinson and his friends. Defense lawyer Howard Herman strenuously objected to the prosecution's case, calling it a "triumph by ambush." He accused the police of "torturing, beating, and assaulting" prosecution witnesses who implicated Robinson.

---

**Robinson, Noah,** 1944- , U.S., attempt. mur. The half-brother of the Reverend Jesse Jackson was sentenced to serve the maximum penalty of ten years in prison after being found guilty of attempted murder by a jury in Greenville, South Carolina, on January 28, 1989. Robinson and Jackson shared the same father but grew up in separate households in Greenville. According to press reports, their relationship was "strained."

Noah Robinson, a millionaire businessman in Chicago, owned and operated a construction firm and several Wendy's fast-food restaurants. He also had extensive ties to the powerful El Rukn street gang, active in Chicago for many years. On January 3, 1986, LeRoy "Hambone" Barber, a former employee of Robinson's, was shot to death in a Greenville phone booth. The five assassins, believed to be El Rukns, were allegedly hired by Robinson and paid $10,000 to carry out the gangland murder. Barber's death was witnessed by Janice Denise Rosemond, a Greenville woman who agreed to appear as a federal witness against Robinson. In an effort to silence Rosemond, Robinson allegedly hired El Rukn gang member Freddy Sweeny to kill her before she could take the stand. Janice Rosemond was stabbed by a knife-wielding assailant but survived to testify. Three members of the gang also testified that they were a part of the five-man hit team sent by imprisoned El Rukn chieftain Jeff Fort to shoot Barber. On January 28, 1989, the 45-year-old Robinson was sentenced to prison for ten years for the attempted murder of the prosecution witness. Circuit Court Judge James Moore declared a mistrial in the Barber case after the jury failed to agree on a verdict.

Robinson was freed on bond, pending an appeal with the high court of South Carolina. His troubles were far from over, however. On October 27, a federal grand jury in Chicago handed down a fifty-six-count indictment against Robinson, charging him with "skimming" the profits from three Wendy's restaurants he controlled. Between 1984 and 1989, Robinson and his employees were alleged to have routinely closed down the cash registers an average of six hours a day in order to conceal $650,000 in receipts. Additionally, the indictment identified Robinson as an intermediary in narcotics deals. Two of his brothers, George and John, were also named, in separate racketeering, mail, and wire fraud counts. The charges were handed down on the strength of government wiretaps and El Rukn witnesses who linked Robinson to another El Rukn plot, the assassination of Robert Aulston, a friend of former Chicago mayor Eugene Sawyer. Aulston, a former business partner of Robinson, had fallen out of favor. On October 30, U.S. Magistrate Elaine Bucklo ordered Robinson held without bond at the Metropolitan Correctional Center pending trial. Robinson's attorneys argued that the judge's decision was tantamount to a five-year prison sentence, since it would take about that long for the case to be prepared and tried.

---

**Rochester (New York) Serial Killings,** 1988-1989, U.S., (unsolv.) mur. The body of a young woman was discovered washed up on the shores of Lake Ontario near Sodus Point, New York, on the morning of December 1, 1989. Police did not identify the woman and would not comment on whether they believed her death was related to a string of twelve unsolved deaths of women in the Rochester, New York, area over the previous two years. The corpse was unclothed, like many of the other bodies found since March 1988. Many of the cases had characteristics in common. Most of the women were prostitutes, and at least ten of these spent much time near Lake and Lyell avenues, areas notorious for prostitution in Rochester. Most of the victims were drug addicts. At least six of the victims were found within walking distance from where they lived or worked. Nearly all had arrest records and were estranged from their families. The Monroe County medical examiner ruled seven of the deaths homicides and said that of those, four were suffocated, one was shot, and two were beaten to death. The cause of death in four of the other cases was not determined. One victim died after being hit by a car. The city police believe that as many as three people may have been responsible for the killings, but a single person may have committed as many as five of the murders,

The victims were black, white, and Hispanic, and ranged in age from 22 to 46. Identified victims included Kimberly D. Logan, 30; June Stotts, 29; Patricia Ives, 25; Viola Brown, 22; Rosalie Oppel, 46; Maria Welch, 22; Linda Lee Hymes, 35; Anna Marie Steffen, 27; Elizabeth A. Gibsons, 29; Dorothy M. Blackburn, 27; and Nicola A. Gursley, 24.

Rochester police, working in conjunction with the FBI and their Violent Criminal Apprehension Program, assembled a chilling psychological profile of the killer after carefully reviewing other serial murders across the country, including those committed by Ted Bundy, Kenneth A. Bianchi, Randy Kraft, and the Green River Killer. In each case, there were common traits. "Most are grown up in body, but they're like emotional 12-year-olds," explained Rochester psychiatrist Dr. Russell Barton. "They are inconsiderate and demanding. But they put on a good show. They con people." According to police chief Terry Mangin of Spokane, Washington, who had tracked the Green River killer for years, this type of murderer does not just quit. "Psychologists and psychiatrists say there's little or no known track record for rehabilitation or retirement on their part," said Mangin. "There's no evidence that killers just sort of retire."

---

**Rockwell International Corp.,** prom. 1989, U.S., consp.-fraud. In 1982, a malfunction developed in the $1.2 billion NAVSTAR satellite navigation system, developed for the U.S. Air Force by Rockwell International Corp. Rockwell billed the Air Force $500,000 to correct the system, and the company was also secretly reimbursed by a subcontractor. Company auditors discovered the duplicity and informed the government, placing the blame on two employees, 46-year-old Robert L. Zavodnik and his supervisor, Donald H. Carter, 60. On January 18,1989, at the U.S. District Court in Los Angeles before Judge Consuelo B. Marshall, representatives of Rockwell entered conditionally guilty pleas for fraud and conspiracy in the attempted cover-up. On March 6, the giant defense contractor was fined a record $5.5 million and ordered to pay $446,248 in restitution. The company was also placed on five years probation. In earlier trials, Zavodnik, who was fired from his job in October 1986, pleaded guilty to the fraud and agreed to testify against Carter. Carter was acquitted of wrongdoing, but was later forced to leave the company.

---

**Rodriguez, David,** 1971- , U.S., mur. The worried mother of 19-year old Stephanie Martinez reported her daughter missing on May 6, 1995, after she failed to appear in her Port Lavaca, Texas, home. Police in nearby Victoria, Texas, began searching for the missing woman and later found her bones in a park. She had been killed. Her common-law husband, David Rodriguez, with whom Martinez had had a son, was also missing, and Victoria police began searching for him.

More than six months later, on December 22, 1995, a handsome young man with considerable charm approached two women who were eating hamburgers at a fast-food restaurant in Austin, Texas. One of the women, 41-year-old Rosita Becerra, left with the young man and was not seen again. Her body was found floating in Town Lake inside Austin by fishermen. Becerra, like Martinez before her, had been murdered, her killer striking her so many times that he had knocked the right eye out of its socket.

David Rodriguez was identified as the young man with whom Becerra had gone off. He was then wanted on auto theft and other charges. Police tracked him down to the home of a cousin in Austin. Brought in for questioning, Rodriguez quickly broke down and admitted murdering Martinez and Becerra. On June 5, 1996, after pleading guilty to killing Becerra, Rodriguez was sentenced to prison for life. The next day he pleaded guilty to having murdered Martinez and received a second life sentence, both life sentences to be served concurrently. He would be eligible for parole in forty years.

---

**Rodriguez, Francisco,** 1967- , U.S., drugs-mur. Calling him a "scourge on society," Judge Ronald J. Aiello of the State Supreme Court of New York sentenced convicted killer Francisco Rodriguez to thirty-seven and a half years to life in prison on February 15, 1989. Prior to his conviction for the murder of New York police officer Robert Venable, Rodriguez had been arrested nine times on charges ranging from larceny to auto theft. Just forty-two days before the Venable shooting, the 22-

year-old Brooklyn crack dealer had been granted his parole.

On September 22, 1987, Venable and six other transit policemen were responding to call made by a resident of Pitkin Avenue in Brooklyn about a gunman in the neighborhood. Venable was searching the area when Rodriguez and another man emerged from a building and began shooting. The 35-year-old police officer was struck in the head with a bullet from a 9-mm semi-automatic pistol and died instantly. Rodriguez fled into the building after being struck by two police bullets. He was arrested in a third-floor apartment where police officers found a quantity of crack and some handguns. Judge Aiello handed Rodriguez a twenty-five years to life sentence for Venable's killing, and a twelve-and-a-half year sentence for drug possession. The defendant will not be eligible for parole until he has passed his 60th birthday. "You put your poison, your drugs, on the streets and life has become cheap," Aiello said. The courtroom was packed with transit police officers and the relatives of the victim. After hearing the sentence they broke out into spontaneous applause.

---

**Rodriguez, Gilberto José,** See: **Medellin Cartel.**

---

**Rodriguez Gacha, José Gonzalo** (AKA: El Mexicano), 1947-1989, Col., drugs. According to a report in the U.S. business magazine *Forbes*, Colombian drug trafficker José Gonzalo Rodriguez Gacha was one of a handful of people in the world worth a billion dollars. The former pig farmer from Pacho, Colombia, who accumulated untold riches, owned eighty ranches, commercial property in large Colombian cities, a radio station, a bus company, and a popular discotheque. Rodriguez Gacha was also listed as an owner of the Los Millonarios professional soccer team, and a high-rise building in Bogota, which contained his investment company. In July 1988, Gonzalo Rodriguez Gacha and six other drug traffickers were indicted in absentia by a federal grand jury in Miami and charged with importing 1,350 pounds of cocaine into the U.S.

Described by U.S. authorities as the number two man in the Medellin drug cartel, then the most dangerous drug-running organized crime operation in the world, Rodriguez Gacha and his cohorts operated with impunity until Colombian president Virgilio Barco announced a general crackdown against the cartel leaders following the assassination of presidential candidate Luis Carlos Gálan Sarmiento on August 18, 1989. In the next few months, Barco demonstrated his commitment to ending the drug barons' reign of terror in Colombia by confiscating the estates of Rodriguez Gacha, Pablo Escobar Gaviria, and Jorge Luis Ochoa, the founders of the cartel. The U.S. Justice Department presented a "most wanted" list of drug traffickers to Colombian officials. Prominent on this list was the name of José Gonzalo Rodriguez Gacha, who suffered the greatest financial losses as a result of the government crackdown. In August, the police seized control of the Bogota office center, where they impounded the records of Coordinadora Comercial Imnitada, the drug gangster's holding company, which controlled fifty other firms.

The government posted a $625,000 reward for his cap-

ture, but Rodriguez Gacha somehow managed to remain one step ahead of the law. Attempts to nab him at his lavish estate in Pacho or other locales around the country inevitably failed when paid informants and corrupt law enforcement officers tipped him off in advance. "All levels of the military and the police are riddled with informants," said one U.S. military official.

President Barco's unwillingness to compromise with the leaders of the cartel was met with disapproval by a large segment of the Colombian population who favored a national referendum on the drug war. There were fears raised that Rodriguez Gacha was secretly providing funds to start up his own pro-drug political party. Several candidates who were allied to the cartel were elected to public office in five towns and in the Magdalena Valley. Rodriguez Gacha and Escobar Gaviria were accused of orchestrating two major attacks on the Colombian government. On November 27, 1989, an Avianca Airlines jet exploded in mid-air just outside Bogota, killing the 107 people on board. On December 8, a bomb exploded at the federal investigative police headquarters in downtown Bogota, killing sixty-three people and injuring an additional 1,000. This and other similar terrorist attacks were believed to be the work of the Medellin Cartel, in which Rodriguez Gacha figured prominently. Public opinion began to turn against the drug trafficker following his terrorist acts.

The government was desperate to imprison the cocaine baron and the national police set an intricate trap for Rodriguez Gacha near Covenas, a Caribbean port 360 miles north of Bogota. First, in early December, a judge freed Freddy Rodriguez Celades, the gangster's 17-year-old son, who had been jailed for three months for various drug offenses. A handpicked team of police officers trailed the youth to his father, who was in a rural area between the towns of Tolil and Covenas. Cornered by the national police on December 15, Rodriguez Gacha and his guards attempted to shoot it out. Rodriguez Gacha, his son Freddy, and fifteen other people were killed in the gun battle. "The operation to locate Rodriguez Gacha was an intelligence operation of great care," General Carlos Arturo Casadiego, assistant director of the national police, said. Upon hearing the news, President George Bush called Barco to express his congratulations to the Colombian police. See: **Extraditables**; **Medellin Cartel**.

---

**Rodriguez, Julio,** See: **DeJesus, Jose M.**

---

**Rodriguez Orjela, Miguel Angel,** See: **Medellin Cartel.**

---

**Rodriguez Pineda, Eduardo,** 1972-, U.S., mur. Eduardo Rodriguez Pineda was sentenced on October 14, 1989, to thirty years in jail after he was convicted of shooting Rio Grande river rafter Michael Heffley on November 19, 1988. Pineda, 17, was one of four people who stood on the Mexican side and shot across the border. In accordance with international law, he was tried in the U.S., in Texas. (Editor's note: Details about

Michael Heffley's death can be found under his name in the *Encyclopedia of World Crime*, Vol. II.)

---

**Roeder, Michaela**, 1958- , Ger., attempt. mansl.-mansl. Between 1984 and 1986, seventeen elderly patients at a hospital in Wuppertal, West Germany, died after being given a lethal injection. Police arrested Michaela Roeder, a nurse who admitted the killings, but claimed they were acts of compassion. Nicknamed the "angel of death," Roeder was tried for six counts of manslaughter, as well as attempted manslaughter and mercy killing. Due to lack of evidence, eleven other charges were dropped. The prosecution sought life imprisonment, but on September 11, 1989, after an eight-month trial, Roeder was found guilty on all counts and sentenced to eleven years in prison.

---

**Rogers, Michael**, 1970- , and **Rogers, Angeline**, 1969- , U.S., felon. child abuse. An 11-year-old boy walking without a coat and barefoot over icy roads to the police station in Brillion, Wisconsin, on November 17, 1997, staggered into the precinct headquarters to beg officers to save his sister from the torture inflicted upon her by his parents, Michael and Angeline Rogers. The crying boy told lawmen that he and his four siblings had been terribly beaten by his parents and that his 7-year-old sister had been locked in a dog cage.

Police responded by sending officers to the Rogers address where they, indeed, found the girl locked in the cage in a cold, dark basement. She had been confined in this cage night after night without food, heat, or bathroom privileges. Michael and Angeline Rogers were arrested and charged with several counts of felony child abuse. The children were placed in foster homes as the couple awaited trial.

Before her trial, Angeline Rogers admitted her guilt, saying that had been "overwhelmed" by her daughter's refusal to cooperate and had allowed her husband Michael to beat the children and lock up her 7-year-old daughter in a dog cage. Both Michael and Angeline Rogers were convicted of felony child abuse and faced up to forty years in prison. Then, incredibly, Judge Steven Weinke, in a Chilton, Wisconsin, court, sentenced the couple only to a year, to be served in the county jail on September 11, 1998. Further, Weinke decreed that the couple should be allowed to leave the jail for up to sixty hours a week to go to work and to seek counseling.

The leniency Weinke showed to two beasts, who have no right to call themselves parents, in this author's opinion, was a miscarriage of justice. In not sending these vicious child abusers to prison, Weinke sent the wrong message to abusers everywhere. If he were forced to cram himself into a small dog cage and be compelled to sleep hungry every night in his own excrement, he might better realize the gravity of his irresponsible sentence. Weinke should be removed from the bench.

---

**Rogers, Sharon Lee**, prom. 1989, U.S., (unsolv.) bomb.-terr. A pipe bomb concealed inside a van belonging to Sharon Lee Rogers, wife of U.S. Navy captain Will C. Rogers III, ex-

ploded on a crowded San Diego thoroughfare on March 10, 1989, as she escaped from the vehicle just seconds before it caught fire. San Diego police and FBI officials believed the bomb was planted by a pro-Iranian terrorist group seeking to avenge the July 3 downing of an Airbus A300 in the Persian Gulf. Captain Rogers, piloting the guided missile cruiser *U.S.S. Vincennes*, mistakenly ordered the Iranian jet shot down after fearing that his ship was under aerial attack from an F-14 fighter plane. A total of 293 people died in the Gulf explosion. Rogers and his officers were cleared of any wrongdoing by a naval board of inquiry. Later that month, his wife complained of receiving threatening calls from a man with a Middle Eastern accent. "Are you the wife of the murderer?" the caller asked her, just before she hung up.

According to a spokesman from the FBI, the van explosion was the first episode of domestic terrorism since 1983. According to Oliver "Buck" Revell, assistant director of the FBI, a "hard-core" group of 200 to 300 Iranians belonging to the Revolutionary Guards (a Beirut-based anti-U.S. terrorist group) had slipped into the country as students.

In the wake of the bombing incident, the Rogers were taken into protective custody. The La Jolla Country Day School where Mrs. Rogers had taught fourth grade, bought out her contract for the following year, fearing other terrorist acts against her.

---

**Rojas, Luis Kevin**, 1976- , U.S., mur. (wrong. convict.) Two groups of arguing teenagers fell to a shoving match on lower Broadway, near Waverly Place, in Manhattan, New York, at 2 a.m. on November 18, 1990. A teenager wearing a Day-Glo orange jacket pulled a gun and fired it into the air. The other group of teenagers began to run off as this youth handed the gun to a friend wearing a green jacket. This youth fired at the fleeing teenagers and his fire wounded 17-year-old Rudy Quesada in the leg. Another bullet slammed into the neck of 19-year-old Javier Bueno, and he died three weeks later.

The shooter in the green jacket was never found, but the boy wearing the orange Day-Glo jacket was located and arrested. He was 18-year-old Luis Kevin Rojas, who was convicted in 1991 of second-degree murder and given a 15-year to life sentence. The conviction was achieved primarily through the testimony of several of the teenagers who had fled the scene, all saying that Rojas had been the man in the Day-Glo jacket who had handed off the gun to the shooter.

Police officers also testified that they picked up Rojas, a native of Union City, New Jersey, a few minutes after the shooting at a PATH station (a rapid transit rail system running between New York and New Jersey) at West Ninth Street. He was wearing a Day-Glo jacket, only the orange side had been reversed. Rojas, when police questioned him, said that he had reversed his jacket and was wearing the burgundy side outward so that he would not get the jacket dirty.

Rojas had insisted that he was innocent and had been having dinner with a friend at the time of the shooting. His attorney, David Fronefield, put up a weak defense and was later criticized for ineptitude by an appellate court. A New Jersey paper interviewed one of Rojas' teachers who said that Rojas' involvement with a murder was utterly "impossible," and went on to describe a gentle and good student who had no criminal background and had never been involved in any violence.

Reading this article, Priscilla Read Chenoweth, a 68-year-old widow and retired lawyer, came to believe that Rojas had been wrongly convicted. She began to investigate the case, asking lawyers and retired detectives to help her in proving that Rojas was innocent. It was a long and arduous crusade that took several years. Meanwhile, she met Rojas in prison and when his mother died, she became his surrogate mother. He sent her cards on Mother's Day and she told him to cut his hair and carried a sport coat in her briefcase for him to wear in court.

Chenoweth began with contacting a retired Manhattan detective named Dennis O'Sullivan, who specialized in solving unsolved cases. O'Sullivan became so involved with the Rojas case that he put up his own house to provide bail for Rojas when he was awarded a new trial. Before that happened, Chenoweth and O'Sullivan enlisted the aid of another retired police officer, Mike O'Connor, who later tracked down John Apel, a PATH police sergeant. Apel recalled with certainty that he watched Rojas just miss a train as it left the station, and, research later determined that that train departed the station at 2:03 a.m. The shooting in Greenwich Village occurred a half mile away at 2:07 a.m., evidence that proved that Rojas could not have been at the site of the shooting.

Tina Mazza, at Chenoweth's urging, served as Rojas' appeals lawyer and she presented the evidence unearthed by Chenoweth's investigators to the Appellate Division in 1995. It overturned Rojas' conviction, and he was freed on bail. Prosecutors, however, insisted on retrying him, believing that they would win a second conviction on the testimony of the teenagers who had stood witness against Rojas at his 1991 trial.

Criminal attorney Jethro M. Eisenstein, who had donated his services at the urging of Chenoweth, went to court and not only brought forth policeman Apel to testify but provided another witness, William Davis, who was present at the 1990 shooting and described the man in the Day-Glo jacket as having a ponytail and the body of a weightlifter and that he had earlier told police that Rojas, an undersized youth of 125 pounds, was the wrong man.

A jury agreed and Rojas, after spending more than four years in prison for a crime he did not commit, was found not guilty on all counts. His acquittal was brought about by many selfless persons, investigators, researchers and attorneys, and chiefly a little gray-haired lady named Priscilla Read Chenoweth, a woman of dogged persistence and iron faith.

---

**Roldan Betancur, Antonio**, 1946-1989, Col., assass. On July 4, 1989, while on his way to deliver a speech condemning political violence, Governor Antonio Roldan Betancur of Antioquia, whose state encompasses lands controlled by the Medellin drug cartel, was killed by a car bomb. The remote-controlled bomb exploded as Roldan Betancur's car passed a second, booby-rapped vehicle. Three bodyguards and two bystanders were killed in the explosion, which extensively damaged at least a dozen private residences. See: **Extraditables**; **Medellin Cartel**.

---

**Roman, Marcos**, 1939- , U.S., arson-mur. On the afternoon of January 27, 1989, Mary Ann Roman handed her estranged husband Marcos a one-way plane ticket back to New Jersey and told him never to come back. Although the couple were divorced, he had continued to reside in their Sulphur Springs, Florida, home after agreeing to pay $200 each month in rent. The living arrangements were strained to the breaking point when Roman began making sexual advances to his stepdaughter, Diane Roman, 26. At that point, Mary Ann decided the time had come for Marcos to pack his things and leave. "We gave him a ticket and told him to go to New Jersey," Mary Ann recounted. Instead of leaving quietly, the 50-year-old man went outside to the tool shed to retrieve a can of gasoline.

Roman returned to the house, splattered the kitchen floor with the gasoline, and flicked his lighter. "We didn't think he would do it," Mary Ann explained. "It was like an explosion. It all went up at once. Diane came toward me all on fire. I told her not to run and to get on the floor in the living room." Mary Ann managed to extinguish the flames, but after seven operations, Diane Roman died sixty-three days later.

Marcos Roman was indicted for attempted manslaughter, first-degree murder, and arson. He went on trial in the Tampa courtroom of Judge John P. Griffin on September 5, 1989. Under Florida state law, the crime of arson constitutes first-degree murder if a person dies, regardless of the defendant's intentions at the time the fire started. Roman maintained all along that he never intended to harm anyone with his "little fire." "I didn't light no fire in the kitchen, as God is my witness!" he told the jury. Roman could not adequately explain just how the fire started. Two days later, on September 7, the jury found him guilty on all charges. Following the jury's recommendation, Judge Griffin sentenced Roman to life in prison, with parole eligibility after he served at least twenty-five years.

---

**Rooney, William E.** 1925- , U.S., fraud. Between 1975 and 1987, William Rooney, a 64-year-old businessman from the Chicago area, bilked 3,500 senior citizens of as much as $28 million in principal and interest by selling nine-month notes he claimed would pay interest at 5 percent above the lending rate. Rooney then used the money to develop a ranch and horse farm in Florida. When his firm filed for permission to reorganize under federal bankruptcy laws on March 3, 1989, investigators suspected a Ponzi scheme. (In Ponzi schemes, investors are paid off with the money acquired from others.) He was indicted in June on charges of fraud and brought to trial before Judge John Nordberg at the U.S. District Court in Chicago. Following a plea arrangement, Rooney agreed to plead guilty to three charges if the others were dropped. The plea was entered on June 28, along with an agreement to pay $12 million in restitution to his victims. On August 15, 1989, Judge Nordberg upheld the agreement and sentenced Rooney to ten years in prison. Rooney was also sentenced to five years' probation and ordered to perform 1,000 hours of community service.

---

**Rose, Axl**, 1962- , U.S., prop. damage-asslt. The lead singer with the rock band Guns N' Roses, was found guilty of assault and property damage in a St. Louis, Missouri, court in November 1992. Rose, while performing in a 1991 St. Louis concert, smashed a microphone on stage and then dove into the audience, injuring several persons. Rose was sentenced to two years' probation and ordered to pay $50,000 in fines to social service organizations.

---

**Ross, Ricky** (AKA: Freeway Ricky), 1957- , U.S., drugs. One of the most notorious drug peddlers in California in the early 1990s, Ricky "Freeway Ricky" Ross met with Oscar Blandon, a narcotics trafficker and reportedly a civilian leader of a CIA-backed guerrilla group, purchasing 220 pounds of cocaine from Blandon and paying Blandon $169,000 for the drugs.

Blandon, it turned out, was a government informant who testified against Ross, clinching Ross' March 1996 drug conviction in San Diego, California. Ross' attorneys asked U.S. District Judge Marilyn Huff to set aside the conviction, claiming that Ross was acting on behalf of the CIA in a covert operation involving the buying and selling of cocaine to benefit the Nicaraguan contras, who were being supported by the CIA in the early 1980s.

Judge Huff refused to set aside Ross' conviction and sentenced him to life in prison on November 19, 1996, a mandatory sentence because of Ross' two prior drug convictions. Said Judge Huff: "The conduct of Ross ... is not excused by any so-called tenuous ties to the CIA. It does not give him a free pass for the rest of his life to further addict people because of something that may have happened in the early 1980s." Also See: **CIA**.

---

**Rostenkowski, Daniel**, 1928- , U.S., polit. corrupt. Fat-gutted, big-boned and with the face of a bumpy Idaho potato, U.S. Congressman Dan Rostenkowski was for four decades a pillar of the Democratic Party and a powerhouse Illinois politician. As the Chairman of the House Ways and Means Committee for fourteen years, Rostenkowski rammed through one tax bill after another, which helped to further drain the pocket-books of U.S. citizens everywhere, and kept him in the lime-light as one of the most powerful men in the world.

Though he brought Chicago, Illinois, his power base, new roads and buildings, along with thousands of jobs, he, like most of his Washington ilk, was nothing more than a power-hungry, self-serving crook whose insufferable arrogance and disdain for decent government brought about his own well-deserved ruination. Typical of Rostenkowski's tax dollar allocations was how he put aside $500 million to build stadiums for the Chicago White Sox and the Chicago Bears. The latter team, due to impasses with government officials, did not get a stadium, but Rostenkowski then rechanneled $75 million to improve the nation's waterways, but where did that go? To the restoration of Navy Pier in Chicago, Illinois, a pier that sits on a waterway called Lake Michigan.

A hulking, obnoxious creature, Rostenkowski wheeled and dealed in Washington with imperialistic abandon. He swaggered in and out of posh restaurants gulping vintage wine and wolfing down fat steaks. In the words of the Chicago *Tribune*, he was "brusque as a bully," and projected an image that said, "I'm important and you're not." He proved that in the manner by which he allocated millions of tax dollars. At one point, Rostenkowski later admitted, he provided enough money to rebuild the Kennedy Expressway in Chicago, "and I threw in an extra $50 million. [Gov. Jim] Edgar asked me what he should do with the extra money. I told him he could plant palm trees if he wanted to. That was the way the game was played."

The face of arrogance—Dan Rostenkowski, once powerful U.S. Congressman, convicted of mail fraud in 1996.

To be sure, Rostenkowski reveled in his power, which brought him into the inner circles of government and the confidences of senators, world dignitaries and presidents. He did not begin his career inside such lofty realms, but started as a grunting precinct worker in his old 32nd ward in Chicago. He was elected to Congress with the help of Chicago Mayor Richard J. Daley and climbed the political ladder in Washington. Once he headed the Ways and Means Committee, Rostenkowski began to play fast and loose with government funds and the law itself.

Federal investigators, however, had long scrutinized the high-rolling congressman. In May 1994, Rostenkowski was indicted on seventeen counts, including a charge that he exchanged stamps for cash, made improper purchases of such items as rocking chairs and ashtrays (which Rostenkowski later claimed were gifts to friends, acts that broke House regulations but not federal laws), and paying "ghost payrolls" with federal funds. In this last charge, it was stated that Rostenkowski paid more than $500,000 in fraudulent salaries from 1971 to 1992.

Before being brought to trial, Rostenkowski pleaded guilty to two counts of mail fraud and misuse of taxpayers' funds. He was sentenced to seventeen months in federal prison and served only thirteen months of this sentence. Upon his release, the swaggering Rostenkowski was unrepentant. He referred to himself as a "political" prisoner and claimed that the only reason he pleaded guilty was to spare himself and his family the expense and aggravation of a trial. Most believed that he pleaded guilty to lesser charges in order to avoid being convicted of the many more serious charges for which he had been indicted. He faced a prison term of thirty or more years of hard time if convicted on those charges. Through his prison term and upon his release, Rostenkowski continued to enjoy his almost $99,000-a-year pension funds. (He also owned extensive properties in Chicago and in trendy Lake Geneva, and owned memberships in exclusive clubs.)

Interviewed upon his release from prison, Rostenkowski bristled at being asked if he was sorry that he had committed the crimes that had sent him to jail. "What is it with you reporters, about contrition," he snapped. "I mean what do you want? Do you want somebody to walk around with a towel, a crying towel?" Prison had taught Rostenkowski nothing.

He wallowed in the memory of his former political power, later saying: "With the all the legislation that I passed, with all the history that I've written with respect to the economics of the country, they're always going to say there's a felon named Danny Rostenkowski. That's going to be the obituary."

---

**Roston, Scott Robin**, 1953- , U.S., mur. Karen Waltz met chiropractor Scott Roston while working as his masseuse in Boynton Beach, Florida. The soft-spoken, attractive young woman "definitely did love him," according to a co-worker at the Hunter's Run resort, but she also wanted the finer things out of life that Roston seemed capable of providing. "I don't feel she knew him that well ... but I guess she felt like she knew what she was doing." Following a whirlwind courtship, Karen left her job in Florida and flew to Santa Monica, California, in December 1987 to be with Roston. During her Christmas holiday in California, the couple became engaged. She returned to Florida to announce her upcoming marriage to her family. Shortly before their wedding in Las Vegas on February 4, Karen took up permanent residence in California.

On February 6, 1988, Karen and Scott embarked on a honeymoon cruise to the Bahamas on board the *Stardancer*, moored in San Pedro. Just seven days out of port, Roston reported to the ship's officers that his wife had been swept overboard by a strong gust of wind. The Coast Guard pulled the body from the water the next day. Roston was arrested on February 14 and charged with strangling his wife and throwing her body overboard. He denied the charge, telling prosecutors that Karen had been murdered by two Israeli agents who had been following him ever since he had written a book detailing his experiences in the Middle East. The book was titled *Nightmare in Israel*, and in it he accused the government of arresting him on false burglary charges and then subjecting him to torture in a mental hospital. The two Israeli nationals could not be tracked down by the defense lawyers, but government prosecutors produced one of the men during deliberations at the Los Angeles federal court, which began in March 1989. The Israeli said he was a photographer but denied any connection with either the Rostons or his own government, saying he was on vacation.

The jury was not swayed by allegations of a conspiracy, and Roston was convicted on March 22, 1989, and sentenced to life in prison. He currently resides in the federal penitentiary at Marianna, Florida.

---

**Rouse, William**, 1965- , U.S., mur. The shotgun murders of well-to-do Bruce and Darlene Rouse of Libertyville, Illinois, on the night of June 5-6, 1980, sent a shock wave through this bedroom community just outside of Chicago. The Rouse family typified what was then the American dream—hard work producing upscale luxury. Bruce Rouse, a workaholic, began with one Standard service station and, over a twenty-year period, built a chain of gas stations. The profits allowed him to build a thirteen-room home on a large tract of land in Libertyville, replete with swimming pool and a recreation room filled with electronic games for his children, Kurt, Robin, and William.

The three Rouse children (left to right), Kurt, Robin and William (back to camera), shown in 1980 after their parents were murdered in their Libertyville home; William finally confessed to the killings fifteen years later.

For his daughter Robin, Bruce Rouse built a small stable on his property where Robin kept two horses. His two sons, however, proved to be argumentative. The grew their hair long in the hippie fashion of the day and smoked marijuana. Kurt, the oldest, was thrown out of the house so many times that he took up residence in a small shack on the sprawling Rouse property. Over the shack's door he hung a sign reading "Kurt's Place." He continued arguing with his parents and, following their murder, he was considered the prime suspect in the killings.

On the night of the killings, the children, all of whom were later shielded under a protective legal umbrella of expensive lawyers, heard nothing, they said. Kurt said he was in his shack asleep. Robin said she came home from a dance and went to sleep. William, then 15, said he was asleep in his room. No one heard the violent explosions of a shotgun repeatedly fired, no one.

The shotgun and some unidentifiable bloody clothing were later found by police in a nearby river, but no fingerprints could be lifted from the gun. The case went into limbo and the Rouse children split up their parents' $2 million fortune and went their own ways. Fifteen years later, in October 1995, William Rouse was arrested in Key West, Florida, in connection with a recent bank robbery. Rouse had settled in Key West years before and had squandered his inheritance. He was living on a houseboat with some friends, one of whom was charged with robbing a local bank.

Hearing of Rouse's arrest, Lt. Charles Fagan of the Lake County (Illinois) Sheriff's Department flew to Florida and interviewed William Rouse, then 31. He had always been a suspect in the killing of his parents and Fagan wasted no time in confronting Rouse, telling him to "put the demons to rest." Surprisingly, in a taped interview, Rouse nodded and calmly stated: "I shot my dad." He went on to say that on the night of the murders, he had returned from working at one of his father's gas stations and was drunk and high on marijuana. His mother ordered him to stop drinking and smoking the drug and he became enraged. "I decided I was going to get rid of my mom," he told Fagan.

As his parents slept, William Rouse said, he climbed the stairs with a shotgun. He beat and shot his mother to death and when his father awoke and looked at him, he shot his father, but he kept moving. Rouse then lashed out at his father with a hunting knife, repeatedly stabbing him until "he quit moving."

Rouse was extradited to Chicago where he stood trial and, after a two-week jury trial, was convicted on August 10, 1996. He was sentenced to eighty years in prison, forty years on each murder count for which he was convicted. Judge Victoria A. Rosetti looked down at Rouse from the bench to see that he was unresponsive to the sentence. She then said: "You did the most hatefully shocking thing when you took that shotgun and, at close range, shot your mother, who brought you into this world ... and then shot your father ... You not only took their lives, but you took your own."

---

**Routier, Darlie**, 1970- , U.S., mur. An intruder, Darlie Routier said, crept into her Rowlett, Texas, home, just outside of Dallas, on the night of June 6, 1995, and stabbed her two little boys to death while they slept. Police found 5-year-old Damon and 6-year-old Devon dead, each with many knife wounds. Detectives were suspicious of Routier from the beginning of the investigation, particularly since they could find not a single trace of evidence pointing to a home invader.

**Darlie Routier (left), being taken to Death Row in Texas in 1997, after being convicted of murdering her two small sons.**

When evidence turned up that Routier had used a butcher knife from her own kitchen to kill her two sons, she was brought to trial in Kerrville, Texas, on January 6, 1997, her attorneys getting a change of venue because of the heavy pretrial publicity in the case. Prosecutors told a jury that Routier murdered her sons in a fit of rage over the family's financial difficulties and because of her weight problems. They linked the murder weapon to her.

Convicted, Routier was sentenced to death by a jury on February 4, 1997, becoming the seventh woman on Texas' Death Row. State District Judge Mark Toile polled the jury to see if its four-hour decision was unanimous. One by one, all of the jurors raised their hands to signify their agreement with the death sentence.

---

**Roveal, Chicqua**, 1973-1996, U.S., suic.-mur. Living in a cramped apartment at the Edenwald Houses project in New York City, Chicqua Roveal struggled to maintain her three children from two separate marriages without the support of the

fathers who did not live with her. Her mother, who had been in prison several times for many crimes, moved in with her on November 23, 1996. That night, because of the mother's presence, Roveal's current boyfriend broke off with her.

The next morning, Roveal dressed her three children—Andre and Andrea, 7-year-old twins, and her 2-year-old son, Shando, and took them to the roof of the 15-story building. She pushed each one of the children off and then jumped herself. Roveal and her son, Andre, died upon impact, but Andrea and Shando somehow managed to survive. Police found no suicide note. Roveal's mother told officers that her daughter had been depressed for some time and had stated to her: "You brang me in, so take me out."

---

**Royster, John,** 1948- , U.S., mur. Debt-ridden insurance executive John Royster, 41, shot his former girlfriend, Willye Jean Dukes, to death with a twelve-gauge shotgun on a crowded Grand Central Station platform in New York City on January 7, 1988. He then shot her sister, Diane Dukes, nearly severing her left arm with the blast.

Diane still had not regained full use of her arm when Royster went to trial on May 23, 1989. In an attempt at an insanity plea, Royster defended himself by describing his existence prior to the shooting as a sort of twilight zone. The assistant district attorney characterized Royster's plea as a "story of self-pity," and Manhattan Supreme Court Justice Juanita Bing Newton called the shooting an "execution, sadistic and inhuman." On July 7, Royster was sentenced to consecutive sentences of twenty-five years to life for murder.

---

**Ruby Ridge**, See **Weaver, Randall.**

---

**Rudolph, Eric Robert**, 1966- , U.S., bomb.-mur. A carpenter, Eric Rudolph was raised in the backwoods of the Missouri Ozarks, learning the radical ideology of the Christian Identity movement, a white supremacist group, from his mother. As he matured, he reportedly had dealings with the anti-government group known as the Aryan Nations, based in Idaho, an organization that sought to exert its influence over the sporadic militia movements throughout the U.S. Rudolph drifted in and out of some of these militias and right-wing anti-black, anti-abortion and anti-government organizations for a dozen years.

Rudolph from childhood was raised to survive in the wilds. As a teenager he was an expert woodsman and hunter and was a survivalist who was at home in the most untamed wilderness. He served in the U.S. Army from 1987 to 1989, discharged with the rank of private. Rudolph had had an undistinguished military career and had no criminal background. He learned how to build bombs through his contacts with various hate organizations and first surfaced on January 29, 1998, when the New Women All Women Health Care abortion clinic in Birmingham, Alabama, was bombed, killing an off-duty policeman who was guarding the clinic, and injuring another, blowing a crater in the ground and shattering windows in the surrounding area.

A 1989 gray Nissan pickup truck with North Carolina plates was seen leaving the bombing site in Birmingham and this was traced to Rudolph, a resident of Murphy, North Carolina, where he lived in a mobile home. The truck was found abandoned in Andrews, North Carolina, on February 8, 1998. By that time, the FBI had assembled a profile on Rudolph that linked him to the Centennial Olympic Park bombing in Atlanta, Georgia, on July 27, 1996, which killed one person and injured dozens of others. (The Bureau had mistakenly pinpointed Richard Jewell as a suspect in this bombing).

Further, the FBI attributed the Atlanta bombings of the Northside Family Planning Services abortion clinic on January 16, 1997, and the Otherside Lounge, a gay and lesbian nightclub, to Rudolph. He was placed on the Bureau's Ten Most Wanted list and scores of state and federal agents began a widespread manhunt to capture him. Civilians were encouraged to participate in the dragnet after a

**Eric Robert Rudolph, wanted by the FBI for several bombings in 1997 and 1998—he vanished inside the Great Smoky Mountains.**

$1 million reward was offered for information leading to Rudolph's arrest.

Rudolph's mother and brothers, who had moved to North Carolina from Florida in the early 1980s, refused to talk to authorities but an older brother, Daniel Rudolph, of Charleston, South Carolina, sliced off his own hand with a power saw in March 1998 and videotaped the gruesome act as a form of protest against the FBI's accusations and the media's coverage.

The much-wanted Rudolph, however, had vanished into the Great Smoky Mountains National Park, or into the even more impenetrable Nantahala National Forest, these vast, deep-forested regions stretching from western North Carolina and into Tennessee and western South Carolina. The FBI believed that Rudolph had planned long in advance of his terrorist bombings to retreat into these regions, where he had provisioned caves or small cabins.

Rudolph was reported to have emerged from the wilds on July 7, 1998, when he approached George Nordmann, a man he knew in Andrews, North Carolina, asking him to provide him with food and batteries. He was also seen in the local store in this town, where he bought a slice of pizza, three quarts of beer and a phone card. The clerk in the store described the once clean-shaven Rudolph as wearing a beard, his long hair tied in a pony tail. His clothes were soiled and he smelled so bad that the clerk had to hold her nose when waiting on him. He was seen to go across the street to a gas station where he made several calls on the phone card.

On July 14, 1998, Rudolph again contacted Nordmann, offering him five $100 bills for supplies. Nordmann refused but Rudolph later returned and stole Nordmann's 1977 Datsun pickup that was loaded with canned goods, leaving the money

behind. The pickup was later found abandoned in a campground.

To many in the backwater region, Rudolph became a folk hero, a lone wolf defying the might of the federal government, and FBI officials believed that he was receiving help from those who empathized with him. Hundreds of manhunters were sent into the Great Smoky Mountains after Rudolph, but the dense woods and underbrush slowed their movements. The search went on and on for months into 1999 and, at the time of this writing, Rudolph remains at large, now almost a mythical fugitive. Also See: **Aryan Nations**; **FBI**; **Jewell, Richard**.

---

**Ruhuna, Joachim**, 1934-1996, Burundi, assass. Joachim Ruhuna, the archbishop of Gitega, Burundi, was reportedly assassinated on September 9, 1996, after the Hutu rebels blew up his car. The burned-out hulk of the auto was found in smoking ruins and blood and the charred body of one of the car's six passengers was discovered on a rural road outside of Gitega.

Ruhuna had been openly critical of the warring Hutu and Tutsi tribes and condemned the widespread violence practiced by both sides in an ongoing civil war. Burundian officials reported that a church deacon had found the bishop's burning car and stated that he had seen the bodies of Ruhuna, his driver, two nuns and two children inside the blazing car. He said he tried to save the passengers, but was unable to get them out of the burning car. He went to a nearby village to get help and by the time he returned with soldiers, all the bodies, except that of one nun, had been mysteriously removed.

---

**Ruiz Massieu, Francisco**, d. 1994, Mex., assass. Francisco Ruiz Massieu was shot to death while addressing a large crowd outside a hotel in Mexico City, on September 28, 1994. The Mexican presidential hopeful was assassinated by a lone gunman, Daniel Aguilar, who simply walked up to the candidate and shot him dead with a Tec-9 semiautomatic pistol. Widespread conspiracy theories abounded for many years that government officials had been involved in the assassination. Investigators assembled enough evidence to convict Raul Salinas de Gortari, brother of the former president of Mexico, for the crime in 1999. Also See: **Mexico**; **Salinas de Gortari, Raul**.

---

**Runnels, Rick**, See: **Kurz, Leonard.**

---

**Rushdie, Salman**, prom. 1989, Iran, heresy. An Indian author living in London, Salman Rushdie published a book called *The Satanic Verses*, in which he challenged and ridiculed the Islamic fundamentalists who took over the government of Iran. This brought down upon his head the wrath of Iran's leader, Ayatollah Ruhollah Khomeini, who pronounced an Islamic *fatwa* (edict) on February 14, 1989, calling for Rushdie's death. A reward for his murder in the amount of $2.5 million was later posted by right-wing fundamentalists in Iran, sending the author into hiding and making a worldwide bestseller out of a book that would have otherwise created little attention. Rushdie went into hiding and was sought for a decade by Iranian death squads.

On September 28, 1998, two senior Iranian clerics in Tehran reaffirmed the death sentence for the author. Stated Ayatollah Mohammad Fazel: "I heard that England is under the illusion that the *fatwa* against the apostate Rushdie will be revoked. This *fatwa* is irrevocable and cannot be changed at any time." Rushdie remains an anonymous person, reportedly moving furtively from one hideout to the next at the time of this writing.

———————————

**Russian Mafia**, 1990s. With the collapse of communism in the former Soviet Union and in Eastern Europe in the late 1980s, the rebirth of the profit motive combined with weak democratic governments conspired to help in the creation of what has come to be euphemistically called the Russian Mafia. Unlike the well-organized and family-structured Italian-Sicilian Mafia, which went into decline in the 1990s, the Russian Mafia was a loose-knit organization of hundreds of criminal gangs controlling drugs, prostitution, gambling, and the smuggling of illegal arms and aliens, producing billions in illicit funds.

Particularly active were the gangs in St. Petersburg and Moscow in Russia. They murdered almost at will, eliminating politicians and businessmen who refused to accept bribes and work with them in taking over Russian businesses, banks and industries. The ruthlessness of the Russian Mafia is so feared that prostitutes from Lithuania to Russia never seek police aid in trying to shed their seamy occupations. Thousands of young women are literally held in bondage as sex slaves serving in thousands of bordellos controlled by the Russian Mafia. Those women who think to escape this miserable disease-ridden life are murdered.

The ranks of the Russian Mafia were peopled by former members of the dreaded KGB (the Soviet Union's secret police and counterintelligence agency), athletes, and army veterans of the Afghan war. In addition to every major city in Russia, members of the Russian Mafia control all the rackets in Poland and the Czech Republic, and, to a lesser degree, Romania and Hungary. In the Baltic states, for decades under the domination of Soviet Russia, when police and the military resisted the Russian Mafia, they were attacked by heavily armed paramilitary groups of the Russian Mafia. More than fifty bombs were exploded in Estonia by the Russian Mafia in 1993 to bring local officials into line.

Throughout Eastern Europe and in Russia, all car thefts and the sales of stolen cars, particularly expensive BMW and Mercedes Benz autos, came under the complete control of the Russian Mafia. Peter Grinenko, a New York police detective who had been fighting the inroads made by the Russian Mafia into the U.S., stated: "There's no fight against the Russian Mafia in Russia. The Mafia *is* the system."

In 1996, CIA Director John Deutch reported that 70 to 80 percent of private businesses in Russia paid huge amounts of extortion money to Russian Mafia thugs and that the criminal organization was seriously jeopardizing U.S. investments in the country. Further, at this time, the smuggling and steal-

ing of nuclear fuels by members of the Russian Mafia became widespread, aimed at the construction of nuclear weapons by anti-Western terrorist organizations. Deutch went on to state that leaders of the Russian Mafia were transferring as much as $1.5 billion a month from illegal profits into Western banks in massive money-laundering operations.

Illinois Congressman Henry Hyde reported that 30 percent of the Russian parliament had strong ties to organized crime. Another report held that Russian Prime Minister Viktor Chernomyrdin was in thick collusion with the Russian Mafia and that he had built a $5 billion fortune by skimming money from gas and oil deals overseen by the Russian Mafia. The FBI, which had opened an office in Moscow in 1994, could track little day-to-day operations of the Russian Mafia in that it assigned only three agents to that field office. The Bureau undertook to train Russian law enforcement officers in democratic law enforcement techniques that stressed "an element of human dignity," according to FBI Director Louis Freeh. "We talk about human rights and civil rights—the necessity of police to protect human dignity."

The Russian Mafia, by 1998, had established footholds in more than fifty countries, with its members spreading throughout the U.S., concentrating illegal operations in New York, Chicago, New Orleans, and Los Angeles. Many top ranking members of the Russian Mafia immigrated to the U.S. in the 1990s and used their professional backgrounds to create enormous financial swindles. Two such Russian Mafia members were Michael and David Smushrevich, one a graduate of the Moscow Missile Construction Institute, the other a practicing physician.

These two had the considerable financial help of members of the Russian Mafia in St. Petersburg. As soon as they became citizens of the U.S., they set up a string of fraudulent employment agencies where immigrating Russians paid them large amounts of cash in return for lucrative jobs in the U.S., jobs that didn't exist.

The Smushreviches then began establishing foreign exchange operations that falsely claimed to Belorussian and Ukrainian firms that they could obtain dollars for almost worthless Russian rubles at an equal rate of exchange. When the Russian firms grew suspicious, the brothers simply shut down their operations and began the largest health-care swindle in U.S. history, chiefly in California. Here they set up more than 350 phony front firms to falsify insurance billings that totaled more than $1 billion.

Employing telemarketing operations, the brothers promised patients free medical examinations, then sent them to sleazy mobile clinics they ran where expensive tests were conducted, charging health insurance firms about $8,000 per person. Hundreds of millions rolled into the coffers of the Smushrevich brothers. They lived in high style, buying Beverly Hills mansions, driving about in Rolls Royces and giving extravagant parties for Hollywood's glitteratti. Both were finally exposed, tried, convicted and sent to prison, but not before enriching themselves and fattening the coffers of the Russian Mafia with hundreds of millions of dollars. Also See: **Churbanov, Yuri**; **FBI**; **Starovoitova, Galina**; **Tatum, Paul**.

# S

**Saadeh, Munir**, d. 1989, Leb., assass. Munir Saadeh, a senior official of the Red Crescent organization, was shot to death on October 17, 1989, by gunmen as he rode in an ambulance outside the Am Hilweh refugee district east of Sidon, Lebanon. The Red Crescent is run by the mainstream Palestinian group Al Fatah, which Saadeh was also a member of, and police speculated that the assassins were members of a more radical rival Palestinian group.

---

**Safebet, Operation**, See: **Operation Safebet.**

---

**St. Charles, Pamala**, See: **Lowry, Donald.**

---

**St. Pierre, Bobby,** See: **Wilson, Barry.**

---

**Salaam, Yousuf**, See: **McCray, Antron.**

---

**Salah, Mohammad**, 1953- , Israel-U.S., money laund.-terr. Israeli police arrested Mohammad Salah, a naturalized U.S. citizen, interrogating him at length on February 11, 1993, in a high-security prison on the West Bank. He stood accused of supervising a vast money-laundering network. Convicted after admitting that he had illegally channeled funds to Hamas, a Palestinian terrorist group, Salah was imprisoned until November 1997. Upon his release, Salah returned to his home in Bridgeview, Illinois. At the time of his release, Salah recanted his confession and denied having anything to do with funding terrorist activities through money-laundering schemes.

On June 9, 1998, FBI agents seized $1.4 million in seven bank accounts and two safe deposit boxes owned by Salah and the Quranic Literary Institute in Oak Lawn, Illinois. The Quranic Literary Institute, the North American Islamic Trust in Plainfield, Indiana, and a housing development company operating in three Illinois communities—Tinley Park, Lombard and Naperville—were all named as part of the Islamic group conspiring to launder money and funnel these funds to Hamas in supporting its terrorist activities. Ahmad Zakhi Hammad, an author and scholar of Islamic Studies at the University of Chicago, was named as the leader of the Islamic group heading the money-laundering conspiracy, and surgeon and real estate developer Tamar Al-Rafai and Salah as co-conspirators. Salah awaits trial at the time of this writing. Also See: **Hamas.**

---

**Saldivar, Efren**, 1970- , U.S., Case of mur. "He was sensitive, goofy and insecure," recalled a boyhood friend of Efren Saldivar, a 28-year-old therapist who confessed to killing forty to fifty persons. On March 11, 1998, Saldivar arrived at the Glendale, California, police headquarters to answer questions about a mysterious death at the Glendale Adventist Medical Center where he worked. Hooked up to a lie detector, Saldivar, only minutes before the test started, began to nervously spew forth a four-hour confession that detailed the killing of as many as fifty persons in the last eight years.

The brown-haired, heavy-set Saldivar described how he either cut off the air supply of elderly patients or injected them with drugs that caused paralysis. Saldivar stated that all of his victims were unconscious when he terminated them and that they had written orders on their charts that stated, "Do not resuscitate."

Saldivar related how he began killing patients in 1989 by turning off their air supply, suffocating them. He went on to state that he became more aggressive in dispatching elderly patients in 1992 after viewing a TV news magazine, copying the technique reported by the TV show: He began injecting patients with lethal quantities of morphine or Pavulon or succinylcholine chloride, causing paralysis to muscles and thereby halting the ability of the patient to breathe. He said he quit the mercy killing in 1997 when he came to believe that other hospital employees were suspicious of him after so many persons died on his shift. Police asked Saldivar if he considered himself an "angel of death." The therapist replied, "Yes."

Held on suspicion of murder, police were compelled to release Saldivar within forty-eight hours. They had no evidence to support the confession, including the bodies themselves. Saldivar promptly disappeared. Investigators began digging into Saldivar's background and the respiratory units of three other hospitals where he had worked within the last decade.

Glendale Adventist Medical Center not only fired Saldivar after the news of his confession broke, but released four other therapists in its respiratory unit. Saldivar, born in Brownsville, Texas, had moved with his family to Tujunga, California, living in a Hispanic-Asiatic community in eastern San Fernando Valley. He attended Verdugo High School and was remembered as being an average student. Some recalled that Saldivar did organize blood drives and reported how painful surgery was after having undergone a minor operation.

Saldivar's brother later stated that the former hospital technician denied ever having made a confession to Glendale police. Investigators were still studying the bizarre case at the time of this writing, but Saldivar remains uncharged.

---

**Saldivar, Yolanda**, 1961- , U.S., mur. In the early afternoon of March 31, 1995, the most popular singer of Mexican-American teenagers, Selena Quintanilla Perez, staggered from a Days Inn motel room in Corpus Christi, Texas. She lurched into the lobby clutching her chest and gasping "She shot me, she shot me." The 23-year-old Grammy-winning singer died at Memorial Medical Center a short time later.

Police responding to the alarm from motel employees found 34-year-old Yolanda Saldivar sitting in a pickup truck with a gun to her head. For almost ten hours police pleaded with the woman to surrender. Saldivar finally gave herself up and was taken into custody, later charged with first-degree murder.

The defendant was the president of Selena's fan club and served as a manager of one of the singer's boutique shops in San Antonio, Texas. According to Selena's father, Saldivar had embezzled funds from the store, and when Selena confronted her at the motel to tell her that she was fired, the woman "went bananas."

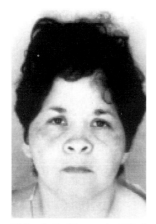

More than 30,000 fans flocked to Selena's lavish funeral in Corpus Christi. Thousands more protested when Saldivar was later found guilty of murdering the singing idol and was not given a death sentence, but life imprisonment.

**Yolanda Saldivar, who killed the popular Tejano music star Selena.**

---

**Sale, Lyndahl Earl,** 1965- , U.S., mur. On May 17, 1989, the mutilated body of 28-year-old Connie Powell was discovered on the beach in the coastal town of Orange Beach, Alabama. Her throat had been slit and she had been repeatedly beaten with a blunt instrument. Police discovered that she had been seen with 24-year-old Lyndahl Sale shortly before her death. Two days later, Sale was arrested for her murder. He admitted that he had stabbed Powell, but only after being provoked. The couple had met in Pappy's Lounge, a Pensacola, Florida, bar, shortly before closing time. Powell, a mother of two children, was employed at a local photography company. Sale offered her a ride on his motorcycle.

According to Sale, they then went to the beach to go "skinny-dipping" and afterwards they had intercourse. Sale said they began to argue, and Powell hit him in the back of the head. "I'm not sure how the argument started. I'm not sure what it was about," Sale said. He had an eight-inch hunting knife in a sheath, and as

**Lyndahl Earl Sale, convicted of murder and sent to prison for life in 1989.**

the quarrel intensified the couple wrestled over the knife. Sale was nicked by the blade and then allegedly lost control and stabbed and bludgeoned Powell to death. "I got close enough to hit her again and got the knife. She hit me in the face ... she hit me and I just blew up and cut her," he added. Within forty-eight hours Sale was arrested and incarcerated at the Baldwin County Jail.

In June 1989, Sale was indicted for murder, rape, and sodomy. He was brought to trial in December at the Baldwin County Courthouse in Bay Minette, Alabama, before Judge Charles Partin. Prosecutor David Whetstone sought the more serious charge of capital murder, which could have resulted in

the death penalty. "The mere fact a woman rides with a man does not mean she consents to have sex with him ... ," Whetstone argued in his closing statements to the jury. "If this was an act of passion, if she consented in this activity, he would've made another date with her."

Defense attorneys David Simon and Mitch Kemmer, while admitting their client's guilt, sought the lesser charge of murder because the event was not premeditated. They also contended that the rape and sodomy charges should be dropped because of the woman's questionable background. On December 15, 1989, the six-man, six-woman jury convicted Sale of the lesser murder charge and he was sentenced to life imprisonment. "We're extremely happy," said David Simon. "We feel like the jury looked at the evidence and despite the gruesome nature of the killing itself, they did their duty and followed the law."

---

**Salem, Wail**, 1965- , U.S., Case of fraud. One of the largest food stamp fraud rings in Chicago history, according to federal and state authorities, was engineered by Palestinian Wail Salem. The odd thing about this case was that prosecutors were, for more than seventeen months, accusing a dead man of the crime. On July 18, 1996, Salem, while on a trip to the Middle East, died in Ramallah. A death certificate for Salem was issued by the Interior Ministry of the Palestinian Authority, one that stated that Salem had died of cardiac arrest only four days after he arrived in the city.

In the summer of 1997, Amal Salem, the dead man's wife, went to a Chicago attorney, asking him to file insurance claims against her husband's life that amounted to more than $2.5 million. But when attorney Douglas Wellman went to Prudential Insurance to press the claims, he was told by an insurance executive, "I can assure you that he's not dead."

To be sure, Salem resurfaced in Chicago, Illinois, in November 1997. His wife then asked attorney Wellman to drop the insurance claims. A very much alive Salem was then arrested on December 2, 1997, charged with leading a family fraud ring that bilked the government out of about $12.5 million. Salem, who operated a string of Chicago grocery stores in Muslim enclaves, along with his wife and several family members, reportedly bought food stamps on the black market at 70¢ per $1 coupon, and then turned in the stamps to the government to receive full cash value.

Salem, following his indictment in 1998, denied faking his own death to collect insurance funds, saying that he had been held hostage and his death erroneously reported by his captors. Yet he could not explain why, when arrested, he was found to be carrying pieces of identification that bore six different names, including three Jordanian passports. Madeleine Sullivan Murphy, the assistant U.S. attorney prosecuting the food stamp fraud, dismissed Salem's abduction excuse to explain away his faked death while, at the same time, he obtained one of his many passports. Stated Murphy: "I don't understand how he was able to shower, put on a tie, smile for an I.D. photo and not alert someone he was kidnapped."

Also, authorities pointed to the fact that, after reportedly managing his release from his abductors, Salem traveled back to the U.S. by a circuitous route that took him to Spain, Cuba and Mexico before he again stepped foot into the U.S. in late 1997, a former kidnap victim who took seventeen months to return to a wife who had filed for his insurance benefits, without ever notifying her or his many relatives that he, indeed, was alive.

Salem, his wife and several relatives await trial at the time of this writing while officials busy themselves with hunting down the estimated $12.5 million the reported swindlers took out of their enormous food stamp scam.

---

**Salinas de Gortari, Raul**, 1947- , Mex., drugs-polit. corrupt.-assass. Under the administration of President Carlos Salinas de Gortari, from 1988 to 1994, Mexico saw unprecedented increases in political and law enforcement corruption and the rise of Mexican drug cartels to billion-dollar operations. Although Carlos Salinas was never directly prosecuted for illegal activities, his older brother, Raul Salinas, was for years suspected to be the bag man for the administration, taking millions in bribes from the drug cartel bosses, as well as engineering the assassination of Jose Francisco Ruiz Massieu on September 28, 1994.

Ironically, Ruiz Massieu was the number two man after Carlos Salinas in Mexico's ruling Institutional Revolutionary Party (PRI), and was Salinas' hand-picked successor. Yet, there was bad blood between Carlos and Raul Salinas and their former brother-in-law, Ruiz Massieu, who had divorced the sister of the Salinas brothers. More insidious was the long-standing belief that although Carlos Salinas had picked Ruiz Massieu to succeed him to the presidency, Raul Salinas, the administration's "enforcer," had marked Ruiz Massieu for death.

The reasons for Raul Salinas' actions remain unclear, but speculation held that revenge for divorcing the Salinas sister was not the main motive for arranging the assassination of Ruiz Massieu, that the presidential hopeful was thought to be uncooperative in secretly supporting the powerful drug cartels that had turned Mexico, with massive political and police aid, into a "narco country," where almost every top official collusively worked with the drug bosses who, in turn, channeled millions of dollars back to these officials in bribes, one of these being Raul Salinas (and, by inference on the part of some Mexican authorities, his brother Carlos).

The 1994 assassination of Ruiz Massieu occurred outside a Mexico City hotel just after the victim gave a political speech. A lone gunman, Daniel Aguilar, walked up to Ruiz Massieu and shot him to death, then meekly surrendered to officers who were nearby. The murder appeared to be staged, many claimed, and smacked of a widespread conspiracy. Aguilar, sent to prison for life, would not reveal the existence of a conspiracy, but prosecutors and investigators doggedly pursued this theory until collecting enough evidence to convince then President Ernesto Zedillo to order the arrest of Raul Salinas on February 28, 1995.

Shortly after the arrest was announced, Carlos Salinas went into European exile, later settling in Ireland. His brother remained in jail awaiting trial. Endorsing the claim that Salinas masterminded the Ruiz Massieu assassination was Fernando Rodriguez Gonzalez, who admitted that he organized the murder for Salinas, employing Aguilar and others. He testified against Salinas at his trial, as did others. Salinas was convicted of being behind the murder plot on January 21, 1999 and given the maximum term of fifty years in prison by Judge Ricardo Ojeda Bohorquez.

Raul Salinas, brother of Mexico's President Carlos Salinas, convicted in 1999 of masterminding the murder of politician Francisco Ruiz Massieu; he went to prison for fifty years.

Further, it was revealed by Mexican officials that Raul Salinas had sent more than $90 million in bribes he had received from Mexican drug cartel bosses to secret Swiss bank accounts. He had also sent $23.4 million to banks in England. These funds were seized by officials in both countries and held for disposition by Mexican authorities.

The conviction and imprisonment of Raul Salinas was seen as a rare victory of law and order in chaotic Mexico. Jose Ortiz Pinchetti, who had briefly served in the Interior Ministry under Carlos Salinas, applauded the verdict and sentence, stating that Salinas was "the one tangible representative of a regime that hurt the nation ... Before, we would never have been able to crack a president's inner circle. And to convict someone so close to the president—his brother, no less—turns a new page in Mexican justice." Also See: **Mexico**; **Ruiz Massieu, Jose Francisco**.

---

**Salinas, Roel**, 1936- , **Martinez, Miguel**, 1979- , and **Alvarez, Ruben**, 1981- , U.S., mur. Arnold Mireles was more than civic-minded. He loathed the garbage-strewn, drug-infested area that made up his neighborhood on Chicago's South Side. To clean up his neighborhood, Mireles led a group of concerned citizens in planting "Victory Gardens." Further, he identified polluters by dragging into Housing Court owners of dilapidated or drug-infested buildings. One of these, according to police, was Roel Salinas, who hired Miguel Martinez and Ruben Alvarez to kill Mireles because he had documented building code violations that had cost Salinas hundreds of dollars over the years in cleanup and court costs.

Mireles was shot to death on the night of December 29, 1997. Police arrested Salinas, Martinez and Alvarez a short time later, and they were charged with Mireles' murder in 1998. All three await trial at this writing. On July 11, 1998, Chicago Mayor Richard Daley and more than 100 residents of Mireles' neighborhood dedicated a vacant lot to the victim's memory, one that was green and blooming as the result of trees, shrubs and plants that had been earlier planted by the slain Mireles.

---

**Salizar, Alberto**, See: **Chavez, Juan R.**

---

**Salman, Ahmad**, 1953-1997, U.S., suic.-mur. Struggling with debt he felt he could not overcome, Ahmad Salman, a native of Syria and a resident of Simi Valley, California, thought to end his problems by the mass murder of his family and his own self-destruction. On the morning of May 27, 1997, Salman's neighbors were startled to see one of his 5-year-old twin sons frantically running about the front lawn of the Salman home. The neighbor then saw the 44-year-old Salman appear with a rifle and methodically shoot his boy to death. He had by then already killed his 28-year-old wife, Nebela, his 3-year-old son and his other 5-year-old twin son when they attempted to flee over a fence. Police arriving at the scene found Salman dead of a self-inflicted gunshot wound; he was curled up with his rifle on the back lawn of his home.

---

**Salvi, John C. III**, 1972-1996, U.S., mur. A lonely, bespectacled figure, John C. Salvi III had been raised a Catholic in Massachusetts and in Florida. He developed an intense hatred for adherents of abortion, and his oft-repeated opinions on this subject were so vocal and full of anger that he had few friends willing to listen to his tirades. Moving to southern New Hampshire, where he became an apprentice hairdresser, Salvi took many trips to Boston, where he became a fringe member of the anti-abortion groups, but he alienated himself from leaders by loudly denouncing these groups as being ineffective and not doing enough to stop abortions.

John Salvi then began making plans to do something more himself. According to prosecutors, he purchased a rifle and customized the weapon in order to make it easy to hide. He stockpiled ammunition and regularly practiced his marksmanship at a shooting range. On December 30, 1994, Salvi, dressed all in black, packed his semiautomatic .22-caliber rifle into his pickup truck and drove to the Planned Parenthood Clinic in Brookline, Massachusetts, a suburb of Boston.

Upon entering the abortion clinic, Salvi immediately shot and killed 25-year-old Shannon Lowney, the receptionist, and wounded three other persons waiting in the reception area. He then returned to his pickup and drove two miles along the same street in Brookline to the Preterm Health Services Clinic. Again, with methodical precision, Salvi entered the reception area and shouted: "This is what you get! You should pray the rosary!" Despite her pleas for mercy, he killed 38-year-old Lee Ann Nichols, the receptionist, shooting her ten times, and wounded two others in the waiting area.

Eluding a widespread dragnet, Salvi drove his pickup to Norfolk, Virginia, where, the following morning, he fired shots at an abortion clinic, fortunately injuring no one. Arrested, he was returned to Massachusetts for a trial that caught the attention of a nation gripped by a raging debate over abortion. Charged with two murders and the attempted murder of five others, Salvi, at a 1995 competency hearing, was judged sane enough to stand trial. But at that time, and throughout his 1996 trial, J. W. Carney, Jr., Salvi's court-appointed attorney, insisted that his client was not a sane man.

Salvi had for some time claimed that he was nothing more than a self-appointed warrior fighting a lone war against a massive anti-Catholic conspiracy led by the Ku Klux Klan, the Mafia, and Freemasons. Defense experts testified at his trial that Salvi was a paranoid schizophrenic with fixed delusions, auditory hallucinations and confused reasoning.

John C. Salvi III, who killed two abortion clinic workers in 1994, took his own life in a prison cell in 1997.

The defendant was nevertheless found guilty and sentenced to two life terms to be served at the Massachusetts Correctional Institution at Cedar Junction in Walpole, Massachusetts. Ann Marie Salvi, the defendant's mother, protested, saying that her son was mentally ill and should have been sent to a psychiatric hospital, not a prison. On November 29, 1996, Salvi was found dead in his cell, a suicide. He had tied a plastic trash bag from the wastepaper basket in his cell around his head and had suffocated to death.

Carney stated that his former client had several times before his imprisonment tried to kill himself and that "he was a seriously ill young man suffering from a mental illness that was not being treated and was not being medicated." He went on to state that by sending his client to prison instead of a medical facility, the state had made "a political decision."

A relative visited Salvi a day before his death and found him disheveled and babbling incoherently, demanding that he be given the address of the Pope in Rome. Following Salvi's death, his mother stated: "My young John is gone, but there are others who will suffer in prison instead of a mental hospital, where they belong."

Ruth Nichols, the mother of Lee Ann Nichols, one of the receptionists Salvi had shot to death two years earlier, had no sympathy for Salvi: "He was a bad boy who grew up to be a bad man. God have mercy on his soul." Oddly, by taking his own life, Salvi, under state law, was cleared of the two murders for which he had been convicted. That law dictates that charges be dismissed if a defendant dies before his court appeals can be heard.

---

**Sanchez, Antonio**, See: **Ochoa Sánchez, Arnaldo.**

---

**Sanchez, George Anthony**, 1961- , U.S., rape. Known as the "ski mask rapist," George Sanchez, a sewage worker in San Jose, California, was responsible for the rapes of twenty-six women in nine Bay Area communities from February 1985 to November 1987. Sanchez indiscriminately attacked females of all ages, the youngest being 16, the oldest 84.

Sanchez "scouted" women living near churches or church-operated schools, keeping his victims under surveillance until they were alone, then raping the women and stealing their cash and valuables before fleeing. Sanchez gave his victims' jewelry to his wife, Clara, 28.

The couple was apprehended in 1988. Clara Sanchez was charged with receiving stolen property. George Sanchez waived his right to trial with the provision that the charges against his wife be dropped. In September 1988, Judge Paul R. Teilh found Sanchez, 27, guilty of 115 crimes.

In June 1989, Sanchez was sentenced to 406 years in prison. Some of Sanchez's victims were present at his sentencing and broke into tears of gratitude at the heavy sentencing. Margo Smith, deputy district attorney for Santa Clara County, who had prosecuted Sanchez, stated that he "is a man who deserves to be in prison for life without the possibility of parole. He did not cut, bruise, or slice or murder (his victims), but what he's taken away from them can never be replaced."

**Sánchez Santa Cruz, Elizardo; Abi Cobas, Hiram;** and **Jérez, Hubert**, prom. 1989, Cuba, slander. Early in the morning of August 6, 1989, Cuban security police arrested three outspoken human rights activists for their declarations against the Fidel Castro regime. Taken into custody and charged with slander were Elizardo Sánchez Santa Cruz, the head of the Cuban Commission of Human Rights and National Conciliation; Hiram Abi Cobas, the acting head of the Human Rights Party; and Hubert Jérez, the head of the newly formed José Marti Human Rights Organization. Since 1987, Sánchez had been given the freedom to contact foreign journalists to voice his displeasure with the Cuban government. He was even allowed to visit the U.S. for a few weeks in 1988. However, the access was tempered following an April 1989 visit by Soviet President Mikhail S. Gorbachev when sixty dissidents were temporally detained. In late July, Sánchez, Abi, and Jérez told *Washington Post* reporter Julia Preston that the executions of four convicted Cuban drug dealers were, in reality, political assassinations, and that their bodies were illegally withheld from their families. On November 24, Sánchez was sentenced to two years in prison, while Abi received eighteen months.

**Sanders, Charles**, See: **Andrews, Jesse James**.

**Sandlin, Jan Barry**, 1952- , U.S., mur. In 1971, 4-month-old Mathew Golder fell from his crib in his Georgia home. Investigators determined that the boy's 2-year-old sister, Tracy, who was in the crib with him, somehow pushed the infant from the crib and he was accidentally killed in the fall. For twenty-seven years Tracy Rhame lived with the haunting guilt of her brother's death, but never came to believe that even as a small child she was capable of injuring her sibling.

Through her insistence, the child's body was exhumed and examined. A pathologist's 1997 report determined that the child had suffered injuries causing his death that could not have resulted in his falling from a crib, that he had, indeed, been beaten to death. The boy's father, Jan Barry Sandlin, who was by then serving a life term in a Florida prison for armed robbery, was charged with the murder of the infant and, after two trials (the first resulting in a mistrial), was convicted and given a life sentence by Judge Hilton Fuller.

On September 26, 1997, a jury in Atlanta, Georgia, convicted Sandlin on the prosecutor's argument that he had beaten the infant to death while his wife and 2-year-old Tracy were out of the house, gone to a laundromat to wash clothes. When they returned, Sandlin, according to prosecutor Lee Ann Mangone, told his wife to put away the clothes and then put the unwitting Tracy into the crib and the infant's body on the floor

**Jan Barry Sandlin, convicted in 1997 of murdering his 4-month-old son twenty-six years later; he set up his 2-year-old daughter for the 1971 death.**

next to it to make it appear that Tracy had thrown the child to the floor.

Sandlin never appeared on the witness stand for his own defense. His attorney, Corrine Mull, told the jury that the infant's mother, Kathy Almon, was the real killer. Mull likened Almon's actions to Susan Smith, who murdered her two young sons in South Carolina. The jury found this argument unconvincing. Also See: **Smith, Susan**.

**Sannon, Evens**, See: **Lucien, Patrick**.

**Santacruz Londono, José**, See: **Medellin Cartel, The**.

**Santana, Deborah**, See: **Benkowski, Judith**.

**Santana, Juan**, 1961- , U.S., mur. On July 7, 1988, Juan Santana, a 27-year-old chronic felon, shot and wounded Ernest Davis during a robbery attempt on a New York City street. The act was witnessed by 42-year-old Alphonso Barclay Deal, the senior clerk of the New York Supreme Court, who, armed with a gun and badge, left his home to confront Santana. Deal announced he was a police officer and ordered Santana to drop his weapon. Santana placed the pistol in his waistband and started to raise his hands, but as Deal approached, Santana quickly drew the gun and fatally wounded Deal with a gunshot through the heart. As he fell, Deal shot Santana four times, but the felon survived to be arrested and charged with murder, as well as the earlier assault and robbery. Santana was convicted on all counts, and on April 10, 1989, he was sentenced by Justice Edwin Torres in the New York Supreme Court to twenty-five years to life for the murder of Deal and another twenty-year consecutive sentence for the assault and robbery of Davis.

**Santana, Raymond**, See: **McCray, Antron**.

---

**Santiago, Maria Victoria**, 1978- , and **Rivera, Jorge**, 1979- , U.S., Case of tamp. with evid.-obstruct.-mur. Maria Santiago of New York City went to police on December 4, 1998, to hysterically report the abduction of her 20-month-old daughter, Victoria, saying that a stranger snatched her child in a crowded subway and ran away with the girl. Detectives began searching for the girl, but were confounded in their hunt by conflicting stories told by Santiago. Suspicious, investigators focused their attention on the mother, who then broke down and told police where to locate the child.

Victoria Santiago's body, her feet jutting from a black plastic bag, was found floating just off the shore of Brooklyn, New York, only hours after her mother attempted to perpetuate the fake kidnapping. A baby carriage bobbed in the tide next to the child's corpse. On December 5, 1998, the 20-year-old Santiago was charged with second-degree murder and her boyfriend, 19-year-old Jorge Rivera, was charged with tampering with evidence and obstruction of justice—he reportedly attempted to hinder the investigation. Both await trial at this writing. Police stated that the hoax was not dissimilar to that perpetrated by Susan Smith, who drowned her two young sons in South Carolina in 1994. Also See: **Smith, Susan**.

---

**Santillanes, Henry**, 1954- , and **Maestas, Victor**, 1980- , and **Lesly, Cynthia**, 1956- , U.S., mur. A caretaker of a small ranch near Ojito Frios, New Mexico, Henry Santillanes was patrolling the area on September 8, 1994. He found 37-year-old Charles Pacheco, a local rancher, and his wife and nephew on the ranch and ordered them off the spread. Pacheco explained that he was only looking for firewood. Santillanes had been drawn to the arroyo when he heard the whine of a chain saw and discovered that Pacheco was cutting a dead tree.

Santillanes later told authorities that he ordered Pacheco to stop cutting, but that Pacheco put down the chain saw and reached for his rifle, which was leaning against a nearby tree. He said he then fired a warning shot from atop a hillock about twenty feet from Pacheco. Santillanes said he then fired a second shot in self-defense, the bullet striking Pacheco, a mortal wound.

Pacheco's wife and nephew, both unarmed, later said they ran behind their pickup truck while Santillanes fired another shot at them with his .270 caliber rifle. They then jumped into the pickup and raced off, reporting the shooting when they reached the small town of Ojito Frios, about twenty miles south of Las Vegas, New Mexico. They said that Pacheco had been shot down in cold blood. Deputies drove to the ranch where Santillanes worked and arrested him on charges of murder.

Investigators had found three .270-caliber shells at the scene of the killing. All the evidence, and the testimony of Pacheco's relatives, pointed to Santillanes' eventual conviction. Moreover, Santillanes had a long criminal background and had been imprisoned for aggravated battery with a deadly weapon. Through family and friends, he was able to post bond and was released from jail pending trial. Santillanes promptly fled, remaining at large for three months while lawmen, including posses on horseback, searched the wild outback of New Mexico for him.

Detectives finally tracked down and recaptured the fugitive in a mobile home in Las Vegas on March 13, 1995, returning him to prison. At the time, Santillanes was found with a packet of cocaine and the drug charge would be added to those of murder and escape. Santillanes believed that only an expensive lawyer could possibly free him, but he had no funds to hire such an attorney. According to police, he then hatched a deadly scheme to obtain those funds.

On April 9, 1995, 35-year-old Angela Bergman was reported missing from her Las Vegas, New Mexico, home. That very same day, her body was dragged out of Storrie Lake in the Santa Fe National Forest, near Las Vegas. She had been stabbed once in the heart. Police went to Bergman's mobile home on Montezuma Street to interview 36-year-old Cynthia Lesly. Bergman, who was Santillanes' former wife, lived with her lesbian lover, Lesly, at the mobile home, along with her son, Victor Maestas, who was also the son of the imprisoned Santillanes.

At first Lesly, who was a home health care nurse, as was Bergman, insisted that Bergman had gotten drunk and wandered off, stating: "She left the house intoxicated last night and that's the last we saw of her." Investigators found the murder knife and a bloody blanket along the shore of Lake Storrie, but no other clues. Bergman had no known enemies and, without a single suspect, the case came to a momentary standstill. Then detectives revisited Lesly and, under intense interrogation, she broke down crying, saying that Bergman's son had argued with his mother about his father's imprisonment, grabbed a knife and fatally stabbed her. Stated Lesly: "He [Maestas] looked at me and said, 'We did it, we did it. We killed her. We killed her all right.'"

Lesly went on to admit that she had helped Maestas take the body in the bloody blanket to Storrie Lake and dump it into the water. Maestas was arrested and charged with his mother's murder. He remained silent, refusing to confess. Brought before Judge Eugenio S. Mathis on May 2, 1995, Maestas pleaded innocent. He was ordered to stand trial as an adult and was imprisoned in the very jail holding his father.

The scheme Santillanes had hatched completely backfired, according to investigators, who believed that he had directed his son to kill his former wife in order to collect on a $250,000 insurance policy, one that had Victor Maestas as the sole beneficiary. With that kind of money, officials were convinced, Maestra could hire a high-priced lawyer to get his father released from prison. In the end, both went to prison and stayed there.

Henry Santillanes was tried for the murder of Pacheco in June 1995 and was convicted. He was sentenced to twenty-seven years in prison, becoming eligible for parole in 2008. On August 29, 1995, Victor Maestas threw himself on the mercy of the court, and, facing the reduced charge of second-degree murder in the death of his mother in a plea-bargain arrangement, was sentenced to only six years in prison by Judge Mathis. Both father and son were sent to the New Mexico State Penitentiary in Santa Fe.

**Santos Vasquez, Jose**, See: **Valdez, Salvador**.

---

**Sarsour, Salem Rajah al-**, 1969- , Israel, terr.-mur. Consumed with hate for Israelis, Palestinian Salem Rajah al-Sarsour, 29, sought to wreak his vengeance upon them through murder and terrorism. To that end, according to his own later statements and those of Israeli officials, Sarsour, in late August 1998, went by night to the Israeli army post near Tel Rumeida, intending to bomb it with homemade Molotov cocktails, but found the place vacant. He then climbed the fence of the Jewish settlement nearby and crept up on a mobile home occupied by 67-year-old Schlomo Raanan.

Seeing Raanan through a window, Sarsour broke inside and stabbed him to death. He then fled back to Palestinian-controlled Hebron. A short time later, Sarsour reported his murder to officials heading the terrorist group Hamas, and was immediately welcomed into the organization. He was inducted into the elite military (terrorist) wing and taught the grim art of grenade-throwing.

The first Hamas-backed terrorist act committed by Sarsour, accompanied by at least six Hamas members, was an attack on an Israeli army post in Hebron on September 30, 1998. Sarsour and his companions hurled grenades at Israeli soldiers, wounding fourteen of them, as well as injuring eight Palestinian passersby. Israeli and Palestinian authorities arrested the six accomplices, but Sarsour escaped. He surfaced on October 19, 1998, to lob several grenades at the Beersheba bus terminal, which was packed with Israelis. He wounded sixty-seven persons, including twenty-four Israeli soldiers.

Sarsour was seized as he tried to flee. He claimed that he had acted alone, quickly confessing that he had participated in the September 30 attack and the killing of Rabbi Raanan. He went on to say that he originally intended to attack Israelis in Jerusalem, but went to Beersheba to seek construction work and when he failed to get a job, he became frustrated and, instead of taking a bus home, he began throwing grenades at Israelis. As Sarsour attempted to flee, a bus driver ran after him and beat him senseless until police arrested the terrorist.

Sarsour's vicious attack created an international furor and halted the Israeli-Palestinian peace talks in Maryland. Sarsour was taken into custody and openly confessed his crimes. Hamas, once their terrorist was in custody, then took responsibility for the Beersheba grenade attack in a fax to Reuters news service. Stated a representative of the Izz el-Deen al-Qassam Brigade (the armed wing of Hamas): "One of our heroic fighters carried out a heroic operation on Monday morning in the town of Beersheba, which targeted a crowd of enemy soldiers." Sarsour awaits trial at this writing. Also See: **Hamas**.

---

**Satcher, Michael Charles**, 1968-1997, U.S., mur. The many users of jogging trails and exercise paths throughout Washington, D.C., were shocked to hear that the body of Anne Elizabeth Borghesani, a paralegal and recent Tufts University graduate, had been found on the Custis Trail near Rosalyn on March 31, 1990. She had been jogging to her 23rd birthday party when she was raped and murdered. Her attacker stabbed her twenty-one times and left her corpse naked from the waist down in an office building stairwell.

Not until August 1991 did police have a solid suspect in the Borghesani murder. Officers arrested Michael Charles Satcher, a resident of Southeast Washington who worked as a furniture mover. At the time, three women identified Satcher as a man who attempted to attack them with a knife wrapped in a shirt along the Arlington trail. He was soon charged with the murder of Borghesani after DNA and semen traces were linked to him, along with another sexual assault committed on the same night that Borghesani was murdered.

The DNA evidence was strong enough to convict Satcher in a 1991 Arlington trial. Following his death sentence, Satcher's lawyers challenged the DNA evidence, saying that it was faulty, but experts and appeals courts disagreed. The U.S. Supreme Court refused to overturn the conviction and sentence in a 7-2 vote and Virginia Governor George Allen refused to commute Satcher's execution. On December 9, 1997, Satcher, protesting his innocence to the last, was put to death by lethal injection, a form of execution he had requested. (Condemned prisoners in Virginia, since January 1, 1995, have the choice of either dying by electrocution or lethal injection. No one since that time chose to die in the electric chair.)

---

**Savage, James Hudson,** 1963- , U.S., rape-mur. An Australian aborigine who was adopted by Christian missionaries and brought to the U.S. when he was 7 years old was convicted of raping and murdering a Melbourne, Australia, woman named Barbara Ann Barber behind her Brevard County, Florida, interior design studio on November 23, 1988. Savage was found guilty of first-degree murder, robbery, and sexual assault on November 21, 1989, by a Circuit Court jury in Rockledge, Florida.

The case received considerable pre-trial publicity when Savage's biological mother insisted that her son had been wrongly taken from her under the terms of a discontinued program that once allowed aborigine children to be placed in the homes of white adoptive parents. Savage was only 4 months old when he was adopted. Aboriginal rights advocates urged the Australian government to intervene on Savage's behalf, but Australian Consul Ira Lindeman remained noncommittal during trial deliberations in Florida. Despite pressure from the activist groups, Savage was sentenced to death in January 1990.

---

**Savino, Joseph John III**, 1959-1996, U.S., mur. A cocaine addict, Savino served six years for a robbery in New York before he was paroled in 1988 to the state of Virginia. It was here that Savino found employment, working for wealthy contractor Thomas McWaters of Bedford County, Virginia, Savino, a handsome, dark-haired man, moved into McWaters' home where, for seven years, he was the homosexual lover of his employer.

Though he allowed McWaters to support him, Savino grew increasingly resentful of his role of male prostitute and later stated that McWaters hounded him for sex night and day. When Savino began to refuse McWaters, his employer threatened to have his parole revoked unless he complied. This was the story Savino told police after McWaters was found bludgeoned to death in his home on November 29, 1988. Police picked up Savino in Roanoke, Virginia, after he apparently attempted to flee.

Convicted of slaying McWaters, Savino was sentenced to death. His execution was carried out on July 17, 1996, at the state prison in Jarratt, Virginia, a relatively short period of time from his sentence to execution in that most condemned prisoners today have extended their life spans by an average of fifteen or more years through seemingly endless appeals.

Before his execution, Savino stated, "I'm sorry for what happened to Tommy McWaters. I did not kill McWaters. I'm sorry. The Commonwealth has chosen to punish my family. I hope my family and my friends know that I love them. I will finally be at peace." It took some time to give Savino the peace he sought since executioners found it difficult to find a vein in his arm into which they could inject the lethal solution that would kill him. Savino's long mainline drug addiction had ruptured and altered many of the veins in his arms.

---

**Sawoniuk, Anthony**, 1921- , Brit., war crimes-mur. A resident of Domachevo, Belarus, during the German occupation in 1942, Anthony Sawoniuk was a member of the local police department. Following the war, he migrated to England, where he worked for the British railroad. Years after he retired, Nazi hunters identified Sawoniuk as a police guard who, with others, lined up fifteen naked Jewish women before an open pit and mowed them down with submachine guns. One of these women was personally shot by Sawoniuk, according to witnesses who testified against him during his 1999 trial in London.

The jury at the Old Bailey also found Sawoniuk guilty of shooting another Jewish woman, one of three women who were shot in the backs of their heads before being pushed into an open grave in December 1942. Judge Humphrey Potts sentenced Sawoniuk to life in prison on April 1, 1999.

---

**Sawyer, Anthony**, See: **Barbier, Susan**.

---

**Sayed, Rafaat el**, 1946- , and **Portofaix, Gaston**, prom. 1989, Swed., fraud. In 1964, Rafaat el Sayed immigrated from Egypt to Stockholm, Sweden. Within fifteen years, Sayed had parlayed himself into a high-ranking position in the biotechnical field, faking a doctorate degree. In 1981, he purchased a large but shaky Swedish firm, Fermenta A.B., and within a few years was celebrated for turning the company into a successful pharmaceutical operation. He went on to develop an enormous empire in the field.

It was then learned that Sayed's degree was a phony; this led investigators to look deeper into his affairs and those of Fermenta. Sayed, with the help of Gaston Portofaix, Fermenta's chief financial officer, had doctored records and annual reports to make it appear that Fermenta was showing great profits, when in reality it was nothing but a shell. Investors were duped into investing huge sums in the firm. Moreover, Sayed, after learning that a negative report on Fermenta was about to be made public, sold off large numbers of shares through insider trading.

In 1987, when Fermenta's stock became almost worthless, Sayed declared bankruptcy and prepared to flee Sweden. He was arrested on May 25, 1988. On July 19, 1989, Sayed was convicted of fourteen counts of swindling Fermenta investors, perjury, insider trading, and fraud in the largest white-collar case ever brought before a Swedish court. Sayed was sent to prison for five years.

---

**Sayeed, Rubiya**, 1967- , India, kidnap. vict. The fierce religious differences that have separated Indian Muslims and Hindus since the British created Pakistan in 1947 manifested themselves in the kidnapping and threatened murder of a Kashmir Muslim woman. The woman, 22-year-old Rubiya Sayeed, daughter of Mohammed Sayeed, the home minister, was abducted at gunpoint on December 8, 1989, as she returned from a hospital in Sanagar, where she was completing her internship. Shortly after the abduction, the Jammu and Kashmir Liberation Front (JKLF) took responsibility and said that they would kill Sayeed if five political prisoners were not released.

The JKLF, which was founded in 1965, sought either to gain complete independence from India or a union with Pakistan for Jammu and Kashmir, the only Indian state with a Muslim-majority population. Although negotiations extended past the kidnappers' December 11 deadline, Rubiya Sayeed was not harmed. On December 13, Sayeed was released by her captors after the government released the five Kashmiri Muslim militants. One of the freed militants, Hamid Sheikh, a high-ranking member of the Kashmir Liberation Front injured in an earlier confrontation with police, had to be delivered via ambulance. The other four militants freed by the Kashmir government were identified as Noor Homanaad Kaiwal, Mohammad Altaf Bhat, Sher Khan Azad, and Javed Ahmed Zargar. Mohammed Sayeed, whose appointment by newly elected prime minister Vishwanath Pratap Singh was intended to appease the Kashmir Muslim population, is responsible for, among other things, law and order. While riots broke out in the streets of Sanagar during celebrations of the militants' victory, the Kashmir government was severely criticized for capitulating to the militants' demands.

---

**Scarfo, Nicodemo** (AKA: Little Nicky), 1929- , U.S., org. crime-mur. Nicodemo Scarfo, boss of one of the nation's most powerful organized crime families, was sentenced to serve fifty-five years in prison on May 13, 1989, for the murder of Frank "Frankie Flowers" D'Alfonso two years earlier. Scarfo was also ordered to pay a $500,000 fine after being found guilty on federal racketeering charges. Flowers was gunned down on a Philadelphia street corner for failing to show the proper "respect" for Scarfo when he decided to cut his boss out of a share of the profits and for joining a rival mob faction.

---

**Scheer, Manfred,** 1945- , Ger., fraud. More than 11 million gallons of diluted wine were the subject of a fraud engineered by Manfred Scheer, a 44-year-old wine merchant from Moselle Valley, Germany. Between 1977 and 1982, Scheer and several others created what they called a high-quality German wine by mixing sugar syrup with cheap French and Italian table wine. Official wine tasters were fooled by this ersatz wine, pronouncing the concoction top quality. More discerning connoisseurs examined the wine in late 1989 and determined that Scheer's product was, at best, medium quality and, at worst, tasted like a wine-flavored beverage. Scheer and two others were tried and convicted of fraud in Mainz, Germany. On December 11, 1989, Scheer was sentenced to seven and a half years in prison for his scam.

---

**Scherr, Nicholas**, 1965- , and **Stroh, James II**, 1965- , U.S., rape-mur. As the divorce of James Stroh II deepened, bitter memories flooded back, including Stroh's darkest secret, one that his mother-in-law made public to police officials. Her ex-son-in-law-to-be, the lady said, had committed a rape-murder, along with another boy, more than fifteen years earlier. Stroh's estranged wife echoed the tale, saying that her husband had told her that at age 15, he and Nicholas Scherr, who was 16 at the time, had raped and murdered 18-year-old Candace Rough Surface, a Sioux Indian girl living on South Dakota's Standing Rock Indian Reservation, on August 2, 1980.

Stroh, a resident of Wisconsin, often visited his relatives in Mobridge, South Dakota, when his father, a former resident of that town of 4,100 people, took the family back for periodic reunions. The white people of Mobridge, a resort town known for its good hunting and fishing, distanced themselves from their impoverished Sioux neighbors in nearby Kenel, a town of 6,100 Lakota Sioux, the very tribe that had spawned Sitting Bull and war chief Crazy Horse, who had defeated and almost annihilated the 7th Cavalry under George Armstrong Custer on the Little Big Horn River in Montana in 1876.

The glory of the Sioux had long fled. In 1980, the plight of the Sioux living in Kenal was dismal. The lack of employment and meager government subsidies had reduced the Indians to destitution. Alcoholism was rampant among its members, and their children looked forward to an unpromising future. One of these was Candace Rough Surface. At 18, she began visiting local bars and was a regular at now-defunct Joker's Wild Bar, which made a practice of serving low-level beer to underage teenagers.

On August 2, 1980, 15-year-old James Stroh II, who had arrived to visit his cousin, Nicholas Scherr, was taken out on the town by the muscular, sandy-haired Scherr, who came from one of the most prominent families in Mobridge. The boys went to the Joker's Wild bar and there met Candace Rough Surface. They were seen leaving with her and that was the last anyone saw of the girl for ten months.

The badly decomposed body of Rough Surface was found on the banks of a receding river by a ranch hand. An autopsy disclosed that the girl had been savagely beaten, raped, and then shot five times in the head and back with a .22-caliber weapon. A widespread search for evidence turned up some shell casings and a piece of some eyeglasses that had belonged to the victim, but there the matter rested until Stroh's relatives began talking fifteen years later (revelations that prompted many to ask why Stroh's wife and mother-in-law, harboring their dark secret for years, did not immediately go to the authorities when first hearing of the killing).

Stroh was interviewed by Wisconsin investigators and later South Dakota detectives. He quickly cut a deal for a lesser sentence, agreeing to testify against his cousin, Nicholas Scherr, who was arrested and charged with first-degree murder in the death of Candace Rough Surface. He was set free on a $200,000 bond to await trial, but this was expected, as his family could afford the bail. The Scherr family in Mobridge, South Dakota, had been long held in high esteem. Scherr's older twin brothers had gone to the 1988 Olympics and one of them had earned a bronze medal for wrestling.

To honor the Olympic winner, Mobridge town fathers renamed the local sports arena Scherr-Howe Arena, the second name being that of an Indian artist, the overall name designed to bridge the great cultural gap between whites and Indians in the area. The disclosure that Nicholas Scherr stood accused of murdering a helpless Indian girl in 1996 widened that gap by leagues.

Scherr's fate was sealed by his cousin's statements when he testified that he and Scherr had picked up Candace Rough Surface at the bar and then took her to a party at a mobile home outside of Mobridge. Someone grabbed at the girl during the party and she became angry, demanding that Scherr take her home. He, Stroh, and the girl then left in Scherr's pickup.

Stroh told officials that Rough Surface shouted at both boys and threatened them. When she slapped Scherr, he stopped the truck, dragged her outside and knocked her to the ground. Scherr then raped her, Stroh said, and then ordered him to sexually attack the girl. Stroh said he complied only because he feared his cousin, who was then in a rage and had retrieved a gun from the pickup. When Stroh finished with the girl, Rough Surface lay on the ground and Scherr shot her three or four times. He then handed the gun to Stroh and ordered him to shoot the girl. Stroh admitted that he fired a single bullet into the victim.

Scherr then tied the body to the pickup, Stroh stated, and dragged it for about a mile to a river, where he tossed the corpse into the water. The next day, Stroh returned to Wisconsin with his family. Years later, Stroh said, he told his wife about the rape-murder and swore her to secrecy. His divorce had unraveled that secret. Scherr was not tried, however, pleading guilty to second-degree manslaughter on May 7, 1996. The 31-year-old Scherr appeared in a Selby, South Dakota, courtroom on May 22, 1996, and was sentenced to 100 years in prison.

---

**Scherzen, Kevin and Kyle**, See: **Archer, Christopher**.

---

**Schmitz, Jonathan**, 1970- , U.S., mur. In one of the most blatant manipulations of an unsuspecting guest on a TV talk show, Jonathan Schmitz appeared on NBC's Jennie Jones Show on March 6, 1996, after being told that he had a secret admirer. He believed, according to his defense attorneys later, that he was about to meet the woman of his dreams. Instead, Schmitz walked onstage in front of a live audience to discover that his secret admirer was Scott Amedure, a 32-year-old homosexual who lived in Schmitz's home town of Bloomfield Hills, Michigan, a suburb of Detroit.

Jonathan Schmitz, right, as he is uncuffed in a Michigan court where he stood trial for killing a gay admirer who was foisted upon him by the Jennie Jones TV talk show.

Schmitz, 24, who had broken up with his girlfriend some months earlier, was eager to begin a new relationship with another female. He spent $300 on new clothes to impress his new admirer before leaving to appear on the Chicago-based TV show. Once he walked onto the stage, Jennie Jones introduced him to his "secret admirer," Amedure, telling the confused guest: "You have to be flattered." (The 24-year-old Schmitz later told police that when he saw Amedure, a person he barely knew, he felt "sick to my stomach.")

Schmitz cracked a nervous smile and replied: "Yes, but I am a heterosexual. I'm not interested."

Although the show was never aired, Schmitz apparently brooded about being blindsided and humiliated by Jennie Jones and her producers. Three days after the TV show taping, on the morning of March 9, 1996, Schmitz went to Amedure's residence and shot him to death, unleashing two shotgun blasts into his chest. Fifteen minutes later, Schmitz called 911 to report the killing, telling the 911 operator that "He [Amedure] f----- me on national TV."

Charged with murder, Schmitz was convicted and, on December 4, 1996, was sentenced to twenty-five to fifty years in prison. The matter did not end there. Jennie Jones came under terrific fire as being responsible for publicly humiliating Schmitz and prompting the murder. Jones emphatically denied any such responsibility, saying that the killing "had nothing to do with the show ... This was not an ambush show."

Jones had appeared during Schmitz's trial and gave ambiguous and evasive answers packed with "I don't recall," "I don't remember," and saying that, even though she was a TV talk show host receiving a huge salary, she had no part in the selection of guests for the show and did not even know the topic of shows until a few hours before taping began. In a later civil suit brought by Amedure's relatives, the show was found liable for bringing about the murder, and millions were awarded in damages. Also See: **Media and crime**.

TV talk show host Jennie Jones who denied "ambushing" Schmitz on her program and prompting his murderous response; NBC later lost a civil suit and millions in damages.

---

**Schoonover, Kathryn**, 1948- , U.S., Case of attempt. mur. On August 23, 1998, police in Marina del Rey, California, were called to the local post office after witnesses reported a woman at a post office counter wearing protective gloves as she took powder from a container marked "poison" and placed this into envelopes. As 50-year-old Kathryn Schoonover emerged from the post office, she was arrested and booked on investigation for attempted murder. Schoonover had attempted to mail more than 100 letters to persons she knew, letters that apparently contained small amounts of cyanide packaged to appear like free samples of a nutritional supplement.

Investigators later reported that Schoonover, a cancer patient, may have nurtured a grudge against doctors and police and attempted to murder several persons by mailing the packages of cyanide, a poison so lethal that if swallowed even in small amounts can produce death within minutes by causing asphyxiation. Schoonover, a resident of Carpinteria, sixty-five miles east of Los Angeles, was living in her van at the time of her arrest. She appeared to have a working knowledge of chemicals and compounds. Schoonover awaits trial at this writing. Several of her poison-packed letters were addressed to members of the West Covina Police Department.

---

**Schwartz, Joseph W.**, 1971- , U.S., child abduct. A predator on the Internet, 27-year-old Joseph W. Schwartz made contact with an 11-year-old girl in Schaumburg, Illinois. When she responded to his message, he asked her, "U like older guys?" The girl became frightened and told her mother, who then assumed the girl's identity in an ongoing Internet conversation. The mother, in her daughter's name, agreed to meet with Schwartz at a convenience store in Schaumburg where, Schwartz later admitted, he planned to kidnap the girl. The mother alerted Schaumburg police, who arrested Schwartz when he showed up at the store for the rendezvous. On September 1, 1998, Schwartz pleaded guilty to attempted child abduction, and Judge Karen Thompson Tobin sentenced him to three years in prison. Also See: **Internet**.

---

**Scott, David Lynn III**, 1971- , U.S., rape-mur. After two days of unexplained absence from her job as a librarian for the Riverside, California, library, the director called the mother of Brenda Gail Kenny on September 12, 1992, saying that Kenny had not showed up for work and that she had not answered the many calls placed to her separate residence. Kenny's mother drove to her daughter's Canyon Crest apartment, and, using her own key, entered the residence only to discover the place ransacked and her daughter on a bed, murdered, stabbed and beaten to death.

Moreno Valley police were summoned and it was soon determined that the 38-year-old librarian had been sexually assaulted before she was savagely murdered. Her killer had struck her with a heavy instrument so hard that her teeth had been driven into her sinuses. A few weeks later, while police were still hunting for Kenny's killer, an attractive woman in her mid-20s living in a Canyon Creek apartment reported that a man crept into her home and raped her.

The intruder wore a mask and was dressed all in black, wearing the traditional garb of the Japanese ninja warrior of the medieval era. He carried two razor-sharp swords, the victim said. After sexually assaulting his victim, the attacker casually sat on the edge of the bed and quizzed his victim about her sex life, talking with her for more than two hours before he left through the window, taking with him all the cash in the young woman's purse.

The press dubbed the rapist-killer the "Ninja Prowler," and increased their efforts to locate him. Only days later, a young nurse called police to say that a man wearing a ninja costume and a mask had entered her Moreno Valley apartment through an unlocked window and, while she pretended to be asleep, rifled her purse, taking her credit cards and cash and then leaving without molesting her. This invasion was followed by two more rapes in Moreno Valley by a man the victims described as the ninja prowler, saying that he called himself a "hit man" and "a ninja warrior."

More attacks followed and in most instances, the intruder forced his victims at sword point to discuss their sex lives before stealing cameras, tape decks and radios, along with cash and credit cards. On November 3, 1992, an office worker in Riverside, California, reported that an intruder had raped and robbed her and that he had worn all black and carried knives, swords and a chrome-plated .45-caliber handgun. The victim, who had been raped and sodomized, told police that her attacker tried to impress upon her his abilities in the martial arts.

On January 17, 1993, a 39-year-old teacher and his 22-year-old girlfriend returned to their apartment in Canyon Crest to find a burglar ransacking their residence. He wore a mask and was dressed in the black costume of a ninja warrior. He flashed a sword in their direction, saying: "You must not move."

The teacher ignored the order and bravely dove for the intruder, struggling with him. As they rolled and punched each other, furniture was overturned and smashed. The intruder stabbed the teacher before fleeing. A neighbor, an Air Force sergeant, came running and followed the intruder into the street, where the burglar turned and, clutching a chrome-plated gun, squeezed off a shot, the bullet whizzing past the sergeant's head. When others joined the chase, the burglar turned again and hurled two sharp-pointed disks at them, these being "throwing stars" reportedly used by ninjas. The intruder escaped into the darkness.

The teacher was rushed to a hospital with a punctured lung, but survived. Meanwhile, police realized that they had a serial rapist-killer who would apparently dare anything. Just after the attack on the teacher, police received a call from an informant who said they knew who the Ninja Prowler was and gave officers an address. On January 21, 1993, officers went to the home of David Lynn Scott III, a young black man living in the 1800 block of Graham Street. Inside the apartment, police found ninja costumes, swords, knives and a chrome-plated handgun. Also found were items taken from the many rapes and robberies in Moreno Valley.

The 22-year-old Scott, who worked in a movie theater, was charged with eighteen felonies that occurred during the eight break-ins between September 1992 and January 1993. He pleaded innocent to all charges and was brought to trial in November 1997. Though witnesses could not positively identify Scott as their attacker because he had worn a mask, the stolen items found in Scott's residence brought about his January 8, 1998, conviction of Kenny's murder and the attempted murder of the teacher and his girlfriend.

While attending the penalty phase of his trial, on January 23, 1998, Scott, while being escorted back to his jail cell, broke free from his guards and dashed down a corridor of the court house. He was recaptured by guards as he tried to get into an elevator. On January 28, 1998, the jury returned its decision: David Lynn Scott III, ninja rapist and murderer, was to die in San Quentin's gas chamber.

---

**Scott, Felecia**, 1967- , U.S., mur. Felecia Scott took her pregnant friend, 17-year-old Carethia Curry, out to buy a pizza on January 31, 1996, in Tuscaloosa, Alabama. When they returned to Scott's home, she shot Curry twice in the head, killing her, and then performed a crude Caesarian operation, cutting out a mature fetus. She then wrapped Curry's corpse in a plastic container and took it to Jefferson County forty miles distant, rolling it down a ravine. Curry was reported missing on February 1, 1996. Her body was found on March 14, 1996.

By that time, Scott, who had been obsessed with having a child, was already in custody. Following the murder of Curry, Scott had returned to her father's home in Norcross, Georgia. She was arrested on a custody charge and taken back to Tuscaloosa, where she gave conflicting reports about the child she first claimed to be her own and then later stated, "No, it's not my baby. It's Carethia's baby." Convicted of murder, Scott was sentenced to life in prison without the possibility of parole on December 14, 1998, by Judge Gay Lake, Jr., who described Scott's crime as "heinous, atrocious, cruel and premeditated."

**Scott, Randolph**, 1951- , U.S., asslt.-mur. A 3-year-old Lowell, Massachusetts, boy who died in Boston Hospital on May 1, 1989, bore so many marks of abuse that the expert who examined him could not record them all. Shortly after Hanif Sutton died, police arrested 38-year-old Randolph Scott, the live-in boyfriend of the boy's mother, Rosalyn Rochester. Rochester told police that Scott frequently beat her and had increased the beatings of her son in the last couple of months before the boy died, ostensibly because the child was not adapting to toilet training. Scott, a heroin addict, also frequently forced Rochester to work as a prostitute to earn money to support his drug habit.

At Scott's trial, which began on December 6, 1989, Rochester testified that she went out to work as a prostitute on the night of April 29, and when she returned, found her son comatose. The prosecution contended that the boy had died of a massive blow to the head. After two days of testimony, Scott pleaded guilty to second-degree murder and received a mandatory life sentence. Scott also pleaded guilty to charges of assaulting both Rochester and Sutton and was sentenced to three concurrent nine- to ten-year sentences. Scott's decision to plead guilty came after testimony from Dr. Eli H. Newberger, a pediatrician and child abuse specialist who had examined Hanif before the boy died. Newberger testified that he found innumerable bruises and puncture wounds on the boy's body, stretching from his hairline to his thighs.

**Scott Todd**, See: **McClary, David.**

**Scroggins, Gregory Scott**, 1962- , U.S., attempt. mur. While investigating a dispute between two male roommates in Smyrna, Georgia, in January 1989, David Crook, a Cobb County policeman, was attacked by one of the men, Gregory Scott Scroggins, 27. Scroggins, who was later found to be a carrier of the AIDS virus, bit officer Crook. Although medical experts state that there have been no confirmed cases of the AIDS virus being transmitted through saliva, a Marietta, Georgia, jury, after deliberating for three hours, found Scroggins guilty of attempted murder on October 20, 1989. Scroggins was given a 10-year prison sentence.

**Scudi, John**, 1944- , U.S., obstruct. of just.-perjury-adultery. A Navy veteran of three decades who rose to the rank of rear admiral, John Scudi was charged in 1998 with having improperly awarded Navy contracts without properly seeking competitive bids, these contracts, worth millions, going to a consulting firm headed by a woman with whom Scudi had an longstanding adulterous affair. Tried by the Navy in a closed hearing in Norfolk, Virginia, Scudi was found guilty of obstruction of justice, perjury and adultery. His sentence, however, was lenient: Scudi agreed to early retirement at a reduced pension and thirty days of house arrest. The sentence was severely criticized by those pointing to the lack of morality in the services, one that reflected the amoral behavior of President William Jefferson Clinton. Also See: **Clinton, William Jefferson.**

**Seaholm, Cameron**, 1967- , U.S., rape-mur. Cameron Seaholm, 22, and Denise Duerr, 21, had known each other since attending high school in Garden Grove, California. Their friendship came to an end on April 19, 1989, when Seaholm unexpectedly showed up at Duerr's home. The young woman was standing in an open garage as Seaholm entered. Seaholm later admitted that he intended to hit Duerr on the head, but she turned at the sound of his approaching footsteps, and, instead of trying to knock out his victim, Seaholm produced an icepick and stabbed the startled woman to death. He then raped her corpse, sexual assault being Seaholm's original motivation.

A man walking a dog in a Riverside County canyon near Corona, close to the Orange County line, found Duerr's half-naked body and notified police. Investigators soon realized that Duerr's car was missing and it was later found parked at the Lake Elsinore home of Seaholm's stepfather. Seaholm was arrested and charged with the young woman's brutal murder. In September 1989, Seaholm pleaded guilty to first-degree murder, realizing that he might face a life term if convicted of rape, according to prosecutors. On December 7, 1989, Seaholm was sentenced to twenty-five years to life in prison by Judge Dennis Myers.

**Secord, Richard V.**, 1932- , U.S., perj. In May 1989, former Air Force Major-General Richard Secord was indicted for his role in the Iran-Contra scandal. Secord served as Oliver North's "intermediary" during the 1985-86 negotiations with the Iranians that culminated in a secret arms deal with a diversion of the profits to the Nicaraguan Contras. Secord was a business partner of Iranian-born businessman Albert Hakim, who brought North, Robert "Bud" McFarlane, and CIA Director William Casey into contact with the Iranian government. Prosecutors in the Iran-Contra case charged Secord and Hakim with concealing $1.5 million in hidden profits in Swiss bank accounts. At least $13,800 of this money was used to purchase a home security system for North. In addition, a $200,000 trust fund was established for North's children. The security system and the Swiss bank account were gratuities given to North for steering the arms deals to Secord and Hakim, though North claimed at the time that he did not know where the money came from.

Secord appeared as the lead-off witness before the congressional Iran-Contra committee in May 1987. On June 10, he denied any knowledge of arms profits benefiting North. Unlike other witnesses who appeared before the investigators, Secord did so without a grant of immunity. On May 11, 1989, he was indicted on nine criminal charges of lying to and obstructing a congressional investigation. Defense attorney Thomas C. Green labeled the charges as "vindictive and contrary to any notion of fair play." Prosecutor Lawrence E. Walsh replied that "this is a very forthright act by a grand jury, which looked into certain matters and concluded that an indictment should be filed."

Facing a possible five-year prison sentence and $250,000 in fines, Secord and his attorney agreed to cooperate with prosecutors in future Iran-Contra cases in return for his agreement to plead guilty to one felony count. The government then dropped eleven other counts against him. Appearing before U.S. District Judge Aubrey Robinson on November 8, 1989, Secord said that his previous statements were not "candid," adding that he lied because of a "misguided effort to prevent further criticism of Colonel North" and himself.

Secord's plea-bargain arrangement earned him two years' probation. The sentence was handed down on January 24, 1990, by Judge Robinson, who said that the crime itself did not warrant a prison term. Immediately afterward, Secord issued statements that censured former president Ronald Reagan for failing to "take the heat" for the scandal. Secord said that Reagan's actions were "cowardly." He reserved his strongest remarks for Prosecutor Walsh, a man he labeled as a "monster at large in our criminal justice system." Secord vowed to challenge the statute on the books that allowed for the appointment of special prosecutors. See: **Iran-Contra Scandal.**

---

**Seda, Heriberto** (AKA: Zodiac Killer), 1970- , U.S., mur. A Brooklyn shooting on June 18, 1996, would not have been more than a routine domestic quarrel had not a curious detective investigated further to discover that the man under arrest was the notorious Zodiac killer who had terrorized New York in 1990. A family dispute erupted when 26-year-old Heriberto Seda reportedly shot his teenage half-sister in the back for running around with members of a notorious gang.

**New York's infamous Zodiac killer, Heriberto Seda, under arrest in 1996.**

When police were summoned to Seda's third-floor Brooklyn apartment, they were met by gunfire. Seda held off police in a raging gunfight for almost four hours before he surrendered. One of the detectives inspecting Seda's apartment after the gunman was taken into custody examined the strange scrawls on paper strewn about the apartment and recognized them as those of the mysterious Zodiac killer who had been widely sought six years earlier.

The Zodiac killer had shot four persons, one fatally, on the Queens-Brooklyn border and in Central Park. The shootings had occurred on Thursdays, twenty-one days or a multiple of twenty-one days apart. The killer wrote taunting letters to the police, saying that he would kill someone born under each of the twelve astrological signs, thus earning the sobriquet of the Zodiac killer (not to be confused with the Zodiac killer who had terrorized San Francisco decades earlier).

Zodiac had shot a Scorpio, a Gemini, a Taurus and a Cancer, somehow learning the signs from the victims. So wide was the 1990 panic that New Yorkers were warned by the press not to divulge their birth dates to strangers. Police went on extra alert every three weeks in anticipation of Zodiac striking again. After a June 21, 1990 shooting, however, the killer vanished.

When Seda was confronted with evidence from his apartment, he broke down and confessed that he was Zodiac, saying that he had been seized by "a sudden urge" to strike randomly and that he learned of his victims' astrological signs only "by chance." Seda was convicted of the 1990 shootings on June 24, 1998. He was sent to prison for life.

---

**Segarra Palmer, Juan,** 1950- , **Ramirez Talavera, Norman,** 1957- , **Comacho Negron, Antonio,** 1944- , and **Maldonado Rivera, Roberto,** 1936- , U.S., rob. On September 12, 1983, Wells Fargo guard Victor Gerena, 25, pulled out his revolver and pointed it at his fellow guards, demanding that they stand back as he loaded $7.1 million in currency from a West Hartford, Connecticut, depot into his car. The money weighed 900 pounds, but Gerena succeeded in padding it into the trunk and back seat before driving off, never to be seen again.

Gerena's Wells Fargo heist was the second largest in U.S. history and remained unsolved until August 30, 1985, when FBI agents arrested thirteen suspects in Puerto Rico. Only a fraction of the stolen money—$80,000—was ever recovered. The rest, it is believed, was given to Los Macheteros (the machete wielders), a militant left-wing group committed to severing all political and economic ties between Puerto Rico and the U.S. The Los Macheteros spent roughly $1 million. An additional $2 million was diverted to Cuba, and some $4 million was tucked away into hiding places. The robbery was masterminded by Juan Segarra Palmer, a member of Los Macheteros. Segarra enlisted Gerena to the cause, whom the FBI believes escaped to Cuba with $2 million.

The thirteen members of Los Macheteros were arrested on the strength of electronic surveillance carried out by the FBI. Since the people whose voices were captured on tape addressed each other using code names, it was probable, according to defense attorneys, that the government was guilty of mistaken identity. The first four defendants in the case appeared before Judge T. Emmet Clarie in West Hartford. Norman Ramirez Talavera, Roberto Maldonado Rivera, Antonio Comacho Negron, and Segarra were formally charged with robbery, conspiracy, weapons violations, and transportation of stolen money. Segarra explained that he had firsthand knowledge of the heist, but denied any direct involvement in the case. On April 10, 1989, the five-and-a-half-month-old trial ended when the four men were found guilty. Conspiracy charges brought against a fifth man, Carlos Ayes Suarez, were subsequently dropped.

In June, defendants Ramirez, Comacho, and Maldonado were sentenced to prison for fifteen years. For masterminding the Wells Fargo heist, Segarra received sixty-five years from Judge Clarie. Speaking through his attorney, Leonard Weinglass, Segarra accused the government of prosecuting him because of his political beliefs. The Harvard-educated nationalist said he "never expected" to receive justice.

---

**Sellers, Sean,** 1970-1999, U.S., mur. Though he showed a smiling, benign face to the world through prison bars, became a born-again Christian as is the wont (ploy, say some) of condemned prisoners, wrote an autobiography and comic books, and produced journals for the Internet designed to aid wayward youths, Sean Sellers, many believed, was nothing more than a conniving killer trying to prolong his life through the ruse of redemption. In 1985, when four months past his 16th birthday, Sellers began practicing Satanism in the bedroom of his parents' home in Oklahoma City, Oklahoma. He became preoccupied with murder and told a friend, "I want to see what it feels like to kill somebody."

On September 8, 1985, Sellers randomly picked out store clerk Robert Bower, shooting him to death. Six months later Sellers shot and killed his mother and stepfather, Vonda and Paul Leon Bellofatto, as they slept. He then went to the home of a friend, where he hid the murder weapon, later telling police that he had spent the entire night with his friend. Sellers returned to his own house the next morning to dramatically fake the finding of the bodies.

The murders were soon attributed to Sellers and he was brought to trial, where his defense attorneys claimed that he had lost touch with reality, that Satanism and his addiction to the video game Dungeons & Dragons had perverted his mind and reason and compelled him to murder his parents. The prosecution dismissed this argument, saying that Sellers had long premeditated the killings, including that of the store clerk, and that he had specifically murdered his parents because he wanted to be free of parental supervision. A jury agreed with the prosecution and convicted him. Sellers was then sentenced to death.

For thirteen years, Sellers filed his many appeals and enhanced his prison image by becoming a born-again Christian. He authored a self-serving autobiography and comic books that he said were aimed at aiding youths and cautioning them not to follow his errant path. Moreover, he wrote journal entries and poetry, which he sent to friends, who, in turn, established a web site for Sellers.

When asked why he should have his own web site and why anyone should be interested in anything he had to say, Sellers likened his journals to the adolescent diaries of Anne Frank, written while she and her family were in hiding from Nazi persecutors. By so positioning himself, Sellers cleverly attempted to portray himself as a victim. This Anne Frank certainly had been. Sellers, however was not the victim in his case; he was the perpetrator, the killer of an innocent clerk and his own parents.

Sellers clogged his web site with musings, homespun philosophy, amateurish poetry and even a so-called "confession," which, in the words of the Washington *Post*, offered "more of a justification for the murders than a reason." He went on to say that his mother verbally and physically abused him as a child, a comment that drew fire from Bellofatto family members and investigators who worked on the 1985 murders committed by Sellers. Said Ron Mitchell, a homicide inspector for the Oklahoma City Police Department: "One of the first things you look at is the home environment. People who knew him [Sellers] portrayed him as a confused kid unable to express emotions. But nobody said a word about abuse."

Born-again Christian, big brother to troubled youths, abused as a child, multiple personality disorder (MPD)—all

these were calculated excuses and ploys by Sellers to forestall and hopefully overcome his death sentence, said Bellofatto family members. Lorne Bellofatto, son of the slain Lee Bellofatto, stated, "I'm just appalled that he can go on the Web and write a lot of untruths and half-truths. He has had twelve years to become a skilled writer and what he has written is a phenomenal fictionalized story. It's fantasy."

As the date of his death sentence approached, Sellers launched a media blitz, which included appearances on such tabloid TV talk shows as "Geraldo" and "Oprah." He also made what was loosely termed a "confession" to *People* magazine. All of it was designed to portray him as a thoroughly reformed person whose death would deprive many troubled youths of his guiding light philosophy. Others argued that Sellers' execution would also serve to enlighten these youths to the consequences of taking the life of another.

On the eve of Sellers' execution, his defense attorneys filed last-minute appeals with the U.S. Supreme Court, which refused to hear the case, and the 10th Circuit Court of Appeals, which rejected the bid for commutation. Oklahoma Governor Frank A. Keating also refused to pardon Sellers. Finally, just after midnight on February 4, 1999, Sellers was put to death at the Oklahoma state prison at McAlester.

---

**Sendero Luminoso,** See: **Shining Path, The.**

---

**Shakur, Tupac,** 1971-1996, U.S., sexual moles.-mur. (vict.) Tupac Shakur was born into poverty in New York. His mother was jailed on a bombing charge while she was pregnant with him and when she was a member of the terrorist group the Black Panthers (she was later acquitted of the charge). His father was reportedly shot to death, but claimants to Shakur's millions later came forth to covet paternity to the gangsta rapper. Writing street poetry while attending the High School for the Performing Arts in Baltimore, Maryland, Shakur at first extolled black womanhood and reflected respect for elders.

Then Shakur began making rapper songs for Death Records and his tone followed the money trail, one which portrayed women as bitches and advocated the murder of cops, violence and anarchy. Millions of disenfranchised black youths responded by buying Shakur's records and, in turn, making him a millionaire. He could not, however, escape his roots or the philosophy of violence he and his record bosses promoted. He began carrying a gun and shooting at people.

In 1993, he was charged with rape. He was later convicted and imprisoned. Free on bond—his record bosses put up $1.6 million for his bail—Shakur appealed the sentence. At the time he went to Las Vegas, where he and his entourage attacked a man outside the MGM Grand Hotel on September 7, 1996. Hotel security video cameras recorded Shakur and others punching and kicking the victim, reportedly a member of the West Coast black gang called the Crips.

Shakur's boss and head of Death Row records, Marion "Suge" Knight, who was reportedly a member of the L.A. gang the Bloods, had somehow brought about the encounter with

**Gangster rapper Tupac Shakur, shown spitting at reporters in 1994 after his indictment for rape; he was murdered in 1996.**

the Crips gang member outside the hotel, according to one report. Some hours later on the night of September 7, 1996, Knight was driving his BMW down a Las Vegas street, with Shakur standing up through the sun roof and four other associates in the car. A white Cadillac came abreast of the moving BMW and its occupants fired at the BMW. Shakur was mortally wounded and taken to a hospital.

Shakur had had two fingers shot off and had received serious wounds to his lung and intestines. He died at the University Medical Center in Las Vegas on September 13, 1996, consumed by the violence that he had urged in his lyrics. His killers were never identified. Also See: **Gangster Rappers**.

---

**Shamburger, Ronald Scott**, 1972- , U.S., mur. A senior college student at Texas A&M University at College Station, Texas, Ronald Shamburger, who had had a strong Christian uprbringing, suddenly began burglarizing the homes of fellow students in September 1994, taking cash and credit cards. One of his victims was Lori Ann Baker, the daughter of a wealthy Texas businessman. An attractive girl, Baker had briefly dated Shamburger, but broke off with him when he began to get emotionally involved.

Shamburger repeatedly broke into Baker's home, which had been built for her by her father, to steal her money, credit cards and other valuables. On the night of September 29, 1994, he again slipped into Baker's home but found the girl asleep in her bedroom. When Baker unexpectedly awoke, Shamburger shot her once in the forehead, killing her.

At about this time, Victoria Kohler, Baker's roommate, entered the apartment and Shamburger came at her in the darkness, throwing a blanket over her and sitting on her, asking if she was able to identify him. Kohler said no and Shamburger led her to Baker's car, putting her into the trunk. He then returned to the apartment, where he retrieved a butcher knife, which he used to probe the ugly wound in Baker's head until he retrieved the bullet that had killed her. He then soaked the place with gasoline and set it afire to eradicate his fingerprints.

He had, however, foolishly left the keys to his car on the bed, and the erupting flames prevented him from retrieving them.

When he ran outside, a campus policeman identified him as he raced from the scene of the burning building, as did Baker's brother, who lived nearby and responded to the fire. Firefighters arrived to extinguish the blaze and find Lori Baker's corpse. Shamburger's car was found nearby, as was Kohler, who escaped the trunk of Baker's car. Within a short time, Shamburger was identified and taken into custody, charged with murder. He was convicted in a speedy trial, with several on-the-scene witnesses identifying him in court. Shamburger was sentenced to death and awaits execution at this writing.

---

**Shamji, Abdul,** 1932- , Brit., perj. Forced to leave Uganda under pressure from dictator Idi Amin, Abdul Shamji arrived in England and began his meteoric rise as a self-made millionaire. As head of the Gomba Group, an expanding conglomerate, Shamji was dubbed a business genius and was elected vice president of the Conservative Party's Small Business Bureau. Through his political connections, Shamji built a huge business empire, largely with money borrowed from the Johnson Matthey Bank, taking out loans in excess of £20 million, £5 million of which Shamji personally guaranteed. Shamji lived regally at Coombe Hill, an estate near Kingston, Surrey. Over the years he had acquired Wembley Stadium along with several theaters and hotels in London. He was considered an inventive tycoon.

In September 1984, the Johnson Matthey Bank collapsed. In February 1986, Shamji was questioned about his firm's debt to the financial institution. "He lied like a trooper," said Judge Kenneth Richardson in 1989 when reviewing perjury charges against Shamji. At the time, Shamji denied having any bank accounts and claimed that his assets were inconsequential. Investigators revealed, however, that the tycoon had at least twenty substantial bank accounts in Switzerland, India, Luxembourg, and England through which millions of pounds had been funneled.

Unpaid loans taken by Shamji's firms were thought to have contributed to the subsequent collapse of the Johnson Matthey Bank, although Gomba repaid £22 million to the bank. During the 1986 hearings, Shamji denied having any Swiss bank accounts and insisted that his last active bank account in the U.S. was in 1973. At Shamji's 1989 perjury trial, prosecutor Oliver Sells stated that the tycoon had lied "to make it appear that he, personally, had few assets ... He took great care to bury all trace of his assets," so that his creditors could not get at his funds.

In October 1989, the multi-millionaire was placed on trial in London's Central Criminal Court for perjury and was convicted. He appeared shocked as Judge Richardson sentenced him to a 15-month prison term and ordered him to pay £28,000 in prosecution costs. Stated Judge Richardson: "Perjurers are not easily brought to justice, and when they are, they must be punished. Their lies seriously undermine the administration of justice."

---

**Shapiro, Michael I.**, 1955- , and **Cole, Terry L.**, 1955- , U.S., computer crime. For purely competitive reasons, Terry Cole, news director, and Michael Shapiro, assistant news director, from WTSP-TV in Tampa, Florida, decided to break into the computer system of a rival station in order to access and retrieve newsworthy stories to increase the ratings of WTSP. Shapiro was arrested on February 7, 1989, and Cole was arrested on April 11. Both were charged with fifteen counts of computer fraud and one count of conspiracy. Shapiro, 33, was a former staff member at the competitor station, WTVT, Channel 13. He resigned in October 1988 to accept a position with WTSP. Two months later, he broke into his former employer's computer files for the first time. "Shapiro used the computer at Channel 10 to access Channel 13's news computer, and looked at the information it had on it," explained Christian Hoyer, chief assistant State's Attorney in Hillsborough County. "Everything dealing with the news operation was on it."

The break-ins were designed to enhance ratings for WTSP, which consistently lagged behind Channel 13—news powerhouse in the Tampa-Petersburg market. The fraud was discovered on January 12 by Jim Hooper, the morning news producer for Channel 13. The computer break-in was engineered from Shapiro's apartment, according to police investigators. Each facing seventy-six years in prison, the two newsmen pleaded no contest before Judge Edward H. Ward of the Circuit Court of Hillsborough on May 18, 1989. Shapiro and Cole were both sentenced to five years' probation and ordered to perform 250 hours of community service in addition to making five presentations to media groups about their role in the matter. Both men were fired from WTSP as a part of a reorganization aimed at restoring credibility and improving morale within the news division.

---

**Shaw, Delbert**, See: **Sledge, Justin**.

---

**Shaw, Ronald**, 1966- , U.S., fraud. A claims adjuster for Colonial Penn Insurance Co. from 1991 to 1997, Ronald Shaw, over a four-year period, added the names of friends to insurance claims, forging police reports and medical bills so that it appeared they had been involved in real accidents where those actually involved were unaware of the other parties listed. In this insurance scheme, Shaw, a resident of Plainfield, Illinois, bilked his own company out of $219,000, splitting the proceeds with his friends.

In 1998, an anonymous tip to Colonial Penn caused the firm to conduct its own internal investigation, which revealed Shaw's scheme. Bruce Losardo, 31, of Plainfield, and 39-year-old William Whitcomb, of Bolingbrook, Illinois, both being part of the scheme, pleaded guilty and were given four years' probation and ordered to pay $1,000 restitution. Shaw pleaded guilty in November 1998 and was sentenced to four years in prison on January 13, 1999.

---

**Sheelen, Donald D.**, 1947- , and **Golden, Vincent P.** prom. 1989, U.S., fraud. In January 1989, the Regina vacuum cleaner company of Rahway, New Jersey, released a financial report claiming earnings of $10.9 million on sales of $181.1 million. But the company failed to report appliances that had been returned, creating a $16.8 million loss. When confronted by auditors, company President and Chief Executive Officer Donald D. Sheelen and Chief Financial Officer Vincent P. Golden admitted they had supplied false information to stockholders and the Securities and Exchange Commission. On February 8, 1989, at the U.S. District Court in Newark, New Jersey, before Judge Nicholas H. Politan, Sheelen and Golden pleaded guilty to charges of mail and securities fraud. On May 25, Sheelen was sentenced to one year in a halfway house, fined $25,000, and ordered to perform 500 hours of community service during each of his five years of probation. Golden received six months in a halfway house, a $12,500 fine, as well as the 500 hours of annual service over the same probationary period. The admissions were devastating to Regina. The company sued Sheelen for $25 million following the February disclosures and, in April, filed for protection under Chapter 11 of the Bankruptcy Codes. In May, Regina was purchased by Electrolux Corporation, a Georgia appliance manufacturer.

---

**Sheinbein, Samuel**, 1981- , U.S., Case of mur. Samuel Sheinbein, according to Maryland authorities, murdered 18-year-old Alfredo Enrique Tello, Jr., then dismembered and burned the body before dumping the remains into a garbage bag inside of an Aspen Hill garage in Montgomery County, Maryland, in September 1997. Three days after Tello's mutilated corpse was discovered, Sheinbein's parents, Sol and Victoria Sheinbein, sent their son to Israel, where he claimed Israeli citizenship—his father had been born in Palestine before Israel had become a state—and, through his lawyers, demanded protection against extradition. Under a 1978 law, no Israeli can be extradited to another country.

Sheinbein and his parents had clearly banked on the protection of the Israeli extradition law in preventing Sheinbein from being returned to Maryland to face a murder trial. The results of this action were vol-

Samuel Sheinbein at a hearing in Jerusalem; Israel's high court refused to allow his extradition to the U.S. to face murder charges in Maryland.

canic, creating an international incident that strained U.S.-Israeli relations to the breaking point. Secretary of State Madeleine Albright formally asked that Sheinbein be returned to the U.S., as did U.S. Attorney Janet Reno. Both requests were stubbornly turned down.

Israel's Supreme Court ruled that it not only recognized Sheibein's citizenship, even though the accused man had never before lived in the country, but that Sheinbein could not be extradited to the U.S. The response in the U.S. Congress to this controversial decision was a threat to cut off all financial aid to Israel, but this proved to be a tempest in a teapot. Israeli officials indicated that Sheinbein might be indicted for the Tello killing in Israel and tried there. This proved to be the case. On August 24, 1999, Sheinbein, in a plea-bargain agreement, confessed to killing Tello and was sentenced to 24 years in an Israeli prison.

Said the mother of the slain Tello: "How can anyone understand this ridiculous decision not to return Sam Sheinbein back to Maryland to face his crimes? This is a person who brutally murdered and dismembered my only child."

---

**Shelton, Ronnie,** 1962- , U.S., asslt.-rape-rob.-kid. On October 5, 1989, Ronnie Shelton, 27, was sentenced to 1,449 to 3,195 years—the longest sentence in the history of Ohio—following his conviction on 220 counts of rape, assault, kidnapping, and robbery. Between 1983 and 1988, Shelton raped twenty-nine women and molested a girl in several West Side Cleveland neighborhoods. He was arrested in 1988 after a joint effort by the Cleveland Police Department, suburban police, and the FBI's Behavioral Science Unit identified him as the attacker.

On trial before Common Pleas Judge Richard McMonagle, Shelton pleaded not guilty by reason of insanity, claiming his mental condition was the result of a fall from a roof. Testifying for Shelton, psychologist Emanuel Taney stated that Shelton was a compulsive rapist who should be remanded to a mental institution. In addition, the jury heard testimony from all thirty victims, and on October 4, after four days of deliberation, they found Shelton guilty on all counts. Before his sentencing the following day, Shelton admitted his crime to some of the twelve victims present in the courtroom, but denied he was a mass rapist. Upon receiving the record sentence, he pleaded to be put to death with a lethal injection of sodium pentothal, an option not available in Ohio. His defense attorney optimistically predicted that Shelton could be eligible for parole in fifteen years. But prosecutor Timothy I. McGinty countered that he hoped to introduce legislation named after Shelton that would guarantee the life imprisonment without parole for anyone convicted on more than four counts of rape.

---

**Sheppard, Mark Arlo,** 1972-1999, and **Graham, Andre,** ? - , U.S., mur. On November 28, 1993, cocaine dealers Mark Sheppard and Andre Graham entered the home of Richard and Rebecca Rosenbluth in Chesterfield County, Virginia. They shot Rosenbluth twice in the head and fired four bullets into the head and neck of his wife, then robbed the home and fled. Quickly identified and arrested, Sheppard and Graham turned on each other. Graham received a life term and Sheppard was sentenced to death. He was executed by lethal injection on January 20, 1999. Sheppard had complained through his lawyers that Virginia's new "fast track" appeals law unconstitutionally denied him due process others received for lesser crimes. The 4th U.S. Circuit Court of Appeals denied the motion.

---

**Shera'ie, Mohammed**, prom. 1989, Saud., mur. For no apparent reason, Mohammed Shera'ie murdered an Arab woman and her two children in Jizzan. Shera'ie was quickly apprehended, convicted, and sentenced to death by decapitation. On June 16, 1989, the executioner stood over the condemned man and lifted his sword, about to behead Shera'ie. At that moment, Mohammed Yehia Faqihi, the husband of the murdered woman, shouted,"Listen, I have forgiven you for the murder of my wife and children, whom you will meet before God."

The executioner put down his sword and the condemned man was removed from the block, led through a huge throng that had assembled to witness his execution, and placed in a cell. Since the husband of the slain woman had forgiven the killer, Shera'ie, under Islamic law, could not be executed and his death sentence was revoked.

---

**Sherwin, James T.** See: **Jefferies, Boyd L.**

---

**Shields, David J.**, 1933- , U.S., polit. corrupt.-brib. After spending thirty-five years as a lawyer and twenty years on the bench as a presiding judge in Chicago's Chancery Court, Judge David J. Shields was convicted of taking a $6,000 bribe to stall a pending case, which had been secretly filed by FBI agents in a 1988 government sting operation. On March 2, 1992, Shields was sentenced to three years and one month in prison by U.S. District Judge Ilana Rovner. Shields was the sixteenth Cook County judge to be sent to prison on federal corruption charges since the mid-1980s.

---

**Shifflett, Melvin Irving**, 1952- , U.S., kid.-rape-mur. A man who had a long history of sexually abusing women, Melvin Shifflett, of Stafford, Virginia, met 20-year-old Patricia E. Smith in a bar in Tysons Corner, Virginia. After leaving the bar with Shifflett on the night of October 30, 1978, the waitress and aspiring model vanished. Her body was found three weeks later, on November 21, 1978, in a remote spot along Old Waterford Road near Leesburg, Virginia. The corpse was partially clothed and an autopsy determined that Smith had been strangled to death.

Police interviewed Shifflett about the disappearance and death of Smith, but he was released. In 1979, Shifflett was again visited by police officers, but this time he was arrested

Melvin Shifflet, serial rapist-killer, shown in a Virginia courthouse in 1996.

and charged with sodomizing and stabbing a 21-year-old Woodbridge, Virginia, woman. He was convicted and sent to prison, serving ten years before being released. In November 1994, Shifflett abducted a woman from her home in Prince William County, taking her to a nearby parking lot, where he sexually attacked her. He was in the process of smothering the woman when two of Shifflett's friends intervened.

Convicted, Shifflett was sent to prison for eighty-five years. While serving this sentence, Shifflett was charged in July 1995 with robbing and strangling 39-year-old Deborah L. Emerey, a resident of Quantico, Virginia, on May 22, 1994, then tossing her body into the Potomac River. Tried for the Emerey slaying, Shifflett was convicted and given a life sentence in 1996.

---

**Shikiba Ei**, See: **Japan Stock Scandal.**

---

**Shinda, Somesha** (AKA: John Coleman), 1953- , U.S., child molestation-rape-kid. Between September 1987 and February 25, 1988, eleven school girls from South Central Los Angeles were accosted by Somesha Shinda, a former karate instructor who selected his victims as they walked to school. Shinda, who went by the name of John Coleman, was observed by a suspicious mother as he tinkered with an automobile engine near the intended victim's home. The woman recorded Shinda's license plate number and then followed him down the street as he jogged after her daughter. However, she was unable to prevent her daughter from being sexually molested. In October 1988, Shinda was convicted on twenty-two counts of rape, kidnapping, and child molestation. He was sentenced to serve 127 years in the state prison by Los Angeles Superior Court Judge Ernest Hiroshige on February 7, 1989.

---

**Shining Path, The** (Sendero Luminoso), prom. 1970s-80s, Peru, terr.-mur. Since the group was founded in 1970 by Abimael Guzmán, a philosophy professor from the University of Huamanga, the Maoist rebel group Shining Path (Sendero Luminoso in Spanish) has waged an endless campaign of terror and violence against the Peruvian government. In 1980, their attacks against polling places in outlying regions resulted in the election of the first civilian president after twelve years of military rule. In 1989, the Shining Path stepped up its efforts to oust the moderate government in anticipation of the national elections scheduled for November 12. "The Sendero terror campaign is more widespread now than in any previous year, and it is widespread throughout Peru," commented a U.S. government official.

In April, the group effectively closed down the country's mining and farming regions during a three-day "armed strike." One million Peruvians heeded the call, resulting in a total cut-off of food, electricity, and export minerals from the Andean provinces to Lima. The year 1989 was the most bloody on record. By October, 1,016 civilians and 293 soldiers and policemen had perished as a result of political violence caused by the guerrillas. On October 29, the Shining Path executed three rural mayors, bringing to 123 the number of public officials killed in 1989. The politicians were targeted for death in an attempt to undermine the electoral process. "Fifty percent of the voters in those areas will probably not be able to vote," commented Agustin Mantilla, the minister of the interior. "They are killing some and giving others a time frame in which they will be killed if they don't resign," added Senator Enrique Bernales. "Everyday we are getting calls and letters from people saying they are resigning their candidacies."

It is estimated that the Shining Path had 4,000 members. Much of their income was derived from Peru's $3-million-a-year cocaine industry. The group served as a kind of broker, demanding taxes from the traffickers while fighting for better prices for the growers. Also See: **Guzmán, Abinael.**

---

**Shinozuka, Yoshiro**, 1924- , U.S., Case of crimes against humanity. On June 25, 1998, 74-year-old Yoshiro Shinozuka, a Japanese businessman and former member of the old Japanese Imperial Army during World War II, arrived at Chicago's O'Hare Airport, ostensibly to speak at an Asian historical group meeting. He was detained by the Immigration and Naturalization Service and was ordered to take the next plane back to Tokyo by officials from the U.S. Department of Justice. Shinozuka's name was on a U.S. federal "watch list" of Japanese citizens who were suspected of having committed crimes against humanity during World War II.

Though never tried following the war, Shinozuka had been a member of the infamous Unit 731 biological warfare group that had dissected live POWs and civilians during the war without the use of anesthesia during experiments. Many of these hapless victims were culled from the more than fifteen million civilians who died in China from torture and neglect during the 14-year occupation of China by Japan, beginning with Japan's ruthless takeover of Manchuria in 1931.

Shinozuka's lawyer, who accompanied the suspected war criminal, attempted to argue with U.S. officials and he, too, was ordered to return to Tokyo. This was the first time since World War II that the U.S. government had barred a Japanese citizen for suspected crimes against humanity during World War II.

---

**Shinto, Hisashi,** See: **Japan Stock Scandal.**

---

**Shirley, Nellie Ruth**, 1959- , U.S., crim. trespass. Obsessed with talk show host David Letterman, Nellie Ruth Shirley several times visited the TV star's home in New Canaan, Connecticut. She was arrested on September 28, 1998, as she sat in Letterman's driveway, waiting for him to arrive. She was charged with criminal trespass and convicted. Judge Harold Dean sentenced Shirley to a year's probation on December 1, 1998, and ordered her to undergo psychiatric examination. Only weeks earlier, 46-year-old Margaret Ray, who had been arrested several times for stalking Letterman at his Connecticut home, committed suicide in Colorado.

---

**Shoemake, Larry Wayne**, 1943-1996, U.S., mur. Race hatred and the reestablishment of Nazi supremacy were the apparent motives for Larry Wayne Shoemake's murderous rampage in a Jackson, Mississippi, shopping mall frequented mostly by blacks. On April 12, 1996, Shoemake, armed with four assault weapons, a shotgun, two handguns and a great deal of ammunition, began shooting black people around the PoFolks Restaurant.

Taking refuge in the abandoned eatery, Shoemake began shooting black passersby at random, killing D. Q. Holyfield, 49, and seriously wounding seven others, including Pamela Berry, a black reporter for the Jackson *Clarion-Ledger* who had been sent to site to cover the ensuing battle between Shoemake and the police.

It was several hours before the furious fusillade from the restaurant ceased and only after the building broke into flames. It was some time later when police dragged the charred body of Shoemake from the gutted building. He had either been killed by police fire or had committed suicide when the flames closed in about him.

Found next to his body were two AK-47 assault rifles, a MAC-11 assault weapon, an AR-15 assault rifle, a shotgun and two handguns. A good deal of unused ammunition was stacked on the floor next to the weapons. Police also found in Shoemake's home a number of messages from the killer, all advocating neo-Nazi and racist views. Police spokesman Lee Vance later stated that "it appeared that he sort of expected that his house would be searched by authorities in the aftermath." Police concluded that Shoemake's fiery rampage had been prompted by his uncontrollable hatred for blacks.

---

**Shubiao, Luo**, 1955-1995, China, mur. A convicted serial killer who murdered twelve young women in Canton, China, from 1990 to 1994, was executed by firing squad on January 20, 1995. The 40-year-old Shubiao had been a truck driver who picked up unsuspecting young females, offering them rides. He then raped and killed them, cutting up their bodies and dumping the remains in trash bins throughout Canton. Police discovered the remains and, in one case, managed to follow the bloody trail to Shubiao's vehicle, which was splattered with the blood of his many victims.

---

**Shukry, Ahmed,** 1963- , Israel, mur. On September 7, 1989, Ahmed Shukry, a 26-year-old Palestinian, attacked construction worker Michael Eshtener, 38, at a Tel Aviv building site. Two days later, on September 9, Shukry boarded an Israeli bus and, as the bus neared a cliff on the Jerusalem-Tel Aviv highway, stabbed the driver and attempted to steer the bus off the cliff. He was subdued before the bus went over the edge.

At the same site, another Palestinian had forced a bus off the road on July 6. At that time, sixteen Israelis, two Canadians, and an American tourist were killed. In Tel Aviv, on October 25, 1989, Shukry pleaded guilty to murdering Eshtener and attempting to kill the 51 bus passengers. He was sentenced to life imprisonment plus twenty years. In the event Shukry is paroled in 2009, he must begin his additional 20-year sentence.

---

**Sicari, Salvatore**, See: **Sledge, Justin**.

---

**Sikh Terrorists,** 1982- , India, terr. Since 1982, a group of radical Sikhs, claiming discrimination by the government of India, have killed more than 5,000 people in the quest for a separate nation to be called Khalistan, or "Land of the Pure." Numerous incidents occurred during 1989 in their continuing quest for independence. On February 21, two police officers were killed during clashes in the Punjab state, and on June 25, Sikh terrorists armed with automatic rifles killed twenty-three members of the right-wing National Self-Reliance Group and wounded another twenty-seven at a public park in Moga. Two police officers were also killed. The attack was prompted by attempts to make Hinduism the official religion of India. On August 18, a bomb exploded on a crowded bus in the village of Chintpoorni, killing fifteen Hindu pilgrims and wounding twenty others. The same day, seventeen people were killed near Amritsar amidst the tensions and continuing quest for political and religious separatism.

---

**Silva, Sofia**, See: **Lisk, Kati**.

---

**Silva, Tony**, 1960- , U.S., illegal import of protected. wildlife. One of the nation's top ornithologists and a world-renowned rare bird expert, Tony Silva, of North Riverside, Illinois, pleaded guilty in Chicago to illegally importing protected wildlife from South America. He reportedly had been smuggling South American parrots into the U.S. from 1986 to 1991. On November 18, 1996, Silva was sentenced to seven years in prison by Judge Elaine Bucklo, who rejected the pleas from Silva's attorneys that their client had smuggled rare parrots into the U.S. to protect them from poachers and traders.

Many of the rare birds died en route to the U.S. in Silva's smuggling operations, including hyacinth macaws, Toco toucans and Queen of Bavaria conures. They had been stuffed into cardboard containers or suitcases with false bottoms without food, water or fresh air. Bucklo also sentenced Silva's mother, Gila Daoud, also of North Riverside, to twenty-seven months in prison for assisting her son in the illegal transportation of rare birds.

---

**Simmons, Ronald Gene,** 1941- , U.S., mur. On February 11, 1989, Ronald Gene Simmons, who killed fourteen family members, including his wife and seven children, outside of his Clarksville, Arkansas, home, was sentenced to die by lethal injection. Johnson County (Arkansas) Circuit Judge John Patterson delivered the verdict, and it came just three hours after a jury convicted Simmons on a second wave of murder indictments. In May 1988, Simmons was sentenced to death for the murders of two co-workers, Kathy Kendrick and James D. Chaffin. After the decision was handed down, defense attorney Robert Irwin characterized Simmons as a man whose motive "was not to avoid arrest, but to satisfy a base, primeval and vile human passion." Simmons proved this point when he assaulted prosecutor John Bynum in the courtroom shortly before the jury began its deliberations. (Editor's Note:

Complete details of this case can be found in the Encyclopedia of World Crime, Vol. IV.)

---

**Simms, Ian,** 1957- , Brit., mur. The case of Ian Simms takes its place alongside only two others in British history in which murderers were tried and convicted without the corpus delicti. Simms, a 32-year-old Lancashire tavern operator, became a suspect in the disappearance and suspected murder of 22-year-old Helen McCourt. McCourt, an insurance clerk, passed the George and Dragon, Simms' tavern, on her way home from work every day. When she had not returned home and had not called on February 9, 1988, her mother notified police. In canvassing the neighborhood, the police questioned Simms. Their suspicions were immediately aroused when Simms began shaking and stuttering as he spoke.

On closer questioning, it was found that Simms could not account for his whereabouts on the evening the crime was committed. He was also implicated by two scratches on his neck. In the weeks that followed, no body was found, although eventually a bloodied jacket of Simms' was found along with McCourt's bloodied clothing on a river bank some few miles away. In the ensuing investigation, police uncovered additional evidence linking Simms to the murder; one of McCourt's earrings, covered in blood, was found in the trunk of his car and bloody fingerprints were discovered on his bedroom door. DNA tests indicated that the blood found on Simms' door was 14,500 times more likely to belong to a child of McCourt's parents than to any randomly chosen person. This was one of the first times DNA testing had been used to identify a murder victim in England.

Simms was charged with first-degree murder. During the trial, he denied killing the woman, although he admitted that he had kissed and fondled her on a previous occasion. He explained the physical evidence against him by saying that someone was trying to frame him. The prosecution explained the disappearance of the body by supposing that Simms had fed McCourt's body to rats along the river. Simms was found guilty of murder and, on March 14, 1989, was sentenced to life in prison.

---

**Simon, Stanley,** See: **Wedtech Scandal.**

---

**Simpson, James,** 1967-1995, U.S. mur. On April 3, 1995, only a few hours after singer Selena had been buried in Corpus Christi, Texas, 28-year-old James Simpson, armed with two pistols, walked into the Walter Rossler Co., a soil-testing company in Corpus Christi, and, while shouting profanities, began shooting people. Shot and killed by Simpson were Walter Rossler and his wife Jo Ann, both 62, and three other employees.

Before going to the company, at about 4:25 p.m., Simpson stopped in one area and began firing an automatic pistol from the window of his red compact car. Shannon Bean, who was just then opening his garage door, was startled by the gunshots and stared at the gun Simpson was holding. "He was firing like he was testing it out," Bean later stated. "I started yelling at him and that's when he took off."

Simpson then drove to the Rossler firm and began his carnage, going from desk to desk with guns in each hand, shooting employees. He had worked at the firm from September 1993 to September 1994. Neighbors heard the shots and stepped from their homes to see people running pell-mell from the Rossler building.

As police sirens could be heard in the distance, Simpson held one of the pistols to his head and blew out his brains. He was one of many former disgruntled employees in the last decade who sought revenge against being laid off by shooting employers and fellow employees.

---

**Simpson, O(renthal) J(ames)**, 1947- , U.S., Case of mur. The murder trial of former football player, actor and promoter O.J. Simpson was the most widely publicized in American history, with millions glued to TV sets and avidly reading printed reports on the case as it unfolded day by day. It was not "the trial of the century," as the media promoted it, but a rather shoddy, sad tale of two brutal murders and a black millionaire suspect whose black attorney managed to win him acquittal by flagrantly using race as the key issue, playing to an almost all-black jury.

The prosecution essentially botched its presentation of the mountain of circumstantial evidence at its command. The defense tried the Los Angeles Police Department instead of defending its client. And the trial judge, Lance Ito, a smug, limelight-seeking jurist, was so overindulgent with attorneys that, in

O. J. Simpson, shown on the day he was booked on charges of murdering his ex-wife Nicole and Ronald Goldman, June 17, 1994.

the opinion of this author, he unnecessarily prolonged an already lengthy trial and vastly contributed to the wasting of millions of dollars in taxpayer money.

Ito had been a prosecuting attorney with little will to seek the death penalty in capital cases. In one instance when prosecuting a serial killer, Ito made sure that defense attorneys got hold of a witness to one of the murders, a witness who asked the jury for mercy, instead of the death sentence. The killer was given a life sentence. When presiding over the trial of colossal swindler Charles Keating, Jr., Ito threw out half the charges against the savings and loan thief.

When hearing the pretrial motions for the Menendez brothers, Ito sealed the grand jury findings and thus muzzled arguments for the prosecution. Before becoming a judge, Ito pridefully placed on his car a license plate that read "7 Bozos, 33," referring to the California Supreme Court judges. When he himself became a judge, Ito got rid of the plate. At the start, Ito said he was not in favor of televising the trial. He not only allowed a TV camera in the courtroom, albeit with a fixed point of view that prevented viewers from seeing the jurors and key

**Denise Brown, shown standing next to a photo of her slain sister, Nicole Brown Simpson, who suffered for years as the abused and battered wife of O. J. Simpson.**

evidence produced, but, during the course of the trial, gave a five-part TV interview to Tritia Toyado on a local Los Angeles station.

Ito took advantage of this situation to condemn the incarceration of Japanese in America during World War II, as well as promote his own career. Ito flagrantly likened his public status to that of Cher and Madonna. It was apparent then and now that, unlike most jurists, Ito reveled in the limelight.

From the day of the murders, June 12, 1994, until Simpson's acquittal on October 3, 1995, the world watched as the defense, led by attorney Johnnie Cochran, whipped up race hatred to the boiling point. When the not guilty verdict was announced, most of white America reeled in shock, believing Simpson to be guilty; most of black America rejoiced, insisting upon Simpson's innocence. To this day and for decades to come, these attitudes, woefully, will probably not change. The Simpson case did more to destroy race relations in America than the Dred Scott decision.

The killer or killers of Nicole Brown Simpson and Ronald Goldman, viciously slain some time during the night of June 12, 1994, have not been found at this writing, despite O.J. Simpson's vow (upon his release) that he would not rest until the killer or killers were brought to justice. When slaying Nicole Brown Simpson and Ronald Goldman, the killer apparently hid in the bushes outside Nicole's Brentwood, California, condominium at 875 S. Bundy. When she appeared outside, either to respond to the doorbell rung by Ronald Goldman (who was reportedly returning her glasses from a restaurant where he worked as a waiter) or summoned by the killer himself, the murderer most probably attacked her from behind, driving a knee into her back, pulling her head backward with an armlock over her face and then reaching around with a large, razor-sharp knife to slash her throat so deeply that she was almost decapitated. He then drove the knife into her breasts many times.

The blood spurting from her undoubtedly shot away from the killer because of the murder position he had selected (much the same way Jack the Ripper killed most of his victims).

Police believed that Goldman was most likely killed afterward, coming upon the scene as Nicole was being murdered, and was killed because he was able to identify the killer. He was slashed to death. At 9:50 p.m. the waiter left the Mezzaluna Restaurant, where Nicole Simpson and her family, except for O.J. Simpson, had earlier dined, intending to return a pair of eyeglasses she had forgotten. His death was later signaled, according to the prosecution, by the "plaintive wail" of a neighborhood dog.

A neighbor of Nicole Simpson's, Pablo Fenjves, was distracted from watching

**Ronald Goldman, slashed to death at the same time Nicole Brown Simpson was murdered on June 12, 1994.**

TV by the sound of loud barking or wailing from a dog. His condominium backed onto the one owned by Nicole Simpson. The barking went on for about an hour. He later fixed the time the dog began wailing at about 10:15 or 10:20 p.m. This was the time fixed for the murders. There were others in that Brentwood neighborhood who also heard the strange wail of the dog. (Brentwood was packed with famous people or relatives of famous people, including a close friend of Nicole's, Candace Garvey, and her former baseball star husband Steve; Carl Colby, son of former CIA director William Colby; and Leif Tilden, who had played the part of Donatello in the first Ninja Turtle movie.)

Louis Karpf and Eva Stein, who were also Nicole's neighbors, pinpointed the sound of the wailing dog at about 10:15 p.m. The dog, as it turned out, belonged to Nicole, a white Akita dog named Kato, a name that also belonged to the long-haired houseguest of O.J. Simpson's, the unemployed Brian Kaelin.

The dog Kato was found wandering outside of Nicole's condominium about 11 p.m. by Steven Schwab, who thought the dog was lost. Kato, Schwab later described, kept turning up the walkway toward Nicole's condominium, barking, then turning back to Schwab as if trying to get him to follow him. Instead, Schwab took the dog home with him, where neighbors Sukru Boztepe and his wife took the dog on a walk a short time later, looking for its owner. As Kato approached Nicole's condominium, it pulled hard on the leash, leading the Boztepes up the walkway, where they saw Nicole's body sprawled in a pool of blood.

O.J. Simpson, the accused murderer, had picked up some fast-food hamburgers with Kaelin at 9:30 p.m. that night and then reportedly returned to his estate at 360 N. Rockingham Avenue, Brentwood. From that point until 11 p.m., Simpson could provide no alibi or witnesses who supported his claimed whereabouts. He said later that he was sleeping, resting up for a long-planned trip to Chicago.

Also planned was a limousine ride to the Los Angeles Airport. The limo appeared twenty minutes earlier than expected at Simpson's estate. Its driver, Allan William Park, entered the Simpson estate and waited. While waiting, he later stated, he noticed that Simpson's white Bronco was not parked in front of the estate as later claimed by the defense.

Park would also later testify that he saw Kaelin walking about the grounds around 10:30 p.m., using a flashlight, as if searching for something or someone. At 10:45 p.m., Park also testified, he saw a well-built six-foot black man weighing, according to his estimation, about 200 pounds, rapidly cross the grounds in front of him and go to the front door. He said he could not make out the man's facial features. After the man entered the house, the house lights went on.

A few minutes later, Park said, he went to the front door and rang the bell. He got no answer. At about 11 p.m., Simpson finally responded, saying that he had been sleeping and that he would be outside soon. Simpson did appear with several bags, ready to go to the airport. One well-packed black hand-bag Simpson kept close to him. This bag reportedly vanished at the L.A. Airport when Simpson was waiting to check his bags and standing next to a large garbage container. Then Simpson caught the 11:45 p.m. flight to Chicago.

A few hours later, Los Angeles Police Detective Philip Vannatter called the home of Marcia Clark, a deputy district attorney, telling her of a horrible double homicide in Brentwood and that he needed a search warrant. "It's O.J. Simpson," Vannatter said.

"Who's that?" Clark responded.

"The football player? *Naked Gun?*"

"Phil, I'm sorry. I don't know him."

Vannatter explained further, how Simpson was a legendary football player, a movie star, the man who was seen in television ads jumping over luggage for Hertz rent-a-car. He went on to say how blood had been found on the door handle of Simpson's white Bronco, there was blood on the driveway of his Rockingham estate, and that a bloody glove had been found on the estate by Vannatter's junior associate, Detective Mark Fuhrman.

"Jesus," Clark finally said, "it sounds like you've got enough for filing (an arrest warrant), much less a search warrant."

Vannatter got his search warrant. He and other detectives then began to build a case against Simpson, who was in Chicago. Simpson himself was awakened earlier in his hotel room in Chicago by LAPD Detective Ronald Phillips, who used the kitchen phone in Simpson's home to call him at 6:05 a.m., June 13, 1994.

As soon as Simpson picked up the phone, Phillips said, "I have some bad news for you. Your ex-wife, Nicole Simpson, has been killed."

Simpson's first words were, "Oh, my God, Nicole is killed. Oh, my God, she's dead."

When Simpson became distraught, according to Phillips, the detective said, "Mr. Simpson, try to get hold of yourself.

I have your children at the ... police station. I need to talk to you about that."

Simpson then asked to speak to his adult daughter, Arnelle. He instructed her to pick up his children from the police station, his daughter, Sidney, age 8, and his son, Justin, age 6. He then resumed his conversation with Phillips, which lasted five minutes.

Phillips later testified that he never mentioned to Simpson that Nicole had been murdered. The detective later stated in court that Simpson never asked if his ex-wife had been murdered. He never asked when she had been killed or how she had been killed or any other details of her death. Just after he hung up the phone, Phillips talked with Mark Fuhrman, who reported finding a bloody glove on the Simpson estate.

Phillips did not call the coroner until 6:50 a.m., alerting him to the double murders, and again at 8:10 a.m., asking that someone from the coroner's office go immediately to the crime scene on Bundy. Simpson returned to Los Angeles to attend his wife's funeral. When Simpson met with police, he was not immediately told that he was a suspect in the case. Not until the morning of June 17 did Simpson learn that he was about to be arrested for murdering Nicole and Ronald Goldman. This information was given to him by his defense attorney, Robert Shapiro.

Shapiro and Simpson were then in the home of Simpson friend Robert Kardashian, who had held on to some luggage Simpson had taken with him on his trip to Chicago. After Simpson was told that he was going to be arrested, he went upstairs to say goodbye to family members. He then vanished with his burly friend, Al Cowlings.

According to Cowlings, he drove Simpson to the cemetery where Nicole was buried, hiding Simpson's white Bronco in an orange grove. Simpson made three calls on his cellular phone from that area before he and Cowlings fled after seeing a marked police car in the area. Police by then were frantically searching for Simpson and put out a public bulletin describing his car.

Two motorists responded to the police alert at 6:25 p.m., reporting that the Bronco was on the San Diego freeway. The infamous chase then ensued, with dozens of police cars catching up to the Bronco and pursuing it. Police ordered Cowlings, who was at the wheel, to pull the car over to the side of the freeway. He did so. Officers drew their weapons as they approached the Bronco.

Cowlings yelled, "F— no!" He slammed his fist against the driver's door, shouting, "He's got a gun to his head!"—referring to Simpson, who sat in the back seat. With that, Cowlings sped off, the police in pursuit, but in a wave of squad cars that blocked all lanes behind the Bronco and remaining at a respectful distance, strange, even bizarre behavior for police attempting to catch a murder suspect who was attempting to avoid arrest.

More than ninety million persons in the U.S. and around the world were glued to the televised police chase (or motorcade), watching the slow chase, which seemed to go on forever, until the Bronco turned slowly into the driveway of Simpson's Brentwood estate, where he and Cowlings finally got out of the car. Simpson was taken into custody and the

481                                                                                    - Simpson

Bronco was immediately inspected. It was apparent to officers that O.J. Simpson had attempted to flee the country. Items found on him and in his car at that time—these items were never made part of his subsequent trial—included his passport. Also found was $8,750 in cash and six checks in a sealed envelope. In addition, a fake beard and a mustache was found in the car, one which prosecutors believed Simpson would employ in his flight to another country. None of these items were introduced as evidence in the case against O.J. Simpson.

Oddly, Vannatter and his partner, Tom Lange, later entered these items not as Simpson's property and evidence but as the property of Al Cowlings. The chase itself was never presented to the jury at Simpson's trial. All of this, according to prosecutor William Hodgman, was a judgment call on the part of the police and the D.A.'s office. Said Hodgman later, "If you knew some of the evidence we were dealing with, you would understand what the cost-benefit analysis was." It was a poor call at that, as events later showed.

The prosecution was made up of Marcia Clark, who had never lost a case; William Hodgman, a veteran trial prosecutor; and Christopher Darden, a young black prosecutor who was portrayed by the defense as an "Uncle Tom." It was Darden who would later, bravely, take most of the abuse heaped upon the prosecution by black defense lawyer Johnnie Cochran, an attorney noted for consistently winning when defending blacks accused of various crimes. His formula was simple. He almost always played the race card to black jurors, insisting that his clients were the victims of race hatred and prejudice.

Cochran had successfully defended black singer Michael Jackson in a child molestation case, one that was reportedly settled out of court for $20 million. He also represented black drug suspect Rodney King, who was videotaped as he was mercilessly beaten by LAPD officers, and won for him a $40 million settlement. Cochran was not originally part of Simpson's "Dream Team" of defense lawyers, hired at unspecified millions in fees.

The case was first headed by Shapiro. F. Lee Bailey was brought in at Simpson's request. It was later stated that Simpson wanted a superstar lawyer like Bailey to match what he considered his own status, that of a superstar. A few days after his arrest, according to Cochran, Simpson began calling him at home. "The whole thing was," Cochran later stated, "he wanted to get out and get this over with by Halloween [of 1994] so he could go trick-or-treating with his kids." It seemed to some that Simpson's only concern was his release and returning to life as usual, rather than any deep concern for solving the murder of his ex-wife.

In addition to Cochran, Bailey and Shapiro, Simpson's monolithic defense team included Alan Dershowitz, who functioned as an adviser and who, in case Simpson was found guilty, would lead the attack on appeal. It was Dershowitz who appealed the conviction of Claus von Bulow for the murder of his millionaire wife and won him freedom on technicalities. Simpson called Dershowitz his "God forbid" lawyer, meaning "God forbid I am found guilty." Dershowitz, who never let the world forget that he was a Harvard professor, promoted himself through his academic position almost every time he appeared on TV. Remaining in Cambridge, Massachusetts with his research team (made up of his students), Dershowitz viewed the televised case on a special split screen monitor and sent in advice via a fax machine that was at the defense table.

The defense team at first was showered with publicity, the wrong kind. It appeared that Shapiro had taken insult at being demoted from lead lawyer when Cochran was brought in by Simpson. He and the temperamental, flamboyant Bailey fell to arguing over the direction the defense should take. Bailey, for instance, was the only one who argued that Simpson should take the stand, telling the accused, "You've got great charisma. You'll blow them away." He also resented Cochran's undeviating intention to play the race card, to portray the prosecution as the white oppressors to a famous black athlete. Shapiro later went on TV to denounce this tactic as his fellow defense team lawyers ridiculed him shamelessly.

The real reason for Shapiro's demotion, however, was undoubtedly based on the fact that early on in the trial he proposed a plea-bargain arrangement, one where Simpson would plead guilty to manslaughter. (Shapiro was known as "The Prince of Plea Bargains.") This was seriously considered by Simpson and his attorneys and then abandoned, mostly due to Bailey's insistence; Cochran stayed out of this debate, merely listening, it was later reported.

The prosecution, though it had at hand more circumstantial evidence than similar trials, accepted defeat as early as July 1994, less than three weeks after the double murder, when Marcia Clark concluded that, as an American hero, O.J. Simpson was "an unconvictable defendant." Moreover, according to one report, she said at that time that "they've filed this case downtown, which means they're going to get a downtown jury. A black jury will not convict this defendant. Forget it. It's all over."

Yet the prosecution went ahead with one of the most expensive trials on record, playing out legal battles and grandstanding for the television camera Judge Ito had allowed in his courtroom. Ito himself proved to be one of the most blatant publicity seekers in the whole shoddy mess.

Ito was not unflappable. He focused upon details apparently to impress the court, but so much so that he often forgot procedures. He was so upset about one juror being televised that he forgot to ask the defense for certain witness information. Prosector William Hodgman objected thirteen times to Cochran's wild opening arguments that, rather than focusing on his client's defense, attacked the prosecution and the police department. Ito ignored the objections and let the defense ride roughshod.

A maverick judge on courtroom behavior from his judicial beginnings, Ito made a point of wearing a pair of weathered jogging shoes into court. On the bench, Ito controlled the courtroom through a special television monitoring screen, which allowed him to inspect every corner of the courtroom through security cameras hidden in the ceiling dome.

One of Ito's many pet peeves was chewing gum in his courtroom. Three times, while peering at his special monitor he saw the jaws of reporters moving and had an officer chastise the newsmen for chewing gum. One might wonder, since Ito was spending so much time monitoring the conduct of everyone in court, how he could stay focused on the actual trial.

Ito's relationship with chief prosecutor Marcia Clark was strained from the start. Clark later said that she felt she had to pretend to play a submissive role with Ito. She was not alone. Defense attorney Peter Neufeld later related how he and others on the defense team were compelled to go to Ito's chambers to cater to his "petty needs."

Neufeld portrayed Ito as an egomaniac, one who was "so concerned with his status as a celebrity, his willingness to entertain personalities in his chambers, to show the lawyers little videotapes of skits on television." On one occasion, Ito had the defense lawyers in his chambers to show them a video he had recently taped from Jay Leno's "Tonight Show," which parodied the trial under the title of "The Dancing Itos."

This incident later caused Neufeld to state, "He had thought it [the Leno show] was great and loved it and wanted all of us to see it in chambers. You may find that amusing on a personal level, but I can assure you that on a professional level it is so unacceptable, for a judge who is presiding over a murder where two people lost their lives in the most gruesome and horrible fashion, and where a third person has his life on the line, to bring the lawyers into chambers to show them comic revues." Ito went so far as to tell the lawyers Simpson jokes he had heard. "I found it deplorable and I was shocked," Neufeld said.

The ego of the lawyers and the judge, however, were nothing compared with the raging, bullish ego of the defendant. Simpson bossed his lawyers about mercilessly, paying millions for the privilege of posing as dictator, of course. He dictated the course of his defense and the positioning of his attorneys from his jail cell and in court. Not until one of his former long-time friends, Ron Schipp, testified in court, however, did Simpson realize that he was in real jeopardy.

Schipp, a fellow black, testified that he had been a close friend of both Simpson and Nicole. A one-time LAPD officer, Shipp had taken classes on domestic violence and at one time, at Nicole's request, had counseled both of them on Simpson's long history of physical abuse of Nicole. Shipp testified that at that time, he told Simpson that he fit the pattern of an abuser. More damaging, Shipp went on to say that he went to Simpson's house on the night he had returned from Chicago and, despite the fact that his ex-wife had just been brutally murdered, Simpson laughed and admitted to Shipp that he had thought of killing Nicole. Shipp quoted Simpson as telling him, "You know, to be honest, Shipp. I've had some dreams of killing her."

Cochran's assistant, defense attorney Carl Douglas, attacked Shipp in a bullying cross-examination, bringing up the fact that Shipp was a recovered alcoholic and claiming he was not a close friend of O.J. Simpson but merely a Simpson groupie. This tactic backfired, most observers agreed, causing the quiet-speaking Shipp to appear sympathetic and believable rather than less credible. Simpson, a shrewd observer himself, realized this, and ordered that Douglas was never again to cross-examine witnesses. That night he held a conference call with Dream Team members and shouted, "I'll decide who the running backs are in this game!"

In the meantime, to shore up his defense fund, Simpson received a $1 million advance from Little, Brown for a quicky tell-nothing book titled *I Want to Tell You*, a book he dictated to

Lawrence Schiller from his jail cell. This was only the beginning of Simpson's self-serving promotion. He autographed photos and other Simpson memorabilia to glean more millions, including an audiotape that said nothing about the trial but, like all the other propaganda he produced, brought in a great deal of money because of the trial. He was literally earning a fortune on the murders of Nicole and Ronald Goldman and receiving over the course of the trial more than 300,000 letters from fans.

As the trial proceeded, the defense tried several approaches, one being that others had killed Nicole Brown Simpson and Ronald Goldman, not their client. Simpson's attorneys implied that both had been victims of a drug buy gone wrong, or of drug dealers avenging non-payment or some sort of betrayal, all of this linked to Faye Resnick, one-time Nicole confidante who was extremely hostile toward Simpson and who had written her own book and made a great deal of money from the case, a book that incensed Judge Ito. Resnick had stated in her book that her friend Nicole had told her that Simpson was going to kill her. Ito personally wrote many letters to the media requesting that no publicity be given to the book, stating that it might prejudice potential jurors. Extending this logic to the media at large would be the same as asking that the trial have no publicity whatsoever for the same reason.

The drug connection advocated by Cochran was a far-fetched scenario, one that was never supported by any facts or actual links to a drug-inspired murder. It was just another defense smokescreen. Defense attorneys offered up the wild statements of Mary Ann Gerchas, who said that she had seen four men running from the murder scene about the time the victims had been killed. Gerchas was later thoroughly discredited as a bad-check artist who had been charged with fraud by several persons and companies. In addition, Gerchas was being sued by Marriott International, Inc. for $23,000 in unpaid room charges.

Cochran told the jury that he would call Gerchas (he did not) and some two dozen witnesses who would support the story about suspicious persons prowling about in Nicole's neighborhood on the night of the murder. Cochran was typically running off at the mouth. He did not disclose the names of these witnesses or call them, which was in violation of a 1990 requirement which demands that the defense turn over to the prosecution all the names of witnesses and their written statements. Judge Ito did nothing about this egregious, disingenuous behavior by Cochran.

Next, the defense attempted to unseat Allan Park's statements about Simpson's Ford Bronco not being present when he arrived at Simpson's estate to take him to the airport. Defense attorneys brought forth Rosa Lopez, a maid who lived next door to Simpson. Lopez, in halting English, claimed that Simpson's Bronco was parked at the estate at the time when prosecutors said he was murdering Nicole and Goldman. (Lopez was long in getting to court. She was ordered to leave a Las Vegas gambling casino to attend the trial in Los Angeles.)

Under pressure from prosecutor Chris Darden, Lopez admitted that she had lied several times in giving information on passport visas and in other instances. She, like Mary Ann Gerchas, was discredited; in fact, some observers stated that she appeared to be a "bought witness," especially when it was learned that the defense was providing her expenses.

On a day-to-day basis, the defense appeared to be losing ground. Simpson's attorneys fought hardest against the introduction of any evidence concerning Simpson's longtime abuse of his former wife. That shameful record, it was finally learned, coursed through seventeen years of the Simpson marriage, and it was a horrid litany of physical and mental abuse by a sadistically domineering O.J. Simpson. The record shows that Simpson beat his wife mercilessly and subjected her to ridicule, embarrassment and public degradation. He treated her as a possession, a thing, dehumanizing and disgracing her whenever his dark whims urged. It is the record of a crude, morally deficient bully intent upon inflicting physical and mental pain upon a long-suffering spouse who had told friends that she expected Simpson to someday lose all control and murder her.

Prosecutors found a great deal of the abuse evidence in Nicole Simpson's safe deposit box. It contained a record of all of Simpson's attacks on her, along with color photos showing her bruised and battered face from a 1989 attack for which Simpson was booked. Nicole's careful chronicle of her husband's abuse was assembled for her divorce case two years prior to her murder, but since Simpson continued to visit and terrorize her after the divorce, she kept the evidence, in case, some said, her husband might eventually murder her as she believed.

In 1986, Nicole wrote, Simpson "beat me up so bad at home, tore my blue sweater and blue slacks completely off me." Nicole's sister, Denise, echoed her sister's grim chronicle, saying that she witnessed many of Simpson's abuses of Nicole. In one instance, Denise Brown recalled how she told Simpson that he took her sister "for granted," which caused a fight. "Pictures started flying off the walls," Denise later testified, weeping, her voice trembling. "Clothes started flying down the stairs. He grabbed Nicole and told her to get out of the house. He picked her up and threw her against the wall. He picked her up and threw her out of the house. She ended up falling on her elbows and her butt."

In 1987, Denise recalled, she and a friend accompanied Nicole and Simpson to a Santa Ana bistro, The Red Onion. There, at the crowded bar of the restaurant, Simpson grabbed Nicole's crotch and shouted, "This is where my babies come from and this belongs to me!" The prosecution added that later that night Nicole asked a friend to drive her home in Simpson's Rolls Royce. As the car began to drive away, Simpson slapped his wife and pushed her out of the car and onto the pavement.

In 1988 Nicole's chronicle recounted an incident where she, her daughter Sidney, and her mother and sister attended a "Disney on Ice" show. Simpson, she wrote, was incensed, accusing Nicole of excluding him from the family outing. He got drunk and then went berserk, calling the two-months pregnant Nicole "a fat pig ... You're a slob! I want you out of my f------g house ... I want you to have an abortion with the baby."

Nicole reportedly responded by saying, "Do I have to go tonight? Sidney's sleeping. It's late."

Simpson, Nicole stated, retorted, "Let me tell you how serious I am. I have a gun in my hand right now. Get the f--- out of here."

Nicole Simpson woke her sleeping daughter, packed some clothes, and left. The key to understanding Simpson's motive for murder, one which somehow slipped through the perception of the prosecution, was in the locked fixation Simpson had for being ostracized or shut out (especially in public events, where he could strut the star).

The identical scenario occurred on the night of the 1994 double murders. Simpson was totally rejected by the entire Brown family on the night of his daughter's recital—all of them said he was "not invited" to a celebration party at the Mezzaluna Restaurant—a white family he had enriched by supporting his wife in style, by reportedly funding her father's enterprises, by paying for college expenses for her sisters. Now all of them, these ungrateful whites, were rejecting him, O.J. Simpson, no longer the superstar, merely a black man with money.

Moreover, that night (and not revealed until after the trial), waiting for him on his answering machine was a message from his attractive girlfriend, Paula Barbieri, that she was breaking off their relationship. (It was reported that Barbieri was with Michael Bolton on the night of the murders.) Another rejection from a white woman to a black man who had given her expensive gifts and trips. He had tried to enter the white world, lived inside of its Brentwood majesty, but gnawing on him— beyond his own bone marrow ego and vanity—was the fact that he was nothing more than a black man with money, mostly a black man who was being rejected by the whole of the white power structure, which he had sought for years to enter.

Simpson struck out against these whites, it is the author's opinion, by brutally slaying Nicole and the young white man who suddenly appeared at her doorstep. (It mattered not whether Goldman was Nicole's lover, friend or merely an acquaintance—he was there, a witness to the gore.) This was the white race card the prosecution did not play in response to Cochran's black race card. It certainly would have done little good with a predominantly black jury whose black members were bent on believing from the beginning, irrespective of the reasons they later gave for the acquittal, that a black man—one of their own black heroes—was being unfairly tried by a system Cochran portrayed as white and persecutional.

Had Simpson premeditated the murder, waiting until the right opportunity, a scheduled trip to leave town, and the correct provocation, another gross insult to his pride and ego by being shut out? He was certainly prepared. He certainly had the right tool. Simpson had purchased a knife, a fifteen-inch stiletto, from a Los Angeles cutlery store in May 1994, it was reported. (This was not brought into evidence by the prosecution.) He had told Shipp how he had dreamed of murdering his wife. The family rejection of him served as the catalyst that prompted his plan into action.

In 1989, Simpson beat his wife so badly that he was booked for assault and battery, the charges later dropped. This was the incident where Nicole took pains to have her bruised and battered face photographed. Following that incident, Simpson wrote to Nicole, "Let me start by expressing to you how wrong I was for hurting you. There is no exceptible [sic] excuse for what I did."

Though Simpson later shrugged at accusations of his being jealous of his ex-wife, claiming to be happily attached to Barbieri (when he knew that Barbieri had already broken off with him), his abuse of Nicole continued long after their divorce. On October 25, 1993, only eight months before Nicole was murdered, she called 911 to report that Simpson had barged into her home and was terrorizing her. The 911 tape, played in court, was chilling as it recorded Nicole telling the operator that "It's O.J. Simpson. He's going f———g nuts!" In the background the court could hear Simpson screaming, cursing, banging things about.

To all of this, Johnnie Cochran responded by saying that these were merely domestic arguments. He portrayed the violent history of O.J. Simpson's wife-beating as somehow nothing more than family spats, not the fist-pounding, body-throwing events that they actually were. According to the Los Angeles *Times*, Cochran himself had been accused by a former wife, as being a wife abuser. In divorce proceedings against Cochran twenty-eight years earlier, his former wife, Barbara Berry, accused him of assaulting her. Cochran shrugged a denial, saying that these charges were merely used as leverage in a divorce. (Berry reportedly stated that she was writing a book about her life with Cochran, joining a never-ending list of authors linking themselves to this notorious case.)

About the same time Cochran was fending off accusations of being a fellow wife-beater, a national TV talk show presented a woman named April Levalois, who insisted that while Cochran was still married to Berry, he was the lover of Levalois' mother who bore his illegitimate son, Jonathan Cochran.

The prosecution then introduced what it considered its strongest and most telling evidence. The first of these salient artifacts was a pair of black, bloodstained gloves. The left-handed glove had been found at Nicole's Bundy St. address, near the bodies. The right-handed glove had been found on a walkway near the guest house on Simpson's estate. Both gloves had been found by Detective Mark Fuhrman, who was in the company of other detectives when the gloves were found. The gloves, DNA analysis later confirmed, contained blood from Simpson, Nicole and Goldman.

A bloody sock containing Nicole's blood and found on the floor of Simpson's lavish bedroom was introduced. A navy-blue knit watch cap containing hairs from the head of a black man was found on the grounds of Nicole's residence. Some of Simpson's blood, DNA evidence later stated, was found at the murder site and more at Simpson's estate, including blood from Nicole and Goldman. More bloodstains were found inside the white Bronco. Then there were bloody shoe prints (the size of which later matched Simpson's size) leading from the murder scene on a walkway to the alley.

The defense attacked this evidence. Barry Scheck, a reported DNA expert, paraded so-called DNA experts before the court who reported that the LAPD lab experts handling the DNA and other blood analysis were sloppy, their procedures slipshod. The defense went so far as to say that some of the blood samples taken from O.J. Simpson following his arrest were missing, more than what would make up normal "spillage" in DNA testing.

The thrust of this statement went to a full-blown claim by the defense that all of Simpson's bloodstains had been planted by a conspiracy of racist policemen and perhaps LAPD lab people, and that the chief racist cop was none other than Detective Mark Fuhrman. It was later shown that Fuhrman was, indeed, a racist who repeatedly used the word "nigger" to describe blacks, but it was never shown how this man was able to plant all of the drops of Simpson's blood throughout the Bundy and Rockingham areas, in the white Bronco, and that he also planted and then discovered the gloves, that he planted the knit cap and the bloody sock.

Fuhrman was, however, a prosecution witness who first appeared to be cool and unflappable on the witness stand. Tapes he recorded years earlier when talking to a writer about a proposed book of fiction revealed him to be one who hated blacks. The destruction of Fuhrman's credibility was complete and the most telling blow to the prosecution.

Then, in a dramatic and bold move, Cochran had his client actually try on the gloves before a riveted jury. His method in doing so was unorthodox. Those putting on gloves compress their fingers and cup their hands so as to be able to slip into gloves that are normally tight-fitting. When Simpson tried the gloves, he kept his fingers wide apart, spreading his palms so that the gloves did not go on easily. He kept his fingers spread so that the gloves appeared not to fit, without snuggling the bottom ends over his palms. It was a colossal bluff that worked, since the prosecution did not take exception to the manner in which Simpson performed this procedure.

So effective did Cochran believe this demonstration to be that he harped on it until the very end of the trial, carping in his final summation a glib coinage: "If it doesn't fit, you must acquit." He repeated this phrase over and over while wearing a copy of the knit cap that had been placed in evidence, as if to contemptuously mock the evidence. And always, with almost every statement, was Cochran's insistence that O.J. Simpson was the victim of a white conspiracy.

The prosecution, on the other hand, put up a list of what it thought were convincing arguments for the jury to convict, but Marcia Clark's summation was timid, tentative, weak, unconvincing, as if she was listening to her own words of a year earlier—"A black jury will not convict this defendant. Forget it. It's all over."—and she appeared unenthusiastic, fearful of failure.

Missing from the prosecution's summation was any mention of Simpson's fantastic flight for freedom and the money, passport and false identity inside the Bronco that would pave the way for his escape. Missing was any mention of the stiletto he had purchased a month before the murders. Missing was an argument showing how Simpson had purposely manipulated the gloves to make them appear not to fit. Missing was a precise timetable that would show that O.J. Simpson had enough time to commit murder and then return to his estate before flying to Chicago. Missing were all of the abuse offenses committed by Simpson against his wife (who had called the Sojourn shelter only five days before her death to say that Simpson was going to kill her).

The International Chiefs of Police had statistics to prove that most women—1,400 of them a year, on average—who were murdered were killed by men who knew them and that most of them were victims of consistent spousal abuse. None of that mattered to a jury of nine blacks (mostly women), two whites and one Hispanic. In less than four hours after merely glanc-

**In one of the most dramatic moments of O. J. Simpson's murder trial, the accused tries on the murder gloves in court, awkwardly spreading his fingers to make it appear that the gloves do not fit.**

ing at the mountain of evidence, the jury acquitted Simpson. Its verdict was not made public for twenty-four hours on order of Judge Ito so that all the lawyers could be present in court, or so he said. Another reason for this delay may have been Ito's typical playing to the TV gallery in order to have the dramatic moment captured on prime time.

The verdict was read on October 3, 1995. Simpson, who had spent 473 days in jail and had defended himself at a cost of unreported millions, was set free. The trial itself had cost more than $9 million and was the most watched event in television history. Judge Lance Ito had seen to it that the trial lasted as long as it did.

Half of the trial time was consumed by endless, unimportant sidebar conferences with lawyers whom Ito allowed to squabble, argue, attack and insult each other. He grandstanded throughout the trial, seeking to impress anyone who would listen to his non-legal comments, which, for the most part, were neither learned nor enlightening. As a jurist, Ito was a disgrace, and, in the opinion of this author, should have been removed from the bench.

The jurors showed themselves unconcerned with the evidence. Brenda Moran, a black female jurist, labelled all of the evidence of Simpson's spousal abuse "a waste of time." One young juror posed for *Playboy*, several wrote books, all played to the media. Though they later claimed to have reached a verdict on the evidence, it was apparent that the almost all-black jury released O.J. Simpson because he was black. "It was payback," one observer stated, "for the unfair Simi Valley decision to release the cops who beat Rodney King, and for all of the LAPD oppression of blacks in Los Angeles."

One of the most repulsive reactions to the verdict was a group of televised (by NBC) black women watching TV to hear the verdict. They were all victims of marital abuse, all residing in a battered women's retreat. When the not guilty verdict was announced, the women leaped from chairs, threw their hands in the air in jubilation and screamed their joy. All that mattered to them was that a fellow black had triumphed, not justice.

The reaction to this strange and apparently unevaluated verdict was to deeply divide whites and blacks as never before, and it most likely convinced an able presidential candidate, Colin Powell, that his chances of being elected were considerably lessened by the racial division that had been drawn by the verdict. More than 80 percent of the more than 220 million whites in America believe to this writing that Simpson is guilty. Roughly 80 percent of the eighteen million blacks in the U.S. believe Simpson not guilty.

Everyone except the murder victims profited by this trial. Network television had captured viewers by the untold millions and benefited enormously. Simpson won his release, while his defense attorneys were enriched by his millions. Prosecutors Marcia Clark and Christopher Darden received multimillion-dollar contracts for books and movies about their rather uninteresting lives. Instead of the dismal failures they really were, the prosecutors were looked upon as beleaguered, heroic figures, but such is the warped perception of media-created images. The choked-up conduct of Clark and Darden during a prosecution press conference at the trial's conclusion was embarrassing and, to some observers, obviously feigned. Instead of heaping kudos on these people, District Attorney Gil Garcetti should have pointed out their ineptitude in failing to use evidence at hand to convict O.J. Simpson. But then, Marcia Clark had announced that inevitable failure more than a year earlier.

Simpson's own conduct following the trial did anything but convince his detractors that he was innocent. He had vowed upon his release that he would spend the rest of his life seeking the killer or killers of his ex-wife and Ron Goldman. That was the last time he mentioned that crusade. On the night of his release, he returned to his Brentwood estate, where he held a champagne party to celebrate his freedom, laughing and drinking with fawning friends, hardly the expected conduct of an aggrieved wrongly accused husband.

He was seen thereafter flitting about the country to play golf at the best courses, courting new friends even among the startled strangers who saw him driving past them in golf carts. Simpson, however, did not escape his actions altogether; he next had to face civil lawsuits brought against him for damages from the Goldman family. He dodged depositions in that case, but in January 1996 accepted a reported $3 million payment to appear on a video in which he talked about the trial, attacking Marcia Clark and trying to dispute the evidence brought against him, particularly the DNA analysis.

It appeared at that time that Simpson was still attempting to regain the favor of the power structure that once made him a millionaire. The tape, however, was viewed as a staged affair, one where Simpson simply answered questions that met his beforehand approval. There was no cross-examination. It was a kangaroo court where Simpson retried his own case and turned the facts in whatever direction suited his purpose. Newsman Ross Becker, who was hired to act as Simpson's questioning stooge in this rigged scenario, was interviewed after its completion and was asked if he felt that Simpson lied to him during the staged videotaping. Becker replied, "Sure, sure." Simpson did not mention his quest for the real killers of his ex-wife on the video, nor did he state that he would be offering any portion of the $3 million he received for doing the tape as a reward for the apprehension of that killer or killers.

Many esteemed criminologists and prosecutors throughout the U.S. generally agreed that Simpson had gotten away with murder. Not the least of these was the brilliant prosecutor Vincent Bugliosi, who had won 105 out of 106 felony jury trials while working for the district attorney's office in Los Angeles, including the notorious Charles Manson case of the Tate-LoBianca slayings of 1969. Said Bugliosi of Simpson in 1996, "I've known a lot of murderers, but this guy is the most audacious murderer I've ever known. I'm convinced that he feels that he had a right to kill Nicole and that she did something to warrant the murder."

**A jubilant O. J. Simpson, following his acquittal for murder in his Los Angeles criminal trial in 1995; he was later found guilty in a civil trial of causing the deaths of Nicole Brown Simpson and Ronald Goldman.**

Simpson's audacity flared throughout the subsequent wrongful death civil suit brought against him by the Goldman family in the murders of Nicole Brown Simpson and Ron Goldman. This time, most of the evidence improperly introduced or not introduced at all in Simpson's criminal trial was presented in masterful fashion by Goldman family lawyer Daniel Petrocelli. He deposed Simpson and continually caught him in stated inconsistences. (Simpson repeatedly lied to Petrocelli in stating that he had never hit or struck or abused his dead wife.)

A key piece of Petrocelli's evidence was a single photo of Simpson wearing size-12 Bruno Magli shoes, the same shoes that had reportedly left a bloody imprint at the scene of the Nicole Simpson-Ronald Goldman murders. Only 299 pairs were sold in the U.S. between 1991 and 1993, and Simpson emphatically denied that he ever owned, let alone wore, such shoes, describing them as "ugly." The single unclear photo of Simpson wearing such shoes at a September 26, 1993 football game at Rich Stadium in Buffalo, New York, was discredited by Simpson's lawyers, who stated that the photo was a fake.

Then Petrocelli found an entire series of photos taken of Simpson at the same event that were crystal clear, and by blowing up the photos he was able to pinpoint the identification of the rare shoes: Indeed, at that time, Simpson was wearing size-12 Bruno Magli shoes. He had been caught in a lie, another lie his lawyer, Robert Baker, could not undo. Baker took the unsavory approach of attacking the victim, attempting to portray the slain Nicole Brown Simpson as a promiscuous woman, a drug-taking alcoholic who abused her chil-

dren by subjecting them to the company of drug dealers and perverts. His attack backfired; the jury refused to believe his argument.

Petrocelli then worked in the evidence that the black jury in the criminal trial had ignored, but this time he effectively nailed that evidence to O.J. Simpson's guilt. On February 4, 1997, the jury in the civil trial found Simpson guilty on all eight counts brought against him and that he was guilty of the wrongful deaths of Nicole Simpson and Ronald Goldman. The victims' families were awarded $33.5 million in damages.

Simpson immediately scurried about to liquidate assets, but he eventually lost everything, including his resplendent Brentwood estate, which he had occupied for twenty years (six bathrooms, a tennis court, waterfalls, and an Olympic-sized pool). His money gone, his prestige and fame reduced to the stigma of murderer, O. J. Simpson even lost custody of his two young children, according to a November 10, 1998 appellate court decision in Santa Ana, California, based on the civil court decision that found Simpson responsible for the murder of his ex-wife.

---

**Singer, Jerry,** 1952- , U.S., mur. On April 7, 1988, three people were stabbed to death in an apartment complex in the Old Town area of Chicago. Two managers of the complex, 29-year-old Cynthia Graeber and 37-year-old Alice Wendt, were attacked by Jerry Singer, a 36-year-old former mental patient they were in the process of evicting because he was three months behind on his rent. Dr. Francis Conrad, a 51-year-old Washington, D.C, psychiatrist, who was helping his daughter look for an apartment at the building, became the third victim when he came to the aid of the two women. Singer was arrested and charged with three counts of first-degree murder. An hour before the assault, Singer had attempted to buy a riot shotgun and a two-foot Marine knife from a local arms dealer, but had to settle for a five-inch hunting knife.

Singer was brought to trial in June 1989 before Judge James Bailey at the Cook County Criminal Court in Chicago. Defense attorneys Crystal Marchigiana and Kevin Smith attempted to portray Singer as a man legally insane who thought a "psychic" was controlling his life and the apartment managers were attempting to persecute him. They claimed that the attempt to obtain five months' rent before he occupied the apartment—the demand that precipitated the final confrontation—was something that would not have been asked of a normal tenant. Prosecutors John Eannace and Patrick O'Brien countered that if Singer was really insane he wouldn't be able to move into one of the more affluent areas of the city. On June 29, 1989, the jury agreed with the prosecutors and rejected the insanity defense, disagreeing that Singer was mentally ill, and declared him guilty of the three murders. Singer himself sought the death penalty, but on August 29, he was sentenced to life imprisonment without the possibility of parole.

---

**Singleton, Lawrence**, 1928- , U.S., rape-mur. Neighbors of Lawrence Singleton in Tampa, Florida, came running to his driveway in February 1997, after someone gave the alarm that

Singleton was trying to kill himself. David Sales and his son pulled Singleton out of his white van. He had attached a dryer hose to the van's exhaust pipe and was lying in the back of the sealed vehicle, resting on two pillows. Sent to a psychiatric hospital for evaluation, he was released, and nine days later, on February 19, 1997, Singleton was charged with the gruesome slaying of a prostitute.

Singleton by then was exposed as the brutal monster who had raped Mary Vincent, a 15-year-old hitchhiker, in 1978, chopping off her forearms and leaving her for dead. Given a fourteen-year sentence for this heinous crime, he served only a little more than eight years of his term and was released in 1987, but so many California communities protested his presence that Singleton was removed to a facility just outside of his former prison, San Quentin, to live out his parole period. A former merchant seaman who had been divorced twice, Singleton earned time off his sentence by working as a teacher's aide while in prison.

Lawrence Singleton, who had served time for raping and chopping off the arms of a teenage girl, is shown at his 1998 murder trial; he was convicted and sentenced to death for stabbing a Tampa woman to death.

In 1988, Singleton returned to his boyhood home of Tampa, Florida, but his monstrous reputation preceded him. Those who knew of his criminal past shouted obscenities at him, and a car dealer went so far as to offer him $5,000 and one-way airfare if he would leave the state. TV crews harassed Singleton, a burly man who drank grain alcohol out of milk cartons. At one point he told reporters, "I'm not the beady-eyed monster you guys have made me out to be."

Singleton moved several times, eventually going to live with his brother in the working-class suburb of Orient Park. When David Sales realized just who he had saved from committing suicide, he stated, "When I found out, the first thing I thought was should I have left that man in [the fume-filled van]."

On February 19, 1997, Paul Hitson, a painter who had been working on Singleton's house, heard a woman scream. Hitson entered the house and saw Singleton struggling with a naked woman. "He was strangling her or something," the painter later told reporters. Running from the house, Hitson called police. Officers arriving within minutes found Singleton at the front door covered with blood. He told police that he cut himself while slicing vegetables, but peering past him, officers could see the blood-smeared naked body of a woman on the living room floor.

The dead woman, who had been stabbed numerous times, was Roxanne Hayes, a 31-year-old mother of three who had a long criminal career, including ninety-nine arrests in the last eleven years for prostitution and drugs. Booked on murder, Singleton was led from a Tampa police station on February 20, en route to court, telling a reporter, "They framed me the first time [on the rape of Mary Vincent], but this time I did it." He could say little else, police stated, since he had been caught red-handed.

Singleton had several times slipped through the cracks of the judicial system. Though he had registered as a convicted sexual offender, he was not monitored. Two years after moving back to Tampa, in 1990, Singleton was arrested for stealing a $10 camera from a drugstore. He was jailed for sixty days. A few months later he stole a $3 hat from a Wal-Mart store and was sent to prison for two years. In February 1997, Singleton was again arrested for stealing an $87 electric drill. It was after this arrest that he tried to commit suicide.

Brought to trial in 1998, Singleton was confronted in court by Mary Vincent, the teenager he had raped and mutilated in 1978. Then 34, Vincent, wearing prosthetic hooks, described how she had run away from her Las Vegas, Nevada, home and was hitchhiking outside of San Francisco when Singleton picked her up, promising to drive her to Los Angeles. He then raped her and used an ax to chop off her forearms, then left her for dead in a culvert near Modesto, California. Vincent told how she walked naked for two miles to a ranch, holding what was left of her arms up to slow the flow of blood.

Singleton was later picked up and sent to San Quentin for his savage crime, although he continued to maintain that he had been framed in the Vincent case. Despite his earlier admission that he "did it," in the Hayes case, Singleton took the witness stand to state that he killed Hayes in self-defense, that she attacked him with a knife and he struggled with her. He could not explain how the victim suffered seven stab wounds in the struggle.

Convicted of murdering Hayes on February 20, 1998, Singleton faced punishment that could bring him death. Assistant State's Attorney Jay Pruner told the jury that the two attacks on Vincent and Hayes were enough to give Singleton a death sentence. Said Pruner, "Separated by twenty years and thousands of miles, two women, unrelated except by the tragic connection to Lawrence Singleton, got into Mr. Singleton's van. Mary Vincent accepted a ride in 1978. Some twenty years later Roxanne Hayes got into a van driven by Mr. Singleton and she, unlike Mary Vincent, did not survive her meeting."

Countered Singleton's defense attorney John Syke, "This trial is not a matter of vengeance or for you to clean up California's mistakes from twenty years ago, but whether that old man dies a natural death or we take him out and kill him."

On April 14, 1998, Lawrence Singleton was sentenced to death by Judge Bob Mitcham, who stated, "This was an unprovoked and senseless killing. We are living in times worse than Sodom and Gomorrah."

---

**Singleton, Scott** (Andre Paul Reich), 1956- , Brit., mur. In July 1991, 17-year-old Lynne Rogers, after having lost her job at a London insurance brokerage, sent out resumes to several travel agencies, hoping to land a job with one of these firms. She received a call from a man who said he represented a travel firm and arranged to meet him at Charing Cross Station in London. Rogers failed to return home from the meeting. Her body was discovered by a ditch digger on September 9, 1991, near the village of Rotherfield, about fifty miles south of London.

An autopsy revealed that Rogers had been strangled. An odd bite mark was found on her chin, one indicating that her attacker had several teeth missing and those remaining were at irregular angles. Police, however, were stymied for months in identifying the killer. Then detectives received a call from an anonymous informant who told them that Rogers' killer was 35-year-old Scott Singleton, who operated a car spray-painting business in London.

Singleton ran a one-man operation that was less than successful. He had officially changed his name from Andre Paul Reich to Scott Singleton because he felt the latter name sounded like the name of a movie star. He lived in a fanciful world, claiming to be related to Baron Manfred von Richthofen, the celebrated "Red Baron," Germany's great flying ace of World War I.

Charged with murdering Rogers, Singleton was brought to trial in 1992. Prosecutors described how he had intercepted one of Rogers' applications for a job and then impersonated the manager of a travel firm, inveigling her to a meeting at Charing Cross Station, where he abducted her and later killed her, burying her body in a shallow grave outside the village of Rotherfield.

Singleton offered no defense and refused to utter a word in court as he listened to how forensic scientists had matched the bite mark on Rogers' chin to his dental charts and teeth. Experts also matched fibers found on the corpse to those of Singleton's car. This evidence brought about Singleton's conviction. He was sentenced to life in prison.

---

**Sinhalese People's Liberation Front.** See **Wijeweera, Rohana.**

---

**Sinks, Theodore,** 1940- , U.S., mur. On January 13, 1989, Theodore Sinks, 49, a maintenance supervisor for the *Daily News* of Dayton, Ohio, was convicted of the murder of his wife, Judy, when on November 20, 1987, he beat her with a blunt object and then strangled her with five loops of rope.

Sinks stuffed the corpse into a barrel and, with the help of an unwitting aide, carted the barrel to a seventh-story utility room at the offices of the newspaper where he and his wife both worked. Sinks then buried the body in the concrete floor of the utility room. The body was found five months later. Sinks was sentenced to fifteen years to life in prison.

---

**Sledge, Justin,** 1981- , **Brooks, Donald, Jr.,** 1980- , **Shaw, Delbert,** 1979- , **Brownell, Wesley,** 1980- , **Thompson, Daniel,** 1981- , and **Boyett, Grant,** 1979- , U.S., Case of mur. Sometime in 1997, three teenage boys who had been reading a book of spells went into some woods outside of Pearl, Mississippi, in attempt to cast a spell that would, they mused, summon a demon. The three boys, Luke Woodham,

Wesley Brownell and Daniel Thompson, recited the words of the spell from the book and shortly thereafter, they stated, the wind blew and a dog howled in the distance. The three nervously fled the woods and returned home.

Following this experiment, according to one report, the three youths were visited by Grant Boyett, who asked if they had summoned him, he being the demon, as was later claimed. Delbert Shaw, another friend, later told the boys that Boyett could get the youths anything they wanted—cars, money, girls—and all it would cost them was their immortal souls. Boyett, an undersized and unattractive person, was nevertheless gifted with persuasive and manipulative talents and he urged the group—which included Thompson, Brownell, Shaw, Woodham, Justin Sledge and Donald Brooks, Jr., to organize a Satanic cult.

Boyett reportedly encouraged the boys to deceive their parents, torture animals and thieve whatever they could. He convinced Brooks to use his father's credit cards to charge more than $10,000 in computer equipment. Brooks had second thoughts and told his father, who managed to cancel most of the orders. He convinced his son to cooperate with police, and the boy told officers in Pearl, Mississippi, about Boyett and the so-called Satanic cult.

Most of the boys soon quit the cult, except for Luke Woodham, who seemed to come under Boyett's spell. According to one report, Boyett told Woodham that he should look upon his dog as the spirit of a girl who had jilted him and take vengeance on the animal, kicking and beating it. To that end, Woodham tortured his dog to death. Further, Woodham went on to murder his mother and then kill two classmates at his school on October 1, 1997.

Following Woodham's arrest, police also arrested Sledge, Brownell, Boyett, Shaw, Thompson and Brooks, charging them with conspiracy to commit murder. Each was held on $1 million bond. At that time, Justin Sledge released a letter that he said Woodham had given to him on the morning of the murders, one that said, "I am not insane. I am angry. I killed because people like me are mistreated every day. I did this to show society push us and we will push back."

In the end, all charges were dismissed against everyone except Woodham, the killer, and his supposed catalyst, Grant Boyett. Charges of being an accessory before the crime are still pending against Boyett at the time of this writing. Ironically, the boy who had informed on the cult, Brooks, was charged by prosecutors reportedly under pressure from the local press. His lawyer, James Bell, of Madison, Mississippi, put together a 15-person defense team at his own expense—criminologists, investigators, other legal experts—to prove his client innocent, finally forcing the authorities to drop charges against Brooks. Also See: **Woodham, Luke.**

---

**Sleeman, George,** 1931- , U.S., embez. In 1984, auditors investigating the books of the Bennington (Vermont) School District discovered a $2 million deficit. After following a labyrinthine paper trail, authorities arrested school superintendent George Sleeman. The 58-year-old Sleeman was later convicted of embezzling the missing funds for personal gain. On January 18, 1989, Sleeman was sentenced to three to seven years in prison. His embezzlement of public funds was described as "the most widespread case of public corruption in Vermont history."

---

**Slepian, Barnett**, 1946-1998, U.S., mur. (vict.) Barnett Slepian, an affluent abortion doctor and native of Amherst, New York, was shot and killed in the kitchen of his home on October 23, 1998. The sniper, apparently hiding in shrubbery behind the house, shot Slepian through a window with a single rifle bullet when returned from synagogue and just after he had greeted his four sons, ages 7 to 15.

Police were unable to immediately identify a suspect in the shooting, but pointed out that they had notified abortion doctors in upstate New York and eastern Canada to be on guard, since four abortion doctors had been shot within a few days of Veteran's Day, November 11. Officials believed there was some sort of connection to that date. Slepian's practice was located in Buffalo, New York, the scene of violent anti-abortion demonstrations in 1992 by hundreds of members of to Operation Rescue.

Rewards totaling $250,000 in the U.S. and Canada were posted for the arrest of Slepian's killer, but no leads developed until early November when authorities stated that they were looking for 44-year-old James Charles Kopp, a Vermont man with a history of anti-abortion activities. Kopp's car was reportedly seen for several weeks before the October 23 shooting of Dr. Slepian, and it was conjectured that Kopp may have been the man seen jogging near Slepian's home on the morning of the shooting.

Kopp had reportedly been arrested for anti-abortion activities in Long Island, New York; Burlington, Vermont; and Pensacola, Florida. In January 1999, Kopp was reportedly in Mexico, having been driven there by a female friend. A Customs Service videotape showed the woman's car returning from Mexico. FBI Director Louis Freeh, on a visit to Mexico at that time, asked Mexican officials to aid the Bureau in its search for Kopp.

---

**Slocum, Brian**, 1979- , U.S., mur. In 1997, 18-year-old Brian Slocum, of Ft. Pierce, Florida, strapped 2-year-old Brittany Vinson into a car seat and then kicked her into a swimming pool. The drowned girl was the daughter of Christina Vinson, Slocum's girlfriend at the time. When arrested, Slocum confessed to police that he had murdered the little girl because "she got on my nerves." Slocum later denied that he ever admitted to killing the girl. He later still said that police had coerced the confession from him and that Brittany Vinson had died in the pool from an accident.

Charged with murder and brought to trial in St. Lucie County, Slocum took the witness stand and attempted to win over the jury by telling its members that he had been abused as a child and was the son of an alcoholic father who abandoned him, a tired old excuse that utterly failed to mitigate his crime and prevent his conviction. On November 25, 1998, the jury took only thirty minutes to recommend a life sentence. Judge Marc Cianca then sentenced Slocum to life in prison without the possibility of parole.

---

**Smallwood, Frederick Baker, Sr.**, 1944- , U.S., mur. On August 31, 1995, police in Hampton, Virginia, were called to the home of 50-year-old Debra Smith Mortimer Smallwood, a respected high school science teacher who had inexplicably committed suicide. Investigators found Smallwood near a small desk, half her head blown away by a single shell from a Smith & Wesson Glock 40-caliber pistol. Her husband, 51-year-old Frederick Baker Smallwood, Sr., a heavy-set, balding man with a dark mustache, explained that he was sitting in the room with his wife when she reached for the gun and shot herself to death.

Detectives thought it odd that there was little blood on the gun, only a few flecks of gore, especially since the bullet had blown away half the victim's head and splattered blood for several feet around the desk. Forensic experts examining the gun later found no fingerprints on the weapon. Smallwood's hands had been dusted for gunpowder residue and none was found to have been on his hands when detectives first arrived on the scene.

Police looking into the dead woman's background found no history of mental instability or depression, no psychological problems. Debra Smallwood had been well-liked by the staff at her high school and by her students. She was a gifted teacher and nothing in her life suggested that she would take her own life. Detectives simply refused to believe she had committed suicide and began to focus their attention on her husband.

Smallwood had dated his wife when they both attended Hampton High School in the 1960s, but upon graduation they went their separate ways. Smallwood attended Christopher Newport College, the College of William and Mary at Williamsburg, and the Southern Seminary Extension of Ohio College. After completing graduate work at William and Mary, Smallwood was ordained a Baptist minister, becoming the pastor of the Menchville Baptist Church in Newport News, Virginia. He resigned in 1973, becoming the pastor of the New Hope Baptist Mission in York County. He later worked in pastoral positions in Buffalo, New York.

For five years, 1981-1985, Smallwood left the church and sold pharmaceuticals in North Carolina. He later moved to Albany, Georgia, where police had, at one time, charged him with being in possession of Tylenol III without a prescription, charges that were later dismissed. Some time in 1994, Smallwood returned to Hampton, Virginia, where he again met Debra. The couple married on June 19, 1994. It was his second marriage and her third. Smallwood moved into his wife's comfortable townhouse and began seeking a ministry.

Detectives learned that during her courtship with Smallwood, Debra had spent several thousand dollars on unaccounted-for expenses. She had also spent more than $1,200 on phone bills. Only eight days before she died, Debra Smallwood had named her husband the beneficiary of her $340,000 life insurance policy, but she had incorrectly filled out the application, and when her husband later filed for the benefits, he was told that no payment could be made since the application was invalid.

Then detectives interviewed some of the victim's friends to learn that she had lunched with them only an hour before she went home and reportedly killed herself. They said the woman was in fine spirits and had gotten a call at the school from her husband, who told her that he was depressed because a relative of his had died in Georgia. She hurried home to be with him.

When this story was repeated to Smallwood, he denied making any such statements to his wife about a dead relative. He said that he had been upset at the time he made the call because he believed his wife would be lunching with him. Police also found Smallwood's 911 call curious and, listening to the tape, heard him say that "someone" had shot herself, and that he had gotten into a quarrel with "a friend" who had shot herself. It seemed strange that Smallwood would refer to his wife as an ambiguous "someone" and "a friend."

Smallwood continued to give police conflicting reports about his wife's death. He at first told officers that he was not looking at Debra when she suddenly picked up the gun and shot herself. He then said that he saw that she had "a crazy look in her eye." He later said, "What if I told you that there was a struggle [for the gun]?"

Investigators then learned that Debra had written a note shortly before her death in which she agreed to give Smallwood a no-fault divorce and that he was to repay her all the money she had given to him. Moreover, Smallwood, they learned, had bilked thousands of dollars out of his wife, as well as two other women he had been seeing at the same time he was married to Debra. It was then learned that Smallwood was a suspect in the death of 34-year-old Rita Craft of Albany, Georgia. Like Debra Smallwood, she had been a teacher. She had named Smallwood the executor of her estate. Albany police came to believe that Smallwood had dosed Craft with drugs to bring about her death so he could seize her assets.

Though prosecutors had largely a circumstantial case against Smallwood, he was brought to trial and was convicted of his wife's murder. Smallwood was sentenced to prison for life by Judge Wilford Taylor.

---

**Smart, John**, 1952-1998, U.S., resist. arrest. A wealthy San Francisco advertising executive, 46-year-old John Smart was found struggling with a woman in his Mercedes-Benz convertible while parked in San Francisco's skid row area on October 6, 1998. When officers ordered Smart to stop struggling with the woman and get out of his car, he became argumentative. He got out of the car and then walked back to it ostensibly to retrieve some identification papers.

Instead, Smart jumped behind the wheel and drove directly at an officer, pinning him against a parking meter. This officer and others arriving at the scene opened fire, killing Smart. The advertising executive had been a senior officer in the San Francisco office of Interbrand, a firm specializing in naming products such as Rogaine and Prozac.

---

**Smart, Pamela**, 1968- , U.S., mur. After meeting at a college Christmas party, Pamela Wojas and Gregory Smart began going steady. They married about three years later. Gregory cut off his long hair and took a job with an insurance firm. Pamela got a job doing public relations for a school. To celebrate a banner year of sales, Smart decided to throw a big party in his Derry, New Hampshire, home and then take his wife on a Florida vacation. He never had the party. On May 11, 1990, as Smart returned from work to his townhouse, he was shot once in the head and killed.

Pamela Smart returned from a school board meeting more than an hour later to find her husband's body and then run hysterically through the

**Pamela Smart, who was sentenced to prison for life for conspiring to murder her husband.**

townhouse complex, screaming for help. Three days later she placed roses on her dead husband's coffin before it was lowered into its grave. Though she gave the appearance of a grieving widow, police were suspicious of Pamela Smart from the beginning. The Smart townhouse had been ransacked, and Smart reported that cash and compact discs had been taken. She later tried to reinforce this story by telling the Derry *News*, "I am absolutely convinced that someone was burglarizing our home and Greg just walked in."

A teenage student at the school where Smart worked then went to the police to say that he had overheard some of his classmates talking about how they had killed Gregory Smart. Then the father of one of those students, Vance Lattime, discovered that one of his guns had been taken from a collection and he turned it over to police on June 10, 1990. Ballistics experts matched the gun with the bullet that had killed Smart. Vance Lattime, 18, was arrested and charged with murder, along with 17-year-old Patrick Randall and William Flynn, a 16-year-old long-haired youth who was reported to be Pam Smart's lover.

Cecelia Pierce, a 16-year-old student aide who worked with Smart, told police that she had caught Flynn and Smart in bed together and that she had overheard both planning to kill Gregory Smart. Cecelia agreed to be wired by the police and when she met with her friend, Smart revealed the entire plot to her in a damning tape that was later used to convict Smart and send her to prison for life. Flynn, the actual shooter, and the two other youths were also sent to prison.

Smart's motive for killing her husband, other than to continue having sex with Flynn, was rather ambiguous. At one point, she told a friend that she felt that Gregory was holding her back from a blossoming career on TV. She had once told her mother, "I'm going to be another Barbara Walters. I don't know how I'm going to do it, but that's my goal in life."

---

**Smith, Albert**, 1957-1989, U.S., suic.-mur. An error in judgment on the part of an assistant prosecutor from the Brooklyn, New York, District Attorney's office permitted a felon to walk out of court on his own recognizance, kill a policeman, and then kill himself. Albert Smith of Brooklyn was arrested on May 5, 1989, and charged with five felony counts, including the abduction of his estranged lover, Joyce Vassel. Smith was arraigned at the Brooklyn Criminal Court, where prosecutors requested a $250 bail. Judge Amy Herz Juviler, however, released Smith with the promise that he would return to court on the appointed day of his hearing. Phil Caruso, head of the police union, criticized District Attorney Elizabeth Holtzman, explaining that a higher bond—normally $1,500—is attached to more serious crimes such as kidnapping. Assistant prosecutor Meryl Bronson, however, was beginning her first day on the job and committed an error of omission that permitted Smith to go free. Holtzman later suspended Bronson.

On May 29, police from the Empire Boulevard station were notified by a resident of an apartment building on Hawthorne Street that a gunman was holding another resident, Joyce Vassel, hostage. The gunman was Smith, and Vassel, a former girlfriend, had filed the original kidnapping charges against him. When officers Jeffrey Herman and William Lynch appeared at the door of the apartment, the 32-year-old Smith began shooting. Herman was fatally shot and died a short time later at Kings County Hospital. Vassel was slightly wounded by two bullets.

One of the most intensive manhunts in recent years was launched by the New York City police. A week later, on June 4, a team of detectives cornered Smith in a Brooklyn apartment. A dozen officers wearing bullet-proof vests entered the building and were preparing to knock down the door of the apartment when they heard a single shot from inside. Officers found Smith sitting against a bedroom wall, shot once in the head.

---

**Smith, Andrew Lavern**, 1960-1998, U.S., mur. The 500th execution carried out in the U.S. since the death penalty was reinstated in 1977 occurred on December 18, 1998, when Andrew Lavern Smith was given a lethal injection at the state prison in Columbia, South Carolina. Smith had murdered his elderly cousins, 86-year-old Christy Johnson and Johnson's wife, 83-year-old Corrie, in 1983. The killer had rented a house from the couple and became enraged when they refused to loan him their car. He stabbed Christy Johnson twenty-seven times and Corrie seventeen times.

---

**Smith, Arthur G.** 1933- , U.S., mur. In October 1988, a native of Alhambra, California, Arthur Smith, was convicted of the 1980 murder of his wife after this previously unsolved killing was determined to be one of two deaths in a contract murder. In a move to avoid the death sentence, Smith admitted the killing and agreed to testify against Los Angeles police officer William Leasure, who, Smith said, had put out the contract for two murders. On May 19, 1989, Superior Court Judge John Reid sentenced the 56-year-old Smith to life in prison.

---

**Smith, Bryan,** See: **Waldron, John.**

---

**Smith, Charles**, 1943- , U.S., mur. A successful dentist in upscale River Forest, Illinois, Dr. Charles Smith was undergoing a bitter divorce with his wife, Nancy, when, in June 1996, he apparently planned to murder her. Smith waited for his wife to return from work, and when she entered her home, he attacked her with a baseball bat, hitting her forty-seven times, most of these blows striking her head. One of Smith's two daughters witnessed this lethal attack and begged her father to stop before calling 911. Paramedics rushed the battered Nancy Bator Smith to a hospital, where she died a short time later.

Convicted of murder in 1998, Smith was sentenced to sixty years in prison by Cook County Judge Thomas Tucker on September 10, 1998. Before Smith was packed off to prison, Judge Tucker told him, "You had the American dream—a good education, a nice home, a wife, and God's greatest gift, two children." He then stated that Smith had turned into a "demon" who had destroyed everything in his life.

---

**Smith, Douglas Alan**, 1964- , U.S., mur. Convicted in April 1998 of the brutal 1995 beating death of 68-year-old Samuel Ambrose in Phoenix, Arizona, Douglas Alan Smith faced twenty-five years to life in prison. Smith, claiming to suffer from a painful form of epilepsy in which the brain deteriorates into a vegetative state, begged to be put to death rather than live out an unbearable existence in prison. His court-appointed public defender, Jamie McAlister, sought to have her client's wishes granted. McAlister was removed from the county defender's office and she promptly resigned. She then entered private practice and was appointed Smith's attorney. McAlister then petitioned the court to grant Smith's request to receive the death penalty. Her petition was denied.

---

**Smith, Eric**, 1974-1996, U.S., resist. arrest. A six-foot one-inch, 240-pound wrestler, Eric Smith, 22, of Joliet, Illinois, was confronted by Forest View police officers on April 9, 1998. At the time, the car in which policemen Peter Bernal and Robert Lawruk were riding was hailed by 66-year-old Lillie Pruitte, the grandmother of Smith. The Smith family car was stopped on the shoulder of the southbound lanes of Chicago's Stevenson Expressway.

Smith at that moment was reaching for keys, which his mother, the third occupant of the car, had thrown to the side of the road. As he did so, Smith was sideswiped by a passing car. When Officer Bernal approached, Smith attacked him, struggling with him for his weapon, which was still in its holster. Officer Lawruk, seeing that Smith was striking his partner and attempting to grab his gun, pulled his own weapon and fired several times, killing Smith. Family members of the slain Smith lodged a complaint with police, charging excessive force. An internal investigation was launched that exonerated Lawruk and Bernal and concluded that there "was clearly a justifiable use of deadly force."

---

**Smith, Gary Allen** (AKA: The Polite Bandit), 1944- , U.S., rob. Dubbed the "Polite Bandit" by Long Beach (California) police because of the courtesy he showed his robbery victims, 45-year-old Gary Allen Smith was sentenced to serve twenty-eight years and eight months in prison by Van Nuys Superior Court Judge Alan B. Haberon on December 1, 1989. Smith, who was turned in by his mother after police linked the license plate of her car to the auto used in several area robberies, was arrested in April at a Tarzana drug treatment center. He pleaded guilty to a string of thirty armed robberies committed in the San Fernando Valley in the spring of 1989.

---

**Smith, Joseph Frank** (AKA: Ski Mask Rapist), 1953- , U.S., rape. After reportedly committing many rapes in San Antonio, Texas, Joseph Frank Smith was convicted of raping the same woman twice in 1983. He was known at that time as the Ski Mask Rapist because he always wore a ski mask when attacking his victims. Smith agreed, as part of his sentence, to undergo chemical castration. He was sent to Johns Hopkins University in Baltimore, Maryland, where he was treated with chemicals designed to suppress his sexual appetite. Smith later moved to Richmond, Virginia, where he worked as a truck driver, but the chemical castration performed upon him appeared to be a failure when he was again arrested and charged with attacking a Richmond woman in June 1993.

Smith confessed to the attack, one of seventy-five police believed he committed since 1987, and was convicted on November 25, 1998 of breaking and entering, aggravated sexual battery and two counts of attempted sodomy. Facing sixty years in prison and a $200,000 fine, Smith awaits sentencing at this writing.

---

**Smith, Joseph R.**, See: **Roberts, John H., Jr.**

---

**Smith, Michael,** See: **Woods, Kevin.**

---

**Smith, Robin** (AKA: The Bogeyman), 1956- , Scot., blk. Convicted blackmailer Robin Smith of Edinburgh said he was "very sorry" for attempting to blackmail four large pharmaceutical firms and a candy company. "I have been stupid," the 33-year- old divorced man said. "I saw it on TV."

In 1989, Smith wrote a series of threatening letters to the companies demanding payment of £625, 000 or he would contaminate their products with blood samples infected with the AIDS virus. One such letter, written to Procter & Gamble in May, was accompanied by a contaminated bottle of shampoo and a syringe. "This time it's glass and hair remover. But believe me I have more potentially lethal cocktails. Take a syringe infected with HIV AIDS blood and you have a time bomb, and if the papers get their hands on it, they will have a field day," he said.

The police arrested Smith on June 1 after a telephone call he placed to Procter & Gamble was traced to a public telephone booth. A small quantity of the contaminant and several newspaper accounts describing the manner in which the money should be paid were found in his home. Smith was placed on trial at the High Court in Perth in September. He pleaded guilty to five charges of attempting to extort money from the pharmaceutical firms of Safeway, Littlewoods, Procter & Gamble, and Elida Gibbs, as counsel Allan Turnbull attempted to portray his client as a "lonely, unhappy man, who had little understanding of the consequences of his actions." Lord Justice Coulsfield of the High Court in Edinburgh ordered Smith to jail for five years.

---

**Smith, Roland**, 1944-1995, U.S., mur. A racist to the marrow, Roland Smith, a black man living in Harlem, hated whites, believing that they had forced him to fight in Vietnam in what he termed was a "colonial" war. He also believed that whites had driven all the black store owners out of business on 125th Street in Harlem. Smith had a record of violent crime dating back to 1966, when he was first arrested for gun possession. In 1967, he was sentenced to four years in prison for resisting the draft.

At that sentencing, Smith shouted at the judge, "I deny my citizenship! I, my people, my race are treated like slaves here!" When released from prison, Smith became a janitor for a Bronx apartment building. He lived in a small basement apartment and spent his leisure hours reading Communist literature that was supplied to him by Glen Stupart, a black electronics store operator, his only friend.

Smith kept to himself, writing poetry and collecting Communist pamphlets that littered his apartment. When his building accidentally caught fire and was gutted in late November 1995, Smith was devastated at having lost his writings and books. Moreover, he could no longer sell his African artifacts on 125th Street after police kicked out all of the street vendors in response to complaints from store owners.

Believing this to be the act of white Republican politicians, Smith's rage consumed him. When he heard the rumor that whites were behind the eviction of the black owner of a record store, he swore revenge. Actually, the eviction notice was delivered by representatives of Freddy's Fashion Mart on behalf of a black Pentecostal Church, the United House of Prayer, the real owner of several buildings on the block, including the one housing Freddy's and its next-door neighbor, the Record Shack, which had been operating for twenty years.

On December 8, 1995, Smith, armed with automatic weapons, burst into Freddy's Fashion Mart, and, after allowing black customers to flee, began shooting whites. He next set the place on fire. As the flames shot up all around him, Smith ranted and raved, then killed himself by firing a bullet into his own chest. Seven died in what the press later termed the "Harlem Massacre," although none of them, ironically, were white. In addition to Smith, a black security guard died, along with five Hispanic women and a Guyanese man.

---

**Smith, Stephen,** 1965- , U.S., rape-mur. On January 7, 1989, Dr. Kathryn Hinnant was strangled and beaten to death after being sexually assaulted while working extra weekend hours at Bellevue Hospital in New York City. Hinnant, five months pregnant at the time of her death, was a native of Lake City, South Carolina, who had moved to New York following her graduation from the University of South Carolina in 1982 and practiced at several hospitals before taking a job at Bellevue in 1987. Fifty detectives were assigned to the case and a $30,000 reward was offered for the identification of her killer.

On January 9, police arrested 23-year-old Stephen Smith and charged him with murder and rape. Smith, a homeless man, who in the summer of 1988 tried to commit himself to Bellevue's psychiatric ward but was turned away, was secretly living in a storage closet in the hospital. Smith attacked Hinnant while wearing a stolen hospital gown and returned to his cubicle with her wallet, wristwatch, and mink coat.

A search turned up these personal possessions, and Smith was apprehended a short time later at a nearby homeless shelter. Smith denied the charges, but he did admit to ten earlier arrests. In May, DNA tests of blood and semen samples positively identified him as Hinnant's attacker.

Smith was tried in October 1989 before Justice James Leff at the New York State Supreme Court in Manhattan. He admitted to the crimes but pleaded innocent by reason of insanity. On October 30, the jury found Smith guilty of murder, rape, robbery, and sodomy, and on November 20 he was sentenced to fifty years in prison.

---

**Smith, Susan**, 1971- , U.S., mur. To everyone living in Union, South Carolina, Susan Smith was cheerful, bright and caring. "She was the best friend and the best mother," said one of her friends. This same 23-year-old woman, however, on Oct. 25, 1994, murdered her two small sons. On that day, Smith strapped her two boys, 3-year-old Michael and 14-month-old Alexander, into their car seats. She drove to a nearby lake, got out of the car and watched silently as the burgundy Mazda Protege rolled down a boat ramp and slowly sank in the dark waters. Her children drowned, still strapped to their car seats, as the waters engulfed them.

Smith slowly walked to a nearby house and told the occupants that her car had been stolen with the boys inside. The carjacker, she said, was a black man wearing a stocking cap. The peaceful town of Union exploded in anger. A shocked nation heard Smith's tale as she appeared for nine days on network TV, including a special appearance on the Today Show. She pleaded with the unknown kidnapper to return her children to her. She made a point of talking to her young sons, telling them that she loved and missed them.

To some these TV appearances did not ring true. Although Smith *sounded* like an aggrieved mother, she shed no tears. When first appearing on TV, Smith did not show signs of hysteria, as one might expect from any normal mother. Some astute viewers asked, "Why is this woman alive?" Any normal mother would have sacrificed her life to prevent a kidnapper from taking her children, or, at the very least, have gone with the abductor to protect those children.

Suspense was heightened when Smith released (rather perversely) a videotape showing her children at play and once again appeared before a duped public to plead for the return of

her boys. Again and again Smith appeared on TV, calmly begging for the lives of the two children she had already murdered.

Law enforcement agents found something wrong at the beginning. Smith's original statements seemed at odds with her story. She had been driving to see a friend on the night of the kidnapping, she had said. The friend was interviewed and told police that he had not expected to see Smith that night. She claimed that after she left home at about 6 p.m. that night, she first went to a Wal-Mart Store. None of the employees at the store recalled seeing her or her two sons.

Susan Smith, who murdered her two small sons in 1995 and was sent to prison for life.

Smith also stated that she stopped her car at a deserted intersection while waiting for a green light. Officers quickly learned that the intersection had a constant green light that was tripped red only when another car approached on the interconnecting street, a street that saw very little traffic. FBI agents then insisted that Susan Smith take a lie detector test. The polygraph report was inconclusive, except for Smith's response to one question, "Do you know where your children are?" The machine's indicator hands, which draw the responses, became erratic when she gave her answer.

Sheriff Howard Wells had suspicions from the beginning. After three days of investigation, he termed the case "impossible." The nation continued to hang on every whispered word uttered by Susan Smith, who was joined by her estranged husband, David, in begging the mythical kidnapper to return her boys. Thousands of viewers wrote the Smiths letters of condolence. Thousands more in many states began searching for the boys.

The woman went on pleading and hoodwinking everyone, although her husband also became suspicious of her, he later stated, questioning her lack of sincere emotion. (Smith had filed for divorce from David only a few weeks earlier on October 7, 1994.) Finally, on November 7, Smith gave up the charade and admitted her guilt to Sheriff Wells.

Smith led Wells and officers to the lake, pointing to the spot where her car and the boys were located. The auto. with the dead little boys still strapped to their car seats, was hauled from eighteen feet of water. Placed under arrest, Smith now became the object of loathing and hatred. As she was being transferred from the Union jail to another, undisclosed location (for her own protection), a large crowd assembled. The very people who had, days earlier, shown her sympathy and support now cursed her. "Baby-killing bitch!" screamed a mother who held her own small child in her arms.

At her 1995 trial, many reasons were given for Smith's murder of her children. One report held that she was a sexually abused child herself and that had warped her moral perceptions. Another had it that Smith expected to marry Thomas Findley, the 27-year-old son of the richest man in town. So sure of this was Smith that she had filed for divorce. Then Findley sent her a note in which he broke off the relationship, reportedly stating that he did "not want the responsibility of children."

It was clear that Smith's plans to escape her blue-collar life into one of luxury and ease had utterly failed. She would have to raise her children alone, now that she had filed for divorce from her husband, David, who later said that he never wished to see his wife again. Smith's trial was brief. Her lengthy confession clearly showed her guilt. She had murdered her boys, she said "because of my romanticized and financial situation ... I've never been so low." She was convicted of two first-degree murder counts. She received from the court, however, that which she had denied her children—mercy. Susan Smith was sent to prison for life.

---

**Smyth, Brenden**, 1926- , Ire., sexual abuse. The Catholic Church in Ireland came under nationwide criticism for allowing one of its priests, Rev. Brenden Smyth, to continue molesting young people over a thirty-six-year-period—seventy-four sexual offenses involving twenty children. When Smyth's offenses first came to the attention of Catholic officials, the only action taken was to move Smyth from one parish to another, lecture the cleric and hope he would reform.

Smith did not reform, sexually abusing youths both in the Republic of Ireland and in Northern Ireland. Officials in Northern Ireland had requested Smyth's extradition from the Republic, but were put off by purposeful delays on the part of Attorney General Harry Whelehan. When this obstruction of justice was exposed in 1994, the government collapsed with the resignation of Prime Minister Albert Reynolds.

Smyth was finally extradited to Northern Ireland, where he was convicted of sexual molestation and sent to prison for four years. When Smyth returned to the Republic, he was arrested and charged with molesting twenty children over a period of three decades. He was convicted and, on July 25, 1997, the 71-year-old Smyth was sentenced to twelve years in prison.

---

**Snoop Doggy Dog**, See: **Broadus, Calvin**.

---

**Snyder, Brenda J.**, See: **Parental Child Murder**.

---

**Snyder, Douglas**, 1949- , U.S., child porn. A successful businessman in Tennessee, Douglas Snyder began an Internet correspondence with someone he believed to be a 14-year-old girl, a contact he had made in an Internet sex chat room in April 1997. If fact, Snyder was talking in cyberspace with Michael Sullivan, a special investigator for the police department in Naperville, Illinois. Believing he had arranged a sexual assignation with the girl, Snyder arrived by train in Naperville on July 17, 1997, and was arrested and charged with child pornography. He confessed to sending a photo to Sullivan in May

1997, that depicted a 15-year-old girl having sex with an adult male and also admitted possessing other photos of children engaged in sex, some as young as 5 years old. On August 6, 1998, Snyder was sentenced to four years in prison by DuPage County Judge Thomas Callum, who also ordered Snyder to register as a sex offender.

---

**Soffiantini, Guiseppe**, 1936- , Italy, kidnap. (vict.). Some time in July 1997, Guiseppe Soffiantini, a wealthy businessman in Brescia, Italy, was seized by a gang of kidnappers and held for eight months before being released, minus a piece of his right ear. The release of Soffiantini was considerably obstructed by the Italian postal department and Italian prosecutors. In 1991, a newly established law prohibited anyone from dealing directly with kidnappers, and the bank accounts of families of kidnap victims were automatically frozen in such instances.

Prosecutors absolutely forbade the Soffiantini family from negotiating with the kidnappers, and the post office further compounded the problem when delivering the ransom demands, delaying these notes by weeks due to miserable service. Worse, when the kidnappers sliced off part of their captive's ear and sent it as proof that they had, indeed, kidnapped Soffiantini, the post office took weeks to deliver the grisly evidence.

Though prosecutors ordered family members not to negotiate with the kidnappers, the family went public and soon a note from the kidnap victim was delivered, one in which Soffiantini stated, "I am asking my sons to pay for my rescue, not the Italian government, and still less any Italian prosecutors." After Soffiantini's message was made public, prosecutors relented, unfroze the family assets, and a $2.3 million ransom was paid. Soffiantini was released in February 1998. His kidnappers were never identified, but it was believed that they were members of the Calabrian Mafia, known as *Ndrangheta*, who were headquartered in Oppido.

---

**Soldiers of Justice**, prom. 1989, Belg., terror-mur. A pro-Iranian Muslim group calling itself the Soldiers of Justice claimed responsibility for the assassination of two prominent religious leaders in Brussels, Belgium, on March 29, 1989. Abdullah Ahdal, the Saudi Arabian Imam of the Brussels mosque and the spiritual leader of the Islamic community in the Netherlands, was gunned down with Salim Behir, who was in charge of the mosque's social welfare activities. Both men were shot inside the Muslim holy site by the Soldiers of Justice, who vowed harsh retaliation against the Saudi royal family, whom they accused of "promoting Israel's policies."

Middle East observers believed that the attack was carried out by the followers of the Ayatollah Ruhollah Khomeini, who had previously issued a death order against Salman Rushdie, author of *The Satanic Verses*, a book considered blasphemous by the Nation of Islam. On February 20, Ahdal had publicly criticized Rushdie's death sentence to reporters from the Belgian RTBF network. "One should not have done that," he said. "Rushdie should have first appeared (before an Islamic tribunal). He should have explained himself. He should have been asked to repent." The Belgian police reported that the 36-year-old Ahdal had received a series of death threats following the airing of the broadcast.

---

**Somali Executions**, prom. 1988-1989, Somalia, terr.-geno. The ongoing violence in the horn of Africa took a new turn in the late 1980s when intra-tribal warfare came to Somalia. In the past, Somalia was regarded as relatively unburdened by tribal rivalries, but suddenly clan affiliation emerged as an excuse for brutality, including military atrocities against civilians.

Among the instances of violence reported was the killing of at least 450 people in religious rioting in the capital city of Mogadishu following the July 9 assassination of Bishop Salvatore Pietro Colombo, an Italian national who was spiritual leader of Somalia's tiny Catholic minority. At least 5,000 civilians were murdered by the Somali army between December 1988 and September 1989, most of them in the north, where the Somali Ishaak clan mounted a civil war. Ishaak rebels attacked the government-held town of Burao in May 1988. In vengeance, the Somali army began rounding up Ishaaks from the port city of Berbera. According to eyewitness accounts, five to fifty Ishaak men were beheaded each night. Robert Gersony, a civilian consultant to the U.S. State Department, documented human rights abuses, such as soldiers beheading small children and the bayonetting of an old man searching for water. Gersony's report further documented attacks by the Somali army and air force on Ethiopian refugees fleeing the civil war in that country. He estimated that hundreds were killed in the attacks.

The rebels, too, committed atrocities, including raids on non-Ishaak Somali refugees from Ethiopia in which more than 400 defenseless civilians were killed, and the court-martial-sanctioned murder of at least fifty prisoners of war. The aftermath of the Mogadishu rioting was the execution of forty-six civilians and the arrest of prominent Muslim leaders. In response to the carnage, the U.S. government froze $55 million of foreign aid earmarked for the desperately poor nation, and human rights organizations around the world condemned the administration of President Mohammad Siad Barre.

---

**Somerman, Andrew I.**, 1975- , U.S., terr. threats. Between November 1996 and April 1997, Lincoln and Braeside schools in Highland Park, Illinois, received six bomb threats that caused the schools to be evacuated and their after-school basketball games to be cancelled. The latter is exactly what the caller wanted to happen. He turned out to be 22-year-old Andrew Somerman, an assistant coach with the Bernard Weinger Jewish Community Center in Northbrook, Illinois.

Somerman confessed that he had made the calls so that he would not have to face the pressure of coaching the team for the three days when the head coach was absent. No bombs were ever found and no injuries reported. Somerman, of Buffalo Grove, was found guilty of making terrorist threats and sentenced to nine months work release by Lake County Judge Stephen Walter on December 19, 1998.

---

**Spaeth, David**, 1966- , U.S., rape-mur. A long-haired, bearded laborer, David Spaeth lived in Apple Valley, Minnesota, with his girlfriend and dog. He lived by his criminal wits, mostly through petty burglaries, working as a laborer at times. In 1984, he was convicted of two burglaries and receiving stolen goods and was sent to prison for a year. In 1987, Spaeth, prowling a Bloomington, Minnesota, neighborhood, saw the glow of a TV set in a home and broke inside, clubbing a girl with a brick. Captured, he was sent back to prison to serve thirty-eight months.

In July 1994, Bloomington detectives were once again at Spaeth's doorstep, entering with a search warrant. "What is this about?" Spaeth asked the investigators. "You tell us," one of them replied, as they rummaged through his apartment. They took custody of a pistol, a burglary kit, some clothes and a pair of dirty sneakers. Then they handcuffed Spaeth and told him that he was under arrest, charged with the murder of 37-year-old Linda Larson, who had been found raped and murdered, beaten to death, by her husband in the early morning hours of July 6, 1994.

As Spaeth was being driven to police headquarters, detectives bluntly told him that they had all the evidence they needed to convict him of Larson's rape-murder. His car had been seen near the victim's home on Portland Avenue, he was told. Spaeth shrugged and said that he had had an argument with his girlfriend on the night of the murder and that he had driven about, drinking with a friend, before returning home about 4 a.m. When he was examined at headquarters, Spaeth was found to have scratches on his chest he could not explain.

The girlfriend supported Spaeth's story, saying that he came home about 4 a.m., and the drinking buddy supported his story about driving around and drinking on the night of July 5-6, 1994, but the friend said he left Spaeth near Portland Avenue, close to Larson's home, a half hour before she was murdered. All of this was circumstantial evidence that did not place his client at the murder scene, Spaeth's lawyer argued at the murder trial, which took place in February 1995 before Judge William Posten.

Evidence that did place Spaeth at Larson's home was then presented. DNA samples of semen taken from the leg of the victim, were identified as being Spaeth's. Moreover, one of his sneakers perfectly fit a shoeprint left outside the Larson home. Spaeth was promptly convicted and then sentenced to forty-four years in prison.

---

**Spain, Troy**, See: **Starr, Robert III**.

---

**Spanbauer, David E.**, 1940- , U.S., rape-mur. Deputies from Langlade County, Wisconsin, were notified that the body of a young girl had been found on July 9, 1994, under some brush in a ditch near the town of Antigo. The girl was identified as 12-year-old Cora Jones. A coroner's report showed that she had been raped and then strangled to death. Another girl, 10-year-old Ronelle Eichstedt, of Ripon, Wisconsin, who disappeared on August 22, 1994, while riding her bicycle, was also found raped and strangled, her partly clothed body found in Iowa County, about 100 miles from Ripon.

Of the many investigators working on these two cases, one detective noticed a report of July 3, 1994, that stated a woman riding a bicycle in Waucapa County, Wisconsin, was sideswiped by a maroon car and thrown from her bike. The driver, the report stated, got out of the car and confronted the woman with a gun, but when another car approached he got back into his car and drove off. The detective took special note that this incident occurred only a short distance from where Cora Jones had disappeared.

A short time later, the community of Appleton, Wisconsin, was plagued by a number of rapes by a burly unidentified man. An Appleton resident, 21-year-old Trudi Jeschke, was raped and murdered by someone who had intruded into her home. Then, on November 14, 1994, a prowler attempted to break into a home in the town of Combined Locks, Wisconsin, but the homeowner chased him to his maroon car, tackling him and holding him for police.

Detectives were soon interrogating the prowler, 54-year-old David E. Spanbauer, an overweight man wearing glasses. He denied being a prowler, saying that he was out for a walk. He was nevertheless arrested and jailed, charged with attempted burglary. Police soon discovered that Spanbauer, a resident of Oshkosh, Wisconsin, had a record of sexual offenses dating back to 1960, having spent most of his adult years in prison. He had been paroled a few years earlier after having served time for rape.

Spanbauer said he had nothing to do with the rapes and the murder of Jaschke in Appleton. When asked about sideswiping the woman in Waucapa County on July 3, 1994, he said, "It isn't what you think. I was just asking directions. It sure wasn't an abduction."

When detectives received the details of Spanbauer's first arrest in 1960, they realized they were dealing with anything but a person with a benign nature. He had broken into a home in Green Bay, Wisconsin, on February 21, 1960, and was caught while raping a young babysitter. When the couple interrupted him by returning home early, Spanbauer fled, but not before shooting. The homeowner chased him and Spanbauer shot him in the face. Caught in Milwaukee later, he was found guilty of the home intrusion in Green Bay, along with the rape of a 12-year-old girl in Appleton, Wisconsin, and sent to prison for seventy years.

After serving twelve years, Spanbauer was released in 1972. Within a year he had raped a woman in Madison, Wisconsin, and was sent back to prison. Released again, he was arrested for burglary and went once more behind bars.

One of the interrogators asked Spanbauer to tell him about Cora Jones, saying, "You killed that little girl. We know it. And you know it. We are giving you the opportunity to tell your side of the story."

To the surprise of detectives, Spanbauer calmly replied, "I did do it." He then described how he had placed the body of Cora Jones in the ditch after raping and strangling her. He also described how he had abducted Ronelle Eichstedt and murdered her, driving to Iowa County to dump the body. Spanbauer, who was later charged with murdering Trudi Jeschke, was convicted of all three slayings.

Spanbauer was brought before Judge John Bayorgeon for sentencing on December 19, 1994. At that time, District Attorney Vincent Biskupic stated, "He is evil. He is a horror. He is a monster at the same time. He's pathetic, worthless and a complete coward. There is no penalty that this state has that is severe enough." (Wisconsin has no death penalty.) Judge Bayorgeon then sentenced Spanbauer to three life sentences, plus 403 years, with no possibility of parole.

---

**Spence, Craig,** 1940-1989, U.S., Case of pros.-drugs-suic. A Washington lobbyist, renowned for his flamboyant style and the air of mystery he created around his life, was found dead in a Boston hotel, an apparent suicide. After beginning his career as a journalist covering the Vietnam War, Craig J. Spence arrived in Washington in the 1970s and within a decade transformed himself into an important Washington influence-peddler for Asian business interests. His friends included numerous celebrities in journalism and politics. His world of influence started falling apart in the summer of 1989, when the Washington *Times* identified him in a series of articles as a frequent client of a Washington homosexual escort service that was under investigation by the Secret Service, the District of Columbia police, and the U.S. Justice Department. The articles alleged that Spence spent as much as $20,000 in one month for male prostitutes for himself and business associates.

In July 1989, Spence was arrested in a New York City hotel room in the company of a man he identified as a prostitute; he was subsequently charged with illegal possession of a weapon and possession of illegal drugs. Spence told police that he had met the man in Times Square and taken him back to his hotel, where, after an argument, the man took Spence's own gun and robbed him. In the months prior to his death, Spence told people that he had AIDS and also began spreading the unlikely story that he worked for the CIA. In addition to linking Spence with the homosexual escort service, the accusatory articles in the *Times* also claimed he had provided drugs to friends, been party to blackmail schemes, and bribed a White House security guard who stole White House china for him and admitted Spence and three other men into the White House for an unauthorized midnight tour.

On November 4, 1989, Spence registered at the Ritz-Carlton Hotel under an assumed name. Six days later, when hotel maids were unable to enter the room, firemen cut through the door and found Spence on the bed dressed in a tuxedo, dead of an apparent drug overdose. No suicide note was found in the room, but scrawled on a mirror in black marker was a note that read,"Consider this my resignation, effective immediately." The charges made against Spence had not been resolved by year's end, and it appeared that they might never be resolved. The federal government had withdrawn its subpoena on Spence before his suicide.

---

**Spik, Vincent,** 1961- , U.S., Case of mur. A resident of Findlay Township, Pennsylvania, 37-year-old Vincent Spik called police on June 4, 1998, telling an operator, "I've just killed my children." Police arrived to find Spik waiting for them. Inside his home, they found his 5-year-old twins, Robert and Emily, lying in pools of blood. Emily was by then already dead and Robert died on the way to the hospital.

Spik, whose wife, Susan, was at work as a bank clerk, told police that he had killed his children with a sledgehammer because he could not find the Power Ranger masks he knew his children would want to take to their day care center that day and knew they would become upset. When they did become upset, he killed them, according to the police. Spik awaits trial at this writing.

---

**Spokane (Wash.) Serial Killings**, 1997-1998, U.S., mur. A number of streetwalkers in Spokane, Washington, began to disappear in 1997, their bodies later turning up in shallow graves in and about the city. Five prostitutes were from Spokane, another was found in Tacoma. All had been shot to death. Police searching for the serial killer believe that for some reason, he murders in series of threes. Three victims were killed within a short period in 1997 and three more within a short period in 1998.

The serial killings were chillingly reminiscent of the so-called Green River killings of the 1980s, when 49 women were murdered in western Washington, a series of killings never solved. Spokane police have stated that the Spokane murders and the Green River murders are not related. The killer or killers of the Spokane women has not been apprehended as of this writing.

---

**Spotz, Mark**, 1972- , U.S., rob.-mur. A high school dropout, Mark Spotz became a professional criminal while in his teens. He committed many burglaries and robberies and was finally caught and sent to a Pennsylvania prison. Paroled, he moved to Altoona, Pennsylvania. A thug and terrorist, he was seen to threaten people with guns and physically attacked others, but he always seemed to escape convictions because witnesses, apparently intimidated by Spotz, refused to testify against him. Typical was Spotz's attack on his girlfriend in December 1993, when he tried to smother her because she ran away from him. She managed to escape and Spotz was arrested and charged with aggravated assault, but his girlfriend refused to testify against him, saying that she did not want to see him returned to prison.

In late January 1995, Spotz and his brother, Dustin Spotz, fell to arguing. The argument ended when Dustin stabbed Mark twice and Mark Spotz, firing a 9 mm semi-automatic handgun, pumped two bullets into Dustin Spotz's chest. As his brother lay dying, Mark Spotz stood over him, sneering, "There you go, pussy." He then spat onto the face of his dying brother.

With that, Spotz went on a murder spree. On February 2, 1995, he and a girlfriend flagged down 41-year-old Penny Gunnet, pretending he had car trouble. When Gunnet stopped her car, Spotz shot her in the head, killing her. He then robbed her and got into her car, which he used to run over his victim. Driving to another county, Spotz pulled the same trick, flagging down 52-year-old June Ohlinger. He shot her in the head,

robbed her, and dumped her body into a creek, then drove off in her car, which, like Gunnet's, he later abandoned.

A short time later, the 17-year-old girl who had been with Spotz at the time of the two killings left him (she said she had remained with him only because she feared for her life and fled at the first opportunity). She went to a police station and identified Spotz as the killer of Gunnet and Ohlinger.

As police now searched for Spotz, the killer struck once more. On February 3, he flagged down Betty R. Amstutz, 71, near Carlisle, Pennsylvania, shooting her to death, robbing her and driving off in her Chevrolet. This time, however, he did not escape. Spotz had stolen Amstutz's credit cards, and when he used one of these to pay for a motel room in Carlisle, police closed in and arrested him without incident. Spotz was convicted of the murders and was sentenced to death. He awaits execution at this writing.

---

**Sprout, Operation**, See: **Operation Sprout**.

---

**Spunaugle, Delpha**, 1955- , and **Woodward, Edwin Davis**, 1957- , U.S., mur. For several years, Delpha Spunaugle had been urging her alcoholic lover, Edwin Davis Woodward, to murder her husband, Dennis Spunaugle, the successful owner and operator of a T-shirt shop in Edmond, Oklahoma. Finally, after she bought him a six-pack of beer, Woodward agreed to do the killing. He, with the considerable help of heavy-set Delpha Spunaugle, beat Dennis Spunaugle to death, reducing his body to a bloody pulp. They then drove along County Line Road and dumped the body into a creek.

On August 17, 1993, Delpha Spunaugle called police to file a missing person's report, saying that her husband, following a quarrel, had left their home and had not returned. Spunaugle's body was found three days later on August 20, 1993. Investigators learned, from witnesses who had overheard Delpha talking in a bar and other places to Woodward, that she had wanted him to kill her husband. Detectives tracked down Woodward and he promptly confessed to the murder, saying that Delpha had given him a six-pack of beer and later a twenty-dollar bill to kill Dennis Spunaugle, but that she had helped him beat the victim to death.

Delpha Spunaugle was then arrested and charged with the murder. At first she pretended no knowledge of the crime, but a short time later she told officials that she had been present when Woodward killed her husband, but that she was afraid to report the murder because Woodward was the head of a powerful Satanic cult and its members were everywhere, watching her. So frightened was she of the cult, she said, that when Woodward ordered her to drink her husband's blood following the murder, she lapped it up like a dog.

This incredible tale was immediately discounted by police and prosecutors. Edwin Davis Woodward was a hopeless drunk who had no cult followers. Both were found guilty of first-degree murder. Woodward was sentenced to prison for life. Delpha Spunaugle was sentenced to death. She awaits execution at this writing in Oklahoma's Mabel Bassett Correctional Center.

---

**Squillacote, Theresa Maria**, 1958- , **Stand, Kurt Alan**, 1955- , and **Clark, James Michael**, 1948- , U.S., conspir.-attempt. espion-illegal. obtain. defense doc. Three former college campus Marxists, Theresa Squillacote, Kurt Stand and James M. Clark, were arrested and held without bail on charges of conspiring to spy on U.S. defenses for twenty-five years, on October 4, 1997. A February 17, 1998 indictment specified that all three, who had met at the University of Wisconsin in Milwaukee, Wisconsin, in the 1970s and formed a Marxist cell, had been providing U.S. defense secrets to East Germany for more than two decades.

Prosecutors stated that the three had a seething hatred for the U.S., and would spy for any country hostile to the U.S., including East Germany, the Soviet Union (and later Russia), and South Africa. All three were recruited by East Germany in the mid-1970s, paid to seek jobs in and around the U.S. government, and steal and smuggle classified government documents to East German spymasters.

Clark, a private investigator when arrested, had been a paralegal with the U.S. Army and, after being recruited by Squillacote and Stand, who later married and became residents of Washington, D.C., stole secret defense documents and passed these to his associates, who, between 1979 and 1984, delivered them to East German spies. The secret documents involved personnel records from the U.S. Department of State, including CIA agents secretly assigned to the department, and classified information about chemical weapons manufactured at the Rocky Mountain Arsenal. Using the code names of "Jack" and "Brother Michael," Clark passed documents, photos and notes, often hidden inside dolls, to East German agents.

Clark had long believed that the FBI was monitoring his every move and he was correct in that assumption. For some time, the Bureau tape-recorded Clark as he paced in his apartment and declared that his home was bugged. Following his indictment, Clark, in a plea-bargain agreement that would bring him a prison sentence of between thirteen and twenty years, agreed to testify against Squillacote, then a lawyer at the U.S. Department of Defense, working at the Pentagon, and her husband, Kurt Stand, a labor union representative.

Squillacote, who was hired as an attorney by the Defense Department in 1991, was trapped in an FBI sting when, in January 1997, she turned over Defense Department secrets to a person she thought to be a secret agent for the government of South Africa. The alleged South African spy was really an undercover FBI agent.

The documents Squillacote turned over to him described a number of secret arms transactions that took place between various governments during 1994, and reports assessing the strength of U.S. troops at many worldwide locations and the speed at which these forces could be deployed to combat zones throughout the globe. One of the documents contained data on U.S. nuclear weapons. The FBI sting on Squillacote began in the fall of 1996, when Squillacote was given a fake letter from a South African official who was also a prominent member of the Communist Party.

On October 23, 1998, Squillacote and Stand were convicted of conspiracy, attempted espionage and illegally obtaining national defense documents. Squillacote, the ringleader of the spy ring, professed her "profound regret" for her espionage activities on January 22, 1999, before she was sentenced by a judge in Alexandria, Virginia, to twenty-one years and ten months in prison. Her husband, Kurt Stand, stated, "I do take responsibility for what we have done." He was then sentenced to seventeen years and six months behind bars. Prosecutor Randy Bellows had urged long prison terms for the spies, saying, "These defendants made a choice to betray their country."

---

**Squires, Gerland,** 1978- , U.S., aggrav. assault. In June 1997, a blood test found that Gerland Squires, a 21-year-old private in the U.S. Army, was an HIV carrier. Her commander at the Aberdeen Proving Ground in Maryland, where she was stationed, ordered Squires to use a condom when having sex and to inform all of her sex partners that she was an HIV carrier and could possibly transmit AIDS to them. Squires had had or was having sex with nine men, six enlisted men and three civilians. She did not inform any of her sex partners that she had tested positive with the HIV virus and continued to have sex with four of the men. She also did not use a condom nor ask her sex partners to employ the protective device.

Later charged with having continued unprotected sex, Squires was tried and found guilty. She wept on the witness stand, saying that she continued her unprotected sexual activities because she was confused and frightened at having HIV and was terrified of passing the virus on to her daughter. Moreover, she feared rejection if she told her sex partners that she had the deadly virus. After pleading guilty to aggravated assault, Squires was sentenced to three years in a military prison on January 19, 1999. Her rank was reduced from private first class to private. Squires, upon her release from prison, will receive a bad conduct discharge.

---

**Sri Lanka Massacre**, 1989, Sri Lanka, terr.-geno. Ethnic violence flared up again in 1989 between the Hindu Tamil faction, which accounts for 18 percent of Sri Lanka's population, and the Sinhalese majority, which controls both the army and the government. On February 28, 1989, the Liberation Tigers of Tamil Eelam staged a commando raid against a group of unarmed Sinhalese peasants living in the rural Polonaruwa district village of Welikande. At least thirty-seven persons were slaughtered by the Tigers. The following day a spokesman from the group phoned the Associated Press to deny responsibility for the atrocity. Few doubted the Tiger involvement in this, the third such massacre to be carried out against Sinhalese peasants in 1989.

On February 11, thirty-six persons were either shot to death or stabbed in Dutuwewa. Seven more were killed in a similar attack just eleven days later in Sinhapura. On December 21, 200 young men were shot to death or carved up in Hambantota, 115 miles south of Colombo. One villager said, "I counted sixteen bodies in one spot." The Tamil Hindu faction has waged a relentless war since 1983 in an effort to gain a separate and independent homeland apart from the Sinhalese, most of whom are Buddhists.

---

**Stack, Richard**, 1956- , U.S., mur. On Mother's Day, 1980, Richard Stack of Chicago, Illinois, beat his 24-year-old wife, Carol Ann, and his 13-month-old son, Richard, Jr., with a pool cue. When the cue broke, he used a knife to complete his savage attack, murdering both mother and child. When police arrived, Stack was hanging from a window, eating glass and mumbling about being possessed by demons. He was tried twice, his attorneys insisting that he was insane at the time of the killings, but Stack was convicted in both instances.

Both previous convictions, however, were thrown out and new trials ordered by the Appellate Court, which ruled that prosecutors had made prejudicial statements to the juries. Stack was tried a third time in a bench trial before Cook County Circuit Judge Themis Karnezis. At this trial, prosecutors introduced new evidence to prove that Stack was not insane at the time he killed his wife and young son, that he was trying to feign insanity, this claim being supported by witnesses who said Stack had told them he would "beat the rap" by using an insanity defense. Judge Karnezis found Stack guilty on October 8, 1996, sentencing him to two life terms on November 5, 1996.

---

**Stacy, James**, 1937- , U.S., prowling-sex. moles. The career of one-time leading Hollywood actor James Stacy, who had been married to actresses Connie Stevens and Kim Darby in the 1960s, went rapidly downhill after his motorcycle was struck by a drunk driver on September 28, 1973. Stacy and a girl he had just picked up were thrown from the bike. The girl bled to death from a severed leg. Stacy survived, but his left arm and leg were amputated.

Hollywood gave a gala to raise money for Stacy's expenses, an affair attended by Frank Sinatra and Barbra Streisand. More than $100,000 was raised and Stacy got to the podium on a crutch to say, "Because of you, I'll smile again. I'm gonna do good things with the money." The former TV player on such popular series as *The Adventures of Ozzie and Harriet* and *Lancer* had little or no film or TV career left. He began getting into trouble, particularly with young girls.

In November 1995, Stacy was convicted of sexually molesting an 11-year-old girl in his house at Meiners Oaks, California, about seventy miles north of Los Angeles. He was convicted at the same time of prowling when he entered the nearby home of two teenage sisters and terrorized them. On March 5, 1996, the wheelchair-bound Stacy appeared in court to be sentenced to six years in prison. He is presently serving that term in California's Chino Men's Prison.

---

**Stager, Barbara T.,** , 1949- , U.S., mur. On February 1, 1988, Russ Stager, a 40-year-old high school teacher in Durham, North Carolina, was shot to death with one bullet to the head from a .25-caliber handgun as he lay in his bed. His wife, 39-year-old Barbara Stager, initially reported her husband's death to be a suicide, but later claimed that she had accidentally shot him as she was removing the gun from beneath a pillow. Mrs. Stager had been married once before, and in March 1978 her first husband, James Larry Ford, had died in a similar incident. She claimed his death was a suicide also, but later insisted that

Ford had accidentally shot himself while cleaning his gun. Following Stager's death, police found a tape recorded three days before his death in Stager's high school office. A voice purported to be that of Stager stated that he suspected Ford had been killed and that he knew that Barbara Stager had forged his signature on bank documents. The voice also related details of discovering his wife with another man. Russ Stager told his first wife, Jo Lynn Ellen Snow, to "look into it" if anything ever happened to him.

Barbara Stager was arrested on the charge of murder and brought to trial in May 1989 before Judge J.B. Allen at the Lee County Superior Court. Prosecutor Eric Evenson introduced a videotaped reenactment of Stager's death as Barbara Stager attempted to convince the jury that the shooting was accidental. But she changed her story of how she extracted and subsequently fired the weapon after watching the videotape. The audiotape found at the high school was also introduced, as well as details of the demise of her first husband. If the death was ruled accidental, Stager would receive $165, 000 in insurance benefits. Defense attorney William Cotter produced a witness who claimed that Mrs. Stager's blood-soaked nightshirt indicated an attempt to save her husband. But the nightshirt had mysteriously disappeared, and on May 17, 1989, after seven days of testimony and less than an hour of deliberation, the jury found Barbara Stager guilty of first-degree murder and two days later sentenced her to death.

---

**Stains, Graham Stewart**, 1941-1999, **Stains, Philips**, 1989-1999, and **Stains, Timothy**, 1991-1999, India, mur. (victims) Radical Hindus, accusing Christian missionaries of attempting to convert Hindus to Christianity, went on a murderous rampage, destroying twelve Christian churches. One report claimed that twenty-four Hindu temples were also burned. Graham Stewart Stains, a native of Australia, was one of those missionaries attacked; he had worked as a missionary helping lepers in India for thirty-four years.

On the night of January 22, 1999, Stains was asleep in his Jeep, along with his two young sons, Philips, 10, and Timothy, 8, outside the village of Manoharpur, 620 miles southeast of New Delhi, near a makeshift Christian church. About forty persons gathered around the Jeep at midnight and doused it with kerosene, then set it ablaze. Stains and his sons were trapped inside and burned to death. Those who tried to help Stains and his sons escape the burning vehicle were beaten up and driven off. Five persons were arrested for the gruesome attack, these being members of the radical Hindu sect Bajrang Dal. Others were still sought at the time of this writing.

---

**Staley, Ernest** (AKA: Polo), 1959- , U.S., drugs. On June 1, 1989, Ernest "Polo" Staley was convicted at the U.S. District Court in Tallahassee, Florida, of dealing crack cocaine. The 30-year-old Staley headed a drug ring that netted him more than $25,000 a week as he handled all manufacturing and distribution until his arrest in April 1988. Staley, also charged with possession of a firearm, attempted to buy his freedom by offering a witness the choice of $10,000 or a luxury car in exchange for their agreement to refuse to testify against him. On August 15, 1989, Judge William Stafford sentenced Staley, a first-time offender, to life imprisonment without the possibility of parole. Defense attorney Robin Rosen thought the sentencing excessive because Staley had no past criminal record, but prosecutor Mike Moore stated the penalty was within the federal guidelines.

---

**Stand, Kurt**, See: **Squillacote, Theresa**.

---

**Stano, Gerald Eugene**, 1951-1998, U.S., mur. One of the worst serial killers in the U.S., Gerald Stano murdered, by his own admission, forty-one women, mostly in the 1970s. His victims were slain in many states, including New Jersey, Pennsylvania, and Georgia. Most were killed in Florida. Stano, a short-order cook, mostly preyed upon runaway girls, college students and young working women on the streets of Daytona Beach and throughout Florida. He picked them up and, and, for the most part, stabbed them to death.

Stano was convicted and sentenced to die for stabbing to death 17-year-old Cathy Lee Scharf, of Port Orange, Florida, on December 14, 1973. After dumping her body in a drainage ditch in Brevard County, Stano admitted that he cleaned up and then went roller skating. Scharf's body was found at the Merritt Island National Wildlife Refuge near Titusville on January 19, 1974. On December 29, 1975, Stano, a dark-featured, burly man with a powerful physique, choked and drowned Susan Bickrest, a 24-year-old waitress he had picked up. Stano was also convicted and sentenced to death for this murder.

On November 12, 1977, Stano shot and drowned 23-year-old Mary Kathleen "Cathy" Muldoon, a student at Community College in Daytona Beach. Apparently Stano cornered Muldoon on a secluded stretch of New Smyrna Beach, killing her there before fleeing. He was convicted and sentenced for this third murder. He received six life sentences for six other murders. The last homicide committed by Stano reportedly occurred on April 1, 1980, when he was apprehended after attacking a prostitute with a can opener and acid.

Shortly after this arrest, Stano began to recite a murder litany, confessing to the murder of 20-year-old swimming star Mary Carol Maher, who vanished after leaving a Daytona Beach nightclub. She was stabbed to death, her body found on January 20, 1980. The remorseless serial killer admitted to murdering forty-one women in all.

After filing seemingly endless appeals stretched out for almost twenty years, Stano's execution was finally set for March 23, 1998. Before he was led to Florida's electric chair, the serial killer gobbled down a Delmonico steak, baked potato, and mint chocolate chip ice cream, washed down with two bottles of pop. He was tired-looking when led into the death room, no doubt because he had not slept a wink the night before.

Several family members of victims watched the burly Stano strapped into the chair. As the lethal charges were sent into his body, several witnesses nodded approval. "Die, you monster," said Raymond Neal, one of the witnesses. His twin sister, Ramona Neal, was one of Stano's many victims, her body found

beaten and strangled to death in a ditch in 1976.

The use of the electric chair was then in some debate. Pedro Medina had been electrocuted in 1997 and the chair, in use for seventy-five years, apparently short-circuited, causing flames to shoot from the top of Medina's head. A move to get rid of the chair by the Florida legislature failed, and the electric chair was used again to execute Stano.

Stano had refused to make a final statement, but following his death, his lawyer circulated a letter the serial killer had left to be read after his death. In it, Stano claimed that "I was not strong enough. I confessed to crimes I did not commit. Now I am dead and you do not have the truth." He had earlier recanted his lengthy and detailed confessions, saying that his admissions had been coerced by police. He also blamed his eight murder convictions on a crooked cop.

John Maher, brother of Mary Carol Maher, slain by Stano, had urged the legislature of Florida to speed up executions and suggested that first- and second-time convicted felons be forced to watch videos of executions like that of Stano. Following the serial killer's electrocution, Maher stated with tears in his eyes (not for Stano, but in remembrance of his murdered sister), "He couldn't even remember some of his victims. Can you imagine forgetting that you killed somebody?" Also See: **Stano, Gerald Eugene**, Vol. IV.

---

**Starovoitova, Galina**, 1946-1998, Rus., assass. (vict.) One of the most outspoken and liberal opponents of the old Communist regime and its holdover adherents in Russia, Galina Starovoitova was the founder of the political action group Seyernaya Stolitsa, or Northern Capital. This grass-roots organization presented many new liberal candidates who particularly opposed Vladimir Yakovlev, the city governor of St. Petersburg. In addition to virulent opposition from the old Communists in Russia, Starovoitova alienated the ruthless Russian Mafia, led by former members of the KGB and ex-military officers. She had exposed corruption among ruling politicians and linked them to the Russian Mafia.

Starovoitova was a member of St. Petersburg's intellectual community. She had always been poor, and even after she became a member of the Duma (the Russian parliament), she lived modestly, taking a subway to work and residing in a small apartment. She had greatly influenced Russian President Boris Yeltsin in turning away from communism to a policy of reform and pro-Western democracy. She had attacked the power-grabbing Communists and the criminals infesting the city who were, for the most part, directed by leaders of the Russian Mafia.

A great crusader with a following that believed she could be elected president of Russia in the year 2000, Starovoitova entered her apartment building in St. Petersburg on the night of November 20, 1998, along with her aide, Ruslan Linkov. Both were attacked by what was later termed a "team of contract killers." Starovoitova was shot dead and Linkov was seriously wounded. Upon hearing of the assassination, Boris Yeltsin ordered a full-scale investigation by the interior minister, who was also chief of Russian intelligence, and the prosecutor general, telling them to take urgent measures in solving the assassination. Though a rifle and pistol were found in the entranceway of Starovoitova's apartment building where she was slain, her killers have not been apprehended at this writing.

Starovoitova's death caused widespread anger and grief among her followers. On the day following her assassination, thousands of pensioners and students gathered in St. Petersburg's Palace Square to weep and praise their lost leader. Igor Artemyev, the city's liberal vice governor, stated, "The city seems to be involved in a redivision of property. Bandits want to get this property and power and kill everybody who stands in their way—not only businessmen, as before, but also politicians who interfere with them." His meaning was clear. Starovoitova stood in the way of the Russian Mafia and was assassinated because of that opposition.

---

**Starr, Robert III**; **Spain, Troy**; and **McCranie, Jimmy**, prom. 1996, U.S., conspir. In April 1996, Robert Starr III, Troy Spain and Jimmy McCranie, all Georgia residents, were arrested and charged with conspiring to use bombs on roads, vehicles, bridges, power lines and federal law enforcement officials. Prosecutors also charged that the three, all claiming to belong to a self-styled militia group in Georgia, planned to rob federal armories and drug dealers in order to finance a "war" against the government. All three were convicted of conspiracy on November 6, 1996, and received prison sentences.

---

**Starrett, Richard Daniel**, 1960- , U.S., kid.-sex. asslt.-mur. In February 1989, the family of 17-year-old Shari Dawn Teets of Lexington, South Carolina, placed an advertisement in a local paper to sell their waterbed. The ad was answered on February 6 by Richard Daniel Starrett, an engineering technician and family man. Starrett arrived at the Teets' home when Shari was alone. After examining the waterbed as if he were interested, he drew a gun and forced Shari to return with him to his apartment in Martinez, Georgia, a suburb of Augusta, just across the state line. There he held her for four days, much of the time handcuffed in a closet. She escaped on Saturday morning, February 11, and led police back to Starrett's residence. Starrett had fled, but police found criminology textbooks detailing how police investigate serial crimes—particularly kidnapping and child molestation; a collection of pornographic magazines and videotapes, including tapes of himself assaulting women; and books about serial killer Ted Bundy. Lexington County, South Carolina, Sheriff James Metts said the preliminary investigation showed Starrett "was having trouble at work and at home and developed a serious drinking problem."

Starrett was arrested on February 15 by Harris County, Texas, sheriff's deputies conducting a routine license plate check on cars at an interstate rest stop outside Houston. A barefoot Starrett was sleeping in his red sports car with a 38-caliber handgun on the seat between his legs. A deputy aimed a 12-gauge shotgun at him before they woke him. Starrett waived his right to challenge extradition and returned east, where he faced investigations in six states. In cooperating with police, he led South Carolina authorities to a creek in rural Newberry

Kidnapper and killer (shown in wheelchair after a prison hunger strike) Richard Daniel Starrett, sent to prison for life in 1989.

County, northwest of Columbia, where he had abandoned the body of 15-year-old Jean Taylor McCrea after abducting, raping, and shooting her to death just before Christmas 1988. He also confessed to sexual assaults in the Columbia, Charleston, and Atlanta areas, seven in all. He was formally charged on February 17 with kidnapping and raping a 12-year-old girl from Lexington County, South Carolina, on June 21, 1988. He was indicted on March 10 by a Richland County, South Carolina, grand jury on four counts of kidnapping and one count of criminal sexual conduct for his activities in and around Columbia. The day Starrett pleaded not guilty to those charges, Charleston County, South Carolina, officials presented warrants for his arrest on charges of first-degree burglary, kidnapping, and criminal sexual conduct. The charges were based on an incident in June 1988 in which a Charleston woman was handcuffed and videotaped as she was being assaulted by a man who answered an ad in the paper—Starrett's usual modus operandi. He later faced nine criminal counts in Columbia County, Georgia, where he lived.

In March 1989, Starrett went on two hunger strikes and attempted suicide by slashing his wrists after his wife filed for divorce. A South Carolina state psychiatrist diagnosed Starrett as suffering from depression but determined that he still could distinguish right from wrong. A second psychiatrist, Dr. Harold Morgan, stated that Starrett's crimes stemmed from paraphilia, a compulsive sexual disorder that constituted an unusual form of mental illness. Morgan recommended counseling and hormonal therapy to control Starrett's sex drive.

The prosecutors had prepared to present another side of Starrett. Their investigations showed he had researched police procedure to learn how to leave less evidence and how to make his crimes against children look more like missing-person cases than abductions. At least twice, Starrett had passed up opportunities to assault girls because he recognized the possibility of being caught. Authorities believe he passed up other opportunities because when he showed up at one would-be victim's door, she was not as pretty as he had expected. Although he had no prior arrests, Starrett used aliases to rent locations he could use as crime scenes, and planned his assaults for occasions when he knew his wife would be out of town. Authorities believe these details indicated that Starrett was calculating in his approach, rather than driven by uncontrollable impulses.

The prosecutors, however, did not need to present evidence in Columbia, for when Starrett went to court there on June 19, he pleaded guilty but mentally ill, and remarked before sentencing that he was tormented by "anguish, remorse, and self-hatred." Circuit Judge J. Ernest Kinard, Jr. gave him the maximum of life in prison for kidnapping and twenty years for criminal sexual conduct, to be served consecutively.

Starrett was also arraigned in the city of Lexington, South Carolina, on July 6, but was not charged in the death of Jean McCrea. When her name was mentioned in court, he covered his ears and fell to the floor, sobbing, "Don't say her name."

Starrett pleaded guiltShari y in Columbia to the kidnappings of the unidentified 12-year-old and of Shari Teets. He received two more life sentences, to be served consecutively. He was on another hunger strike and had to be wheeled in and out of the courthouse in a wheelchair due to weakness from hunger. His mother speculated that the self-imposed fasting was an act of penance. She repeated doctors' suggestions that her son's behavior might have been rooted in two concussions sustained during childhood that caused him headaches and damaged his growth.

---

**Steckel, Brian D.,** 1969- , U.S., rape-arson-mur. A man driving along a street in Prices Corner, Delaware, on the afternoon of September 2, 1994, saw smoke coming from the Driftwood apartments. The driver stopped his truck and raced to the building. Seeing a woman inside, he called to her to crawl on the floor to the front door, but flames blocked her path. The hysterical woman could only cry out, "Help me! Please help me!" Another man appeared and tried to smash through the windows. Again the roaring, blistering flames drove them back as the woman disappeared inside the blaze.

Firefighters arrived and put out the fire, finding Sandra Dee Long, a 29-year-old data inputter, dead inside the building. She was discovered to be have been five months pregnant. While officials were investigating the deadly fire, editors of the Wilmington *News Journal* began receiving calls from a man who identified himself as the "Driftwood Killer," and who said that he had raped and killed Sandra Long. Further, he promised that he would kill another woman and even gave her name to an editor.

The editor called Delaware police, but they had little to go on other than the unsubstantiated statements of the anonymous caller. They did contact the woman the caller had named, offering her protection. Detectives were surprised that the woman then told them she believed the caller was a man named Brian D. Steckel. The woman explained that Steckel had been mak-

ing obscene phone calls to her and she had filed a criminal complaint with the police, and that the complaint, if the officers checked, could be found in their own files.

Indeed, the complaint against Steckel had been filed. Having no other suspects, investigators began a widespread search for Steckel, learning that he was an unemployed drifter and had even lived for a time at the Driftwood Apartments and on the same floor as Sandra Long. After an extensive manhunt, police found Steckel sitting on the curb of a street in a drunken stupor. He was jailed and charged with killing Long. While in custody, Steckel told officials that he had killed a number of women and girls, but his stories never checked out. He was apparently building his ego by pretending to be a terrifying serial killer.

In the case of Sandra Long, however, Steckel's remarks proved to be accurate. He said he had stayed with a friend for two nights at the Driftwood Apartments, observed Long and decided to sexually attack her. He went to her apartment and rang the bell and when she answered, he identified himself as a neighbor and asked to use her phone. She let him inside and he immediately attacked her, choking her with a nylon stocking and a tube sock, then sexually attacking her with a screwdriver. He said she bit him and crawled to another room. He lit the curtains of her bathroom on fire and fled, letting the woman burn to death.

In September 1996, Steckel was brought to trial in Superior Court in Wilmington, Delaware. Dental experts who had taken impressions of Long's teeth testified that her teeth matched the bite marks found on Steckel's fingers. Then FBI Special Agent Paul Cowley testified that DNA evidence placed Steckel at the scene of the fire. Blood drops found outside Long's door in the hallway of the apartment matched those taken from the defendant. According to the testimony of Dr. Richard T. Callery, medical examiner of Delaware, the bite marks on Long's buttocks matched the impressions of Steckel's teeth.

The jury found Steckel guilty of several counts of rape, arson and murder. When Steckel was brought before Judge William C. Carpenter, Jr., he had already compounded the crimes for which he had been found guilty. While in prison awaiting trial, Steckel had written seventy-five letters in which he threatened to kill people, including witnesses scheduled to testify against him and the chief prosecutor in his case. Steckel was sentenced to death.

---

**Steibel, Kurt,** 1941-1989, U.S., suic.-mur. On December 8, 1989, before setting fire to his Belleville, Illinois, home, 48-year-old Kurt Steibel shot and killed his wife, Carolyn, his daughter, Cindy Townley, and his 1-year-old grandson, Eric Townley. When firefighters arrived to fight the blaze, Steibel, waiting outside with a gun, fired on them, then committed suicide by going back into the burning house. His charred body and those he had shot to death were found later. No motive was ever discovered in this multiple slaying.

---

**Steinberg, Joel,** 1942- , U.S., mansl. Hedda Nussbaum met Joel Steinberg in 1972. Nussbaum was a successful author of children's books and Steinberg a criminal lawyer in New York City. The two became lovers and moved in together. According to Nussbaum, Steinberg began beating her in 1977. Despite his legal work, Steinberg was later depicted as a man deeply involved in illegal activities, including drug abuse, illegal weapons possession, and frequent, violent assaults on Nussbaum and others; he was even accused of practicing law without a valid license, as he had tricked his way out of having

New York lawyer Joel Steinberg (at right, with his attorneys in court during his trial) was convicted and sent to prison in 1989 for killing his 6-year-old adopted daughter two years earlier.

to take the New York bar examination.

In 1981, when she was 19, Michele Launders gave birth to an illegitimate daughter, Usa, and gave her up for adoption. Without filing for legal adoption, Steinberg took charge of the girl, raising her as his own and Nussbaum's. Usa Steinberg died of injuries at the age of 6, in November 1987. Steinberg claimed that she fell and hit her head on a cabinet. He said that he blamed himself for not recognizing that she needed medical attention, but that he never hit Usa. Nussbaum left Steinberg at the time of Lisa's death, turning state's evidence against him. She produced photos of herself with her face beaten almost beyond recognition. She told stories of his violent temper. In the ten years he abused her, Nussbaum said Steinberg blackened her eyes innumerable times, broke sixteen of her ribs, and at least once nearly killed her. According to her version of events the night of Lisa's death, Steinberg beat the girl severely, went to dinner with a friend, used cocaine, and then called for help only after Lisa had been unconscious for twelve hours.

The case made national headlines and galvanized public opinion on the subject of child abuse. After Steinberg was convicted of first-degree manslaughter on January 30, 1989, the Manhattan Supreme Court was deluged with letters from around the country urging Justice Harold Rothwax to impose the maximum penalty. Steinberg's defense was his insistence on a claim of innocence. He constantly repeated that he would never do anything to harm the little girl he loved and that he never lifted his hand to Hedda Nussbaum. He claimed that Nussbaum, who moved into the Four Winds Hospital in Katonah, New York, where she received psychiatric treatment to offset her years of

abuse, was being influenced by hospital staff members to turn on him. He also accused one juror of attempting to influence the other jurors to vote against him. Nussbaum was reportedly furious at what she called his lying with a straight face when he claimed he never beat Lisa.

Steinberg's sentencing was attended by Michele Launders, three of the jurors who had voted to convict, and Graceann Smigiel, the natural grandmother of another child Steinberg and Nussbaum had unofficially adopted. In passing the maximum sentence of eight-and-one-third to twenty-five years and a $5,000 fine, Justice Rothwax stated, "There is nothing in the record to mitigate the extreme callousness and harshness of (his) conduct.

Hedda Nussbaum, an author of children's books, while attending the murder trial of her common-law husband Joel Steinberg.

His extraordinary narcissism and self-involvement, his extreme need to control everyone ... led him to become the instrument of Lisa's death. I strongly and emphatically recommend against parole."

---

**Steinbrenner, George M., III**, 1930- , U.S., consp. George Steinbrenner, the outspoken and controversial owner of the New York Yankees baseball team, was pardoned by outgoing president Ronald Reagan on January 18, 1989. In 1974, Steinbrenner negotiated a plea-bargain arrangement with the government, whereby he agreed to plead guilty to two felony and misdemeanor counts charging him with conspiracy to violate federal election laws. He had also attempted to coerce the employees of his American Shipbuilding Company into lying to a federal grand jury about his $100,000 contribution to President Richard Nixon's 1972 reelection campaign. Additionally, Steinbrenner was accused of making illegal corporate contributions to the campaigns of Senators Daniel Inouye (D., Hawaii), and Vance Hartke (D., Indiana). "Everybody has dents in his armor," Steinbrenner often said.

Steinbrenner paid a $15,000 fine and therefore avoided a jail sentence. He was the first executive from the private sector to be charged with a felony crime by the special Watergate prosecutor. At one time, Steinbrenner was a popular fund-raiser within Democratic circles, but following his conviction he distanced himself from the political process.

---

**Stephens, Jason**, 1974- , and **Cummings, Horace**, 1974- , U.S., rob.-kidnap.-mur. On June 2, 1997, Jason Stephens and Horace Cummings broke into a Jacksonville, Florida, home, robbing the place and kidnapping Robert Sparrow III, the 3-year-old son of the homeowner. After brutally killing the boy, Stephens and Cummings fled, but were caught separately in a statewide manhunt. Both were found guilty and sentenced to death.

**Stewart, Brian**, 1966- , U.S., mur. A hospital technician in St. Charles, Missouri, Brian Stewart was forever threatening people that he could kill them with an injection of "something." When his wife threatened to divorce him in 1992, Stewart told her, "You won't need to look me up for child support anyway because your child is not going to live very long." He reportedly went to the hospital where his son was receiving treatment and stole HIV-infected blood, injecting this into his own son, who was later diagnosed as having life-threatening AIDS.

At his 1998 trial, Stewart's wife testified about her husband's threat. A letter was read from her hospitalized 7-year-old son, who by then was being fed through a stomach tube and had lost most of his hearing. It stated, "I feel mad. I think he shouldn't ever be out of jail ... Why did he do such a bad thing to me?"

Prosecutor Ross Buehler then constructed a circumstantial case against Stewart, eloquently telling a jury that "the circumstantial evidence is like a number of strings that weave together and make a rope. It's a very strong rope that bears the weight of a conviction." A jury agreed with Buehler's evidence and convicted Stewart of first-degree assault.

On January 8, 1999, Judge Ellsworth Cundiff sentenced Stewart to life imprisonment, telling him, "My thought is, injecting a child with the HIV virus really puts you in the same category as the worst war criminal. I believe that when God finally calls you, you are going to burn in hell from here to eternity." At this writing, Stewart's son is still alive, but should he die of the AIDS virus, Stewart will be charged with murder and could face the death penalty.

**Steyn, Nicholas**, 1956- , S. Afr., Case of mur. Since the abandonment of white apartheid in South Africa and the takeover of political power and the government by the black majority under Nelson Mandela, outbreaks of racial violence have increased. In the area around Benoni, South Africa, a number of white farmers have been murdered, reportedly by blacks who had formerly worked for these landowners. Racial tension was running high in April 1998 when white farmers banded together to form armed groups that patrolled their lands at night against intruders.

One of these farmers, 42-year-old Nicholas Steyn, saw several blacks crossing his property on April 11, 1998. He stepped from his home, according to one account, and fired a shot that killed a 6-month-old black girl being carried on the back of her cousin, who was wounded. Steyn was jailed, refusing bail, saying that he feared for his life if he were released. He awaits trial for murder at this writing.

**Stone, Michael**, 1956- , Ire., terr.-mur. Reportedly an activist for Protestant paramilitary groups in Northern Ireland, Michael Stone, in March 1988, attacked an Irish Republican Army (IRA) funeral at Belfast's Milltown Cemetery. Scores of mourners were attending the funeral of three IRA members, who had been killed in an abortive bombing attack in Gibraltar. Among the mourners were members of the IRA's legal political wing, Sinn Fein.

Stone, attempting to assassinate the Sinn Fein members, fired shots and lobbed grenades in their direction. He missed his targets and fled through the cemetery, firing into the crowd of mourners as he dodged behind a tombstone. Stone's bullets killed three people attending the funeral. Stone, a Protestant, was later apprehended, tried, and convicted of these three murders, as well as the murders of three other Catholics. On March 3, 1989, he was sentenced to life imprisonment.

**Storm, Mark**, 1967-1997, U.S., suic.-mur. A riverboat pilot, Mark Storm was having psychiatric problems and had sought help, checking himself into the Hillcrest Behavioral Health Services at the Ohio Valley Medical Center in Wheeling, West Virginia, in early March 1997. He was reportedly being treated for stress and panic disorder. On March 6, 1997, Storm left the hospital on his own initiative and returned home to his wife and two children to attend a birthday party. A neighbor attending the party described Storm's behavior at that time as "stressed out and quiet."

Storm later produced a 9mm semiautomatic pistol and began shooting his family members, killing his 26-year-old wife, Betty, and his daughters, Jessica, 8, and Megan, 3. He then drove more than two miles to his boyhood home on Wheeling Island, where he shot and killed his 59-year-old mother, Roberta Myles, as she sat in a wheelchair, and his 32-year-old brother, Benjamin. He then went to a spot along the Ohio River where he had fished as a child and shot himself. His body was later pulled from the waters.

**Stouber, Elaine,** 1927- , and **Aprigliano, Frank**, 1928- U.S., fraud. New York City residents Elaine Stouber, one-time aide to Brooklyn borough president Abe Stark, and her husband, Frank Aprigliano, a clerk at the United Nations, convinced several hundred of their neighbors that for considerable secret investments, they could receive huge profits from "insider" investment schemes. These schemes, as outlined by Stouber and Aprigliano, included secret commodity and real estate investments with an Arab sheik, a mythical business in Peru, and the complete rebuilding of Brussels, Belgium.

The couple took in an estimated $3.9 million from Brooklyn residents, mostly elderly or retired persons in the Canarsie and Flatlands sections. To convince their neighbors and friends to continue their investments, Stouber and Aprigliano actually paid off some of their earlier investors, who, upon seeing considerable profits, reinvested and were used as unwitting shills to influence others to invest.

Complaints about the Stouber-Aprigliano deals caused their arrests. On October 4, 1989, both pleaded guilty to charges of defrauding more than 200 people. On December 14, Manhattan Federal Judge Robert Sweet sentenced Stouber and Aprigliano to two and a half years in prison. Stated Judge Sweet to the more than forty victims who were in court at the time " ... there is no free lunch. Deals that are too good to be true, as in this case, turn out to be false and fraudulent."

Many of the victims in the courtroom were critical of the

decision, stating that he had been too lenient with Stouber and Aprigliano. Judge Sweet is on record as having called for the legalizing of drugs, which caused one female victim of the confidence tricksters to shout, "This is a judge who doesn't want to arrest people for crack (cocaine)!"

---

**Straing, Ricky Lynn**, 1967- , **Morris, Wesley Tyrone**, 1973- , and **Garland, Tavis Zavan**, 1968- , U.S., mur. A farm worker driving a tractor along West Duncan Road in Union County, North Carolina, on June 14, 1993, found a badly decomposed body later identified as Douglas Effird. The dead man, a 32-year-old Union County resident who had recently been paroled from prison, where he had been serving a term for voluntary manslaughter, had been beaten to death. Police found no clue leading to suspects, but an anonymous tip led them to arrest Ricky Lynn Straing, Wesley Tyrone Morris and Tavis Zavan Garland, all black, like the victim.

These three suspects were interrogated separately and Garland quickly revealed that he, Straing and Morris had picked up Effird in Spring Hill, a drug-infested area, and that when he attempted to buy crack and would not pay the price, the three men beat him up and then stuffed him in the trunk of their car. They then drove about, getting high on alcohol and drugs. When Effird began banging on the lid of the trunk, Straing and Morris got out of the car, opened the lid, and beat Effird to death with a folding chair. They then dumped his body alongside a rural road.

Straing was tried and convicted of Effird's murder on August 4, 1994. He was sentenced to life in prison. Morris was convicted in October 1994, and also was sent to prison for life. Garland, who had cooperated with prosecutors, received a twenty-year sentence.

---

**Stramaglio, Ralph F., Jr.**, 1952- , U.S., theft. In June 1992, 84-year-old Ralph Stramaglio, Sr., died of natural causes at his home in McHenry, Illinois. His son, Ralph F. Stramaglio, instead of reporting his father's death, took the body to the Chequamegon National Forest in Medford County, Wisconsin, hiding it in a shallow grave. From that moment on, Ralph Stramaglio, Jr., continued to perpetuate the lie that his father was still alive in order to receive and cash out his father's Social Security and Railroad Retirement benefits.

For about three years, the father's checks were deposited in his own account and the money was withdrawn by his son, who spent it in supporting his mother and sister. Then, in October 1995, hunters discovered the skeletal remains of Ralph Stramaglio, Sr., leading to his son's arrest. Convicted of federal theft, Ralph Stramaglio, Jr., was sentenced to fourteen months in federal prison on April 5, 1996, and ordered to pay a fine of $2,000 and restitution in the amount of $38,000.

---

**Strasser, Steven**, See: **Mieske, Kenneth M.**

---

**Stratton, Richard**, 1942-1989, U.S., mur. A business dispute between two former partners culminated in murder at the headquarters of Police Officers Promotions, an El Paso, Texas, firm that sponsored fund-raising activities to benefit local law enforcement agencies. On October 16, 1989, Richard Stratton armed himself with a .38-caliber revolver and set out to square accounts with his one-time associate, Norman Montion, a police detective. During the past year, Montion had bought out Stratton's share of the business after the two men failed to resolve a fundamental "disagreement over management of the company."

Stratton arrived at Police Officers Promotions and opened fire. Montion and an employee, Sergio Munoz, were shot and killed. A third man, John Ely, was wounded. Before Montion died from his wounds he fatally shot Stratton. Detectives later discovered that Stratton had also shot and killed his 35-year-old wife, Elva, at the couple's home prior to his rampage.

Company funds had turned up missing in March, which led to the falling out, according to sources close to the investigation. At the time of the shooting, Stratton was employed by a competitor, the El Paso Police Association. A search of police records revealed that Stratton was an ex-convict who had served eight years in a California prison for manslaughter before his parole in 1975. Seven years later he was hired by the El Paso Municipal Police Association, which had full knowledge of his criminal past.

---

**Strawberry Murders**, 1986-1989, U.S., (unsolv.) mur. In Los Angeles street slang, a "strawberry" is a prostitute who trades sex for drugs. From 1986 through 1989, there were several strawberry killings. Most of them are still unsolved. This has led to protests from community groups, such as the Black Coalition Fighting Back Serial Murders, which demonstrated in February 1989 to put pressure on the Los Angeles Police Department to protect black women, who have been the predominant victims of the wave of violence, and to bring the killer or killers to justice. Coalition leader Margaret Prescod alleged that the women her group had interviewed, survivors of the attacks, indicated that their assailant was "some sort of law officer."

An apparent break in the case came on February 24, 1989, when police stopped a car driven by Los Angeles County Sheriff's Deputy Rickey Ross on a routine traffic stop. Ross was off-duty and had no police identification with him. He was with a prostitute, who claimed that they had been smoking crack together. Upon searching the car, an unmarked county police vehicle assigned to Ross, they found a 9-mm semi-automatic pistol. They arrested Ross for driving under the influence, but when he submitted to chemical testing, his system was found to be free of intoxicants.

Despite the fact that technicians in the ballistics lab had to pry the gun open to load it, they found that it matched the murder weapon that fired the shots that killed three prostitutes the previous year. Ross was charged with the murders of 27-year-old Judith Simpson, whose body was found October 14, 1988; 35-year-old Cynthia Walker, found November 18, 1988; and 24-year-old Latanya Johnson, found December 11, 1988. Although Ross was an eighteen-year veteran sheriff's deputy with a nearly unblemished record, other allegations quickly surfaced. A search of his house revealed firearms he confiscated in arrests but had not turned in to the department. Old friends and acquaintances noticed a change in his behavior—a deeply religious man, Ross had recently stopped his ministerial work among the inmates in jail. He had moved his family into an expensive home, and his wife had been seen driving a Mercedes-Benz. He also asked a friend to stencil the name "Mad Dog" onto his motorcycle helmet.

Still, several details in the case did not add up. People who knew him well still attested to Ross's character. Ross issued a statement in May explaining that the gun was an old service revolver that he stashed in the trunk of the car when he was issued a new one three years before. Later, an eyewitness came forward to say that she saw a woman shoot one of the prostitutes, Cynthia Walker, to death.

Ross was released on May 15. An independent ballistics expert, Charles Morton of Oakland, California, proved that the previous ballistics report was faulty and that Ross's gun did not match the murder weapon after all. The prostitute with him at the time of his arrest proved to be an unreliable witness who kept changing her story and was motivated to lie to avoid a jail term. The strawberry murders remain unsolved.

**Streitferdt, Thomas**, 1929- , U.S., sex. abuse-rape. The Reverend Thomas Streitferdt reportedly told church members the devil forced him to sexually assault a teenage babysitter and his wife's niece in 1957. He then left New York City's East Orange Pentecostal Church, and in 1964 became head of the 700-member True Church of God in East Harlem. Between May 1985 and February 1987, Streitferdt assaulted three female members of his congregation who met with him in his basement office for counseling. Streitferdt was charged with sexual abuse, sodomy, and rape involving a 16-year-old girl, the rape of a 21-year-old woman twelve days before he performed her marriage ceremony, and with two counts of sexually abusing a 40-year-old woman. Under direct cross-examination, Streitferdt admitted that he kissed and embraced the 40-year-old in a "pastorly gesture of affection," but denied any sexual contact with the other victims. Prosecutor Alejandro Schwed called Streitferdt "a wolf in sheep's clothing," and went on to describe the suffering caused to the victims, one of whom became a runaway, another who suffered nightmares, and a third who attempted to kill herself after developing ulcers.

Streitferdt, who demanded from his church members more than 30 percent of their wages, lived in a $1.4 million estate in Long Island. The 60-year-old minister continued to preach even after his May 26, 1989, conviction on three counts of sexual abuse and one count of rape (he was acquitted on one count of rape and sodomy in the case of the 16-year-old) and received overwhelming support from his remaining parishioners. On July 7, before Manhattan Supreme Court Judge Franklin Weissberg, Streitferdt was sentenced to one to three years for each sexual abuse charge and five to fifteen years for rape, to be served consecutively. "With faith in God I have hopes in my complete vindication," Streitferdt said.

**Strickland, Leonard**, See: **Moore, Armand**.

**Stroh, James II**, See: **Scherr, Nicholas**.

**Strohmeyer, Jeremy Joseph**, 1979- , U.S., sexual asslt.-mur. One of the most ruthless murders in recent times—the 1997 rape and strangulation murder of a 7-year-old girl—was committed by Jeremy Joseph Strohmeyer, an honor student from Long Beach, California. Though outwardly easygoing and affable, Strohmeyer's mercurial temper often flared into violence. He hoarded child pornography, visiting web sites on the Internet to obtain this material, according to prosecutors, and even stated to an Internet chat room, "I fantasize about having sex with 5- and 6-year-old girls all the time."

Strohmeyer's father was in prison and his biological mother was in a mental institution. Strohmeyer's few friends at Woodrow Wilson High School in Long Beach described him as "intelligent" but "dangerous," and a girl who dated him briefly stated that Strohmeyer appeared to be a nice person, but that his mood dramatically changed when he did not get his own way. On a date with this girl, Strohmeyer was rebuffed and, according to the girl, "punched me with his fists, leaving bruises." He later wrote in this girl's yearbook, "Live life to its fullest today cause we'll probably all be dead tomorrow."

In a pathetic attempt to draw attention to himself, as well as provide cheap shocks, Strohmeyer took to mutilating his body, piercing his tongue with a stud, piercing his left ear and inserting a long silver earring, piercing the nipples on his chest with studs. These vicious body ornamentations really declared Strohmeyer's low self-esteem, rejection of his own higher intelligence, and his contempt for civilized behavior. Worse, and more ominous, his willingness to injure himself was an indication, no matter how oblique, that Jeremy Strohmeyer was willing to injure others.

Two weeks before he was to graduate high school, Strohmeyer and a friend, David Cash, traveled to the Primadonna Resorts (now called the Primm Valley Hotel) on the California-Nevada state line in the last week of May 1997. The boys caroused in the casinos, with Strohmeyer seeking out strangers to shock by lifting his T-shirt to show his pierced nipples, sticking out his tongue at females to displayed his studded tongue, telling them that he was from Long Beach, California. At one point they were reported to casino security officers for urinating on video machines.

While Strohmeyer and Cash were making nuisances of themselves, Leroy Iverson and his two children entered the Primadonna Resorts, shortly after midnight on May 25, 1997. Before Iverson went to play blackjack, he told his son to take care of his younger sister, 7-year-old Sherrice Iverson. Iverson, a resident of Los Angeles, had custody of his children at the time while his wife battled for custody in the courts. The children headed for the arcade as Iverson entered the gambling casino.

Several times the little girl wandered off, but her brother found her and brought her back to the arcade. At one point, however, she vanished. A little before dawn that day, a female casino employee went into the women's washroom. When she went to clean out the handicapped stall, she gasped. Sherrice Iverson was there, sitting upright on the toilet, her dress pulled up to her waist, her underpants gone. She was dead.

Police soon swarmed into the casino. Detectives notified Leroy Iverson, who stood stunned as his daughter's body was removed to the coroner's office, where it was quickly determined that the little girl had been raped and strangled to death. Hundreds of visitors were questioned in the next two days, but the videotapes taken from more than 300 security cameras in the three casino-hotels of the resort turned up the killer. Caught on tape was a dark-haired youth shown walking toward the washroom with Sherrice Iverson. This image was flashed across the TV screens of the West Coast, and soon police received calls identifying the youth as Jeremy Joseph Strohmeyer.

Strohmeyer was picked up at his home in Long Beach as he was leaving through a side door. He at first denied having been at the Primadonna Resorts, but he changed his story when detectives told him that videotapes showed him playing with Sherrice Iverson at the Primadonna and then following her into a women's restroom. Further, he was told that witnesses were on hand who would identify him as the repulsive youth who had gone about showing his pierced tongue and nipples.

Extradited to Las Vegas, Nevada, and held for trial, Strohmeyer told investigators that he had killed the girl. He said, "I was playing hide-and-seek with her, and we were throwing spitballs at one another." When she threw a "Caution Wet" sign at him, which struck his leg, he went into a rage, Strohmeyer said, and he chased her into the women's washroom. He said he grabbed her and forced her into a stall for the handicapped, holding his hand over her mouth.

As she struggled, he said, he lifted her to the top of the toilet, tearing away her pants and undergarments. In her terror, the girl urinated all over him and this further incensed him, Strohmeyer admitted. He took her black boots off and threw them into the toilet and then sexually assaulted her, still holding his hand over her mouth. He said that while he was raping the girl, three women came into the washroom and subsequently left. One other person also appeared, Strohmeyer later stated, and that was his friend, David Cash.

Cash would state that he had gotten worried about what Strohmeyer might do and went into the washroom, going into the stall next to the one occupied by Strohmeyer and Sherrice Iverson. He said he leaned over the partition and touched the rapist's forehead, telling him to leave the girl alone, but became frightened when Strohmeyer gave him a devastating look and left. Cash said he went to the pool outside and waited for his friend.

Strohmeyer finally joined him, Cash said, sitting down next to him in a pool chair. Cash asked him what he did to the girl. "I killed her," Cash quoted Strohmeyer as saying. Cash had done nothing about the murder. He did not interfere when his friend was raping the helpless girl and he did not try to stop Strohmeyer from hurting the girl, other than his lame remark about leaving her alone. Further, once Strohmeyer told him he had killed the girl, David Cash did not go to the authorities. (Cash was never charged in the murder, the state of Nevada having no "Good Samaritan" law, which would have caused him to be charged for not coming to the assistance of a victim.)

Later, Strohmeyer would say that he killed the girl as an act of compassion, that, because he had cupped his hand over her nose and mouth so tightly, her breathing became labored. He said that he thought she had been "brain damaged," and so, to ease her suffering, he simply choked her to death.

Strohmeyer's September 1998 trial was brief, even though his attorney, Leslie Abramson, who had defended the Menendez brothers, tried to portray her client as a troubled youth who had come under the spell of evil influences. Strohmeyer himself said that he could not even remember killing Sherrice Iverson, that he was in "a drunken and drugged haze" at the time of the murder. By that time, Strohmeyer had, through Abramson, pleaded guilty to the murder in a plea-bargain arrangement.

Abramson stated that she would aid anyone who wanted Cash held accountable for not preventing the murder, which drew fire from Cash's attorney, Mark Werkman, who stated, "She should save her indignation and outrage for the conduct of her own client, who just pleaded guilty to murdering a 7-year-old girl."

On October 14, 1998, Strohmeyer appeared in a Las Vegas court, where he stated, "I am truly sorry. If I were given the opportunity to exchange my life for Sherrice's and bring her back, I would not hesitate, not even for a second." He was then sentenced to life in prison. Many believed that Strohmeyer's chances in prison were slim; child killers must invariably be protected against the wrath of other inmates.

In Northern California at that time, David Cash had become a student at the University of California at Berkeley. Hundreds of protestors had demanded that he be expelled, but university officials stated that they had no grounds to throw Cash out of the school.

---

**Stroud, Danny Joe**, See: **Roth, Brian David.**

---

**Strozzi, Wayne,** 1953-1989, U.S., mur. Following his release from the Colorado State Penitentiary in October 1987, Vietnam veteran Wayne Strozzi became increasingly angry and despondent over the direction his life was taking. Strozzi was described as suffering from a "post-traumatic stress disorder" brought on by his wartime experiences in Southeast Asia. Strozzi served thirteen months in prison on cocaine charges. When he was released, he discovered that his wife was seeing someone else.

On January 3, 1989, Strozzi went on a rampage. He assaulted his estranged wife, Barbara Strozzi, at her apartment, and then proceeded to the Riverhouse Restaurant in Loveland, Colorado, where he threatened to kill all twenty patrons unless the police provided him with a getaway car and safe passage to Libya. For nearly an hour Strozzi held them at bay while police snipers from the SWAT team lined up outside. The marksmen opened fire from strategic positions outside the restaurant. Strozzi shot and killed waitress Sally Mills and wounded two officers before police bullets struck the gunman, fatally wounding him. Forty-five-year-old Fenton Crookshank, who was attending a Lion's Club meeting in the restaurant, was accidentally shot to death after he fled from a bathroom window. Police said that they had ordered Crookshank to halt, but when he refused they took aim and fired. Crookshank was a former principal at a Nebraska high school.

---

**Strydom, Barend Hendrik**, 1966- , S. Africa, mur. A member of a militant South African resistance group, aimed at fomenting a "war" between the white Afikaners and the black majority, was sentenced to death on May 25, 1989, for the slaughter of eight people in central Pretoria on November 15, 1988. Barend Strydom, a member of the "Wit Wolwe" (White Wolves) faction of the rightist Afrikaner Weerstandsbewg (Resistance Movement), entered a predominantly black area in the theater district of Pretoria and opened fire with an automatic pistol. Eight persons were killed in the assault and sixteen others were wounded before Strydom was apprehended by police after a chase through the streets of the city. Strydom's motives were tied to the racist views of the group to which he belonged. Police attributed several bombing attacks against anti-apartheid churches to the White Wolves.

Strydom's trial in Pretoria in May 1989 was attended by 700 spectators, many of whom were sympathetic to Strydom. "What amazes me is that there are people who support what he (Strydom) has done," commented Reverend Elliot Khumalo, a black minister in attendance at the trial. Robert von Tonder, head of the right-wing Borstast Party, called Strydom a "super patriot." "What he's done is a symbolic act, an act of protest." A physician who was called on to testify at the trial explained that Strydom had a "psychopathic personality" and believed that the killings were a part of a "propaganda show." In handing down his sentence, Supreme Court Justice Louis Harms said that "mass murder and racial murder will never be tolerated in this court. He (Strydom) was worse than any terrorist." The trial took place at the same court where black resistance leader Nelson Mandela was convicted of sabotage twenty-five years earlier.

---

**Stuart, Charles**, 1960-1990, U.S., mur. Like many another killer before and after him, from Carl Otto Wanderer to Susan Smith, Charles Stuart found the idea of having a child so repellant that he murdered to escape the responsibility. Stuart made a very good living by selling expensive furs in Boston. When his wife Carol, 30, informed him that she was pregnant, Stuart went to pieces. He first suggested that she have an abortion.

Carol Stuart, however, wanted very much to have a child and told her husband that she intended to give birth. A short time later, on the night of October 23, 1989, Stuart unexpectedly drove through a predominantly black neighborhood in Boston. His car was stopped, he later reported, by a black gunman "with a raspy voice" who fatally shot his wife and wounded him by shooting him in the abdomen.

Stuart called police on his car phone, saying to the 911 operator, "My wife's been shot. I've been shot." A few minutes later, he moaned on the phone to the operator, "Oh, man, it

hurts ... My wife has stopped gurgling. She's stopped breathing." Police and paramedics finally located the Stuart car and rushed both Stuart and his wife to a hospital. Carol Stuart was dead on arrival. Her child, however, was delivered in a Caesarian operation and was born alive. He died a short time later.

Three days later, Stuart collected $82,000 from his wife's life insurance. (Another report had it that he collected as much as $500,000 from other recent policies he had taken out on Carol's life.) Because of his eagerness to collect the insurance money and his lack of apparent grief over his wife's death, detectives grew suspicious of Stuart. Also, Stuart's story did not ring true to police, and investigators began to look into his background. (It is normal for police investigating homicides to keep in mind a grim but accurate statistic—that 30 percent of all women who are murdered are killed by their husbands.)

They began by interviewing members of Stuart's family. His 23-year-old brother, Matthew, after several interviews, finally admitted to officers that Stuart had given him a gun and some jewelry following the shooting. He had thrown the gun away, said the brother, tossing it over a railroad trestle spanning the Pines River in Revere, Massachusetts, but it was recovered and ballistics matched the bullets in Carol Stuart to the gun.

It was now evident that Stuart had killed his own wife, taken her jewelry in a fake robbery and turned over both jewelry and gun to his brother for safekeeping while all the while blaming the murder on an anonymous black killer. Upon hearing that he was to be arrested, Stuart drove to a Boston bridge and jumped into the Mystic River, taking his own life, rather than wait for the conviction that would surely result from the evidence police had collected. Also See: **Smith, Susan**; **Wanderer, Carl Otto**, Vol. IV.

---

**Sturgill, Crystal**, See: **Cornett, Natasha**.

---

**Stutzman, Eli,** 1951- , U.S., mur. The residents of Thayer County, Nebraska, dubbed the child "Little Boy Blue." Police investigators from this rural farming community did not know the little boy's name or where he came from when they pulled the frozen, lifeless body out of a ditch on Christmas Eve 1985. He was clad only in a pair of baby-blue pajamas, which gave rise to the nickname. It was a local mystery that would remain unsolved for two years.

Meanwhile, the 9-year-old boy was buried in a cemetery in Chester, Nebraska The inscription on the headstone read, "Matthew," meaning "gift of God," and it was paid for, in part, by the members of the community. Thayer County Sheriff Gary Young spent the next two years following nearly 1,000 blind leads until the first real break in the case came on December 1, 1987. An anonymous Wyoming woman sent Sheriff Young a snapshot of 9-year-old Daniel Stutzman, an Amish boy, who was raised in Apple Creek, Ohio. Daniel was traveling with his father, Eli, along Interstate 80 during the Christmas holiday in 1985. The father told his boy that they were going back to Ohio to visit the family. But when Stutzman arrived, Daniel was not with him. Stutzman, a drifter who had been treated for depression, explained that Daniel had elected to remain in Wyoming so he could go skiing. "He never seemed nervous or upset," explained a resident of the small Amish community in Ohio, "so there was no reason to doubt him." At the end of January, Stutzman left Apple Creek. In July, friends and relatives in Ohio received word from Stutzman that his son had been killed in a car accident. Andy Gingrich, the boy's uncle, visited Lyman, Wyoming, but could not locate the grave site. He immediately contacted the couple that Danny had supposedly been living with, but was surprised to learn that Stutzman had apparently enrolled the youngster in an Ohio public school.

On December 14, 1987, the Nebraska police confirmed that "Little Boy Blue" was indeed Daniel Stutzman after comparing a palm print on Daniel's third-grade report card with the remains. Medical and dental records confirmed the findings. Eli Stutzman was arrested that same day in Azie, Texas, and charged with child abuse. He told authorities that Daniel had died from a throat infection during the trip to Ohio. Out of a gnawing sense of fear, he decided to throw the body into a roadside ditch. The whole story seemed incredible to Young. "You don't leave a 9-year-old boy in a ditch for the animals to chew on," he said. "That's out of the dark ages. Since day one I have felt there was something more to this, but I can't put my finger on it."

As the investigation unfolded, the police soon linked Stutzman to the May 12, 1985, murder of his onetime roommate, Glen Albert Pritchett, in Austin, Texas. Shortly after the body was found, Stutzman took Daniel out of school and headed to Wyoming because, as he explained, the authorities had asked the boy if his father had sexual relations with Pritchett. "It really upset him, so I decided to have him stay with friends until things were squared away." At his first trial in Hebron, Nebraska, on January 11, 1988, Stutzman pleaded guilty to misdemeanor charges of abandoning a body and concealing a death. He was sentenced to eighteen months in prison. In July 1988, while serving his sentence, Texas authorities indicted him for the 1985 murder of Glen Pritchett. Stutzman was convicted on August 1, 1989, and was sentenced to serve forty years in prison by a judge in Austin.

---

**Sugg, Shawn**, 1968- , **Miokovic, Andrew**, 1977- , **Reda, Danielle**, 1972- , **Dobbs, Eric**, 1975- , Swed., viol. of hate crime law. The rock band Max Resist, based in Michigan, appeared at a rock concert in Stockholm, Sweden, on January 3, 1998. The musicians had agreed to perform for free as long as the sponsors paid for their expenses. During the performance, band members and some in the audience began shouting the Nazi slogan "Sieg Heil!" This prompted police to arrest band members Shawn Sugg, Andrew Miokovic, Danielle Reda, and a fan, Eric Dobbs, for violating Sweden's hate laws. All were sentenced to a month behind bars at Kronoberg Remand Prison.

---

**Suh, Catherine Diana** (Suh Hae-Sung; AKA: Kasia Kane; Tiffini Escada), 1969- , U.S., mur. America meant only one thing to Catherine Suh, getting the best of everything and getting it as soon as possible. Dining in the finest restaurants, driving the most expensive cars, having designer clothes and jewelry, and living in luxury apartments were Suh's ultimate goals. She achieved all those ends while in her 20s, accomplishing one other feat in her clawing climb to riches—cold-blooded murder.

Suh was born Suh Hae-Sung in South Korea on May 2, 1969, to affluent parents. Her father, Suh Yoon Myunt, was a captain in the army of dictator Park Chung Hee; her mother, Tai Sook, was a working pharmacist who later changed her name to Elizabeth Suh. She and her brother, Andrew, younger by five years, enjoyed luxuries Korean children only dreamed about—a large house, good food, tailored clothes of brocaded silks and their own nanny, who was chastised if Suh or her brother ever suffered a fall that bruised a knee or elbow.

Park's oppressive dictatorship, however, was on shaky ground and Suh's fa-

Chicago's "dragon lady," Catherine Suh, who arranged for her brother to kill her lover, then fled to Hawaii; she went to prison for life.

ther decided to immigrate with his family to America, settling in Chicago in 1976. By 1979 Park was dead from an assassin's bullet and the Suhs had moved into small but comfortable living quarters in the West Peterson Park district on Chicago's Northwest Side. Suh's parents worked long hours as punch press operators for a manufacturing firm that hired Koreans at low wages. No longer were Suh and her brother treated as children of wealth. The brocaded robes had long since been sold, although Suh's memory of her pampered years fiercely lingered in her mind, so much so that as a teenager growing up in Chicago she resolved to somehow reclaim the luxury of her childhood, no matter the cost.

Suh's lot in life began to improve when her parents opened and successfully ran a dry-cleaning shop in Evanston, an upscale suburb just north of Chicago. The family moved into better living quarters and there was suddenly extra money for Suh's better lifestyle. At age 17, she was finishing high school, buying designer clothes and working out in an expensive North Side health club. It was here, in the spring of 1987, that she met the tall and attractive Robert W. Koron, Jr., who had graduated Holy Cross High School in River Grove and had gone on to Triton College to study engineering.

The 25-year-old Koron had dropped out of school and had gone on cross-country trips before taking a job at the health club as an instructor. Suh attracted the macho Koron and the pair soon struck up a torrid romance. Suh was not satisfied with Koron's personality. She wanted a more urbane, sophisticated man and to that end she subtly converted the outdoorsy Koron to a businessman. He suddenly began wearing custom-made suits and talking about investment opportunities. Then he changed his name to Robert O'Durbaine. To his family, he became an altogether different person, someone his brothers and sisters knew had been drastically altered by the scheming, manipulative Suh, who had moved in with their brother.

Suh's entrepreneurial ambitions culminated in the fall of 1987. She was brimming with ideas for businesses to buy and operate. She began spending nights in the Gold Coast clubs, where she cultivated "business contacts." O'Durbaine came to believe that she was cheating on him; he was thinking of breaking off the relationship. Then an event took place that drastically changed the lives of Catherine Suh and Robert O'Durbaine.

On the morning of October 6, 1987, O'Durbaine picked up Suh at her family's home. They planned to go to breakfast and called the dry-cleaning shop to see if Suh's mother wanted them to bring her any food. The shop at the time was operated by Suh's mother, Elizabeth, her father having died of stomach cancer in 1985. When Elizabeth did not answer the shop phone, Suh and O'Durbaine went to the Evanston shop to find police swarming about the place.

Elizabeth Suh was dead, a murder victim. Her killer had literally slashed the woman to pieces, stabbing her thirty-seven times before slitting her throat. When detectives went to the Suh home, they found the place a shambles, as if someone had been desperately looking for something. A photo of Elizabeth Suh had been turned over on the mantlepiece.

Police initially attributed Elizabeth's death to a berserk robber who had come to loot the dry-cleaning shop, but when they found the Suh house ransacked, their suspicions turned toward Catherine Suh. The turning over of Elizabeth's photo was one key to that suspicion. Suh had had a difficult time with her mother for months. Elizabeth Suh had repeatedly quarreled with her daughter about her dating a Caucasian, O'Durbaine, insisting that she see only Korean boys. Moreover, she refused to provide her daughter with anything more than a small allowance.

It was quickly surmised that Catherine Suh had brutally murdered her mother to maintain her relationship with O'Durbaine, as well as to obtain the $400,000 from an insurance policy on Elizabeth Suh's life, along with another $400,000 from the family estate. Speculation had it that she (perhaps with O'Durbaine's help) killed her mother, then raced to her house, where she tore the place apart looking for the insurance policy and the estate papers.

Nothing could be proved against either Catherine Suh or O'Durbaine. Both insisted that they were together having breakfast when Elizabeth had been killed. A short time later, Suh was awarded the insurance and estate money. She, her brother Andrew and O'Durbaine then occupied the Suh home, buying expensive clothes and a new Mercedes. They began living the high life, spending their time in the better Chicago restaurants and nightclubs, all of which disturbed the tightly-knit Korean community of Chicago, more than 100,000 clannish citizens who viewed open lifestyles by Korean females as disgraceful conduct.

It was that mold that Catherine Suh sought to break. She wore designer dresses, sped about in her Mercedes and flaunted her wealth to disapproving neighbors. She hired a maid to take care of the house and then worked with O'Durbaine to run the dry-cleaning shop, an operation that proved uninspiring. They

sold the shop, then went into rehabilitating properties on the Near North Side. They then bought a nightclub, the Club Metropolis, in the northwest suburb of Glenview.

In 1991, knowing the Korean community disapproved of her, Suh insisted that she, O'Durbaine and her brother Andrew, then a senior honor student at the exclusive Loyola Academy in Wilmette, move to Bucktown, a Yuppie community of young go-getters like themselves. They took a large house and remodeled it at considerable expense, adding a sunken living room, a large glass atrium, an elaborate goldfish pond in the back patio and a sophisticated security system.

Like everything else, Suh began to tire of O'Durbaine. They argued almost all the time and she often attacked him, attempting to claw his face with her long fingernails, which she habitually painted blood red. At such times, O'Durbaine would grab her wrists and push her away. She began pushing him, striking him, screaming in Korean at him. Both began having affairs.

Then, on the night of September 25, 1993, it became Robert O'Durbaine's time to die. About 7 p.m. that night, neighbors in the 1600 block of North Hermitage heard a number of shots coming from the back of Suh's house. Police were called and they soon found O'Durbaine in the garage, which faced an alley. He lay in a spreading pool of his own blood, shot several times. His killer appeared to be a thief. His wallet and Jeep Laredo were missing.

Catherine Suh ostensibly learned of the murder the next morning when she called the house for messages. Police detectives drove to Glenview to pick her up; she had stayed with a lover overnight, she said. She seemed unconcerned about O'Durbaine's death, never bothering to ask how he had been killed or whether or not he had suffered. In fact, she sneered in talking about him, saying he was a bad gambler who had run up large debts that had caused them to sell the Glenview nightclub a month earlier for $125,000, taking a considerable loss on her investment. (The suggestion to police was obvious; O'Durbaine had been murdered for welching on gambling debts to syndicate gamblers who had apparently taken what money was on the victim and stole his car as an afterthought.)

With no evidence to charge her with the crime, police released Suh, who returned to the Hermitage house, accompanied by her lover, a real estate developer. Friends went to the garage to clean up the blood and gore left by the killing (using a shovel, according to one account) while Suh lay in bed reportedly weeping over the death of O'Durbaine. Apparently someone had told Suh that her lack of emotion over the death of her longtime lover made her appear suspicious. When she attended the wake and funeral some days later, she wailed so loudly—noticeably without tears—that O'Durbaine's relatives asked her to quiet down. Further, when O'Durbaine's relatives cremated his remains and buried them, Suh arrived too late for the ceremony. She threw herself down on the ground and began to claw at it, picking up chunks of sod and asking how far down her ex-lover's ashes were buried. When she was told six feet, she gave up.

Detectives saw through it all. A month later, Suh was summoned to police headquarters. An investigator directly accused her of engineering O'Durbaine's murder, telling her that they had picked up a recording she had left on her own phone answering machine on the night of the murder, one wherein she stated that her car had broken down in Glenview and asked O'Durbaine to pick her up, thus luring him to the garage, where someone was waiting to kill him.

Suh, who was dressed in tight-fitting black satin slacks and a breast-hugging lamé blouse, smiled at the detective questioning her. She admitted making the call, but denied knowing anything about the murder. Then she said that her real estate lover might have killed O'Durbaine out of jealousy. When that failed to work, she suggested that the victim had been murdered by a mob man to whom O'Durbaine owed large gambling debts. The detective shrugged off the suggestion. Growing desperate, Suh then offered the investigator money to drop her as a suspect, saying, "You name your price."

The next day Suh was charged with conspiracy to commit first-degree murder. She was held on $150,000 bail, which was put up by her brother Andrew, who sent the cash from Los Angeles. Only two hours after she was released, Suh was back at the Hermitage house, frantically boxing her clothes and personal effects, a hauling company removing all her belongings. She destroyed all of O'Durbaine's personal effects. When she left the house, Catherine Suh ceased to exist. She was now Kasia Kane, resident of a chic Lake Point Tower apartment.

On November 10, 1993, Andrew Suh finally made his way back to Chicago. En route, he was stopped by DEA agents at the Dallas-Fort Worth Airport, who thought he was acting suspiciously. The small black bag he was carrying was searched but no drugs were found. Instead, detectives found $56,000 in cash. DEA officers notified Chicago police, who picked up Andrew when he arrived. Andrew Suh was not made of the kind of steel ingrained in his sister Catherine. He almost immediately broke down and confessed to murdering O'Durbaine at his sister's insistence. She had wanted her lover dead for months, Andrew said, kept carping about when he, Andrew, "would take care of Robert."

Andrew had hesitated. He was then a college student in Boston, but Catherine had called him repeatedly, demanding that he murder her ex-lover. She was now head of the family, he said, and, according to Korean custom, she had to be obeyed. He agreed to kill O'Durbaine, flying from Boston under the alias of Jean Choi. He was dressed in dark clothes when, according to his sister's plan, he crept into the garage of the Hermitage address, waiting with gun in hand. "Shoot him more than once," Catherine Suh had emphasized to him. "You have to make sure that Robert is dead."

Suh then began calling O'Durbaine with the lie that her car had broken down and she needed to have her onetime lover pick her up. Apparently, O'Durbaine did not come home until late, because Andrew waited and sweated in the stifling garage for more than five hours. About 7 p.m., however, he told police, O'Durbaine walked into the garage and Andrew shot him in the head. He shot him again as his victim crashed toward the concrete floor. The killer then filched O'Durbaine's wallet and stole the Jeep to make the murder appear to be part of a robbery.

After throwing the gun into a dumpster, Andrew parked the Jeep on a dark Bucktown street, then took a cab to the airport. As he flew back to Boston, he recalled for police, he

smelled gunpowder on his hands and chest. Booked for murder, Andrew Suh's bond was set at $250,000. His sister did not come to his rescue as he had for her. His bail was reduced, however, when a priest from Loyola Academy pleaded his case and he was released.

Andrew Suh's fortunes then went into a steep decline. Within months he had joined a gang of thieves and was selling drugs. He had planned to rob a Lake Zurich bank, but the plan was thwarted. He sold guns and was arrested with four others for a robbery committed in the summer of 1994. Back in jail, he was held without bond, awaiting his trial for murder. His sister, however, went on living out her fantasy life, going to nightclubs and seducing eligible bachelors.

She had sold the Hermitage house to a lawyer and then inveigled a gullible divorcé into an affair. The new lover knew her only as Kasia Kane, a fellow resident of Lake Point Towers. He took her to plays and fashionable restaurants like the Pump Room, and made sure that she was always supplied with champagne. Then he hired her for his graphics design firm but soon discovered that she was not interested in sales or work of any kind. She spent her time talking to friends on the phone and taking four-hour lunches.

Throughout 1995 Suh continued to network her way to the side of well-to-do men. A 60ish international financier met her and took her to dinner at the exclusive Ambria club but grew nervous when he saw a pearl-handled revolver snuggled inside of his date's designer purse. "Why are you carrying a gun?" he asked her.

"A young woman can't be too careful in the dangerous city," she replied.

On another date with a young businessman, Suh said her father had abused her as a child, that he beat her incessantly and even sexually molested her while her mother sat by without objecting. She said she hated her parents. To another young man she said her father had been killed by Chinese gangsters. As her murder trial loomed ever closer and time began to run out, Suh frantically lived the high life, selling one expensive car, buying another. When the lawyer representing her brother filed a suit against her for misappropriating Andrew's $350,000 trust fund, Suh bought herself a Jaguar and went on a spree. She then hired one of Chicago's best criminal defense attorneys, Patrick Tuite.

When consulting Tuite in preparation for her trial, she appeared nervous. She then bought a book that described how to change identities. A few days later Suh was haggling in an auto dealership, where she was attempting to sell her Jaguar. The salesman offered her $8,000. "Make it $8,500 and I'll meet you later," she said in her most seductive voice.

"I'm married," replied the salesman. "It's $8,000."

Suh took the money home with her and stuffed it into a Chanel bag along with other cash and jewels, and then fled to Hawaii. Her brother Andrew was then convicted of murdering O'Durbaine and given a 100-year prison sentence. His Dragonlady sister was convicted in absentia and sentenced to prison for life. While her brother went behind bars, Suh surfaced in Kailua Kona, where she rented a comfortable condominium under the name of Tiffini Escada, an alias she created from the names of her two favorite stores. She quickly picked up a muscular, blond trainer named Kelmer Beck and the two began an affair. Suh then convinced Beck to move with her to Hawaii's prestigious One Waterfront Tower, which overlooked magnificent Honolulu harbor. When he objected to the expense, Suh told him that living life at the highest level would compel his income to rise to meet it.

A month later Suh took her lover to a posh restaurant and, after a few drinks, proposed that they marry. Beck was stunned but impressed. "She was a millionairess with the class of a billionairess," he told one reporter. Suh's season in the sun came to an abrupt end when, on the night of January 27, 1996, while watching television, she saw herself profiled on the program "America's Most Wanted." When Beck came home, she appeared agitated. When he went to sleep, she stole $3,000 he had hidden and, at dawn, told him that she had to leave for home to help with a family crisis.

With that Catherine Suh once again disappeared. She had not left Hawaii, however, but had merely blended into the community's poverty-level society. When her money ran out on March 8, 1996, she called Honolulu police, telling them where to pick her up. Detectives found her standing next to a phone booth at the YWCA. She was barefoot, wearing a dirty T-Shirt and cut-off jeans. Her bland pieface was absent of makeup. Her nails were clogged with dirt and the long black hair she had once had so expensively coiffed was a rat's nest of straggly, greasy strands.

Detectives noticed a recent, livid scar over one eye. Suh explained that she had sliced away a telltale mole to further disguise herself. As she was led away, police realized that she was bleeding from a thigh injury where she had inflicted a knife wound. She was nevertheless as arrogant as ever. When a female detective attempted to handcuff her, Suh slapped her hand away. At the station, one detective asked where she had been hiding. "Don't insult me with questions like that!" Suh snapped back.

Obviously attempting to create an image of insanity, Suh began stabbing herself in the buttocks while in a holding cell. She next tried to attack a police psychiatrist during an examination. When she was being extradited back to Chicago, Suh smeared herself with suntan oil, believing that she would be able to slip from the grasp of escorting detectives. All her ploys failed.

She was brought into court on June 26, 1996. Judge John Morrissey reaffirmed her life sentence for murder, then asked if she had any remarks to make to the family members of her victim. With that the brothers and sisters of Robert O'Durbaine, nee Koron, stood up in court. The once glamorous Catherine Suh, looking diminutive in her prison blues, never gave them a glance as she was led from the court to begin serving out her life in prison.

---

**Sullivan, Eugene R.,** See: **Kaub, George H.**

---

**Sullivan, Joe Harris,** 1975- , U.S., burg.-asslt.-rape. Judge Nicholas Geeker of the Pensacola Circuit Court pronounced 14-year-old Joe Harris Sullivan hopelessly incorrigible and then sentenced the youngster to a life term without parole for twice raping an elderly woman at knifepoint on May 4, 1989. Sullivan, a habitual criminal, had a police record that included convictions for burglary and assault. "He is beyond help," Judge Geeker told the court. "The juvenile system has been utterly incapable of doing anything with Mr. Sullivan." Florida state law does not allow for a prisoner to receive parole if he or she received a life term under the guidelines applying to capital cases. If he had actually killed the 74-year-old Pensacola woman, he would have been eligible for parole in twenty-five years. After hearing the verdict of the court, Sullivan showed absolutely no remorse. "He didn't have any reaction at all," said defense attorney Mack Plant. "He was just kind of emotionless."

---

**Sun, Michael,** See: **Chia, Michael Su.**

---

**Sunder, Mangit,** See: **Batth, Rajinder Singh.**

---

**Suszkin, Tatiana,** 1971- , Jerusalem, commit. racist acts. Tatiana Suszkin, a 26-year-old extremist Jewish woman, plastered walls with posters showing the prophet Mohammed as a pig in the Palestinian town of Hebron in December 1997. Her actions prompted bloody clashes between Israelis and Palestinians. The outrage also caused widespread protests by Muslims in Iran and Bangladesh. Suszkin was arrested and charged with committing racist acts, as well as supporting a terrorist organization, attempted vandalism, and endangering life by throwing rocks at Arab motorists. Suszkin was convicted on December 30, 1997, and was sent to prison. She had defiantly stated, "I have no regrets for what I have done."

---

**Sutherland, Cecil S.,** 1954- , U.S., rape.-mur. In hearing the death sentence handed down in the case of his 10-year-old daughter, a murder victim, Dennis Schulz stated, "I hope this sends a message to those who perpetrate crimes against children. I hope they find out this is what will happen to them." On June 13, 1989, Cecil Sutherland, a career criminal, was sentenced to death in Richland County, Illinois, for the rape-murder of Amy Rachelle Schulz. "Her death was brutal, violent, and terrible," said Kathleen Alling, the state's attorney who prosecuted the case. "The final hour of her life with this vile killer is too terrible to imagine. The defendant can be accurately described as a sexually perverted sadist. He has no compassion for human beings."

Sutherland abducted Schultz on July 1, 1987, while she was looking for her dog. Her body was found the next day in an oil field not far from the family home in Dix, Illinois. Amy's throat had been slashed and there was evidence of sexual assault. At the time, Sutherland was living in an area only a few hundred feet away from the Schulz family.

Police investigators uncovered a spate of forensic evidence, including dog hair, pubic hair, and fibers from an automobile tire. Sutherland first emerged as a suspect when Montana officials contacted the Jefferson County authorities during an identification check. The suspect was well known in Montana, where he was arrested in the fall of 1987 for sniping at passing vehicles in the Glacier National Park with a .22-caliber rifle. For shooting at a federal worker and endangering the lives of motorists, Sutherland was sentenced to serve fifteen years in Leavenworth Penitentiary. The accused was brought back to Olney, Illinois, in rural Marion County, where he went on trial for first-degree murder, aggravated kidnapping, and sexual assault on May 11, 1989. Following a twelve-day trial, the jury voted to convict Sutherland on May 23. The defendant showed no remorse when Judge Lehman D. Krause read the verdict aloud.

**Cecil S. Sutherland, sentenced to death for rape and murder.**

---

**Sutherland, William**, 1970- , U.S., home invas.-attemp. mur. A 28-year-old guard at the Pontiac (Illinois) Correctional facility, William Sutherland became enraged when his wife, Elaine, separated from him, taking their 5-year-old daughter with her. In April 1997, Sutherland invaded the home in which his estranged wife and daughter were living, shooting his wife eight times while she slept, and then shooting his daughter, who was being cradled in her mother's arms. Both victims survived. Sutherland was convicted of home invasion and attempted murder in August 1998. On September 28, 1998, Judge Colleen McSweeney Moore sentenced Sutherland to ninety years in prison, saying, "It's my intent and hope that you never ever leave the penitentiary except in a wooden box."

---

**Swann, James E., Jr.**, 1964- , U.S., Case of mur. Between February 23 and April 19, 1993, James E. Swann, Jr., using a shotgun, murdered four persons and wounded another five people in random attacks—his victims were both black and white—in northwest Washington, D.C. A tall, lean black man, Swann had long earlier manifested mental problems. His neighbors at Oxon Hill, Maryland, called him "crazy," since he was forever shouting at squirrels. He held jobs occasionally but was quickly released after exhibiting strange behavior. At one point he was a security guard in a large drugstore, where he walked down aisles backward because he feared being "ambushed."

On March 23, 1992, Swann purchased a Mossburg 500 C 20-gauge pump action shotgun at a K-Mart in Oxon Hill. His purchase was approved because he had no criminal record or criminal convictions and had never been committed to a mental institution. Maryland law also demanded that the purchaser of any weapon also have a valid state driver's license. Swann did not; his driver's license had been issued in New Jersey. The shotgun was nevertheless sold to him.

In February 1993, Swann took his shotgun into some woods near the home of his sister where he was living and began target practicing. Someone hearing the racket called the Prince George's County Police. Officers arrived to take the gun away from Swann, who promptly bought another shotgun. Five days later, the police returned the shotgun to Swann, who then returned the second shotgun he had purchased and got his money back.

At about this time, Swann went to New York, where, according to psychiatrists later examining him, he said he got in touch with "spirits," "witches" and "the forces of creation." He said he then talked with long-dead African kings and queens, as well as Martians, and, in particular, the ghost of Malcolm X. It was Malcolm X, said Swann after his arrest and confinement in a mental institution, who ordered him to go to Washington, D.C. "on the civil rights side of town"—the northwest side—and "blow their heads off."

Swann somehow purchased a new Tercel and cruised about Washington, D.C.'s northwest side. He parked his car and walked into a barbershop, blasting a patron to death. He fired randomly at men and women, wounding five of them. Two of these victims lost eyes. On March 23, 1993, Swann drove down an alley in Mount Pleasant and spotted a young woman walking her dogs. He shot and killed her, then drove off. He had murdered 28-year-old Bessie Hutson, the daughter of career diplomat Thomas Hutson. In all, Swann murdered four persons and seriously wounded another five.

Shortly after Swann's arrest, officials realized that they had a lunatic on their hands. He was officially diagnosed as a paranoid schizophrenic and was judged not guilty by reason of insanity. (In England such judgments are more correctly termed "guilty, but insane." The U.S. terminology in such cases is misleading, "not guilty" meaning innocent, that the person did not commit the crime, when in fact Swann was guilty of committing his shootings.) Swann was committed to St. Elizabeth's Hospital in New Jersey, where many criminally insane killers reside, including Howard Unruh, who shot and killed thirteen persons within twelve minutes on the streets of Camden, New Jersey, on September 9, 1949. Taxpayers continue to pay $450 a day to maintain the existence of serial killer James E. Swann, Jr. Also See: **Unruh, Howard**, Vol. IV.

---

**Swanson, Carl**, 1964-1993, U.S., mur. A little after 9 a.m., on May 21, 1993, Carl Swanson, a 29-year-old resident of Sturgis, South Dakota, arrived in the small town of Hosmer, just as his 25-year-old wife, Donna, was leaving her home with their three children. Swanson shot and killed Donna Swanson, their 6-year-old daughter Tabatha, and their 3-year-old son James. He then fled with his 17-month-old son Joel. Police arrived at the site of the shooting to find Donna and Tabatha Swanson dead. James was alive and was rushed to a hospital, where he later died. By that time, his father and younger brother Joel were also dead. An hour after the inexplicable shooting, deputies found Carl Swanson's car stopped on county road 253. He had shot and killed his infant son and himself.

---

**Swindall, Patrick L.** 1981- , U.S., perj. In 1987, U.S. Representative Patrick L. Swindall negotiated with an undercover Internal Revenue Service (IRS) official to secure an $850,000 loan to finance a home he was building. The IRS agent told Swindall that drug money would likely be used for the loan. The congressman accepted a check for $150,000 from Herriberto Figueroa, alias Charles LeChasney, but then returned it. On February 2, 1988, Swindall testified before a grand jury that he did not know the loan involved drug money. However, trial evidence included a taped discussion between Swindall, the IRS agent, and LeChasney, who was later convicted for conspiracy to launder money.

Swindall, a representative from suburban Atlanta, Georgia, was indicted for perjury on October 17, shortly before the November 8 election. He asked for, and received, a quick trial before District Court Judge Robert L. Vining, Jr. But after Swindall sent a campaign newsletter that discussed the case to voters, including some jurors, Judge Vining declared a mistrial. Swindall, elected to two-year terms in 1984 and 1986, lost the 1988 election.

On June 20, 1989, before Federal District Judge Richard C. Freeman, Swindall was convicted of nine counts of perjury. He was defended by Richard Hendrix and prosecuted by U.S. Attorney Robert Barr. Swindall was found guilty of telling eighteen deliberate, willful lies to the grand jury, including saying that he did not consent to take the money and that he did not know the loan involved money laundering for drug operations. On August 28, 1989, Swindall was sentenced to one year in prison and fined $30,450.

# T

**Taborsky, Petr**, 1963- , U.S., theft. The strange case of Petr Taborsky, who was convicted of theft and sent to a Florida prison, began in 1987 when he was a student at the University of South Florida. To help pay for his tuition, Taborsky took a job in the university lab that paid $8.50 an hour. Taborsky and others were being paid at the time from a $20,000 grant from a subsidiary of Florida Progress, the local power company. The research conducted by Taborsky and others was to determine if bacteria could be employed to extract ammonia from clinoptilolite, a clay used to filter water.

When it appeared that the experiment was not working, the project was cancelled and Professor Robert Carnahan reassigned Taborsky to other chores. Taborsky, however, continued his experiments on clay after hours and eventually discovered what he thought was the solution by heating clay to high temperatures. Taborsky went to Professor Carnahan and a representative of Florida Progress, explaining his discovery without specifying too many details.

The Florida Progress representative told him that his idea could be "worth millions." Taborsky asked what his share would be. Carnahan told him, "Nothing." His superior explained that since he had been initially paid to work on the project, he was a salaried employee and his discovery belonged to the university. He then told Taborsky, according to one report, that if he turned over his notes regarding his discovery, he would be rewarded with a staff job at Florida Progress.

Taborsky balked, refusing to turn over notes dealing with his research. University police were then ordered to seize the notes, but Taborsky had hidden them. He was charged with grand theft of trade secrets and arrested. Noreen Segrest, attorney for the university stated, "It is irrelevant to us who invented [the process]. We own it."

Brought to trial in 1990, Taborsky was found guilty of grand theft, even though the notes and ideas had been his. He was given a year's suspended sentence, a year of house arrest, and fifteen years' probation. Taborsky was also forbidden by the trial judge to profit from his notes or use his invention in any way.

Taborsky defiantly filed for a patent on his invention and this was granted in 1992 by the U.S. Patent Office. By that time, Carnahan had obtained and studied Taborsky's notes and filed for a joint patent for the university and Florida Progress. When told that its patent application had been rejected because two patents had been awarded to Taborsky, university officials appealed to the courts. Taborsky was ordered to assign his patents to the university or be sent to prison.

Stubbornly, Taborsky refused and was sentenced to three-and-a-half years in a Florida state prison. He was put to work with road crews, wearing shackles as he cleared brush. In 1996, Taborsky filed an appeal that was turned down. Governor Lawton Chiles offered Taborsky a pardon, which the researcher turned down, vowing to complete his sentence, which he did, being released in 1997.

**Tadesse, Sinedu**, 1977-1997, U.S., mur. An Ethiopian immigrant whose family had struggled against oppression in their native country—her father, a teacher, spent two years in prison—Sinedu Tadesse worked hard to earn a high school scholarship and admission to Harvard University. She worked hard, but found it difficult to deal with what she termed "social problems," because of her race and background.

These emotional problems apparently increased during Tadesse's junior year at Harvard and she reportedly sought help from the school's counseling center. Her emotional condition, however, continued to deteriorate. Tadesse, according to one account, then desperately turned to her dormitory roommate, Trang Ho, a brilliant Vietnamese immigrant who had graduated at the top of her class at a Boston high school and had entered Harvard with a full scholarship.

When Trang Ho informed Tadesse that she had decided to room with someone else the next year, the Ethiopian girl went berserk. On May 28, 1995, Tadesse killed Ho in their room, stabbing her forty-five times. She then committed suicide by hanging herself in the bathroom.

---

**Tadic, Dusan**, 1956- , U.S., Bosnia, war crimes. After he had been identified as a war criminal for acts committed during Bosnia's 1992-1995 war, Dusan Tadic was tracked down and arrested in Germany in 1996. The former cafe owner, karate expert and concentration camp guard was brought before a United Nations tribunal at The Hague in 1997. Tadic was charged with eleven counts of crimes against humanity and war crimes, including beatings, torture and murder. He was specifically accused of killing two Bosnian Muslims. Found guilty, Tadic, a Bosnian Serb, was sentenced to ninety-seven years in prison on July 14, 1997.

---

**Taggart, Arthur**, 1930- , U.S., sex. abuse. In 1956, Arthur Taggart opened Camp Running Deer, a Kentucky summer camp for boys. At the camp, Taggart insisted on nudity, explaining that campers should experience the heritage of Indian lore and wilderness. In 1968, he was convicted of having sexual contact with two pre-adolescent boys. In 1987, Taggart was arrested in Addison, Illinois, after two young boys claimed he molested them in his van. Camp Running Deer closed after Taggart was charged with sexual abuse, and an investigation into his activities at the camp turned up further improprieties.

On April 14, 1989, with thirty-five sexual molestation charges pending against him in Kentucky, Taggart appeared in a Wheaton, Illinois, courtroom before Du Page County Circuit Court Judge John J. Bowman. Taggart claimed that he was on a camping trip in Indiana at the time the Illinois boys said they were molested and said prosecutors were trying to frame him to cover up an unlawful search of his van. Judge Bowman rejected Taggart's claims and sentenced him to forty-five years in prison. "Why don't you just change it to a death sentence, with immediate execution?" Taggart asked Bowman after sentencing. Taggart will be eligible for parole in 2010.

**Taggert, David,** See: **Bakker, Jim.**

---

**Taggert, James,** See: **Bakker, Jim.**

---

**Takaishi Kunio,** See: **Japan Stock Scandal.**

---

**Tallios, Joseph**, 1966- , U.S., arson. In June 1997, Joseph Tallios, in a scheme to burn down a home he owned on Chicago's Southwest Side to collect insurance money, set fire to a house on Komensky Avenue. Aiding him in the arson plot was Tallios' brother-in-law, 33-year-old Pat Wiest. Both men ransacked the house to make it appear that a burglary had taken place. They then soaked the place with gasoline, but an explosion prematurely ignited the blaze, which entrapped and killed Wiest.

Tallios was charged with arson and posted a $30,000 bond. He then disappeared. Tried in absentia, Tallios was convicted of arson in November 1998. He was sentenced, also in absentia, on December 9, 1998, to forty-five years in prison. The fugitive, however, had not been apprehended at the time this writing.

---

**Tamashiro, Lee,** 1968-1989, U.S., suic-mur. After his love affair broke up, Lee Tamashiro of Rolling Hills, California, went to the home of his former girlfriend, Stephanie Collins, 20, and shot her, along with her mother, Karen Collins, 46. In the attack on March 28, 1989, Karen Collins was wounded but managed to stagger to a next-door neighbor, where she called police. When officers arrived, they found Stephanie Collins shot dead and Tamashiro also dead, shot through the head, an apparent suicide. Tamashiro left two notes with undisclosed text, one for his family and one for his victim's family.

---

**Tamez, Amado,** See: **Corthron, Casey Dean.**

---

**Tamiami Trail Strangler,** See: **Conde, Rory Enrique.**

---

**Tan, Tak Sun**, 1977- , **Chan, Jason**, 1978- , and **Lim, Indra**, 1978- , U.S., rob.-mur. Three members of the Lazyboys (or Lazyboyz), a Los Angeles street gang specializing in home invasions and carjackings, spotted a man in his carport behind his Chinatown apartment on the night of February 25, 1996. Tak Sun Tan, Jason Chan and Indra Lim approached the man and, during the course of a botched robbery, shot and killed him. Their victim, it turned out, was none other than 55-year-old Haing S. Ngor, a physician and Cambodian actor who had won an Oscar for his role in the 1984 film *The Killing Fields.*

Ngor was a gynecologist and obstetrician who escaped Cambodia in 1980, five years after he had been trapped by the Khmer-Rouge, who had seized power in 1975. He had witnessed the wholesale slaughter of his countrymen by Commu-

nist dictator Pol Pot. Early reports of Ngor's murder speculated that he had been the victim of a political assassination. This was soon dispelled by investigators, who quickly determined that he was, sadly, just another victim of street gang violence.

Tan, Chan and Lim were placed on trial and convicted of first-degree murder and robbery on April 16, 1998. All were given long prison terms. The trial of these three gang members was unusual in that three juries deliberated the three separate trials at the same time and in the same room.

---

**Tang Mihong**, ? -1998, and **Zhao Jian**, ? -1998, China, smug. While the economies of many Far East countries plunged during the 1990s, mostly brought on by Japan's financial collapse due to its estimated $500 billion in bad loans (made to many Yakuza members), China, on the other hand, maintained the value of its currency. This, in turn, created the potential for huge profits for smugglers bringing cheaply bought goods from foreign markets into China. By 1998, 15 percent of China's imports were smuggled goods, amounting to an estimated $30 billion each year.

Two of China's most brazen smugglers were Tang Mihong and Zhao Jian, who ran a vast computer smuggling ring the length of China from 1992 to 1995. Tang, the general manager of the Beijing Huilu Computer Development Co., and his assistant, Zhao Jian, along with many accomplices at research institutes and trading firms, imported foreign electronic goods worth $6.8 billion, and of these shipments, at least ten huge loads were smuggled past customs offices throughout China.

In July 1998, Chinese state police and customs agents launched a widespread crackdown, imprisoning thousands of smugglers and arresting hundreds of customs agents for taking bribes. Tang Mihong and Zhao Jian, considered to be the country's foremost smuggling offenders, were ensnared in the crackdown. Both were convicted of smuggling and, on December 6, 1998, Chinese officials announced that Tang Mihong and Zhao Jian had been executed.

---

**Tashjian, Ralph**, 1948- , U.S., fraud. Record industry executive Ralph Tashjian pleaded guilty in May 1989 to charges of tax fraud, obstruction of justice, and violating federal regulations while bribing radio station employees to play records in an effort to make them hit singles. Tashjian admitted providing both money and cocaine to California radio station personnel in exchange for the air time. On December 11, 1989, U.S. District Court Judge Pamela Ann Rymer sentenced Tashjian to sixty days in a halfway house, 500 hours of community service and three years of probation, and fined him $100,000. Tashjian was employed by record promoter Joseph Isgro, who was indicted for fraud December 1 for redirecting record company funds allocated for legitimate promotional purposes to pay off station personnel.

---

**Tateoka Sejichi,** See: **Japan Stock Scandal.**

---

**Tatum, Paul**, ? -1998, Rus., mur. Since Russia abandoned communism and turned to a free, capitalist society, its economy has been plagued by more than 8,000 gangs that have flourished in all of its major cities. By 1996, these gangs, loosely dubbed the Russian Mafia, had control of half of the country's stock exchanges and 60 percent of the nation's banks. According to Russian officials, about 80 percent of the country's businesses paid tribute to ruthless gangs. If anyone resisted the extortion, they were tortured and killed.

**American businessman Paul Tatum, who was shot to death in a Moscow subway station by members of the Russian Mafia on November 3, 1996. He is shown standing before the Radisson Hotel in Moscow, of which he owned 50 percent; he was in a hot dispute over ownership at the time of his death.**

Police in Russia were paid so miserably—about $100 a month for the average officer—that lawmen were easily bribed by members of the Russian Mafia. In 1995, an internal probe into its ranks by Moscow police revealed more than 1,500 cops as having been corrupted by gangster bribe money.

Worse, the government itself contributed to the criminal takeover of the Russian economy by wildly taxing businesses and individuals, affixing unreasonable rates that often soared beyond 100 percent of a company's profits, which invited, if not compelled, rampant tax evasion on the part of millions of Russian citizens and businessmen, as well as foreign investors. Banks controlled by the Russian Mafia then used their clients' tax evasion to leverage extortion payments. In a 1996 report to the U.S. Congress, FBI Director Louis Freeh stated that most American businesses operating in Russia were compelled to pay up to 30 percent of their profits to the Russian Mafia.

Despite this chaotic state of affairs, Paul Tatum, a middle-aged businessman and entrepreneur from Oklahoma, believed that great legitimate fortunes were to be made in the new Russian democracy. To that end, he, with Russian partners, built the Radisson Slavyanskaya Hotel in Moscow, the first truly Western hotel in Russia, one brimming with all the modern conveniences and luxuries to be found in any first-class hotel in America.

Following the opening of the Radisson-Slavyanskaya Hotel, Tatum and his Russian partners fell into a control dispute. The American businessman chose to settle the matter as he would have done in the U.S., by taking it to court, despite the fact that he had been warned not to do so.

The court battle was long and bitter, but Tatum refused to back down. He claimed 50 percent ownership of the lucrative Radisson Slavyanskaya Hotel, the other half owned by a Mos-

cow City agency. On November 3, 1996, as he descended into a Moscow subway station, Tatum was suddenly confronted by a young machine–gun wielding assassin who fired several bursts into him, killing him on the spot. The murderer fled and was not, at the time of this writing, apprehended.

Most Russian and American authorities believed that the killing had been a contract murder ordered by Tatum's foes and carried out by a Russian Mafia hit man who was paid the going murder rate of $6,000. A reporter who attempted to probe into the Tatum killing was cornered inside a room at the Radisson Slavyanskaya Hotel and beaten senseless by a gang of Russian Mafia toughs who promised to return shortly and kill him. He managed to get to the American Embassy, which aided him in fleeing the country.

---

**Taufield, Arnold**, 1935-1989, U.S., (unsolv.) mur. Arnold Taufield, a successful art dealer who ran three galleries in Manhattan, New York, was shot and killed on May 13, 1989, by a lone gunman who stopped him outside his Greenwich Village Allstate Art Gallery. The killer, a tall, thin man wearing a black jacket with a white cross on it, fired a single bullet into Taufield's head at 8:45 p.m., but did not bother to loot his victim's body. If he had, he would have found $18,000 in cash.

Taufield was en route to his three galleries to pay his twenty employees, who preferred cash payments in order to avoid check-cashing delays. Taufield never worried about carrying cash, even in this crime-ridden area, according to his partner, Irving Schneider, "... because he was macho, very macho. He wasn't fearful. You know the story. You never think it will happen to you. That's how he thought." The unknown killer's motives remain a mystery, although it has been speculated that this was either a killing for hire or a murder committed by someone who certainly knew the victim and bore him a deep-seated grudge.

---

**Taylor, John Merlin**, 1937-1989, U.S., suic.-mur. Early on the morning of August 11, 1989, postal worker John Merlin Taylor of Escondido, California, shot his wife, Elizabeth, to death with a handgun before he went to work. He entered the Orange Glen postal substation at 7:30 a.m. and, armed with enough ammunition for an extended siege, he murdered two co-workers—38-year-old Richard Berni and 56-year-old Ron Williams—and wounded a third before shooting himself in the head.

Taylor, 52, was a veteran letter carrier who had won numerous awards for his work and was described as well-liked by his colleagues. Speculation on the cause of his sudden outburst of violence focused on the increasing level of job-related stress, a previous divorce in which he was characterized as drunk and abusive, and an incident during his youth when his sister shot their drunken father to death to protect their mother. A friend said that Taylor had discussed a similar shooting spree just two days earlier.

---

**Taylor, Kenneth**, 1959- , U.S., Case of armed rob.-armed sex. rob.-rape. From January to July 1998, ten vicious rapes were committed by a lone intruder in hotels and motels throughout the Orlando-Kissimmee, Florida, area. The last attack occurred in a Kissimmee hotel where a British couple were staying. They had called the lobby for an iron and had left their room door ajar. The rapist entered and forced the man and woman at gunpoint to perform sexual acts. He then raped the woman and stole their cash and valuables before leaving.

The rapist in the attack on the British tourists was identified as Kenneth Taylor, a 39-year-old Orlando resident. Arrested at his home on July 16, 1998, Taylor denied the robbery-rape, stating that he was in Georgia laboring as a construction worker at the time of the attack. Taylor awaits trial at this writing.

---

**Taylor, Lonnie**, 1952- , U.S., sex. asslt.-attempt. mur. A 37-year-old suburban Chicago, Illinois, man who received government disability compensation was convicted of slashing and sexually assaulting a prostitute. In his statement to police, Lonnie Taylor stated that he picked up the 31-year-old woman on February 6, 1989, on Chicago's West Side. After binding her hands and feet, Taylor raped the woman and mutilated her with a pocketknife before dumping her out of his truck naked and still bound in below-freezing temperatures. The woman required over 200 stitches to close wounds on her abdomen, breasts, buttocks, and right calf. In Cook County Criminal Court, Judge Michael Bolan, calling the crime "heinous," ordered Taylor held on $1 million bond. Taylor who had a criminal record that dated back twenty years, was convicted of one count of attempted murder, three counts of aggravated sexual assault, and one count of armed robbery. He was sentenced on January 23, 1990, to forty years in prison.

---

**Taylor, Michael Douglas**, 1954- , U.S., pris. esc.-rob. Chicago native Michael Taylor escaped with four other prisoners from the Orange County, California, jail on November 20, 1988, by using a rope made of tied-together sheets to climb down from the roof of the four-story building. A fifth escapee was captured after breaking his leg in a fall when the sheets ripped. Accused murderer Eleazar Gonzales turned himself in Thanksgiving Day, and the two other fugitives, Steven Wilson and Richard Fluharty, were arrested in Denver, Colorado, in early December. Only Taylor remained at large, with police theorizing that he was the mastermind behind the breakout.

Michael Taylor was known for his methodical, well-planned jewelry store robberies in which he controlled his accomplices' moves and timed their actions. Since 1987, he was believed to have robbed more than twenty Southern California jewelry stores of approximately $2 million in merchandise. In February 1989, Taylor and another man were believed to have abducted Elsa Pacini from her Chicago home and driven her to her brother's jewelry store in suburban River Grove, where they forced her to turn over diamonds and gold. Police found Pacini blindfolded, gagged, and tied to a chair in a nearby motel

On May 20, 1989, Taylor was arrested in Rapid City, South Dakota, trying to sell jewelry from the River Grove robbery. An FBI agent involved in tracking Taylor acknowledged help from tips that came in after Taylor was featured on the television show "America's Most Wanted" on May 7. A viewer called to say that Taylor was living in Portland, Oregon, under the name of Michael Prescott. The alias, added to his profile in the National Criminal Information Center network, led to his identification in Rapid City.

---

**Taylor, Renee,** 1969- , U.S., mur. Renee Taylor, 20, of Chicago, Illinois, smothered her 5-month-old daughter in June 1988, because the child would not stop crying. After pleading guilty to the murder, Taylor was sentenced to fifty years in prison by Cook County Criminal Court Judge Michael Toomin. Judge Toomin stated that he imposed the fifty-year prison term on Taylor to make sure that upon her release she would no longer be of childbearing age and could therefore not repeat her brutal act.

---

**Tenney, Edward L.,** 1959- , U.S., burg.-mur. On September 22, 1998, a jury in Kane County, Illinois, recommended the death sentence for 39-year-old Edward L. Tenney, who was convicted the previous month for the murders of Virginia Johannessen, 76, and Jill Oberweis, 56, of Aurora Township, Illinois. In January 1993, Tenney burglarized the home of Johannessen and Oberweis, shooting both of them to death.

---

**Terrorism**, 1990s. Terrorism in the 1990s increased across broad fronts and in isolated areas throughout the world. By the mid-1990s, several countries had been pinpointed as state sponsors of terrorism, including Cuba, Libya, Sudan, Syria, Iraq, Iran and North Korea. The U.S. and the United Nations applied sanctions against these rogue nations, blocking billions in assets.

The U.S. spent $5.7 billion in combating terrorism in 1996 and $6.7 billion in 1997, increased to $9.4 billion in 1998. In the U.S., the two chief agencies fighting terrorism, cooperating with more than forty other federal agencies, were the CIA, which was responsible for gathering and disseminating information on terrorism in foreign countries, and the FBI, responsible for gathering data on domestic terrorism.

The most devastating acts of terrorism in the U.S. in the 1990s included the truck bomb explosion in the garage of New York's World Trade Center on February 26, 1993, which took the lives of six persons and injured more than 1,000 others, and the blowing up of the Alfred P. Murrah Federal Building in Oklahoma City, Oklahoma, on April 19, 1995, resulting in the deaths of 168 persons and the wounding of hundreds of others. Two U.S. embassies were also ruthlessly bombed in Kenya and Tanzania in August 1998, with hundreds killed and wounded, an attack by Arab extremists led by Osama bin Laden.

Abroad, one of the worst terrorist acts of the 1990s occurred in 1995 when nerve gas was released into the subway system of Tokyo, Japan, which took a half dozen lives and injured thousands more. These acts were attributed to fanatical cult members belonging to Aum Shinri Kyo. Thousands of cult members, along with their sinister leader, were tracked down and imprisoned.

**Two police photos of Ramzi Ahmed Yousef, the mastermind behind the World Trade Center bombing in New York in 1993.**

The most infamous of international terrorists during the 1990s included Illich Ramirez Sanchez, better known as Carlos, or the Jackal, who, after a worldwide manhunt, was finally tracked down in Sudan in 1994 by French agents and returned to Paris, France, where he was convicted of murder and many terrorist acts and sent to prison for life. Also apprehended was Ramzi Yousef, an Iraqi national who was the mastermind behind the World Trade Center bombing and who was sent to prison for life.

Also in custody by 1999 were two Libyan terrorists, Abdel Baseet ali al-Megrahi and Lamen Khalifa Fimah, who were held responsible for the 1988 bombing of Pan Am Flight 103 over Lockerbie, Scotland, although the real organization behind this worst of plane bombings was the Popular Front for the Liberation of Palestine (PFLP), the same organization that supervised Osama bin Laden's 1998 bombings of the U.S. embassies in Kenya and Tanzania.

The leading Palestinian terrorist, Abu Nidal (Sabri al-Banna), was also pinpointed as hiding in Libya in 1998, reportedly stricken by a fatal illness. He, however, was not captured. Also remaining at large was the Palestinian terrorist and close friend of Yasir Arafat, Mohammad Abbas, who masterminded the 1985 hijacking of the cruise ship *Achile Lauro* and numerous other terrorist acts.

**Timothy McVeigh, shown in V-neck prison uniform, who bombed the federal building in Oklahoma City, Oklahoma, in 1995 and was sentenced to death for his horrendous terrorist act.**

In the U.S., individual terrorist bombers plagued the public and law enforcement agencies, the worst of these being the Unabomber, who had mailed dozens of lethal bombs across the country and was responsible for several deaths and many injuries. He was finally identified as Theodore Kaczynski, a Montana hermit, who went to prison for life in 1998. The bombing of the Centennial Park in Atlanta and the many bombings of abortion clinics, for which the much-hunted Eric Rudolph has been blamed, further evidenced widespread domestic terrorism in the U.S., as well as the hundreds of church burnings in the Middle West and South during the 1990s.

**The Unabomber, Theodore Kaczynski, one of the worst lone terrorists in American history, who was sent to prison for life in 1998.**

In late 1998, the threat of spreading lethal biological agents such as anthrax came to reality. Dozens of letters threatening anthrax—the present-day equivalent of a bomb scare—were sent to government offices, courthouses, schools, and places of business. On Christmas Eve 1998, employees of a department store in Palm Desert, California, herded about 200 customers into a parking lot, ordered them to remove all their clothes, and then rinsed them down with a bleach solution because someone had called the store with an anthrax threat. The call turned out to be a hoax, as have been dozens of others. Still, authorities properly insist, each threat must be taken seriously.

In January 1998, President Clinton asked that $2.8 billion more be added to the U.S. anti-terrorism budget, warning that "we must be ready" for terrorist attacks against computer systems and chemical and germ warfare employed by terrorists. As the century closed, it was evident to global leaders that the most dangerous threat to the world community was terrorist nations and the terrorists they spawned, who would stop at nothing to achieve their fanatical political or religious ends.

New laws with strict punishments for terrorist acts were passed, such as the Anti-Terrorism and Effective Death Penalty Act of 1996 in the U.S. Moreover, billions were put aside in all leading countries to combat terrorists, with government agencies and special anti-terrorist military groups dedicated to the suppression of still flourishing terrorists and terrorist groups. It is a nightmare war still being waged.

Also See: **Abu Nidal**; **Aum Shinri Kyo**; **Church burnings**; **Cuba**; **Iran**; **Iraq**; **Libya**; **Lockerbie, Scotland**; **Kaczynski, Theodore**; **McVeigh, Timothy** (Oklahoma City bombing); **Ramirez Sanchez, Illich**; **Rudolph, Eric Robert**; **U.S. Embassy bombings**; **World Trade Center bombing**.

---

**Terry, Narkey Keval**, 1970- , U.S., invol. manslt. Narkey Terry, who worked at the CIA in Langley, Virginia, as a computer operator for a private contractor, was driving to work on April 17, 1996, along the George Washington Memorial Parkway when he became involved with another motorist in a duel that led to the deaths of three persons. At 6 a.m., Terry was seen on the parkway near National Airport, driving a red 1994 Jeep Cherokee only a foot behind a 1988 Chevrolet Beretta sedan driven by Billy M. Canipe, Jr.

For seven miles, Terry drove at an estimated 80 m.p.h., jockeying for position with Canipe. At 6:15 a.m., Canipe, who was driving in the right lane, reportedly cut in front of Terry, who was in the left lane. Canipe lost control of his car and shot across a four-foot grass median into a Ford Taurus driven by 49-year-old George A. Smyth, Jr. The Beretta was driven backward into the path of Terry's Cherokee, which slammed into it at high speed, ripping away the Beretta's midsection, which became an airborne missile that crushed a Dodge Caravan driven by 41-year-old Nancy O'Brien.

Canipe, Smyth, and O'Brien were all killed upon impact. Terry survived to be charged with reckless driving and two counts of involuntary manslaughter. He was convicted and sentenced to thirteen years in prison, a conviction that sent a message to the hundreds of thousands of aggressive drivers across the U.S. who risk their lives and those of countless others in reckless driving along the nation's highways.

---

**Texas Tub Murders**, See: **Prescott, Wendie Rochelle**.

---

**Thipyaso, Chamoy**, prom. 1989, Thai., fraud. Known as the "queen of underground investments," Chamoy Thipyaso and seven associates ran private, or "underground," banks, taking deposits from 16,231 residents of Bangkok, Thailand, and accumulating millions of dollars. Thipyaso was arrested on charges of defrauding her customers and was convicted of failing to pay the 6.5 percent monthly interest she promised clients. For this mammoth swindle, Thipyaso and her seven aides were each given 141,078 years in prison by the Bangkok Criminal Court.

---

**Thomas, Dennis** (AKA: Heat Wave Rapist), 1955- , U.S., rape. On the night of August 19, 1988, 33-year-old Dennis Thomas crawled through the open window of a Chicago, Illinois, home, put a knife against the neck of a sleeping 24-year-old woman, and raped her in her bed. After he fled, family members flagged down a police car and described the assailant. Police arrested Thomas three blocks away, hiding under shrubbery and ditching a towel he had stolen from the home. Near him lay the knife he used in the attack.

Thomas's arrest ended a series of break-ins, rapes, and attempted rapes that had plagued the Chicago neighborhood. Thomas was charged with two other rapes and two attempted rapes during that summer of record-breaking heat, leading police to dub him the "Heat Wave Rapist." In 1976, he had been convicted of robbery, burglary, and drug offenses, and was on parole from a 1984 rape conviction at the time of his arrest. Thomas was convicted on June 12, 1989, and was sentenced to life in prison.

---

**Thomas, Robert**, See: **Jordan, Yolanda**.

---

**Thomas, Ruth,** 1952- , **Wrighton, Sara**, prom. 1989, and **Burns, Robert,** 1970- , Brit., rob.-attempt. mur. Ruth Thomas, an assistant matron in a Southport, England, nursing home, devised a scheme to take over several nursing homes, as well as rob some of its occupants. In one scheme, Thomas and her companion, Sara Wrighton, who was also a care assistant, tried to wrest control of the Sharon Jewish Rest Home in Southport by lacing the tea of matrons with strong sedatives and then attempting to have the matrons sign over control of the homes to them. This failed, as well as another bizarre plan in which Thomas enlisted the aid of a youthful thug, Robert Burns.

Burns was sent to the flat of elderly Abraham Rosenfield, who had newly arrived at the Sharon home. His personal effects and cash, Thomas learned, were still in his apartment in Manchester. Thomas sent Burns to the flat, where the young thief stole more than £19,000 of the old man's savings. When Rosenfield got suspicious, Thomas tried to kill him with Wrighton's help. First, the pair mixed a lethal cocktail for the old man, one made up of dangerous drugs, and then tried to force Rosenfield to drink it. When he resisted, Thomas lost all patience and smashed a whiskey bottle over the retired tailor's head.

Rosenfield survived and managed to summon help. Thomas, Wrighton, and Burns were arrested. After standing trial in Liverpool, Thomas was convicted of robbery and attempted murder and sent to prison for ten years. Wrighton received a four-and-a-half-year term and Burns was placed on probation for two years.

---

**Thomas, Walic Christopher**, 1965- , U.S., rob.-mur. Kenneth Dale Tuttle, a 27-year-old college student living in Greensboro, North Carolina, was found murdered September 11, 1995, in a home he shared with a roommate. A burly man, Tuttle stood almost six feet and weighed more than 220 pounds. Yet he had apparently been overpowered by an even stronger man, who tied Tuttle's hands behind his back with a phone cord and then stabbed him to death. There were multiple wounds in Tuttle's neck and chest.

Greensboro police were informed of the murder by the roommate when he returned home late to find Tuttle's body. Detectives learned that a color TV, some of Tuttle's clothes, and the victim's bank card and 1990 Nissan Sentra were missing. It was a only a short time later when the Nissan was found parked on Pearson Street and a woman getting into the car was detained. She stated that the car belonged to her boyfriend, 30-year-old Walic Christopher Thomas.

Thomas had a long criminal background that trailed back to the 1980s. In 1989, he was convicted of stabbing the mother of one of his friends in a botched robbery of her house. He was sent to prison for fourteen years, but was released in September 1994, after serving only five years because of overcrowding in the prisons. Within five months, Thomas entered a convenience store and held up the clerk at gunpoint, taking $108. He was arrested but then released on his written promise to the judge that he would appear for trial.

Thomas robbed a woman of her purse at gunpoint in April 1995 and was jailed under a $25,000 bond. A judge, however, reduced the bail to $500, which Thomas paid. He was again released. The following month, Thomas was arrested for rape, but was freed by a judge who accepted only his written promise to appear for trial.

Quickly tracked down and arrested for murdering Kenneth Tuttle, Thomas was brought to trial in 1996. His palm print was matched to one found in Tuttle's kitchen. Further, Thomas, who stood six-feet-one-inch and weighed 170 pounds, was proved to be powerful enough to overwhelm his victim. Prosecutors also proved that it was Thomas who had stolen Tuttle's bank card and car. A videotape recording made at a cash station clearly showed Thomas attempting to use the stolen card only hours after Tuttle's slaying. Also clearly visible in the background was Tuttle's Nissan.

Thomas' lawyers mounted a weak defense. Their client appeared surly and defiant in court, at one point snarling, "I didn't participate in a killing! I didn't kill nobody!" A jury disagreed with him, not only finding Thomas guilty of Tuttle's slaying, but recommending that he be put to death. On August 9, 1996, Judge Howard Greeson, Jr., sentenced Thomas to death. As he was being led away, the killer shouted, "I'll be back!" What probably prompted that deluded statement was Thomas' former ability to time and time again slip through the cracks of the judicial system. In his case, all the cracks were now sealed. Thomas awaits execution at this writing.

**Thompson, Daniel**, See: **Sledge, Justin**.

**Thompson, Eugene Frank, Jr.**, 1968-1989, U.S., suic.-mur. Wielding a MAC-11 machine pistol, Eugene Frank Thompson, Jr. went on a rampage on March 24, 1989, in Littleton, Colorado, a suburb south of Denver. Thompson, who was wanted for a number of burglaries committed in Jefferson County, abducted a woman, forcing her to drive to her parents' house, where he stole another vehicle, drove to a different neighborhood and held a man, woman, and child hostage before raping the woman and again escaping in a stolen car. After ramming a state patrol car, he fled on foot to an area duplex. During a door-to-door search, two sheriff's deputies were shot. A SWAT team led by Arapahoe County Sheriff Pat Sullivan then lobbed flash grenades into the duplex. Officers rushed the house and Thompson unleashed a savage fire from his submachine gun. As he retreated, Thompson shot the female hostage in the back, then ran to the second floor, where he shot himself in the head. Thompson was dragged from the building and later died in the hospital.

**Thompson, Robert**, See: **Venables, Jon**.

**Thornton, Floyd, Jr.**, ?-1997, and **Thornton, Rebecca**, ?-1997, U.S. prison esc.-mur. In a daring prison break attempt, Rebecca Thornton tried to free her husband, Floyd Thornton, Jr., from Arizona's state prison in Florence on July 9, 1997. Mrs. Thornton had apparently been planning with her husband, an inmate on Death Row, to break him out of prison for some time. Parking near the prison, Rebecca Thornton, carrying two guns, met her husband just outside the prison gate. He had managed to cut the leather shackles that bound him and somehow get beyond the gate.

Guards in the towers, however, were already shooting at the couple. Thornton, who was by then wounded, was overheard to shout to his wife, "I'm sorry things went wrong—shoot me! Shoot me!" Rebecca Thornton reportedly sprayed several bullets into her husband from an automatic weapon before she herself was killed by a fusillade of gunfire from the guard towers. Inside of Mrs. Thornton's car, guards found camping gear, two more handguns, ammunition and clothing.

**Tibetan Riots,** 1989, Tibet, mob. vio. In 1989, the worst outbreak of civil unrest in Tibet in thirty years claimed the lives of at least a dozen people, though Tibetan sources maintain that the death toll was much higher. Tibet, an autonomous region of China, enjoyed forty years of independence from 1911 to 1951 when the Communist Party took control of the government. In 1959, the Dalai Lama was ousted in the wake of the separatist uprising and driven into permanent exile in India along with 100,000 of his followers. The anti-Chinese riots began in the city of Isasa on March 5, 1989, just five days before the thirtieth anniversary of the 1959 uprising, in which 87,000 people died.

The 1989 rioting began when thousands of Tibetans began burning and looting Chinese and Muslim stores in the Old City. Barricades constructed from overturned tables served as shields for the rioters, who assaulted any Chinese citizen on the street. Incidents of gunfire between the heavily armed police and rioters were reported, although Tibetans denied the rumors. The violence continued for three days before the Chinese government declared martial law. Some 300 people were arrested during the crackdown that followed. On September 13, the Chinese courts sentenced ten Tibetans to prison for terms ranging from three years to life for instigating a riot and spying on behalf of the Dalai Lama.

**Tigner, Charles**, 1956- , U.S., rape. Charles Tigner, a Chicago resident and a three-time convicted sex offender, met an attractive 24-year-old woman from Oak Brook, Illinois, as she stepped from a Near North Side nightclub on November 8, 1986. She appeared confused and told Tigner that she could not find her car. Tigner offered to help her, and when they located her car, Tigner asked for "a lift," stating that he only lived a short distance away.

Instead of directing the woman to his residence, Tigner hoodwinked her into driving onto an expressway and eventually to a dead-end road, where Tigner seized the woman and raped her. He was convicted of another rape after this attack and sentenced to nineteen years in prison. While serving this term, Tigner was charged with the rape of the Oak Brook woman and was also convicted of this offense, despite his plea at his trial that he was "a nice guy" who was "only helping" the woman find her car. Criminal Court Judge Michael B. Getty disagreed in sentencing Tigner, calling him "a menace," and ordered that he serve another twenty-six years in prison after finishing the first term of nineteen years.

---

**Timmendequas, Jesse**, 1961- , U.S., rape-mur. Seven-year-old Megan Kanka lived in Hamilton Township, New Jersey, on a quiet, tree-lined street that was both peaceful and predictable. The heinous crimes of brutal felons were unknown to this community, and those who lived there felt safe. Yet, across the street from Megan Kanka's comfortable home lurked a predator waiting for his chance to strike, watching Megan's every move, looking for an opportunity where the child would be isolated and vulnerable. That opportunity presented itself to this beast of prey on the evening of July 29, 1994.

Megan, wearing a pink and blue shorts outfit, asked her mother if she could go down the street to play with a friend. Maureen Kanka approved, and that was the last time she saw her daughter alive. As Megan went down the street, Jesse Timmendequas, who lived diagonally across the street from the Kanka home, watched the child stroll from sight, then re-appear a short time later after she could not find her friend.

Timmendequas lived with two other child molesters in that house, all three of these convicted felons having met in a prison housing compulsive sex offenders. Timmendequas had been convicted twice and imprisoned for sexually attacking a 5-year-old girl in 1981 and for attempting to sexually molest a 7-year-old he had strangled into unconsciousness in 1982.

As Megan Kanka went past his house, Timmendequas struck up a conversation with the girl. She knew he had a puppy and asked about him, saying that she loved dogs. He told her that she could see the puppy, but would have to come inside his house and into his bedroom. Once inside the bedroom with him, Timmendequas, according to his later confession, began to fondle the girl. When she resisted, he punched her head, inflicting serious head injuries, then strangled her with a belt. He then ripped away her shorts and raped her. When he discovered that Megan was still breathing, Timmendequas wrapped two plastic bags over her head, suffocating her. He then bundled up her body and took it to Mercer County Park, dumping the half-naked girl in high grass.

When Megan did not return that night, her parents began a frantic search, which was later joined by neighbors and eventually police. Some of the neighbors knew that one of the three men living in the house diagonally across the street from the Kankas had served time for sexually molesting a child. This led police to that house, where they questioned Joseph Cifelli, who had served nine years in prison for sexually molesting a child.

Satisfied that neither Cifelli nor another man had been involved, detectives turned their attentions to Jesse Timmendequas, who promptly broke down and confessed to sexually attacking and murdering Megan Kanka. The next morning he led officers to the spot in Mercer County Park where he had hidden the body. At his May 1997 trial, prosecutors brought forth a dental expert who matched Megan's

teeth impressions to bite marks found on the palm of Timmendequas' hand. Moreover, the defendant did not dispute his detailed confession to the police; in fact, Timmendequas never took the stand.

Timmendequas' attorney, public defender Barbara R. Lependorf, did not challenge the facts. They were irrefutable. She asked the jury to "separate your emotions—your natural, your normal human emotions—and divorce those emotions from your mind." This, of course, was an impossibility. Lependorf later introduced a weary defense for her client, one used time and again by recidivist child molesters and child killers, that they themselves had been molested as children, as if this mitigated their crimes. Timmendequas had been sexually abused as child by his father, Lependorf pointed out, a brutal, sadistic father who had also molested his siblings, and a mother who beat him regularly, once breaking his arm.

The jury was unmoved. Timmendequas was convicted of rape and first-degree murder in Trenton, New Jersey, and was sentenced to death on June 20, 1997. The defendant said nothing when hearing the verdict, only rapidly blinked his eyes behind thick glasses. He was ordered by Judge Andrew J. Smithson to be held in solitary until the day of his execution. Timmendequas awaits that execution at this writing, while his attorneys file appeals.

Five months following Megan Kanka's slaying, the New Jersey legislature passed the first Megan Law, requiring all sex offenders to register with the police of their local community and that their identities and addresses be publicly posted. In May 1996, President Clinton signed a federal Megan's Law, which was passed unanimously in the House of Representatives. Most states presently have a Megan's Law, which repeatedly beat back challenges, even those stating that applying such a law retroactively before the law took effect is unfair to the sex offender.

Hamilton Township, New Jersey, vowed never to forget Megan Kanka. The house where Jesse Timmendequas and two other sex offenders lived was purchased by the local Rotary Club. It was torn down piece by piece, its foundation uprooted and buried. It was dedicated as a small park called "Megan's Place," a plot of verdant ground now, with shade trees, flowers, a fish pond and an area for little girls to play hopscotch. And there is a watch that ends the night here, a staunch vigil by neighbors and police that fiercely guards this little hallowed sanctuary against the stalking beasts of prey. Also See: **Megan's Law**.

---

**Timmons, Ronald,** 1958- , and **Bolden, Henry,** 1959- , and **Clark, Kevin,** 1961- , U.S., mur. In the late 1970s, the crimes committed against the elderly in New York City by two teenagers sparked nationwide attention, and led to the enactment of tough legal statutes designed to punish underage offenders regardless of age. Ronald Timmons, his twin brother, Raymond, and Henry Bolden repeatedly terrorized the elderly residents of a Bronx housing development. Ronald was eventually captured and sentenced to prison for ten years after being convicted of stealing $1 from an 82-year-old woman. Bolden was imprisoned after a jury found him guilty of robbing an 85-year-old man in 1976. As a result of the Timmons case, state legislators passed laws permitting minors to be prosecuted as adults for crimes deemed abhorrent by society standards.

Both Timmons and Bolden served ten years in jail before their release in 1987. On August 21, 1987, Timmons, Bolden, and Kevin Clark, killed three people during an attempted robbery. The three men were arrested and went on trial at the Bronx Supreme Court in June 1989. After three days of deliberations, they were found guilty. On August 3, Timmons and Bolden were each sentenced by Justice Fred Eggert to serve 112 and a half years in prison. (Editor's Note: Complete details of this case can be found in the *Encyclopedia of World Crime,* Vol. IV.)

**Tinning, Marybeth Roe**, 1943- , U.S. mur., Joseph and Marybeth Tinning appeared to their neighbors in Schenectady, New York to be friendly and good-hearted. They lived their entire married life in the city. The only peculiarity attached to them was that they moved about with abnormal consistency. They were forever seeking a new apartment. Another fact concerning the couple was more alarming. Marybeth Tinning had nine children, and all of them died before reaching the age of 5.

Dr. Thomas F.D. Oram, after routinely checking Mrs. Tinning, began to look into the strange deaths of her children, beginning with Joseph Tinning, Jr., who died in 1973, and ending with the couple's ninth child, Tammi Lynne, in 1985. Oram concluded that "there is only one explanation for all this, and it has to be smothering."

Mrs. Tinning was brought in for questioning, but refused to admit anything. It was proved that her first child, Jennifer, had, indeed, died of natural causes in 1972. This was not the case with the remaining eight children. Marybeth, after several confrontations with authorities, finally broke down and stated, "I smothered each of them with a pillow because I am not a good mother."

Tinning was brought to trial and was convicted of second-degree murder. The court stated that she had "a depraved indifference to human life." On October 1, 1987, she was sent to prison to serve a 25-year sentence.

**Tinsley, Darnell Lee**, 1974-1998, U.S., rape. On August 8, 1998, police in Alexandria, Virginia, fatally shot 24-year-old Darnell Lee Tinsley after chasing him from a Duke Street apartment complex. Tinsley pulled a gun, which provoked officers to fire. A woman had called police a short time earlier to report that a man matching the description of a serial rapist plaguing Montgomery County, one responsible for at least four rapes, was lurking in the building area.

Tinsley was found to be carrying a large quantity of condoms and latex surgical gloves, as did the Montgomery County serial rapist. Police believed that the rapist used these items to prevent DNA and fingerprint evidence from linking him to the crimes. Tinsley, of Burtonsville, would certainly have known about such criminal identification procedures in that he was married to a female police officer.

**Tinsley, Steven**, 1957- , U.S., rob. On May 4, 1995, Steven Tinsley, of Chicago, Illinois, earned long prison sentences by pleading guilty to robbing seven banks in Chicago and five banks in Springfield, Illinois, and St. Louis, Missouri. At the time Tinsley was enacting his robbery spree, he was on supervised release, dating back to October 1994. Tinsley had served four years in prison for a 1990 conviction of robbing four Chicago-area banks. He was known as the "Apologetic Bandit," because he would say he was sorry to tellers emptying their cash drawers. Before he left each bank, Tinsley stated, "Have a nice day."

**Titone, Dino**, 1960- , U.S., kid.-mur. A cold-blooded killer who spent several years on Illinois' Death Row was spared execution because of a corrupt judge and his equally corrupt lawyer. On December 12, 1982, Dino Titone, of Elgin, Illinois, accompanied by Joseph Sorrentino and Robert Gacho, met with two drug pushers, 39-year-old Aldo Fratto and his 26-year-old nephew, Tullio Infelise. After receiving a large supply of cocaine, Titone and Sorrentino kidnapped Fratto and Infelise, driving them in Fratto's car to a rural spot in unincorporated Lemont Township. There they fatally shot Fratto and Infelise, stuffing them into the trunk of Fratto's car.

The killers then hitched a ride back to Chicago with Robert Gacho and his girlfriend, Kathryn DeWulf, in DeWulf's car. En route Titone laughed and bragged about shooting the two men, describing how they had begged for mercy before he and Sorrentino shot them. Hours later, a DuPage County Forest Preserve ranger found Fratto's abandoned car and heard someone inside the trunk yelling to be released. Inside the trunk he found Fratto dead and Infelise, though wounded many times, still alive.

Infelise lived for seventeen hours and before dying said that Robert Gacho had had two hitmen shoot Fratto and himself. His statements led detectives to the doorstep of Kathryn DeWulf, who escaped being charged as an accessory to the murders by informing on Gacho, Titone and Sorrentino, who were all arrested and charged with murder. All three were convicted in 1984, Gacho and Sorrentino sent to prison for life. Titone was sentenced to death by Cook County Circuit Court Judge Thomas Maloney in November 1984.

In a subsequent corruption probe of the Chicago courts, Operation Greylord uncovered the fact that Judge Maloney had taken a bribe from Titone's attorney, Bruce Roth, in order to acquit Titone in a bench trial. But instead of rendering an acquittal, Judge Maloney found Titone guilty and sentenced him to death. On August 4, 1989, Titone signed an affidavit stating, "I am not sure why Judge Maloney convicted me after the case had been fixed, but Roth indicated to me that a deal had been made. I believe I was convicted either because Roth failed to live up to his end of the bargain and pay Judge Maloney the $10,000 or because Judge Maloney was scared about Greylord and his reelection and wanted to prove that there was no fix."

The $10,000 bribe money had been provided by Titone's father, Salvatore Titone, who stated that Roth had originally demanded $60,000 to fix his son's case, but that all he could put together through savings, loans and selling off family jewelry was $10,000. All of this resulted in Roth's conviction for bribery, extortion and racketeering. He was sent to prison for ten years in 1987. Judge Maloney was also convicted and sentenced in 1994 to fifteen years and nine months in prison and ordered to pay a fine of $200,000.

Titone, by that time, had won a new trial. In 1990, Judge Earl Strayhorn vacated Titone's death sentence. Titone was not brought to trial until 1998, and he was again convicted. On October 13, 1998, Titone was sentenced to life in prison by Criminal Court Judge Daniel Locallo. His life was spared because of the actions of a crooked lawyer and a venal judge.

---

**Tjibaou, Jean-Marie**, 1936-1989, New Caledonia, assass. Jean-Marie Tjibaou, leader of the Kanak Socialist National Liberation Front of New Caledonia, was shot and killed by hardline separatist Djubelly Wea on May 5, 1989. Tjibaou, a one-time Catholic priest, had led the separatist group for a number of years in overthrowing the French government in France's most troubled territory. In June 1988, Tjibaou negotiated a peace settlement between his political faction and French officials, one which brought an end to the long and bloody warfare between the island's radical sect and French commandoes, and that called for independence by 1998.

Wea, a member of Tjibaou's most radical sect, Palika, opposed the truce. Tjibaou and Yeiwene Yeiwene, an aide, arrived at a cave where nineteen of their followers had been slain a year earlier by French commandoes liberating hostages taken by the separatists. Wea Tjibaou approached the two men and fired point blank, killing both. Two French commandoes, who were guarding Tjibaou and Yeiwene, then opened fire and killed Wea.

---

**Tokyo (Jap.) Poison Gas Attacks** (1995), See: **Aum Shinri Kyo**.

---

**Tolerton, Kenyon Battles**, 1956- , U.S., rape-mur. The partially clad body of a 14-year-old girl was found in a rural area near Byers, Colorado, on September 1, 1993. The dead girl was not immediately identified, but a coroner's report determined the cause of her death. She had been strangled and stabbed to death after having been raped. A composite sketch of the girl was broadcast on Denver TV stations, and this drew a response from the victim's father, who identified her as Cissy Pamela Foster, who had been missing since August 27, 1993.

Foster, a Denver resident, was known to have been reckless in accepting rides from strangers. One of her friends told an investigator that only a few days before she disappeared, Foster got out of a car and joined some of her girlfriends. When asked who had given her a lift, Foster merely shrugged and said she didn't know the man. One of the officers probing the Foster death thought he recognized the handiwork of a killer involved in an almost identical slaying thirteen years earlier.

The officer had been part of an investigating team of the Arapahoe County Sheriff's Department examining the July 28, 1980 rape and murder of 22-year-old Donna Ursula Waugh, of Englewood, Colorado. She had been reported missing ten days

earlier. Waugh's killer was tracked down. He was Kenyon Battles Tolerton. Brought to trial, he pleaded guilty to second-degree murder on October 2, 1981, and was sentenced to ten years in prison. He was paroled on February 10, 1991.

This was not Tolerton's first serious criminal offense. He had, in 1976, tried to kidnap a young woman in an Akron, Ohio, shopping mall, but a bystander had overpowered him. He had received a fifteen-year prison term for that offense, but in October 1976, his sentence was suspended and he was placed on probation. Four years later, Tolerton murdered Waugh. Following his 1991 parole, Tolerton had attempted to molest several women and was the suspect in several Denver-area rapes. He became the prime suspect in Foster's rape-murder.

Detectives learned that while Tolerton was a prisoner in the Colorado State Penitentiary for the Waugh killing, samples of his blood were automatically requested before his final parole hearing. Tolerton provided these samples on October 16, 1990. Using these samples, DNA experts compared them with a swab taken from Foster. It was a match. Tolerton was arrested and charged with Foster's murder. He was convicted on DNA evidence and sentenced to life in prison.

---

**Tomassi, David**, 1954- , U.S., kid. On December 23, 1983, David Tomassi kidnapped his two young sons from their mother's Michigan home, later claiming that the boys were being abused by their mother, whom he had recently divorced. For eleven years, Tomassi moved through five states and Canada, raising his sons. He was finally located in upstate New York, and arrested and charged with kidnapping on October 4, 1994. His sons were then attending a college preparatory school, and when their father was tried in a Pontiac, Michigan, court, the boys both pleaded with Judge David Breck not to send Tomassi to prison, saying that he was a good and loving father. Judge Breck, however, thought to set an example of Tomassi and send a message to all those guilty of parental kidnapping by sentencing Tomassi to the maximum term of one year in prison.

---

**Tonkovich, Dan; Tucker, Larry;** and **Boettner, Si**, prom. 1989, U.S., extor. When West Virginia Governor Gaston Caperton took office in January 1989, he said the state was in a serious "ethical crisis" as allegations of widespread political corruption threatened to undermine the effectiveness of the government. In Mingo County, some forty local police officers, fire fighters, administrators, and even school officials had been indicted or faced convictions on charges ranging from bribery to vote stealing, to running a drug market. The corruption extended to the state legislature, as the former president of the Senate, Dan Tonkovich, was sentenced to five years in prison on December 15, 1989, for extorting $5,000 from a corporation seeking to influence the passage of a bill legalizing casino gambling. Tonkovich, one of three powerful Democratic leaders implicated in the scandal, pleaded guilty to the charges and, in addition to his prison sentence, was fined $10,000.

Two other legislators, Larry Tucker and Si Boettner, were also convicted on similar charges. Tucker, also a former Senate president, received a six-month sentence and a $20,000 fine for extorting bribes from a state lobbyist interested in the gambling legislation. Boettner, former Senate Majority leader, was given five years' probation and ordered to perform 250 days of community service after failing to report $4,100 in income he received from a lobbyist in 1985. The state treasurer, A.J. Manchin, resigned earlier in the year to avoid an impeachment trial on charges of gross mismanagement. An audit discovered nearly $300 million missing from an investment fund.

**Tornay, Cedric**, 1975-1998, Vatican, mur. Violence was unknown within the confines of the Vatican, a city-state within Italy and headquarters of the Roman Catholic Church. Before the modern era, the last known killing in the Vatican occurred in 1848, when Count Pelligrino Rossi, Vatican prime minister to Pope Pius IX, was assassinated during the political upheaval that led to the unification of Italy. All had been tranquil and orderly since then, until May 4, 1998, when two senseless murders and a suicide occurred within the ranks of the Pope's prestigious Swiss Guards.

On that date, Cedric Tornay, a 23-year-old Swiss guardsman, apparently incensed at not receiving a medal he expected to be awarded to him, went to the apartment of his commander, Alois Estermann, and shot and killed him, along with Estermann's Venezuelan-born wife, Gladys Meza Romero, 49, then killed himself. Tornay was also reportedly incensed at having received a letter of reprimand from Estermann for staying out all night.

The 43-year-old Estermann had earlier that day been named as the new commander of the Swiss Guards, an elite 100-member guard unit whose resplendent uniforms had been designed by Michelangelo. The Swiss Guards were established in 1506 by Pope Giulio II to keep order during Papal events and guard the entrances to the Vatican. A plainclothes detachment, along with some Swiss Guards, accompanied the Pope on foreign trips. Estermann had made thirty such trips with Pope John Paul II.

Investigators reported that Tornay, a corporal with the Swiss Guards for three years, had shot Estermann and Romero and then himself, the gun he used, a Swiss-made 9mm SIG, being found beneath his body. All three bodies were fully clothed when found. An autopsy revealed Tornay was suffering from a cyst on the brain, which may have made him mentally unstable and brought about the murders and suicide.

Pope John Paul II celebrated a mass for the Estermanns, while Cardinal Angelo Sodano, the Vatican's secretary of state, asked for divine forgiveness for Tornay, whom he profiled as an example of human fragility. Estermann, a veteran with the Swiss Guards for eighteen years, was held in high esteem by Pope John Paul II. Estermann had been following the Pope's car in 1981 when it traversed Vatican Square as Mehmet Ali Agca, a Turkish assassin, shot and wounded Pope John Paul II. Estermann heroically climbed aboard the car and shielded the Pontiff with his body as the Pope was rushed to a hospital.

**Toro-Aristizibal, Amparo**, See: **David, Shmuel.**

**Toro-Aristizibal, Jaime**, See: **David, Shmuel.**

**Torrence, Michael**, d.1996, U.S., mur. On September 6, 1996, Michael Torrence, who had been convicted and condemned for the murder of three persons, was executed in South Carolina. Torrence had murdered Charles Bush and Dennis Lollis during a 1987 robbery in Midlands, South Carolina. He stabbed Lollis nineteen times and choked Bush to death with a dog chain. A month later, he murdered Cynthia Williams, a prostitute from Charleston, whom he said was his girlfriend.

**Torres, Leslie**, 1971- , U.S., rob.-asslt.-attempt. mur.-mur. During an eight-day period in January 1988, 17-year-old Leslie Torres killed five people and wounded six in New York City's East Harlem. On the evening of January 7, he robbed a store and shot to death the owner, Pablo Amaya Rojas, and wounded an employee, Juan Corona. Torres was captured trying to elude police the following day. He was charged with murder, attempted murder, weapons violations, robbery, and assault.

Torres' defense attorney maintained that abuse of crack cocaine had caused Torres to go insane, and that his $500-a-day habit forced him to steal. Manhattan Assistant District Attorney Kristine Hamann called Amaya's murder an "execution" and stated that under New York law, voluntary use of narcotics is invalid as a defense against a felony murder charge. On February 27, 1989, after nineteen minutes of deliberation, the jury found Torres guilty on all charges. Acting New York Supreme Court Justice Herbert Altman, convinced Torres would kill again if he were ever released from prison, sentenced him to a minimum of sixty years and ten months, making him ineligible for parole until he is at least 77 years old.

**Toto, Frances**, 1945- , U.S., attempt. mur. In 1984, several attempts were made on the life of Tony Toto, a pizza parlor owner in Allentown, Pennsylvania. Assailants hit Toto on the head with a baseball bat, placed a trip wire at the top of some stairs, which caused him to take a nasty fall, and finally, on two separate occasions, he was shot twice. The shootings occurred while Toto slept after consuming soup that had been drugged. His soup had been dosed by none other than this wife, Frances, the person behind the murder attempts. Toto miraculously survived both shootings, and Frances was finally revealed to be the catalyst behind the many murder attempts on the life of her husband.

Frances Toto confessed to sending hired killers to murder her husband so she could be with a secret lover. She was convicted and sent to prison, although her husband, an admitted ladies man, held her blameless and even paid for her attorney's fees. He visited her regularly in prison, bringing along the couple's four children. When she was released in 1989, Toto welcomed Frances back to their Allentown home. The 43-year-old Toto was philosophical about his wife's attempts on his life, saying, "I think that if you find the right person, you have to stick with it." Shortly after Frances' release, director Lawrence Kasdan announced plans to make a movie about the Totos titled *I Love You to Death*.

---

**Tracy, Mary Ellen** (AKA: Sabrina Aset), 1942- , and **Tracy, Wilbur,** 1928- U.S., pros. Mary Ellen Tracy of west Los Angeles engaged in sex with more than 2,000 men because God and her husband told her to. "Anything God wants from me, I will give Him" explained the 47-year-old housewife who went by the name of Sabrina Aset, guru of the Church of the Most High Goddess. "If He wants me to be monogamous, I'll be monogamous," said Tracy. "If He says go have sex with 20,000 men, I'll do it."

Tracy started the religion with her husband, Will, who compared himself to the Mormon prophet Joseph Smith, who was persecuted for his beliefs. Wilbur Tracy believed that he had revived the "world's oldest religion," one that dates back to the time of Cleopatra. At the Tracys' Church of the Most High Goddess, women were elevated to the role of "high priestess," and were required to "absolve" the sins of the male parishioners during sexual rituals. Police maintained that the Tracys operated a thinly disguised prostitution ring, as the men were required to make cash contributions in order to engage in the cleansing sexual rituals.

The church, run from the couple's home near Beverly Hills, California, was permanently closed down on April 17, 1989, following Mary Ellen's arrest on prostitution charges. The Tracys appeared before Los Angeles Municipal Court Judge Marion Obera on September 22, 1989. Deputy Public Defender Maureen J. Tchakalian asked Judge Obera to exercise leniency, given the fact that the Tracys were first-time offenders. "There are first-time prostitutes and those who are convicted for the first time," Obera noted. "And I feel Mrs. Tracy is in the latter category." Mary Ellen was sentenced to serve ninety days in jail and fined $3,000. She was also ordered to undergo an AIDS test and to attend AIDS education classes at the Sybil Brand Institute for Women. Wilbur Tracy received the maximum sentence of 180 days in jail and a $1,000 fine for running a house of ill repute. Freed on bond, Mary Ellen was re-arrested later in the year for a probation violation. She was sentenced to 360 days in jail on December 11, 1989.

---

**Trepanier, Peter T.,** prom. 1989, U.S., attempt. mur. Peter T. Trepanier launched a one-man crime wave from December 1986 to January 1987 by sniping at residents of Cumberland and North Smithfield, Rhode Island, wounding four persons. Trepanier also broke into six houses and set another three houses on fire. Arrested and convicted on twenty-seven felony counts, Trepanier was sentenced to eighty years to life by Judge Dominick Cresto in February 1989.

---

**Trie, Yah Lin,** See: **Yah Lin Trie**

---

**Truman, Allen Lee**, 1947- , U.S., child molestation. Scoutmaster and civic leader Allen Lee Truman, who was named Citizen of the Year in 1988 in Galt, California, a suburb of Sacramento, turned out to be anything but a model resident. Truman, who headed a Scout group, was accused of molesting the youths in his charge. Brought before Sacramento Superior Court Judge Jack Sapunor, Truman admitted that he had molested nine boys, forcing them to stand naked when they misbehaved, and bathing others, washing their genitals.

When arrested, Truman told police, "I do what I do because I'm searching for satisfaction. When I'm helping the boys, I need to feel needed and loved in return." Truman also pointed out that he was dropping out of all Scouting activities. In a plea-bargaining maneuver, Truman pleaded no contest before Judge Sapunor in an attempt to obtain a minimum eight-year sentence. Judge Sapunor, however, rejected the deal, labeling Truman's child molestations as "horrendous," and pointing out that the scoutmaster had scarred many of the boys for life.

Five of the boys were so traumatized that they were sent to counseling. Another was placed in a mental institution for evaluation, and still another had wholly rejected men, including his own father, as a result of Truman's molestation. Judge Sapunor sentenced Truman to ten years in state prison, the maximum sentence.

---

**Tsegaye, Emmanuel**, 1956-1989, U.S., suic.-mur. Emmanuel Tsegaye, a 33-year-old Ethiopian immigrant, attempted to take his own life numerous times. On February 15, 1989, he finally succeeded, but not before claiming the lives of three of his Bethesda, Maryland, co-workers.

In October 1988, Tsegaye was hired as a credit card bill collector and, according to bank policy, his fingerprints were submitted to the Maryland State Police, who would determine if he had a criminal record. Although such requests were typically answered within ninety days, the results of the Tsegaye inquiry were not returned until several months later. If the results had been received sooner, bank officials would have learned that in 1984 Tsegaye threatened a Montgomery County police officer with a butter knife and attempted to steal his gun. If bank officials were able to legally examine Tsegaye's medical files, they would have learned that he had been committed to Maryland's Clifton T. Perkins Hospital Center for the criminally insane. They would also have known that Tsegaye had been arrested and tortured during the 1970s political unrest in his native Ethiopia, and had recently been tormented by disembodied voices. In a letter to Circuit Court Judge David L. Cahoon in 1984, Tsegaye described the nature of his problem. "I used to hear voices both from space and as exact repeated words responded by people towards me about my thoughts, or things that were in my mind. In other words, I used to hear a person speaking from the distance about the things I was thinking or thoughts," he wrote.

On February 15, 1989, the day after he had been reprimanded for making a personal phone call during work, Tsegaye arrived at work armed with a handgun. He went into the offices of the credit card collection department, where he had worked for less than a year, and opened fire at random. He fired five rounds from a six-shot gun, killing Cynthia Mitchell, 28, Tanya Walker, 23, and Mahasty Agha-Kaim, 29. Tsegaye seriously wounded 22-year-old Edward James Johnson before he killed himself.

---

**Tucker, Jim Guy**, 1943- , U.S., conspir.-fraud. According to David Hale, a small-time investment banker in Little Rock, Arkansas, he, former Arkansas governor Jim Guy Tucker, and James McDougal hatched a scheme in 1985 to use proceeds from a bogus $825,000 real estate deal to infuse $500,000 into a small business investment firm owned and operated by Hale. Hale's statements were made at Tucker's trial in April 1996, and he further implicated President William Jefferson Clinton, stating that Clinton, when he was governor of Arkansas, pressured him into making an illegal $300,000 loan to his business partners in a real estate scheme called Whitewater. (Clinton's response to this accusation was that it was a "bunch of bull.")

**Jim Guy Tucker, former governor of Arkansas and political backer of President Clinton, convicted of fraud in 1996.**

Hale's testimony was heard at the trial of Jim Guy Tucker when he stood accused of conspiracy and fraud. The investment banker also stated that Tucker and McDougal told him they needed money and McDougal added that "we're going to have to clean up some members of the political family," meaning that they had to take care of then-Governor Bill Clinton. Bill Watt, who had performed some legal chores for Hale, also testified that Hale had told him during the money-juggling scheme that Clinton was pressuring him to close the phony $825,000 deal so that he could "help his friends."

Tucker was convicted of fraud and conspiracy and, on August 19, 1996, was sentenced to four years' probation. Presiding in a Little Rock, Arkansas, court, U.S. District Judge George Howard, Jr., could have imposed ten years of hard time in prison for Tucker, but due to Tucker's failing health—a chronic liver condition—he gave him a lenient term, saying that "a sentence requiring imprisonment would be as cruel as the grave." Also See: **Clinton, William Jefferson**; **McDougal, James and Susan**; **Whitewater**.

---

**Tucker, Karla Faye**, 1960-1998, U.S., mur. From early childhood, Karla Faye Tucker, of Houston, Texas, proved herself a vicious and dangerous person. She dropped out of seventh grade and by the age of 8 had begun smoking marijuana. Two years later she was shooting heroin and thieving while traveling with a small-time rock band. At 15, she married, but this union broke up and Tucker supported herself as a prostitute.

By the time Tucker was in her early 20s, she was a confirmed drug addict, ingesting all manner of drugs, particularly amphetamines (speed). In 1983, she met Danny Garrett at a doctor's office in Houston, Texas, where both of them regularly obtained illegal prescriptions for drugs. After staying up for three days and while high on speed, according to her later statements, Tucker and Garrett decided to visit a friend, Jerry Lynn Dean, planning to steal his motorcycle and possibly kill Dean. She and Garrett had talked to several friends of going on a murder spree, of "offing people" who ran drug labs.

Tucker also later admitted that she harbored hatred for Dean because he once dripped motorcycle oil on her living room carpet and had torn up a photograph of her mother. Tucker and Garrett, both high on drugs, or so they later claimed, arrived at Dean's Houston home before dawn on June 13, 1983. Tucker began arguing with Dean and then wrestling with him.

When Dean appeared to be getting the better of Tucker, Garrett intervened, striking Dean repeatedly on the head with a hammer. Tucker later stated that she wanted Dean to stop making a "gurgling" noise, so she grabbed a pickax (she and Garrett had brought the pickax and hammer along for the purpose of killing Dean) and began viciously striking Dean in the back, making horrible wounds. Tucker later bragged to a friend that she had "come with every stroke" (had a sexual orgasm).

As Dean fell dead, Tucker noticed a figure cowering beneath a blanket. Tucker hit the blanket-clad figure several times. Pulling the blanket back, she discovered Deborah Thornton, who was estranged from her husband and had been staying with Dean. Garrett then killed Thornton, according to Tucker.

Both Tucker and Garrett were quickly arrested and charged with murder. Tucker testified against Garrett, who was convicted of murdering both Dean and Thornton. (He died in 1993 of a liver ailment while awaiting his second trial in this case.) Tucker, however, was convicted only of killing Dean. She was sentenced to death and, while on Texas' Death Row, she embraced religion and became an evangelist and an apostle against drugs, making videotapes and giving speeches about the evils of drug use. Further, she married the prison chaplain (although the union was never consummated).

For fourteen years Tucker fought off execution, claiming to be a thoroughly reformed person. She promoted her evangelism and her redeemed life on TV talk shows and enlisted the aid of Pat Robertson and other evangelists, who tried to persuade Texas authorities to commute her death sentence. A week before her scheduled execution on February 3, 1998, Tucker wrote to the Texas Board of Pardons and Paroles, "Even though I did murder ... that night and not think anything of it back then, it is now the one thing that I regret most in life ... And in the frame of mind I am in now, it is something that absolutely rips my guts out as I think about it."

Richard Thornton, the 48-year-old husband of the slain Deborah Thornton, believed, as did many others, that Tucker was merely acting the redeemed soul to save her life. Said Thornton, "It's all 'Sweet Karla Faye, Miss Saint' ... She is not wanting her life—she wants back on the streets, in the bedroom with her husband."

Death penalty opponents held rallies on Tucker's behalf and many religious leaders asked that her sentence be commuted, saying that Karla Faye Tucker had been transformed into a good person. Further, they pointed out, no woman had been executed in recent times since the execution of Margie Velma ("Death Row Granny") Barfield, who was executed in North Carolina in 1984, even though she, too, had insisted that she was a different person after having become a born-again Christian. Texas, in fact, had not executed a woman since hanging Chipita Rodriguez in 1863 for killing a horse trader.

All of the arguments and appeals failed in the end. On February 3, 1998, 38-year-old Karla Faye Tucker was strapped onto a gurney in the Death Room of the Huntsville, Texas, penitentiary and given a lethal injection, which stopped her heart. She became the 145th person executed in Texas since that state resumed the death penalty in 1982.

---

**Tucker, Larry**, See: **Tonkovich, Dan**.

---

**Tucker, Leslie**, 1937- , U.S., Case of child moles. Leslie Tucker, a 61-year-old U.S. mail carrier, was arrested for molesting a 7-year-old girl in Park Forest, Illinois, on August 11, 1998. Residents called police after they spotted Tucker holding the girl and fondling her and exposing himself to her as he pinned her and her bicycle next to his postal truck. Following Tucker's arrest, the girl told police that he had assaulted her.

Upon his arrest, Tucker told Will County officers that he had been delivering mail for fifteen years and, before that, had been in the grocery business for thirty years. Married with children, Tucker had been a resident of Crete, Illinois, for more than forty years. Released on a $150,000 bond, Tucker was suspended without pay by the U.S. Postal Service.

Tucker was arrested a second time on August 27, 1998, and charged with sexually assaulting another child, a 5-year-old girl, sometime between May 1 and August 17, 1998 (the latter date being after Tucker was released on bond), while she was in the driveway of her Park Forest home. Facing seven to fourteen years if convicted in the first charge and thirty years in the second, Tucker awaits trial at this writing.

---

**Tucker, Russell William**, 1967- , U.S., asslt.-rob.-mur. Richard Byron Wall, a 35-year-old cab driver, was found mortally wounded by a gunshot, lying beside his cab on a four-lane highway near Winston-Salem, North Carolina, on November 1, 1994. Witnesses who stopped their car to aid Wall saw a tall black man with a Jamaican accent leave the scene—he said he was going to find an ambulance. Wall was rushed to a hospital, where he died.

Detectives searched for the missing black man, who was presumed to have been Wall's passenger and killer, but they turned up no clues. Then, on December 8, 1994, a shooting occurred outside a Super K-mart Center in Winston-Salem, when a shoplifter shot and killed store security guard Maurice T. Williams before he fled down the street. Two policemen gave chase and the bold thief emptied his gun at the officers, riddling their patrol car and wounding both of them. The officers were taken to a hospital, where they recovered.

Meanwhile, an all-points bulletin went out for the K-mart shootist. He was picked up a short time later and identified as 27-year-old Russell William Tucker, a small-time thief and drugster. He was charged with murdering Williams, robbing the K-mart store and feloniously assaulting the two police officers. On January 31, 1996, Tucker, in a plea-bargain deal, confessed to murdering cab driver Wall. He was sentenced to twenty-three to twenty-seven years in prison by Judge Jerry Cash Martin.

In the K-mart killing of the guard Williams, however, prosecutors would cut no deal. Tucker was convicted of this killing and sentenced to death. Upon hearing this sentence on February 21, 1996, Tucker leaped to his feet and inexplicably shouted, "God is great!" He had been feigning mental illness, and this last demonstrative act was thought to be only more of his charade. Tucker was led off to North Carolina's Death Row, where he currently awaits execution.

---

**Tuggle, Lem David, Jr.**, 1952-1996, U.S., mur. Twice convicted of murder, as well as robbery and numerous prison breaks, Lem David Tuggle was 19 when he picked up 18-year-old Shirley Mullins Brickey at an American Legion dance and took her to an abandoned house at Seven Mile Ford, outside Marion, Virginia, on the night of September 11, 1971. The next day Brickey was found in the house, strangled by a bedsheet. Tuggle was tracked down, convicted of second-degree murder and sent to prison for twenty years.

Paroled on July 10, 1981, after serving less than half of his sentence, he was sent back to prison in 1982 for parole violation, then paroled again in 1983. On May 29, 1983, Tuggle picked up Jessie Geneva Havens, a 52-year-old grandmother, at a dance at the same American Legion Lodge in Marion, Virginia, where he had picked up Shirley Brickey twelve years earlier. Havens disappeared and was later found murdered. Tuggle was sent back to prison, this time with a death sentence.

On December 12, 1996, Tuggle, weighing more than 300 pounds, was brought into the execution chamber at Jarrat, Virginia. It took seven prison guards to lift the overweight killer onto a gurney, where he was strapped down. Before he was given the lethal injection that would take his life, Tuggle looked at those witnessing his execution and grimly uttered his last words, "Merry Christmas." He was pronounced dead a few minutes later.

---

**Tuilefano, George**, See: **Leuluaialii, Kenneth**.

---

**Tullis, Patrick**, 1959- , U.S., mur. In February 1987, Patrick Tullis was released from Menard Correctional Center in Illinois after serving two and a half years for aggravated battery. While in prison, Tullis stabbed another inmate for reportedly making sexual advances toward him—an act that caused three more months to be added to his existing sentence. Upon his release, Tullis moved to the North Side of Chicago. Here, according to his later statements, Tullis attacked John

Tolbert, 25, after Tolbert made sexual advances. On April 5, 1987, Tullis wrapped a phone cord around Tolbert's neck and strangled him to death. Tullis then tied the body, hand and foot, and placed it in a dumpster behind his Sheffield Avenue home.

Three weeks later, on April 29, 1987, Tullis was again sexually attacked, this time by Raymondo Hernandez, 43, according to his later claim. Wielding a knife, Tullis stabbed Hernandez twenty-one times, then placed the body beneath some CTA tracks on Ashland Avenue. On July 12, police finally tracked down Tullis and questioned him about the Hernandez slaying. He confessed to the killing, adding details about his killing of Tolbert. After reaching a plea-bargain agreement, Tullis was convicted of murdering Hernandez and committing manslaughter in the case of Tolbert. Cook County Criminal Court Judge Robert Boharie sentenced Tullis to fifteen years for manslaughter in the Tolbert case and a consecutive forty-five-year term for the murder of Hernandez.

---

**Turco, Frank J.**, See: **Helmsley, Leona.**

---

**Turford, Rose Marie**, 1960- , and **Stevens, Carolyn**, 1965- U.S., rob. In a real-life replay of the fatalistic and fanatical feminist movie *Thelma and Louise*, Rose Marie Turford, a registered nurse and mother of three children, teamed up with drifter Carolyn Stevens to rob gullible men seeking female companionship through a phony dating service Turford and Stevens ran in the Texas cities of Houston and Galveston in the early 1990s.

Turford, who was married to a computer company executive, took ads for a fake dating service, then quizzed male callers as to their positions and wealth. When she found what she thought to be a well-to-do victim, she and Stevens visited the caller's home, holding him up at gunpoint and stealing all the cash and valuables in sight. Also, while Stevens held the victim in his home at gunpoint, Turford would take the victim's bankcard to cash stations and loot the victim's account.

The two women thus robbed dozens of men for a two-year period, 1994-1995, until their scheme was exposed and they were arrested. Stevens quickly cut a plea-bargain deal on February 22, 1996, that brought her a minimum sentence for testifying against her friend. Turford, on the other hand, received the maximum penalty of thirty years in prison.

---

**Turkowski, Mark**, 1973- , U.S., aggrav. batt. of a child-aggrav. kid.-imperson. of pol. off.-attempt. mur. Mark Turkowski approached an 11-year-old boy on a bicycle in South Kiwanis Park in Brookfield, Illinois, on September 26, 1995, telling the boy that he was an undercover police detective and that he needed the boy's help, asking him where teenagers held parties. The boy took him to some nearby woods. Turkowski then grabbed the boy by the neck and choked him into unconsciousness. As the boy lay on the ground, Turkowski slammed a brick repeatedly onto the unconscious boy's face, breaking his eye sockets and jaw.

Just then the boy's friends arrived on bicycles and Turkowski fled. He was picked up by police a short time later and identified as the assailant. At the time of his arrest, Turkowski was covered with the boy's blood. (The boy was rushed to a hospital, where he successfully underwent reconstructive surgery.)

Charged with aggravated battery of a child, aggravated kidnapping, impersonating a police officer and attempted murder, Turkowski pleaded guilty to all charges shortly before his 1996 trial was to begin. He was sentenced to sixty years in prison on December 9, 1996, by Judge Frank DeBoni. He will not be eligible for parole until serving fifty-one years of his sentence.

---

**Turner, Ike**, 1932- U.S., drugs. The one-time husband of singing star Tina Turner (née Anna Mae Bullock), Ike Turner was addicted to cocaine for years. A native of Clarksdale, Mississippi, Turner began performing as a singer in 1948, then met Tina Turner when she was a 16-year-old in the 1950s, teaming up with her and going on to rock music stardom.

Drugs, however, tainted Turner's life with uncontrollable addiction from 1974 onward. He once spent $100,000 on cocaine, he said, in a two-month period in 1989. So devastating was the drug to Turner that it destroyed his septum, the cartilage that divides the nostrils. Drugs also destroyed Ike Turner's 14-year marriage to Tina, who divorced him in 1978, stating that "I thought he was bad before; the cocaine started making him evil." Turner was arrested in 1989 for drug possession and given a four-year sentence at the Men's Colony at San Luis Obispo, California.

---

**Turner, Luther**, 1958- , U.S., rob.-mur. The body of Reverend George Williams was found in his Nichols, South Carolina, home on August 11, 1994. The elderly clergyman was found to have been stabbed nineteen times, but a motive—the home was not disturbed or looted—for the crime was not evident. Also, none of the fingerprints found in the Williams home led to the identification of the killer.

In February 1995, Barbara Windham, a middle-aged woman living in Marion County and close to where the Reverend Williams had been murdered, was reported missing. Her home had been ransacked and almost everything of value had been taken, including her car. A short time later police unearthed witnesses who stated that they had seen Windham in the company of a muscular man named Luther Turner, and that Turner was driving about in Windham's car following her disappearance.

Turner, it was discovered, had been convicted of murder and sent to prison for twenty-four years, but had been paroled after serving only ten years. He had been released only a few months before Williams was murdered. Turner was tracked down and arrested for the Windham murder. The victim's car was located and Turner's fingerprints were found inside of it. Turner at first denied having anything to do with Windham's disappearance, but then broke down and admitted killing her and hiding her body in a swamp. Though the body was never found, Turner was nevertheless convicted of murdering Windham and then stealing her valuables and car.

While he awaited trial for the Windham killing, Turner bragged to a cellmate that he had also killed the Reverend Williams, but he never gave a reason for this killing. Turner was convicted in two separate trials for murdering Williams and Windham. He was sentenced to two separate life terms.

---

**Turra, Anthony**, 1937-1998, U.S., org. crime-attempt. mur. A boss of a drug gang in Philadelphia, Anthony Turra was indicted, along with his son Louis and three others, of plotting to murder Joseph "Skinny Joey" Merlino. Because of ill health—he suffered from cancer, emphysema and congestive heart failure—Anthony Turra was allowed to go free on bond during the trial. He moved from his home in South Philadelphia to court every day while confined to a wheelchair. On March 18, 1998, while Turra was preparing to leave for court, a man wearing a ski mask and dressed all in black, reportedly a mob hit man, suddenly appeared outside Turra's home and shot him dead.

---

**Tyburski, Leonard**, 1944- , U.S., mur. On July 8, 1967, science teacher Leonard Tyburski, 24, married Dorothy J. Barker, 19, in Detroit, Michigan. The couple had two daughters, Kelly and Kim, and by 1985 were living in Canton Township, Michigan. According to Tyburski's later confession, he and his 37-year-old wife had an argument on September 28, 1985, and he killed her. He apparently struck her on the head with a blunt object and then put her body in the basement freezer because he "loved her and didn't want to part with her." Tyburski reported his wife missing on October 2. The case remained unsolved and was treated as a missing persons case.

After her mother's disappearance, Kelly Tyburski had a recurring nightmare that her mother was locked up or tied up. Then she realized that the freezer, which had frequently been used, remained locked after her mother vanished. About 1 p.m. on January 2, 1989, Kelly, 19, forced open the lock and discovered her mother's body. She called a friend, who drove the Tyburski sisters to the police station. On January 3, police arrested 45-year-old Leonard Tyburski. He confessed and was held without bond. On June 26, 1989, a jury found him guilty of murder, and on July 12 he was sentenced to twenty to forty years in prison.

---

**Tyson, Mike**, 1967- , U.S., rape-asslt. One-time heavyweight boxing champion of the world, Mike Tyson was convicted of raping an Indiana woman in 1991 and served three years in prison for the offense. A product of the gutter, Tyson learned nothing from his prison time. When he emerged, he displayed this same brutish and savage character, being accused of a sexual assault on a Gary, Indiana, woman in 1996.

That same kind of jungle-like savagery was again displayed by Tyson in 1997 when he fought Evander Holyfield for the heavyweight title. Frustrated at losing round after round to the superior Holyfield, Tyson bit off part of Holyfield's ear and was disqualified. He was later barred from the ring and fined $3 million for his vicious ring behavior.

A millionaire many times over, Tyson found it impossible to conform to the laws of society. His maniacal temper flared again in August 1998 when, following a minor traffic accident in Maryland, Tyson went berserk and attacked two motorists. On February 5, 1999, Tyson appeared in a Rockville, Maryland, courtroom and was sentenced to a year in prison by Judge Stephen Johnson, who typified Tyson's assault on the motorists as "potentially lethal road rage." Judge Johnson said that Tyson "repeatedly speaks and acts compulsively and violently."

Tyson typified the kind of boxer that presently dominates the ring—uneducated, sadistic, violently anti-social and utterly savage, a wild beast better penned up in a cell than set loose on the streets, let alone allowed into a boxing ring, where he could viciously maim and mutilate opponents. Tyson, more than any other boxer of recent times, represented the moral collapse of a long-corrupted sport.

**Former heavyweight boxing champion Mike Tyson, sent to prison for rape in 1991 and sent back to prison for assault in 1999.**

---

**Tyson Foods**, prom. 1990s, U.S., perj.-illegal gifts. Tyson Foods, the Arkansas poultry giant that backed President William Jefferson Clinton in his two successful bids for office, came under scrutiny in 1994 when then-Secretary of Agriculture Michael Espy, the first black man to hold that high office, was accused of accepting bribes in the form of expensive gifts from Tyson. In 1993-1994, Espy and his department were considering applying regulations against Tyson that could have cost the company millions of dollars.

Following a four-year probe of Tyson led by Kenneth Starr, Tyson lobbyist Jack Williams was found guilty of lying to investigators, and Archie Schaffer III, a Tyson corporate spokesman, was found guilty on two counts of illegal gift-giving. Both Tyson representatives faced long prison terms after they were found guilty on June 26, 1998. Espy was tried in December 1998 and was found not guilty in a controversial verdict. Also See: **Espy, Michael**.

# U

**Ulla, Saber Abu el-**, and **Ulla, Mahmoud**, Egypt., terr.-mur. Following the September 18, 1997 terrorist attack against a busload of tourists in Cairo, Egypt, Saber Abu el-Ulla and his brother, Mahmoud Ulla, were arrested for the crime. The brothers had attacked the bus containing German tourists as the vehicle was parked outside a Cairo museum. They killed the Egyptian bus driver and nine tourists, wounding another twenty-six persons in the bus, which they riddled with bullets from automatic weapons and then firebombed.

Saber Abu el-Ulla, a former mental patient in a Cairo asylum, and his brother, Mahmoud, were brought to trial in Cairo in October 1997, locked in a steel cage, behind which they shouted and rattled the wire. Both pleaded guilty on October 11, 1997. They were later sentenced to death.

---

**Unabomber, The**, See: **Kaczynski, Theodore**.

---

**Union Carbide Poisonings**, 1984-1989, India, crim. neg. Several criminal complaints were filed against Union Carbide in Bhopal, India, after a 1984 gas leak from that plant killed an estimated 3,300 people, the worst industrial disaster in the country's history. In 1989, the government ordered the firm to pay $470 million in damages, $45 million to be paid by Union Carbide's Bhopal subsidiary and the remainder to be paid by its parent company in Danbury, Connecticut.

---

**University of Oklahoma Scandal**, 1989, U.S., drugs-rape-asslt. Five members of the University of Oklahoma football team were indicted for criminal activity during the first two months of 1989. On January 13, Jerry Parks, a defensive back, was charged with shooting with intent to injure following an altercation with teammate Zarak Peters. On January 21, team members Glen Bell, Nigel Clay, and Bernard Hall were charged with first-degree rape following an incident in their dormitory. On February 13, FBI agents concluded a six-month investigation when they arrested starting quarterback Charles Thompson, 21, for selling cocaine. All five athletes were suspended from the football team, as well as from the university.

On April 27, 1989, at the U.S. District Court in Oklahoma City before Judge Ralph Thompson, Charles Thompson pleaded guilty to the charge of conspiring to distribute cocaine. On August 30, Thompson was sentenced to two years in prison and was also required to submit to three years of drug testing following his release. On May 15, Jerry Parks pleaded no contest to wounding Peters and was sentenced to three months in prison. On November 17, Clay and Hall were convicted of rape and five days later were sentenced by Judge Preston Trimble to ten years in prison and fined $10,000. Bell, the third defendant in the rape trial, was acquitted.

---

**Uno, Sosuke**, 1923-1998, Jap., prost. First elected to Japan's Diet (parliament) in 1960, Uno later served as the country's Defense Agency director general, trade minister and foreign minister. In 1989, Uno became premier of Japan after a bribery scandal forced his predecessor, Noboru Takeshita, to step down. Uno's own administration became one of the shortest in Japan's history. After only sixty-nine days in office, Uno was forced to resign after prostitution charges were leveled—that he had paid a geisha to become his mistress. Uno remained in Japanese politics until 1996, when he retired. He died at age 75 of lung cancer on May 19, 1998, in the hospital at Moriyama, Shiga prefecture, about 230 miles southwest of Tokyo.

---

**U.S. Embassies bombings**, 1998, Ken./Tanzan., terr.-mur. One of the worst foreign terrorist attacks against the U.S. occurred when two U.S. embassies in Nairobi, Kenya, and Dar

**A U.S. Marine guard orders a cameraman to move back from the still smoldering ruins of the U.S. Embassy in Nairobi, Kenya, on August 7, 1998, after a terrorist blast took the lives of 225 persons, including twelve Americans.**

es Salaam, Tanzania, were bombed on August 7, 1998, both gigantic explosions taking place within seconds of each other at 10:40 a.m. The bomb in Tanzania exploded some distance from the U.S. Embassy, thanks to the building having been constructed far from the street. Eleven Tanzanians were killed and many injured. In Nairobi, however, the explosion was catastrophic, claiming the lives of twelve Americans and 213 Kenyans. The entire building next to the embassy was collapsed by the massive explosion and hundreds of windows in scores of buildings nearby were blown out, causing more than 5,000 persons to be injured by flying glass.

Almost immediately after the smoke cleared, American intelligence and other foreign agencies scurried to identify those behind the horrific bombings. Investigators were at a loss to identify the culprits until the apprehension of Mohammed Sadeek Odeh, also known as Abdull Bast Awadh and Mohammad Sadig Howaida. Odeh had been arrested by Pakistani officials on August 7, 1998, the very day of the explosion, after arriving in Karachi, Pakistan, from Nairobi. After being promptly extradited back to Nairobi, Kenya, Odeh was relentlessly interrogated by Kenyan investigators, as well as interrogation experts from the FBI who had flown to Nairobi from the U.S.

At first, Odeh would admit nothing, even though he had earlier told Pakistani officials that the bombings had been ordered by Osama bin Laden, an errant 42-year-old Saudi Arabian millionaire and terrorist leader. Bin Laden, whose father was a billionaire in Saudi Arabian construction, had studied engineering in England. Backed by his father's millions, bin Laden, a shrewd investor, amassed his own fortune—between $200 and $300 million. He volunteered his services to the CIA in the Afghan war against Soviet Russia, financing and organizing his own mountain guerrillas, who defeated the Russians at almost every turn.

Following the war, bin Laden reorganized his Afghan forces into his own terrorist organization, which he called the Islamic Front for Jihad Against Jews and Crusaders. He was suspected of being behind the bombing of the World Trade Center in 1993, the prime suspect in that case, Ramzi Ahmed Yousef, convicted of the bombing in 1996. Yousef had reportedly been captured in a bin Laden family guest house in Pakistan.

**Multimillionaire Saudi terrorist leader Osama bin Laden directed bombings of the U.S. Embassies in Nairobi and Dar es Salaam on August 7, 1998.**

In studying the background and rigid Islamic beliefs of Osama bin Laden, it became apparent to this author that bin Laden had become as fanatical a terrorist as the mystical figure he sought to emulate—the Old Man of the Mountain (Hasan ibn-al-Sabah), creator of the Order of the Assassins, an eleventh-century killer cult seeking to murder the Christian leaders of the Third Crusade, which invaded the kingdoms of Islam. (This explains why bin Laden labeled his organization against "Crusaders.")

Since the early 1990s, bin Laden posed as an "agriculturalist," and began expanding his terrorist organization into Egypt, Saudi Arabia and Sudan. Saudi officials became so unnerved by his activities that he was "denaturalized" in 1991. In 1994, Saudi authorities froze many of his bank accounts for fear that bin Laden would employ these millions to fund terrorism inside Saudi Arabia.

Bin Laden then moved to the Sudan where, through a front, he invested in, the Military Complex, an industrial compound in Khartoum, where the plant for Shifa Pharmaceutical Industries was located. It was in this plant, U.S. officials later claimed, that the deadly nerve gas VX was to be produced and then later used in terrorist attacks against the U.S. and its allies.

Bin Laden's terrorist activities intensified throughout the 1990s. In addition to funding the bombing of the World Trade Center, bin Laden was pinpointed as the person behind several bombings of U.S. facilities in Saudi Arabia in 1995 and 1996, although these attacks still remain officially unsolved. The U.S. pressured Sudan to expel him (and his three wives) in 1996. He then established a terrorist training compound at Zhawar Kili, Afghanistan, near the Pakistan border. Bin Laden had long

The U.S. Embassy in Dar es Salaam, Tanzania, after a terrorist bomb blew away part of the compound's wall; eleven Tanzanians were killed.

endeared himself to the fundamentalist Islamic Taliban regime controlling Afghanistan and its leader, Mullah Mohammad Omar.

From his mountain retreat, bin Laden granted interviews and publicly condemned Western "non-believers," telling a reporter from the ABC-TV network that U.S. forces should "leave Saudi Arabia or die." He proudly led this reporter and others on a tour of his terrorist compound, which boasted anti-aircraft missile systems, radar, and a sophisticated communications systems allowing bin Laden to uplink faxes and video by satellite and to tap into the Internet. It was from this remote staging area that bin Laden ordered the bombings of the U.S. embassies in Africa.

Once U.S. intelligence had pinpointed bin Laden's stronghold, President Clinton retaliated on August 20, 1998, ordering American warships in the Red Sea to launch cruise missiles into Khartoum, utterly destroying the Shifa Pharmaceutical plant. At the same time, U.S. warships in the Arabian Sea unleashed long-range Tomahawk missiles that targeted bin Laden's camp at Zwahar Kili. The damage inflicted was reported to be considerable, but bin Laden, according to several accounts, survived the attack. One of the reasons why the camp was targeted was to disrupt a conference of many top-level Islamic terrorists who were to meet on that day, including members of the Islamic Jihad.

U.S. intelligence was not able to determine if, indeed, the conference had taken place, but it was believed that among those scheduled to attend were representatives of the PFLP (Popular Front for the Liberation of Palestine), a terrorist arm of the Al Fatah Council (as is Islamic Jihad), which is directly linked to the Palestine Liberation Organization and Yasir Arafat. Although he was profiled as the director of the August 1998 bombings, it was obvious to trained observers that bin Laden's posturing and threats, his willingness to give interviews and be photographed and filmed in his Afghanistan hideout, made him too much of a public figure to be the actual mastermind of the bombings. To trained observers, bin Laden was simply another high-profile PFLP front man. None of the real Islamic terrorist leaders in the past two decades would ever think to seek the limelight.

The Islamic terrorist leaders have always opted for the shadows, as has been the case with Abu Abbas (Mohammed Zaidan Abbas; AKA: Abu Khalid), the insidious PFLP leader and one of Arafat's foremost aides and advisers, who engineered the Black September killings of the Israeli Olympic team in 1972, the seizing of the cruise ship *Achille Lauro* in 1985 and the destruction of Pan Am Flight 103 over Lockerbie, Scotland, in 1988. The bomb that destroyed the plane was placed by two of Abbas' hand-picked terrorists who for years took refuge in Libya, guests of Muammar Qaddafi. It was Abbas who directed countless terrorist attacks against Israel, usually from Lebanon bases, as well as numerous skyjackings through the 1970s and 1980s.

By the mid-1990s, the PFLP/Al Fatah had flattered the strutting, arrogant bin Laden into taking up their terrorist causes. Bin Laden's gnawing vanity, these shrewd manipulators knew, would insist that he take center stage as the successor to the legendary Old Man of the Mountain (which undoubtedly explained bin Laden's proclivity for residing in mountaintop caves). Bin Laden would not only help fund PFLP operations, but would happily take credit for its heinous crimes in the name of "holy Jihad."

There could be no doubt that bin Laden certainly represented the terrorist arm that launched the August 1998 embassy bombings, but he was not the catalyst that inspired those deadly attacks; that distinction belonged most certainly to the PFLP, which has historically directed and approved of almost all major Islamic terrorist attacks against the U.S. and Israel in the last three decades. Through this attack, a PFLP message was sent to both the U.S. and one of its most ardent allies, Israel: Give up the territories along the West Bank demanded by the Palestinians and Arafat, and give them up quickly.

The historical precedent, modus operandi and motive for the August 1998 bombings in Kenya and Tanzania were deeply rooted to the PFLP, not to the publicity-seeking bin Laden. Two months before the attacks in Nairobi and Dar es Salaam, on June 19 and June 21, 1998, two bomb attacks in Beirut were made by PFLP terrorists, a car bomb killing two persons and, two days later, rocket-propelled grenades that were exploded near the U.S. Embassy, which brought about no injuries. These attacks were symbolic demonstrations against the U.S. to compel America to further pressure Israel into giving up West Bank territory. Prime Minister Benjamin Netanyahu's government, despite U.S. pressure (and Hillary Rodham Clinton's unofficial public remark that "Palestine deserves to be a state"), resolved not to give up territory until the Palestinians (Arafat) cracked down on terrorism.

The PFLP's answer was to order bin Laden's attacks in Africa, returning to the very city, Nairobi, where the PFLP had exploded a tremendous bomb on December 31, 1980, destroying the Zionist-owned Norfolk Hotel, an explosion that killed between sixteen and twenty persons and injured another eighty-five. In that explosion, as well as those of August 7, 1998, the PFLP left its calling card—traces of Semtex, an explosive manufactured in Czechoslovakia and used consistently by the PFLP in its terrorist bombings over the years.

The 1980 and 1998 bombings followed an identical attack plan, a vehicle packed with explosives driven close to a parking area before the explosives were detonated. The 1980 Nairobi bombing was conducted by the PFLP in retaliation for the successful raid by Israeli commandos at Entebbe four years earlier when Israeli hostages were rescued. (More than irony can be found in the fact that only one fatality among the commandos was inflicted by the PFLP terrorists—that of its heroic leader, Col. Netanyahu, the brother of Israel's former prime minister.)

Moreover, the August 1998 attacks against U.S. embassies occurred in the year marking the fiftieth anniversary of Israel as a sovereign state, the U.S. being one of the first nations to acknowledge it as such. To Yasir Arafat, the PFLP and its allied terrorist groups, Israel and the U.S. were one and the same, a common enemy; they were the "Jews and Crusaders" Osama bin Laden has vowed to destroy. Bin Laden, despite his menacing threats, was not the present-day Old Man of the Mountain—that dubious distinction belonged to Yasir Arafat, who uttered not a word of condemnation for those who set off the deadly African explosions.

Intensive searches and manhunts for the terrorists resulted in the September 21, 1998 arrests in Tanzania of two men identified as part of bin Laden's terrorist organization—Mustafa Mahmoud Said Ahmed, an Egyptian, and Rashid Saleh Hemed, a Tanzanian. Both men were charged in Dar es Salaam with eleven counts of murder, the number of deaths brought about by the Tanzanian bombing. On November 4, 1998, Osama bin Laden was indicted by a federal grand jury in New York for directing a worldwide terrorist network that launched the August 7, 1998 bombings in Nairobi and Dar es Salaam. The charges also named bin Laden's group, Al Qaeda, as the one directly responsible for the bombings, specifying that Al Qaeda maintained terrorist cells in Kenya, Tanzania, Britain and the U.S.

In addition to Odeh, who was arrested and charged with the blast in Nairobi the day after the Kenyan explosion, authorities located Mohamed Rashed Daoud al-'Owhali in a hospital where he was being treated for wounds from the bombing and placed him under arrest as one of the terrorists who helped set off the bomb. Two more men, Wahid Hage and Fazul Abdullah Mohammed were also arrested and charged with the Nairobi bombing. All of these suspects held low level positions in bin Laden's organizations, according to officials. Mamdough Mahmoud Salim, however, who handled some of the group's finances, was located in Germany in December 1998, and U.S. extradition efforts were made to have Salim sent to the U.S. for trial, negotiations that were incomplete at the time of this writing.

# V

**Valencia Garcia, Carlos Ernesto**, See: **Extraditables.**

---

**Van Den Borre, Rudy Albert**, 1963- , U.S., mur. Belgian Army Sergeant Rudy Albert Van Den Borre worked as a chauffeur and clerk for his country's embassy in Washington, D.C., until January 3, 1989, when he had a fight with his male lover, got on a bus, and went to Florida. In Fort Lauderdale, Van Den Borre met 36-year-old Michael Egan, an airline ticket agent, and 52-year-old Gerald Simons, a cab driver. In separate incidents, Van Den Borre murdered both men on a Fort Lauderdale beach by firing a single shot to the head. He taunted police detectives with phone calls that gave clues to the killings, telling them, for example, where to find Egan's car. At other times, he begged them to catch him before he killed again. He gave himself up to Fort Lauderdale police on January 12.

Van Den Borre cooperated extensively with police. He explained that his motive for the murders was revenge against his lover in Washington, and he consented to videotaped reconstructions of the crimes. Wrangling over diplomatic immunity extended only to the question of whether he would be tried in Belgium or the U.S. The matter was settled when the Belgian embassy waived immunity because prosecutors for the state of Florida, which officially supports capital punishment, agreed not to seek the death penalty. On August 15 and August 23, Van Den Borre was convicted of first-degree murder in the Broward County court of Circuit Judge Russell E. Seay, Jr., who sentenced Van Den Borre to two consecutive life terms in prison, guaranteeing that he will not be eligible for parole for at least fifty years.

---

**Van den Breer, Brian**, See: **Garner, Roy.**

---

**Vargas, Alfredo Enrique**, d.1997, Jamaica, assass. Venezuela's ambassador to Jamaica, Alfredo Enrique Vargas, was shot and killed on November 6, 1997, while lying in his bed inside his Kingston apartment. His wife and two children were in the embassy apartment when Vargas was shot by an unknown assailant. A single and fatal bullet had been fired into his chest. Nothing was disturbed in the apartment and nothing was stolen. An economist before joining Venezuela's diplomatic service, Vargas's father had also been ambassador to Jamaica years earlier. Investigators examining the crime scene could not determine how the assassin got into the secured area.

---

**Vargas Escobar, Diego**, 1933-1989, Col., (unsolv.) mur. Radio journalist Diego Vargas Escobar, working in the drug capital of Medellin, Colombia, stepped from his office on October 17, 1989, as two motorcycles shot past him on the street, both riders firing automatic weapons. The 56-year-old Vargas Escobar was struck by several bullets and killed instantly. Vargas Escobar, who directed a radio program titled Radio Buenos Dias Medellin,

was conducting a broadcast campaign against the drug cartel in cooperation with the government. Vargas was the third journalist believed murdered by Medellin drug lords in 1989.

---

**Varisco, Enzo**, See: **Gambino, Francesco.**

---

**Vaugh, Carolin L.**, See: **Hubbard, Brenda L.**

---

**Venables, Jon**, 1983- , and **Thompson, Robert**, 1983- , Brit., mur. Security cameras in a crowed Liverpool, England, mall recorded, in February 1993, the very nightmare that haunts all parents. Two 10-year-old boys, Jon Venables and Robert Thompson, were shown walking away, hand-in-hand, with 2-year-old James Bulger after the toddler wandered away from his mother while she shopped in a butcher store. Venables and Thompson took Bulger a half mile distant to a construction site and there beat him to death next to a railroad embankment, leaving his body to be run over by a train.

An eyewitness to the murder was ironically another mother who had just rescued her own toddler from two older boys. The Bulger slaying enraged the people of Great Britain, where such heinous crimes are unheard of, England having one of the lowest murder rates in the world. The 10-year-old culprits found little or no sympathy for their callous actions. A grandmother being interviewed about the crime by BBC-TV leaned toward the camera and said, "To be honest, I would bloody hang them!"

Venables and Thompson were later tried as adults, convicted of the murder and given fifteen-year prison sentences. They won an appeal on May 2, 1996, two High Court judges ruling that the sentences imposed upon the two boys by Home Secretary Michael Howard were "unlawful" and ordering the boys to a youth detention center until they reached maturity.

---

**Venditti, Veronica**, 1966- , U.S., attempt. mur. On October 24, 1997, Veronica Venditti faced a twenty-year prison sentence after she was convicted of attempting to murder her 12-year-old son, Jason. A native of Henderson, Nevada, the 31-year-old Venditti had driven with her son to Lake Meade, Nevada, on June 24, 1997. She had earlier given her son some sedatives, which caused him to fall asleep in the back seat of the car.

After parking on a lonely road near Lake Meade, Venditti hooked up a hose to the car's exhaust pipe and fed this through a partially opened window. She then sat in the front seat, waiting for the fumes to kill her and her son. Unexpectedly, Jason Venditti somehow awoke from his stupor, crying out, "Mom, I can't see or breathe." He struggled with the car door and managed to open it. As he stood up in the fresh air, he swooned, falling backward toward the ground, but just at that moment a park ranger, Gary Sebade, who had spotted the parked car and was investigating, caught the boy in his arms.

Then Veronica Venditti came stumbling and coughing out of the car. Ranger Sebade stated later that Venditti was sobbing and uncooperative as she stumbled toward him. He noticed that she had written on her forearm in black ink the words, "God forgive me." Venditti told the ranger, "Don't tell him [Jason] what's going on. I don't want him to know." Both Venditti and her son were rushed to a hospital, where they were given separate care. Venditti, once she reached the hospital, reportedly never asked about the condition of her son. (Jason Venditti would fully recover.)

During her trial for attempted murder, Venditti told a Nevada jury that she wanted to take her son "to a better place," where he would not have to experience the kind of physical and sexual abuse she had endured throughout her life. She then stated that she had no idea that she would try to take her son's life until she reached Lake Meade. Defense lawyers argued through witnesses that Venditti had a personality disorder that caused her to attempt to take her son's life, as well as her own.

Prosecutors however, successfully argued that she had followed a premeditated plan, that Venditti had earlier planned to take Jason to Lake Meade and that she had purchased the hose and other paraphernalia to effect the suicide-murder. Said prosecutor Robert Daskas, "It was pure luck that he [Jason] woke up, realized that he couldn't breathe and had to escape from the car. It was also pure luck that a park ranger happened to see what was happening."

---

**Venezuelan Riots,** prom. 1989, Venez., mob vio. Venezuelan President Carlos Andres Perez, in office only two weeks, announced to the Venezuelan people on February 26, 1989, that strict economic austerity measures, including a 90 percent hike in gasoline prices and a 30 percent increase in bus fares, were imperative if the government was to pay off its $32 billion foreign debt. The announcement sparked three days of rioting in the Venezuelan capital of Caracas, which left 300 people dead and more than 2,000 wounded. It was Venezuela's worst riot in decades.

The austerity package Perez said was required to obtain an International Monetary Fund loan also called for price hikes, a widespread slashing of subsidies, the freeing of interest rates, and a floating currency—which would result in higher prices for imports. A day after the chaos began, Perez ordered an overnight curfew and sanctioned martial law. By the third day, people lined up to buy groceries while others looted department stores and supermarkets. All schools were closed. Public transportation was halted. Litter and trash clogged city streets, which one local paper described as "a giant garbage pail." A week after the rioting, Perez charged industrialized nations with being inflexible in insisting on debt repayment from Venezuela without regarding the nation's inability to pay. "I hope this painful sacrifice by our country will serve for the leaders of the industrial powers to reflect that we are not exaggerating when we say the crisis is serious," he said. Meanwhile, the violence in Venezuela caused other Latin-American leaders to wonder what might happen in their countries. The U.S. offered Venezuela a $450 million loan and Spain gave the struggling country a $50 million loan.

---

**Vernon, Michael**, 1973- , U.S., rob.-mur. On December 19, 1995, Michael Vernon entered the Little Chester Shoe Store in the Bronx, New York, planning to rob the place. He asked to see a pair of size 13½ boots, but when the attendant, as he later said, gave him "a hard time," he produced an automatic weapon and began firing at everyone in the store. Vernon killed five persons and wounded another four people before he was captured by police.

While awaiting trial, Vernon's violent background surfaced through the statements of Ronald Rodriguez, a housing patrolman. Rodriguez told NYPD officials that three times he urged members of the 47th Precinct Detective Squad to take Vernon's statements, and that detectives ignored the requests. According to Rodriguez, when Vernon, five months before the "Bronx Massacre," had been arrested for misdemeanor assault, he offered to talk about a sniper attack on two policemen. Vernon also admitted to Rodriguez that he had murdered a cab driver in 1993. Five detectives in the 47th Precinct denied ever having talked with Rodriguez about Vernon.

At his 1997 trial, Vernon claimed that he was insane at the time of his 1995 robbery-murders. On October 24, 1997, Vernon was found guilty by a New York jury of five counts of first-degree murder and four counts of attempted murder. He was sent to prison for life.

---

**Vesco, Robert Lee**, 1935- , Cuba, fraud-illicit economic activities. The top financial swindler of modern times, Robert Lee Vesco masterminded insider trading and established a Wall Street stock empire in the 1970s, fleeing the U.S. after he was charged with embezzling more than $224 million from stockholders in November 1972. Vesco first fled to San Jose, Costa Rica, where, for five years, he fought off efforts by the U.S. Department of State to have him extradited.

After an attempt on his life, Vesco was ordered to leave Costa Rica. He went to the Bahamas, where he reportedly recouped more than $50 million he had secreted in Bahamian banks. Next he moved to Cuba, where, in 1982, he was protected by the Communist dictatorship of Fidel Castro, reportedly paying off Castro with millions for the state-sponsored sanctuary.

**Robert Vesco, who swindled $224 million and fled the U.S., finally hiding out in Communist Cuba, where, in 1996, he was convicted of fraud and sent to prison for thirteen years.**

Vesco continued to live in splendor, even in poverty-ridden Cuba. He and his Cuban-born wife, Lidia Alfonsa Lauger, lived in an elegantly furnished villa, maintaining a lavish yacht and a private airplane. Instead of living out his life in comfort, however, the fugitive could not resist the urge to swindle. With the help of some Cuban lab researchers, Vesco developed a drug called TX. He attempted to market the drug abroad, claiming that it would eliminate AIDS.

In May 1995, Vesco and his wife were arrested and charged with crimes against the Cuban state, specifically fraud and illicit economic activities. At his August 1996 trial, Vesco gave a long and rambling account of his marketing activities involving TX, denying any guilt, as did his wife. Both were convicted on August 26, 1996. Vesco was sentenced to thirteen years in prison and his wife Lidia received a nine-year sentence. Also See: **Vesco, Robert Lee**, Vol. IV.

---

**Vineland, New Jersey,** 1989, U.S., mob vio. Four people were injured, twenty-three arrested, and nearly forty businesses and twenty cars damaged when at least 200 blacks and Hispanics rioted on August 29, 1989, in Vineland, New Jersey, after the city's chief of police called the fatal police shooting of a black youth "justifiable homicide." Samuel C. Williams, 26, was shot to death on August 27 by white police officer Paul Letizia after Williams allegedly threatened Letizia with a steel bar. Letizia, a seven-year veteran, had been trying to arrest Williams on drug and weapons charges. The event was the first suspect shooting in Vineland, and in an attempt to end the violence, Mayor Harry Curley said neither the shooting nor the rioting signalled underlying racial problems in the city.

---

**Vinson, Michele**, See: **York, Thomas.**

---

**Virginia Beach Riots,** 1989, U.S., mob vio. Officials from the National Association for the Advancement of Colored People (NAACP) blamed Labor Day weekend rioting in Virginia Beach, Virginia, on overzealous state troopers and National Guardsmen. The September 3, 1989, riot began in the city's central business district along the waterfront and spread to other parts of town. Virginia Beach, a predominantly white resort area, had been inundated with thousands of vacationing students, many of them members of fraternities and sororities from black colleges on the East Coast.

The disturbance, marring a decades-long tradition, began shortly after 2 a.m. when crowds of students along the waterfront confronted local police, already dressed in riot gear. Police, saying the youths were blocking traffic, began forcibly pushing them from the street. The students began breaking windows in retaliation, and the violence escalated. At least 100 stores were damaged and dozens more looted during the rock-throwing melee. At the request of Mayor Meyera E. Oberndorf, National Guardsmen were called in to quell the riot. The authorities arrested 160 people, amidst growing criticism from black leaders that the students were targets of racial harassment. "Most of the students feel they were not wanted in this city or welcomed by the city," said Jack W. Gravely of the Virginia chapter of the NAACP. As the celebration became more and more popular with students, it grew less popular with Virginia Beach residents, who requested increased police security each year.

Acting in response to complaints filed by the NAACP, the FBI agreed to review videotapes of the clash between police and students to see if the officers were guilty of using excessive force.

**Visor, Randy**, 1970- , U.S., reck. homicide. On the night of October 17, 1997, three 16-year-old girls from Naperville, Illinois, were returning from pre-homecoming festivities. Their car passed an intersection at New York Avenue and Eola Road in DuPage County when it was struck broadside by a car driven by Randy Visor. All three girls—Allison Matzdorf, Jenni Lynn Anderson, and Jennifer Roberts—were killed upon impact, as was 27-year-old Anna Pryor, who was riding in the passenger seat of Visor's car. Visor himself survived.

Police arrested Visor shortly after coming upon the grisly scene. He had a blood alcohol level nearly twice the legal limit. In other words, Visor was drunk. Tried in June 1998, Visor was convicted of reckless homicide. On August 14, 1998, Visor was sentenced to thirteen years in prison.

---

**Vitale, Francis, Jr.**, prom. 1997, U.S., theft. A lifelong fascination with antique clocks caused Francis Vitale, Jr., an executive with Englehard Corp., to steal more than $12.5 million from his firm. On September 30, 1997, Vitale pleaded guilty in a Newark, New Jersey, courtroom to wire fraud and tax evasion. In addition to a prison sentence, Vitale was ordered to pay the Internal Revenue Service about $3 million.

Vitale stole millions from his firm in order to purchase 140 rare antique clocks from European dealers, having these clocks shipped to a store in New Jersey, which he ran on the side. Vitale had sold more than 200 clocks through Christie's at auctions in New York and London in 1996, raising more than $7.2 million. One eighteenth century clock was purchased for $431,400. In that same year, Englehard Corp. fired Vitale from his position as vice president of strategic development after an internal audit revealed missing funds under his control.

---

**Volgares, Jack**, 1955- , U.S., child endanger.-kid.-mur. A resident of Ironton, Ohio, Jack Volgares abused his 7-year-old stepdaughter, Seleana, shouting at her for the slightest offense. He began yelling at her for doing dishes improperly one night in 1997, causing her to wet her pants. He then violently shoved her and the girl went into convulsions, then lost consciousness and died during the night.

After Volgares discovered his stepdaughter dead, he, with the help of this 28-year-old wife, Mona Volgares, secretly dumped the body in a trash can and then buried the can in the backyard of their home. A short time later the family left town, but relatives working in the yard noticed a strong odor and dug up the body.

On December 5, 1997, Volgares was convicted of murder, child endangerment, three counts of kidnapping and the illegal cultivation of marijuana. He was sent to prison for life.

---

**Vreeland, Jason**, See: **Koskovich, Thomas J.**

# W

**Wachtler, Sol**, 1930- , U.S., blk.-attempt. ext. As chief justice of New York's Court of Appeals, Sol Wachtler was thought to be the exemplary judge, rendering what were thought to be landmark decisions on civil rights for women and the handicapped, on free speech and in banning discrimination. Yet this same judge came to symbolize monumental judicial misconduct, exercising his enormous powers in the most vile and degenerate manner, reducing himself to a lowlife blackmailer and would-be extortionist. His victims were his former mistress and her child.

Judge Wachtler was an imposing figure on the bench, as handsome as any TV judge, with a luxurious head of hair, chiseled features, and a mellifluous baritone voice that commanded attention and respect. He was invariably decisive and knowledgeable, and he was often referred to by the press as "the prince of jurists." Yet beneath the black robe lurked another Sol Wachtler, one who emerged in shadows in 1991.

At that time, Wachtler, who had been married for forty-one years to his wife, Joan, was dumped by his mistress of several years, Joan Silverman, a stunning brunette and one of New York's leading socialites. Silverman, a divorcé, was also one of the leading GOP campaign fund-raisers and a personal friend of President George Bush, who had at one time nominated her for the ambassadorship to Barbados.

Silverman was also a stepcousin to Mrs. Joan Wachtler. She and Sol Wachtler met after Wachtler became the executor of her stepfather's $24 million estate. Silverman and Wachtler began seeing each other and often appeared together in public, but since Silverman was related to Wachtler's wife, few questioned the relationship. In 1991, however, Silverman broke off the affair.

Wachtler responded by making several angry phone calls. Then silence. Some months later, in April 1992, Silverman began receiving phone calls at her Manhattan apartment from someone using electronic devices to disguise his voice. The caller demanded payment for reportedly compromising photos and tapes of Silverman "with a man." The same proposition was made in several letters Silverman received. Silverman's 14-year-old daughter, Jessica, received a condom in the mail on May 11, 1992, from the blackmailer, along with a letter the FBI later stated was full of "offensive sexual references." Finally, the blackmailer specifically told Silverman to place an ad in the New York *Times* to arrange for the payment of $20,000.

Silverman then went to her friend, FBI Director William Sessions, asking for his help. Sessions diverted an entire contingent of agents to the case. Silverman then placed the ad in the *Times* on October 1, 1992, as the caller had instructed (and with the approval of the FBI), arranging to pay the $20,000 for the photos and tapes. The ad gave an unlisted number, which the FBI wire-tapped and monitored around the clock.

On October 3, 1992, the blackmailer called the unlisted number, threatening Silverman once more. The call was traced to the mobile phone in the state-owned car of Judge Sol Wachtler. The calls kept coming from Wachtler as he attempted

**Sol Wachtler (second from left), shown with other retired judges at the 150th anniversary of New York's Court of Appeals in 1997; Wachtler, former chief justice of the court, had been convicted and sent to prison for blackmail, extortion and attempted kidnapping.**

to arrange a pickup of the blackmail money, but soon this turned to extortion and then a kidnapping threat.

On October 7, 1992, Wachtler called Silverman to tell her, "God damn, you better understand me. You're gonna get a letter from me and you better ... do what it tells you to do or ... you're not gonna see your daughter again, you hear me? I'm a sick and desperate man."

The calls kept coming as Silverman, following FBI instructions, took her time in making arrangements for the payoff. This delay incensed Wachtler, who called Silverman again on October 28, 1992, still believing he was protecting his identity through the electronic phone device that distorted his voice. In the October 28 call, Wachtler stated, "If you f--- up ... I promise you it will cost you $200,000 to get your daughter back. How does that suit you?"

The payment was finally set for November 7, 1992. Wachtler told Silverman that he would drop off the incriminating material in a Manhattan alley after he received the $20,000 payment. From the moment Judge Wachtler left his offices in Albany, New York, he was trailed by FBI agents who followed him for 200 miles to the Upper East Side of Manhattan. Here, Wachtler reportedly called an employee of a hair salon close to Silverman's apartment building and offered "a big tip" if that employee would pick up a manila envelope containing the blackmail and extortion payoff.

Wachtler himself never retrieved the money. Instead, after trying to disguise himself by putting on a cowboy hat, he gave $10 to a cab driver to deliver an envelope to Silverman that contained only another threatening letter. He then began driving to his home in Manhasset on Long Island via the Long Island Expressway, FBI agents tailing him. At that time the agents contacted Michael Chertoff, U.S. Attorney for Newark, New Jersey (some of Wachtler's letters to Silverman had been posted from this area), who was in charge of the case. When Chertoff was told that Wachtler was heading home, he told the tailing FBI agents, "Arrest him."

Taken into custody, Wachtler was taken to a medical facility, where he was handcuffed to a psychiatric ward bed for three days before he was formally placed under house arrest, confined to his Manhasset home, and ordered to wear an electronic monitoring bracelet about his ankle. About this time, he called Richard Simons, who had become acting chief judge of the Appeals Court, officially resigning from his judicial post and asking for forgiveness for what he had done to the court's reputation.

Tried for blackmail, extortion and attempted kidnapping (in the instance of threatening to abduct Silverman's daughter), Wachtler was convicted and sent to prison. He served only thirteen months behind bars, however. His attorneys blamed Wachtler's crimes on stress, too many pills and a breakdown of his faculties. Moreover, Wachtler, like most prestigious men sent to prison, emerged with lessons to teach about prison life and the errors of his own ways. In reality, he was a convicted felon promoting himself on the strength of his former judicial stature, a once-illustrious reputation he had permanently smashed. That was the only lesson to learn from Judge Sol Wachtler.

---

**Wagge, Robert**, See: **Schwerin, Russell.**

---

**Wagner, Waltraud**, 1959- , **Leidolf, Rene**, 1969- , **Mayen, Stefanie**, 1939- , and **Gruber, Maria**, 1961- , Aust., mur. Four auxiliary nurses working at Lainz General Hospital in Vienna, Austria, were found guilty of murdering perhaps more than 100 elderly patients from 1982 to 1989, but only after their serial murders were slowly unraveled. All four nurses had been employed at the hospital for many years. Waltraud Wagner, the apparent leader of the group, had been working at Lainz General for almost a decade.

The women cared for elderly patients in the hospital's Ward D, which was made up of open areas and some cubicles where patients were confined to iron beds. Most of these elderly patients were terminally ill, but Wagner and her friends, Rene Leidolf, Stefanie Mayen and Maria Gruber, helped them along into eternity, simply because these patients annoyed them, demanded too much attention or too consistently wet their beds.

To rid themselves of these pesky patients, Wagner and her friends simply administered death in the form of "oral hygiene," or what Wagner called "the mouthwash." In this murder technique, Wagner or one of the others would pinch the nostrils of the patient and pour a large glass of water down his or her throat. Unable to breathe, the lungs would fill up and the patient would literally drown. If patients struggled, the other nurses would hold down their arms and legs. Usually when this was done, Wagner and the others would draw screens around the bed of their in-

tended victim, shielding their actions from others in the open ward.

Death certificates were routinely made out without question in these instances. It was not uncommon for water to be found in the lungs of the dead elderly patients. This murder method was abandoned in early 1989, however, when Wagner felt that she and the others were being watched. Indeed, they were. Sometime earlier the four nurses, as was their habit, went to a local pub to down steins of beer when their shift was over. At one point, they began discussing their victims and how they had reacted as they were being murdered.

Sitting with his back to them at the next table one night was one of Lainz Hospital's leading physicians, Dr. Franz Pensdorfer. He was shocked to hear the nurses describe in detail how they killed their elderly patients. Pensdorfer immediately hired a private detective, first as a worker, then as a patient, to keep Wagner, Leidolf, Mayen and Gruber under surveillance.

When Wagner thought she and the others were being observed, she changed the modus operandi of the murders. From February 1989 onward, she and the other nurses began injecting patients with fatal doses of insulin, glucose and soporifics. Hospital security had been tightened by then and the four nurses were closely watched. When it was determined that a disproportionate number of deaths were occurring in Ward D when the four nurses were on duty, and that insulin in large quantities had been found in many deceased patients, the four nurses were arrested and charged with murder. Wagner was the first to confess to the murders, detailing how she and her fellow nurses had slain their patients.

Dr. Alois Stacher, head of the Vienna hospital system, announced at a press conference that dozens of patients at Lainz Hospital had been killed over a seven-year period (1982-1989). This news shocked the nation and caused thousands of Austrians to immediately begin checking on their elderly loved ones who were patients in hospitals and nursing homes. Stacher had taken great care to state that the murders were not "mercy killings."

"These nurses enjoyed killing," Stacher said, "because it gave them extraordinary power over life and death. They killed patients who had become a nuisance to them, who had angered them, or who posed special problems. At first, the killings were one every two or three months, but later rose to one a month, until their [the nurses] remarks were overheard in that bar and an investigation began."

Stacher went on to describe how the "drowning" technique had been employed. He then stated that Wagner had admitted to at least twenty-two murders, as many as she could remember. Wagner admitted, Stacher said, that she often worked alone, but many times had the help of the other three nurses when killing patients. He concluded ruefully, "So many were killed that Wagner could only remember a handful!" The actual death count from these hospital serial murders was never fully realized, but estimates had it that more than 100 persons had been slain.

All four nurses were brought into a Vienna, Austria, court in March 1989 and were found guilty of numerous murders. Wagner was sentenced to life in prison, as was Leidolf. Mayen was sent to prison for twenty years and Gruber was given a fifteen-year sentence.

**Wahiid, Zakii**, 1955- , U.S., mur. A resident of Aurora, Illinois, Zakii Wahiid was convicted of first-degree murder in December 1996, found guilty by a Kane County jury of killing his girlfriend, Mona Lee Vaughn, after terrorizing her over a two-year period. Wahiid had been sentenced to prison for thirty-eight years. The Illinois Appellate Court, however, in November 1998, set aside Wahiid's conviction on the grounds that the defendant was denied his rights under the state's Speedy Trial Act, which requires prosecutors to bring a defendant to trial within 120 days of his arrest.

In Wahiid's case, he was not brought to trial until 397 days after his arrest. Under the law, the defense must request or explicitly agree to a continuance, and apparently in Wahiid's case this did not happen. The state planned to have the Appellate Court reconsider its ruling and, failing that, appeal the matter to the Illinois Supreme Court. Should those appeals fail, Wahiid, a convicted murderer, could walk free from his jail cell at Stateville Prison thirty-five years before his sentence is due to end. State appeals are still pending at this writing.

**Wainwright, Anthony Floyd**, See: **Hamilton, Richard Eugene**.

**Walden, David**, 1965- , and **Daniels, Shawn**, 1956- , civil rights viol. In September and October 1991, and on the night of January 20, 1992, in dark celebration of Martin Luther King's birthday, David Walden and Shawn Daniels, two white men, drove through the predominantly black neighborhoods of St. Louis, Missouri, spraying more than fifty black persons with Kool-Aid from a high-pressure fire extinguisher.

Not only did Walden and Daniels repeatedly commit these hate crime attacks, but, in their September 1991 attack, they videotaped their victims, many of whom were knocked down by the high-pressure spray. At the time of this attack, Walden and Daniels shouted out racial slurs at their victims and laughed as they sprayed them to the ground. The video was taped at the time by a third occupant of the car, Deanna Powers, then married to Walden.

Walden, of Ellisville, Missouri, and Daniels, a resident of Fenton, Missouri, were charged with civil rights violations and, on February 10, 1995, pleaded guilty in U.S. District Court in St. Louis, facing one-year prison sentences and fines. According to the U.S. Department of Justice, there are about 500 such hate crimes occurring in the U.S. each year.

**Waldholtz, Joseph**, 1947- , U.S., fraud. Joseph Waldholtz, the husband and campaign manager for Enid Greene Waldholtz, U.S. Congresswoman from Utah and once a rising star in the GOP, was indicted on May 2, 1996, for fraud in writing numerous worthless checks in early 1995 to make it appear that there were substantial deposits in two separate bank accounts belonging to Waldholtz and his wife. Rep. Waldholtz had filed for divorce from her errant husband three days after Waldholtz

disappeared on November 11, 1995. He resurfaced six days later to be arrested for fraud.

Waldholtz had already been jailed on March 28, 1996, charged with stealing $600,000 from his grandmother. He apparently defrauded his wife's relatives of millions, and was thought to have illegally financed his wife's 1994 campaign.

On the day Waldholtz was charged with bank fraud, Enid Greene stated that she was innocent of her husband's crimes, saying that he had "criminally victimized a long line of people who trusted him," and she applauded his indictment, adding that it was "the first step toward justice in that regard." In March 1996, Rep. Waldholtz announced that she would not seek a second term.

On November 7, 1996, Joseph Waldholtz pleaded guilty to bank fraud, failing to report campaign contributions, making false statements to the federal election agency (which caused his wife to file a false 1993 tax return), and was sentenced to thirty-seven months in prison. Enid Greene was present at the sentencing, her political career in ruins. She wept, then stated, "I needed to be here today to end this chapter of my life ... He [Waldholtz] is a very sick man ... I don't get any satisfaction from [the sentencing]."

**Waldron, John**, 1959- , and **Smith, Bryan**, 1969- , and **Eshom, Paul**, 1957- , U.S., rob.-mur. Twenty-six-year-old Kathy Waldron of McHenry County, Illinois, threw her husband, John, out of their house in August 1988 out of frustration with his cocaine addiction. On September 6, Waldron used cocaine and alcohol with his friends, Bryan Smith, 20, and Paul Eshom, 32. When they ran out of drugs, they decided to rob a convenience store to get money.

Eshom supplied handguns for the three and drove them to a gas station mini-mart in unincorporated Lake County just outside the Chicago suburb of Wheeling. Smith and Waldron went inside and took $226 from the cash register. Waldron shot attendant Thomas Goings, 26, at point-blank range with a .44-caliber revolver. "The guy looked at me like I was scum, so I shot him," Waldron said later. The three bandits drove to suburban Rolling Meadows, where they purchased more cocaine. Smith and Waldron were arrested eighteen hours after the minimart killing when they held up six people outside a pizzeria in Wheeling.

Eshom agreed to turn state's evidence against Waldron on January 23, 1989, in return for lighter sentencing. Smith pleaded guilty the following May 10 and also agreed to testify against Waldron. Eshom received a twenty-year sentence, but Smith got the maximum for armed robbery under Illinois law, sixty years. Waldron went on trial in June. The jury needed only six and a half hours of deliberation to find him guilty. The jury deadlocked in their four-hour deliberation about capital punishment, with nine jurors favoring Waldron being put to death and three opposing it. As the jury must be unanimous to impose the death penalty, Circuit Judge William Block announced on July 27 that Waldron would serve life without possibility of parole on the murder charge, plus sixty years on the armed robbery charge—the stiffest sentence allowable in Illinois next to death.

**Walgreen, Loren**, prom. 1998, U.S., drugs-prost. Loren Walgreen, the daughter-in-law of the retired chief executive of the Walgreen's drugstore chain, had a history of drug abuse. which was exposed in May 1997 when she left her 2-year-old son unattended to buy heroin from an undercover Chicago police officer. She was arrested and convicted of child endangerment and attempted possession of a controlled substance. Sentenced to jail, Walgreen's sentence was reduced to eighteen months of probation and 180 days of home confinement in November 1997.

On October 7, 1998, however, Walgreen was again arrested, this time for prostitution, as she solicited two undercover Cook County Sheriff's officers, getting into their car in Cicero, Illinois, and offering sex for $40. Walgreen, who had already lost a custody battle for her two young children (who went to live with her former in-laws, Charles Walgreen III and his wife Kathleen), was sentenced to a year in prison on January 11, 1999, for prostitution, not completing her court-ordered drug treatment and violating her curfew.

---

**Walker, Neville George**, 1954- , and **Chignell, Renee Melanie**, 1970- , New Zea., mur. Renee Chignell's former classmates in the western suburbs of Auckland, New Zealand, described her as a young woman who was extremely self-possessed, attractive, outgoing and popular. No one believed her to be the kind of girl who would end up working in a massage parlor as a "bondage and domination" (B & D) mistress for older men. In 1988, she went to work as "Sasha," indulging the fantasies of wealthy men who frequented the vice district of Remuera. Chignell earned $100-$200 per session. "She loved it," recalled a co-worker. "She was a natural and really enjoyed her work. She was hungry for the money, too—that's why she set up her own business."

Chignell's live-in boyfriend, Neville George Walker, a concrete layer, did not approve of her activities. "I don't even go to massage parlors," he said. "I wouldn't waste my time or money." He did not interfere, however, hoping that Chignell could earn enough money so that they could leave New Zealand at some future time. Walker later told police that he was not involved in the business directly, even though his name appeared in a newspaper advertisement promoting Chignell's services. Peter Plumley-Walker, a cricket umpire who noticed the ad in the paper, dropped by the couple's residence on January 27, 1989, for a private B & D session with "Mistress Dominique" (Chignell). During the session, 19-year-old Chignell chained the man to the wall of the bondage room. During the sexual antics that followed, Plumley-Walker died. Neville Walker later told police that he believed the man had suffered a heart attack. Failing in his attempt to revive the 51-year-old umpire with cardiac massage, Walker panicked. He packed the body into the car and drove to the Walkato River in Taupo, where he dumped Plumley-Walker.

On April 29, Neville Walker and Renee Chignell were arrested and charged with murder. A medical examiner believed the cause of death resulted from compression to the neck. The trial began before Justice Hillyer and a jury of seven women and five men in Auckland on December 1, 1989. At issue was

whether there was ample evidence to convict the couple on a charge of willful murder. "The defense case is that this was accidental death," explained Stuart Grieve, counsel for the defense. "There was no intent to kill. It was not murder, not manslaughter—it was accidental death." Prosecutor Bruce Squire contended that evidence showed that Plumley-Walker's murder "was not inconsistent with death by drowning." On December 21, the pair were convicted of murder and sentenced to life in prison.

---

**Wallace, Amanda**, 1965-1997, U.S., suic.-mur. Like many unmarried minority women, Amanda Wallace, single and black, found it impossible to cope with parenthood. She had lived a loveless, abused childhood, and when raising her two small children in Chicago, she had repeated bouts with mental instability. Chicago officials filed many documents detailing Wallace's psychotic behavior, wild rages and explosive violence. Her son Joseph was the subject of her wrath to the point where he was placed in a foster home in Park Ridge, Illinois. There, Joseph Wallace received loving care from foster parents Michael and Faye Callahan.

Yet, Joseph was returned to his mother's care under the guidelines of the family preservation movement by the Illinois Department of Children and Family Services (DCFS), despite desperate pleas from the Callahans and their warnings that Wallace was not only an unfit mother but dangerous.

A few months later, on April 19, 1993, Amanda Wallace, in a fit of rage over her son's conduct, had him stand on a stool and tied a cord around his neck, the other end of which was tied to an overhead beam. As his baby brother played on the floor beneath him, 3-year-old Joseph saw his mother wave goodbye to him and then kick the stool from beneath his slender frame. He dangled in space, strangling to death as Amanda Wallace looked on.

Arrested and charged with murder, Wallace was sent to prison. On Saturday, August 2, 1997, Wallace tore a strip of cloth from her robe in her cell at Dwight Women's Prison and strangled herself. She was found alive and rushed to a hospital, where she died the following day.

---

**Wallace, Andre**, 1979- , U.S., mur. On January 17, 1994, 39-year-old Herbert Handy was house-sitting for a real estate firm at 825 N. Lawndale Avenue in Chicago, Illinois, when he spotted Andre Wallace, who, according to prosecutors, was then acting as a lookout for a drug dealer. Handy and Wallace got into a verbal argument, which continued when Handy entered the house and shouted down to Wallace from a second-story window, challenging him to break into the locked home. Wallace climbed inside the building through a rear window to be confronted by Handy, who was holding a baseball bat. Wallace shot Handy three times, killing him, according to statements he later gave police.

Police first arrested Wallace at about 8 p.m. on January 19, 1994, taking him to the Harrison area police station, where he was reportedly held inside a locked interrogation room, not charging him with Handy's arrest until the following morning at 4:30 a.m. Wallace was convicted of Handy's murder in 1996 and given a 26-year prison sentence.

On September 21, 1998, however, Wallace's attorney won an appeal from the Illinois Appellate Court which ruled that Wallace, 15 years old at the time of his arrest, had been held illegally at the time of his confession. The conviction was reversed and sent back to a lower court. The court held that officers did not have probable cause to arrest Wallace before his incriminating statements and that his presence at the police station "escalated to an involuntary seizure prior to his formal arrest." The Wallace case remains undetermined at this writing.

---

**Wallace, George Kent** (AKA: The Paddler), 1941- , U.S., mur. In February 1987, the body of 15-year-old William Eric Domer of Fort Smith, Arkansas, was found in a pond near Pocola, Oklahoma. He had been stabbed and beaten to death. In November 1990, 14-year-old Anthony McLaughlin, who had earlier disappeared from Van Buren, Arkansas, was found dead, stabbed and beaten, in the very same pond outside Pocola, Oklahoma, where the Domer boy had been found three years earlier. George Kent Wallace was identified as having been seen with the McLaughlin boy shortly before his disappearance. He was picked up and brought in for questioning, and a strong case was put together that saw him convicted.

In 1991, Wallace was given the death penalty in Oklahoma. He was also thought to have murdered two boys in North Carolina in the 1970s, when he worked in that state as a truck driver. Wallace's modus operandi was to drive about and look for young boys who were hitchhiking or were isolated from friends. He would stop his car and tell the boy that he was a police officer investigating a burglary and order the boy into his car for questioning. Once inside the car, if he believed no no one was watching, Wallace then drove the unsuspecting boy to a remote area and murdered him. Sometimes he would simply paddle the boys he picked up as a warning not to hitchhike and then release them. He thus earned the moniker "The Paddler." Wallace presently awaits execution in Oklahoma.

---

**Wallace, Henry Lewis**, 1966- , U.S., rape-mur. Over a two-year period, 1992-1994, Henry Lewis Wallace, a black man, raped and murdered nine North Carolina women, also black, selecting victims that mostly worked at fast-food restaurants where employee turnover was high. When these women vanished, few took notice. Police identified Wallace as a suspect and charged him with the murders. On January 7, 1997, Wallace was convicted in Charlotte, North Carolina, of twenty-eight felonies and nine counts of murder. He was sentenced to death.

---

**Wallace, John**, 1944-1989, U.S., mur. John Wallace arrived for work at the Coca-Cola West Metro Sales Center in Marietta, Georgia, on July 7, 1989, only to be told by his supervisor that he was being fired after twenty-three years as a route salesman. Apparently it was too much for the 45-year-old Georgian to bear. Wallace cleaned out his locker and left the plant, only to return a short time later carrying a handgun. He turned the gun on the two men responsible for his dismissal, Maurice McCluskey and Al Parsons, and shot both of them in cold blood.

Wallace then took a hostage at gunpoint and barricaded himself inside the company office for the next seven hours while the police attempted to negotiate with him. The standoff ended early the next morning after a canister of tear gas was fired into the building. John Wallace agreed to surrender to authorities, but when he emerged from hiding, he brandished two guns and began firing wildly at police. The shots were returned, and one of them cut down Wallace in his tracks. The critically wounded gunman was removed to Cobb General Hospital, where he later died. The hostage was unhurt.

---

**Wallace, Lawrence**, 1970- , and **Peacock, Taki**, 1978- , U.S., kid.-mur. Lawrence Wallace and Taki Peacock, two black thugs living on Chicago's South Side, stalked 60-year-old Rufus Taylor, the black owner of a successful electrical firm. Taylor caught the attention of Lawrence and Peacock while driving about in his 1990 black Jaguar, a car both men intended to steal.

In August 1995, Lawrence and Peacock went several times to Taylor's South Side home, but left because neighbors appeared to be watching them. Some time later the pair returned and slipped inside Taylor's garage, waiting for him to return from work. When he did, they held him at gunpoint and robbed him, then ordered him into the Jaguar and drove off.

Stopping in Riverdale, Illinois, Wallace and Peacock allowed Taylor to get some things from the trunk of his car. As he reached down to retrieve his jacket, Wallace shot him in the face. The thieves then drove away, believing Taylor dead. Though the bullet had entered his carotid artery and jugular vein, Taylor still managed to stagger 400 feet to an intersection, where he hailed a motorist. Rushed to a hospital, he died three days later, but not before identifying his kidnappers and killers.

Both Wallace and Peacock were convicted of kidnapping and murder, and on August 26, 1998, Wallace was sentenced by Judge Richard Samuels to life in prison. Peacock, the day earlier, was sentenced to eighty years in prison. Prosecutor Kathy Bankhead summed up the case: "It was a horrible waste and a senseless crime."

---

**Wallace, Stephen**, See: **Privaky, Seth Stephen**.

---

**Wallach, E. Robert**, 1934- , and **Chinn, W. Franklyn**, 1942- , and **London, Rusty Kent**, 1943- , U.S., rack. E. Robert Wallach, a friend and legal adviser to former Attorney General Edwin S. Meese III, entered a plea of not guilty to a twenty-one-count indictment stemming from his employment as a consultant with Wedtech Corporation, the Bronx military contractor charged with illegal influence peddling in government contracts. The charges against Wallach, a 55-year-old San Francisco personal injury attorney who acted as Wedtech's "mole in Washington," included racketeering, conspiracy, fraud, and receiving illegal payments and payoffs. Wallach's co-defendants, W. Franklyn Chinn, 47, and Dr. Rusty Kent London, 46, also pleaded not guilty to the twenty-one-count indictment. The men were tried in Manhattan.

The bulk of the evidence presented in the trial, which began on April 28, 1989, were memoranda and letters written by Wallach to Edwin Meese. Wallach's correspondence was so copious that U.S. District Judge Richard Owens requested at the end of the trial's first week that the prosecution cease reading the documents into the court record verbatim and summarize them instead. In the second week of July, Meese made an unexpected appearance to testify on Wallach's behalf. He denied being asked by Wallach for, or giving, special treatment to Wedtech while in his post as counselor to President Ronald Reagan or as attorney general. Meese, who had known Wallach since they were law students together in the 1950s, was cleared of any wrongdoing in the ongoing Wedtech scandal. Wallach was alleged to have defrauded Wedtech by concealing his lobbying fees within false legal fees.

After three months of testimony, a jury deliberated seven days before finding Wallach guilty on August 8 of racketeering and fraud, but acquitted him of a second racketeering conspiracy charge. The jury found Wallach guilty of illegally receiving $425,000 of the $525,000 that the prosecution claimed he had received from Wedtech to gain Edwin Meese's help in obtaining government contracts. He was ordered to forfeit the $425,000. Chinn and London were convicted of racketeering, racketeering conspiracy, and fraud in connection with over $1 million worth of payments made to them by Wedtech.

All three defendants were sentenced on October 16, 1989. Wallach received six years in prison and a fine of $250,000. Chinn was sentenced to three years in prison and was fined $100,000. London was sentenced to five years in prison and was fined $250,000. London and Chinn were also ordered to forfeit the $1.1 million they received from Wedtech. See: **Wedtech Scandal.**

---

**Walther, Stephen**, See: **Compean, Aaron F.**

---

**Wang, Stephen,** 1965- , and **Cronin, Jerome B.**, 1965- , U.S., fraud. Stephen Wang met Jerome B. Cronin when they were undergraduates at the University of Illinois in 1986. Both men became stockbrokers, Cronin in Chicago and Wang on Wall Street. On January 31, 1989, U.S. District Court Judge Richard Owen of New York ordered Wang to repay $127,585 and Cronin to repay $20,000, which they made on illegal inside trades by sharing information between their offices. Neither admitted to any wrongdoing under the agreement, but Cronin allegedly dealt in securities of at least six companies using information that Wang had given him. Wang was convicted of fraud in October 1988 and sentenced to three years in prison. (Editor's Note: Complete details of this case can be found in the *Encyclopedia of World Crime,* Vol. IV.)

---

**Wang Youcai**, 1966- , and **Qin Yongmin**, 1954- , China, Case of endangering state security. In mid-December, 1998, Wang Youcai and Qin Yongmin, two of China's leading dissidents, were charged with endangering state security. Both Wang and Qin had attempted to set up the China Democracy Party, an opposition party to the Communist dictatorship which had ruled China since the late 1940s after the fall of Chiang Kai-Shek's regime. Wang, the actual founder of the new party, had been a student at Beijing University in 1989, and had taken part in the pro-democracy demonstrations in Tiananmen Square, which had been ruthlessly suppressed by the Communists. For his role in that political uprising, Wang had served a year in prison, 1991-1992.

Chinese dissident Wang Youcai, tried and sent to prison in China for attempting to start a political party opposed to the country's Communist dictatorship.

Wang was charged with "colluding with foreigners" in attempting to set up the opposition party, illegally sending e-mail to "foreigners," and using a computer which had been purchased with "foreign money." His ally, Qin, was not even given a copy of the indictment against him before he and Wang were brought to a closed trial where the press was barred and no

Qin Yongmin, longtime political activist in China, who was imprisoned for trying to set up a democratic party with Wang Youcai in 1998.

news of the ongoing events was reported. Both men were given prison terms. Also See: **China**; **Chinese Democracy Protests, 1989**.

---

**War Crimes, Yugoslavia**, 1990s. In the savage civil wars encompassing many Yugoslavian provinces and separate Slavic states throughout the 1990s, unspeakable atrocities were committed on both sides, but mostly, according to most reports, by Serbian or Croatian forces or individuals who sought to eradicate Muslims in the national federation through what they loosely termed "ethnic cleansing." They committed war crimes or crimes against humanity that included mass murder, rape, and wholesale destruction of villages and towns. So oppressive was Serbia's role in this "ethnic cleansing" that it led to United Nations (U.N.) sanctions and later widespread bombings of Serbian military strongholds and the Yugoslavian capital, Belgrade, in 1999, and the labeling of militant Yugoslavian president Slobodan Milosevic as the leading war criminal.

Of the thousands of documented war crimes, the most notorious committed by Bosnian Serbs, in fact the worst since World War II, was the mass extermination of 7,500 Muslim men and boys taken by Serbian forces in the town of Srebrenica. In 1996, 480 bodies of those taken from this town and slaughtered were exhumed, but it took U.N. investigators more than two years to discover the whereabouts of the bodies of the remaining victims. Investigators, aided by U.S. (NSA) satellites that can locate bodies decomposing underground, finally discovered the remaining corpses. They had been dug up with giant earthmovers by the Serbs and reburied as far as ten miles from the original site of executions. About a dozen such secret burial sites with telltale discolored earth and riddled with land mines were uncovered by U.N. investigators on May 12, 1998.

Many Serbian, Bosnian and Croatian leaders were later indicted by a U.N. international tribunal in The Hague, which meted out justice for war crimes and crimes against humanity in Yugoslavia during the prolonged civil wars in many provinces. These included Radovan Karadzic, a Bosnian Serb leader who stood accused of genocide; Ratko Mladic, commander of the Bosnian-Serb army, accused of genocide; Simo Zaric, a Bosnian Serb, accused of expelling hundreds of non-Serbs from Bosanski Samac; Mirjan Kupreskic, a Bosnian Croat, who was accused of murdering a man and then burning his family alive in the village of Ahmici; Marinko Katava, a Bosnian Croat accused of murdering his Muslim and Croat neighbors in Vitez; Radovan Stankovic, a Bosnian Serb who was a police officer in Foca and who was accused of establishing a rape motel into which young Muslim women were herded and each attacked by dozens of Serbs; Veselin Sljivan, a Serbian officer teaching at the Belgrade Military Academy, who was accused of attacking a hospital in Vukovar; and Gojko Jankovic, a Bosnian Serb accused of supervising gang rapes of Muslin women in Foca.

The atrocities, massacres and crimes committed in strife-torn Yugoslavia were not confined to Serbs, Croats or Bosnians. Muslims, too, were found guilty of such crimes. Indicted by the U.N. international tribunal were Hazim Delic and Esad Landzo, bosnian Muslims who guarded Serb prisoners at Celebici prison and who were accused of murdering prisoners. So, too, were Zejnil Delalic and Zdravko Mucic. Also See: **Dokmanovic, Slavko**; **Erdemovic, Drazen**; **Furundzija, Anto; Gagovic, Dragan; Jelisic, Goran; Krstic, Radislav; Tadic, Dusan.**

---

**Ward, Julie,** 1960-88, Kenya, Case of (unsolv.) mur. British tourist and amateur photographer Julie Ward, 28, was reported missing by friends in the Masai Mara game reserve in Kenya on September 6, 1988. Julie's father, John Ward, a wealthy hotelier from Suffolk, England, flew to Kenya to find his daughter. Shocked to find that no rescue operation had been mounted, he used his own resources to hire five airplanes and a helicopter to provide aerial reconnaissance of the 565-square-mile game preserve.

The Masai Mara is one of the largest wildlife preserves in the world. Half a million North American and European visitors visited the preserve in 1988, bringing $360 million into the Kenyan economy, making tourism the largest industry in this struggling third-world country. Government officials put a high priority on making tourists feel safe in the preserve, restricting their movements and warning them not to leave their motor vehicles because of the dangerous animals that roam freely there.

Julie Ward was nearing the end of an extended vacation that took her to various parts of Africa. She was an experienced traveller who was well aware of the rules of survival in the bush. On September 2, she arrived at the Masai Mara range accompanied by Glen Burns, an Australian marine biologist she had met in Kenya. When their Jeep broke down the next day, Ward and Burns camped overnight at the nearby Mara Serena lodge. There was an airstrip nearby, from which Burns got a flight to Nairobi in the morning. He promised to arrange for a fuel pump to be delivered while Ward waited with the Jeep.

The car trouble was discovered to be an electrical problem and was easily fixed. Late in the afternoon of September 6, Ward drove off alone to the Sand River Camp to pick up some tents she had left there before continuing to Nairobi. Camp attendant David Nchoka later admitted that he forged her signature in the park registry, which placed her departure at 2:37 p.m., because, he said, "she forgot to do so." She told the other campers that she planned to spend the night in the Keekkorok Lodge a few miles to the north, and make the main journey to the capital the next morning. Her friends, concerned for her safety, warned her against making the trip alone. She was reported missing when she did not arrive at the lodge.

The privately financed search led to the discovery of her remains several miles southeast of Sand River Camp, on a line parallel to the Tanzanian border. Searchers found her lower jaw, which had been cut through in the center, and part of her left leg. Her charred bones were discovered in a campfire and had distinct scars on them. After the discovery of her body, chief game warden Simon Makallah joined the search and found Ward's abandoned Jeep within a few hours. It was mired in the mud of a dried-up riverbed. Scrawled in mud on the top of the jeep was the distress signal "SOS." The car was dredged from the riverbed, then washed and examined. As a result, any forensic evidence that may have been recovered from it was destroyed.

In the car were provisions, including food, beer, binoculars, a map of the park, and athletic shoes. Among the ashes found with Ward's remains were a pair of sandals, shreds of her clothing, and canisters for camera film. The riverbed was half a mile from the main road and six miles from where the bone fragments were found. No one could account for why she had left the road. Warden Makallah testified that a Jeep should have been able to negotiate the riverbed easily, unless the front wheel drive were disconnected. The gas tank was half empty, although the vehicle had supposedly been driven only thirty-two miles since its last fill-up, and a utility gas can was missing.

A postmortem report on the bone fragments contained ambiguities. The original typewritten report by Dr. Adel Youssef Shakir, an Egyptian pathologist, noted that the bones were "cleanly cut," but these words were replaced by "torn and cracked," crudely typed over them. Kenya's chief pathologist, Dr. Jason Kaviti, acknowledged that he personally altered the document to clarify what his assistant Shakir meant to say in his limited English. British diplomat John Ferguson met with Dr. Shakir on September 21, and Shakir told him, "It was clear from my postmortem examination, beyond any doubt, that both the lower left leg and the jaw had been cleanly cut, probably with a sharp instrument such as a panga, before an attempt to burn them had been made." Chemical analysis of the ashes revealed that her dismembered body had been burned with gasoline and that she had been killed less than forty-eight hours before her body was found seven days after she disappeared.

Nevertheless, the police investigation led by Kenyan CID superintendent Munchiri Wanjau concluded that Julie Ward spent at least one night with the disabled Jeep in the riverbed before setting off into the bush for help, then was attacked and devoured by wild animals at the site where her bones were recovered.

Only John Ward's dogged efforts kept the case from being closed. He insisted on investigating the inconsistencies in the case, which led to an inquest on August 9, 1989. One of the first witnesses was wildlife photographer Paul Weld-Dixon, a friend of Julie Ward. He testified that Dr. Shakir had shown him her bones and stated that "the leg and jawbone have been severed with a sharp instrument ... That makes it a case of murder."

The second day of the inquest brought the revelation that camp attendant Nchoka had been secretly questioned by Kenyan police, but not arrested. Police Superintendent Wanjau accused Nchoka of murder but because of insufficient evidence was unable to hold him. More startling information came forth when the inquest was told that nomadic Masai tribesmen reported hearing screams on the night of September 12, six days after Julie Ward disappeared and the day before her scant remains were found. They were also said to have found a body, but further details were not forthcoming, and the Masai were believed to have moved on into Tanzania long before the inquest was convened.

John Ward's barrister, Byron Georgiadis, introduced medical evidence showing that Julie Ward was alive until September 12. The remains were sent to a Cambridge University pathologist, Professor Austin Gresham, who later reported that Julie Ward had most certainly been decapitated from behind, and her leg and lower jaw had been severed with a sharp instrument.

Simon Makallah took the stand, and soon came to look more and more like a suspect. When asked why he did not mount a search for Ward immediately upon her being reported missing, he claimed that neither he nor most of his dozens of rangers knew how to drive. After further questioning, which brought out discrepancies in his earlier testimony, Makallah finally admitted he could drive, but that he had no license, and lied because he wanted to avoid prosecution. He could not explain how he knew Ward's Jeep was disabled without having examined it, nor how he was able to immediately find her body after her Jeep was discovered miles away. It was also discovered that Makallah had been called to Nairobi for a private conference with President Daniel Arap Moi.

As details of the case emerged, it became more and more an embarrassment to the Kenyan government and a source of international friction between Kenya and Britain. Diplomatic concerns arose in London as to whether backing John Ward against the Kenyan police might alienate what it regarded as the only friendly country left among its former African colo-

nies. The Kenyan government itself faced the difficulty of its biggest industry being damaged by news of another death on the game preserve—three other tourists were murdered in July 1988, and naturalist George Adamson soon after. Kenyan officials admitted that the case ought to have been investigated as a murder from the beginning, rather than covered up. Kenyan public opinion, which at first accepted the police findings, swung gradually to John Ward's side.

Chief Magistrate Mango ruled on October 27, 1989, that Julie Ward's death was murder by person or persons unknown. However, he went on to say that he saw no reason to investigate the matter further. The preponderance of evidence indicated that Ward was abducted from her Jeep on September 6, 1988, held for six days, then killed on September 12, and her Jeep left in the riverbed after her death to cover the tracks of the killer or killers. No further investigation was ordered. Still, John Ward regarded the finding as a victory, and stated that he had a far higher opinion of Kenyan justice due to Magistrate Mango's courage and integrity in making a politically difficult ruling. Encouraged by the decision, he continued his pressure on authorities to reopen the case. After spending more than a year of his time and over $100,000 of his own money, John Ward learned on December 12, 1989, that Kenyan police were beginning a full murder investigation, fifteen months after the victim's death.

A final mystery remained, less gruesome than the first. In early September 1989, as part of his private investigation, John Ward visited the last site where his daughter was known to have camped. On the spot where Julie was last seen alive were a bunch of cellophane-wrapped, freshly watered flowers. "The site was almost deserted," John said. "I have no idea who left the flowers or why."

---

**Ward, Levern**, See: **Williams, Jaqueline Annette**.

---

**Ward, Paul** (AKA: Hippo), 1964- , Ire., drugs-mur. In June 1996, Veronica Guerin, a well-known Irish crime reporter, came under physical attack from drug dealers she was exposing in the media. The 36-year-old journalist had been beaten several times and even shot in the leg by thugs trying to silence her. Yet, she continued exposing criminals in Dublin, Ireland. As her car was idling at a stop sign, two men on a motorcycle, Paul "Hippo" Ward and Charles Bowden, came to a stop next to Guerin's car and fired several pistol shots at her, killing her instantly.

Both men were identified, arrested and convicted. Bowden was given a prison sentence and Ward, the actual killer, was sentenced to life in prison on November 27, 1998. Guerin was the first reporter ever to be killed in Dublin. Her murder caused authorities to crack down on the criminal networks operating in the city.

---

**Wardell, Gordon**, 1952- , Brit., mur. Staff workers entering the offices of the Woolwich Building Society at Nuneaton, Warwickshire, England, on September 12, 1994, found the company safe open. More than $30,000 and some blank checks were missing. So, too, was Carol Wardell, the manager. Her half-naked body was found by a motorist later that day sprawled on the grass along a roadway twelve miles from Nuneaton. Police quickly learned that Carol Wardell had been choked to death. They also learned that no forced entry had been made into her offices; that she had, in fact, entered the building at 5:22 a.m., using her personal coded key number; and that she had used her own keys to open the company safe.

Police believed that Carol Wardell had been kidnapped, forced to open the doors of her office and the company safe, and that the kidnapper had then looted the safe and forced Wardell to accompany him, killing her and dumping her body along the road outside of Nuneaton. Officers next went to the victim's home where, to their surprise, they found Gordon Wardell, dressed only in his underwear; he was bound and gagged. Once released, Wardell told a weird story.

On the night of September 11, 1994, he said he had driven to the town of Coventry to mail a letter for his wife and when returning he stopped in a pub for a few drinks. When he arrived home he smelled tobacco smoke, which he thought odd, since neither he nor his wife smoked. When he entered the living room he was shocked to see a man wearing a clown's mask and holding a knife to his wife's throat. Three other men then jumped him, punched and kicked him, pinning him to the floor before knocking him out with some strange-smelling chemical. He remembered nothing more, until police arrived ten hours later to release him. (A clown's mask was later found some distance from the Wardell home, but this was later determined "planted evidence," to throw police off the track.)

Investigators were immediately suspicious in that they knew of no drug, not even chloroform, that would keep anyone unconscious for ten hours. Also, there were no burns or abrasions on the sensitive parts of Wardell's nose that would have been left by a chemical. There was no sign of the fierce struggle between Wardell and his attackers and there were no fingerprints to be found in the home, other than those of Wardell and his wife. Wardell did bear a slight bruise to his stomach where he said one of the intruders had kicked him, but he showed no other signs of the intense beating he said he had been given by the intruders.

Another discrepancy found by detectives was the fact that an automatic cash dispenser in Carol Wardell's office had not been touched, and it had contained much more cash than the safe. A professional gang of thieves would not have made such an oversight. Wardell himself was the primary suspect in the robbery-murder. This was strengthened when police learned that Wardell had never held a steady job and was much in need of cash. In fact, his wife's death would enrich him by $200,000 from her insurance policy, plus her considerable pension would be paid to Wardell by her employer on the event of her death.

Police followed Wardell to note that once he thought he was out of surveillance, he no longer limped from his reported beating, and did not employ the temporary walking stick he used when meeting the press and sobbingly detailing his awful ordeal and his wife's terrible murder. When Wardell arrived at the insurance company headquarters to claim his wife's policy, however, he once again affected the limp and employed the cane.

Then police unearthed Wardell's criminal record dating back to when he was 17 and earned a four-year prison sentence for viciously attacking a teacher's wife in her car with her children present, stabbing her in the neck and almost killing her; she managed to escape with her children by driving off when Wardell momentarily got out of the car, and rushed to a hospital, where a transfusion saved her life.

Also, police learned that Wardell had been visiting Coventry, Birmingham and other towns in the Midlands to keep company with prostitutes throughout the twelve years of his marriage to Carol Wardell. Brought to trial in 1995, Wardell was found guilty of murdering his wife and was sentenced to life imprisonment.

---

**Warmus, Carolyn**, 1964- , U.S., mur. Carolyn Warmus, while attending the University of Michigan, began forming a number of strange attachments to unavailable men. One graduate student even had to ask a court to issue a restraining order against her in 1984 after he was married, but she continued to bombard the man with letters. Warmus moved east to live in Westchester County, New York, where she formed another attachment to a married man, Paul Solomon, a teacher at Greenville Elementary School, where Warmus also worked as a teacher.

Instead of rebuffing Warmus, however, Solomon developed a sexual relationship with her in 1987. Warmus was invited to dinner at the Solomon home, where an unsuspecting Betty Jeanne Solomon was the affable host. Warmus even took the Solomons' daughter on a ski trip. This friendly atmosphere evaporated when Solomon tried to break off the affair. Warmus responded in January 1989 by going to the Solomon apartment in Edgemont, New York, and pumping nine bullets into Betty Jeanne Solomon.

Police investigating the murder of Mrs. Solomon suspected Warmus, who initially claimed that at the time of the murder she had driven to the Treetops Restaurant in Yonkers, New York, to meet Solomon, and that they had had sex in her car. For several months thereafter police kept an eye on Warmus but did not have enough evidence to arrest her. Meanwhile, Solomon had acquired a new girlfriend, and Warmus wrote more than a dozen letters and cards to him, one of them saying, "You are the most important thing in my life."

Prosecutors had been steadily building a circumstantial case against Warmus. Knowing that Mrs. Solomon had been shot with a .25-caliber pistol, officers tracked down a private detective named Vincent Parco. The detective said that he had been hired by Warmus years earlier to trail one of her boyfriends and that, shortly before the murder of Betty Jeanne Solomon, he had sold Warmus a .25-caliber pistol for $2,500.

Though the weapon was never found, Warmus was brought to trial and convicted on largely circumstantial evidence. She was sent to prison for twenty-five years. A 1992 made-for-TV movie, *A Murderous Affair: The Carolyn Warmus Story*, drew fire from Warmus' attorney, who stated that the film might prejudice the appeals he was filing on his client's behalf.

**Washington, Thomas**, 1968- , U.S., mur. After a South Side Chicago man was thrown out of his own house because of his crack cocaine addiction, 71-year-old Olivia Williams, a good Samaritan, offered Thomas Washington shelter, allowing him to live in the upstairs apartment of her two-flat residence. In response, in August 1996, Washington sneaked into Williams' apartment, stabbed his elderly host a half dozen times, then beat her to death with a blunt instrument.

Washington then took her body into his upstairs apartment, where he hid it for several days while he sold off Williams' belongings and furnishings to pay for his drug habit. Police were alerted by neighbors, who reported Williams missing and the fact that her possessions were being sold on the street. Officers found the woman's decomposing body stuffed into a trash can in the back of her building. They promptly arrested Washington and charged him with murder. He was convicted and sentenced to forty years in prison on July 1, 1998, by Judge Vincent Gaughan.

**Washington, Troy**, 1965- , U.S., rape-mur. A former installer for Barksdale Interior Design, a San Diego, California, firm, Troy Washington was laid off by its owner, Deborah Barksdale, an attractive 38-year-old divorcé. Washington, by his own later admission, had stolen Barksdale's key to her North Rim Court condo in an upscale community north of San Diego with the purpose of using it to gain entrance to Barksdale's apartment, where he planned to disguise himself and then rape the shapely woman he had so long desired.

On the Friday night of November 2, 1990, Washington went to Barksdale's apartment wearing dark clothes and a ski mask. He used the stolen key to gain entrance and found Barksdale asleep. He sexually assaulted her, but when she fought him and tried to tear away the ski mask, Washington strangled her. He then took her body into the attached garage and stuffed it into the trunk of Barksdale's car. He stole her money, credit cards and keys to make his crime appear to be a robbery and then left.

Police were called by Barksdale's employees when she failed to show up for work the following Monday. Officers investigated but found nothing in the missing woman's apartment for two days, until checking her car. Forcing the trunk, they found Barksdale's body, naked from the waist down. A check of the neighborhood yielded two reports of a "tall, black man" seen near Barksdale's apartment on Friday night. A security guard in the area said he not only saw the man, but had written down the license plate number of the man's 1989 Pontiac Le Mans.

This allowed detectives to track down Washington easily and bring him into a police station for questioning. After about an hour, Washington shook his head, then said, "Oh, hell, I might as well kill myself." He then admitted raping and murdering Barksdale. He went on to say that "a voice" told him to "put on a mask and rape her. When you're done, walk out. She'll never know what happened."

Charged with rape and murder, Washington was brought to trial in 1992. His lawyers argued that he was temporarily insane at the time of the crime, but court-appointed psychiatrists convinced a jury that Washington was sane. Prosecutors pointed out that Washington's plan was calculating and premeditated, that he stole Barksdale's key long in advance of the crime, and that he had planned for some time to rape the single woman, if not kill her for laying him off. Washington was convicted, and on March 13, 1992, he was sentenced to life imprisonment.

**Wasserstein, Jack**, 1902-1989, U.S., suic-mur. A gathering of elderly women watched in horror as 87-year-old Jack Wasserstein pumped three bullets into his estranged wife, Evelyn, at the May Company Department Store restaurant in Los Angeles on June 21, 1989. A second later, he turned the gun on himself as fifty senior citizens scurried for the exits.

Wasserstein had been married to Evelyn for thirteen years. It was the second marriage for both of them. The elderly couple's relationship began to deteriorate in February 1989, when Wasserstein suddenly stopped talking to his wife. In early March, according to statements given by friends and acquaintances, Wasserstein began yelling at her incessantly and accused the 79-year-old woman of stealing his money.

Evelyn Wasserstein filed for divorce shortly afterward, but Jack kept forcing his way back into their home. Matters stood at an impasse until Evelyn joined her friends for a card game at the May Company's fifth-floor dining room on Wilshire Boulevard, a favored rendezvous for the senior citizens. Nobody paid much attention to Wasserstein as he silently made his way into the restaurant and opened fire. Evelyn Wasserstein was shot in the neck and chest and was pronounced dead on arrival at a local hospital. Her husband died instantly of a single gunshot wound to the head.

**Waterhouse, Alan**, 1952-1998, U.S., mur. On October 10, 1998, Alan Waterhouse, who suffered from multiple sclerosis and was confined to a wheelchair, crawled into the apartment across from his own in Mt. Pleasant, Pennsylvania. Waterhouse clutched a gun, apparently intent on shooting Cheryl Barnhart, whom he had formerly dated. Instead he found Barnhart's 9-year-old son, Jeremy, and her 14-year-old daughter, Cori, who was with a girlfriend.

Waterhouse shot and killed Jeremy Barnhart, wounded Cori Barnhart, and then crawled back into his own apartment. When police arrived, he began shooting at them and threatening to blow them up. To prove his point, he threw a stick of dynamite out of his apartment window, but it failed to explode. As police closed in, Waterhouse killed himself.

**Weaver, Randall** (AKA: Randy), 1948- , and **Harris, Kevin**, 1968- , U.S., weapons viol. A hero to the militia movement in the early 1990s, Randall Weaver, a white separatist, resided in a cabin in Northern Idaho near Ruby Ridge, with his wife Vicki, his 14-year-old son, and Kevin Harris, a friend. In 1992, Weaver and Harris were charged with weapons violations. Federal agents stated that Weaver had illegally hoarded a large cache of weapons (with the implication being that these weapons would later be used to attack government agencies). On August 21, 1992, FBI agents and U.S. Marshals under the command of FBI Special Agent Larry Potts surrounded Weaver's cabin and ordered him and his family to surrender.

Instead of capitulating, Weaver and his friend Kevin Harris exchanged fire with the agents. This firefight continued for some time, with U.S. Marshal William Degan being killed, reportedly by Harris. The federal agents also fired fatal bullets into Weaver's 14-year-old son. As the siege continued, the agents also shot and killed Weaver's wife, Vicki. These killings were later attributed to FBI sharpshooter, Lon Horiuchi. The standoff continued until August 31, 1992, when Weaver and Harris finally surrendered.

Weaver and Harris were tried and acquitted in a federal court in 1993, but the matter did not end there. Weaver sued the federal government on several charges, including wrongful death in the shootings of his wife and child. In August 1995, Weaver was awarded a $3.1 million settlement by the U.S. Department of Justice. The siege at Ruby Ridge, however, went on capturing headlines. The case continued to anger residents in Boundary County, Idaho, where the Ruby Ridge shootout took place, and in many other areas of the country where the FBI raid took on the appearance of overkill or even persecution.

In September 1997, Denise Woodbury, prosecutor for Boundary County, announced that she would charge Lon Horiuchi, the FBI sharpshooter, with manslaughter in the deaths of Vicki Weaver and her son. She also brought a charge of murder against Kevin Harris in the death of U.S. Marshal William Degan. This brought forth staunch support for Horiuchi from FBI Director Louis Freeh, who said the sharpshooter had his "total support and confidence."

Although the FBI had been given a clean slate for Ruby Ridge in a U.S. Department of Justice report issued in 1997 (which specified that sharpshooter Horiuchi had committed no federal crime), lingering allegations had it that agent-in-charge Larry Potts and his deputy Danny Coulson had conspired to cover up the mismanaged operation and had even enacted an illegal shoot-to-kill order right from the beginning of the siege, which resulted in the deaths of Vicki Weaver and her son.

Potts eventually provided an undated memo as proof that he never approved of the shoot-to-kill order, a document Potts claimed he had dictated to an FBI secretary. One report held that investigators had Potts' memo examined by forensic experts who determined that it had been created after the fact and, worse, the FBI secretary stated that she could not recall typing the memo. All of this was labelled "absurd" by Potts' attorney. Potts would later leave the FBI and become a member of a private investigative agency.

The state trial in Idaho was short and to the point. Charges brought against Kevin Harris by prosecutor Woodbury were dismissed by Magistrate Quentin Harden on October 2, 1997. Charges against FBI sharpshooter Len Horiuchi were also dismissed.

**Webb, Walter Anthony**, 1954- , U.S., mur. On October 9, 1994, the bodies of 64-year-old James W. Graves and 51-year-old Aurora Carney were found in Graves' office in the small town of Rector, in northeastern Arkansas, close to the Missouri line. Graves' daughter, who was stopping by to visit her father, found the bodies, her father, lying on the floor clad only in boxer shorts and his long-time lady friend, Carney, a resident of nearby Kennett, Missouri, slumped in a chair wearing only a negligee. She called police and officers soon determined that both victims had been shot to death.

Graves was one of the most important men in Rector, a leading real estate broker who owned several farms and cotton gins. His family and friends had no idea who would want to kill him. Arkansas State Police then visited Carney's ex-husband, who said he had not seen his former wife in some time. He told investigators that his ex-wife had been seeing a man named Walter Anthony Webb, who owned used bookstores in Kennett and in Jonesboro, Arkansas. He said that his wife was a recovering alcoholic. (This was true and known to detectives by then since they had learned Carney and Graves were both alcoholics and had met at an Alcoholic Anonymous meeting.)

Detectives interviewed Webb in Kennett; he seemed genuinely shocked upon hearing the news of Carney's murder. Webb admitted that he had been seeing Carney for years, but that they had their "ups and downs," because of her alcoholism and he also believed that she used drugs. He said he knew Graves, too, because he was a rehabilitation nurse who aided Graves when he fell off the wagon. Officers told Webb to stay in town.

Webb did nothing of the kind. He fled to New Orleans where his van was later found abandoned. A search of the city revealed no clues as to his whereabouts. Then police received a tip from a woman who said that she had gotten two calls from Webb from Florida on October 21 and October 26. He told the woman that he was on the verge of suicide and admitted that he had been present when Graves and Carney were murdered.

Then State Police Investigator Dale Blalock found the murder weapon—which had been tossed into a creek—a .38-caliber weapon which matched the bullets fired at close range into Graves and Carney. The gun belonged to Graves. Webb was formally charged with the murders of Graves and Carney. A police dragnet was set up for Webb, one that was joined by the FBI. Webb, however, made arrangements through a lawyer to turn himself in on January 3, 1995.

Webb's trial began in Paragould, Arkansas, in November 1995. Prosecutors contended that Webb had killed the couple in a jealous rage. Webb took the stand to say that he had confronted the pair in Graves' office-home in Rector and that Graves waved a pistol at him as he staggered about half drunk. Waving the pistol, Graves fired off a shot that accidentally killed Carney, Webb said, and then he and Graves struggled for the gun, which went off three times, one of the bullets killing Graves, the other shots going into the floor. Webb said he then fled the scene, taking the gun and throwing it into a creek.

Prosecutor Brent Davis tore apart Webb's testimony, providing forensic evidence that proved that both Graves and Carney had been killed execution style and that both had been shot at close range, that Webb had fired bullets into the left sides of their heads, blasts so close that they left visible powder burns. Davis also showed a foot-by-foot floor plan of the murder room. There were no bullets fired into the floor, as Webb had claimed.

Moreover, Davis added, there was no struggle between Webb and Graves. Webb stood six-foot-three-inches and weighed 240 pounds. Graves was six inches shorter and weighed only 154 pounds. Webb knew that Graves had a gun and where it was kept from information given to him by Carney. When he entered Graves' office, he obtained the gun and simply executed the couple in a jealous rage. A jury of nine women and three men took three hours to deliberate before returning a guilty verdict. Judge David Burnett sentenced Webb to two life terms in the Judge David with no possibility of parole.

---

**Webb, Troy Lynn**, 1967- , U.S., rape-rob. (wrong. convict.) After serving seven years of a 47-year prison term, 29-year-old Troy Lynn Webb was released with apologies from the state of Virginia for his wrongful conviction for a rape and robbery that occurred in January 1988. Webb had been convicted for robbing and raping a Virginia waitress, based on blood samples and the waitress' eyewitness statements.

Insisting that he was wrongly convicted, Webb, in September 1996, wrote to the Innocence Project at Yashiva University's Benjamin N. Cardoza School of Law in New York. Lawyer Barry Scheck, who had helped to destroy a jury's confidence in the DNA evidence offered in the O.J. Simpson trial, and who was connected with the project, undertook Webb's case.

More sophisticated DNA analysis was applied to Webb's case, new technology that can test and identify factors within the genetic code of organic material. The new test was conducted by the state Division of Forensic Science. Webb had been convicted on a less sophisticated blood serology test conducted from a semen stain on the victim's clothing. The new DNA test proved that the semen could not have come from Webb and Virginia authorities had no choice but to release Webb, despite the fact that the waitress' testimony identified Webb as the assailant.

---

**Webster, Bruce C.**, See: **Hall, Orlando Cordia**.

---

**Wedtech Scandal**, prom. 1989, U.S., brib.-polit. corr. For nearly a decade the Wedtech Corporation of New York was considered to be a trendsetter of American entrepreneurship— a minority-run firm that set an example for small businesses seeking to make their mark in society. Wedtech was founded by John C. Mariotta, the son of Puerto Rican immigrants. Mariotta started his defense-contracting business in a renovated garage in 1965. Ten years later, Wedtech was awarded a series of special no-bid contracts through a Small Business Administration program for minority businesses. By 1985, the company was receiving over $400 million in contracts. But in April 1986, government investigators turned the searchlight on Wedtech activities and discovered that company officials had

retained their minority status through extortion, political payoffs to politicians, and considerable legal pressure. Wedtech was no longer a minority firm, though Mariotta had made a private agreement in 1983 to purchase enough shares of stock to give him controlling interest. The bill for the shares did not come due until 1985, which constituted a fraudulent arrangement in the opinion of government investigators. Wedtech went bankrupt after the investigation started, and 1,500 workers lost their jobs. For years, Wedtech officers had looted the company of its assets. Stocks worth $24 million were sold and the money deposited in FHJ Associates, a company that existed only to pay off lobbyists for Wedtech contracts and to bribe inspectors, union officials, and government officials. Wedtech officers also walked off with $13 million in salaries and bonuses. Due to their greed, everyday operations at the company depended on money from new contracts, since they already had spent or taken available assets.

The trail of dirty money and corruption extended all the way to the White House where Attorney General Edwin C. Meese III was censured for his close ties to E. Robert Wallach, a San Francisco lawyer convicted on four counts of racketeering and fraud on August 9, 1989. Wallach was accused of taking $425,000 in consulting fees for arranging lucrative no-bid contracts for Wedtech in 1981. "They (Wedtech) paid everybody," explained Bronx district attorney Mario Merola, who prosecuted the case. "They thought that was the way of doing business." Wallach was described as the company's "mole" in Washington.

In 1989, nearly two and a half years after Wedtech filed for bankruptcy, Representative Robert Garcia (D-New York) was convicted of extortion and conspiracy for receiving $178,500 in illegal monies from the company. Garcia and his wife introduced former Wedtech vice chairman Mario Moreno to Governor Rafael Hernandez Colon of Puerto Rico in an effort to help him obtain a contract to build ferryboats there. At a private meeting on a terrace in Old San Juan on September 23, 1985, Garcia assured Moreno that everything was going according to plan. Wedtech received the bid, valued at $1.29 million, but the company went bankrupt before any actual work could be performed. Moreno pleaded guilty to charges of conspiracy, bribery, and grand larceny and was sentenced to serve eighteen months in prison. His testimony on behalf of the prosecution helped convict both Representative Garcia and his wife.

Several other prominent Wedtech figures were sentenced to prison in 1989. In August, W. Franklyn Chinn, a former consultant and director, was convicted of fraud and racketeering for using $1.1 million to promote the company's stock. Chinn was a partner of Wallach, and was advanced through the ranks largely through his influence. Federal Judge Richard Owen sentenced Chinn to three years in prison and ordered him to pay a $100,000 fine.

Dr. Rusty Kent London, a Wedtech consultant who was convicted of fraud and racketeering in conjunction with Chinn's scheme to promote company stock, received five years in prison and a $250,000 fine. Bronx Borough president Stanley Simon, who helped Wedtech gain approval from the Board of Education for a lease, allegedly received, in return, $20,000 in campaign kickbacks. He was sentenced to five years and fined $70,000. Other Wedtech figures found guilty and sent to prison included Vito J. Castellano, former commander of the New York State National Guard, one to three years for tax evasion and falsify records; Bernard G. Ehrlich, former head of the 42nd Infantry Division of the New York National Guard, six years and a $222,000 fine for extorting Wedtech stock valued at $1.8 million; Fred Neuberger, former Wedtech president, sentenced to two years and three months for bribery, grand larceny, and falsification of records; Michael B. Mitchell and Clarence Mitchell III, two former state senators from Maryland who accepted $100,000 in bribes for helping steer an investigation away from their Uncle Parren, chairman of the House Small Business Committee. Michael and Clarence Mitchell each received two-and-a-half years in prison and fines of $7,000 and $6,000, respectively.

By the end of October, the government had convicted twenty-eight of twenty-nine Wedtech defendants. Only one conviction was overturned, that of Lyn Nozfiger, who served as one of President Ronald Reagan's aides. (Editor's Note: Complete details of this case can be found in the *Encyclopedia of World Crime*, Vol. IV.) See: **Wallach, E. Robert.**

---

**Weeding, David A.**, 1950- , U.S., rape-mur. The testimony of two women raped fifteen years earlier by convicted California rapist-murderer David Weeding was presented to the jury deciding the penalty for his later conviction. Weeding, 39, was convicted late in November 1989 of the attempted forcible rape of 25-year-old Vickie Linn Petix and the stabbing murder of her husband, Steve Petix. According to testimony given by Petix, on May 20, 1988, Weeding appeared at the door of her El Cajon, California, apartment, claiming to be a member of the building's maintenance staff. Once in the apartment he attacked her, ripping off her clothes with a knife. Petix's husband, a reporter for a local newspaper, came home in the middle of the attack. While Vickie Petix ran for help, her husband struggled with Weeding, who fatally stabbed him.

During the penalty phase of Weeding's trial, the prosecution produced as witnesses two Texas women whom Weeding had raped in 1975 and 1976 while he was serving in the military. Weeding had been convicted of the two rapes, sentenced to twenty-five years in prison, and was paroled after ten years. After Weeding's 1989 conviction, the jury was asked to consider whether he should be given life in prison or death in the gas chamber. The jury deliberated for two and a half days before sentencing Weeding on December 11, 1989, to life in prison without parole.

---

**Weinberg, Sheldon,** 1925- , and **Weinberg, Ronald,** 1947-, and **Weinberg, Jay,** 1954- , U.S., consp.-fraud. Brooklyn dress shop owner Sheldon Weinberg left the garment industry in 1975 when the lease on his shop ran out. He and his sons, Ronald and Jay Weinberg, then set up a medical corporation, though none of them had any medical training. They started a clinic, called the Bedford-Stuyvesant Health Care Corporation, which they founded with a $400,000 loan in 1976, hiring a medical staff to provide health care to the poor people of the area. The Weinbergs later took another loan for the same amount

to open a similar clinic in the Bushwick neighborhood, also in Brooklyn. At the height of their success in 1984-88, the Weinbergs employed twenty-five doctors and twenty-five members of a support staff, and the clinics generated $200,000 a week in false claims.

From 1980-87, the Weinbergs' clinics received between $31 million and $32 million in Medicaid reimbursements. About half of these reimbursements were later determined to be fraudulent. "It was an unprecedented scam in size and sophistication," said James A. Durkin, New York state supervisor of Medicaid claims. "They used an ingenious trick, a computerized system to invent phantom records and services for actual patients." Altogether, the Weinbergs submitted nearly 381,000 fraudulent claims, covering services allegedly rendered to some 3,000 Medicaid patients.

Prosecution witness Dr. David Z. Beldengreen, a dentist who worked at one of the clinics from 1979 to 1984, and who testified to lessen his own culpability in an unrelated Medicaid fraud case, said that the Weinbergs paid him at least $5,000 a week for generating false claims for them. In addition, Jay Weinberg used second-floor clinic offices to run a securities-trading business, whose employees were paid from clinic funds. Jay was indicted under securities laws for failing to register as a stockbroker. Ronald Weinberg also used clinic parking facilities as the garage for his limousine-rental business.

The family that had once lived modestly on the dress shop proceeds quickly learned to enjoy big money. In 1983, Sheldon Weinberg had a house built in Boca Raton, Florida, valued at $2.5 million. He bought a Rolls-Royce and other luxury cars. Sheldon and Jay both maintained apartments in Trump Towers in Manhattan; the rent on Sheldon's apartment was $180,000 per year. The investigation of the Weinbergs began in 1986, when Dr. Beldengreen was arrested and agreed to give evidence against them. All three Weinbergs were indicted in 1987 and convicted in November 1988. They were sentenced on January 10, 1989. Brooklyn Supreme Court Justice Ruth Moskowitz sentenced Jay Weinberg, whom prosecutors regarded as the criminal mastermind, to eight and one third to twenty-five years. She gave Ronald five to fifteen years, and Sheldon was sentenced to seven to twenty-one years in absentia because he jumped bail on the eve of the sentencing. He forfeited a quarter of a million dollars bond for doing so.

Sheldon and his wife, Roslyn Weinberg, were captured four months later in Scottsdale, Arizona. They were featured on the television series "Unsolved Mysteries" on May 18, 1989, after which phone calls offering tips on the couple's whereabouts came flooding in, according to New York State Medicaid prosecutor Edward Koriansky. The Weinbergs had not seen the program themselves, and were taken by surprise when the FBI showed up at their door later in the evening. Sheldon was extradited back to New York to serve his prison term. When Roslyn followed by commercial jet on May 20, federal agents confiscated $105,000 in cash and an unspecified amount of jewelry from her at New York's LaGuardia Airport.

As a result of the Weinberg case, new methods of detecting Medicaid fraud were developed, including computerized verification of patient visits and random requests by mail for verification of services from the patients themselves.

**Weiner, Christopher**, 1981- , U.S., sex. asslt. A popular football player at Trumbull High School in Trumbull, Connecticut, 17-year-old Christopher Weiner was convicted in July 1998 for sexually assaulting a 14-year-old girl. A jury found that Weiner, on the night of February 7, 1997, during a birthday party for another teenager, had forced the girl to sexually fondle him. The girl claimed Weiner had raped her. Weiner was sentenced to three years in prison and expelled from school.

**Welch, David** (AKA: Moochie), 1958 , U.S., mur. David "Moochie" Welch had a long criminal history before he committed six murders on December 8, 1986. Welch had been convicted of sodomy, rape, assault with a deadly weapon, and, while in prison, assault and battery on guards and jailers. Welch had lived briefly with Dellane Mabrey. Together Welch and Mabrey had a child. According to his later statements, a family feud was the cause of his pre-dawn murder rampage on the Mabrey household in east Oakland, California, in 1986.

At that time, Welch stormed into the Mabrey home firing an Uzi assault rifle. He shot and killed Dellane Mabrey, 17; Sean Orlando Mabrey, 21; Dwayne Miller, 4; Valencia Morgan, 3; Kathy Walker, 34; and Darnell Mabrey, 20. Upon his conviction on June 19, 1989, a jury recommended the death penalty for Welch. Alameda County Superior Court Judge Stanley Golde upheld this recommendation, sentencing Welch to death. Judge Golde stated, "There is no circumstance which extenuates the gravity of this crime. His (Welch's) entire life is a life of violence."

**Wendorf, Heather**, 1981- , **Ferrell, Roderick Justin**, 1980- , **Anderson, Howard Scott**, 1980- , **Cooper, Dana**, 1977- , and **Remington, Sarah** (AKA: Shea, Charity Lynn Keesee), 1980- , U.S., mur. In the fall of 1996, Roderick Justin Ferrell, 16, got a call from Heather Wendorf, a 15-year-old he had known at high school in Eustis, Florida, before he had moved back to his home town of Murray, Kentucky. Wendorf, according to Ferrell's later testimony, asked him to help her steal her parents' sports utility vehicle so that she could run away from home.

Ferrell, accompanied by 16-year-old Howard Scott Anderson, 19-year-old Dana Cooper and 16-year-old Sarah Remington, left Kentucky and traveled to Eustis, Florida, twenty miles northwest of Orlando. Ferrell, a troubled youth whose own mother had schooled him on vampirism and had recently been convicted of sexually molesting a 14-year-old boy, was confronted on November 25, 1996, by Wendorf's parents when he and the others tried to run off with Wendorf. Ferrell, using a crowbar, beat Richard Wendorf and Naomi Ruth Wendorf to death. He then burned a "V" on Wendorf's stomach before he and the others fled in Wendorf's utility sports vehicle.

The bodies were found the next day by Jennifer Wendorf, the couple's older daughter. By then Heather had run off with Ferrell and his vampire cult, driving the Wendorf's 1994 Ford Explorer. As the teens headed west, they stopped one night in a graveyard where Ferrell conducted vampire rituals; he and Wendorf, it was later reported, drank each other's blood. Ferrell acted out the part of a vampire leader, his hair shoulder-length and wearing a black trenchcoat. He carried a wooden stick and boasted immortality as a vampire. Heather Wendorf blindly followed him, dying her hair purple and wearing fishnet stockings and a dog collar around her neck.

Tracked to Baton Rouge, Louisiana, the vampire gang members were arrested on November 28, 1996, and jailed, all charged with the murders of the Wendorfs. The gang had been pinpointed after Sarah Remington called her mother in South Dakota, asking that she send money to her. The mother contacted authorities and then, when her daughter called back, told her to go to a motel and have the clerk call her to have the bill charged to her credit card. When the clerk called, the mother was then able to give police the exact location where the gang was hiding.

By then Ferrell and Howard Scott Anderson had been identified as the actual culprits of the vampire clan, which claimed more than thirty members in Kentucky where they had busied themselves with such bestial and cretinous activities as breaking into animal shelters, stomping puppies to death and dismembering them.

All of the gang members were extradited to Florida. Cooper, the only adult of the group, was tried and received a jail sentence. Only the two boys, Ferrell and Anderson, however, were tried for the murders of the Wendorfs. Ferrell, with the others testifying that he performed the actual killings after "going crazy," was convicted after pleading guilty and was sentenced to death in the electric chair on February 27, 1998. Anderson was sentenced to life in prison. Wendorf and the other teenagers were remanded to a youth facility.

Ferrell, on the eve of his death sentence, stated that he resented being called a "vampire cult leader," even though he still believed he was a vampire. He did not still believe, however, that he was immortal. He urged teenagers not to follow his path, saying, "I want them to see that this is real life and that it has consequences."

**Wentzel, LeRoy and Sheila**, See: **Brown, Patricia Gayle**.

**Wesbecker, Joseph T.**, 1942-1989, U.S., suic-mur. The Standard-Gravure Company of Louisville, Kentucky, hired Joseph T. Wesbecker to work in its printing plant in 1970. Several years later, Wesbecker was diagnosed as suffering from manic depression, also known as bipolar disorder, and alternated between periods of suicidal depression and intense excitement. He sought psychiatric treatment for his symptoms, which included anxiety, blurred vision, confusion, dizziness, headaches, demented anger, physical tremors, and sleep disorders. Other workers noticed that Wesbecker exhibited paranoia, and noted his fixation on guns and his fondness for *Soldier of Fortune* magazine. Co-worker James R. Lucas notified company officials that Wesbecker had shown him a handgun he carried in a bag and said he would shoot any supervisor who talked to him about anything but work. The officials did not take Lucas' warning seriously. When psychiatric treatments proved unsuccessful for Wesbecker, Standard-Gravure placed him on disability leave in August 1988.

On September 14, 1989, Wesbecker returned to the plant "looking for bosses" with an AKA-47 assault rifle and a 9-mm semiautomatic pistol. Confronting former co-worker John Tingle, he said, "I told them I'd be back. Get out of my way, John. I told them I'd be back." Tingle and other employees ran to a bathroom and locked Wesbecker out. Wesbecker took an elevator upstairs to the third- floor offices, where, ironically, the executives he sought were absent. He began firing at anyone who happened to be there, working his way downstairs and shooting everyone he encountered in the stairwell. When Wesbecker arrived at the pressroom where he once worked, he turned the pistol on himself. Wesbecker had murdered a total of eight employees and wounded twelve before shooting himself to death. Another person, who was not shot, had a heart attack brought on by the carnage. It was the worse mass killing in the U.S. in one day since the August 20, 1986, massacre of fourteen postal employees by a fellow worker at a post office in Edmond, Oklahoma.

---

**West, Frederick**, 1942-1995, Brit., mur. On January 1, 1995, Federick West, of Gloucester, England, was found dead in his cell at Winson Green Prison near Birmingham, an apparent suicide. West had died only days before he was to be tried for the murders of twelve girls and women whom he had reportedly murdered and then buried in and around his house. West's victims, all killed between 1970 and 1987, included his first wife and two of his daughters. Police had dug up nine bodies in West's back yard and three others in nearby areas.

---

**Weston, Russell Eugene, Jr.**, 1957- , U.S., mur. Rusty Weston heard voices and saw suspicious characters lurking everywhere about his Montana hermit's shack. Like Theodore Kaczynski, Weston had gone west to a remote area near Rimini, Montana, where he lived a reclusive life, often returning to his ancestral home in Valmeyer, Illinois, to visit his family. In Remini, Weston complained to his few friends that federal agents had planted land mines around his property and that the satellite dish owned by his friend Ken Moore was being used to spy on him. He would stand next to the dish and wave his arms and shout, "They are watching me from Washington!"

Weston, who had a long record of mental illness, had once been to Washington and returned to his father's farm in Valmeyer with stacks of newspapers and reports, saying that he was going to work for the CIA. His grandmother laughed at him, later telling reporters that her grandson was "a schizophrenic, and he gets it in his head he's something big."

On July 23, 1998, Weston, after an exhausting drive from Montana, arrived once more at the family farm in Valmeyer. He spent the day shooting and killing a dozen pet cats near the woodshed. When his father found the bodies, he ordered his son off the farm. Weston left, but he took his father's .38-caliber Smith & Wesson handgun when he climbed into his 1983 Chevrolet S-10 pickup and headed for the very center of his personal aggravation—Washington, D.C.

It is 755 miles from Valmeyer to Washington, D.C., and Weston apparently drove that distance without stopping, reaching the capital the next day. After parking his pickup in front of the north side of the Capitol Building, Weston joined a line of tourists entering the building through the Document Room door. He approached Capitol Police Officer Jacob J. Chestnut, 58, who was giving directions to a father and his 15-year-old son. Without warning or explanation, Weston fired a bullet into Chestnut's head, killing him on the spot.

As Weston rushed past him down the hall, going through an metal detector and toward the Majority Whip Suite occupied by Tom DeLay and his staff, Capital Policer Office Douglas B. McMillan fired at Weston. He missed his mark as the man rapidly moved past him, as he chased a screaming woman who ran down the hall in front of him. As he dashed forward, Weston shot and wounded 24-year-old Angela Dickeron, a tourist.

Hearing the first shot fired by Weston and McMillan's fire, 42-year-old John M. Gibson, a Capitol Police special agent, ordered everyone in DeLay's suite to get down on the floor and under or behind desks. He then drew his weapon and stepped into the hall just as the screaming woman reached him. Weston was behind her. Gibson pushed the woman out of the way. Gibson pointed his weapon at Weston and shouted, "Drop your weapon!"

Weston fired a shot that struck Gibson in the chest but the intrepid officer held his ground, and then both men exchanged fire at point blank range. Gibson's bullets struck Weston in the stomach and in both legs. Both men then collapsed. McMillan by then had caught up to Weston. He looked over to see Gibson motionless on the hallway floor and then he pointed his weapon at Weston's head, telling the still-moving killer, "Don't move! You've shot two of my men!"

Weston was rushed to a hospital where he was in critical condition, but he survived his wounds. Chestnut and Gibson were taken to the morgue. Both officers were dead. Gibson's courageous actions had undoubtedly saved the lives of many persons and he was later posthumously decorated for his valor. His murderer, Weston, however, never went to trial. After extensive psychiatric examinations, Weston was ruled unfit to stand trial on April 22, 1999, by U.S. District Court Judge Emmet Sullivan, who sent the killer to a mental institution. Another madman in a country increasingly populated by madmen had brought maniacal violence and death into the very nerve center of the American government.

---

**Wetherell, Nicci**, 1980- , **Jones, Daniel**, 1982- , **Burden, Patrick**, 1982- , **Hargett, James**, 1979- , and **Glynn, Brandi**, 1979- , U.S., Case of mur. According to police in Bellevue, Nebraska, a pack of mindless and bestial teenagers slashed to death one of their own friends on September 29, 1998. A week earlier, Scott Catenacci, 19, and his friends Nicci Wetherell, 18, Daniel Jones, 16, Patrick Burden, 16, James Hargett, 19 and Brandi Glynn, 19, had begun to experiment with partner swapping sex, or group orgy sex. When Catenacci, a six-foot-one-inch, 250-pound youth, attempted to have sex with Nicci Wetherell, however, she rejected him and the angered Catenacci slapped her and roughed her up.

The group then planned to have its revenge on Catennaci by killing him, according to police, enticing the unsuspecting Catennaci to a remote spot beneath the Bellevue Bridge where "someone" was to pay $400 for his laptop computer. When Catenacci showed up to make the deal, he was greeted by Jones, Burden, Hargett, Wetherell and Glynn, all wielding knives. They reportedly slashed him to death. In a later TV interview, Brandi Glynn told a reporter from her jail cell that following Catenacci's slaughterhouse death, one of her male co-conspirators, his hands soaked with the victim's blood, hugged and kissed her, saying, "I love you." Glynn hugged and kissed him back, stating, "I love you."

The five accused killers, along with Glynn's estranged husband, Christopher Glynn, who allegedly knew of the plot, but said nothing to the authorities, were placed under arrest and jailed pending their trials for first-degree murder. They all await trial at the time of this writing.

---

**Wetterling, Jacob Erwin,** 1978- , U.S., abduc. (unsolv.) Until tragedy struck on October 22, 1989, the small farming community of St. Joseph, Minnesota, was considered to be an ideal place for a child to grow up in. The streets were relatively crime free, and parents had few concerns about the safety of the children in their community. Then an 11-year-old boy was carted off by a masked gunman as he made his way home from a local convenience store with his brother and a friend.

Jacob Wetterling, his 10-year-old brother, Trevor, and their pal, Aaron Larson, 11, were on their bicycles returning from a store where they had rented a video on the evening of October 22, when a middle-aged man brandishing a handgun suddenly appeared out of the shadows and ordered them to lie on the ground. He asked them what their ages were, and then grabbed 11-year-old Jacob. Aaron and Trevor were told to run into a nearby field as fast as they could, or risk being shot. The boys headed toward the Wetterling home where they told a neighbor woman, who was baby-sitting Carmen Wetterling, Jacob's younger sister, while his parents were attending a party. The Wetterlings were notified immediately, thus setting in motion the most intensive manhunt in Minnesota state history. "I have no rational, logical idea," Jerry Wetterling said of his son's disappearance. "Just in hindthought, I hope it wouldn't be because I am a chiropractor or because I'm president of the local NAACP or a member of the Bahai faith. I have no enemies and I've never been threatened." By midnight, the FBI was working on the case. The following morning pictures of Jacob were circulated around town and on local TV stations. The abduction of the sixth grade boy soon blossomed into a full blown media event. In St. Paul, the 3M Corporation flew in cartons of white ribbons that were distributed to townspeople. Governor Rudy Perpich called on 200 members of the Minnesota National Guard to assist local law enforcement agencies by conducting a search.

The FBI proceeded on the theory that the kidnapper was a local man—perhaps a former mental patient—who intended no physical harm. "If we didn't think he was alive, we wouldn't be working at this pace," explained agent Byron Gigler. But with each new lead came additional frustration. A call placed to the missing children's network several weeks later sent the agents scurrying back to St. Joseph, where they were told they could find Jacob. Like so many other tips, it proved false. A composite sketch of the suspect was published in December, resulting in 400 new leads. Stearns County Sheriff Charles Grafft had reason to believe that the kidnapper was the same individual who sexually molested a boy from nearby Cold Spring, Minnesota, in 1988. The man wanted in the Wetterling case was identified as a white male, standing approximately five-feet, eight-inches, between the ages of 40 and 50. He wore dark clothes and spoke in a "raspy" voice. "There's enough similarities that we're hot on his trail," Grafft said.

**A police composite of the kidnapper who abducted 11-year-old Jacob Wetterling in St. Joseph, Minnesota, on October 22, 1989.**

The Wetterling case received extensive media attention and was discussed on several nationally syndicated television shows including "A Current Affair," "Inside Edition," "Good Morning America," and the "Geraldo Rivera Show." Minnesota's professional sports teams, the Vikings, Timberwolves, and North Stars, did what they could to keep the plight of Jacob alive in people's minds, but by year's end hope began to fade. The investigation cost Stearns County an estimated $208,000—money augmented by fundraising efforts coordinated by local TV stations and private citizens' groups. Local lawmakers sought financial relief from the Minnesota legislature.

What began as a full-scale investigation has now been left in the hands of the Stearns County Sheriff's Department, which continues to follow up on occasional leads. The case remains unsolved.

---

**Weyls, Scott L.,** See: **Bivens, Gerald.**

---

**Wheeler, Michael L.,** 1958- , U.S., mur. Fifteen-year-old runaway Autumn Marie Chinn, who lived with a foster family from the Portland, Oregon, suburb of Forest Grove, was last seen alive on June 6, 1989. Her body was found in the Tualatin River about fifteen miles west of Portland on June 17. Her skull was fractured and her jaw broken, apparently with a heavy rock.

Several days later, a TV police bulletin announced that 31- year-old Michael Wheeler was being sought in connection with the crime. Wheeler surrendered to police but denied any knowledge of the murder. A witness, Don Gellings, claimed Wheeler told him he had picked the girl up at an amusement park on June 6 and killed her the same day. Gellings said Wheeler had taken him to the murder site and shown him a bloody stone he allegedly hit the girl with when she said something he did not like. Wheeler insisted he was innocent throughout his trial, but on April 13, 1990, he was sentenced to life in prison, with a minimum twenty-five years before becoming eligible for parole.

---

**Wheelock, Thomas**, 1977- , and **York, Peter**, 1977- , U.S., Case of rob.-mur. Thirty-year-old Rodrigo J. Cortez, a family man with a 3-year-old son, had worked for five years as a guard for Armored Transport of Oakland in Oakland, California. On the morning of November 24, 1997, he kissed his wife goodbye while she lay half asleep. "I didn't open my eyes," Marlene Cortez said later. "I didn't know it was going to be the last time."

That day Cortez had agreed to work overtime and was paired for the first time with another guard, 20-year-old Thomas Wheelock, who had been working for Armored Transport for about two months. Later that day, Cortez was found dead, curled in a fetal position inside the armored car in which he had been riding with Wheelock. He had been shot several times in the neck. His partner, Wheelock, along with about $300,000, was gone.

Police were later able to reconstruct events from the testimony of 20-year-old Peter York, a former roommate of Wheelock's, as well as statements from York's brother, Robert. After making several stops in the Oakland area, Wheelock pretended to be ill and asked Cortez, who was driving the armored car, to pull over. When Cortez did so, Wheelock fired several shots into Cortez with a 9mm semiautomatic pistol. He unloaded all the cash into a car that had been purposely parked near the spot where Wheelock had asked Cortez to pull over. But the car would not start. Wheelock moved the cash back into the armored car and then, while the dead Cortez lay inside, drove twenty-five miles north to his home town of San Ramon, California.

Wheelock left the bloodied armored car near an auto-parts store where he once worked and hid the $300,000 nearby. He next appeared at the Danville, California, home of his friend Peter York, tapping on York's bedroom window. York was not at home. To his brother Robert, Wheelock nervously stated that "he had done something horrible." Robert York went to his laundry room and talked with Wheelock, who mentioned the words "armored" and "I did it."

Wheelock then asked Robert York to loan him his car, but York refused. Wheelock then suggested that he pretend to steal the car and York report it as stolen. Robert York again refused. Wheelock then left, taking a cab to the Game Station Arcade in Walnut Creek, California, where his friend Peter York worked as a security guard. It was about 10:30 p.m. when Wheelock arrived to blurt out his story to Peter York. The two then drove back to San Ramon, where they loaded the hidden cash into York's car and then fled to Sacramento.

The two men had long planned the armored car heist, according to police, working out the robbery while the pair were enjoying a cruise on a Royal Caribbean liner, a free trip for two, which York had won in a contest. The cruise ended the day before Wheelock killed Cortez and robbed the armored car. Both men had worked together as security guards at the Game Station Arcade in Walnut Creek in the summer of 1997,

before Wheelock was fired in August 1997 by arcade owner Jenny Spinello, who later said that she let Wheelock go because she believed he was stealing funds. Following the armored car robbery, Spinello said that she had planned to "phase out" York as a guard because of his poor job performance.

Once in Sacramento, York dropped Wheelock and most of the cash off at a Motel 6, then returned to his home in Danville ($4,000 in cash was later found in Peter York's home). Meanwhile, Wheelock purchased a used Ford Bronco in Sacramento, paying for the car in cash. Police had pinpointed Wheelock's whereabouts—the car dealer had identified Wheelock from photos broadcast on local TV and had notified authorities. Oddly, Wheelock had not bothered to hide his identity, using his own name when renting the room and buying the car.

Before dawn, a SWAT team burst into the Motel 6 room that had been rented by Wheelock, but he was not present. Officers found about $270,000 in cash from the robbery stuffed in paper bags beneath the mattress. Wheelock's whereabouts was not known to the police at that time and it was uncertain as to how he eluded capture. By that time, Wheelock was driving northward. His car broke down near Red Bluff, California, about eighty miles north of Sacramento. Highway Patrol Officer Richard Barr stopped to help Wheelock, not knowing he was a fugitive. Wheelock's car was towed to Fred's Auto Clinic where mechanic Harvey Miller repaired the Bronco's broken fuel pump. Wheelock was soon on his way.

While California police conducted an intensive manhunt throughout Northern California for Wheelock, he drove eastward and out of the state. On November 27, 1997, Thanksgiving Day, he was stopped near Centerville, Utah, at 12:30 p.m., by a highway patrolman who charged Wheelock with a minor offense, having improper registration plates. The arresting officer recognized the fugitive and he was arrested and taken to the Davis County Jail in Farmington, Utah, held there for extradition back to California. Wheelock waived his extradition rights and was returned to California where he was imprisoned, along with his friend and co-conspirator, Peter York, both charged with robbery and murder. (Robert York was not charged.)

A day before Wheelock's capture in Utah, police in California were shocked to get reports that the man they most wanted then was appearing on the syndicated "Judge Judy" television show. On November 26, 1997, the show, taped in October 1997, was aired on San Francisco's KRON-TV. Wheelock appeared before the TV judge with his former fiancee, Amy Baugham, arguing over the custody of a car they had jointly purchased earlier. The TV judge asked Wheelock why he had not kept up the payments on the car and he bluntly replied, "Because I'm a bum ... I couldn't keep a job very long." During this show, Wheelock also argued with Baugham for more visitation time with his young son.

Judge Judy churlishly responded, "Why would I want to expose a 2-year-old child to a bum?"

"I cannot tell you that," Wheelock replied.

Wheelock and York await trial at the time of this writing.

---

**Whigham, Mark**, See: **Braun, Roger Tracy**.

---

**Whitacre, Mark**, See: **ADM**.

---

**White, Melvin James II**, See: **Curl, Darron Deshone**.

---

**White, Richard**, 1959-1998, U.S., Case of bomb.-mur. On December 30, 1997, the United Methodist Church in Oakwood, Illinois, a small town in mid-state and close to the Indiana border, was inexplicably bombed, killing church worker Brian Plawer. Five months later, on May 24, 1998, the First Assembly of God Church in Danville, Illinois, was also bombed, an explosion that injured thirty-four persons. The church in Danville was only seven miles from the church bombed earlier in Oakwood.

Four days following the Danville explosion, investigators who had been working on the two church bombings, believed they had pinpointed the bomber and were en route to question 39-year-old Richard White of Danville. They were too late. Before detectives arrived at the home of White's mother, on May 28, 1998, the suspect blew himself to pieces with a powerful bomb inside of a garage, an explosion described by police as accidental. White had not, officials concluded, committed suicide.

White, who had a long history of mental illness, had harbored a deep-seated grudge against health care workers who had participated in the rescue and treatment of his brother, Randy Shotts, who suffered lifelong spinal injuries from a 1986 swimming accident. Some paramedics, White believed, had dropped his brother during rescue operations and had permanently crippled him. White took his revenge, according to officials, by bombing the two churches that the health care people regularly attended.

Bomb experts, following the garage explosion that took White's life, linked the two church bombing to the bomb that went off inside White's garage. Examining a burn pit outside White's garage, experts found what was described as trace evidence of a metallic and fiber composition similar to evidence found at the two churches previously bombed. White was known to be a skilled mechanic and had earlier displayed an ability to construct and detonate explosive devices.

---

**White, Nathaniel**, 1960- , U.S., mur. Six females were reported missing from small towns near Poughkeepsie, New York, over an 18-month period in 1991-1992. Police searched for these missing persons but to no avail, until Poughkeepsie police received an anonymous tip to interview 32-year-old Nathaniel White, a resident of Walkill, New York. Officers visited White who gave inconsistent answers to questions about Angelina Hopkins, a 23-year-old Poughkeepsie resident who had been missing since July 20, 1992, along with her cousin Brenda L. Whiteside. Suspicious of White, officers arrested him for using stolen license plates and driving without a license, charges strong enough to hold White until he could be further questioned about the missing Hopkins.

While White was detained at police headquarters, his background was checked. He had graduated Poughkeepsie High School in 1979 and had finished a year at Bowie State College in Maryland. After serving three years, 1981-1984, in the Army, White was honorably discharged with the rank of sergeant. He held odd jobs after his discharge, until robbing a convenience store in 1986, receiving a three-year prison term. Released in 1989, he was charged with physically abusing his girlfriend in September 1990, but the charges were dropped.

On April 17, 1991, White abducted a 16-year-old girl in Walkill, holding her at knifepoint and sexually assaulting her, telling her that if she did not cooperate, "I'll cut your throat and kill you." The girl managed to escape and report White, who was charged with kidnapping and rape. Prosecutors offered to drop the serious felony charges if White pleaded guilty to unlawful imprisonment, a misdemeanor. He did, and received a prison term of nine months, plus twelve months for parole violation.

Paroled on April 23, 1992, White was kept under closer supervision, with parole board personnel visiting him at his home and with White reporting regularly to his probation officer. He was given a drug test on July 3, 1992, which he passed. This is all Poughkeepsie police had on the man they held in custody. Officers interrogated White for thirteen hours. Finally, White told them that he had kidnapped and murdered Angelina Hopkins. To their shock, they also heard White quickly confess to five more kidnapping-murders.

White ticked off his slayings with precision accuracy and chilling detail. He confessed to kidnapping, raping and murdering six females. He was not apparently motivated by race selection when it came to his victims. White, who was a black, had killed one white woman and five black females. He said he had killed 29-year-old Juliana Frank of Middletown, New York, on March 25, 1991, a month before he was sent back to prison for attacking the 16-year-old girl.

On July 10, 1992, less than three months after his latest prison release, he entered the Middletown, New York, home of 34-year-old Laurette Huggins Reviere, raping and stabbing her to death and leaving her naked body to be found a short time later. On July 29, 1992, White kidnapped 27-year-old Adraine Marcette Hunter of Middletown, New York, raping and stabbing her to death, and then dumping her naked body at the outskirts of Goshen, New York, where it was discovered on July 29, 1992.

White led officers to the graves of these three women, after he had already taken detectives to the graves of three other women on August 4, 1992, those of 14-year-old Christine M. Klebbe, of Goshen, New York, who had been kidnapped, raped and stabbed to death by White before he dumped her naked body in Waywayanda, New York, a few miles south of Middleton, New York; 20-year-old Brenda L. Whiteside, of Elmsford, New York; and Whiteside's cousin, 23-year-old Angelina Hopkins.

Police were able to link the six murders to White because of his unusual murder "signature," the manner in which he killed and mutilated each corpse with a knife and a blunt instrument and the way in which he positioning the bodies. White further illustrated his modus operandi when being interviewed in his cell by NBC. Before millions of shocked viewers White stated that he had been inspired to kill his first victim, after seeing the movie *Robocop*. Immediately after seeing this movie, White abducted Juliana Frank, his only white victim, and followed an irresponsibly detailed murder shown in the film.

Said White, "The first killing was from Robocop I or Robocop II with a man in it named Cain. I seen him cut somebody's throat, then take a knife and slit down the chest to the stomach and left the body in a certain position. With the first person I killed [Frank], I did exactly what I seen in the movie."

The killer went on to describe his feelings at the time of murder, "While I'm doing it, I enjoy it. It's like it stimulates me or something and then it seem like a dream and after it's over, that's when the remorse comes." He added that he had struggled with himself to stop the killing, but he found it impossible to control his urge to murder the women after they got into his car.

White went to trial before a jury of eleven men and one woman on March 11, 1993. The defense argued against admitting White's confession, saying that he was unduly pressured into making statements in a 13-hour grilling. Police statements insisted that White had been given food and a nap before he took officers to the hidden gravesites of his victims and that, in fact, he was casually munching on a slice of pizza as he pointed out some of the hiding places.

On April 12, 1993, the jury took only a few hours to find White guilty on six counts of first-degree murder. On May 26, 1993, White was given six consecutive twenty-five years to life sentences, for a total of 150 years minimum to be served. Judge Berry told Nathaniel White upon sentencing, "I find you to be the perpetrator of the most vicious, evil, senseless, brutal acts."

------

**White Slavery**, 1990s, Eastern Europe/Far East. With the collapse of communism in Russia and its allied Eastern Bloc nations, the economies of these countries plummeted to poverty level. Hundreds of thousands of unemployed women in their late teens to their late 20s turned to prostitution to support themselves and their families. Of the 200,000 prostitutes working in Germany by 1996, half of these women were from Eastern Europe, mainly Russia, Ukraine, Poland and Hungary. More than seventy percent of prostitutes in the Netherlands were from the same regions.

In the Ukraine, young, attractive females were ensnared into white slavery by answering ads that promised a minimum of $400 a month in salary for working as "hostesses" in clubs in the Far East. To these women, where the average salary was little more than $40 a month, the opportunity seemed great. Thousands applied and were given air far to Tokyo where they were met by brutal pimps who immediately took them to brothels where they were guarded night and day and gang raped repeatedly until they became the sex slaves of the brothel owners. Having no papers or income, these women were truly white slaves to widespread prostitution rings that also operated in Brussels and Amsterdam.

One applicant for a "hostage" job was typical. A statuesque woman from Russia, she was interviewed, but was asked no questions about her professional background or education—

she was a bookkeeper—but she was told that she might be too tall for the job that awaited her in Japan. She was asked to take off her shoes and was then approved for the "hostess" job. She signed a contract that guaranteed her a high-paying salary, a contract printed in English, Japanese and Russian. Before this woman flew to Tokyo, however, she met a friend who had just returned from Japan, a woman who told her how she had been held in Japan as a white sex slave, until she managed to escape and borrow money for her return trip to Russia. The applicant cancelled her flight to Tokyo.

Hampering police in combating widespread white slavery is the fact that prostitution is legal throughout most of Western Europe and prostitution is haphazardly prosecuted in Japan. When police do crack down on the most notorious white slavery clubs, only low-level employees and the women themselves are caught in the roundups. The owners and operators of the white slavery networks, all members of the international underworld and many of these being millionaire owners of legitimate enterprises, are never present at such raids and invariably escape arrest, let alone identification.

------

**Whitewater**, 1994-1997. A muddied Arkansas real estate scandal, Whitewater was a scheme developed by James McDougal and his wife Susan McDougal, who invited their friends Bill and Hillary Rodham Clinton to participate. The scheme involved taking huge loans to develop a large tract of undeveloped Arkansas land known as Whitewater. Charges were made that the McDougals and others, including the Clintons, had illegally benefited from illicit loans made to the Whitewater Development Corp. These charges persisted to the point where the Clintons, by then in the White House, were thought to be directly involved in the illegal scheme. U.S. Attorney General Janet Reno responded by appointing Robert Fiske as independent counsel to investigate Whitewater on January 20, 1994.

A court order of August 5, 1994, replaced Fiske with Kenneth Starr, who was named independent counsel to investigate Whitewater by a three-judge panel. The Clintons, chiefly Hillary Rodham Clinton, began to complain that the panel was made up of Clinton's political enemies and was out to blacken the name of the president. (Hillary Clinton's much publicized broad accusations would continue throughout her husband's two terms in office, statements that insisted that all of the many charges brought against her husband, from political corruption to sexual offenses committed in the White House, were the creation of a "right-wing conspiracy.")

James McDougal's operations in Arkansas were shady throughout the 1980s. He began a thrift, Madison Guarantee, which failed in 1989, costing taxpayers more than $60 million. His wife, Susan McDougal, began a public relations firm that took a $300,000 loan from an Arkansas firm operated by David Hale, a loan Hale later insisted Bill Clinton pressured him into making. Part of the loan to Susan McDougal's firm was used to buy a piece of large property later deeded to Whitewater. The loan was never repaid.

The Rose Law Firm in Little Rock, Arkansas, where Hillary Rodham Clinton had worked, was involved in handling papers and documents for Whitewater, but by the time Kenneth Starr and his investigators tried to obtain much of this documentation, it had vanished. Jeremy Hedges, a courier for Rose Law Firm, later testified that many documents having to do with the Clintons and Whitewater had been shredded, including files maintained by presidential adviser Vincent Foster, who committed suicide in July 1994. Foster had been a partner at Rose Law Firm and he had handled most of the documents concerning Whitewater, especially those in connection with his friends Bill and Hillary Clinton.

Although several former Clinton associates—James McDougal, David Hale, former Arkansas governor Jim Guy Tucker—were convicted of conspiracy, fraud and other charges in various illegal financial deals, Starr was unable to secure enough evidence in the Whitewater scandal to charge President Bill Clinton and his wife Hillary. The scandal, in which considerable investment dollars were lost, has stigmatized the Clintons to this day. Also See: **Clinton, William Jefferson**; **McDougal, James**; **Tucker, Jim Guy**.

---

**Whittington, Ernest**, See: **Peters, Colin**.

---

**Wijeweera, Rohana**, 1943-1989, Sri., terr. Leader of the Sinhalese People's Liberation Front (JVP), Rohana Wijeweera, 47, was the most wanted man in Sri Lanka. Wijeweera's terrorist organization was reportedly responsible for murdering almost 10,000 people in the country since 1987, chiefly politicians, civil servants, and family members of security forces hunting the JVP.

Wijeweera attended college in the U.S.S.R. during the 1960s. He returned to Sri Lanka in 1971, where he attempted to topple the government in an armed revolt that failed, and was jailed for six years. Once released, Wijeweera led the JVP in open elections. When the rebels were rejected by the electorate, the JVP threatened to kill anyone who voted.

Following his capture by an army patrol on November 12, 1989, Wijeweera agreed to order his top lieutenants to surrender to government troops. The next day, Wijeweera led them to his organization's headquarters in the country's capital, Colombo, where he met with his one-time aide, H.B. Herath. An army spokesman later stated that Herath resisted turning over information about the JVP, pulled a gun, and shot Wijeweera. Members of the army patrol, in turn, shot Herath. Other sources later claimed that both Wijeweera and Herath were simply murdered by the patrol as soon as Herath and others showed themselves. Wijeweera's wife and children were taken into "protective custody."

Following Wijeweera's death, vigilante death squads and the security forces attacked and killed dozens of JVP members. In October 1989, seven members of a policeman's family were murdered by JVP terrorists and, in retaliation, vigilantes seized twenty-four JVP members and cut their throats, leaving the bodies strewn across a road in Kandy.

---

**Wike, Warfield Raymond**, 1956- , U.S., abduc-rape-mur.

A 33-year-old machinist convicted of murdering a 6-year-old girl and raping her sister swore vengeance against the prosecutor who put him away. After learning of the jury's decision to send him to the Florida electric chair, Warfield Raymond Wike made threats against Assistant State's Attorney Kim Skievaski. His statements prompted Judge Ben Gordon of the Circuit Court in Milton, Florida, to order Wike shackled and handcuffed during his sentencing hearing on June 21, 1989.

Wike was arrested and charged with the September 22, 1988, abduction-murder of the Pensacola girl, and the rape of her 8-year-old sister. The victims were taken to a wooded area near Allentown and assaulted with a knife. The surviving girl identified Wike as the man who carried her away from her parents' home, a charge Wike vehemently denied. Doubts were raised by the defense when a second eyewitness failed to identity Wike. FBI lab tests of hair and sperm were equally inconclusive, and no concrete motive could be established by the district attorney's office for the tragedy. Nevertheless, a jury found Wike guilty of murder and sentenced him to die. In addition, Judge Gordon imposed three concurrent prison sentences totaling sixty-nine years for the rape and attempted murder charges, and for kidnapping the children from their parents.

---

**Wildhaber, Dennis**, 1974- , and **Pfingsten, James**, 1973- , U.S., mur. Malynda Waddell, an attractive 16-year-old brunette who attended the Visual Performing School in St Louis, Missouri, and who aspired to be a Hollywood actress, was reported missing in March 1993. Her purse was found on March 13, 1993, alongside Interstate Highway 44, outside of Webster Grove, Missouri. Then her car, a 1985 Tempo, was found abandoned but in good order and with no signs of foul play. One of Waddell's friends told police that she and Waddell had been cruising about St. Louis on the night of Waddell's disappearance and that they had spent some hours listening to rock music at an apartment shared by Dennis Wildhaber and James Pfingsten.

Wildhaber, who wore his straggly hair shoulder-length and had a cadaverous face, told police that he and his roommate, Pfingsten, had been with the girls for a few hours, but that the girls had gone home. Police were suspicious and told the youths that they would want to question them further. When officers returned to see both men, they discovered that the pair had fled. St. Louis police put out an all points bulletin for the arrest of Wildhaber and Pfingsten.

Within a few days, St. Louis officers handling the case were contacted by the Santa Rosa County Sheriff's Department in Pensacola, Florida. They were informed that Wildhaber and Pfingsten were being held on suspicion of murder. St. Louis detectives flew to Pensacola and first interviewed Pfingsten, who seemed to be the more docile of the pair, telling him that he was suspected of killing Waddell and that he could be executed for the murder.

Pfingsten quickly confessed that he had been present when Wildhaber kidnapped Waddell, raped the girl, slit her throat and then he and Wildhaber had dumped the body along the Meramec River between Tyson Park and Times Beach, Missouri. In an effort to save himself from the death penalty, Pfingsten offered to testify against Wildhaber.

Police, meanwhile, searched the area along the Meramec River with dogs and soon uncovered Waddell's body. Her throat had been slit, just as Pfingsten had said. Both Wildhaber and Pfingsten were charged with murder. Before his December 1, 1994 trial was to begin, Wildhaber accepted a plea-bargain deal and confessed to the kidnapping, rape and murder of Waddell. He was sent to prison for life. Pfingsten refused to accept a plea-bargain deal and went to trial. He was found guilty on May 1, 1995, and was sentenced to prison for life.

---

**Wilkening, Karen,** 1946- , U.S., pros. Karen Wilkening ran a $150-per-visit call girl ring from her condominium in Linda Vista, California, before her arrest in May 1987 for soliciting an undercover San Diego policewoman to become one of her call girls. In September of that same year, she conspired with her attorney, Buford "Bo" Wiley, to flee to the Philippines in order to escape prosecution, and protect her clients from "further embarrassment." Wilkening remained there until May 1989, when she was extradited back to San Diego at a cost of $20,000. The police were anxious to question her about the unsolved murders of forty-two women, most of them street prostitutes who were slain between 1985 and 1989. Wilkening was not considered to be a suspect in any of the cases, but the police believed there was a possible link between her and 23-year-old Donna Gentile, who was found strangled in East County in June 1985. Gentile was involved with two San Diego police officers at the time of her death.

Wilkening's attorney, Steven Carroll, asked the court to be lenient with his client. He pointed out that Wilkening had undergone nearly three months of solitary confinement at the Las Colinas jail. According to her testimony, Wilkening's arms were shackled to a chain encircling her waist every time she went to the bathroom. "It was extremely excessive," Carroll said.

The former madame was sentenced to serve three years and eight months at the California Institute For Women at Frontera on November 29, 1989. In addition, Judge Jesus Rodriguez of the Superior Court imposed a $1,500 fine. "I don't know how I'll be perceived once I get out but I'll probably think about moving from here," Wilkening told reporters. "I really want to make a difference."

---

**Wilkinson, Philip Edward**, 1968- , U.S., mur. On July 28, 1991, the bodies of 38-year-old Judy Faulk Hudson, her 19-year-old daughter Crystal, and her 11-year-old son Larry Martin, Jr., were found in their Fayetteville, North Carolina apartment. All had been horribly bludgeoned to death with a heavy instrument. Police found the apartment unlocked, a glass sliding door ajar through which the intruder probably entered. They could find no clues leading to the identity of the killer.

Then, on January 9, 1992, Fayetteville police received a call from military police at Fort Bragg, North Carolina, about ten miles distant. They were informed that Philip Edward Wilkenson, a private stationed on the base, had confessed to killing the Hudson family members. He told authorities that he

was peeping into windows on the night of the murder and spotted Crystal Hudson sleeping on the couch wearing only a T-shirt and shorts. He entered the apartment through the sliding glass doors that were open and began caressing the girl. She woke up and screamed and then he hit her with a heavy bowling pin he had picked up outside. He kept hitting her. He then went into another bedroom and used the bowling pin to crush the skulls of Judy and Larry Hudson.

Three years later, Wilkinson went to trial. It was brief. Against the advice of his attorneys, he pleaded guilty, saying, "I threw my life away, and I threw away the lives of three innocent, precious people for nothing." He was sentenced to death on September 15, 1994.

---

**Williams, Annie Laurie**, 1922- , U.S., mur. Annie Laurie Williams worked in a dimestore in Pasadena, Texas, and her young sons, Calvin and Conrad were often in the care of babysitters. On the night of February 16, 1955, Williams returned home to find her sons asleep, or so she thought until she checked. They were both dead, having consumed a bottle of barbiturates, or so she later told authorities. She panicked, she said, and dismembered their bodies, then packed them into boxes, which she buried. The bodies were later discovered and Williams was tried for murder, defended by the famous criminal attorney Percy Foreman. Instead of being sent to the electric chair, Williams was sent to prison for life.

Williams was paroled to a halfway house on November 26, 1980, on the condition that if she displayed good behavior, she would receive her final release in a year and a half. Williams, however, simply got into a cab, then took a bus to California. Once in the Golden State, she changed her name to Laurie Sheldon, learned word processing and got a secretarial job at the community college in Yosemite. She later married a widower, James Allen, and became Laurie Allen.

Just short of her seventy-fifth birthday, on April 11, 1997, a local sheriff, who had received a tip as to "Laurie Allen's" real identity, arrested her. Annie Laurie Williams was sent back to prison for parole violation.

---

**Williams, Anthony,** 1966- , U.S., rape. Serial-rapist Anthony Williams was sentenced to serve forty-five years in prison on January 4, 1990, by Cook County Criminal Court Judge Shelvin Singer for a series of sexual assaults committed in Chicago's Rogers Park neighborhood in June and July 1987. Williams typically gained access to the women's apartments by cutting a hole in the screen or removing a window late at night while the victims were asleep.

The defendant was originally charged with two counts of aggravated sexual assault and one count of home invasion for the rape of a 34-year-old Rogers Park woman on July 19, 1987, after he was arrested with a stolen purse in his possession. However, the first trial in April 1989 ended in a mistrial when the jury failed to arrive at a verdict. The state attorney's office, armed with a variety of forensic evidence, prosecuted Williams a second time. The second trial resulted in Williams' conviction.

**Williams, Bennie, Jr.**, 1965- , U.S., rob. One of the most prolific and inventive lone bank robbers in recent Illinois history, Bennie Williams reportedly robbed twenty-one banks from 1997 to 1998, mostly in suburbs around Chicago. He used a variety of disguises when entering banks, sometimes wearing a large bandage that covered most of his face. On one or more occasion, Williams was videotaped by bank security cameras as he arrived in a limousine outside the bank. Wearing a wig and dark glasses, he dashed inside, held up the bank, then raced back to the limousine.

Williams was finally tracked down to a motel in Chicago and, after a chase, was apprehended with about $5,000 in cash on his person. He was convicted of robbing twenty banks on January 16, 1999.

**Williams, Glenn,** 1970- , U.S., mur. Nineteen-year-old Glenn Williams, a member of the Corbet Street gang of Roxbury, Massachusetts, was convicted by a Suffolk County jury of second-degree murder on October 10, 1989. On December 25, 1988, Inacio Mendes, 43, was shot in the chest and arm as he stood in the kitchen of his Roxbury home. The shots were actually intended for Mendes' stepson Mervin Reese, the alleged leader of the Humboldt Boys gang. The evidence showed that gang warfare between the two rival factions prompted Williams to boast that he was going to be "shooting up Homestead Street," where Mendes lived. The murder weapon, a .38-caliber handgun, was later found on the floor of a car in which Williams had been sitting.

Suffolk Superior Court Judge Robert W. Basks sentenced Williams to life in prison. Williams will not be eligible for parole until 2004.

**Williams, Jacqueline Annette**, 1967- , and **Caffey, Fedell**, 1973- , and **Ward, Lavern**, 1972- , U.S., mur. Lavern Ward, a black man and resident of Wheaton, Illinois, who had fathered a child with Debra Evans, a white woman, had also impregnated Evans with a second child. Ward's cousin, Jacqueline Annette Williams, also a resident of Wheaton, wanted to have a child and Ward promised that he would deliver the Evans' baby to her. To that end, Ward, Williams and Fedell Caffey, Williams' boyfriend, went to Evans' Addison apartment on the night of November 16, 1995.

The trio killed Evans and then cut her full-term baby from her womb. They also brutally killed Evans' 10-year-old daughter Samantha and abducted her 7-year-old son Joshua, whose body was found dumped in a Maywood, Illinois alley the next day. Evans and her two older children were white. A third child, 2-year-old Jordan, who was also Ward's child, was left with the bodies of his mother and older brother and sister when the savage killers fled.

Police quickly caught up with the killers, finding the newborn child alive and in Williams' home. Jacqueline Williams was the first to go on trial. She was shown to be a calculating and sinister person who hatched the plan to steal Evans' child.

Three Illinois killers who murdered a woman and her children, then cut her full-term child from her womb (left to right): Lavern Ward, sentenced to life in prison; Jacqueline Annette Williams, sentenced to death; Fedell Caffey, sentenced to death.

Williams was convicted of first-degree murder on March 20, 1998. She was later sentenced to death. Williams carped to the press, "There was not one black juror on my side. It's not fair. I got screwed around. They just want to see three blacks die for killing three whites."

Lavern Ward was convicted and sentenced to life in prison. Fedell Caffey, of Schaumburg, Illinois, the person who actually murdered Evans and cut her baby from her womb, was convicted of first-degree murder on November 10, 1998. Described by a prosecutor as a "cold-blooded murderer of defenseless women and children," Caffey was sentenced to death in January 1999. The killings of the Evans family by Williams, Ward and Caffey remains one of the most heinous and vile crimes on record.

**Williams, Matthew and Roger**, See: **Gardner, Joseph**.

**Williams, Roger**, 1956-1996, U.S., mur.-suic. On February 19, 1996, a Monday night, Roger Williams, of Welch, West Virginia, drove to nearby Mohegan to his sister-in-law's home to pick up his 20-year-old daughter Angela. She refused to go with her father because he had been drinking. Williams, a truck driver who worked long transcontinental hauls, was rarely home and when he did return, he wanted his daughter with him. Normally, they had a close relationship, except when Roger Williams was drinking. At that time, his whole nature changed. He became surly and threatening.

On Tuesday morning, February 20, Williams called his sister-in-law's home, demanding that Donna Williams bring his daughter home immediately. He then grabbed a rifle and a semiautomatic pistol and drove along West Virginia 7 to meet them. When he spotted the car driven by his sister-in-law, Williams stopped and began firing at the car. He shot 43-year-old Donna Williams several times, killing her. Her son, 18-year-old Richard Williams, was shot in the arm and he staggered to a nearby house to get help. He was later taken to a hospital where he died.

Williams had also shot his daughter in the arm, apparently by accident. He put her into his car and drove to a nearby mountaintop where for several hours, he apparently tried to stop the bleeding by tearing his own shirt and using this as a bandage. A short time later, police surmised, he shot and killed

Angela Williams by firing a bullet into her head. He then fired another bullet into his own head. Police found both bodies late in the day. No reason was ever forthcoming that would explain William's sudden eruption of murderous violence.

---

**Williams, Scott Martin,** 1960- , U.S., rape-mur. Thirteen-year-old Jennifer Moore of suburban Novato, California, became the fourth San Francisco Bay area girl to disappear in less than a year when she failed to return home from a shopping mall where she stopped to get an ice cream cone on the evening of April 13, 1989. Over 20,000 leaflets were circulated throughout the Bay Area as volunteers frantically searched for the missing girL

Moore's nude body was found partially concealed in garbage bags by a passing motorist at the side of Novato Boulevard in Marin County four days later. Religious tracts in one of the bags led police back to the Bethel Baptist Church, which Moore attended. There they discovered similar trash bags in use. They arrested volunteer groundskeeper and church deacon Scott Martin Williams, 29, who confessed to Novato police on April 21 to raping, strangling, and beating the girl on the head with a baseball bat in the church library. Police found blood stains on the floor, which had been hastily covered with coffee.

Williams was charged with murder and could have faced capital punishment under the "special circumstances" clause of California law because the murder was committed under two unusual circumstances—murder during a rape and murder connected with lewd and lascivious behavior with a person under 14. However, he was sentenced on September 14, 1989, to life imprisonment without possibility of parole. No connection between Williams and the disappearance of Ilene Misheloff, 13, in February, Amber Swartz-Garcia, 9, who was kidnapped outside her Pinole, California, home in June, and Michaela Garecht, 10, who was abducted outside a Hayward market in November, could be made. "People are a little more guarded today and more aware," commented Police Chief Jim Rose of Dublin, California, where the Misheloff kidnapping took place.

---

**Willmott, Donna Jean**, See: **Marks, Claude.**

---

**Wilson, Barry,** 1959- , **St. Pierre, Bobby,** 1963- , and **Gibons, Jacqueline,** 1962- , U.S., consp.-mur. In 1982, Benjamin and Sybil Gibons considered pressing charges against their daughter Jacqueline's lover, Barry Wilson, after they suspected him of breaking into their Skokie, Illinois, home. At that time, Wilson, who had met Jacqueline Gibons while she lived in a group home for girls, devised a plot to kill his lover's parents.

Wilson recruited Bobby St. Pierre into the plot, to do the actual killing. St. Pierre broke into the Gibons' home on July 29, 1982. When Benjamin, 62, arrived at 6 p.m., he was bludgeoned to death with a claw hammer. A short time later, Sybil called Jacqueline and asked her to pick her up from the train station. When Sybil, 60, entered the home, she was also killed.

The three conspirators wrapped up the bodies and put them in St. Pierre's car. He drove to Albuquerque, New Mexico, and left the bodies in a remote area, where they were found a week later. He was arrested in Arizona, and Jacqueline and Wilson were arrested in Skokie.

St. Pierre, 26, was convicted on two counts of murder and given the death penalty. On June 26, 1989, Jacqueline, in a plea-bargain agreement, pleaded guilty to the murder of her mother and conspiring to murder her father. In exchange for avoiding the death sentence by pleading guilty to the lesser charge of conspiracy, she agreed to testify against Wilson. On November 6, 1989, Cook County Criminal Court Judge Richard Neville sentenced Wilson, 30, to life in prison without parole. The next day, Jacqueline, 27, was sentenced to sixty-five years in prison.

---

**Wilson, Betty,** 1946- , **Lowe, Peggy,** 1946- , and **White, James D.,** 1951- , U.S., mur. To inherit her husband's $6.3 million fortune, Betty Wilson conspired with her twin sister, Peggy Lowe, to have Dr. Jack Wilson murdered. To that end, the sisters agreed to pay $5,000 to part-time carpenter James D. White to kill the 55-year-old eye surgeon. White beat and stabbed Wilson to death in his Huntsville, Alabama, home. A short time after the killing, the conspiracy fell apart. White was identified as the killer and he agreed to testify against the sisters in exchange for a life term. Betty Wilson was found guilty of first-degree murder on March 3, 1993 and sentenced to life imprisonment, a fate that also befell her sister, Peggy Lowe.

---

**Wilson, Brandon,** 1978- , U.S., mur. Shortly before 8 p.m., on November 14, 1998, 9-year-old Matthew Louis Cecchi, was escorted to a cinderblock restroom in a campground at Oceanside Harbor, California, by his aunt. Cecchi, from Oroville, in Northern California, was attending a family reunion at the campgrounds. The boy went inside while the aunt waited outside. A teenager then entered the rest room and came out within minutes. Worried, the aunt went inside to find her nephew's throat cut; he was bleeding to death from fatal stab wounds and died a short time later.

A hunt for the youth who had entered the washroom resulted in the arrest of Brandon Wilson, who was seen running from the washroom. A transient

**Brandon Wilson, who confessed to murdering 9-year-old Matthew Ceechi in Oceanside, California in November 1998.**

from St. Croix Falls, Wisconsin, the 20-year-old Wilson freely admitted killing Checchi, giving police interrogators exact details of the murder. He was charged with first-degree murder and held without bond.

On November 17, 1998, just after his public defender, Curt Owen, had entered a not guilty plea, Brandon Wilson faced a bevy of media reporters and suddenly shouted as he stared wide-eyed into cameras, "I'm guilty! I did it. I did it. I killed him. I killed the little boy."

Prosecutor David Rubin told the press that Wilson had told police that he had intended "to go on killing until he was stopped." Wilson was charged with murder under special circumstances, that of lying in wait and using a knife, which qualified him for the death penalty. Wilson awaits trial at this writing.

---

**Wilson, Earl D. and Harriette**, See: **Butcher, Jake**.

---

**Wilson, Jackie Barron**, 1967- , U.S., kid.-rape-mur. A Dallas County jury took only eight minutes to give the death penalty to child killer Jackie Barron Wilson on September 27, 1989. Wilson, a 22-year-old bricklayer, was convicted on September 22 of the abduction, rape, and murder of 5-year-old Lottie Margaret "Maggie" Rhodes. Rhodes' body was found by a truck driver on a rural road the morning of November 30, 1988. The child had been sexually molested, beaten, asphyxiated, and run over by a car, after being abducted from her bedroom in an Arlington, Texas, apartment complex the previous evening.

According to testimony given during the trial, Wilson's fingerprints showed up on shards of glass from the window in Rhodes' room. Other evidence linking Wilson to the murder were car tire tread marks on the child's back and legs that matched the tires on the car Wilson was driving that evening. Wilson, who maintained his innocence throughout the trial, became a suspect when police learned that he had once lived in the same apartment complex and knew her babysitter. He was sentenced to death by injection.

---

**Wilson, James W.**, 1969- , U.S., mur. Nineteen-year-old James Wilson, an unemployed recluse who surrounded himself with books on crime, emerged from his isolation on September 26, 1989, armed with a .22-caliber nine-shot revolver. He entered a Greenwood, S.C., elementary school cafeteria where he opened fire, killing a student and wounding a teacher. Next he went into a girls' restroom to reload his gun. When teacher Kat Finkbeiner tried to keep him from leaving the room, Wilson shot her in the mouth and hand. Then he went to a third-grade classroom and opened fire, killing an 8-year-old girl and wounding five other students. Wilson threw his empty pistol on the floor and was ordered by Finkbeiner to raise his hands and wait until the police arrived.

In April, Wilson pleaded guilty but mentally ill to two counts of murder. He was convicted of murder and on May 9 was sentenced to die in the electric chair. (Editor's note: For more information on this case, see the *Encyclopedia of World Crime*, Vol. IV.)

---

**Wilson, Johnny Lee**, 1965- , U.S., mur. (wrong. convict.)

The home of 79-year-old Pauline Martz in Aurora, Missouri, caught fire in 1986. Inside the home, bound and gagged, Mrs. Martz had been beaten and was left to die by a thief who also set the house on fire. A large crowd assembled before the burning house at the time, and within the onlookers was a retarded janitor named Johnny Lee Wilson. According to another person in the crowd at that time, Wilson made incriminating remarks about the murdered woman.

These statements, along with Wilson's so-called confession to police, served as enough evidence to convict him in 1987 and send him to prison for life. The conviction did not set well with some prosecutors who brought the details of the case to Missouri Governor Mel Carnahan, who, for more than a year, reviewed the so-called "evidence" that convicted Wilson.

During that period, the witness in the crowd at the burning of the Martz house had recanted those statements. Moreover, Carnahan came to the conclusion that police interrogators had fed Wilson details about the Martz robbery and murder, and that they had "manipulated a weak mind" into confessing a crime he did not commit.

On September 29, 1995, Governor Carnahan pardoned Wilson, stating, "It is clear that Johnny Lee Wilson's confession is false and inaccurate. Furthermore, there is no evidence to corroborate or substantiate it. Quite to the contrary." Wilson, after eight-and-a-half years behind bars, stepped from the gray walls of Jefferson City Correctional Center with tears in his eyes, saying in a sobbing voice, "I didn't do what they said. I'm glad it's over. I feel wonderful, absolutely wonderful."

---

**Wilson, Otis**, See: **Moore, Armand.**

---

**Wilson, Robert Swayne**, See: **Howard, Kenneth Daniel.**

---

**Wilson, Terrance**, See: **ADM.**

---

**Wind, Timothy**, See: **Koon, Stacey.**

---

**Wingate, Dale**, 1947- , U.S., fraud. In 1995, the U.S. Immigration and Naturalization Service (INS) conducted a sweep of illegal aliens in the Moline, Illinois area, and unearthed several illegal immigrants working in a meatpacking plant. One of these was 33-year-old Martha Oncebay, a native of Peru. Upon checking her background, officials noted that false information about Oncebay that allowed her to stay in the U.S. had been provided by Dale Wingate, an INS official living in Chesterton, Indiana.

Further checking revealed that Oncebay had delivered twin daughters in Peru and had arranged for Wingate and his wife, Susan to adopt the girls. She illegally migrated to the U.S., with Wingate's help and connivance, and delivered another child, a boy, whom the Wingates also adopted. The Wingates had one biological son, Jason, who was a U.S. Marine by the time that Oncebay was exposed.

Wingate and his wife could not have more children after Jason, even though they wanted a large family. Wingate used his position with the INS to illegally adopt three of his four Peruvian-born children and then aid one of the mothers, Oncebay, to illegally remain in the U.S., in exchange for her allowing the Wingate's to adopt her children. In his defense, Wingate stated that he had not been motivated by greed or money, but had only wanted to build a larger family.

Convicted of fraud and illegally aiding several aliens to remain in the U.S., as well as aiding in the issuance of a Social Security card to one of the Peruvian mothers, Wingate was sentenced to fifteen months in prison on November 26, 1996, in a Hammond, Indiana, federal court by U.S. District Judge James Moody.

---

**Wise, James**, 1959- , and **Cochrain, Matthew**, 1959- , U.S., Case of mur. Frederick Hughes, a 49-year-old Vietnam War veteran, who worked periodically on construction and lived in a homeless camp in Orlando, Florida, had been buying drinks and hamburgers for his fellow workers for some days in January 1996. Hughes, it was evident to his friends, James Wise and Matthew Cochrain, both 39, was not a well man. He continually coughed up blood from severe emphysema and was racked by pain from advanced stages of cirrhosis of the liver.

On January 26, 1998, as Hughes, Wise and Cochrain munched hamburgers and downed drinks in Orlando's Tiffany Inn, Hughes told his friends that he no longer wanted to live. He found it difficult to work, let alone breathe, he said, and he hated his life, working to exhaustion all day and curling up in a chicken coop in a homeless camp at night. He was in pain and sought relief, so he begged his friends to kill him, or so Wise and Cochrain later told police.

Cochrain refused to kill Hughes, but Wise borrowed a gun from a friend and then he and Hughes staggered out of the bar, going toward the homeless camp. About forty-five minutes later Wise returned, telling Cochrain that he had fulfilled Hughes' desires. Cochrain then, according to Hughes' wish, or so he later said, went to the camp and burned the body and buried the remains.

On January 28, 1998, Cochrain turned himself into police and told the whole story. Wise was later picked up and even both men insisted that they had performed a mercy killing, police charged both men with murder. They await trial at this writing.

---

**Wise, Johnnie**, 1926- , **Grebe, Jack Abbot**, 1955- , and **Emigh, Oliver Dean**, 1935- , U.S., conspir. Three Brownsville, Texas, men—Johnnie Wise, 72, Jack Abbot Grebe, 43, and Oliver Dean Emigh, 63—were arrested at Olmito, Texas, on July 1, 1998, and charged with conspiracy to use weapons of mass destruction against federal agencies. The three men, reportedly connected to the defunct Texas militia separatist group, Republic of Texas, had allegedly sent threatening e-mail to federal officials with the intent to kill the directors of the FBI and the IRS.

U.S. Magistrate John Black refused to release the three men on bond, dismissing arguments from their defense attorneys that the trio had no criminal backgrounds and posed no threat. Black also issued a gag order prohibiting any discussion of the case with the media by prosecuting and defense lawyers. No motives were given by FBI officials, nor was it revealed what kind of weapons had been seized, if any. The defendants await trial at this writing.

---

**Withers, Michael Keith**, 1964- , Aus., attept. mur. On October 23, 1996, Michael Keith Withers faced a long prison term after being convicted of attempted murder in Sydney, Australia. In one of the most bizarre crime stories in Australian history, prosecutors related how Withers and his partner and wife, Stacey Larson, had been championship ballroom dancers. Then, as the team lost its lustre and failed to win contests, Withers, according to prosecutors, got so fed up that, on November 29, 1994, he doused his wife Stacey with gasoline and set her on fire.

**Michael Withers, an Australian ballroom dancer who set his wife-partner on fire when they began to lose contests in 1995.**

Larson barely survived the horrible murder attempt with most of her body burned. She appeared in court to testify against her vicious attacker almost completely swathed in bandages, her grotesque appearance shocking TV viewers and newspaper readers who saw her picture.

A physician testifying in court described how Larson's flesh was so badly burned that, following the attack, he had to slice through the tightly stretched burned skin without being able to give his patient an anesthetic to prevent her fingers from dying from lack of circulation. So graphic was the doctor's descrip-

**Stacey Larson, wife and dance partner of Michael Withers, who is shown wearing the body bandage that covered her horrible burns after her husband tried to burn her alive.**

tion that the jury foreman grew white-faced, groaned and then fainted in the West Australian Supreme Court.

---

**Wong, Chi Wai**, 1944- , U.S., drugs. Chi Wai Wong, a major Hong Kong drug trafficker, was convicted on January 17, 1989, by a federal jury in Los Angeles of possession of sixty-six pounds of heroin and intent to distribute 1,400 grams of heroin. Wong was arrested by U.S. Drug Enforcement Agency (DEA) agents at the Los Angeles International Airport on June 16, 1988. U.S. Customs officials discovered the shipment during a routine inspection of the air freight. The seizure, worth $72 million, was the largest ever intercepted in Southern California.

---

**Wood, Amber Lynn**, See: **Kay, Virginia Marie**.

---

**Wood, Angela**, See: **Ballinger, Jay**.

---

**Wood, Catherine,** See: **Graham, Gwendolyn.**

---

**Wood, James Thomas**, 1970- , U.S., mur. On Christmas Eve, 1994, James Thomas Wood, a crack cocaine addict who had been charged with armed robbery in Tennessee in 1989 and with theft in Hartford County, Maryland in 1991, stabbed to death 55-year-old Reverend Samuel Nathaniel Booth in Middle River, a suburb of Baltimore, Maryland. The next day, December 25, 1994, Wood called state police, admitting that he had killed a minister in a "robbery gone wrong."

The 24-year-old Wood was picked up and charged with murder after he admitted that he had gone to Booth's home, a trailer behind his small Christian Faith Tabernacle Church in Middle River, and tried to rob Booth, whom he killed when the victim resisted. Before he went to trial in Baltimore Circuit Court in December 1995 before Judge Christian M. Kahl, however, Wood had changed his story. He claimed that Booth had been selling him cocaine and was also a user. He said that the two had collected several hundred dollars worth of cocaine and consumed it during a drug binge party.

Booth had then ordered Wood out of his trailer, refusing to give him more crack cocaine, he said, and a struggle ensued with Wood kicking and punching Booth, then grabbing a six-inch kitchen knife and using this to stab Booth to death. He admitted that he had taken $77 from Booth's wallet and some of the crack cocaine they had not consumed.

Wood also claimed in court through his attorneys that Booth had made a homosexual advance and that he had reacted violently. Defense attorneys also argued that Wood was too stoned to have a clear intent to kill. The jury of six women and six men, however, believed prosecutor James Gentry, Jr., who insisted that Wood had committed a premeditated murder in connection with his robbery of the minister and that Wood's claim of Booth being a crack cocaine addict like himself was nothing more than a smokescreen that sullied the reputation of the minister. On December 15, 1995, Wood was convicted of murdering Booth. He was sentenced to life in prison and another twenty years was added for the robbery.

---

**Wood, Randy Lee**, See: **Gambill, Curtis**.

---

**Woodham, Luke**, 1981- , U.S., mur. "I remember I woke up that morning and I'd seen demons that I always saw when Grant told me to do something." That was how 17-year-old Luke Woodham described his first waking moments of Octo-

ber 1, 1997. The "Grant" he referred to was 19-year-old Grant Boyette, a friend of Woodham's since January 1997. At that time, Boyette and a number of other teenage boys in tiny Pearl, Mississippi, formed a Satanic cult, with Boyette as the reported cult leader. No one, however, except Woodham, if his later statements were to be believed, ever came under Boyette's spell.

When Woodham, a tall, big-boned boy who wore glasses and looked somewhat "nerdy" to his friends, broke up with his girlfriend, 16-year-old Cristina Menefee, Boyette, said Woodham later, used the devastating event to manipulate him, telling him that "I was gutless, spineless and that if I didn't do it [kill her], I was nothing. I could have gotten over it, but Grant wouldn't let me."

On October 1, 1997, Woodham woke up and went into the bedroom of his mother, 50-year-old Mary Woodham. There he killed her, slitting her throat and stabbing her fourteen times with a butcher knife, then beating her with an aluminum baseball bat. "I just closed my eyes and fought with myself," Woodham later said about killing his mother, "because I didn't want to do any of it. When I opened my eyes, my mother was lying on her bed dead ... I didn't want to kill my mother. I just wanted her to understand."

After killing his mother, Woodham slipped a rifle beneath a trenchcoat and went to Pearl High School where he was a member of the junior class. He said the demons summoned by Grant Boyette talked to him, "They said I was nothing and I would never be anything if I didn't get to that school and kill those people." Once in the hallway of the school, he sought out his former girlfriend, Cristina Menefee. Finding her he shot her almost point blank in the chest, killing her. "I shot Cristina and I don't know why I shot the others," Woodham said later. "It just happened."

Woodham's second victim was Lydia Dew, whom Woodham had escorted to the prom in 1997 and who was a close friend of Menefee's and was standing close to her. He fired a bullet into Dew's arm that passed into her chest and killed her. He then went down the hall, selecting seven other victims at random. He recognized Alan Westbrook and walked toward him.

Westbrook, seeing the gun in Woodham's hands, began to run away from him, but tripped and fell. Woodham caught up with him, stood over him and cursed Westbrook for turning his back on him. He then shot Westbrook in the back as he lay prone. The bullet missed Westbrook's spine by less than an inch. "I tried to get up, but I couldn't," Westbrook later remembered, "so I just laid there." He would survive.

To Adam Scott, a student who witnessed Woodham's shooting rampage, but who escaped unharmed, the episode was "like a horror movie ... We were standing there in the commons and I heard a loud boom and everything got real quiet ... I saw him [Woodham] walk up to the first girl and pull out a gun and shoot her." In all, Woodham shot nine classmates, killing two and wounding seven others. The shooting rampage stunned the small town of Pearl, a community of 20,000 working-class people located just east of the capital, Jackson, Mississippi.

Brought to trial in 1998, Woodham's attorneys pleaded their client insane at the time of the killings, pointing out that Woodham had been a troubled loner all his life, looking for love and being rejected, first at the age of 2 when his parents divorced, then later, when friends, and finally his girlfriend, Menefee, also rejected him. His only associate was the sinister Grant Boyette, leader of the Satanic cult he called "Kroth," the real person to be blamed for the killings, said the attorneys.

Tim Jones, assistant district attorney, said that Woodham, who had a superior intellect—an I.Q. of 116—had premeditated his murders and was alone guilty of those killings. Woodham loudly sobbed in open court as Jones stated, "He's mean. He's hateful. He's bloodthirsty. He wanted to kill her [his mother]. Murder was on this boy's mind."

On June 5, 1998, Woodham, who was tried as an adult, was found guilty of murdering his mother and was sentenced to life in prison. On June 12, Woodham was convicted of killing Menefee and Dew and wounding the seven other students. He was given two more life sentences and twenty years each for the attempted murder of the seven others. Luke Woodham's response was to say that "I am sorry for the people I killed and the people I hurt ... The reason you don't see any more tears is I have been forgiven by God." He described his murders as "sick and evil. If they could have given the death penalty in this case, I deserve it."

Before he left the court for a lifetime inside a barren prison cell, Woodham faced Cristina Menefee's grandmother, Nita Lilly, who rose in court to say to him, "You initiated a chain of events across these United States that's wreaked havoc on our children." When Woodham left the court, Lilly turned to a reporter and said, "He's a genetic waste." The reported catalyst for the mass murders and shootings, Grant Boyett, was charged with conspiracy and awaited trial at this writing. Also See: **Sledge, Justin**.

---

**Woods, Dorothy**, 1942- , U.S., fraud. Dorothy Woods, the "Welfare Queen" of Los Angeles, was sentenced to five years probation by Superior Court Judge Lillian Stevens on February 1, 1989, after Woods pleaded guilty to collecting $450 in benefits for a teenaged son who did not live with her. In 1983, the 47-year-old Pasadena woman was convicted of fraud after receiving $377,000 in welfare benefits by listing nonexistent children and using aliases. At the time, it was the largest welfare fraud case in U.S. history.

---

**Woods, Jerrol**, 1948- , U.S., Case of burg.-mur. On May 5, 1998, the husband of 30-year-old Dr. Kerry Spooner-Dean, found his wife dead in their Oakland, California, home. She was lying in a pool of blood in her kitchen, two knives still protruding from her back. Though a $50,000 reward was posted for the arrest and conviction of the killer, police reportedly solved the case with their arrest of 50-year-old Jerrol Woods, who had been released from prison in 1996 and whose criminal record for robbery, rape and other charges dated back to 1975. Woods awaits trial at this writing.

---

**Woods, Kevin,** 1953- , and **Bawden, Barry,** 1958- , and **Smith, Michael,** 1954- , Zimbabwe, bomb. Three former members of a Rhodesian military unit were sentenced to prison for forty years each after being found guilty of attacking the headquarters of the African National Congress (ANC) with South African commandos in Harare in 1986. Michael Smith and Kevin Woods both received the death sentence in 1988 after they were convicted of blowing up an ANC building in Bulayow that same year. The sentences against Woods, Smith, and Barry Bawden, were handed down on June 9, 1989.

---

**Woodward, Edwin Davis**, See: **Spunaugle, Delpha**.

---

**Woodward, Louise**, 1977- , U.S., Case of mur., manslght. A teenager from Elton, England, just outside Liverpool, Louise Woodward went to the U.S. in 1996, where she worked as an au pair for two doctor-parents, Sunil and Deborah Eappen, caring for their infant son, Matthew Eappen and his 2-and-a-half-year-old brother, Brendan, in their Newton, Massachusetts, home. On February 4, 1997, Woodward called 911 to report an injury to Matthew, saying that the baby had stopped breathing. Paramedics arrived to take the baby to a hospital where he remained in a coma. He died five days later, on February 9, 1997, reportedly from a skull fracture prosecutors later insisted had been the result of Woodward's violently shaking the child and then slamming the 8-month-old boy "to a hard surface."

Woodward was initially charged with assault, but the charges were upgraded later to murder. In a highly publicized trial watched on cable TV by millions of mostly women (there were reports of women quitting their jobs so that they could stay glued to the gavel-to-gavel coverage offered by cable Court TV), Woodward was convicted by a jury of second-degree murder. Defense attorney Barry Scheck, who had gained fame as one of the "dream team" defense attorneys in the O.J. Simpson case, had led the defense of Woodward, presenting photographic evidence that the victim had suffered a skull fracture some considerable time before the 911 call was placed by Woodward. He was later criticized as introducing this evidence too late in the trial to make an impact upon jurors.

The Woodward case spawned a debate between Woodward's supporters and the millions of working mothers who agonized over the care of their own small children by irresponsible or even vindictive nannies. The case also caused widespread purchases of video systems to be installed in homes where parents could monitor the actions of babysitters.

In England, support for Woodward was widespread and in the U.S., thousands contributed to a defense fund (which accumulated to $400,000) for Woodward. Woodward had not helped her own case when admitting to arresting officers that she may have been "a little rough" with Matthew Eappen, and that she might have earlier dropped him "a few feet" to the floor. Her trial had been further dramatized by Scheck, who insisted that his client not be tried on manslaughter charges but either be convicted of first- or second-degree murder or be acquitted, a gamble that did not pay off. She was convicted of second-degree murder and sentenced to life in prison, a jury decision that shocked Woodward's thousands of supporters in the U.S. and in England.

Further heightening the suspense of this case was the defense argument before Middlesex Superior Court Judge Hiller B. Zobel that the conviction was excessive and that Woodward should receive reduced charges. Again, the public remained glued to television sets while Zobel pondered his decision in early November 1997. Zobel announced that decision in a unique manner, posting his determination on the Internet so that all could see that he had decided to reduce the charges against Woodward to manslaughter and her life sentence to the time already served, 279 days in prison.

Woodward was released, but ordered to remain in Massachusetts while the case was appealed to the state supreme court by prosecutors who were enraged at Zobel's decision, stating that he had overstepped his authority. On June 16, 1998, the Massachusetts Supreme Court upheld Zobel's decision and, to the joy of her supporters and the anger of her detractors, Woodward was allowed to return to her home in Elton, England.

Upon her arrival in England, Woodward stated, "I feel great sorrow for the death of baby Matthew, but like I've said time and time again, I had nothing to do with his death." She was widely criticized at the time, as were her parents, for profiting from Matthew Eappen's death. It was reported that her parents, Susan and Gary Woodward, had received £40,000 ($67,000) from the London *Daily Mail* for Louise Woodward's life story, money the Woodwards claimed had been used for Louise's defense.

Sunil and Deborah Eappen, meanwhile, had filed a wrongful death suit against Woodward in civil court on June 16, 1998. On that date, a day before Woodward departed for England, U.S. District Court Judge William G. Young ordered Woodward to disclose any money-making deal she might receive as a result of her notoriety. Said Deborah Eappen at that time, "There is right and there is wrong. It is wrong for her to profit in any way for what she did to Mattie." The wrongful death suit filed on behalf of the Eappens asked for millions of dollars in compensation.

A settlement in the wrongful death suit was reached on January 29, 1999, before the case went to trial. Woodward was barred from profiting from her story. In England, Paul Barrow, Woodward's attorney, stated, "Louise has always maintained that she has no intention to profit from her story, and Louise continued to maintain her innocence." If Woodward ever makes any money relative to the Eappen death, the court decreed, she was to donate those funds to UNICEF, the international children's charity.

---

**World Trade Center bombing**, 1993, U.S., terr.-mur. A Ryder rental truck was driven into the underground parking area of New York's World Trade Center on February 26, 1993. The truck was packed 1,200 pounds of explosive material, along with three cylinders of hydrogen gas. The entire truck was one huge bomb and when it exploded, six persons were killed and more than 1,000 others were injured. Officials evacuated the twin towers of more than 50,000 persons and then inspected the near-catastrophic damage the bomb had made.

The terrorists, engineers determined, had planned to blow up the support columns and base structure of one of the WTC

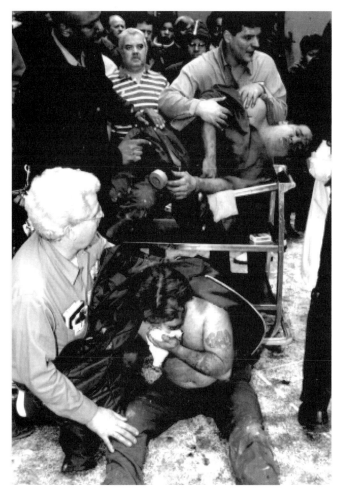

**Some of the injured victims of the World Trade Center bombing in New York on February 26, 1993.**

towers so as to topple it into the other, thus killing tens of thousands of persons. They almost succeeded at their gruesome task. Engineers worked night and day to support the weakened columns to avoid a collapse. The terrorists knew, it was surmised, that the twin WTC towers sit on a large landfill, which is primarily a mud basin and the bomb was positioned so that it could blow a hole in the mud fill. Had that occurred, the Hudson River would have crashed through the opening and flooded lower Manhattan.

From the beginning, senior law enforcement officials felt that the bombing was the work of Iraq, a state-sponsored act of terrorism, knowing that all such massive bombings have been in the past the work of well-established terrorist groups such as the IRA, the Popular Front for the Liberation of Palestine or other such organizations that are secretly backed by terrorist states such as Libya, Iraq and Iran. Pinpointing the insidious agents working for these fanatically right-wing Islamic countries, however, proved to be another matter. In the instance of the World Trade Center bombing, however, investigators were lucky enough to find a solid clue inside the enormous rubble left by the explosion.

On February 28, 1993, investigators uncovered a three-foot piece of truck chassis that had been hurled from the center of the blast. An identification number on the chassis led agents to a truck rental agency in Jersey City, New Jersey, the firm

**FBI photos of Ramzi Ahmed Yousef, the mastermind behind the 1993 World Trade Center bombing; he went to prison for life, as did others in the terrorist plot.**

that had, on February 23, rented the Ryder truck to Mohammed Salameh, a resident of the Little Egypt section of town. Salameh was a 25-year-old Islamic fundamentalist and follower of Sheik Omar Abdel Rahman, the blind fundamentalist leader of fanatical Islamic groups in Manhattan.

Salameh refused to forfeit the $400 deposit he had placed on the truck. When the money-grubbing terrorist appeared to report the vehicle stolen and collect his deposit on March 4, he was arrested by FBI agents. On that same date, agents arrested Ibrahim Elgabrowny in his Brooklyn, New York, apartment, where they found bomb-making materials. Elabrowny did not go gentle into custody, but kicked and punched agents as they struggled to subdue him. His address appeared on Salameh's New York driver's license. Six days later, on March 10, agents located and arrested Nidal Ayyad in Maplewood, New Jersey. Ayyad was a chemical engineer and friend of Salameh's who, according to officials, had the expertise to make the bomb that exploded at the World Trade Center.

At the core of official suspicion was Sheik Omar Abdel Rahman, a blind Egyptian cleric who often preached at a storefront in Jersey City, New Jersey, ceremonies attended by Salameh and Ayyad. Salameh was also a regular visitor to the prison that housed Sayyid Nosair, who was acquitted of the 1990 assassination of Rabbi Mein Kahane in New York, but who went to jail on weapons charges. Salameh, Elabrowny and Ayyad were all indicted for the bombing on March 17, 1993.

Sheik Omar Abdel Rahman, on the following day, denied having anything to do with the World Trade Center bombing. To one reporter, he said, "Did anyone intercept any kind of a letter or any kind of written statement or anything else? I'm asking, what is the clue that they [law enforcement agents] have based their accusations on?"

Two more suspects, Mahmud Abouhalima and Bilal Alkaisi, were arrested in connection with the bombing on March 24-25, 1993, but by then the mastermind of the bombing, Ramzi Ahmed Yousef, a 26-year-old Iraqi, had been identified. He was indicted in absentia on March 31, 1993 for the bombing. By June, the media reported that Emad Salem, a translator and bodyguard for Sheik Omar Abdel Rahman, was identified as an FBI informer. Salem had gone wired for many months among the Islamic fundamentalists working with Rahman and

others who planned the WTC bombing and other terrorist acts. Sheik Rahman himself was indicted and imprisoned for the bombing on August 25, 1993.

The chief suspect, Ramzi Ahmed Yousef, however, was still at large. The FBI made Yousef one of its top public enemies and a worldwide search ensued for him. A 20-man FBI team finally ran him down in Pakistan and returned him to the U.S. on February 8, 1995, where he was convicted of planning and executing the World Trade Center bombing. According to one of the eleven suspects indicted in the bombing—Siddig Ibrahim Siddig Ali, who had turned state's evidence—Yousef and one other man actually drove the rented Ryder truck into the lower parking area of the World Trade Center, parking it in a spot where Yousef felt the bomb would do the most damage.

In the end, all of the indicted Islamic fundamentalists were convicted of the bombing and sent to prison, Yousef and four others for life. Up to the time of its explosion, the horrendous bomb planted in Manhattan's World Trade Center was the worst terrorist act committed in the U.S., one far surpassed in loss of human life by the bomb that wrecked the federal building in Oklahoma City, Oklahoma in 1995. Also See: **McVeigh, Timothy**.

---

**Wright, Daniel,** 1952-1989, U.S., suic.-mur. Daniel Wright had lived with his girlfriend, Agnes Rivera, in Philadelphia for a number of years. In September 1989 Wright moved out of the house after the couple had a violent quarrel. The feud continued to fester and on October 16, 1989, the 37-year-old Wright armed himself with a rifle, a homemade bomb, tear gas, and a flammable liquid and returned home. At 6 a.m. he forced his way inside and fatally wounded Rivera with one shot to the chest. As other relatives fled the house, Wright set off a tear gas container and began firing randomly before going upstairs to his children's bedroom. He fatally shot his 7-year-old son Daniel and his 4-year-old son Maurice before spreading their clothing around the room, soaking it with the flammable liquid and igniting it. As the room filled with flames, Wright fatally shot himself in the neck and fell on top of his sons' bodies. Hours later, when medical examiners inspected Wright's charred remains, they discovered an undetonated black powder bomb in the pocket of his jacket, an indication that the awful destruction could have been much worse.

---

**Wright, Douglas Franklin**, 1940-1996, U.S., mur. After serving twelve years in an Oregon prison for the 1969 murders of a woman and her mother, Douglas Franklin Wright was paroled to murder again. He was convicted and sentenced to death for luring three homeless men from the streets of Portland, to central Oregon on the promise of giving them jobs. Instead, he murdered them. Wright was also charged with killing a fourth homeless man, but that case never went to trial.

The condemned man did not appeal his execution and was scheduled to die on September 6, 1996. A week before he was executed, Wright confessed to kidnapping, molesting and murdering a 10-year-old boy who vanished from his Portland home twelve years earlier. On the last day of his life, Wright listened to Bob Dylan's song, "Knockin' on Heaven's Door," over and over again.

Wright went to his death without making any last remarks, but, as he was strapped onto a gurney in the death room and as he was being given the lethal injection, he mouthed the words "I'm sorry," to the mother of one of his victims; the woman solemnly nodded back to him.

Wright's execution was the first since August 20, 1962, when LeeRoy Sanford McGahuey was executed in Oregon's gas chamber for murdering a child with a hammer. Oregon voters had twice banned capital punishment, in 1914 and in 1964, but they reinstated the death penalty in 1920 and in 1978.

---

**Wright, Dwayne Allen**, 1972-1998, U.S., mur. In October 1989, 17-year-old Dwayne Allen Wright, a resident of Northeast Washington, D.C., went on a five-day shooting rampage, killing a person in Washington, D.C., another in Prince George's County and in Annandale, Virginia. In the last killing, Wright attempted to rape 34-year-old Saba Tekle, a mother of three and when she resisted in the foyer of her apartment, he shot her to death.

Convicted of the Annandale murder, Wright was sentenced to death in Virginia. As his execution date, October 14, 1998, approached, several anti-death penalty groups went into action, as did Wright's lawyers, who appealed to Virginia Governor James S. Gilmore III to commute Wright's sentence to life imprisonment.

Many groups protested Wright's execution on the grounds that he had been a 17-year-old when he committed the murders and that the state had not executed anyone since 1924 for crimes committed while a minor. On the day of execution, African American religious and civic leaders—Wright was a black man—marched to Richmond's Capitol Square to protest the execution and asked that the governor show clemency.

In their appeal to the governor, Wright's attorneys stated that the jury at Wright's trial should have been informed in detail how Wright had suffered brain damage as a child and that he was a borderline retarded person. Governor Gilmore was unmoved and unconvinced by the arguments. He responded by stating that Wright's final appeal "fails to raise any substantially new issue." He went on to say that he remained focused on the rights of Wright's victim, an Ethiopian immigrant whom Wright spotted when she drove past him on a highway and whom he stalked to her Annandale apartment.

Said Gilmore, "Saba Tekle's hopes and aspirations for herself and her three children died with her on the stairs of her apartment building when Wright shot her in the back as she fled his attempted rape ... Today, he is 26. He is not a child nor is he a model prisoner." Gilmore went on to add that Wright had been punished while in prison for making a knife and for assaulting other prisoners. On the same day Gilmore rejected the appeals of Wright's attorneys, the same appeals were rejected by the U.S. Supreme Court.

On the day of his execution, Wright met with his mother, two brothers and an aunt. He then ordered his last meal—pizza, a cheeseburger, french fries and apple pie. He entered the death chamber at Greensville Correctional Center at Jarratt, Virginia,

and was asked if he had a final statement. "My attorney has my statement," Wright said coldly. He was then strapped down on the gurney and given a lethal injection. Wright was pronounced dead at 9:15 p.m.

---

**Wright, Gary,** 1955- , Brit., fraud. Financial woes on the British Stock Exchange compelled 34-year-old Gary Wright of London to gamble with his clients' money in order for him to maintain an ostentatious lifestyle. In the end he came up short, and was sent to jail for two years by Judge Hordern of the Queen's Court on November 15, 1989.

Wright was a principal stockbroker for the firm of Spencer, Thornton, and Northcote. His yearly income was placed at £250,000—until the disastrous 1987 stock market crash impacted the fortunes of the company. In an attempt to recoup his losses, Wright began placing bets at the race tracks. The money was derived from his clients' accounts. Wright hoped to use part of his winnings to cover his bets. The scheme was kept secret from his friends and family until a colleague at the investment firm noticed that a large number of customers had piled up a number of mysterious debts. Following a police investigation, Gary Wright was arrested. Wright pleaded guilty to nine charges of obtaining property by deception and false accounting.

---

**Wright, Malcolm,** See: **Burmeister, James II**.

---

**Wrighton, Sara,** See: **Thomas, Ruth.**

---

**Wuornos, Aileen Carol** (AKA: I-75 Killer), 1957- , U.S., rob.-mur. Between 1989 and 1990, Aileen Carol Wuornos, a drifter and prostitute (she listed her occupation as "professional call girl"), murdered by her own count seven men. She hitch-hiked along Florida's I-75 Highway, being picked up by men she would rob at gunpoint and then order the drivers to turn off at lonely areas where she killed them. She later took delight in recalling how she shot one of her male victims six times, including a coup de grace to the head "to put him out of his misery."

The victims undoubtedly picked up Wuornos at night and one would suppose them to be in drunken stupors to invite this monster into their cars, for in the broad light day they would have seen a horridly repulsive creature with greasy, straggly, dirty-blonde hair, cracked and lined skin, decaying teeth, jowls and wattles, a beer gut and the hands of a lumberjack. She was the lowest of diseased whores who sought salvation for her vile murders by absurdly posturing herself as a feminist striking back at a male-dominated world that had shown her little pity. In reality, she was a calculating, sinister killer, who premeditated each and every one of her robbery-murders.

Before she was arrested on January 9, 1991, Wuornos, following her sleazy opportunistic instincts, signed a movie deal with Hollywood producer Jackelyn Giroux, who later moronically described Wuornos as being "delightful." Wuornos' life, or the blatantly false representations she made to concoct a phony image of that life, was later made into a tawdry made-for-TV movie. An equally repugnant documentary was also made about her.

Convicted of four of the seven murders she committed, Wuornos was sentenced to death on January 31, 1992. She now awaits her execution on Florida's Death Row, while she files one frantic appeal after another to prolong an utterly worthless life at the considerable expense of the taxpaying public.

---

**Wurst, Andrew**, 1984- , U.S., mur. On the Friday evening of April 24, 1998, 14-year-old Andrew Wurst went to an eighth-grade graduation dance in the small town of Edinboro, Pennsylvania, in the northwest part of the state. As soon as he arrived at the hall, he shot and killed teacher John Gillette on a patio outside a banquet hall. He then entered the hall and continued to fire a .25-caliber handgun registered to his father, several more shots that wounded another teacher and two students. Wurst then left the school, walking into a field, but he was cornered by James Strand, the owner of the hall, Nick's Place, and ordered to drop his handgun. Strand pointed a shotgun at Wurst who calmly obeyed.

Andrew Wurst, 14-year-old boy who shot and killed a teacher from his middle school in Edinboro, Pennsylvania, and wounded three others in April 1998.

Charged with murder, authorities debated whether or not to try Wurst as an adult. His lawyers, who visited with him in jail, stated, "He's devastated. This family [Wurst's] is devastated. Their hearts go out to the Gillette family." (Such lame dog comments had become excruciatingly routine after the recent school shootings in Jonesboro, Arkansas; West Paducah, Kentucky; and Pearl, Mississippi.

Wurst's classmate at Parker Middle School, Trenton Lucas, thought the killer "had a really sick sense of humor ... He would like laugh when he said it: 'I'm going to the dinner dance and kill some people.'" Lucas did not take Wurst's statements seriously. Neither did Ben Mills, who had nicknamed Wurst "Satan," because of his fascination with rocker Marilyn Manson and his violent music.

The teenage killer could give no explanation for the shooting. He did not know the man he killed, 48-year-old Gillette, who had taught at his school for twenty-seven years. According to Ben Mills, Wurst's classmate, "He hated his life. He hated the world. He hated school." Wurst bore an uncanny physical and emotional resemblance to other school shooters such as Luke Woodham, who murdered three persons and wounded seven others in Pearl, Mississippi in 1997. Both boys had mop heads and wore oversized glasses. They were both loners and felt a deep sense of rejection. Also See: **Woodham, Luke**.

---

**Wybrun, Joseph**, 1940-1889, Belg., assass. Jewish leaders in Belgium blamed the October 3, 1989, murder of Dr. Joseph Wybrun of the Coordination Committee for Jewish Organizations on neo-Nazi fanatics anxious to fan the flames of anti-Semitism in this predominantly Catholic country. Wybrun was shot to death as he walked towards his car outside the Brussels University Hospital, where he was head of the immunology department.

Wybrun was an outspoken critic of the Catholic church's decision to build a Carmelite Nunnery outside the former Nazi death camp at Auschwitz. In his visit to Poland, Dr. Wybrun called on the papacy to remove the religious symbols and convent from the Auschwitz memorial. Wybrun was the chairman of the Belgian chapter of the Auschwitz Committee, and was the second ecumenical leader to be gunned down in Belgium in 1989. In April the leader of the Arabic mosque in Brussels was assassinated for publicly condemning the Ayatollah Khomeini's order to kill novelist Salman Rushdie.

---

**Wymer, Steven David**, 1950- , U.S., fraud. An investment adviser and money manager in Newport Beach, California, Steven David Wymer managed more than $1.2 billion through his Institutional Treasury Management firm. Through the years, Wymer, instead of making legitimate investments, operated a Ponzi scheme where he paid off early investors with money from those later investing with his firm. He was convicted in 1991 of swindling more than $57 million from the Jefferson Bank and Trust of Lakewood, Colorado, along with two other entities in that state, Weld County, Colorado, and Investment Trust of Colorado. Wymer received a reduced prison term for cooperating with federal agencies investigating the investment business.

Wymer testified in 1993 in Washington, D.C., before a House panel that the Securities and Exchange Commission did brief inspections of his firm's records, but did not realize (or question) the falsified numbers in those records. Further, Wymer said he was aided in easily moving his clients' money by corrupt stockbrokers who agreed to help shift funds without sending confirmation statements to his clients.

# X-Y-Z

**Xu Lin Wang**, 1972- , and **Xue Nan Wang**, 1971- , U.S., kid. Kuan Nan Chen, the son of a wealthy Los Angeles developer, was kidnapped from the garage of his San Marino home on December 15, 1998, and held in the Los Angeles home, his abductors demanding a $1.5 million ransom for his return. The ransom was to be paid in China's Fujian Province. On January 4, 1999, Fu Shun Chen, the victim's father, delivered $500,000 in ransom money to two men in Fujian Province, who were promptly arrested by Chinese authorities.

At the time his father was delivering the ransom, Kuan Nan Chen was rescued by Los Angeles officers who had located the hiding place of the kidnappers through phone taps and a tip from a neighbor. Kuan Nan Chen was set free unharmed and his kidnappers, Xu Lin Wang, of Temple City, California, and Xue Nan Wang, of New York City, were arrested and charged with kidnapping. If convicted, they would face life in prison. Both await trial at the time of this writing.

---

**Xu Wenli**, 1967- , China, treason. On November 30, 1998, twenty heavily armed policemen in Beijing, China, burst into the home of Xu Wenli, arresting him on charges of treason, and ransacking his house in an effort to find incriminating evidence. The police confiscated Xu's fax machine, phone receipts and other paperwork that might show his deep involvement in the establishment of the China Democratic Party, a political party Xu and others, including Qin Yongmin and Wang Youcai, had been attempting to establish in opposition to the Communist dictatorship of China. Xu had spent more than a decade in prison for his anti-Communist activities. He awaits trial at this writing. Also See: **Wang Youcai** and **Qin Yongmin**.

---

**Yah Lin Trie** (AKA: Charlie), 1952- , U.S., Case of illeg. polit. donations, obstruct. of just. A longtime friend of President Bill Clinton, and former restaurant owner in Little Rock, Arkansas, Yah Lin Trie, called "Charlie," was accused in 1998 of making illegal political donations to the Democratic National Committee in order to have access to President Clinton, and obstructing justice by ordering subpoenaed documents hidden or destroyed. A native of China, Yah had a Taiwanese passport, which was revoked in December 1998, pending his forthcoming trials.

---

**Yakuza**, 1990s, Jap., criminal secret society. The all powerful Japanese secret criminal society known as Yakuza came into existence following World War II, after the so-called disbanding of the dreaded Black Dragon Society, the secret criminal organization that helped Emperor Hirohito engineer Japan into World War II. Yakuza was the extension and outgrowth of the old Black Dragon Society, but, in the last five decades it has grown to enormous proportions, with an estimated national membership of between one and three million persons. Membership included top level government officials, banking and financial leaders, law enforcement and military chiefs. (These leaders, it was reported, were coated with Yakuza tattoos from neck to ankle, which symbolized their status and position within the criminal society.)

During the 1980s, Japan's banking system, with many Yakuza members at the helms of banks, made enormous loans to developers and building firms that were nothing more than fronts for Yakuza operations, loans that the bankers knew would never be repaid. This led to the establishment of ultra-secret banking records where such loans could not be disclosed. By the mid-1990s, intelligence reports had it that the bulk of the top bankers in Japan, chiefly Tokyo, had come under suspicion of being members (high-echelon directors) of the national crime syndicate, Yakuza, and had umbilical ties to Yakuza's enforcement-collection arm, Sokaiya.

The more than $600 billion in defaulted loans, which caused the Far East economic crisis in the late 1990s, were made by bankers and chiefs of securities firms who were Yakuza members themselves, to Yakuza directors of development firms and other businesses in the private sector. In some cases, huge unsecured loans were made directly to Yakuza members. Kunjii Miyazaki, chairman of the Dai-Ichi Kangyo Bank (which claimed to have had more assets than Citibank and Bankers Trust combined) loaned 30 billion yen to Ryuichi Koike, chief extortionist of the Sokaiya. When confronted with this loan by Japanese regulators, Miyazaki excused himself, went to his study and promptly hanged himself.

The Japanese banks had lamely attempted to collect the bad debts by seizing collateral, but this measure utterly failed. One report held that such collections were intended to fail, that such attempts were merely lame-duck gestures by bankers who were themselves Yakuza members attempting to pacify the demands of banking investigators. The regulators themselves may have been Yakuza members, compelled to act because "outsiders" unearthed information on the criminal loans. When Sumitomo Bank *appeared* to aggressively seize collateral for a large outstanding loan in Nagoya, its branch manager, who had been instructed to seize assets, was murdered by Yakuza thugs.

In August 1997, Koichiro Tarutani, an executive of Yamaichi Securities (this firm having "loaned" crime boss Koike 79 million yen), was murdered in Tokyo while walking home, slashed to death as if his killers had employed a Samurai sword—the traditional murder weapon of the Yakuza. (The shopkeeper, who found Tarutani crying for help, stated, "His guts were spilling out. I was so shocked I couldn't sleep that night.") This murder, like so many others dealing with Japan's financial community, remained unsolved. One charge has it that the investigations into such killings were also purposely sluggish, since they were directed by high-ranking police officials who were also Yakuza members.

For years Japanese bankers used Yakuza and Sokaiya members as collection enforcers on bad debts. Real estate developers used Yakuza to forcibly evict tenants from desirous land locations. Over time, however Yakuza placed members inside the banks and then recruited the top banking officials, as well as top officials in real estate, business, manufacturing, finance, securities firms, government, police and the military to its ranks (under penalty of death). The control of the country's finances, banking and government was considered to essentially be in the hands of the Yakuza. Much like the Masons, there are degrees of rank in the Yakuza, signified by the number and type of tattoos to be found on the bodies of Yakuza members, and this would include leading bankers, financiers, and government officials. When Dai-Ichi chairman Miyazaki's body was examined following his suicide, it was reported that his body was coated, from neck to ankles, with Yakuza tattoos.

Japan's Ministry of Finance (MOF) was rife with Yakuza members. MOF had a practice of "arm-twisting" in the back rooms of its government offices. Japan's entire economy was, in intelligence parlance, run "extralegally." A report had it that Hideo Sakamaki, one-time president of Nomura Securities, was a Yakuza, as was Tadashi Okuda, former chairman of the Dai-Ichi Kangyo Bank. The more than $600 billion in loans made by Japanese banks in recent years have gone largely to real estate developers, the bankers and the developers both reportedly being high-ranking Yakuza members. These loans make up more than half of Japan's present bad real estate loans.

Some of the Yakuza-controlled banks attempted to "repackage" their bad debts in the form of bonds to be sold to investors. One overseas deal by Japanese banks involved $1 billion in medium-term notes, which were reportedly backed by Yakuza loan-shark assets, as well as other illegal operations (brothels and opium distribution that trail to Hawaii and Mexico). Japan's ministry of finance had unofficially admitted that the country was in the grip of the Yakuza, one of its top officials stating (off the record), "I do not think it can be rooted out."

From all reliable reports, Japan's economy and, specifically, its banking system, is, at the time of this writing, thoroughly corrupted by and infected with the criminal organization, Yakuza, making it impossible to place any real value on the yen or the dollars ostensibly controlled by Japan's banks. Also See: **Aum Shinri Kyo**; **Japan**; **Japan Bank Scandal**.

---

**Yamashita Tokuo**, 1920- , Japan, morals. In early August 1989, Japan's prime minister, Uno Sousuke, was replaced by Kaifu Toshiki after Uno's extramarital affairs were revealed. Kaifu had vowed his regime would uphold higher moral standards, but less than a month later, on August 24, his chief cabinet secretary, Yamashita Tokuo, announced his resignation after admitting he had an affair with a cocktail waitress. Yamashita, 69, acknowledged his liaison with an unnamed 21-year-old woman, which occurred between 1984 and 1987, after a newspaper reported that he had given the woman $21,000 in hush money when he was about to be named to the cabinet. Yamashita denied the monetary allegation, saying that he had given her the money as a gift. He further stated that he told his wife about his indiscretions and that she had forgiven him, but announced his resignation on August 25 to prevent further embarrassment to the Kaifu regime.

---

**Yandle, Joseph**, 1949- , U.S., On June 20, 1972, Joseph Yandle drove a getaway car while an accomplice robbed the Mystic Bottled Liquors store in Medford, Massachusetts. During the course of the robbery, the accomplice shot and killed the store owner, Joseph Reppucci. Yandle was convicted and sent to prison for life, but Yandle won freedom in 1991 after telling the CBS news program, "60 Minutes," that he had committed the robbery under the influence of heroin, which he used to quell nightmares of his harrowing wartime experiences in Vietnam, and to which he was addicted.

The media picked up the story and soon Yandle had the widespread support of the public, including organizations of war veterans. The Massachusetts State Board of Pardons approved of Yandle's 1991 release, which was ordered by then Governor William Weld. On August 26, 1998, Yandle was arrested at his Rutland, Vermont, home and returned to prison for fabricating his war experience.

Records proved that he had been far from the fighting in Vietnam during the war and that he had been a Marine desk clerk stationed in Okinawa and never saw any action, facts that neither researchers for "60 Minutes," nor Massachusetts officials closely checked. Yandle admitted that he "had to find a way to get someone to listen to my plea for commutation. The fact is I just wanted to go home after twenty-three years in prison."

---

**Yarborough, Keith**, See: **Moshoures, Michael**.

---

**Yassin, Ahmed**, See: **Hamas**.

---

**Yilmaz, Mesut**, prom. 1998, Turk., polit. corruption. After a decade of corrupt administrations in Turkey, the government led by Mesut Yilmaz, ostensibly a reformer who had reduced the country's mercurial inflation and eased restrictions on Islamic practices, it was charged that Yilmaz himself, along with most of the members of this administration, had been working hand-in-hand with Turkish gangsters to take over the country's financial institutions. When it was disclosed that Yilmaz had personally helped gangsters take over a large Turkish bank—allegations he denied—the Turkish parliament voted him out of office on November 25, 1998.

---

**York, Thomas**, 1939- , U.S., mur. On July 7, 1989, the testimony of the son and the daughter of Thomas York led to his conviction for the 1981 murder of his business partner, Gail Maher. On April 19, 1981, a bomb exploded in the Just Friends Lounge in Summit, Illinois, killing Maher. York, a former Chicago police officer, then collected $60,000 in business insurance, as well as an additional $50,000 in life insurance from a policy he had secretly taken out on Maher. The circumstances were similar to those in the May 1978 death of York's first wife, Maureen Ann Jurkiewicz, who was shot in the head and left naked in a river. Although their marriage was failing, York had taken out a $104,000 life insurance policy shortly before his wife's death. York was never tried for the murder of his wife, but in 1986 was tried and convicted of Maher's murder, largely on the testimony of his son's parole officer who claimed that Tommy York, as a 9-year-old child in 1981, had witnessed his father assembling a bomb. But in 1988, the U.S. Circuit Court of Appeals overturned York's conviction, ruling that the conversation between the parole officer and the boy was inadmissible evidence.

York was retried in June 1989 at the U.S. District Court in Chicago before Judge Ann Williams, the judge who had earlier allowed the inadmissible evidence. Tommy York, now 17, said he was no longer afraid of his father and reiterated that he had witnessed his father with the components of an explosive device. His sister, Anne York, stated that her father had asked her to provide an alibi for his whereabouts on the night of the tavern bombing. On July 7, 1989, York was found guilty of murder, conspiracy, mail fraud, and obstruction of justice, and on September 8, he was sentenced to forty years in prison.

---

**York, Walter Thomas**, 1976- , **Fox, Kenneth Ray**, 1960- , **Fox, Vickie Jumper**, 1964- , **Anderson, Carlton Eugene**, 1976- , **Trantham, Robert Lee**, 1976- , **Vinson, Michele Shook**, 1974- , and **Hagedorn, Michael Blain**, 1978- , U.S., mur. A group of trailer trash inhabitants of Sylva, North Carolina, gathered in the trailer of Vickie Jumper Fox on the night of April 1, 1994, and beat to death 24-year-old Tony Cecil Queen, for allegedly fondling a child. Kenneth Ray Fox went to the local police to report the beating, saying that it had occurred in the trailer occupied by his estranged wife, Vickie. She, Walter Thomas York, a long-haired 18-year-old, along with teenagers Carlton Eugene Anderson, Robert Lee Trantham, Michele Shook Vinson and Michael Blain Hagedorn, had all participated in the savage beating of Queen.

Actually, as investigators later learned, the seven cretinous killers had kept Queen a prisoner for almost ten days, torturing him slowly to death, burning his genitals with a blowtorch and periodically beating him with mop handles, broomsticks and bats, until he died. The killers who performed this grisly chore to teach Queen not to "mess with kids," then drove his body into the Chattahoocie National Forest in Georgia and dumped it in the wilds.

Kenneth Fox was the first to admit the murder, but he and the others blamed Walter York, the most savage of their group, as being person who literally kicked Queen to death. Brought to trial in 1995, York and Anderson were given life sentences. The rest received fifteen to twenty-five years in prison for their roles in the murder.

---

**Young, Bruce Alan**, 1950- , U.S., rape. A male nurse at Florida's Citrus Memorial Hospital, Bruce Young was discovered by another nurse as he was atop a groggy 15-year-old patient, raping the girl. Young was arrested, and, in a plea-bargain agreement, admitted that he had raped seven patients while they were heavily sedated. He was sentenced to seventeen years in prison and, upon release, he was to serve thirteen more years on probation, on the provision that he never again work as a care giver. The sentence was passed on February 3, 1995 by Judge Hale Stancil in Inverness, Florida.

Young stood in court handcuffed and wearing an orange prison jumpsuit, saying, "I'm pleading guilty to the charges because it's in my best interest." Before he was led off to prison, a husband of one of the victims shouted after Young, "I hope you burn in hell for the evil deeds you've done!"

---

**Young, Julius Ricardo**, 1948- , U.S., mur. A neighbor living in the same Tulsa, Oklahoma, apartment building as Joyland Morgan was asked to check on the 20-year-old Morgan, who had failed to show up for work that day, October 1, 1993. The neighbor went to the upstairs apartment and found the door ajar. Inside the apartment lay the mangled bodies of Morgan and her young son Kewan. Both had been bludgeoned to death, their heads hardly recognizable. A coroner later stated that the two had been beaten to death by either a baseball bat or a lead pipe.

Detectives investigating the murders failed to turn up any suspects until they interviewed the victim's mother, who told them that the only person who might be considered her daughter's enemy was her own boyfriend, 45-year-old Rev. Julius Ricardo Young, who was pastor of the African Methodist Episcopal Church in nearby Boynton, Oklahoma. The mother explained that Joyland had often come between her and Young, stating that he was evil and even claiming that Young had raped her when she was 16-years-old.

Investigators looked into Young's background and discovered that he had a criminal record dating to 1977 when he was convicted of forgery. In 1985, he was convicted of fraud—obtaining money under false pretenses—and sent to prison for five years. When detectives first interviewed Young about the Morgan murder, he appeared to be shocked. They found in his apartment a pair of blood-covered shoes. Young said that the blood had come from his cleaning some fish. The shoes and hairs found in the hands of the victim—Morgan had struggled with her attacker, tearing away some strands of hairs—were sent to a lab for DNA analysis.

The DNA analysis proved that the blood on Young's shoes had been that of Morgan and her son and the hair found beneath the nails of the victim was that of Young. The clergyman was charged with murder and went to trial on September 11, 1995. After ten days, a jury deliberated less than four hours to find Young guilty of both murders. He was sentenced to death by Tulsa District Judge Clifford Hopper. Young awaits execution at this writing.

---

**Young, Massie Linwood** (AKA: Charles Miles Breedlove), 1925-1992, U.S., escaped prisoner. Following a 15-year-marriage, Charles Miles Breedlove died in Greenville, North Carolina, on April 6, 1992. His wife, who knew nothing of his past, and who had trouble in collecting insurance because of a dispute over her dead husband's social security number, hired a private investigator to look into her deceased husband's background. It was then learned that Breedlove, who had never taken out a driver's license and had refused to ever sign a legal document, was really Massie Linwood Young, an escaped convict from a state prison in Fredericksburg, Virginia. Young had escaped in 1963, after serving three years of an 11-year prison term for forgery.

---

**Young, Todd,** 1965- , U.S., weapons-mur. On April 18, 1989, Todd Young, a 24-year-old Queens, New York, man, was convicted of shooting his fiance and then using $2,000 earmarked for their upcoming wedding to purchase cocaine. Young was found guilty of the January 24, 1987, murder of 20-year-old Melanie Hendricks. Young had confessed to police following the murder that Hendricks had become enraged with him after she caught him using cocaine in the bathroom of her parents' house. Later that same evening, the couple, who were to have been married a week later, argued again about the incident. Young told police that he followed Hendricks into the laundry room of their apartment building and shot her twice in the head with a .25-caliber automatic pistol.

After killing Hendricks, Young then called a drug dealer to whom he owed money and asked him to bring more cocaine to him. Young paid the dealer $2,000, which had been given to Hendricks by her grandmother to pay for wedding expenses. Young, also convicted of illegal possession of a firearm, was sentenced on May 24, 1989, to twenty-five years to life in prison, the maximum sentence permitted by law.

---

**Youngerman, David S.,** 1965- , Case of, U.S., attempt. mur. David Youngerman was a genius, so brilliant in mathematics that he earned his doctoral degree at age 16. But his intellect hindered his emotional development, and he attended special schools to overcome dyslexia and various speech impediments. Youngerman blamed his father for his problems, and on October 2, 1985, attempted his revenge by trying to kill his father.

Irwin Youngerman never saw the attacker who entered his Evanston, Illinois, home, slashed his throat and hands, and left him for dead. His son David became a suspect when investigators learned he had quit school and returned to the Chicago area. David fled the area soon afterwards, moving to California where he lived on public aid and performed manual labor. Youngerman, arrested for jaywalking, was returned to Illinois for police questioning. He confessed to the attempted murder, saying that he would have also killed his mother if given the opportunity, and was brought to trial in March 1989 at Cook County Circuit Court before Judge Nicholas Pomaro.

Public defenders Gerald Kirschbaum and Henry Singer presented psychiatric testimony that diagnosed Youngerman as a paranoid schizophrenic who was convinced that his father was evil. Prosecutors Sander Klapman and Toni Winninger said the attack was premeditated, citing an August 1985 incident when Youngerman had returned to the area and bought a knife only to find his parents away from their house. On March 7, 1989, Judge Pomaro ruled David Youngerman innocent by reason of insanity. Youngerman underwent psychiatric evaluation, and in September he was sentenced to the Elgin Mental Health Center for up to fifteen years.

---

**Younis, Fawaz** (AKA: Nazeeh), 1959- , U.S., hijack. On June 11, 1985, members of the Amal terrorist militia organization led by Fawaz Younis, a Lebanese Muslim, stormed and occupied a Royal Jordanian airliner with seventy passengers aboard at the Beirut airport. While four other terrorists beat Jordanian security guards, Younis ordered the pilot to fly to Tunis so he could deliver a statement to the Arab League denouncing the Palestinian occupation of Lebanon. Their attempt to land was blocked by Tunisian officials, and the hijackers returned to Beirut where they released the passengers and crew and blew up the aircraft. When it was learned that two Americans were aboard the jetliner, the hijacking became a U.S. crime under a 1984 statute that protects American citizens anywhere in the world. The FBI captured Younis on September 13, 1987, on a yacht in the Mediterranean after agents lured him into an alleged drug deal. Younis was brought to Washington, D.C., and ordered to stand trial in October 1989 before U.S. District Court Judge Aubrey Robinson. Younis stated that he was merely following orders and that he had no knowledge that the plane was to be destroyed. He denied being a terrorist and said that the beatings of the Jordanian guards would have been worse if he had not intervened. On October 4, 1989, Younis was found guilty of taking hostages, aircraft piracy, and conspiracy and sentenced to thirty years in prison. He was found innocent on charges of assaulting the passengers and of the destruction of the aircraft.

---

**Youseff, Ehyin Mohammed,** 1972- , U.S., manslght. Relatives of Dr. William McCoy Yates, a wealthy 42-year-old black parapsychologist living in a luxury home in the resort community of River Bend, North Carolina, became concerned when Yates disappeared on March 6, 1992. The relatives searched through the doctor's home, but found nothing. Then one of the relatives saw a bloodsmear on the trunk of Yate's Mercedes sedan. Police were called and officers pried open the trunk to find Yates stuffed inside. He had been bludgeoned to death.

A check of Yates' carports revealed that one of the seven luxury cars he owned, a BMW, was missing. It was later found abandoned. On it and on the trunk of the Mercedes, police found fingerprints that were later linked to 20-year-old Ehyin Mohammed Youseff, a black youth with a criminal record. Youseff had been charged with robbing at gunpoint a student on the campus of North Carolina State University on October 28, 1991, and had been locked up in the Raleigh, North Carolina, jail. He had previously been charged with many assaults and theft.

A search for Youseff was conducted but he evaded capture until May 5, 1994, when Youseff, who had been working in a Washington, D.C. health club and living under an assumed name in that city, turned himself into D.C. police who had charged him with larceny. D.C. police identified Youseff through his fingerprints and, in response to the outstanding murder warrant for him issued in North Carolina, contacted officers of that state. Youseff was returned to Raleigh to stand trial for the Yates killing.

Before he went to trial, Youseff cut a deal with prosecutors. He confessed to murdering Yates, but claimed that he had been driven to murder by Yates himself, an aggressive homosexual who hounded Youseff for sex. Said Youseff, "He [Yates] worshipped Satan in every aspect of his life and he tried to get me to sell my soul to Satan." He said that Yates knew of his criminal background and threatened to have him arrested. Youseff said that Yates coerced him into having homosexual sex with him, until he finally rebelled and beat Yates to death, then stuffed his body into the Mercedes and fled with the BMW.

On June 2, 1992, Youseff pleaded guilty to second-degree manslaughter and was sentenced to twenty years in prison. He is now serving that sentence at the Central Prison in Raleigh, North Carolina.

---

**Yun, Juwhan**, 1941- , U.S., consp. On January 12, 1989, Juwhan Yun, a 48-year-old Korean businessman from Short Hills, New Jersey, was arrested by U.S. Customs agents near Newark International Airport and charged with conspiring to illegally export 125 tons of the lethal gas SARIN, allegedly to be sold to the government of Iran. An odorless, colorless nerve gas, SARIN causes death shortly after inhalation or absorption through the skin. Yun, president of Komex International Corporation, which exported legal munitions, had been dealing with the undercover agents since June 1988 in an attempt to legally purchase a variety of weapons. On January 6, 1989, Yun told an agent that the nerve gas would be shipped from the port of Baltimore, but on January 11, the night before his arrest, he cancelled the deal. In May, Yun was tried at the Federal District Court in Newark, New Jersey., before Judge H. Lee Sarokin. Defense attorney Stephen Dratch claimed that Yun was a licensed arms dealer who had been entrapped by agents who had refused to provide him with legitimate arms unless he participated in the nerve gas scheme. Prosecutor Mark S. Olinsky countered that Yun was aware of the nerve gas' toxicity and the illegality of dealing with a potentially hostile government, and that he had been motivated by his own greed. The jury concurred, and on May 19, 1989, Yun was found guilty of conspiracy. On September 10, he was sentenced to thirty months in prison.

---

**Zahnd, Kimberly**, See: **Holly, Christopher**.

---

**Zakrzewski, Edward**, 1963- , U.S., mur. Tech. Sgt. Edward Zakrzewski, stationed near Shalimar, Florida, pleaded guilty in March 1996 to hacking his family to death with a machete. Zakrzewski murdered his 34-year-old wife Sylvia, his 7-year-old son, Edward, Jr., and 5-year-old daughter, Anna. On April 19, 1996, Judge G. Robert Barron sentenced Zakrzewski to die in Florida's electric chair.

---

**Zamarreno, Manuel**, 1956-1998, Spain, assass. On June 25, 1998, ETA guerrillas parked a motorcycle on a residential street in the Basque town of Renteria, Spain, and, as town councilor Manuel Zamarreno walked past the bike, the bomb was detonated, killing the Popular Party politician. The following

day, tens of thousands took to the streets of Madrid, Seville, Bilbao and San Sebastian in protest over the latest separatist assassination.

Zamarreno, who had often been threatened by ETA terrorists, became the twelfth politician in Spain within the year to die because of his opposition to the separatists. Members of the Popular Party demanded that the Basque National Party break off all association with Herri Batasuna, the legal political wing for ETA. This the Basques refused to do, knowing that their

**Basque town councilor Manuel Zamarreno, assassinated in Renteria, northern Spain, on June 25, 1998.**

party members in parliament were instrumental in holding the balance of power in Spain's minority government.

---

**Zamora, Diane**, 1978- , and **Graham, David**, 1978- , U.S., mur. During their freshman year in high school, Diane Zamora and David Graham, residents of the small town of Mansfield, Texas (pop. 22,000, south of Forth Worth), met and became engaged. Both were top students at their separate schools, Graham at Mansfield High and Zamora at Crowley High. Both became enamored of each other and then obsessed with each other. Super achievers, Zamora and Graham were honors students who also excelled in athletics. She wanted to become an astronaut and he dreamed of flying warplanes. They both got part of their wish with scholarships, Zamora to the Naval Academy in Annapolis and Graham to the Air Force Academy. They planned to marry upon graduation from their highly prestigious military colleges. That was not to be.

Graham had met an attractive blonde, 16-year-old Adrianne Jones, who was also a member of his school's track team. During the long bus rides across the far stretches of the Texas prairies to track meets, Graham and Jones held lengthy conversations and soon began seeing each other. On November 4, 1995, Graham and Jones were in Lubbock, Texas, 250 miles away from their hometown. There they had sex, according to a later statement by Graham.

After struggling with guilt for about a month, Graham confessed his infidelity to Zamora who became livid. As Graham later wrote: "This precious relationship we had was damaged by my thoughtless actions, the only thing that could satisfy her [Zamora's] womanly vengeance was the life of the one who had, for an instant, taken her place."

Zamora and Graham agreed that Jones had to pay with her life for coming between them. They made a murder plan; Graham would pretend to pick up Jones on a date and drive her to Joe Pool Lake near Grand Prairie, Texas, and there they would break the girl's neck, then weight her body down with barbells and sink it in the lake. They premeditated the murder of a young innocent girl and carried out their plot on December 3, 1995, when Graham picked up Jones, who thought she was going on a date.

Lurking in the trunk of Graham's car was Zamora. The back seat had been loosened so Zamora could see Graham behind the wheel and Jones sitting next to him. When Graham neared the lake on a lonely road, he motioned to Zamora who climbed into the back seat where she began screaming at Jones. Graham tried to break Jones' neck, but was unsuccessful, later stating, "I realized too late that all those quick, painless snaps seen in the movies were just your usual Hollywood stunts."

**Honor student and Annapolis mid-shipman Diane Zamora, who masterminded the Texas murder of her sexual rival in 1995 and who, along with her lover and co-killer, David Graham, went to prison for life in 1998.**

Zamora, however, swung a barbell onto Jones' head, but the spunky girl still had fight left in her and crawled out through the window of the car door. Zamora's blow to the head had nevertheless fractured Jones' skull and damaged her brain. She staggered to a barbed wire fence, then collapsed. "I knew I couldn't leave the key witness to our crime alive," Graham later wrote. He produced a Russian-made 9mm Makarov pistol he had brought along and fired two bullets into the girl. One bullet smashed into Jones' forehead, square between the eyes. (It was never made clear what brought about Jones' death; the coroner stated in an autopsy report that she might have been dead from the blow to her head before the bullet was fired into her brain.)

With Jones dead, Graham and Zamora embraced. They told each other, "I love you." They left and Jones' body was found the next day, but police had no clue as to who might kill the popular student, who was, like Graham and Zamora, an honor student. Graham was known to have dated Jones and was questioned, but he was not considered a suspect. Another boy, a 17-year-old drugstore clerk, was arrested, but he was released in January 1996.

Meanwhile, Graham and Zamora went on with their lives, graduating high school with honors. An article about the pair appeared in the Fort Worth *Star-Telegram*, one that described the pair as the "best and the brightest" of the area, a wholesome couple who had met four years earlier at a Civil Air Patrol Meeting, and how they planned to attend Annapolis and the Air Force Academy, that they would both study physics and, on August 13, 2000, would marry to begin a blissful life together as man and wife.

Both Graham and Zamora went off to their colleges, but Zamora, who roomed with two other girls at an Annapolis dormitory, could not resist talking about the murder, or, at least, hinting about it. Early in the morning of August 25, 1996, one of Zamora's roommates asked about the clean-cut looking young man in the photo Zamora kept on her nightstand. Zamora told her friends how Graham was at the Air Force Academy in Colorado and how they planned to marry upon graduation. She then added cryptically, "He'll always be faithful, because I'll always have something on him."

One of the girls said jokingly, "Well, what did you do, commit murder?"

Zamora's response was echoed by her roommate, Jennifer McKearney when she went to authorities at Annapolis, Maryland, saying that Zamora had admitted that she and her boyfriend had killed a girl who had gotten between them. Officials at Annapolis then began calling small towns around Fort Worth, to see if any teenage girl had been slain within the last year. Grand Prairie police responded by telling them that, indeed, a girl, Adrianne Jones, had been killed. Police from Grand Prairie arrived at Annapolis on August 30, 1996 to question Zamora.

Zamora was cool-headed as detectives questioned her, saying that she had not really killed anyone, that she had made up the story for her roommates to get attention, to impress them. It was a foolish thing to do. The detectives returned to Texas, but a short time later Zamora took a leave of absence and flew to Colorado where she met with Graham.

Detectives from Grand Prairie then arrived to question Graham and he passed off the story about Zamora's confession as a young girl trying to impress her friends, nothing more. He was asked to take a polygraph test and did so. He failed. The detectives then aggressively questioned Graham, and he admitted to the murder, writing out a detailed confession.

Zamora, who had returned home to Mansfield, was arrested and jailed, charged with murder. She spent most of her time awaiting trial by either crying or doing hundreds of sit-ups and then collapsing into exhaustion. Graham was extradited from Colorado and placed in the men's wing of the Tarrant County Jail, also charged with murder. Neither of the accused had any contact with each other as they awaited trial, each on a $250,000 bond.

Zamora was tried first in February 1998. Small in stature, she played the innocent little girl in court; her manner of dress was obviously intended to portray her as a bewildered young girl—she wore dresses and outfits more befitting a 14-year-old, not the woman of 20 who stood before the court. Throughout the trial, Zamora attempted to put all the blame for the murder on Graham, saying that she was manipulated by him and that she was his helpless victim, swayed by his money and intimidated by his constant demands for sex.

Then witnesses came forward to state how Zamora had boldly told them how she killed Jones. Zamora accused the witnesses of lying or being confused. In the end, a jury of five women and seven men believed she had masterminded the murder and convicted her on February 17, 1996. She received an automatic life sentence with no hope of parole for forty years. Graham was tried next and was convicted on July 24, 1996. He, too, was sentenced to life imprisonment with no hope of parole for forty years. Prosecutors had not sought the death penalty at the request of Jones' parents.

Following Graham's conviction, two brothers of the slain Adrianne Jones stood in court to see their sister's killer be led off to prison. Justin Jones, 16, stated: "I can't hate an animal, for they are ignorant, dumb and blind." His 13-year-old bother Scott then added as he choked back tears: "He ruined so many lives, so many families, and, unlike my brother, I can hate an animal, and I can hate David Graham."

**Zayas, Carlos**, 1949- , U.S., mur. On October 20, 1980, a teenager named Terry Meenan vanished from her Philadelphia home. Her partially clothed body was found on November 7, 1980, in a vacant lot in Philadelphia. Her cause of death was uncertain; a coroner attributed death to a possible drug overdose. Seven years later, on October 20, 1987, 13-year-old Lisa Fobare was reported missing from her Philadelphia home. She was found dead beneath some underbrush in a wooded area of Northeast Philadelphia on November 15, 1987. Her body, like that of Terry Meenan, was partially clothed, her bra wrapped around her neck. Duct tape covered her mouth. An autopsy determined that she had suffered several skull fractures.

Investigators interviewed Fobare's relatives and her mother told officers that her former boyfriend, Carlos "Ed" Zayas, although he had no sexual contact with her daughter, was a suspicious character, that he had seduced her babysitter and that she had broken off with him. Officers looked into Zayas' background and discovered that he had also been seeing Terry Meenan at the time of her 1980 disappearance.

Zayas was questioned, but gave detectives no information they might use to charge him with the Meenan and Fobare deaths. Before his van could be searched, Zayas fled the country. In his absence, investigators searching his home found duct tape similar to that used to seal the lips of Lisa Fobare. Next, a witness came forward to say that Zayas had admitted killing Terry Meenan years earlier, that he choked her to death while they were having sex and he "was at the height of passion."

After locating Zayas and his wife hiding out in Puerto Rico, Philadelphia detectives flew to San Juan and then to the village were Zayas was staying. He was arrested and returned to the U.S. He was convicted of murdering Terry Meenan in September 1989, and was given a life term. He then pleaded guilty to murdering Lisa Fobare and, on September 10, 1990, he was given a second sentence of life imprisonment.

**Zhao Jian**, See: **Tang Mihong**.

**Zhao Ming**, 1948-1996, China, abduct.-slavery. From 1989 to 1994, Zhao Ming and several gang members abducted 119 women from several provinces in China and sold these females, some as young as 15, to farmers seeking wives to bear them sons. The going price for a woman was about $25,000. Appearing before the Fuyang Intermediate People's Court in Anhul province, Zhao and seven of his gang members were all sentenced to death on April 24, 1996.

Three more gang members were also sentenced to death, but were given two-year suspended sentences. (Under Chinese sentencing, these defendants, if proven to be model prisoners within two years, would have their death sentences reduced to life terms.) A short time after sentencing, Zhao and the seven others were summarily shot to death.

**Zhu Jianguo**, 1957-89, China, embez. Fearful that the new policy of "openness" in Communist China would foster escalating crime, the hardliners in the government sent a clear signal to democratic dissidents in January 1989, when they summarily executed two criminal offenders. In Beijing, Zhu Jianguo was put to death for the crime of embezzlement. The 32-year-old salesman was found guilty of embezzling 180,000 yuan ($50,000) in public funds. A few weeks later, arsonist and murderer Li Jitao was shot to death by police. See: **Li Jitao.**

**Zilk, Helmut**, 1927- , Aust., Case of espionage. Helmut Zilk, the mayor of Vienna, Austria, from 1984 to 1994, was accused in October 1998 of having been a spy for Czechoslovakia's Communist secret police in the 1960s. Zilk had been a liberal mayor, a Social Democrat who had supported immigration and had incurred the wrath of many right-wing Austrian groups. He had been threatened with assassination many times during his terms of office and, in December 1993, a bomb blast tore away most of his left hand. A lengthy investigation conducted by Austrian authorities determined that there was no substance to the allegations against Zilk and, on December 4, 1998, it was announced by an official of the Czech Republic that Zilk had been cleared.

**Zimbabwe riots**, 1998. The do-nothing regime of Robert Mugabe, who led the country's fight for independence that ended in 1980, and who had clung to power as a lifetime president ever since, increased taxes on an already financially strapped population of largely black citizens. When food prices rose dramatically, thousands of protestors clogged the streets of Harare, Zimbabwe, on January 19, 1998.

Many protestors became looters, tearing through the shopping centers, seizing food and other goods, while wrecking shops. Troops were called in and, within several days, eight persons had been killed and dozens more injured. More than 2,300 persons had been arrested. The riots signaled an end to Mugabe's popularity and heralded the end of his inept dictatorial regime.

**Zink, Rudolph**, 1928- , U.S., attempt. mur. Rudolph Zink was arrested in June 1998 in his Deerfield, Illinois, home, charged with attempting to arrange for the murder of his roommate, Bruce Derrickson. Zink had paid an undercover police officer $500 to kill Derrickson, promising to give the would-be contract murderer another $5,000 once the job was done. Following his arrest, Zink posted bond and promptly fled to California, where he was located and returned to Illinois. Zink pleaded guilty to attempted murder and, on October 29, 1998, was sentenced to six years in prison.

**Zinn, Herbert D., Jr.,** 1971- , U.S., fraud. In 1988, a computer hacker code-named "Shadow Hawk" pirated computer programs valued at more than $1 million from NATO, the U.S. Defense Department, a U.S. government computer installation in Burlington, Vermont, and from Bell Laboratory computers in Naperville, Illinois, and Warren, New Jersey. "Shadow Hawk" entered his name on an electronic bulletin board that led federal investigators to the home of 17-year-old Herbert Zinn, a high school dropout who lived in Chicago. Zinn was arrested after officials obtained a search warrant and found fifty-two AT&T computer programs in his home. Zinn was brought to trial at the U.S. District Court in Chicago before Judge Paul Plunkett, and on February 14, 1989, became the first person convicted under the federal Computer Fraud and Abuse Act of 1986. Because he was a juvenile at the time of the crimes, he was sentenced to nine months at a South Dakota juvenile detention center, fined $10,000, and placed on probation for two and a half years.

---

**Zodiac Killer**, See: **Seda, Heriberto**.

---

**Zorig, Sanjaasuregiin**, d.1998, Mongolia, assass. (victim) A minister in the ruling Democratic Coalition of Mongolia and a probable candidate for prime minister, Sanjaasuregiin Zorig was stabbed and axed to death in his Ulan Bator home on October 2, 1998. Zorig had been one of the Mongolian leaders who led the successful democratic revolt in 1990 that overthrew a Stalinist regime of seven decades. Zorig's assassins were not apprehended and the motive for the killing was unclear. Reports held that Zorig had been murdered by members of organized crime or because of a private business deal.

---

**Zucker, Craig**, 1963- , U.S., child porn. In September 1995, Craig Zucker, of Gurnee, Illinois, a former Sunday school teacher and father of a young daughter, was brought to court in Chicago and charged with distributing child pornography over the Internet through a website called Innocent Images. FBI agents posing as America Online subscribers, were able to locate Zucker after reviewing his website, which offered pornographic photos of children.

Zucker, an accountant whose wife ran a daycare center out of their Gurnee home (there were no reported incidents of children in her care being involved in her husband's child pornography), was placed on two years' probation on November 20, 1996, and was ordered to undergo extended sexual counseling.

# CHRONOLOGY: 1989-1998

Note: The following ten-year chronology is a selective time-line representing the most important worldwide events in criminal justice throughout the decade.

## 1989

### January 1

**MURDER: Dade City, Fla.** Three residents of a retirement home were bludgeoned to death and three others were injured when an elderly man went on a rampage. Henry Thomas, 88, was arrested in Tampa, and was charged with two counts of first-degree murder.

**MURDER: New Delhi, India** Politician Mukesh Sharma ordered a street theater troupe to end a performance of a play, which supported a rival candidate. When Safdar Hashmi, the play's director, refused, he was fatally beaten by more than 100 people.

### January 3

**MURDER: Nuangola, Pa.** Eric Cottam, 14, died after his family went without eating since Nov. 22, 1988, and his unemployed parents refused to spend any of their $3,700 savings, money they said was for church tithes. Larry and Leona Cottam were convicted of third-degree murder on Sept. 8.

**TORTURE: London, England** Amnesty International released a report charging that many political prisoners in Turkey died in custody and were frequently tortured.

### January 4

**MURDER: Tampa, Fla.** Rufus Ford Jr., 22, was indicted in the Nov. 10, 1987, shooting death of his wife, Sybil Ford, 23, whose death had been previously ruled a suicide.

### January 5

**ABDUCTION: Los Angeles, Calif.** Christi Daniels, 19, and Kenneth Ceasar, 23, both students at California State Northridge, abducted Czarian Ramsey, 18, from her Sherman Oaks apartment, and threatened her at gunpoint. Daniels believed that Ramsey had stolen $18,000 worth of clothing from her residence on Jan. 3. Daniels, Ceasar, and a third person were arrested by sheriff's deputies in South Central Los Angeles.

**THEFT: Bensenville, Ill.** Public Armored Car, Inc. was barred from transporting cash and other valuables for the Secretary of State's office in Illinois following an FBI probe into the disappearance of more than $2 million that belonged to the Federal Reserve Bank of Chicago.

### January 6

**ASSASSINATION: New Delhi, India** Kehar Siagh, 53, and Satwant Singh, 25, two Sikh extremists who were convicted of the 1984 assassination of Prime Minister Indira Gandhi, were hanged.

**EXECUTION: Iran** Nine people convicted of drug smuggling were hanged on Jan. 6 and 7 in Kerman, Zahedan, and Mashhad.

**MURDER: Pago Pago** American Samoa Fugitive David Davis, 44, was arrested in Pago Pago and charged with the July 23, 1980, murder of his wife Shannon Mohr, 25, at their farm outside Pittsford, Mich. A tip from a viewer who watched the television program "Unsolved Mysteries" led to the arrest of Davis at Tafuna International Airport. The accused murderer had been missing since 1981.

### January 8

**MURDER: St. Albans, S.C.** Nineteen-year-old Mark Southern McCallister was held without bond in the shooting deaths of six people whose bodies were found outside St. Albans. He was charged with two of the deaths and suspected of the other four slayings. Three of the victims were the children of McCallister's 46-year-old girlfriend, Carol Jean Rutherford.

**MURDER: Wilmington, Del.** Robert P. Hughes, 21, was arrested several hours after allegedly fatally shooting two McDonald's Restaurant staff during a robbery in Chester County, Pa.

### January 9

**FRAUD: Chicago, Ill.** William F. Powers, 47, and Donald Ceaser, 43, both executives of the defunct First Financial Savings and Loan of Downers Grove, were sentenced to prison for three and six years respectively, for defrauding the business of $2. 6 million.

**MURDER: Will County, Ill.** Alan Todd Peters, 18, pleaded guilty after strangling his mother, Peggy Ann Tutor, 38, and putting her body in a freezer on Apr. 17, 1985. Peters, whose two previous convictions have been overturned, was sentenced to fifteen years for voluntary manslaughter and three years for concealing a homicide.

**RIOT: Beijing, China** Yang Wei, a 33-year-old biologist who was imprisoned by the Chinese government in December 1987 for his role in anti-Communist demonstrations, was released after serving nearly two years in detention. Yang had earned a master's degree in the U.S. at the University of Arizona and was planning to return there to begin work on his doctorate when he was arrested.

### January 10

**ASSASSINATION: Canberra, Australia** An unknown gunman assassinated Assistant Commissioner Cohn Winchester, 55, of the Sydney Police Department outside his home in Canberra. Winchester, who was shot execution-style, was scheduled to appear as a witness in a drug trial involving several alleged key figures of the Italian Mafia.

**EXECUTION: Baghdad, Iraq** Massoud Rajavi, leader of the People's Mujaheddin, accused Iranian officials of executing 1,107 political prisoners beginning after the July 1988 Iran-Iraq cease fire supported by the United Nations.

**MURDER: Athens, Greece** Magistrate Constantinos Androulidakis was shot in the arm and leg outside his home. Police believed Androulidakis was the victim of a leftist organization's attempt to intimidate judges.

**THEFT: Kauai, Hawaii** A 14-year-old Berkeley, Calif., boy removed $120,000 in cash from a relative's home and used the money to treat his friends to a birthday party, which included a trip to Hawaii. Police in Kauai recovered $111,000 when they picked up the youth and two companions at the airport.

### January 11

**MURDER: Skokie, Ill.** Paul Latture, 39, was sentenced to serve fifty years in prison for the Dec. 17, 1986, murder of 66-year-old Meyer Harris. Latture delivered some medicine to the Harris apartment, where he stabbed the victim with a steak knife and assaulted his 67-year-old wife, Yetta.

**POLITICAL CORRUPTION: Moscow, U.S.S.R.** Viktor Smirnov, former second secretary of Soviet Moldavian's Communist Party, was arrested in connection with allegations of political corruption.

### January 12

**DRUGS: Chicago, Ill.** A member of the narcotics trafficking Herrera family was arrested by police. Eighteen-year-old Silvestre Valdez was taken into custody and $13 million worth of cocaine was impounded. It was the largest drug seizure on record in Chicago.

### January 13

**ASSAULT: Cleveland County, Okla.** Oklahoma University football player Jerry Parks reportedly shot his teammate, Zarak Peters, after a quarrel about a cassette tape. Parks, who was charged with shooting with intent to injure, was suspended from the university.

**THEFT: Arcadia, Calif.** Forty-year-old Asatour Nagapetian and Palmen Arsoff, 48, were arrested for allegedly running an auto theft operation that may have involved up to 30 valuable automobiles.

### January 14

**KIDNAPPING: Brussels, Belgium.** A group calling itself the Socialist Revolutionary Brigade allegedly abducted 69-year-old former Belgian prime minister Paul Vanden Boeynants outside his residence in Brussels. He was released on Feb. 14 after a sizeable ransom, thought to be between 100 million and 200 million francs, was paid by family members.

**SEXUAL ASSAULT: Wheaton, Ill.** Frank Post, 36, was found guilty of the Mar. 12, 1988, sexual assault of a woman abducted from a mall parking lot. She was assaulted for six hours before Post released her.

### January 15

**DRUGS: Wyandanch, N.Y.** A 10-year-old boy and his 14-year-old companion were arrested and charged with selling crack cocaine from the back of a bicycle to residents of Wyandanch, N.Y. The 10-year-old was held in the Nassau County Juvenile Shelter.

### January 16

**HOOLIGANISM: Prague, Czechoslovakia** Vaclav Havel, playwright and well-known dissident, was arrested during a demonstration at Wenceslas Square for human rights and charged with hooliganism.

### January 17

**KIDNAPPING: New York, N.Y.** Manhattan resident Francisco Cruz was abducted Dec. 30 by a kidnapping ring while on his way to an appointment in Queens. The 38-year-old immigrant from the Dominican Republic was held in a Queens building on a $500,000 ransom. Cruz was released unhurt on Jan. 17 after police arrested nine suspects. None of the ransom had been paid.

**MURDER: Salem, Ore.** Oregon Corrections chief, Michael Francke, 42, was stabbed to death outside department headquarters here. The investigation into the murder was focused on Frank E. Gable, 30, who is imprisoned at the Coos County Jail on unrelated charges. According to inmate Mike Keerins, Gable admitted to killing Francke while both men were incarcerated.

**RACKETEERING: Chicago, Ill.** A grand jury brought fraud indictments against eighteen former employees of the First Commodity Corp. of Boston. Chief among the charges were accusations of federal racketeering and conspiracy.

### January 18

**DISORDERLY CONDUCT: Los Angeles, Calif.** John Arthur Junot, 40, who had planned a "symbolic assassination" of George Bush prior to his election as president, was convicted of disorderly conduct for possessing a starter's pistol at a Bush rally.

**FRAUD: Beijing, China** Deng Pufang denied allegations of financial impropriety. Pufang, the son of Chinese leader Deng Xiaoping, founded the company Iaang Hua, which was the center of a financial scandal last year in which government officials allegedly provided donations to Deng's welfare fund.

**FRAUD: Los Angeles, Calif.** Twenty-five-year-old Thomas Leonard Balla, who defrauded companies out of more than $686,000, pleaded guilty to mail fraud.

**FRAUD: New York, N.Y.** Kuang Hsung Joseph Chuang, former chairman of Golden Pacific Bank, and former vice president Theresa Shich were convicted of conspiracy and fraud. The two diverted $15 million in deposits by issuing fake certificates of deposit not federally insured and using the profits to cover failed loans and other risky ventures.

**MURDER: Chicago, Ill.** A new hearing was ordered to determine whether convicted murderer Juan Caballero, 28, was adequately represented by counsel during the penalty phase of his trial in 1980. Caballero, a former street gang member, was sentenced to die for the Feb. 24, 1979, stabbing murders of three youths in a North Side alley.

**THEFT: Paris, France** German art student Florian Fielder, 28, was arrested and charged with the theft of rare paintings valued at $3. 2 million. The art pieces were removed from the Carnavalet Museum, the Petit Palais, the Guimet Museum, and the Marmatton Museum in Paris.

### January 19

**DRUGS: New London, Conn.** Bruce Lloyd, 51, and Michael Friedman, 40, two psychologists who ran a counseling practice for cocaine addicts, were arrested for possessing cocaine.

**MURDER: Forsyth, Ga.** Georgia resident Darrell Bowden, 23, was arrested and charged with the stabbing death of Frank F. Fowle III, 42, who traversed the country reciting literature in coffee houses and on university campuses.

**MURDER: Spanish Town, Jamaica** A man was shot dead and two women were injured when two men fired into a group of people in a neighborhood thought to oppose Prime Minister Edward Seaga's party. Seaga supporter Altiman "Milo" Chambers, 37, was charged with murder.

### January 20

**FRAUD: Paris, France**. The continuing probe into alleged insider trading involving the French state-owned metals firm Pechiney, resulted in the resignation of a senior official in the Ministry of Finance. Alain Boubil, whose role in the $13 billion dollar purchase of U.S. conglomerate Triangle Industries fueled rumors of official impropriety, announced his resignation from the cabinet.

**MURDER: Chicago, Ill.** Robert Longbine, a 30-year-old homeless man, was charged with the murder of David Sass, 38, when fire swept through an abandoned bus that had been converted to a temporary shelter. Longbine allegedly set fire to the bus in retaliation against the owner of the lot.

### January 21

**MURDER: Melville, N.Y.** Two police officers were shot and wounded at the Times Square Mall in Melville, N.Y., while trying to arrest a murder suspect. Officer Peter Kelly and Detective Sergeant Kevin Cronin, 37, were only slightly injured when Leslie Eugene Sage, 32, opened fire on them in the mall. Sage, wanted for murder by the Suffolk County Police, was shot in the groin and removed to an area hospital.

**MURDER: Newhall, Calif.** Eighteen-year-old Alphonso Tapia was arrested in connection with the Jan. 20 fatal shooting of 15-year-old gang member Miguel Jiminez of San Fernando.

**MURDER: Warsaw, Poland** The Reverend Stefan Nieddielak, 74, was found dead in his apartment. The Solidarity supporter, who had reported receiving death threats on Jan. 20, was found with a broken back.

**RAPE: Oklahoma City, Okla.** A 20-year-old woman was raped in the athletic dormitory, allegedly by three members of Oklahoma University Sooners football team. The three players, identified as Nigel Clay, Bernard Hall, and Glen Bell were charged with first-degree rape. Clay and Hall were each sentenced to ten years in prison on Nov. 22, 1989, and each fined $10,000. Bell was acquitted of the same charge.

**RIOT: Lorton, Va.** Officials quelled one of the most severe riots ever to occur at the District of Columbia prison. Inmate Andre Drake, 26, was fatally stabbed and inmate Jerry Gill, 36, was stabbed and injured. Fire damaged some buildings.

### January 22

**BRIBERY: Rio de Janeiro, Brazil** U.S. jet setter Peter Tripp, 40, agreed to return to Rio de Janeiro to appear as a witness in a bribery investigation involving a Brazilian police officer, who allegedly received a bribe from the operator of a charter boat, which sank in turbulent waters off of Botafogo on Dec. 31, 1988. Tripp was one of a handful of survivors. He told local authorities that the craft was allowed to proceed out onto the sea despite turbulent waters and heavy winds.

### January 23

**ASSASSINATION: Athens, Greece**. Sixty-one-year-old Supreme Court deputy prosecutor Anastasios Venarthos was fatally shot outside his home. The left-wing May 1 Revolutionary Organization claimed responsibility for the shooting.

**ASSAULT: Sacramento County, Calif.** Joseph Prigley, 22, slashed another inmate with a homemade knife in the exercise yard of Folsom Prison. When he refused to stop fighting, guards fatally shot him.

**MURDER: Chicago, Ill.** Twenty-two-year-old Gregory Turner of Chicago was convicted of murdering his grandmother with a meat cleaver because she refused to give him money to purchase cocaine. The murder of 59-year-old Lillian Broome occurred in the woman's South Side apartment in November 1987.

### January 24

**EXECUTION: Starke, Fla.** Convicted serial killer Theodore Bundy was put to death in the electric chair for murdering 20, possibly more, young women between 1974 and 1979.

**MURDER: Los Angeles, Calif.** David Brooks "Let Loose" Cole, a member of the Rolling 60s Crips gang, was convicted of first-degree murder in the February 1987 drive-by shooting of 10-year-old Dominique Blackshear. Cole was sentenced to 27 years to life in prison.

**MURDER: New York, N.Y.** Fourteen-year-old Preston "Little Man" Simmons was shot and killed at the Castle Hill Houses, a housing project, by rival drug dealers. Despite his age, Simmons was a major supplier of marijuana to neighborhood residents of the East Bronx.

**POACHING: Massachusetts.** Ten people were arrested for killing black bears and selling their gall bladders, which are believed to be an aphrodisiac in the Far East.

**RACKETEERING: Chicago, Ill.** FBI agents walked through the corridors of Chicago's futures exchanges, handing out more than 200 subpoenas to employees as Operation Sourmash, Chicago's largest investigation of stock corruption, continued to expand.

### January 25

**BURGLARY: Jackson, Miss.** The Mississippi State Supreme Court upheld the conviction of Clyde Ashley Jr., 44, who was sent to jail for the Jan. 15, 1986, theft of two cans of sardines from an Osyka, Miss., grocery store, but ordered a new sentencing hearing after deciding the crime did not merit life in prison. Ashley spent 23 years behind bars for a series of burglaries before receiving parole in December 1985.

**MURDER: Santa Monica, Calif.** A high-speed car chase between Santa Monica police and two street gang members resulted in the shooting death of Daniel Villa, 19, identified as a member of the Sotels. The second suspect was hospitalized and charged with murder in a drive-by shooting. Police were attempting to arrest the two for involvement in the shooting when the car chase ensued.

**TERRORISM: Jerusalem, Israel** Four Jewish editors, whose newspaper was funded by a radical faction of the Palestinian Liberation Front (PLO), were convicted of membership in a terrorist organization. Yaacov Ben Efrat was sentenced to 30 months in prison. Michael Schwartz and Asaf Adi were sentenced to 18 months and Roni Ben Efrat was sentenced to nine months in prison.

### January 26

**BRIBERY: New York, N.Y.** An investigation into the political tie-up in the New York City community school boards resulted in the indictment of five officials from districts 9 and 12 in the Bronx. Aurella Greene, 54, her husband, the Reverend Jerome A. Greene, 47, both Democratic district leaders were indicted along with Harold Chapnick, 56, former school superintendent; Curtis Johnson, 59, president of the District 9 board; and Jose M. Craz, 41, a member of the District 12 board on charges range from theft to bribery.

**PROSTITUTION: El Cerrito, Calif.** The mother of a 12-year-old girl and a 9-year-old boy was arraigned after allegedly giving the children drugs, forcing them into prostitution, and using the profits to buy drugs.

**ROBBERY: Downey, Calif.** Two armed robbers lowered themselves through the roof of a Bank of America branch and made off with a couple of bags of money despite the presence of the FBI and Los Angeles County Sheriff's deputies. The two suspects were arrested a few moments later by members of the sheriff's SWAT team. One of the men was identified as Charles Lee Hayes, 55.

### January 27

**FRAUD: San Francisco, Calif.** J. William Oldenburg, 50, former chairman and owner of the State Savings and Loan Association in Salt Lake City, Utah, was indicted along with three of his officers on charges of conspiring to defraud the business of $26. 5 million in 1984. The savings and loan was purchased by Oldenburg for the sum of $10.5 million, but it folded in 1985 and Oldenburg was later sued by the federal regulatory agency. Other officers named in the indictment were Nicholas

L. Muccino, 59, James Rossetti, 52, and Martin L. Mandel, 44.

**MURDER: Des Plaines, Ill.** Seventy-year-old Loona Andresen was formally arrested and charged with the Dec. 14 mercy killing of her 77-year-old husband William, a cancer patient. Andresen reportedly stabbed the ailing man 50 times before turning the knife on herself in a botched suicide attempt.

**RACKETEERING: New York, N.Y.** Two drug dealers linked to the 1988 "Pizza Connection" case, were charged with attempting to arrange the murder of Manhattan U.S. Attorney Rudolph W. Giuliani. Federico and Salvatore Spatola were charged with engaging in a "racketeering enterprise" to commit murder for hire in order to protect their drug trafficking network.

**ROBBERY: Chicago, Ill.** Polish speaking Southwest Side resident Chris Sanocki was arrested and charged with three bank robberies between Dec. 1, 1988 and Jan. 13. Sanocki made off with $12,050 in cash from three institutions before he was identified in the pages of Zgoda, the daily Polish foreign language newspaper here.

### January 28

**MURDER: Johannesburg, South Africa** Racial violence flared up in Davidsonville, on the outskirts of Johannesburg, when a 14-year-old boy was stabbed to death. A suspect was arrested, but an angry throng forced his release. A riot ensued, resulting in injuries to four people. The murder suspect was later re-arrested.

### January 29

**ARSON: DeKalb, Ill.** A fire, thought to have been set by an arsonist, broke out in the Holmes Student Center of Northern Illinois University, resulting in $25,000 damage.

**ASSAULT: Garden Grove, Colo.** Paige Richelieu was speaking with police at her home after reporting that her 20-year-old boyfriend, Dennis Gonzales, had beaten her. During the discussion, Gonzales apparently came to the home and drew a toy gun. The officers fatally shot him.

**BATTERY: Chicago, Ill.** Pompillo Ortiz's bizarre behavior prompted firemen responding to a call to contact police. Ortiz, 41, who reportedly attacked an officer with a screwdriver, was charged with aggravated battery.

**MURDER: New York, N.Y.** Yusef Abdullali Ranman of Riverhead, Long Island, was charged with a series of sniper shootings in 1988 that killed one person and injured three others. When Ranman, 20, was arrested on Jan. 28, he admitted to the New York shootings and to two other shootings in Kansas City, Mo., in 1987. The self-described "Rambo-like" commando was diagnosed as a paranoid schizophrenic and found unfit for trial on Apr. 19.

### January 30

**MISSING PERSON: Dublin, Calif.** Thirteen-year-old Ilene Misheloff became the third Bay Area school girl to disappear in six months. Police believe that she was abducted while walking home from the Wells Middle School.

**MURDER: Los Angeles, Calif.** Three men tied up Lee Gottstein, 57, and his wife Sylvia Carruth, 45, who ran a cocaine distribution ring, and a 33-year-old woman, who had earlier been raped, doused them with gasoline and set them on fire. The rape victim survived, and Derek Bloodworth, 26, Lonnie Lewis, 29, and his brother Jerome Martin, 22, were charged with the crime.

### January 31

**FRAUD: Washington, D.C.** Special task forces in Chicago, New York, Kansas City, Denver, San Francisco, and Los Angeles were created to further the investigation and prosecution of corruption in futures trading and sales of stocks.

**HIJACKING: Costa Rica** A Costa Rican Ace Airline B-727 destined for Medellin, Colombia, was hijacked by Alvin Antonio Siu, a Nicaraguan Indian exile. The suspect was arrested in Costa Rica.

**PRISONS: London, England** At Wandsworth Prison, 200 police officers filled in to preserve order after 100 prison employees went on strike on Jan. 29.

### February 1

**DRUGS: New Haven, Conn.** Carlos Restrepo, 38, of the Medellin drug cartel was sentenced to serve 40 years in federal prison after being convicted of moving about $13 million in cocaine proceeds through a dummy corporation set up in the U.S.

### February 2

**CORRUPTION: Beverly, Hills, Calif.** The California Supreme Court suspended Judge Charles Boags, 59, without pay for his improper dismissal of parking fines involving cars owned by himself, his son, and his son's friend.

**HOMICIDE: New York, N.Y.** Robert Wallace, 21, convicted of criminally negligent homicide for killing Daniel Klagsbrun, 24, with a karate kick to the neck, was sentenced to one and a third to four years in prison.

**MURDER: New York, N.Y.**, Radames Ortiz, a 24-year-old Brooklyn police officer, was indicted for the Jan. 23 slaying of Stephen Kelly Sr., killed during a traffic dispute with the off-duty officer.

**MURDER: Santa Ana, Calif.** Ruben Valle, the first person ever in Orange County to be found guilty of murder as a result of a traffic death, had his conviction overturned. The stolen van that Valle drove while being pursued by police struck another car, killing two teenagers on Dec. 19, 1984.

### February 3

**DRUGS: Los Angeles, Calif.** Former Drug Enforcement Administration agents Darnell Garcia, 41, John Jackson, 40, and Wayne Countryman, 45, were indicted by a federal grand jury on charges of cocaine and heroin trafficking, and stealing drugs from Drug Enforcement Administration vaults where evidence was stored.

**MURDER: Acquitla, El Salvador** The tortured bodies of Mario Antonio Flores Cubas, 32, a student at the National University, and his friend Jose Gerardo Gomez, 23, were found by the side of the road near this city.

### February 4

**ROBBERY: Chicago, Ill.** Three masked gunmen and an ex-employee of W.H. Smith Co., a concessions company at O'Hare International Airport, robbed the company safe of $40,000.

### February 5

**POLICE BRUTALITY: Sao Paolo, Brazil** Eighteen inmates died of asphyxiation after being forced into one four-by-ten-foot cell by local police following an unsuccessful escape attempt from the city jail.

### February 6

**ASSASSINATION: Philippines** Communist rebels shot and killed army major Antonio Manalo and his bodyguard in a suburb outside Manila.

**FRAUD: New York, N.Y.** Law partners Leonard Messinger, 48, and Michael Oshatz, 51, were convicted of creating partnerships in the 1970s that were used by investors to claim unlawful tax deductions totalling more than $1.6 billion.

**MANSLAUGHTER: London, England.** Bette Cohen, 57, convicted of manslaughter after she battered to death her 62-year-old friend Irene Solomon in 1986, was ordered to remain in a mental hospital for an unlimited time.

**SEXUAL ABUSE: New York, N.Y.** Thirty-seven-year-old Paul Weiner, a grad-school music teacher who was earlier charged with molesting a 10-year-old girl, was also charged with molesting her on two previous occasions.

**SEXUAL ASSAULT: Nassau County, N.Y.** Former FBI agent Richard Taus, 45, was charged with sexually assaulting 10 boys during the last five years.

**SMUGGLING: Los Angeles, Calif.** Francisco Ernesto Jerez, 30, and Francisco Salvador Martin Panameno, 29, the pilot and co-pilot of an El Salvadoran airliner, pleaded innocent to charges that they attempted to smuggle weapons out of the U.S.

### February 7

**FRAUD: Rochester, N.Y.** A New York Supreme Court justice temporarily barred Power Securities Corp. from soliciting new business in the state, due to charges that the penny-stock brokerage had defrauded investors.

**RAPE: New York, N.Y.** Wayne Booker, 27, a suspect in as many as ten Queens rapes, was arrested and charged with two earlier rapes.

### February 8

**DRUGS: Los Angeles, Calif.** Dion Floyd, 27, a member of the Grape Street Crips gang, was convicted of conspiracy and drug distribution.

**FRAUD: Chicago, Ill.** The U.S. Court of Appeals rejected the arguments of Joseph R. Cosentino Sr. and Robert H. Patterson that their 1986 convictions of defrauding the Kenilworth Insurance Co. were outside the limits of use of the mail fraud statute.

**FRAUD: New York, N.Y.** Government securities traders Jon Edelman, 43, and Bernhard F. Manko, 48, were indicted for conspiracy to defraud the Internal Revenue Service of $511 million in phony tax losses and helping others to lie on their tax returns.

**MURDER: New York, N.Y.** Keith Muckle of Roosevelt, Long Island, was arrested and charged with the murders of his mother, Althea Muckle, 58, and his 31-year-old sister, Michelle, at the family home. The 30-year-old former mental patient was also charged with the attempted murders of his sister Rene and her husband Darnell Hill.

### February 9
**ARSON: Paterson, N.J.** Forty-one-year-old Thomas A. Peters, curator of the Paterson Museum for more than 15 years was arrested and charged with setting fire to the building on Jan. 20.

**DRUGS: Chicago, Ill.** The arrests of Pilar Gutierrez, 42, Alberto Rincon, 31, and Juan Barriga-Barejas, 33, culminated in a day-long investigation into a local drug ring. The Drug Enforcement Administration agents recovered $332,000, cars, jewelry, and drugs.

**DRUGS: Puerto Vallatra, Mexico** Fugitive murderer Glen S. Godwin, 30, who escaped from Folsom Prison in 1987, was arrested on drug charges.

**FRAUD: Cook County, Ill.** A grand jury indicted three doctors and two pharmacists on charges of defrauding Medicare of more than $350,000 through false prescriptions and treatment the patients never received.

**MISSING PERSON: Gainesville, Fla.** Tiffany Sessions, a 20-year-old University of Florida student, disappeared after notifying her roommate that she was going for a walk.

**MURDER: Belfast, Northern Ireland** Thirty-three-year-old Roman Catholic Tony Fusco was killed by a gunman riding a motorcycle through Smithfield Square.

**MURDER: Evanston, Ill.** Tadeusz Skowron, a 40-year-old Polish immigrant, became the fifth Chicago-area cab driver to be found murdered in seven months.

### February 10
**ATTEMPTED MURDER: Kankakee, Ill.** Thirty-six-year-old Steven Autry, a suspect in the shooting of a Chicago teacher, was arrested when he went to a hospital following his suicide attempt.

### February 11
**FRAUD: New York, N.Y.** Bronx state senator Israel Ruiz was dropped from the state's payroll after being convicted of federal bank fraud for filing a false application to secure a bank loan.

**MURDER: Yonkers, N.Y.** Thirty-eight-year-old Casimiro Cedeno shot and killed Migdalia Diaz, his 33-year-old estranged wife, and then turned the gun on himself. Cedeno died in a hospital early the next morning.

### February 12
**MURDER: Greenwood, Miss.** After his father threatened to whip him with a belt, Johnny Dewayne Daniels, 17, allegedly shot and killed him. He was arrested and held on $50,000 bond.

**RIOT: Islamabad, Pakistan** Thousand of people, demanding that the U.S. ban *The Satanic Verses* by British author Salman Rushdie, rioted outside a U.S. government build-

ing. Five people were killed by police and at least 65 were injured.

### February 13
**BRIBERY: Chicago, Ill.** After he admitted that he had paid police officers to deliver dead bodies to his funeral home, Michael Harrington was sentenced to one year of probation and a $10,000 fine.

**DRUGS: Oxford, Miss.** Thirty-seven-year-old Sylvester Kyles, mayor of Shaw, Miss., agreed to enter a drug treatment program and resign his office nearly a year after he pleaded guilty to selling cocaine.

**MURDER: Chalantenago, El Salvador** Dr. Alejandra Bravo Betancourt, 35, and 14-year-old nurse Rosibel Dubon were found beaten and shot to death, allegedly by the Atlacatl Battalion, an elite group of the Salvadoran army.

**MURDER: Lima, Peru** Saul Cantoral, leader of the General Federation of Mine Workers, was abducted and shot to death, allegedly by right-wing death squads.

### February 14
**ARSON: New York, N.Y.** A Harlem apartment building was set afire, killing one woman and injuring eight other residents. Frances Perez, 34, was arrested in the Bronx. Authorities said she set the fire after an argument over a crack purchase.

**DRUGS: Mays Landing, N.J.** Atlantic City drug ring leader Hakeem Abdul Shaheed, 29, was arrested as he tried to leave the state and was charged with heading an organization that sold over $1 million worth of cocaine a month.

**DRUGS: Woodland Hills, Calif.** Police arrested five suspects including Myron Keene, 47, of New York, and confiscated more than 970 pounds of cocaine from two vehicles.

**ESCAPE: New York, N.Y.** Convicted robbers Elias Hernandez, 27, and John Santiago, 34, escaped from the Arthur Kill Correctional Facility in Staten Island, by hiding in a garbage-filled dumpster when a city sanitation truck made a pickup.

**MURDER: Santa Rosa, N.M.** Michael R. Ardila, a 19-year-old New Jersey fugitive, was arrested by police and charged with the stabbing death of Tony Pompelio, 17, and the abduction of 16-year-old Donna Shaban.

**TERRORISM: Tehran, Iran** Ayatollah Ruhollah Khomeini issued a death sentence for Salman Rushdie, author of *The Satanic Verses*.

### February 15
**DRUGS: Chicago, Ill.** Cheryl Tillman, 22, was arrested and charged with drug possession after she was stopped for a traffic violation and police saw plastic bags on the seat beside her. They confiscated 1,519 grams of cocaine and marijuana from her car.

**ESCAPE: New York, N.Y.** Escaped prisoner John Santiago, 34, was recaptured in the Bronx without incident. Santiago fled from the Arthur Kill Correctional Facility with Elias Hernandez, 38, earlier in the week. Hernandez was not apprehended.

**FRAUD: Cook County, Ill.** A grand jury indicted Terry

Brooks, 38, Mozelle Braun Sr., 58, and 41 others on charges that they defrauded $228,000 from insurance companies. Members of the ring allegedly filed claims for faked or imaginary car accidents.

**MURDER: New York, N.Y.** Twenty-one-year-old Miriam McKenzie of the Prince George Hotel in midtown Manhattan was charged with the murder of her 3-year-old son for allegedly submerging the child in a tub of scalding hot water on Mar. 22.

**MURDER: Roselle, N.Y.** Fugitive Gene Allen Wasson, 41, was arrested and ordered back to Louisiana to stand trial for a 1984 slaying. Wasson was apprehended as a result of being profiled on the "America's Most Wanted" television program.

### February 16

**DRUGS: New York, N.Y.** An undercover investigation resulted in the arrests of nine city corrections officers and two others, charged with attempting to smuggle cocaine to prison inmates.

**FRAUD: Los Angeles, Calif.** Fifty-three-year-old Alvin A. Deshano, accounting director for the Anaheim-based Carl's Jr. fast-food chain, was indicted on charges of securities fraud by using insider trading tactics to avoid a more than $7,000 stock market loss for parent company Carl Karcher Enterprises.

**FRAUD: New York, N.Y.** Broadway producer Adela Hoizer, 54, was arrested in Manhattan and charged with bilking two investors out of $280,000 in a bogus money-making scheme in which she falsely claimed to be the wife of millionaire David Rockefeller.

**FRAUD: Paris, France.** Seventy-year-old businessman Roger-Patrice Pelat and four others were charged with fraud in France's widening insider trading scandal. Pelat, a close friend of President Francois Mitterand, died on Mar. 7, before the case went to court.

### February 17

**ESCAPE: Orange County, Calif.** Convicted murderer Ivan Von Staich was acquitted by an Orange County jury for his Jan. 26, 1986, escape from jail. Staich contended that he was beaten by his jailers and was escaping only to save his life.

**RAPE: Chicago, Ill.** Chicago Police arrested 16-year-old Shabazz Muhammed on Chicago's far South Side for a series of rapes committed between Jan. 7 and Feb. 15.

### February 18

**FRAUD: Mexico City, Mexico** Eduardo Legoretta Chauvet, chairman of Operadora de Bolsa, one of Mexico's largest brokerage firms, another Operadora broker, and two other brokers from Mexicana de Valores y Invers were indicted on charges of illegal trading and criminal fraud.

**ROBBERY: New York, N.Y.** Robert Fischetti, 29, owner of a Greenwich Village bar was in critical condition after being shot in a robbery attempt by Calvin Johnson, 28, of Brooklyn.

### February 19

**MURDER: Chicago, Ill.** While walking in the Brighton Park area near midnight, two men were attacked by four to six others carrying baseball bats. Gonzalo Hernandez, 19, was killed and his friend was seriously injured.

### February 21

**DRUGS: Chicago, Ill.** The FBI arrested 70-year-old Joe Wing, a key figure in an international drug ring based in New York's Chinatown. Wing, the ring's Chicago connection, was tied to Fok Leung Woo, better known in New York as Peter Woo.

**DRUGS: New York, N.Y.** The New York State Court of Appeals ruled that a Customs search of Ecuadorean drug courier Julio Luna, 48, at Kennedy Airport in 1985 was legal. Cocaine was found strapped to Lena's ankles.

**DRUGS: New York, N.Y.** Seventy-one-year-old Chinese businessman Fok Leung Woo, known as Peter Woo, was arrested and charged with overseeing a heroin ring that has landed hundreds of pounds of heroin on New York streets. Forty-two other suspects were arrested worldwide for their participation in a ring that stretched from the U.S. to Hong Kong. Woo entered a guilty plea in federal court on Aug. 18.

**FRAUD: Chicago, Ill.** The U.S. Court of Appeals upheld the 1986 conviction of Tamara Jo Smith, 28, who was convicted of bank and wire fraud based on voice identification or "spectograms." The court ruled that the so-called voiceprints were used as valid evidence.

**MURDER: Harlow, England.** The trial began for Michael Hays, 21, accused of murdering his baby in May by overdosing the infant's formula with salt.

**MURDER: Johannesburg, South Africa.** Two bodyguards assigned to protect Winnie Mandela, wife of the anti-apartheid leader Nelson Mandela, were arrested and charged with the murder of 14-year-old Stompie Seipei. The men were identified as Jerry Richardson and Jabu Sithole.

**MURDER: London, Ontario** Police found the bodies of Peter and Evelyn Nixon, who had been dead in their home for about a week. Peter Nixon, 58, an international art dealer suspected in a million-dollar art theft, apparently killed his 55-year-old wife and then himself.

### February 22

**ASSAULT: Huntington Park, Calif.** A 15-year-old boy, apparently carrying out a gang initiation rite, stabbed a 15-year-old girl on the grounds of Huntington Park High School, then calmly boarded his school bus. He was arrested and charged.

**FRAUD: Chicago, Ill.** Samuel W. Sax, 55, and Charles B. Hall, 56, former executives of the defunct United of America Bank in Chicago, were charged with making insider loans and misapplying bank funds before the business folded in 1984. Both men agreed to plead guilty.

**MURDER: Johannesburg, South Africa.** Zakhele Mbatha, 21, confessed to the Jan. 27 murder of Dr. Abu Baker Asvat, a leading anti-apartheid activist. Mbatha said robbery was his motive, but Asvati's death has been linked to a scandal involving the alleged abduction of four youths by Winnie Mandela's bodyguards.

### February 23

**FRAUD: New York, N.Y.** Eight employees of the Department of Motor Vehicles in New York were arrested and charged with selling phony driver's licenses and auto registration certificates for prices ranging from $50 to $1,600.

**MURDER: Kingston, N.Y.** Jeffrey Allen Dawson, 29, was sentenced to twenty-five years to life for the murder of 19-year-old Anna Kithcart. Dawson and his accomplice Joseph Kiernan, 41, were arrested on July 15, 1988.

**RAPE: Indianapolis, Ind.** The County and Township Committee of the Indiana House voted unanimously to recommend passage of a bill that would allow a convicted rapist to have his sentence suspended if he agreed to be castrated.

**SEX ABUSE: Indianapolis, Ind.** The medical license of Dr. Pravin D. Thakkar, 38, was suspended after twelve female patients claimed he engaged in sexual acts with them. Two patients filed lawsuits claiming Thakkar impregnated them and then performed abortions without their consent or knowledge.

### February 24

**ASSAULT: Phoenix, Ariz.** Thirty-two-year-old Douglas Kirkpatrick, son of former United Nations ambassador Jeane Kirkpatrick, was arrested on charges of aggravated assault involving his live-in girlfriend.

**BURGLARY: New Canaan, Conn.** An obsessed fan of entertainer David Letterman, Margaret Ray, 36, was arrested a fourth time for breaking into Letterman's home. She was charged with burglary, larceny, trespass, and possession of marijuana and ordered to seek psychiatric care.

**ESCAPE: New York, N.Y.** Michael DiCarluccio, 28, held on charges of attempted murder of three police officers, escaped Riker's Island Prison by hiding in a garbage truck on its way to a Queens landfill.

**KIDNAPPING: Los Angeles, Calif.** Five people, including 70-year-old Thomas Carver, were charged with the 1988 conspiracy to kidnap 74-year-old millionaire Jean Fay Drexler as part of a plot to gain control of her estate. Carver was Drexler's attorney.

**LAW ENFORCEMENT: New York, N.Y.** Chief administrative law judge William E. Vandiveer, 65, resigned from his post after it was alleged that he had made racially derogatory statements and harassed a homosexual superior.

**MURDER: Nablus, West Bank** Six Palestinian men were arrested for murder after they dropped a concrete block from a roof onto the head of Israeli soldier Binyamin Meisner on Feb. 24. All six were sentenced to 15 years to life in prison on July 19.

**MURDER: Westchester County, N.Y.** After being jailed for shoplifting, partially paralyzed 43-year-old Vietnam veteran Donald Zamfino was allegedly beaten to death with his own cane by another inmate.

**RIOT: Bombay, India** A march protesting the publication of the book *The Satanic Verses* by British author Salman Rushdie became a riot. At least 12 people died and 40 were injured as rioters and police exchanged fire.

**SEXUAL ASSAULT: Chicago, Ill.** Aron Hazzard, 51, was sentenced to 45 years in prison after being convicted of raping a 2-year-old girl in August 1988.

**THEFT: Pittsburgh, Pa.** John Sackman, 25, a guard at a United Parcel Service depot, was arrested and charged with stealing as much as $1 million worth of parcels.

### February 25

**BURGLARY: Chicago, Ill.** Police arrested Cortez Dixon, 25, for burglary after the owner of a restaurant he had burgled found him stuck in a barbecue vent the next morning. Although Dixon had entered the restaurant through the vent, he was unable to escape the same way.

**MURDER: Los Angeles, Calif.** Jasmine Guevara, 11, was killed and her aunt was wounded in a drive-by shooting. Police arrested two 16-year-old suspects, members of a Central American gang.

**MURDER: New York, N.Y.** Barbara Chiles, a 42-year-old bank teller, was handcuffed to two other women and shot in the head while burglars ransacked her apartment.

### February 26

**ROBBERY: New York, N.Y.** Three men followed 17-year-old Keith Headley and 19-year-old John Carpio from a Manhattan disco, robbed them, and then fatally shot Headley in the chest with a sawed-off shotgun.

### February 27

**EXTORTION: Geneva, Switzerland** Four former Du Pont Co. employees, who claimed to have taken the secret of spandex manufacture, were arrested after trying to extort $10 million from company representatives.

**MURDER: Broward County, Fla.** Gilbert Anthony Hall, 26, was arrested in connection with the 1981 kidnapping, rape, and murder of 11-year-old Christine Anderson. Hall was tied to the crime through accomplice Frank Maxwell's written confession, not delivered to the Ft. Lauderdale police until after Maxwell died in a car accident in December 1988.

**MURDER: Sasairna, Colombia** Emerald dealer and drug trafficker Gilberto Molina and 17 others were killed when 50 gunmen stormed a dinner party at his ranch, handcuffed the 18 men, and shot them.

**RAPE: Chicago, Ill.** Forty-two-year-old Stephen Montgomery, who pleaded guilty to raping a 77-year-old woman in July 1988, was sentenced to 18 years in jail.

### February 28

**ARSON: New York, N.Y.** The offices of *The Riverdale Press*, a Bronx daily newspaper, were firebombed with a Molotov cocktail. Authorities believed that the action may have been retaliation for an editorial that supported author Salman Rushdie.

**BOMBING: Berkeley, Calif.** Protesters threw firebombs through display windows of two bookstores selling Salman Rushdie's novel, *The Satanic Verses*.

**MURDER: Waterloo, Calif.** Lawrence J. Carnegie, business partner of Michael Blatt, sports agent and former interim manager of the Seattle Seahawks, was murdered, allegedly by two former college football players hired by Blatt.

### March 1

**MURDER: Chicago, Ill.** Ted Light, 19, was arrested and charged in the 1987 crossbow murder of a transient, following the Feb. 28 release of another suspect.

**MURDER: Dallas, Texas** Randall Dale Adams, 40, whose story of being wrongly convicted and sentenced to death for the 1976 murder of police officer Robert Wood was recounted in the documentary *The Thin Blue Line*, had his conviction overturned. He was released from prison three weeks later.

**RAPE: New York, N.Y.** Hospital security guard Jose Figueroa was arrested and charged in the Jan. 21 rape of a psychiatric patient and for the assault of a 30-year-old woman at the Manhattan hospital where he worked. A second suspect, Reynold Rayes, was arrested Mar. 8.

**SEXUAL ASSAULT: Glen Ridge, N.J.** At least eight teenagers watched while five members of the city's high school football team allegedly assaulted a 17-year-old retarded girl. The assailants were arrested on May 24.

**SMUGGLING: Los Angeles, Calif.** Immigration and Naturalization Service officials arrested 31 illegal aliens at the Los Angeles airport, bringing the week's total to 206.

**WEAPONS VIOLATION: Los Angeles, Calif.** The city council of Los Angeles' ban on the sale and possession of assault weapons, including military-style assault weapons and short-barreled shotguns, went into effect.

### March 2

**KIDNAPPING: New York; N.Y.** Police arrested two men who, in a Brooklyn robbery attempt, took a 5-month-old baby hostage while his parents leaped through a window to escape the gunmen. The baby was recovered after his father dropped off the ransom.

**KIDNAPPING: Pasadena, Calif.** Raymond Kenneth Singer, under investigation for the murders of four prostitutes, was arrested in connection with the kidnapping of two other prostitutes in 1988.

**LOOTING: Caracas, Venezuela** Rising food prices sparked riots and widespread looting in which an estimated 200 people were killed. Martial law was imposed on Feb. 28.

**MURDER: Kinnelon, N.J.** The written confession of Frank Maxwell, delivered to police after his death in December 1988, tied Anthony Rodriguez to the kidnapping, rape, and murder of 11-year-old Christine Anderson. Rodriguez was released on May 18 due to insufficient evidence to charge him with involvement. A second suspect, Gilbert Anthony Hall, was arrested on Feb. 27.

**MURDER: New York, N.Y.** Samuel "Baby Sam" Edmonson, 28, Johnny Ray Robinson, 28, and Victor Breland, who allegedly ran a Brooklyn crack cocaine ring worth $11 million a year, were indicted under the New York Organized Crime Control Act and charged with nine murders and six attempted murders. Three other gang members also were indicted.

**MURDER: New York, N.Y.** Brooklyn drug dealer Gerald Spencer, 27, was convicted of the 1987 murder of another drug dealer and the attempted murder of a rookie police officer and a bystander. Police arrested him in a clothes dryer in Miami, Fla.

**MURDER: San Francisco, Calif.** The California Supreme Court reversed the death sentence of Bronte Lamont Wright, who was convicted of the 1981 robbery and murder of a 7-year-old Sunday school teacher from whom he took $5.

### March 3

**MURDER: New York, N.Y.** Plainclothes police officer Robert B. Machate, 25, was fatally shot in Brooklyn as he grappled with a suspect. He was the first officer to die in the line of duty in New York in 1989. Renaldo Rayside and Kurt Haneiph were arrested shortly after the shooting and were charged the next day.

**ROBBERY: New York, N.Y.** Chris Gilyard, 16, allegedly robbed and slashed Hasidic Jews Shoshna Rabkim and her son in Brooklyn. A group of 20 to 30 Hasidic men assaulted Gilyard in retaliation. Gilyard was charged with assault, robbery, and possession of a deadly weapon.

### March 4

**DESECRATION: Chicago, Ill.** Suzy Willhoft, a 40-year-old schoolteacher from Arlington, Va., was the first person charged with violation of the Illinois statute prohibiting desecration of the U.S. flag after she stepped on the flag that was part of an exhibition at the School of the Art Institute.

**MURDER: Mishawaka, Ind.** Alan L. Matheney, 38, imprisoned in 1987 for eight years for battery of his wife, Lisa Marie Bianco, allegedly beat her to death with a shotgun when he was released from prison on an eight-hour furlough. He was sentenced to death.

### March 5

**MURDER: New York, N.Y.** John Miller was shot to death in a Brooklyn apartment where he was house-sitting. Neighbor Clarence Nesbitt, 64, heard the shots, opened his door, and was shot dead also.

**MURDER: Spartanburg, S.C.** Justin L. Turner, five, was sexually assaulted and strangled. He was found in a camper near the home of his father and stepmother, Pamela K. Turner, who was later charged with his murder.

**RIOT: Lhasa, Tibet** More than 100 were wounded and 11 people died in a riot that broke out when Chinese policeman shot at marchers in an unlawful Buddhist parade.

**TERRORISM: Damascus, Syria** Terrorist Ahmed Jabril, leader of the Popular Front for the Liberation of Palestine, issued a statement wherein he vowed to kill British author Salman Rushdie.

### March 7

**MURDER: New York, N.Y.** Jeffrey Taylor, 23, was convicted of the May 1988 murder of Isabel Gonzalez, 53, who was robbed and beat to death.

**MURDER: Van Nuys, Calif.** Reecy Clem Cooper was acquitted of murder but still remains charged with conspiracy along with four other men, in connection with the slaying of Detective Thomas C. Williams, who was killed as he picked up his son from a day care center.

**MURDER: West Orange, N.J.** Barbara Loftus was found strangled in her home after reportedly arguing with her 16-year-old son, who became the prime suspect.

### March 8

**DRUGS: Bloomington, Ill.** Myles Connor Jr. was arrested for allegedly selling a kilogram of cocaine. He pleaded guilty on Nov. 22 to drug charges and theft charges involving paintings worth $400,000 stolen from Amherst College.

**FRAUD: Seattle, Wash.** Isabel Anderson, the witness whose testimony convicted Luis Gillespie of sexually abusing a 3-year-old, and a companion, were arrested after demanding $500,000 from defense attorneys in exchange for her testimony in Gillespie's retrial.

**MURDER: Chicago, Ill.** Eddie Ward was charged with murder after he confessed to using a sweat sock to strangle his girlfriend, Cynthia Adams, 23, their daughter, Marshanika Ward, 18 months, and Adams' daughter, Roteshia Lane, 7.

### March 9

**CONSPIRACY: Newark, N.J.** Former mayor of Wayne, N.J., Louis V. Messercola pleaded guilty to conspiracy with former planning board member A. Thomas Acquaviva. The two attempted to extort $50,000 from Cosden & Sons Inc., a developer who sought permission to build an $18 million condominium development.

**EMBEZZLEMENT: New York, N.Y.** Conrad Mauge, 54, Wayne Fortune, 33, Robert Bowden, 56, and Terence Kennedy, 61, former staffers at the AIDS Outreach Program, were indicted on charges after allegedly diverting $350,000 from the program for their own use.

### March 10

**KIDNAPPING: Los Angeles, Calif.** Five people were arrested after allegedly kidnapping Maria del Refugio Sanchez, 33, and her 3-year-old daughter, Yesenia, and holding them for $150,000 ransom.

**PERJURY: Harare, Zimbabwe** Zimbabwe defense minister Enos Nkala announced his resignation after he admitted lying to a judicial inquiry. A car he bought for $15,000 was resold for $45,000, a violation of prices established by the government.

**THEFT: New York, N.Y.** George Athanasatos and Ronald Corteselli were arrested in connection with the theft of art treasures valued at $3.5 million from six museums.

### March 11

**ESCAPE: Devon, England** John Corbett, 40, and Ian Oppenshaw, 22, who had escaped from Dartmoor Prison, were arrested less than one mile from the prison when a woman called police after they asked for and were given tea.

**KIDNAPPING: Jackson, Miss.** Newton Alfred Winn, a lawyer, was arrested in connection with the July 26, 1988, kidnapping of Annie Laurie Hearin, 72-year-old wife of millionaire Robert Hearin. Winn was charged with perjury, conspiracy, and extortion by mail.

### March 12

**RAPE: Chicago, Ill.** Anthony Anderson, 24, a convicted robber, allegedly raped a woman on her way to church and took $5, her car, coat, and shoes.

### March 13

**DRUGS: Chicago, Ill.** Attorney Manina M. Harper, 34, was arrested and charged with smuggling cocaine and marijuana to prison inmates incarcerated at the Cook County Jail.

Harper served as an instructor at the John Marshall Law School.

**MURDER: Pasadena, Calif.** Hugo Beltran, 31, accused of the 1987 murder, rape and robbery of 73-year-old artist Helen Kennedy, was acquitted.

**PRICE FIXING: Los Angeles, Calif.** Waste Management of California, Inc., the local branch of the national disposal firm, agreed to plead no contest to charges of price fixing and anti-trust violations. The firm agreed to pay a record $1 million fine.

**RACKETEERING: Washington, D.C.** An out-of-court settlement was reached between the Justice Department and the Teamster's Union, whereby the mob-infiltrated union agreed to purge its leadership of individuals associated with organized crime.

### March 14

**FRAUD: Lake Barrington, Ill.** Real estate developer James Russell Scarborough was indicted by a federal grand jury in Wisconsin on two counts of wire fraud and three counts of submitting false to a federally insured financial institution in an attempt to secure $3.9 million in loans.

**MURDER: Newport Beach, Calif.** William D. King, a rare coin dealer who was allegedly bilking several investors of $1 million, was critically wounded by unknown gunmen in his shop, the Newport Coin Exchange. Two other people were killed execution style. In May, King was arrested for operating a second firm without a telemarketing license.

**ROBBERY: Markham, Ill.** Markham police officers Brandon Adams, 25, Michael Stewart, 31, and Walter Eubanks, 25, were charged with invading the home of suspected drug dealer Jube Roberts, and his wife Sheila. According to testimony, $57,000 in cash and valuables were stolen.

**WEAPONS VIOLATION: Washington, D.C.** Anti-drug czar William Bennett announced an immediate suspension on the import of AK-47s and other semi-automatic weaponry into the U.S. A permanent ban was given final approval by President George Bush on July 7.

### March 15

**ASSAULT: West Covina, Calif.** Phyllis Patricia Shademan, 29, pleaded not guilty to two counts of attempted murder and two counts of assault, stemming from alleged attack against her two small children, aged 7 and 6, with a kitchen knife.

**HARASSMENT: Norwalk, Conn.** Margaret Ray, arrested in talk show host David Letterman's house for the fourth time, was ordered to undergo further psychiatric testing.

**KIDNAPPING: Bloomington, Ind.** Financially strapped hotel owner Arthur J. Curry, 41, was charged with abducting Gayle T. Cook, a wealthy Chicago woman who lived south of the Indiana University campus. She was rescued unhurt the next day.

**MURDER: Albany, N.Y.** Convicted cop-killer Gary McGivern was paroled from the Otisville State Prison after serving 21 years for the murder of a Westchester deputy sheriff on the New York Thruway in 1968.

**MURDER: San Sebastian, El Salvador** Major Mauricio Beltran and Lieutenant Arnaldo Vasquez were indicted on murder charges, for the Sept. 21, 1988 massacre of ten farmers in the town of San Francisco.

**RACKETEERING: Newark, N.J.** Reputed Genovese crime figure Matty "the Horse" Ianniello, 68, entered a plea of guilty to racketeering and conspiracy charges at the Newark Federal Court.

## March 16

**ASSAULT: New York, N.Y.** Sandra Lewis was rescued by police in her Queens Village apartment following a tense hostage situation. The woman was held at gunpoint by Charles Scott, her former boyfriend, who was angry because she had filed assault charges against him on Feb. 11.

**FRAUD: Rockford, Ill.** Three executives from the Sundstrand Corp. of Rockford were indicted on charges of defrauding the U.S. government. Named in the indictment were Joseph J. McCarthy, Ralph G. Hamann, and Ray John Chapel Jr.

**MURDER: Cicero, Ill.** Monico Campos was convicted of killing his 24-year-old pregnant wife, Victoria, and their unborn child on New Year's Eve, 1987. The Cicero man was sentenced to serve 35 years in prison.

**THEFT: New York, N.Y.** Nedy Torres was arrested by Transit Authority policeman Peter Brown for selling stolen bus transfers in the Bronx. Torres stabbed Brown with a syringe, raising concerns that the needle was contaminated by the AIDS virus. On Apr. 10, Torres agreed to submit to an AIDS test and share the results with Brown.

**THEFT: New York, N.Y.** Patrick Phillips, controller of the Good Samaritan Hospital, entered a guilty plea to charges that he stole $25,000 from the hospital between 1983 and 1987.

## March 17

**KIDNAPPING: New York, N.Y.** The Allious Gee family of North Carolina was abducted at gunpoint in the Hell's Kitchen neighborhood of Manhattan by Victor Otero, 39. Otero ordered them to drive him to Long Island, where he left them at the side of the road. Otero surrendered the next day and was charged with attempted murder, kidnapping, robbery, and weapons possession.

**MURDER: Calumet City, Ill.** Todd Hinko, 20, of Hammond, Ind., was charged with the Oct. 19, 1988 robbery of a Calumet City mini-mart that resulted in the murder of Catherine Marie Hoch, 34, an employee of the store.

**MURDER: New York, N.Y.** Former Black Panther Party member Richard "Dhoruba" Moore was granted a favorable preliminary ruling by Justice Peter J. McQuillan of the State Supreme Court who ruled that the key witnesses in his 1973 murder trial "would have been successfully impeached" if the defense had certain critical evidence in hand at the time. Moore was convicted of murdering two policemen with a machine gun.

**SEXUAL ABUSE: Portugal Cove, Canada** Two former parish priests were charged with molesting young boys in their care. The Reverend James Hickey, who served at the parish of St. John's in Portugal Cove, Newfoundland was arrested in January 1988. In a separate incident, Brendan Foley, 43, was charged with four counts of sex abuse on Mar. 17.

## March 18

**ASSAULT: New York, N.Y.** Sharon Amsterdam, a 21-year-old student from John Jay College in Manhattan, was shot twice in the back of the neck while riding on a subway train. The assailants stole her earrings.

**MURDER: Milwaukee, Wis.** Maximillion Adonnis, convicted in 1976 of conspiracy to commit extortion, was shot and killed in Giovanni's Restaurant, where he was the manager. An unidentified woman was seriously wounded.

**SUICIDE: Villa Park, Ill.** David Bullock, 24, barricaded himself in the bathroom and shot himself to death when police arrived at his home to arrest him in connection with the 1983 murder of Jeanne Coyne in Hillside, Ill.

## March 19

**ARSON: Jersey City, N.J.** Sam Tagliarinni, 74, his wife, Florence, 51, and their three children were killed when someone started a fire in an empty apartment in their building.

**MURDER: Chicago, Ill.** Ronald Parker, 34, was charged with the stabbing death of his son, 17-year-old Julius, in the parking lot of the Ickes housing development where the father lived.

## March 20

**ESCAPE: Pretoria, South Africa** Four black political dissidents escaped from a detainment hospital and took refuge in the West German Embassy in Pretoria. After receiving written government assurances they would not be arrested, Ephraim Nkoe, 28, Clive Radebe, Job Sithole, and Mpho Lekgoro left the embassy.

**MURDER: Boston, Mass.** Judge Charles Grabau dismissed murder charges against Albert Lewin, a 33-year-old Jamaican accused of murdering Detective Sherman Griffiths, 36, during a Feb. 17, 1988, drug raid. Grabau cited "egregious misconduct" on the part of the prosecution team and the police.

**MURDER: Jonesborough, Ireland** Chief Superintendent Harry Breen and Superintendent Bob Buchanan of the Royal Ulster Constables were ambushed and murdered allegedly by members of the South Armagh "brigade" of the Irish Republican Army.

**MURDER: Santa Ana, Calif.** Nine-year-old Nadia Puente was found murdered near the Griffith Park Observatory, 11 hours after she was abducted by a man while walking home from school. Richard Lucio Dettoyos, 31, was arrested on Apr. 1 and admitted to police that he had killed her.

## March 21

**BOMBING: Islamabad, Pakistan** A bomb exploded near the British Council Library, doing slight damage to surrounding buildings. Police linked it and the Feb. 27 bombing in Karachi to Muslims protesting against British author Salman Rushdie.

**SEXUAL ASSAULT: Los Angeles** Officer Stanley Yorikazu Ranabe, 32, of the LAPD was charged with burglary and taking indecent liberties with a 14-year-old Hollywood girl on two separate occasions. He was sentenced to serve two years in prison on July 20, 1990.

**TERRORISM: San Diego, Calif.** FBI agents arrested

William Albert Risley, 50, and charged him with making at least 100 bomb threats beginning in 1985 to various airlines operating out of California and Detroit, Mich.

### March 22

**ASSAULT: Culver City, Calif.** Two men, who attempted to flee from police after stealing a car, were shot and killed for resisting arrest. The dead men were identified as 17-year-old Jorge Jaramillo of Silver Lake, and Amir Abedi, 18, of the San Fernando Valley.

**EXECUTION: Huntsville, Texas** Leon King, 44, was put to death by lethal injection for the Apr. 10, 1978, beating death of Michael Clayton Underwood, 26, who was abducted with his girlfriend from a Houston nightclub and robbed of $11.50.

**MURDER: Chicago, Ill.** Dennis Johnson, who was already charged with aggravated battery for allegedly beating 3-month-old daughter Sierra in February 1988, was indicted for murder after the girl died of her injuries on Feb. 11.

**MURDER: Poughkeepsie, N.Y.** Sixteen-year-old Brian Britton shot and killed his father, Dennis, 44, his mother, Marlene, 42, and 8-year-old brother, Jason, following a quarrel over his school attendance. Britton's 18-year-old sister escaped after being wounded.

### March 23

**BURGLARY: St. Petersburg, Fla.** James Edward Burgess, 31, was apprehended and charged with burglary after getting stuck in a chimney while trying to enter a doctor's office.

**MURDER: Valley Stream, N.Y.** Robert Golub, 21, was arrested and charged with the Mar. 3 slaying of his neighbor, Kelly Tinyes, 13. Her mutilated body was found in a storage bin in the Golub residence on Long Island.

**THEFT: Torrance, Calif.** James McGrail, 52, was extradited to the U.S. from Australia, and was charged with theft. The restaurateur had used bogus checks in order to steal $250,000 shortly before he fled the country in 1982.

### March 24

**SEXUAL ASSAULT: Glen Ridge, N.J.** Five teenagers, suspected of assaulting a 17-year-old retarded girl on Mar. 1 with a broom handle and a miniature baseball bat, were arrested.

**SUICIDE: San Francisco, Calif.** Death Row inmate Ronald E. Fuller, 35, convicted of the murder of cab driver Barry W. Cravey in 1982, hanged himself with a torn bedsheet at San Quentin Prison.

### March 25

**CONSPIRACY: Los Angeles, Calif.** Operation Rescue founder Randall Terry and 251 members of his pro-life organization were jailed on felony charges during demonstrations. Most spent Easter Sunday in jail.

**ESCAPE: Wisconsin** Police found escaped convict Ronald R. Plummer, 40, and his girlfriend, Lisa Bonvillain, 31, in a farmhouse, both semi-conscious from an apparent drug overdose. Plummer had escaped from custody the day before, robbed a video store, and shot a police officer.

**ROBBERY Pomona, Calif.** A man, who gained access to 90-year-old Jessie Moody's apartment on Feb. 7 by impersonating a police officer, returned, this time in a nurse's aide's uniform, claiming he was returning money stolen before. The man beat Moody and searched her home for more money, but found nothing.

### March 26

**DRUGS: California** Richard Wallstrum was convicted of running a $33 million cocaine ring for 10 years between South America and California.

**EXTORTION: New York, N.Y.** Apprehended in a phone booth while making a bomb threat to Pan American Airlines, Scott Sasonkin, 23, who had been arrested seven times before for the same type of charge, was ordered to undergo a psychiatric evaluation.

**MURDER: New York, N.Y.** Four men, two armed with handguns, stormed the Body and Soul Social Club in the Prospect-Lefferts Gardens section of Brooklyn. The men opened fire killing Reynaldo McCarthy, 20, and wounding eight others.

**MURDER: New York, N.Y.** Anthony Perry, a 25-year-old ex-convict released only 12 days earlier, stabbed and killed Roy Lee Jr., 13, an innocent bystander who had stopped to watch Perry argue with others about a street basketball game in Queens.

**THEFT: New York, N.Y.** Deloshea Dehart, 28, and Jonathan McNeil, 24, were arrested for disconnecting Brooklyn fire alarm telegraph lines with the intention of selling the wire's valuable copper content to construction companies.

### March 27

**MURDER: Central Islip, N.Y.** The bodies of Joanne Johnson and her children, Octavin and Lavar Toney, 12 and 9, were found by Johnson's estranged husband in separate rooms of their house, apparently killed execution-style.

**MURDER: Tucson, Ariz.** In one of the city's worst mass murders, five men were found shot to death in an apparent drug-related execution.

### March 28

**BRIBERY: Tokyo, Japan** Takashi Kato, 59, former deputy minister of labor in Japan, was charged with accepting shares as bribes to help persuade the ministry not to add more stringent laws in 1984 regarding employment information magazines, a stance benefiting Recruit Information Co.

**EXECUTION: San Francisco, Calif.** A stay of execution was ordered for Charles Rodman Campbell, 34, sentenced in Washington State for killing two women and a girl, thus halting the first possible hanging in the U.S. since 1965.

**FRAUD: Washington, D.C.** Former Litton Industries employee James Carton, acting under the False Claims Act, which encourages employees to reveal the fraudulent activities of their employers, brought charges against Litton for defrauding the federal government out of an estimated $25 million.

**MURDER: New York, N.Y** Two unidentified women apparently coerced Monique Rivera, 22, into accompanying them on a car ride with her 6-week-old infant, Andre. Rivera's battered and strangled body was found two days later. The baby was missing.

**THEFT: New York, N.Y.** Mark Silver, a 32-year-old podiatrist, pleaded guilty to stealing $75,000 from New York's Medicaid program over a three-year period.

### March 29

**ARSON: New York, N.Y.** Ronald A. Scaglionie, 45, was convicted of setting fire to a Bedford-Stuyvesant health clinic in an attempt to cover up a $16 million Medicaid fraud scheme.

**ASSASSINATION: Ankara, Turkey** Abdurrezzak Ceylan, a Turkish opposition deputy from a southern province, was shot and killed in Parliament. Other deputies from Ceylan's province, Idris Arikan and Zeki Celiker, accused each other of the crime.

**ASSASSINATION: Brussels, Belgium** Gunmen shot and killed Muslim cleric Abdullah al-Ahdal, 36, and Salem el-Behir, a 40-year-old librarian, after al-Ahdal spoke out against Ayatollah Ruhollah Khomeini's sentence of death on author Salman Rushdie.

**FRAUD: Chicago, Ill.** Grand jury indictments resulting from the Operation Double Dip welfare fraud investigation named Cherry Ann Berry, 40, charging her with receiving $93,859 during a period when she was employed.

**MURDER: Bogota, Colombia** Gunmen shot and killed lawyer Hector Giraldo Galvez, who had investigated the murder of an anti-drug cartel newspaperman.

**MURDER: Sonora, Mexico** The tortured and mutilated bodies of nine people were found on an abandoned ranch near the Mexican-U.S. border town of Agua Prieta owned by Hector Fragoso. Three more bodies were found in a well on Apr. 1.

**RACKETEERING: New York, N.Y.** A federal grand jury indicted Drexel Burnham Lambert Inc. executive Michael Milken on charges of racketeering and breaking securities laws by using investors' funds to finance mergers and to control financial markets. He pleaded not guilty on Apr. 7.

### March 30

**ABDUCTION: Chicago, Ill.** Hellice Robinson, an 8-year-old girl, was reported missing after a witness saw her being forced into a man's car on her way to school.

**MURDER: Boston, Mass.** Suspect Kien Vinh Ly, 23, wanted in the shooting of an off-duty Los Angeles deputy marshal, was arrested in Chinatown.

### March 31

**ATTEMPTED MURDER: New York, N.Y.** Police arrested Catherine Papadakos, who shot her son Charles Papadakos, 30, after they argued about his drug use.

**FRAUD: Alexandria, Va.** Defense consultant Fred Lackner, on trial for getting classified information by bribing a Navy official, pleaded guilty.

**FRAUD: Dallas, Texas** Carol C. Peeler and Albert E. Johansen, former securities executives of Hillcrest Equities, pleaded guilty to criminal tax fraud.

**LAW ENFORCEMENT: Arlington, Texas** Police officer Bryan Farrell, 25, was dismissed after Dallas police found notches on the gun Farrell used to kill three suspects in seven months.

**MURDER: New Bedford, Mass.** The body of 26-year-old Mary Rose Santos, the apparent eighth victim of a serial killer, was found.

**RAPE: Chicago, Ill.** Veteran Chicago police officer Dennis Zancha, 39, was indicted and charged with the Mar. 13 rape of a neighbor and the Jan. 20 attempted rape of a female police officer.

### April 1

**KIDNAPPING: Central Islip, N.Y.** Joseph Amorosa, 50, was charged with kidnapping and weapons possession after he allegedly pulled a gun on two men and accused them of selling him sick pigeons.

### April 2

**MURDER: Los Angeles, Calif.** Darris Garvin, 37, who attempted to foil the North Hollywood theft of a neighbor's pickup truck by four teenagers, was shot and killed as he chased them. Police arrested three of the suspects on Apr. 12.

**MURDER: New Rochelle, N.Y.** Leslie Gordon Jr., 32, was shot and killed by police after he pointed a toy Uzi submachine gun at police and threatened to shoot.

**THEFT: New York, N.Y.** Police arrested 13 men, two related to reputed mobster John Gotti, for the possession of stolen car parts used in a car repair shop in Queens.

### April 4

**CONSPIRACY: Pomona, Calif.** Thomas A. Gionis, 35, estranged husband of 32-year-old Aissa Wayne, the late John Wayne's daughter, was arrested and charged with arranging a pistol-whipping assault on his former spouse and her friend.

**RAPE: Long Beach, Calif.** Postal clerk Tom Yang, 33, was charged with raping the 10-year-old daughter of a Long Beach woman who was allegedly offered $10,000 in return for the girl's hand in marriage. Yang lived in the same house with the woman.

### April 5

**DRUGS: Chicago, Ill.** Federal marshals confiscated $3.5 million worth of property from suspected cocaine and heroin dealer Jonathan and Clara Penny.

**DRUNK DRIVING: Huntington, N.Y.** Joseph J. Hazelwood, 42, captain of the *Exxon Valdez* and wanted for criminal charges in connection with the oil tanker, surrendered to authorities at his Long Island home. Bail on the Alaskan warrant was set at $500,000. He was released on bond the following day.

**FRAUD: Los Angeles, Calif.** Businessman James P. Lund, 67, was arraigned on felony charges of fining a false tax return and forgery for his alleged pocketing of more than $3 million in unemployment and worker's compensation fees for dead employees.

**LAW ENFORCEMENT: Inglewood, Calif.** Burglary suspect Javier Salvador Arreola, 23, was shot and killed by police after a 100-mile chase at speeds of up to 100 m.p.h.

**MURDER: Fort Lauderdale, Fla.** Twelve-year-old Arva Betts was indicted on charges that she killed her 2-year-old half brother and beat her 15-month-old half sister, both of whom she had to baby-sit every day.

**ROBBERY Chicago, Ill.** Ex-convict Kenneth Carter, 23, was sentenced to 20 years in jail for the robbery and beating of Donald Valentini, a church volunteer, just before mass.

**ROBBERY Salem, Ore.** The Oregon Court of Appeals ruled that cowboy boots can be considered weapons. Todd Bell's appeal on a robbery conviction, which he claimed was too severe, was denied because he used his boot to kick a woman in the chest.

## April 6

**BATTERY: Chicago, Ill.** Timothy Klavanowitch, 23, convicted of aggravated battery for throwing a female hitchhiker out of his van when she resisted his advances and then running over her, was sentenced to three years in prison.

**FRAUD: Kansas City, Mo.** George Pettengill Bowie, 64, former chairman of Transit Casualty Co., a high-risk insurance company, pleaded innocent to charges that he left $3-$4 billion worth of claims unpaid.

**MURDER: Westport, Conn.** Marcus Singer, 20, was arrested for the murder of his father, retired ophthalmologist Bernard Singer.

## April 7

**BLACKMAIL: Rayleigh, England** A jar of contaminated baby food was discovered, starting a flood of tampering incidents against two of Britain's leading baby food manufacturers, H.J. Heinz Co. Ltd. and Cow and Gate Ltd.

**CONSPIRACY: San Diego, Calif.** Multimillionaire businessman Richard T. Silberman, 59, and three other men were arrested on money laundering charges after an FBI sting operation uncovered links between the Chicago mob and southern California. Silberman is a Democratic Party fundraiser and is married to a San Diego County Commissioner.

**MURDER: Oakland, Calif.** James Richard Garrett, 49, of San Francisco was arrested by FBI agents in Oakland and charged with murdering his mother, Grace Reever Garrett, 79, with a pickax on Mar. 23 in an attempt to gain control of her estate.

**MURDER: Vienna, Austria** Nurse's aide Waltraud Wagner, 30, and three others were arrested after admitting to the killings of at least 49 patients in the Lainz Hospital.

**RACKETEERING: New York, N.Y.** Michael Milken, Drexel Burnham Lambert Inc. executive, pleaded not guilty to 98 counts of securities fraud and racketeering.

**ROBBERY: Gardena, Calif.** Bank teller Alexander V. Manansala, 29, disappeared along with $400,000 from the Republic Bank where he worked.

## April 8

**DRUGS: Guadalajara, Mexico** Mexican officials arrested top cocaine trafficker Miguel Angel Felix Gallardo, 43, and the entire police force of the city in Culiacan, Felix Gallardo's base of operations.

**MURDER: Palacios, Texas** Duc Nga Nguyen, 27, was killed in a shootout with police after he killed a judge and wounded a police officer who told him he was applying for a driver's license on the wrong day.

## April 9

**ATTEMPTED MURDER: Santa Monica, Calif.** Psychiatric patient Larry Anthony Taylor, 27, was arrested after he allegedly stabbed social worker Shirley Ann Sauerwein, 44.

## April 10

**HIJACKING: Miami, Fla.** Two armed Haitian men hijacked a Missionary Aviation Fellowship plane at Cap Haitien and demanded to be flown to Miami, where they surrendered to authorities.

**LAW ENFORCEMENT: Fort Worth, Texas** Convicted for accepting a vacation in Florida, former Bronx congressman Mario Biaggi, 71, began a two-and-a-half-year jail sentence. Biaggi was also convicted for involvement in the Wedtech scandal, and received an additional eight-year sentence.

**RACKETEERING: Newark, N.J.** Anthony (Fat Tony) Salerno, 78, facing charges of racketeering and extortion for trying to control the sand-pit business of Morris County, pleaded guilty.

## April 11

**FRAUD: Los Angeles, Calif.** Janet Faye McKinzie, 39, and five others were indicted on bank fraud and other charges after allegedly bilking the North America Savings and Loan Association of more than $16 million in 1987 in a plot headed by the bank's founder, Duayne D. Christensen.

**LAW ENFORCEMENT: Chicago, Ill.** Operation Risky Business, an undercover sting operation in which police officers pose as drug dealers, began. Within three weeks of its initiation, 72 arrests had been made.

**MURDER: Chicago, Ill.** Eddie Lee Jimmerson, convicted forger, was arrested and charged with the Apr. 6 strangulation of Myra Adams.

**MURDER: Matamoros, Mexico** Twelve bodies were unearthed as the search continued for reputed drug ring leader Adolfo de Jesus Constanzo, 26, and Sara Maria Aldrete, 24, honor student and high priestess of Constanzo's drug trafficking cult, in connection with the ritual murders of 15 people.

**MURDER: Pomona, Calif.** Arnold Lloyd, 47, fatally shot Michael Stephenson, 20, after Stephenson tried to take the tires from his car.

**THEFT: White Plains, N.Y.** Accountant Nicholas Shepis, 50, pleaded guilty to charges involving the theft of $200,000 he had collected from his clients to be used to pay sales tax liabilities.

## April 12

**ARSON: Peoria, Ill.** Joe Pickens, 34, a homeless man, was indicted on two counts of arson and nine counts of murder after a fire at an apartment complex killed two mothers and seven children.

**DRUGS: Maywood, Ill.** Corey Shorter, 20, and Felicia O'Neal, 17, were arrested in a police raid in which three automobiles, more than $200,000 worth of heroin and cocaine, and $3,678 cash were confiscated.

**MURDER: Albany, N.Y.** Richard Ruff, 52, previously sentenced to four to 12 years for two counts of attempted sodomy of his stepdaughter, was indicted for the sodomy and hanging of his 11-year-old first cousin, William Ruff, whose body was found Sept. 1, 1957. Ruff was later sentenced to life in prison.

**MURDER: Jerusalem, Israel** Rabbi Moshe Levinger, 54, head of a right-wing Jewish nationalist group, was indicted on charges that he killed Khayed Salah, 42, while randomly shooting at a shop after his car was stoned by Palestinians. Levinger was sentenced to five months in jail on May 1.

**THEFT: Zurich, Switzerland** Twenty-one paintings were stolen from the Koetser Gallery. On May 1, Belgians Rene De Grove, Martine Wins, and Thierry Houze were arrested and charged with possession of internationally transported stolen goods.

### April 13

**BRIBERY: New York, N.Y.** Peter Tully was arrested in an investigation into allegations of bribes given to city health inspectors to overlook code violations. Seventeen other restaurateurs have been arrested and 46 inspectors have been found guilty of extortion thus far.

### April 14

**MANSLAUGHTER: Strathclyde, England** Kelly Lynch and Lorraine Simpson, both 11, took Brian Simpson's two Rottweiler dogs for a walk. The dogs suddenly turned on the girls, killing Kelly. Authorities had the Rottweilers destroyed and continued an investigation into the incident.

**MURDER: New York, N.Y.** John Chang, 58, fatally shot his son, Jenn Ju Chang, 22, after an argument about a video cassette recorder that disappeared from their home in Queens.

**MURDER: Sonoma County, Calif.** Ramon Salcido, 28, allegedly left his Boyes Hot Springs house and went to a dump, where he cut the throats of his three daughters, one of whom survived. He then murdered his mother-in-law, Marian Richards, 42, his wife, Angela, 24, her two sisters, and a fellow winery worker.

**MURDER: Trent, England** Carl Powis, 23, who allegedly murdered Joseph Parkes, 72, father-in-law of Member of Parliament George Stevenson, was remanded in custody.

**ROBBERY Costa del Sol, Spain** Ronald Knight was arrested and later charged in connection with the 1983 robbery of Security Express involving £5 million.

**SEXUAL ABUSE: Edenton, N.C.** The first suspect was arrested in connection with the alleged sexual abuse of children from September 1988 through January 1989 at the Little Rascals' Day Care Center run by Robert Kelly Jr., 41, and his 34-year-old wife Elizabeth, who have been charged.

### April 16

**PIRACY: Songkhla, Thailand** Pirates murdered 130 Vietnamese refugees by bludgeoning and shooting them, and then burning their boat, leaving one survivor, Pham Ngoc Minh Hung, 23.

**RAPE: Los Angeles, Calif.** A 15-year-old girl was abducted and taken to a home where she was repeatedly raped and assaulted for six days by at least three men. She managed to escape on Apr. 22 but was picked up by three other men and again raped before being rescued. Antonio Diaz, 18, one of the men

who picked her up on Apr. 22 was arrested, as were a 16- and a 17-year-old boy.

### April 17

**BOMBING: Indianapolis, Ind.** Erin Bower, 5, lost most of her left hand and injured her eye and abdomen after a pipe bomb concealed in a toothpaste container in a K Mart department store exploded. Her mother was slightly injured.

**BOMBING: Wiesbaden, Germany** One official died and another was critically injured when a radio bomb went off at federal police headquarters. The bomb was similar to the one that exploded on Pan Am Flight 103 over Scotland on Dec. 21, 1988, killing all 259 passengers on board.

**MURDER: Washington, D.C.** The U.S. Supreme Court said it would deliberate the reversed conviction of Bernard Harris, whose 1984 confession that he fatally stabbed girlfriend Thelma Staton was ruled inadmissible because it was taken during an unlawful arrest.

### April 18

**FRAUD: Cook County, Ill.** Former Glenview, Ill., residents George and Esther Apostol were indicted on charges of theft and securities fraud after allegedly using $180,000 entrusted to them for investments to make personal purchases.

**FRAUD: Switzerland** Adnan Khashoggi, Saudi Arabian prince and aide to Libyan leader Muammar Qaddafi, was arrested after the U.S. requested his extradition on charges that he allegedly helped hide the assets of deposed Philippine leader Ferdinand Marcos and his wife, Imelda.

**MURDER: Jerusalem, Israel** Four masked Arab youths broke into the West Bank home of Palestinian Nadira Boulus, 43, and stabbed her to death, believing that Boulus had collaborated with Israeli agents.

**MURDER: Montgomery, Ala.** Lee Artis Carter, 36, was arrested after his wife and three children were found murdered in their home.

**MURDER: New York, N.Y.** Kenneth Combs, 45, angry after his wife called him lazy, fatally struck her with his fists and a broom handle. For three weeks police believed Combs' story that he accidentally killed her when he was swinging at insects. Combs was arraigned on May 11 after making a confession.

**MURDER: New York, N.Y.** In Nassau County, Pedro Llamas, 21, was convicted of the fatal stabbing and beating of his homosexual lover, Luis Moran, 32, in 1987. Llamas said Moran wanted too much sex. Llamas received a 25-year to life prison sentence.

### April 19

**CONTEMPT: Waterbury, Conn.** Richard C. Dobbins Jr., a possible juror in the triple murder case of Donald Couture, shouted "Guilty" when his name was called. Dobbins was arrested for contempt, fined $100, and sent to jail for 10 days. The 66 others who arrived for jury selection were afterwards disqualified.

**RAPE: New York, N.Y.** A gang of nearly three dozen youths on a "wilding" spree, viciously raped and assaulted a 28-year-old Wall Street investment banker while she was jogging near the West Bridle Path in Central Park.

**SABOTAGE: Caribbean Sea** Forty-seven crew members on board the Navy battleship U.S.S. *Iowa* lost their lives during a routine training exercise off the coast of Puerto Rico when a gun-turret exploded. Investigators suspected that 25-year-old sailor Clayton Hartwig, who died in the blast, may have deliberately sabotaged the ship.

*April 20*

**ASSAULT: Des Plaines, Ill.** A Cook County court convicted George Matuska, 52, of aggravated assault, resisting a police officer, and possessing a firearm without a license after Matuska assaulted two workers of the Illinois Citizen Animal Welfare League who attempted to remove a pet skunk from his Des Plaines home. Matuska, who also shot at the workers and missed, was acquitted of attempted murder charges.

**FRAUD: New York, N.Y.** Frank Shannon, 56, director of the British division of the Nissan Motor Co., pleaded guilty to charges that he gave the Securities and Exchange Commission false statements about his role in a penny stock fraud.

**MURDER: St. Petersburg, Fla.** David White Jr., 22, son of a CBS executive, was shot to death near the campus of Eckerd College, where he was a student, in an apparent robbery attempt.

**MURDER: Tucson, Ariz.** Hector Fragoso, 45, was arrested outside Tucson on suspicion of murder. Fragoso was the suspect in 12 drug-related murders that occurred at an abandoned ranch in Mexico in March.

*April 21*

**ARSON: Joliet, Ill.** Former mental patient Larry C. Williams, 38, was charged with setting fire to the Joliet Public Library, causing more than $1 million in damages.

**MURDER: Nebraska** Yale Booska, 21, was arrested and charged with grand theft auto and the murder of Charles Washington, 61, a Los Angeles car salesman. Booska escaped to Nebraska after admittedly shooting Washington during a demonstration drive. He was arrested near Grand Island in the stolen vehicle and extradited to California.

**RAPE: New York, N.Y.** Four suspects were charged in the brutal rape of a 28-year-old Wall Street investment broker who was jogging in Central Park when the attack occurred Apr. 19. Charged with attempted murder, rape, and assault were Raymond Santana, 14, Anton McCray, 15, Kevin Richardson, 14, and Steve Lopez, 15.

*April 22*

**MURDER: Mission Viejo, Calif.** Deborah Ann Werner, 40, and three accomplices identified as Carrie Mae Chichester, 20, Charles L. Clemmons, 20, and Miguel Ruiz, 21, were arrested on suspicion of murdering Werner's 72-year-old father. David Werner, a retired stockbroker, was smothered to death then stabbed at the family home.

*April 23*

**ASSAULT: London, England** The Criminal Injuries Compensation Board awarded Jacqueline Jones, 21, a sum of £200,000 for injuries sustained in 1970 when she was assaulted by Michael Rowley during a home invasion at her residence in Allerton. Rowley is serving two life sentences for the savage attack upon Jones, whose lips were stapled shut with a fork by Rowley after he beat her sister to death.

**MURDER: Riverhead, N.Y.** Opening statements were made in the trial of 17-year-old Martin Tankleff, accused of killing his adoptive parents, Seymour Tankleff, 62, and Arlene Tankleff, 54, on Sept. 7 with a dumbbell and knife.

*April 24*

**ASSAULT: San Francisco, Calif.** Controversial TV talk show host Morton Downey Jr. was allegedly assaulted in the men's room at the San Francisco airport. Downey blamed the attack on three people he described as skinheads. An eyewitness doubted the veracity of the story and police found no suspects.

**ROBBERY New York, N.Y.** Three bandits, who police believed were responsible for holding up 20 transit station token-booths in Brooklyn, were arrested following a gun battle with police. The suspects were identified as Paul Taylor, 31, David Thigpen, 25, and Kevin Reeves, 26.

*April 25*

**DRUGS: Chicago, Ill.** Mario Lettieri, 47, the owner of a West Side butcher shop, was indicted with former police officer Nedrick Miller and seven other people in connection with a $1 million drug ring they allegedly operated in a local hotel.

**MURDER: Dayton Beach, Fla.** James Richardson, 53, was released from Daytona prison where he was serving a life sentence for poisoning his seven children with pesticide. A judge ruled that prosecutors had suppressed evidence during Richardson's 1967 trial.

**MURDER: Long Beach, Calif.** Pia Wright, 19, and her boyfriend, Mario King, 21, were charged with murder and child abuse in the beating death of Wright's two-and-a-half-year-old son.

*April 26*

**FRAUD: Beverly Hills, Calif.** Insurance agent Julian Barton, 60, was named in a 54-count criminal indictment charging him with bilking 18 investors out of $3.8 million.

**FRAUD: New York, N.Y.** Convicted stock speculator Ivan Boesky's plea for an early release after having served one year of a three-year sentence was refused by U.S. District Court judge Morris E. Lasker.

**MURDER: New Bedford, Mass.** A serial murderer claimed his ninth victim since July, an unidentified woman found strangled to death along Interstate Highway 195. The other victims were disposed of in the same manner, along rural highways. The women were all connected in some way to prostitution or drugs.

**MURDER: Tampa, Fla.** Newton Carlton Slawson, 34, was indicted for the Apr. 11 murders of a co-worker's family: Gerald Wood, 23, his pregnant wife Peggy, 21, and their two children. Slawson, who was reportedly discharged from the military for a "personality disorder," claimed Gerald Wood tried to force him to take cocaine.

*April 27*

**DRUGS: Chicago, Ill.** Former Austin District patrol officer Nedrick Miller, 62, sheriff's police sergeant Joseph Neeley, 60, and five others were arraigned on charges that they operated a major West Side drug ring.

**DRUGS: New York, N.Y.** The owner of the Kissena Pharmacy, three pharmacists, and two doctors were charged with selling phony prescriptions for medicine to known drug addicts for between $15 and $20.

**MURDER: Fort Worth, Texas** Ricky Lee Green, 28, was arrested and charged with the sexual mutilation murders of four people. His wife Sharon was also indicted for taking part in the murders.

**RAPE: New York, N.Y.** Yusef Salaam, 15, and Raymond Santana, 14, allegedly involved in the Apr. 19 Central Park rape, were indicted. The charges included rape, attempted murder, and assault.

### April 28

**MURDER: New York, N.Y.** The body of a newborn infant was discovered in an alleyway where it lay for nearly two days because passersby thought it was a doll. Nineteen-year-old Maridily Benetez admittedly dropped the baby from her second-story apartment after giving birth because she feared the reaction of her family, who did not know she had been pregnant.

**MURDER: Prince George County, Md.** Kirk Bruce, convicted of killing two of five victims a 1988 Landover multiple murder connected to a crack ring, was sentenced to death in Maryland's gas chamber, becoming the state's nineteenth Death Row inmate.

**PERJURY: Chicago, Ill.** U.S. District Court Judge Ann Williams sentenced 36-year-old sports agent David Lueddeke to 26 months in jail for lying to a grand jury about alleged payments made to Cris Carter, an All-American receiver from Ohio State University.

**THEFT: Fresno, Calif.** Following an eight-year manhunt, the FBI arrested Home Wayne Carter, 60, a former civilian employee of the U.S. Navy who allegedly stole 17 blank Treasury checks from the Naval Construction Battalion Center in Port Hueneme. Carter had been charged in 1982 with government theft after reportedly cashing more than $1 million in checks.

### April 30

**MURDER: Lakeville, Ind.** The Reverend Robert Pelley, 38, of the Olive Branch United Brethren Church, his wife Dawn, 32, and their two children were found shot to death in their home outside South Bend.

**MURDER: Port Orchard, Wash.** Seventeen-year-old Michael Monroe Furman was arrested for the murder of Ann Presler, an 85-year-old widow who was bludgeoned to death in her garden. Kitsap County Prosecutor C. Danny Clem decided to push for the death penalty in this case, despite Furman's age.

### May 1

**ASSASSINATION: Manipay, Sri Lanka** T. Panchalingam, a senior representative of the government, was shot by an assailant. The Liberation Tigers of Tamil Eelam, who were discussing possible negotiations with the government, claimed responsibility.

**MURDER: Florence, Calif.** When a car pulled out in front of Charles Padilla, 57, he honked his horn. The other driver stepped out of his car, walked back to Padilla, and shot him dead in front of the victim's two grandchildren.

**RAPE: Malibu, Calif.** Yoon No Yoon, 31, was arrested for the Apr. 19 attempted rape of a woman who arranged to meet him in a local restaurant. Police found Yoon carrying a glass vial that contained his dismembered finger that he had intended to give the woman as a token of remorse for his actions.

### May 2

**DRUGS: Chicago, Ill.** Doctors performed surgery on Kayode Olujare, 33, to remove 49 packets of 90 percent pure white heroin which he had ingested as a means of smuggling. Olujare had passed 32 more packets, but one packet had burst, putting him in danger of death. He was charged with possession.

**MURDER: Whitely Bay, England** Robert Sartin, a 22-year-old civil servant, was arraigned for the murder of Kenneth Mackintosh after he was arrested for an Apr. 30 shooting rampage in which 14 others were injured.

**RAPE: New York, N.Y.** A 38-year-old woman was assaulted and raped by three men on the roof of a Brooklyn apartment building and then thrown off the roof. She survived. Kelvin Furman, 21, Tyrone Prescott, and Darron Decoteau, 16, were charged on May 5.

**ROBBERY Chicago, Ill.** Patricia Bass, 21, who took part in the robbery of a bar which resulted in the murder of its owner, was sentenced to 30 years in prison.

**ROBBERY Chicago, Ill.** Two armed men rushed an armored truck as a guard emerged from the passenger door. They unloaded 10 to 15 bags of money—an estimated $140,000—to two other men, who loaded it into a getaway car. The robbers drove away under gunshots from the armored car driver.

**ROBBERY Torrance, Calif.** Paul Mooneyham, 41, was arrested after witnesses recognized his car as being the getaway vehicle in a bank robbery earlier that day. Mooneyham was also wanted for suspicion in at least nine other Southern California robberies.

### May 3

**FRAUD: Washington D.C.** David Rivers and John Clyburn were indicted on charges of arranging city government contracts to be awarded to friends.

### May 4

**MURDER: New York, N.Y.** Pet shop owner Vincent Becchinelli, 44, was shot to death while waiting to make a deposit at a bank. The robber fled with several thousand dollars.

**RAPE: Tallahassee, Fla.** The state Supreme Court upheld an appeals court decision that Lee Curtis Davis, 46, should not have been sentenced to life for the rape of a 13-year-old handicapped girl because the girl was not, by legal definition, physically helpless.

**THEFT: Utah** While two guards slept in the bunk section of an armored car, the driver, Jared Layne Gray, 26, stole $2.5 million and disappeared.

### May 5

**MURDER: Skokie, Ill.** George Saro, 34, Adel al-Sakhria, 28, and Johnny Mirza, 23, were found guilty of the May 29, 1985, murder of Chicago motel manager, Mohammed Shamin, whom they beat to death while robbing the Acres Motel.

### May 6

**MURDER: Mexico City, Mexico** Adolfo de Jesus Constanzo, 27, alleged leader of a drug-smuggling cult thought responsible for 15 murders, was shot to death after reportedly directing a fellow cult member to kill him and Martin Quintana Rodriguez, 25, alleged top cult figure, during a police raid. Constanzo's "high priestess," Sarah Maria Aldrete and three others were arrested afterwards.

### May 7

**MURDER: Catania, Sicily** Five armed men entered a hospital and shot ex-convict Francesco Cazzetta, 36, to death as he recovered from a failed attempt on his life two days before.

### May 8

**MANSLAUGHTER: Rockford, Ill.** Melanie Green, 24, was charged with involuntary manslaughter and delivery of a controlled substance to a minor, becoming the first person convicted of killing a child by using cocaine during pregnancy. A grand jury later refused to indict Green.

**MURDER: La Plata, Md.** Kirk Bruce, 27, was sentenced to death, four life terms, and 130 years in prison for the Jan. 22, 1988, murders of five people in Landover.

**MURDER: San Francisco, Calif.** The state Supreme Court upheld the death sentence of Andre Burton, 26, convicted of murdering an elderly woman who attempted to aid her son when Burton robbed him.

**TORTURE: Buenos Aires, Argentina** Former air force commander Orlando Ramón Agosti, who was convicted in 1985 of being involved in eight tortures, finished his three-and-a-half year prison sentence and was released.

### May 9

**ABDUCTION: Melbourne, Australia** Four children were released with minor injuries when Turkish immigrant Sereffettin Hurseyin, 32, surrendered to authorities after an eight-hour siege at a public school, during which Hurseyin had been armed with gasoline and a revolver.

**ASSAULT: Wheaton, Ill.** Robert W. White, 38, was convicted of aggravated assault for the Dec. 20 attack against Wheaton North High School assistant principal Philip A. Stough, who had called White to the school to discuss discipline for the man's son.

**MURDER: Chicago, Ill.** Convicted of raping and straggling 19-year-old Latrina Humphries, Wade Frazier, 29, was sentenced to 80 years in prison.

### May 10

**MURDER: Boston, Mass.** Alfred J. Hunter, 42, shot and killed his wife, then stole a plane and flew over the city of Boston for three hours, indiscriminately firing an automatic weapon at targets on the ground.

**RAPE: New York, N.Y.** The defendants in the Central Park rape case—Raymond Santana, 14, Kevin Richardson, 14, Steve Lopez, 15, Antron McCray, 15, Yusef Salaam, 15, and Kharey Wise, 16—all pleaded not guilty to charges that they raped and beat a Wall Street executive in Central Park on Apr. 19.

### May 11

**ASSAULT: New York, N.Y.** Two drug dealers shot Lloyd Daniels, a 21-year-old basketball hopeful who was planning to begin negotiations for a contract with the Washington Bullets professional team. The shots were the result of a dispute over an $8 overdue drug payment.

**DRUGS: Chicago, Ill.** In what was to be a final blow to a resilient, suburban-based cocaine ring, Drug Enforcement Administration agents raided six houses, seizing drugs and cash and arresting Mario Lloyd, 29, Gregory Hawkins, 34, and Andrew Jefferson, 50.

**ESCAPE: Chicago, Ill.** Roger Sexton, 28, pleaded guilty to killing a Cook County corrections officer when he attempted to escape from incarceration. He was sentenced to nine years in prison.

**KIDNAPPING: Wiesbaden, West Germany** Welshman Allan Rees, 37, was charged with the 1983 abduction of a Lufthansa Airlines manager in Bolivia, a crime for which he was sentenced in absentia in Bolivia for 22 years and six months in prison.

**MURDER: Scotch Plains, N.J.** After taking a taxi from New York City to New Jersey with her boyfriend, 18-year-old Laurie Ann Cuzzolino realized she could not pay the $100 fare. Instead, she allegedly killed cab driver Harish Kakar, 36, with a .38-caliber pistol.

**POLICE BRUTALITY: Hayward, Calif.** Police officers Eric Ristrim and Marie Yin saw David St. John, 37, place what they thought was an illegal weapon, a nunchakus, in his pocket. When he did not hand it over, they beat him without identifying themselves. The officers discovered that St. John was blind, and the "weapon" was a collapsible white cane.

**ROBBERY: Sylmar, Calif.** A viewer, who saw Archie Michael Wolf's face on a TV news story about Los Angeles' 12 most-wanted bank robbers, called the police and told them where Wolf lived. Wolf, 35, may have been involved in 27 Southern California heists.

### May 12

**BOMBING: Athens, Greece** The Greek Supreme Court upheld a U.S. extradition order for Mohammed Rashid, 39, wanted for the 1982 bombing of a Pan American Airlines airplane that killed one and injured 15. The order was delayed in July.

**MONEY LAUNDERING: New York, N.Y.** Authorities arrested 12 of 16 people connected to drug lord José Santa Cruz Londoño's Cali, Colombia, drug cartel, and charged them with laundering $100 million from New York cocaine sales to Colombia and Panama.

**MURDER: Las Vegas, Nev.** A jury found former Los Angeles police officer Steven Homick, 48, guilty of the Dec. 11, 1985, killing of oil heiress Bobbie Jean Tipton, her maid Marie Bullock, and deliveryman James Myers.

**MURDER: Mineral County, Mont.** Montana deputies on horseback tracked down David L. Schoenecker, 48, and held him for the murder of his wife, Gail Schoenecker, 40, in Anaheim, Calif. Schoenecker sent a letter to the Orange County (Calif.) *Register* confessing to the crime and giving the body's location.

**MURDER: New York, N.Y.** During an annual review of open cases, Bronx detectives linked through fingerprints convicted rapist Herbert Hoover White, 35, to the case of Eileen McHale, 21, raped and murdered on Sept. 13, 1980. White confessed to the crime during interrogation.

**ROBBERY Bethesda, Md.** A branch of Crestar Bank and the Maryland National Bank were robbed. Thomas Springer, 40, former press secretary to Representative Toby Roth, was later charged.

### May 15

**MURDER: Los Angeles, Calif.** Reputed gang member Gilbert Munoz, 20, believed to be the triggerman, was arrested for the murder of Juan "Chaka" Enriquez, 18, a high school football and wrestling captain.

**POLICE BRUTALITY: Washington, D.C.** In a 9-0 vote, the U.S. Supreme Court ruled that victims in police brutality lawsuits need only to prove that the officer acted unreasonably, not "maliciously and sadistically," widening the definition of brutality.

### May 16

**ASSASSINATION: Beirut, Lebanon** A car bomb killed Grand Mufti Sheikh Hassan Khaled, 68, a Sunni Muslim leader, and at least 21 bystanders. Eighty others were also wounded.

**EXTORTION: Alexandria, Va.** Lester Hummer was indicted on 14 counts of extortion. Hummer, 47, is accused of trying to coerce the Coca Cola Co. into paying him $2 million to keep him from poisoning the company's products.

**FRAUD: Washington, D.C.** Kerry A. Hurton, 24, a former paralegal in New York law firm Skadden, Arps, Slate, Meagher & Flom, and five investors were charged with insider trading by passing information about a future buyout.

**MURDER: Los Angeles, Calif.** Natividad Flores, 26, and her boyfriend, Alejandro Lara, 29, pleaded not guilty to murder in the beating death of 8-year-old Alba Susanna Flores. The girl's charred body was found May 11 in a park miles from her home.

**SMUGGLING: Houston, Texas** U.S. Customs agents arrested four people and seized $1.8 million worth of computer equipment in connection with a smuggling ring that was illegally exporting high-tech equipment to Eastern bloc countries.

### May 17

**ESCAPE: Springville, Ala.** Roy Andrew Rafos, 42, who escaped from the Morris County, N.J., jail in 1975 after he was convicted of urinating in public, was arrested. His conviction carried a five-year sentence.

**ILLEGAL DUMPING: New York, N.Y.** A grand jury indicted Brooklyn medical company Plaza Health Laboratories and its vice president Geronimo Villegas, 49, on charges of dumping vials containing a hepatitis virus into New York waterways.

**THEFT: London, England** John Patrick Naughton, 47, suspected of selling paintings from £30 million worth of art stolen from Sir Alfred Beit three years ago, was arrested.

### May 18

**CHILD MOLESTATION: Simi Valley, Calif.** Cartoonist Dwaine Tinsley, 43, author of the "Chester the Molester" strip in *Hustler* magazine, was arrested and booked for investigation of child molestation.

**EXECUTION: Jackson, Ga.** Convicted murderer Henry Willis III was put to death in the electric chair. He shot Ray City police chief Ed Giddens in 1976.

### May 19

**FRAUD: Omaha, Neb.** Franklin Credit Union manager Lawrence King, 44, formerly praised for his charitable activities, was arrested with his wife, Alice King, and charged with fraud and violating tax laws. The credit union is missing an estimated $41.8 million.

**MURDER: Sacramento, Calif.** Sheriff's deputies found the body of 10-year-old Robin Cobb, a few feet away from where they later found the body of her father, Stephen Cobb, 42, who left a suicide note after killing her.

### May 20

**CHILD ABUSE: New York, N.Y.** After trying to reclaim her 2-year-old she had left at a hospital, Emmanuelle Jedone, 18, was arrested for child abandonment and reckless endangerment.

**CONSPIRACY: Madrid, Spain** Juan Miguel Bengoechea and Ramón Ferrero received 20 and 12 years in jail respectively for their part in the 1981 "toxic syndrome," in which contaminated cooking oil killed more than 600 people and made 25,000 ill.

**MURDER: Bogota, Colombia** Francisco Javier Monsalve Arango, 31, a judge who had investigated paramilitary groups, was shot to death by four gunmen.

### May 22

**ATTEMPTED MURDER: Tacoma, Wash.** Earl K. Shriner, 39, was charged with the rape, beating, attempted strangulation, and sexual mutilation of a 7-year-old boy.

**MURDER: Will County, Ill.** Opening statements were given in the trial of David DeMarco, 36, charged with soliciting jailed El Rukn gang member Anthony Echols to murder his former wife Joanne DeLoach so DeMarco could get custody of the couple's 6-year-old daughter.

### May 23

**MURDER: Long Beach, N.Y.** Elizabeth Menard, 23, an unemployed nurse's aide from Queens, was arrested and charged with murder for the death of Glenn Warshaw, 32, during an attempted robbery.

### May 24

**ASSAULT: New York, N.Y.** Robert Woods, 13, was

stabbed in the back by a fellow classmate during the lunch recess in a Bronx school. LeRoy Whitchett, also 13, was arrested and was to be charged as an adult.

**EXECUTION: Huntsville, Texas** Stephen Albert McCoy, 40, was executed by lethal injection for raping 18-year-old Cynthia Johnson and then aiding Gary LeBlanc and James Paster kill the stranded motorist Jan. 1, 1981.

**MURDER: La Paz, Bolivia** Two missionaries from Utah, Todd Ray Wilson, 19, and Jeffrey Brente Ball, 21, were gunned down by communist guerrillas outside their home in suburban La Paz.

**TERRORISM: Los Angeles, Calif.** Trial began for Tina Marie Ledbetter, 26, accused of writing nearly 6,000 letters to actor Michael J. Fox, most including death threats to Fox, his wife, and child.

**WAR CRIMES: Nice, France** A French war criminal hidden by right-wing church officials since the end of the war, Paul Touvier was arrested at a Catholic priory. Touvier, 74, was one of France's most notorious collaborators.

## May 25

**BRUTALITY: Jerusalem, Israel** Israeli soldiers Yitzhak Adler, Ron Hakhel, Arye Luzzato, and Yitzhak Kabudi were found guilty of brutality but were acquitted of manslaughter in the beating death of Palestinian Ani al-Shami in the Occupied Gaza Strip on Aug. 22.

**GAMBLING: Mineola, N.Y.** A $300-million-dollar-a-year sports gambling ring was smashed, and 68 people were arrested in a pre-dawn police raid. The leaders of the gambling ring were linked to the Gambino crime family.

**MURDER: Dallas, Texas** Bus driver Chauncey Plummer was charged with murder after he shot David Hayden, who attempted to use someone else's bus pass in order to avoid paying the $1.50 fare.

**MURDER: London, England** Marie Burke, a 63-year-old U.S. Embassy diplomat, was found stabbed to death in her apartment.

**MURDER: Olleros, Peru** Twenty-four-year-old Edward Bartley of Buckley, England, was executed by Peruvian leftist guerrillas in the town square of this Andean village. The motive for the shooting was not clear.

## May 26

**EXECUTION: Altmore, Ala.** Michael Lindsey, 28, was put to death in the electric chair for the Dec. 14, 1981, murder of Rosemary Zimlich Rutland, 64, in Mobile.

**MURDER: Johannesburg, South Africa** Judge Jan Basson sentenced 14 blacks to death for the Nov. 13, 1985, murder of black police officer Jetta Lucas Sethwala during a period of racial unrest. The condemned prisoners were part of the "Uppington 26."

**SEXUAL ASSAULT: New York, N.Y.** Elementary school principal Gustavo Torres, 60, was arrested for sexually abusing an 11-year-old girl in a classroom.

## May 27

**HIJACKING: Miami, Fla.** Cuban-born Pedro Rene Comas Baños, 37, hijacked a Miami bound American Airlines jetliner in Dallas, and ordered the craft to fly to Havana. The plane landed in Florida, and the hijacker surrendered to the FBI.

## May 28

**ARSON: Los Angeles, Calif.** Police investigators confirmed that the devastating fire that leveled the Pan Pacific Auditorium was the work of an arsonist. Forty-two-year-old transient Mark Kamansky was arrested; he was later released due to lack of evidence.

**ASSAULT: La Verne, Calif.** Neo-Nazi skinheads William R. Killackey, 21, his sister Amy Killackey, 19, Scott Wilson, 28, and Timothy Zaal, 25, were arrested after attacking a couple they believed was Jewish and a black man who came to their aid.

## May 29

**ATTEMPTED MURDER: Milwaukee, Wis.** Three Milwaukee women, Deborah Lee Kazuck, 26, Ramona Estelle Barry, 27, and Catherine Ann Lipsham, 22, lured a male acquaintance to their apartment and then assaulted him with an ax. The crime was done to "prove" Kazuck's "love" for Jack the Ripper.

**MURDER: Springfield, N.J.** Yale University honor student Rolando Marcello, 24, went on a murderous rampage and killed his mother, a brother, and two other people in his back yard. Police believed the unprovoked assault was triggered by depression or illness.

## May 30

**ABDUCTION: New York, N.Y.** Thirty-five-year-old Migdalia Pagan was imprisoned at Riker's Island for lying about the location of her son, a leukemia patient who was taken from the Sloan-Kettering Cancer Center by his father. Pagan was freed two-days later when husband David returned with the boy.

**DRUGS: New York, N.Y.** Justice William T. Martin, 37, of the New York State Supreme Court located in the Bronx was indicted on charges of tax evasion, cocaine possession, and perjury.

**FRAUD: White Plains, N.Y.** Dr. Ronald Klein, 30, a Westchester County podiatrist, entered a guilty plea to charges that he stole $1 million in false Medicaid claims.

**MURDER: New York, N.Y.** Police officer Jeff Herman, 25, was fatally shot in the Flatbush section of Brooklyn allegedly by freed kidnap suspect, Albert Smith, 32.

## May 31

**ASSAULT: New York, N.Y.** Computer technician Eliezer Silber, 40, was assaulted by as many as nine members of a strict Orthodox Hasidic movement that took exception to published reports in the *Panim Chadashot* of an internal dispute within the sect. Silber was mistaken for Chaim Shaulson, the publisher.

**DRUGS: Los Angeles, Calif.** Fugitive drug dealer Stanton Garland, 60, the alleged powerful head of the "French Connection" drug ring, was arrested after 17 years as a fugitive.

**FRAUD: Chicago, Ill.** Edward Johnson, 26, Joseph Fricano, 29, and James Zavacki, 31, of the General Finance

Corp. were indicted on charges of obtaining 72 fraudulent loans totaling $286,582 in order to repay gambling debts to bookie Paul C. Bagwell.

**MURDER: North Chicago, Ill.** Ricky Irby Sr., 27, and Sheila Smith, 26, were arrested for the 1984 poisoning of their son, who was force-fed sulfuric acid in an attempt to fraudulently sue Ross Laboratories, a baby-formula manufacturer.

**SABOTAGE: Phoenix, Ariz.** Mark L. Davis, 39, David Foreman, 42, and Marc A. Baker, 37, of "Earth First" were arrested and charged with conspiring to sabotage power lines that supply energy to the Palo Verde nuclear plant.

### June 1

**MURDER: Midlothian, Va.** John Emil List, 63, whose mother, Alma, wife, Helen, and three teenage children were found dead in their Westfield, N.J., home on Dec. 7, 1971, was arrested in connection with their murders.

### June 2

**FRAUD: Los Angeles, Calif.** Salvador Cano, 38, and four others were arrested for rendering illegal medical care in four clinics. Two others surrendered on June 5.

**MURDER: Wheaton, Ill.** Circuit Judge Edward Kowal denied a move to bar murderer Brian Dugan's confession from a retrial for Alexandro Hernandez and Rolando Cruz, accused of killing Jeanine Nicarico, 10, in 1983.

**ROBBERY Los Angeles, Calif.** Doyle Ray Jones, 44, was convicted in connection with the 1986 armed robbery of six San Gabriel Valley restaurants, allegedly stealing between $100,000 and $150,000.

### June 3

**MURDER: Baltimore, Md.** Frank "Born" Pruitt, 19, was arrested in connection with the Queens, N.Y., drug-related murders of Jahar Bellamy, 18, and Tyrone Lee, 17.

### June 4

**ASSAULT: Madison, Wis.** Vincent Lee Mott, 25, stabbed his ex-girlfriend, Ellen Kell, injured three others with rifle shots, and died when he lit a pipe bomb that went off in his hands.

**MURDER: Calcutta, India** The first of seven homeless people was killed during a three-month period. The killer was dubbed "Stoneman" because he smashed their heads with concrete slabs.

### June 5

**FRAUD: Chicago, Ill.** The Reverend T.L. Barrett, who allegedly operated pyramid schemes to defraud members of his congregation of about $3 million, was directed to give titles held by his church, church property, and $48,000 to a receiver.

**MURDER: Los Angeles, Calif.** Manuel Bonilla, 22, was arraigned and charged with child sexual abuse and the murder of Johanna Gutierrez, two, his girlfriend's child whose body was found June 1. Maria Gutierrez, 22, was charged as an accessory after the fact and with child abuse.

**ROBBERY Chicago, Ill.** Rowena Leonard, 45, allegedly demanded $500,000 from the Michigan Avenue National Bank, threatening to set off a bomb. Leonard tried to shoot herself to evade capture after a silent alarm was activated. She was indicted for armed violence and armed robbery.

**THEFT: Pleasanton, Calif.** Timothy Loggins, 20, was released from jail after serving five weekends and writing "If I don't own it, I won't take it," 10,000 times, a sentence imposed by Judge Ronald Hyde after Loggins was convicted of auto theft.

### June 6

**KIDNAPPING: Hanno, Japan** Ayako Nomoto, five, was the fourth girl to be kidnapped from the Tokyo suburb. Nomoto, Mari Konno, four, the first victim who vanished Aug. 22, 1988, and a third were found dead.

**MURDER: Chicago, Ill.** Bryant Long, 29, allegedly suffocated one of his two children because they were crying while he was watching a TV soap opera. The other child died after Long reputedly set a fire under their bed to hide the crime.

**MURDER: Chicago, Ill.** Mervyn Wright, 25, a convicted burglar, received an 80-year prison sentence for the September 1987 murder of off-duty policeman Gregory Edwards, 27, during an attempted burglary.

**SEXUAL ABUSE: New York, N.Y.** Jose Santiago, 21, of Coney Island, was arrested and charged with 124 counts of sexual abuse, sodomy, and endangering the welfare of children.

### June 7

**MURDER: Hebron, Occupied West Bank** Ziad Abu Ras, a 30-year-old Palestinian, was fatally attacked and his body suspended in chains from a telephone pole.

**MURDER: Mexico City, Mexico** Alleged drug smuggling cult high priestess Sara Maria Aldrete, 24, and cult members Omar Francisco Orea Ochoa and Alvaro de Leon Valdez pleaded not guilty to charges of committing 15 mutilation murders, the victims of which were discovered Apr. 11 on Matamoros ranch.

### June 8

**MURDER: San Francisco, Calif.** The death sentence of 31-year-old David Leslie Murtishaw for the murders of three University of Southern California film students in 1978 was restored. The California Supreme Court ruled that the sentence, struck down as improperly applied, was still the intention of the jury.

### June 9

**ABDUCTION: Yellowstone National Park, Wyo.** Brett Hartley, 18, allegedly took three park staffers and five visitors hostage at a visitor center for about three hours. None were hurt and he later surrendered.

**ASSASSINATION: San Salvador, El Salvador** Jose Antonio Rodriguez Porth, 73, minister of the president and closest advisor of President Alfredo Cristiani, was fatally shot with two bodyguards as he was leaving his house.

**MURDER: New York, N.Y.** Eddie Davis, 31, was found guilty of murder and attempted robbery in the shooting death of Raymond Vizcaino, 36, in August 1986.

**POLLUTION: Washington, D.C.** An affidavit of the Justice Department accused Rocky Flats nuclear weapons plant workers in Colorado of dumping toxic chemicals in November 1988 into two creeks that feed Denver area drinking water sources.

**RAPE: Chicago, Ill.** Corbette Johnson, 33, a convicted rapist, was sentenced to 110 years in prison for the January 1988 robbery and rape of a woman he drove from a bus station while pretending to be a taxi driver.

**THEFT: Coral Gables, Fla.** Joaquin Capestany, 56, an accountant for New York City's Department of General Services, was arrested after he allegedly stole $1 million from the city using their computerized accounting system.

### June 10

**ASSAULT: New York, N.Y.** Kevin Coyne, 37, an off-duty transit police detective, allegedly went into a Brooklyn Heights bar where he pointed his gun at customers, demanded a drink, and seriously injured one customer with a shot fired at close range.

**MURDER: Long Beach, Calif.** Duncan Anderson, 23, was shot and killed while trying to chase a man who had just robbed his girlfriend of $3,000.

**MURDER: Los Angeles, Calif.** Nineteen-year-old J.C. Metoyer was arrested for suspicion of raping and shooting two Inglewood women, one of whom died, and a 14-year-old girl on June 3.

### June 12

**ARSON: Evanston, Ill.** A $75,000 bond was set for Helen Johnson, 54, who confessed to setting her parents' house on fire because she was angry that her stepfather beat her mother. Johnson was charged with two counts of arson.

**ATTEMPTED MURDER: New York, N.Y.** Peter Thomas, under orders to stay away from his wife after shooting at her, stabbed her 23 times at her Medford, Long Island, home. She escaped, and he was charged with attempted murder and criminal contempt for violation of the protection order.

**FRAUD: New York, N.Y.** Thirteen people were charged in Brooklyn in connection with an operation in which false vehicle registrations were issued to drug dealers for stolen cars that were used to carry cash and narcotics.

**MONEY LAUNDERING: New York, N.Y.** Daniel Pagano, reputedly involved in loansharking and gambling as the Genovese crime family boss for Westchester and Rockland counties, was arrested for allegedly trying to launder money.

**MURDER: Van Nuys, Calif.** Nova Marcia Thompson, 34, pleaded not guilty to murder and child abuse charges in connection with the June 9 death of 18-month-old Jasmine Lynn Sanders, whom Thompson had been baby-sitting.

**POLITICAL CORRUPTION: Chicago, Ill.** Edward Emond, 51, Streamwood village manager from 1982 to 1988, was convicted of mail and income tax fraud, extortion, and racketeering for corrupt political practices. His wife, Maxine, Earl Mink, and Raymond Seifert were also convicted.

### June 13

**ASSASSINATION: Mexico City, Mexico** Jose Zorrilla Perez, former head of Mexico's Federal Security Directorate

from 1982 to 1985, was arrested and charged for involvement in the May 30, 1984, assassination of Manuel Buendia, a well-known journalist.

**MANSLAUGHTER: London, England** Robert Johnson, 29, convicted of manslaughter, was sentenced to a 10-year prison term for shaking his 3-year-old son, Liam, who died on Dec. 25, 1987.

**RACKETEERING: San Francisco, Calif.** San Jose Federal District Court Judge Robert P. Aguilar was indicted for racketeering after allegedly plotting to alert Abe Chapman, 83, if the FBI investigated him and trying to influence a judge in Michael Rudy Tham's probation violation hearing. Chapman and Tham were also indicted.

**THEFT: New York, N.Y.** Chester Blondonville Jr., 27, was arrested after allegedly stealing four bearer bonds from Paine Webber and using his girlfriend's estranged husband's name to put the bonds in a bank account. The husband, Ricardo Smith, 34, who had been arrested, was cleared of charges.

**WEAPONS VIOLATION: Chicago, Ill.** Police discovered weapons worth more than $100,000 at the home of Eric Johnson, 41, who was charged with unlawful possession of explosives and unlawful use of weapons.

### June 14

**ESCAPE: Staffordshire, England** David Blood, 24, charged with attempted murder in the September 1988 stabbing of police officer Mark Crooke, 23, escaped from Tamworth police station after apparently breaking some bars.

**FORGERY: Chicago, Ill.** Perry Figueroa, 24, Steve Price, 33, and six others were indicted on forgery charges as alleged members of three counterfeiting operations that distributed fake transit passes.

**FRAUD: Belleair, Fla.** Former New York City policeman David Greenberg, 45, well-known for his 1960s undercover work, and two others were arrested. They were charged in Brooklyn, N.Y., with insurance and mail fraud after altering records following the burglary of his videotape business.

**FRAUD: New York, N.Y.** John A. Mulheren Jr., 39, was indicted in Manhattan on charges of conspiracy and securities fraud for allegedly obtaining inside stock information in exchange for manipulating Gulf & Western Inc. stock.

**MURDER: Chicago, Ill.** Henry Kaczmarek, 38, was found guilty of burglary, armed robbery, home invasion, and murder after beating and stabbing to death his 86-year-old neighbor, Millie Nielsen, in April 1987.

**MURDER: Newport News, Va.** Thomas Hart, 22, was found stabbed and beaten to death. His wife, Sabrina Hart, 18, was charged with murder and officials sought to try a 17-year-old, allegedly involved in the murder, as an adult.

### June 15

**CONTEMPT: Jim Thorpe, Pa.** Charles Petro, who weighed 311 pounds, was found in contempt of court for gaining 85 pounds in a year. Petro was directed to lose 50 pounds by Sept. 9 when it became apparent that he was unable to work to meet child support payments.

**FRAUD: Chicago, Ill.** Danny Omar Cherif, 35, and William Bronec Jr., 36, were indicted in connection with insider trading information allegedly stolen from the First National Bank of Chicago.

**ILLEGAL DUMPING: Glen Ellyn, Ill.** Peter Letsos, was fined $7,500 and sentenced to 200 hours of community service and two years' probation for pouring gasoline into a storm sewer without a permit.

**MURDER: New York, N.Y.** A body with no hands or head was discovered in the Bronx. The victim was thought to be Bruce Bailey, 54, chairman of the Columbia Tenants Union, who was reported missing June 14.

**MURDER: Rowland Heights, Calif.** Leslie Benevides, 39, allegedly shot and injured a woman believed to be his girlfriend, fatally shot two others, then drove to a former girlfriend's home, where he was arrested after passing out in a lawn chair.

**MURDER: Spring Branch, Texas** Sarah Lee Murray, 75, was found strangled and hidden in a freezer in her apartment. Her daughter, Jolene O. Dale, 46, was arrested in Cambridge, Ohio, on a warrant for a 1986 burglary and later charged in Houston with murder.

**ROBBERY: Turweston, England** Terence Ward, a bank manager, his family, and Nigel and Mandy Saunders were held hostage by armed robbers who forced bank cashier Angela Ward, 18, to use her keys to gain access to a Barclays Bank in Bloxham. The robbers stole, 26,000.

### June 16

**ASSAULT: New York, N.Y.** Wellington Chang, 59, was shot in the jaw as he walked into the middle of a shootout between gang members in Chinatown.

**DRUGS: Everett, Mass.** Officials arrested Frank Imbruglia, 57, for possession of narcotics. Joseph L. Sturnaiuolo, 24, and Vincent M. Marino, 28 were arrested on weapons charges. Officials also found a paper with the license number and color of the car owned by Francis P. Salemme, who was the victim of an attempted murder 12 hours earlier.

**GAMBLING: New York, N.Y.** Police arrested three New Jersey men and charged them with running a Manhattan gambling ring that profited $44 million a year and might be linked to the Genovese crime family.

**MURDER: San Fernando, Calif.** Dawn Michelle Rodriguez and Socorro Mauricio, both 20, pleaded not guilty to the murder of Elizabeth Valdivia, also 20, who was beaten to death with a baseball bat. The three women had been good friends.

**MURDER: Wabasha, Minn.** The state Supreme Court upheld the second-degree murder conviction of Jo Ann Hennum, 48, who killed her abusive husband Nov. 28, 1986, while he slept after beating her during a drunken rage. Her sentence, however, was reduced from eight-and-a-half years in prison to four-and-a-half years.

**RIOT: Kazakhstan, U.S.S.R.** Riots in various cities, including Marneuli and Novy Uzen, between ethnic groups of Georgians and Azerbaijanis began and continued for the next ten days.

### June 18

**MURDER: Chicago, Ill.** Dana Feitler, 24, a graduate student, was forced by a gunman to withdraw $400 from a cash machine and was then shot in the head. She died July 9. Suspect Lee Harris, 34, was arrested on Oct. 27.

**MURDER: New York, N.Y.** Victor Bell, 27, who was hired as a home care attendant while out on bail for burglary, was charged with the beating murder of 87-year-old William Brockmeyer.

**MURDER: New York, N.Y.** Shawn Brown, 22, was arrested for murder in the stabbing death of his stepfather Ronald Butts, 44, who held a knife to the throat of Shirley Brown, 44, Shawn's mother, while high on drugs.

**MURDER: New York, N.Y.** Police arrested Robert Williams, 21, and charged him with the stabbing death of his grandmother, Donada Petrus, 60, who was killed after she refused to give Williams money.

### June 19

**ASSAULT: New York, N.Y.** Police arrested Ulysses Williams, 19, of Queens and charged him with assaulting subway passengers in as many as 10 attacks with a knife and a metal pipe.

**ESCAPE: Leicester, England** John Kendall, 38, involved in a helicopter escape from Gartree prison, was given an additional seven years in prison. Accomplices Andrew Russell, 27, and Sydney Draper, 41, received 10-and four-year sentences, respectively.

**EXECUTION: Carson City, Nev.** Multiple-murderer William Paul Thompson, 52, was executed by lethal injection for the 1984 murder of 28-year-old transient Randy Waldron in Reno. Thompson had also been convicted of killing two brothers camping near Auburn, Calif., and may have murdered up to three other people in New York, Kansas, and Oklahoma.

**LAW ENFORCEMENT: Boston, Mass.** A court ruling by U.S. District Judge Rya W. Zobel ordered that $4 million worth of property belonging to suspected drug dealer Lionel Laliberte, 38, be confiscated by the government.

**MURDER: Quezon City, Philippines** Police arrested Donato Continente, 27, and issued warrants for six others in connection with the Apr. 21 shooting death of U.S. Army Colonel James "Nick" Rowe.

### June 20

**COMPUTER CRIME: Chicago, Ill.** Leslie Lynne Doucette, 35, was indicted on charges of violating computer laws after federal authorities raided homes nationwide to break up a ring of hackers who stole credit card and telephone numbers.

**FRAUD: Boston, Mass.** Raymond D. Pollard and Edward E. Dockray were charged with defrauding Massachusetts investors of nearly $800,000.

**MURDER: Monument Beach, Mass.** After Howell Glyn Morris, 72, learned he had cancer, he called police and told them he had killed his wife and their cat and planned to kill himself. He was dead when officers got to his home and found the bodies.

### June 21

**ASSAULT: Zaragoza, El Salvador** Sister Mary MacKey, 73, a U.S. nun of the Sisters of Charity of the Incarnate Word, was shot in the head as she travelled from San Salvador, by one of six men in a pickup truck.

**ATTEMPTED MURDER: New York, N.Y.** Police officer Paul Yurkiw, 34, wearing a bulletproof vest, stopped to help a disabled motorist and was shot three times. Suspect Shawn Boyd, 23, from Hackensack was arrested on July 21.

**ATTEMPTED MURDER: Palermo, Sicily** Bodyguards discovered a bomb with a 100-meter impact force outside the summer villa of Giovanni Falcone, 50, a leading Mafia investigator.

**FRAUD: Duluth, Minn.** Convicted former governor of Illinois Dan Walker, 66, was released from his seven-year prison sentence after citing model behavior and bad health.

**MONEY LAUNDERING: Boston, Mass.** Two people were arrested in connection with the $700-million money laundering ring through the National Mortgage Bank of Greece. Twelve others were also arrested nationwide as part of "Operation Zorba." The next day charges were brought against National Mortgage.

**MURDER: Lincoln, Maine** A judge ruled that Trey Emery, 17, a suspect in the 1988 murder of Heather White, 8, could be tried as an adult.

**RAPE: Highland, La.** A rapist attempted to attack a woman, but was frightened off by a noise. He went on to assault eight other women in the same neighborhood. Police arrested a suspect, Robert Glover, 40, on Nov. 21.

### June 22

**BRIBERY: Melbourne, Australia** Anthony Aloi, 31, a Victoria radio sales manager, was arrested and charged with offering a $110,000 bribe to Tasmanian member of Parliament Jim Cox.

**KIDNAPPING: Arnhem, Netherlands** Kidnap victim Colonel Karel Van de Hieft, 56, was killed during a shootout between his captor, West German Stefan Krueger, 33, and Dutch police. Kreuger was arrested.

**MANSLAUGHTER: London, England** The P&O European Ferries Corp. was charged with corporate manslaughter stemming from the March 1987 capsizing of the *Herald of Free Enterprise*, a disaster which claimed 193 lives. Two employees and five former employees were also charged.

**MURDER: New York, N.Y.** Joseph Wolske, 17, pleaded guilty to murdering a man who sexually accosted him in 1982.

### June 23

**ARSON: Bethany, Conn.** Volunteer fire fighter Michael A. Legge, 19, and his friend Brian S. Golembowski, 22, were arraigned on first-degree arson charges after they admitted firebombing Carbolabs Inc.

**FRAUD: Chicago, Ill.** Leroy Brooks, 49, was arrested by Chicago Police for bilking an 82-year-old widow of $267,000. The investment fraud Brooks was charged with is known as a "pigeon drop."

**MURDER: New York, N.Y.** Thirteen-year-old Mack Morton turned himself in and was charged as an adult with murder. Three days earlier in the Bushwick neighborhood he had apparently stabbed to death Roscoe Cooke, 55, who had earlier assaulted his grandfather.

**SEXUAL ABUSE: London, England** Peter Nunn, 52, who claimed to be gifted with mystic powers, was sentenced to life in prison for luring youngsters to his home and then sexually abusing them.

### June 24

**PIRACY: Songkhla, Thailand** Two fishermen were arrested two days after two others were arrested for the Apr. 16 attack upon Vietnamese refugees in the South China Sea. The men were charged with murder, attempted murder, attempted rape, and robbery for having killed 130 people, which they admitted doing.

### June 25

**ASSASSINATION: Lahore, Pakistan** Unidentified gunmen opened fire on a car and killed Safdar ul-Haq Dogar, a member of the Punjab province ruling Islamic Democratic Alliance, and two other passengers in the auto.

**MURDER: Rano, Philippines** Thirty-nine villagers, who were attending Sunday worship service at the United Church of Christ, were killed by Communist guerrillas.

### June 26

**ROBBERY: Boston, Mass.** A payroll guard, who was picking up money from the Boston *Herald* newspaper, was robbed at gunpoint apparently by David Smith, 22, and David Morrison, 33, who were arrested.

**THEFT: New York, N.Y.** Suspected art thief, criminal fence, and forger Joseph Cinque, 51, was arrested in his apartment. Some 43 works of art, including originals by Marc Chagall and Joan Miro were found inside.

### June 27

**FRAUD: Chicago, Ill.** The Reverend Columbus Ewings, 57, and his daughter, Shirley, 33, were indicted for insurance fraud. They had collected close to $1 million in false insurance premiums on his niece Debra Sue, who died in 1987. He recruited other people, besides Shirley, to pose as Debra in order to collect benefits.

**MURDER: Tamworth, N.H.** Timothy Eldridge, 21, was found guilty of shooting to death Travis Wiggin, 15, with a high-powered pistol, in a dispute over Eldridge's former girlfriend.

### June 28

**ASSAULT: Caernarvon, Wales** Police Constable David Cecil Owen, 39, was sentenced to jail for a month, for beating a motorist during a traffic stop. The officer suspected that Michael Williams was concealing an air rifle in his car.

**MURDER: New York, N.Y.** Seven reputed members of the Gambino family's DeMeo assassination squad, Carlo Profeta, Sol Hellman, Joseph Testa, Anthony Senter, Douglas Rega, Ronald Ustica, and Salvatore Mangialino, were convicted of racketeering and murder.

**MURDER: St. George's, Grenada** Diplomat John Butler, 33, of the U.S. Embassy, and Acting Police Commissioner Cosmos Raymond were shot and killed by Grafton Bascombe, a police official who went on a rampage. Bascombe was killed by other police officers immediately afterward.

**POLLUTION: Providence, R.I.** Captain Iakovos Georgoudis of the Greek tanker *World Prodigy* was arrested and charged with violating federal pollution laws as a result of spilling 420,000 gallons of oil into Narragansett Bay.

**ROBBERY: Chicago, Ill.** Donald Ray Bennett, 45, known to police as the "leaping bandit," was sentenced to 50 years in prison without parole for five robberies committed in 1987.

**WEAPONS VIOLATION: Bonn, Germany** German police raided the Rheineisen Chemical Products Co., accused of arranging the shipment of 257 tons of thionyl chloride to Iran, to be used in manufacturing mustard gas.

### June 29

**FRAUD: Chicago, Ill.** Don Scott, 47, of Illinois Tool Works, pleaded guilty to defrauding the Defense Department of $874,000 in phony claims on U.S. Navy submarine navigational parts.

**FRAUD: New York, N.Y.** The Reverend Al Sharpton, 34, known for his outspoken and flamboyant manner in crusading for the rights of Tawana Brawley, who had been allegedly raped, was arrested on charges of theft, fraud, and tax evasion.

**MURDER: Wynnum, Australia** A domestic dispute in this suburb of Brisbane, compelled a 26-year-old man to go on a shooting rampage. Before he turned the .303-caliber rifle on himself; the gunman murdered Police Detective Timothy Handran, and a 2-year-old girl.

**VANDALISM: Austin, Texas** Paul Stedman Cullen, 25, the man accused of poisoning the 500-year-old Treaty Oak tree in Austin, was arrested by police.

### June 30

**ATTEMPTED MURDER: Shenandoah County, Va.** Fugitive robber and kidnapper Grant Douglas Snowden, 20, was arrested after fleeing Brookline, Mass., where he allegedly stabbed and wounded Donna DiNisco, 25, before stealing her car. Snowden is a suspect in the murder of Elizabeth Ann MacIvor, 24, a Georgia woman.

**RAPE: Baltimore, Md.** Eugene Dale, 31, of South Baltimore was convicted of rape and handgun charges in connection with the rape of a 13-year-old girl. Dale was also charged with the Oct. 13, 1988, rape and murder of 12-year-old Andrea L. Perry.

**TAX EVASION: New York, N.Y.** Dominick Volpe and his wife Sharon, both 40, pleaded not guilty to filing false tax returns. The couple is accused of running a prostitution ring, composed of 400 beeper-equipped women.

### July 1

**DRUGS: South Lake Tahoe, Calif.** Mayor Terry Trupp, 46, and four others were indicted on charges of drug trafficking and money laundering. Trupp was arrested, along with his wife and 16 others, on June 11.

**MURDER: Joliet, Ill.** Three inmates of the Stateville Correctional Center fatally attacked corrections officer Lawrence Kush Jr., 24, with metal pipes. They were indicted on July 12.

### July 3

**EMBEZZLEMENT: Northampton, England** Police began searching air and seaports for Elizabeth Sheil, a 44-year-old accounts clerk who disappeared three days before, 120,000 was discovered missing from the postal office where she worked.

**FRAUD: Mexicali, Mexico** The Institutional Revolutionary Party was charged with election fraud by opposing parties after PRI won elections in four out of five states.

**MURDER: Jonesboro, Ga.** Martha Ann Johnson, 34, was arrested and charged with killing her four children from 1977 to 1982, deaths blamed on natural causes or accidents. Johnson is charged with smothering them in attempts to keep her husband from leaving her.

**MURDER: New York, N.Y.** Eddie Williams, 30, charged in the 1987 murder of grocer Koo Jik Young, allegedly killed William Johnson, 24, while out on bail. Police said Williams, known as "El-Son", was the founder of the A-Team drug gang.

**RAPE: New York, N.Y.** Lorenzo Rojas, 21, was arrested as a suspect in five rapes, five attempted rapes, and one sexual assault, all of which took place in the last six months on girls between the ages of nine and 14 years old in Brooklyn and Queens.

**RIOT: Bophuthatswana, South Africa** Approximately 2,000 people were arrested after nine policemen were killed during an attempt to stop a rally protesting the forced incorporation of their tribal homeland and their loss of citizenship once the land was taken over by the government.

**THEFT: Chicago, Ill.** Walter Poole, 34, and four accomplices were charged with the attempted theft of a $100,000 sculpture, "La Ronde" by sculptor Bill Barrett, which commemorated the 100th anniversary of the Metropolitan Water Reclamation District.

### July 4

**ASSASSINATION: San Pedro Sula, Honduras** Two gunmen shot and killed labor leader Salomón Vallecilo, 34, as he left his house to go to work.

**ASSAULT: New York, N.Y.** Nearly 30 white men chased and assaulted a group of eight black men from a Rosedale, Queens schoolyard, shouting racial epithets. James LaGreca, 17, Robert Gadoro, 25, Gary Santanastasi, 24, and Michael Sims, 22, were arrested and charged in connection with the attack on July 10.

**THEFT: New York, N.Y.** Two workers from the Happy Trails Riding Center were charged with grand larceny after they stole two quarter horses, rode them to a Bronx park, and treated children to rides until patrolling policemen rounded them up.

### July 5

**DRUGS: Miami, Fla.** Luis Santacruz Echeverri, 35, suspected to be a leader of Colombia's Cali drug cartel, was arraigned on drug trafficking charges. The arraignment took place inside prison, for fear confederates would try to free him.

**EMBEZZLEMENT: Chicago, Ill.** Timothy Sirmer, 31, was charged with embezzling $2.2 million from the Pershing Co. in order to pay for a $450,000 home and cocaine purchases.

**FRAUD: Dallas, Texas** Former president and director of

Northpark Savings Association in suburban Richardson, Bob R. Franks pleaded guilty to charges he diverted $138,000 from the institution and used the funds for his personal benefit.

**HIJACKING: Srinager, Kashmir** Alleged Sikh extremists hijacked an Indian Airlines A-300 Airbus en route to New Delhi, forcing its detour to Pakistan. The Sikhs, threatening to blow up the plane, demanded $25 million and the release of political prisoners.

**MURDER: Boston, Mass.** After Thomas V. Fowler Jr., 76, a patient at Winthrop Community Hospital, died from complications resulting from strangulation with his oxygen tube, William Fitzmeyer, 43, who had been a patient in Fowler's room, was charged with his murder.

**MURDER: Los Angeles, Calif.** Nathan Trupp, 43, pleaded innocent after allegedly shooting to death Armando Torres, 18, and Jeren Beeks, 27, two security guards for Universal Studios who would not allow him to see actor Michael Landon on Dec. 1, 1988.

**MURDER: Pasadena, Calif.** Wei Wen Wang, 19, was convicted of murder, attempted murder, and robbery. Wang killed two undercover agents in 1988 during a drug deal.

**MURDER: Westchester, N.Y.** Ronald Appling, 19, was charged with the strangulation death of 15-year-old Ann Marie Sullivan. Both were residents of Hawthorne Cedar Knolls, a treatment center for emotionally troubled children.

**THEFT: Chicago, Ill.** Police arrested five men who were allegedly trying to steal a $100,000 bronze sculpture by dismantling it and placing the parts into a van.

**THEFT: Wyalusing, Penn.** Paul Mueller, 42, was arrested and charged with stealing $20,000 worth of cattle gallstones, valued as aphrodisiacs in Asia, from the meat packing company he worked at.

## July 6

**BURGLARY: London, England** The house of Prince Jefri, the brother of the world's richest man, the Sultan of Brunei, was burgled of $6 million in cash and jewelry.

**CONSPIRACY: New York, N.Y.** Clemard Joseph Charles, 66, his son, and two other men were arrested in Queens in connection with the Banque Commerciale Haiti fraud, which used a fake bank to siphon off money from other financial institutions.

**DRUGS: Long Beach, Calif.** Police arrested four men and confiscated $111 million worth of cocaine. The men were charged with drug possession and conspiracy to distribute cocaine.

**EXECUTION: Cairo, Egypt** Heroin smuggler Anwar Hossein, 27, was hanged, the first drug smuggler executed in Egypt.

**MANSLAUGHTER: London, England** Albert Thompson, 72, pleaded guilty to manslaughter in the death of his 75-year-old wife, who had a fatal stroke after he tried to strangle her.

**MURDER: New York, N.Y.** Christine Forsyth, 21, was charged with second-degree murder after she slashed the throat of the infant she had just given birth to in the stall of the drugstore where she worked.

**SEXUAL ASSAULT: Markham, Ill.** The Reverend Paul Hall, 43, convicted of sexually attacking the 17-year-old boy who was his foster son in 1987, was sentenced to four years in prison. Hall, director of a youth service, resigned his position July 11.

**TERRORISM: Abu Ghosh, Israel** Abdel Hadi Ghanem, a 23-year-old Arab from the West Bank, was arrested after he grabbed the wheel of a crowded bus, forcing it to overturn in a ditch seven miles from Jerusalem. Fourteen people were killed and 27 injured.

## July 7

**MURDER: Dallas, Texas** Richard Grissom Jr., a paroled burglar and auto thief wanted in the possible murders of as many as five women in Kansas, was arrested at Dallas/Fort Worth International Airport.

**MURDER: Danbury, Conn.** Michael T. Mebert, 19, and Mark L. Brooks, 20, were arrested for the murder of Dean Lockshiss, a student killed in a New York robbery which netted $4.

**MURDER: Lawrence, Mass.** George Gurney pleaded not guilty to charges of murder and attempted murder after his ex-wife, Miriam Stolz-Gurney, 48, identified him as the gunman who shot and killed her lover, Roger Whittemore, 51, and left her for dead.

## July 8

**CONSPIRACY: Dothan, Ala.** Former Army Lieutenant Colonel Kenneth Lee Landon, 47, was convicted of passing military secrets to a Defense Department contractor.

**MURDER: Israel** Palestinian Jamal Nasir, 31, was stoned to death and four passengers in his car injured when they were attacked by a mob enraged by the July 6 bus crash allegedly caused by Palestinian Abdel Hadi Ghanem.

## July 9

**MURDER: Chicago, Ill.** Ronald Pugh, 18, was killed by two gunmen who mistook him for another teenager. Police arrested Carl Dawkins, 17, who allegedly ordered the killing, Gynovel Jones, 15, and Rasaki Emmanuel, 16.

**MURDER: Pittsburgh, Pa.** Ronald Byrd, 30, manager of the singing group New Edition, allegedly shot to death Anthony Bee, security chief for the opening band, Guy. The two groups reportedly had been feuding while on tour together.

## July 10

**ASSAULT: Providence, R.I.** While facing rape and firearms charges, Stephen G. Rollins, saying he felt his lawyer, Robert Testa, could not defend him adequately, beat up Testa in court. Testa was ordered to continue to defend Rollins.

**BOMBING: Mecca, Saudi Arabia** One person was killed and 16 others wounded by two explosions outside the city's Grand Mosque during the annual Muslim pilgrimage.

**FRAUD: New York, N.Y.** Marcus Schloss & Co. was convicted on charges of conspiracy and securities fraud, while the company's arbitrage head, D. Ronald Yagoda, was acquitted.

**KIDNAPPING: Plymouth, N.H.** Susan Dessert, 32, and John H. Rose, 36, were arraigned on charges they kidnapped two female hikers, assaulting one, and threatening to kill them in Waterville Valley.

**MURDER: Elizabeth, N.J.** John Emil List, 63, pleaded not guilty to the murder of his mother, wife, and three children, who were found dead in their Westfield, N.J., home on Dec. 7, 1971.

**MURDER: New York, N.Y.** Nermina Huseinovic, 15, was charged with killing Saka Srdanovic, 28, while trying to resist his advances. Srdanovic was the cousin of her fiance.

## July 11

**CHILD MOLESTATION: West Covina, Calif.** Leslie Humberto Tompkins, 46, was charged with having fondled as many as 20 students in his fourth-grade class. A plea of not guilty was entered for Tompkins.

**MURDER: Crown Point, Ind.** Robert Paul Olsen, a 30-year-old Iowa carnival worker, was charged with the strangling of 8-year-old Geneva Morris on July 4.

**PROSTITUTION: Chicago, Ill.** Prosecutors charged that Rose Laws, 54, with her son, Kenneth Laws, 33, and his wife, Linda Lou Laws, 31, ran a prostitution ring that catered to local businessmen from eight expensive apartments.

**THEFT: Chicago, Ill.** Alleged bigamist William R. Dickens, 58, was arrested for theft warrants in Louisiana and Texas. It was suspected that Dickens had at least seven wives and several girlfriends located across the U.S.

## July 12

**COUNTERFEITING: Phoenix, Ariz.** Richard Perez, 39, was arrested after he attempted to persuade a U.S. Secret Service agent to accept $1 million in counterfeit bills created on a photocopier for 500 pounds of marijuana.

**FRAUD: Hauppauge, N.Y.** Thomas Brazier and Albert Iannuzzi, both 44, and 11 others were indicted as part of a conspiracy to defraud a Brookhaven, Long Island, federally subsidized housing program.

**LAW ENFORCEMENT: Spokane, Wash.** Police searched two residences of William Jay Stevens II, a possible Green River killer suspect, allegedly responsible for at least 48 deaths. Officers seized police uniforms, badges, hundreds of videotapes, and 29 firearms. Stevens was cleared as a suspect in November.

**MURDER: Los Angeles, Calif.** Defendants in the "Cotton Club" murder case, alleged cocaine dealer Karen DeLayne "Lanie" Greenberger, 42, and bodyguards Alex Marti, 27, and William Mentzer, 39, were ordered to stand trial for the May 13, 1983, murder of producer Roy Radin, 33.

**MURDER: Luxiol, France** Fourteen people were killed and 10 injured, including the gunman, Christian Dornier, 31, who drove through this village in his car and fired at villagers, before he was arrested. His mother and sister were among the dead.

## July 13

**ASSASSINATION: Sri Lanka** Appapillai Amrithalingam and Vettivelu Yogeswaran, leaders of the Tamil United Liberation Front, were killed by gunmen most likely tied to the rival Liberation Tigers of Tamil Eelam. Security guards killed the three gunmen.

**BOMBING: La Ceiba, Honduras** Seven U.S. military police officers were wounded by a bomb thrown at them by an unidentified attacker. The leftist Morazanista Liberation Front later claimed responsibility.

**DRUGS: Cuba** General Arnaldo Ochoa and three other officers were executed after being found guilty of several offenses, chiefly drug smuggling.

**DRUGS: New York, N.Y.** Major General Vech Pechborom, former commander of an anti-terrorist unit in Thailand, was indicted on charges he smuggled heroin into the U.S. by arranging for couriers to pass through customs unsearched.

**MANSLAUGHTER: New York, N.Y.** For the first time, a female correction guard was charged with an inmate's death when Denise Whyte, 26, was accused of hitting Franklin Straker, 54, in the head with a flashlight. Straker lapsed into a coma and later died.

**OBSTRUCTION OF JUSTICE: Columbia, S.C.** Social services caseworker Frank Edson was indicted on charges of obstruction of justice and falling to report child abuse after he did not investigate a report of sexual abuse of 8-year-old Brett Hall, who later died of AIDS.

## July 14

**DRUGS: London, England** Three-quarters of a ton of cannabis resin, estimated to be worth, 2 million, was seized from a warehouse by police who also arrested Tanios Bassili, 29, and 11 others.

**MURDER: Chicago, Ill.** James Kluppelberg, 24, was convicted of setting a fire that killed five children and their mother and leveled two South Side homes. While awaiting sentencing, Kluppelberg was mistakenly released from jail Oct. 7, but was rearrested Oct. 11 in Macon, Ga.

**MURDER: Gan Yavne, Israel** Building contractor Zalman Shlein, 64, was stabbed and beaten to death during an argument over money. Two 16-year-old Palestinians confessed to the killing.

**THEFT: London, England** After picking up $1.5 million in foreign currency from a TAP Air Portugal flight for delivery, guard Philip Cedric Wells of Chalmers Security Systems Ltd. and his cargo disappeared. Police thought he may have been abducted.

## July 15

**BOMBING: Kabul, Afghanistan** A truck bomb exploded, killing at least nine people and injuring 49 others.

**KIDNAPPING: Colombia** Norbeto Rodriguez, brother-in-law of Venezuelan president Carlos Andres Perez, was abducted near the Venezuela-Colombia border.

**RIOT: Abkhazia, U.S.S.R.** At least 11 people were killed and more than 100 wounded following two days of violence provoked by economic strife, territorial grievances, and ethnic discord in this region of Soviet Georgia.

## July 16

**MURDER: New York, N.Y.** Queens restaurant manager Mon Hsiung Ting, 32 and customer Anthony Gallivan, 31, were murdered and two others wounded in what police believed was connected to a surge of killings by Chinese-American extortion gangs.

**MURDER: Old Windsor, England** The body of CB radio enthusiast Dennis Wallis, 49, the victim of a vicious knife attack, was found floating in the Thames River. Joyce Warns, 46, and her daughter Tricia, 19, were charged with the murder.

### July 17

**ABDUCTION: Sacramento, Calif.** Candi Talarico, 4, and Meuy Han Saefong, 5, were rescued following the arrest of Kenneth Michel, 32, who was arrested after a motorist saw him trying to abduct a child and got his license plate number.

**MURDER: St. James, N.Y.** Lea Greene, 35, was fatally stabbed in the neck while sleeping in her bed. Thomas Lydon Jr., 21, later admitted to the killing, saying he felt "a sense of power." Lydon and Daniel Toal, 20, were charged with the crime.

### July 18

**EXECUTION: Iran** Thirteen drug dealers were hanged throughout the country, bringing the total number of people executed here for drug trafficking to 700 since January.

**MURDER: Ashland, Miss.** Lee A. Allen, 42, was given two consecutive life sentences and a concurrent life term after pleading guilty to three murders on Mar. 8, 1988. On July 21, he admitted to another murder and assault committed the same day in Alcorn County for which he was sentenced to life in prison plus 20 years to run concurrent with his previous sentence.

**MURDER: Burlington, N.C.** Blanche Taylor Moore, 56, was arrested and charged with the arsenic murders of her husband James Taylor, 45, in 1973, and a boyfriend Raymond C. Reid in 1986. Moore is also accused of attempting to poison her current husband, the Reverend Dwight W. Moore.

**MURDER: Lancashire, England** The charred body of 9-year-old Annette Poole was found in a field behind her home. The Lancashire CID focused its investigation on John Geoffrey Heeley, 30, whose description matched the killer's.

**MURDER: Los Angeles, Calif.** Actress Rebecca Schaeffer, 21, was shot to death after opening the door of her apartment for the gunman. On July 19, Robert John Bardo, 19, reportedly an obsessed fan, was arrested in Tucson, Ariz., for unrelated offenses, but implicated himself in Schaeffer's shooting.

### July 19

**BRIBERY: Chicago, Ill.** State Representative James DeLeo, 37, was indicted by a federal grand jury for failing to report alleged bribe money he received, on federal tax forms. DeLeo became the first lawmaker connected with the Operation Greylord investigation into judicial corruption.

**DRUGS: Cook County, Ill.** Patrolmen Louis Messina, 36, of Bellwood and Predrag Loncar, 30, of Hillside were indicted on several charges including providing protection for a drug sale conducted as part of a government sting operation.

**FRAUD: New York, N.Y.** Arms dealer Adnan Khashoggi, 53, was arraigned on charges of fraud and obstruction of justice for his allegedly aiding deposed Philippine leader Ferdinand Marcos and his wife, Imelda, secretly hide assets from the U.S. government.

**LAW ENFORCEMENT: Norwell, Mass.** State police arrested 10 men near a rest stop as a part of a general crackdown against homosexual activity in the area. The police were accused of selective harassment by gay activists.

**MURDER: Roxbury, Mass.** Donald Ghee, 48, was charged with the murder of his girlfriend, Karen Jackson, 24, whose body was found in the trunk of his car by a tow truck operator after Ghee was arrested for drunk-driving on July 4.

**TERRORISM: Madrid, Spain** Colonel José Maria Martin and Major Ignacio Baragus were murdered in their automobile, allegedly by members of the Basque separatist group E.T.A.

**TRESPASS: Atlanta, Ga.** Randall Terry, 30, the national director of the anti-abortion group Operation Rescue, was sentenced to two years in prison after refusing to pay a $1,000 fine for his role in a staged protest at the Democratic National Convention in 1988.

### July 20

**MURDER: Buffalo, N.Y.** Police arrested Barbara James, 28, and charged her with the murders of her two children, 18-month-old Victoria, and 6-month-old Brittany.

**MURDER: New York, N.Y.** Krist Gjidoda, 22, and his brother Mark, 26, formerly of Yugoslavia, were arrested in Queens in connection with the unrelated murders of two Hispanic men on Apr. 23, and May 5, 1982.

**RIOT: Window Rock, Ariz.** Two people were killed and 11 wounded in an outbreak of violence between the supporters of ousted Navajo tribal chairman Peter MacDonald, and police on the Indian reservation. Supporters of MacDonald, who has been accused of accepting bribes, were marching on tribal headquarters when the fight broke out.

**SEXUAL ASSAULT: Plainville, Conn.** Seventy-nine-year-old Dr. John Iannotti, former health director, was arrested and charged with sexual assault.

### July 21

**BATTERY: Chicago, Ill.** Nekenge Power, 17, was charged with breaking the arms and legs of 3-week-old Jasmine Blunt in an attempt to stop Jasmine, who was sharing a room at Mercy Hospital and Medical Center with Power's 11-month-old son, from crying.

**DRUGS: Brevard County, Fla.** State troopers arrested Darien Cedric Wright, 23, after finding 2 kilograms of cocaine and 263 grams of crack in his car. The arrest was made as part of a sting operation, Operation CoFlaMe, involving 15 states from Florida to Maine.

**KIDNAPPING: North Amityville, N.Y.** A 30-year-old Wyandanch woman was abducted and forced to shoplift items from a local mall, or risk rape or death. Juan Solla, 19, and Ralph Elliott, 16, were arrested and charged with the crime.

**MURDER: Los Angeles, Calif.** Two people were killed and two people wounded by a masked gunman who shot at members of a Bible study group at Mount Olive Church of God in Christ. Albert Lewis Jr., 33, and Anthony Oliver, 27, were charged with the attack.

**THEFT: Boston, Mass.** An auto theft ring was smashed, and 14 people were indicted following 22-month investigation by three state agencies and the FBI.

*July 22*

**ATTEMPTED MURDER: Raymond, N.H.** Clifton Reid, 34, was arrested, following a four-hour standoff with police, and charged with firing shots at a passing car from the front window of his house.

**ESCAPE: Los Angeles, Calif.** Inmate Keith Lee Williams, 28, awaiting trial for armed robbery, escaped from the Los Angeles County Central Jail, after lowering a rope made from bedsheets down three stories.

**MURDER: New York, N.Y.** Three gunmen, possibly Asian gang members, shot and killed Kimberly Lewis, 20, and wounded her friend, Anthony Woodcock, 19, in Broadway Park.

**MURDER: New York, N.Y.** Bernie Pollard, 26, was arrested and charged with the murder and robbery of Yvonne Harris, 34, who was stabbed to death July 17.

**MURDER: Peshawar, Pakistan** Retired Lieutenant General Fazle Haq, former governor and Chief Minister of the North West Frontier Province was arrested for allegedly ordering the 1988 murder of Allama Arif al-Hussaini, a Shia Muslim spiritual leader.

*July 23*

**ASSASSINATION: Polhengoda, Sri Lanka** Themis Guruge, 60, chief state censor and head of the Sri Lanka Broadcasting Co. was shot and killed by unknown assailants. It was reported that Velupillai Prabakaran, founder of the Liberation Tigers of Tamil Eelam, was also killed.

**MURDER: Comanche County, Okla.** Michael Frank Greene, 37, a suspect in a robbery spree begun July 19, in which four people were killed and two wounded in Kansas, Oklahoma, and Texas, was arrested after he checked into the Comanche County Hospital complaining of a sore back.

*July 24*

**ASSAULT: Akron, Ohio** Kimberly Richmond, 17, eight-and-a-half months pregnant, was set on fire, apparently by her father, Joseph Richmond, 41, who was charged with the crime. The child was born unhurt.

**MURDER: New York, N.Y.** City corrections officer Darryl Jerome Smith, 26, arrested July 23 for allegedly attempting to rob a male prostitute, was charged with two shooting deaths committed June 23

**MURDER: Raton, N.M.** Greg Francis Brown, 28, was arraigned on a charge of murder following the shooting death of a Springer store clerk.

*July 25*

**CORRUPTION: Washington, D. C.** Congressional subcommittee hearings investigating the financial affairs of Ronald Saranow, former head of the Internal Revenue Service criminal investigation division in Los Angeles, got under way.

**DRUGS: Illinois** Operation White Night, an undercover police investigation in three Chicago area counties, resulted in the arrest of 21 suspects charged with selling illegal drugs to officers.

**DRUGS: Islamabad, Pakistan** The reputed godfather of the Pakistani heroin trade, Haji Iqbal Baig, 55, surrendered to members of Pakistan's Narcotics Control Board.

**MURDER: Pasadena, Calif.** Eric Beauchamp, and Raed Abujaber, both 21, pleaded not guilty to the shooting death of Grossmont College (San Diego) tennis player David Young, 21, on July 19.

**MURDER: Stockport, England** Daniel Jones, 7, and his sister Suzanne, 5, were found murdered in their beds, victims of lethal injection.

**SEXUAL ASSAULT: Acton, Mass.** Former Boy Scout leader Edward Bishop was arrested and charged with sexually assaulting two teen-age boys in his care.

**VANDALISM: Marbelehead, Mass.** Vandals spray-painted anti-Semitic writings and Nazi swastikas on windows and walls of Temple Emanu-el and the North Shore Jewish Community Center.

*July 26*

**COMPUTER CRIME: Syracuse, N.Y.** Cornell University student Robert Tappan Morris, 24, was indicted on one felony count of fraud, after allegedly crippling a nationwide network of computers with a virus he planted in the software.

**FRAUD: New York, N.Y.** Manhattan psychiatrist Robert H. Willis, 50, was indicted on mail fraud and securities fraud charges, stemming from insider information concerning shares of Bank America common stock he received from a patient.

**MURDER: Lowell, Mass.** More than nine years after nursing student Marianne Alexander, 22, was found beaten to death Feb. 8, 1980, her next door neighbor Roland Douglas Phinney, Jr., 45, was arrested and charged.

*July 27*

**BOMBING: Yangon, Myanmar** Three members of the opposition National League for Democracy were sentenced to death for the July 7 bombing of the Syriam oil refinery.

**BRIBERY: New York, N.Y.** Contractor Antonio "Tony" Rodriguez was indicted on a felony charge of bribery for allegedly attempting to bribe a labor union official over a lucrative city contract.

**MURDER: Kenya** Marie Esther Ferraro, 49, was shot and killed and one man was wounded when a group of robbers ambushed a tour van of Americans in a game park.

**MURDER: Lakeland, Fla.** Two-year-old Bradley Gene McGee had his head repeatedly thrust into a toilet and then he was beaten with pillows into unconsciousness. He died the next day and his mother, Sheryl McGee Coe, 20, and his stepfather, Thomas Coe, 22, were charged with his death.

**MURDER: Riverside, Calif.** Juanito Pascua Purugganan, 29, and his wife Michelle, 20, were arrested and charged with the stabbing death of Doug Timm, 29, who composed musical themes for television shows.

*July 28*

**DRUGS: Langlade County, Wis.** The posting of a sign that read "Narcotics Inspection Ahead" by police led to 20 arrests of people who were seen discarding drugs along highway 55.

**DRUGS: San Diego, Calif.** Roy Williams was arrested in connection with the death of fellow Compton Community College student Lina Aldridge, 19, whose body was found in the trunk of a car, apparently the victim of a cocaine overdose.

**ROBBERY: London, England** Frederick Foreman, 57, was extradited from Spain to face charges in connection with the 1983 robbery of almost $10 million from a securities firm.

**ROBBERY: London, England** John McCabe, 57, in a 1,100-page statement, pleaded guilty to at least 37 robberies, 18 burglaries, 41 thefts, and 27 firearms violations during a four-year period.

**THEFT: Shaker Heights, Ohio** Former Cleveland mayor Carl Stokes, 61, was acquitted on charges he stole $17.25 worth of dog food from a local pet store.

## July 29

**MISSING PERSON: Moscow, U.S.S.R.** French-Armenian poet and art collector Garig Basmadjan left his Moscow apartment for a meeting and never returned, fueling speculation that he was abducted by the Russian Mafia.

**MURDER: Buenos Aires, Argentina** Basketball star Eddie Pope, 23, was arrested for the murder of his girlfriend Nirvana Ercoli, 30, after landing atop Ercoli when the two fell from the fifth floor window of Ercoli's sister's apartment. Pope apparently beat both women before throwing Ercoli out the window.

**MURDER: Tampa, Fla.** Deaf-mute Brian Charles Hodge, 24, was arrested and charged with the sexual assault and murder of 14-year-old Karl Phillip Heiland.

## July 31

**DRUGS: Middlesex, Mass.** John Mele, 22, who has been linked to the attempted murder of reputed mob figure Francis P. "Cadillac Frank" Salemme, 55, in June, pleaded guilty to cocaine trafficking.

**FORGERY: Los Angeles, Calif.** Anthony Gene Tetro, 39, described as the country's biggest forger of paintings, was charged with 44 counts of forgery and one count of conspiracy. Authorities found 250 forged works at Tetro's home.

**INCEST: London, England** A 55-year-old man convicted of engaging in sex with his daughter when she was 11, had his three-year prison sentence increased to six years by the Court of Appeal, in a broad-based ruling that permits the courts to increase sentences considered too lenient.

**MURDER: Chicago, Ill.** Police Officer Elijah Harris, 51, was fatally shot during a routine frisk search of a 16-year-old boy. Andrew Jordan was charged in the shooting. Harris died Nov. 16.

**MURDER: Hudson. Mass.** The body of David Orin, 41, who worked as a software engineer for the Digital Equipment Corp., was found tied and manacled to his bed.

**MURDER: North Charleston, S.C.** The state Court of Appeals ruled that the state corrections and highway departments were not responsible for 1984 rape and murder of Shirley Mae Mack, 47, by Frank Middleton, 21, a convict who walked away from a minimum security road crew.

**TERRORISM: Beirut, Lebanon** U.S. Marine Lieutenant Colonel William R. Higgins, 44, was hanged by his Lebanese captors, reportedly the Iranian-backed Hezbollah, or Party of God.

## August 1

**DRUGS: Guatemala City, Guatemala** Officials arrested Jose Fernando Minero Navas, an employee of Guatemala's anti-corruption office, as he was about to board a plane bound for Miami with a suitcase containing 55 pounds of cocaine.

**DRUGS: Washington, D.C.** Congress voted to spend an additional $1.7 billion in 1990 on anti-drug programs.

**MURDER: Dade City, Fla.** Kimboy Bo Partain, 15, Christopher Henry Kelly, 15, and Kurtis Ray Martin, 14, were charged with first-degree murder for the beating of Billy Olgeves Downing, 47, who was left unconscious on railroad tracks and decapitated by a train.

## August 2

**FRAUD: Chicago, Ill.** A continuing investigation into corruption in the Chicago futures market netted indictments against 46 traders and brokers, with the majority of the indictments against traders in Japanese yen and soybean futures trading pits.

**MURDER: Elmont, N.Y.** James Due, 22, was indicted for second-degree murder in the death of his estranged wife, Erica Due, 20, who had obtained an order of protection against him in 1987. Due allegedly strangled and stabbed her to death.

**MURDER: Essen, Germany** Trial began for Hans-Jurgen Rósner, 31, Dieter Degowski, 32, and Marion Loblich, 34, accused of robbery, kidnapping, and the murder of two hostages in 1988.

**MURDER: New York, N.Y.** Brandon Hawkins and Harvey Armwood, both 17, were charged in connection with a three-day robbery spree that left one man dead and five wounded. Hawkins was charged with murder.

**RACKETEERING: Chicago, Ill.** Martin J. Dempsey, 52, and James D. Nowak, 47, were indicted on charges of trading violations involving illegal soybean trades. The men pleaded innocent to the charges.

## August 3

**DRUGS: Salt Lake City, Utah** Football players Cedric Riles, 21, Errol Martin, 21, Sean Henderson, 20, and Clyde French, 24, were arrested and charged with conspiracy and cocaine distribution.

**LAW ENFORCEMENT: Essex County, N.J.** Twenty-four-year-old police officer Keith Neumann was killed during a drug raid in which a fellow officer's 12-gauge shotgun went off accidentally, hitting Neumann in the chest.

**LAW ENFORCEMENT: Hudson, N.Y.** Three police officers raided the apartment of 34-year-old Bruce Lavoie in search of drugs. One of the officer's guns allegedly misfired and Lavoie was killed. On Sept. 14, Lavoie's family filed suit against the police department.

**MURDER: Chicago, Ill.** Police charged 32-year-old Earl Hampton with the murder of Carol Thomas, 39, who was shot when she refused to give up her purse.

**MURDER: Wilmington, Del.** Lonnie Vincent "Dinky" Williams Jr., 21, accused of a Silver Spring, Md., rape in May, was arrested in connection with the murders of Dwayne E. and Marilyn K. Novak, who had accused him of kidnapping their daughter, 21-year-old Lisa Novak.

**THEFT: Chicago, Ill.** Four men suspected of trafficking in stolen auto parts were indicted as a result of a three-year investigation, "Operation Chi-Ring," in which 55 people were indicted.

## August 4

**ARSON: New York, N.Y.** Han Tak Lee, 54, was arrested in connection with the fire that killed his 20-year-old daughter, Ji Yun Lee, at a religious retreat in Pennsylvania.

**DRUGS: London, England** Thomas Wisbey, 59, and James Hussey, 56, received ten and seven years in jail, respectively, for cocaine trafficking. The men had previously served prison sentences for their part in the Great Train Robbery.

**DRUGS: Lowell, Mass.** Christine J. Dickie, a 66-year-old grandmother charged in November 1988 with cocaine trafficking was arrested and charged with cocaine and amphetamine possession.

**DRUGS: Sacramento, Calif.** Justin Wolf, 47, a state Department of Social Services ombudsman, was arrested and charged with illegal marijuana cultivation after police found 65 marijuana plants in his house.

**FRAUD: Albany, N.Y.** Podiatrists Dr. Jacqueline Porter and Dr. Michelle Donaldson were indicted on charges of fraudulently billing Medicaid for more than $166,000.

**ILLEGAL TRADE: Tokyo, Japan** Prometron Technics Corp. president Hirokuni Matsuda was charged with illegally selling equipment to East Germany which could be used in the construction of nuclear reactor rods.

**MONEY LAUNDERING: Boston, Mass.** A federal grand jury indicted seven men and two corporations on charges of conspiracy to defraud the federal government in a money-laundering scheme allegedly involving $1 million in drug profits. Edmond P. La France, 44, was arrested.

**MURDER: New York, N.Y.** Michael Milan, 23, was arrested in connection with the stabbing death of his father, 50-year-old Maximo Milan. While police were being notified, Milan escaped through a window, jumped into the ocean, and began swimming. Milan threatened to drown police as a boat caught up with him, a mile from shore.

**PERJURY: New York, N.Y.** Joseph DeVincenzo, 46, accused of using a city minority hiring organization as a shield for political patronage, was indicted on 11 counts of perjury.

**ROBBERY: Chicago, Ill.** Audrey Owen, 54, was shot in the face following a robbery by four juveniles, including a gun-wielding 14-year-old, who were arrested after at least three robbery attempts.

**SEXUAL MISCONDUCT: Washington, D.C.** The House Ethics Committee announced an inquiry into the conduct of Representative Gus Savage, 63, who was accused of accosting a female Peace Corps volunteer during Savage's March 1988 visit to Zaire.

**TAX EVASION: Suffolk County, N.Y.** Sheldon Levine, an independent gasoline distributor convicted of evading $38 million in taxes, was sentenced to three years in prison and ordered to pay more than $1 million in fines.

**THEFT: San Francisco, Calif.** Police arrested Steven Lyman Rivas, 28, who, posing as a busy physician, stole more than $1 million in Rolex watches. Rivas would ask to try on a watch, excuse himself, and then leave the store wearing the watch.

## August 5

**ASSASSINATION: Diffun, Philippines** Mayor Romulo Liclican was fatally shot by unidentified gunmen.

**MURDER: New York, N.Y.** Police arrested Matias Reyes in connection with the rape and murder of Lourdes Gonzalez, 24, on June 14. A suspect in four other rapes, the 18-year-old Reyes was caught by two men after allegedly committing a fifth rape.

**PIRACY: Kuala Lampur, Malaysia** Pirates attacked a boat carrying 84 Vietnamese refugees, and killed 40 men. After abducting women and children, they sank the boat, leaving 13 survivors, who were discovered by fishermen.

## August 6

**FRAUD: Chicago, Ill.** Dr. Henry Pimental, 52, Dr. Chowdary Adusumilli, 50, Dr. Nathan Potkin, 74, two unlicensed medical workers, and a pharmacist, were indicted for defrauding Medicaid of more than $500,000.

**MURDER: Phoenix, Ariz.** James William Stuard, a 52-year-old gardener and former boxer, was arrested in connection with the beating deaths of three elderly women and the attempted murder of another.

**WEAPONS VIOLATION: Hollywood, Calif.** While making a routine traffic stop, police arrested Earl Pridgon, 26, and Eric Peterson, 24, for the possession of a machine gun, handguns, ammunition, and other weapons.

## August 7

**CHILD ABUSE: Boston, Mass.** Former Boy Scout leader Edward Bishop, 53, was indicted on charges that he transported children across state lines for sexual purposes. He was arrested on July 26 for abusing two members of his troop.

**CHILD ABUSE: Boston, Mass.** Albert C. Schwarz was indicted on charges that, as a foster parent, he sexually abused boys in his care.

**CONSPIRACY: Boston, Mass.** Udo W. Kloepper, 43, and Margrit Eustachi, 35, were indicted on charges of conspiring to transport a child from Germany to Massachusetts for purposes of sexual activity. Kloepper allegedly filmed Eustachi as she assaulted her 10-year-old son.

**MURDER: Boston, Mass.** A new trial was ordered for 20-year-old Raji W. Guyton, convicted and sentenced to life for the 1985 robbery and murder of newspaper vendor Stanley Cymbura. The court ruled that Guyton's conviction was based on illegally obtained statements and evidence.

**MURDER: Santa Monica, Calif.** The jury that convicted 33-year-old Dean Phillip Carter in July of burglary, rape, and the 1984 murders of three women recommended that he be executed in the gas chamber.

**RAPE: Dorchester, Mass.** Brian Hughes, 23, was arrested as the last of three suspects in the April rape of a 14-year-old girl who, while allegedly speaking to Hughes, Michael D. Gudzevich, and Philip E. Davis on a telephone party line, was persuaded to run away from home.

*August 8*

**ARSON: Lynn, Mass.** The Ben Crest Plaza rooming house burned, leaving three people dead and 17 injured. Investigators suspected arson in the fire.

**FRAUD: Chicago, Ill.** Thomas Braniff, 33, James G. Sledz, 24, and Brian E. Sledz, 29, became the first to plead guilty to fraud charges in the Justice Department's investigation of corruption at the Chicago Mercantile Exchange and the Chicago Board of Trade.

**FRAUD: San Francisco, Calif.** U.S. District Court judge Stanley A. Weigel ruled that Southwest Marine Inc. acted "with intent to deceive, manipulate, and defraud" the U.S. Small Business Administration and the U.S. Navy in an attempt to win a government contract.

**MURDER: Middlesex County, Mass.** Daniel T. Sama, 28, was convicted of first-degree murder in the Dec. 21 stabbing death of his friend, 44-year-old Kenneth Grace in Waltham, Mass. The two had met in a halfway house for recovering alcoholics, and Sama's defense was that he was drunk at the time.

**MURDER: New York, N.Y.** Ricardo Colon, a 34-year-old homeless man, was killed when four teenagers chased him onto subway train tracks, where Colon was electrocuted.

**MURDER: New York, N.Y.** Anti-drug crusader Maria Hernandez, 34, was fatally shot in the head through her bedroom window in Brooklyn, William "Willy Bundle" Figueroa, 26, and Hector "Harry" Santiago, 24, were arrested Sept. 13 as suspects in the case.

**MURDER: Vancouver, Wash.** George Daniel Lucas, 27, was arrested in connection with the murder of his 54-year-old housemate, Leonard J. Mullen.

*August 9*

**BOMBING: Karnal, India** At least 14 people were killed and 36 wounded when a bomb planted on a bus exploded. Sikh extremists were suspected in the terrorist act.

**KIDNAPPING Ridgefield, N.J.** Victor Guzman, 24, and his uncle, 42-year-old Guillermo Ayala, were arrested in connection with the abduction of 12-year-old Trudy Marie Walker. The two men were arrested after a state trooper saw the girl near a car in a Jersey Turnpike Service Area.

**MURDER: Rolling Meadows, Ill.** Cook County courts tried to close one of the oldest murder cases on the docket as the second trial started for 50-year-old Ralph Harbold, accused of the 1981 stabbing of Park Ridge businessman Frank Paul.

**MURDER: San Antonio, Texas** Suspected drug trafficker 59-year-old Ruben Zuno-Arce, brother-in-law of former Mexican president Luis Echeverria, was arrested in connection with the murder of Drug Enforcement Administration agent Enrique Camarena Salazar. He was later granted limited immunity in exchange for his testimony.

**ROBBERY: Nashville, Tenn.** Police arrested high school physical education teacher Carolyn Sue Turner and charged the 34-year-old with five Nashville-area bank robberies, allegedly committed during her summer vacation.

*August 10*

**CONSPIRACY: Boston, Mass.** A grand jury indicted Richard C. Johnson, Peter E. Maguire, Martin P. Quigley, Gerald V. Hoy, and Christina Leigh Reid on charges of conspiring to violate the arms export control act in a scheme to sell advanced weapons to the Irish Republican Army.

**DRUGS: Forrest County, Miss.** Suspected crack cocaine dealer James Earl Mays, 33, telephoned 911 to find out if he was among the 101 people being sought in a recent drug charge indictment. Mays, unaware that his address was recorded when he called, was located by police and arrested.

**DRUGS: Horsham, England** Thirty-year-old British jockey Allan Mackay was arraigned along with five other men on charges of conspiracy to smuggle £7 million worth of cocaine into England.

**DRUGS: New York, N.Y.** During an undercover drug buy, 24-year-old police officer José Ortiz was shot twice in the back. Dwayne Frederick, 21, Curtis Frederick, 25, and Alson Schmidt, 21, were arrested and charged in the assault.

**FRAUD: Rio de Janeiro, Brazil** A federal judge handed down indictments of Naji Robert Nahas, a key speculator, and 10 other Brazilians, on charges of starting the June 9 stock market crash. Nahas allegedly bounced a $29 million check payable to a brokerage house.

**KIDNAPPING: Waukegan, Ill.** Yvette Hamtak's 5-day-old daughter was abducted from Victory Memorial Hospital. Police located the child that evening and arrested Barbara Chrushshon, 40, who had disguised herself as a nurse and carried the baby away.

**MONEY LAUNDERING: New York, N.Y.** Police arrested Guillermo Gomez, 42 and Zoraida Estrada, 40, and broke up what was believed to be the largest drug money laundering operation in the Northeast U.S. Nine others in connection with the ring were apprehended.

**MURDER: Escondido, Calif.** Postal carrier John Merlin Taylor, 52 shot and killed his wife, and drove to work and killed two co-workers before he turned the gun on himself. Authorities said Taylor's self-inflicted injury left him "brain dead."

**MURDER: Raton, N.M.** At a preliminary hearing, mass murder suspect Gregg Francis Braun, 28, confessed to slaying convenience store clerk Geraldine Valdez on July 23. Braun said his cocaine use had worsened his violent tendencies.

**MURDER: Wyandotte, Mich.** Lawrence DeLisle, 28, was charged with murder and attempted murder after he drove the family car into the Detroit River with his wife and four children on board. His wife survived but the children died.

**ROBBERY: San Francisco, Calif.** Richard L. Dunbar, 34, walked into a branch of Bank of America and handed a teller a note explaining that he was robbing the bank. Officers wrestled Dunbar to the ground and only then realized that he was blind. He said he felt safer in jail than on the city's streets.

*August 11*

**FRAUD: Los Angeles, Calif.** U.S. District Court Judge Mariana R. Pfaelzer upheld the constitutionality of a fraud case against Northrop Corp., a government contractor accused of overcharging the government by at least $2 billion on the B-2 stealth bomber project.

**MURDER: Dallas, Pa.** William Jackson Prater, 70, serving a life sentence for his conviction in the 1969 murder of

Joseph Yablonski, an opponent of the United Mine Workers, and his family, died in his cell of natural causes.

**MURDER: New York, N.Y** High school student Duane Lewis, 18, was fatally shot in the back on the first day of the Brooklyn public school year.

**MURDER: Saffron Walden, England** Eighteen-year-old Stephen Hambleton was remanded into custody in connection with the murder of Evelyn Hambleton, his mother, at their home in Little Walden, Essex.

**MURDER: Tokyo, Japan** Tsutomu Miyazaki, 26, was arrested in connection with the abduction and murder of 5-year-old Ayako Nomoto. He later confessed to killing Ayako and four other girls to "fulfill his necrophiliac fantasies."

*August 12*

**MURDER: New York, N.Y.** An unidentified gunman entered a Queens bar, approached 31-year-old Edgar Otadlora and 32-year-old Arturo Rodriguez, shot them, and fled. Otadlora died from his head wound.

**POLICE BRUTALITY: New York, N.Y** Police officers Gabriel Guerrero and John Martini, both 24, pleaded innocent to charges that they beat 21-year-old Andre London and hurled racial epithets at him on Oct. 28, 1988.

*August 13*

**MURDER: Chicago, Ill.** Clarence Gaunt, 27, told police that 11-month-old Benjamin Miller accidentally fell into a tub of hot water. Police believed Benjamin, who later died of his injuries, was purposely held in the tub. Gaunt pleaded not guilty Sept. 22 to charges of murder.

**ROBBERY: Chicago, Ill.** Police arrested Steven Triplett, 18, Robert Cary, 28, Jimmy Townsend, 30, and Charles Staples, 17, in connection with two Brinks robberies at Peoples Gas Light & Coke Co. offices. The men were also suspected in four armored car robberies.

*August 14*

**ABANDONMENT: Nashua, Mass.** David Fischer, 37, left his 3-day-old daughter at the emergency room entrance hospital. After attendants discovered the infant, they radioed the description of Fischer's van to police, who arrested him almost immediately. When Fischer's live-in companion, Susan B. Wall, 37, arrived to post bail, she was arrested for conspiring to abandon their child.

**ASSAULT: Miami, Fla.** Police officers shot and killed Rolando Rodriguez, 59, after he threatened them with a machete and threw a knife at one of the officers.

**DRUG: Boston, Mass.** Edward K. O'Brien, 44, a highly decorated Drug Enforcement Administration agent, was arrested at Logan International Airport with 62 pounds of cocaine and charged with possession and intent to distribute drugs.

**DRUGS: Houston, Texas** A federal indictment named 16 people as participants in a drug "pipeline" operating between Joliet, Ill., and Texas. Among those taken into custody were alleged ringleaders George Rodriguez, Sr. of Joliet, and Alberto Banuelos of Benito, Texas.

**ESCAPE: Dumfries, Scotland** Thomas Gordon and Jack Roy, both 19, escaped from the Dumfries Young Offenders'

Institution. Gordon was serving a life sentence; Roy was being held indefinitely.

**FRAUD: Chicago, Ill.** Michael Sidel pleaded innocent to charges of wire and mail fraud, becoming the seventeenth trader from the Chicago Mercantile Exchange's Japanese yen futures pit to be arraigned in the continuing federal fraud investigation.

**KIDNAPPING: London, England** Victor Cracknell, 32-year-old son of a well-to-do businessman, was kidnapped, held for five days for £1 million, and freed after his family paid about 142,000 to the kidnappers. Police arrested six people and recovered most of the money.

**KIDNAPPING: Richmond, Md.** Dean Ashley Lambey, 34, and Daniel T. Depew, 28, were arrested in connection with a plot to kidnap a young boy, sexually exploit him, and then kill him for a "snuff" videotape.

**MONEY LAUNDERING: Atlanta, Ga.** A Panamanian bank, Banco de Occidente, pleaded guilty to charges of laundering money obtained through illegal drug transactions.

**MURDER: Boston, Mass.** The Supreme Judicial Court ruled that even though there was serious police misconduct in the handling of the case of Albert Lewin, Lewin, 33, must still stand trial for the shooting death of police detective Sherman Griffiths.

**MURDER: Gardiner, Maine** Twenty-one-year-old Byron N. Raines was arrested on charges of abducting Margaret C. Shaw, 35, and her children, killing the woman, and leaving the children with the body.

*August 15*

**ATTEMPTED MURDER: New York, N.Y.** After screaming a racial epithet at a black couple outside a cinema in Manhattan, 60-year-old David Schor, who is white, retrieved a 45-caliber gun and shot at them as they were running, hitting instead 28-year-old Alex Bujaki.

**MURDER: Chicago, Ill.** Sarah Cardona, 30, was stabbed 12 times by a man she let into her apartment to use the bathroom. Cardona died from the wounds. Forty-one-year old suspect John Childress, who had served a prison sentence for murder and rape, was later arrested.

**MURDER: New York, N.Y.** Franklin Rivera turned himself in to police for allegedly raping, beating, stabbing, and strangling 39-year-old Ruth Velez, who he surprised during a burglary.

**MURDER: Portland, Ore.** Otto Rene Alvarado, 25, Amanda Orozco Lima, 24, and Gloria Orozco Lima, 26, were shot to death in their apartment. Alvaro Israel Alvarado, 25, Amanda Lima's common-law husband, was charged with the crime.

**POLICE BRUTALITY: Chicago, Ill.** Fourteen-year-olds Calvin McLin and Joseph Weaver, both black, were beaten by a group of white residents after Chicago police officer Kathleen Moore and her partner, James Serio, stopped the youths for an alleged curfew violation. McLin claimed that Moore hit him and Weaver after the officers dropped the youths off in a hostile all-white neighborhood.

**VIOLATING EXCLUSION ORDER: Londonderry, Northern Ireland** Thirty-nine-year-old American lawyer Martin Galvin was arrested for violating a government order after he held a news conference with an official of the Sinn Fein wing of the Irish Republican Army. Galvin had been banned from Britain in 1984 for "encouraging violence."

### *August 16*

**ASSASSINATION: Bogota, Colombia** Forty-three-year-old Carlos Valencia Garcia, a court magistrate who denied court motions by reputed Medellin drug cartel leader Pablo Escobar Gavaria and top cartel member Gonzalo Rodriguez Gacha, was fatally shot as he was leaving work.

**FRAUD: Massachusetts** Alan N. Scott, of West Roxbury, was arrested after allegedly using an electronic system for tax filing to fraudulently file for 45 income tax refunds.

**FRAUD: Seattle, Wash.** Bruce J. Rice, 42, president of Rice Aircraft Inc., pleaded guilty to mail fraud and conspiracy in connection with an alleged kickback plan in which competitors' bids were learned and used parts were sold as new for use in planes. Rice was sentenced later to a four-year prison term.

**MURDER: Baton Rouge, La.** Louisiana governor Buddy Roemer commuted the death penalty to a life term in prison with no possibility of parole for 35-year-old Ronald Monroe, convicted of the 1977 fatal stabbing Lenora Collins.

**MURDER: Florida** Jeffrey Lynn Feltner, 26, a former nursing home employee, was arrested on murder charges for the death of Doris Moriarty in Daytona Beach. Feltner was indicted in October for first-degree murder in the death of Sarah F. Abrams, a Melrose, Fla., nursing home resident.

**MURDER: Los Angeles, Calif.** Opening statements began in the trial of Stewart Woodman, 39, who, with his brother Neil Woodman, 45, allegedly hired "ninja assassins" to kill his parents in 1985.

**SEXUAL ASSAULT: Nashua, N.H.** Forty-year-old Gerald Hill was arrested when a 12-year-old boy identified him as the man who had just forced him into a rooming house at knife point and had sexually assaulted him. The youth was describing the ordeal to a police officer when Hill walked by.

### *August 17*

**DRUGS: New York, N.Y.** Dominick Davanzo and Alfred Talavera, 33-year-old policemen assigned to a Harlem housing project precinct face drug charges in connection with their alleged attempt to steal cocaine from a drug dealer.

**MURDER: New Orleans, La.** The U.S. Court of Appeals struck down a ruling that directed $9.4 million compensation be paid to relatives of Sandra Black by *Soldier of Fortune*. The magazine ran an ad by John Wayne Hearn, who was hired by Black's husband to kill her.

**MURDER: Stockton, Calif.** Dang Cha Xiong, a Laotian refugee recently released after he was jailed on child abuse charges, killed his wife, Bao Cha, and himself after holding her and their seven children hostage for more than six hours.

**ROBBERY: Ogle County, Ill.** Richard Bloomquist, Ron Fredman, and Patricia Noble-Schenk, three backers of Lyndon LaRouche, were indicted for theft, robbery, burglary, and intimidation after allegedly stealing $80,000 in securities and cash from an elderly woman between Apr. 12 and May 15.

### *August 18*

**ASSASSINATION: Bogota, Colombia** Forty-six-year-old Senator Luis Carlos Galán, a presidential candidate, was slain outside of Bogota at a political rally, the last victim in a 48-hour period of assassinations that included a magistrate and a police colonel.

**ASSASSINATION: Colombia** Colonel Waldemar Franklin Quintero, police chief detachment in the province where Medellin is located, was assassinated. Nicolas Gonzalez Cardona, reputed pilot for the Medellin cartel, and eight others were arrested later for questioning in the murder.

**ATTEMPTED MURDER: Cambridge, England** Seventeen-year-old Simon Carter was brought before a court on charges of attempting to use rat poison to kill his stepmother and father.

**DRUGS: Los Angeles, Calif.** Roceo Campo, 26, Angelo Alviro, 41, and three other Colombian nationals were arrested in three separate incidents on suspicion of possession of a controlled substance and police confiscated a total of 2,068 pounds of cocaine.

**ESCAPE: Holdrege, Neb.** Inmates Freddie Gonzales, 42, and Ralph P. Brown, 30, were arrested after their wives, Patricia A. Gonzales, 41, and Rebecca Brown, 26, hijacked a helicopter and aided them in an escape from the Arkansas Valley Correctional Center, outside Pueblo, Colo.

**ESCAPE: Palm Springs, Calif.** Forty-year-old Modesto Benigno Perales, a former Los Angeles policeman, was arrested after he escaped from the Big Springs, Texas, prison camp, where he was serving time for conspiracy to possess and distribute cocaine.

**FRAUD: Los Angeles, Calif.** Donald A. Wright Jr., 25, and 10 others were charged with tax and mail fraud in connection with a kickback scheme and the false billing of hospitals for services and products that were not delivered.

**MURDER: Chicago, Ill.** Angela Rhonda Hines, 17, and Kevin Marshall, 15, were arrested and charged with armed robbery and murder hours after the shooting of 29-year-old pizza delivery driver Juan Avila. Marshall allegedly robbed Avila to obtain $94 owed in restitution ordered by a court.

**MURDER: Monrovia, Liberia** Major General Gray Allison received the death penalty from a military court for planning the Mar. 31 murder of policeman Melvin Pyne so his blood could be used in a ritual to aide in a coup against President Samuel Doe.

**ROBBERY New York, N.Y.** Darryl Waters, 27, was charged with grand larceny, assault, burglary, and robbery in connection with a series of robberies between May 10 and June 24 on Long Island and in Queens involving elderly victims.

### *August 19*

**ESCAPE: Springfield, Mass.** Barry Ray, 27, convicted of larceny, was apprehended after disappearing Aug. 18 from the Robinson Correctional Institution in Enfield, Conn. Ray unknowingly approached an off-duty guard from the facility at a pay phone and asked for money. The guard recognized Ray and phoned the police emergency number.

**MURDER: Denver, Colo.** The U.S. Tenth Circuit Court

of Appeals handed down a stay of execution for William Andrews, 34, three days before the execution. Andrews was convicted in the 1974 torture and slayings of three people in an Ogden, Utah, robbery.

**MURDER: New York, N.Y.** Daniel Rakowitz, 28, allegedly stabbed and dismembered Swiss dance student Monika Beerle, 26, whom he met on Aug. 3, when she tried to force him to leave her apartment. He confessed on Sept. 18.

*August 20*

**ASSAULT: California** Jose Alfredo Velasco, 25, allegedly kicked his pregnant former girlfriend, Valerie Morales, in the stomach after an argument with her new boyfriend, who fathered the child. Velasco was charged in the beating and for intentionally causing the death of a fetus.

**DRUGS: Somerville, Mass.** Richard F. "Teensie" Huard Jr., 25, was arrested for possession of heroin. He briefly escaped the next day while en route to court, but he was apprehended in Stoneham.

**LAW ENFORCEMENT: Colombia** About 4,000 people were arrested throughout Colombia as officials searched for drug smugglers and those involved in the Aug. 18 assassination of Luis Carlos Galán in a crackdown outlined Aug. 19 by President Virgilio Barco.

**MURDER: Beverly Hills, Calif.** Jose B. Menendez, 45, chairman of music and video distributor LIVE Entertainment, Inc., and his wife, Kitty, were shot dead at close range at their home. Their sons, Erik, 18, and Lyle, 21, were later charged.

**MURDER: Kora National Reserve, Kenya** George Adamson, 83-year-old British conservationist devoted to studying lions, and two assistants were slain when Adamson tried to help a friend accosted by armed Somali bandits. Abdi Osman Sheuri and two others were arrested.

**SEXUAL ASSAULT: Nashua, N.H.** Romuald Vaillancourt, a coach for the Nashua Youth Soccer League, was arrested and charged with sexual assault after allegedly fondling two players between August 1988 and June 1989.

*August 21*

**ASSAULT: New York, N.Y.** Herman McMillan, 42, was arrested on charges of physically and sexually assaulting his nine children, ranging in age from four months to 16 years. His 34-year-old wife, Frances, was arrested for endangerment and assault.

**BOMBING: Sheffield, England** Eileen Caulton, 47-year-old international gem businesswoman, was wounded seriously after she opened a package bomb at her apartment, where an arsonist struck five weeks earlier. Barry Thomas Caunt, 28, Terry Thornton, 58, Peter Stuart Fletcher, 45, and two others were arrested.

**DRUGS: Colombia** In a government crackdown on drugs police raided drug traffickers' estates and confiscated cars, cattle, and aircraft. More than 11,000 people were arrested in three days, including Eduardo Martinez Romero, reputed Medellin drug cartel finance chief.

**WEAPONS VIOLATION: Philippines** Dominique C. Adams, a 22-year-old American, was arrested by customs po-

lice after they discovered 70 pistols in her luggage. Arms dealer Richard Pedrioli, Adams' reputed contact, was later arrested in California.

*August 22*

**ASSASSINATION: Oakland, Calif.** Huey Percy Newton, 47, co-founder of the Black Panther Party organized in the 1960s to fight racism in this city, was found shot to death.

**ASSAULT: London, England** Jeremy Hicks, 28, received a six-year sentence for injuring Catherine Macksey, whom he met through a "lonely hearts" ad. Hicks burned Macksey with a cigarette and slashed her with a wine glass when she would not have sex with him after a date. She jumped from a second-story window to escape.

**ATTEMPTED MURDER: Wilmington, Calif.** Paul Turner, a 50-year-old transient, was charged with stabbing 14-year-old Nathan Maciel. Turner was apprehended by police through the efforts of Maciel's mother, who located Turner by talking to transients in the park where her son was stabbed.

**ESCAPE: Indianapolis** William "Pops" Kerns, 67, a convicted counterfeiter, forged a pass to leave a pretrial custody facility, where he was being held on counterfeiting charges, and escaped.

**MURDER: Chicago, Ill.** Marina Justice, 44, was robbed of $4 and killed in a purse snatching, allegedly by convicted robber 31-year-old Warren Murdock, who confessed. Justice died on Aug. 23.

**MURDER: Los Angeles, Calif.** Jerry Weber, 49, was shot and killed as he withdrew $40 from a cash machine. On Dec. 19, police arrested Nicholas James Williams, 18, in connection with Weber's shooting and robbery.

*August 23*

**BURGLARY: Marion County, Fla.** Eddie Johnson, former Atlanta Hawks basketball player, was arrested on charges that he burglarized two Florida homes.

**CONSPIRACY: Morristown, N.J.** Dale Berra, 32-year-old former baseball player and son of Hall of Fame baseball player, Yogi Berra, was charged with cocaine possession and conspiring to violate narcotics laws.

**CRIMINAL JUSTICE: Reno, Nev.** A district court judge ruled that a suit could be filed against rock band Judas Priest for its alleged use of subliminal messages, which were judged exempt from constitutional protection under freedom of speech.

**DRUGS: Barranquilla, Colombia** Bernardo Londono Quintero, 40, was arrested and charged with cocaine trafficking. Authorities called him one of the top ten drug shippers of the Medellin drug cartel.

**DRUGS: Danville, Ill.** Four Pontiac Correctional Center guards and one Illinois Youth Center guard were arrested for drug possession in the ongoing Operation Whiteshirt aimed at ending drug distribution from guards to inmates.

**FRAUD: Los Angeles, Calif.** Forty-five-year-old Sanford A. Habalow pleaded guilty to fraud in concealing a $120,000 campaign contribution which was used against the election effort of a Republican senator.

**GAMBLING: New York, N.Y.** Baseball commissioner A. Bartlett Giamatti and Cincinnati Reds manager Pete Rose reached an agreement that permanently suspended Rose from baseball for suspicion of betting on his own team.

**HIJACKING: Algiers, Algeria** Said Djamel, who was placed on an Air France jet after being expelled from France, hijacked the plane for an hour, but when he was denied landing permission in Tunis, he surrendered to police in Algiers, the flight's original destination. The 30-year-old's "weapons" were a bar of soap and a shaving cream can hidden under his jacket.

**KIDNAPPING: Tulkarm, Occupied West Bank** Shaul Mishaniya, a 46-year-old Bat Yam jeweler, was kidnapped by masked Palestinians. He was found alive and unharmed the next day at the bottom of a well.

**MURDER: Suffolk County, Mass.** On the grounds of constitutional violations, new trials were ordered for Leo Cunningham, 26, and Lynn and Michael Riley, both 26, previously convicted of the 1984 murder of Michael Maronski, a high school student.

**RACKETEERING: Chicago, Ill.** Chicago Board of Trade broker Howard J Goberstein, 33, pleaded innocent to 127 counts of racketeering and violating the Commodities Exchange Act.

**ROBBERY: Miami, Fla.** John R. Johnson, 48, and his wife Jacqueline Johnson, 42, were arrested as suspects in an Aug. 11 Green Bay, Wis., jewelry store robbery. The couple had disappeared on Jan. 12, 1988, the day his trial on unrelated drug trafficking charges was to start.

**THEFT: Chicago, Ill.** Sherwin Pomerantz, accused of stealing $486,500 between 1980 and 1982 from companies he worked for as a payroll agent, pleaded not guilty. He was arrested July 29 while on a business trip from Israel, where he had worked since 1982.

### August 24

**DRUGS: Bogota, Colombia** In a renewed effort against the drug cartels, police seized 2 tons of cocaine after a raid on a drug-processing laboratory, bringing the total confiscated to 6 tons.

**DRUGS: Erie County, N.Y.** John J. Battaglia, 60, was indicted on drug charges by a grand jury, which indicted seven others allegedly involved in shipping cocaine from Los Angeles to the East Coast.

**EMBEZZLEMENT: Boston, Mass.** A federal magistrate ruled that fugitive banker George Koskotas could be extradited to Greece to face charges of embezzling $200 million from the Bank of Crete.

**MURDER: Hartford, Conn.** Banker Diane Gellenbeck, 37, was abducted from a parking garage and shot to death on a golf course. Police arrested 27-year-old Daniel James Webb, already facing rape, kidnapping, and assault charges, in connection with her death.

### August 25

**ASSASSINATION: Oakland, Calif.** Tyrone Robinson, 25, member of the West Coast Black Guerilla Family gang, was arrested for the murder of 1960s civil rights activist Huey P. Newton. Robinson claimed to have shot Newton in self-defense after he confronted Newton for allegedly stealing drugs from fellow gang members.

**ASSAULT: Dorchester, Mass.** Police officers Dwight Allen, 28, and Alan James, 30, were arrested on charges that they robbed a series of men in Dorchester, after telling them they were renegade policemen.

**ATTEMPTED MURDER: Athens, Ala.** The conviction of AIDS-infected inmate Alan Brock, 31, who was charged first with attempted murder and then assault for biting a prison guard, was reversed.

**ATTEMPTED MURDER: New York, N.Y.** Armored truck guard Billy John Hackworth was shot during a $500,000 robbery. His partner, Wycliff Warner, who drove Hackworth to the hospital, later confessed to shooting him and robbing the truck himself.

**CONTEMPT: Washington, D.C.** William A. Borders Jr., a disbarred lawyer, was jailed for contempt for refusing to testify against Alcee Hastings, a federal judge undergoing impeachment proceedings.

**DRUGS: Cudahy, Calif.** Authorities arrested three people and confiscated more than 400 pounds of cocaine worth $75 million.

**MURDER: Chicago, Ill.** Police arrested Patrick Carr, 22, as a suspect in the Aug. 7 shooting of 45-year-old auto dealership owner Joseph Tostado, who was shot in a holdup and died Aug. 21 of his injuries. Carr also was identified in connection with three other armed robberies.

**MURDER: Los Angeles, Calif.** One person was shot and killed and three were wounded in a gang shoot-out at a stoplight in an unincorporated area. Mike Thomas, 27, the driver of one of the cars, was arrested on charges of murder, attempted murder, and weapons possession.

**MURDER: San Francisco, Calif.** A state appeals court reduced the convictions of Timothy White, 27, Donny Clanton, 24, and David Rogers, 24, from murder to involuntary manslaughter. The three had been convicted of beating to death John O'Connell in a 1984 "gay-bashing" spree.

**MURDER: Stroudsburg, Pa.** Cameron R. Kocher, 10, pleaded not guilty at his arraignment for the fatal shooting of 7-year-old playmate, Jessica Ann Carr, as she rode a snowmobile in a neighbor's yard on Mar. 6. He is to stand trial as an adult.

**THEFT: Buena Park, Calif.** James Clark, 49, was arrested and charged with stealing more than $500,000 from pay phones in 24 states over a period of eight years.

### August 26

**ASSAULT: San Juan, Puerto Rico** Filberto Ojeda Rios, 55, was acquitted on eight charges of opening fire on FBI agents in 1985. Ojeda was held pending a trial on federal charges in a 1983 Wells Fargo armored car robbery in Hartford, Conn.

**MONEY LAUNDERING: Roslyn Heights, N.Y.** N.Y John and Deysi Posada were arrested and charged with laundering $48 to $50 million yearly for the Medellin drug cartel. Police found $4 million in cash in their apartment.

**MURDER: Denver, Colo.** The convictions of David Lane and Bruce Pierce, white supremacists who killed Jewish radio talk show host Alan Berg in 1984, were upheld by a court of appeals.

*August 27*

**ARSON: St. Regis Mohawk Reservation, N.Y.** Antigambling forces burned a casino scheduled to open on the reservation. More than 500 people clashed as state police set up roadblocks outside the reservation.

**MURDER: Los Angeles, Calif.** Maria Navarro, 27, a family friend, and two of her aunts were shot to death by Navarro's estranged husband, Raymundo Navarro, 26. A 911 dispatcher was told that Raymundo had threatened to kill Maria, but the dispatcher allegedly refused to send police to Maria's home. Surviving family members later filed a suit against the county.

**MURDER: Punjab, India** Alleged Sikh militants armed with automatic weapons stopped a train and shot at passengers aboard, killing 20 and injuring 30.

**MURDER: Quezon City, Philippines** Police arrested another suspect in the Apr. 21 killing of U.S. Army colonel James (Nick) Rowe. Juanito Itaas is one of seven people believed to have participated in the murder. Another was arrested June 19.

**MURDER: Rome, Italy** Ludovico Ligato, former head of Italian railways, was shot to death by unidentified gunmen as he stood outside his villa.

**MURDER: Walasmulla, Sri Lanka** Gunmen thought to be leftist rebels shot to death five members of a policeman's family and burned their bodies by setting the house on fire.

**MURDER: Washington, D.C.** Ronald E. Turner, a 31-year-old transient, was arrested and charged with the rape and murder of Ella Starks, a homeless woman who was stabbed and choked to death with an umbrella.

*August 28*

**POLITICAL CORRUPTION: Belgrade, Yugoslavia** Fifteen ethnic Albanians, including former Communist Party leader Azem Vlasi, were charged with counter-revolutionary activities for allegedly instigating protests and strikes in Kosovo province.

**RACKETEERING: Lyons, Ill.** Police officers Lieutenant Donald Kroft and William Teeter were arrested and charged with racketeering for accepting sex and bribes to overlook prostitution at a strip joint, My Uncle's Place.

*August 29*

**FRAUD: Boston, Mass.** King Yon Yee, a 40-year-old prosecution witness against 17 Boston officials involved in a towing scam, was arrested and charged with fire insurance fraud. Yee was released on $1,000 cash bail.

**HIJACKIING: Frankfurt, Germany** Czech teenagers Stefan Macicko, 17, and Dusan Styck, 16, were sentenced to two years' probation for the Mar. 29 hijacking of a Malev Airlines jetliner from Prague's Ruzyne Airport to West Germany.

**MURDER: Dallas, Texas** Jeffrey Mark Woodson, 35, was shot to death in his North Dallas home, the victim of an alleged drug-related killing. Police believed Woodson was a major distributor of the drug Ecstasy.

**WEAPONS VIOLATION: Chicago, Ill.** Alleged gang leader Willie Lloyd, 38, was given a three-year sentence for the illegal use of a gun by a felon. Lloyd was convicted in 1973 of having killed a police officer in Iowa.

*August 30*

**ABUSE: Tifton, Ga.** Ola Mae Thomas, 27, was arrested and charged with imprisoning her 18-year-old daughter Betty Faye Green in a room of their mobile home. The girl weighed only 42 pounds when she was found after police responded to a call from a social worker.

**DRUGS: Chicago, Ill.** Nineteen people were arrested and charged with drug trafficking, following a coordinated operation by local FBI and Drug Enforcement Administration offices. Victor Velazquez, 43, was identified as the ringleader.

**EXECUTION: Richmond, Va.** Convicted murderer Alton Waye, 34, was put to death in the electric chair for the 1977 rape and murder of Lavergne B. Marshall, 61, at her farm house.

**EXTORTION: Concord, N.H.** Former state representative Charles T. McMahon pleaded not guilty to charges of extorting $1,000 to $10,000 from two auto dealers in return for favorable treatment from the Salem Planning Board of which he was a member.

**KIDNAPPING: Los Angeles, Calif.** A federal grand jury indicted Rolando Peralta, a chiropractor, his secretary Socorra Contreras, and her boyfriend with arranging the abduction of Maria Robleto, a 22-year-old student at the University Technological School in Mexico City.

**MURDER: Salem, Va.** Gary Lee Colby, 42, was arrested and charged with the Apr. 9, 1977, murder of Beverly A. Autiello. The woman was battered to death at her home in Haverhill, Mass.

**TREASON: Lusaka, Zambia** Lieutenant General Christon Tembo and three other military leaders were charged with treason for allegedly plotting to overthrow President Kenneth Kaunda's regime.

*August 31*

**DRUGS: Sturbridge, N.Y.** Carlos Asenio and Miguel Medina were arrested by New York State Police trooper Richard Rollins, who discovered 500 grams of cocaine with a street value of $500,000 in their car after stopping them for speeding.

**ILLEGAL OPERATIONS: Pasadena, Calif.** David Sconce, 33-year-old operator of the Lamb Funeral Home in Pasadena, entered a plea of guilty to 21 criminal offenses, including desecrating corpses and conducting mass cremations. He was also charged with hiring individuals to beat up three competing morticians.

**MURDER: Boston, Mass.** Darin N. Bufalino, 28, of Revere, Mass., pleaded not guilty to murdering Vincent J. DeNino, 27, who was found in the backseat of a car on Feb. 29, 1984.

**MURDER: Boston, Mass.** Nine alleged gang members were indicted on charges from theft to murder. Mervin Reese, 19, alleged leader of the Humboldt gang, and Steven Howard, 17, of the Academy Homes gang were charged with receiving a motor vehicle and attempted murder, respectively.

**MURDER: Los Angeles, Calif.** A mistrial was declared in the case of 47-year-old Harvey Rader, a car dealer from Reseda accused of murdering Sol and Elaine Salomon and their two children at their San Fernando Valley home in 1982.

**ROBBERY: Chelmsford, Mass.** Robert Burke, 23, Frank Bolduc, 51, and Francis Larkin, 55, arrested in connection with a $300,000 robbery of a Wells Fargo truck, pleaded not guilty.

Paul Cresta, 37, a fourth suspect wounded in the robbery attempt, was hospitalized and did not appear in court.

### September 1

**CORRUPTION: Los Angeles, Calif.** Sergeant Robert Sobel and eight sheriff's deputies were relieved of their duties in an ongoing probe into allegations that the officers used money seized in drug raids for personal gain.

**COUNTERFEITING: Arcadia, Calif.** Nicolas C. Tano, 61, was arrested apparently while in the process of printing phony $10 and $20 bills. Police also seized nearly $1 million in counterfeit paper and equipment for counterfeiting.

**DRUGS: New York, N.Y.** Rocio Gallego, Luis Edwardo-Franco, Jorge Lopee, and Sergio Castro-Munoz had their drug convictions overturned on the grounds their trial judge may have displayed "ethnic prejudice. " New trials were ordered for all except Castro-Munoz.

**FRAUD: Newark, N.J.** Jack Colbert, 37, and his brother Charles Colbert, 42, were indicted on charges of washing cancellations off postage stamps and reselling them through a mail-order business they ran from Somerset County Jail where the two were imprisoned for an earlier crime.

**FRAUD: Washington, D.C.** William J. Sands, former military contract consultant, pleaded guilty to selling inside information about a $100 million Pentagon-proposed contract to the Unisys Corp.

**MURDER: Caddo Parish, La.** Evidence of eight gruesome murders was allowed to be submitted by prosecutors trying Nathaniel Code, 33, for the murder of four members of the Vivian Chaney family in 1985.

**MURDER: Wheaton, Ill.** In the retrial of Alejandro Hernandez and Rolando Cruz, accused of the Feb. 25, 1983, rape and murder of 10-year-old Jeanine Nicarico, the judge allowed the defense to submit the confession of convicted murderer Brian Dugan as evidence.

### September 2

**ARSON: Adairville, Ky.** Bill Sircy, 22, Angela B. Estep, Sherri Davenport, 19, and Danny Smith, 22, returned to the newly renovated Smith Grove A.M.E. Zion Church, and carried out the final requirement of their sentence: an apology to the congregation for setting fire to the 11-year-old church in May 1986.

**BOMBING: Bogota, Colombia.** A bomb demolished the offices of the newspaper *El Espectador*, wounding none of the staff or bystanders but injuring more than 70 passengers on two buses passing by.

**DRUGS: Portland, Ore.** Authorities seized 25 tons of hashish, valued at $156 million, found aboard the *Lady Brigid*, an oil rig supply ship. Seven men on the ship were arrested, including the owner, Sidney M. Lewis, 51.

**MURDER: Troy, N.Y.** Marian F. Allen, 68, was arraigned on a charge of second-degree murder after confessing to killing her baby boy, the result of an extramarital affair, and burying him in her back yard 37 years ago.

### September 3

**ATTEMPTED MURDER: Chicago, Ill.** Albert Hogan,

61, was arrested for allegedly shooting police officer Alex Horstein, 35, through the door of an apartment during a drug investigation, hitting Horstein in the leg.

**DRUGS: New London County, Conn.** One hundred pounds of marijuana was discovered when a state trooper smelled a sweet odor coming from the trunk of a car he had pulled over. Stephen T. O'Neill, 38, the car's driver, was arrested and charged with possession.

**MURDER: Ferriday, La.** Thomas Martin, 37, who allegedly killed his live-in girlfriend, Roxie Clark, placed her body in a car, ordered her two sons to get in the back seat, and drove from Denton, Texas, was arrested after stopping at his mother's home.

**MURDER: Gautier, Miss.** The body of April Sherry Turner, 7, was found strangled to death near her home. Henry Lee Harrison, 33, was charged Sept. 4 with April's murder.

**MURDER: Melbourne, Fla.** Rogers David Mansfield, 62, a dean at Brevard Community College, was arrested only hours after authorities discovered the body of his wife, Lillian June Mansfield, 68, in a Marion County, Mo., grave. Mansfield was charged with having killed his wife in August.

### September 4

**KIDNAPPING: Houston, Texas.** Tracy Levis, 24, who had held a hunting knife to the throat of her 15-month-old son Brandon Duke, was arrested by police following a 13-hour standoff.

**MURDER: Sri Lanka.** The bodies of four people, bound together, were found floating in the Kelani River near Colombo. The deaths brought the toll to at least 50 killed, or found dead, in the past two days.

**MURDER: Vicenza, Italy.** Four Americans, three of them soldiers of the U.S. Army, were charged with beating to death Johnny Boateng, 32, of Ghana outside the Palladium disco near here.

**TERRORISM: Medellin, Colombia.** Rafael Arango Cuartas, 27, was killed and 14 others were wounded by a gunman dressed in fatigues who opened fire on an airport waiting room. The gunman was killed when police and troops returned fire.

### September 5

**CRIMINAL JUSTICE: San Francisco, Calif.** In rejecting an appeal by Death Row inmate Ronald Lee Bell, 40, the state Supreme Court ruled that statistical under-representation of minorities among prospective jurors was not sufficient grounds for a racial bias challenge in a trial.

**FRAUD: Dallas, Texas.** Patrick G. King, former president of the defunct Vernon Savings and Loan Association, was convicted of making illegal contributions to politicians and using thrift money to pay for topless dancers.

**FRAUD: New York, N.Y.** Robert M. Freeman, 47, former partner handling risk arbitrage at the investment firm Goldman, Sachs & Co., pleaded guilty to charges he used inside information to trade on stocks.

**POLICE BRUTALITY: Mitchell's Plain, South Africa.** White riot police allegedly beat student demonstrators who had been given permission to protest in this township outside

Capetown. Two officers were acquitted of assault charges on Oct. 12.

**RAPE: Cambridge, Mass.** Suspended state trooper Robert Monteiro, 25, pleaded not guilty to charges he forced a woman to have sex with him in exchange for not ticketing her for speeding, and for offering other women the same bribe.

*September 6*

**ATTEMPTED MURDER: Montbello, Colo.** A 30-year-old woman survived an attack by her next-door neighbor, who robbed, raped, beat, and stabbed her before setting her house on fire. Donnie E. Russell, 18, was arrested in Oklahoma City, Okla., on Sept. 7.

**DRUGS: Boston, Mass.** Local, state, and federal authorities broke up a cocaine ring with the arrest of 12 men, who allegedly distributed drugs for a major cocaine cartel in Medellin, Colombia.

**ESCAPE: Cumbria, England.** Forty-five-year-old convict Edward Hutchinson escaped from Haverigg Prison.

**FRAUD: Bern, Switzerland.** Lebanese businessman Khalil J. Ghattas was extradited to West Germany to face charges of fraud in a scam that cost Kloeckner & Co. $303 million.

**MONEY LAUNDERING: Bogota, Colombia.** Eduardo Martinez Romero, 36, was extradited to Atlanta, Ga., to face money laundering charges. Martinez Romero, believed to be the Medellin cocaine cartel's financial brains, was the first person extradited to the U.S. from here in more than two years.

**MURDER: Chicago, Ill.** Dorothy Williams, 37, was arrested for the murders of Mary Harris, 97, found dead July 25 and Lonnie Laws, 79, killed Dec. 5, 1987, at a senior citizens complex. Williams apparently also stole money from the victims to support a heroin habit.

**MURDER: Fresno, Calif.** Suspected smugglers shot and killed undercover Border Patrol agent Keith Connelly, 42, and wounded his partner, Ted Jordan, 42. Three men and a woman were later apprehended.

**MURDER: Linden, Ala.** For scheming to kill his adoptive mother with a rattlesnake, Reginald Wayne Pope, 37, was convicted of criminal solicitation after contacting snake handler Keith Davis.

**MURDER: Los Angeles, Calif.** Seven-year-old Lamont Compton and Melvin Morris Gentry, 17, were shot and killed and a woman injured when two men opened fire with AK-47 semi-automatic rifles. George Williams Jr., 26, was arrested Sept. 8 in connection with the shooting.

**MURDER: New York, N.Y.** A grand jury indicted Joseph Fama, 18, as the triggerman in the Aug. 23 racially motivated killing of Yusuf Hawkins, 16, in Bensonhurst. Keith Mondello, 18, and Pasquale Raucci, 19, were indicted earlier. By Oct. 16, James Patino, 24, Charles Stressler, 21, Joseph Serrano, 19, and Steven Curreri, 18, had also been indicted. Curreri was not charged with murder.

**MURDER: Oxted, England.** Julia Phillips, 31, was remanded to a mental hospital, charged with the Sept. 5 suffocation murders of her two children, Robert, 5, and Claire, 3.

**MURDER: Shrewsbury, England.** Patricia Robinson, 41, was charged with the murder of her husband James Robinson, 42, between July 1 and Sept. 4. Their son, Terence Robinson, 19, was also charged with helping dispose of the body underneath the family's patio in Hanwood.

**RIOT: South Africa.** Twenty-nine anti-apartheid demonstrators were allegedly killed by police during protests against parliamentary elections in townships surrounding Cape Town.

*September 7*

**ATTEMPTED MURDER: Chicago, Ill.** Police officers shot and wounded parolee Jerome Wilson, 35, as he held a woman hostage with a gun to her head. He was charged with attempted murder and seven counts of armed robbery for having held up seven people earlier.

**ATTEMPTED MURDER: Los Angeles County, Calif.** Christopher Mack, 23, was wounded by gunfire from a passing car. Police nearby returned fire, and wounded suspects Jeffrey Howard, 26, and Devlyn Cole, 21. Both were charged with attempted murder as was Ricky Lewis, 24.

**BRIBERY: San Francisco, Calif.** Hotel magnate Donald Werby, 63, was indicted on charges of allegedly bribing pregnant 18-year-old Amelia Becker, who was to testify against him in an earlier case, in which he was accused of having sex with teenage girls and supplying them with drugs.

**CRIMINAL JUSTICE: Washington, D.C.** A four-month investigation into the Apr. 19 explosion in the U.S.S. *Iowa* gun turret, which killed 47 sailors, cleared Gunner's Mate Third Class Kendall L. Truitt, 21, of any wrongdoing.

**FRAUD: Chicago, Ill.** Harry O. Patten III, 39, a soybean futures trader on the Chicago Board of Trade, pleaded guilty to aiding in a trade after the Board's closing bell. Fellow trader Kenneth Gillen, 29, also pleaded guilty to a separate misdemeanor charge.

**KIDNAPPING: New Brunswick, N.J.** Thirteen-year-old Veglio Jiminez was abducted and taken to Puerto Rico, where police officers there recognized the boy and his abductor, Ivan Figueroa, 35, from FBI wanted posters. Figueroa was arrested and Jiminez was returned home safely after six weeks.

**MURDER: Dortmund, West Germany.** Irish Republican Army members shot and killed Heidi Hazell, 26, as she sat in her car, mistakenly believing she was a British soldier.

**MURDER: San Francisco, Calif.** The state Supreme Court ruled four to three that a drug provider can only be charged with second-degree felony murder when there is a "high probability" that his supplying the drug would be deadly to the victim.

**MURDER: Warwick, R.I.** A 15-year-old was arrested for the brutal stabbings of his neighbors, Joan Heaton, 39, and her daughters Jennifer, 10, and Melissa, 8, whose bodies were found Sept. 4.

**RAPE: Chicago, Ill.** Diane Daniels, 30, William Patterson, 31, and Courtney Hicks, 36, were charged with participating in the rape and assault of a 25-year-old pregnant woman, who was sexually assaulted by as many as nine people on Sept. 6.

**ROBBERY: La Roche-sur-Yon, France.** Jean-Jacques Guillon, 28, believed to be the famed Lo Grand Bleu or Gerard Roblochon who escaped police by riding an old bicycle, was arraigned on robbery charges after his arrest as he attempted to rob his tenth bank in six months.

**SEXUAL ABUSE: Springfield, Mass.** Edward B. Ellis, 40, owner of the Mohawk Theater, pleaded innocent to charges he transported a child across state lines for sexual purposes.

### September 8

**FRAUD: Chicago, Ill.** Treasury bond futures trader John Myskowski, 36, pleaded guilty to one count of prearranged trading and one count of mail fraud.

**LAW ENFORCEMENT: Khan Yunis, Gaza Strip.** A 13-year-old Palestinian, Akran Zaki Hamdan, was shot and killed by Israeli troops during a stone-throwing protest.

**MURDER: Tampa, Fla.** Thomas Michael Wicklace, 44, Jay Michael Hickerson, 33, and Bryan Keith Williams, 26, were arrested in connection with the Apr. 19, 1985, murder of 1-year-old Billy Rosebud, after a newspaper article on the open case sparked information from a prison inmate.

**THEFT: New York, N.Y.** Dr. Juan B. Suros, 48, was indicted on charges of stealing rare coins worth more than $1 million from the American Numismatic Society.

### September 9

**ATTEMPTED MURDER: West Covina, Calif.** Martha Araceli Alspuro, 25, and Hector Ubaldo Soto, 22, were arrested for alleged attempted murder, child abuse, and sexual abuse after the woman's 2-year-old daughter was hospitalized.

**GAMBLING: Los Angeles, Calif.** In a crackdown on illegal sports bookmaking operations, police arrested Barbara Tullos, 45, her husband Nick Tullos, 49, Robert Raff, 68, his son Edward Raff, 31, and Carlita Smith, 59.

**MURDER: Dorchester, Mass.** John A. Keniston, 35, was arrested and charged with the stabbing death of his roommate, Ernest Jordan, 46.

**ROBBERY: Los Angeles, Calif.** Security guard Aundra Spencer, 29, chased bank robbery suspect James Ernest Davis, 44, for more than a block before apprehending him. Police placed Davis under arrest and gave Spencer an application to become a police officer.

### September 10

**MURDER: DuPage County, Ill.** William Timothy Leahy, 53, allegedly tracked down and stabbed to death Aaron Mitton, 30, with an 11-inch hunting knife following a traffic altercation on the Eisenhower Expressway, west of Chicago.

**MURDER: Los Angeles, Calif.** Luis Palacio was arrested for allegedly shooting to death two women who shared an apartment in Studio City.

**PRISONS: Washington, D.C.** The U.S. prison population increased by 46,004 inmates in the first six months of 1989, the highest margin of increase on record, bringing the total population to 673,565, according to Bureau of Justice statistics.

### September 11

**DRUGS: Grand Junction, Colo.** The local police department seized more than 1,000 pounds of cocaine, the largest in state history. Three men were charged in the case.

**DRUGS: London, England.** David Widdowson, 31, Rupert Elliott, 50, John Hodner, 43, and Alan Felton, 46, were remanded into custody for allegedly importing 7 million worth of cannabis resin through Ipswich Docks.

**DRUGS: Washington, D.C.** Jury selection began in the trial of Rayful Edmond III, accused of operating one of the area's largest drug rings and suspected in more than 30 drug-related murders, and 10 co-defendants.

**MONEY LAUNDERING: Atlanta, Ga.** Eduardo Martinez Romero, 36, extradited from Colombia Sept. 6 and suspected of being the financial wizard of the Medellin drug cartel, pleaded not guilty in federal court to charges of money laundering.

**MURDER: Cambridge, Mass.** Charges were dropped against Donald Sleeper, 34, in connection with the stabbing death of Joseph Pires. Later in the day police arrested Juan Carlos Sorto, 38, and he was charged with the crime.

**MURDER: Northern Ireland.** Ulster Defense Regiment privates Andrew David Smith, 29, Andrew Neville Browne, 25, and civilian Edward Charles Jones, 25, were charged with the August murder of Loughlin Maginn, a Roman Catholic. Browne also was charged with having killed Liam McKee at Lisburn in June.

**MURDER: Troy, N.Y.** Lisa Fikkle, 24, pleaded not guilty to killing her stepmother Carol Fikkle, 42, who was stabbed more than 100 times and beaten for allegedly kicking Muffin, the family poodle.

**THEFT: New York, N.Y.** Charles Trotter, 22, was arrested and charged with the theft of 300 pounds of copper cable belonging to the Metro-North Commuter Railroad.

### September 12

**ASSASSINATION: Windhoek, Namibia** Anton Lubowski, 37, the only white leader of the South West Africa People's Organization independence movement, was shot and killed. A former South African police drugs squad defective, Ferdi Barnard, 31, was arrested as a suspect in Johannesburg, South Africa.

**DRUGS: Atlantic Ocean** Four people were arrested and 1,600 pounds of cocaine was recovered when the Coast Guard, working with the Customs Service and the Drug Enforcement Administration, seized the fishing boat *Lorick*. The day before, authorities seized the *Nerma*, a Danish freighter, arresting 13 people and recovering 1,100 pounds of cocaine.

**DRUGS: Los Angeles, Calif.** Dario DiCesare, 46, was arrested by Drug Enforcement Administration agents and police officers after allegedly throwing 12 kilograms of cocaine in a trash dumpster and attempting to run down the agents with his car.

**KIDNAPPING: Devon, England** Keith Rose, 40, was remanded into custody for the kidnapping of businessman Victor Cracknell, who was held for a £1 million ransom.

**MURDER: Bilbao, Spain** Luis Reina Mesonera, owner of a fish store, was killed in a parcel bomb explosion mistakenly sent by the Basque separatist group E.T.A.

**MURDER: Los Angeles, Calif.** Rifka Cason, 29, was fatally shot in the head, apparently by her 72-year-old father Leonard, who could not stand to see his daughter sink into a life of prostitution and drug abuse.

*September 13*

**ASSAULT: Washington, D.C.** Michael A. Feaster, 30, was indicted on assault charges after forcing a 13-year-old boy to engage in sex with him, with the knowledge he was infected with the AIDS virus.

**CRIMINAL JUSTICE: Los Angeles, Calif.** The Los Angeles Superior Court ordered the Torrance Police Department to pay an additional $82,500 on top of a $5.9 million judgment to the family of Kelly Rastello, 19, who died in a 1984 vehicular collision with Sergeant Rollo Green.

**DRUGS: Baton Rouge, La.** A state trooper found 350 pounds of cocaine, valued at $17 million, inside a car he had pulled over for speeding. Two men from South America were arrested.

**EXTORTION: Los Angeles, Calif.** Newspaper publisher Tae Il Yi, 28, and Cha Chi Ya Hong, 21, and Nuumoto Leuto, 20, were arrested and charged with extorting payments from Koreatown businessmen who were threatened with arson.

**THEFT: Enfield, Conn.** George L. DeDemonicis, 44, pleaded guilty to larceny charges after attempting to steal a woman's used underwear by telling her she would receive new underwear for the old.

*September 14*

**DRUGS: Budapest, Hungary** Police uncovered 62 pounds of heroin valued at $1.6 million, stored in a West German-bound peanut truck, marking the country's largest seizure of heroin. The 37-year-old Turkish driver was arrested.

**DRUGS: Depew, N.Y.** Darlene O'Hara, 27, was arrested and cocaine, marijuana, and drug paraphernalia was seized after her 8-year-old son saw President George Bush's talk on drugs and told police.

**MURDER: Charlestown, Mass.** Mark R. Smith, son of this city's alleged mob leader, was arrested in connection with the Apr. 25, 1987, murder of Kevin J. Martell, 25, who was shot four times in the head.

**MURDER: Lancashire, England** John Simons, 44, was charged with the Aug. 12 murder of Drocketts Restaurant chef Andrew Maddocks, 22.

*September 15*

**DRUGS: Denver, Colo.** Hector Fragoso Burgueno, 47, wanted in connection with 12 torture-murders in March near Agua Prieta, Mexico, was indicted along with Walter Bruce Wood and Shirley Wood and four others for conspiracy to smuggle marijuana and cocaine into Colorado between December 1985 and June 1987.

**FRAUD: Lubbock, Texas** A mistrial resulted in the case of D.I. Faulkner, James L. Toler, and five others charged with conspiracy to defraud five savings businesses of $135 million after allegedly overstating property values and getting loans based on those values.

**MURDER: Boston, Mass.** Matthew Rosenberg, 20, convicted when he was 14 for the October 1983 kidnapping and murder of his 5-year-old neighbor, Frank Kenneth "Kenny" Claudio, was denied release from custody transferred to an out-of-state program for adult sexual offenders.

**MURDER: Fort Worth, Texas** Amy Lynn Thatcher, 14, was forced into a car as she walked to school. On Sept. 16, Kenneth Reed Smith, 20, was arrested and led police to Thatcher's body, found strangled and sexually assaulted. Smith was also charged in an Aug. 19 sexual assault of a 13-year-old girl.

**MURDER: Los Angeles, Calif.** Exclusive fashion designer Ruben Panis, 57, was found strangled in his home and his two cars were gone.

**ROBBERY: Los Angeles, Calif.** Three armed men robbed $500,000 worth of jewelry from Bullock's department store.

*September 16*

**DRUGS: Worcester County, Mass.** Hector Compres and Rubi David, 31, were arrested when police discovered a pound of cocaine after stopping the two for a traffic violation.

**EMBEZZLEMENT: Nevada** Jonn Aiden, 22, Trinity Mine employee, was charged with conspiracy and embezzlement for allegedly taking more than one ton of silver from the mine, located about 90 miles northeast of Reno.

**KIDNAPPING: Tilff, Belgium** Bank manager Guy Jeuris, Marie-Madeleine Bolland, and her two children were taken hostage by gunmen who intended to rob the bank. Jeuris escaped, so the gunmen held the others for six days until $720,000 ransom was paid and a getaway car provided. One gunman claimed he was Philippe Delaire, 28, who escaped in April from a French prison.

**MURDER: Buenaventura, Colombia** Guillermo Gomez Murillo, reporter for the Bogota newspaper *El Espectador*, was fatally shot at his parents' home. The paper was bombed Sept. 2 and its editor killed by drug smugglers in 1986.

*September 17*

**BOMBING: Cali, Colombia** A shopping center and two banks were bombed, killing one security guard.

**MURDER: Danby, Vt.** George Peacock, 76, and his wife, Catherine, 73, were discovered stabbed to death. Officials thought they were slain on Sept. 14.

*September 18*

**DRUGS: Connecticut** Louis Atherton, 51, was arrested and charged with distributing cocaine. His New London minimall was confiscated as collateral against a bond for his half brother, Alberto Howe, who had been charged with possession of and intent to distribute cocaine and left the state after Atherton's arrest.

**ESCAPE: East Kilbride,** Scotland Jonn McHugh, 37, sentenced to a life term in prison for murder, was arrested after his Sept. 16 escape from Hartwood Hospital, a psychiatric facility in Lanarkshire.

**FRAUD: Oklahoma City, Okla.** Charles J. Bazarian Jr. was charged, here and in Los Angeles, Calif., with defrauding two now-defunct Orange County, Calif., savings and loans and the Department of Housing and Urban Development after allegedly using promissory notes for real estate with overstated value as collateral to secure loans.

**MURDER: Los Angeles, Calif.** Anthony Jerome Gardner, 19, who frequently reported to police drug activity in his neighborhood, was killed in an apparently random drive-by shooting. A 17-year-old youth was arrested Dec. 9 as the alleged triggerman.

**MURDER: New York, N.Y.** Joseph Fama, 18, James Patino, 24, Keith Mondello, 18, Pasquale Raucci, 19, and Joseph Serrano, 19, pleaded innocent to charges of murder in the Aug. 23 slaying of Yusuf Hawkins in Bensonhurst, Brooklyn.

**SUICIDE: Temple Terrace, Calif.** Cathy Heiland, 34, the mother of Karl Heiland, 14, whose body was found July 27 in a ditch after allegedly being strangled and raped by Brian Charles Hodge, 24, committed suicide.

*September 19*

**BOMBING: Niger** A bomb exploded on board the French airline UTA Flight 772 as the DC-10 jetliner was airborne over a desert and killed all 171 passengers and crew.

*September 20*

**CONSPIRACY: Liverpool, England** Douglas Wood, 38, and his accountant, Anthony Ashton, 39, were convicted for conspiring to murder a teenager, whom Wood thought forced his son to go out on a boat. The son died in a boating accident.

**EXECUTION: Huntsville, Texas** James Paster, 44, a former Elvis Presley impersonator, was executed for the contract murder of Robert Edward Howard, 38, in Houston for which he received a $1,000 payment and a motorcycle from Howard's former wife.

**JUDICIAL MISCONDUCT: Montpelier, Vt.** William Hill, 72, retired state Supreme Court justice, was found guilty of judicial misconduct by the state Supreme Court after he used his influence to try to hasten an investigation of Jane Wheel, an assistant judge at the time.

**MURDER: Brisbane, Calif.** The nude body of Cheryl Chambers, 34, was found, bringing to seven the number of prostitutes slain in the San Francisco Bay Area within eight weeks, apparently by the same killer.

**MURDER: Portland, Maine** The state Supreme Court denied a request for release from custody of the Department of Mental Health and Mental Retardation by Bryce Worcester, 35, ruled innocent by reason of insanity of murder in the Dec. 3, 1974, shootings of Duane and Shirley Worcester, his father and stepmother.

**MURDER: Santa Monica, Calif.** Stanley Bernard Davis, 27, was convicted of auto theft, arson, kidnapping, robbery, and murder in connection with the Sept. 30, 1985, abduction and murder of Brian Edward Harris, 20, and Michelle Anne Boyd, 19. Davis was also convicted of the 1984 kidnapping and robbery of David Kingsmill.

**POLITICAL CORRUPTION: Athens, Greece** Andreas Papandreou, former prime minister, was ordered by Parliament to stand trial before a special court on charges of accepting the proceeds of a crime, receiving bribes, and breach of faith in connection with an alleged $210 million bank embezzlement.

**RACKETEERING: Illinois** Leonard Keller was charged with currency reporting violations and racketeering after reputedly using currency exchanges to launder money presented by undercover officials as cocaine profits. Eleven others were charged in the scheme and 67 currency exchanges nationwide were seized.

**RAPE: Cambridge, Mass.** Kevin Watkins, 24, formerly a Harvard Law School student, was indicted on assault and battery and rape charges after allegedly attacking a woman on Dec. 11, 1988, when she went to get a videotape that showed her nude.

**TRESPASS: Braintree, Mass.** Robert Jabaily, Paul Shinney, Paul Shanhan, and Wayne Martin were arrested on trespassing charges alter they blocked traffic entering Clean Harbors Inc., where a toxic-waste incinerator may be installed.

*September 21*

**ASSASSINATION: Beirut, Lebanon** Nazem al-Kaderi, 73, a Sunni Muslim legislator in the Lebanese Parliament was shot to death by three gunmen who also killed Kaderi's police bodyguard and wounded two bystanders.

**DRUGS: Tampa, Fla.** Patricia Margaret Ryan, 24, an AIDS-infected prostitute, was ordered to jail for 30 months on a charge of cocaine possession, after failing to comply with her earlier sentences of probation and house arrest.

**FRAUD: New York, N.Y.** Joseph LaSala and Susan Paisley of Astradyne Computer Industries Inc., entered guilty pleas to charges they falsified documents in order to quality Medicaid recipients for government aid.

**FRAUD: New York, N.Y.** Shayne Walters, 32, a salesman for R.R. Donnelley & Sons, the Chicago-based printer for *Business Week* magazine, pleaded guilty to charges that he engaged in insider trading based on stock tips he received from the "Inside Wall Street" column.

**FRAUD: Santa Ana, Calif.** Defense contractor Swedlow Inc. was indicted on charges of falsifying inspection reports in order to diminish the seriousness of cracks in the windshields of B-1B bombers. Norman Gene Nixon, 53, a vice-president of the firm was also named in the indictment.

**MURDER: El Capitan State Beach, Calif.** Phillip Bogdanoff, 49, was shot dead at this secluded nude beach. His wife, Diana Bogdanoff, 41, her daughter, Stephanie Joy Allen, 18, and Allen's boyfriend, Brian Keith Stafford, 21, were arrested.

**POLITICAL CORRUPTION: Zurich, Switzerland** Former Justice Minister Elizabeth Kopp was charged with violating the state secrecy laws after she warned her husband that he should resign from Shakarchi Trading Co., which was under investigation for drug money laundering.

*September 22*

**DRUGS: Wrentham, Mass.** Amalie Ragusa, 56, her sons John, 27, and Bruno, 18, and seven others were arraigned on drug charges stemming from a cocaine distribution ring operating from Ragusa's suburban home.

**FRAUD: Los Angeles, Calif.** Reputed mobster Martin Taccetta, 38, was charged with establishing a bogus company, Ollinor Video Products Inc., for the purpose of defrauding competing companies of $1 million in videotape equipment used to produce pornographic films. Three others were also charged.

**MURDER: Kansas City, Mo.** Bryan Sheppard, 18, was indicted on charges he set off an explosion that killed six area firefighters. Sheppard reportedly started the fire in order to steal explosives from a construction site.

**MURDER: Markham, Ill.** Merrionette Park police officer Thomas Medeiros, 32, was charged with the shooting death of Kenneth Wayne, 23, a bystander during a bungled drug rip-off. Also charged were Medeiros' brother Steven, 23, and Larry Lietz, 27.

**MURDER: New York, N.Y.** Maurice Quinton, 60, was charged with the stabbing death of Wendy Strong, 26, his live-in girlfriend who was apparently killed during a fight.

**MURDER: Orange Free State, South Africa** The body of Frank Budd, father of international distance runner Zola Budd, was found shotgunned to death in his farmhouse near Bloemfontein.

**MURDER: Richmond, Va.** The state Supreme Court upheld the rape and murder convictions of Timothy W. Spencer, 26, who was found guilty of killing Susan Tucker and Debbie Dudley Davis in 1987. His conviction was based on DNA evidence.

**MURDER: Shelby County, Ala.** Samford University student Rex Bartley Copeland, 20, was found stabbed to death at his apartment. He was apparently killed during an argument with his debate coach, William Lee Slagle, 42, who fled and sent confessions to officials.

### September 23

**ASSAULT: Dorchester, Mass.** Tien Lou, 30, and Nhieu Nguyen, 35, were arrested following a bizarre shooting incident in which Lou was accused of ramming his vehicle into a parked car belonging to Nguyen, who retaliated by opening fire with a gun.

**ASSAULT: New York, N.Y.** Dr. Efrain Go, 37, was stabbed four times with a barbecue fork after a woman walked into the Bronx-Lebanon Hospital and asked for the head doctor. Roberta Nardine was charged with the wounding.

**DRUGS: Chicago, Ill.** Police confiscated 352 pounds of marijuana concealed in suitcases carried by Gusavo Mora, 27, Ramone Silva, 25, and Rafael Salinas, 21, who were arrested as they stepped off a plane at O'Hare International Airport arriving from Tucson, Ariz.

**LAW ENFORCEMENT: New York, N.Y.** Police fatally shot Howell Freeman, 27, and wounded Jorge Garcia, 36, a bystander caught in a crossfire between police and attempted robbery suspects, Freeman and Cahill Berry, 24, who escaped. Also wounded were the would-be victim, Patrick Hyde, and officer Michael Hinrichs, 27.

**MURDER: California** Gang violence resulted in the deaths of Richard Trevino and Jose Juan Espana, both 19, in two unrelated incidents. Lashawnte Taylor, 18, was arrested for the Trevino shooting.

### September 24

**MURDER: New York, N.Y.** The bodies of 19-month-old Carmen "Elsie" Santana and her baby sitter, 41-year-old Jaunita Bodre-Guzman, were found in the Bronx apartment building in which they lived one day after the two had disappeared. Neighbor Ricardo Corbin, 24, was charged with the killings on Sept. 28.

**MURDER: Pomona, Calif.** Cornelio Perez Ruiz, 18,

Vincent Salazar, 20, and Eduardo Cruz, 17, were shot and killed by three to six men riding in a small truck.

### September 25

**MURDER: Lyons, Ill.** John Cazzato, 48, was found shot dead in the parking lot of a tavern, while his apparent assailant, Raymond Ricci, 40, was found wounded following a shootout between the two men, who reportedly had a long-standing feud.

**ROBBERY: Bolton, England** A masked gunman stole a car, robbed 80 from off-license operator Zahir Ahmed, stole a second and third car, and then a fourth after forcing Richard Palframan into the trunk. Palframan escaped shortly after, but the gunman continued his spree, stealing a fifth car, attempting to steal three more, firing at another car, and locking the driver of the fifth stolen car, Barton Hansen, in that trunk for more than eight hours before fleeing.

### September 26

**DRUGS: Brockton, Mass.** Josephine Pellegrini, 23, was indicted on drug distribution charges for ingesting cocaine when she was pregnant, becoming the first Massachusetts woman charged with harming an unborn child. Her live-in boyfriend, Aaron Jackson, 26, was indicted on charges of burning the child's feet.

**DRUGS: Washington, D.C.** Keith Jackson, 18, was arrested and charged with distributing the same crack cocaine that President George Bush held up on television to underscore the seriousness of the U.S. drug problem. The drug was seized across the street from the White House.

**MOB VIOLENCE: Randolph County, Ill.** Inmate James Bailey, 34, was shot and killed and 21 others wounded when a prison fight erupted at the Menard Correctional Center.

**MURDER: Arnhern Land, Australia** Aboriginal artist Dick Ngueli Ngueli, alias Muru Muru, and four members of his family were found shot to death at their camp in the Northern Territory.

**MURDER: Philippines** William Thompson, 45, and Donald G. Buchner, 44, both retired from the U.S. Air Force, were shot and killed apparently by Communist guerrillas 12 miles from Clark Air Base.

**RAPE: New York, N.Y.** Accused of being Brooklyn's Bicycle Rapist, Willie Gonzalez, 25, was arrested and charged with having committed a series of rapes between Jan. 16 and Apr. 10.

**TERRORISM: New York, N.Y.** Accused Palestinian terrorist Mahmmoud Abed Atta Ahmad, 36, was ordered extradited to Israel to stand trial for an Apr. 12, 1986 machine gun attack on a civilian bus traveling through the Occupied West Bank.

### September 27

**BRIBERY: Boston, Mass.** Retired Boston police detective Joseph Lundbohm pleaded not guilty to charges that he received bribes from a North End bookmaker linked with the Angiulo crime family.

**FRAUD: New York, N.Y.** Sheldon Kanoff, 53, and Albert

Weiss, 44, both former presidents of F.D. Roberts Securities Inc., pleaded guilty to fraud and conspiracy. Both admitted defrauding investors of $68 million through their defunct penny stock brokerage firm.

**MURDER: St. Clair County, Ill.** Jolaine Lanman, a 34-year-old pregnant woman, was found shot to death with her 3-year-old son. Dale Anderson, 38, was charged with the murders.

**PRISONS: San Antonio, Texas** Attorney General Richard Thornburgh revealed plans to construct 3,000 new federal prison cells using money and assets seized from drug trafficking.

**RAPE: Los Angeles, Calif.** Paul Garcia, 38, Yolanda Garcia, 28, and Margarita Ruvalcaba, 30, accused of imprisoning and raping two female Salvadoran refugees in the back of a camper, pleaded not guilty.

**THEFT: Beverly Hills, Calif.** Police detectives raided art galleries in the San Fernando Valley, Orange County, and here, seizing at least 1,700 possible forgeries. Frank de Marigny, 38, was charged with grand theft.

### September 28

**EXECUTION: Johannesburg, South Africa** Convicted murderers, Alfred Ndela, 24, and Nafton Mchunu, 25, were given a stay of execution by the Supreme Court.

**EXTORTION: Philadelphia, Pa.** Bruno Skerianz, 52, pleaded not guilty to charges that he extorted $10 million from E.I. du Pont de Nemours & Co.

**FRAUD: Gainesville, Fla.** Sports agents Gerald Gratenstein, John Kasber, Glenn Halt, and Greg Latimer pleaded guilty to charges that they made secret payments to former football and basketball players during the players' college careers.

**MURDER: New Milford, Conn.** Eighteen-year-old Dawn March, who later claimed to be possessed by demons, allegedly threw her 5-month-old daughter into the Housatonic River.

**RACKETEERING: New York, N.Y.** Lorenzo "Fat Cat" Nichols, 32, who once allegedly controlled cocaine distribution in southeastern Queens, pleaded guilty to racketeering charges involving two murders.

### September 29

**CHILD ABUSE: Tampa, Fla.** Rufus Ford Jr., 23, already charged with his wife's murder, had his Sept. 21 conviction for abusing his 2-year-old daughter, who died from her injuries, set aside and a new trial ordered.

**DRUGS: Los Angeles, Calif.** More than 21 tons of cocaine was seized from a warehouse in the Sylmar neighborhood, marking the largest such seizure in history. Federal authorities also recovered more than $10 million in cash and arrested three suspects, including James Romero McTague. Carlos Tapia Ponce, 68, and two others were arrested in Las Vegas, Nev., on Sept. 30.

**DRUGS: Los Angeles County, Calif.** Twenty people were arrested, $180,000 in cash was seized, and small amounts of cocaine was recovered by sheriff's deputies and FBI agents.

**EXTORTION: Chicago, Ill.** Alleged organized crime enforcer Frank Schweihs, 59, and co-defendant Anthony Daddino, 60, were convicted of extorting money from a pornographer in the city's Old Town neighborhood.

**MURDER: Los Angeles, Calif.** Suk Kyung Baek, 30, surrendered to police after allegedly murdering his wife Kwang Kim, 28, her mother, Jun Eui Kim, 65, and wounding his wife's sister, Kwang Shin, 35, and his 15-year-old nephew.

**SUICIDE: Dannemora, N.Y.** Christopher Shipman, 28, serving 20 to 40 years for the kidnapping, rape, and attempted murder of a 5-year-old girl, was found hanged in his jail cell at the Clinton Correctional Facility, an apparent suicide.

### September 30

**ESCAPE: East Sussex, England** Convicted murderer Richard Dennick, 22, escaped from Lewes prison, apparently by using a rope fashioned from blankets.

**HIJACKING: New York, N.Y.** Haitian soldiers Edouine Noel, 24, Nicolas Mormil, 23, and Jean Charlston Beinamie, 23, were arrested at Kennedy International Airport when American Airlines Flight 658 landed, carrying 224 passengers and the three hijackers who sought political asylum.

**ROBBERY: Chicago, Ill.** Darshell Armour, 29, was arrested and charged with attempted robbery for allegedly attacking James Ahern, 57, who, though hampered by arthritis in his legs and feet, managed to throw his attacker down a flight of stairs before hailing police.

### October 1

**ESCAPE: Bridgewater, Mass.** Three convicted rapists escaped from a treatment center for the sexually dangerous. Authorities later recaptured John R. McCabe, 25, and James LeBlanc, 28, at a Wareham, Mass., boarding house.

**LAW ENFORCEMENT: New York, N.Y.** FBI agents shot and killed off-duty firefighter Steven Lopez, 38, during a confrontation with agents in which Lopez pulled out an assault rifle. Described as mentally disturbed, Lopez believed the FBI were tapping his phones and had robbed his apartment.

**MURDER: Harrisburg, Pa.** One of the FBI's 10 most wanted fugitives, Pedro Luis Estrada Jr., was apprehended by police after a viewer who saw Estrada featured on the television show "America's Most Wanted." Estrada was wanted in connection with three drug-related murders in New York, N.Y.

**MURDER: South Oak Cliff, Texas** Witnesses said church deacon Gerald King, 30, shot and killed two other deacons, Jack Earl Ray, 51, and Artis Weaver, 60, and wounded a third shortly after services ended at the Living Testimony Baptist Church. King was arrested Oct. 5 in Dayton, Ohio.

**ROBBERY: Hollywood, Calif.** After committing a string of robberies at several Melrose Avenue restaurants, Ronald Hopson, 33, and Paul Cohen, 37, were arrested at the Hollywood Seven Star Motel and charged with 11 holdups during the past several months.

### October 2

**ASSAULT: New York, N.Y.** High on cocaine, 39-year-old Sergio Vega admittedly mutilated his sleeping wife's hands with a machete, then drove through the Bronx in a car, hitting a 1-year-old girl and a 35-year-old woman. Vega eventually crashed into the 34th precinct stationhouse and surrendered to police.

**ATTEMPTED MURDER: New York, N.Y.** A Queens Supreme Court justice ruled that the testimony of Mildred Greene, 61, who was murdered Oct. 4, 1987, three days after giving an eyewitness account of a gun battle would be admissible in court in the case against Derrick Kornegay, 23, in his trial for Greene's murder.

**MURDER: Wausau, Wis.** Lori Esker, 20, was charged with murder for the strangling death of former schoolmate Lisa Cihaski, 21, who was soon to be engaged to William Buss, the man that Esker apparently wanted to marry herself. Esker pleaded not guilty on Dec. 1.

## October 3

**ASSASSINATION: Arauca, Colombia** Catholic Bishop Jesus Jaramillo Monsalve, 72, was abducted and killed, along with the Reverend Jose Munoz Pareja. The National Liberation Army, a group led by a former priest, was suspected of the killings.

**DRUGS: Bogota, Colombia** The Supreme Court upheld President Virgilio Barco Vargas' order that suspected Colombian drug traffickers could be extradited to face charges in the U.S.

**DRUGS: Cedar Lake, Ill.** Police arrested Arid "Sleepy" Hardy Rivera, 37, the leader of a 16-member drug ring known as the "Balloon People", so named because they used colorful balloons to transport cocaine and heroin. Other ring members, all of whom used the names of the Seven Dwarfs to hide their identities, were also arrested.

**ROBBERY: Long Beach, Calif.** Robert Michael Graham, 33, known as the "Mr. Magoo Bandit" because of his thick eyeglasses, was arrested along with getaway driver Kraig Fujinaka, 30, minutes after robbing a Great Western Savings bank. Graham was wanted for 22 other robberies in the past seven months.

**SEXUAL ASSAULT: Skokie, Ill.** Scott Welty, 39, suspended from his duties as a high school teacher, was indicted on charges he beat and sexually assaulted a 14-year-old girl in April 1987. The girl recognized her attacker when she walked into his classroom on the first day of the new school year.

**SEXUAL MISCONDUCT: Anchorage, Alaska** Police raided an administrative meeting at Bartlett High School and over the next two days searched for documents to be used in the investigation of Gordon Carlson, 44, a teacher accused of having sexual relations with a 17-year-old student.

## October 4

**ATTEMPTED MURDER: Topsham, Maine** Former nursing home employee Olian Small, 36, was indicted on charges of attempted murder for allegedly trying to kill an 81-year-old woman by tying a knot in her oxygen tube.

**COMPUTER CRIME: Levittown, N.Y.** A 15-year-old boy, Brian Hatten, was arrested for using his personal computer to access the computer system at Grumman Corp., a defense and aerospace contractor. No damage was done, but the boy was able to gather information from Sept. 5 to Oct. 3.

**DRUGS: Gulf of Mexico** The U.S. Coast Guard confiscated 5 tons of cocaine aboard the Panamanian chartered *Zedom Sea* off the Yucatan peninsula. The cocaine was valued at $525 million—the third largest drug seizure in U.S. history. Eight men and one woman aboard the ship were arrested.

**DRUGS: Harlingen, Texas** Police officers seized 9 tons of cocaine, worth $1 billion, in the second largest drug seizure in U.S. history. Two Mexican nationals and a San Antonio man were also arrested.

**DRUGS: Luxembourg City, Luxembourg** Adaline Brigitte Garcia, the wife of former Drug Enforcement Administration agent Darnell Garcia, 42, charged with drug trafficking and money laundering, was arrested with Maria Angie Zuniga on charges of concealing a $3 million European bank account.

**FRAUD: Los Angeles, Calif.** The owners of Ramona Savings & Loan in Orange, Donald P. Mangano Sr., 52, and John L. Molinaro, 48, were convicted of bank fraud and conspiracy for their part in the failure of the company in September 1986.

**RAPE: Fort Lauderdale, Fla.** A jury acquitted Steven Lamar Lord of rape because the 22-year-old victim was wearing clothing that suggested she "asked for it," according to one juror. Another juror said, "She was up to no good the way she was dressed."

**THEFT: Chicago, Ill.** Charges were dismissed against two employees of Peoples Gas Light and Coke Co. after Nathaniel King revealed to authorities that the allegations of stealing gas meters was an elaborate hoax. Eventually charges were dropped against the 30 other employees supposedly involved in the scheme.

## October 5

**ASSAULT: Anaheim, Calif.** Fifteen-year-old Cory Robb walked into a Loara High School drama class armed with a 12-gauge shotgun, ordered the teacher out of the room, and took the class hostage. Robb wounded one student, 15-year-old Tony Lopez. Robb surrendered to police after 40 minutes.

**MURDER: New York, N.Y.** Six-year-old Zainab Abdussalaam was pushed to her death from a tenth-floor window, her 3-year-old brother, Husein, was also pushed, but survived, and her mother, Ameenah Abdussalaam, 32, was about to push her 1-year-old sister out the window when passing firefighters broke into the apartment and stopped her. The woman apparently planned on pushing all five of her children out and then following them.

**MURDER: Oakland, Calif.** The naked body of prostitute Sharon F. Frazier, 23, was discovered hanging from a walnut tree in a city park. Frazier was the sixth prostitute in two months to be murdered, but police were unsure the deaths were the work of a serial killer.

**MURDER: Skokie, Ill.** Peter Weber, 20, was reindicted on charges of concealing a murder in the Oct. 27, 1988, death of his girlfriend, Marie Pompilio, 18. The new charges were added to an earlier indictment charging Weber with the murder.

**RACKETEERING: Newark, N.J.** An indictment unsealed in court charged Leo M. Eisenberg, 68, Richard S. Cannistraro, 36, and Richard O. Bertoli, 56, with operating a penny stock fraud scheme that bilked customers of more than $10 million.

**RAPE: New York, N.Y.** Jermain Robinson, 15, agreed to testify against six of the accused rapists in the Apr. 19 Central Park jogger rape case in return for a promise that he would receive no more than a year in jail.

## October 6

**BRIBERY: New Haven, Conn.** Advertising agency Young & Rubicam Inc., its New York branch president Arthur R. Klein, and a former vice president, Thomas Spangenberg, were indicted on charges involving a kickback scheme which allowed the agency to win the Jamaica Tourist Board account in 1981. Two Jamaican officials and ad agency vice president Steven McKenna were also indicted.

**CHILD MOLESTATION: Palatine, Ill.** A 15-year-old mentally disabled girl was allegedly sexually assaulted in a van operated by the Little City Foundation. Child care worker Nathaniel Evans, 33, was later charged with the incident.

**FORGERY: Chicago, Ill.** A grand jury indicted Mary Smith on charges of using the identity and teaching credentials of a former friend, Lynda Haig, 42, to work in public schools since December 1987.

**MURDER: Los Angeles, Calif.** Kent Derek Parish, 21, and Ronald Lewis Fort, 20, were charged in connection with the shooting death of Richard Ronald Davis, 19, who was trying to sell his sports car when he was killed by two men posing as buyers in September.

**MURDER: Providence, R.I.** Arthur Stanley, 23, was charged with the bludgeoning death of his father, Noah Stanley, 51, after he confessed to the crime which resulted from a fight over the use of the family car.

**MURDER: Silver Spring, Md.** Calvin A. Stafford, 32, was charged with the murder of his roommate, Anita Faye Bowling, 28, who was allegedly strangled, her body placed in a dumpster, and later incinerated.

**MURDER: Somerville, Tenn.** Diane Oakley, 38, wife of slain high school coach Kenny Oakley, 42, was charged with conspiring with her 16-year-old lover, David Britt, to murder her husband. Britt, already charged with the killing, was an inmate at the John S. Wilder Youth Development Center, where Mrs. Oakley worked as a teacher's aide.

**THEFT: White Plains, N.Y.** Sherman Krisher, 27, former curator for the Museum of Cartoon Art in Rye, was sentenced to five years' probation, 500 hours of community service, and pay $45,000 restitution after confessing to stealing more than 100 pieces of art from the museum.

## October 7

**ASSAULT: New York, N.Y.** Suspect Dwight Johnson, 19, was charged with the shooting of 24-year-old police officer William Chisholm, whose fiancee was Johnson's former girlfriend.

**ESCAPE: Chicago, Ill.** Convicted arson murderer James Kluppelberg walked free from jail after his records were changed to allow a $25,000 bond posted though a judge had ordered him held without bail. He was rearrested in Macon, Ga., on Oct. 12, and the officer who allegedly doctored the records, Robert Velasquez, 31, was charged with official mis-

conduct on Oct. 18.

**EXECUTION: Iran** The government hanged 31 people convicted of drug trafficking, bringing the total number of executed drug dealers since Jan. 1 to more than 800.

**MURDER: Clackamas County, Ore.** The nude body of Deborah Sue Spicer, 27, was seen hurled off a cliff into the Clackamas River by a bearded man. An autopsy showed she died of multiple stab wounds and trauma from the fall.

**MURDER: Worcester, England** Drug abuse and AIDS counsellor, Elizabeth Page-Alucard, 41, was found bludgeoned to death in her office run by the national charity, Turning Point. David Laurence Bingham, 30, was later charged with her murder.

**TERRORISM: White Bear Lake, Minn.** The Ukranian family of Vladimir and Ekaterina Doroshkevich, who recently fled the Soviet Union because of religious persecution, began receiving death threats by phone. Vandals later burned a cross on their lawn and sprayed graffiti on the walls of the church that sponsored the Doroshkevich's resettlement.

**THEFT: Dorchester, Mass.** David Joyner, a 26-year-old homeless man, stole an empty Massachusetts Bay Transportation Authority bus and led police on a five-minute chase before being stopped and arrested. The bus driver had left the bus briefly at a station to use the bathroom.

## October 8

**BOMBING: East London, South Africa** Trevor Tutu, son of Archbishop Desmond M. Tutu, was arrested at the airport here for threatening to blow up the airplane he was aboard. In August Tutu was sentenced to 18 months in prison for staging a bombing hoax at the Johannesburg airport on Dec. 31.

**DRUGS: Port Newark, N.J.** Federal agents confiscated nearly 900 pounds of cocaine hidden in a 13-and-a-half ton load of apples being trucked from Los Angeles to New York. Truck driver Segundino Reyes Flores, 36, and Carlos Arturo Ceron, 33, were arrested.

## October 9

**MURDER: Llanelli, England** Robert Naylor, 37, was charged in the stabbing death of his 32-year-old brother, John.

**MURDER: Mooresville, Mo.** Cattle ranchers Ray and Faye Copeland were arrested for conspiracy to commit theft for their roles in an alleged cattle buying operation. Authorities later began a search of their home and property to uncover clues in the disappearance of three transients, who had worked for the couple, after a former employee saw a human skull and a leg bone at the Copeland farm.

## October 10

**ASSAULT: New York, N.Y.** Anthony Sorrentino, 18, James E. Hynes, 17, and Joseph Guben, 16, were arrested for the Oct. 8 anti-Semitic beating of Jewish Brooklyn College students Juhoshua Fogel and Steven Weisberg.

**BOMBING: Anderson, Ind.** A 16-year-old student was arrested and charged with making two pipe-bombs that were detonated at Anderson High School.

**DRUGS: Bogota, Colombia** Jose Rafael Abello Silva, 34, believed to be the fourth-ranked leader of the Medellin drug cartel, was arrested. He was extradited to the U.S. on Oct. 29 to face drug trafficking charges.

**DRUGS: Chicago, Ill.** Chrisondra Bibbs, 46, a Chicago elementary school teacher, and her husband Donald Bibbs, 48, were among nine people arrested and charged in connection with a drug ring smuggling heroin from Nigeria to the U.S.

**DRUGS: Los Angeles, Calif.** Hugo Fernando Castillon, 32, James Romero McTague, 41, Romero Mauricio Monroy, 36, and Miguel Chavez, alias Miguel Gonzalez, 34, were arraigned on drug trafficking charges related to the record cocaine seizure of 21.4 tons on Sept. 29.

**DRUGS: Newark, N.J.** Drug Enforcement Administration agents arrested two people and seized 871 pounds of cocaine worth $40 million from a truck containing apples from California and Washington.

**FRAUD: New York, N.Y.** Jeffrey Feldman, 42, and Paul Foont, 40, were indicted on charges of involvement in a tax-fraud ring from 1979 to 1985 that generated false tax writeoffs totalling more than $4 billion.

**KIDNAPPING: Framingham, Mass.** Gary Porter, 39, surrendered to authorities after allegedly kidnapping his girlfriend, 37-year-old Sharon Feinberg, for the second time on Oct. 8. Porter had reportedly abducted Feinberg on July 22 from the Marlborough pharmacy where she worked.

**MURDER: Attleboro, Mass.** Eric A. Avellar, 29, pleaded not guilty to charges that he killed his infant son, who died with a fractured skull and broken ribs.

**MURDER: Brockton, Mass.** The body of 18-year-old Michelle Foster was found. Her boyfriend, Paul Kent Stockwell, 20, was arrested on Oct. 11 and charged with strangling her.

**MURDER: Medellin, Colombia** Gunmen killed advertising manager Martha Lux Lopez Lopez, 36, and circulation manager Miguel Arturo Soler Rodriguez, 46, both of *El Espectador,* an anti-drug cartel newspaper.

**RAPE: New York, N.Y.** State Supreme Court justice Thomas Galligan issued a gag order to attorneys involved in the Central Park "wilding" rape trial of six youths accused of assaulting a 28-year-old investment banker.

**VANDALISM: Wakefield, Mass.** Bickford G. White Jr. and Craig S. Cooper, both 19, were charged with spraypainting anti-Semitic, white supremacist symbols and phrases on buildings and cars. The graffiti was found hours before the beginning of Yom Kippur.

## October 11

**FRAUD: Window Rock, Ariz.** Peter MacDonald, suspended chairman of the Navajo Indian tribe, was charged with 107 criminal offenses including election law violations, bribery, fraud, and extortion.

**MURDER: Chicago, Ill.** Two teenagers entered a math classroom in Harper High School and stabbed to death Chester Dunbar, 16, in front of his classmates and teacher.

**MURDER: Glen Burnie, Md.** The body of Gladys Faye Beauchamp, a 37-year-old Baltimore woman, was found near a bicycle path. Police suspected her killer was connected with a series of rapes and robberies in the area.

**MURDER: Seattle, Wash.** The remains of Andrea Marion Childers, believed to be the forty-first victim of the Green River Serial Killer, were found near the Seattle-Tacoma International Airport. Childers had been missing since 1983.

**MURDER: Staining, England** The body of 82-year-old Jim Parkinson was found, apparently beaten to death by a burglar.

**SMUGGLING: Romania** Dr. David Ormerod, a 27-year-old British geology lecturer, was arrested for trying to smuggle an ethnic woman out of Romania. His parents later paid a £15,000 fine and he was released.

## October 12

**CHILD ABUSE: Teesside, England** Stephen Smith, 27, was sentenced to three years in prison for forcing bleach down the throat of a 14-month-old child he was babysitting.

**ESCAPE: London, England** Robert Taylor, 32, held on armed robbery charges, was arrested after escaping while being transferred to a hospital Aug. 9. Police surrounded the house where he was before he gave up peacefully after nine hours.

**KIDNAPPING: Northwich, England** Brothers Christopher and Ian Medland were charged with the September kidnapping of Alan Frew, an ICI executive.

**MURDER: Bloemfontein, South Africa** Chris Barnard, 26, confessed to the Sept. 22 murder of Frank Budd, athlete Zola Budd's father.

**MURDER: Los Angeles, Calif.** Juan Gilberto Hernandez-Parra and four others were indicted on charges in the 1985 torture-murders of John Walker, 38, and Albert Radelat, 35. The two men were mistaken for Drug Enforcement Administration agents.

**TERRORISM: Paris, France** Enzo Calvitti, Anna Mutini, and Dario Faccio, suspected members of the Red Brigades, were arrested.

**TRESPASS: Los Angeles, Calif.** Controversial comic Andrew Dice Clay was arrested on charges of trespassing at Ben Frank's restaurant, six years after the owner had banned him from entering the 24-hour diner.

## October 13

**DRUGS: Cali, Colombia** Victor Eduardo Mera Mosquera, 36, convicted in absentia in the U.S. for drug trafficking five years ago, was arrested by police.

**DRUGS: New York, N.Y.** Kevin Ashley, 23, was arrested on assault charges after a mob attacked five construction workers helping police arrest Keith Smalls, 20, on drug charges. Three of the workers were injured.

**MURDER: Boston, Mass.** Darin F. Bufalino, 28, indicted for the 1984 murder of Vincent DeNino, 27, was extradited from Spain. DeNino was shot for refusing to pay a $10,000 drug debt.

**MURDER: San Francisco, Calif.** Frankie Don Huie Jr.'s plea of "homosexual panic" was rejected by a state appeals court. Huie, convicted of the 1987 murder of Steve Mayeda, claimed his actions were prompted by a homosexual advance and he had acted out of fear and in self-defense.

## October 14

**CRAB MOLESTATION: Palatka, Fla.** Four men began serving their "sentence" for having taken crab traps from the St. Johns River. Each agreed to walk back and forth over a St. Johns River bridge carrying signs which read, "It is a felony punishable by prison and-or a $5,000 fine to molest crab pots. I know because I molested one."

**DRUGS: Bogota, Colombia** Roberto Carlini Arrico, 37, Bernardo Pelaez Roldan, 44, and Ana Rodriguez de Tamayo, 50, were turned over to U.S. marshals and extradited to Miami, Fla., for drug trafficking charges. Pelaez Roldan was already convicted in absentia in Detroit, Mich., in 1984.

### October 15

**CRIMINAL JUSTICE: South Africa** Walter Max Ulyate Sisulu, 77, who had been imprisoned for 26 years, and seven other political activists were released from prison.

**DRUGS: Yucatan, Mexico** Ten men, including Luis Alfredo Aguilar Castro and Ricardo Isunza Ochoa who are nephews of two leading Medellin cocaine cartel leaders, were arrested at a clandestine airstrip where a drug ring was based.

### October 16

**FRAUD: Chicago, Ill.** Former state's attorney aide Joanne Kucinski, 41, pleaded guilty to election fraud charges, becoming the twenty-first Democratic precinct worker to do so since the 1986 petition drive for a nonpartisan mayoral election.

**MURDER: Livingston County, Mo.** The bodies of Paul Jason Cowart, 21, and John W. Freeman and Jimmie Dale Harvey, both 27, were discovered buried on a farm here. Each man had been shot in the head with a small-caliber bullet and at one time had been employed by Ray and Faye Copeland. The Copelands were under arrest on charges of conspiracy to commit theft in a cattle buying scheme.

**ROBBERY: Boynton Beach, Fla.** Derick Grace, 22, and Robert Lee Jackson Jr., 21, allegedly committed a robbery, led pursuing police through Palm Beach and Broward counties, ditched the stolen car, and kidnapped the driver of another car they stole. Jackson was arrested after the kidnapped driver escaped and identified Jackson for police. Grace was arrested when Jackson gave police the name of the motel where Grace was staying.

### October 17

**BOMBING: Bucaramanga, Colombia** Four employees of the Vanguardia Liberal were killed and seven others were wounded when a car bomb exploded outside the paper's offices. The newspaper has joined other papers in condemning drug traffickers.

**MURDER: Medellin, Colombia** Hector Jimenez Rodriguez, 55, a High Court judge, was shot dead, allegedly in retaliation of accused drug traffickers extradited to the U.S.

**WAR CRIMES: La Habra, Calif.** Bruno Karl Blach, 69, was arrested at his home after he was indicted in West Germany for allegedly killing three prisoners during a trip in April 1945 to the Austrian Mauthausen concentration camp. West Germany asked for extradition.

### October 18

**CHILD MOLESTATION: Los Angeles, Calif.** Charles Chavez, 33, was arrested and charged with four counts of lewd conduct involving children. Chavez was a driver for a day care center.

**DRUGS: New York, N.Y.** Shu Yan Eng, 42, known as Ah Shu and one of New York City's largest heroin distributors, was arrested and a restaurant and ice cream store were seized. Three alleged top aides were arrested Oct. 19.

**FRAUD: Indianapolis, Ind.** Joseph W. Cirillo, 37, a real estate agent who allegedly falsified Department of Housing and Urban Development (HUD) applications, and Garry W. Newman, 36, a former HUD closing agent accused of embezzlement, were indicted for fraud.

**MURDER: Austin, Texas** A request for parole was denied nurse Genene Jones, convicted in 1984 of injecting Chelsea Ann McClellan with a fatal dose of succinylcholine. The 15-month-old died Sept. 17, 1982.

**MURDER: Herford, England** Stephen Powell, 26, was remanded in custody on murder charges involving 2-year-old Michaela Woodhouse.

**MURDER: New York, N.Y.** Wesley Degeneste, 26, was arrested in connection with a robbery at the Brooklyn home of Angela Finkelstein, 23, who was murdered with her sister-in-law, Loren Naraine, 18.

**ROBBERY: Charleroi, Belgium** Two armed men robbed the post office of $6. 6 million in the largest reported Belgium robbery. Money from the Belgian National Bank had just been brought to the post office.

**TERRORISM: Jerusalem, Israel** Asman Mar'a, a 23-year-old Palestinian who pleaded guilty to 27 charges of guerrilla acts, was sentenced to a 27-year prison term by a military court.

### October 19

**BOMBING: London, England** Gerard Conlon, 35, Patrick Armstrong, 39, Paul Hill, 35, and Carole Richardson, 32, known as the "Guilford Four", were released from prison after serving 14 years for a 1974 Irish Republican Army bombing that they did not commit.

**ROBBERY: England** Thomas Gerald Corey, 31, former Partington, constable was freed on bond after his conviction for planning a robbery that netted 11,000 was appealed. Three other officers were suspended and a new inquiry was launched.

### October 20

**DRUGS: Indiana** Police arrested 201 alleged drug dealers and confiscated 160 pounds of marijuana, weapons, automobiles, and cash in 29 northern and northwestern communities in the states's largest coordinated raid ever.

**MURDER: Portland, Ore.** Heidi Dozier, 21, was strangled and bludgeoned to death allegedly by Brian Douglas Hessel, 34, who had forced her to commit sodomy before killing her.

**MURDER: South Africa** A stay of execution was granted to Butana Almond Nofomela, 32, a former policeman convicted of murdering a white farmer. Nofomela claimed he was a member of a South African security police death squad and could disclose important information.

**PERJURY: Washington, D.C.** U.S. District Court Judge

Alcee Lamar Hasting, 51, was convicted by the Senate of eight articles of impeachment for conspiracy and perjury.

**SMUGGLING: Brownsville, Texas** Fernando Macias, director of Customs Service at the Port of Brownsville and two international bridges, was arrested on charges of smuggling food, clothing, liquor, and saddles into the U.S.

## October 21

**CONSPIRACY: England** Rodney Whitchelo, 42, was charged with conspiracy to extort 1. 25 million from a subsidiary of H.J. Heinz Co., by poisoning baby food.

## October 22

**BOMBING: Lesbos, Greece** Michalis Pavlis, 33, died when a bomb exploded as he tried to plant it in a theater where Constantine Mitsotakis, leader of the New Democracy Party, was scheduled to speak.

**FENCING: White Plains, N.Y.** William So, a Queens jeweler, was arrested and charged with "selling or offering for sale articles and parts of an endangered or threatened species." Police seized 170 elephant ivory pieces.

**MURDER: Antelope Valley, Calif.** Ten-year-old Thomas Hernandez was shot dead in the home of a 12-year-old boy, who was staying with another friend while his parents were away. The 12-year-old was later charged with murder.

## October 23

**EXILE: Santiago, Chile** Labor leaders Manuel Bustos and Arturo Martinez were pardoned by President Augusto Pinochet. They were freed after serving 404 days of a 541-day internal exile imposed after they called for a general work stoppage.

**EXTORTION: Los Angeles County, Calif.** John Scotto, 28, lawyer and son of a member of the Gambino organized crime family, was indicted on forgery and extortion charges for allegedly trying to extort $176,000 from four individuals.

**FORGERY: Los Angeles, Calif.** David and Karen Missman, owners of a now-bankrupt real estate investment firm, pleaded not guilty to charges of forgery, grand theft, and securities violations.

**ILLEGAL WASTE STORAGE: New York, N.Y.** The South Nassau Communities Hospital in Oceanside was fined $20,000 for unlawful storage of infectious waste between May 5 and 12.

**MANSLAUGHTER: Chelsea, Mass.** Luis Rivera, 18, drove a stolen car into a taxi, killing his girlfriend Elizabeth Ramon, and taxi passenger, Florence Bush, and injuring eight others. Rivera was charged with manslaughter and negligent homicide.

**MURDER: Albany, N.Y.** Robert McLaughlin, 29, was awarded $1.935 million as reparations for serving six years in prison for a December 1979 murder that he did not commit.

**MURDER: Boston, Mass.** Carol Stuart was shot dead allegedly by her husband, Charles Stuart, who reported the incident as a robbery. On Jan. 4, 1990, Charles committed suicide when his brother informed police that Charles had killed Carol, who was pregnant at the time of her death.

**MURDER: Dublin, Ireland** A court directed that Paul Magee, 41, held in Ireland for a June 1981 escape from the Crumlin Road jail in Belfast, be extradited to Northern Ireland, where he would serve a life term in prison for the 1980 murder of an SAS captain.

**MURDER: Roxbury, Mass.** Aaron Watts, 21, allegedly broke the back window of a car and fatally shot James Moody, 29, in the neck.

**PORNOGRAPHY: Illinois** Edward Davis, 41, was charged with reproduction of and possession of child pornography after officials discovered videotapes in his home.

**SEXUAL ASSAULT: Markham, Ill.** Benjamin Valentine, 21, was convicted of sexually assaulting a 12-year-old and attempting to sexually assault the girl's mother after he broke into their home. Three police officers who waited outside the apartment for 27 minutes before they entered because they feared for the safety of the girl and her brother, were disciplined.

**THEFT: Barnstable, Mass.** Charles N. Rogers, 21, stole a police car and engaged local and state police in a 30-minute chase through six towns. When Rogers was arraigned, the judge ordered him to undergo psychiatric tests.

## October 24

**DRUGS: Brockton, Mass.** Police Chief Richard J. Sproules, 45, was arrested and charged with stealing cocaine from a police station evidence room beginning in 1984. He was later indicted on charges for embezzling $74,000 in city monies.

**MURDER: Jacksonville, Fla.** Brad Evans, 34, who served 14-and-a-half years of a 199-year term for the murders of white teenagers Stephen Lamont Roberts and Stephen Orlando was paroled. The youths were slain by members of the Black Liberation Army in an effort to incite racial violence.

**RACKETEERING: Chicago, Ill.** Wentworth District policeman Elbert Elfreeze, 55, pleaded guilty to racketeering and conspiracy charges for accepting $4,550 in payoffs from South Side drug dealers and gambling operators. He and 12 other policemen were indicted in 1988 in the reputed protection operation.

**RAPE: Chicago, Ill.** Donald Williams, 27, was charged with raping and robbing three women between Oct. 5 and Oct. 10, 1988, in three separate downtown locations.

**THEFT: Los Angeles, Calif.** Edwin Lopez, 26, thought to be a member of a group of thieves trained in South America, was arrested in connection with the Aug. 25 theft of $900,000 worth of jewels taken from a saleswoman for Van Lightner Jewelry in Van Nuys.

**THEFT: Los Angeles, Calif.** Lee Sonnier, a 42-year-old Beverly Hills art dealer, was charged with grand theft for not delivering artwork sold for about $872,000. Another art broker, Frank de Marigny, was arrested in September for forgery and grand theft in a widening Southern California art fraud scandal.

**TRESPASS: Memphis, Tenn.** Betty Gloyd, falsely arrested on Aug. 20, 1988, at Elvis Presley's mansion, Graceland, was awarded $65,500.

## October 25

**ARSON: Chicago, Ill.** Timothy Sayers, 17, son of former

Chicago Bears football star Gale Sayers, was charged with attempted arson for allegedly pouring a flammable liquid inside Kenwood Academy high school.

**ASSAULT: Washington, D.C.** Ohio senator John Glenn, 68, was punched in the jaw allegedly by Michael Breen, 31, who was charged with assaulting a member of Congress.

**MONEY LAUNDERING: Los Angeles, Calif.** The cash vault assistant manager at Security Pacific National Bank, Jose O. Lopez, 27, five fellow bank employees, and two others were arrested for allegedly conspiring to launder $364,000.

**MURDER: Grapevine, Texas** Lawrence Barfield, 38, was found shot and wounded in his apartment, where authorities also found the mutilated body of Veronica L. Stone, 22, who Barfield apparently killed before attempting to take his own life.

**MURDER: Livingston County, Mo.** The body of transient farm worker Wayne Warner was found buried under several bales of hay on a farm where Ray Copeland had once worked as a farmhand. Warner, who had been shot in the head, was the fourth body unearthed here in the continuing investigation of Ray and Faye Copeland.

## October 26

**DRUGS: Costa del Sol, Spain** Kristan Bennett, 20, was arrested with two Turkish men after police seized 109. 2 kilograms of heroin valued at 42 million, believed to be this country's largest single heroin seizure.

**DRUGS: Jacksonville, Fla.** Jack Carlton Reed, 59, allegedly linked to convicted Colombian drug lord Carlos Lehder Rivas, and two others were convicted of drug smuggling, while two others were acquitted.

**FRAUD: Wheaton, Ill.** Dr. Irving Starkman, 56, was convicted on four counts of theft and six counts of conspiracy to commit theft for filing about $200,000 worth of phony accident claims.

**MURDER: Boston, Mass.** The body of convicted drug smuggler and reputed Mafia associate John E. Zullo was found inside his car with bullet wounds to his head.

**MURDER: Chicago, Ill.** Omar Dixon, 20, was sentenced to 30 years in prison for the 1984 murder of 17-year-old high school basketball star Benjamin Wilson. The shooting occurred after Wilson accidentally bumped Dixon and his friend, William Moore, outside the school building. Moore fired the shots that killed Wilson after Dixon gave verbal encouragement.

**MURDER: Green Bay, Wis.** Randy C. Bockorny, 35, and his wife, Debra L. Bockorny, 34, were arrested in connection with the Oct. 7 murder of Deborah Sue Spicer, 27, in Clackamas County, Ore. The couple later pleaded innocent to the charges.

**MURDER: New York, N.Y.** Katrina Buchanan, 22, was arrested and charged with second-degree murder for killing her 2-year-old son by allegedly forcing pepper into his mouth and nose.

**MURDER: Ottawa, Canada** The Supreme Court approved the extradition to California of Charles Ng, 28, who has been charged with at least 12 sex and torture murders committed in 1984 and 1985. Ng was imprisoned on a Canadian charge of shooting a security guard.

**RAPE: New York, N.Y.** Long Island school bus driver

Robert Izzo, 39, was indicted on 143 counts of sexually assaulting 16 kindergarten pupils he transported to school.

## October 27

**ASSASSINATION: Medellin, Colombia** State leader of the leftist Patriotic Union, Gabriel Jaime Santamaria, was shot and killed by a gunman who was himself killed by security guards.

**LAW ENFORCEMENT: Chicago, Ill.** Chicago police and federal agents seized the reputed headquarters of the El Rukn street gang following federal indictments of 65 gang members and associates on charges ranging from racketeering and narcotics to murder.

**MURDER: Lake Tahoe, Calif.** The body of Dorothy Greene, 52, was found floating in the water here with a bullet wound to the head. Police later arrested and charged John Aldon Colwell, 42, with the murder.

**MURDER: New York, N.Y.** Albert Rielly, 44, was found guilty of the shooting death of his wife Annette Rielly, 47, based in part on testimony provided by his 6-year-old son.

## October 28

**MURDER: Marietta, S.C.** The dismembered body of Kathy Kessler Arnold, 31, was found stored in plastic bags in a freezer. Daniel R. Hill, 21, Julia Redding, 29, and her husband David B.D. Redding, 32, were charged with the killing.

**RAPE: New York, N.Y.** Johnny Vick, 30, was charged with rape and sodomy for allegedly dragging a woman from a nearly empty subway platform and raping her at knifepoint.

## October 29

**BURGLARY: Howard County, Md.** Richard Makofski, 35, who once made a videotape on burglary methods to be used in police training, was arrested in connection with more than 1,000 break-ins in Florida.

## October 30

**BRIBERY: Boston, Mass.** Raymond Chia Chi Cheng, 55, a reputed leader of an Asian organized crime syndicate on the East Coast, was indicted on charges of attempting to bribe an Immigration and Naturalization Service official.

**FRAUD: Philadelphia, Pa.** The trial began for General Electric Co., accused of defrauding the Defense Department of $10 million in military contracts.

**KIDNAPPING: Joliet, Ill.** Inmate Mark LaRue, 36, surrendered to officials at the Stateville Correctional Center and released unharmed the four prison employees he had held hostage for more than four hours.

**THEFT: Fairfax, Va.** Suspected serial rapist Randall Lee Breer, 28, was sentenced to ten years in prison for the theft of a car in December.

## October 31

**ASSAULT: Hackensack, N.J.** Nine security guards who worked the Oct. 11, 14, and 15 concerts for the rock group Grateful Dead at the Meadowlands Sports Complex pleaded not guilty to charges of assault relating to the injuries received by five people. Adam Katz, 19, died from his injuries.

**BRIBERY: Chicago, Ill.** Patrolman Willie Smith, 42, pleaded guilty to receiving a $5,200 payment from an undercover police officer who posed as a corrupt officer connected to an illicit gambling operation. Alleged bookmaker Thomas Dillon, 67, pleaded guilty to racketeering and extortion charges.

**FRAUD: Los Angeles, Calif.** Joseph Kasparoff, 55, owner of Super K and J.K. Precision Machining Inc., and Harold Geyer, 71, pleaded guilty to setting up a tax fraud scheme. Frank Calta, 40, pleaded guilty earlier to similar charges.

**RAPE: New York, N.Y.** Charges were dismissed against Clarence Thomas, 14, who was accused with seven other youths of taking part in the Apr. 19 "wilding" attack in Central Park in which a female jogger was raped and severely beaten.

### November 1

**CONTEMPT: Los Angeles, Calif.** Cynthia Garvey, former television celebrity and former wife of former baseball star Steve Garvey, had a 126-day jail sentence suspended after being found guilty in October of 42 counts of contempt for violating a child visitation order.

**LAW ENFORCEMENT: Florala, Ala.** Phillip James, 21, wanted for allegedly having shot and wounded Essex County, N.J., police officers Jerry DelSordo and George Bello on Oct. 26, was shot and killed by Covington County police after a high-speed car chase. James' half-brother and accomplice Alvin Gregory, 24, was arrested later.

**MURDER: Vancouver Lake Park, Ore.** The body of 4-year-old Lee Joseph Iseli, whose disappearance Oct. 29 led to a massive search operation, was found.

### November 2

**MONEY LAUNDERING: New York, N.Y.** Erasmo Taveras, Raul Quiroz, and Pedro Alegria were indicted for illegally transferring money to the Dominican Republic and Latin America through an unlicensed company.

**RAPE: Northampton, England** Trial began in the case of police constable Brian Walker, 43, accused of raping a female police officer in July 1988.

### November 3

**BOMBING: Washington, D.C.** An appeals court ruled that the evidence used against three people accused of bombing the Capitol and other government buildings does not violate the "double jeopardy" clause in the Fifth Amendment. The ruling allowed the government to proceed with its prosecution of Susan Rosenberg, Timothy Blunk, and Alan Berkman.

**DRUGS: Crofton, Md.** Russell J. Hibler, a psychologist for the National Security Agency, his wife Susan M. Hibler, both 43, and their two children were arrested on charges of drug trafficking.

**MURDER: Chicago, Ill.** Robert Lee Mitchell, alias Billy Jackson, was arrested for the 1960 murder of his former girlfriend, Billie Marie Redmon Phillips, in Dallas, Texas..

**MURDER: Chicago, Ill.** Noah Robinson, half brother of the Reverend Jesse Jackson, was indicted by a grand jury on charges of hiring El Rukn gang members to commit a murder.

**MURDER: Roxbury, Mass.** Michael P. Caputo, 39, pleaded not guilty to charges he murdered Helen Caputo, 42,

his estranged wife, and Angelina Papastamos, 69, his mother-in-law, on Sept. 1.

### November 4

**DRUGS: Bogota, Colombia** Hotel owner and reputed member of the Cali cocaine cartel Guillermo Juan Delgado Bueno, 54, was extradited to the U.S. on cocaine trafficking indictments.

**ESCAPE: Los Angeles, Calif.** Convicted rapist Christopher Rambert was recaptured after he escaped on Oct. 1 from a Massachusetts facility for the sexually dangerous.

**MURDER: Los Angeles, Calif.** Rick Hutchins and Ralph Lopez were killed In unconnected gang-related drive-by shootings.

### November 5

**MURDER: Los Angeles, Calif.** Miguel Sanchez, 19, was beaten to death with baseball bats by five teenagers who stopped his car at an intersection. Joffrey Deleon Lagadia, 18, was arrested in connection with his death.

**MURDER: Nottingham, England** Matthew Fowkes, 10, was shot through the throat with a projectile fired from an airgun. Ian Walters, 20, was charged with the murder.

**MURDER: Rio de Janeiro, Brazil** Carlos Maguinho Barbosa, 14, allegedly shot and killed Angela Machado, 36, a bystander, in a gun battle between Maguinho and a rival gang member.

### November 6

**KIDNAPPING: New York, N.Y.** Twelve-year-old Danny Wong was abducted, and then released unhurt near a Bronx subway station. The boy's father, Shih Min Wong, was arrested and charged with the July 17 shooting of Yu Sheng Zheng, 49. His confession came out during questioning by police concerning the boy's disappearance.

**MURDER: Atlanta, Ga.** Twenty-year-old William Maurice Porter, one of two men charged with abducting, raping, and killing 27-year-old Julie Love, pleaded guilty. Emmanuel Fitzgerald Hammond, believed to be the gunman, had pleaded innocent.

**MURDER: Joliet, Ill.** Trial began for Matthew Taylor, 20, one of three youths accused of killing Charles Layfield, 57, in 1988, who died when an 11-pound concrete chunk thrown from an interstate overpass crushed his skull.

**MURDER: Nashville, Tenn.** Oscar Frank Smith, 39, was charged with the Oct. 1 murder of his estranged wife and his two stepsons.

**MURDER: Wheaton, Ill.** Pamela Knuckles, convicted for the 1984 murder of her mother, Nancy Knuckles, was given another trial. Her 1985 guilty plea was based on her belief that a trial by jury was a death penalty risk.

### November 7

**ESCAPE: Hagerstown, Md.** Former Judge Paul W. Ottinger, 74, who failed to report on Sept. 1 to serve a state prison sentence after completing a federal sentence for fraud, surrendered to authorities.

**MURDER: Chicago, Ill.** Fugitive Samuel Earl Dillon

turned himself in to police after seeing himself featured on the TV show, "America's Most Wanted." Dillon was charged in connection with two 1981 murders.

**MURDER: Los Angeles, Calif.** A Superior Court judge turned down a motion to grant Kevin Dykes a new trial. Dykes was convicted of a 1986 murder based on evidence given by jailhouse informants.

**THEFT: Lawrenceville, Ga.** Donna Leeper, 43, was charged with theft and making a false statement after she collected $1,400 from school faculty and PTA members by claiming her daughter had leukemia.

### November 8

**CHILD ABUSE: New York, N.Y.** Geraldine Clay was arrested and charged with trying to sell her 11-day-old baby for $100 at the Port Authority bus terminal.

**CRIMINAL JUSTICE: Cook County, Ill.** Cook County Circuit Court Judge Donald O'Connell ruled that the relatives of the victims shot by Laurie Damm in May 1988 may file lawsuits against the woman's parents charging negligence.

**GAMBLING: Chicago, Ill.** Reputed mobsters Dominic Cortina, 64, and Donald Angelini, 63, were among seven people charged with running a multimillion dollar sports betting operation.

**MURDER: Carrollton, Ky.** Jury selection began in the trial of Larry Mahoney, 36, charged with 27 counts of murder, endangerment, assault, and driving under the influence. In 1988, he allegedly hit a church bus carrying children, killing 27 passengers.

**MURDER: Juneau, Wis.** Chad Goetsch, 19, was charged with killing his mother, Carolyn Goetsch, and wounding his father, state representative Robert R. Goetsch, with arrows shot from a hunting bow. He pleaded not guilty on Dec. 19.

**MURDER: Rosharon, Texas** Valerie Susan Taylor was charged with the stabbing death of her 4-year-old daughter Meara Brooke Taylor. Taylor allegedly became enraged when the girl accidentally broke a music box.

**MURDER: Waterbury, Conn.** Luis Robles, 35, was indicted in connection with the Aug. 4 shooting of David Morrison in Brooklyn, and with four murders in October 1988.

### November 9

**DRUGS: Mexico** Jorge Humberto Chalarca Cortes, allegedly a representative in Mexico for the Medellin drug cartel and who allegedly brought 50 tons of cocaine into the U.S., was arrested.

**DRUGS: New York, N.Y.** Elementary school principal Matthew Barnwell, 53, was arrested and charged with buying two vials of crack cocaine. His arrest touched off an investigation into corruption in the New York school system.

**ESCAPE: Boston, Mass.** Kike Secarra, 29, and Myles Gedes, 24, escaped from the Deer Island House of Correction. Secarra was serving a five-year term for manslaughter.

**FRAUD: Chicago, Ill.** Richard Lowrance, who worked as a broker in the Eurodollar pit of the Chicago Mercantile Exchange was charged with insurance fraud after he allegedly conspired with Judd Hirschberg to have his late model Mercedes Benz automobile stolen.

**FRAUD: London, England** Eleven persons were arrested and charged with fraud stemming from a share rigging scheme in the Blue Arrow Company's 1987 take over of Manpower. Corporate defendants in the case include: County NatWest, UBS Phillips & Drew Securities, and NatWest Investment Bank Ltd.

**MANSLAUGHTER: London, England** Mark Allen, 23, was convicted of arson and manslaughter, after he hired two thugs to set fire to the residence of Victor Johnson and his wife Audrey, who complained about the loud rock music he played. The couple perished in the blaze.

**MURDER: New York, N.Y.** Lucrezia Gentile, 37, of Brooklyn confessed to Supreme Court Justice Ronald Aiello that she had drowned her two-month-old son, admitting her earlier story, that the child was abducted from his stroller, was false.

**MURDER: Waukegan, Ill.** Bond was denied for Jared Fitch and Harold Hains, two Navy men indicted for the murder of Mark R. Mueller, who was battered to death with a baseball bat while fishing off the Waukegan lakefront.

**THEFT: Grasse, France** Three men were charged with the $17 million theft of artwork belonging to Pablo Picasso's daughter. Fernand Laugier, Serge Clouzeau, and Daniel Jaguin were accused of stealing the artwork from the Picasso villa in Cannes.

### November 10

**ASSAULT: Los Angeles, Calif.** Warren Lawson, 41, was arrested after a computer check revealed a 13-year-old arrest warrant. Lawson escaped from the Alabama State Prison in 1976 and remained a fugitive until he was picked up for assaulting his girlfriend.

**MURDER: Grundy County, Ill.** Keith Woyciechowski was charged with the murder of his 22-year-old finance, Kimberly Yeates, two years after she was found beaten to death in Morris, Ill.

**MURDER: Rochester Hills,** Mich. General Motors executive Glenn B. Tarr and his wife Wanda were shot to death, and their home ransacked during a robbery attempt. Their bodies were dumped in a nearby park.

### November 11

**ABDUCTION: Los Angeles, Calif.** Jose Guzman, 23, and Carlos Valenda, 22, were arrested on kidnapping charges after they allegedly abducted Blanca and Carlos Gonzales, aged 9 and 7. The children were apparently being smuggled into the U.S. from Mexico, but when the children's father failed to come up with the extra cash to complete the deal, the two men fled with the youngsters.

**DRUGS: Dover, Delaware** The Drug Enforcement Administration announced the arrest of Nathan Thomas, 23, and his brother Victor, 32, who conspired to smuggle 66 pounds of cocaine from Howard Air Force Base in Panama into Dover. The drugs were valued at $3 million.

**MURDER: Chicago, Ill.** Off duty prison guard Michael Young was shot to death outside a South Side chicken restaurant. Darryl Jefferson, 23, and James Harrison, 20, were charged with first-degree murder.

**MURDER: Montreal, Canada** Olympic swimmer Victor Davis, 25, was deliberately run down by three youths who had verbally taunted his girlfriend outside a convenience store. Davis later died from internal injuries.

**MURDER: Naples, Italy** Six members of a Camorra gang allegedly entered a Naples ice-cream parlor and tavern on the east side of the city and shot to death five people. The number of Camorra-related deaths in 1989 soared to 200.

### November 12

**GAMBLING: Chicago, Ill.** During a police raid, Donnell Jackson was arrested and charged with running an illegal gambling parlor. Bobby Porter was charged with drug possession, and 49 others arrested were charged with patronizing a disorderly house.

**LAW ENFORCEMENT: Hartford, Conn.** Lester J. Forst, a public safety official, resigned amid charges that he illegally taped conversations between defendants and their lawyers.

**MURDER: Kansas City, Mo.** A 14-year-old was arrested in connection with the shooting death of Frederick Jones, 11, who was found outside a suspected drug house.

**MURDER: New York, N.Y.** Seventeen-year-old Michael Allen was arrested and charged with the murder of Queens honor student Donald White.

**MURDER: New York, N.Y.** Allen Cole was arrested and charged with the murder of his wife, Sharyn Cole. She was beaten to death with wine bottles and a wooden mallet on her 44th birthday.

**MURDER: New York, N.Y.** Janet Pierro, 33, was shot to death in her car in Harlem, apparently trying to purchase drugs. Her 4-year-old son was found in the back seat unharmed. Police charged Myron Morton with Pierro's murder.

### November 13

**CONSPIRACY: Los Angeles, Calif.** Former bank president Roger McGinnis, 52, pleaded guilty to charges that he falsified credit information for organized crime figures so five Las Vegas casinos would approve credit lines for them.

**LAW ENFORCEMENT: Cape Town, South Africa** Police lieutenant Gregory Rockman and 12 others were arrested during a protest against Rockman's transfer orders. In September, Rockman, classified under apartheid laws as mixed-race, had compared the behavior of a squad of all-white riot police to "wild dogs." He was suspended from the force.

**MURDER: Chicago, Ill.** In a plea-bargain agreement, abused wife Barbara Lange pleaded guilty to killing her husband, Peter Lange, by stabbing him once in the back.

**MURDER: Cook County, Ill.** Kevin Young, 29, and Thomas Carter, 25, were charged with the murders of Thomas Kaufman, 58, a security guard, and Dan Williams, 25, whom they had suspected of raping a friend.

**MURDER: Nashville, Tenn.** Forty-two-year-old William Clark Dugger was charged with the Aug. 24 murder of 28-year-old Robin Boswell.

**MURDER: New York, N.Y.** While being taken to Rikers Island jail, murder suspect Jay "Stoney" Harrison allegedly stole a gun from a police locker and shot to death his escorts, Queens detectives Richard J. Guerzon and Keith L Williams. He was arrested later that day.

**ROBBERY: Brookline, Mass.** William "Willie" Bennett, a black man, was arraigned on an armed robbery charge in connection with an Oct. 2 robbery of a video store. Bennett became a prime suspect in the highly publicized murder of Carol Stuart.

### November 14

**CRIMINAL JUSTICE: Philadelphia, Pa.** A federal lawsuit ended with the city of Philadelphia agreeing to pay 336 black men a total of $50,000 for being harassed by police in 1988.

**MISSING PERSON: Riverside County, Calif.** A deputy coroner identified skeletal remains found scattered across a canyon as those of 7-year-old Charitie Careins, who was reported missing from a family camping trip on Aug. 6, 1988.

**MURDER: Castries, St. Lucia** Leroy McDoom, a mentally disturbed man, was arrested and charged with killing Judith Taylor, a U.S. tourist who was hacked to death with a machete.

**MURDER: Chillicothe, Mo.** Cattle farmers Ray Copeland, 75, and his wife Faye, 69, were charged with three counts of murder in the deaths of three former employees whose decomposed bodies were discovered in a barn on a Livingston County farm on Oct. 14.

**ORGANIZED CRIME: Boston, Mass.** Reputed Mafia leaders Robert Carrozza, Vincent M. Ferrara, and Joseph Russo were arrested on charges of conspiracy to extort $500,000 from two bookmakers.

**POLITICAL CORRUPTION: Sacramento, Calif.** Assembly Speaker Willie Brown and Assemblywoman Cathie Wright were cleared of charges alleging they attempted to have the 27 traffic tickets written against Wright's daughter dismissed.

**THEFT: Tyler, Texas** Merwyn Nichols, 49, convicted of shoplifting $10 worth of beef brisket, was sentenced to life in prison by a jury which cited his extensive criminal record.

**VANDALISM: Los Angeles, Calif.** In the second episode of church vandalism in a month, stained glass windows in the Immanuel Presbyterian Church were broken with candlesticks.

### November 15

**MURDER: Garland, Texas** Daniel Hittle, convicted of killing his parents in 1973, was arrested and charged with shooting to death police officer Gerald Ray Walker, 4-year-old Christy Condon, her mother Mary Alice Gross, Richard Joseph Cook Jr., and Raymond Scott Gregg.

**MURDER: Louisburg, N.C.** Katrina McKay, 20, was charged with the murders of her three children, who were stabbed, mutilated, tied together with cord, and left on a neighbor's doorstep. The children were all under the age of three.

### November 16

**LAW ENFORCEMENT: Scottsdale, Ariz.** More than 60 federal agents and Phoenix police officers seized control of two luxury hotels partially owned by the failed Lincoln Savings and Loan Association and run by Lincoln's former head Charles H. Keating Jr.

**MURDER: Chicago, Ill.** Declaring that "the party was over," Lucius O'Banner, 51, shot and killed Rico Warwick, 34, and wounded Lucille Walker, 46.

**SMUGGLING: Washington, D.C.** Two Americans and three South Africans were indicted on charges of conspiring to smuggle U.S. missile-guidance equipment worth $50 million to South Africa via Israel.

*November 17*

**EXECUTION: Atmore, Ala.** Arthur James Julius, 43, was executed in the electric chair for the 1978 rape and strangulation murder of his cousin while on an eight-hour work-release pass from prison where he was serving a life sentence for a 1972 murder.

*November 18*

**DRUGS: Bogota, Colombia** Manuel Palma, 49, indicted in Miami, Fla., on drug trafficking and money laundering charges in 1987, and Robert James Sokol, 29, indicted in Greensooro, N.C., on drug conspiracy charges in 1984, were extradited to the U.S.

**DRUGS: Boston, Mass.** Police seized 220 single-dose bags of heroin and arrested Eleanor Thistle, 49, her daughters Elizabeth, 22, and Charlotte, 30, and their alleged grandfather Lois Santiago, 65, and seven others.

**EMBEZZLEMENT: Mesa, Ariz.** Louis Fowler, 35, living under the alias William David Rice, was arrested in connection with the theft of $5 million in funds stolen when Fowler was an accountant for the California State Water Resources Control Board. His former wife, Jill Baume, 26, was arrested in Citrus Heights, Calif.

**MURDER: Providence, R.I.** Carol Taylor, 41, who gave her 5-year-old daughter, Shanna, methadone to help relieve the child's cold, was charged with murder when Shanna died from the drug.

*November 19*

**MURDER: Gaza Strip** The "Tel Aviv Strangler," responsible for killing three Arabs and four Jews, was apparently taken into custody when Israeli soldiers arrested Palestinian Mohammed Halabi, 32.

**MURDER: Highland Park, Ill.** Former Chicago narcotics detective Salvatore "Sam Cee" Canzoneri, 61, was found shot to death in an apparent organized crime killing.

*November 20*

**ASSASSINATION: Madrid, Spain** The right-wing Anti-Terrorist Liberation Group claimed responsibility for the murder of Josu Muguruza, a member of the ETA, a Basque terrorist group, who was about to be sworn in as a member of the Spanish Parliament. A second man, Inaki Esnaola, was wounded in the attack.

**ESCAPE: Los Angeles, Calif.** Jamil David Jacome-Iza, 25, who was wanted in Mexico on a murder charge, escaped from the U.S. Immigration and Naturalization Service agents who were taking him to a deportation hearing.

**MURDER: Los Angeles, Calif.** Lonnie Lewis, 29, his brother Jerome Martin, 22, and Derek Bloodworth, 26, were charged with the grisly murders of Lee Gottstein, 57, and his wife, Sylvia Carruth, 45, who ran a cocaine ring from their home. The couple was robbed, doused with gasoline, and set on fire Jan. 30.

**MURDER: York County, Maine** Roy Irwin Abbott of Denton, Texas, surrendered to Maine authorities and was charged with the shooting deaths of his two sons, Roy Jr., 6, and 3-year-old Rooney Irwin.

**RAPE: Braintree, Mass.** Bridgewater State College student Matthew Crowley was charged with raping an 11-year-old retarded boy, who was placed in his care at the Children's Physical Developmental Clinic.

*November 21*

**BURGLARY: Fremont, Ohio** Burglary suspect Robert Chavez, 19, cut off his body cast and fled from his mobile home, shortly before he was scheduled to appear in court to answer charges of aggravated burglary and felonious assault. Chavez was shot by police on Nov. 21.

**FRAUD: Wheaton, Ill.** Consumer fraud charges were filed against William Godwin of Manitowoc, Wis., who swindled 22 people out of $125,000 through his Global Fisheries investment scheme.

**MURDER: Oise, France** Frederic Blancke, 22, confessed to the murder of Fiona Jones, a British schoolteacher who disappeared on Aug. 14. Blancke's confession was detailed, but he would not reveal what he had done with the victim's body.

**MURDER: Uchiza, Peru** The body of Tampa *Tribune* reporter Todd C. Smith, 28, was found in a public square. He had been kidnapped Nov. 17 at the airport here, apparently by Shining Path guerrillas and strangled to death.

**POLITICAL CORRUPTION: Manila, Philippines** Former public highways director Rolando Mangubat was sentenced to 3,576 years in jail for acts of corruption.

**POLITICAL CORRUPTION: New York, N.Y.** Representative Robert Garcia was indicted on bribery and extortion charges in connection with his role in the Wedtech scandal.

**SEXUAL ASSAULT: Chicago, Ill.** Therapist Richard Quinlan, 37, was convicted of sexual assault after administering an unauthorized pelvic examination to a female patient at Humana Hospital in suburban Hoffman Estates.

**THEFT: Baltimore, Md.** Marilyn Louise Harrell, dubbed "Robin HUD" for embezzling $5.6 million from the government and then turning it over to the needy, was indicted in the widening scandal involving the Housing and Urban Development Department.

*November 22*

**BRIBERY: Miami, Fla.** Alfredo Duran, the former chairman of the Florida Democratic Party, was indicted on charges of bribery and conspiring to violate the Federal Foreign Corrupt Practices Act. Duran pleaded not guilty to the charges.

**CORRUPTION: New York, N.Y.** David Murray, former commanding officer of the Nassau County Police Department, pleaded not guilty to a 59-count indictment charging him with using officers and civilian employees for his own personal use.

**FRAUD: Waukegan, Ill.** Reputed con-artists Vincent Woodard, 28, Jordan Russell Jr., 47, and Linda Russell, 40, were arrested and charged with attempting to swindle a 72-year-old woman of her life savings in what is known as the "pigeon drop."

**MURDER: Chicago, Ill.** Cynthia and David Dowaliby were charged with the Sept. 10 murder of their daughter Jaclyn, whose body was found four days later in a field in Blue Island.

**MURDER: Kurunegele, Sri Lanka** South Korean engineer Jun Her Choi was murdered by Sinhyalese radicals after he tried to stop them from burning his company's vehicles.

**MURDER: New York, N.Y.** Korean national Hong Din Park was stabbed in the forehead by an assailant wielding an umbrella.

**RAPE: Dorchester, Mass.** Shaun Adams, 19, and Gus D. Warren, 49, were arrested for allegedly raping and torturing two female roommates after a dispute over an $80 debt.

### November 23

**ASSAULT: Rissen, West Germany** Matthias Rust, who landed his aircraft in Moscow's Red Square in 1987, was arrested after allegedly stabbing an 18-year-old student nurse who refused his advances.

**ATTEMPTED MURDER: Uttar Pradesh, India** Political leader Sanjay Singh was shot and wounded by an armed gang near his family's home in Amethi. Singh was a candidate for a seat in the state assembly.

**BOMBING: Paris, France** Pro-Iranian terrorist Fouad Ali Saleh, and 17 others were indicted for a series of bombing attacks in 1986 that killed 13 persons and injured 250 others.

**DRUGS: Magdalena River Valley, Colombia** Fugitive drug lord Pablo Escobar Gavaria narrowly escaped a police manhunt at a ranch he allegedly owned, but two bodyguards were killed and 55 associates were rounded up in the dragnet.

**MISCONDUCT: London, England** Dr. James Sharp was charged with professional misconduct after offering a false cure for the AIDS virus.

**MURDER: Livingston County, Mo.** The body of Dennis Kevin Murphy was recovered from a well on a farm where Ray Copeland had once worked as a farmhand. The corpse is the fifth discovered in this county after the Oct. 9 arrest of Ray and Faye Copeland on charges of conspiracy to commit theft in a cattle buying scheme.

### November 24

**BOMBING: Bogota, Colombia** A bomb exploded on an Avianca jetliner en route to Cali. Cocaine traffickers are suspected of planting the bomb which claimed 11 lives.

**BOMBING: Peshawar, Pakistan** Three Palestinians returning from a mosque were killed by a remote controlled bomb set off by Communist guerrillas.

**BRIBERY: Tokyo, Japan** The trial of former vice minister Takashi Kato, 59, opened in the Tokyo District Court. He is one of several figures implicated in an influence-peddling scandal that disgraced the government of Prime Minister Noboru Takeshita.

**MOB VIOLENCE: New Delhi, India** Thirty-six people were killed in the latest wave of election violence. Police fired on angry crowds and hurled tear gas canisters on the second day of parliamentary voting.

**MURDER: Canton, Ohio** Moses Williams, 36, was charged with the murder of Elsie Jackson, who attempted to intercede in a dispute between her son and four men over a drug buy.

**MURDER: London, Canada** Fugitive murderer Joseph Shepherd was deported back to the U S. where he was wanted in conjunction with the slaying of two teenage girls in Tellico Plains, Tenn.

**MURDER: Newcastle, Canada** Convicted murderer Allan Legere was re-captured following his escape from prison in May. He was seized near the town of Nelson-Miramichi.

**RIOT: Harrisburg, Pa.** Prison inmate William Diggs was charged with rioting at the Camp Hill State Prison, following a disturbance on Oct. 25 and 26 that caused $15 million in damages.

### November 25

**MURDER: Gary, Ind.** Linda Bownes, 42, and her two daughters Gena and Lesa Mabon were murdered in their home in the Tarrytown section of the city.

**MURDER: Miami, Fla.** Carlos Rueben Eiber was charged with shooting to death Marlen Schlesinger, 66, after she accused him of using her money to pay his gambling debts.

**MURDER: Sambag, Philippines** Filipino farmer Pelagio Caro was one of nine rural villagers arrested and charged with the massacre of 12 worshippers in a crowded church.

**ROBBERY: Boston, Mass.** Michael J. Miele, 45, and Michael Walters, 39, were arrested and charged with robbing the Reading Cooperative Bank. They were picked up as they walked out of the branch.

### November 26

**BOMBING: Santiago, Chile** A 16-year-old was killed and widespread damage was reported when a bomb was detonated by a group calling itself the Manuel Rodriguez Patriotic Front.

**LAW ENFORCEMENT: New York, N.Y.** Police Detective Robert Nugent shot and killed suspected drug dealer Julio Rosa, 17, in a Harlem apartment.

### November 27

**ARSON: Kankakee, Ill.** Bernon Howery, 38, was arrested and held without bail for the murders of four young children, three of them his own, who were trapped inside a house that he allegedly set on fire.

**GAMBLING: Chicago, Ill.** A gambling ring was broken up in suburban Oak Park, and its proprietor, Lamont Howard, 39, was arrested and charged with running an illegal game.

**MURDER: Acme, Wash.** The body of college student Amanda Stavik, missing for two days, was found floating in the Nooksack River.

**MURDER: Phoenix, Ariz.** Murder charges were refiled

against James Robison for the 1976 car bomb slaying of newsman Don Bolles. The Arizona Supreme Court overturned his original conviction in 1977.

**MURDER: Sandpoint, Idaho** James Pratt, 30, was sentenced to death for the murder of U.S. Forest Service Agent Brent Jacobson. Pratt's brother Joseph received a sentence of life in prison.

**MURDER: Washington, D.C.** The U.S. Supreme Court ordered a new trial for Richard Delmar Boyer, 31, the so-called "Halloween II" murderer who allegedly killed an elderly Fullerton couple in 1982. The court decided that the police had violated Boyer's civil rights.

*November 28*

**EMBEZZLEMENT: New York, N.Y.** Patrick J. Kelly, the former manager of Manhattan's trendy Water Club restaurant, was ordered to pay a $135 million penalty for embezzling $485,000 in funds between 1983 and 1986.

**EXTORTION: Sacramento, Calif.** Karin Watson, 42, a top Republican fund raiser in California, pleaded guilty to charges that she tried to coerce undercover FBI agents posing as businessmen to pay a sizeable campaign contribution to two legislators.

**MURDER: Bexar County, Texas** Though a body was never found, Thomas James Fisher, 42, was convicted of murdering his live-in girlfriend Barbara Baughman, 32, in November 1988.

**MURDER: Concord, N.J.** Kenneth E. Johnson, 37, was one of three men charged with the July 28, 1988, murder of Sharon G. Johnson, the wife of the suspect. Johnson allegedly hired Anthony Pfaff and Jason Carroll, both 19, to abduct and murder the pregnant woman.

**MURDER: Glasgow, Scotland** The longest murder trial in Scottish history ended with the convictions of Thomas Collins, 25, John Paul McFayden, 24, and Ricardo Blanco, 26. The three men were found guilty of murdering drug courier Paul Thorne, 26.

**MURDER: Hartford, Conn.** Dennis Coleman, 21, of Glastonbury, Conn., was sentenced to 34 years in prison for the Aug. 5, 1987, murder of Joyce Aparo, whose death was allegedly ordered by her 15-year-old daughter Karin, who claimed her mother abused her.

**MURDER: Miami, Fla.** Charles Harry Street, 34, allegedly shot and killed police officers Richard Boles, 41, and David Strzalkowski, 34, as they attempted to prevent him from throwing rocks at a trailer park. Street had previously served eight years in prison for attempted murder.

**MURDER: San Mateo, Calif.** Twenty years after 8-year-old Susan Nason of Foster City was bludgeoned to death, real estate agent George Thomas Franklin Sr., 50, was taken into custody after his daughter decided to report him to police.

**MURDER: Vancouver, Wash.** Accused child murderer Westley Allan Dodd, 28, pleaded not guilty to three counts of first-degree murder, stemming from the Sept. 4 deaths of Cole Neer, 11, his brother William, and Lee Joseph Iseli, 4.

**THEFT: Brady, Texas** Billie Sol Estes, who made a name for himself in the 1960s through his connections with former President Lyndon B. Johnson, was indicted with five other people who allegedly tried to steal trade secrets from the Loadcraft Co., a manufacturer of cargo trailers.

*November 29*

**EXECUTION: Washington, D.C.** The U.S. Supreme Court ordered a temporary stay of execution for condemned murderer Dalton Prejean, who murdered a Louisiana state police officer in 1976 when he was 17.

**FRAUD: Window Rock, Ariz.** Suspended Navajo Chairman Peter MacDonald was charged with conspiracy, bribery, extortion, fraud, and election-law violations in connection with a scheme to receive kickbacks from firms doing business with the Indian tribe.

**JUDICIAL MISCONDUCT: San Francisco, Calif.** The California State Supreme Court upheld the ruling of the Judicial Performance Commission and ordered Judge Kenneth L. Kloepfer removed from the bench for falling to uphold the rights of criminal defendants.

**MURDER: Waukegan, Ill.** Navy men Jared Fitch and Harold Haines III, both 19, pleaded not guilty to the Oct. 26, 1988, murder of Mark Mueller, 33.

**SEXUAL ABUSE: New York, N.Y.** Frank D. Carr, 45, was arrested and charged with taking indecent liberties with two 7-year-old girls during the time he worked as a gym teacher at Junior High School 22 in the Bronx.

**SEXUAL ASSAULT Chicago, Ill.** Police officer Patrick Lawrence, 25, was indicted on charges of sexual assault and sexual abuse after he allegedly gave cocaine to and had sex with a 15- and 18-year-old.

*November 30*

**BOMBING: Bad Homburg, West Germany** Alfred Herrhausen, who headed up the powerful Duetsche Bank A.G., was killed in a bomb blast that demolished his car. The Red Army Faction claimed responsibility.

**CONSPIRACY: Washington, D.C.** John B.G. Roberts III, an executive with the Unisys Corp. pleaded guilty to charges of making illegal contributions to various lawmakers who influenced the defense budget.

**EXTORTION: Boston, Mass.** Robert F. Carrozza, Vincent M. Ferrara, and Joseph Russo, alleged members of a Boston crime family, pleaded not guilty to charges that they extorted money from Boston bookmakers.

**FRAUD: Los Angeles, Calif.** Record promoter Joseph Isgro was indicted on mail fraud and drug trafficking charges after allegedly paying off various radio employees with cocaine in a payola scandal.

**MONEY LAUNDERING: Philadelphia, Pa.** Bahrudin Bijedic, the Yugoslavian consul in Chicago, was one of five men indicted for laundering $500,000, which was deposited in several foreign banks.

**RAPE: Natchez, Miss.** Emotionally distraught over the breakup of his marriage, Larry Bates entered a kindergarten class where he raped and beat two teachers in the presence of 19 children. He then shot and wounded his estranged wife Adria, a teacher's aide, before being subdued by police.

**THEFT: Galveston, Texas** Former head librarian Emil Frey, 62, was charged with the theft of five rare books from the

Moody Medical Library. The books were valued at between $750 and $20,000 a piece.

**THEFT: Los Angeles, Calif.** Craig Warner, 40, was arrested and charged with the 1978 theft of hundreds of Nepalese and Tibetan art objects dating back to the eighth century.

## December 1

**BOMBING: Springfield, Mass.** Prosecutors said they would not re-try Raymond and Patricia Levasseur and Richard Williams, three radicals accused of bombing a Suffolk County courthouse in April 1976. The first trial—the most expensive in Massachusetts history--ended in a mistrial on Nov. 29.

**CONSPIRACY: Chicago, Ill.** Former Chicago stock trader Melanie Kosar, 26, pleaded guilty to federal conspiracy charges of prearranged trading and cheating customers at the Chicago Board of Trade.

**DRUGS: New York, N.Y.** Brooklyn drug lord Delroy "Uzi" Edwards was sentenced to seven consecutive life terms for ordering and participating in six drug-related killings.

**EXTORTION: New York, N.Y.** Queens school board officials Samuel Granirer, 48, and James Sullivan, 37, were indicted on charges of extortion, bribery, and fraud. Granirer pleaded not guilty and Sullivan pleaded guilty to coercion and mail fraud.

**FRAUD: Portland, Ore.** Loan broker Albert Yarbrow was convicted of fraud, conspiracy, and other charges in connection with the failure of the State Federal Savings and Loan Association of Corvallis, the largest institutional failure in Oregon's history.

**MANSLAUGHTER: Chicago, Ill.** Donald Volkman, 54, the drunk driver who killed Herbert Knechtel, 80, inventor of Frango Mints sold by Marshall Field's department store, was sentenced to three-and-a-half years in prison.

**MURDER: Los Angeles, Calif.** Durrell Dewitt Collins was sentenced to 27 years to life imprisonment for the Jan. 31, 1988, murder of Karen Toshima, who was shot when Collins fired on rival gang member Tyrone Swain.

**MURDER: New York, N.Y.** Former Dominican Republic police officer and drug dealer Bienvenido Castillo was convicted of killing undercover narcotics officer Christopher Hoban. Castillo's alleged accomplice, Flavio Prophete, was acquitted.

**MURDER: Newburyport, Mass.** James B. Carver was sentenced to two consecutive life terms and 15 to 20 years in prison for setting fire to a Beverly, Mass., rooming house in 1984, killing 15 people.

**MURDER: Norwich, England** Former Conservative lawyer Michael James, 49, was sentenced to four years in prison after he beat to death Philip Goldspink, 52, his wife's lover, in November 1988.

**ROBBERY: Los Angeles, Calif.** Gary Allen Smith, called the "Polite Bandit," was sentenced to 28 years and eight months in prison, after pleading guilty to a string of 30 robberies.

**TERRORISM: West Germany** Nationwide roadblocks were set up to apprehend two suspects in the car bombing assassination of Deutsche Bank executive Alfred Herrhausen on Nov. 30 in Bad Homburg. The Red Army Faction claimed responsibility.

**VIGILANTISM: Bronx, N.Y.** Bernhard H. Goetz refused to appear in court to answer a $50 million lawsuit filed by Darrell Cabey, one of four youths Goetz shot in 1984 in a New York subway.

## December 2

**BOMBING: Colchester, England** A car bomb explosion injured Army Sergeant Andrew Mudd and his wife. Mudd helped thwart the 1984 assassination attempt on Sinn Fein leader Gerry Adams, and authorities believed the Irish Republican Army set the bomb as part of a Christmas terror campaign.

**MURDER: Dover, Del.** Richard W. Lynch Jr., was acquitted of killing Joseph and Beverly Gibson of Hasletteville, Del. In a separate trial, his wife, Joyce Lynch, was found guilty of the murders and of abducting the Gibsons' infant son Matthew, for which she was sentenced to life in prison.

**MURDER: Los Angeles, Calif.** Harold Veo, 76, known as the "Angel of Main Street" for his efforts on behalf of the homeless and unemployed along Skid Row, was fatally beaten inside the employment agency where he worked.

**MURDER: New York, N.Y.** Larry Davis, 23, was acquitted of the 1986 murder of alleged Harlem drug dealer Victor LaGombra. The decision was Davis' third acquittal on charges of murder or attempted murder since October 1988.

**MURDER: Round Rock, Texas** Thirteen-year-old cheerleader Kelly Brumbelow was stabbed 97 times by 12-year-old neighbor and close friend Terrence Sampsan, who admitted killing Kelly.

**MURDER: Vernon Hills, Ill.** Donald J. Bartel, 21, and Christopher R. Porter, 22, were charged with first-degree murder, armed violence, and armed robbery. The two allegedly robbed, beat, and killed gas station attendant George Wilson Jr., 46.

**MURDER: Waterville, Maine** Leonide L. Michaud Sr., 77, who suffered from a terminal illness, was shot to death in his hospital bed by his 47-year-old son Leonide Jr., who then attempted suicide with the same gun.

## December 3

**MURDER: Boston, Mass.** Alphonsus King, 36, was arrested and charged with the stabbing death of his 75-year-old friend Ellison Wynn.

## December 4

**BLACKMAIL: Tokyo, Japan.** Four people, who learned the Fuji Bank allegedly loaned money to right-wing gangsters, were arrested for blackmailing $3.5 million from the bank.

**BRIBERY: San Francisco, Calif.** The state Supreme Court ordered Torrance attorney Barry G. Sands, 45, disbarred after he allegedly tried to pass a $400 bribe to a Department of Motor Vehicles hearing officer.

**CRIMINAL JUSTICE: Belfast, Northern Ireland** The Court of Appeal attached an extra three years to the five-year sentence already imposed on convicted child rapist Cyril David Workman, 27.

**DRUGS: Dallas, Texas.** Jim Humphreys, 40, was arrested on drug and conspiracy charges after a federal agent recognized his picture in the newspaper. Humphreys headed up an advocacy group for people wrongly convicted of crimes.

**ESCAPE: Barstow, Fla.** Barry Leslie Dyson, 27, charged with several rapes in the south Lakeland area, was shot and killed by a guard when he tried to escape from the Polk County Jail.

**MURDER: Cook County, Ill.** Joseph Slode, 68, was convicted of second-degree murder in the shooting death of Willie Ferrell, 51, who had punched him.

**MURDER: Gary, Ind.** Murder charges were filed against Terance Ballard, 22, Ivory M. Bryant, 22, and Ray Williams for the Nov. 24 murders of Linda Bownes, 42, and her 22-year-old twin daughters Lesa and Gena Mabon.

**MURDER: Los Angeles, Calif.** Theda Demon Rice, 54, was arrested and charged with the apparent beating death of her 4-year-old grandson Daniel Hillman.

**POLITICAL CORRUPTION: Sacramento, Calif.** Jury selection began for the corruption trial of state Senator Joseph B. Montoya, the first legislator indicted in the 4-year-old FBI probe of state government.

**TERRORISM: Uppasala, Sweden** Mohammed Abu Talb was named by the District Court as a suspect in the Dec. 21, 1988, bombing of Pan Am Flight 103, which exploded over Lockerbie, Scotland.

### December 5

**DRUGS: California.** Authorities arrested seven people and seized $100,000 in cash, more than 2 pounds of heroin, and nearly half a ton of cocaine, valued at $130 million, in an operation extending from the San Joaquin Valley to Culver City.

**INSURGENCY: Johannesburg, South Africa.** Police arrested five right-wing extremists who planned to assassinate key political leaders, including President F.W. de Klerk and ministers R.F. Botha, Adriaan Vlok, and Magnus Malan.

**MURDER: Los Angeles, Calif.** Robert John Bardo, the allegedly obsessed fan and accused killer of actress Rebecca Schaeffer, was ordered to stand trial for her July 18 murder.

**MURDER: San Jose, Calif.** Pit bull owner Michael Berry went on trial for the 1987 mauling death of 2-year-old James Soto, who was attacked by the dog while it allegedly guarded a marijuana crop.

**PERJURY: Charlotte, N.C.** Sam Johnson and John Wesley Fletcher, former PTL ministry associates, were indicted on charges of perjury for their grand jury testimony in the case against minister Jim Bakker.

**POLITICAL CORRUPTION: Berlin, E. Germany.** Erich Honecker, former East German head of state, was placed under house arrest along with several associates due to allegations of corruption within the Communist Party.

**RAPE: Atlanta, Ga.** Steven Lamar Lord, acquitted in a Florida rape trial in which the jury foreman claimed the woman "asked for it," was sentenced to life in prison after pleading guilty to raping a woman in Decatur, Ga.

**ROBBERY: West Goshen, Pa.** A man dressed as Santa Claus handed a teller at the Fidelity Bank a note claiming he was armed, and sang "We Wish You a Merry Christmas" as the teller filled his bag with cash. The robber escaped with an undetermined amount of cash.

### December 6

**ASSAULT: Chicago, Ill.** A woman who was sexually attacked by seven men during a concert at the International Amphitheater on Dec. 29, 1981, received $1.2 million from Showtime Security and Crowd Control, Rainbow Productions, and the amphitheater.

**BOMBING: Bogota, Colombia** At least 45 people were killed and nearly 400 injured when a bus loaded with 1,000 to 3,000 pounds of (dynamite exploded across the street from police intelligence headquarters. The blast was blamed on Colombian drug traffickers.

**DRUGS: Iran.** Kiyumars Abu, the director of Iran's anti-narcotics division, announced that 14,000 suspected drug smugglers had been arrested since March. Nine hundred were expected to be executed.

**DRUGS: Los Angeles, Calif.** Richard V. Winrow was sentenced to life in prison without parole for possessing 5-and-a-half ounces of crack, marking only the second use in the U.S. and the first in California of the severe 1988 federal narcotics law.

**DRUGS: Washington, D.C.** Rayful Edmond III was convicted of running a drug ring that supplied 30 percent of the city's cocaine. Ten cc-defendants were found guilty of assisting him.

**DRUGS: Washington, D.C.** The Justice Department announced that Medellin cartel drug lord Jose Gonzalo Rodriguez Gacha had bank accounts totaling $61, million in Austria, Britain, Luxembourg, Switzerland, and the U.S., where the assets are frozen.

**EXTORTION: Burbank, Calif.** After trying to see talk show host Johnny Carson in an apparent attempt to extort $5 million from Carson, Ken Orville Gause, 36, was arrested.

**FRAUD: Lompoc, Calif.** Former Wall Street investment mogul Ivan Boesky, 52, was released from the Lompoc Federal Prison Camp, and ordered to complete his sentence at a hallway house in New York.

**FRAUD: Ottawa, Canada** Former Indian Affairs Minister John Munro, 58, was charged with 34 counts of fraud and breach of trust for allegedly arranging a $13 million grant for the Saskatchewan Indian Corp.

**KIDNAPPING: New York, N.Y.** Fairlene Walton, 25, was charged with kidnapping and endangering a child's welfare after abducting the 5-year-old son of her friend, Esther Pass, and using the boy to panhandle money in order to by crack cocaine.

**MURDER: Chicago, Ill.** Alonzo Eaton, 17, suspected of killing his girlfriend, Kimberly Hunt, 20, found on Dec. 4, was arrested en route to the Children's Memorial Hospital, where Hunt's 3-year-old son, who identified his mother's killer for police, was recovering from five stab wounds.

**MURDER: Los Angeles, Calif.** Police found the body of Alexandria Hickman, 24, and then found the body of Deborah Converse, 42, when they received no answer after knocking on the apartment door next to Hickman's. The victim's neighbor, Martin Anthony Navarette, 24, was arrested and charged in connection with the stabbing deaths.

**MURDER: Montreal, Canada** Marc Lepine killed 14 women and wounded 13 at the University of Montreal's engineering school, then killed himself with a hunting rifle. In a suicide note, Lepine blamed feminists for having ruined his life. The shooting rampage was the worst in Canadian history.

**ORGANIZED CRIME: Peoria, Ill.** Louis Lomas, 27, a ranking member of Chicago's El Rukn street gang, was arrested at the Greater Peoria Airport in connection with his October indictment for narcotics and weapons violations, intimidating witnesses, and racketeering.

**RIOT: Jersey City, N.J.** Inmate Kenneth Johnson, 28, was killed and six guards injured in a riot at the Hudson County Jail. Johnson's death apparently resulted when a guard mistakenly loaded his shotgun with live ammunition.

**WAR CRIMES: Buenos Aires, Arg.** Fugitive Nazi war criminal Johann Olij Hottentort, 68, was arrested thirty-nine years after fleeing a German jail. He was convicted in absentia and sentenced to 20 years in prison for turning over members of the Dutch Resistance to the Nazis.

### December 7

**ARSON: Pasadena, Calif.** Timothy Loxson, 26, was arrested in connection with an arson fire which caused $5 million in damages to a condominium construction site and a nearby townhouse complex. Loxson was released on Dec. 8 due to lack of evidence.

**BOMBING: Belfast, Northern Ireland** Twenty-nine people were injured by a car bomb explosion in a suburban shopping district. The Irish Republican Army telephoned a warning to a radio station 20 minutes before the blast.

**BURGLARY: Albany, N.Y.** John Leslie Hill, 50, who escaped from a Florida prison in 1988, pleaded guilty to breaking into the governor's mansion on Nov. 29, 1988.

**MANSLAUGHTER: Miami, Fla.** Police officer William Lozano was found guilty on two counts of manslaughter in the deaths of two black men whom Lozano shot when they allegedly tried to run him over with a motorcycle. The killings resulted in three days of rioting in Miami's black communities.

**MURDER: Pasadena, Calif.** William Wang, the triggerman for a heroin ring, was sentenced to life in prison without parole for killing two undercover federal drug agents and wounding a third in February 1988.

**MURDER: Topeka, Kan.** Tyrone Baker, 19, and Lisa Ann Pfannenstiel, 18, were charged with 19 felonies, including first-degree murder, aggravated kidnapping, and aggravated robbery in the murders of three Westboro residents.

**ORGANIZED CRIME: Chicago, Ill.** Albert Tocco, reputed south suburban crime boss, was convicted on 34 counts, including extortion, racketeering, filing false income tax returns, and obstruction of justice.

**RIOT: Poland** Riots broke out at four prisons housing repeat offenders after Parliament denied amnesty to hardcore felons. Inmates at Goleniow and Czarne, where four prisoners were killed, gave up on Dec. 9.

**SEXUAL ABUSE: New York, N.Y.** Brooklyn school teacher Anthony Romain, 42, was arrested and charged with molesting three female students aged 9 to 11 at Public School 59.

**SUICIDE: Southampton, N.Y.** Dr. Rodney Thorp Wood, convicted of soliciting students to have sex with his wife in a phony research project, was found dead in his home, shot through the head in an apparent suicide.

### December 8

**ABDUCTION: Van Nuys, Calif.** Babysitter Alicia Lopez, 22, was arrested in connection with the abduction of 3-year-old Hector Vasquez, who was found unharmed in Tijuana, Mexico, where Lopez had apparently abandoned him after having an argument with Hector's mother.

**CORRUPTION: Washington, D.C.** Loral Corp. pleaded guilty to three felony counts of fraud and conspiracy for hiring a federal defense consultant to influence the Pentagon in Loral's bid for two multi-million dollar defense contracts.

**FRAUD: New York, N.Y.** Eugene Laff, former chairman of defunct Hans Securities, was convicted on five counts of stock manipulation, conspiracy, mail fraud, and obstructing a Securities and Exchange probe.

**KIDNAPPING: Srinagar, India.** Rubaiya Sayeed, daughter of Indian home minister Mufti Mohammed Sayeed, was kidnapped by the Kashmir Liberation Front, a group seeking secession from India. She was released Dec. 13 when the government released five separatists.

**LAW ENFORCEMENT: Richmond, Va.** While trying to post bail for a friend charged with an unrelated crime, Kevin L. Jones, 20, was arrested by police who compared him to his most wanted picture hanging on the wall of the station.

**MURDER: Buxton, N.D.** Farmer Wayne Nygaard, 42, allegedly shot and killed his wife Carol, 40, and his 11-year-old daughter Kate before shooting himself.

**MURDER: Dallas, Texas** Fernando Garcia was sentenced to death by lethal injection for the rape and strangulation murder of 3-year-old Veronica Rodriguez.

**MURDER: New York, N.Y.** Christopher Foster, 16, who had escaped from a Louisiana psychiatric hospital was charged with the stabbing death of Chris Zacharopoulos, 26, an ad agency employee.

**MURDER: Spanaway, Wash.** Air Force employee Ronald Burris, 45, apparently killed his former wife, his two daughters, and his wife's new husband, and then committed suicide, reportedly because he was denied visitation rights.

### December 9

**MURDER: Houston, Texas.** Craig Neal Ogan, 35, an informant for the Drug Enforcement Administration, allegedly shot and killed police officer James Charles Boswell reportedly during a hysterical fit.

**MURDER: Los Angeles, Calif.** A 17-year-old youth, arrested in a Watts boarding house, was held as a suspect in the Sept. 18 drive-by shooting death of 19-year-old Sheriff's Department volunteer Anthony Jerome Gardner.

### December 10

**CORRUPTION: Chicago, Ill.** Former Circuit Judge Wayne Olson, 58, convicted for accepting bribes in the Operation Greylord investigation, lost an appeal to reduce his 12-year jail sentence. Olson pleaded guilty to fraud, extortion, and racketeering.

**LAW ENFORCEMENT: Los Angeles, Calif.** Patrick Shanahan, 19, a fan of the rock group the Grateful Dead, died from injuries sustained during his arrest at a concert. Police contended he died of a drug overdose, while the Los Angeles County coroner ruled the death a homicide.

### December 11

**CRIMINAL JUSTICE: Boston, Mass.** The Supreme Judicial Court ruled that lie detector or polygraph test results cannot be used as evidence in a state criminal trial, reversing a 1-year-old position.

**CRIMINAL JUSTICE: Van Nuys, Calif.** Superior Court Judge James M. Coleman ruled that DNA analysis, known as "genetic fingerprinting," had gained sufficient scientific acceptance to be used as evidence in a Los Angeles County trial.

**DRUGS: Miami, Fla.** Former Bolivian interior minister Lois Arce Gomez was extradited here from Bolivia to stand trial on drug trafficking charges stemming from a 1983 indictment.

**FRAUD: Mainz, W. Ger.** Manfred Seheer and two other men who, from 1977 to 1982, sold 11 million gallons of cheap wine mixed with sugar syrup and labeled it as prize-winning German wine, were sentenced to prison terms of at least six years.

**MONEY LAUNDERING: Los Angeles, Calif.** Argentine Raul Silvio Vivas pleaded not guilty to charges that he laundered $250 million in cocaine money through store fronts in New York and Los Angeles.

**MURDER: Los Angeles, Calif.** Ruben Zuno Arce, 59, the brother-in-law of former Mexican president Luis Echeverria, was indicted for conspiring to kidnap and murder U.S. drug agent Enrique Camarena.

**MURDER: New York, N.Y.** Geraldine Mitchell, 24, and George Chavis, 34, were arrested and charged with beating to death Mitchell's 3-year-old son, burying his body, and reporting him missing on Apr. 28.

**MURDER: New York, N.Y.** Howard "Pappy" Mason, leader of a multi-million dollar crack cocaine racket, was found guilty of drug trading, conspiracy, and murder for ordering the death of rookie police officer Edward Byrne.

**NEGLIGENCE: Chicago, Ill.** Schoolbus driver Bobbette Corner, 35, was charged with contributing to the neglect of children when, lost on her route, she allegedly deserted seven children, telling them, "You're gifted, you figure out what to do."

**RIOT: New York, N.Y.** The state appeals court overturned the convictions of William Bollander, Thomas Farino, and James Povinelli, who were found guilty of second-degree riot in the second trial following the Howard Beach racial attack.

**SEXUAL ASSAULT: Skokie, Ill.** Tony Adams, 25, convicted Oct. 24 of sexually attacking a 20-year-old woman in an elevator of the Cabrini-Green housing project, was sentenced to an extended 50-year term in prison because of the brutality of his attack.

**TAX EVASION: San Diego, Calif.** Nancy Hoover Hunter was found guilty of tax evasion, though the jury did not convict her on 192 counts of fraud and conspiracy resulting from a multi-million dollar Ponzi scheme Hunter allegedly conducted with J. David Dominern.

### December 12

**ASSAULT: New York, N.Y.** Supreme Court justice Jeffrey Atlas ruled that tape recordings of conversations held in Mafia boss John Gotti's clubhouse can be used against Gotti in his assault and conspiracy trial, scheduled to begin Jan. 8.

**BOMBING: Chicago, Ill.** William English, 20, convicted of firebombing the home of a black schoolteacher in February 1987, was sentenced to 12 years in prison.

**CHILD ABUSE: Spokane, Wash.** Former Catholic priest John Bauer, 53, wanted in connection with a child pornography ring, was arrested after he fled Los Angeles, Calif., while on $1,000 bail.

**FRAUD: Suffolk County, Mass.** Willie C. Veal Jr. and 16 others were arrested in connection with a $1 million insurance fraud ring involving an auto shop and false accident claims.

**MURDER: Bogota, Columbia** A prosecutor, a judge, and a bank official were killed, apparently in an effort by drug cartel assassins to thwart extradition of drug traffickers to the U.S.

**MURDER: Brockton, Mass.** Therese Rogers was acquitted by a jury of the murder of her boyfriend, Walter E. Quinn Jr., who had abused Rogers and her 9-year-old daughter for 16 months before she stabbed him to death on July 13, 1987.

**MURDER: Chicago, Ill.** Michael Daniels was convicted of the August 1987 rape and murder of Brigitte Andersen based in part on DNA testing of sperm found on the victim's underwear. This was the first conviction in Illinois based on genetic testing.

**MURDER: Dade City, Fla.** Convicted serial killer Michael Lee Lockhart, imprisoned on death row in Huntsville, Texas, for the strangulation murder of Jennifer Colhouer, received a third death sentence for killing a 14-year-old Florida girl.

**MURDER: Guadalajara, Mexico** Rafael Caro Quintero and Ernesto Rafael Fonseca Carrillo of the Guadalajara drug cartel were each sentenced to 40 years in prison for planning the death of U.S. Drug Enforcement Administration agent Enrique Camarena.

**RACKETEERING: Los Angeles, Calif.** Record promoter Ralph Tashjian was sentenced to 60 days in a substance abuse center and fined $100,000 after pleading guilty to reduced payola charges and admitting he gave radio stations cocaine in exchange for airplay.

**RAPE: Pensacola, Fla.** Fourteen-year-old Joe Sullivan, was sentenced to life in prison without parole for twice raping an elderly woman when he was 13.

**SUICIDE: Lebanon, Tenn.** Tennessee secretary of state Gentry Crowell, whose office was in the midst of a scandal over illegal gambling on charity bingo games, attempted suicide by shooting himself in the mouth. He died on Dec. 20.

**TAX EVASION: New York, N.Y.** Hotel queen Leona Helmsley was sentenced to four years in prison and fined $7.1 million for tax evasion.

### December 13

**ASSAULT: Burbank, Ill.** Former Boy Scout leader Thomas Hacker, convicted on two counts of aggravated sexual assault for attacking an 11-year-old Boy Scout in 1986 and in 1987, was sentenced to two 50-year prison terms.

**BRIBERY: Tokyo, Japan** Hisashi Shinto, 78, former chairman of Nippon Telegraph and Telephone, pleaded not guilty to bribery charges in the fourth trial connected with the Recruit Cosmos shares-for-favor scandal.

**DRUGS: Lewiston, Idaho** Victor Smith, 23, the former vice president of a Just Say No to drugs chapter, was sentenced to 60 days in jail and fined $1,000 for possessing cocaine and not paying taxes on it.

**FRAUD: New York, N.Y.** The GAF Corp. and senior executive James T. Sherwin, 55, were found guilty on eight counts of stock fraud for attempting to manipulate Union Carbide Corp. stock when their takeover bid failed.

**FRAUD: San Francisco, Calif.** Financier J. William Oldenburg was found guilty on one count of fraud for bilking the since-failed State Savings of Salt Lake City of $26.5 million.

**MURDER: Blue Island, Ill.** Constantina Branco was sentenced to 10 years in prison for soliciting policeman Ronald Tellez to kill her husband, George Archer Mueller, in 1986.

**MURDER: Chicago, Ill.** Peter Saunders, convicted of murdering Elisa Totoni, was sentenced to life in prison without parole and a consecutive 30-year sentence for robbery and attempted rape. Saunders was 16 at the time of the murder.

**MURDER: Huntsville, Texas** Death Row inmate Clarence Lee Brandley, convicted of the 1980 rape and strangulation murder of a teenager, was freed two years after a judge ruled he was tried unfairly.

**MURDER: Long Island, N.Y.** Christopher Loliscio, 20, was arrested and charged with the rape and murder of Jessica Manners, 14, who was found dead Mar. 26, strangled with her own bra.

**ROBBERY: Fox River Grove, Ill.** Robert A. Maro, 28, a suspect in eight bank robberies, was arrested after a security guard at a Lynwood bank reported a license plate number of a suspicious car to police.

### December 14

**BRIBERY: Memphis, Tenn.** Charles McVean, promoter of robot-jockey horse races, was indicted on charges that he paid a lobbyist $24,000 to convince Senator Randy McNally to vote for legalized pari-mutuel betting.

**DRUGS: New York, N.Y.** Drug lord Thomas Mickens was sentenced to 35 years in prison on federal charges of drug conspiracy, money laundering, and tax fraud.

**MURDER: Baton Rouge, La.** The Louisiana Pardon Board recommended that Gary Tyler, 31, sentenced to life in prison for the 1974 shooting death of a Ku Klux Klansman, be given an early release.

**MURDER: Riverhead, N.Y.** Nurse Richard Angelo was found guilty of murder, manslaughter, and criminally negligent homicide in the deaths of four hospital patients. Angelo injected the victims with Pavulon to induce illnesses so he could act as hero and revive them.

**ORGANIZED CRIME: Boston, Mass.** Joseph A. "J.R." Russo was denied release on the grounds that he was likely to become a fugitive. Russo, a suspected Mafia boss, and four others were indicted Nov. 16 on charges of racketeering and extortion.

**THEFT: Cook County, Ill.** Former insurance agent Leo Fornelli, 26, was sentenced to six months in jail and 30 months' probation and fined $12,000 alter he pleaded guilty to stealing $645,556 in investors' money.

### December 15

**BOMBING: Miami, Fla.** Prominent criminal attorney Gino P. Negretti, 71, was critically injured when his car exploded. Negretti has represented defendants in several cases involving the city's Cuban-American community.

**CHILD ABUSE: Los Angeles, Calif.** Jurors in the McMartin molestation trial returned 24 sealed verdicts in the 65 counts against Peggy McMartin Buckey and Ray Buckey, charged with molesting 11 children in their nursery school.

**CHILD MOLESTATION: New York, N.Y.** David MacLeod, 45, producer of the film *The Pick-up Artist*, was charged with criminal solicitation and endangering the welfare of a child for allegedly soliciting teenaged boys for sex.

**CORRUPTION: New Orleans, La.** New Orleans district attorney Harry Connick was indicted on charges that he aided a Louisiana bookmaker and his illegal gambling business by providing him with copies of gambling records.

**DRUGS: Boston, Mass.** Michelle A. Ross, 26, her sister, Elizabeth Ross, 35, and a cousin, Lynn Ross Ward, 20, were arrested and charged with selling cocaine at the Boston Coast Guard station, where Michelle Ross' husband was an officer.

**DRUGS: Covenas, Colombia** Gonzalo Rodriguez Gacha, the second most important drug lord in the Medellin cartel, was killed, along with his son Fredy, aide Gilberto Rendon Hurtado, and 14 others, during a police raid.

**DRUGS: New York, N.Y.** Nelson Cuevas Ramirez, 55, a suspected member of a Colombian cocaine cartel, was extradited from Bogota and indicted for drug trafficking. He and three others allegedly attempted to smuggle 244 pounds of cocaine through a county airport on Apr. 14, 1987.

**EXTORTION: Charleston, W. Va.** Former sate senate president Dan Tonkovich, convicted of extorting $5,000 from a company that sought to legalize casino gambling in West Virginia, was sentenced to five years in prison and fined $10,000.

**FRAUD: Chicago, Ill.** Debra Hartmann, John Scott Korabik Jr., and Kenneth Kaenel were convicted of wire and mail fraud in connection with the June 1982 murder of Hartmann's millionaire husband, Werner Hartmann. Mrs. Harmann collected $700,000 in insurance.

**MOB VIOLENCE: Chile.** A woman was killed in Temuco, and dozens injured among the 589 arrested in Santiago during celebration demonstrations following the election of opposition leader Patricio Aylwin on Dec. 14. Another 281 people were arrested in Vina del Mar.

**MURDER: Los Angeles, Calif.** Irene Franco was raped and murdered and her boyfriend severely beaten when three gunmen forced their way into the couple's car at a drivein theater and abducted Franco.

**TERRORISM: Bloemfontein, South Africa** Activists Moses Chikane, 41, Patrick Lekota, 41, Gcinumuzi Malindi, Pope Molefe, 37, and the Reverend Tom Manthata, 49, were released from prison after their convictions for treason and terrorism were overturned by the Appeals Court.

*December 17*

**ABDUCTION: Oceanside, Calif.** Seven-year-old Leticia Hernandez was allegedly abducted from her home and was seen several hours later in Buckman Springs with an unidentified man.

**ASSASSINATION: Cairo, Egypt** The attempted assassination of Interior Minister Zaki Badr went awry when a truck bomb prematurely exploded before Badr's car drove by the site. A man who fled the scene was arrested nearby.

**BOMBING: Mountain Brook, Ala.** Federal Appeals Court Judge Robert S. Vance was killed instantly, and his wife seriously injured, when a package mailed to his home exploded.

**CORRUPTION: Ebensburg, Pa.** Cambria County Judge Joseph O'Kicki, 59, was found guilty of bribery, corruption, and official oppression. O'Kicki solicited and accepted bribes from employees, defense attorneys, and defendants.

**HIJACKING: Fukuoka, Japan** Air China Flight 981, en route from Beijing to New York, was hijacked by Zhang Zhenhai, 35, who ordered the plane flown to South Korea. The plane landed in Japan where Zhang was pushed from the plane through an open door onto the tarmac. He was hospitalized and arrested.

**MURDER: Los Angeles, Calif.** Daphne Brownlee, 25, and her boyfriend, Gregory McClain Jenkins, 34, were arrested in connection with the stabbing death of Brownlee's blind aunt, Helen Duvalle, 75, whose diamond ring was pawned for drug money.

*December 17*

**MURDER: Atlanta, Ga.** The U.S. Circuit Court of Appeals threw out the 1983 murder confession of Gerald Eugene Stano, 38, that led to two of three death sentences Stano received for the murders of Susan Bickrest, 24, and Mary Kathleen Muldoon, 23. The court stated that Volusia County (Fla.) Circuit Judge James Foxman denied Stano his right to legal counsel in accepting the confession.

**RAPE: West Bradenton, Fla.** Work-release inmate Gilbert S. Diamond, 30, was arrested within 10 minutes after he allegedly forced his way into a home and raped a woman while on his way to his job as a dishwasher in a local restaurant.

*December 18*

**BOMBING: Savannah, Ga.** Alderman Robert Robinson died three hours after a mail bomb exploded in his office. Atlanta, Ga., officials intercepted another bomb sent to a circuit court official several hours earlier.

**DRUGS: Dyfed, England** Former police officer Gareth Jones, 47, Barry Williams, 42, and David Craythorne, 40, were arraigned on charges of smuggling £2.5 million worth of marijuana from Spain to England.

**DRUGS: Salem, Mass.** Sergeants Lorenzo E. Hill, 35, and Charles Rehal, 37, and patrolman Garrett J. Lynch, 41, were arrested and charged with conspiracy to distribute cocaine, bringing to four the number of Salem police officers arrested on drug charges since June.

**FRAUD: New York, N.Y.** Wall Street stock speculator Salim B. "Sandy" Lewis was sentenced to three years' probation and fined $250,000 after pleading guilty to manipulating Fireman's Fund Corp. stock.

**MURDER: Hadley, Mass.** Sharon Galligan, a 20-year-old University of Massachusetts student, was stabbed to death in her car parked in a mall parking lot. Her body, lying upside down with one foot visible, went unnoticed for 21 hours.

**MURDER: Los Angeles, Calif.** Dr. Milos Klvana was convicted on nine counts of second-degree murder in the deaths of eight infants during high-risk births outside a hospital between 1982 and 1986.

**MURDER: San Francisco, Calif.** The state Supreme Court upheld the death sentence of Michael Anthony Jackson, 34, convicted of the August 1983 murder of West Covina police officer Kenneth Scott Wrede. Jackson claimed he was not responsible for the murder because he was under the influence of PCP.

*December 19*

**ABDUCTION: Los Angeles, Calif.** Zennie Joanna McGowan, 23, and Michele Thomas, 24, were seized by a man driving a van along the Pacific Coast Highway. McGowan escaped, but Thomas was driven away by the assailant. It was the third and fourth reported area abduction in less than a week.

**ASSASSINATION: Johannesburg, South Africa.** Supreme Court Justice J.C. Kreigler granted the release of former police officer Calla Botha, detained since Nov. 30 for questioning in the assassination deaths of white left-wing activists David Webster and Anton Lubowski.

**ESCAPE: Springfield, Mass.** Nancy McKay, 24, an inmate who escaped from Niantic State Prison in Connecticut by trading places with a visitor, was captured with an accomplice, Kevin Bailey, 21.

**EXTORTION: Wilmington, Del.** Argentines Bruno Skerianz, Raul Armando Giordano, and Antonio Ruben Inigo and two others were convicted of attempting to extort $10 million from the Du Pont Co. in exchange for stolen trade secrets of the manufacture of Lycra.

**FRAUD: Chicago, Ill.** Edward M. Boden Sr., Edward M. Boden Jr., and Roger Walsh Jr., the former owners of Bodine's Inc., pleaded guilty to fraud charges for allegedly conspiring to market millions of gallons of adulterated orange juice between 1978 and 1985.

**MURDER: Lester Prairie, Minn.** Philip Cole, 29, who allegedly shot to death police officer Michael Hogan while being questioned about shoplifting, surrendered to police following a lengthy standoff.

**PERJURY: Torrance, Calif.** Former police officer Mark Holden, 30, was ordered to stand trial on charges of conspiracy to obstruct justice and one count of conspiracy to falsely charge another with a crime for allegedly lying about the May 1988 shooting of Patrick J. Coyle.

**THEFT: Boston, Mass.** Former Malden Police Chief James M. Keohane was sentenced to five years in prison for buying a stolen civil service promotional exam in 1983.

*December 20*

**BURGLARY: Monrovia, Calif.** Clad in a Santa Claus costume, Sergeant Don Lacher, 35, arrested burglary suspects David Villalobos, 26, and Anna Marie Gallegos, 29.

**CHILD ABUSE: Liberty, Mo.** Ernest Parks, 32, was indicted on charges of child abuse and sexual abuse committed against two children that he and his wife, Cheryl Parks, 31, were babysitting. Mrs. Parks was also indicted on a child abuse charge.

**DRUGS: Panama City, Panama** U.S. troops landed in Panama to arrest Panamanian dictator General Manuel Antonio Noriega, who had been indicted in Miami and Tampa, Fla., on drug racketeering charges stemming from his relations with the Medellin drug cartel in Colombia. On Dec. 24 Noriega sought political asylum at the Vatican's embassy.

**ESPIONAGE: Seoul, South Korea** South Korean legislator Suh Kyung Won was sentenced to 15 years in prison for spying for North Korea.

**FRAUD: Washington, D.C.** Nelson and William Hunt, former billionaires who were charged with commodities manipulation for their attempt to corner the world's silver market in 1979 and 1980, agreed to a $10 million fine and a ban from U.S. commodities trading.

**RIOT: Seoul, South Korea** Police tear-gassed some 700 rioting students at Yonsei University, who demanded the release of jailed radical student leader Im Chong Suk.

**MURDER: Chicago, Ill.** Tony Bay, 34, and Rodney Ivy, 17, were indicted on charges of robbery and murder in the Nov. 21 killings of Robert Nelson, 67, and William Brown, 58.

**MURDER: Chicago, Ill.** Evelyn Claiborne, who hired a hit man in 1977 to kill her abusive husband, was given clemency and pardoned after serving 12 years in prison.

**MURDER: Exeter, N.H.** Christopher Wells, 19, pleaded guilty to the Jan. 21 stabbing deaths of his father, James, 49, and his brother, Kevin, 15, and then setting the family home ablaze.

**MURDER: Los Angeles, Calif.** Fred "Fat Fred" Knight, an admitted gang member, was acquitted of murder charges arising from the 1984 "54th Street Massacre" in which five youths were killed.

**MURDER: Moncks Corner, S.C.** Pamela K. Turner was charged with murder in connection with the sexual assault and strangulation of her 5-year-old stepson, Justin L. Turner.

### December 21

**BOMBING: Uppsala, Sweden** Mohammed Abu Talb, the prime suspect in the 1988 bombing of Pan Am Flight 103, was sentenced to life imprisonment for bombing a synagogue and airline offices in Copenhagen and Amsterdam. Abu Talb's three co-defendants were also imprisoned.

**BRIBERY: Birmingham, Ala.** State representative Pat Davis was convicted on two counts of taking money to influence legislation. Representatives John Rogers and Jim Wright were also tried and were found not guilty.

**FRAUD: Detroit, Mich.** Former civilian deputy chief of the Detroit Police Department Kenneth E. Weiner was arrested and charged with a fraudulent metals investment scheme that bilked investors of thousands of dollars.

**FRAUD: New York, N.Y.** An appeals court upheld 119 of 564 counts against state senate minority leader Manfred Ohrenstein and three other senate officials charged with using legislative payroll for "no show" jobs during the 1986 legislative elections.

**GAMBLING: New York, N.Y.** New Hyde Park, Long Island, fire chief Harold Hugli, 42, James Colosi, 50, and Frederick Falvo, 42, were arrested and charged with running a $10 million-a-year sports betting service.

**MANSLAUGHTER: Carrollton, Ky.** Larry Mahoney was convicted on 27 counts of second-degree manslaughter in the worst drunk-driving accident in U.S. history. Twenty-seven people were killed when Mahoney's truck, on the wrong side of the interstate, struck their church bus.

**MURDER: Chicago, Ill.** Police charged Paul Gilmore, Maurice James, and a 16-year-old youth with the murder of Denise Farmer, a hospital security guard killed in her apartment in June 1989.

**MURDER: Frontera, Calif.** Leslie Van Houten, one of Charles Manson's followers, was denied parole for the eighth time for the Tate-La Bianca murders in 1969.

**MURDER: New York, N.Y.** A stray bullet killed Elaine Olmo, 50, who had volunteered to patrol her South Bronx apartment building in an effort to deter neighborhood crime.

### December 22

**BOMBING: Hagerstown, Md.** Criminal Court Judge John P. Corderman, 47, was seriously injured when a parcel bomb exploded in his apartment. Authorities claimed the bomb was "substantially" different, and had no connection to the earlier Southern mail bombs.

**DRUGS: Du Page County, Ill.** Daniel Elston, 39, was convicted of auto theft and illegal possession of 109 grams of cocaine, which was found among the ashes of his wife, who died Oct. 7, 1988.

**LOOTING: Panama City, Panama** After U.S. troops had secured the capital in an effort to extradite dictator General Manuel Antonio Noriega, the city's shopping district was overrun by looters, creating more than $600 million in damages.

**MANSLAUGHTER: Santa Clara, Calif.** Michael Berry, the owner of a pit bull that killed 2-year-old James Soto, was acquitted of second-degree murder but convicted of involuntary manslaughter.

**MURDER: Harrisburg, Pa.** The state Supreme Court ruled the conviction of Jay C. Smith, 60, invalid because the judge at his trial allowed the jury to hear hearsay evidence. Smith, a former principal, had been sentenced to death for the 1979 murder of teacher Susan Reinert and her two children.

**MURDER: Munster, Ind.** Bruce McKinney of Phoenix, Ariz., was arrested in connection with the Nov. 9 slaying of Munster, Ind., businessman Donald Levine and his wife, Marsha. McKinney was a former employee.

### December 23

**ARSON: Los Angeles, Calif.** Arson investigators suspected that a series of fires that gutted sections of a Westwood neighborhood were deliberately set. Part of a 14-story residential condominium was destroyed.

**ESCAPE: Plymouth, Mass.** Johnny Roy Oliver, 17, and Brian Lopilato, 20, both awaiting trial for separate crimes, overpowered a guard and escaped from the Plymouth County House of Correction. Lopilato was recaptured Dec. 26.

**EXECUTION: Taloqan, Afghanistan** Syed Jamal Agha, a commander of the fundamentalist Hizb-i-Islami guerrilla group, and several others were hanged for killing some 30 moujahedeen rebels during the summer.

**KIDNAPPING: Riverside, Calif.** Luther Loatman, 36, was freed after spending two days in the trunk of his car, during which time his abductors apparently conducted drug transactions from the car.

**MURDER: Dryden, N.Y.** Tony and Delores Harris and their children, Shelby, 15, and Marc, 11, were found dead in their home. Each family member was tied up, shot in the head, doused with gasoline, and set on fire.

**MURDER: Philadelphia, Pa.** Mark Martinez Jr., 17, and Mark Christian, 26, were convicted for the murder of two teenage brothers, Cornell and Anthony Williams, who failed to return the receipts of $500 worth of crack.

**MURDER: Vitoria, Brazil** Gabriel Mayra, a French Roman Catholic priest, was found shot to death, the victim of an apparent robbery.

**RAPE: Los Angeles County, Calif.** Frank Palomino, 37, was arrested and charged with the abduction and rape of a 16-year-old Mexican girl who had come to the U.S. seeking work. Under the pretense of finding her a job, the girl was taken to Tijuana, Mexico, and raped.

## December 24

**DRUGS: New York, N.Y.** Victor Eduardo Mera-Mosquera, convicted in absentia of smuggling and distributing more than a ton of cocaine, was extradited to the U.S. from Colombia.

**MURDER: Santa Ana, El Salvador** Five people were killed and 45 injured when Julio Retana threw a grenade onto a dance floor at a party he had not been allowed to enter because he was drunk. Retana was among the dead.

**MURDER: Van Nuys, Calif.** Anna Alfaro, 22, was dragged from her family's home and shot to death just two days after reporting to police that her former boyfriend, Ruben Dario Garcia, 20, had threatened her. Garcia was charged with the killing Dec. 28.

**RIOT: Bogota, Colombia** Six prison inmates were killed and five guards injured when police stormed a La Picota jail cell block that had been taken over by inmates.

**SMUGGLING: Bangkok, Thailand** Tsuyoshi Shiwara, 20, was arrested and charged with attempting to smuggle 98 turtles and 185 Oriental lizards in his suitcases. He was convicted the next day and given a three-month suspended sentence and fined $100.

## December 25

**CHILD MOLESTATION: Los Angeles, Calif.** Simon Bermudez, 37, a former aide at the Echo Park Recreation Center day-care, was charged with molestation and lewd conduct. Another former aide, Charles Chavez, 33, was arrested Oct. 18 on similar charges.

**DRUGS: Panama City, Panama** Lieutenant Colonel Luis del Cid, 46, an associate of deposed dictator General Manuel Antonio Noriega, was flown to Miami, Fla., to stand trial on drug-related charges after he surrendered and was arrested by Drug Enforcement Administration agents.

**EXECUTION: Bucharest, Romania** Ousted President Nicolae Ceausescu and his wife Elena were executed following a secret trial before a military tribunal in which both were found guilty of "grave crimes" against Romania, including ordering the massacre of thousands of protesters and stealing more than $1 billion from the country. The trial was conducted by Romanians who had taken power in the days since being fired upon by government security troops in Timisoara on Dec. 17.

**MURDER: El Sereno, Calif.** An exchange of gunfire between neighbors at a Christmas party left Tommy Frajio, 29, dead. Police arrested Johnny Vega, 21, and Robert Jones, 31, in connection with his death.

**MURDER: Jerusalem, Israel** Army Colonel Yehuda Meir was ordered to face a court-martial on charges that he told his troops to beat and break the legs of 20 bound and gagged Palestinian rock-throwers in January 1988. Meir resigned from the army in April.

**MURDER: New York, N.Y.** Felix Agosto, 25, and Angel Silva, 31, were arrested and charged with the death of 11-year-old Elford Verette, who was killed Dec. 24 by a stray bullet fired from across the street.

**MURDER: New York, N.Y.** In successive drive-by shootings, Ebony Williams, 18, and Lysa Biffle, 26, were killed on the same street. Before she died, Biffle gave birth to a boy. On Dec. 29, Eric Reed, 17, and Dwayne Faust, 16, were arrested and charged with the killings.

**MURDER: Waterbury, Conn.** The body of Julia Ashe, 22, who disappeared Dec. 16, was found bound and gagged and partially submerged in the Mad River.

## December 26

**DRUGS: Seattle, Wash.** Forty-three-year-old Brian Peter Daniels, perhaps the largest single U.S. supplier of Southeast Asian marijuana, pleaded guilty to smuggling nearly 200 tons of marijuana into the U.S.

**DRUGS: West Azerbaijan, Iran** Members of the Islamic Revolution Committees seized 247 pounds of heroin, valued at $7.5 million, and arrested 24 people after breaking up three heroin-smuggling rings.

**EXECUTION: Colombo, Sri Lanka** Saman Piyasiri Fernando, the last senior leader of the Sinhalese People's Liberation Front, was executed along with 67 others in a government crackdown against the militant nationalist group.

**FRAUD: Portland, Maine** Michael Denton, a 29-year-old contractor, pleaded guilty to charges that he conspired to defraud federal agencies by filing false claims about energy-saving improvements.

## December 27

**DRUGS: Panama** U.S. forces arrested Mike Harari, 62, a former Israeli intelligence official, who trained General Manuel Antonio Noriega's security force. Harari was suspected to have deposited Noriega's drug profits in Israeli banks.

**MURDER: Fremont, Calif.** Michael K. Doeschot, 27, was arraigned on charges of murder in the death of Graham

Glickfeld, 31, whom Doeschot allegedly ran over with a car. Glickfeld apparently asked Doeschot to kill him and offered him money to do it.

**ROBBERY: Aix-en-Provence, France** Seven robbers stole 7 million francs from an armored van they had damaged with a grenade. As the gunmen fled, they opened fire with a machine gun on a crowd of shoppers. No one was hurt.

**ROBBERY: Los Angeles, Calif.** Two armed men gagged and handcuffed the owners and five employees of the Rope Mine Jewelry Corp., and then stole nearly $1 million in gold dust, bars, and chain jewelry.

### December 28

**COUNTERFEITING: Phoenix, Ariz.** Eighteen people were indicted in a "worldwide conspiracy" of money-laundering and violation of trademark laws in the manufacture of counterfeit name-brand athletic shoes.

**ESCAPE: Los Angeles County, Calif.** Prisoners Raymond Vansandt, 35, David Jeffrey, 30, Kimberly Rodenborg, 19, and Frank Gonzalez, 46, escaped while being driven to Los Angeles by David and Ellen Hollie, representatives of a private extradition company.

**MURDER: Boston, Mass.** William Bennett, the prime suspect in the shooting of Charles and Carol Stuart, was picked out of a line-up by Charles Stuart. The Stuarts were allegedly abducted, robbed, and shot. Carol Stuart, who was pregnant, died.

**MURDER: Chicago, Ill.** Robert Williams, 36, was indicted on charges that he stabbed to death his roommate, Willie Epps, 48, during an argument.

**MURDER: Dover, N.H.** William Lepine, 37, a former Somersworth city official, was sentenced to 43 years to life in prison for trying to kill his former wife and her boyfriend by setting fire to the building in which she lived. The fire killed Dwayne Chubb, 26, another resident of the building.

**MURDER: Naples, Italy** Ahmet Gulduoglu, a Turkish security guard, apparently shot and killed his friend, Vincenzo Di Scala, alsò employed at the Turkish embassy. Gulduoglu, a former soldier who reportedly was mentally unbalanced, then killed himself.

**SUICIDE: Vienna, Austria** Marin Ceausescu, eldest brother of Romania's slain ruler, Nicolae Ceausescu, hanged himself in the Romanian Trade Mission.

**TERRORISM: Atlanta, Ga.** A group calling itself Americans for a Competent Federal Judicial System claimed responsibility for the four Southern mail bombs and threatened further attacks on black leaders for "savage acts of violence by black men against white women."

**THEFT: Sullivan County, Mass.** John Fairbanks, 66, a former district court judge, was indicted on charges of stealing $1.8 million from the trust funds of clients in his private law practice.

### December 29

**ASSAULT: Lakeland, Fla.** Sisters Sheila C. and Sherry C. Gill, both 30, were arrested on charges of tampering with a witness and assault with a firearm after they allegedly threatened Carl Kyte regarding an upcoming murder case at which he was to testify.

**DRUGS: Medellin, Colombia** The Colombian military arrested drug trafficking suspect Jose Ocampo Obando—allegedly fifth in power in the Medellin drug cartel—after seizing 3 tons of dynamite from cocaine traffickers planning to attack police.

**MURDER: Chicago, Ill.** Felefia Thomas, 33, was indicted on charges that on Dec. 11 he stabbed to death his wife Marion Griffin-Thomas, 33, and then tried to burn her body.

**MURDER: San Francisco, Calif.** U.S. federal appeals court ruled that the government of Taiwan is liable for the October 1984 murder of U.S. journalist Henry Liu, 52, whose killer was linked to Taiwan's military intelligence chief, Wong Hsilin, now imprisoned in Taiwan for the killing.

**OBSTRUCTING A FLIGHT PATH: Los Angeles, Calif.** Alcide Chaisson, 69, was arrested and charged with using a mirror to blind pilots taking off and landing at the Crystalaire Airport. Chaisson said he was averse to planes flying over his property.

**RAPE: Boston, Mass.** Boston police officer Joey A. Brewer was convicted in a Superior Court of the Oct. 22, 1988, rape of a 15-year-old girl in the back seat of his police cruiser.

**ROBBERY: Cambridge, Mass.** James J. McCormick, 50, Benjamin Wonsch, 49, and four other men of a U.S. Canadian robbery ring were arrested in an office above the Coolidge Bank and Trust Co., which they were allegedly going to rob.

**WEAPONS VIOLATION: East Detroit, Mich.** Eric Norman Sanderson, 46, was arrested and charged with probation violation and weapons possession after he threatened to kill a woman, with whom he had had an affair, and her husband.

**WEAPONS VIOLATION: Los Angeles, Calif.** Mailman Floyd Bertran Sterling, 34, was charged with cruelty to animals and carrying a concealed weapon for allegedly shooting to death a German shepherd named Skippy.

### December 30

**MURDER: New York, N.Y.** Steven Pleasants, 30, was shot to death during a fight outside a Manhattan nightclub. Another man was killed and a third wounded, but the gunman escaped.

**ROBBERY: Albany, N.Y.** A man driven in a cab to the First American Bank told the cabby, Carl Olson, Jr., to wait for him while he robbed the bank. Olson alerted police, who arrived alter the man had fled with $10,000.

**DRUGS: Washington, D.C.** U.S. Supreme Court chief justice William H. Rehnquist stated in his annual year-end report that Congress needs to create more federal judgeships to handle the escalating caseload of drug-related trials.

**MURDER: Panama City, Panama** Panama's attorney general, Rogelio Cruz, announced that the country's new government would charge deposed dictator General Manuel Antonio Noriega with murder for 10 officers killed in an Oct. 3 military coup.

# 1990

## January 1

**MURDER: Narsaq, Greenland** An 18-year-old student shot and killed seven persons and wounded another with a semi-automatic weapon during a New Year's Eve Party at a dormitory.

## January 2

**ASSAULT: London, England** Kenneth Aymer was sentenced to six months in prison for ordering his pit bull to attack a couple at a party on December 28, 1989. The dog was ordered destroyed.

**BOMBING: Belfast, Northern Ire.** The IRA claimed responsibility for the car bombing deaths of a taxi driver and Ulster Democratic Party member Harold Dickey.

**MURDER-SUICIDE: Los Angeles, Calif.** Philip L. Saylor shot and killed his lover, Steven C. Jenkins, who was dying of AIDS at Cedars-Sinai Medical Center, and then shot and killed himself.

**MURDER: Ripley, Tenn.** Ule Reynolds, an 82-year-old barber, confessed to the murders of two deputy sheriffs. Reynolds was found sitting on a gun in the squad car of his victims.

## January 3

**DRUGS: Panama City, Panama** General Manuel Antonio Noriega left the Vatican Embassy and surrendered to U.S. authorities to face drug trafficking and money laundering charges in the U.S.

**MURDER: London, England** Andreas Savvas was convicted of attempted murder for pushing a woman into the path of a speeding fire truck.

**MURDER: St. Charles, Mo.** Charles Crewse was arrested for conspiring to commit murder by allegedly offering another man $1,000 to kill his former girlfriend by injecting her with the AIDS virus.

**SEXUAL ASSAULT: Chicago, Ill.** Eric Clark was sentenced to 15 years in prison for the 1982 kidnapping and sexual assault of a 10-year-old girl. The sentence was to run concurrently with a 10-to-25-year sentence for Clark's 1985 rape of a 12-year-old girl.

## January 4

**MURDER: Boston, Mass.** Charles Stuart, who had killed his wife Carol for insurance money in October 1989, while driving with her in his car through a black community, and then blamed the slaying on a mythical Negro gunman, learned that he was about to be arrested for the murder scheme and leaped to his death from a bridge in Boston harbor.

**MURDER: Sudan** The mass murder of more than 2,000 rebel villagers in Sudan by pro-government Arab militia was reported this date. In late December 1989, two members of the Shilok tribe killed their Moslem employer which prompted the local militiamen to destroy everyone in the village with machine guns.

**PRISON RIOT: Leopoldov, Czech.** Inmates not included in a general amnesty rioted and took control of parts of the penitentiary.

## January 5

**DRUGS: Brooklyn, N.Y.** Claudia Mason, mother of convicted drug dealer Howard "Pappy" Mason, was sentenced to 10 years in prison for drug possession and conspiring to take over her son's crack business.

**MURDER: Kansas City, Kan.** Seven cult members sought in connection with five April 1989 murders of a Kirtland, Ohio, family, were arrested. Cult leader Jeffrey Lundgren and five others remained at large. Lundgren, his wife Alice, and his son Damon, would be taken into custody on January 7, 1990, in National City, California.

**MURDER: Rochester, N.Y.** Arthur Shawcross, convicted of strangling an 8-year-old girl, pleaded not guilty to charges that he murdered and mutilated eight local women since his 1987 parole.

**MURDER: St. Louis, Mo.** Reginald Perry was convicted of murder in the stabbing death of his father, civil rights activist Ivory Perry. He would be sentenced to life in prison on February 16, 1990.

**RAPE: Norcross, Ga.** John Charles Whipple, a suspect in five Will County, Illinois, rapes, was arrested and charged with three rapes and one attempted rape. Whipple admitted to police that he committed all nine acts.

**SEXUAL ASSAULT: Ventura, Calif.** Dwaine Tinsley, the cartoonist who created the *Hustler* magazine cartoon character "Chester the Molester," was convicted of molesting a teenage girl. He was sentenced to six months in prison on May 3, 1990.

**TAX EVASION: Milwaukee, Wis.** Lynette Harris and Leigh Ann Conley, twins who appeared in *Playboy* magazine, were arrested in court for not paying taxes on about $1 million in cash gifts from millionaire David Kritzik between 1984 and 1987.

## January 6

**DRUGS: Monterey, Mex.** Americans John Bradley and Joseph Brandall Evans were arrested after they ran a roadblock and police found 220 pounds of marijuana in their surfboards.

**MURDER: Victorville, Calif.** Brian Keith Framstead, who set himself on fire after a highway patrolman pulled his car over, was arrested for the murder of his ex-girlfriend, Tammy Marie Davis.

**MURDER: Wickenburg, Ariz.** The body of Carrie Gaines was discovered in a mine shaft. She was reportedly murdered by her husband, Robert Earl Gaines, and accomplice Steven Allen Simpson, who were arrested on January 4, 1990.

## January 7

**BURGLARY: Portland, Ore.** Howard Prink shot and killed Billy Yahnson, an unarmed 15-year-old boy who was burglarizing his home. Prink was not charged under Oregon law which allowed the use of deadly force against an intruder in certain circumstances.

**MURDER: San Salvador, El Sal.** President Alfredo Cristiani announced that members of the military had been responsible for the murders of six Jesuit priests and two others in late November 1989, because the priests had denounced civil rights abuses on the part of government forces and had supported a negotiated settlement with leftist guerrillas to end the long-running civil war.

### January 8

**MURDER: Norwalk, Conn.** Richard B. Crafts, convicted in November 1989, of murdering his wife and shredding her body with a wood chipper, was sentenced to 50 years in prison.

**ROBBERY: Kingston, Can.** Prisoner Robert Walker, released on a six-hour parole, got drunk with his guard in a bar, then walked across the street and robbed a bank before being recaptured.

**SECRET POLICE: East Ger.** An official for the East German government, which had promised to disband its secret police organization in December 1989, announced that 60,000 secret police members (out of an original 85,000) were still on government payrolls.

**SEXUAL ASSAULT: Minneapolis, Minn.** Christopher Tsipouras, a bodyguard for rapper LL Cool J, was sentenced to 10 years in prison for sexually assaulting a 15-year-old girl, following an August 1989 concert.

### January 9

**ASSASSINATION: Lima, Peru** Enrique López Albujar, former defense minister, was shot and killed, apparently by Shining Path terrorists. Police detained 15,000 people in their search for the killers.

**KIDNAPPING: Paris, Fr.** Olivier Groues, president of Rank Xerox-France, was shot and critically wounded by police who stormed his office after a former employee held him and four co-workers hostage for seven hours.

**MURDER: Palatka, Fla.** Jeffrey Feltner was sentenced to life in prison for smothering a nursing home patient, after confessing that he murdered seven patients in order to publicize poor nursing home conditions.

### January 10

**DRUGS: Houston, Texas** Gosie Mbachu was arrested for drug smuggling by customs agents at Houston Intercontinental Airport after an X-ray showed his stomach contained 42 condoms filled with heroin.

**DRUGS: Tehran, Iran** Convicted of smuggling drugs, 31 persons were hanged in a mass execution.

**JUDICIARY: Washington, D.C.** The U.S. Supreme Court ruled 5-4 to reaffirm its exclusion of illegally obtained evidence in a criminal trial, with the exception that such evidence could be used to contradict testimony in court by a defendant.

**MURDER: Phoenix, Ariz.** Leary Frederick Darling was sentenced to 25 years in prison for stabbing two persons to death and wounding three others. In a separate Phoenix case, Michael Anthony Sanders, who pleaded guilty to beating to death a blind woman and her parents, was sentenced to life in prison.

**SECRET POLICE: East Ger.** An official in East Germany's new political coalition stated that the government was forming a new secret police organization.

**TERRORISM: London, England** Danny Morrison, senior official of Sinn Fein, was charged with terrorism and conspiracy to commit murder.

**TERRORISM: Tocata, Peru** Nine people were killed by Shining Path terrorists.

### January 11

**EXECUTIONS: Guangzhou, China** Declared guilty of crimes ranging from rape to murder by a People's Court, 31 persons were executed.

**FRAUD: Switz.** Gerald L. Rogers, convicted in 1982 of defrauding U.S. investors of more than $90 million, and who had escaped in 1987 after he was allowed to remain free pending sentencing, was located and arrested.

**MURDER: Chicago, Ill.** Alicia Abraham, who allowed her live-in boyfriend, Johnny Campbell, to torture her two oldest sons, was convicted of the murder of one boy and the aggravated battery of the other.

**MURDER: New York, N.Y.** Bienvenido Castillo, a drug dealer convicted of murdering undercover narcotics officer Christopher Hoban, was sentenced to 57 years in prison.

**SEXUAL ASSAULT: Loveland, Colo.** Raymond Mickelic, an artist suspected of committing 500 sexual assaults on children over a 10-year period, turned himself in to the police.

### January 12

**BOMBINGS: San Juan, Puerto Rico** Pipe bombs exploded in a U.S. Marine Corps recruiting office and a Westinghouse Electric Company store.

**BURGLARY: County Meath, Ire.** Burglars stole five paintings estimated to be worth £1 million from 13th-century Dusany Castle.

**DRUGS: Jacksonville, Fla.** Jack Carlton Reed, a Medellin cocaine cartel pilot convicted of conspiracy to distribute cocaine, received two consecutive life terms.

**MURDER: Fairfax, Va.** Tammie Lynn Smith pleaded guilty to attempted murder after poisoning her 2-year-old son in order to convince her husband to return from Army duty in Germany.

**SECRET POLICE: East Ger.** Hans Modrow, premier of East Germany, stated that no new secret police organization would be organized before the national elections were held. Modrow admitted that the secret police had continued to spy on political opponents to communism.

### January 13

**ASSAULT: New York, N.Y.** Actress Viveca Lindfors, 70, was slashed across the neck on a Greenwich Village street by a gang member who had attacked another pedestrian only minutes earlier. Suspect Peter Bedford would be arrested on January 20, 1990.

**MURDER: San Salvador, El Sal.** President Cristiani announced that one colonel, two lieutenants and six enlisted men (including one soldier still being sought) had been indicted for murdering six Jesuit priests and two others.

**MOB VIOLENCE: Baku, Azerbaijan** Anti-Armenian mobs, mostly youths, stormed through the Armenian section of town, destroying Armenian shops and homes; thirty persons, mostly Armenians, were killed in the riots.

*January 14*

**DRUGS: Bogatá, Colombia** Officials ordered the arrest of Gilberto Rodriguez Orejuela, the alleged leader of the Cali cocaine cartel, on charges of money laundering and drug trafficking.

**MURDER: San Clemente, Calif.** Keith Eugene Goodman, an ex-convict who allegedly preyed upon pen pals he made while in prison, was arrested for murdering four gay men in two states.

*January 15*

**DRUGS: London, England** Jockeys Alan Mackay and Frank Curley were charged with membership in a £7 million international drug smuggling ring.

**MOB VIOLENCE: East Ger.** A crowd of more than 100,000 persons who had gathered outside the headquarters of the East German security service (secret police) for a peaceful rally to oppose the organization of another secret police organization turned violent; thousands of protestors stormed into the headquarters of the security service, destroying the interior and burning thousands of documents, particularly dossiers put together by security agents on political opponents.

*January 16*

**DRUGS: Los Angeles, Calif.** Honduran drug lord Juan Ramon Matta Balleseros was sentenced to life in prison without parole.

**FORGERY: Hartford, Conn.** Art forger Robert L. Trotter was sentenced to 10 months in prison and ordered to donate four of his forgeries of 19th century paintings to a group of students for study.

**MURDER: Clarksville, Ark.** Wendell Ayers was charged with murder for burning automobile dealer George G. Lancer to death with hydrochloric acid.

**MURDER: Lake County, Ind.** George Frances Swetkey was charged with murder after admitting he shot and strangled Deputy Sheriff Gary Rosser and Rosser's wife.

*January 17*

**BURGLARY: Eidsberg, Norway** Burglars used a truck to escape with a 1,400-pound bank teller machine worth $27,000 to obtain the $16,200 in cash contained in the machine.

**MURDER: Beaverton, Ore.**: Yoshio Morimoto was arrested and charged with strangling his wife and two children.

*January 18*

**CHILD MOLESTATION: Los Angeles, Calif.** After the longest and costliest trial in U.S. history (33 months, 60,000 pages of transcript, a cost of $15 million), Peggy McMartin Buckey and her son Raymond Buckey, who operated the McMartin Pre-School in Manhattan Beach, California, were found not guilty on fifty-two counts of child molestation. Charges against five other defendants in the case had been dropped. The jury criticized the manner in which children had been interviewed about possible molestation, saying that it appeared that they had been asked leading questions.

**DRUGS: Washington, D.C.** Marion Barry, Jr., the controversial black mayor of Washington, D.C., was arrested by local police on drug charges. Barry was reportedly lured to the Vista International Hotel in downtown Washington by a female friend and former model in an FBI sting. Barry was shown later on an FBI tape as he bought crack cocaine from an undercover agent, stuffed this into a pipe and smoked it.

**MALFEASANCE: Bulgaria** Former Communist party boss Todor Zhivkov, was put under house arrest, charged with malfeasance of his office and with misappropriating government property and funds.

**ROBBERY: Brooklyn, N.Y.** FBI agents and police fatally shot Joseph Mangine and Joseph Coluccio after the two robbed a bank.

*January 19*

**DRUGS: Washington, D.C.** Mayor Marion Barry was arraigned in U.S. District Court on one charge of willfully possessing cocaine.

**EXTORTION: New York, N.Y.** Former U.S. Representative Robert Garcia and his wife, Jane Lee Garcia, convicted of extorting $76,000 from Wedtech Corp., for help in obtaining government contracts, were sentenced to three years each in prison.

**MURDER: San Salvador, El Salvador** Nine soldiers (three officers and six enlisted soldiers), one of whom was still being sought, were indicted in El Salvador, for the murders of six Jesuit priests and two others on November 16, 1989. All were reported members of the terrorist group, FMLN. Sergeant Antonio Avalos and Private Oscar Amay initially admitted to the shootings.

**MURDER/RAPE: New Orleans, La.** Steven Quatreving was convicted of murdering and raping a retarded woman in a case that represented the city's first use of genetic test results as legal evidence.

**MURDER: Spartenburg, S.C.** Gerry Douglas Kerpan was charged with the 1977 Lake County, Illinois, abduction and killing of 12-year-old Lisa Slusser after confessing to FBI agents.

**RAPE: Cleveland, Ohio** James E. Cornell was sentenced to two life terms and nine consecutive four to 10 years for the repeated sexual assault of three boys under 13 who lived with Cornell's brother and their mother.

*January 20*

**MURDER: Bronx, N.Y.** Wayne A. Wilson, while coming to the aid of his mother, was shot and killed by two thieves who had forced their way into her apartment.

**ROBBERY: Los Angeles, Calif.** Edward Leigh Hunt, Jr., a former armored car guard who admittedly stole $651,000 in 1988, turned himself into the FBI.

*January 21*

**DRUGS: Flagstaff, Ariz.** Five men were arrested on drug charges for allegedly flying 907 pounds of marijuana from Mexico to Pulliam Airport.

**RAPE: San Leandro, Calif.** A 12-year-old boy admitting raping his 5-year-old stepsister and claimed that a television show depicting a couple making love inspired him.

**RIOT: Srinagar, India** The Indian army killed more than 25 people and wounded at least sixty more persons demonstrating for the independence of Kashmir, the only state in India with a Muslim majority.

*January 22*

**FRAUD: Syracuse, N.Y.** Robert T. Morris, charged with creating a computer "worm" that crippled the Internet computer network, was convicted of computer fraud.

**MURDER: Caernavon, Wales** Soap opera actor Clive Roberts was sent to prison for life for the March 1989 murder of his girlfriend, TV production assistant Elinor Roberts.

*January 23*

**MURDER: Brevard County, Fla.** James Hudson Savage, an Australian aborigine, was sentenced to death and to two life terms for the murder, rape and robbery of Barbara Ann Barber.

**RAPE: Dallas, Texas** Donald Ray Gray was arrested and charged with kidnapping and rape for two of six attacks on areas school girls.

**SEXUAL ASSAULT: Chicago, Ill.** Clifton Davis, a 70-year-old man with a history of sexual offenses, was charged with sexually assaulting a 12-year-old girl.

**WAR CRIMES: Los Angeles, Calif.** Bruno Karl Blach, accused World War II concentration camp guard, was extradited to West Germany to face charges of killing three prisoners in 1945.

*January 24*

**ASSASSINATION: Panama City, Panama** American William Joyce, finance director of the Panama Canal Commission, was fatally shot by home invaders. Joyce will die the following day.

**FRAUD: Alexandria, Va.** Richard Marcinko, retired Navy commander of an elite anti-terrorist squad, was found guilty of conspiring to defraud the government of $113,000 in kickbacks on a hand-grenade contract.

**MURDER: Miami, Fla.** The body of Arik Afek, an Israeli businessman with ties to the Medellin drug cartel, was discovered in the trunk of a car at Miami International Airport.

**MURDER: Riverhead, N.Y.** Richard Angelo, a former nurse convicted of killing four elderly patients by injecting them with Pavulon, was sentenced to 50 years in prison.

*January 25*

**DRUGS: Rockdale County, Ga.** Edward Lee Timberlake was sentenced to life plus 25 years and William Preston Broome received 60 years in prison and both were fined $1 million for cocaine trafficking.

**MURDER: Blakely, Ga.** Nelson Earl Mitchell was sentenced to death for the 1986 murder of Iron City Police Chief Robert Cunningham after Cunningham stopped his brother for speeding.

**MURDER/ROBBERY: White Hall, Jamaica** Five persons were shot to death by four men who broke into their home demanding money and marijuana. Police believed that the killings resulted from a drug-smuggling disagreement.

**MURDER/SUICIDE: Appleton, Wis.** Todd Longsine, 19, killed his 14-month-old son and his wife Bonnie, 18, then committed suicide.

*January 26*

**FRAUD: Tuba City, Ariz.** Navajo leader Peter MacDonald, Sr., and 40 co-defendants were ordered to stand trial on charges of defrauding the tribe of $33.4 million.

**MURDER: Cobb County, Ga.** Raymond Miller was sentenced to life in prison for murdering his 26-year-old daughter after she refused to continue their incestuous relationship.

**WAR CRIMES: Sydney Aus.** Ivan Timofeyevich Polyukhovich, 73, was charged with complicity in the deaths of 850 Jews during World War II, marking Australia's first prosecution of an alleged Nazi war criminal.

**THEFT: Salt Lake City, Ut.** Former Air Force security guards Brian David Roth and Danny Joe Stroud received prison terms of 10 years and 37 months, respectively, for stealing three fighter jets worth $10 million.

*January 27*

**GENOCIDE: Bucharest, Rom.** Four former high-ranking officials in Nicolae Ceausescu's regime went on trial, charged with the deaths of hundreds of people during the December 1989 revolution.

*January 28*

**BOMBING: Londonderry, Northern Ire.** A teenager was killed and eight other persons injured when an IRA bomb exploded during a march commemorating the 18th anniversary of Bloody Sunday when British troops killed 14 Catholic demonstrators.

*January 29*

**EMBEZZLEMENT: Baltimore, Md.** Private escrow agent Marilyn Louise Harrell, appearing in federal court, pleaded guilty to embezzling $4.75 million that was earmarked for the U.S. Department of Housing and Urban Development. She also confessed that she had under-reported her income for 1987. In her defense, Harrell had earlier claimed that she had given much of what she embezzled to the poor and to many charities, and that she had earned the nickname "Robin HUD." Harrell, said prosecutors, had been "her own biggest charity."

**MALFEASANCE: Bulgaria** Former Communist boss Todo Zhivkov, accused of malfeasance of office and stealing government property and money, was sent to prison.

**MURDER: Beatrice, Neb.** Thomas Winslow was sentenced to 50 years in prison and Ada Joann Taylor to 40 years for the 1985 rape and murder of 68-year-old Helen Wilson. Three others received 10-year sentences.

**RAPE/MUTILATION: Tacoma, Wash.** Trial began for Earl Shriner, charged with raping and mutilating a 7-year-old boy. He will be convicted on February 7, 1990.

*January 30*

**FRAUD: Dallas, Texas** Connie Arvidson was convicted of conspiracy and mail fraud in a $2 million counterfeit coupon scheme. Co-defendant David Rees was convicted of conspiracy.

**KIDNAPPING: Careri, Italy** A group calling itself the Anonymous Kidnappers released Cesare Casella, whom they had held for two years.

**MURDER: Atlanta, Ga.** The trial of Emmanuel Fitzgerald Hammond, a black man charged with murdering Julie Love, a white teacher, began under tight security.

### January 31

**BOMBING: Kabul, Afghanistan** A car bomb exploded killing five persons and injuring 105 more outside the government's official press organ, Bakhtar Information Agency.

### February 1

**MURDER: Bankok, Thailand** Three Saudi Arabian embassy employees were shot and killed in two apparently coordinated attacks near the embassy.

**MURDER: Lewiston, Id.** Bradley R. Thomasson, 17, was convicted of killing his parents, reportedly after a family fight over his using the family car.

**PIRACY: Barisal, Bengal** Twenty-five pirates hijacked a river ferry bound for Dhaka, killing three policeman.

**ROBBERY: Milford, Conn.** Edward M. Aranjo and Ellen M. Marks, accused of committing 24 robberies, were arrested after a shoe store robbery in which a clerk was stabbed.

### February 2

**EXECUTION: Riyadh, Saudi Arabia** Two Thais and a Saudi were convicted of rape, robbery and murder and were beheaded.

**GENOCIDE: Bucharest, Rom.** A military court convicted four top aides of deposed Communist dictator Nicolae Ceasescu of genocide. The four, including Emil Bobu, ranked third in the Ceasescu regime, were all sentenced to prison for life.

**MURDER: Portland, Ore.** Mark Thomas was sentenced to life imprisonment for killing prostitute Traci Lee Thomson and conspiring to kill a key witness to the slaying.

**MURDER: Tampa, Fla.** Deaf-mute Brian Charles Hodge was sentenced to life in prison after pleading guilty to the murder and rape of 14-year-old Karl Heiland.

### February 3

**DRUGS: Guaduas, Colombia** Officials seized more than 200 guns and $2.5 million in drug money on the property of slain drug lord Jose Gonzalo Rodriguez Gacha.

**EXECUTION: Accra, Ghana** Nine men found guilty of armed robbery were executed by firing squad.

**KIDNAPPING: Brooklyn, N.Y.** Two-day-old Steven Earl Penda was abducted from a hospital nursery. Utopia Quinones was charged after the baby's safe return on February 4

**MURDER: Clarksdale, Miss.** Anthony Carr and Robert Simon were charged with the execution-style murders of a family of four found earlier in their burning farmhouse. Willie Lee Henderson, who will be arrested February 4, was also charged with the killings.

### February 4

**MURDER: Fukuoka, Japan** Masaru Himuro surrendered to police after reportedly strangling his 70-year-old neighbor because she refused to clean up after stray cats she fed.

**MURDER: Denver Colo.** The body of Dion Granados who apparently hanged himself, was found. The bodies of his wife Christine and his 11-week-old son, Dion, Jr., were found in the family's home.

**TERRORISM: Cairo, Egypt** Palestinian terrorists attacked a bus carrying Israeli academics and their wives en route to Cairo on the main highway east of the city, killing eight and wounding another seventeen persons.

### February 5

**MURDER: Cleveland, Ohio** Arthur Halloran killed his ex-wife, Katherine Clark, outside her workplace and was shot to death by police.

**MURDER: Greenburgh, N.Y.** Schoolteacher Carolyn Warmus was indicted for shooting to death her lover's wife, Betty Jeanne Solomon.

**MURDER: Los Angeles, Calif.** Obstetrician Milos Klvana was sentenced to 53 years to life in prison for the deaths of eight infants and a fetus.

**RAPE: Naples, Italy** U.S. Navy enlisted men Patrick R. McCoy and Brian T. Vaugh were sentenced to four years in jail for raping a Naples woman in September 1988.

**RIOT: Leipsig, East Ger.** A weekly demonstration for German unity was disrupted by hundreds of neo-Nazi skinheads who Marched through the city yelling "Sieg Heil," and smashing windows.

**TERRORISM: Kan Yunis, Israel** Jamil Rizik El-Bayouk and his pregnant wife Intissar were stabbed to death by masked Palestinians who suspected them of collaborating with Israel.

### February 6

**ASSAULT: Waitangi, New Zeal.** A radical female, Maori, was arrested after she threw a wet cloth at Queen Elizabeth II during Waitangi celebrations commemorating the founding of modern New Zealand.

**MANSLAUGHTER: Birmingham, Ala.** Doris Franklin and Eddie James Amous were charged with manslaughter for allowing their 5-month-old daughter to starve to death while they went on a drinking spree.

**MURDER: Pontiac Mich.** Susan Farrell was sentenced to life in prison for the sledgehammer murder of her husband while her son, Robert Baker, received 40 to 60 months in prison as an accessory after the fact.

### February 7

**COUNTERFEITING: Tokyo, Japan** Bank of Japan officials and the Ministry of Finance admitted that inside their vaults were counterfeit gold coins amounting to $71 million.

**KIDNAPPING: Hattiesburg, Miss.** Florida lawyer Newton Alfred Winn was convicted of extortion, conspiracy to kidnap, and perjury in the 1988 disappearance of 74-year-old Annie Laurie Hearin.

**MURDER: Ocotal, Nicaragua** Orlando Canales Sandoval, armed with a rifle, entered the home of Maura Huete, shot six persons to death, injured a seventh and kept several others hostage for six hours before surrendering.

**MURDER: Santa Ana, Calif.** Reputed Mafia underboss Michael Anthony Rizzitello was convicted of attempted murder and mayhem.

### February 8

**DRUGS: Miami, Fla.** U.S. District Court Judge William Hoeveler announced that deposed Panamanian dictator Manuel Noriega would stand trial for drug-trafficking.

**MURDER: Cuzco, Peru** American Charles John Williams was found shot to death in the ancient ruins.

**MURDER: Fort Worth, Texas** A jury which heard a tape recording of the murder victim's dying words took 12 minutes to find Martin Stovall guilty of killing his estranged wife by backing her into a drill bit, dousing her with gasoline and setting her on fire.

**MURDER: Washington, D.C.** Marlon A. Chin was sentenced to 115 years to life in prison for two murders and other felonies.

### February 9

**BRIBERY: New York, N.Y.** Advertising agency Young & Rubicam, Inc. was fined $500,000 for bribing foreign officials in an attempt to keep the Jamaican tourism account.

**MURDER: Allentown, Pa.** Dennis Counterman was sentenced to death after being convicted of the 1988 burning deaths of his three sons.

**MURDER: London, England** Carol McDonald was sentenced to four years in jail for conspiracy to murder her lover's common law wife.

**SMUGGLING: Chula Vista, Calif.** U.S. Customs, the DEA and the California Highway Patrol revealed the results of Operation Hydra, in which seven smuggling rings were broken and more than $3.2 million in fenced items were confiscated.

### February 10

**MURDER: Tuxtla Gutierrez, Mex.** Wealthy landowner Roberto Zenteno Rojas was sentenced to 30 years in prison for murdering a farm workers' leader he said was responsible for disputes over his land.

**MURDER/ROBBERY: Las Cruces, N. M.** Two young girls, their father and a third girl were murdered by two robbers who forced them and three other people into a bowling alley office. The gunmen then set the building on fire and fled.

**ROBBERY: New York, N.Y.** Armed robbers attacked three unarmed Bloomingdale's security guards and stole at least $500,000 in cash receipts.

### February 11

**PRISON RELEASE: South Africa** Nelson Mandela, imprisoned (in 1964) in South Africa, for more than twenty-seven years for plotting to overthrow the government and for terrorist activities, was released. He urged that pressure be applied against the white minority government.

**TERRORISM: Takasaki, Japan** A right-wing activist was arrested for firing several shots in former Prime Minister Yashuhiro Nakasone's campaign office.

### February 12

**FRAUD: Dallas, Texas** Former insurance salesman Jerry Hugh Mudd was sentenced to 16 years in prison for defrauding investors out of more than $9 million.

**MURDER: Decatur, Ga.** James D. "Mac" Sumpter was convicted of murdering his 25-year-old wife, Lois, who was shot in the back while fleeing her abusive husband.

**MURDER: Tulsa, Okla.** Eugene Mervin Sides was convicted of the 1989 murders a prominent Osage Indian couple.

### February 13

**KIDNAPPING: Bloomington, Ind.** Arthur Curry, former part-owner of two Michigan hotels, was convicted on four of five counts connected with the kidnapping of millionaire Gayle Cook.

**KIDNAPPING: Prince George, Can.** Three gunmen were arrested after holding 11 students hostage on a school bus.

**MASS EXECUTIONS: Moscow, Rus.** Officials of the KGB, the secret police of the former Soviet Union, announced that 786,098 persons had been summarily executed under the brutal Communist dictatorship of Joseph Stalin.

**MUTINY: Manila, Philippines** Former Lieutenant Colonel Reynaldo Cabauatan was sentenced to 12 years' hard labor for leading troops against army headquarters in a 1987 coup attempt against President Corazon Aquino.

### February 14

**KIDNAPPING: Lumberton, N.C.** Activist Eddie Hatcher was sentenced to 18 years in prison after pleading guilty to holding 20 people hostage in a newsroom to protest alleged police involvement in drug dealing.

**MURDER: Akron, Ohio** Edward Swiger, Jr. was convicted in the murder of fellow fraternity brother Roger Pratt, whom he allegedly abducted and beat to death to prevent Pratt from implicating him in burglary and arson.

**SEXUAL ASSAULT: Dallas, Texas** James Michael Olander received two life sentences for sexually assaulting two young boys.

**TERRORISM: Tehran, Iran** The Iranian government officially reaffirmed the death sentence against *Satanic Verses* author Salmon Rushdie one year after Ayatollah Ruhollah Khomeini first issued the death decree and five days after Iran's fundamentalist spiritual leaders renewed the sentence.

### February 15

**DRUGS: Cartagena, Colombia** In a drug summit attended by the presidents of Bolivia, Colombia, Peru and the U.S., accords were signed where all four countries promised to work together in the war against illegal drug-trafficking. President George Bush, who arrived and departed under tight security, ignored warnings that he might be attacked when attending the meeting. Coca in the production of cocaine was mostly produced in Bolivia and Peru, with Colombia acting as the chief manufacturing center, its drug lords operating the multi-billion-dollar Medellin and Cali cartels.

**DRUGS: Singapore** Officials extended the use of the death penalty to include those convicted of trafficking in cocaine, marijuana and opium.

**DRUGS: Washington, D.C.** Mayor Marion Barry, Jr., was indicted by a federal grand jury on five counts of cocaine possession and three counts of perjury.

**MURDER: Beit Furik, Israel** Mohammed Khatabeh, an admitted informer for Israel, was publicly slashed to death by Palestinian radicals.

**MURDER: Chicago, Ill.** Johnny Campbell and Alicia Abraham were sentenced to life in prison for the torture murder of Abraham's 4-year-old son, Lattie McGee. In a separate Chicago case, Howard Wiley, called an "American urban terrorist" by prosecutors, was sentenced to death by lethal injection for the murders of his girlfriend, Donna Rucks, and Rucks' daughter and sister.

### February 16

**BOMBING: Brussels, Belg.** At least 40 students were injured when a bomb exploded in a college lecture hall.

**KIDNAPPING: Pamplona, Spain** Businessman Adolfo Villoslada, kidnapped by Basque ETA terrorists three months earlier, was released unharmed after a ransom of approximately $2.2 million was paid.

**MURDER: Koru, Kenya**: The burned body of Kenya's foreign minister, Robert Ouko, was found four miles from his home in a sugar cane field. Officials announced that he had been murdered.

**MURDER: Miami, Fla.** Leroy Strachan was charged with the 1946 murder of police officer John Milliedge, who was Miami's first black policeman.

### February 17

**BOMBINGS: Roswell, Ga.** Small bombs exploded in two grocery stores. After four stores received bomb threats, police evacuated shoppers. No injuries were reported.

**DRUGS: Khartoum, Sudan** A military court sentenced Hamid Mohamed Hamad to death by hanging for trafficking in hashish.

**FRAUD: Miami, Fla.** Kentucky dentist Joseph James Brown was arrested and charged with wire fraud by undercover FBI agents for allegedly killing racehorses for a share in insurance money.

**RIOT: Belfast, Northern, Ire.**: Sixty-three persons were injured when rioting erupted between Catholic and Protestant soccer fans.

### February 18

**PRISON ESCAPE: Paris, France** A convict was killed and another critically injured when a line lowered into a prison yard from a helicopter snapped during an attempted escape.

**RAPE: New York, N.Y.** Reginald Darby, a security guard at Columbia University was arrested for allegedly raping a student at knifepoint in an off-campus dormitory.

### February 19

**MURDER: Billericay, England** Mrs. Oi Tai Ngai was charged with murdering her four children.

**MURDER: Moratuwa, Sri Lanka** The body of journalist Richard de Zoysa washed up on a beach two days after he was abducted by gunmen.

**MURDER: Philadelphia, Pa.** Donovan Grant and Michael Gaynor were convicted of murder and sentenced to life imprisonment for their involvement in a 1988 shootout that killed 5-year-old Marcus Yates.

### February 20

**DRUGS: Kansas City, Kan.** Eleven persons were indicted, including Fire Captain Gilbert L. Dowdy, and accused of running a cocaine operation that netted $50 million annually.

**MURDER: Cardiff, Wales** Partially deaf Timothy Robson was told via sign language that he had been sentenced to life in prison for raping and murdering a deaf woman.

**MURDER: Milton, Fla.** Self-proclaimed exorcist Mary Nicholson was convicted of murder and aggravated child abuse in the 1988 starvation death of a 4-year-old girl Nicholson claimed was possessed by demons.

### February 21

**EMBEZZLEMENT: Montgomery, Ala.** Cy Walker pleaded guilty to embezzling $2 million in federal housing funds.

**MURDER: Bililiban, Philippines** American geologist John Robert Mitchell, his wife, Marilou Chatoo, and her father, Silvino Chatoo, were shot to death by Communists guerrillas.

**MURDER: Des Moines, Ia.** Daniel Clarkson was convicted of murder in the August 2, 1988 beating of Miland Van Mill, a homeless Vietnam veteran.

### February 22

**BRIBERY: Norfolk, Va.** Officials at Mid-Atlantic Coca-Cola Bottling Company were indicted on a charge of conspiring to swindle the government through bribery to get Navy cola contracts.

**DRUGS: London, England** Eight men were found guilty of conspiracy to smuggle £18 million worth of marijuana from Africa into England.

**DRUGS: Washington, D.C.** Melvin D. Butler, a drug dealer for the city's largest cocaine ring, was sentenced to life in prison.

### February 23

**KIDNAPPING: Wiesbaden, West Ger.** Briton Alan Rees was sentenced to 13 years in prison for kidnapping and extortion in the 1983 abduction of a Lufthansa manager in Bolivia.

**MURDER: Bay Minette, Ala.** Clayton Joel Flowers, 17, became the youngest person to receive the death penalty since capital punishment was ruled acceptable in 1976 when he was sentenced for a murder he committed when he was 15.

**MURDER: Nevada Ia.** Ruben Deases, 18, was convicted of the May 28, 1989 murder and decapitation of his brothers' girlfriend, Jennifer Ann Gardner.

**RAPE: Detroit, Mich.** Paulette Dale, convicted of criminal sexual conduct for letting her boyfriend repeatedly rape her 12-year-old retarded daughter, was sentenced to 20 to 40 years in prison.

**SEXUAL ASSAULT: Omaha, Neb.** Omaha *World-Herald* newspaper columnist Peter Citron was charged with sexually assaulting two children.

*February 24*

**DRUGS: Kuala Lumpur, Malaysia**: Abdullah Zawawi Yusoff was the 248th person sentenced to death by hanging for drug trafficking since 1975.

**MURDER: Phoenix, Ariz.** Former Phoenix Cardinals football player Darryl Usher and Chiquita Burt were shot and killed by Craig Gardner, Burt's estranged husband, who then shot and wounded himself in the head.

**MURDER: Washington, D.C.** Two gunmen entered a nightclub and killed three men and left two seriously wounded in a shootout in which one of the gunmen, Michael Jones, was also killed.

*February 25*

**MURDER: Pleasanton, Calif.** Manuel Villegas Oller, who shot and killed two maids and wounded another at a motel on February 23, 1990, critically wounded a policeman when officers closed in on him, then shot himself in the head.

*February 26*

**MURDER: Chicago, Ill.** Convicted murderer and rapist Mark Johnson was found guilty in the May 1984 killing of Cherry Wilson.

**MURDER: Las Vegas, Nev.** Cornelius Gunter, lead singer of the rhythm and blues group The Coasters, was shot to death while driving his car.

*February 27*

**ARSON: Tokyo, Japan** Police believed that radicals who opposed the expansion of Tokyo's airport set fire to the home of construction company president Teruzo Yoshino.

**BOMBING: Madrid Spain** Madrid's High Court president Fernando de Mateo Lage was critically wounded when a mail bomb exploded.

**FRAUD: New York, N.Y.** Former chairman of the defunct Haas Securities Corporation, Eugene Laff, received a five-year prison sentence for altering the price of penny stocks.

**RAPE: Houston, Texas** Abram Montoya, Jr., 23, was sentenced to life in prison for rape and attempted murder. Montoya was apprehended after he dropped his wallet near the Ship Channel where he tried to drown one of his female victims.

*February 28*

**JUDICIARY: Washington, D.C.** The U.S. Supreme Court ruled 7-2 that police arresting a suspect in his home could conduct a warrantless search of the premises to determine whether or not they were in danger and that any evidence seized at this time could later be used against the defendant. The court also ruled 5-4 that Pennsylvania's death penalty, requiring a death sentence if a jury determined that a murder was committed with at least one "aggravating" circumstance and no "mitigating" circumstance, was constitutional.

**MURDER: London, England** Former hitman for Ferdinand Marcos, Victor Castigador, was sentenced to 25 years in prison for torching two arcade employees.

**MURDER: Mexico City, Mex.** Former Interpol chief Miguel Aldana Ibarra was arrested on weapons and drug charges. Aldana Ibarra had already been indicted for the murder of U.S. Drug Enforcement Administration agent Enrique Camarena Salazar.

**MURDER: Brigham City, Ut.** Billy Cayer was the fourth defendant found guilty in the beating death of co-worker Miguel Enrique Ramirez. All four defendants, including William Cummings, Ray Cabututan and Donald Brown, were tried separately and sentenced to five years to life in prison.

*March 4*

**MOB VIOLENCE: Ciskei, South Africa** Black nationalists overthrew the government in Ciskei, and widespread arson and looting ensued, leaving twenty-seven persons killed.

*March 5*

**MOB VIOLENCE: Ciskei, South Africa** Government troops were sent into the homeland to quell rioting and random murders.

**MURDER: Winter Haven, Fla.** Andrew Lee Golden, who had murdered his wife, Ardelle, in September 1989, applied for the collection of $200,000 in insurance on her life. Golden would be convicted and condemned in 1991.

*March 6*

**MOB VIOLENCE: South Africa** Black activists of the once proscribed African National Congress led riots in several homelands, clashing with government troops.

**TAX EVASION: Del Mar, Calif.** Convicted of tax evasion in an $80 million Ponzi scheme, Nancy Hoover Hunter, former mayor of Del Mar, California, was sentenced to ten years in prison.

*March 7*

**MASS SHOOTINGS: Bophuthatswana** As an estimated 50,000 persons Marched on a government office, police opened fire and killed seven people, wounding another 450 persons.

**MURDER: Luecadia, Calif.** Police raiding a drug house captured Cheri Dale, who confessed to the January 25, 1990, murder of Susan Tayler in San Diego.

*March 9*

**IRAN-CONTRA: Washington, D.C.** Oliver North appeared as a prosecution witness in the trial of John Poindexter, the former national security adviser to President Ronald Reagan, who was being tried in federal court for his role in the Iran-Contra scandal. Poindexter was charged with lying to Congress in connection with its investigation into the Iran-Contra affair. North, apparently attempting to shield Poindexter, stated: "No one told me to lie to Congress."

*March 12*

**IRAN-CONTRA: Washington, D.C.** Appearing at the trial of John Poindexter in the Iran-Contra affair, Oliver North testified that he had seen Poindexter destroy an order signed by President Reagan which reportedly authorized U.S. participation in arms sales to Iran.

*March 18*

**THEFT: Boston, Massachusetts** The Isabella Stewart

Gardner Museum was robbed of twelve near priceless works of art valued at more than $100 million. The theft was the largest in the history of art and included the taking of two Rembrandt paintings, including the artist's only seascape, a Degas, a Vermeer, and a Manet. None of the paintings was insured, according to museum officials, since annual premiums would cost more than the museum's yearly budget.

*March 21*

**IRAN-CONTRA: Washington, D.C.** Federal Judge Harold Greene ruled that President Reagan would not be required to provide his presidential diaries in defense of John Poindexter, who was being tried for lying to Congress in the Iran-Contra affair.

*March 22*

**IRAN-CONTRA: Washington, D.C.** Edwin Meese III, former U.S. Attorney General, who had headed a U.S. Department of Justice investigation of the Iran arms sales, testified for the defense in John Poindexter's trial that Poindexter had not attempted to conceal information about the arms sales from Congress.

**NEGLIGENCE: Anchorage, Alas.** Joseph Hazelwood, former captain of the oil tanker *Exxon Valdez*, was found guilty of the negligent discharge of oil when his ship dumped almost eleven million gallons of oil into Prince William Sound, Alaska on March 24, 1989. He was acquitted of criminal mischief and two other charges. Hazelwood, appearing in a state court, was sentenced to 1,000 hours of community service and ordered to make token restitution of $50,000.

*March 25*

**ARSON: New York, N.Y.** Police arrested Julio Gonzalez in New York City, charging him with deliberately setting fire to a Bronx social club, where eighty-seven persons perished from burning or asphyxiation in a blazing inferno. The club, which had been ordered closed in 1988, lacked sprinklers, fire exits and emergency lights. It was a popular hangout for Hispanics; most of those killed were immigrants from Honduras.

*March 26*

**MASS SHOOTINGS: Sebokeng, South Africa** Police opened fire on a large crowd of anti-government demonstrators, killing seven persons and wounding hundreds of others.

*March 27*

**MURDER/TERRORISM: Lebanon** William Robinson, a U.S. missionary, was slain in the Israeli-designated "security zone" in Lebanon by Palestinian terrorists to deter the establishment of Israeli settlements.

*March 31*

**MURDER: Washington, D.C.** Paralegal Elizabeth Borghesani, who was jogging to her 23rd birthday party, was raped and murdered by Michael Charles Satcher, who stabbed his victim 21 times. Satcher would be sentenced to death for this killing in 1997.

*April 1*

**MANSLAUGHTER: Houston, Texas** The trial of Jolene Dale, accused of killing her mother, began. Dale was found guilty of voluntary manslaughter and sent to prison for sixty years.

*April 7*

**CONSPIRACY: Washington, D.C.** John Poindexter was convicted of making false statements to Congress, obstructing Congress and conspiracy to obstruct Congress. Poindexter was the highest ranking official to be convicted in the Iran-Contra affair.

**MURDER: Milwaukee, Wis.** Errol Lindsey, 19, vanished from his home; he would be murdered by serial killer Jeffrey Dahmer.

*April 9*

**BOMBING: Downpatrick, County Down, Ire.** IRA terrorists exploded a bomb which wrecked two vehicles of a British army patrol on a country road near Downpatrick, County Down, killing four British soldiers.

*April 10*

**TERRORISM: Middleast** Arab terrorists released three hostages—a French woman, her Belgian companion, and daughter, who were kidnapped on a Mediterranean cruise two years earlier.

*April 13*

**MURDER: Portland, Ore.** Michael L. Wheeler was convicted of murdering 15-year-old Autumn May Chinn, who had disappeared on June 6, 1989. Wheeler was sentenced to life in prison.

*April 17*

**MURDER: Philadelphia, Pa.** Police responding to a murder report, found John DiGregorio in his apartment covered with blood and, in the kitchen, the body parts of his daughter Carol whom he admitted murdering and dismembering a short time earlier.

*April 18*

**JUDICIARY: Washington, D.C.** The U.S. Supreme Court ruled 6-3 that states could make unlawful the possession of child pornography, even in private homes, this being the first time the court banned the possession of pornography. (Eighteen states already had laws prohibiting the possession of child pornography.)

*April 20*

**TAX EVASION: Cincinnati, Ohio** Baseball player Pete Rose pleaded guilty to two counts of filing false tax returns in U.S. District court. He had been banned from baseball in 1989 for gambling. Rose agreed to pay $366,000 in back taxes and interest.

*April 22*

**TERRORISM: Beirut, Lebanon** Robert Polhill, a 55-

year-old American taken hostage by pro-Iranian terrorists two years earlier, was released.

### April 23

**CRIME LEGISLATION: Washington, D.C.** The Hate Crimes Statistics Act was signed into law by President George Bush. Under this law the federal government would maintain records of crimes committed by persons motivated by racial, ethnic or sexual prejudice.

### April 24

**FRAUD: New York, N.Y.** Michael Milken, the so-called "junk bond king" at the securities firm of Drexel Burnham Lambert, Inc., who had prodded the corporate takeover boom of the 1980s, pleaded guilty in U.S. District Court to six counts involved with securities fraud, agreeing to pay a record $600 million in fines and restitution. Milken pleaded guilty to conspiracy, aiding and abetting the filing of a false statement with the Securities and Exchange Commission, and assisting the filing of a false tax return. More serious charges were dismissed against Milken and all charges against his brother, Lowell Milken, in exchange for his plea, were also dismissed.

### April 26

**ASSASSINATION: Bogatá, Colombia** Carlos Pizarro Leongomez, a presidential candidate, was shot to death on board an Avianca Airlines flight which had just departed Bogatá. Leongomez's bodyguards killed the assassin. A short time later, an anonymous caller claimed that the murder had been carried out on orders of the drug cartels.

### April 30

**BRIBERY: Washington, D.C.** DuBois Gilliam, a former deputy assistant secretary of the U.S. Department of Housing and Urban Development, testified before a House Government Operations subcommittee that HUD was corrupt and that he alone had accepted more than $100,000 in bribes from developers and consultants seeking to do business with HUD. Gilliam, who had earlier been convicted and sent to prison, implicated another HUD secretary, Samuel Pierce, stating Pierce had been involved in widespread bribery, a charged denied by Pierce's attorneys.

**TERRORISM: Beirut, Lebanon** Frank Herbert Reed, a fifty-seven-year-old American abducted by Arab terrorists almost four years earlier, was released.

### May 1

**KIDNAPPING: Liberia** Liberian radicals kidnapped Peace Corp volunteer David Kelley and three relief workers who were working in local villages.

**MURDER: Daly City, Calif.** Paul Bellazain reportedly shot and killed a bicyclist and wounded a freeway driver and two policemen in a forty-five minute rampage before he was wounded by police and taken into custody.

**MURDER: Elizabeth, N.J.** John Emil List was sentenced to five consecutive life terms for killing his mother, his wife and three children in 1971.

**MURDER: Flagstaff, Ariz.** Paul Gardner, 20, received two life terms for killing his parents.

### May 2

**ASSASSINATION: Milan Italy** Adriano Sofri and Giorgio Pietrostefani, leaders of a left-wing revolutionary organization, were sentenced to 22 years in prison for the 1972 murder of Milan police chief Luigi Calabresi.

**BRIBERY: Washington, D.C.** Convicted of taking bribes while an official at HUD, DuBois Gilliam continued his testimony before a House subcommittee, stating that Kansas City developer Hector Barreto was granted $500,000 for a trade center project that had originally been rejected by HUD.

**MURDER: Carmel, N.Y.** Mark Brooks, the son of a police officer, was sentenced to 37-and-a-half years to life for murdering a Hofstra University student and robbing him of $4.

**ROBBERY: Hong Kong** Four robbers stole $1.9 million worth of jewelry from a shop in a prominent hotel.

**WAR CRIMES: Buenos Aires, Argen.** Josef Franz Leo Schwammberger, 78, who reportedly killed thousands of persons in Nazi concentration camps, was extradited to West Germany to stand trial on charges of mass murder and torture.

### May 3

**MURDER: Chicago, Ill.** David Dowaliby was convicted of murdering his adoptive daughter two days after his wife, Cynthia, was acquitted of the same charges.

**MURDER: London, England** Gerald Dowden was found guilty of killing his 5-year-old stepson, Daniel Vergauwen. In a separate London murder trial this date security guard Ronald Ross was sentenced to life in prison for strangling to death Denise Davis who was working late in the office building where Ross worked.

**RAPE: Denver, Colo.** Babysitter Donnie E. Russell was found guilty of rape, torture and attempted murder of his employer, Daling Collier.

### May 4

**ARSON: Edinburgh, Scotland** William Simpson was sentenced to life in prison for setting fire to a cottage just hours after he was released from a 12-year prison term.

**CHILD MOLESTATION: Indianapolis, Ind.** Former elementary school principal Michael G. Barger was found guilty of molesting a 12-year-old girl.

**EXECUTION: Starke, Fla.** Jessie Tafero, 43, was executed for the 1976 murders of two policemen. A faulty component in the electric chair caused flames to rise from Tafero's head.

**MURDER: Olongapo, Philippines** U.S. Marine Sgt. John Fredette was shot to death near the Subic Bay Naval Base. Two men were arrested and charged with the killing.

**MURDER: Painesville, Ohio** Sharon Bluntschley, a member of Jeffrey Don Lundgren's cult, pleaded guilty to conspiracy to commit aggravated murder for her part in the murders of Dennis Avery, his wife and their three children.

**MURDER: Tyler, Texas** Former police chief Thomas Lardner and two former deputies were given prison terms ranging from 10 to 28 years for the December 1987 murder of Loyal Garner, Jr., a black prisoner who was beaten to death by the white officers.

*May 5*

**ASSAULT: Nantes, France** Jean-Marie Lupin was charged with aggravated assault after he allegedly beat to death Daniel Droniou for interrupting Lupin's conversation in a public telephone booth.

**KIDNAPPING: Italy** Carlo Celadon, 20, was released after being held hostage for more than two years in the southern Calabria region, ending the longest ransom kidnapping case in Italy's history. Celadon's father had reportedly paid a ransom of $4 million.

**MURDER: Blairsville, Ga.** Ronald Dexter Radford was convicted and sentenced to death for the July 28, 1989 rape and murder of 11-year-old Jeannie Marie Densberger.

**MURDER: Jackson, Miss.** Reginald Donald was sentenced to life in prison after confessing to the October 27, 1988, rape and murder of a mentally retarded woman, Alice Louise Ryan.

**MURDER; Philadelphia, Pa.** Leonard Christopher was charged with the stabbing murder of a mentally handicapped woman, who police believed to be the eighth victim in a string of killings.

*May 6*

**BOMBING: Pakistan** A bomb exploded in the toilet of a passenger train, killing 21 persons and injuring another 30 people.

**MURDER: Los Angeles, Calif.** Joel Darren Sanders turned himself in to police and was charged on suspicion of murder in connection with the shooting death of 13-year-old Angel Hernandez on a city bus.

**ROBBERY: San Francisco, Calif.** At least 10 people were robbed in two days by "oil can bandits," who slicked the road with oil and then attacked and robbed drivers of the cars that spun to a stop.

*May 7*

**MURDER: Baltimore, Md.** Donnie Wise Brown surrendered to police and was charged with first-degree murder, after he allegedly shot his infant son to death.

**MURDER: Birmingham, Ala.** Gregory Terrell Long, 18, was shot to death by a 16-year-old in an argument over a call in a basketball game.

**MURDER: Dallas, Texas** Genaro Ruiz Comacho was sentenced to death for the May 1988 murder of David Wilburn. Comacho was also suspected of killing four other persons, including a mother and her 3-year-old son.

**RAPE: Champaign, Ill.** Vincent Lipscomb, whose conviction for aggravated criminal sexual assault in an attack on a college student was based on DNA testing, was sentenced to 24 years in prison.

*May 8*

**MURDER: Kansas City, Mo.** After numerous threats Benjamin Escareno shot and killed his ex-wife Martha Valencia in her restaurant and then shot and killed himself.

**POLITICAL CORRUPTION: Charleston, W.Va.** Former three-term governor Arch A. Moore, Jr., pleaded guilty to political corruption charges.

*May 9*

**BOMBING: Amritsar, India** Four persons were killed and as many as 41 injured when alleged Sikh separatists detonated two bombs that destroyed two busses.

**BURGLARY: Memphis, Tenn.** Bank janitor Jesse Mormon was charged with burglary after allegedly trying to drill holes from the women's restroom into the vault.

*May 10*

**ASSASSINATION: Santiago, Chile** Luis Fontaine Manriquez, retired national police colonel, was shot and killed by two gunmen.

**DRUGS: Cairo, Egypt** Judge Gamal Abdel-Halim of the Cairo Criminal Court sentenced 12 people to death for smuggling and distributing 10 tons of hashish and 858 pounds of opium.

**KIDNAPPING: Tallahassee, Fla.** Babysitter Kenneth M. Cole II was charged with kidnapping after he allegedly abducted 5-year-old Nicole Ravesi from her Massachusetts home and held her in Florida for 39 days.

*May 11*

**BOMBING: Manila Philippines** Eight people were killed and 82 injured when an explosion and fire gutted a Philippine Airlines jet as it awaited takeoff. Officials believed a bomb had caused the explosion.

**EXECUTION: Potosi, Mo.** Winford Lavern Stokes, 39, was executed by lethal injection for the 1978 stabbing and strangulation murder of Pamela R. Benda.

**ILLEGAL GOODS: Vega Baja, Puerto Rico** FBI agents seized $11 million worth of cars, boats, homes and other goods bought by residents who found $43 million buried in drums on the farm of reputed drug trafficker Ramón Torres Gonzalez.

**MURDER: Florence, Ariz.** Michael Apelt, a West German citizen, was convicted of murdering his wife, Cyndi, to collect $400,000 in life insurance.

**MURDER: South Bend, Ind.** Alan L. Matheney, who beat his ex-wife to death during a prison furlough on March 4, 1989, was sentenced to die in the electric chair.

*May 12*

**BOMBING: Philadelphia, Pa.** Sarah Scott, 71, and her two grandchildren were killed when an explosion destroyed a home suspected of being a storehouse for drug money. Police found thousands of dollars in cash.

*May 13*

**MURDER/TERRORISM: Philippines** Communist terrorists shot and killed two U.S. airmen, John H. Raven and James C. Green, near Clark Air Force Base.

**MURDER: St Regis Indian Reservation, Canada** Four men were arrested in connection with the deaths of two Mohawk Indians killed in fighting between pro- and anti-gambling factions.

*May 14*

**BOMBING: London, England** Seven persons were injured when a bomb planted by the IRA exploded in a flower bed outside a British army office.

**MURDER: Hamilton, Ohio** Tarvie Collins, the son of a Ku Klux Klan leader, was indicted on a charge of aggravated murder in the shooting death of black teenager Roy Lee Printup, Jr. Collins pleaded innocent by reason of insanity on May 23, 1990.

*May 15*

**FRAUD: Baltimore, Md.** Computer consultant Leonard Rose, Jr., a member of a computer hackers group, was indicted for his alleged part in a scheme to steal and distribute software from AT&T Unix systems.

**MURDER: Bozeman, Mont.** Brett D. Byers, who allegedly shot and killed two fellow freshmen in his dormitory, was arrested after a car chase and charged with deliberate homicide.

**MURDER: Des Moines, Ia.** Roy Finch, convicted of stabbing Diane Laurence 225 times, was sentenced to prison for life for the 1989 murder.

*May 16*

**MURDER: Chicago, Ill.** Renaldo Hudson was sentenced to death for the 1983 stabbing death of Folke Peterson, 72, who was tortured for more than eight hours.

**MURDER: West Bank, Israel** Ahmed Mohammed Abu Nijima, a Palestinian believed to have been collaborating with Israeli authorities, was found strangled near his home.

**RACKETEERING: New York, N.Y.** Michael and Joseph Agnello and Michael DeLuca, reportedly linked with the Gambino crime family, were convicted of selling stolen car parts to body shops in Brooklyn and Queens.

*May 17*

**FRAUD: Chicago, Ill.** Businessman Morton Scherl received a 16-year prison term after pleading guilty to tax fraud and the theft of $741,000 in pension funds.

**EXECUTION: Huntsville, Texas** Johnny Ray Anderson, 30, was executed for the 1981 killing of his brother-in-law in order to collect insurance money.

**MURDER: New York, N.Y.** Joseph Fama was convicted of second-degree murder in the racially-motivated killing of 16-year-old Yusuf Hawkins in Bensonhurst, in August 1989.

*May 18*

**BOMBING: Lahore, Pakistan** Ten people were killed and 54 wounded when a remote-control bomb was detonated in a shopping area as police came to investigate a suspicious-looking wooden box.

**MURDER: Cleveland, Ohio** Eric Miller was sentenced to 36 years to life in prison for the October 1989 shooting death of David Smith and the attempted murder of another man.

**MURDER: Naples, Italy** Three armed men began shooting at a family apartment party, killing Gennaro Pandolfi and his 18-month-old son Nunzio, whom he held in his arms.

**RIOT: Kwangju, South Korea** Riot police used tear gas to disperse thousands of demonstrators honoring the tenth anniversary of the Kwanju uprising that left 200 people dead.

The rioters retaliated by hurling broken sidewalk blocks at the police.

*May 19*

**DRUGS: Tulsa, Oklahoma** A key figure in the Medellin drug cartel, Jose Abello Silva, was convicted on federal drug charges. On May 29, 1990, he was sentenced to 30 years in prison and fined $5 million.

**MURDER: Brooksville, Fla.** Russell Coats, a 19-year-old white was beaten to death by a group of blacks. John W. Smith and five others were arrested.

**TREASON: Ethiopia** Major General Hailu Gebre-Michael and 11 other top military officers were found guilty during court martial trials for involvement in a coup attempt. They were all sentenced to death and later executed.

*May 20*

**MURDER: Centerville, Tenn.** Donald Givens, a teacher at Hickman County High School, was arrested after allegedly shooting to death assistant principal Ron Wallace and starting a fire in the school.

**MURDER: Gaza Strip** A mentally unbalanced Israeli, Ami Popper, 21, a former Israeli soldier, opened fire on Arab construction workers, killing seven and wounding 10 others before being subdued. Ensuing riots left seven more dead.

*May 21*

**ASSASSINATION: Srinagar, Kashmir** Islamic leader Maulvi Mohammed Farooq, 45, was assassinated.

**MURDER: Portland, Ore.** Jeffrey S. Winchester pleaded guilty to aggravated murder for the October 1989 strangulation of Ronald E. Bailey. Winchester was sentenced to life in prison.

**MURDER: Sinaloa, Mexico** Human rights activist Norma Corona Sapienz was shot to death after three armed men in a pickup stopped her car.

*May 22*

**FRAUD: New Orleans, La.** Arco Oil & Gas Co. was ordered to pay $2 million in damages after being found guilty of defrauding Kelly Oil Co.

**KIDNAPPING: Austin, Texas** Ray Logan and Ronald Wayne Thompson were arrested and charged with kidnapping a man they suspected of burglary and beating him until he confessed.

*May 23*

**ARSON: West Hartford, Conn.** Developer Vincent A. Roberti was charged with conspiracy to commit arson for a fire at one of his condominium units.

**MANSLAUGHTER: Preston, England** An 11-year-old boy who killed his 70-year-old father after years of physical and psychological abuse, pleaded guilty to manslaughter due to provocation.

**MURDER: Chicago, Ill.** Michael Savickas, son of a state senator, was sentenced to 28 years in prison for the 1988 murder of Thomas Vinicky.

**MURDER: Monrovia, Liberia** The bodies of six soldiers

who had been hacked to death were dumped at various locations in the capital city.

## May 24

**CHILD MOLESTATION: Decatur, Ga.** Catholic priest Anton Mowat received a six-year prison sentence and nine years' probation after pleading guilty to the molestation of four altar boys.

**MURDER: Hawthorne, Calif.** Eleven-year-old William James Tillett was kidnapped and murdered while walking home from school.

**MURDER: Philadelphia, Pa.** Louis DeLuca, an associate of the Scarfo crime family, was shot and killed in his car by two gunmen.

**MURDER: Phoenix, Ariz.** James William Stuard was convicted of the serial murders of three elderly women and the attempted murder of an 81-year-old woman.

## May 25

**BOMBING: Oakland, Calif.** Radical environmentalists Darryl Cherney and Judi Bari, were arrested for investigation of possession of explosives.

**FRAUD: Honolulu, Hawaii** Stefan Paal, suspected of being a former Nazi SS guard at Auschwitz concentration camp, was charged with visa fraud.

**MURDER: Johannesburg, South Africa** Jerry Musivuzi Richardson, a bodyguard for Nelson Mandela's wife, Winnie, was convicted of beating to death 14-year-old James "Stompie" Mokhetsi Seipei in 1988, reportedly on Winnie Mandela's orders. He will be sentenced to death on August 8, 1990.

## May 26

**EXECUTIONS: Henan, China** Eleven convicted train robbers were executed, each with a bullet to the back of the head, immediately following their convictions.

**MURDER: Beverly Hills, Calif.** Daniel Guil, a Swiss transient, was arrested for the murder of taxi driver Dane Whittenberg.

**MURDER: West Palm Beach, Fla.** A person disguised as a clown handed Marlene Warren flowers and balloons before shooting her as her sons watched. She died from her wounds on May 29, 1990.

## May 27

**MURDER: Clondalkin, Ireland** American Mormon missionary Gale Stanley Critchfield was stabbed to death while walking to his home, located just outside of Dublin.

**MURDER: Racine, Wis.** Runaway Diana Jo White, 14, was shot to death while walking with a group of her friends. Melvin Arthur was charged with her murder.

**TERRORISM: Roermond, Netherlands** A unit of the IRA shot and killed two vacationing Australian lawyers, Stephan Melrose and Nick Spanos, believing them to be British soldiers.

**ROBBERY: Paris, France** Three gunmen stole $900,000 worth of antique jewelry from a shop across from the Louvre museum.

## May 28

**BOMBING: Jerusalem, Israel** A 72-year-old man was killed and nine people injured when a bomb exploded in a crowded shopping district. Fatah Uprising claimed responsibility.

**CAPTURE: Mesa, Ariz.** Richard Kevin Hawlay, who had escaped from police custody while awaiting trial on an attempted murder charge, was apprehended by a K-Mart security guard while trying to shoplift a pair of tennis shoes.

## May 29

**KIDNAPPING: Libreville, Gabon** Augustin Boumath, president of the Gabonese National Assembly, was kidnapped by a group of armed men.

**MURDER: Indianapolis, Ind.** Kevin M. Caldwell was sentenced to 63 years in prison for the 1988 murder of Sharon L. Turner.

**MURDER: Milwaukee, Wis.** Serial killer Jeffrey Dahmer murdered Raymond Lamont Smith, a 33-year-old ex-convict.

## May 30

**EXECUTIONS: Hong Kong** Eight Hong Kong citizens convicted of peddling 28 pounds of heroin were hanged, the highest number executed in a single day.

**MURDER/SUICIDE: Chicago, Ill.** Unemployed sheet metal worker Hermino Elizalde reportedly doused his five children with gasoline and set them on fire before taking his own life.

**RAPE: Dallas, Texas** Gilbert H. Escobedo, who admitted committing 35 rapes and 100 burglaries since 1985, was sentenced to 10 life prison terms.

**TERRORISM: Israeli coast** PLO terrorists attempted raids along the coast of Israel, but Israeli troops wrecked the attacking speedboats, killing four and capturing twelve of the raiders. Yasir Arafat denied any PLO involvement.

## May 31

**MURDER: Los Angeles, Calif.** Gang leader Virgil Byars was sentenced to 49 years to life in prison for the 1982 fatal drive-by shootings of two rival gang members. The sentence ended the longest active criminal case in Los Angeles County.

**TERRORISM: Karachi, Pakistan** Thirty people were killed and at least thirty more injured when gunmen fired at a bus with automatic weapons.

## June 4

**DRUGS: Washington, D.C.** Marion Barry's trial on drug charges began. The mayor of Washington, D.C., faced eleven counts involving cocaine use and three felony counts of lying to a grand jury.

**JUDICIARY: Washington, D.C.** The U.S. Supreme Court ruled 8-1 that police did not have to provide a Miranda warning as to rights against self-incrimination in the case of jailed suspects who confess to undercover police officers posing as fellow inmates, determining that such law enforcement tactics constituted "strategic deception," not "coercion."

**MOB VIOLENCE: Osh, Kirghizia** Riots and fighting between Kirghiz citizens and Uzbecks erupt over the allocating of a large plot of land for Kirghiz residents.

**SUICIDE: Detroit, Mich.** Dr. Jack Kevorkian, a pathologist who became notorious for assisting those wanting to commit suicide and who would later go to jail for this practice, aided Janet Adkins of Portland, Oregon, in using his suicide machine. Kevorkian later told police that he drove Adkins in his van to a park where he inserted an intravenous needle into her arm. She then pushed a button that fed a fatal combination of drugs into her bloodstream. Adkins suffered from Alzheimer's Disease and reportedly took her own life with the consent of her husband.

*June 5*

**MURDER: San Diego, Calif.** Linda Blackburn, a 38-year-old homeless person, was found dead in Balboa Park; she had been sexually assaulted and then strangled to death. Her killer, James Nimblett would be tracked down to Sacramento on August 3, 1990, and later sent to prison.

*June 7*

**MOB VIOLENCE: Osh, Kirghizia** Continued rioting and fighting resulted in the deaths of forty-eight persons.

*June 10*

**MURDER: Derry, N.H.** Police received a gun from the father of 18-year-old Vance Lattime which was matched to bullets that killed Gregory Smart on May 11, 1990. Lattime and two other teenagers had murdered Smart at the behest of the victim's wife, Pamela Smart, who was sent to prison for life.

*June 11*

**CONSPIRACY: Washington, D.C.** John Poindexter was sentenced to six months in prison for his role in the Iran-Contra affair, the first defendant involved in the scandal to be sent to jail

**JUDICIARY: Washington, D.C.** The U.S. Supreme Court ruled 6-3 that an anonymous tip provided sufficient grounds for suspicion in permitting police to legally stop and question a suspect.

*June 13*

**DRUGS: Washington, D.C.** Mayor Marion Barry, being tried on drug charges, announced that he would not seek a forth term because his dependence on drugs and alcohol prevented him from undergoing another political campaign.

**MOB VIOLENCE: Bucharest, Romania** After protesting students established a tent city in the downtown section of the city, riot police attacked the area, driving out 200. Thousands of students rioted, burning police headquarters. Police and paramilitary forces opened fire on the students, killing four persons and wounding more than 200 others.

**MOB VIOLENCE: Osh, Kirghizia** Continued rioting between Uzbeks and Kirghiz natives brought the death toll to 148.

*June 14*

**MOB VIOLENCE: Bucharest, Romania** More than 10,000 miners entered the city to drive out protesting students. The miners ransacked the headquarters of two opposition par-

ties, wrecked the offices of the leading newspaper and set up barricades throughout the city.

*June 16*

**MURDER: Woodbridge, Va.** Michael Carl George, a longtime child molester, tortured and murdered 15-year-old Alexander Sztanko. George would be executed for his gruesome crime in 1997.

*June 19*

**DRUGS: Washington, D.C.** Attorneys for Marion Barry argued in opening statements at his trial that FBI agents had entrapped Barry into using cocaine so that they could videotape him before his January 1990 arrest.

*June 22*

**EMBEZZLEMENT: Baltimore, Md.** Marilyn Louise Harrell, a private escrow agent who pleaded guilty on January 29, 1990, to embezzling $4.5 million which had been earmarked for HUD, was sentenced to forty-six months in prison and was ordered to pay $600,000 in restitution.

*June 25*

**POLITICAL EXILE: Beijing, China** Physicist Fang Lizhi and his wife Li Shuxian, two dissidents who had led the 1989 pro-democracy uprising and who had entered the U.S. Embassy to escape arrest following the crackdown by Communist officials, flew to London on a U.S. Air Force plane.

*June 27*

**MURDER: Allen County, Ohio** Ryan Young, 16, vanished, his car found on a lonely road. His body would be found eight days later and his killers, Richard Joseph and Jose Bulerin would later be tracked down and convicted, Joseph receiving a death sentence and Bulerin sent to prison for life.

*June 28*

**DRUGS: Washington, D.C.** Prosecutors in the Marion Barry drug trial showed the video tape of Barry smoking crack cocaine in a Washington hotel in January 1990. Defense attorneys claimed that the tape reenforced their claim that Barry had been entrapped.

*July 2*

**FRAUD: New York, N.Y.** Mrs. Imelda Marcos, the wife of former Philippines President Ferdinand Marcos, was found not guilty of fraud, racketeering and obstruction of justice charges in a federal court. Her co-defendant, Saudi billionaire Adnan Khashoggi, was also found not guilty. Marcos was accused of looting $200 million from the Philippines treasury and purchasing, with Khashoggi's help, many office buildings in the U.S.

*July 3*

**MOB VIOLENCE: Mecca, Saudi Arabia** After seven persons fell from a bridge at the entrance to Mecca Tunnel (500 yards long and twenty yards wide), more than 50,000 persons inside the tunnel panicked and stampeded, suffocating or trampling to death 1,426 persons.

## July 6

**MOB VIOLENCE: Tirana, Albania** Riot police attacked more than 100,000 pro-democracy demonstrators; hundreds were injured.

## July 17

**MURDER: Adairsville, Ga.** Tried three times and convicted of murdering a 12-year-old girl, Darrell Gene Devier had his death sentence once more redocketed in the 11th U.S. Circuit Court. The Devier case was one of the most prolonged appeals process in Georgia history.

## July 19

**TAX EVASION: Cincinnati, Ohio** Banned baseball player Pete Rose, was sentenced to five months in jail, fined $50,000, and ordered to perform 1,000 hours of community service, following his April 20, 1990 conviction of filing false tax returns.

## July 20

**BOMBING: London, England** The London Stock Exchange was bombed by IRA terrorists, who gave warning, allowing the safe evacuation of more than 300 persons; no one was injured.

**CONVICTIONS SUSPENDED: Washington, D.C.** Oliver North's three convictions stemming from his role in Iran-Contra—deceiving Congress, receiving an illegal gratuity and destroying government documents—were set aside by a three-judge Appeals Court panel, stating that North had been granted immunity for his testimony and that witnesses against him had improperly used that testimony against him.

**JUDICIARY: Washington, D.C.** U.S. Supreme Court Justice William Brennan, who had served on the court for thirty-four years, announced his immediate retirement.

## July 24

**BOMBING: Armagh, Northern Ireland** IRA terrorists were blamed for the explosion of a bomb that killed three policemen in a car and a Catholic nun.

## July 27

**CHILD MOLESTATION: Los Angeles, Calif.** Raymond Buckey, who had been earlier acquitted of fifty-two counts of child molestation with his mother, Peggy McMartin Buckey, operators of the McMartin Pre-School in Manhattan Beach, California, and who was retried on eight counts of child molestation, faced a deadlocked jury.

**COUP ATTEMPT: Trinidad and Tobago** Prime Minister Arthur Robinson and other members of the government were seized by black Moslem rebels attempting to seize power and held as hostages. Robinson was shot in the leg.

## July 28

**COUP ATTEMPT: Trinidad and Tobago** Rebels attempting to seize power released the wounded Prime Minister Arthur Robinson and other hostages.

## July 30

**BOMBING: Hankham, East Sussex, England** An IRA bomb claimed the life of Ian Gow, 53, a Conservative member of the British parliament who had repeatedly condemned the IRA. Gow had been a close friend and adviser to British Prime Minister Margaret Thatcher.

## August 1

**CHILD MOLESTATION: Los Angeles, Calif.** All charges against accused child molester Raymond Buckey were dismissed by Superior Court Judge Stanley Weisberg.

**COUP ATTEMPT: Trinidad and Tobago** After a failed attempt to seize power, 113 rebels surrendered to government troops; thirty persons had been killed in the abortive coup.

**MURDER: Detroit, Mich.** Lawrence DeLisle was sentenced to life in prison for killing his four children and trying to kill his wife by driving the family car into a river.

**MURDER: Tallahassee, Fla.** Roswell Gilbert, 81, was granted clemency by Governor Bob Martinez after serving five years of a life sentence for the mercy killing of his sick wife.

**TERRORISM: Trinidad** Muslim terrorists in Trinidad, after seizing Prime Minister Arthur N.R. Robinson and others, surrendered to local authorities, releasing their hostages.

## August 2

**BOMBING: Tyre, Lebanon** Eight persons were killed and 75 others injured when a car bomb exploded near an office occupied by Syrian-backed Amal military personnel.

**MURDER: Los Angeles, Calif.** Abelino Manriquez was charged with murder in connection with a year-long killing spree that left seven persons dead.

## August 3

**MURDER: Los Angeles, Calif.** Donal McKinsey, 52, the owner of a nursery, was shot and killed by two robbers after refusing to surrender his $10,000 Rolex watch.

## August 4

**DRUGS: Miami, Fla.** Police discovered $12 million worth of cocaine in a van that had been involved in a minor accident and abandoned by its driver.

## August 5

**BURGLARY: London, England** A burglar was arrested at the home of Labor Party leader Neil Kinnock in what was the second invasion of Kinnock's home in six days.

**MURDER: Charlotte, N.C.** Police officer Terry Lyles was fatally shot while escorting to jail Calvin Christmas Cunningham whom he had earlier arrested for threatening his girlfriend. Cunningham had apparently secreted the murder weapon in the back seat of the police car.

**MURDER: New York, N.Y.** An unidentified murderer shot and killed John Myers after quarreling over the use of a public phone in a subway station.

## August 6

**EMBEZZLEMENT: Truro, England** Clifford Porter was sentenced to three years in prison for embezzling $167,590 from a firm where he was employed as a financial controller.

**MURDER: Atlanta, Ga.** Sean Reynard Patmon was sentenced to life plus 20 years in prison after pleading guilty to the murder of policeman Joseph E. Davis.

**MURDER: Cleveland, Ohio** Cedric Wendell Payne was sentenced to life in prison for the October 1989 murder of Wayne Price.

**MURDER: Evanston, Wyo.** Alvin "Hap" Russell III was sentenced to life in prison for aiding and abetting condemned killer Mark Hopkinson in the 1977 murder of Jeffrey Lynn Green.

**MURDER: Israel** Jewish youths Lior Tubul and Ronen Karamani were found stabbed to death between Jewish and Arab settlements. The murders touched off violent attacks against Arabs for the next three days.

**ROBBERY/MURDER: Montezuma, Ga.** Bank teller Tish Hall was shot and killed by a robber who then demanded money from the remaining tellers and fled. Walter Lee Brown was arrested on August 8, 1990, and charged with the crime.

### August 7

**KIDNAPPING: Rio de Janeiro, Brazil** Mauro Goncalves de Oliveira, the suspected leader of a kidnapping ring responsible for more than 30 abductions was killed in a shootout with police.

**MURDER: Farwell, Texas** Diane Lumbrera was indicted on charges of killing her three daughters. Two sons and a niece also died while in her care.

**MURDER: San Jose, Calif.** A relentless search by the mother of Gus Henry Hoffman, who was stomped to death and had his motorcycle stolen on July 4, 1978, led to the conviction of Michael Allen Hodges, Richard Morris Dollar and John Michael "Slug" Stelle.

### August 8

**ROBBERY: Lugano, Switzerland** A drug addict infected with the AIDS virus was sentenced to three years in prison and barred from the country for 15 years for trying to rob a jewelry store with a contaminated syringe.

**MURDER: Santa Monica, Calif.** Christian Brando, son of famed actor Marlon Brando, pleaded not guilty to killing his sister's boyfriend, Dag Drollet.

**TERRORISM: Damascus, Syria** Shiite Moslems released Emmanuel Christen, a Swiss Red Cross worker who had been held hostage in Lebanon for more than ten months. A group calling itself the Palestinian Revolutionary Squads, took credit for the abduction.

### August 9

**MURDER: Kansas City, Mo.** James R. Clark was sentenced to 30 years in prison for the 1988 murders of reputed drug dealer Johnny Strange and two others.

**MURDER: Marietta, Ga.** Neva Jane Veitch, a former member of the Ku Klux Klan, was sentenced to prison for life after admitting that she had killed her husband in order to collect $50,000 in insurance money.

**MURDER: New York, N.Y.** Earl Imbert, an out-of-work actor suffering from AIDS, was arrested and charged with

murder after reportedly beating to death his visiting mother, Leona Imbert, and then setting himself on fire.

**RIOTS/LOOTING: Trujillo, Peru** Four persons were killed during rioting and looting that erupted in protest of President Alberto Fujimori's austerity plan.

**THEFT: Crete, Greece** Six British tourists were sentenced to prison terms ranging from 20 days to nine months for shoplifting.

### August 10

**DRUGS: London, England** Leroy Francis and his brother Ivan, also known as Ivan Thomas, were each sentenced to seven years in prison for selling crack and heroin.

**DRUGS: Washington, D.C.** Mayor Marion Barry was found guilty on one count of possessing crack cocaine, but a mistrial was declared when the jury deadlocked on 12 other counts.

**FRAUD: Los Angeles, Calif.** Matthew Lothian, Lester Charles Thompson and Mark Stephen Ott were convicted of fraud in connection with a $5 million telemarketing scheme in which hundreds of people were sold worthless rights to precious metals.

**RIOTS: Port Elizabeth, South Africa** Two persons were killed in rioting which had been going on since August 6 and had claimed a total of 42 lives.

**SEXUAL ASSAULT: Edinburgh, Scotland** Robert Black was sentenced to life in prison for the abduction and sexual assault of a 6-year-old girl.

### August 11

**DRUGS: Medellin, Colombia** Police killed the Medellin drug cartel's number two man, Gustavo de Jesus Gaviria, in a gunfight that erupted after police raided an upper-class home.

**TERRORISM: Sri Lanka** Tamil rebels killed at least 119 persons with machine guns and machetes throughout several villages in retaliation for the killing of 33 Tamil citizens by Moslems.

### August 12

**RIOT: Chateauguay, Canada** Seventy-four people were injured when thousands protested against the Mohawk Indian barricade of the Mercerier Bridge connecting Montreal to its suburbs. Protestors threw objects at police who were guarding the bridge.

### August 13

**BOMBING: Lima, Peru** Four people were wounded when a 90-pound car bomb exploded at the presidential palace while President Alberto Fujimori was inside. Two other bombings in Peru killed three persons and injured another 19.

**KIDNAPPING: Lebanon** Elio Erriquez, a Swiss orthopedic technician with the Red Cross, was released by Palestinian terrorists who had held him hostage since October 6, 1989.

**MURDER: Cleveland, Ohio** Wolford L. Berry, Jr. was sentenced to die in the electric chair for the December 1, 1989 shooting death and robbery of baker Charles Mitroff. An accomplice, Anthony Lozar, 18, was sentenced to 53 years in prison.

**MURDER: Harrisonville, Mo.** Joseph B. Denti, 17, who shot and killed his parents in their home on October 31, 1989, was sentenced to two consecutive life terms in prison.

**MURDER: Kenny Lake, Alaska** Charles Thurman Sinclair was arrested in connection with seven murders at coin shops throughout the U.S. and Canada since November 1986.

### August 14

**MURDER: Cornwall, England** The bodies of Leslie Ann Fleming and her son Timothy, who had just celebrated his 10th birthday, were discovered after they had been beaten to death with a hammer.

**MURDER: Dallas, Texas** Daniel Joe Hittle, who allegedly killed seven persons since 1973, was sentenced to die by lethal injection for the murder of Garland, Texas, police officer Gerald Walker.

**MURDER/KIDNAPPING: Riyadh, Saudi Arabia** Kimberley Hinkson, an American who was pregnant, and her 10-year-old daughter, were shot and killed after a suspected drug trafficker seized their car and entered into a high-speed chase and gun battle with police.

**TERRORISM: Damascus, Syria** Shiite Moslems released a second Swiss Red Cross worker who had been held hostage in Lebanon for more than ten months.

### August 15

**RIOTS: South Africa** Street battles between two opposing black anti-apartheid factions continued for a fourth day, bringing the death toll to more than 139 persons.

**SEXUAL ABUSE: Independence, Mo.** Vincent P. Elbert was convicted of sodomy and sexual abuse of a 4-year-old girl. His wife, Louetta, pleaded guilty to a charge of sexual abuse and was sentenced to five years' probation.

### August 16

**DRUGS: Kentucky** Four county sheriffs were arrested for allegedly taking bribes to protect marijuana and cocaine traffickers in the state.

**MURDER: Vancouver, Wash.** Skinheads Melissa McEathron, 13 and Mark E. Stevenson, 17, were arrested for the beating murder of fellow skinhead David R. Lindley, 19.

**RAPE: Oshkosh, Wis.** Mark A. Peterson pleaded not guilty in the rape of a woman who claimed to have multiple personalities. Peterson insisted that one personality consented to have sex in his car.

**TERRORISM: Dusseldorf, West Germany** Terence Gerard McGeough, an IRA bomber accused of wounding 45 people in two bombings, was placed on trial.

### August 17

**MURDER: Bartow, Fla.** Thomas Coe was sentenced to life in prison for murdering his 2-year-old stepson, Bradley McGee, by dunking his head in a toilet.

**MURDER: Fairfax County, Va.** A policeman checking the car of Charles E. Baeza, following a routine traffic stop, found Baeza's wife, Ruth Baeza, dead in the back seat of Baeza's car. Baeza was charged with murder.

### August 18

**ASSAULT: Wunsiedel, West Germany** Forty-six people were arrested after fighting broke out between leftist protestors and right-wing extremists celebrating the anniversary of the death of Nazi Rudolf Hess.

**BATTERY/RAPE: New York, N. Y.** Two black teen boys and one Hispanic teenager were convicted of raping a 28-year-old Manhattan investment banker who had become known as the Central Park Jogger, in an April 1989 attack in Central Park. The woman, a year after the vicious attack—she had been struck repeatedly with rocks and a pipe after being gang raped—had little or no memory of the attack, having lost her sense of smell and suffering from double vision and an inability to walk.

**MURDER: South Prairie, Wash.** The nude body of 11-year-old Shanno Potter was found eight days after her disappearance. Michael W. Sanchez, who helped in the search for the missing girl, was arrested and charged with Potter's murder after her bloodstained swimsuit was found on Sanchez's property.

### August 19

**DRUGS: Exeter, England** Ten people were arrested after police seized £2 million worth of cannabis resin at a gas station.

**HIJACKING: Karachi, Pakistan** Eleven Soviet inmates, who hijacked a plane on a domestic flight over Siberia, surrendered to Pakistani officials.

**WAR CRIMES: Berlin, East Germany** Josef Schwamm-berger, 78, a commandant of concentration camps during World War II, and once listed as one of the ten most wanted Nazi war criminals, was indicted in the deaths of more than 3,400 persons.

### August 20

**MURDER: Los Angeles, Calif.** Jimmy Joe Gregory entered the City of Industry police substation and held officers at bay for 90 minutes while he confessed to the murders of his 27-year-old daughter and her boyfriend, whose bodies were later found in Gregory's car.

### August 21

**MURDER: New York, N.Y.** Fred Weldon, a former butcher suspected of the December 17, 1976, murder and dismemberment of his wife, was tracked down and arrested by Detectives Victoria Myers and Rolf Rehbein, who specialized in old, unsolved cases.

### August 22

**ESPIONAGE: Los Angeles, Calif.** The third trial began for FBI agent Richard W. Miller, accused of passing secret documents to a Soviet woman with whom he was having an affair.

**MURDER, Huancayo, Peru** Two Mormon missionaries were shot and killed while on their way to a church member's home.

**ORGANIZED CRIME: Tokyo, Japan** Police raided an office of Yakusa members and for the first time announced a crackdown on the most powerful crime organization in the country, but this raid was thought to be only a token gesture.

### August 23

**MURDER: Kansas City, Mo.** Waretta Blair pleaded guilty to suffocating her boyfriend, Pablo Gomez, an alleged Cuban drug dealer who threatened to cut off her supply of crack, and was sentenced to 10 years in prison.

**RAPE: Dallas, Texas** Timothy Kehoe was sentenced to life in prison after a jury watched a 72-minute videotape that Kehoe recorded while he beat and raped a 25-year-old woman.

### August 24

**MURDER: Jackson, Miss.** Mondrick Bradley, 18, who was confined to a wheelchair, was charged with murder after he and a 13-year-old boy allegedly shot and killed Janie Howell during a robbery.

**MURDER: Wausau, Wis.** Lori Esker, once crowned dairy princess, was sentenced to life in prison for the strangulation murder of Lisa Cihaski over a farmer they both loved.

**SEXUAL ABUSE: London, England** Robert Tickner, the deputy headmaster of a special school, was sentenced to four years in prison for the sexual abuse of four teenage boys.

### August 25

**MURDER/ROBBERY: South Bend, Ind.** Three employees of an Osco Drug Store were found shot to death, the victims of an apparent robbery.

**TERRORISM: Beirut, Lebanon** Brian Keenan, 52, a Belfast-born teacher who had been held for four years as a hostage, was released by a group calling itself the Organization of Islamic Dawn.

### August 27

**FRAUD: London, England** Former Guinness PLC Chairman Ernest Saunders and three other businessmen were convicted of fraud in connection with the brewery's take-over of a Scottish distiller. Saunders and two other defendants were sentenced to jail terms ranging from one to five years in prison.

**MURDER: Chicago, Ill.** Businessman Lonnie Branch was fatally shot during an apparent robbery after refusing to give his assailant a match.

**KIDNAPPING/SEXUAL ASSAULT: Olathe, Kan.** Patrick E. Schweiger pleaded guilty to aggravated kidnapping and aggravated sodomy in the February 18, 1990, abduction of two 11-year-old boys.

### August 28

**MURDER: Gainesville, Fla.** The bodies of University of Florida students Tracy Inez Paul and Manuel Taboada, both 23, were found at the Gatorwood Apartments, the fourth and fifth victims of a serial killer. Danny Rolling, a smalltime burglar and thief, would confess to all five Gainesville student murders in 1994 and would be sentenced to death.

### August 29

**MURDER: Painesville, Ohio** Cult leader Jeffrey Don Lundgren was found guilty of kidnapping and murdering Dennis and Cheryl Avery, and their three daughters.

**TAX EVASION: Milwaukee, Wis.** Leigh Ann Conley, a former *Playboy* model turned high-priced prostitute, convicted of failing to pay taxes on $398,000 she received for sex, was sentenced to five months in prison and ordered to stay away from men until her term began.

### August 30

**ASSASSINATION: Brooklyn, N.Y.** Vander Beatty, a former state senator seeking election to the Democratic State Committee, was shot to death in his campaign headquarters.

**CHILD MOLESTATION: Salem, Ore.** Norman Dutcher Powers, who had been accused of molesting six children and who claimed to have AIDS, was arrested, ending a nationwide search.

**MURDER: Sydney, Australia** Paul Anthony Evers allegedly shot and killed a man who ridiculed him for being on welfare and then proceeded to kill four more people in the public housing project where he lived before surrendering to police.

### August 31

**EXECUTION: Potasi, Mo.** George C. Gilmore, 44, who was convicted of killing five people during a 1979 crime spree in St. Louis, was executed by lethal injection.

### September 7

**RAPE: Chicago, Ill.** John Willis, who had been dubbed "The Beauty Shop Rapist," because he had reportedly raped a number of women in South Side beauty shops on May 2, 1990, was convicted and given concurrent sentences of 100 years and 45 years.

### September 8

**ILLEGAL EXPLOSIVES: Philadelphia, Pa.** Postal employees accidentally dropped a box which spilled out live grenades and an artillery shell. The explosives were taken to a remote area by a police bomb squad and detonated. The illegal explosives had been sent from France to a Chambersburg, Pennsylvania, address.

### September 9

**ASSASSINATION: Liberia** President of the Republic of Liberia, Samuel K. Doe, 38, who had murdered his predecessor in 1980, was himself assassinated. His mutilated body would later be put on display.

### September 10

**MURDER: Chicago, Ill.** The body of Arron Ranson, 18, who had been shot and killed in a gang fight, lay in state at a South Side funeral parlor when two rival gang members slipped into the room where the body was on display and sliced off one of the body's ears, a final act of gang mutilation and revenge.

### September 11

**THEFT: Linthicum, Md.** William Longthorne, 64, a

mechanical engineer who had fled Saddam Hussein's invading army in Kuwait and had returned home only hours earlier, was held up by a lone gunman who stole his last possession, a $200 watch.

### September 17

**ROBBERY: Miami, Fla.** Xavier Suarez, mayor of Miami, was in his home playing with his children when two armed men entered the house and robbed his wife and another women and then fled when Suarez appeared with a gun, shouting at the thieves.

### September 18

**FRAUD: Los Angeles, Calif.** Charles Keating, Jr., head of the Lincoln Savings and Loan Association, along with three other executives, were indicted for fraud and deceiving elderly investors who purchased uninsured high-risk bonds, a massive financial swindle involving $250 million.

### September 20

**MURDER: Philadelphia, Pa.** John DiGregorio was found guilty of manslaughter. He had killed and dismembered his mentally unstable daughter Carol. DiGregorio was sentenced to four to ten years in prison.

### September 21

**ASSAULT: Washington, D.C.** Columnist Jack Anderson, walking a dark street, was attacked by a mugger, hit on the head with a pipe and then robbed. Anderson later stated: "I've prowled the streets of Washington in the dark of night for many years, but this is the first time anything like this has ever happened."

### September 22

**EXECUTION: Starke, Fla.** James William Hamblem, who was convicted of killing the owner of a Jacksonville lingerie store during a robbery on April 24, 1984, was executed in the state's electric chair. Hamblem had years earlier wisecracked that it would be "spiffy" to be electrocuted, but when his time came, he cowered and quaked and had to be restrained.

### September 28

**ASSASSINATION: Manila, Philippines** A Filipino general and fifteen soldiers were convicted of killing Benigno S. Aquino, Jr., in 1983, and were all sent to prison for life.

### October 2

**HIJACKING: Guangzhou (Canton), China** In an attempt to seize a Chinese airliner, two armed hijackers demanded that the plane be flown to Taiwan or Hong Kong. As the plane attempted to land, a struggle for the control of the airplane occurred and the plane crashed into two planes on the ground, one filled with passengers, the other empty. Chinese officials reported that 132 persons in both planes had been killed and another fifty persons had been injured.

### October 8

**MOB VIOLENCE: Jerusalem** Thousands of Palestinians assembled near the wailing wall to protest the threat of one of their mosques being razed by a Jewish group. More than twenty Jewish citizens and policemen were struck by rocks and police fired into the mobs, killing between seventeen and twenty-one Palestinians.

### October 16

**MURDER: Colorado** Before being released from the Colorado State Penitentiary, Kenyon Battles Tolerton routinely gave a blood sample to officials. This preserved sample was later matched by DNA analysis to blood samples found on the murdered 14-year-old Cissy Pamela Foster in 1993, evidence that brought about Tolerton's life imprisonment.

### October 20

**DRUGS: Washington, D.C.** Marion Barry, the black mayor of Washington, D.C., was sentenced to six months in prison and fined $5,000 after being convicted of possessing cocaine. Federal Judge Thomas Penfield Jackson said that Barry's conviction and sentence set an example for other public officials and that Barry had given "aid, comfort and encouragement to the drug culture at large."

### October 22

**TERRORISM: Portland, Ore.** A group of supremacist terrorists calling themselves members of the White Ayran Resistance, were found liable by a Portland, Oregon, jury of inciting the 1988 beating death of an Ethiopian man. Damages were assessed against the leaders of the group in the amount of $12.5 million, along with the two skinheads responsible for the beating.

### November 2

**MURDER: San Diego, Calif.** After making a key to his employer's home, fired employee Troy Washington sneaked into the house of 38-year-old Deborah Barksdale, who owned a design firm, and raped and murdered her. Washington would be sent to prison for life in 1992.

### November 4

**MURDER: Greensboro, N.C.** Police responding to a 911 call by Thomas Boczkowski found his wife Elaine dead, apparently from drowning in her bathtub. Boczkowski would later stand trial for his wife's murder, and be convicted in 1996.

### November 5

**MURDER: New York, N.Y.** Rabbi Meir Kahane, founder of the Jewish Defense League which advocated aggressive self-defense by Jews, was shot and killed in a mid-Manhattan hotel after giving a speech by El Sayyid A. Nosair, a native Egyptian who had become a U.S. citizen. Nosair also wounded two others before being shot and wounded.

### November 18

**MURDER: New York, N.Y.** Two teenage gangs began fighting on lower Broadway near Waverly Place and one youth fatally shot 19-year-old Javier Bueno. Luis Kevin Rojas was wrongly convicted for this killing and sent to prison, but would later be freed through the research and legal efforts of a volunteer team headed by 68-year-old retired lawyer Priscilla Read Chenoweth.

### November 20

**MURDER: New York, N.Y.** El Sayyid A. Nosair was indicted for the murder of Rabbi Meir Kahane.

**MURDER: Russia** Andrei Chikatilo, one of the Soviet Union's worst serial killers was arrested by military police following a massive manhunt. After a week of intense interrogation, Chikatilo finally broke down and admitted to murdering fifty-two persons in the 1980s, most of his victims being young girls. He claimed that he could not find sexual release until he murdered his victims. He was summarily executed, shot in the back of the head in small room of a prison basement. A superior made-for-cable film, *Citizen X* (1995) was faithfully based on this chilling case.

### November 21

**FRAUD: New York, N.Y.** Former "junk bond" king Michael Milken was sentenced to ten years in prison for securities fraud by District Court Judge Kimba Wood.

### November 24

**MURDER: Buena Park, Calif.** Contract killer Neill Matzen beat to death Donna Connaty in her home and, nine days later, shot and killed the man who hired him to murder his wife, Richard Connaty. Matzen would later be sentenced to life in prison.

### December 3

**JUDICIARY: Washington, D.C.** The U.S. Supreme Court ruled 6-2 to further restrain interrogation of criminal suspects by police, disallowing questioning once a suspect asked for legal representation, and continuing thereafter only when the suspect's attorney was present. This ruling expanded upon the court's 1966 landmark ruling, Miranda vs. Arizona, which had been extended in a 1981 ruling (Edwards vs. Arizona).

### December 15

**MURDER: Brazil** A rancher and his son were convicted of the murder of Chico Mendes, an environmentalist who had been shot and killed in 1988, after his fight to save the rain forests of Brazil from wholesale destruction by Brazilian ranchers.

# 1991

### January 6

**COUP ATTEMPT: Haiti** Roger Lafontant, former head of Haiti's dreaded Ton Ton Macoutes, the terrorist secret police under former dictator Duvalier, attempted to seize control of the government, seizing the presidential palace with armed supporters.

**MURDER: Crizzo Springs, Texas** Benjamin "Doc" Murray, sheriff of Dimmitt, Texas, was stabbed and shot to death in his own home by intruders who turned out to be Jose Garcia Briseno and Alberto Gonzalez, two thieves who lived nearby and who were suspected by Murray of several bur-

glaries. Gonzalez went to prison for life and Garcia Briseno was sentenced to death.

### January 7

**COUP ATTEMPT: Haiti** Roger Lafontant, would-be government usurper and former chief of Haiti's Ton Ton Macoutes, was captured along with his supporters by government troops. More than 70 persons were killed during rioting following the coup attempt.

### January 8

**JUDICIARY: Washington, D.C.** The U.S. Supreme Court unanimously ruled that convicted prisoners testifying in federal court were to be paid the same $30-a-day fee as received by other federal witnesses, this decision overruling a ruling by a federal appeals court that upheld federal policy against paying witness fees to convicted prisoners.

### January 9

**MURDER/ROBBERY: Florida** Prostitute and serial robber-killer Aileen Carol Wuornos was arrested and charged with murdering seven men who picked her up on Florida I-75.

### January 14

**MURDER: Tunis** Two PLO leaders were shot dead, along with a bodyguard, by rival Arab terrorists.

### January 21

**MURDER: Belanglo State Park, Australia**. Simone Schmidt, a 21-year-old German tourist, was one of the first of many hikers to disappear inside the national forest. Her remains would be discovered in October 1992. She had been killed, investigators later learned, by Ivan Robert Marko Milat, one of Australia's most sinister serial killers.

### January 27

**MURDER: Chimayo, N.M.** Police officers began a massive manhunt for 29-year-old Ricky Abeyta, a skilled hunter, in the mountainous area after he reportedly killed a policeman and a sheriff's deputy attempting to serve a restraining order on him, as well as five other persons, members of the same family, including a 5-month-old child.

### February1

**FRAUD: Lincoln, Neb.** Found guilty of fraudulent check cashing, 18-year-old Freedom A. Hunter, was sentenced to six months in prison. Hunter had somehow obtained the driver's license of Tim Holt and a lost or stolen check book belonging to a Lincoln couple. He wrote a check payable to Tim Holt for $275, but when he went to cash it, the teller at the bank was the very Tim Holt who had lost his license.

### February4

**MURDER/DRUGS/ORGANIZED CRIME: New York, N.Y.** Prosecutors announced that they would seek the death penalty for reputed Mafia hit man Thomas "Tommy Karate" Pitera, arrested in June 1990 and held without bail. Pitera, prosecutors stated, was the boss of a Bonanno family crew responsible for widespread drug distribution and drug-related murders. He had been indicted for the murder of two men and was thought to be responsible for the deaths of another two dozen persons.

### February5

**MURDER: Bartow, Fla.** George Trepal, 42, a computer programmer, chemistry enthusiast and MENSA high-IQ club member, was convicted of poisoning his neighbor to death because of loud music, barking dogs and other annoyances. Trepal spiked several bottles of Coca-Cola with thallium nitrate, a highly toxic and banned heavy metal, and slipped the soda into the kitchen of his next-door-neighbor, 41-year-old Peggy Carr. After sipping Coke from one bottle, Carr lapsed into a three-month coma and later died. Two of her sons got sick but recovered.

### February7

**TERRORISM: London, England** IRA terrorists fired three mortar shells at 10 Downing Street, residence of British Prime Minister, but no one was injured.

### February9

**MURDER: New York, N. Y.** Burglar John Howard was found guilty of killing a 90-year-old woman when he refused to give her heart medication while she was having a seizure and Howard and others were burglarizing her apartment. He was sentenced to 30 years to life.

### February10

**MURDER: Colorado** Kenyon Battles Tolerton, after serving ten years for second-degree murder, was paroled. In less than three years, Tolerton would murder another woman and be sent back to prison for life.

### February14

**MURDER: New York, N.Y.** Trial began for 30-year-old Daniel Rakowitz, a busboy, drug-peddler, self-styled messiah and former mental patient, who was charged with murdering and dismembering his girlfriend, 26-year-old Monika Beerie, a go-go dancer in September 1989. Rakowitz had reportedly led police to a Port Authority bus terminal locker where he showed officers a bucket of flesh and bones packed in cat litter, the remains of the victim.

### February15

**ASSAULT: Montgomery, Ala.** The Alabama Supreme Court ruled that sisters Robbie Jean McCorkle and Marita M. McElwey, convicted of tarring and feathering Elizabeth Jamieson McElwey at gunpoint in March 1981, had to pay compensation of $35,000 to Elizabeth McElwey. One of the sisters, Marita M. McElwey, had been married to Dr. John McElwey, divorcing him in 1975, and became incensed at Elizabeth McElwey when she became Dr. McElwey's second wife, which led to the tarring and feathering incident.

### February16

**DRUGS: Medellín, Colombia** Drug-trafficking terrorists exploded a car bomb, killing twenty-two and injuring another 140 persons near a bullfighting ring.

### February18

**BOMBINGS: London, England** IRA terrorists bombed two railways stations, Victoria and Paddington terminals, killing one person and injuring another forty people.

### February23

**BRIBERY: New Orleans, La.** District Judge Robert Collins pleaded innocent to charges that he accepted bribes from a drug smuggler who was cooperating with the FBI in a probe of the New Orleans judiciary. Judge Collins entered the plea during a break from hearing cases in his own courtroom.

### February25

**LARCENY: New York, N.Y.** Steven Romer, a 55-year-old Manhattan attorney, surrendered to authorities, charged with first-degree larceny in absconding with $15 million of his clients' money. Romer, missing since New Year's Eve, 1990, told police that he was run off the highway while en route to Kennedy Airport that night, and that he had been kidnapped and beaten by two men, held hostage until he managed to escape. Romer refused to answer questions about the missing money, according to Assistant District Attorney Roslynn Mauskopf.

**MURDER: London, England** Neighbors responding to screams released 30-year-old Dassa Jackson from a locked garage where she had been forced to inhale corrosive fumes and her body was horribly burned. She died later that day in a bizarre murder plot hatched by her husband, Cecil Jackson, who went to prison for life.

### February26

**DRUGS/WEAPONS VIOLATIONS: New York, N. Y.** Christopher Clemente, a black Ivy League student who had worked his way out of a Harlem ghetto and was convicted of peddling crack cocaine and armed with several illegal weapons, was sentenced to 15 years to life.

### February27

**MURDER: San Francisco, Calif.** Artie Mitchell, a 45-year-old pornographic film entrepreneur, heard a prowler and told his stripper girlfriend Julie Bajo to call 911 and then hide. She heard shots a few minutes later as Mitchell was shot to death in the hallway of his home. His brother and business partner, Jim Mitchell, 47, was later charged with the killing.

### February28

**MURDER: Santa Monica, Calif.** In an emotionally-charged scene, actor Marlon Brando testified on behalf of his son, Christian, who was charged with the killing of his sister's lover, Dag Drollet.

### March 3

**FRAUD/INCOME TAX EVASION: New York, N.Y.** Manhattan attorney Vincent J. Catalfo, 57, was indicted for bilking his court-appointed mentally retarded ward of $45,000 left to Mark Leyden, a victim of Down's syndrome, and in looting the estate left to Leyden for which he was the executor and received a court-awarded fee of $25,000. Catalfo was also charged with evading taxes on more than $770,000 in income.

**POLICE BRUTALITY: Los Angeles, Calif.** Four LAPD officers, led by Sgt. Stacey Koon, were captured on video tape by George Holliday (shooting the scene from a window of his home) as they beat with nightsticks a black motorist, Rodney Glenn King. The two-minute tape showed King being beaten and kicked by the policemen and was later shown on local and national television, causing a nationwide outrage against the police brutality.

*March 14*

**POLICE BRUTALITY: Washington, D.C.** U.S. Attorney General Richard Thornburgh, in response to the Rodney King beating by LAPD officers, said that the U.S. Department of Justice would review this incident and other recent complaints about police brutality.

*March 15*

**POLICE BRUTALITY: Los Angeles, Calif.** The four white LAPD officers who were shown on video tape beating black motorist Rodney King were indicted on charges that included assault with a deadly weapon and inflicting bodily injury.

*March 25*

**MURDER/KIDNAPPING/RAPE: Middletown, N.Y.** Juliana Frank, 29, was kidnapped and sexually attacked before being murdered by serial rapist-killer Nathaniel White. Frank would be the first of six women White would murder in 1991-1992.

*March 26*

**JUDICIARY: Washington, D.C.** The U.S. Supreme Court ruled 5-5 that use of a coerced confession in a criminal trial did not automatically void a conviction, this decision changing a 1967 precedent that a coerced confession could never be held as a "harmless error."

*March 30*

**RAPE: Palm Beach, Fla.** William Kennedy Smith, the 30-year-old nephew of Senator Edward Kennedy (D-Mass.), reportedly raped a woman at the Kennedy family estate.

*March 31*

**ASSAULT: Phoenix, Ariz.** Danny Bonaduce, 31, the former "Danny Patridge" of the popular television series, "The Patridge Family," and a disc jockey with KKFR-FM, was arrested for beating a transvestite prostitute.

*April 1*

**JUDICIARY: Washington, D.C.** The U.S. Supreme Court ruled 7-2 that criminal defendants could object to race-based preemptory challenges of jurors from prosecutors, irrespective of the race of the defendant or the juror.

*April 4*

**RAPE: Palm Beach, Fla.** William Kennedy Smith was identified as the man who raped a woman at the Kennedy estate. In a complaint signed by the victim, the woman stated that she and another woman had met Kennedy, his uncle and his cousin, Patrick Kennedy, in a Palm Beach bar and had been invited to the Kennedy estate where William Kennedy sexually assaulted her.

*April 5*

**RAPE: Palm Beach, Fla.** Medical student and nephew of Senator Edward Kennedy, William Kennedy Smith denied that he had raped a woman at the Kennedy family estate on the night of March 30.

*April 14*

**BURGLARY/MURDER: Gilchrist County, Fla.** John Christopher Mayo and Thomas Edward "Teardrop" Robertson (he had a tattoo of a teardrop beside his left eye), two young burglars, slipped into the home of 73-year-old Jesse Maxine Briggs with intent to burglarize the place when they were interrupted. Mayo reportedly took Briggs' shotgun away from Briggs and beat him to death with it. (Both were later convicted in a Trenton, Florida trial in 1993.)

*April 16*

**JUDICIARY: Washington, D.C.** The U.S. Supreme Court ruled 6-3 to apply more restricted standards to challenges filed by state prisoners arguing the constitutionality of their convictions.

**RAPE: Palm Beach, Fla.** Two news organizations, NBC News (April 16), and the New York *Times* (April 17), revealed the name of the woman who had filed a complaint against William Kennedy Smith for rape. The identification was universally condemned by women's rights organizations, stating that female rape victims are often unfairly stigmatized after being identified.

*April 17*

**KIDNAPPING/SEXUAL ASSAULT: Walkill, N. Y.** Serial rapist-killer Nathaniel White abducted a 16-year-old girl and sexually assaulted her at knifepoint before she managed to escape and inform police. White would later be sent to prison for this attack. White had already murdered another female, Juliana Frank, on March 25, 1991.

*April 23*

**JUDICIARY: Washington, D.C.** The U.S. Supreme Court ruled 7-2 that evidence discarded by a fleeing suspect had no protection under the Fourth Amendment's guarantee against illegal search and seizure.

*April 24*

**NEGLIGENCE: Anchorage, Alaska** U.S. District Judge H. Russell Holland rejected a plea-bargain arrangement made in March 1991 between Exxon Corp. and the U.S. Department of Justice which related to the *Exxon Valdez* oil spill in Alaska in 1989, stating that the $100 million in fines the oil company agreed to pay for its criminal negligence did not "adequately punish" Exxon and would not "achieve deterrence."

### April 25
**MURDER: Greensboro, N.C.** Shot three times, the body of Frederic Brown, a business professor at Guilford County Community College, was found next to his car outside of the city. Brown was the victim of a contract killer hired by his wife Patricia Gayle Brown, who would go to prison for life.

### April 29
**JUDICIARY: Washington, D.C.** The U.S. Supreme Court ruled 6-3 to prohibit prisoners from filing certain kinds of petitions without paying the $300 filing fee. The court also changed its rules to deter the filing of "frivolous" appeals by indigent prisoners.

### May 2
**MOB VIOLENCE: Borovo Selo, Croatia** Serbians living in Croatia wanting to join their country to Yugoslavia, clashed with Croatians in armed shootouts which left twelve policemen and three civilians dead and dozens more wounded.

**CHILD MOLESTATION: Bushnell, Fla.** Judge John W. Booth awarded custody of two teenagers to Billy Williams, not recognizing Williams as the man he had sentenced to ten years' probation in 1989 for an indecent assault on an 11-year-old girl. (The judge was informed of Williams' background four days later and the custody was revoked.)

### May 8
**HANDGUN LEGISLATION: Washington, D.C.** The U.S. House of Representatives voted 239-186 to pass the Brady Handgun Violence Prevention Act, which required a seven-day waiting period for the purchase of any handgun in the U.S., allowing police to check the background of any prospective buyers. The National Rifle Association had vigorously lobbied against the passing of the Brady bill.

### May 9
**RAPE: Palm Beach, Fla.** Following a six-week investigation, William Kennedy Smith, nephew of Senator Edward Kennedy, was officially charged with a felony count of sexual battery.

### May 11
**RAPE: Palm Beach, Fla.** William Kennedy Smith surrendered to police and was booked on a charge of rape; he was released after posting bond.

### May 13
**JUDICIARY: Washington, D.C.** The U.S. Supreme Court ruled 5-4 that suspects arrested without warrants could be held for 48 hours while awaiting the ruling from a judge to determine if the arrest was proper.

**KIDNAPPING: Johannesburg, South Africa** A South African judge branded as a terrorist Winnie Mandela, wife of Nelson Mandela, leader of outlawed African National Congress, finding her guilty of kidnapping four youths, who had been taken to her home and beaten for not supporting her political cause. She was sentenced to six years in prison the following day, but she would never serve a day behind bars, being fined and put on probation.

### May 20
**JUDICIARY: Washington, D.C.** The U.S. Supreme Court ruled 7-2 that in certain cases states could limit an accused rapist's ability to present evidence about his prior sexual relationship with the alleged victim.

### May 21
**ASSASSINATION: Sriperumbudur, Madras, India** While campaigning once more for political office, Rajiv Gandhi was approached by a woman who had concealed a bomb, according to police, and exploded the device, killing Gandhi, herself and fifteen other persons. Gandhi had become India's prime minister in 1984 after his mother, Indira Gandhi, had been assassinated by her own bodyguards. His grandfather, Jawaharlal Nehru, had also served as India's prime minister.

**TERRORISM: Addis Ababa, Ethiopia** Mengistu Haile Mariam, president and dictator of Ethiopia, who had led a hardline Marxist government employing terrorism, fled the country as rebels approached the capital of Addis Ababa.

### May 23
**JUDICIARY: Washington, D.C.** The U.S. Supreme Court ruled 7-2 that a suspect who permitted police to search his vehicle for narcotics also gave implicit permission to search closed containers in the car's passenger compartment.

### May 24
**MURDER: Milwaukee, Wis.** Serial killer Jeffrey Dahmer murdered 31-year-old Tony Hughes, a deaf-mute from Madison, Wis.

### May 26
**BOMBING: Thailand** An Austrian Boeing 767-300 jetliner exploded over the jungle in Thailand, killing all 223 persons on board; a terrorist bomb was suspected, but this allegation remained unproven.

### May 27
**MURDER: Milwaukee, Wis.** Konerak Sinthasomphone, a Laotian immigrant, ran naked and bleeding into the arms of three police officers who, unable to understand his language, turned him back to his host for the night, Jeffrey Dahmer. A few hours later Dahmer murdered and dismembered the Laotian youth.

### May 30
**JUDICIARY: Washington, D.C.** The U.S. Supreme Court ruled 6-3 that police could search bags, suitcases or other containers in the trunk of a car, overturning a 1979 precedent requiring warrants for luggage searches.

### May 31
**RAPE: Palm Beach, Fla.** William Kennedy Smith en-

tered a plea of not guilty in the charge of rape (sexual battery) filed against him.

## June 3

**JUDICIARY: Washington, D.C.** The U.S. Supreme Court ruled 5-4 that a promise of impartiality from potential jurors in criminal cases was sufficient enough to protect a defendant's Sixth Amendment rights to a fair trial and that a judge need not question jurors about what they had heard or read about the crime.

## June 13

**JUDICIARY: Washington, D.C.** The U.S. Supreme Court ruled 6-3 that a suspect in a criminal case represented by an attorney could, could, under certain circumstances, be questioned by police about a second, separate crime without the attorney being present, this ruling further limiting the rights of suspects guaranteed by the court's 1966 landmark decision of Miranda vs. Arizona.

## June 15

**DEATH SENTENCES: Kuwait City, Kuwait** Six persons were condemned to death for working as political allies to invading Iraq forces during the Gulf War. All six had worked for a newspaper published by Iraq.

**MURDER: Burlington, Ontario, Canada** Leslie Mahaffey, 14, disappeared. She would be taken in and sexually tortured, then murdered by Paul Bernardo, who would be sent to prison for life.

**TERRORISM: Punjab, India** Violence erupted during India's national election; terrorists fired on two passenger trains and killed 76 persons.

## June 17

**JUDICIARY: Washington, D.C.** The U.S. Supreme Court ruled 5-3 that prisoners filing challenges against the constitutionality of prison conditions, such as filthy washrooms and unsanitary dining areas, had to prove the conditions resulted from deliberate indifference by prison officials.

## June 19

**DRUGS: Medellín. Colombia** Following the passing of a Colombian law that prohibited the extradition of Colombian nationals, Medellín drug lord Pablo Escobar Gaviria surrendered to authorities. He had been indicted for drug trafficking and murder, but, under the new law, he could not be sent to the U.S. for trial. Escobar was sent to a facility especially built for him in Envigado, Colombia, not far from his massive drug operations in Medellín, a place more like a posh home than a prison. U.S. officials stated that Escobar's arrest would have little effect on the flow of cocaine out of Colombia.

## June 20

**JUDICIARY: Washington, D.C.** The U.S. Supreme Court ruled 6-3 that police searching for drug traffickers, with permission, could board buses and search passengers' luggage, without violating the Fourth Amendment guarantee against illegal search and seizure.

## June 21

**JUDICIARY: Washington, D.C.** The U.S. Supreme Court ruled 6-3 to tighten restrictions on the rights of state prisoners appealing their cases in federal courts.

## June 25

**FRAUD: Chicago, Ill.** Joseph Pierre, 40, was indicted for an immigration scam wherein he reportedly arranged phony marriages for 17 foreign nationals to wed U.S. citizens, so the immigrants could obtain "green cards," charging the immigrants large fees for the sham marriages. Prosecutors claimed that Pierre also conspired to aid illegal immigrants in making false statements to the U.S. Immigration and Naturalization Service in order to obtain resident alien status.

## June 26

**DEATH SENTENCES: Kuwait City, Kuwait** The six persons condemned to death on June 15 for collaborating with Iraq forces during the Gulf War, had their sentences commuted to life in prison.

## June 27

**JUDICIARY: Washington, D.C.** U.S. Supreme Court Justice Thurgood Marshall, a one-time pioneering civil rights lawyer, announced his retirement when a successor was appointed. Marshall expressed his disappointment with the court's conservative trend in recent years.

## June 30

**MURDER: Milwaukee, Wis.** Serial killer Jeffrey Dahmer murdered 20-year-old Matt Turner of Chicago. Dahmer had lured Turner to his apartment and then killed him, sodomized him after death and then, according to his own later admissions, dismembered and cannibalized the corpse.

## July 5

**BANK FRAUD: International** The Bank of Commerce and Credit International (BCCI), which had offices in 69 countries and was controlled by Sheik Zayed bin Sultan Al Nahayan in Abu Dhabi in the United Arab Emrites and which had pleaded guilty to money laundering schemes, was closed down in seven countries, including the U.S., by bank regulators.

## July 9

**POLICE BRUTALITY: Los Angeles, Calif.** Warren Christopher, a former deputy secretary of state, who had been appointed to head a special commission looking into excessive use of force by police officers, released its findings. The commission, appointed by L.A. Mayor Tom Bradley and Police Chief Daryl Gates, studied more than 2,000 cases of alleged excessive use of force by police officers and concluded that officers were encouraged to "command and confront, not to communicate." The internal investigation was sparked by the beating of motorist Rodney King by four LAPD officers. As part of the report's conclusion, the commission recommended that a "a major overhaul" of the police disciplinary system by enacted and that Chief Gates resign.

### July 11

**CHILD PORNOGRAPHY: Chicago, Ill.** Steven Meschino, 39, on parole for distributing and reproducing child pornography, was arrested on new child pornography charges and held on a $500,000 bond.

**PRISON PAROLE: North Carolina** Anthony Hipps, convicted of an ax murder and sent to prison for life, was paroled, his released mandated by prison overcrowding, according to officials. Four years later Hipps would kill a 17-year-old girl in Spencer, N.C. and be sentenced to death.

### July 18

**POLICE SHOOTINGS: Jerusalem** Judge Ezra Kama, heading an Israeli judicial inquiry into the violence that had erupted at Temple Mount in October 1990, reported that at least seventeen Arabs had been killed after Palestinians had provoked a clash with Israeli border police, but he blamed the police for indiscriminately using live ammunition to fire into the crowds.

### July 22

**MURDER: Milwaukee, Wis.** Serial killer Jeffrey Dahmer was arrested and charged with murder after police found human body parts littering his apartment.

**LAW ENFORCEMENT: Los Angeles, Calif.** Police Chief Daryl Gates, in response to an internal police commission report that criticized his "get tough" policies, announced that he would resign in April 1992, if a replacement could be found to fill his position.

### July 23

**BANK FRAUD: International** Robin Leigh-Pemberton, governor of the Bank of England, stated that the Bank of Commerce and Credit International (BCCI) had committed "fraudulent conduct on a world-wide scale," and that its top executives were implicated in wrong-doing.

### July 24

**MURDER: Milwaukee, Wis.** Police stated that 31-year-old Jeffrey Dahmer had confessed to murdering eleven men, most of them homosexuals whom he lured to his apartment where he drugged and strangled them and then dismembered their bodies. He also admitted that, in some instances, he cannibalized the remains.

### July 25

**MURDER: Milwaukee, Wis.** Jeffrey Dahmer, one of the worst serial killers in recent times, was charged with four counts of homicide.

### July 26

**POLICE NEGLIGENCE: Milwaukee, Wis.** Three Milwaukee police officers who had, in May, encountered a beaten and bloodied 14-year-old boy who had just escaped from serial killer Jeffrey Dahmer and who was later murdered by Dahmer that night after police turned the boy back to him, were suspended.

### July 28

**MURDER: Fayetteville, N.C.** The bodies of 38-year-old Judy Faulk Hudson and her two children were found bludgeoned to death. Their killer, Philip Edward Wilkinson, a private stationed at nearby Fort Bragg, later confessed to the murders and was sentenced to death.

### July 29

**BANK FRAUD: International** A state grand jury in New York, N. Y., indicted the Bank of Commerce and Credit International (BCCI) on charges of fraud, theft and money-laundering.

**MURDER: Hollis, N.C.** An elderly couple, William Fred Davis and his wife Margaret, were found bludgeoned to death in their home. Their killer, Phillip Lee Ingle, was executed in 1995.

### July 31

**TERRORISM/MURDER: Lithuania** Six Lithuanian border guards were slain by terrorists, who challenged Lithuania's claim of independence from the Soviet Union.

### August 8

**HOSTAGE RELEASED: Beirut, Lebanon** British journalist John McCarthy, kidnapped and held hostage since 1986 by Islamic Jihad, a Shiite Moslem terrorist organization, was released to carry a letter to U.N. Secretary General Javier Pérez de Cuéllar, a letter stating that all hostages would be released if Palestinian and Lebanese prisoners were also set free.

### August 9

**MURDER: Mecklenburg County, Va.** Kenneth Gray Via was reported missing near John H. Kerr Dam after he went off to fish. His body was later found and his killer, dam worker Stuart Duke, Jr., was found guilty and sent to prison for life.

### August 11

**HOSTAGES RELEASED: Beirut, Lebanon** Edward Austin Tracy, an American who has been held for five years by Lebanese terrorists, was released. Only hours earlier, French hostage Jèrome Leyraud, abducted a week earlier, was released by the same terrorist group.

### August 13

**BANK FRAUD: International** Because of their alleged involvement with the BCCI fraud, former secretary of defense and Democratic Party sachem Clark Clifford and his protegé Robert Altman (husband of actress Lynda Carter) stepped down as chairman and president of First American Bankshares, which had come under control of BCCI.

**MURDER: Chicago, Ill.** Virginia Griffin, 44, visited a small park in Rogers Park on the North Side of Chicago. She was found dead the following morning, stabbed 32 times and sexually violated. Ralph Andrews, her killer, who reportedly murdered and sexually attacked more than a dozen women in several states over the past decade, was convicted and sentenced to life in prison.

### August 15

**ASSAULT: Waukegan, Ill.** Because he wanted to quit a

Waukegan, Illinois, street gang, Keith Smith was beaten sense-less on the orders of gang leader Francisco Aguirre, 23, who had three members of his gang punch, kick and stomp Smith in a Waukegan park while he timed the assault. Smith lay co-matose in a hospital for 58 days, but testified against his at-tackers in December 1991; Aguirre and three others were con-victed and imprisoned.

### August 19

**ARSON: New York, N.Y.** Cuban immigrant Julio Gon-zalez was found guilty of arson, felony murder, murder with depraved indifference to human life and assault in the deaths of 87 people who perished in a 1990 fire he set, one that con-sumed the Happy Land Social Club in the Bronx. Gonzalez had set the blaze following an argument in the club with his ex-girlfriend.

**RIOTS/CIVIL RIGHTS VIOLATIONS: Brooklyn, N. Y.** Widespread rioting by blacks began when Gavin Cato, a 7-year-old black boy was run over and killed by a car driven by a Hasidic Jew. Hasidic Jew Yankel Rosenbaum was murdered that night in retaliation for Cato's death, a murder for which Lemrick Nelson was later charged.

### August 30

**PRISON RIOT: Talladega, Ala.** Federal agents stormed the Federal Correction Institution, freeing nine hostages from prison inmates and capturing 121 rioting prisoners.

### September 3

**ATTEMPTED MURDER: Channelview, Texas** Wanda Webb Holloway was found guilty of trying to hire a hitman to kill the mother of a girl who was a rival of Holloway's daugh-ter in competition for a place on the local school's cheerleading squad. Holloway believed that by murdering the mother the girl would be so distraught that she would fail in her tryouts and that her own daughter would win the cheerleading spot.

### September 4

**ATTEMPTED MURDER: Channelview, Texas** Wanda Webb Holloway was sentenced to a 15-year prison term for attempted murder.

### September 5

**DRUGS: Miami, Fla.** Former Panamanian dictator Manuel Noriega, who had been arrested for drug laundering and trafficking two years earlier, went on trial, charged with help-ing Colombian drug lords transport huge amounts of cocaine.

### September 6

**IRAN-CONTRA: Washington, D.C.** Clair George, former director of operations at the CIA, was indicted for ly-ing to Congress and a grand jury during its investigation of the Iran-Contra arms sales. The indictment was based upon the testimony of another CIA official, Alan Fiers, who had headed the CIA's Latin American operations and who had earlier pleaded guilty to having lied to Congress in the Iran-Contra affair.

**MURDER: Milwaukee, Wis.** Two police officers who had turned over a murder victim to serial killer Jeffrey Dahmer were fired from the police force.

### September 8

**MURDER: League City, Texas** The skeletal remains of a young woman were found in a field; pathologists determined that the woman had been murdered; she was one of more than 30 unsolved disappearances and killings that occurred from the mid-1980s through the 1990s near Interstate 45, between Galveston and Houston, Texas.

### September 9

**MURDER: Gaston, N.C.** E.Z. Willis and his wife Sarah, an elderly couple, were found bludgeoned to death. Phillip Lee Ingle, would be found guilty of these murders and the slayings of another elderly couple and be executed in 1995.

**MURDER: Rotherfield, England** The body of 17-year-old Lynne Rogers was discovered by a ditchdigger. Her killer, Scott Singleton, would later be sent to prison for life.

### September 11

**MURDER: Winter Haven, Fla.** To cover the murder of his wife, Andrew Lee Golden filed a wrongful death suit against the city, stating that his wife drove into Lake Hartridge off a boat ramp that was not properly lighted and caused her death.

**PRISONERS RELEASED: Israel** Acting on the prom-ise from Hezbollah, a Palestinian terrorist group, that it would identify Israeli soldiers taken years earlier, Israeli officials re-leased 51 Palestinians and returned the bodies of nine others.

### September 12

**BODIES IDENTIFIED: West Bank** Hezbollah, the Pal-estinian terrorist organization, confirmed that two Israeli sol-diers taken captive in 1986 were dead and a third body was returned, this information exchanged for the release of 51 Pal-estinian terrorists by Israel.

### September 13

**MURDER: Bath Township, Ohio** The remains of 19-year-old Steven Hicks, who had been murdered in 1978 by serial killer Jeffrey Dahmer, were identified after a coroner's examination.

**MURDER: Phoenix, Ariz.** Police arrested six persons and charged them with the slaying of nine people at a Buddhist temple outside the city.

### September 16

**DRUGS: Miami, Fla.** Prosecutors opened the trial against former Panamanian dictator Manuel Noriega by stating that he had intended to make Panama a center of cocaine manufactur-ing and distribution. Fifteen of Noriega's co-defendants had already pleaded guilty in plea-bargain agreements and would later testify against their former chief, Noriega.

**IRAN-CONTRA: Washington, D.C.** District Judge Gerhard Gesell declared that the case against Oliver North, who was involved with the Iran-Contra arms sales, was "ter-minated," with all charges dismissed.

*September 17*

**BANK FRAUD: International** Ghaith Pharaon, a front man for the corrupt Arab-owned BCCI banking system, admitted that he had purchased Independence Bank in Encino, California in 1985, for approximately $23 million, claiming then that he was making the purchase with his own money and for himself, when, in truth, he had been acting on behalf of BCCI. Pharaon was fined $37 million, according to an announcement by the U.S. Federal Reserve Board.

*September 19*

**LAW ENFORCEMENT CRIME DATA SYSTEMS: Chicago, Ill.** Computer consultant Richard E. McDonell reported to Cook County Citizens Advisory Law Enforcement Committee that scores of criminals were returned to the streets with pending charges against them because state, country and city computer data systems do not exchange information efficiently. McDonell cited several cases to prove his point, including an injunction against a man ordered to stay away from his estranged wife and who was picked up by police in front of her home and then released because a search of city files failed to show the injunction; an hour later the man murdered his wife.

**TORTURE: Camp Lejeune, N.C.** In an illegal initiation ceremony, veteran Marines sadistically pinned emblems of the Corp into the bare flesh of helpless recruits, a private video tape recording this unspeakable torture. Although the offenders were reportedly disciplined, such bestial conduct reflected an increased moral indifference by top U.S. commanders to military codes of conduct

*September 21*

**ROBBERY: San Antonio, Texas** The Texas Commerce Motor Bank was robbed of more than $242,000, a lone gunmen forcing two tellers to open a safe inside the unguarded bank on a Saturday morning. Through careful and cautious investigation, San Antonio detectives pinpointed the culprits, Lisa Michelle Silvas, one of the tellers, and her boyfriend, Jack Nealy, a distinguished member of the city police force. Both were sent to prison.

*September 24*

**HOSTAGE RELEASED: Beirut, Lebanon** Pro-Iranian terrorists released British hostage Jack Mann, 77 and in poor health, to Syrian officials. Mann had been held for more than two years.

*September 25*

**MOB VIOLENCE: Bucharest, Romania** Thousands of unemployed workers demanding pay raises and better working conditions rioted, causing police to use tear gas and gunfire. After three days of rioting, three persons were left dead and 137 others were injured.

*September 28*

**MURDER: San Salvador, El Salvador** A jury found Col. Guillermo Alfredo Benavides Moreno guilty of ordering a Salvadorian military squad to kill six Jesuit priests, a cook and her daughter, in 1989.

*September 30*

**COUP: Haiti** Jean-Bertrand Aristide first freely-elected president, was ousted from power in a bloody coup between a military cabal and Aristide's supporters which saw twenty-six persons killed and 200 wounded. Aristide flew to Venezuela to begin his exile.

*October 2*

**MURDER: Lebanon, Ind.** John Mason, who had hired a contract killer to murder his ex-wife, Patricia, to rid himself of alimony payments, was sentenced to fifty years in prison.

*October 8*

**MURDER: Winter Haven, Fla.** Andrew Lee Golden went on trial for the murder of his wife. He would be found guilty of killing Ardelle Golden for her life insurance policies.

*October 16*

**MURDER: Killeen, Texas** George Hennard, of Belton, Texas, armed with two 9-mm semiautomatic pistols, drove his pickup through the front window of Luby's Cafeteria, then began shooting everyone in sight, killing twenty-two persons instantly and fatally wounding another before a policeman wounded Hennard. The mass murderer went into the restaurant's washroom and there killed himself. The death toll was the highest in mass murder committed in U.S. history.

**MURDER: McKinney, Texas** Jim Brunette, head of a local brokerage firm, was abducted and murdered by Casey Dean Corthron and Amado Tamez. Tamez was later sent to prison for 40 years and Corthron, the actual killer, to life.

*October 18*

**MURDER/ROBBERY: Fountain Valley, Calif.** Kathy Lee, 47, who arrived at a CompUSA store to visit her 18-year-old son, who worked there, interrupted a robbery and was shot and killed by one of the armed men holding employees at bay. William Clinton Clark and two others were arrested. Clark was convicted of the murder and sent to prison for life in 1996.

*October 21*

**HOSTAGE RELEASE: Beirut, Lebanon** Jesse Turner, an American professor of mathematics at Beirut University College, was released from captivity by Islamic Jihad, a Palestinian terrorist group that had held Turner hostage for more than five years.

*October 23*

**JUDICIARY: Washington, D.C.** Clarence Thomas was sworn in as the 106th U.S. Supreme Court justice, replacing Thurgood Marshall, who had retired.

*October 28*

**ROBBERY: Raleigh, N.C.** Ehyin Mohammed Youseff robbed a student on the campus of the University of North Carolina at gunpoint and was locked up. Youseff, who had a long record of assaults and theft, would go on to murder a fellow black, Dr. William McCoy Yates, who became his benefactor.

*October 29*

**MURDER: Winter Haven, Fla.** Andrew Lee Golden, convicted of murdering his wife in order to collect insurance money, was sentenced to death. His response was a sneer and the comment: "Who cares?"

*November 4*

**MURDER: Fayetteville, N.C.** Helissa Hayes and her two small sons were found strangled in their mobile home. Their killer, Earl Richmond, Jr., was later identified and convicted of the multiple murders.

**MURDER: New York, N. Y.** The trial of Arab terrorist El Sayyiud Nosair began. Nosair stood accused of the November 1990 shooting and killing of Meir Kahane, a rabbi and former head of the Jewish Defense League. Nosair will be found guilty only of assault with a deadly weapon and be sentenced to a term of seven to 22 years in prison.

*November 5*

**SUSPICIOUS DEATH: Canary Islands** Robert Maxwell, the publishing czar who controlled the Macmillan publishing group and the Mirror Group newspaper group in England, drowned while his yacht was cruising through the islands. His death was suspected as having been caused by foul play, but Spanish authorities later and unconvincingly reported that Maxwell, who was about to see his financial empire crumble, had probably suffered a heart attack and fell overboard.

**TAX FRAUD: Manila, Philippines** A day after she had voluntarily returned to the Philippines after five years of exile, Imelda Marcos, the wife of the now deceased Filipino dictator Ferdinand Marcos, was arrested on charges of tax fraud involving money allegedly seized by her and her husband during Marcos' presidency. She was released after posting bail.

*November 14*

**BOMBING/TERRORISM: Washington, D.C./Scotland** Two Libyans working with the PFLP to place the bomb on board Pan Am Flight 103, which exploded over Lockerbie, Scotland on December 21, 1988 and killed 270 persons, were indicted in the U.S. and also in Scotland. The two were Abdel Basset Ali Megrahi, the former Libya Airlines security chief at Malta and Amin Khalifa Fhimah, the airline manager. They reportedly secured luggage tags and substituted a bomb-packed suitcase for another before the plane took off from Malta.

*November 15*

**IRAN-CONTRA: Washington, D.C.** John Poindexter's conviction for lying to Congress, obstructing Congress and conspiracy was overturned by the U.S. Court of Appeals for the District of Columbia on grounds that witnesses testifying against Poindexter had been unduly influenced by Poindexter's statements to Congress in 1987. Also on this date, Elliot Abrams, a former top Reagan official who had earlier pleaded guilty of withholding information from Congress during the Iran-Contra hearings, was sentenced to two years' probation and ordered to perform 100 hours of community service.

*November 16*

**CRIME BACKGROUND SCREENING: Washington, D.C.** In an effort to curb the hiring of convicted felons, Postmaster General Anthony Frank announced that all applicants for postal positions would be screened by law enforcement and military agencies.

*November 18*

**HOSTAGE RELEASE: Beirut, Lebanon** Islamic Jihad, an Arab terrorist organization in Lebanon, released Terry Waite, who had been a representative of the Archbishop of Canterbury in the Middleast and who had originally been sent to negotiate the release of hostages in 1987, when he himself was taken hostage. Also released with Waite was Thomas M. Sutherland, former dean of agriculture at American University in Beirut, who had been held hostage since 1985.

*November 21*

**MURDER: Chicago, Ill.** In savage murders intended to silence witnesses, the mother, sister and aunt of jailed child molester Sanatone Moss stabbed Emma Jones and her 11-year-old daughter Diandra to death. Moss was later sentenced to death for ordering the murders and his relatives sent to prison.

*November 26*

**IRAN-CONTRA: Washington, D.C.** Duane Clarridge, a former CIA official, was indicted on seven counts of lying to Congress about the diversion of money from arms sales to the Nicaraguan contras.

*November 29*

**MURDER: Sydney, Australia** John Wayne Glover, convicted of the serial killing of six elderly women, was sentenced to six life terms without the possibility of parole.

*December 1*

**HOSTAGES RELEASED: Beirut, Lebanon** The Israeli-supported South Lebanon Army released 25 Arab hostages.

*December 2*

**HOSTAGE RELEASED: Beirut, Lebanon** Arab terrorists released Joseph Cicippio, an American who had been held hostage.

*December 3*

**HOSTAGE RELEASED: Beirut, Lebanon** Arab terrorists released American Alann Steen, who had been held hostage. He, like his fellow prisoner Joseph Cicippio, released a day earlier, had suffered permanent injuries at the hands of their brutal captors.

*December 4*

**FRAUD: Los Angeles, California** Charles Keating, Jr., head of the defunct Lincoln Savings and Loan and other corrupted financial institutions, was found guilty on seventeen counts of securities fraud. Keating and others had induced more than 17,000 U.S. investors to purchase $250 million in uninsured bonds.

**HOSTAGE RELEASED: Beirut, Lebanon** Terry Anderson, a former Associated Press reporter who had been held hostage for seven years by Arab terrorists, was released.

*December 11*

**RAPE: Palm Beach, Fla.** William Kennedy Smith, nephew of Senator Edward Kennedy, who stood trial for raping a woman at the Kennedy estate, was found not guilty of sexual battery by a jury.

*December 18*

**EXTORTION: Chicago. Ill.** Organized crime boss Gus Alex, 75, and three of his lieutenants were indicted for extorting hundreds of thousands of dollars from area businesses from 1983 to 1989.

*December 19*

**BANK FRAUD: New York, N.Y.** Officials for the corrupted Bank of Credit and Commerce International (BCCI) plea-bargained the criminal charges of international bank fraud by agreeing to the demands of the U.S. Department of Justice and the New York District Attorney's Office to forfeit all of its U.S. assets, about $550 million, and support two U.S. banks BCCI had purchased and were then in a weakened position. The plea-bargain did not include charges still pending against BCCI officers.

**RAPE: Palm Beach, Fla.** Although she had been shielded during the trial of her accused rapist, William Kennedy Smith, the reported victim identified herself in a television interview as Patricia Bowman.

*December 21*

**MURDER: New York, N. Y.** Egyptian immigrant El Sayyid Nosair, accused of murdering Rabbi Meir Kahane at a hotel in 1990, was acquitted of first degree murder by a jury, although he was found guilty of assault with a deadly weapon and was sentenced to seven to twenty-two years in prison.

*December 22*

**MURDER: Beirut, Lebanon** An anonymous caller contacted Lebanese authorities to tell them where to find the body of Lt. Col. William Higgins, who had been slain years earlier by Arab terrorists.

*December 24*

**ARMED RESISTANCE: Calhoun, Ky.** Edna Lee Evans, who had served 12 years in a Missouri prison for murder and who had shot a deputy sheriff near Calhoun, Ky., where he had relocated, was ordered to surrender by sheriff's deputies, but he raised a shotgun in their direction and was shot and killed by an officer standing nearby.

*December 27*

**MURDER: Beirut, Lebanon** An anonymous caller contacted Lebanese authorities to tell them where to find the body of CIA officer William Buckley, slain by Arab terrorists.

*December 30*

**MURDER: Portland, Ore.** Scott William Cox, a 28-year-old truck driver, was charged with murdering two prostitutes and, according to prosecutors, was the suspect in the murders of another twenty women who frequented truck stops across the country.

# 1992

*January 4*

**MURDER: New York, N.Y.** Members of a black teenage gang who terrorized a tourist family on a subway platform, killing one, were sentenced to 25 years in prison.

*January 5-6*

**BOMBING: Northern Ireland** IRA terrorists attacked civilians working at a British army base with a bomb that killed eight persons and wounded another six people as they were riding home.

*January 9*

**MURDER: Fayetteville, N.C.** Philip Wilkinson, a private stationed at Fort Bragg, admitted to authorities that he had murdered Judy Faulk Hudson and her two children. He would be sentenced to death in 1994.

*January 10*

**BOMBING: London, England** IRA terrorists exploded a bomb less than 300 yards from 10 Downing Street, the prime minister's residence. No one was injured.

*January 15*

**DEPORTATION: New York, N.Y.** A court ruled that Joseph Doherty, reputed IRA terrorist and convicted killer of a British soldier, who had taken refuge in the U.S., was not entitled to political asylum and was ordered deported back to Britain.

*January 20*

**CIVIL RIGHTS VIOLATIONS: St. Louis, Mo.** David Walden and Shawn Daniels, two white men, drove through black communities, spraying black residents with Kool-Aid from a high pressure fire extinguisher and shouting racial slurs. Both would later be imprisoned.

*January 30*

**MURDER: London, England** Going on trial at the Old Bailey, Cecil Jackson was allowed to defend himself in the murder trial of his wife, Dassa, who had been burned to death with acid in one of the most gruesome killings of recent times.

*January 31*

**MURDER: Florida** Serial killer and highway prostitute Aileen Carol Wuornos was sentenced to death for killing seven men along state highway I-75.

*February 10*

**RAPE: Indianapolis, Ind.** Mike Tyson, former heavyweight boxing champion, was convicted of raping Desiree Washington, one of the contestants at the Miss Black America beauty pageant in July 1991. In addition to rape, the jury found Tyson guilty of two criminal counts of deviant conduct.

**MURDER: Georgia** Carnival worker Kenneth Daniel Howard was found guilty burglary and murdering Edgar Couch in Lawrenceville. He was sent to prison for life.

*February 14*

**ROBBERY: San Antonio, Texas** Jack Nealy, a policeman on the city force who robbed the Texas Commerce Motor Bank of $242,000, was sentenced to 15 years in prison. His accomplice and lover, Lisa Michelle Silvas, who worked as a teller at the bank, received a 12-year sentence.

*February 15*

**MURDER: Milwaukee, Wis.** Jeffrey Dahmer, who had confessed to murdering fifteen boys and young men, as well as dismembering and cannibalizing their body parts, but who had initially pleaded innocent by reasons of insanity, was found by a jury to be sane.

*February 16:*

**MURDER: Elmhurst, Ill.** Unemployed truck driver Kenneth Kopecky, who had been stalking Karen Erjavec for months, hid behind some shrubbery until the 24-year-old Erjavec and her boyfriend, Glenn Beach, arrived at Beach's home. Kopecky, wearing camouflage clothes then shot Beach five times and Erjavec once, killing both. He later fled to White Plains, Michigan, tracked down by police at the Konteka Motel, but before Kopecky could be taken into custody, he killed himself.

**TERRORISM: Southern Lebanon** Israeli helicopter gunships fired on a motorcade, killing Sheik Abbas al-Musawi, one of the leaders of Hezbollah (Party of God), a known terrorist organization.

*February 17*

**MURDER: Arlington, Va.** Handyman Angel Francisco Breard entered the home of a neighbor, Ruth Dickie, 39, raping and killing her. He would be executed for this slaying in 1998.

**MURDER: Milwaukee, Wis.** Serial killer Jeffrey Dahmer, who had confessed earlier to murdering fifteen boys and young men, was sentenced to fifteen consecutive life terms in prison.

*February 20*

**MURDER: Las Vegas, Nev.** The bodies of roommates Laurie Jacobson and Denise Lizzi were discovered; both had been murdered. Their killer, Michael Rippo would later be convicted and sentenced to death.

**MURDER: London, England** Wife killer Cecil Jackson—he had trapped her inside of a garage, releasing toxic fumes that burned away her flesh—was convicted and sentenced to life in prison.

*March 2*

**POLITICAL CORRUPTION: Chicago, Ill.** After being convicted of taking $6,000 in bribes, former judge, David J. Shields, was sentenced to prison for three years.

*March 7*

**MURDER: Indiana** Gerald Bivens, a career thief, was convicted of murdering William H. Radcliffe, a minister, at a reststop outside of Lebanon, Indiana on Jan. 16, 1990, for the $20 Radcliffe was carrying. Bivens was sentenced to death the following day.

*March 12*

**MURDER: Torrington, Conn.** Philomene Farnham, 94, was found beaten to death in the living room of her home by a neighbor. Her 88-year-old brother, Just Fournier, who suffered from Alzheimer's disease, was charged with his sister's murder.

*March 15*

**MURDER: Yerington, Nev.** Police hunting for the killer of two young women in Las Vegas, tracked down Diana Hunt, who had used the credit cards of one of the victims. Hunt quickly implicated Michael Rippo as the murderer.

*March 17*

**BOMBING: Buenos Aires, Argentina** A powerful car bomb exploded at the Israeli embassy, killing 14 persons and wounding another 252 people. It was reported that the bomb had been planted by Islamic terrorists.

*March 21*

**THEFT/MURDER: Chicago, Ill.** In a precedent-setting case involving Illinois' Speedy Trial Act, Yolanda Jordan, accused of killing a newlywed couple in a high speed escape following a 1991 store theft, was ordered released because she had been held overlong, 407 days, before being brought to trial on this date.

*March 23*

**TERRORISM: Libya** Although Libyan officials announced that two suspects in plane bombings of 1988 (Lockerbie, Scotland) and 1989 (Niger), would be turned over the members of the Arab League, the two terrorists were not turned over and remained protected by Libya.

*March 26*

**RAPE: Indianapolis, Ind.** Mike Tyson, former heavyweight boxing champion, convicted of rape, was sentenced to six years in prison and was ordered to pay a fine of $30,000.

*March 31*

**TERRORISM: New York, N.Y.** The U.N. Security Council voted to impose sanctions on Libya if two terrorists suspected of bombing Pan Am Flight 103 in 1988 and anther plane bombing in 1989, were not turned over by April 15.

*April 2*

**ORGANIZED CRIME: Brooklyn, N.Y.** John Gotti, reported head of the Gambino crime family in New York, was convicted in U.S. District Court of murder, extortion and obstruction of justice, along with other crimes. Convicted with Gotti was codefendant Frank Locascio. One of Gotti's lieutenants, Salvatore "Sammy the Bull" Gravano, testified against his former mob boss, saying that Gotti was involved with ten murders (Gravano himself admitted to nineteen killings), in exchange for a prison sentence not to exceed twenty years.

**TERRORISM: Libya** Libyan mobs in Tripoli attacked several embassies of countries that had voted to place sanctions on Libya if that country did not turn over two terrorists suspected of bombing Pan Am Flight 103 over Lockerbie, Scotland in 1988 and other terrorist acts.

### April 2 (to May 4)

**FRAUD: Washington, D.C.** Fifty-three members of the House of Representatives announced that they would not be seeking reelection—a record since World War II. Although many gave varied reasons for their decision, it was believed that most thought their upcoming campaigns would be overwhelmed with their involvement with the writing of overdrafts at the scandal-ridden House bank. Vin Weber (R, Minn.) stated that he refused to put his family through what he expected would be a "vicious, negative" campaign. Weber had written 125 overdrafts at the House bank.

### April 6

**ESCAPED PRISONER: Greenville, N.C.** Massie Linwood Young, an escaped prisoner from a Virginia prison, died under the assumed name of Charles Miles Breedlove.

### April 9

**DRUGS: Miami, Fla.** Manuel Noriega, former dictator of Panama, was convicted in U.S. District Court of racketeering, drug trafficking and money laundering. The first foreign head of state to be convicted by a U.S. jury, Noriega had been seized by U.S. troops during the 1990 American invasion of Panama. During his trial, Noriega had been tied to the Medellin drug cartel by many drug traffickers who testified against him, including former aides.

### April 10

**BOMBING: London, England** IRA terrorists exploded a bomb inside of a van parked in the city's financial district, killing three people and injuring 91 others. A second bomb exploded in northwest London, but caused no injuries.

**FRAUD: Los Angeles, Calif.** Charles Keating, Jr., who headed one of the biggest securities swindles in U.S. history, was sentenced to ten years in prison and fined $250.000.

### April 15

**TAX EVASION: Lexington, Ky.** New York hotel magnate, Leona Helmsley, who had been convicted of tax evasion, entered the federal prison in Lexington to begin serving a four-year prison term. Her pleas to avoid prison because of poor health were ineffective.

**TERRORISM: Libya** Sanctions were put into effect against the rogue nation of Libya which had refused to turn over two terrorists thought responsible for the bombing of Pan Am Flight 103 over Lockerbie, Scotland in 1988. Many countries refused to allow commercial planes to fly to Libya, other countries expelled officials at Libyan embassies and consu-

lates, and Russia said it would withdraw 1,500 advisers from the country.

### April 16

**FRAUD: Washington, D.C.** The House of Representatives Ethics Committee released the names of 303 Congressmen who had written overdraft checks on the House bank.

**MURDER: St. Catherines, Ontario, Canada** Kristen French, 15, vanished as she was returning home from school. She had been abducted and tortured by serial sex killer Paul Bernardo, then horribly murdered. Bernardo would later go to prison for life.

### April 17

**MURDER: Belanglo State Forest, Australia** Caroline Clarke, 21, a British tourist, disappeared while hiking. Her decomposing body was found the following September. She was a victim of serial killer Ivan Robert Marko Milat.

### April 18

**ASSAULT: Dallas, Texas** Impatient for crowds to clear away from the path of his Cadillac, Henry Earl Miles drove his car into a crowd of pedestrians, injuring twelve people and fatally wounding church janitor Kenneth McDonald. Miles was charged with aggravated assault.

### April 19

**MURDER: Belanglo State Forest, Australia** Joanna Walters, 22, a British tourist, vanished while hiking through the state park. Her body was found in September by other hikers. It was later proved that Walters had been murdered by serial killer Ivan Robert Marko Milat.

### April 20

**MOB VIOLENCE: Buffalo, N.Y.** Violence broke out between anti-abortion members of Operation Rescue and pro-abortion factions protecting the city's six clinics where abortions were performed.

### April 21

**EXECUTION: San Quentin, Calif.** Robert Alton Harris, who had viciously shot two teenage boys to death in 1978, and who had desperately filed every kind of known appeal to preserve his life, was executed in San Quentin's gas chamber.

**FRAUD: Washington, D.C.** Malcolm Wilkey, who had been appointed to investigate the house bank which had tolerated the flagrant writing of overdrafts by U.S. Congressmen, subpoenaed the financial records of all House members' accounts over a 39-year period. Wilkey said he had uncovered evidence of a "classic check-kiting scheme."

### April 23

**MURDER: New York** Serial killer Nathaniel White was paroled after serving a short term for abducting and molesting a 16-year-old girl.

### April 29 (through early May)

**MOB VIOLENCE: Los Angeles, Calif.** Following the

acquittal this date of four white LAPD officers by a mostly white jury in Simi Valley of the notorious beating of black motorist Rodney King, blacks in South Central Los Angeles erupted in rioting, looting and murder. Fifty-two persons were slain in the massive rioting that lasted into early May, and more than 600 buildings were set on fire. Blacks by the thousands looted stores and stopped and beat white motorists at random. Hundreds were jailed and some given long prison terms for their vicious attacks. Marine and Army units, supported by the National Guard were brought into Los Angeles to restore order. An estimated $1 billion in damage was done by the rioting blacks.

### April 30

**MOB VIOLENCE: U.S.** In a half dozen cities, blacks rioted at the news of the acquittal of the four white LAPD officers who had beaten black motorist Rodney King. In San Francisco, 1,100 persons were arrested. In Miami, Seattle and Atlanta, disturbances were widespread, and in Las Vegas two persons were murdered.

**MURDER: Edmonton, Canada** Ho Ming Chan was convicted of the 1985 murder of his wife Lisa, a killing he staged in order to make it appear that she had been slain by intruders, so that he could collect $100,000 in insurance money. Ho went to prison for life.

### May 2

**MOB VIOLENCE: Buffalo, N. Y.** Mob violence plaguing the city from anti-abortion and pro-abortion factions, resulted in the arrests of 597 persons for trespassing, disorderly conduct and resisting arrest.

### May 10:

**EXECUTION: Joliet, Ill.** After his attorneys had exhausted seemingly endless appeals, petitions, and other process-strangling legal tactics, serial killer John Wayne Gacy, murderer of at least thirty-four persons, was executed by lethal injection.

### May 11

**BLACKMAIL: New York, N.Y.** A blackmailer sending messages to socialite Joy Silverman in which he demanded she pay $20,000 or risk the exposure of compromising photos, sent Silverman's 14-year-old daughter, Jessica, a condom, along with "offensive sexual references," according to the FBI. The blackmailer was later identified as none other than Sol Wachtler, chief justice of New York's Court of Appeals, who had had a prolonged affair with Silverman.

### May 17-19

**MOB VIOLENCE: Bangkok, Thailand** More than 100,000 demonstrators rioted against the military regime of Premier Suchinda Kraprayoon, with government troops firing into crowds. An estimated 48 persons were killed and 600 more were wounded or missing.

### May 19

**ATTEMPTED MURDER: Long Island, N.Y.** Teenage call-girl Amy Fisher, in order to eliminate her sexual rival, shot and wounded Mary Jo Buttafuoco, wife of her paramour, Joseph Buttafuoco. Fisher's highly publicized case saw her sentenced to five to 15 years in prison for attempted murder. When asked at the time why she so desperately wanted to be on TV, Fisher reportedly replied: "Because I want to make a lot of money and buy a Ferrari."

### May 20

**EXECUTION: Jarratt, Va.** Despite a widespread publicity campaign to save the life of convicted rapist-murderer Roger Coleman (he had raped and killed his sister-in-law in 1981), including a cover story in *Time* magazine, Coleman, after failing a polygraph (lie detector) test allowed by Virginia Governor L. Douglas Wilder, was sent to the electric chair.

**KIDNAPPING/MURDER: Van Buren, Ark.** Amanda Dee-Ann Craig, 11, vanished while walking home from school. She had been abducted, molested and murdered by serial killer Vernon Lynn Hopper, who would be convicted of this killing in 1994.

### June 1

**KIDNAPPING/MURDER: Tulsa, Okla.** Serial killer and child molester Vernon Lynn Hopper abducted and murdered 11-year-old Roxie Moser. He would lead officers to her remains in the Lincoln National Forest near Roswell, N.M. in 1994.

### June 2

**MANSLAUGHTER: Raleigh, N.C.** Ehyin Mohammed Youseff pleaded guilty to manslaughter in the death of Dr. William McCoy Yates, whom he had killed and robbed on March 6, 1992.

**SEXUAL ASSAULT: U.S. Navy, U.S. Marines** Secretary of the Navy, H. Lawrence Garrett III, announced that disciplinary action would begin against 70 officers, Navy and Marine fliers who had attended the September 1991 convention of the Tailhook Association, a private organization, and who had reportedly gotten drunk and had sexually harassed, abused and even attacked 26 women in a Las Vegas, Nevada hotel, including fourteen female military officers.

### June 8

**MURDER: Paris, France** Atef Bseiso, considered to be a PLO terrorist by Israeli intelligence (the Mossad), was shot dead outside of his hotel.

**MURDER: Seattle, Wash.** Insurance salesman Joseph Mehling was sentenced to prison for life after a botched murder attempt on the life of his wife which resulted in the cyanide deaths of two other persons.

### June 16

**BURGLARY: Georgia** Carnival worker Bobby Edward Perez, who had burglarized the home of Edgar Couch in Lawrenceville, while his partner, Kenneth Daniel Howard, murdered Couch (and went to prison for life), was sentenced to 15 years in prison.

### June 17

**HOSTAGES RELEASED: Beirut, Lebanon** The last

two known hostages held by Arab terrorists in Lebanon, Heinrich Struebig and Thomas Kemptner, German workers who had been taken prisoner in 1989, were released.

### June 18

**MURDER: Laredo, Texas** Jose Garcia Briseno, a professional burglar, went to trial for the murder of Sheriff Benjamin Murray of Dimmitt County, Texas. He would be convicted and sentenced to death.

### June 23

**ORGANIZED CRIME: Brooklyn, N.Y.** Crime boss John Gotti and henchman Frank Locascio were both sentenced to life in prison, after having been convicted of murder, extortion and obstruction of justice.

### June 25

**FRAUD: London, England** Kevin Maxwell, son of multimillionaire publisher Robert Maxwell, was arrested and charged with conspiracy to defraud and theft totaling $251 million. He was set free on $925,000 bail.

### June 26

**SEXUAL ATTACK: U.S. Navy, U.S. Marines** Navy Lt. Paula Coughlin met with President George Bush to tell him that she had been sexually assaulted by twenty Navy and Marine pilots at the Tailhook Association convention in a Las Vegas hotel in September 1991. On this date, after it was revealed that Secretary of the Navy H. Lawrence Garrett III had been nearby during the time of the sexual attacks on women, Garrett took "full responsibility" for the scandal and resigned.

### June 29

**ASSASSINATION: Algeria** Mohammed Boudiaf, 73, president of Algeria (installed in January 1992 after a coup), was shot in the back of the head and killed by terrorists as he was delivering a speech.

### July 5

**RAPE: Costa Mesa, Calif.** James Bridle, who preyed upon elderly women, attacked 70-year-old Madge Rhodda in a restaurant washroom, but fled when another customer appeared. Bridle was sentenced to prison in 1993, his victim giving him a Bible before he was led away to begin a 17-year sentence.

### July 7

**MURDER: Elkin, N.C.** The strangled body of 30-year-old Nona Kay Stanley Cobb was found. This was only one of a dozen murders attributed to serial killer Sean Patrick Goble, who later went to prison for life.

### July 10

**DRUGS: Miami, Fla.** Former Panamanian dictator Manuel Noriega, who had been convicted of drug trafficking and other crimes, was sentenced in U.S. District Court to forty years in prison by Judge William Hoeveler.

**MURDER: Middletown, N.Y.** Serial killer Nathaniel White raped and murdered Laurette Huggins Reviere in her home.

### July 17

**THEFT: New Orleans, La.** Police videotaped a couple that appeared to embrace every few yards down a street when, in fact, the man, Donald Simmons, 53, a skilled locksmith, was busy stealing coins out of parking meters. "They embraced and the meter seemed to disappear between them," said a police spokesman. "Then they walked to the next meter. As Simmons embraced his female companion, 38-year-old Cheryl Collins, he opened the meter, removed the coins and slipped the money to Collins who put the change into a bag strapped to her body under her skirt. After their arrest, Simmons, according to police, admitted that he had been working the meter theft since 1985.

### July 19

**ASSASSINATION: Palermo, Sicily** Paolo Borsellino, 54, an Italian prosecutor responsible for convicting many Mafia members, was murdered, blown up in his car as he visited his mother.

### July 20

**MURDER: Houston, Texas** Kynara Taylor, 7, and 10-year-old Kristin Wiley were stabbed to death in their home, their eyes gouged out. Police were unable to located the killer until next-door-neighbor Rex Mays became a suspect. He later admitted the double murder.

**MURDER/KIDNAPPING: Poughkeepsie, N.Y.** Angelina Hopkins, 23, and Brenda L. Whiteside, 20, both disappear; they had been abducted, raped and murdered by serial killer Nathaniel White.

### July 21

**PRISON ESCAPE: Envidgado, Colombia.** Drug lord Pablo Escobar, a billionaire drug trafficker who had agreed to be imprisoned with is top aides in a luxury enclosure on the promise that he would not be extradited to the U.S. to face charges, learned he was about to be transferred to a military prison. Escobar and his henchmen took guns from guards, then held prison officials hostage.

### July 22

**PRISON ESCAPE: Envigado, Colombia.** Pablo Escobar, billionaire drug lord, escaped from his minimum security prison through a tunnel with seven other prisoners, while his men held off troops attacking the prison. Six persons were killed.

### July 23

**MURDER: Dallas, Texas** Terri Edwards, a 21-year-old health care director at Baylor University Medical Center, vanished, along with her car. The next day, Roy Glen Harris, Jr., was found driving Edward's auto, its back seat stained with blood. He was arrested and charged with the missing woman's death.

*July 28*

**BANK FRAUD: New York, N.Y.** Sheik Kamal Adham, former chief of Saudi Arabian intelligence, after agreeing to cooperate with federal investigators, pleaded guilty to conspiring with officials of the Bank of Credit and Commerce International (BCCI) to illegally purchase in 1982 the First American Bankshares Inc., the largest bank in Washington, D.C. Adham paid a $105 million fine.

**MEDIA AND CRIME: New York, N.Y.** Time Warner announced that, following complaints and demonstrations from police associations and widespread criticisms from public officials, it was dropping the song "Cop Killer," from its album *Body Count* by rapper Ice-T which was about to be released. Ice-T reportedly asked that the song be deleted after a storm of protest over lyrics that advocated the murder of policemen. Like most of the current gangster (gangsta) rap songs of this era, the theme was anti-establishment, anti-social, anti-law and order, stemming from many so-called "artists" who proved to be little more than street thugs themselves.

**MURDER: Catania, Sicily** Giovanni Lizzio, 47, who had been heading investigations into Mafia extortion rackets, was slain by Mafia killers.

*July 29*

**BANK FRAUD: Washington, D.C., New York, N.Y.** Clark Clifford, a prominent member of the Democratic Party since the administration of President Roosevelt, along with Robert Altman—both men had been top officials for the First American Bankshares Inc.—were indicted on charges that they had purposely misled banking regulators as to BCCI's control of First American. Robert Morgenthau, Manhattan District Attorney, also announced that Clifford and Altman had been indicted on several charges, including conspiracy and bribery. He stated that four others, all BCCI officials, had also been indicted and that BCCI had defrauded investors of $5 billion.

**MURDER/KIDNAPPING: Middletown, N.Y.** Serial killer Nathaniel White abducted, raped and murdered 27-year-old Adraine Marcette Hunter, dumping her body at the outskirts of Goshen, N.Y.

*August 4*

**MURDER/KIDNAPPING: Waywayanda, N.Y.** Serial killer Nathaniel White, who had already confessed to kidnapping, raping and murdering six women, led police to the burial site of 14-year-old Chistine M. Klebbe, whom he had abducted and killed.

*August 9*

**MURDER: Allentown, Pa.** In the first of many murders committed by serial killer Harvey Robinson, 29-year-old Joan Mary Burghardt was bludgeoned to death.

*August 12*

**CRIMINAL VANDALISM: Newport News, Va.** An Amtrak train was derailed, injuring 74 passengers. Federal investigators reported that criminal vandalism to a vital switch caused the wreck.

*August 13*

**MURDER: Sarajevo, Yugoslavia** ABC-TV news producer David Kaplan, 45, was shot in the back and killed by a sniper firing into a caravan carrying Milan Panic, prime minister of Yugoslavia.

*August 15*

**MURDER: Dallas, Texas** A fisherman found a human head at the Trinity River bottoms, the body part later identified as belonging to Terri Edwards, 21, who had disappeared on July 23. Her killer had already been named as Roy Glen Harris, Jr.

**MURDER: Las Vegas, Nev.** Diana Hunt, who had been present when two young woman had been murdered by Michael Rippo, pleaded guilty to robbing one of the victims of her credit cards and was sentenced to 15 years in prison.

*August 17*

**MURDER: Waukegan, Ill.** Holly Staker, 11, was raped and stabbed to death while baby-sitting. Her killerwas later identified as Juan A. Rivera.

*August 25*

**BOMBING: Rostock, Germany** In an effort to drive out foreigners, neo-Nazis bombed a hotel housing refugees seeking asylum from communism. No serious injuries occurred.

*August 31*

**WEAPONS VIOLATIONS/ARMED RESISTANCE: Ruby Ridge, Id.** White separatist and gun advocate Randall "Randy" Weaver surrendered to authorities, following a long siege of Weaver's remote, barricaded cabin in northern Idaho by U.S. marshals and FBI agents attempting to arrest him as a fugitive on gun charges. His wife, Vicki, and his 14-year-old son, Samuel, along with deputy marshal William Degan, were killed during the siege. Weaver, a hero to right-wing militias and terrorist groups in the Far West for his defiance of gun laws, along with associate Kevin Harris, will later be acquitted of all charges in a jury trial. Harris allegedly shot and killed Degan; Vicki Weaver was killed by FBI sharpshooter Lon Horiuchi who was exonerated in a Department of Justice report.) Horiuchi will be indicted in the deaths of Vicki and Samuel Weaver, and, three years later, in August 1995, the Weaver family will be awarded a $3,100,000 settlement by the Department of Justice for the deaths of Weaver's wife and son.

*September 7*

**MASS MURDER: South Africa** Among hundreds of protestors, 24 persons were machine gunned to death by Ciskei troops supporting an oppressive military regime.

*September 8*

**MURDER: Savage, Md.** While video taping his wife, Pamela, and 2-year-old daughter, Sarina, as they were about to drive to preschool, Biswanath Basu inadvertently caught on camera two men, Bernard Eric Miller, 16, and 26-year-old Rodney Eugene Solomon, as they stole his wife's pale gold BMW. They threw the child who was strapped into a car seat onto the road—she was uninjured—and drove off, dragging Mrs. Basu more than a mile to her death, until dislodging her by purposely crashing into a fence. (Mrs. Basu had caught her arm in a car strap.) Both Miller and Solomon were captured at a roadblock a short time later and charged with murder.

### September 9

**BANK FRAUD: Washington, D.C.** The U.S. Department of Justice announced that some of the 329 current and former members of the House of Representatives who had written overdrafts at the House Bank had been cleared of any wrongdoing.

### September 10

**EMBEZZLEMENT/MISUSE OF PUBLIC FUNDS: Washington, D.C.** Joanna O'Rourke, former manager of the House Post Office, was indicted on charges of embezzlement and misuse of public funds.

### September 12

**MURDER: Riverside, Calif.** Brenda Gail Kenney, a 38-year-old librarian, was found raped and stabbed to death in her apartment. Her slayer, serial rapist-killer David Lynn Scott III, was sent to prison for life in 1998.

### September 13

**TERRORISM: Peru** Abimael Guzmán Reynoso, leader of the Shining Path terrorist organization of Peru, was captured after a 12-year search, along with about a dozen of his top aides. Guzmán's decade-long terror campaign had cost 25,000 lives and $22 billion in damages.

### September 15-16

**MURDER: Chicago, Ill.** After buying cocaine and getting high on drugs and alcohol, Philip N. Faraone and John J. Chomer used a large concrete brick to crush the head of their friend, John Kopansky, who had fallen asleep. After robbing Kopansky, Faraone and Chomer fled. Before dying, Kopansky identified his attackers. They were later apprehended and sent to prison.

### September 17

**EMBEZZLEMENT/MISUSE OF PUBLIC FUNDS: Washington, D.C.** Joanna O'Rourke, former manager of the House Post Office, pleaded guilty to embezzling government property and misusing public funds.

### September 22

**MURDER: Dallas, Texas** Casey Dean Corthron was convicted of kidnapping, robbing and murdering his former employer, Jim Brunette, a broker in McKinney, Texas. Corthron would be sentenced to life in prison on September 29.

### October 1

**BLACKMAIL: New York, N.Y.** According to instructions from a blackmailer (who was later identified to be Sol Wachtler, chief justice of the New York Court of Appeals), socialite Joy Silverman placed an ad in the New York *Times* which arranged for the payment of $20,000 in exchange for reported compromising photos and tapes, an ad which was approved by FBI agents working with Silverman to expose the blackmailer.

**MURDER: Los Angeles, Calif.** Career criminal Andre Stephen Alexander was arraigned for the murder of Secret Service agent Julie Cross, killed by Alexander at a drug stakeout on June 4, 1980. Alexander would be convicted and sentenced to death four years later.

**TERRORIST ATTACK: Assiut, Egypt** Terrorist gunmen fired at a Nile cruiser carrying 140 German tourists. Three Egyptian crew members were injured.

### October 2

**BRIBERY: Brazil** Fernando Collar de Mello resigned as president of Brazil while facing charges of complicity in a multimillion dollar bribery scheme. His wife was also under investigation on charges that she had embezzled huge amounts of money from a charity she operated.

**MURDER: National City, Calif.** The bodies of Don Freeman, 64, and his 62-year-old wife Glenda, were found in their home. Both had been shot to death by their son, Kenneth Freeman in an effort to take over his father's lucrative truck repair business and collect on insurance policies so he could lavish money on nude dancers at the seedy strip clubs he frequented. Freeman would go to prison for life.

**PRISON RIOT: Carandiru Penitentiary, Sao Paulo, Brazil** Following a riot at Carandiru Penitentiary in Brazil's commercial capital of Sao Paulo, state police stormed the institution, initially reporting that eight prisoners had been killed in the attempt to restore order and herd inmates back into their cells. Surviving prisoners, however, informed investigators and relatives that the police attack had been a mass slaughter, that attacking officers machine-gunned prisoners at random as they fled back to their cells and even shot them to death once they had returned to their cells, shouting: "Your time has come!" Wounded prisoners were then dragged from their cells to a prison workshop where attack dogs were unleashed, the animals savagely tearing the bleeding prisoners to pieces. Officials later posted the true fatality list of prisoners: 111 inmates dead, this being a conservative estimate. In response to a public outcry, Governor Luis Antonio Fleury fired the chief of state security who ordered the attack.

### October 3

**BLACKMAIL: New York, N.Y.** The man blackmailing socialite Joy Silverman for $20,000 in exchange for purported compromising photos and tapes phoned Silverman and the call was traced to the mobile phone in the state-owned car of Judge Sol Wachtler, chief justice of the New York Court of Appeals, who was Silverman's former paramour.

**TERRORISM: Arnstadt and Dresden, Germany** Thousands of neo-Nazis marched through the streets demanding that foreigners leave Germany and shouting "Germany for Germans!"

*October 7*

**BLACKMAIL/KIDNAPPING: New York, N.Y.** Judge Sol Wachtler, who had been attempting to blackmail his former mistress, socialite Joy Silverman, made a call to Silverman which was monitored by the FBI and in which he threatened Silverman to conform to his demands or suffer the kidnapping of her daughter, 14-year-old Jessica Silverman.

**TERRORISM/TREASON: Lima, Peru** Abimael Guzmán Reynoso, the leader of the Maoist guerrilla movement known as Shining Path, was sentenced to life in prison after being convicted of treason, countless murders and millions in destruction over the last decade. His trial judge wore a hood over his head so as not to be identified.

*October 8 (through December 7)*

**MURDER: Riverside, Calif.** Orlando Romero and Christopher Self went on a murder-robbery rampage through Riverside, Beaumont, Moreno Valley and Perris, California, a crime spree that lasted almost two months in which they committed three murders and 16 other felonies. Both were tried and convicted in 1996 and were sentenced to death.

*October 9*

**NUCLEAR THEFT: Russia** An engineer in a Russian nuclear plant was arrested just before leaving for Moscow to sell to terrorists 1,539 kilos of highly enriched uranium (HEU).

*October 10*

**TERRORISM: Ayacucho, Peru** This village was obliterated and 44 residents slaughtered by members of the Peruvian terrorist group, Shining Path, in retaliation for the life imprisonment of their leader, Abimael Guzmán Reynoso, three days earlier.

*October 14*

**HOSTAGES: U.S.** Ex-hostages Joseph Cicippio and David Jacobsen filed suit against the government of Iran, claiming that their abductions and others were directed and financed by Iran in order to force the U.S. into freeing frozen Iranian assets.

*October 20*

**MURDER: Waukegan, Ill.** Following an intensive police interrogation, murder suspect Juan A. Rivera confessed to raping and murdering 11-year-old Holly Staker in August 1992. He would be tried twice and convicted and finally sentenced to life in prison.

*October 21*

**TERRORIST ATTACK: Egypt** A tourist bus was ambushed by terrorists who killed a British woman and injured two British men.

*October 27*

**MURDER: Sasebo, Japan** Sailor Allen Schindler, stationed on board the aircraft carrier USS *Beleau Wood,* was found dead in a public restroom near the U.S. Navy base. Schindler had been killed, his body mutilated. A short time earlier, Schindler had announced the fact that he was homosexual,

incurring the anger of many shipmates. Two other U.S. sailors, Terry M. Helvey and Charles E. Vins stood accused of the killing.

*October 28*

**BLACKMAIL/KIDNAPPING: New York, N.Y.** Judge Sol Wachtler, in attempting to blackmail his former mistress, Joy Silverman, who was working with the FBI, called to threaten Silverman once more, telling her that if she did not follow his instructions she would have to pay "$200,000 to get your daughter back."

*November 2*

**MURDER: Dallas, Texas** Trial began for Roy Glen Harris, Jr., who shortly plea-bargained a life sentence for the July 23, 1992, killing of Terri Edwards.

*November 3*

**MURDER: Riverside, Calif.** A female office worker reported being raped by an attacker dressed all in black and carrying knives. He would later be identified as serial rapist and killer David Lynn Scott III, who was dubbed the "Ninja Rapist," by the press.

*November 5*

**MANSLAUGHTER: Detroit, Mich.** Malice Green, an unemployed black man, struggled with two officers questioning him outside a crackhouse. The policemen, Walter Budzyn and Larry Nevers, reportedly struck Green over the head with flashlights, killing him. Both were later tried for murder. Nevers was convicted, but his conviction was overturned. Budzyn was convicted of manslaughter in 1998.

*November 7*

**BLACKMAIL: New York, N.Y.** Judge Sol Wachtler, chief justice of the New York Court of Appeals, who had been blackmailing his former mistress Joy Silverman for months, arranges to pick up a $20,000 payoff in exchange for reputed compromising photos and tapes, but, after driving from his Albany, New York, offices to Manhattan to pick up the money—the FBI monitored Wachtler's actions for weeks—Wachtler paid someone to deliver a package to Silverman and another unwitting person to pick up the payoff, all the while wearing disguises, before he began driving to his Manhasset home on Long Island. He was arrested and charged with blackmail and extortion. Wachtler later went to prison, serving only 13 months behind bars before being set free.

**MURDER: Morrow Bay, Calif.** Lynwood "Crazy Jim" Drake III killed his 80-year-old landlord Andy Zatko with a shotgun at the beginning of a murder spree that would see Drake eventually kill himself.

*November 11*

**MURDER: Chicago, Ill.** Delbert Heard stormed into the apartment of his ex-girlfriend, Natalie Wilson, and shot her, her lover, Kenneth Seals, and her cousin, Zita Jones. Heard would be sentenced to death in 1996 for the three killings.

*November 12*
 **TERRORIST ATTACK: Qena, Egypt** Terrorists ambushed a tourist bus in Qena, wounding five German tourists and two Egyptians.

*November 27*
 **COUP ATTEMPT: Caracas, Venezuela** Insurgents denouncing President Carlos Andres Perez as undemocratic and indifferent to his nation's millions of poor people, took over a television station and two air bases and then bombed the presidential palace by air. Government forces overwhelmed the insurgents, after 169 persons were reported killed in the fighting.

*December 6*
 **MOB VIOLENCE: Ayodhya, India** Militant Hindus used sledgehammers and bare hands to tear down a Moslem mosque which they claimed stood on a site that was the birthplace of the Hindu deity Ram, a site where they intended to build their own temple. Violent clashes between Hindu and Moslems ensued.

*December 9*
 **IRAN-CONTRA: Washington, D.C.** Clair George, former director of operations at the Central Intelligence Agency (CIA), was convicted on two felony counts of giving false testimony to congressional committees.

*December 13*
 **MOB VIOLENCE: Northern India** As a result of Hindus tearing down a Moslem mosque in Ayodhya in Northern India, riots and widespread destruction between Moslems and Hindus resulted, according to a government report, in the deaths of 1,210 persons, with another 4,600 injured.

*December 15*
 **MURDER: Texas** Serial killer Vernon Lynn Hopper was convicted of murdering two women; he would later confess to the abduction and murders of two small girls in Arkansas and Oklahoma.

*December 17*
 **MURDER: Trenton, N.J.** Kristin Huggins, a 22-year-old artist, was kidnapped and murdered by Ambrose Harris, who was convicted and condemned in 1996.

*December 24*
 **IRAN-CONTRA: Washington, D.C.** As one of his last acts, President George Bush pardoned six former public officials who had figured in the Iran-Contra scandal, the most prominent of these being Casper Weinberger, the former Secretary of Defense, who was facing a January 1993 trial. Bush stated that "whether their actions were right or wrong," these men had not been motivated by personal gain, but by patriotism. Also pardoned were Clair George, Duane Clarridge and Alan Fiers, all former CIA officials, Robert McFarlane, former national security adviser, and Elliott Abrams, former assistant secretary of state.

*December 28*
 **KIDNAPPING: Long Island, N.Y.** John Esposito, a neighbor of 10-year-old Katie Beers, kidnapped the girl and held her captive, for sixteen days, chained to a wall in his basement, before police freed her.

*December 29*
 **BRIBERY: Brazil** President Fernando Collor de Mello, only hours after an impeachment trial began to oust him from office for accepting bribes in exchange for government contracts, officially resigned from office.
 **MURDER: Portland, Ore.** Artist Chantee Woodman, 23, left her apartment and went to a downtown nightclub; her body was found the next day, dumped along U.S. Highway 26. She had been shot and raped. Her attacker, Cesar Barone, who killed another woman the following year, would be identified and sentenced to death in 1994.

*December 30*
 **BRIBERY: Brazil** The Brazilian senate voted 76-3 to convict former President Fernando Collor de Mello of accepting bribes in exchange for government contracts.
 **MURDER: Charleston, S.C.** Joseph Gardner led a group of other men in the gang rape and murder of Melissa Ann McLaughin, 25, a killing for which Gardner would later be condemned to death.

# 1993

*January 5*
 **EXECUTION: Washington** Convicted child molester and killer Westley Allen Dodd was hanged, the first person so executed in the U.S. since 1965

*January 6*
 **BANK FRAUD: Los Angeles, Calif.** Charles H. Keating, Jr., was convicted for a second time on 73 counts of fraud and racketeering in connection with his failed Lincoln Savings & Loan Association. Keating's son, Charles H. Keating III, was also convicted on 64 counts. The jury stated that the Keatings had defrauded investors and regulators and had diverted money from Lincoln Savings for their own use.

*January 8*
 **ASSASSINATION: Bosnia** Hakija Turajlic, one of three Bosnian deputy prime ministers, was assassinated after a U.N. vehicle in which he was riding was halted. Serbian military leaders later apologized, saying that an overanxious Serbian draftee responsible for the killing had been detained.
 **BANK FRAUD: Los Angeles, Calif.** Charles H. Keating, Jr., who was already serving a term in prison for violating California securities laws, was sentenced to twelve years and seven months in prison as a result of his January 6 conviction.
 **MASS MURDER: Palatine, Ill.** Seven workers at a Brown's Chicken and Pasta fast food restaurant were found slain at the hands of unknown robber-killers, a mass murder

that would go unsolved.

**TERRORISM: The Hague, Netherlands** A board of inquiry reported that more than 20,000 Muslim women in Bosnia and Herzegovina have been raped and impregnated by mostly Serbian terrorists in an effort to drive them from their homes and to propagate the Serbian race.

*January 17*

**ASSAULT/BURGLARY: Canyon Crest, Calif.** A 39-year-old teacher returning to his apartment with his girlfriend interrupted a burglar all dressed in black who had ransacked the place. Following a struggle in which the teacher was stabbed by the intruder, the burglar fled, escaping from several neighbors who tried to stop him. He was later identified as David Lynn Scott III, a serial rapist-killer who was dubbed the "Ninja Rapist," because of his clothes and weapons.

*January 21*

**LAW ENFORCEMENT: Harris County, Texas** Michael Griffith, a deputy with the sheriff's department, was fired for beating up his girlfriend. Griffith would be convicted in 1995 of robbing and murdering flowershop owner Deborah Jean McCormick.

**MURDER/RAPE: Riverside, Calif.** Police arrested David Lynn Scott III, the infamous "Ninja Rapist," who would be sentenced in 1998 to die in San Quentin's gas chamber for the many rapes and murders he committed.

*January 22*

**LAW ENFORCEMENT: Scappoose, Ore.** Famed FBI agent Ramon Stratton, 64, died of a heart attack at his home. Stratton, who began as a clerk at the FBI at the age of 16, went on to become one of the Bureau's most effective agents, breaking several kidnapping cases, including that of Minnesota socialite Virginia Piper, solving that case only days before the statute of limitations was to expire.

**PRISON RELEASE: Bedford Hills, N.Y.** Jean Struven Harris, who had murdered her former lover, millionaire diet doctor Herman Tarnower, on March 10, 1980, was paroled following heart surgery. She went on to give lectures and write books about aiding female prisoners.

*January 25*

**MURDER: Langley, Va.** A shootist began firing on CIA employees as they arrived by car at the entrance to agency headquarters. Two persons, Frank Darling and Lansing Bennett, were killed, and three others were wounded before the killer fled. He was later identified as Mir Aimal Kasi, a Pakistani terrorist. A worldwide manhunt for Kasi would ensue almost immediately.

*January 27*

**ABDUCTION/RAPE: Texas** Serial rapist Vernon Lynn Hopper was sentenced to two 99-year terms for two separate rapes. He was later discovered to by the kidnapper and killer of two children.

*February 4-5*

**MOB VIOLENCE: Zaire** In a clash over the worthiness of newly-issued government currency, President Mobutu Sese Seko, who had issued the money, and Premier Etienne Tshisekedi, who pronounced the currency worthless, thousands rioted over a two-day period which resulted in more than 1,000 deaths and thousands more in injuries.

*February 6*

**ORGANIZED CRIME: Milwaukee, Wis.** Frank Balistrieri, 74, who was named in 1963 by federal officials as the boss of the Mafia/syndicate in Wisconsin, died in his home of a heart attack. Balistrieri had served only 15 months in prison for extortion and he had steadfastly denied his role in organized crime, once saying to a reporter: "The first time I heard the word 'Mafia,' was when I read it in the newspapers."

*February 8*

**MURDER: Wisconsin** Serial child molester and killer James A. Duquette was convicted of abducting, raping and killing 14-year-old Tara Kassens of Mequon, Wisconsin in 1987, and was given a third life term in prison (he had earlier been convicted of murdering two others).

*February 9*

**TAX EVASION: Los Angeles, Calif.** Marvin Mitchelson, famed celebrity divorce lawyer, was convicted of tax evasion.

*February 10*

**MURDER: Langley, Va.** FBI agents searching for Mir Aimal Kasi, who had killed two CIA employees and wounded another three outside of CIA headquarters in January, located the murder weapon in Kasi's abandoned apartment in Reston, Va.

*February 11*

**LAW ENFORCEMENT: Washington, D.C.** Newly-elected President Bill Clinton nominated Janet Reno for the post of U.S. Attorney General. Reno, who had been the chief state prosecutor in Miami, Florida since 1978, would prove to be one of the most controversial Attorney Generals in recent history.

**MONEY LAUNDERING: West Bank, Israel** Mohammad Saleh, a U.S. citizen was arrested and charged with laundering money for the Palestinian terrorist group Hamas. He would be sent to prison and released in 1997.

*February 15*

**EXTORTION/Miami, Fla.** Deborah Pereira, 31, of Hialeah, Florida, pulled alongside a car driven by Joseph Elizarde, after Elizarde had switched lanes in front of her. She flashed a fake police badge, saying "I'm a police officer," and ordered him to pull over. When Elizarde rolled down his window to reveal his uniform—that of a police lieutenant, Pereira drove off. Elizarde pursued her. Pereira admitted that she had been pretending to be a police officer in order to extort money from traffic violators. She was arrested for extortion and impersonating a police officer. Two packets of marijuana and crack cocaine were also found in her car, along with a .38-caliber revolver, and she was also charged with obstruction of justice, carrying a concealed weapon and drug violations. Pereira shrugged at the drug charges, reportedly saying: "What's wrong with that? All cops smoke pot."

### February 19
**DRUGS: Levy County, Fla.** Else Christensen, a 79-year-old medical office worker, was found guilty of running marijuana from Texas to Florida. She would be sent to prison.

### February 20
**DRUGS: Goddard, Kan.** George Marquardt, 47, a self-taught chemist obsessed with creating designer drugs and working out of his home laboratory, was arrested for producing fentanyl, a highly toxic and deadly anesthetic which was sold on the street as artificial heroin. Many junkies in New York City reportedly began dying from the use of fentanyl in 1991. Marquardt, who had been arrested for producing methamphetamines in Oklahoma in 1978, admitted to a judge in Wichita that he was a producer of "clandestine" drugs. He had earlier stated in an interview that drug making excited him because of "narcotics agents chasing you all over the land. It's a fantasy made real."

### February 24
**RIOTING/LOOTING: Mogadishu** Mobs of rioters and looters created widespread destruction and looting, along with firing guns for more than six hours in challenge to the presence of U.N. peacekeeping forces that eventually fired back at the rioters.

### February 25
**THEFT/DRUGS: San Diego, Calif.** A transient out of money, 32-year-old Michael Starling, spotted a man trying to extinguish a fire inside his car. The man had already removed his dog from the burning auto and was bending over flaming seats, beating out the fire when Starling ran behind him and plucked his wallet from his pocket. A passing policeman apprehended Starling, recovering the wallet and its content, but also discovering a cocaine pipe on Starling who was charged not only with grand theft but with possessing drug paraphernalia.

### February 26:
**BOMBING: New York, N.Y.** A powerful bomb exploded in the parking garage beneath the World Trade Center. Six persons were killed and more than 1,000 were injured in the worst terrorist attack on U.S. soil to date. Several Islamic terrorists, including mastermind of the bombing, Ramzi Ahmed Yousef, will later be sent to prison for life.

**MANSLAUGHTER: London, England** After enduring decades of abuse from her husband of 57 years, Mabel Hyams, 79, beat her spouse to death with a bedpan. She was convicted and given a suspended sentence.

**TERRORIST ATTACK: Cairo, Egypt** A terrorist bomb in a crowded coffee shop exploded, killing three persons, a Turk and a Swede, as well as an Egyptian. Twenty other persons were injured.

### February 27
**AUTO THEFT: Toledo, Ohio** Paramedics arrived at the home of Jimmie King, Sr., to take him to a hospital after he had suffered a stroke, but when they took him to the street on a rolling stretcher, they discovered their ambulance had been stolen. A short time later Stanley Fleetwood, 31, a Toledo native, was arrested after he had crashed the ambulance into the city traffic engineering building, after a police chase. Fleetwood was jailed, charged with grand auto theft. Patient King was taken to the hospital in another ambulance and survived his stroke.

### February 28:
**BOMBING: New York, N.Y.** Investigators luckily discovered a three-foot piece of chassis blown from the truck bomb exploding at the World Trade Center on February 26. The chassis part yielded an identification number that led to the identification of the Ryder truck, its rental agency and the terrorist who rented the vehicle, the key evidence that eventually led to the arrest, conviction and imprisonment of the terrorists.

**WEAPONS VIOLATIONS/ARMED RESISTANCE: Waco, Texas** David Koresh, a self-styled religious cult leader (he insisted that he was the reincarnation of Jesus Christ), heading a group calling itself the Branch Davidians, resisted arrest by federal officers charging the cult with possession of illegal weapons. The Davidians, barricaded inside a rural compound of interconnecting buildings outside of Waco, Texas, reportedly fired upon attacking ATF (Bureau of Alcohol, Tobacco and Firearms) agents as they attempted to storm the place. Six persons were killed, including four federal agents, and fourteen others were wounded. It was later reported that Koresh had ordered his top lieutenants, all heavily armed, to hold his followers in line by force; many Davidians, women and children mostly, were reportedly threatened with murder if they attempted to escape the compound.

### March 1
**WEAPONS VIOLATIONS/ARMED RESISTANCE: Waco, Texas** More than 400 federal agents participated in the siege of the Branch Davidian cult compound. Cult leader David Koresh (Vernon Howell) arrogantly defied agents to attack and seize the enormous cache of illegal weapons held by him and his followers. Koresh again said that he was Jesus Christ.

### March 2
**ORGANIZED CRIME: New Orleans, La.** Mafia/syndicate crime boss Carlos Marcello, 83, died of natural causes at his suburban residence. Marcello, who began as an associate to Florida crime boss Santo Trafficante in the 1930s, later went on to control widespread syndicated operations, particularly open gambling in New Orleans, Jefferson Parish and in the Mississippi coastal towns during the 1940s. He reportedly was involved in plans to assassinate President John Fitzgerald Kennedy, but these allegations were never proven.

**WEAPONS VIOLATIONS/ARMED RESISTANCE: Waco, Texas** David Koresh, leader of the Branch Davidians, told authorities that he and his followers would evacuate their barricaded compound if his 58-minute taped monologue was aired over TV and radio. Several stations did play the rambling, almost incoherent speech by the self-appointed religious guru, but Koresh later reneged on his promise, saying that God told him to wait.

### March 3

**MURDER: Huntsville, Ala.** Betty Wilson was found guilty of hiring James D. White to kill her millionaire husband, Dr. Jack Wilson, in order to acquire his $6.3 million estate. Instead, the 46-year-old Wilson went to prison for life.

### March 4

**BOMBING/TERRORISM: Jersey City, N.J.** Police arrested Mohammed Salameh, a follower of Sheik Omar Abdel Rahman, the blind spiritual leader of radical Islamic groups in New York, and reportedly one of the architects of the February 26 bombing of the World Trade Center. Salameh, a Jordanian-born Palestinian, had rented the Ryder truck (police had found remnants of the yellow Ford van after the bombing and traced it to a Jersey City rental agency) three days before the explosion. Salameh told the rental agency that the truck had been stolen following the bombing and when he appeared at the agency to collect his $400 deposit, he was arrested. Also arrested this date in Brooklyn, N.Y., was a second suspect in the bombing, Ibrahim Elgabrowny, who resisted officers searching his apartment for incriminating bomb materials.

**COMPUTER FRAUD: Las Vegas, N.M.** Wayne Steffan, 21, a New Mexico Highlands University student, pleaded guilty to breaking into the school's computer system to change his and other students' grades. He was ordered to pay $4,900 in restitution and forfeit his computer to the state attorney general's office for use in law enforcement.

**KIDNAPPING/RAPE: Los Angeles, Calif.** Wayne Taira, 33, who was known as the "imposter rapist," because he often impersonated a police officer when kidnapping and raping his victims, was sentenced to 322 years in prison for nine kidnapping-rapes in southern California in 1986-1987.

### March 8

**AGGRAVATED ASSAULT: Dallas, Texas** Henry Earl Miles, who had purposely driven into a crowd of shoppers in April 1992, killing one person and injuring many others, was given eight 10-year prison terms.

**ANIMAL CRUELTY/DOG KIDNAPPING: Menomonie, Wis.** Rodney A. Larsen, 38, pleaded guilty to tying his neighbor's basset hound to his truck and dragging the animal to its death at speeds in excess of 50 m.p.h. Larsen was sentenced to two years' probation and ordered to pay $2,000 to the Dunn County humane society.

### March 10

**BOMBING/TERRORISM: Maplewood, N.J.** Nidal Ayyad, a chemical engineer and associate of Mohammed Salameh, was arrested in his apartment. Police stated that Ayyad had the know how to make the bomb exploded at New York's World Trade Center on February 26.

**MURDER: Pensacola, Fla.** Dr. David Gunn, who operated an abortion clinic, was shot and killed by abortion foe Michael Griffin, 31, who surrendered to police and admitted the murder. Griffin was a member of Rescue America, an organization opposing abortion. Its director, Don Teshman, upon hearing of Gunn's killing by Griffin said that the shooting was unfortunate, but added that "it's also true that quite a number of babies' lives will be saved." Griffin was later convicted and sent to prison for life.

### March 11

**MURDER/RAPE: New York** Serial rapist-killer Nathaniel White, who had abducted, raped and murdered at least six women in and around Poughkeepsie, N.Y., went on trial. He said his murders were inspired by the movie, *Robocop*.

### March 12

**BOMBINGS: Bombay, India** Several bombs were exploded at the Bombay Stock Exchange, where fifty persons were killed, and, within ninety minutes, at banks, government offices, hotels a shopping complex and an airline office.

**LAW ENFORCEMENT: Washington, D.C.:** Janet Reno was sworn into office as the first female to become the U.S. Attorney General. One of her first major decisions would be to determine the course of action against the Branch Davidian cult resisting federal officers outside of Waco, Texas. Her decision would prove to be a disaster.

**WEAPONS VIOLATIONS/ARMED RESISTANCE: Waco, Texas** Federal agents besieging the Branch Davidian compound cut off electrical power to the buildings.

### March 13

**MURDER: St. Louis, Mo.** Malynda Waddell, an aspiring actress, was reported missing. Her body was later found along the Meramec River. She had been raped and her throat had been slit. Her killer, Dennis Wildhaber, along with accomplice James Pfingsten, were tracked down and later received life terms in prison.

### March 14

**WEAPONS VIOLATIONS/ARMED RESISTANCE: Waco, Texas** Federal agents besieging the Branch Davidian compound concentrated floodlights on the interconnecting buildings throughout each night.

### March 15

**ATROCITIES: San Salvador, El Salvador** A U.N. commission report made available this date, following interviews with more than 20,000 Salvadorans over several years, concluded that the Nationalist Republican Alliance (ARENA), the ruling party, was linked to death squads that murdered countless victims in the twelve-year civil war that ended in 1992. The commission linked the 1989 murders of six Jesuit priests and two women to General René Emilio Ponce, who had already offered to resign. The report also stated that Roberto D'Aubuisson, founder of ARENA, had probably ordered the 1980 assassination of Archbishop Oscar Arnulfo Romero. The assassinations of many public officials were linked by the commission to the left-wing Farabundo Marti National Liberation Front

**BOMBINGS: Bombay, India** Bombay police reported that they had arrested two men and charged them with the bombings of March 12.

**WEAPONS VIOLATIONS/ARMED RESISTANCE: Waco, Texas** Two of David Koresh's followers left the Branch Davidian compound to negotiate with federal officers but no headway was made.

*March 16:*

**TERRORIST ATTACK: Cairo, Egypt** Five tourist buses were damaged outside Egyptian Museum when a terrorist bomb exploded.

*March 17*

**BOMBINGS: Calcutta, India** Bombs exploded in two apartment buildings which killed eighty persons.

**BOMBING/TERRORISM: New York, N.Y.** Three suspects arrested earlier in connection with the February 26 bombing of New York's World Trade Center—Mohammed Salameh, Ibrahim Elgabrowny and Nidal Ayyad—were all indicted for the terrorist bombing.

**MURDER: Chicago, Ill.** Rhonda Falkner, a 15-year-old who had reportedly been abused by her mother, shot and killed her mother, Beatrice. She would be tried as an adult and convicted of second-degree murder in 1995, being sent to prison.

**ROBBERY/MURDER: Baltimore, Md.** Drug addict Warner Hill murdered his landlady, 74-year-old Jeromia O'Neal, bludgeoning her to death to steal her money. He was convicted and sent to prison for life in 1995.

*March 18*

**BOMBING/TERRORISM: New York, N.Y..** Sheik Omar Abdel Rahman denied that he had been involved in the bombing of the World Trade Center on February 26.

*March 19*

**BOMBINGS: Calcutta, India** Another bomb exploded in a train station. Calcutta police stated that a Muslim family in the city with links to organized crime had been part of the bombings of March 17 and March 19. All toll, more than 300 persons had been killed in bombings occurring in Bombay and Calcutta this month, with 1,100 more persons injured.

**JUDICIARY: Washington, D.C.** U.S. Supreme Court Justice Byron White announced that he would retire after the court's 1992-1993 term.

*March 20*

**ATROCITIES: San Salvador, El Salvador** In response to a U.N. report of March 15, 1993, that identified the parties behind numerous atrocities committed during the country's twelve-year civil war, ARENA, the ruling party, along with other right-wing factions, supported the National Assembly's decision to announce an amnesty for anyone who had committed atrocities during the war, a move that blocked any prosecution for human rights abuses.

*March 23*

**MURDER: Washington, D.C.** James E. Swann, Jr., who had gone on shooting spree which resulted in the deaths of four persons and the wounding of another five, shot and killed 28-year-old Bessie Hutson as she walked her dog in an alley. She was the daughter of career diplomat, Thomas Hutson.

*March 24*

**ASSAULT: Tacoma, Wash.** Margaret Rose Mayberry became the first prostitute in the state to be charged with assaulting a customer because she failed to disclose the fact that she was infected with the deadly AIDS virus.

**BOMBING/TERRORISM: New York, N.Y.** Mahmud Abouhalima, who had been turned over to U.S. officials by Egyptian authorities, was arrested upon his arrival by plane. He was another suspect in the bombing of the World Trade Center in February 26, having been seen with another bombing suspect, Mohammed Salameh, on the morning of the bombing.

*March 25*

**BOMBING/TERRORISM: Newark, N.J.** A day after turning himself in to agents in FBI offices, Bilal Alkaisi, was arrested in connection with the World Trade Center bombing of February 26. Alkaisi had been seen at a storage shed in New Jersey, where materials used to make explosives had been stored. A timing mechanism was later found in Alkaisi's apartment.

*March 28*

**DRUGS: Washington, D.C.** The U.S. Department of Justice announced that drug trafficking convictions accounted for one-fifth of all felony convictions in the U.S. during 1990, up from 13 percent four years earlier. State courts convicted 168,000 persons of trafficking in illegal drugs, twice the number of convictions on the same charges in 1986. Another 106,000 persons were convicted in 1990 of possessing illegal drugs. Almost half of the convicted drug traffickers were sent to prison, compared with 37 percent four years earlier.

*March 30*

**DEATH SENTENCES: Bosnia** Two Serbian terrorists were sentenced to death by firing squad on orders of a military tribunal that had found them guilty of mass rape and genocide against Muslims.

**WEAPONS VIOLATIONS/ARMED RESISTANCE: Waco, Texas** Three followers of David Koresh's Branch Davidian cult who had earlier left the compound were indicted for conspiracy to murder federal officers in the February 28 shootout that left four federal agents dead.

*March 31*

**BOMBING/TERRORISM: New York, N.Y.** Ramzi Ahmed Yousef was indicted in connection with the bombing of the World Trade Center on February 26, although Yousef was not then in custody and it was not then known if Yousef was even in the U.S. Yousef had shared an apartment with Mohammed Salameh, another suspect in the bombing. Yousef was by then thought to be the mastermind behind the bombing.

*April 1*

**MURDER: Chicago, Ill.** Olivia Dawson, a 32-year-old prostitute, was killed when an arrow was shot into her chest. Her bizarre killer, Lee Curtis, would later be tracked down and sent to prison.

**TERRORISM: Washington, D.C.** The U.S. indicted four Palestinians on charges that they plotted to blow up the Israeli Embassy in Washington, D.C. as part of a terror campaign against Jews in the U.S. and abroad by the Abu Nidal network.

*April 2*

**MANSLAUGHTER: Sonora, Calif.** Ellie Nesler, whose son had reportedly been molested, along with several other young boys, by Daniel Mark Driver, shot and killed Driver in a courtroom as he awaited trial. Nesler's vigilante action would spur a national debate for years to come. She was sentenced to ten years in prison for manslaughter in 1994, but released in 1997.

*April 10*

**ASSASSINATION: Johannesburg, South Africa** Chris Hani, an official with the South African Communist Party was fatally shot in the driveway of his home. On the same day, police arrested Januzu Walus, a Pole who had become a South African citizen, and confiscated a pistol in his possession which proved to be the weapon used to assassinate Hani.

*April 11*

**PRISON RIOT: Lucasville, Ohio** When guards at the Southern Ohio Correctional Facility (Ohio's only maximum security prison) went to break up a fight between prisoners in the recreational yard, eight guards were taken hostage. This began an eleven-day siege between prison officials and guards and 450 barricaded prisoners who demanded improvements of conditions within the prison.

*April 12*

**MURDER: Jackson, Miss.** Neo-Nazi Larry Wayne Shoemake invaded a restaurant and began shooting black people, killing one and wounding seven others before police arrived and a gun battle ensued in which Shoemake was killed (or committed suicide) as the restaurant caught fire.

**PRISON RIOT: Lucasville, Ohio** Prisoners who had taken over cell blocks at Southern Ohio Correctional Facility on April 11, released the bodies of six inmates who had apparently been beaten to death by other prisoners. A seventh prisoner was found dead within a cell in an adjoining cell block the next day.

**TAX EVASION: Los Angeles, Calif.** Celebrity divorce lawyer Marvin Mitchelson, who had been convicted of evading taxes in February, was sentenced to 30 months in prison and ordered to pay $1.8 million in restitution.

*April 14*

**MOB VIOLENCE: Johannesburg, South Africa** Demonstrations designed to honor the memory of Chris Hani, assassinated on April 10, turned violent as mobs ran amuck; eight persons were killed and hundreds more were injured.

**PRISON RIOT: Lucasville, Ohio** Officials were told by rioting prisoners barricaded in cell blocks at the Southern Ohio Correctional Facility that they would begin killing one of the eight guards they held hostage every day until their demands were met.

*April 15*

**PRISON RIOT: Lucasville, Ohio** Prisoners at Southern Ohio Correctional Facility killed one of the eight guards they were holding hostage, throwing his body outside of a barricaded cell block.

*April 17*

**ASSASSINATION: Johannesburg, South Africa**. Clive Derby-Lewis, leader of the Conservative Party, was arrested in connection with the assassination of Chris Hani, who was killed on April 11.

**POLICE BRUTALITY: Los Angeles, Calif.** A federal jury found two of the four LAPD officers who beat black motorist Rodney King guilty. Officer Laurence Powell, who had struck most of the blows, was found guilty of violating King's right to be free from an arrest made with unreasonable force and his superior, Sgt. Stacey Koon, was found guilty of permitting the violation to happen. Officers Theodore Briseno and Timothy Wind were acquitted. Though 6,500 police officers, along with National Guard troops and other units were on standby alert, the verdict caused no uproar in the black communities of Los Angeles.

*April 19*

**MURDER: Chicago, Ill.** Amanda Wallace hanged her 3-year-old son Joseph for misbehaving. Sent to prison, Wallace committed suicide in her cell in 1997.

**WEAPONS VIOLATIONS/ARMED RESISTANCE: Waco, Texas** ATF and FBI officers stormed the Branch Davidian compound, firing tear gas into the buildings which were defended by heavily armed cultists led by David Koresh. The buildings were set afire, reportedly by the sect's fanatical diehard leaders and at Koresh's instructions, and the resulting inferno claimed the lives of seventy-two cultists. Koresh and some of his lieutenants were later found with bullets in their heads, apparent suicides, according to reports. U.S. Attorney General Janet Reno, who ordered the frontal attack by federal agents, was later severely criticized for mishandling the siege and final assault on the compound. Many felt that the cultists could have been induced to surrender if other tactics had been employed. The destruction of the Davidian compound later served to inspire terrorist-bomber Timothy McVeigh to destroy the Alfred P. Murrah Federal Building in Oklahoma City, Oklahoma, killing 168 persons, the worst terrorist attack in U.S. history.

*April 21*

**PRISON RIOT: Lucasville, Ohio** Warden Arthur Tate promised to review the complaints of prisoners who had taken over cell blocks at the Southern Ohio Correctional Facility on April 11. The 450 prisoners then surrendered. Two more bodies of inmates were then discovered. A total of nine prisoners and one guard had been killed during the riot and siege.

*April 22*

**ILLEGALLY DIVERTING FUNDS: Montgomery, Ala.** A jury found Governor Guy Hunt guilty of illegally diverting more than $200,000 from a non-profit inaugural fund to his personal accounts, money that Hunt then spent on himself. As required by his conviction, Hunt resigned.

**MURDER: London, England** Stephen Lawrence, an 18-year-old black youth was knifed to death by five white teenagers as he waited for a bus. Three of the reported killers were later tried, but acquitted in a case that caused a national uproar and increased racial tensions throughout England.

*April 23*

**ASSASSINATION: Colombo, Sri Lanka** Opposition leader Lalith Athulathmudali was shot and killed by a lone gunman during a political rally.

**SEXUAL ASSAULT: Washington, D.C.** The scores of sexual assaults occurring at the notorious 1991 Tailhook Association convention at the Las Vegas Hilton was summarized in a 300-page report. The report was based upon 2,900 interviews and was prepared by acting Pentagon Deputy Inspector General Derek Vander Schaaf. The report, released this date by the U.S. Department of Defense, stated that 83 women and seven men were assaulted in one form or another by 175 former and present Navy and Marine fliers. The report stated that victims were "groped, pinched, fondled," and "bitten" by their attackers and that oral sex and sexual intercourse was performed in front of others, all of this contributing to a "general atmosphere of debauchery. The report concluded that "Tailhook 91 is the culmination of a long-term failure of leadership in naval aviation."

*April 24*

**ASSASSINATION: Sri Lanka** Police produced the body of a man they said was the gunman who shot and killed political leader Lalith Athulathmudali on April 23.

**BOMBING: London, England** An IRA bomb exploded in the financial district, killing one person and wounding 44 others.

*April 28*

**MURDER GUN: Lewes, England** Wallis and Wallis auctioneers sold the purported .44-caliber Smith & Wesson revolver used by Bob Ford to shoot and kill America's most infamous western outlaw, Jesse Woodson James. The buyer, with a postal bid of $164,000 was identified only as a gun collector named J. McGee. There was considerable controversy about the gun before the auction. It was claimed that the revolver had been stolen from a Missouri museum in 1968. Further, some questioned the authenticity of the weapon.

**ROBBERY: Fukuoka, Japan** A man wielding a knife slashed one of two guards in a bank car stopped at a signal light, then made off with $1.6 million in cash. The biggest similar heist occurred in 1988 when $2.85 million was stolen from a cash delivery car in Kobe, Japan.

*April 30*

**ATTEMPTED MURDER: Schaumburg, Ill.** A 14-year-old girl, her 21-year-old boyfriend, James R. Hale, and another 14-year-old girl were arrested after plotting to kill the girl's father with a mixture of household chemicals and then use his bank card to loot his bank account and hold a celebration party at a hotel. Police were tipped off to the plot when the plotters approached a man and tried to enlist his aid, offering him $3,000 if he would help them murder the father. The girls were remanded to a juvenile facility and Hale was jailed pending trial.

*May 1*

**ASSASSINATION: Colombo, Sri Lanka** A terrorist riding a bicycle with explosives strapped to his body, blew himself and 24 others to pieces, including Ranasinghe Prema-dasa, president of Sri Lanka, at a May Day political rally. The assassination was reportedly made in retaliation for the killing of Lalith Athulathmudali, a political opponent to the Premadasa regime.

*May 3*

**MURDER: Yokosuko Naval Air Base (Tokyo), Japan** Airman Apprentice Terry Helvey, a crew member of the aircraft carrier U.S.S. *Belleau Wood*, pleaded guilty to the October 1992 murder of fellow crewman Allen Schindler, who had announced to his shipmates that he was homosexual. While the ship was anchored at Sasebo, Japan, Helvey and Charles Vins, another crew member, encountered Schindler in a public toilet. Helvey, apparently with Vins help, beat Schindler to death in what was later termed a hate crime (although Helvey claimed Schindler had been repeatedly harassing him with unwanted homosexual advances). Vins testified against Helvey and received reduced charges and a minimal prison term.

*May 4*

**DISORDERLY CONDUCT: Columbus, Ga.** Seven 6th-grade students—four boys and three girls—were arrested on disorderly conduct charges and released to the custody of their parents. The students, twelve and 13-years-old, had plotted for months to "eliminate" their teacher because she had disciplined them. They had dumped chemicals into her tea, trip her on school stairways, and had smuggled weapons into class to use on her. The teacher was made aware of the plot only a week before the arrest of the students. The teacher, who had taught at Georgetown Elementary School for 20 years, was never confronted with a weapon, did not trip down the stairs, nor did she get sick from the tainted tea.

*May 6*

**BOMBING/TERRORISM: New York, N.Y..** Mohammed Ahmad Ajaj was arrested in connection with the bombing of the World Trade Center, becoming the seventh suspect in the case. Ajaj arrived in New York in September 1992 with instructions on how to construct a bomb like the one employed at the World Trade Center, authorities stated.

**BURGLARY: Miami Beach, Fla.** Three young men broke into the home of Police Chief Phillip Huber and began ransacking the place until driven off by shots fired by Huber, who had been awakened by the noise. All three burglars were captured a few blocks away. Burglars had recently plagued homes of influential citizens in the Miami area; burglars had invaded the home of Jeb Bush, son of the former President, and several times burglarized the home of Miami Mayor Xavier Suarez.

**MURDER: Dearborn, Mich.** Postal worker Larry Jasion, who had reportedly been passed over for promotion, opened fire at a post office, killing one person and wounding three others. Only hours later in Dana Point, Calif., another postal worker, who had been dismissed seven months earlier, opened fire in a post office, killing a letter carrier and wounding a clerk. Since 1986, 32 persons have died in similar post office rampages. A spokesman for the National Safe Workplace Institute in Chicago later stated that the 740,000 postal workers in the U.S. were under great strain because of autocratic management and the introduction of high-tech equipment requiring constant concentration and creating stress.

*May 7*

**ILLEGALLY DIVERTING FUNDS: Montgomery, Ala.** Former governor of Alabama, Guy Hunt, who had been convicted on April 22 of illegally diverting funds for personal use from a non-profit organization, was sentenced to perform 1,000 hours of community service and pay $211,000 in restitution and fines.

*May 9*

**BANK THEFT: Hartford, Conn.** A fake automatic teller machine was removed from a shopping mall, one which high-tech thieves had installed in order to obtain customer bank passwords and identification so that the thieves could later loot their accounts. Authentic bank teller machines elsewhere in the mall were dismantled by the thieves in order to increase use of the fake equipment. Early discovery of the phony machine prevented any bank losses by customers.

*May 13*

**MURDER STATISTICS: Washington, D.C.** The U.S. Department of Justice released a report, that was a year in research, which stated that there was no racial bias in the sentencing of defendants. The report stated that blacks were given slightly longer prison sentences, but whites were more frequently sentenced to death. Among those eligible for capital punishment, 16 percent of whites were sentenced to death, compared to 10 percent of blacks. Overall, the report found that 63 percent of people arrested on murder charges were ultimately convicted of homicide, 19 percent of first-degree murder, 22 percent of second-degree murder or other murder charges, and 22 percent of voluntary manslaughter.

**RAPE: Austin, Texas** Joel Rene Valdez was found guilty of raping a woman after consuming a case of beer and entering her bedroom carrying a knife. Valdez' attorneys attempted to defend their client by saying that the woman gave her consent because she gave Valdez a condom. The victim stated that she did this only because she feared contracting the fatal HIV virus.

*May 15*

**ABDUCTION: Paris, France** A terrorist took six children hostage in a nursery, but he is killed was French police commandos who caught him sleeping. The children were rescued without injury.

*May 17*

**DRUGS: Cleveland, Ohio** State officials stated that 45 percent of non-violent drug abusers sent to conventional prisons should receive alternative sentences to regional prisons, halfway houses or electronic house arrest in order to ease overcrowded prisoners which were at 175 percent capacity.

*May 19*

**"TRAVELGATE": Washington, D.C.** Seven staff members of the White House travel office were fired. It would later be stated that Bill and Hillary Clinton got rid of these workers in order to replace them with family members and cronies from their native state of Arkansas and when their scheme was uncovered, asked the FBI to doctor a report on the travel office so that the report would make it appear that the firings were supported by the Bureau.

*May 21*

**MURDER: Hosmer, S.D.** Carl Swanson shot and killed his 25-year-old wife Donna and his three children, later shooting himself.

*May 22*

**ASSASSINATION/TERRORISM: Cairo, Egypt** A court sentenced six Muslim terrorists to death and two others to life sentences for attacks on tourists and plotting to assassinate Egyptian officials.

*May 23*

**JUSTIFIABLE HOMICIDE: Baton Rouge, La.** In a controversial trial, Rodney Peairs was found not guilty of murdering a 16-year-old foreign exchange student, Yoshihiro Hattori, who had come to Peairs' front door with another boy, seeking the location of a party. Peairs, thinking the youths were burglars, held a gun on them and ordered them to freeze. When Hattori, who did not understand English, appeared not to comply, Peairs fatally shot him. Peairs attorneys argued that their client had "an absolute right" to defend his home. The jury agreed. News of this verdict in Japan caused widespread criticism of American justice.

*May 24*

**ASSASSINATION: Guadalajara, Mexico** Cardinal Juan Jesús Posadas Ocampo arrived to greet a representative of the Vatican at the Guadalajara airport; the Cardinal's limousine was caught in the crossfire of two rival drug gangs, resulting in the Cardinal's death, along with six others. Posadas' limousine may have been mistaken for that of a drug cartel boss who had been marked for murder. Police arrested two suspects but most of the gunmen escaped.

**LAW ENFORCEMENT DATABASE: Los Angeles, Calif.** Because of an expected $100 million budget cut, Sheriff Sherman Block announced that his unique computerized gang-tracking system would shut down. The system, widely used by law enforcement agencies, listed names, nicknames, descriptions and addresses of 119,000 gang members.

## May 25

**ILLEGAL IMPRISONMENT: Guatemala** President Jorge Serrano Elías, under the guise of "purging the state of corruption," imprisoned scores of his political opponents.

## May 27

**BOMBING: Florence, Italy** The Uffizi Gallery, one of the world's great art museums, was severely damaged when a car bomb exploded. Five persons were killed and more than twenty others were seriously injured. Three paintings by minor artists were destroyed and damage was done to about thirty other paintings. Masterpiece works by Michelangelo, Botticelli and others were undamaged in that they were protected by shatterproof glass. Though police never apprehended the bombers, officials theorized that the explosion was the work of the Mafia which was signaling to police that even though hundreds of Mafiosi had recently been arrested and tried, the criminal brotherhood was still very much to be feared.

**MURDER: Yokosuko Naval Air Base (Tokyo), Japan** Terry Helvey, who had pleaded guilty to murdering homosexual shipmate Allen Schindler on May 3, was sentenced to life in prison.

## May 28

**MANSLAUGHTER: Orlando, Fla.** Miami Police officer William Lozano, who had been charged with two counts of manslaughter in the shooting deaths of two blacks in 1989, was acquitted. Lozano, a Hispanic, shot and killed the two blacks as they fled from a pursuing police car. He killed the driver and the passenger was fatally injured when the cycle crashed. Following the deaths, widespread rioting occurred in Miami's black communities. Convicted of manslaughter in 1989, an appeals court overturned Lozano's conviction in 1991, stating that a jury may have feared than an acquittal might have triggered more bloody rioting. At Lozano's second trial, his attorneys successfully argued that he had acted in self-defense. Lozano's acquittal this date did not prompt any widespread rioting, although some violence did break out in a black Miami neighborhood where five persons were injured and sixty were arrested.

## June 1

**OUSTED DICTATOR: Guatemala** President Serrano, who had illegally imprisoned political opponents was ousted from office by government officials and the military.

## June 2

**MANSLAUGHTER: Bakersfield, Calif.** As an autopsy was performed on the 5-year-old remains of a 3-year-old boy, his parents, DeEtte Stewart and William Bell, who had been living in their car (the boy's remains were found in the trunk), were detained in the Kern County jail on an investigation of manslaughter.

**OUSTED DICTATOR: Guatemala** President Serrano, the deposed dictator of Guatemala, flew to El Salvador and into political exile.

## June 7

**JUDICIARY: Washington, D.C.** The U.S. Supreme Court expanded the "plain view" doctrine by ruling unanimously that police do not need a warrant to seize narcotics, or other illegal objects that are clearly visible. Also, under "plain feel," when a suspect is being frisked by police for concealed weapons, no warrant was needed to seize such weapons.

## June 8:

**MURDER: Philadelphia, Pa.** David Dickson, a former campus guard at Drexel University, was arrested and charged with the 1984 murder of Debbie Wilson, a 20-year-old student. Dickson would later be convicted and sent to prison for the killing, one which he committed so that he could collect the dead girl's sneakers to add to his strange collection.

**MURDER: Providence, R. I.** Christopher Hightower, a one-time stockbroker who murdered a client and his family because the customer complained of his crooked practices, was sentenced to prison for life.

**TERRORIST ATTACK: Cairo, Egypt** Terrorists exploded a bomb near a tour bus on the Pyramids Road in Cairo. Two Egyptians were killed and 22 others were injured, many of these being tourists.

## June 11

**JUDICIARY: Washington, D.C.** The U.S. Supreme Court ruled unanimously that states could impose harsher sentences on defendants convicted of hate crimes, those crimes motivated by religious, racial or other prejudices, since those types of crimes could inflict great harm on victims and society in general.

**MURDER: Chicago, Ill.** George Pittman and his pregnant fiance, Jacqueline Porter were robbed and shot while in their car, Pittman later dying. Igdaliah Graham was later identified as the killer by the surviving Porter and was sent to prison.

**MURDER: Hayward, Calif.** A 15-year-old girl was convicted of murdering her 4-year-old sister after an entry from her diary was read in court which stated: "Dear Diary ... I killed my little sister." The girl, not identified because of her age, reportedly suffocated her younger sibling in a mistaken effort to save her from abuse. The girl was remanded to a state facility, to be held until her 25th birthday.

## June 12

**MURDER: Port St. Lucie, Fla.** The body of Mollie Mae Frazier, an 81-year-old widow, was found in a vacant lot by police, led there by teenagers who told officers that their friend, Victor Brancaccio, had bragged to them how he had murdered the old lady. Frazier had scolded Brancaccio for rapping the vulgar lyrics of the Dr. Dre tune "Stranded on Death Row when he passed her on a street and the 17-year-old pounced on her, beating her, punching her, kicking her, then taking her into the lot and killing her. Brancaccio was convicted and sentenced to life in prison.

## June 16

**MURDER: Paris, France** René Bousquet, an 84-year-old millionaire businessman, was shot dead at his front door by Christian Didier, who then held a press conference before turning himself into police to state that he had murdered Bousquet because he had been a Nazi collaborator during World War II.

### June 18

**JUDICIARY: Washington, D.C.** The U.S. Supreme Court ruled 7-2 that putting a non-smoking prisoner in a cell with a chain-smoking cellmate could constitute "cruel and unusual punishment" under the Eighth Amendment.

### June 20

**ABDUCTION/MURDER: Allentown, Pa.** Charlotte Schmoyer, a 13-year-old newspaper carrier, was abducted from her paper route and killed by serial rapist-killer Harvey Robinson.

### June 21

**ESPIONAGE: Marion, Ill.** Jonathan Pollard, convicted of spying for Israel (providing Israeli intelligence with more than 1,000 classified U.S. documents and satellite photos) in 1986, and sent to prison for life, was transferred from the maximum federal security prison at Marion, Illinois, after spending almost seven years in solitary confinement, to another federal prison in South Carolina.

**JUDICIARY: Washington, D.C.** The U.S. Supreme Court ruled 5-4 that federal courts should refuse to grant habeas corpus review of violations of a defendant's rights during a trial, unless the violation had a "substantial and injurious effect or influence in determining the jury's verdict."

### June 22

**BOMBING: University of California** Geneticist Charles Epstein received a package bomb that blew off several of his fingers when he opened it.

### June 23

**ASSAULT: Manassas, Va.** Lorena Bobbitt sliced off her husband's penis while he was sleeping and launched one of the most sensational and sordid domestic crime cases of the decade.

### June 24

**TERRORISM: New York, N.Y.** FBI agents arrested eight radical Muslims who arrived in New York with plans to bomb several sites in the city, as well as assassinate the secretary general of the U.N., and other officials. Five of the suspects had arrived with Sudanese passports, Sudan being a rogue nation that would later play host to Arab millionaire and terrorist leader Osama bin Laden who would blow up the U.S. embassies in Nairobi, Kenya and Dar es Salaam, Tanzania on August 7, 1998. Of the eight suspects arrested by the FBI, six of these have ties to Sheik Omar Rabdel Rahman and all are considered suspects in the bombing of the World Trade Center.

### June 25

**TERRORISM: New York, N.Y.** Emad Salem, a translator and bodyguard for Sheik Omar Abdel Rahman, was identified as an FBI informer who had secretly taped conversations between Rahman and those under arrest.

### June 28

**JUDICIARY: Washington, D.C.** The U.S. Supreme Court ruled unanimously that the government held limited power in the seizing of assets of convicted criminals by using civil forfeiture law. Such seizures could be considered "excessive" fines under the Eighth Amendment. The court also ruled this date 7-2 that the conclusions of an expert witness need not be "generally accepted" within the scientific community, but the "methods and procedures" involved in reaching such conclusions must be valid.

### June 29

**TERRORISM/NUCLEAR THEFT: Russia** Two seamen were apprehended after stealing 1.8 kilos of highly enriched uranium and before they could sell the HEU to terrorists who planned to construct a nuclear bomb, according to authorities.

### June 30

**RAPE: Allentown, Pa.** Serial rapist-killer Harvey Robinson invaded a home and raped a 5-year-old girl while the girl's mother slept in another room.

**TERRORISM: New York, N.Y.** FBI agents arrested a ninth suspect in the World Trade Center bombing when he arrived in New York; he was charged with conspiracy to transport explosives.

### July 1

**FRAUD: Odin, Minn.** Herbert Saunders, a farmer, was charged with fraud in taking money for milk from one of his cows which he claimed would cure all manner of deadly ills, including cancer and AIDS. Saunders, according to authorities, claimed that by drinking milk from the udder of a cow injected with the patient's blood, a cure would come about. He reportedly sold the cow for $2,500 many times over on the provision that it stay on his farm, and bottles of "treated" milk for between $30 and $35 each.

### July 2

**BOMBING: New York, N.Y.** FBI agents arrested Sheik Omar Abdel Rahman, Islamic fundamentalist leader suspected of organizing the bombing of the World Trade Center.

**"TRAVELGATE": Washington, D.C.** The White House issued a report on the controversy involving the White House Travel Office. Catherine Cornelius, who had been named head of the Travel Office and who was a cousin of President Clinton, was reprimanded for attempting to cast suspicions on former employees of the Travel Office who had been fired by attempting to find wrongdoing by those ex-employees and by seeking to enlist the aid of the FBI by having the Bureau rewrite reports to show these former employees in unfavorable light. Five former Travel Office employees were cleared of any wrongdoing and promised other government jobs.

### July 3

**MURDER: Fort Bragg, N.C.** Sgt. Irvin Graves attacked

and murdered Lt. Lisa Bryant, who had refused to dance with him at a post dance earlier that night. Tried later by military tribunal, Graves would be convicted and given life imprisonment.

**MURDER: Sacramento, Calif.** Serial poisoner Dorothea Puente, who had reportedly killed a dozen people, mostly elderly pensioners living at her San Francisco rooming house (she killed them for their social security checks, burying the bodies in the back yard), went on trial. The 78-year-old killer would be sent to prison for life.

## July 8

**FRAUD: Houston, Texas** Forrest B. Williams, head of FW Marketing Consultants, Inc., was arrested and charged with fraud in a scam whereby hundreds of Houston businessmen paid $100 each for a supposed fire department inspection of their offices and plants.

## July 11

**ABDUCTION/MURDER/SUICIDE: Antioch, Calif.** Joel Souza, 35, distraught over his divorce, barricaded himself inside his house with his two small children and, after a 9-hour police standoff, killed his children and himself.

## July 13

**MURDER: Boca Raton, Fla.** Kim Brunner, an attractive 24-year-old secretary, was murdered while attempting to start her car in a parking lot. Police soon arrested the victim's ex-husband, William Brunner, who had been recently released from jail, after serving time for violating a restraining order obtained by his ex-wife. Brunner had stalked his former wife for several months before fatally shooting her in the head, according to prosecutors who convinced a jury in 1996 to find him guilty of murder. Brunner was sentenced to life in prison.

## July 14

**MURDER/RAPE: Allentown, Pa.** Serial rapist-killer Harvey Robinson sexually attacked and strangled to death 47-year-old Jessica Fortney.

## July 17

**EXECUTIONS: Cairo, Egypt** Five Islamic terrorists found guilty of bombings and mass killings were executed as part of a government campaign to shut down terrorist operations in the country.

**LAW ENFORCEMENT: Washington, D.C.** Attorney General Janet Reno asked FBI Director William Sessions to resign or be fired. Sessions and his wife had come under criticism for reported abuses, including failure to pay taxes for prerequisites provided by the government. Sessions, who had been appointed by President Ronald Reagan in 1987, rejected Reno's ultimatum.

## July 19

**EMBEZZLEMENT: Washington, D.C.** Former Postmaster for the U.S. House, Robert Rota, pleaded guilty to conspire to embezzle public funds and helping embezzlement by House members.

**LAW ENFORCEMENT: Washington, D.C.** President Bill Clinton dismissed William Sessions as FBI Director.

## July 20

**LAW ENFORCEMENT: Washington, D.C.** President Bill Clinton nominated U.S. District Judge Louis J. Freeh of New York City as the new director of the FBI.

**MYSTERIOUS DEATH: Northern Va.** Vincent Foster, deputy White House counsel and close friend of President Clinton, was found shot to death in a park. Though it was reported that Foster, troubled by pressures of the job and recent scandals such as "Travelgate," had committed suicide, other reports held that he might have been murdered. Foster's death remained a mystery.

## July 23:

**MURDER: Rio de Janeiro, Brazil** Several street youths of the many thousands of impoverished children wandering the poverty-stricken areas of Rio were picked up by four members of a private "death squad" and shot in front of the Candeleria Cathedral. The bodies of two more street children were found on the steps of the Museum of Modern Art. One survived to later testify against death squad leader Marcos Vinicius Emmanuel who would be convicted and sentenced to 309 years in prison.

**MURDER: Robeson County, N.C.** James Jordan, the 56-year-old father of famed basketball superstar Michael Jordan, pulled his new car (a Lexus, a gift from his famous son) over to the side of the road to sleep while en route to a Wilmington funeral. He was attacked and murdered, it was later proved, by two thugs, Daniel Andre Green and Larry Martin Demery, who dumped Jordan's body and stole his car. They were later tried, convicted and sent to prison for life.

## July 27

**BOMBINGS: Milan and Rome, Italy** Terrorists (reported Red Brigadists) exploded a car bomb in downtown Milan, killing at least five persons. Another bomb exploded in the center of Rome, injuring 24 persons and damaging the basilica of St. John Lateran, the Pope's See.

**MURDER: Ennis, Texas** Christine Benjamin, 13, and her 14-year-old stepbrother, James King, disappeared from their home. Both teenagers had been abducted and killed by another teenager, Jason Massey, who would be sentenced to death in 1994.

## July 29

**CONVICTION OVERTURNED: Israel** The Israeli Supreme Court overturned the conviction of John Demjanjuk, who had been extradited from the U.S. and convicted in an Israeli court as a one-time guard in German concentration camps known as "Ivan the Terrible." KGB information provided by Russia, however, showed that Demjanjuk, although he had been a concentration camp guard, was not the dreaded "Ivan the Terrible," and that this war criminal had been another Ukrainian, Ivan Marchenko.

**MURDER: Raleigh, N.C.** To eliminate his homosexual rival, Joseph Mannino injected a fatal dose of drugs into Michael

Hunter. He would be convicted of manslaughter and sent to prison.

### July 31

**MURDER/RAPE: Allentown, Pa.** Police set up a trap for serial rapist-killer Harvey Robinson, but when he broke into a home and found an officer waiting for him, he escaped after a shootout. He would later be apprehended, tried, convicted and given three death sentences for the three persons he was known to have murdered.

### August 4

**POLICE BRUTALITY: Los Angeles, Calif.** Stacey C. Koon and Laurence M. Powell, the two LAPD officers convicted by a federal jury in 1993 for the beating of black motorist Rodney King, were sentenced to two-and-a-half years in prison by Judge John Davies who explained the lenient sentence by stating that King had provoked the beating.

### August 5:

**MURDER/ROBBERY: Chicago, Ill.** Eduardo Estremara, a 28-year-old Chicago resident, robbed and shot to death Dmitry Rabin on West Belden Avenue. Estremara will be found guilty of these crimes and sentenced to death following his 1996 trial.

### August 6

**LAW ENFORCEMENT: Washington, D.C.** The U.S. Senate unanimously confirmed President Clinton's nomination of Louis J. Freeh as the new director of the Federal Bureau of Investigation (FBI).

### August 10

**JUDICIARY: Washington, D.C.** Ruth Bader Ginsburg was sworn in as the 107th U.S. Supreme Court Justice.

### August 11

**ANTI-CRIME LEGISLATION: Washington, D.C.** President Clinton endorsed legislation designed to combat crime; he endorsed the Brady bill which required a five-day waiting period for anyone wanting to buy a handgun. Clinton proposed to spend $3.4 billion over the next five years to hire 50,000 more police officers. Clinton also issues an executive order which required stricter licensing of gun dealers and banned the importing of semiautomatic assault-style handguns.

### August 13

**MURDER: San Antonio, Tex.** Cheri Dale, wanted for a brutal killing in San Diego, was detained by police and extradited to California where she stood trial for the ax murder of 25-year-old Susan Taylor. Dale would be convicted and sent to prison.

### August 14

**BANK FRAUD: New York, N.Y.** Clark Clifford, who had been indicted on charges of bank fraud connected to the scandal-ridden Bank of Credit and Commerce International, was not tried because he was thought to ill to stand trial. Co-defendant Robert Altman, was found not guilty of misleading bank regulators and filing false statements.

### August 15

**MASS MURDER: Yanomami Indian Reservation, Brazil** Invading gold miners killed 73 Indians and terrorized whole communities in what was the largest massacre in the country's history.

### August 17

**MURDER: Edmond, Okla.** Delpha Spunaugle reported her husband Dennis missing. Three days later police arrested her and her alcoholic lover, Edwin Davis Woodward, charging them with the murder of Dennis Spunaugle. Woodward was later sent to prison for life and Spunaugle, who had given Woodward a six-pack of beer and $20 to kill her husband, was sentenced to death.

**MURDER: Mission Viejo, Calif.** Jennifer Ji, the beautiful mistress of wealthy Taiwanese businessman Tseng Jyi Peng, was stabbed to death in her luxury apartment, her infant son smothered in his crib. The killer, it was later discovered, was Peng's jealous wife, Lisa Peng, who was convicted on DNA evidence and sent to prison for life in 1996.

### August 18

**ASSASSINATION ATTEMPT: Cairo Egypt** Four were killed and 15 others injured when Islamic terrorists attacked the new Egyptian security chief (he was wounded and survived).

**CHILD MOLESTATION/KIDNAPPING/MURDER: Franklin, N.Y.** Sara Anne Woods, 12, vanished from her home. According to police, Lewis Lent, Jr., a serial child molester, would later confess to abducting, molesting and murdering the Woods child. He would be convicted of this crime and sent to prison for life, although Lent insisted at his trial that he had no part in Woods' death.

**TERRORIST NATION: Washington, D.C.** The U.S. State Department officially notified the government of the Sudan that it would be added to the list of nations that the U.S. regarded as supporters of international terrorism, making Sudan ineligible for all U.S. aid, except that of humanitarian relief.

### August 24

**MURDER: Los Angeles, Calif.** Rapper Calvin Broadus (Snoop Doggy Dog), and a bodyguard, McKinley Lee, reportedly shot and killed Philip Woldermariam, an Ethiopian immigrant, firing three bullets into his back in Woodbine Park as he munched on Mexican food. Broadus and Lee would later be acquitted of the killing.

### August 25

**TERRORISM: New York, N.Y.** Sheik Omar Abdel Rahman was indicted by a federal grand jury on conspiracy charges connected to the February 1993 bombing of the World Trade Center, and other abortive terrorist attacks in the city, as well as the 1990 murder of Rabbi Meir Kahane. Fifteen others were also indicted as part of the Arab terrorist conspiracy, including Sayyid Nosair who had earlier been acquitted of slaying

Kahane in a state court and who now faced the same charge in a federal court.

### August 31:

**MURDER: Niles, Ill.** William Lenius, intending to kill his estranged girl friend, Ellen Marshall, left a toolbox with a bomb inside of it beneath her car. When Marshall drove off, a neighbor, Deborah Conrad, took the toolbox to her home where she gave it to her husband, Wayne Conrad. When Conrad opened to box, the explosion killed him and injured his wife. Lenius will later be convicted and sent to prison for life.

### September 1

**ABDUCTION/MURDER: Byers, Colo.** Cissy Pamela Foster, 14, was found strangled to death. Her slayer, paroled murderer Kenyon Battles Tolerton, would later be sentenced to life in prison for this killing.

### September 3

**CHILD MOLESTATION: Riverside, Calif.** Police stopped a car driven by Nicholas Charles Argante for a routine traffic violation, but a check of the auto proved it to be have been used in many abductions and child molestations from March to May 1993. Argante confessed to his crimes and received a 100-year prison sentence.

### September 4

**MURDER: Peoria, Ill.** Elderly Bernice Fagotte disappeared from her home; she had sponsored a paroled convict, Joseph Robert Miller, who had killed her.

### September 11

**MURDER: Peoria, Ill.** Serial killer Joseph Robert Miller murdered Helen Dorrance, a streetwalker.

### September 13

**MURDER: Florida** Aundra Aikens, a petty thief, shot and killed Gary Colley and Margaret Jagger in a botched holdup in a rest area where the two British tourists had stopped. Aikens would later be sent to prison for 27 years, his crime having all but crippled Florida tourism.

### September 15

**BANK ROBBERY/MANSLAUGHTER: Boston, Mass.** One-time militant opponent of the Vietnam War, Katherine Ann Porter, who had been a federal fugitive for twenty years, turned herself in and pleaded guilty in a State Superior Court in Boston to armed robbery and manslaughter. Power had driven a getaway car during a 1970 Boston bank robbery in which a policeman was shot and killed. Power had disguised her identity when moving to Oregon where she married.

**MURDER: Peoria, Ill.** Streetwalker Sandra Cseznegi, 42, disappeared; she had been killed by Joseph Robert Miller, a serial killer recently paroled from prison.

### September 18

**MURDER: Gainesville, Fla.** In a reported attempt to silence witnesses against him in an arson charge, Richard Anthony Meissner broke into the home of Gina Langevin and Jena Hull, beating and stabbing them, killing Langevin and wounding Hull, who survived to identify him. Meissner would be later caught and sent to prison.

**MURDER: Peoria, Ill.** The bodies of Helen Dorrance and Marcia Logue, streetwalkers, were found by police; they had been sexually assaulted and stabbed to death by serial killer Joseph Robert Miller.

### September 19

**WAR CRIMES: Israel** John Demjanjuk, whose conviction for war crimes had been overturned by the Israeli Supreme Court after the defendant was shown to have been wrongly identified as a war criminal, was released from custody in Israel.

### September 22

**ARSON/MURDER: Muskogee, Okla.** A blazing inferno consumed the home of Curtis Foster, Jr., claiming the lives of his wife and five children. Foster, an ex-convict from Arkansas, was later convicted of purposely starting the fire and murdering his family.

**MURDER: Norfolk, Va.** The strangled body of 17-year-old Sara J. Wisnosky was found under a bridge spanning the Lafayette River. The girl's killer, Derek R. Barnabei, 26, was later tracked down and convicted, sentenced to death in 1995.

**WRONGLY CONVICTED: U.S.** John Demjanjuk, after having been wrongly convicted in Israel of war crimes and then released, returned to the U.S. Demjanjuk had been extradited to Israel by the U.S.

### September 24

**BURGLARY: Boston, Mass.** Long-time fugitive Katherine Ann Power, who had pleaded guilty to bank robbery and manslaughter in a 1970 Boston bank robbery in which a police officer was killed, pleaded guilty to the burglary of a National Guard armory.

### September 26

**MURDER: Peoria, Ill.** The body of streetwalker Sandra Cseznegi was found in a drainage ditch. She had been brutally murdered by serial killer Joseph Robert Miller.

### September 29

**MURDER: Peoria, Ill.** Paroled serial killer Joseph Robert Miller, who had slain at least four women within a month, was arrested by police. He would later be sentenced to death.

### September 30

**LAW ENFORCEMENT: Washington, D.C.** The U.S. Department of the Treasury issued a report in which it sharply criticized top officials of its own ATF (Bureau of Alcohol, Tobacco and Firearms) in their handling of the attack on the Branch Davidian complex in Waco, Texas on February 28, 1993, in which four ATF agents had been killed, along with six cultists. ATF officials in charge of the Waco operation, the report went on, then deceived investigators and Congress by attempting to blame the botched raid on an undercover agent who, in truth, had warned the agents not to make the attack as they had lost the element of surprise. Lloyd Bentsen, Secretary of the Treasury, announced that he had replaced ATF chief Stephen Higgins and suspended five other ATF officials connected with the Waco raid.

## October 1

**CHILD MOLESTATION/MURDER: Petaluma, Calif.** One of California's most ruthless predators, Richard Allen Davis abducted, raped and murdered Polly Klaas.

**MURDER: Tulsa, Okla.** Joyland Morgan, 20, and her young son Kewan, were found murdered in their apartment. Their killer was later identified as Julius Ricardo Young, a minister and the lover of the victim's mother, who would be sentenced to death in 1995.

## October 5

**EMBEZZLEMENT: Washington, D.C.** Jack Russ, former sergeant-at-arms in the House of Representatives, pleaded guilty in a plea-bargain arrangement to embezzlement by a custodian of public funds, wire fraud, and making a false statement on his financial disclosure form, all charges connected to the House bank scandal. Russ agreed to aid prosecutors in their on-going investigation of the Bank scandal.

## October 7

**BANK ROBBERY: Boston, Mass.** Katherine Ann Porter, who had pleaded guilty to robbing a Boston bank in 1970 and manslaughter in the shooting of a police officer at that time, was sentenced to eight to twelve years in a Massachusetts prison.

## October 8

**LAW ENFORCEMENT: Washington, D.C.** The U.S. Department of Justice issued a report which cleared U.S. Attorney Janet Reno of any errors in her handling of the April 19, 1993 assault by federal officers on the Branch Davidian compound outside of Waco, Texas, which resulted in a fire that consumed the cultists and their children. The report stated that no evidence had been found that the cultists were abusing their children which Reno had used as a reason to launch the attack. The report also stated that after tear gas had been fired into the compound, the cultists set off the fire that consumed the complex. (A 1999 report held a completely different view, one in which FBI officials admitted that the fire may have been set off by attacking federal officers who used flammable devices.) In the light of later disclosures, this report served to whitewash Janet Reno, who, in the opinion of this author and other criminologists, had horribly blundered in her handling of the affair.

## October 9

**MURDER: Washington County, Ore.** Martha Bryant, a 41-year-old midwife, was found along a lonely road and rushed to a hospital. She had been abducted, raped and shot; before dying she described her attacker, who was later identified as Cesar Barone, a career criminal who had also murdered another woman in Portland. Barone would later be sentenced to death.

## October 10

**MURDER: Bellwood, Ill.** Shadrach Pitchford, while stalking Nathaniel Jefferson, encountered Jefferson and his friend, Anthony Crothers. Jefferson ran away at the urging of Crothers and, incensed, Pitchford shot Crothers ten times, then beat and kicked him before fleeing. Pitchford would be convicted for this killing in 1996.

## October 15

**SEXUAL ASSAULTS: Washington, D.C.** The Pentagon censured three admirals who had organized the notorious 1991 Tailhook convention at which time scores of women were sexually attacked by drunken Navy and Marine fliers at the Las Vegas Hilton Hotel. One report held that Secretary of the Navy John Dalton had wanted to remove Admiral Frank Kelso, Chief of Naval Operations, who had been one of thirty-five admirals and Marine generals who had attended the Tailhook abomination. Dalton was overruled by Secretary of Defense Les Aspin who decided to retain Kelso as CNO. In the end, twenty-nine admirals, including Kelso, and one Marine general, were sent letters of caution which were not officially placed in their files. [In the opinion of this author, Aspin's apparent disregard for setting and maintaining moral standards in this instance reflected the same kind of moral imbecility practiced by President Clinton five years later in his sexual escapades in the White House. All of the top officers involved, as well as the 175 Navy and Marine fliers who proved themselves moral degenerates through their sexual attacks, were unfit to command anyone or anything. They should all have been sacked without pensions.]

## October 20

**MURDER: Pima County, Ariz.** Virginia Depper, a woman in her sixties, was found bludgeoned to death in her apartment. Evidence pointed to her ex-husband, Dr. Dale Bertsch, as her killer and he was later convicted and sent to prison. Bertsch had reportedly murdered his former wife so he would not have to continue making alimony payments.

## October 28

**SUSPICIOUS DEATH: Beverly Hills, Calif.** Millionairess Doris Duke died under suspicious circumstances at her mansion. Her personal secretary, heavy-drinking Bernard Lafferty, who was named as executor of Duke's $1.2 billion estate, was later accused of murdering his employer, but no case was ever proven against him.

## October 29

**MURDER/RAPE: Chester, England** Serial rapist-killer John Henry Bell was sentenced to life in prison.

## November 4

**MURDER: Belanglo State Forest, Australia** The bodies of two more hikers—Anja Habschied, 20, and her companion, 21-year-old Gabor Neugebauer—were discovered, both murdered. Their slayer, Ivan Milat, one of Australia's most horrendous serial killers, would be caught in 1994 and sent to prison for life.

*November 7*

**NUCLEAR THEFT: Russia** Three Russian naval officers stole 4.5 kilos of highly enriched uranium, reportedly intent on selling this to terrorists who planned to construct a nuclear bomb. The thieves and the fuel were located by authorities six months later.

*November 12:*

**ESPIONAGE: Washington, D. C.** President William Clinton received a request from Israeli Prime Minister Yitzhak Rabin, asking that convicted spy Jonathan Pollard (convicted and sentenced to life in prison in 1986 as a spy for Israel) be released. Clinton refused the request.

*November 13*

**MURDER: Fort Worth, Tex.** The bodies of two college students, Melanie Golchert, 18 and Channing Elizabeth Freelove, 19, were found on a remote road next to their car, both having been shot to death. Police later pieced together a solid case against Darron Deshone Curl and Melvin James White II to prove that they had murdered the girls who had been trying to sell them drugs. Both received long prison terms.

*November 15*

**MURDER: Tucson, Ariz.** Michelle Page Malone, 33, was found in her home strapped to a chair and stabbed to death. Her killer, Robert Joseph Moody, would later be tracked down and be sentenced to death.

*November 19*

**MURDER: Osceola National Forest (Baker County), Fla.** Hunter Don Hill was found dead, shot three times and robbed. His murderer, Jimmie Rae Beagle, who had would also murder another hunter five days later, would later die in a police station shootout in 1998.

*November 24*

**MURDER: Tucson, Ariz.** Patricia Magda, 56, was found stabbed to death in her home. Her cash, credit cards and valuables had been stolen. The perpetrator, Robert Joseph Moody, who had killed another woman less than ten days earlier, would be captured and condemned to death.

*November 28*

**MURDER: Chesterfield County, Va.** Richard and Rebecca Rosenbluth were shot to death by cocaine dealers Mark Arlo Sheppard and Andre Graham. Graham would later be sentenced to life in prison and Sheppard would be executed for the murders on January 20, 1999.

*November 29*

**CHILD MOLESTATION/MURDER: Ukiah, Calif.** Police arrested paroled prisoner and predator Richard Allen Davis at his sister's home, charging him with the October 1, 1993, abduction, rape and murder of 12-year-old Polly Klaas.

*November 30*

**WEAPONS LAW ENACTED: Washington, D.C.** President Clinton signed the Brady bill into law which include a mandatory five-day waiting period for all handgun purchases, ostensibly a period of time in which applicants could be screened for criminal backgrounds.

*December 5*

**CAUSING A CATASTROPHE: West Quincy, Mo.** On July 17, 1993, a wall of sandbags holding back the swollen Mississippi River at West Quincy, Mo., gave way and flooded more than 14,000 acres of rich farmland. This disaster, it was later learned, was caused by 24-year-old James Scott, an Illinois resident, who removed the crucial sandbags. Scott's bizarre explanation for his act was that he brought about the flooding so that he could strand his wife on the other side of the waters and could hold a beer-drinking party without her. Tried and convicted for causing a catastrophe, Scott was sentenced, this date, to life imprisonment.

*December 7*

**MASS MURDER: Garden City, N.Y.** Black racist Colin Ferguson, carrying an automatic pistol, boarded a commuter train at Penn Station and, as the train arrived at Garden City, leaped from his seat, going down the aisles of several cars, selected white passengers to shoot, killing six persons and wounding 19 others.

*December 9*

**DRUGS: Medellin, Colombia** Pablo Escobar, the mutlibillionaire head of the Medellin drug cartel, was tracked down to his hideout and was killed during a shootout with Colombian police commandos.

*December 14*

**MURDER: Greensboro, N.C.** Police received a call reporting the murder of prostitute whose naked body had been dumped into a cemetery. The body of Lois Elizabeth Williams was found in a graveyard a short time later. Her murderer, Robert Sylvester Alston, a serial rapist-killer, was later apprehended and sent to prison for life.

*December 19*

**MURDER: Cayahoga Falls, Ohio** Police arrested Derek R. Barnabei, wanted in Virginia for the murder of a 17-year-old girl, later extraditing him for trial; he would be convicted and receive the death sentence.

*December 27*

**TERRORIST ATTACK: Cairo, Egypt** A tourist bus traveling through old Cairo was attacked by terrorists with a bomb and guns. Eight Austrian tourists and eight Egyptians were injured.

*December 28*

**MURDER: Wilmette, Ill.** Suzanne Olds, 56, the estranged wife of wealthy lawyer Dean Olds, was bludgeoned to death in the attached garage of her posh Indian Hill Estates home. He husband, a prime suspect in the case, was never tried, but Olds' homosexual lover, Helmut Carsten Hofer, a German, was later tried and acquitted of the murder.

### December 31

**MURDER: Humboldt, Neb.** After she complained that John Lotter and Thomas Nissen had beaten and raped her on December 24, 23-year-old Teena Renee Brandon was murdered by both men in retaliation for her police report. Lotter also shot and killed two other persons staying with Brandon. He would later be sentenced to death and his accomplice, Nissen, sent to prison.

# 1994

### January 5

**MURDER: Orange County, Calif.** The sheriff's department called police in Tucson, Ariz. to report that a man named Robert Moody had wandered into a police station in an apparent daze, saying he could not remember his name, but that he fit the description of the man Tucson police were seeking in the murders of two women. Moody was extradited to Tucson.

**WHITEWATER: Washington, D.C.** The White House announced that in late December 1993, the U.S. Department of Justice had subpoenaed documents belonging to President Bill Clinton and Hillary Rodham Clinton, concerning their dealings with James McDougal, an Arkansas businessman and close Clinton friend, who was under investigation.

### January 6

**ASSAULT: Detroit, Mich.** Olympics skater Nancy Kerrigan was attacked by a man who struck her on the right knee and fled. Her leg sorely bruised, Kerrigan would withdraw from the U.S. Figure Skating Championship which she had been favored to win. Instead, her competitor, Tonya Harding won the championship and thus qualified for the Winter Olympic Games scheduled in February.

### January 12

**WHITEWATER: Washington, D.C.** In response to an uproar from Congress, President Clinton asked U.S. Attorney General Janet Reno to appoint an independent counsel to conduct an inquiry into the Clintons' involvement with the failed Whitewater real estate venture which was headed by their close Arkansas friend, James McDougal.

### January 13

**ASSAULT: Portland, Ore.** Sheriff's deputies arrested Shawn Eckhardt, bodyguard for Olympic skater Tonya Harding, along with Derrick Smith, charging them with the January 6 assault on skater Nancy Kerrigan.

**MURDER: Los Angeles, Calif.** A mistrial was declared in the case against 23-year-old Erik Menendez, who, with his brother Lyle, had shot and killed his parents, Jose and Kitty Menendez, in their Beverly Hills home in order to obtain their $14 million estate.

### January 14

**ASSAULT: Phoenix, Ariz.** Shane Stant, believed to be the actual person who carried out the January 6 attack on skater Nancy Kerrigan, surrendered to police.

### January 17

**MURDER: Chicago, Ill.** Herbert Handy, who was house-sitting for a real estate firm, got into an argument with Andre Wallace and Wallace reportedly shot Handy three times, killing him. Police arrested Wallace two days later and held him until the next day in a locked interrogation room until he confessed to the killing. Wallace was convicted in 1996 and given a 26-year prison term, but in 1998, his lawyers successfully argued before the Illinois Appellate Court that their client had been held illegally at the time of his conviction and the case was reversed.

### January 18

**IRAN-CONTRA REPORT: Washington, D.C.** Lawrence Walsh, the independent counsel who had headed the investigation of the Iran-Contra scandal, issued his final report which illustrated how the six-and-a-half-year investigation had cost $37 million and had resulted in charges against 14 men and convictions or guilty pleas in 11 cases. Two of the convictions were overturned and President George Bush pardoned six others who had been tried or were facing trial.

### January 19

**ASSAULT: Portland, Ore.** Jeff Gillooly, former husband of Tonya Harding, was arrested and charged with conspiracy in the January 6 assault on skater Nancy Kerrigan. Gillooly had divorced Harding in 1993, but had reunited and the two were living together.

### January 20

**WHITEWATER: Washington, D.C.** U.S. Attorney General Janet Reno appointed Robert Fiske, a former U.S. Attorney from New York City, to conduct an inquiry into the involvement of President Bill Clinton and his wife Hillary Rodham Clinton in the failed Whitewater real estate scheme headed by close friend James McDougal.

### January 21

**ASSAULT: Prince William Henry County, Va.** Lorena Bobbitt, who had cut off the penis of her husband, John Bobbitt, while he slept, was found not guilty by reason of temporary insanity. Judge Herman Whisenant ordered her to undergo psychiatric examinations.

### January 22

**RAPE: Greensboro, N.C.** Police located a woman who had survived a brutal rape, beating and choking, who described her assailant, a description that led to the arrest of serial rapist-killer Robert Sylvester Alston, who was sent to prison for life.

### January 24

**SEXUAL HARASSMENT: Washington, D.C.** In an inquiry concerned with allegations that Senator Robert Packwood

(R.,Ore.) had committed sexual harassment and other misconduct, federal district court Judge Thomas Jackson upheld a subpoena from the Senate Ethics Committee for Packwood's diaries, particularly all entries from 1989 onward.

### January 25

**CHILD MOLESTATION: Los Angeles, Calif.** Singer Michael Jackson reached an out-of-court settlement with the parents of a 14-year-old boy who had accused him of sexual molestation. The terms of the settlement were not made public, but sources claimed that the amount was between $10 million and $20 million. Although the civil suit ended, Jackson was nevertheless the subject of a continuing criminal investigation.

### January 27

**ASSAULT: Portland, Ore.** Skater Tonya Harding announced that she had learned several days after the January 6 attack on her competitor Nancy Kerrigan that "persons that were close to me," had been involved in the vicious assault. She also admitted that she did not tell authorities what she had discovered until some days later.

### January 28

**MURDER: Los Angeles, Calif.** A mistrial was declared in the case against 26-year-old Lyle Menendez, who, with his brother Erik, had shot and killed his parents, Jose and Kitty Menendez, in their Beverly Hills home in order to obtain their $14 million estate.

### February 1

**ASSAULT/RACKETEERING: Portland, Ore.** Jeff Gillooly, former husband of skater Tonya Harding, pleaded guilty to racketeering charges in planning the January 6 attack on figure skater Nancy Kerrigan, in order to eliminate her from competing with Harding. Gillooly testified that Harding had helped to plan the assault.

### February 2

**WHITEWATER: Washington, D.C.** Roger Altman, deputy Treasury secretary and head of the Resolution Trust Corp. met privately with Hillary Rodham Clinton and several White House aides. The RTC was the federal agency responsible for disposing of the assets of insolvent savings and loan institutions, such as Madison Guarantee, a failed Arkansas S&L which had reportedly funneled illegal funds to Bill Clinton's political campaigns and diverted other funds to Whitewater, the real estate scheme headed by James McDougal, a friend of the Clintons who were also involved in the land development project. In later testimony before the Senate Banking Committee, Altman admitted that he had briefed Hillary Clinton on what actions the RTC could take and was soundly criticized for having discussions about an on-going investigation which involved the Clintons and their possible involvement in illegal activities.

### February 5

**MURDER: Jackson, Miss.** Byron de la Beckwith had escaped conviction in the 1963 murder of Medgar Evers, a NAACP activist killed in front of his Jackson, Miss., home (despite the fact that the murder weapon had Beckwith's fingerprints on it) through two all-white deadlocked juries in 1964. Beckwith was retried and new evidence convinced a jury to convict Beckwith with the Evers slaying. He was sent to prison for life.

### February 8

**SEXUAL HARASSMENT/ASSAULT: Washington, D.C.** U.S. Navy Judge William Vest, Jr., who dismissed charges against three naval officers reportedly involved in the notorious 1991 Tailhook convention in Las Vegas that involved sexual harassment and assault on many females by Navy officers, stated that Admiral Frank Kelso, Chief of Naval Operations, had employed "unlawful command influence" to "manipulate" the investigation "in a manner designed to shield his personal involvement." Kelso had reportedly witnessed numerous incidents of sexual misconduct by his officers and did nothing about it. Kelso angrily denounced the findings of Navy Judge Vest on February 8.

### February 10

**SEXUAL HARASSMENT/ASSAULT: Washington, D.C.** The Navy announced the resignation of Lt. Paula Coughlin, the officer who first exposed the infamous 1991 Tailhook convention in Las Vegas where dozens of U.S. Navy officers sexually harassed and assaulted scores of females. Couglin stated in her letter that the attacks on her and the "covert attacks" that followed when she publicly complained of the sexual harassment, compelled her resignation.

### February 11

**MISUSE OF STATE FUNDS: Fort Worth, Texas** U.S. Senator Kay Bailey Hutchinson (R, Tex.), went on trial, charged with misusing state funds and personnel for political purposes. Hutchinson's lawyers argued that documents obtained in a 1993 raid on her office were inadmissible in that no search warrant had been obtained. Travis County District Attorney Ronnie Earle refused to open the case and Judge John Onion dismissed the charges against Hutchinson.

### February 14

**MURDER: Rostov-on-Don, Russia** Serial killer Andrei Chikatilo, who admitted to murdering 52 girls, boys and women, was executed, shot to death in the basement of a prison. Prior to his November 20, 1990, arrest, Chikatilo had eluded capture for more than a decade. When he confessed to his crimes, the serial killer also admitted that he had mutilated and cannibalized many of his victims.

**MURDER: San Diego, Calif.** Charles Henderson, top salesman for the local Coca-Cola bottling plant, was reported missing. He had been killed by male prostitute Matthew MacDonald, who had reportedly murdered several others in a long criminal career. MacDonald would be sentenced to life in prison for this murder in 1996.

*February 15*

**SEXUAL HARASSMENT/ASSAULT: Washington, D.C.** Admiral Frank Kelso, who reportedly tried to cover up his involvement in the notorious Navy Tailhook convention in Las Vegas in 1991, announced his early retirement from the Navy.

*February 17*

**MURDER: Osceola National Forest, Fla.** William Chistopher Paul and Lauren Kevin Cole murdered camper John Timothy Edwards and raped his 21-year-old sister, who was tied to a tree and also marked for murder, but she managed to escape and later identify the slayers of her brother. Paul and Cole were later sent to prison for life.

**OBSTRUCTING JUSTICE/TAX EVASION: Washington, D.C.** Catalina Vasquez Villapando, a former U.S. treasurer, pleaded guilty to obstructing the investigation and influence peddling at the U.S. Department of Housing and Urban Development (HUD) during the 1980s. Vasquez Villapando was the twelfth person to be convicted or plead guilty in connection with the widespread HUD scandal.

*February 19:*

**TERRORIST ATTACK: Assiut, Egypt** Polish and Taiwanese tourists were injured when the Egyptian train on which they were traveling was attacked by terrorists.

*February 21:*

**ESPIONAGE: Alexandria, Va.** CIA analyst Aldridge Hazen Ames, and his wife Maria del Rosario Casas Ames, were arrested by FBI agents and jailed, charged with espionage. It will later be revealed that Ames had served the Soviets for years as a well-placed mole, selling U.S. secrets to the Russians for millions of dollars, as well as identifying to Soviet spymasters at least nine U.S. spies behind the iron curtain, all of whom were arrested and liquidated.

*February 23:*

**MURDER: Oahu, Hawaii** Kototome Fujita, a millionaire clairvoyant, was found murdered in her posh penthouse apartment which had been set afire by her killer.

**TERRORIST ATTACK: Assiut, Egypt.** Terrorist exploded a bomb aboard an Egyptian train, injuring six tourists—two Germans, two Australians and two New Zealanders.

*February 25*

**MASS MURDER: Hebron, West Bank** Dr. Baruch Goldstein, an American citizen who had become a Jewish settler, walked into the a mosque and shrine known as the Cave of the Patriarchs and, using an automatic rifle, fired indiscriminately into a crowd of worshippers, killing 29 and wounding another 150 persons. Three more people were trampled to death when the crowd panicked. Goldstein was overpowered by Palestinians and beaten to death. Goldstein had been a supporter of the militant Rabbi Meir Kahane, who had been assassinated in New York City in 1990 and who may have committed the massacre in revenge for the Kahane killing.

*February 26*

**MANSLAUGHTER/WEAPONS VIOLATIONS: Waco, Texas** Eleven members of the Branch Davidian cult were tried on various charges. All were found not guilty of murder in the deaths of four federal agents during a February 1993 assault on the Branch Davidian compound, but five cult members were found guilty of aiding and abetting the voluntary manslaughter of federal officers and two members were found guilty of weapons charges.

*March 3*

**MURDER/JAIL ESCAPE: Alachua County, Fla.** While awaiting trial for the murder of Gina Langevin and wounding Jena Hull in 1993, Richard Anthony Meissner escaped the county jail.

*March 4:*

**BOMBING: New York, N.Y.** Four Islamic terrorists found responsible for bombing the World Trade Center on February 26, 1993, were sent to prison for life. The four terrorist killers were Mohammed Salameh, Ahmad Ajaj, Nidal Ayyad and Mahmud Abouhalima. Six more terrorists, including Ramzi Ahmed Yousef, mastermind of the bombing, would later be convicted and sent to prison.

**TERRORIST ATTACK, Nile River, Egypt** Terrorists along the bank of the Nile fired upon a tourist cruiser going down river. A German woman was injured and later died of her wounds.

*March 5*

**WHITEWATER: Washington, D.C.** White House counsel Bernard Nussbaum resigned in a furor over a controversial meeting he and Hillary Clinton and others had had with Roger Altman, a secretary of the U.S. Department of the Treasury, who had advised Clinton on what the department might do relating to the Whitewater investigation. Nussbaum had been severely criticized for removing Whitewater-related papers from the offices of Clinton counsel Vincent Foster who had reportedly committed suicide in 1993.

*March 7:*

**TERRORIST ATTACK: Southern Egypt** Terrorists attacked a tourist train and wounded 11 Egyptians.

*March 7-15*

**MURDER: Bophuthatswana** Whites and blacks battled over elections and dozens were murdered in the political chaos.

*March 10*

**MURDER: Elgin, Ill.** Millionaire Edward Lyng was convicted of stabbing his wife to death in 1977 and was sent to prison for 65 years.

*March 14*

**SEXUAL HARASSMENT/Washington, D.C.** Senator Robert Packwood dropped his court battle to prevent a Senate subcommittee from gaining access to his diaries which purportedly revealed his sexual harassment of female federal employees.

*March 16*

**ASSAULT: Portland, Ore.** Figure skater Tonya Harding pleaded guilty in helping to cover up the plot to injure her competitor Nancy Kerrigan. She acknowledged having conspired with her former husband Jeff Gillooly, and her former bodyguard, Shawn Eckhardt, to conceal from investigators what she knew about the assault. Harding was fined $100,000 and court costs and she agreed to establish a $50,000 fund for the Special Olympics and perform 500 hours of community service. She also agreed to resign from the U.S. Figure Skating Association, which brought an end to her amateur career.

*March 21*

**ASSAULT/Portland, Ore.** Shawn Eckhardt, Tonya Harding's former bodyguard, was arrested with two other men and indicted for the January 6 attack on figure skater Nancy Kerrigan.

*March 23*

**ASSASSINATION: Tijuana, Mexico** Luis Donaldo Colosio Murrieta, the leading candidate of the ruling Institutional Revolutionary Party for the president of Mexico (handpicked in 1993 by President Carlos Salinas de Gortari) was shot in the head by a gunman identified as Mario Aburto Martinez, who was immediately held by police.

*March 25:*

**WRONGFUL DEATH: Boston, Mass.** A thirteen-member SWAT team, part of Boston's Police Drug Control unit, broke into the second-floor apartment of Rev. Accelyne Williams in the city's drug-ridden Dorchester section. Believing the apartment was a center for drugs and illegal weapons, officers chased the terrified Williams into a bedroom where he suffered cardiac arrest. The raiding officers had been misinformed, it was later learned, as to the actual apartment housing drugs and weapons and had stormed into Williams' apartment in mistake. Williams' death later brought an $18 million lawsuit from Mrs. Williams. The city settled for $1 million.

*March 30*

**CAPTURE/Waldo, Fla.** Escaped prisoner Richard Anthony Meissner, who was accused of murdering Gina Langevin and wounding her roommate, Jena Hull in 1993 in Gainesville, was recaptured, found hiding in a trailer.

**MURDER: Oahu, Hawaii** Raita Fukusaku was indicted for the murder of millionaire Kototome Fujita and the kidnapping-murder of her son Goro Fujita in a botched effort to collect a $20,000 ransom. He would be convicted and sent to prison for life in 1995.

*April 8*

**POLITICAL CORRUPTION: Tokyo, Japan** Prime Minister Morihiro Hosokawa, who had been elected in August 1993 on an anti-corruption platform, resigned his office after it was disclosed that he had profited illegally from a 100 million yen loan from a trucking firm in 1982.

**SUICIDE: Seattle, Wash.** Kurt Cobain, 27, lead singer of the rock group Nirvana, committed suicide at his home, after years of struggling with drug addiction.

*April 11:*

**MURDER: Schaumburg, Ill.** Neal Allen visited the residence of his boss, John Ebeling, 52, and began to quarrel. Allen and Ebeling fought and Allen stabbed his boss forty times, killing him. He later called police, claiming self defense. In a controversial 1996 verdict, a jury would free Allen.

*April 19*

**ASSAULT: Los Angeles, Calif.** Rodney King, who had been savagely beaten by LAPD officers in 1991, an attack recorded on video tape and later shown to shocked national TV audiences, was awarded $3,816,535.45 by a U.S. federal jury. (King had turned down a pretrial settlement offer of $1.5 million.)

*April 27*

**EXECUTION: Greensville Correctional Center, Va.** Timothy Spencer, convicted of murdering four women in 1987, became the first person executed who had been convicted almost exclusively on DNA evidence.

**KIDNAPPING/MURDER: Lake City, Fla.** Carmen Gabriella Gayheart, 23, was kidnapped from a shopping center parking lot by two escaped convicts, Richard Eugene Hamilton and Anthony Floyd Wainwright, who later shot her to death. Both men were recaptured and later sentenced to death for killing Gayheart.

*April 28:*

**ESPIONAGE: Washington, D.C.** Convicted turncoat spy Aldridge Ames, who worked for the CIA for years and provided the Soviets with secrets and the identification of U.S. agents in Russia, pleaded guilty to spying for the Soviet Union and Russian, and was sentenced to life in prison. He would spend twenty-one months in solitary confinement before being released into the prison's general population.

*May 4*

**VANDALISM: Singapore** Michael Fay, an 18-year-old American living in Singapore with his mother and stepfather, had been found guilty of vandalism in 1993—he had gone on a spray-painting spree, randomly decorating cars and walls—and had been sentenced to 4 months in prison, a $2,250 fine and he was to received a six-stroke caning. Singapore's low crime rate was attributed to its severe punishments, according to officials, but human rights groups protested the caning on the naked buttocks with a rattan cane, a painful and humiliating punishment that invariably drew blood and left permanent scars. President Clinton appealed the canning, but his plea was rejected this date. The canning was reduced to four strokes, however, and was administered to Fay on May 5, 1994.

*May 6*

**SEXUAL HARASSMENT: Little Rock, Ark.** Paula Corbin Jones filed a sexual harassment suit against President

Bill Clinton, claiming that Clinton, then governor of Arkansas, had made unwanted sexual advances during a meeting with her in an Arkansas hotel room in 1991. Jones demanded a $700,000 settlement from Clinton and an apology from him and Danny Ferguson, an Arkansas state trooper who had reportedly taken Jones to the hotel room to see Clinton.

### May 10

**NUCLEAR THEFT: Munich, Germany** Police discovered 5.6 grams of pure plutonium-239 in the garage of a professional criminal linked to the KGB and Bulgarian terrorists. Officials believed that the nuclear fuel was to be used by terrorists for the construction of a nuclear bomb.

### May 18

**MURDER: Charleston, S.C.** In an effort to locate Ann Lafayette, his estranged girlfriend, James Earl Reed shot Lafayette's parents to death in their home, killing Joseph Lafayette, 51 and his 46-year-old wife Barbara Ann. Reed would be convicted of these murders and sentenced to death in 1996.

### May 20

**MURDER/RAPE: Orange, Calif.** Leanora Wong, 23, was picked up in a bar by a man who was later identified as Edward Patrick Morgan, who later raped and then beat Wong to death.

### May 22

**MURDER: Eagle Vale, Australia** Ivan Robert Marko Milat, one of Australia's worst serial killers, was arrested at his home, charged with killing seven backpackers in the Belanglo State Forest, from 1991 through 1993.

**MURDER: Quantico, Va.** Deborah L. Emerey, 39, was strangled to death and her body was found floating in the Potomac River. Her killer was later identified as Melvin Irving Shifflett, who was charged with the murder in July 1995 while he was already serving a long prison term for another rape-killing. He was convicted of the Emerey slaying in 1996 and given a life term.

### May 24

**MURDER/RAPE: Quincy, Calif.** Edward Patrick Morgan, wanted in the slaying of Leanora Wong, was tracked down and captured by police. He would be convicted and sentenced to death in 1996 for killing Wong.

### May 31

**EMBEZZLEMENT/TAMPERING WITH A WITNESS: Washington, D.C.** Representative Daniel Rostenkowski (D., Ill.), was indicted on 17 felony counts, charging that from 1971 to 1992, Rostenkowski, chairman of the House Ways and Means Committee, and one of the most powerful men in America, had put 14 persons on his payroll who did little or no work, of embezzling $50,000 from the House Post Office, tampering with a witness in the investigation and improperly charged $40,000 in gifts to friends to his congressional expense account.

### June 1

**MURDER: National City, Calif.** Kenneth Freeman was convicted of the 1992 murders his parents in order to inherit their lucrative business and was sentenced to life in prison.

### June 6

**JUDICIARY: Washington, D.C.** The U.S. Supreme Court unanimously ruled that prison inmates attacked by other prisoners should be facilitated in proving that jail officials had been negligent in preventing these attacks.

### June 10

**SEXUAL HARASSMENT: Little Rock, Ark.** State trooper Danny Ferguson filed a denial that he had arranged a May 1991 assignation between Bill Clinton, then governor of Arkansas, and the unwitting Paul Corbin Jones, who claimed that she had been hoodwinked into meeting Clinton in a hotel room where he exposed his privates to her and attempted to sexually molest her. Ferguson claimed that Jones had offered to become Clinton's mistress and had given her phone number to him to pass on to Clinton.

### June 12

**MURDER: Los Angeles, Calif.** Nicole Brown Simpson, the former wife of TV actor and former football star, O.J. Simpson (they were divorced in 1992), along with Ronald Goldman, were slashed to death outside of Mrs. Simpson's Brentwood condominium. The bodies were found early the following morning. O.J. Simpson, who lived two miles away, had left by plane for Chicago after the estimated time of the murders.

**WHITEWATER: Washington, D.C.** Special counsel Robert Fiske took the depositions of President Bill Clinton and his wife, Hillary Rodham Clinton, at the White House, regarding their involvement in the Whitewater real estate scandal. This was the first time a sitting president had responded directly to questions in a legal case relating to his official conduct, and the first time a first lady had given testimony regarding her own conduct in such matters.

### June 13

**MURDER: Los Angeles, Calif.** After being informed by phone of his ex-wife's murder, O.J. Simpson returned to Los Angeles and was questioned by police.

**NUCLEAR THEFT: Bavaria** German police seized 800 milligrams of highly enriched uranium (HEU) which had been smuggled from Prague, Czechoslovakia.

### June 16

**MURDER: Los Angeles, Calif.** O.J. Simpson attended the funeral of his ex-wife, Nicole Brown Simpson, who, along with her friend Ronald Goldman, had been stabbed to death on the night of June 12. Accompanying Simpson at the funeral were his two small children from his marriage with the slain woman.

## June 17

**DISORDERLY CONDUCT: Pensacola, Fla.** Paul Hill, an anti-abortion activist, was arrested for yelling at women entering an abortion clinic. Hill would kill an abortion doctor and another man in July.

**MANSLAUGHTER/WEAPONS VIOLATIONS: Waco, Texas** Judge Walter Smith sentenced five Branch Davidian cult members to 10 years in prison each for aiding and abetting the voluntary manslaughter of federal officers and 30 years on weapons charges. Three other cult members received lesser terms on other charges.

**MURDER: Los Angeles, Calif.** Police issued an arrest warrant for O.J. Simpson, charging him with two counts of murder in the deaths of his former wife, Nicole Brown Simpson and Ronald Goldman. Simpson reneged on a promise to surrender himself and reportedly attempted to flee the country. Police tracked him down on a Los Angeles freeway in a Ford Bronco driven by his friend Al Cowlings, who, by cellular phone, informed officers following in many squad cars that Simpson had a gun to his head and might commit suicide if the police stopped the car. The slow 60-mile pursuit was televised nationally from overhead TV news station helicopters and gripped a huge national viewing audience. Simpson was allowed to slowly return to his home where he sat in the car for more than an hour before surrendering to police. Fake whiskers, along with considerable cash was found in the car, leading police to believe that Simpson had originally intended to flee the country in disguise, evidence that was never introduced into his later murder trial.

## June 20

**MURDER: Los Angeles, Calif.** A plea of not guilty was entered by O.J. Simpson in the murders of his former wife, Nicole Brown Simpson, and her friend, Ronald Goldman, both slashed to death late on the night of June 12.

## June 21

**VANDALISM: Singapore** Michael Fay, the 18-year-old American who had been caned on May 5, 1994, for committing acts of vandalism in 1993, and whose severe punishment had created a worldwide uproar among human rights groups, was released from prison. He was returned to the U.S. on June 22.

## June 23

**MURDER: Brooksville, S.C.** Amy Frink, 20, left her Shallotte, S.C. home to visit her sister in North Myrtle Beach, but failed to arrive. Her naked body was found alongside a lonely road the next day. Her car was found abandoned seven miles away. Frink had been sexually molested, beaten, then stabbed to death and run over by her own car. In July 1998, John Gamble, a prisoner at the Essex County Jail in East Orange, N.J., was charged with the Frink killing, as was John Paul Counts of Ocala, Fla.

## June 27

**PRESIDENTIAL IMMUNITY AGAINST PROSECUTION: Little Rock, Ark.** Robert Bennett, President Bill Clinton's lawyer, filed motions in federal district court that argued for the immunity of Clinton against the sexual harassment lawsuit brought by Paula Corbin Jones and in the Whitewater scandal, saying that presidents were entitled to immunity during their terms to assure that their attention would not be diverted from their constitutional duties.

## June 30

**ASSAULT: Portland, Ore.** Figure skater Tonya Harding was informed that the U.S. Figure Skating Association (USFSA) had taken away her 1994 national championship. Harding had previously pleaded guilty to a conspiracy charge involving the assault on her rival, Nancy Kerrigan. After Kerrigan's debilitating injury, Harding had won the title. The USFSA concluded that Harding had "prior knowledge" of the attack. Harding was also banned from USFSA ranks for life. Four men had confessed to having roles in the assault on Kerrigan.

**JUDICIARY: Washington, D.C.** The U.S. Supreme Court upheld the right of a federal district judge to issue a stay of execution for death-row prisoners who had exhausted their state appeals but who wished to obtain legal representation to pursue a federal appeal, in a 5-4 vote, Justice Blackmun writing the majority opinion.

**MURDER: Virginia Beach, Va.** After robbing the Witchduck Inn, Michael D. Clagett strolled down the bar and shot and killed the owner and three customers, a savage robbery-murder that resulted in Clagett receiving a death sentence in 1996.

**WHITEWATER: Washington, D.C.** Special counsel Robert Fiske reported that he had found no corruption between White House aides and Roger Altman, a secretary of the Treasury who had met with them to discuss the possible outcome of an investigation into the collapse of the Madison Guaranty Savings and Loan in Arkansas by the Resolution Trust Corp. Fiske also stated that he believed that the July 1993 death of former White House aide Vincent Foster had been a suicide, a statement that did not put to rest the widespread rumors that Foster had been murdered to silence him in matters involving the Whitewater scandal.

## July 2

**ABUSE OF POWER/VIOLATION OF CITIZENS' RIGHTS: Tirana, Albania** Ramiz Alia, the last Communist president of Albania who had been forced from office in 1992 by Democratic forces, was convicted of abuse of power and violation of citizens' rights. Alia was sentenced to 9 years in prison. Nine other Albanian leaders, all members of the former Communist regime, had been convicted of similar offenses and imprisoned.

## July 3

**ATTEMPTED ASSAULT: Waucapa County, Wis.** A woman riding a bicycle was sideswiped by a car driven by a man who stopped and got out, making a menacing move toward her before being frightened off by another car. The woman described a car which was later identified as being owned by David Spanbauer, who had killed 12-year-old Cora Jones only a short distance from where the woman was knocked from her bike.

*July 4*

**ATTEMPTED RAPE: Oklahoma City, Okla.** Franklin Delano Floyd, a convicted child molester and escaped convict, attempted to rape a woman whose apartment he was painting, but was interrupted by the woman's boyfriend, who beat him up. Floyd posted bond and was placed in a half-way house, but he then kidnapped a teacher and child from Choctaw, Oklahoma, school and, for this crime was later sent to prison.

*July 6*

**MURDER: Bloomington, Minn.** Linda Larson was found raped and murdered by her husband. Her slayer, David Spaeth, a long-haired unemployed laborer, was later convicted and sent to prison.

**MURDER: Los Angeles, Calif.** At a pretrial hearing policemen testified that they had gone over a fence on O.J. Simpson's property on the night of the murders of his former wife, Nicole Brown Simpson, and her friend, Ronald Goldman, and that they had found a bloodstain on his van which was parked outside of his estate.

*July 7*

**MURDER: Los Angeles, Calif.** Municipal Court Judge Kathleen Kennedy-Powell denied a motion by the defense in the O.J. Simpson case to suppress evidence police officers had obtained during their search of Simpson's estate.

*July 8*

**MURDER: LosAngeles, Calif.** Judge Kathleen Kennedy-Powell stated that there was "ample evidence to establish strong suspicion of the guilt" of O.J. Simpson in the slaying deaths of Simpson's former wife, Nicole Brown Simpson, and her friend, Ronald Goldman, and she ordered that Simpson stand trial on two counts of first-degree murder.

*July 9*

**MURDER/SEXUAL MOLESTATION: Antigo, Wis.** The body of 12-year-old Cora Jones was found beneath some brush in a ditch; she had been raped and strangled to death. Serial rapist-killer David E. Spanbauer would later admit to this killing.

*July 10*

**MURDER: Orlando, Fla.** Shopkeeper Betty Shea was found stabbed to death by a pair of scissors in the back room of her boutique, her cash, credit and bank cards taken. Her killer, Jerry Dale Bobbitt, would later be caught and tried for her murder.

*July 18*

**BOMBING: Buenos Aires, Argentina** A powerful car bomb exploded near a building housing Jewish organizations, killing more than 100 persons.

*July 22*

**MURDER: Los Angeles, Calif.** O.J. Simpson was arraigned on two counts of murder in the slaying deaths of his former wife, Nicole Brown Simpson and her friend Ronald Goldman. Simpson stated that he was "absolutely 100% not guilty."

*July 26*

**BOMBING: London, England** A bomb exploded near the Israeli embassy which injured more than a dozen people.

**WHITEWATER: Washington, D.C.** The House Banking Committee began an investigation into the ties between Bill and Hillary Clinton and the failed Madison Guaranty S&L in Arkansas, that firm's association with the Whitewater land development scheme, in which the Clintons were reported partners, and the alleged improprieties on the part of Roger Altman, a secretary of the Treasury and chief of the Resolution Trust Corporation which was investigating these matters.

*July 27*

**BOMBING: London England** A bomb exploded at an Israeli fund-raising office. Five persons were injured.

*July 28*

**CRIME LEGISLATION: Washington, D.C.** The Senate-House approved a $30.2 billion crime legislation bill that included the hiring of 100,000 new police officers over a six-year period and the building of new state prisons. Backed by the Clinton administration, the cost of the bill would be covered by the elimination of 250,000 federal jobs over a six-year-period. The bill expanded the death penalty to apply to 60 types of crimes and banned 19 types of semiautomatic assault rifles. The bill also contained a popular "three-strikes, you're out" provision, whereby anyone convicted of a federal felony who had two previous serious felony convictions would receive an automatic lifetime prison sentence. Added provisions included the allowing of accusations of past sexual offense to be introduced in federal criminal trials and that a requirement be established whereby communities were notified when a convicted sex offender moved there.

*July 29*

**CHILD MOLESTATION/MURDER: Hamilton Township, N.J.** Jesse Timmendequas, a paroled child molester, enticed 7-year-old Megan Kanka into his home, across the street from Kanka's, to see a puppy. Once inside, Timmendequas molested and choked the little girl to death, later hiding her body in a park. Police were led to the body by the killer, who was sentenced to death in 1997. The girl's death caused a national outcry against child molesters and led to the establishment of Megan's Law wherein all convicted child molesters were identified to their communities.

**MURDER: Pensacola, Fla.** Dr. John Bayard Britton, who performed abortions, and his escort, James Barret, were shot to death, and Britton's wife, June, was wounded, by Paul Hill, an outspoken anti-abortion activist. Hill was arrested.

**WHITEWATER: Washington, D.C.** The Senate Banking Committee began an investigation into Whitewater and the involvement of the Clintons in this land development scheme, along with other Arkansas financial institutions.

### July 30

**MURDER: Pensacola, Fla.** Anti-abortion activist Paul Hill, who had slain two men and wounded a woman outside an abortion clinic the previous day, was charged with two counts of murder, which Hill termed "justifiable homicide."

### August 2

**MURDER: Orlando, Fla.** Felicia Hawkins, 34, was found murdered in her boutique, killed on the same street where another shop owner, 53-year-old Betty Shea, had been killed three weeks earlier. Hawkins had been robbed and her killer, Jerry Dale Bobbitt, a male prostitute, would be sent to prison for life in 1996.

### August 3

**EXECUTION: Varner, Ark.** Three men—Hoyt Clines, Darryl Richley and James Holmes—were executed by lethal injection about an hour apart. All three men had been convicted of murdering the same man in 1981.

### August 5

**MURDER: Phoenix, Ariz.** Wealthy Dr. Dale Bertsch, 64, convicted of murdering his ex-wife, Virginia Depper, so that he would no longer have to pay her alimony, was sentenced to 25 years to life.

**WHITEWATER: Washington, D.C.** A panel of 3 federal judges named Kenneth Starr, who had been solicitor general under President George Bush, as the new independent counsel to investigate Whitewater and other matters having to do with President Bill Clinton and his wife Hillary. Starr replaced Robert Fiske as independent counsel; the decision to replace Fiske by the judges was based on their belief that Fiske was technically an appointee of the administration.

### August 10

**NUCLEAR THEFT: Munich, Germany** Police intercepted at the airport a suitcase shipped from Moscow, one containing lithium-6 and nuclear fuel which, according to officials, were intended for terrorists planning on building a nuclear bomb.

### August 11

**MURDER: Nichols, S.C.** Rev. George Williams was killed by an intruder who stabbed him 19 times. In February 1995, not far from where Williams had been killed, Barbara Windham disappeared from her Marion County home. Luther Turner, a convicted murderer who had been paroled just before these two incidents was later convicted of murdering Williams and Windham and was given two life terms.

### August 14

**TERRORISM: Khartoum, Sudan** Illich Ramirez Sanchez, the international terrorist known as "Carlos," and "The Jackal," was seized by French agents and taken back to France on August 15, 1994, to stand trial for many murders and terrorist acts. French Interior Minister Charles Psqua said that Ramirez Sanchez had claimed to have murdered 83 persons.

### August 17

**WHITEWATER: Washington, D.C.** Many members of Congress criticized Roger Altman, a deputy secretary of the Treasury who had met with Hillary Clinton and other White House aides in a controversial conference to discuss Whitewater and other matters while a division of the Treasury Department was investigating these matters. Altman's response was to resign his position.

### August 19

**SOLICITATION OF CHILD PORNOGRAPHY/ HAVING SEX WITH A MINOR: Chicago, Ill.** Melvin Reynolds, a representative in the U.S. House, was indicted on twenty counts, including witness tampering, solicitation of child pornography and having sex with a minor. Reynolds would be convicted and sentenced to five years in prison in October 1995.

### August 21

**CRIME LEGISLATION: Washington, D.C.** The House of Representatives passed the $30 billion crime bill, 235-195.

### August 22

**MURDER: Iowa County, Wis.** The body of 10-year-old Ronelle Eichstedt, who had been kidnapped from her Ripon, Wis., home, was found raped and strangled. Serial rapist-killer David E. Spanbauer would later admit to this killing.

### August 25

**CRIME LEGISLATION: Washington, D.C.** The U.S. Senate passed the $30 billion crime bill, 61-38.

### August 26:

**TERRORIST ATTACK: Southern Egypt** Terrorists attacked a tourist bus, killing a Spanish boy.

### August 28

**MURDER: Chicago, Ill.** After shooting three teenagers, one of them fatally, Robert "Yummy" Sandifer, a member of the Black Disciples street gang (whose right forearm was tattooed like all members with "BDN III"), was identified by one of the victims and a police dragnet ensued for Sandifer's capture.

### August 31

**MURDER: Myrtle Beach, S.C.** Firefighters extinguishing a blaze in a vacant lot found the partly burned body of Holly Frazier, who had been murdered. Her killers, Michael Moshoures and Keith Yarborough, crack cocaine addicts, pleaded guilty to the murder in 1995 and were sent to prison.

*September 1*

**MURDER: Chicago, Ill.** Leaders of the Black Disciples, knowing police were looking for one of their members, Robert "Yummy" Sandifer, who had shot three teenagers a few days earlier, ordered Sandifer's execution, fearing that if he were picked up, he would implicate them in the August 28 shootings. Two brothers, Craig and Derrick Hardaway, who had been members of the Disciples since the age of ten, were ordered to execute Sandifer. They located their fellow gang member and pretended to drive him to safety, but took him to a pedestrian tunnel at 108th Street and Dauphin Avenue on Chicago's South Side and there Craig Hardaway reportedly fired two bullets into Sandifer's head, killing him. His body was found by police two hours later. Both Hardaway brothers were later convicted of the killing.

*September 2*

**MURDER: Prices Corner, Del.** Sandra Dee Long was trapped inside her burning apartment and burned to death before rescuers could reach her. Brian D. Steckel later confessed that he had attacked the woman and after she fought with him, he set the apartment on fire, causing her death. Steckel was convicted and sentenced to death for this heinous crime.

*September 8*

**MURDER: Ojito Frios, N.M.** Henry Santillanes, a ranch caretaker, shot and killed neighboring rancher Charles Pacheco, and, while awaiting trial, hatched a bizarre murder plot to have his teenage son, Victor Maestas, kill his former wife for insurance money in order to get an expensive lawyer to free him from the murder charge involving Pacheco.

*September 12*

**MURDER: Warwickshire, England** Carol Wardell, manager of Woolwich Building Society in Nuneaton, was reported missing, and the company safe looted. Wardell's body was later found along a highway. Her husband, Gordon Wardell, was found bound in his home, telling police a fantastic story of home invaders who kidnapped his wife, then presumably forced her to open the company safe and later killed her. Police broke down Wardell's story and he was later convicted of the robbery-murder and sent to prison for life.

*September 13*

**RAPE: Dhekelia, Cyprus** Three off-duty British soldiers—Allan Ford, Justin Fowler and Geoff Pernell—knocked a couple from a motorbike, and abducted the woman, Louise Jensen, whom they gang raped and murdered. All three would later be sent to prison for life.

*September 15*

**MURDER: Fayetteville, N.C.** Philip Edward Wilkinson, a former soldier stationed at Fort Bragg, N.C., who had been convicted of murdering Judy Faulk Hudson and her two children, was sentenced to death.

*September 16*

**CRIMINAL POLLUTION: Anchorage, Alaska** In the largest assessment of punitive damages in a pollution case, a federal jury hit Exxon Corp. with $5 billion in punitive damages to be paid to 34,000 fishermen and natives whose livelihoods had been damaged by the massive 1989 oil spill from the *Exxon Valdez*. Joseph Hazelwood, the ship's captain, was ordered by the jury to pay $5,000 in punitive damages.

*September 24*

**MURDER/KIDNAPPING: Arlington, Texas** Lisa Rene, a 16-year-old student was kidnapped from her home and raped, then murdered by a group of men led by Orlando Hall, who was later sentenced to death for the crime.

*September 26*

**MURDER: Los Angeles, Calif.** The first phase of the murder trial of O.J. Simpson on two counts of murder, got underway with the process of jury selection, anticipated as a protracted process because of the difficulty in finding jurors who were not familiar with the notorious case.

*September 26-30*

**THEFT: Charlotte, N.C.** Ivy James Lay, a switch engineer for MCI, along with many confederates across the county, following a final week of investigation, was arrested and charged with stealing more than 100,000 telephone calling card numbers that were used to make more than $50 million worth of long distance calls, the largest fraud of its kind to date. The card numbers were sold to other computer hackers who, in turn, sold them throughout the U.S. and Europe. Lay, a hacker known as "Knightshadow," reportedly created software which trapped calling card numbers from several local and long-distance carriers which came across MCI's switching equipment.

*September 27*

**TERRORIST ATTACK: Hurghada, Egypt** Terrorist gunmen attacked a resort on the Red Sea, killing a German tourist and wounding another.

*September 28:*

**ASSASSINATION: Mexico City, Mexico** Francisco Ruiz Massieu, secretary-general of Mexico's ruling Institutional Revolutionary Party (PRI), was shot and killed outside a hotel by assassin Daniel Aguilar.

**ESPIONAGE: Washington, D.C.** Inspector General Frederick Hitz told the U.S. House Intelligence Committee that 11 present and retired members of the CIA would be sent letters of reprimand because they bore indirect responsibility for the actions of CIA turncoat Aldrich Hazen Ames, who worked as a Soviet spy and identified a reported 55 American agents to the KGB. Hitz stated that no CIA member would be demoted or dismissed. Several committee members stated that the letters of reprimand did not constitute enough discipline.

*September 29*

**BURGLARY/MURDER: College Station, Texas** Ronald Scott Shamburger repeatedly broke into the apartment of Lori Ann Baker, a girl with whom he was obsessed. When Baker awoke on the night of September 29, Shamburger shot her between the eyes, killing her. He was later sentenced to death.

### October 3

**POLITICAL CORRUPTION: Washington, D.C.** Amid accusations that he had taken expensive gifts from Tyson Foods of Arkansas, the country's largest poultry supplier, Michael Espy, Secretary of Agriculture, resigned. Espy, at the time he reportedly received the gifts (his girlfriend had received an academic scholarship from Tyson), was accused of delaying implementation of regulations that might affect Tyson.

### October 4

**DRUGS: San Juan, Puerto Rico** Drug enforcement agents arrested Charles Galletti in his penthouse apartment, charged with drug dealing and money laundering. Galletti had reportedly run one of the largest heroin distributing rings in New York for two decades, before "retiring" to a lavish lifestyle in Puerto Rico, where he oversaw several legitimate business ventures such as restaurants, auto repair shops, a hair salon, a recycling plant and a San Juan firm that provided meals and hangar space for international airlines. At one point during his heroin heyday, prosecutors said, Galletti took $800,000-a-month in profits. He lived lavishly, having condos in Manhattan and Puerto Rico. He had a house at 26 Katherine Court on Staten Island which had five bathrooms, a $100,000 swimming pool with a waterfall and a jacuzzi that could hold 20 people. The day after Galletti was arrested, five of his associates were arrested in New York City.

**PARENTAL KIDNAPPING: New York** David Tomassi was located and charged with kidnapping his two sons from their mother's Michigan home in 1983. Despite pleas from the two boys, who were by then in college and testified that their father had been a kind and loving parent, Tomassi was sentenced to one year in jail by Judge David Breck in Pontiac, Mich., who sought to make an example of anyone kidnapping their children.

### October 5

**MASS MURDER/SUICIDE: Cheiry, Switzerland** Police found 23 members of the Order of the Solar Temple dead, most being bound and bearing bullet wounds, in a house that served as the cult's temple. Investigators found 25 more bodies in three chalets in Granges-sur-Salvan. Among the dead in the chalets were cult founders Joseph di Mambro, and Luc Jouret, a Belgian homeopathic doctor. On the same day and the following morning, Canadian police found 5 more dead cult members in Morin Heights, Quebec, in two neighboring buildings. In all instances, the houses and chalets had been set on fire by timing devices. Jouret had founded the cult in 1984, teaching a ragtag philosophy of Christianity, spiritualism and astrological gobbledygook.

### October 7

**MURDER: Ellis County, Texas** Jason Massey, who bragged to friends that he had tortured more than 200 animals to death and wrote in his diary that he wanted to become a serial killer that would surpass the slayings of California's Richard Ramirez, the infamous "Night Stalker," was convicted of murdering to teenagers, Christina Benjamin, whom he had beheaded, and her stepbrother James King.

### October 10

**MURDER/RAPE: Houston, Texas** Deborah Jean McCormick, owner of a flower shop, was found in her shop, raped and murdered. Her killer was later identified as Michael Griffith, one-time sheriff's deputy, who was later convicted and sentenced to death.

### October 12

**MURDER: Ellis County, Texas** Jason Massey, convicted of brutally murdering two teenagers, was sentenced to death.

### October 14

**KIDNAPPING/MURDER: West Bank, Israel** Israeli commandos attacked a Hamas hideout where Palestinian terrorists were holding Cpl. Nahshon Waxman, a kidnapped Israeli soldier. They found Waxman shot to death and, during the raid, three of the Hamas kidnappers were killed, along with an Israeli soldier. Hamas had kidnapped Waxman and were holding him hostage in an attempt to disrupt the PLO-Israeli peace accords.

### October 19

**BOMBING: Tel Aviv, Israel** A bomb exploded on board a bus and killed more than 20 people, the worst terrorist attack in Israel since 1978. The bombing was attributed to a Palestinian terrorist group.

### October 21

**ESPIONAGE: Washington, D.C.** Rosario Ames, the wife of convicted CIA spy Aldrich Hazen Ames, was sentenced to 63 months in prison for collaborating with her turncoat husband. The couple reportedly received as much as $2.5 million or more from Soviet spymasters for turning over information on CIA operations and for identifying American agents behind the Iron Curtain during the Cold War.

### October 23

**ARSON: Portland, Ore.** Shelley Shannon, of Grants Pass, Ore., was charged with setting a series of fires at abortion clinics in Oregon, Idaho, Nevada and northern California. She was also charged with using acid to create stink bombs at clinics in Chico, Calif., and in Reno, Nevada. Shannon was already imprisoned for shooting a Kansas abortion doctor.

**TERRORIST ATTACK: Egypt** Muslim terrorists attacked a tourist vehicle, killing one British sightseer and wounding three others, including the Egyptian driver.

### October 25

**MURDER: Union, S.C.** Susan Smith, a young mother, told police that an armed black man had taken her car and her two sons who were inside, 3-year-old Michael and 14-month-old Alexander. Smith, and her estranged husband, David, who believed her story, appeared on network TV shows, such as "Today," appealing to the alleged kidnapper to return her sons.

*October 29*

**ATTEMPTED ASSASSINATION/ASSAULT/DESTRUCTION OF FEDERAL PROPERTY: Washington, D.C.** Francisco Duran, a resident of Colorado Springs, Colo. stood on Pennsylvania Avenue and opened fire on the White House with an assault rifle, spraying 27 rounds at the building. President Clinton was inside at the time, watching a football game on TV. Duran was overpowered by bystanders and was charged with attempted assassination, assaulting a federal officer, possession of a firearm as a convicted felon, and the destruction of federal property.

*October 31*

**ASSASSINATION: Mexico City, Mexico** In a non-jury trial, Mario Aburto Martinez, a 23-year-old factory worker, who had confessed to killing Mexican presidential candidate Luis Donaldo Colosio in March, was convicted of the murder and sentenced to 42 years in prison. Rumors had it that even though Colosio had been the hand-picked successor to then President Carlos Salinas, Raul Salinas, the president's brother, had been behind the Colosio assassination.

*November 1*

**MURDER: Winston-Salem, N.C.** Richard Wall, a cabdriver, was found mortally wounded and witnesses saw Russell William Tucker leaving the scene. Tucker later shot and killed Maurice T. Williams, a security guard at a store, and woundinded two policemen who tried to apprehend him. Tucker was later sentenced to death.

*November 3*

**MURDER: Union, S.C.** After appearing on TV for several many days to appeal the return of her two small sons, Susan Smith was arrested and charged with the murder of 3-year-old Michael Smith and 14-month-old Alexander Smith. Police reported that with her two sons strapped inside the car to safety seats, Smith drove her car to the edge of a lake outside of Union, S.C., and allowed it to roll into the water, drowning her boys. Police stated that Smith's motive for the murders was the fact that she had broken up with a wealthy young man in Union who told her that he wanted nothing to do with the children. Smith would later be sent to prison for life.

*November 9*

**MURDER: Missouri City, Texas** Farah Fratta was shot to death in the garage of her home, a killing, police later determined, that was the result of a murder contract ordered by the victim's ex-husband, Robert Fratta, who wanted to avoid alimony payments. Howard Guidry, the actual gunman, Joseph Andrew Prystach, a go-between, and Fratta, were sentenced to death for the murder in 1996.

*November 10*

**KIDNAPPING: Louisville, Ky.** Kidnapper Franklin Delano Floyd was arrested by FBI agents and charged with kidnapping teacher James Davis and Michael Hughes, a child, and was returned for trial to Oklahoma.

*November 14*

**BURGLARY: Combined Locks, Wis.** A burglar breaking into a home was interrupted by the owner who chased the overweight man to his car, tackling him and holding him for police. The burglar was David E. Spanbauer, who later admitted to murdering 12-year-old Cora Jones and 10-year-old Ronelle Eichstedt. He would be convicted of these murders, as well as the slaying of 21-year-old Trudi Jeschke, of Appleton, Wis., and, on December 19, 1994, receive three life terms.

*November 16*

**MURDER: Cornwells Heights, Pa.** Charles Burella was found bludgeoned to death, his throat slit, and his cash and credit cards stolen. Police tracked down Maureen Hollie, who had been taken in by Burella when she and her 3 children were destitute, and Hollie's lover, Carl Gueknecht, to a Las Vegas motel. Both were convicted of the killing and sent to prison for life.

*November 17*

**ATTEMPTED ASSASSINATION: Washington, D.C.** Francisco Duran, who had sprayed the White House with bullets from a semiautomatic assault weapon on October 29, was indicted on a charge of attempting to assassinate President Bill Clinton, along with 10 other felony charges. Duran's co-workers in Colorado Springs, Colo., told investigators that he had intended to "take out" the president.

*November 18*

**MURDER: London, England** Richard Elsey and James Petrolini, convicted of the January 14, 1994, murder of Egyptian businessman Mohammed el-Sayed, were sentenced to life in prison.

*November 21:*

**MURDER: Chicago, Ill.** Police searching for two missing children, found an 11-year-old girl gagged and bound, and the body of 7-year-old Kenneth Wright in the second-floor apartment of Stanley Head, who admitted the murder but would later be held mentally incompetent to stand trial.

*November 22:*

**ROBBERY: Jonesboro, Ark.** Larry Archer, an unemployed factory worker, robbed the MidSouth Bank of Jonesboro of $4,150; he was promptly tracked down and arrested, saying that he had robbed the bank in order to feed his starving family and pay his wife's medical bills—she was dying of ovarian cancer.

*November 23*

**MURDER: Washington, D.C.** Murder suspect Bennie L. Lawson, whose car had been impounded by local police, was released after questioning regarding a recent triple murder. Lawson, angry over losing his car, returned to the station some hours later and fired on officers, killing a policeman and two FBI agents, before he himself was shot to death.

*November 27*

**MURDER: Pensacola, Fla.** Paul Hill, an anti-abortion

activist who had been convicted of the July 29, 1994 murder of Dr. John Bayard Britton and James Barrett, was sentenced to death.

### November 28

**CARJACKING: Chicago, Ill.** In what was the first prosecution in northern Illinois under the federal carjacking law, Juan A. Jackson, Jr., a 25-year-old man from County Club Hills, was sentenced to the maximum term of 9 years for a 1993 carjacking on Chicago's South Side. Jackson and another man, Deon Howard, following the carjacking, used the auto in a failed bank robbery at the Thornridge State Bank in South Holland. Howard was sent to prison for seven years. Jackson received a stiffer sentence because he tried to drive the stolen car over a security officer after the failed bank robbery.

**MURDER: Portage, Wis.** Serial killer Jeffrey Dahmer and another inmate, Jesse Anderson, were bludgeoned to death as they cleaned out a latrine in the correctional facility where they were housed by Christopher Scarver, a Negro prisoner who sought racial revenge in killing Dahmer because he thought the serial killer's victims had been mostly black.

### November 29

**THEFT: New York, N.Y.** Police reported the existence of a female pickpocket they called "The Sexy Bandit," a beautiful woman dressed in a tight-fitting nurse's uniform who got rides from well-to-do middle-aged or elderly men on the desperate plea that she had to get somewhere in a hurry. Once inside of the car, the woman fondled the men suggestively, distracting them and filching their wallets. The female bandit had been successfully working this racket since 1988, according to police, averaging $500 on each occasion. The woman bandit worked Long Island, the five New York boroughs, upstate Westchester County and northern New Jersey.

### December 1

**ATTEMPTED MURDER: DuPage County, Ill.** Wynne Superson, a 40-year-old physician from Bolingbrook, Ill., was convicted of attempted murder and faced a 40-year prison term. Superson had earlier hired a hitman to kill her ex-husband, wealthy Leon Malachinski, also a doctor and resident of Naperville, Ill., who had gotten custody of their two children after an ugly divorce. Superson simply wanted the children back, she told the so-called hitman, offering him $8,000 to murder her ex-spouse. The hitman turned out to be an undercover Naperville police officer who testified against Superson in court.

**DRUGS: New York, N.Y.** Drug agents arrested a man when he attempted to claim a sheepdog which had been shipped from Colombia to John F. Kennedy International Airport. The dog had been carrying five pounds of cocaine in condoms in its belly, which were surgically removed by a veterinarian. (The dog survived, the drug smuggler went to prison.)

**PRISON RELEASE: Schlewig-Holstein, Germany** Irmgard Moeller, one of the worst terrorists in Germany, who had been found responsible for the deaths of three American soldiers in 1972, was released from prison over the objections of the U.S. Department of State.

### December 4

**ROBBERY/MURDER: Port-Au-Prince, Haiti** Francois College, a 25-year-old American bodyguard to U.S. Ambassador William Swing, was arrested and charged with the November 10, 1993 fatal shootings of two Haitian embassy employees and the wounding of another as they left a bank with a $60,000 payroll. College had reportedly taken to the hills following the robbery attempt and was captured after wanted posters for his arrest were circulated among the native villages.

### December 5

**FRAUD: Orange County, Calif.** Robert Citron, treasurer and fund manager for Orange County, California, one of the wealthiest counties in the U.S., resigned his position. Citron would later be charged with fraud in the mishandling of public funds.

**WHITEWATER: Little Rock, Ark.** Property appraiser Robert Palmer pleaded guilty in a U.S. District Court to having conspired in falsifying documents regarding loans made by the failed Madison Guaranty S&L in the 1980s. Palmer agreed to cooperate with Kenneth Starr, the independent counsel investigating the Whitewater land development scandal.

### December 6

**BANKRUPTCY/FRAUD: Orange County, Calif.** In one of the largest bankruptcy filings in U.S. history, Orange County, which lost more than $1.5 billion in bad investments made by its treasurer, Robert Citron, filed for relief. Citron had risked huge amounts of county funds by buying derivatives linked to the success of fixed income securities and depended on falling interest rates. When rates rose, Citron's investments collapsed. Citron would later be charged with fraud.

**WHITEWATER: Little Rock, Ark.** Webster Hubbell, close friend and adviser to President Bill Clinton, pleaded guilty to embezzling more than $400,000 from the Rose Law Firm in Little Rock (where Hillary Rodham Clinton worked at the time as an attorney), and its clients, by submitting false vouchers and bills. Hubbell also pleaded guilty to mail fraud and tax evasion and promised to cooperate in the Whitewater investigation.

### December 8

**MURDER: Los Angeles, Calif.** The jury selection in the O.J. Simpson trial was completed, with eight women and four men selected for the main jury, a racial makeup that was heavily black—eight blacks, two Hispanics, one person identified as half white and half native American and one white. Simpson, accused of slashing to death his ex-wife Nicole Brown Simpson and her friend, Ronald Goldman, in June, would, through his main lawyer, Johnnie Cochrane, repeatedly play the race card in a desperate attempt to win an acquittal.

### December 10-11

**BOMBING: North Caldwell, N.J.** Advertising executive Thomas Mosser went into his kitchen late on December 10 and opened a packaged delivered to his home and was killed when a bomb contained within exploded. This terrorist act was later attributed to the Unabomber, who was subsequently identified as Theodore Kaczynski. Mosser had recently been promoted to a managerial level by Young and Rubicam Inc.

*December 14*
   **NUCLEAR THEFT: Prague, Czechoslovakia** Investigators discovered 2.72 kilos of highly enriched uranium (HEU) in the back seat of a parked car. Police will find another kilo of the same shipment in January 1995, all of this fuel, officials believed, intended for delivery to terrorists who planned to construct a nuclear bomb.

*December 21*
   **BOMBING: New York, N.Y.** Edward Leary, a 50-year-old former computer analyst, firebombed a subway train in the Wall Street district. He will be convicted in 1996 of two subway train bombings which injured fifty persons, including himself, and be sent to prison for 31 to 94 years.

*December 22*
   **CIVIL RIGHTS VIOLATION: New York, N.Y.** Francis Livoti, a NYPD officer, attempted to arrest 29-year-old Antony Baez who had had been playing football with his three brothers and who had twice kicked a football into Livoti's squad car. When Baez struggled with him, Livoti reportedly choked Baez to death. He was later convicted of violating Baez's civil rights.

*December 25*
   **MURDER: Middle River, Md.** Crack cocaine addict James Thomas Wood called police to confess that he had killed Rev. Samuel Nathaniel Booth, in what Wood described as a "robbery gone wrong." Wood would later go to prison for life.

*December 29*
   **MURDER: Fort Worth, Texas** Michael Johnson, who had been acquitted of stabbing a teacher to death in 1989, was himself murdered, shot in the back by street gang members when he refused to give them his athletic jacket.

*December 30*
   **MURDER: Brookline, Mass.** John C. Salvi III, an anti-abortion activist, entered the Planned Parenthood Clinic and shot to death Shannon Lowney, a 25-year-old receptionist, and wounded three others. He then drove to another clinic and killed Lee Ann Nichols, a 38-year-old receptionist, and wounded two others. Salvi would be given two life terms for these killings and commit suicide in his cell in 1996.

# 1995

*January 1*
   **MURDER: Birmingham, England** Frederick West was found dead in his cell at Winson Green Prison, where he was awaiting trial. West stood accused of murdering as many as twelve women, having buried nine bodies in the back yard of his home in Gloucester, England.
   **MURDER: Roanoke, Va.** Following an argument over which branch of service was the toughest, Army or Marines,

Robert Michael May, 27, shot and killed 5 persons, the three men who had been arguing with him at a New Year's Eve party, and two women who witnessed the shootings. According to police, who arrested May a short time later, the killer stated: "I don't know what to say. I shot five people. It was like ... a nightmare. I wish I could just wake up and go on to work and it would be all over."

*January 12*
   **TERRORIST ATTACK, Southern Egypt** Muslim terrorists opened fire on an Egyptian train, wounding two Argentine tourists and four Egyptians.

*January 16*
   **MURDER: Chicago, Ill.** Angelo Roberts, one of the leaders of the Four Corner Hustlers street gang, was found murdered in a car trunk. His killers were not apprehended.

*January 18*
   **MURDER: Los Angeles, Calif.** Judge Lance Ito ruled that the jury hearing the case of O.J. Simpson, accused of murdering his ex-wife, Nicole Brown Simpson and Ronald Goldman, could hear allegations that Simpson had some times attacked and beaten his former wife during their marriage.

*January 20*
   **MURDER: Canton, China** One of the country's worst serial killers, Luo Shubiao, found guilty of murdering at least twelve women, was executed by firing squad.

*January 22*
   **BOMBING: Israel** Two Palestinian terrorists killed 18 Israeli soldiers, a civilian and themselves by exploding a bomb outside a military camp in central Israel. The bomb also injured 65 others. The Islamic Jihad terrorist group claimed responsibility for the bombing.

*January 24*
   **MURDER: Los Angeles, Calif.** Deputy District Attorneys Marcia Clark, the chief prosecutor, and Christopher Darden, told a jury in their opening remarks on the O.J. Simpson case that "a trail of blood" would establish the fact that Simpson had brutally murdered his former wife, Nicole Brown Simpson, and her friend, Ronald Goldman. Darden went on to state that Simpson "killed her because he couldn't have her. And if he couldn't have her, he didn't want anyone else to have her."

*January 25*
   **MURDER: Los Angeles, Calif.** Johnnie Cochran, Jr., chief defense counsel for O.J. Simpson (leading what was called the "Dream Team" of defense attorneys which included Robert Shapiro and F. Lee Bailey), told a jury that there was no "trail of blood" linking his client to the murders of Simpson's former wife, Nicole Brown Simpson and her friend Ronald Goldman, and he stated that the police investigation had been sloppy and that evidence might even have been planted by police. Cochran's defense from the beginning was to attack the police and the evidence. Cochran surprised the prosecution by

saying that he would call 14 witnesses not earlier identified who would support his claims. He would call two witnesses and the credibility of both would be effectively challenged.

### January 30

**BOMBING: Algiers, Algeria** A car bomb exploded on a crowded street, killing 42 persons and injuring another 300 people.

### January 31

**SHOOTING: Los Angeles, Calif.** William Masters, who claimed that he was out for a late-night stroll around his neighborhood while carrying an unlicensed gun in his fanny pack, spotted two men were spray-painting graffiti on a cement column beneath a Hollywood freeway. According to what he later told police, Masters wrote down the license number of the car in which the two men riding. When the men, Cesar Rene Arce, 18, and David Hillo, 20, approached him, demanding the slip of paper and his wallet while one of them brandished a screwdriver, Masters pulled out his gun, shooting the pair, killing Arce and wounding Hillo. The surviving Hillo later claimed that he and Arce never threatened Masters and ran from him when he began firing. Both men had been shot in the back. Los Angeles County District Attorney Gil Garcetti ruled the shooting an act of "justifiable self-defense," and refused to file charges against Masters. His act was heralded as courageous on the part of many, while others likened Masters to the New York vigilante Bernhard Goetz, who shot four black muggers on a subway.

### February 3

**MURDER: Los Angeles, Calif.** Prosecutors had Denise Brown, sister of the slain Nicole Brown Simpson, testify that O.J. Simpson had repeatedly abused Nicole when she was his wife, stating that, on one occasion, the former football player had thrown his wife against a wall and then out of the house.

### February 6

**TERRORISM: New York, N.Y.** Twelve Islamic terrorists were tried in federal court for the 1993 bombing of the World Trade Center. Siddig Ibrahim Siddig Ali, one of the accused, changed his plea from not guilty to guilty, saying that Sheik Omar Abdel Rahman, one of his fellow defendants and nominal leader of the group, and for whom he had served as bodyguard and translator, had played a significant role in the bombing conspiracy. In addition to the UN building in New York, Siddig Ali told the court, the terrorists planned to destroy an FBI office, a bridge and two tunnels.

### February 7

**BOMBING: Islamabad, Pakistan** Ramzi Ahmed Yousef, the Islamic terrorist who masterminded the 1993 World Trade Center bombing was arrested. He will be flown to New York the following day to face trial.

**BANK FRAUD: Troutdale/Gresham, Ore.** David and Terry Gallagher, of Troutdale and Danny Ballow, of Gresham, were arrested by Secret Service agents and charged with defrauding $346,770 from 48 automatic teller machines in several Oregon towns in November 1994. According to agents, the trio used a single stolen ATM card to defraud machines owned by the Oregon Telco Credit Union. Though normally limited to $200 on each withdrawal, the thieves were able to empty out machines because of a computer software glitch, covering the withdrawals by making $820,500 in bogus deposits. The thieves, five in all, made 724 withdrawals in several cities in a 100-mile path through northwest Oregon.

**TERRORISM: West Bank** Israeli officials stated that they were seeking Yehiya Ayash, 28, the mastermind behind many bombings that had killed 55 Israelis and wounded another 200 within the last year. A former engineering student, Ayash was known as Al-Muhandis, "the Engineer," and was hailed as a hero by many Palestinians, although to Israelis, he was nothing more than a cold-blooded killer.

### February 7-8

**MURDER: Los Angeles, Calif.** Prosecutors in the O.J. Simpson murder trial sought to establish the time of the murders of Nicole Brown Simpson and Ronald Goldman at approximately 10:15 p.m., enough time for Simpson to have slashed his victims to death, returned to his own home two miles away, clean the blood from himself, and then take a limousine to the airport to travel to Chicago on a midnight flight.

### February 8

**BOMBING: Rochester, N.Y.** Earl Figley, 57, pleaded guilty to mailing bombs which killed five persons on December 28, 1993, in exchange for a 20-year prison term at a minimum-security prison, and also agreed to testify against his alleged accomplice, Michael Stevens, 54, who reportedly sought vengeance against the family of his girlfriend, Brenda Lazore Chevere because he thought family members were attempting to turn her against him. Chevere remained uninjured by the bombs, but the explosions killed her mother, stepfather and sister, along with two others.

### February 9

**BOMBING: New York, N.Y.** Ramzi Ahmed Yousef, the mastermind behind the World Trade Center bombing in 1993, pled not guilty to 11 counts in federal court.

**RAPE MESSAGE ON INTERNET: Ann Arbor, Mich.** Jake Baker, 20, a student at the University of Michigan, was arrested by FBI agents in the offices of his attorney, David Cahill, and charged with transmitting a threat to injure on the Internet. Baker, according to officials, had posted a message in which he talked of his intent to tie up, rape and sexually torture a female classmate, whose actual name was used by Baker. Held without bond, Baker told reporters that he had a right to post the message.

### February 10

**ATTEMPTED BOMBING/MURDER: Detroit, Mich.** Lawrence Dell, 44, an autoworker, was arrested and charged with mailing a bomb to his estranged wife on February 7; Charlene Dell, 33, who had filed for divorce, suffered shrapnel wounds and burns over half her body when she opened a package sent to her by mail.

*February 15*

**SEXUAL CHILD ABUSE: Andover, Md.** Three Roman Catholic priests, Rev. Alphonsus Smith, 70, Rev. Edward Pritchard, 50, and Rev. Edward Hartel, 58, were arrested and charged with repeated acts of sexual child abuse dating back to 1975.

*February 16*

**MURDER: Tizi Ouzo, Algeria** Islamic terrorists killed Nabila Djahnine, a prominent 35-year-old architect and feminist who led a group called The Cry of Women. The murder followed the on-going pattern to suppress women in Algeria, killing female intellectuals and unveiled women, to support rigid fundamentalist Islamic traditions.

*February 17*

**MURDER: Nassau County, N.Y.** Colin Ferguson, a Jamaican immigrant who had slaughtered six white persons on a commuter train in December 1993—he was black, his crime motivated by racial hatred for whites—was convicted.

**SERIAL KILLER DIES: Durham, England** Michael Lupo, a serial killer who strangled four homosexuals in revenge for contracting HIV, the virus that causes AIDS, died in Frankland Prison from an AIDS-related illness. Lupo, an Italian-born fashion boutique owner, was imprisoned for life after confessing to an eight-week killing spree in 1986, when he strangled four homosexuals in derelict buildings after having sex with them and then mutilating their bodies. Lupo had also attacked two other homosexuals who survived.

*February 26*

**MURDER: Salisbury Township, Pa.** Bryan and David Freeman, two brutish skinheads, stabbed and bludgeoned their parents to death, along with their 11-year-old younger brother. They would both go to prison for life.

*February 28*

**ILLEGAL CAMPAIGN FUNDING: Little Rock, Ark.** A federal grand jury indicted Neal Ainley, former president of the Perry County Bank in Perry, Ark., charging that Ainley had attempted to conceal two 1990 transactions in which the bank transferred $52,500 in cash to a representative of the campaign of then Gov. Bill Clinton.

*March 1*

**BANK FRAUD: Little Rock, Ark.** As part of Kenneth Starr's ongoing investigation into Whitewater, banker Neal Ainley was indicted on charges on hiding cash withdrawals from the IRS.

*March 3*

**FAILURE TO DECLARE FUNDS: Newark, N.J.** Mario Ruiz Massieu, brother of presidential candidate Jose Francisco Ruiz Massieu, who had been assassinated in Mexico in 1994, was arrested at the airport and charged with failure to declare the more than $45,000 he was carrying.

*March 5*

**MURDER: Highland County, Fla.** John N. Canning, the pastor of a church, was arrested for murdering two of his parishioners and looting their bank accounts. Canning would be sent to prison for life.

*March 6*

**OBSTRUCTING JUSTICE: Mexico City, Mexico** Mario Ruiz Massieu was charged with obstructing the investigation into the 1994 assassination of his brother, Jose Francisco Ruiz Massieu.

*March 6-7*

**MURDER: Los Angeles, Calif.** LAPD Detective Tom Lange testified for the prosecution in the O.J. Simpson murder case, that he believed that the same knife had been used in the killings of Nicole Brown Simpson and Ronald Goldman. In cross-examination, defense counsel Johnnie Cochran suggested that the murders had been drug-related and that 2 killers had been involved, but he failed to support these inferences with any evidence.

*March 9*

**MURDER: Los Angeles, Calif.** LAPD Detective Mark Fuhrman stated that he had discovered a bloody glove that matched another glove found at the crime scene outside O.J. Simpson's home on the night of the murders. Defense counsel F. Lee Bailey suggested that Fuhrman could have planted the glove, but he had no evidence to support such a suggestion, let alone a motive for Furhman to have done such a thing.

*March 14*

**MURDER: Los Angeles, Calif.** LAPD Detective Mark Fuhrman, testifying at the murder trial of O.J. Simpson, denied he had made racist statements, a remark later proven to be untrue.

*March 17*

**EXECUTION: Singapore** Flor Contemplacion, a 42-year-old Filipino maid, who had been convicted of murdering another Filipino maid, Della Maga, and a toddler, in 1991, was hanged, an execution which caused an uproar in the Philippines and compelled Singapore to withdraw its ambassador.

**MURDER: Los Angeles, Calif.** LAPD Detective Philip Vannatter testified at the murder trial of O.J. Simpson, that a knuckle on Simpson's left middle finger had been cut and was swollen when examined a day after the murders. Vannatter stated that he believed this wound was responsible for the trails of blood found at the homes of Nicole Brown Simpson and O.J. Simpson. Simpson had earlier told police that he had cut the finger on the day of the murders, though he could not recall how, and that he cut it again in Chicago when he broke a glass after receiving a call from the LAPD informing him of his wife's death.

*March 20*

**NERVE GAS ATTACK: Tokyo, Japan** Members of the Aum Shinri Kyo, a fanatical terrorist organization, planted several packages inside the subway system which emitted a powerful nerve gas (sarin, which can paralyze the central nervous system and cause death). The nerve gas killed 12 persons and injured another 5,500 people. A massive police hunt ensued for the cult leaders.

### March 21

**WHITEWATER: Little Rock, Ark.** Charles Wade, one-time financial manager of Whitewater Development Corp., pleaded guilty in federal district court to 2 counts of fraud. The corporation had, at the time of these committed felonies, been owned in part by then Gov. Bill Clinton and his wife, Hillary Rodham Clinton, a partner in the Rose Law Firm, which handled many of the corporation's business affairs.

### March 22

**MURDER: Los Angeles, Calif.** Brian "Kato" Kaelin, a houseguest at the estate of O.J. Simpson who lived in a small cottage testified at Simpson's murder trial that on the night of the murders of Nicole Brown Simpson and Ronald Goldman, he had dinner with Simpson who told him that he was finished with his ex-wife, and that the two of them returned to Simpson's estate at 9:40 p.m, about 35 minutes before the estimated time the murders occurred. Kaelin stated that, at 10:40 p.m., he heard three loud thumps on the outside wall of the bedroom in his cottage. It was there, where a fence was close to the cottage that the bloody murder glove was reportedly found by LAPD Detective Fuhrman. It was later speculated that Simpson, after eating at a fast-food restaurant with Kaelin, had driven his Ford Bronco to his ex-wife's home, slashed her to death, along with Ronald Goldman, who, it was speculated, came upon the scene, then drove the Bronco back to his estate and entered the grounds by climbing over the back fence that bordered the cottage and that the "thumps" Kaelin had heard was Simpson, striking the cottage wall as he went over the fence.

**MURDER: Nassau County, N.Y.** Convicted black murderer Colin Ferguson—he had slain 6 whites on a commuter train in a burst of racial hatred, was sentenced to 200 years in prison.

**NERVE GAS ATTACK: Japan** Police raid 25 offices of the widespread cult, Aum Shinri Kyo, members of which had released deadly sarin nerve gas in the Tokyo subway system on March 20. Officers seized two tons of chemicals and compounds that could be used to make the sarin nerve gas, along with about $7 million in cash (the cult had raised more than $1 billion to fund its nefarious operations), and publications that predicted mass murders by poison gas.

### March 28

**MURDER: Los Angeles, Calif.** Allan Park, a clean-cut limousine driver, testified at O.J. Simpson's murder trial that he began searching for Simpson's address at 10:22, with instructions to pick up Simpson and drive him to Los Angeles Airport so that he could catch an 11:45 p.m. flight to Chicago. Park stated that he did not see Simpson's white Ford Bronco parked outside the Simpson estate, though the defense insisted that the Bronco was parked there all evening. Park said he rang Simpson's doorbell several times and got no response. He fur-

ther stated that at 10:56 p.m. he observed a black man—he could distinguish the man's features in the shadows—about six feet tall and weighing 200 pounds, go across the lawn and enter the house. Park said that 30 seconds after this man entered the house, he again rang the bell. Simpson responded, saying that he had not heard the earlier bells because he was sleeping. Park helped Simpson load his luggage into the limousine's trunk, but Simpson insisted upon carrying a small black bag; Kaelin also supported this statement.

### March 29

**MURDER: Los Angeles, Calif.** James Williams, a skycap at Los Angeles Airport, testified at O.J. Simpson's murder trial that Simpson boarded the plane for Chicago with only three pieces of luggage. This was two pieces less than what Park stated he had put into the limousine. Park said that while he was at the airport, he noticed a black duffel bag sitting atop a trash can with Simpson standing next to it. The prosecution theorized that the duffel bag contained that small black bag Simpson had insisted on carrying from his home and within that bag Simpson had secreted the murder weapon and his blood-soaked clothes. It was further speculated that Simpson either dumped the duffel bag and its incriminating evidence into the trash can at the Los Angeles Airport, or took it with him as a carry-on and, once in Chicago, disposed of the bag and the evidence.

**NERVE GAS ATTACK: Moscow, Russia** The offices of Aum Shinri Kyo were seized and records confiscated by police cooperating with Japanese authorities investigating the cult's involvement in the sarin gas attack in Tokyo's subway system on March 20. The cult claimed to have as many as 30,000 members in Russia alone.

### March 31

**MURDER: Corpus Christi, Texas** Selena Quintannila Perez, an enormously popular Mexican-American singer, was shot and killed by Yolanda Saldivar, who had headed the singer's fan clubs and had embezzled money from the club funds. Saldivar would later be sent to prison for life.

### April 2

**BOMBING: Gaza Strip** The Islamic Resistance Movement of Hamas exploded a bomb that killed 8 persons and wounded another 30 people. Police reported that the terrorists were assembling a bomb that went off by accident.

### April 4

**ATTEMPTED ASSASSINATION: Washington, D.C.** Francisco Duran, 26, of Colorado Springs, Colorado, was convicted of attempting to assassinate President Bill Clinton by firing several rounds from an assault rifle at the White House in October 1994.

**MURDER: Los Angeles, Calif.** Defense lawyer Barry Scheck in a relentless cross-examination of forensic expert Dennis Fung, originally testifying for the prosecution in the O.J. Simpson trial, got Fung to admit that he had not taken the blood samples but that a trainee had done so and that he himself, as he had earlier testified, had not taken a vial of blood out of O.J.

Simpson's home and put it into a police van. The implication was that the LAPD lab had managed its forensic work in a sloppy, irresponsible manner.

## April 5

**MURDER: Los Angeles, Calif.** Judge Lance Ito, presiding in the O.J. Simpson murder trial, dismissed juror Jeanette Harris, the 6th juror to be excused. Harris later told the press that the jury was already decided, one faction for guilt, the other for innocence. She further said that sheriff's deputies assigned to the jurors were encouraging racial discord.

## April 6

**MURDER: Little Lake Como, Fla.** Police charged Kinghamvong Phimmachack, a Laotian immigrant, with shooting to death his wife, mother-in-law and three young daughters on the night of April 3-4, 1995, and then turning a shotgun on himself. Phimmachack survived the blast.

## April 9

**BOMBINGS: Gaza Strip** Two suicide terrorists killed themselves, along with 7 Israeli soldiers and an American student, and wounded another 45 persons, mostly Israeli soldiers, after they detonated bombs. Both Hamas and Islamic Jihad took credit for the terrorist explosions.

## April 10

**TERRORISM: Jerusalem** PLO Chairman Yasir Arafat reportedly ordered a crackdown on radical Palestinians, and more than 300 were arrested. Of these, Arafat announced, one member of Islamic Jihad had been sentenced to 15 years in prison for recruiting young men to the terrorist organization and encouraging them to become suicide bombers. On the following day, PLO officials announced that a Palestinian clergyman had been given a similar sentence.

## April 11

**ART THEFT: Chicago, Ill.** Calvin Fitch, 35 and Anthony Smith, 34, pleaded innocent to a charge that they stole a painting by Pablo Picasso, the portrait of a man's head entitled "Tete," taken from the Richard Gray Gallery on January 3, 1994. The painting was recovered in the back seat of a car and was valued at $650,000.

## April 18

**MURDER: Brooklyn, N.Y.** Michael Burnett (AKA Michael Raymond), was arraigned on charges in federal court that he hired two men to murder Valerie Vassell, a 32-year-old bank teller who allegedly helped Burnett cash counterfeit checks, and, when the scheme was exposed, agreed to testify against him. Burnett/Raymond had reportedly survived many lengthy prison terms from various illegal schemes by obtaining immunity in exchange for testimony in organized crime cases. In 1971 Burnett received immunity from prosecution by testifying before Senator John McClellan's committee hearings on organized crime, while employing a pseudonym and while wearing a paper bag over his head.

**MURDER: Scottdale, Pa.** Paul Corvin, 61, was arrested and charged with killing one of two newborn infants he had sired with one of his two daughters in 1971.

## April 19

**BOMBING: Oklahoma City, Okla.** A powerful truck bomb exploded outside the Alfred P. Murrah federal building, slicing away half the nine-story building and killing 168 men, women and children, the worst terrorist attack in U.S. history. A short time later, 27-year-old Timothy McVeigh, who would become the prime suspect in the bombing, was arrested near Perry, Oklahoma, and charged with carrying a concealed weapon.

**MURDER: Starke, Fla.** Two Death Row inmates, Edwin B. Kaprat III, and Charlie Street, were stabbed to death at the Florida State Prison recreation yard, but no suspects were immediately charged. Guards only found the bloody home-made knives used to commit the murders. Kaprat and Street had both been sentenced to death for 1990 murders they committed separately.

## April 20

**MURDER: Camden, N.J.** Leslie Ann Nelson, a transsexual also known as Glen Nelson, opened fire with an AK-47 assault rifle on police officers and officials who appeared at her home in an attempt to search it for illegal weapons. Nelson reportedly shot and killed a policeman, a prosecutor's investigator and wounded another officer, before she/he was subdued and taken into custody.

## April 21

**BOMBING: Perry, Okla.** FBI agents charged Timothy McVeigh with blowing up the Murrah building in Oklahoma City on April 19. McVeigh's associate, Terry Nichols, was arrested the same day in Herington, Kansas, and charged with aiding McVeigh in blowing up the Murrah building.

**INCITING RACIAL HATRED: Karlsruhe, Germany** Gunter Deckert, leader of the neo-Nazi National Democratic Party, was sentenced to 2 years in prison, following a conviction on charges that he had incited racial hatred and denied the existence of the Holocaust and that he would publicly repeat his views. Deckert was convicted of organizing a 1991 lecture in which he and U.S. engineer Fred Leuchter insisted that it was impossible for the Nazis to have killed 6 million Jews in World War II concentration camps.

**MURDER: Scottsboro, Ala.** Frank Potts, a migrant farm worker, thought to have murdered as many as 15 persons in several states, was sentenced to life in prison for the 1989 murder of Robert Earl Jines, 19, whose body was unearthed on Potts' farm in northeastern Alabama. Potts was already serving a life term in Florida for sexually assaulting an 11-year-old girl.

## April 24

**BOMBING/MURDER: Sacramento, Calif.** Gilbert Murray, president of the California Forestry Association, was killed by a package bomb which was later determined to have been sent by the Unabomber (Theodore Kaczynski). Murray was the third and final fatality claimed by the Unabomber. Two dozen others were injured and maimed by bombs sent by the Unabomber since 1978.

**EXECUTIONS FOR GENOCIDE: Rwanda** Firing squads executed twenty-two Rwandans who were among the first to be convicted of participating in the Hutu-orchestrated genocidal slaughter of more than 500,000 persons in 1994, these victims being from the mostly minority Tutsi tribe.

**KIDNAPPING: Alem Paraiba, Brazil** Paula Zamboni, 13, was kidnapped outside of her school by five men and held for ransom. Her father was one of Brazil's biggest wholesalers.

**NERVE GAS ATTACK: Tokyo, Japan** Police located the hideout of Hideo Murai, one of the five top leaders of Aum Shinri Kyo, the terrorist cult responsible for the planting of nerve gas packages in the Tokyo subway system that killed 12 persons and injured another 5,500 on March 20, 1995. According to police, Murai acted as the cult's chemist who packaged the deadly sarin gas. As he was being escorted from the hideout, the 36-year-old Murai was fatally stabbed by Hiroyuki Yo, a 29-year-old South Korean, who was reportedly connected with the vast and secret criminal organization known as Yakusa.

### April 28

**MURDER: Littleton, Colo.** Albert L. Petrosky, 35, reportedly suffering marital problems, opened fire in the parking lot of a supermarket, killing three people, including his wife, 37-year-old Terry Petrosky, the store's deli manager, Dan Suazo, 39, the store manager, and Timothy Mossbrucker, a 36-year-old sheriff's deputy, as well as wounding a fourth person. Petrosky was charged with three counts of first-degree murder and one for assault.

**MURDER: Orlando, Fla.** Former boxer Timothy Anderson shot and killed his one-time fight promoter, Rick Parker, while the two met to discuss a project.

### April 29

**THEFT: Portland, Ore.** David Gallagher, one of five men who had looted many ATM cash machines with a stolen card, while on weekend release from jail, was attempting to return about $60,000 of the $346,770 he had helped to steal when he himself was held up by an armed robber, who stole the stolen money. The thief was caught and the stolen money returned.

### April 30

**PRISON ESCAPE: Santa Clarita, Calif.** Fourteen maximum-security prisoners broke out of the Peter J. Pitchess Honor Rancho Facility, 35 miles northwest of Los Angeles, situated between two national forests. Four of the men were almost immediately recaptured and the rest were later hunted down as hundreds of deputies joined the search.

### May 1-5

**MURDER: Los Angeles, Calif.** Gregory Matheson of the LAPD testified at O.J. Simpson's murder trial that any mishandling of evidence in the murders of Nicole Brown Simpson and Ronald Goldman would not have resulted in blood incorrectly matching that of the defendant or the victims.

### May 2

**EXECUTION: Bellefonte, Pa.** Keith Zettlemoyer, 39, who had begged the state to execute him because a brain disease was making his life "a living hell," and after 14 years of failed appeals, was put to death by lethal injection. Zettlemoyer had killed a friend in 1980 who had planned to testify against him in a robbery case. Zettlemoyer, executed at Rockview State Prison, was the first person put to death by Pennsylvania in 33 years.

**MURDER: Kingston, Jamaica** Noel Riley, a handicraft vendor, was convicted of murdering Norris Rayam in June 1994, after Rayam refused to buy his wares. Riley had forced his way into the Ocho Rios villa where Rayam and his wife Lisa were staying. Riley was sentenced to be hanged.

**WHITEWATER: Little Rock, Ark.** Banker Neal Ainley pleaded guilty to illegally transferring loans in 1990 to then Gov. Bill Clinton's campaign.

### May 4

**MURDER: Chicago, Ill** Michael Hodo, a 34-year-old bus boy who had been fired from his job at Army & Lou's restaurant, a Chicago landmark frequented by politicians and powerbrokers, and who had killed Fletcher Smith, the restaurant's co-owner, on October 3, 1994, because Smith would not re-hire him, was sentenced to 55 years in prison.

### May 10

**ASSAULT: Edmonton, Alberta, Canada** In the case against Marilyn Tan, charged with assaulting celebrity photographer Con Boland with HIV-infected blood, one of Tan's friends admitted that she helped Tan obtain the HIV-infected blood which was injected into Boland during a sado-masochistic sex party in 1992. Boland later tested HIV-positive.

**ASSASSINATION: Guadalajara, Mexico** Leonardo Larios Guzman was shot to death by four gunmen in a car as Guzman was leaving home to teach a law class at the a nearby university. Guzman had been one of the chief prosecutors who investigated the 1993 assassination of Catholic Cardinal Juan Jesus Posadas Ocampo.

**KIDNAPPING: Rio de Janeiro, Brazil** More than 40 picked police officers surrounded the hideout where five kidnappers, all Rio police officers, were holding 13-year-old Paula Zamboni for ransom. Three kidnappers were arrested and two escaped. Their hostage was returned to her businessman father unharmed.

**MURDER: Los Angeles, Calif.** Robin Cotton, an expert of Cellmark Diagnostics, testifying in the O.J. Simpson murder trial, showed a match between Simpson's blood and blood found at the scene of the murders of Simpson's ex-wife, Nicole Brown Simpson and Ronald Goldman.

### May 13

**JUDICIARY: Washington, D.C.** The U.S. Supreme Court ruled 8-1 that the federal government's prosecution in crack cocaine cases was not racially biased.

### May 15

**BOMBING/TERRORISM: New York, N. Y.** Kuwait-born Abdul Hakim Murad, 30, along with Ramzi Ahmed Yousef, who was separately convicted of masterminding the bombing of New York's World Trade Center in 1993, was sentenced to life imprisonment without parole and fined $250,000 by U.S. District Judge Kevin Duffy for planting a bomb that killed a passenger on a Philippines Airlines jet in 1994. Murad, a commercial pilot and a resident in Pakistan, plotted to destroy eleven U.S. airliners in 1995, after exploding the bomb on the Philippines plane, which, according to prosecutors, was a test run before launching the all-out terrorist bombings of American airliners.

**CONFESSIONS/GENOCIDE: Rwanda** More than 2,000 prisoners, mostly of the Hutu tribe, confessed to being part of the 1994 genocidal slaughter of more than 500,000 victims who were mostly from the minority Tutsi tribe. Under Rwandan law, defendants (other than the organizers of the genocidal killings) who confessed were eligible for reduced sentences such as life imprisonment. Rwandan Justice Secretary-General Gerard Gahima stated: "Some of them [who confessed] are tired of being in prison. Others know the possibility of being brought to justice is real. They saw the confessions to be in their best interest."

**NERVE GAS ATTACK: Tokyo, Japan** Police at a roadblock outside of the city apprehended Yoshihiro Inoue, head of "intelligence" for the murderer of Aum Shinri Kyo cult. Officers obtained Inoue's notebook which detailed timetables and numbers of passengers using Tokyo's three subway lines where the sarin gas was unleashed on March 20, 1995.

### May 16

**KIDNAPPING: Newark, N.J.** Glenn Harris, a 33-year-old teacher who took 15-year-old Christina Rosado on a cross-country odyssey of cheap motels, casinos and amusement parks, surrendered with his attorneys to the school where he worked and Rosado was a student. Harris was charged with kidnapping, although he claimed he had taken the child to protect her from parental child abuse.

**MURDER: Los Angles, Calif.** Gary Sims of the California Department of Justice testified at O.J. Simpson's murder trial that he had matched Ronald Goldman's blood to a stain on the glove found at O.J. Simpson's estate. The defense tried to suggest that the bloody glove was planted by police or that the DNA analysis was unreliable, a tactic maintained by Simpson's attorneys throughout the trial.

**NERVE GAS ATTACK: Mt. Fuji, Japan** Police and paramilitary units stormed the secret compound of Aum Shinri Kyo, hidden at the base of Japan's most resplendent mountain. Among those captured was the cult's leader, Shoko Asahara, who would later be sent to prison. Arrested with the cult leader were 40 other cultists who were charged with the Tokyo subway gas attack, as well as a June 1994 gas attack in Matsumoto which reportedly killed seven persons and injured 200 more.

**PROSTITUTION: Paris, France** Francesco Smalto, a successful Italian fashion designer, who was convicted of pimping, was ordered to pay a fine of $120,000. Smalto had sent call girls to Omar Bongo, president of Gabon, with clothing deliveries in 1992 and 1993. Gabon was Smalto's biggest customer, spending $600,000 a year with Smalto.

### May 17

**MURDER: Sunnyside, Wash.** Kenneth Arrasmith, a 44-year-old truck driver, shot and killed Ronald and Luella Bingham, for reportedly sexually molesting his daughter.

### May 20

**BOMBING: Kingman, Ariz.** Michael Fortier, a friend of Timothy McVeigh, had implicated McVeigh in the bombing of the federal building in Oklahoma City, Oklahoma, according to news reports. Reports had it that Fortier admitted that he had accompanied McVeigh prior to the bombing when they drove to Oklahoma City to inspect the federal building, McVeigh's bombing target.

### May 22

**JUDICIARY: Washington, D.C.** The U.S. Supreme Court, in a unanimous ruling, stated that, under normal circumstances, when police execute a search warrant, they are required to knock and announce their arrival before entering a house. Reasonable exceptions were thought to be imminent threat of violence or destruction of evidence.

### May 27

**MURDER: Antigua** John Earl Baughman, who had been acquitted of murdering his wife in 1985, took his new wife, Valerie, to the roof of a hotel where they were vacationing, and threw her off, Baughman was convicted and sentenced to death in 1996.

### June 3

**JUDICIARY: Washington, D.C.** The U.S. Supreme Court upheld the use of capital punishment by the military justice system.

### June 7

**TAX EVASION: Little Rock, Ark.** Gov. Jim Guy Tucker was indicted for conspiring to defraud the IRS and the Small Business Administration.

### June 9

**DRUGS: Colombia** Police arrested Cali drug cartel boss Gilberto Rodriguez Orejuela, who, according to U.S. officials, was responsible for smuggling 80 percent of all the cocaine into the U.S.

### June 10

**FRAUD: Havana, Cuba** Robert Vesco, U.S. financier who had defrauded stockholders of hundreds of millions of dollars and who had fled the U.S. in 1973, eventually seeking asylum in Cuba, was arrested for fraud in promoting a newly-developed drug Vesco claimed would cure AIDS, cancer and other deadly diseases.

**JUDICIARY: Washington, D.C.** The U.S. Supreme Court unanimously granted the police wide latitude in using an even minor traffic violation as a reason for stopping a vehicle and searching it for drugs.

*June 15*

**MURDER: Los Angeles, Calif.** Prosecutors asked O.J. Simpson, to try on the pair of gloves that had been entered into evidence, one reportedly found at the murder scene, the other at O.J. Simpson's estate. Simpson spread his fingers wide apart and appeared to struggle into the gloves which were the same brand and size of gloves that had been purchased for him at Bloomingdale's in New York City in 1990 by his then wife Nicole Brown Simpson. Simpson held up his hands, his fingers still spread wide to say twice: "too tight, too tight." The gloves appeared to fit, even though Simpson had awkwardly spread out his fingers in an obvious attempt to make it appear otherwise. Johnnie Cochrane seized upon his client's lame claim, droning to reporters later: "The gloves don't fit." He would later chant to the jury over and over again—"if they don't fit, you must acquit." The prosecution missed its opportunity to properly supervise the trying on of the gloves to prove to the jury that the murder gloves did fit the hands of O.J. Simpson.

*June 24*

**JUDICIARY: Washington, D.C.** The U.S. Supreme Court upheld the government's right to both seek criminal penalties against drug traffickers and to seize the same person's property in an 8-1 decision.

*June 26*

**ATTEMPTED ASSASSINATION: Addis Ababa, Ethiopia** Islamic terrorists fired on the limousine carrying Egyptian President Hosni Mubarak who was on a state visit. The attackers fired from rooftops, on the street and from a speeding Jeep, but they failed to injure the Egyptian leader. Two Ethiopian policemen were killed, along with two of the terrorists and many passersby were wounded.

**MURDER: Miami, Fla.** Rory Enrique Conde, known as the Tamiami Trail Strangler, confessed to murdering six prostitutes. He would later be sentenced to death.

*June 27*

**CONSPIRACY: Decatur, Ill.** FBI agents raided the offices of ADM, in search of evidence that some of its top executives were part of a conspiracy to fix prices.

*June 28*

**JUDICIARY: Washington, D.C.** The U.S. Supreme Court upheld a federal law restricting appeals by death-row inmates.

**TAX EVASION: Washington, D.C.** Webster Hubbell, former associate U.S. attorney general and close friend of Bill and Hillary Clinton, was sentenced to 21 months in prison for tax evasion and mail fraud. He was ordered to pay $135,000 in restitution. Hubbell, documents showed, had defrauded the Rose Law Firm, where Hillary Clinton once worked as a lawyer. Hubbell had embezzled $482,410 from 15 of the firm's clients and had failed to pay $143,747 on this income to IRS.

*June 29*

**ATTEMPTED ASSASSINATION: Washington, D.C.** Francisco Duran, convicted of attempting to assassinate Bill Clinton on April 4, 1995, was sentenced to 40 years in prison.

*July 12*

**MURDER: Los Angeles, Calif.** Robert Heidstra, a defense witness in the murder trial of O.J. Simpson, stated that he was walking his dog near the home of Nicole Brown Simpson and heard two men arguing about 11 p.m., a time period that would preclude Simpson's ability to murder his ex-wife and her friend and return to his estate in time to be driven to the airport. In cross-examination, however, Heidstra admitted that he had seen a white vehicle similar to Simpson's Ford Bronco leave the scene in a hurry about 10:40 p.m.

*July 16*

**HOSTAGES FREED: Iraq** William Barloon and David Daliberti, two defense contractors working in Kuwait and who had apparently crossed the Iraqi border in error and had been arrested, were released with considerable ceremony by dictator Saddam Hussein.

*July 17*

**MURDER: Washoe County, Nev.** Cable installer and one-time Boston cop, David Middleton, 34, was charged with murdering Katherine Powell, a 45-year-old teacher, and Thelma Davila, a 42-year-old porter at the Circus Hotel in Reno, Nev.

*July 22*

**MURDER: Union, S.C.** Susan Smith was found guilty of drowning her two young sons in a lake outside of the city by allowing her car to roll into the water with the boys locked inside.

*July 25*

**BOMBING: Paris, France** Algerian separatists, as part of a terrorist campaign, planted a bomb in a subway car of the metro system which exploded at the Latin Quarter stop, killing 7 people and wounding dozens more.

*July 27*

**CHILD MOLESTATION: Corsicana, Texas.** Catholic Bishop Charles Grahmann, who had been accused of waiting too long in stopping child molestation in his diocese at the hands of former priest Rudolph "Rudy" Kos, addressed parishioners during mass to apologize to the ten men who had been abused by Kos when they were boys. Stated Grahmann: "I want to look into the eyes of each of the victims and say to them from the most intimate part of my being that I am profoundly sorry." The ten men were not present during the mass. They had successfully sued the Catholic Diocese of Dallas, Texas, for $119.6 million.

**PRISON REVOLT: Wrightsville, Arkansas.** Fifteen inmates at the Wrightsville work farm seized two barracks after guards insisted on searching one prisoner for drugs. The prisoners barricaded themselves inside the barracks and held back guards attempting to enter for four hours. When guards broke into the barracks they quickly subdued the prisoners and placed them in cells. All would later be removed to maximum security prisons.

*July 28*

MURDER: Union, S.C. Susan Smith, who had been convicted of drowning her two small sons, was sentenced to life in prison.

*July 29*

MURDER: Cologne, Germany Leon Bor, an Israeli citizen, boarded a tourist bus and shot the driver, then held 26 passengers hostage. He randomly shot and killed an elderly woman who identified herself as a German citizen. After terrorizing the passengers for several hours, Bor was shot and killed by police.

*July 30*

MURDER: Fort Worth, Tex. In a wild shooting spree, John Leslie Wheat, 52, reportedly killed 18-month-old Lacey Anderson, her sister, 6-year-old Ashley Ochoa, and brother, Eddie Ochoa, 8, and also wounded the mother of the children, a Fort Worth policeman and two others.

*July 31*

MURDER: Framingham, Mass. Richard Rosenthal was arrested and charged with killing his wife. The mutilated body of Laura Rosenthal was found in the back yard of the couple's stately home. The victim had been slit with a butcher knife from the throat to her naval and her heart and lungs had been removed and impaled on an 18-inch stake in a nearby garden. According to police, Rosenthal told them his motivation for the savage killing: His wife had scolded him for burning the ziti. "I had an argument," Rosenthal was quoted as saying. "I overcooked the ziti."

*August 6*

DRUGS: Colombia Cali cartel drug boss Miguel Rodriguez Orejuela, whose brother had been arrested months earlier, was taken into custody, charged with shipping cocaine to Costa Rica. Since June 1995, 6 of the cartel's leaders had been arrested.

*August 7*

MURDER: Kankakee State Park, Ill. Christopher Meyer, 10, was abducted and murdered by Timothy Buss, who had a long record of child molestation. Buss would later be convicted of this killing and sentenced to death.

*August 10*

BOMBING: Oklahoma City, Okla. Michael Fortier, who had been implicated in the bombing of the federal building in Oklahoma City, pleaded guilty to transporting stolen firearms, making false statements to the FBI and failing to report a crime.

*August 11*

EXECUTION: Oklahoma Robert Breechen, who had been convicted of murdering a woman, overdosed on sedatives just before he was due to be executed. He was nevertheless revived by a prison physician and the execution was performed on schedule. When asked if this was an ironic gesture on the part of the state, Larry Field, director of Oklahoma's Corrections Department, stated: "Certainly, there's irony. But we're bound by the law, the same law he violated."

LAW ENFORCEMENT: Washington, D.C. FBI Director Louis Freeh suspended four Bureau officials, including agent Larry Potts, after it was disclosed that the Bureau either withheld or destroyed documents relating to the 1992 Ruby Ridge siege in Idaho in which three persons were killed.

*August 15*

WRONGFUL DEATH SETTLEMENT: Washington, D.C. The U.S. Department of Justice agreed to pay $3.1 million to Randall Weaver and his daughters, who had filed a $200 million wrongful death suit against the Department for the shooting deaths of Weaver's wife, Vicki, and son, Samuel, during the FBI's 1992 siege of Randall's cabin in Ruby Ridge, Idaho.

*August 16*

TERRORISM: Lyon-Paris, France An unexploded bomb was discovered on board a high-speed train. Forensic specialists lifted a fingerprint which identified Khaled Kelkal, an Algerian separatist leader and terrorist.

*August 17*

FRAUD: Little Rock, Ark. James McDougal and his ex-wife, Susan McDougal, were indicted by a federal grand jury for arranging fraudulent loans through Madison Guaranty S&L and investment firm, Capital Management Services, to fund business ventures such as the Whitewater Development Corp.

*August 22*

SEXUAL ASSAULT: Chicago, Ill. U.S. Representative Melvin Reynolds was convicted of sexual assault, sexual abuse, soliciting child pornography and obstructing justice. The married Reynolds had carried on an affair with an underage girl who had worked in his political campaign, as well as another underage girl.

*August 24*

ESPIONAGE: China Human rights activist Harry Wu, who had spent 19 years in Chinese prison camps and recorded myriad abuses, was found guilty of spying and expelled from China to the U.S., his adopted country.

*August 29*

BOMBING: Tbilisi, Georgia Eduard Shevardnadze, president of Georgia, escaped an assassination attempt when a terrorist bomb exploded close to his motorcade. Shevardnadze was slightly wounded.

*September 1*

MURDER: Toronto, Canada Paul Bernardo, one of the country's most brutal sex killers, was convicted of murdering of two underage girls. He would be sentenced to life in prison.

*September 6*

EXPULSION: Washington, D.C. The U.S. Senate Ethics Committee recommended 6-0 that Senator Robert

Packwood be expelled from the Senate after finding him guilty of sexual misconduct, influence peddling and obstruction of justice.

## September 11

**MURDER: Oswego, N.Y.** Waneta E. Hoyt was sentenced to 75 years to life in prison for murdering five of her infant children from 1965 to 1971.

## September 19

**TERRORISM: Washington, D.C.** On the recommendations of U.S. Attorney General Janet Reno and FBI Director Louis Freeh, the Washington *Post* published (as well as the New York *Times*) the 35,000-word manifesto which had been sent by the Unabomber (Theodore Kaczynski), in the hope that someone would recognize the writing style of the terrorist and identify him. The manifesto consisted of a rambling intellectual tirade which attacked the Industrial Revolution.

## September 20

**EXECUTION, Joliet, Illinois.** After many appeals and stays of execution, Charles Albanese (1937-1995) was put to death by lethal injection at the Stateville Correctional Center. Albanese had sustained his life for fourteen years in prison through the appeal process after having poisoned three people in his attempt to gain an inheritance.

## September 22

**MURDER: Houston, Texas** Claudette Kibbie, 23, was arrested and charged with murder after she told police that she had killed 3 of her five children since she first gave birth at the age of 13.

**MURDER: Los Angeles, Calif.** Defense counsel in the O.J. Simpson murder trial refused to allow their client to take the stand in his own defense, but Judge Lance Ito allowed Simpson to make a short statement with the jury absent, a statement in which he insisted that he was innocent in the murders of his ex-wife, Nicole Brown Simpson and Ronald Goldman.

## September 24

**MASS MURDER: Cuers, France** Eric Borel, a 16-year-old French youth, entered this village with a hunting rifle and terrorized the town for several hours as he hunted down residents, randomly killing 9 persons and wounding another 8 people before killing himself when he ran out of ammunition.

## September 26

**MURDER: Wilson County, Texas** Dennis Bagwell, 31, was arrested and charged with murdering his mother, 47-year-old Leona McBee and three other females.

## September 28

**MURDER: Pontiac, Mich.** Kenneth Tranchida, 42, was charged with the murder of 23-year-old Tina Biggar, an undergraduate psychology student at Oakland University. (Biggar's body was found on September 21, behind a house where one of Tranchida's relatives once lived.) Biggar was reportedly working as a prostitute in order to gather research on the profession and she had met Tranchida, a drifter, through an escort service. Upon his arrest, police reported Tranchida as saying: "I'm guilty."

**TERRORISM: Lyon, France** French police and commandos located a hideout of Algerian separatists led by Khaled Kelkal, shooting it out with the terrorists, wounding one of three who were captured. Kelkal escaped.

## September 30

**TERRORISM: Lyon, France** French commandos hunting for terrorist Khaled Kelkal found him waiting at a bus stop five miles outside of town. Following a shootout, Kelkal was killed.

## October 1

**BOMBING: New York, N.Y.** Ten Islamic fundamentalist terrorists tried in a federal court, were convicted of a conspiracy to destroy U.S. public buildings and structures. One of their leaders, Sheik Omar Abdel Rahman, a near-blind Egyptian cleric and Islamic fanatic, was convicted of directing the conspiracy, as well as attempting to assassinate President Hosni Mubarak of Egypt. El Sayyid Nossair was convicted of the 1990 murder of Rabbi Meir Kahane (he had been acquitted of state charges in this case in 1991, but convicted at that time of assault). The case against the Islamic bombers of the World Trade Center had been largely won for the prosecution with tapes secretly recorded by undercover FBI informant Emad Salem. One of these tapes revealed four of the Islamic terrorists making a bomb by mixing diesel oil and fertilizer in a Queens, N.Y., garage.

## October 3

**ATTEMPTED ASSASSINATION: Skopje, Macedonia** Terrorists attempted to assassinate President Kiro Gilgorov by firing on his car as he was being driven to the National Parliament Building. Gilgorov was seriously wounded in the head. His driver and three bystanders were killed.

**MURDER: Los Angeles, Calif.** O.J. Simpson faced a jury in his murder trial and was acquitted of the killings of his ex-wife Nicole Brown Simpson and Ronald Goldman. The acquittal was largely attributed to the racial bias of the predominately black jury, which had all but ignored the evidence in the case and followed the lead of Johnnie Cochran, who played the race card throughout the trial and, without evidence of any kind, stated that the LAPD had planted most of the evidence in an attempt to frame his client. Marcia Clark, chief prosecutor, and Christopher Darden were later criticized for presenting an ineffective case against Simpson.

## October 10-11

**SABOTAGE: Phoenix, Ariz.** According to federal investigators, a group calling itself the Sons of the Gestapo, derailed an Amtrak train southwest of Phoenix, The derailment killed one of the 20 crew members and injured 100 of the 248 passengers.

## October 20

**AIR RAGE: Buenos Aires-New York** Gerard Buckley

Finneran, a 59-year-old investment banker, enraged at attendant's who refused to serve him more alcoholic drinks, defecated on a food cart and disrupted service. He was later charged when the plane landed.

## October 23

**MURDER: Houston, Texas** Yolanda Saldivar, who had shot and killed popular Tejano singer Selena Quintanilla Perez in Corpus Christi, Texas, in March, was convicted of first-degree murder. Saldivar, who had headed Selena's fan clubs, had been accused of embezzling $30,000 by the singer before Saldivar shot her.

## October 26

**ASSASSINATION: Malta.** Islamic Jihad leader Fathi Shqaqi was killed by assassins who will not be apprehended. Leaders of the Islamic Jihad, a terrorist organization which had conducted countless attacks on Israel, insisted that Shqaqi's murder was committed by Israeli agents.

## October 27

**POLITICAL CORRUPTION: Seoul, South Korea** Roe Tae Woo, former president of South Korea (1988-1993), admitted that he had taken about $650 million in illegal campaign donations while he was in office. Lee Hyun Woo, director of South Korea's National Security Planning Agency in the Roe administration, also admitted taking and keeping large sums of money.

## November 2

**MURDER: California, Md.** According to police, Navy Ensign Dana R. Collins, 37, who had mental problems, as well as marital difficulties—he had tried to burn down his estranged wife's home and had several times threatened to dismember her—lured Petty Officer 2nd Class Jerry L. Culbreath from his apartment, and held Culbreath in a choke hold before breaking his neck. He then reportedly stabbed Culbreath three times and then dismembered his body with a chain saw, dumping body parts in a school's trash container. Collins had apparently killed Culbreath, who served with him at Putuxent River Naval Air Station in Lexington, Park, Md. out of jealousy. When Collins separated from his wife, it was reported, Culbreath became Mrs. Collins' boyfriend.

## November 4

**ASSASSINATION: Tel Aviv, Israel** Prime Minister Yitzhak Rabin, one of Israel's founding wartime heroes and 1994 Nobel Peace Prize winner, was shot and killed by 26-year-old Yigal Amir, a right-wing activist who was opposed to Rabin's peace negotiations with the Palestinians. Amir shot Rabin three times as he emerged from City Hall after having made a speech to more than 100,000 persons. Rabin was immediately replaced by Foreign Minister Shimon Peres, who had worked closely with Rabin in advancing the peace negotiations with the Palestinians.

**MURDER: Italy** Giulio Andreotti, who had been 7 times premier of Italy, was indicted for the 1979 murder of magazine editor Carmine Pecorelli, who was reportedly attempting

to blackmail Adreotti because of his alleged ties to high-ranking Mafia figures. Four others, including two Mafia bosses and the actual killer were also indicted.

## November 6

**MURDER: Boston, Mass.** Two gunmen walked into a restaurant in the city's Charleston section and opened fire in front of a booth, killing four men and wounding another. Two Boston police detectives, who were in the restaurant at the time of the shooting, followed the gunmen outside and arrested Damien Clemente, 20, and 27-year-old Vincent John Perez.

## November 7

**MURDER: Gary, Ind.** Serial killer Eugene Britt confessed to murdering at least six women and young girls (authorities believed he may have murdered a dozen more). He would be sent to prison for life.

## November 8

**TERRORIST ATTACK: Southern Egypt.** Muslim terrorists fired guns at a passing tourist train and wounded ten persons.

## November 9

**TERRORIST ATTACK: Southern Egypt.** Terrorist gunmen opened fire on a passenger train, wounding two tourists, a Dutch man and a French woman, as well as an Egyptian man.

## November 10

**EXECUTION: Nigeria** Ken Saro-Wiwa and eight of his allies, were hanged after being convicted of inciting the murders of four pro-government civilians. Saro-Wiwa, Nigeria's leading playwright, had long been an opponent of the dictatorial Nigerian regime under Sani Abacha and a severe critic of the country's disastrous environmental policies, particularly the economic exploitation by the Royal Dutch/Shell Group.

## November 13

**BOMBING: Riyadhi, Saudi Arabia** Two bombs exploded at a military and communications center, killing 7 persons, including five Americans (one soldier and four civilians) and injuring 60 others. Of the 200 persons stationed at the complex, most were American advisers.

**WAR CRIMES: The Hague, Netherlands** A war crimes tribunal indicted six Bosnian Croats who were charged with persecuting Muslim civilians, two of these being held responsible for the wholesale destruction of 14 towns and for their involvement in a massacre that claimed 120 people.

## November 15

**MURDER: Lynnville, Tenn.** Jamie Rouse, 17, reportedly walked into Richland High School and opened fire with a rifle, killing Carolyn Foster, a 58-year-old business teacher, and Diane Collins, a 16-year-old student. Wounded was 49-year-old science teacher Carol Yancey. Another teacher and student wrestled Rouse to the ground and held him until police arrived to make the arrest.

*November 16*

**BRIBERY: Seoul, South Korea** Former president Roh Tae Woo was arrested and charged with taking $650 million in bribes.

**FRAUD: Washington, D.C.** Billy Dale, former head of the White House Travel Office, who had been accused of transferring $68,000 to his personal account, proved that this payment was for legitimate reimbursements. A federal jury acquitted Dale of all charges. He had been at the core of what the press termed "Travelgate," a mini-scandal wherein Dale and 6 other Travel Office employees, who were responsible for arranging travel for the press corps that accompanied the president on trips, were summarily dismissed at the oblique direction of Bill and Hillary Clinton, who wanted to replace these workers with their own cronies. Dale had been replaced by Catherine Cornelius, a distant relative of Bill Clinton. The patronage ploys by the Clintons had reportedly so distressed White House aide Vincent Foster that it drove him to suicide (among many other scandals that seemed to enshroud Clinton).

**MURDER: Addison, Ill.** In one of the most gruesome killings on record, Jacqueline Annette Williams, Fedell Caffey and Lavern Ward, in order to get Williams a child of her own, murdered Debra Evans, then cut her full-term baby from Evans' womb, then killed two of Evans' other children. Ward would receive a life sentence for this heinous crime and Williams and Caffey would be sentenced to death.

**MURDER: Torrance, California.** Model and former Los Angeles Raiders cheerleader Linda Sobek was murdered by free-lance photographer Charles Rathbun. The killer will lead investigators to her shallow grave in the San Gabriel Mountains nine days later.

*November 19*

**MURDER: Columbus, Ohio** Jerry Hessler, a 38-year-old bank employee, reportedly went on a shooting spree, killing four persons—Brian and Tracey Stevens and their 5-month-old daughter Amanda, and P. Thane Griffin. In September 1996, while awaiting trial for these murders, Hessler reportedly wrote on the wall of his prison cell that the killings were "not a bad day's work," and "today the score is 4 and 0, but when they execute me it will be 4 and 1. I still have the higher score."

**TERRORIST ATTACK: Aswan, Egypt.** Muslim terrorists opened fire on a tourist train en route to Cairo. The gunmen killed one Egyptian train worker and injured several others.

*November 23*

**MURDER: Sunnyside, Wash.** Kenneth Arrasmith was convicted of shooting to death Ronald and Luella Bingham, who had reportedly sexually assaulted his underage daughter. He would be sentenced to prison for life.

*November 26*

**ARSON/MURDER: New York, N.Y.** In a botched robbery, a gang of thieves sprayed flammable liquid into a subway token booth and ignited it, blowing the booth apart and killing Harry Kaufman, a 50-year-old token book clerk. Police later arrested James Irons, 18, Thomas Malik, 18, and Vincent Ellerbie, 17, charging them with the crime, one which was likened to a scene in a movie, *Money Train*.

*December 1*

**SEXUAL ASSAULT: Palm Beach, Fla.** Howard Steven Ault, who had a long record of sexual child abuse, reportedly molested an 11-year-old girl.

*December 3*

**MILITARY COUP: Seoul, South Korea** Chun Doo Hwan, former president, was charged with having staged a military coup which put him into power.

**MURDER: Joe Pool Lake, Texas** Diane Zamora and her lover David Graham murdered 16-year-old Adrianne Jones, who had been marked for death by Zamora because she had come between her and Graham.

*December 5*

**BRIBERY: Seoul, South Korea** Former president Roh Tae Woo, was indicted for taking $650 million in bribes during his term in office.

*December 7*

**LAW ENFORCEMENT: Atlanta, Ga.** Believing that a shop was being robbed, plainclothes police officers entered a motorcycle shop with drawn guns. A shop employee, thinking the plainclothesmen were robbers, pulled a gun and opened fire. The detectives returned fire and in the ensuing gunfight, Jerry Jackson, a customer in the store, was hit by a ricocheting bullet. He reportedly crawled outside and was killed execution style by one of the detectives, a report later challenged. Two others, including one of the officers, were wounded in the gunfight.

**MURDER: Fayetteville, N.C.** James Burmeister II, a paratrooper at Fort Bragg, N.C., as part of his initiation into a skinhead group, randomly shot and killed two black persons, Michael James and Jackie Burden.

*December 18*

**BRIBERY: Seoul, South Korea** The trial of former president Roh Tae Woo on charges of bribery began. Roh admitted taking $650 million from many sources, but said that he had destroyed all his records and could not remember who had paid him the money. Fourteen others were also charged with being part of the bribery during Roh's administration.

*December 19*

**MASSACRE: Seoul, South Korea** Legislation was passed that cleared the way for the prosecution of Roh Tae Woo and Chun Doo Hwan, former presidents, for the 1980 massacre of prodemocracy demonstrators in Kwangju.

*December 20*

**FRAUD: Salt Lake City, Ut.** A 13-year-old boy called Utah social services to state that he had been abandoned at a bus terminal on his birthday. The news media spread the story and cash gifts and other aid poured in, but authorities then announced that the boy, who had refused to undress for a medical examination, was really a 25-year-old woman named Birdie Jo Hoaks (Hoax?), who had pulled similar scams in other cities, particularly in Vermont. Hoaks was charged with fraud.

**MURDER/ROBBERY: New York, N.Y.** Michael Vernon reportedly entered the Little Chester Shoes shop in the Bronx and, after arguing with a clerk about some sneakers, opened fire on patrons, killing five people, including a mother and her two sons, and wounding three others, before he was shot and wounded by a policeman and taken into custody.

### December 21

**MILITARY COUP: Seoul, South Korea** Roh Tae Woo and Chun Doo Hwan were indicted for staging the 1979 military coup that brought them into power.

**TRANSPORTING POISON: Little Rock, Ark.** Thomas Lewis Lavy, 54, was charged with illegally transporting one of the world's most toxic poisons—130 grams of ricin—into Canada in 1993. Lavy committed suicide in his jail cell on December 23, 1995.

# 1996

### January 4

**MURDER: Pullman, Ill.** The body of 20-year-old Latrice Wood was found in a trash bin. She was the second in a series of four unsolved killings dubbed the Pullman Strangulations.

### January 8

**WHITEWATER: New York, N.Y.** In an article published in the New York *Times*, columnist William Safire, while reviewing the Rose Law Firm documents (or the lack of them) and the White House "Travelgate," labeled Hillary Rodham Clinton a "congenital liar." A White House spokesman later stated that President Clinton had said that he wished he could punch Safire on the nose for making the comment.

### January 9

**MURDER: San Diego, Calif.** Matthew MacDonald, who had preyed upon wealthy, elderly gay men, was sentenced to life in prison for the 1994 murder of Charles Henderson.

**SEXUAL HARASSMENT: St. Louis, Mo.** A three-judge federal panel in the 8th Circuit Court of Appeals by a 2-1 vote reversed a 1994 decision by a federal judge who held that Bill Clinton was immune to lawsuits while being president, thus allowing the 1991 lawsuit filed by Paula Corbin Jones to proceed. Jones insisted that Clinton, while governor of Arkansas, had sexually harassed her in a hotel room.

### January 11

**TERRORISM: Lima, Peru** New York activist Lori Berenson was convicted of treason and working with terrorist groups and sentenced to life in prison.

### January 14

**DRUGS: Monterey, Mexico** Mexican drug agents swarmed into a rural villa and arrested drug cartel boss Juan Garcia Abrego, who would be extradited to the U.S. and there convicted of drug trafficking and sent to prison.

### January 15

**BOMBING: New York, N.Y.** Ramzi Ahmed Yousef, Is-

lamic terrorist and mastermind behind the February 26, 1993 bombing of the World Trade Center, was sentenced to life in prison. Before the sentencing, Yousef screamed: "I am a terrorist, and I am proud of it!" Federal Judge Kevin Duffy held up a copy of the Koran and said: "Your God is not Allah. You worship death and destruction." Yousef had been convicted and sentenced for two crimes, the World Trade Center bombing and an unsuccessful plot to blow up a dozen U.S. airliners in Asia.

### January 17

**BOMBING/TERRORISM: New York, N.Y.** Sheik Omar Abdel Rahman, the ringleader of ten Muslims who sought to bomb the U.N. Building and other U.S. landmarks, as well as assassinate public figures, was sentenced to life in prison, plus 65 years for directing the conspiracy and plotting to assassinate President Hosni Mubarak of Egypt. El Sayyid Nosair was sentenced to life for the 1990 murder of Rabbi Meir Kahane in New York City. Federal Judge Michael Mikasey sentenced the eight others to prison terms of 25 years or more.

### January 24

**ESPIONAGE: Israel** Jonathan Pollard, convicted of spying for Israel in the U.S. in 1986 and serving a life sentence, was granted Israeli citizenship. One report had it that $2,500 a month had been regularly deposited in an Israeli bank for Pollard, money he might claim upon his possible release and relocation to Israel.

### January 26

**MURDER: Philadelphia, Pa.** Multimillionaire John E. du Pont, inexplicably shot and killed David Schultz, who had been hired by the eccentric du Pont to train an Olympics wrestling team. Du Pont, after barricading himself on his estate, eventually surrendered to police.

**TERRORIST ATTACK: Southern Egypt** Terrorists opened fire on a tourist train, killing an elderly Egyptian.

### January 30

**HOSTAGE TAKING: Managua, Nicaragua** About 300 university students demanding increased funding for their institutions seized the Foreign Ministry building and held hostage Foreign Minister Ernesto Lean, and two foreign diplomats. The students were armed with crude weapons but caused no injuries.

**MURDER: Belfast, Ireland** Gino Gallagher, 32, acting chief of staff of the outlawed Irish Liberation Army, a splinter group of the IRA, was shot repeatedly in the back of the head and killed by a gunman who then calmly walked away on a busy street. Witnesses said that the killer was wearing a wig and sunglasses.

### January 31

**BOMBING: Colombo, Sri Lanka** A suicide bomber drove a truck into the gates of the Central Bank, killing 86 people and injuring another 1,400 people. The powerful truck bomb had been made up of more than 400 pounds of explosives. Officials later arrested 2 suspects who were reportedly members of a terrorist group, the Liberation Tigers of Tamil

Eelam, which, since 1983, had been fighting guerrilla warfare and conducting widespread terrorism in an effort to set up an independent state for the Tamil minority in Sri Lanka. By the end of 1995, more than 40,000 lives had been lost in this bloody campaign.

**MURDER: Tuscaloosa, Ala.** Felecia Scott shot and killed her pregnant friend Carethia Curry, then performed a Caesarian operation, removing her victim's newborn child and abducting it. Scott would later be sent to prison for life.

### February 2

**MURDER: Moses Lake, Wash.** Barry Loukaitas, 14, killed three persons and wounded another at Frontier High School before being subdued by a teacher. Loukaitas stated that he had been inspired to kill after reading Stephen King's novel *Rage*, and watching Oliver Stone's movie, *Natural Born Killers*.

### February 3

**MURDER: Vista, Calif.** Joshua Bradley Jenkins, a 15-year-old boy, was suspected of murdering his parents, grandparents and his 10-year-old sister. All five victims had reportedly been stabbed and bludgeoned to death and then dragged into a single room of the family condominium which was set ablaze. Jenkins was seen fleeing the scene in his parents' Mercedes-Benz. He was arrested the following day at a convenience store.

### February 4

**BOMBING: Riyadh, Saudi Arabia** Hassan al-Sarai, a suspect in the November 13, 1995 bombing of the Saudi National Guard training center which killed 5 Americans and 2 Indians and injured scores of persons, was held after being deported from Pakistan.

### February 9

**BOMBING: London, England** A bomb estimated to be about 1,000 pounds exploded beneath an elevated railroad station, killing 2 persons and injuring another 100 people. The bombing, attributed to the IRA, ended the so-called IRA cease fire during which tenuous peace negotiations took place.

**MASS MURDER: Fort Lauderdale, Fla.** Clifton McCree, who had been fired in 1994, stormed into his former workplace and shot and killed five persons and wounded another before he committed suicide.

### February 17

**MURDER: Baltimore, Md.** Following the disappearance of 9-year-old Marvin Wise, police tracked down Shawn Brown, a convicted child molester from New York City who reportedly confessed to killing Wise, and also the murder of 16-year-old Abdul Richards. Brown led police to an abandoned building where the body of Richards was found.

**MURDER: Fort Worth, Texas** Diane Zamora was sentenced to life in prison for the 1995 murder of Adrianne Jones, her rival for the affections of David Graham. Graham, also convicted of the Jones killing, would be sentenced to life in prison on July 24, 1996.

**MURDER: Highland County, Fla.** John N. Canning, a rural church leader who confessed to murdering two of his wealthy parishioners so he could obtain their estates, was sentenced to two consecutive life terms.

**MURDER: Mineola, N.Y.** Mass murderer Colin Ferguson, who had acted as his own lawyer in defense of his shooting spree aboard a New York commuter train in 1993, was convicted of murdering 6 persons and attempting to kill 22 others. He was given a life sentence with no hope of parole.

### February 18

**BOMBING: London, England** A bomb on board a bus exploded, killing one person and wounding another nine people. The IRA claimed responsibility for the terrorist act.

### February 20

**BOMBING: Oklahoma City, Okla.** Federal Judge Richard Matsch granted a defense motion to move the trial of Timothy McVeigh and Terry Nichols, both charged with the April 1995 bombing of the federal building in Oklahoma City, to Colorado, noting that prejudice against the suspects ran high in Oklahoma.

**MURDER: Trenton, N.J.** Ambrose Harris was convicted of the 1992 murder of 22-year-old Kristin Huggins. He was sentenced to death.

**MURDER: Welch, W. Va.** Roger Williams shot and killed his sister, nephew and daughter, then himself, after a family argument.

### February 21

**MURDER: Winston-Salem, N.C.** Russell William Tucker was sentenced to death for killing Kmart guard Maurice T. Williams during a botched robbery; Tucker was already serving a life term for another murder.

### February 23

**ESPIONAGE: Millersville, Pa.** Robert Stephen Lipka, 50, was arrested by FBI agents and charged with selling military secrets to the Soviets during the Vietnam War when Lipka worked for the National Security Agency as an Army enlisted man (1964-1967).

**EXECUTION: San Quentin, Calif.** Serial killer William Bonin, who had murdered at least 21 persons from August 1979 to June 1980, and was known as the Freeway Killer, was put to death by lethal injection. Bonin showed no remorse for his many murders and ravenously ate a last meal consisting of two large sausage and pepperoni pizzas, a six-pack of coke and three pints of coffee ice cream.

**MURDER: Baghdad, Iraq** Hussein Kamel Hussan al-Majid, his brother, Saddam Kamel Hassan al-Majid, another brother and their father were all murdered by a death squad sent by Iraq dictator Saddam Hussein. The Majid brothers had been married to Hussein's two daughters and had defected in 1995, but returned to Iraq after receiving a pardon from their treacherous father-in-law, who then had them killed.

### February 25

**BOMBINBS: Jerusalem/Ashkelon, Israel** A terrorist

killed himself and 27 other people, including 2 American Jewish students, and wounded dozens of others when he exploded a bomb in West Jerusalem. A second bomb exploded in Ashkelon, killing a soldier and the bomber. Hamas, the Palestinian terrorist group, claimed responsibility for both bombings.

**MURDER: Los Angeles, Calif.** Academy award-winning actor Haing Ngor was shot twice and killed as he stood in the driveway of his home by a member of an Asian street gang in a botched robbery. The killer overlooked a cash-filled wallet carried by the 55-year-old Ngor, who apparently resisted giving up a gold chain and locket which contained a photo of his wife who had been killed by the Khmer Rouge in the 1970s.

*February 28*

**MURDER: Rolling Meadows, Ill.** Ronald Kilner, a contract killer, was convicted of the 1988 murder of Diana Rinaldi. He was later sentenced to death. Kilner had been hired to murder Rinaldi by her husband, Joseph Rinaldi, and his friend, Michael Permanian, who were both sentenced to prison.

*March 1*

**WAR CRIMES: The Hague, Netherlands** Judge Richard Goldstone of the U.N. International War Crimes Tribunal charged that Serbian General Djordje Djukic of the Bosnian Serbian army was guilty of committing war crimes against civilians.

*March 3*

**BOMBING: West Jerusalem, Israel** A bomb exploded on a bus and killed 19 persons. The explosion was attributed to Hamas, the Palestinian terrorist organization.

**MURDER/ROBBERY: Albuquerque, N.M.** Three tuxedo-clad employees at a Hollywood Video store—Zachary Blacklock, Mylinh Daothi and Jowanda Castillo—were killed execution style, all shot in the back of the head, during an apparent robbery. Shane Harrison and Esther Beckley were later charged with the murders.

*March 4*

**BOMBING: Tel Aviv, Israel** A bomb exploded in a busy shopping mall, killing 14, including the 2 bombers. Another 19 persons were injured. Hamas, the Palestinian terrorist organization, was thought to be responsible for the bombing.

**WAR CRIMES: The Hague, Netherlands** General Djordje Djukic, who had been captured by Bosnian forces in January 1996, and who was being tried before a U.N. tribunal on charges of war crimes against civilians, pleaded not guilty.

*March 5*

**CHILD MOLESTATION: Los Angles, Calif.** Former actor James Stacy was sentenced to six years in prison for sexually molesting an 11-year-old girl.

*March 6*

**MURDER: Los Angeles, Calif.** Career criminal Andre Stephen Alexander was convicted of the 1980 murder of Secret Service agent Julie Cross. He was subsequently sentenced to death for this killing.

**MURDER: San Diego, Calif.** Beatrice Toronczak, 32, was reported missing. Her boyfriend, Ramon Rogers, 36, would later be charged with Toronczak's murder after police found teeth and fingers in a locker rented by Rogers and identified as belonging to the victim by a medical examiner. Rogers was also charged with killing another former girlfriend, 33-year-old Rose Albano, whose dismembered body had been found on a rural back road near San Diego in 1993. Further, Rogers was charged with killing his former roommate, 29-year-old Ronald Stadt who vanished at the time of Albano slaying.

*March 7*

**BOMBING: Beijing, China** A bomb exploded on a bus, killing 2 persons and injuring many others. Communist authorities blamed "hooligans," but others reported that the bomb had been placed by anti-Communist terrorists.

*March 8*

**MURDER: Honolulu, Hawaii** Catherine Suh, who had been convicted in absentia of the 1993 murder of her boyfriend, Robert O'Durbaine (Robert W. Koron, Jr.), turned herself into local police. She would be sent back to Illinois and then to prison for life.

*March 9*

**MURDER: Bloomfield Hills, Mich.** Jonathan Schmitz, who had three days earlier been surprised in a taping of the Jennie Jones TV talk show with a secret admirer, homosexual Scott Amedure, went to Amedure's home and shot him dead, later telling police that Amedure had "f----- me on national TV." The Jones Show producers were later held liable in a civil suit.

*March 11*

**WHITEWATER: Little Rock, Ark.** The trial of Jim Guy Tucker, and James and Susan McDougal (by then divorced) opened. Tucker and the McDougals, who had been partners with Bill and Hillary Clinton in the Whitewater Development Corp., were accused of having borrowed $3 million under false pretenses from Capital Management, and investment firm that made loans underwritten by the Small Business Administration and from Madison Guaranty S&L, an institution owned by James McDougal that later collapsed. Prosecutor Ray Jahn labeled the trio "collaborators" who schemed to illegally enrich themselves through loans for which they had no eligibility.

*March 13*

**MASS MURDER: Dublane, Scotland** Thomas Hamilton, using four guns, opened fire on a class of kindergarten children in a school gymnasium, killing 16 children and their teacher, and wounding 12 others. One child escaped injury. Dublane killed himself before police could apprehend him. He had apparently been incensed because he had not been reinstated as a boy scout leader after many reports held him responsible for child molestation.

*March 14*

**MURDER: Las Vegas, Nev.** Michael Rippo was sentenced

to death for the 1992 murders of Laurie Jacobson and Denise Lizzi.

**MURDER: San Luis Obispo, Calif.** Three Satan-worshipping teenagers—Jacob W. Delashmutt, 16, Joseph Fiorella, 15, and Royce E. Casey, 17, were arrested and charged with murder, rape, torture and conspiracy in the death of 15-year-old Elyse Pahler. Casey reportedly came forward and led police to the girl's body. The group murdered Pahler as a virgin sacrifice to Satan, according to court records, in order to earn "a ticket to hell."

### March 18

**MURDER: Boston, Mass.** John Salvi III, who had killed 2 receptionists in separate abortion clinics in Brookline, Mass., in December 1994, and wounded five others, was sentenced to 2 life terms, plus 18 to 20 years on assault charges by Superior Court Judge Barbara Dortch-Okara.

### March 20

**MURDER: Van Nuys, Calif.** Lyle and Erik Menendez were found guilty of the 1989 murders of their parents, Kitty and Jose Menendez.

**WHITEWATER: Little Rock, Ark.** Judge George Howard, presiding over the trials of Jim Guy Tucker and James and Susan McDougal, ruled that President Bill Clinton could testify by video tape. Susan McDougal's attorneys had subpoenaed Clinton to testify and rebut allegations by David Hale, a former municipal judge who had pleaded guilty to arranging fraudulent loans through Capital Management that had cost the federal government $2 million. Hale had testified that in 1986, then Governor Clinton had pressured him into making a $300,000 personal loan to Susan McDougal that was misrepresented by a business loan in order to qualify for federal subsidies.

### March 22

**MURDER: Dallas, Texas** Juan R. Chavez, who had killed five persons and wounded another three people in a 1995 murder spree, was sentenced to death.

**MURDER: Gray's Harbor, Ore.** Brian Bassett, 16, was convicted of killing his parents and his 5-year-old brother. He was given three life terms in prison.

**MURDER: Stafford, Texas** Despondent over her strained marriage, Nirmala Devi Katta reportedly shot and killed her husband, her three small children and then committed suicide.

### March 25

**FRAUD: Jordan, Montana** FBI agents surrounded a farm complex housing about 20 persons who belonged to the Montana Freeman anti-tax group, ordering all to surrender and face charges of fraud. The Freemen had conducted seminars in which they had instructed about 800 persons on illegal techniques to defraud the government of taxes and, according to federal charges, had also defrauded banks and other companies of more than $1.8 million. LeRoy Schweitzer and Daniel Petersen, two of the group's leaders, were arrested as they apparently attempted to join the main group.

**WHITEWATER: Little Rock, Ark.** David Hale, a former municipal judge who had reportedly arranged for illegal loans to the McDougals, was sentenced to 28 months in federal prison and fined $10,000 by Judge Stephen Reasoner.

### March 27

**ASSASSINATION: Tel Aviv, Israel** Yigal Amir, who had shot to death Prime Minister Yitzhak Rabin in November 1995, was found guilty by a three-judge panel and sentenced to life in prison.

### March 28

**FRAUD: Jordan, Montana** LeRoy Schweitzer and Daniel Petersen, two of the leaders of the Montana Freemen, were charged with making a death threat against a judge and defrauding banks and firms.

**FUGITIVE: Maywood Ill.** Police searching for a pickpocket questioned a man waiting for a bus and he was identified by a computer check as Richard Bernard Thomas, wanted for shooting a police sergeant in the back five times in an attack by six black militants on a Philadelphia police station in 1970. Thomas, who had been using the alias of Taylor, had been a member of the Revolutionaries, part of the long-defunct Black Unity Council, and had fled to New York, then Chicago, remaining a fugitive for 26 years.

### March 29

**BOMBINGS/MURDER: Johannesburg, South Africa** Nine white neo-Nazis were convicted of murder for a series of bombings that killed 21 persons. Eugene TerreBlanche, leader of the Afrikaner Resistance Movement, insisted that the bombers had committed political crimes and were eligible for amnesty.

**DRUGS: Bogata, Colombia** Juan Carolos Ortiz, reportedly a leader of the Cali drug cartel, turned himself into authorities to face a charge of illegally possessing a weapon. The 33-year-old Ortiz had been arrested in 1994 on charges of murder, kidnapping and extortion and had been released for undisclosed reasons. Earlier this month, Juan Carlos Ramirez, another young Cali cartel leader, also surrendered to police.

**MURDER: Tucson, Ariz.** Robert Joseph Moody was sentenced to death for killing two women in 1993.

**ROBBERY: Lille, France** Four armed robbers were killed and two policemen were wounded when police trapped the thieves along a highway.

### April 1

**ESPIONAGE: Orlando, Fla.** FBI agents arrested Kurt G. Lessenthien, a 29-year-old petty officer and instructor at the Navy Nuclear Power school, charging him with espionage. Lessenthien had reportedly attempted to sell top secret information to a representative of a "foreign government."

### April 3

**BOMBINGS/MURDER: Western Montana** Theodore Kaczynski, a one-time college professor living as a hermit in a remote cabin, was seized by FBI agents who suspected him of being the notorious Unabomber. Kaczynski had been turned in to authorities by his brother, David Kaczynski, who recognized his sibling's writing style in the Unabomber's manifesto published earlier in the Washington *Post* and the New York *Times*.

### April 4

**BOMBINGS/MURDER: Western Montana** Theodore Kaczynski, a former math professor at University of California at Berkeley, was charged with the 3 murders and 23 woundings caused by exploding devices sent by the Unabomber since 1978.

**HORSE-KILLINGS: Chicago, Ill.** Ronald Mueller was sentenced to 12 months in prison for killing horses to collect insurance money. Mueller burned four horses to death in 1973 when driving them from Chicago to Iowa, flipping a lighted match into the trailer carrying them and igniting hay that he had saturated with an accelerant. Mueller had reportedly worked for years with horse trader and con man, Richard Bailey, who was implicated in the murder of candy heiress Helen Vorhees Brach.

**MURDER: Antigua** John Earl Baughman, who had been acquitted of murdering his first wife in 1985, was convicted of murdering his second wife, Valerie Joyce Baughman by pushing her off the roof of a hotel where they were vacationing. Baughman was sentenced to death.

**SEXUAL ABUSE: Frederick County, Md.** D. Carleton Gajdusek, who shared a 1976 Nobel Prize in medicine for proving the existence of a slow virus called kuru, was arrested by FBI agents and charged with sexually abusing one of many young boys Gajdusek had brought to live and study with him from Micronesia and New Guinea.

### April 5

**MASS MURDER: Vernon, British Colombia, Canada** Mark Vijay Chahal, drove to his father-in-law's home and shot and killed nine persons, including his estranged wife, then drove to a motel and committed suicide.

### April 7

**BOMBINGS/MURDER: Western Montana** FBI agents reported that Theodore Kaczynski, charged with the bombings committed by the notorious Unabomber, had been in Sacramento, California, according to hotel records, at the same time bombs had been mailed from that city.

### April 8

**CRUELTY TO CHILDREN: Washington, D.C.** First grade teacher Allison York, 25, was charged with pinning a boy's arms behind him while his classmates beat him. She pleaded not guilty.

### April 9

**MURDER: Bereketa, Madagascar** Nancy Coutu, a 29-year-old Peace Corps volunteer, while riding her bicycle, was struck on the head and killed. Coutu, and environmental volunteer from Nashua, N.H., was the first Peace Corps volunteer murdered since an incident in Bolivia in 1990.

**POLITICAL CORRUPTION: Washington, D.C.** Daniel Rostenkowski, congressman from Illinois and power-ful head of the House Ways and Means Committee, pleaded guilty to two counts of mail fraud. Rostenkowski had been charged with padding his payroll with do-nothing employees (a tradition in his backyard, Chicago, Illinois), buying gifts with cash from his expense account and obstructing justice. Judge Norman Johnson sentenced Rostenkowski to 17 months in prison and fined him $100,000.

**TERRORIST ATTACK: Northern Israel** Hezbollah, the Islamic fundamentalist terrorist organization backed by Iran and Syria, fired rockets into Israel. More than thirty persons were injured.

### April 10

**GENOCIDE: Addis Ababa, Ethiopia** Witnesses at an on-going trial of 71 former Ethiopian officials described in detail the mass executions and genocidal slaughter by military leaders who took over the country in 1974, toppling and assassinating Emperor Haile Selassie, and murdering 1,823 of his followers.

### April 11

**CONSPIRACY: Annapolis, Md.** Midshipman Arthur Sherrod was arrested at the U.S. Naval Academy and charged with conspiring to transport stolen cars from New York and resell them in Maryland. Other Academy personnel indicted in the stolen car theft ring were Arthur Brown, a 1995 graduate; Christopher Rounds, of Baltimore, who had been dismissed from the Academy in 1994; Kenneth Leak, of Westbury, N.Y., who had been dismissed from the Academy in 1995; and Joe Smith, of Jackson, Mississippi, who was on leave from the Academy and awaiting dismissal.

### April 12

**BOMBING/MURDER: Plantation, Fla.** A neighbor boy brought a package into the house of Miledy Cartaya, saying that it had been left outside. When Cartaya opened the package in her kitchen, the blast killed her, injured her two children and blew the neighbor boy out the back of the house. The tremendous blast blew the back and front doors of the house off their hinges and knocked the rear windows out. In a March 31 statement to police, when Cartaya sought a restraining order against her ex-husband, she said he had threatened to blow her up.

**BOMBINGS/MURDER: Western Montana** The FBI reported that agents had found the original manuscript of the Unabomber's manifesto in the cabin occupied by Theodore Kaczynski.

### April 13

**TERRORIST ATTACK: Northern Israel** Hezbollah fired rockets into Israel. Two women and four girls riding in an ambulance were killed when the vehicle was struck by Israeli return fire.

### April 17

**MASSACRE: Maraba, Brazil** Military police opened fire on peasants they were attempting to evict from lands, killing 19 and wounding dozens of others. The slaughter, labeled the

"Maraba Massacre," was graphically captured on video tape and later shown on national television, shocking the nation.

**MURDER: Van Nuys, Calif.** Lyle and Erik Menendez, who had been found guilty in March of the 1989 murders of their millionaire parents, Kitty and Jose Menendez, were sentenced to life in prison.

### April 17-18

**CRIME LEGISLATION: Washington, D.C.** The Senate (on April 17) and the House (April 18) approved an anti-terrorism bill which provided $1 billion over a four-year-period to combat terrorism. The bill included provisions whereby foreigners who were members of terrorist groups would be denied entry into the U.S. and fundraisers for terrorists and terrorist groups could face prosecution. The bill also curtailed opportunities for death row inmates to utilize the habeas corpus process in seeking federal review of convictions.

### April 18

**TERRORIST ATTACK: Cairo, Egypt** Terrorist gunmen opened fire outside of the Europa Hotel in Cairo close to the Pyramids. They killed seventeen Greek tourists and one Egyptian man, wounding another fifteen persons. The outlawed Islamic Group, a terrorist organization bent on undermining the $3 billion to $4 billion tourist trade in Egypt in order to topple the government, took responsibility for the mass slaying, the worst terrorist attack in Egyptian history. Directed by Muslim fundamentalists, the Islamic Group had been responsible for almost all terrorist attacks in Egypt in the previous four years, a bloody campaign designed to replace Egypt's secular government with strict Islamic rule. (Since 1992, eight tourists out of twenty-five foreigners were killed and seventy-three wounded, with more than 900 Egyptians, mostly police officers and terrorists, being killed.) Several suspects were later arrested.

**TERRORIST ATTACK: Northern Israel** Hezbollah fired rockets and mortar shells into Israel. The Israelis returned fire, striking a United Nations base packed with Lebanese refugees. Many refugees were killed, along with several U.N. peacekeepers.

### April 19

**EXECUTION: Smyrna, Del.** James B. Clark, Jr., a recidivist child molester who had shot and killed his parents in 1994, was executed by lethal injection.

**MURDER: Singapore** John Martin Scripps, 35, who had been convicted of murdering Gerard George Lowe, a South African tourist, was hanged. Scripps had also been charged in Thailand in September 1995 for the murders of two Canadians.

**RECKLESS HOMICIDE: Stevens Point, Wis.** Julie Quinn, who suffocated her baby shortly after giving birth on December 21, 1995, was convicted of reckless homicide.

**ROBBERY: Chicago, Ill.** James E. Washington was found guilty of recruiting homeless people to rob two Loop banks and robbing a bank himself in 1995.

### April 21

**ESPIONAGE: Orlando, Fla.** Machinist Mate 1st Class Kurt G. Lessenthien, serving as a first class petty officer and instructor at Orlando's Navy Nuclear Power School, was arrested by FBI agents and investigators from Navy intelligence and charged with espionage. An FBI spokesman reported that "to date, no classified defense information was successfully provided...to any foreign interest or government." This suggested that Lessenthien may have been dealing with an American agent posing as a foreign spy. Lessenthien had served aboard U.S. nuclear submarines.

### April 22

**COMPUTER FRAUD: Los Angeles, Calif.** Kevin Mitnick, a notorious hacker who had been a fugitive for three years and had been tracked down in North Carolina in 1995 by a computer security specialist, pleaded guilty to illegally using stolen mobile phone numbers. As part of the plea bargain between Mitnick and federal prosecutors, the hacker also pleaded guilty to violating probation for a 1988 break-in of Digital Equipment Corp. computers in California.

### April 23

**ATTEMPTED MURDER: Richmond, Calif.** Ignacio Bermudez, a four-month-old baby was nearly beaten to death by a six-year-old child and eight-year-old twins who had entered the unlocked front door of the Bermudez home to steal a bicycle. While searching for the bike, the children overturned the bassinet in which the baby was sleeping, then kicked and beat the infant with a stick, cracking his skull.

**POLITICAL CORRUPTION: Italy** Bettino Crazi, former prime minister, was convicted of political corruption, given an 8-year prison sentence and a fine of $23 million.

### April 24

**ABDUCTION/SLAVERY: Anhul Province, China** Zaho Ming and three of his gang members were sentenced to death for abducting and selling 119 women to farmers seeking sons from 1989 to 1994.

**MURDER: Jackson, Miss.** Kenneth Tornes, a firefighter, reportedly killed his wife at home, then went to a firehouse and opened fire on his supervisors, killing four department officials before he was wounded and captured by police, following a high-speed chase in which several vehicles were wrecked.

**MURDER: Rio de Janeiro, Brazil** The bullet-torn bodies of two more of Rio's impoverished street children, ages eleven and twelve, were found outside the city's Dona Marta shantytown. At the time of these killings, the murder trials of four "death squad" members was in progress.

### April 25

**FRAUD: Chicago, Ill.** Dorothy Rivers, who had established a Hyde Park shelter for homeless families and unwed mothers was charged with defrauding city, state and federal agencies of more than $5 million for almost a decade. She reportedly spent lavishly on herself and family, purchasing expensive cars, giving lavish parties and buying a resort home with funds that should otherwise have gone to the shelter.

### April 28

**PRISON RELEASE: Shanghai, China** Fu Shenqi, one

of the country's leading dissidents, was released from prison after serving three years on charges of "causing trouble."

**MASS MURDER: Port Arthur, Tasmania, Australia** Martin Bryant, a wealthy eccentric, opened fire inside of a restaurant, randomly shooting people inside and outside in the parking lot, killing 32 persons and wounding another 18 persons.

*April 29*

**MASS MURDER: Port Arthur, Tasmania, Australia** Martin Bryant, after shooting 32 people at a restaurant, took 3 persons hostages and held off police until the cottage in which he was hiding was set ablaze. The hostages all died as Bryant was taken into custody.

*April 30*

**MURDER: Chicago, Ill.** Raymond Goldfarb, a 59-year-old lawyer, was shot to death in his Loop office by a client who was apparently disgruntled over his bill in a long-running lawsuit.

**RIOTS: New Delhi, India** Six persons were killed in political riots that preceded parliamentary elections.

*May 2*

**DRUGS: Bogata, Colombia** Prosecutors ordered the arrest of Attorney General Orlando Vasquez, on charges that he took money from the Cali drug cartel, the world's largest illegal drug organization.

*May 5*

**RIOT: Denver, Colo.** Drunken revelers celebrating the Mexican holiday called Cinco de Mayo, turned violent, driving along Federal Boulevard and throwing rocks and bottles at police officers wearing riot gear. At least 75 persons were arrested.

*May 6*

**MURDER: Ventura County, Calif.** Sherri Dally, 35, was kidnapped and taken to a remote spot where she was axed to death, beheaded, her body dismembered and scattered. Charged with her murder was Diana Haun, the 36-year-old lover of the victim's husband, Michael Dally, who claimed to be a witch and occultist and who had made a human sacrifice of his wife, the mother of his two children, as a birthday gift. Haun allegedly tricked Sherri Dally into believing she was a deputy sheriff, handcuffing her and leading her to her car on a trumped up charge, before driving the woman to her horrible death.

*May 7*

**RAPE: Virginia Beach, Va.** Jon C. Bush, 26, an occultist who claimed to be a vampire and who habitually wore a black cape, black nail polish, red contact lenses and fake fangs, went to trial on charges of raping or sexually molesting 13 girls, ages 13 to 16, under the ruse of initiating them into a "vampire club."

*May 9*

**ESPIONAGE: Washington, D.C.** President Clinton received a letter from Benjamin Netanyahu, later Israel's prime

minister, requesting that convicted spy Jonathan Jay Pollard be pardoned. Pollard was sent to prison for life in 1986 after providing classified documents to Israel. Clinton refused to pardon Pollard. Netanyahu will make the same request in September 1998, which will again be denied by President Clinton.

*May 12*

**ESPIONAGE: Moscow, Russia** Richard Dann Oppfelt, a U.S. businessman from Seattle, was ordered expelled on a charge that he had been conducting espionage against Russia.

*May 14*

**HIJACKING: Salt Lake City, Utah** Justin Allgood, 15, shot the driver of a school bus and then drove the bus at high speeds with police in pursuit until he crashed into a house and shot himself to death before police could arrest him.

*May 15*

**SEXUAL HARASSMENT: Washington, D.C.** President Clinton's lawyers appealed to the U.S. Supreme Court, claiming that the president should not have to submit to a suit filed by Paula Corbin Jones and the Court agreed to review the matter, thus effectively postponing the case until after the November 1996 election.

*May 22*

**MURDER: Selby, S.D.** Nicholas Scherr, 31, was sentenced to 100 years in prison for the 1980 murder of Candace Rough Surface, an 18-year-old Sioux Indian girl.

*May 26*

**MURDER: Surry County, N.C.** State policemen found Curtis Swett in his car, shot to death, four bullets fired into his head. Carolyn Louise James, of Winston-Salem, who had briefly dated Swett, was tracked down in New York City and charged with the killing.

*May 28*

**WHITEWATER: Little Rock, Ark.** James and Susan McDougal, who had been partners with Bill and Hillary Rodham Clinton in the Whitewater Development Corp., along with Arkansas Governor Jim Guy Tucker, were convicted of arranging $3 million in fraudulent loans through financial institutions. David Hale, who had been convicted of aiding the McDougals and Tucker after pleading guilty, stated that Bill Clinton had pressured him into arranging for the loans to the McDougals. Susan McDougal had subpoenaed Clinton to testify in rebuttal. Clinton, in video-taped testimony, denied Hale's accusations. Upon his conviction, Tucker said that he would resign his governorship.

*May 30*

**MURDER: Houston, Texas** Pete Kanakidas, 27, reportedly shot and killed Alejandro Cruz Arroyo outside his auto shop when Arroyo appeared with two of Kanakidas' former employees who had earlier beaten him up. According to Kanakidas' attorney, Kanakidas fired in self-defense, believing that Arroyo was going to shoot him. Kanakidas was the first person who held a concealed weapons permit to be charged with murder since the law had gone into effect on January 1, 1996.

### May 31

**WAR CRIMES: The Hague, Netherlands** Drazen Erdemovic, an ethnic Croat who had fought with the Bosnian Serbs, pleaded guilty to charges that he had participated in the 1995 massacre of Muslims in Srebrenica. Erdemovic, who was the first person to be convicted by the special U.N. war crimes tribunal, said that his commanders told him that if he did not slaughter the Muslims, he would be killed himself. Erdemovic agreed to cooperate with the tribunal in its on-going prosecution of war crimes in the Yugoslavian states.

### June 1

**MURDER: Luray, Va.** The bodies of two backpackers, Julianne Williams, 24, of St. Cloud, Minnesota, and Lollie Winans, 26, of Unity, Maine, were found along the Appalachian Trail. The murdered pair made up the eighth and ninth people murdered on the Trail since 1974.

### June 3

**ARSON: Greensboro, Ala.** The Rising Star Baptist Church was burned to the ground, investigators believing that the building was torched by anti-black racists. At least 25 black churches had been torched throughout the South since January 1995.

**MURDER: Ft. Meyers, Fla.** Six gang members belonging to a group calling itself the Lords of Chaos, were arrested and charged with the fatal shooting of a band teacher on April 30, 1996. Kevin Foster and Christopher Black, two of the gang members, were later charged with attempted murder in a bizarre plot to mug employees at Disney World, don their cartoon character costumes and then shoot black visitors with guns affixed with silencers.

**SMUGGLING TRASH: Beijing, China** William Ping Chen, a U.S. citizen, was arrested and charged with importing and dumping 640 tons of U.S. garbage—dirty plastic bags, sewage, used syringes and rubber gloves—at a recycling location outside the city.

### June 4

**BOMBING: Manchester, England** An IRA car bomb exploded in the downtown area, injuring more than 200 persons.

### June 6

**MURDER: Chicago, Ill.** Delbert Heard was sentenced to death for killing three people in 1992.

### June 9

**WAR CRIMES: Zagreb, Yugoslavia** Officials announced the arrest of Zlatko Aleksovski, a Bosnian Croat indicted for war crimes in Muslim civilians in central Bosnia in 1993.

### June 10

**ARSON: Greenville, Texas** The Church of the Living God, with a predominately black membership, was burned

down, along with several empty houses in the town. Mark Anthony Young, 18, a black youth, would confess to the arson in July.

### June 13

**FRAUD/WEAPONS VIOLATIONS: Jordan, Mont.** Several members of the Montana Freemen who had been under FBI siege at a ranch outside Jordan, surrendered to agents who charged them with defrauding banks and possessing illegal weapons.

### June 15

**VEHICULAR HOMICIDE: Worcester, Mass.** A truck smashed into a parked car, killing five members of a New Hampshire family. The truck driver, Austin Kilcollins, of Florenceville, New Brunswick, Canada, was charged with vehicular homicide.

### June 18

**MURDER: Brooklyn, N.Y.** After a four-hour gunfight with police, Heriberto Seda surrendered to police; evidence was found in Seda's apartment which pinpointed him as the lone terrorist known as "Zodiac," who had, in 1990, shot and killed four persons. Before being sent to prison, Seda confessed that the had been moved to kill by a "sudden urge."

**MURDER: Sacramento, Calif.** Theodore Kaczynski, identified as the notorious Unabomber who had killed three persons and injured another 23 persons with mail bombs since 1978, was charged with murdering two persons and injuring another two people in California.

### June 20

**MASS MURDER: Big Sauk Lake, Minn.** Peter Crawford, angry that a property stake had been removed from his land, shot and killed his neighbor, Warren Schoegl, his wife and two children, then killed himself before police arrived.

**MURDER: Montrose, Pa.** Stephen Scher, a successful 56-year-old physician, was arrested and charged with the June 2, 1976 shooting death of 30-year-old Martin T. Dillon, a lawyer and father of two children. Scher and Dillon had gone skeet shooting and Scher later reported that Dillon had fallen down and his gun went off, accidentally killing him. Scher said that Dillon had grabbed his gun and chased a porcupine, but fell awkwardly and the gun discharged, blasting out Dillon's heart. Scher said he was so frustrated and angry that he smashed the gun against a tree. Officials were prodded to exhume Dillon's body and reexamine it by the victim's 76-year-old father, Lawrence Dillon, one-time mayor of Montrose, and who had always suspected Scher of killing his son, especially after Scher married Dillon's widow following Dillon's death.

### June 25

**BOMBING: Dhahran/Khobar, Saudi Arabia** A truck bomb exploded at the entrance of Khobar Towers, a complex housing U.S. personnel, killing 19 American servicemen and wounding 500 hundred more, mostly Americans. Saudi police later reported that a gasoline truck arrived at the eight-story Towers and its driver fled the truck, entered another vehicle and then fled. Police had little time to warn anyone before the truck bomb exploded, gouging out a 35-foot-deep crater. President Clinton ordered the FBI to send investigators to Saudi Arabia, but agents later reported that it was next to impossible to obtain cooperation from Saudi officials in the on-going investigation.

### June 27

**MURDER: Philadelphia, Pa.** Ann Marie Fahey, mistress of wealthy attorney Thomas J. Capano, disappeared after having dinner with Capano, who would be convicted of her murder on January 28, 1999.

**WAR CRIMES: The Hague, Netherlands** The United Nations War Crimes Tribunal indicted eight Bosnian Serb policemen and soldiers for reportedly raping scores of Muslim women in Southeastern Bosnia, the first time the crime of rape was labeled a war crime.

### June 28-29

**TERRORISM: Paris, France** A group of seven nations, led by the U.S. met to support an anti-terrorist plan, that included expanding extradition treaties, controlling the import and export of firearms and the prevention of money-laundering. On the following day, the world leaders warned Serbia that it would face renewed sanctions unless Radovan Karadzic, an indicted war criminal, resigned as president of the Bosnian Serb republic.

### July 1

**CONSPIRACY/TERRORISM: Phoenix, Ariz.** Twelve members of the Viper Militia were arrested by FBI agents and charged with conspiring to manufacture and possess unregistered destructive devices and illegally instructing others in the use of explosive devices to cause disorder and destruction and illegally possessing automatic weapons. Evidence presented by the Bureau included a video tape in which 7 target buildings were shown and how to place explosives in the destruction of those buildings. All 12 pleaded not guilty.

**CELLULAR PHONE NUMBER THEFT: Brooklyn, N.Y.** Abraham Romy and Irina Bashkavich were arrested and charged with possession, distribution and trafficking in access devices. Police stated that the couple used a high-powered scanner from their 14th-floor window sill to steal more than 80,000 cellular phone numbers from passing motorists, the largest such theft in U.S. history.

### July 2

**MURDER: Los Angeles, Calif.** Lyle and Erik Menendez, convicted of the 1989 murders of their millionaire parents, were each sentenced to two consecutive life terms in prison.

**PRESIDENTIAL THREAT: Chicago, Ill.** While President Bill Clinton was visiting the Taste of Chicago, a food festival, he moved through the crowds, shaking hands. When he approached Patricia Mendoza, she said to him: "You suck and those boys died!" She later said she was referring to the 19 American servicemen who died on June 25 following an bombing in Saudi Arabia. Mendoza and her husband, Glenn Mendoza, were both arrested at the request of Secret Service agents and jailed until the following morning, charged with making a threat to Clinton.

### July 3

**MURDER: Indiana** The body of Herbert Baumeister, an Indianapolis businessman thought to have been the serial killer of a dozen gay men, was found in his car at a state park; he had committed suicide.

### July 6

**AIR RAGE: Savannah, Ga,** Gary Lee Lougee, a 40-year-old Georgia native, appeared to be drunk when he boarded a USAir flight bound for Charlotte, North Carolina, shoving a flight attendant who refused to serve him drinks and who had to be subdued by several members of the crew, causing the plane to return to Savannah.

### July 7

**MURDER: Sydney, Australia** Serial killer Ivan Robert Marko Milat was found guilty of murdering 7 backpackers in Belanglo State Forrest and was sent to prison for life.

### July 9

**FALSE STATEMENTS: Washington, D.C.** A grand jury indicted Henry Espy, mayor of Clarksdale, Mississippi, and brother to Agriculture Secretary Mike Espy, charging him with making false statements to obtain a campaign loan in 1993.

**RAPE: Rochester, N.Y.** John Horace, 52, who had been fired from his position as a nurse's aide at the Westfall Health Care Center, was charged with raping a 30-year-old woman who had been comatose since being injured in a 1985 car wreck.

### July 11

**WAR CRIMES: The Hague, Netherlands** The U.N. International Crime Tribunal issued warrants for Radko Mladic, the Bosnian Serb military chief, and Radovan Karadzic, political head of the Bosnian Serbs, charging each with crimes against humanity.

### July 11-12

**BOMBINGS: Moscow, Russia** Two bombs exploded on two trolley buses, one on July 11, injuring 5 persons, a second on July 12, wounding 28 more persons. Police stressed that there was no evidence that the bombings were planted by Chechen separatists or Russian Mafia gangsters. President Boris Yeltsin remarked that Moscow was "infested with terrorists."

### July 12

**BOMBING: Moscow, Russia** A bomb planted on a bus exploded on the busy Prospect Mira, injuring 28 persons, eight of them seriously. This was the third bombing in Moscow since June 11, 1996, which killed one person and wounded scores more. Government officials ordered 1,000 troops into the city to clear the streets of homeless vagrants. Mayor Yuri Luznkov attributed the bombings to Chechen terrorists.

**ROBBERY/SUICIDE: Covington, Ky.** Richard Gutherie, 38, one of four bank robbers belonging to a gang called the "Midwestern Bank Bandits," which had taken more than $200,000 in robberies from banks in Iowa, Kansas, Kentucky, Missouri, Nebraska, Ohio, and Wisconsin in 1994-1995, used a bedsheet to hang himself in his cell. Gutherie and his fellow bandits had mocked the FBI by wearing the Agency's logos when committing their crimes. Gutherie had pleaded guilty on July 3, 1996. Prosecutors had agreed to recommend his sentence be no more than 30 years if he agreed to later testify against three others awaiting trial.

## July 13

**BOMBING: Edmond, Okla.** Kelly Sean Spencer was arrested after a bomb exploded inside his room at the Red Carpet Motel. Police found four pipe bombs inside the room, all of the pipe bombs taped together and having 16 pounds of explosives. Motel manager Bee Bowker reported how Spencer emerged from his room covered with soot, shouting to her: "Call somebody! My air conditioner blew up!" She called police, later saying: "I knew no air conditioner could do that."

**MURDER: Virginia Beach, Va.** Michael D. Clagett was sentenced to death after having been found guilty of robbing a bar and executing four persons on the spot.

## July 13-14

**RIOTS: Belfast, Northern Ireland** Thousands of Catholics rioted for almost two days in protest over marches by Protestants through their neighborhoods, these marches commemorating 17th century battle victories over Irish Catholics by British armies. One person was killed and scores more were injured in the bloody confrontations between police and Catholics.

## July 17

**EXECUTION: Jarratt, Va.** Joseph John Savino III was executed by lethal injection for the 1988 murder of his employer, Thomas McWaters.

**EXPLOSION: Long Island, N.Y.** TWA Flight 800, a jumbo 747 jetliner, just after taking off, blew up over the ocean off Long Island, with all 230 persons on board killed. It was later claimed that the airplane was downed by a missile, accidentally fired by a U.S. military training plane, or by terrorists firing from shore or on a ship at sea, but none of these speculations would be proven.

**ROBBERY: Joliet, Ill.** Darrell Taylor, 35 and 29-year-old Ali R. Robinson, robbed the First National Bank of Chicago branch in Joliet of about $134,000, forcing two bank employees into the vault at gunpoint and used duct tape to tie up the employees, also using the tape to cover their fingers in order not to leave prints. The thieves, as well as Lawanda Corruthers, their getaway driver, were tracked down through their purchases of cars and other luxury items after the robbery. Taylor and Robinson were convicted on November 18, 1996. Corruthers pleaded guilty to lesser charges before the trial of her associates.

## July 17-19

**WAR CRIMES: Belgrade, Yugoslavia** Richard Holbrooke, U.S. assistant secretary of state, and Serbian President Slobodan Milosovic negotiated the resignation of Radovan Karadzic as president of the Bosnian Serb republic and chief of the leading political party, but Holbrooke later stated that he believed Karadzic would attempt to hold power while working behind the scenes.

## July 20

**ASSAULT: Tokyo, Japan** Terrence Michael Swanson, a 20-year-old U.S. sailor assigned to the missile frigate U.S.S. *McClusky* at the Sasebo Naval base, confessed that he had slashed the throat of a Japanese woman in order to steal her purse. (The victim survived after a month of hospitalization.) Swanson had been turned over to Japanese authorities following the assault. Previous to the Swanson case, U.S. personnel were not handed over until indicted, but new accords had been established between U.S.-Japanese officials in response to a widespread uproar in Japan over the brutal rape of a Japanese girl by three U.S. servicemen stationed on the island of Okinawa.

**BOMBING: Tarragona, Spain** A bomb exploded at Reus Airport, injuring 33 persons, most of them British tourists. The bomb was reportedly planted by ETA terrorists.

**GENOCIDE: Bugendana, Burundi** More than 300 members of the Tutsi tribe were slaughtered by invading Hutu tribe members bent on wiping out all Tutsis in a genocidal campaign that had seen more than 150,000 Burundians killed within the last three years, similar to the genocide practiced by Hutus in Rwanda in the early 1990s.

## July 22

**FRAUD/BANK ROBBERY: San Diego, Calif.** Investment broker Thomas W. Collins, convicted of bilking millions from customers in Illinois and who had fled and remained a fugitive for two years, was stopped for questioning in a bank robbery that day (Collins had robbed the bank). As officers approached his car, Collins fatally shot himself.

## July 24

**MURDER: Chicago, Ill.** Fanny Garay, a 7-month-old girl was brought to Columbus Hospital with burns over more than 50 percent of her body and died a short time later. Five days later, her parents, Juan Garay, 25, and his 21-year-old wife Isabel were charged with first-degree murder, police reporting that the couple had submerged their child in scalding water and caused her subsequent death.

## July 26

**HIJACKING: Miami, Fla.** Three Palestinians hijacked a Madrid to Miami Iberian airliner by using a fake bomb and were arrested by FBI agents when arriving in Miami.

**MURDER: Montgomery County, Md.** Bruman Stalin Alvarez pleaded guilty in court to murdering Dr. David Marc Goff, raping and murdering Goff's three daughters and killing Mark Richard Aldridge, the contractor who hired him to paint Goff's house where the slayings occurred on July 20, 1995. Alvarez was given five life terms.

## July 27

**BOMBING: Atlanta, Ga.** A nail-laden pipe bomb hidden inside a backpack was placed in a crowded dancing area in Atlanta's Centennial Olympic Park and exploded a short time later, killing one woman and injuring 111 others. Security guard Richard Jewell will be hailed a hero for spotting the backpack and warning those nearby, but will later be considered a prime suspect by the FBI. The Bureau would later drop Jewell and openly charge Eric Rudolph, a much-wanted fugitive.

**GENOCIDE: Bujumbura, Burundi** More than 150 members of the Hutu tribe were massacred by attacking Tutsi tribesmen in retaliation for the July 20, 1996 attack on a Tutsi village.

### July 29

**MURDER: Tucson, Ariz.** Beau John Green, convicted of murdering and robbing Roy Andrew Johnson, a 58-year-old music professor at the University of Arizona, was sentenced to death.

### August 1

**ARSON: Dillon, S.C.** The AME Church, which had a black congregation, was burned to the ground. Two white youths, Dennis Martin Moody, Jr., and Neil Talbot, both 17, were arrested and charged with the arson on August 4, 1996.

**WHITEWATER: Little Rock, Ark.** Robert Hill and Herby Branscum, Jr., two Arkansas bankers who had been accused of concealing large cash withdrawals made by the 1990 reelection campaign of then Governor Bill Clinton, were acquitted of conspiracy charges and found not guilty on 2 of 9 fraud charges. The jury was deadlocked on other charges. Both had been prosecuted by Kenneth Starr, the independent counsel investigating Whitewater. President Bill Clinton testified on video tape that he had not appointed Hill and Branscum to state agencies in exchange for campaign contributions.

### August 4

**BOMB PLOT: Grossetto, Italy** Prosecutor Piero Luigi Vigna announced that the Mafia had plotted to blow up the leaning Tower of Pisa as part of a strategy to attack the country's monuments in response to a crackdown on the criminal brotherhood.

**MURDER: Doraville, Ga.** Two security guards, Danny Cook and Juventino Silva, were members of the 4,000 Indiana National Guardsmen sent to Atlanta as part of added security for the Olympic Games. Cook and Silva were returning to their quarters after having dinner when someone jumped from some bushes and fired at them, grazing Cook and fatally shooting the 25-year-old Silva. No one was arrested and the reason for the shootings remained a mystery.

### August 6

**MURDER: Wabash, Ind.** David Sholes, 40, reportedly became enraged when a motorcyclist struck the fishing boat he was towing, fatally shot the biker, a bystander and a passing driver. He wounded another person before overturning his truck in his attempt to flee from pursuing police.

### August 7

**MURDER: Pueblo, Colo.** Two Catholic priests, Rev. Tom Scheets and Rev. Louis Stovik, were found stabbed to death in the rectory of the St. Leander Catholic Church. Douglas J.

Comiskey, a parishioner who had lived across the street from the church most of his life, was charged with the murders.

### August 8

**DRUGS: New York, N.Y.** Herbert Huncke, a notorious drug addict, street hustler and burglar who had spent most of the 1950s in jail and whose vicious experiences inspired much of the gutter-life literature of his cronies, Jack Kerouac and Allen Ginsberg (he is credited with coining the tag "Beat Generation"), died of congestive heart failure at age 81. Huncke allegedly gave writer William S. Burroughs his first drug fix. Jerry Garcia, of the Grateful Dead group, reportedly paid Huncke's rent at New York's Chelsea Hotel.

### August 9

**EXECUTION: McAlester, Okla.** Steven Keith Hatch, who had, with an accomplice, killed Richard and Marilyn Douglass, raped their 12-year-old daughter Leslie and wounded their 16-year-old son Brooks, was executed by lethal injection. Leslie and Brooks Douglass were present as witnesses.

### August 10

**FALSIFICATION OF RECORDS: Woodbourne, N.Y.** Mortician Lynn Sullivan was arrested and charged with falsification of records in that he had not cremated or buried many bodies for which he had charged against his services. Several decaying corpses in cheap cardboard boxes were removed from Sullivan's basement and garage.

**KIDNAPPING: Tijuana, Mexico** Mamoru Konno, the 57-year-old president of Sanyo Video Component Corp., USA, was kidnapped after a company baseball game and held for a $2 million ransom. The cash, in unmarked bills, was delivered to the kidnappers by a Mexican state police officer driving a Sanyo company car on the night of August 19. He drove to the La Joya section of Tijuana where he was met by two men who took the ransom money and then told the officer where Konno could be found. Konno was discovered unharmed in an abandoned building. Although Mexican authorities stated that the kidnappers, six Mexicans operating an abduction ring in Tijuana and Ensenada, were responsible, no one was arrested. One report had it that the members of the Tijuana police department were behind the kidnapping. In similar instances, Mexican police, operating in what had become a lawless "narco country," had performed kidnappings.

### August 13

**CHILD MOLESTATION: Chicago, Ill.** Raymond Borkowicz, previously convicted of child molestation, was arrested and charged with molesting a 9-year-old boy after police stopped at his home to remind him to register as a convicted child molester, required under a new state law, and found him with two children.

### August 15

**MURDER: Arlington, Va.** Christopher J. Beck, who had confessed to killing three persons, was sentenced to death.

**MASS MURDER: San Diego, Calif.** Frederick Martin Davidson, a student at San Diego State University, shot and killed three professors whom he believed were about to reject his master's thesis.

## August 17

**MURDER: Algiers, Algeria** More than 100 Muslim militants intent on overthrowing the government reportedly stopped two buses outside the town at a fake police barricade and then proceeded to shoot, stab and ax to death the 63 passengers. The government refused to confirm the report which appeared in the London-based Arabic daily, *Al-Hayai*.

## August 19

**CHILD PORNOGRAPHY ON THE INTERNET: Chicago, Ill.** William G. Kaspar, 25, pleaded guilty to distributing child pornography by computer. Kaspar admitted that he had sent computer images of underage girls engaged in sex to an undercover FBI agent logged onto America Online.

## August 19-20

**WHITEWATER: Little Rock, Ark.** Jim Guy Tucker, found guilty of fraud, was sentenced to four years' probation by federal Judge George Howard, Jr. Tucker was thought to be in failing health. Susan McDougal, Tucker's co-defendant, who was also convicted of Whitewater-related charges, was sentenced to two years in prison the following day. James McDougal was not sentenced; he was reportedly cooperating with independent counsel Kenneth Starr.

## August 21

**TERRORISM: Havana, Cuba** Walter Van der Veer, a U.S. citizen, was arrested and charged with working for "a terrorist group," in that he had smuggled military equipment into Cuba and was planning actions against the government. Van der Veer denied the accusations, saying that he went to Cuba to distribute food and Bibles to the poor.

## August 26

**DEATH SENTENCE: Seoul, South Korea** Chun Doo Hwan, former president of South Korea (1980-1988), convicted of leading a 1979 coup that put him in power, bribery, and the massacre of pro-democracy demonstrators in 1980, was sentenced to death. Former government officials, army officers and business executives, who had all been part of Chun's cabal, were also convicted and received prison sentences.

## August 28

**ORGANIZED CRIME: Brooklyn, N.Y.** Vincent "The Chin" Gigante, head of the Gambino crime family, who had wandered about Greenwich Village in slippers and bathrobe mumbling to himself for years as an act to convince authorities that he was unbalanced, was ruled sane and ordered to stand trial on charges of murder and racketeering.

## August 29

**PROSTITUTION: Washington, D.C.** Sherry Rowlands, identified by the press as a prostitute, had reportedly been paid to sex by Dick Morris, presidential adviser to President Clinton, who let her listen in on phone conversations he had with Clinton. Morris, as the scandal broke, resigned this date.

## September 4

**WHITEWATER: Little Rock, Ark.** Susan McDougal, who had been convicted and sentenced to prison for fraud in Whitewater-related matters, refused to testify before a grand jury still probing Whitewater and was sentenced to jail for contempt by Judge Susan Webber Wright.

## September 5

**MURDER: Virginia Beach, Va.** Dustin Turner, a 21-year-old former SEAL, was convicted of snapping the neck of 21-year-old Jennifer Evans, a college student who had refused to have sex with him. The jury recommended 82 years in prison.

**TERRORISM: New York, N. Y.** Three radical Islamic terrorists were convicted of plotting to blow up 12 U.S. airline flights over the Pacific Ocean. Ramzi Ahmed Yousef, the mastermind behind the World Trade Center bombing was found guilty of ordering five Muslims each to smuggle on board 12 U.S. airliners leaving the Far East in January 1995. Yousef was also found guilty of planting a bomb on a Philippine Airlines plane that exploded and killed 1 person.

## September 6

**DRUGS: Houston, Texas** Police seized a shipment of 12-foot steel cylinders used to compress paper from a Colombian-registered ship and found, crammed into the hollow steel rollers, more than a ton of cocaine with an estimated street value of $100 million. No arrests were made.

## September 8

**PROSTITUTION: Las Vegas, Nev.** Devine Brown, the prostitute arrested with actor Hugh Grant in 1995, was arrested at the MGM Grand Hotel and Casino and charged with loitering for the purpose of prostitution.

## September 9

**ASSASSINATION: Gitega, Burundi** Archbishop Joachim Ruhuna was reportedly assassinated when his car was firebombed and machine gunned outside the village of Gitega.

## September 13

**MURDER: Las Vegas, Nev.** Rapper Tupac Shakur, shot on September 7, 1996, by unknown assailants in Las Vegas while riding in his agent's white Cadillac and standing through the open sun roof, died of his wounds at the University Medical Center.

## September 14

**MURDER: Bunievel, N.C.** Keturah Reese reported her 8-year-old son Justin missing. The boy's body was later found in a remote area. He had been strangled. Upon questioning, Reese admitted killing her son.

## September 15

**RAPE: Andes, N.Y.** Richard Paul Elliott, who had earlier in the month kidnapped, repeatedly raped and held hostage two prostitutes in a dungeon-like room in his Baltimore, Maryland, home, was shot and killed in self-defense by a former business associate.

*September 18*

**MURDER: State College, Pa.** Jillian Robbins, 19, began shooting a rifle at college students on the Penn State campus, killing Melanie Spalla, and wounding Nicholas Mensah, 22. Robbins, who had once served in the Army Reserve, gave no reason for the shootings when taken into custody and charged with murder.

*September 23*

**ABDUCTION/MURDER/RAPE: Newalla, Okla.** Thomas Loveless, Jr. and Michael Foldenauer, both 16, were charged with the abduction, rape and shotgun murder of Tiffany Rebecca Tull, 15, their classmate. Loveless was reportedly the killer, although Foldenauer helped Loveless to abduct the girl and also raped her before Loveless fatally shot Tull in the chest with a 12 gauge shotgun slug.

**CRIME LEGISLATION: Washington, D.C.** As part of a defense bill signed into law by President Clinton, a key provision, unrelated to the military, made it a crime to cross a state line to stalk someone.

*September 26*

**CHILD MOLESTATION/MURDER: Santa Clara, Calif.** Richard Allen Davis, one of California's worst child molesters and killers, was sentenced to death for the 1993 abduction, sexual molestation and murder of 12-year-old Polly Klaas.

*September 28*

**MURDER: Chicago, Ill.** Three persons—Johnny Jones, 46, Marshall Mason, 72 and Erica Chotoosingh, 22—were found shot to death in an upscale Cape Cod home on Chicago's far South Side. Their suspected killer, Edward Graham, was tracked down and arrested at a Las Vegas, Nevada, motel in November 1996.

**POLICE RAIDS: London, England** Police raided the hideout of four IRA members, confiscating army weapons and 10 tons of explosives. In an earlier raid on a London flat, police shot and killed 27-year-old IRA leader Diarmuid O'Neill.

*October 1*

**MURDER: Avon Park Correctional Institution, Fla.** Convicted child killer Donald McDougall was reportedly killed by another inmate, Arba Earl Barr, inspired to the murder by a talk show caller who offered a reward to anyone who killed McDougall.

*October 3*

**KIDNAPPING: Salem, Ore.** Lance Sterling Alexander, wanted for the October 1, 1996 murder of William Jason Mowdy, kidnapped at random 7-year-old Kristina Jacobson, leading police on a high-speed chase while he held a gun to the head of the child. When Alexander's car crashed and overturned, a police sharpshooter shot Alexander dead. Jacobson was rescued with only minor injuries.

**MURDER: Highland Park, Ill.** Richard Grossman, a successful 44-year-old businessman was reportedly stabbed to death by his 17-year-old son, Michael Grossman. While jailed and awaiting trial, Grossman told his attorneys that he was being hounded by "demons" in his cell.

**MURDER: Waurika, Okla.** Heather Rich, a 16-year-old honors student vanished. Her body would later be found dumped across the border in Texas. Her killers were her own classmates, Curtis Gambill, Joshua Bagwell and Randy Lee Wood, who would all be sent to prison for life.

*October 4*

**ADMINISTERING UNSANITIZED BLOOD: Tokyo, Japan** Akihito Matsumura, the 55-year-old former chief of the Health and Welfare Ministry's blood products department, was arrested and charged with allowing unsanitized blood to be given to hemophiliacs, hundreds of whom later died from AIDS. Several others, including Dr. Takeshi Abe, a leading hemophilia specialist, were also arrested.

*October 7*

**BOMBINGS: Lisburn, Northern Ireland** Two car bombs were detonated inside the British Army's heavily defended headquarters, wounding 31 persons. The IRA was held responsible.

*October 8*

**MURDER: South Korea** Two men disappeared after they went off to pick mushrooms. They were later found shot to death, along with a 67-year-old woman who had been beaten and suffocated to death. All three murders were attributed to members of a North Korean submarine that was stranded on the South Korean coast.

*October 9*

**SMUGGLING: Paris, France** Officials announced that a large ring of smugglers trafficking in illegal aliens, had been rounded up, 17 persons in all who had smuggled hundreds of illegal immigrants from Sri Lanka to France and then to Canada in the past 8 years.

*October 11*

**CONSPIRACY: Clarksburg, W. Va.** FBI agents arrested seven members of the West Virginia Mountaineer Militia, charging them with conspiring to blow up federal buildings. An informant within the ranks of the right-wing group had gone to the FBI months earlier to report the group's plans.

*October 12*

**PLOTTING TO SUBVERT THE STATE: Beijing, China** Wang Dan, who had been Number 1 on the Most Wanted police list as a political dissident, was charged with plotting to subvert the state, as had China's longest serving political prisoner, Wei Jingsheng, sentenced to 14 years imprisonment in 1995. Wang Dan had been one of the pro-democracy leaders of the 1989 Tiananmen Square uprising.

*October 14*

**PRICE-FIXING: Chicago, Ill.** Archer Daniels Midland

(ADM), was fined $100 million for conspiring with competitors to fix prices on two agricultural products. Several of its top executives were also convicted and sent to prison.

## October 15

**PRICE FIXING: Chicago, Ill.** ADM, in a plea-bargain agreement, agreed to pay a $100 million fine for price fixing some of its agricultural products.

## October 17

**WRONGFUL DEATH: Santa Monica, Calif.** Though acquitted of murdering his ex-wife Nicole Brown Simpson and Ronald Goldman, O.J. Simpson was sued in a wrongful death suit by the relatives of Ronald Goldman and Nicole Brown Simpson.

## October 19

**PRISON ESCAPE: Florence, Ariz.** Six prisoners escaped from the privately run Central Arizona Detention Center, operated by the Corrections Corp. of America. All six were from Alaska which had a contract to house several hundred prisoners at the institution, and three of these were convicted murderers. All six men were later recaptured.

## October 23

**ATTEMPTED MURDER: Sydney, Australia** Michael Keith Withers was convicted of attempting to murder Stacey Larson, his common-law wife—he had doused her with gasoline and set her on fire—after their ballroom dancing act went into decline.

## October 29

**BOMBING: Atlanta, Ga.** Richard Jewell, who had been relentlessly pursued by the FBI as a suspect in the July bombing of Atlanta's Centennial Park, was finally cleared by the Bureau.

**TAX EVASION: Jerusalem, Israel** Israeli tax officials raided the offices of News Datacom Research, Ltd., a firm owned by media magnate Rupert Murdoch, seizing records and charging that the firm had evaded paying $150 million in taxes.

## October 22

**FRAUD: Chicago, Ill.** Four men were sentenced to prison for defrauding the Chicago Housing Authority of more than $12 million. Sent to prison for 17 years was ringleader Joseph Polichemi, 64. The three others were 54-year-old Lyle Neal, Oscar Olson, a 69-year-old attorney from Wheaton, Ill., and 46-year-old Charles Padilla, a former banker from Lexington, Ky.

**OBSTRUCTION OF JUSTICE: Washington, D.C.** FBI agent E. Michael Kahoe was charged with obstruction of justice in an on-going investigation into FBI wrongdoing and destruction of documents involved in the 1992 FBI siege of Randall Weaver's ranch in Ruby Ridge, Idaho, which resulted in the shooting deaths of 3 persons.

## October 24

**OBSTRUCTING OFFICIAL BUSINESS: Cincinnati, Ohio** Sylvia Stayton, a 62-year-old businesswoman and grandmother of 10, was arrested and charged with obstructing official business and disorderly conduct when she fed coins into several expired meters on a business street. Warned not to put more coins into an expired meter by Officer Edward Johnson, Stayton reportedly stated: "You've got to be kidding." When she inserted more coins into a meter, Johnson handcuffed her and arrested her. Stayton thought she was merely being a good Samaritan in helping strangers avoid parking tickets. The case captured national attention and brought Stayton hundreds of dollars in donations toward in what she called her "legal abuse fund." Johnson's arrest was considered petty, even specious and brought unnecessary ridicule on the Cincinnati Police Department.

## October 24-25

**RIOTS: St. Petersburg, Fla.** Following the shooting of a black motorist by a white policemen, thousands of blacks resorted to rioting and looting as 25 buildings were burned in a 25-block square area. Blacks threw bottles and rocks. A news reporter was seized and beaten and 20 black residents were arrested, charged with looting.

## October 26

**BOMBING: Atlanta, Ga.** The FBI officially notified Richard Jewell, who had been a Bureau suspect in the bombing of Atlanta's Centennial Park, that he was no longer a suspect.

## October 30

**OBSTRUCTING JUSTICE: Washington, D.C.** E. Michael Kahoe pleaded guilty to obstructing justice regarding the FBI siege of the Randall Weaver farm at Ruby Ridge, Idaho in 1992 in which three persons were killed. Kahoe, then chief of the Bureau's Violent Crime and Major Offenders' sections, had destroyed an FBI report critical of the conduct of some of its agents at Ruby Ridge.

## November 1

**MURDER: Cincinnati, Ohio** Gerald Clemmons, a 54-year-old truck driver, was sentenced to death for killing three co-workers in a job-related dispute in December 1995.

## November 3

**MURDER: Moscow, Russia** American businessman Paul Tatum, who had had problems with his partners in the operation of the Raddison Hotel, was shot and killed in a subway station.

## November 4

**MURDER: Anderson, Ind.** Lowell Amos, a General Motors plant manager, was sentenced to prison for life after having been convicted of killing his third wife. (He was thought to have also murdered his own mother and two previous wives for insurance money.)

## November 5

**LAW ENFORCEMENT: Port-au-Prince, Haiti** Police shot and killed five men, one in handcuffs, which was cited in the world press as another example of terrorist tactics practiced by what has been described as a "constabulary of thugs."

The Haitian police force, poorly trained in a four-month crash course by U.S. advisers, following the free election of President Jean Bertrand Aristide (with the help of a strong U.S. military presence in Haiti in 1994), had sadistically beaten prisoners, some to death, and indiscriminately used deadly force, firing after autos (killing a small girl riding in one car).

**MURDER: Seoul, South Korea** U.S. authorities refused to turn over Eric Munnich, a serviceman accused of the September 1996 stabbing to death 44-year-old Lee Ki Sun in a boarding house near a U.S. military base where Munnich was stationed. Munnich reportedly admitted the killing.

### November 6

**CHILD MOLESTATION/MURDER: Ford Lauderdale, Fla.** Longtime child molester Howard Steven Ault was arrested and charged with the abduction, sexual molestation and murder of two young girls. Their bodies were later found in the attic of Ault's home.

**MURDER: St. Louis, Mo.** Kelly McGinnis, 40, who had fatally shot his wife's divorce lawyer, Thomas Meyer, on August 12, 1996, and who bombarded newspapers with letters railing against the "divorce industry," while on the run, was captured after a being featured on the TV show, "America's Most Wanted."

### November 7

**DEATH HOUSE COMMUTATION: Richmond, Va.** Governor George Allen commuted the death sentence of Joseph Payne, who had been convicted of murdering a fellow inmate by setting him on fire, only three hours before Payne was scheduled to be executed. Allen's decision to spare Payne was based upon conflicting testimony in the case—an eye-witness recanted his testimony, four jurors in Payne's case publicly doubted their verdict and the victim's mother asked for clemency.

**SEXUAL HARASSMENT IN THE U.S. MILITARY: Washington, D.C.** Army officials announced that it was investigating a large number of complaints from female soldiers that they had been sexually harassed by non-commissioned and commissioned officers. Two servicemen had been charged with rape. More than two dozen women trainees at the Aberdeen Proving Ground in Maryland had complained of sexual abuse.

### November 9

**ROBBERY: Chicago, Ill.** An armed robber held up the Success National Bank, taking $12,000 from 20-year-old teller Janet Patterson, who then hit the alarm button when the thief ran from the bank. After Patterson gave conflicting information about the robber, investigators probed her relationship to another woman, 21-year-old Valencia Lee, who had made a scene in the bank immediately after the robbery, as a diversion it later turned out. Patterson and Lee later confessed that they had been part of the plot to rob the bank with the armed thief, Victor Orozco, 23, and all three were charged.

### November 10

**THEFT: Quincy, Mass.** Thieves broke into the first presidential library—that of John Quincy Adams—and made off with a half dozen books from the 14,000-book library. One of the volumes was a priceless Bible which had been given to John Quincy Adams who successfully defended the Africans who had killed their slavers aboard the ship Amistad in 1839.

### November 12

**DRUNK DRIVING: Franklin, Tenn.** Jennifer O'Neill was indicted for speeding and drunk driving. The 48-year-old actress had been arrested in March 1996, by a state trooper for driving at the clocked speed of 95 m.p.h. in a 65 m.p.h. zone. At the time she failed a sobriety test.

**MURDER: Newark, Del.** Amy Grossberg and Brian C. Peterson, Jr., murdered their newly-born child, wrapping the body in a plastic bag and dumping it into a trash can.

**SEXUAL HARASSMENT IN THE U.S. MILITARY: Fort Leonard Wood, Mo.** Army officials announced that 3 male sergeants had been charged with the sexual abuse of female soldiers. One non-commissioned officer pleaded guilty this date to improper relations with women trainees.

**TERRORISM: Ciudad del Este, Paraguay** Police burst into a hotel room to arrest Marwan Al Sadafi, also known as Marwan Adib Adam Kadi, a 40-year-old Lebanese who was suspected of being a top terrorist for the Iranian-backed Hezbollah organization and was involved in the 1994 bombing of a Jewish community center in Buenos Aires that killed 86 people and the 1992 attack on the Israeli Embassy in Buenos Aires that killed 29 people.

### November 13

**HOSTAGE-TAKING: Columbus, Ohio** James L. Dailey, an unemployed welder distraught over a disability claim, took three hostages at the Bureau of Workers' Compensation and held them at gunpoint in a 7-hour standoff with police until he was tackled and subdued by a former FBI agent.

### November 14

**MURDER: Wixom, Mich.** Gerald Michael Atkins stormed into the Ford Motor plant and began shooting people at random. He would be sent to prison for life in 1998.

### November 16

**BOMBING: Fairton, N.J.** A woman picked up a package at the local post office and, when opening it in her car, it blew up, blowing out the windows and blasting her legs with shrapnel. No suspects were named.

**BOMBING: Kaspyisk, Russia** A powerful bomb ripped apart a building housing Russian border guard officers, killing 24 persons and wounding eight others. Chechen terrorists were blamed for the explosion.

### November 17

**FRAUD: Santa Ana, Calif.** Former Orange County Treasurer Robert Citron was sentenced to 1 year in prison and fined $100,000 after his conviction of securities fraud and misuse of public funds. Citron had brought the richest county in America to bankruptcy through his uncontrolled investments.

### November 18

**MURDER: Bartow, Fla.** John Zile, 34, who had claimed

that his 7-year-old stepdaughter, Christina Holt, had been kidnapped from a flea market, was found guilty of beating the girl to death and dumping her body behind a Kmart store. Zile admitted killing his stepdaughter because she had soiled her pants.

**SMUGGLING: Chicago, Ill.** Ornithologist Tony Silva was sentenced to seven years in prison for illegally smuggling South American parrots into the U.S.

*November 19*

**DRUGS: San Diego, Calif.** "Freeway Ricky" Ross, one of the state's most notorious drug traffickers, was sentenced to life in prison as a three-time loser.

**KIDNAPPING: San Francisco, Calif.** Marshall Wais, an 80-year-old businessman, was kidnapped and held for eight hours until his abductors collected a $500,000 ransom and then released Wais, giving him $20 for cab fare. Police in wait nearby rammed the getaway van and arrested two suspects.

*November 21*

**EMBEZZLEMENT: Knoxville, Tenn.** George Norman, a brilliant 66-year-old confidence man who had been on the run for 23 years, was arrested by U.S. marshals as he left a motel for dinner with his wife Donna. Norman, had used a dozen aliases since March 13, 1973, when he drove away from Denver, Colorado, in a borrowed car, skipping out on a two-year prison sentence for embezzling more than $500,000 from a now defunct Rocky Mountain Bank. Norman had reportedly made more than $50 million in mostly illegal schemes since that time (he was wearing a gold Rolex watch and his pockets were stuffed with hundred dollar bills when he was taken into custody) and had lived with the jetset for more than two decades, hobnobbing with celebrities and belonging to such exclusive organizations as San Diego's La Costa Country Club. Norman had come to Knoxville to have his $980,000 luxury Monaco motor home serviced when he was spotted by the U.S. marshals.

*November 22-26*

**WRONGFUL DEATH: Santa Monica, Calif.** O.J. Simpson underwent intense questioning from Daniel Petrocelli, an attorney for plaintiffs seeking a wrongful death verdict in a civil trial concerned with the murders of Nicole Brown Simpson and Ronald Goldman, for which Simpson had been acquitted in a criminal trial. Shown a photograph of a bruised and battered Nicole Brown Simpson, Simpson, who had earlier denied ever injuring his former spouse, admitted that he had been "wrongly physical." He denied ever owning or wearing a pair of rare Bruno Magli shoes similar to those which had left bloody imprints at the murder scene and he also denied that he had received a phone call from his former girlfriend, Paula Barbieri in which she told him that she was breaking off their relationship, although phone records suggested otherwise. Petrocelli stated that Simpson had murdered Nicole Brown Simpson was because he blamed her for the breakup with Barbieri (and that Goldman was killed because he arrived at the time Simpson was murdering his former wife).

*November 23*

**MURDER: Chicago, Ill.** Rev. Paul Smith, a retired 65-year-old Catholic priest and school teacher who was partially paralyzed, was bound and gagged by three robbers, the duct tape covering his face causing him to suffocate. Three men, including Smith's caretaker, Burrell Geralds, 36, and Fred and Freeman Carter, were later arrested and charged with the murder and robbery.

**SKYJACKING: Addis Ababa, Ethiopia** Three terrorists skyjacked and Ethiopian airliner, causing a crash-landing which killed 127 of the 175 persons on board.

**TRESPASSING: San Francisco, Calif.** After climbing San Francisco's Golden Gate Bridge to hang banners urging federal protection for 60,000 acres of redwood trees in Northern California, 35-year-old actor Woody Harrelson and eight others were arrested on charges of trespassing, being public nuisances and failing to obey a police officer. Later released, Harrelson and his associates faced fines up to $10,000.

*November 25*

**ASSAULT/ABUSE OF POWER: Jerusalem, Israel** Two Israeli border policemen, David Ben Abu and Tsahi Shmaya, were indicted on charges of aggravated assault and abuse of power. The pair had been arrested a week earlier after officials viewed a video tape showing the policemen kicking and humiliating six Palestinians, forcing them to do pushups and then hitting them in the face.

**MURDER: Eustis, Fla.** Roderick Justin Ferrell, a self-styled "vampire" and cult leader, used a crowbar to beat to death Richard and Naomi Wendorf, while their daughter Heather, who had joined Ferrell's cult, looked on. Ferrell, Wendorf and other cult members were later tracked down and arrested in Baton Rouge, La.

*November 26*

**FRAUD: Laughlin, Nev.** Nicholas Bissell, one-time high profile prosecutor for Somerset County, N.J., who had been convicted of fraud and had fled before sentencing, was tracked down to the Colorado Belle Hotel where he was confronted by U.S. marshals. Before he could be arrested, Bissell put a gun to his head, said: "I can't do ten years," and pulled the trigger, committing suicide.

*November 29*

**MURDER/SUICIDE: Walpole, Mass.** John C. Salvi III, sent to prison for life for the 1994 murders of two abortion clinic receptionists, hanged himself in his cell.

*December 1*

**KIDNAPPING: Pereira, Colombia** Brian Steven Ramirez Ortiz, a 4-year-old, was kidnapped and held for a $5,000 ransom, but the abductors killed the child by bundling him inside a large plastic bag and locking him in a closet, causing him to suffocate. Two suspects were later arrested. Colombia had to this time the highest abduction/kidnapping rate in the world with more than 900 persons kidnapped in 1996, 110 of these being minors.

*December 2*

**FRAUD: Los Angeles, Calif.** Federal Judge Mariana Pfaelzer threw out the federal conviction of Charles Keating, Jr., who had been convicted of racketeering and securities fraud and whose failed Lincoln Savings had caused the collapse of more than 700 savings and loan institutions, compelling a government bailout. Judge Pfaelzer stated that several jurors in the federal trial had become improperly predisposed to the defendant after discussing his 1991 state conviction. The 1991 state trial had been overturned in April 1996 because presiding Judge Lance Ito (who had presided at the overlong O.J. Simpson murder trial) had given improper instructions to the jury. Keating, by this time, had served four years in prison.

**MASS MURDER: Hobart, Australia** Martin Bryant, a 29-year-old gunman who had killed 35 persons and wounded another 19 people in a Tasmanian resort in April 1996, was sentenced to 35 life terms in prison.

*December 3*

**DRUGS: New York, N.Y.** William Drayton, 37, a rapper known as Flavor Flav and a longtime member of the group Public Enemy, was stopped by police as he rode his bicycle against traffic. Found on Drayton was more than 2 pounds of marijuana. He was charged with drug possession.

**RIOTS: Rangoon, Burma** Police and riot police arrested 120 students following prolonged riots stemming from the earlier arrests of 80 students who had demanded the right to organize independent unions on campus.

*December 4*

**ORGANIZED CRIME: Key Biscayne, Fla.** FBI agents arrested Nicholas "Little Nick" Corozzo, 56, as he climbed out of the surf, charging him with loansharking and attempted murder. The arrest was part of a crackdown on the Gambino crime family's operations in South Florida. Eight other members of Corozzo's alleged crime organization were also arrested.

*December 5*

**MURDER: Mexico City, Mexico** Crusading journalist Fernando Balderas, who had exposed widespread political corruption and identified drug cartel bosses was murdered, along with his wife and 3 children.

**MURDER: Newark, N.J.** Amy Grossberg and Brian C. Peterson, Jr., both 18, were indicted on murder charges after their newborn child was found dead in a motel trash bin. An autopsy revealed that the baby had been born healthy, but had died of skull fractures and brain injuries.

*December 7*

**MURDER?: Chicago, Ill.** The body of mystery writer Eugene Izzy was found hanging by a rope from his 13th office window at 6 N. Michigan Avenue. Speculation held that he had been murdered by those he had antagonized while researching a new crime novel, but police believed that Izzy had accidentally hanged himself while trying out a murder technique. The case remains a mystery.

*December 9*

**MURDER: Chicago, Ill.** Lucy Sprague, a 30-year-old student at John Marshall Law School was strangled in her apartment. Dwayne Vinson, 28, a maintenance worker in Sprague's building was charged with the killing.

*December 11*

**BOMBING: Washington, D.C.** The U.S. Air Force cleared General Terry J. Schwalier of any responsibility for the terrorist bombing of the U.S. military camp in Saudi Arabia on June 25, 1996, in which 19 Americans were killed and another 500 wounded, saying that Schwalier had taken responsible steps to protect the base. Hani al-Sayegh, a Saudi citizen, was later arrested and held in Canada as being the mastermind behind the attack.

*December 12*

**EXECUTION: Jarratt, Va.** Lem David Tuggle was executed by lethal injection for the 1982 murder of Jessie Geneva Havens.

*December 16*

**EXECUTION: Jarratt, Va.** Ronald Lee Hoke, Sr., was executed by lethal injection for the 1985 murder of Virginia Stell.

**MURDER: Torrance, Calif.** Photographer Charles Rathbun was sentenced to life in prison for the 1993 murder of model Linda Sobek.

**REDUCTION OF SENTENCES: Seoul, South Korea** An appeals court reduced the sentences given to 2 former presidents on August 26, 1996. Chun Doo Hwan's death sentence was reduced to life imprisonment and the 22 plus years given to Roh Tae Woo was reduced to 17 years. Many others convicted in the corruption case were given suspended sentences and some were acquitted.

*December 17*

**MASS MURDER: Chechnya** In the worst terrorist attack in the 133-year history of the Red Cross, five women, four being nurses, and a construction worker, were shot to death while they slept in a hospital compound. Veeselin Sljivancanin was thought to have led the raid against the hospital.

*December 17-18*

**HOSTAGE-TAKING: Lima, Peru** Fourteen members of the Túpac Amaru Revolutionary Movement (MRTA), led by Néstor Cerpa Cartolini, dashed into the Japanese Embassy during a diplomatic party, taking 490 hostages, many of these being top-ranking international diplomats. The terrorists threatened to kill the hostages unless imprisoned terrorists were released by the Peruvian government.

*December 18*

**EXECUTION; Kabul, Afghanistan** Ghulam Mahmad, convicted of murdering the pregnant wife of Mohammed Alif, a money-lender, during a robbery, was executed by Alif himself, which was allowed under Islamic law. More than 1,000 persons watched as Alif machine gunned Mahmad to death.

**RIOTS: Nairobi, Kenya** Police shot and killed two students who took part in widespread rioting, following the shooting of another student.

### December 23

**HOSTAGE-TAKING: Lima, Peru** MRTA terrorists occupying the Japanese Embassy released 225 of the 490 hostages as a Christmas gesture, but kept the remaining hostages under heavy guard and threat of death while they continued negotiating with Peruvian officials for the release of imprisoned fellow terrorists.

### December 25

**MURDER: Arlington, Texas** School teacher Wendie Rochell Prescott was found murdered in the bathtub of her apartment. She was the second teacher to be murder in the same way and in the same area, Christine H. Vu having been found strangled to death in her bathtub on September 17, 1996. Both unsolved killings were called the "Texas Tub Murders."

**ROBBERY: New York, N.Y.** Thieves followed two priests into the foyer of the famous St. Patrick's Cathedral in midtown Manhattan, and robbed them of $175.

### December 26

**MURDER: Boulder, Colo.** JonBenet Ramsey, a pretty 6-year-old who had won many junior beauty contests, was found dead in the home of her wealthy parents, John and Patsy Ramsey. She had been sexually assaulted and then strangled to death. The case remains unsolved at this writing, one of the most enigmatic murders in the decade, although the Ramseys themselves were all but labeled the killers by a national press obsessed with the case. Police reported no forced entry into the Ramsey luxury home. The parents, shielded by lawyers, did not grant interviews until April 30, 1997.

### December 28

**HOSTAGE-TAKING: Lima, Peru** MRTA terrorists occupying the Japanese Embassy released more hostages, but the Peruvian government took a hard line in negotiations, refusing to release imprisoned terrorists, only offering a safe passage to Cuba for the terrorists.

**TERRORIST THREATS: Beverly Hills, Calif.** Ken Wahl, one-time star of TV's *Wise Guy*, was arrested after reportedly getting drunk and threatening a hotel bartender with a hunting knife. The 39-year-old actor was booked on suspicion of making terrorist threats and released after posting a $150,000 bond.

### December 29

**ESPIONAGE: Pyongyang, North Korea** The Communist government announced by radio its "deep regret" for an incident occurring in September when a North Korean spy submarine ran aground on the South Korean coast and 26 North Korean commandos landed to commit murder and cause havoc. Of these 24 were killed, 1 was captured and 1 remained missing.

### December 30

**BOMBING: Kokrajhar, India** Separatists exploded two bombs beneath the tracks of a packed train as it was about to leave the station, killing 18 persons and injuring 60 others.

# 1997

### January 1

**BOMBING: Tulsa, Okla.** Two containers of flammable liquid were thrown at an abortion clinic, but little damage was done and no injuries were reported.

### January 5

**MURDER: Riverside, Calif.** Two sheriff's deputies were reportedly killed by 36-year-old Timothy Russell when they appeared outside his mobile home in response to a call about a domestic dispute. Russell was taken into custody and charged on two murder counts.

### January 7

**MURDER: Charlotte, N.C.** Serial killer Henry Lewis Wallace was convicted of murdering nine women from 1992 to 1994. He was sentenced to death.

### January 9

**MURDER: Bellevue, Wash.** Alex Baranyi, Jr. was arrested and charged with the murders of four persons—Kimberly Wilson, 20, whose strangled body was found in a park, her parents and sister, found in their home, beaten and stabbed.

### January 10

**ATTEMPTED ASSASSINATION: Ningthoukom, Manipur, India** Separatist terrorists attempted to kill N. Mangising, a Communist member of the Manipu state assembly, killing Mangising's six bodyguards, and injuring Mangising and four soldiers. The attackers were thought to be members of the Peoples' Liberation Army.

**MURDER/ROBBERY: Washington, D.C.** Kenneth Joel Marshall was sentenced to 80 years in prison for killing four employees of a McDonald's restaurant during a 1995 robbery.

### January 16:

**BOMBINGS: Atlanta, Ga.** A bomb exploded outside a building housing the Northside Family Planning Services, an abortion clinic. With police and reporters present, a second bomb exploded a short time later. Six persons were injured, including an investigator. The FBI would later attribute these two bombings to fugitive Eric Robert Rudolph, posting a $1 million reward for his capture.

**MURDER/ROBBERY: Los Angeles, Calif.** Ennis Cosby, the 27-year-old son of comedian Bill Cosby, was shot and killed in a robbery on an off ramp of an L.A. freeway while Cosby was attempting to fix a flat tire on his mother's Mercedes-Benz.

### January 19

**BOMBING: Tulsa, Okla.** Two bombs exploded at the abortion clinic attacked on January 1, damaging the building, but causing no injuries.

*January 20*

**TERRORIST ATTACKS/BOMBING: Algiers, Algeria** Islamic terrorists raided a village south of Algiers, murdering 36 residents, decapitating some of these victims. Hours later, these same terrorists exploded a car bomb outside of a cafe in Algiers, killing more than 30 persons and wounding scores more.

*January 21*

**MURDER: Los Angeles, Calif.** Lorenzo Newborn, Herbert McClain and Karl Holmes, all street gang members who had killed three innocent boys in 1993, were all sentenced to death.

*January 28*

**MURDER: South Africa** Five former police officers admitted to the 1977 beating murder of apartheid foe Steve Biko while he was in police custody. At the time of Biko's death, a false police report stated that Biko had accidentally injured himself while scuffling with officers.

*January 31*

**FRAUD: Seoul, South Korea** Steel magnate Chung Tae Soo, 73, was arrested and charged with defaulting on bank checks and corporate notes totaling $328 million and illegally drawing $51 million from a mutual savings firm which was controlled by his conglomerate.

*February 1*

**DEMOCRATS' FUND-RAISING SCANDAL: Washington, D.C.** The Washington *Post* revealed that Eric Wynn, of New Jersey, who had attended many events held by the Democratic National Committee (DNC) and a campaign contributor who had met President Clinton, had links to organized crime and had been convicted of stock manipulation and had been jailed for fraud and tax evasion.

*February 4*

**FRAUD: Vlore, Albania** After operating a blatant pyramid (or Ponzi) scheme in which early investors were paid returns from deposits of later investors, the Gjallica/Populli pyramid went bankrupt and the government began distributing what funds were left in the fund. Many investors received 60% on their money, but many others received nothing, having lost their life savings.

**MURDER: Newton, Mass.** Louise Woodward, a British au pair working for Sunil and Deborah Eappen, called 911 to say that 8-month-old Matthew Eappen had been injured. She was later charged with killing the child by shaking him and slamming him to "a hard surface."

**WRONGFUL DEATH: Santa Monica, Calif.** Though he had been acquitted in a criminal trial of murdering his former wife Nicole Brown Simpson and her friend, Ronald Goldman, O.J. Simpson was found liable in these deaths. New evidence such as 31 photos showing Simpson wearing Bruno Magli shoes like those that left a bloody imprint at the murder scene and which he at first denied ever owning were put into evidence. Daniel Petrocelli's masterful prosecution on the part of the

plaintiffs made the prosecutors in the criminal trial appear limp and inept. The jury returned a unanimous verdict, awarding the Goldman family $8.5 million in compensatory damages.

*February 5*

**MURDER: Delaware County, Pa.** Multimillionaire John E. du Pont was found guilty of the 1996 murder of David Schultz, a 36-year-old wrestling coach who had been training an Olympic team on the du Pont estate.

*February 6*

**DRUGS: Mexico City, Mexico** General Jesús Gutiérrez Rebollo, chief of the country's top anti-drug agency, resigned after allegations were made that he had taken huge bribes from the Mexican drug cartels.

**EXECUTION: Jarratt, Va.** Michael Carl George, a long time sexual predator, was executed by lethal injection for the 1990 torture-murder of 15-year-old Alexander Sztanko.

*February 7*

**MURDER: Belleville, Ill.** Mary Rae Morgan, 59, was charged with murder in the August 9, 1961 death of 4-year-old Michelle LeAnn Morgan. The girl's death was originally attributed to pneumonia, but Mary Rae's brother, a convicted rapist serving a prison term in Missouri, accused his sister of trying to drown Michelle and then, in a fit of rage, stomping on her stomach until she died.

*February 8*

**MASS MURDER: Raurimu Spiral, New Zealand** A family dispute erupted into mass murder when a gunman killed six persons and wounded five others before fleeing into the woods.

*February 9*

**FRAUD: Vlore, Albania** Government officials charged the director and 11 managers of the Gjallica/Populli Fund with fraud. Premier Alexander Meksi declared a partial state of emergency the following day.

*February 10*

**MURDER: Birmingham, Ala.** Walter Leroy Moody, Jr., was sentenced to death for the 1989 bombing murder of federal Judge Robert S. Vance.

**WRONGFUL DEATH: Santa Monica, Calif.** The jury that found O.J. Simpson liable in the deaths of his former wife Nicole Brown Simpson and her friend Ronald Goldman, awarded $12.5 million to each of the Brown and Goldman families that had sued Simpson, a financial blow to the accused killer that would ultimately see the collapse of his fortune and the loss of his lavish Brentwood estate.

*February 11*

**EXCESSIVE FORCE: Texcoco, Mexico** Claudia Rodriguez, who had shot and killed 27-year-old Juan Miguel Cabrerra when he reportedly tried to rape her, was found guilty of using excessive force (which carries a sentence of from three days to seven years in prison) and then set free by Judge Carlos

S. Cruz Preciado, who fined the woman $256 and ordered her to pay $1,538 in damages to Cabrerra's family.

## February 12

**DEFECTION: Beijing, China** South Korean officials announced that Hwang Jang Yop, a secretary of North Korea's ruling Workers (Communist) Party, had defected to its embassy. Hwang was the highest-level official to ever defect from North Korea.

**DEMOCRATS' FUND-RAISING SCANDAL: Washington, D.C.** The Washington *Post* stated that the Chinese government might have funneled money to the Democratic National Committee (DNC) in order to influence the Clinton administration.

**MISAPPROPRIATED HOLOCAUST FUNDS: Switzerland** In response to international criticism, Swiss banks accused of hiding funds of Holocaust victims, either placed in these institutions or stolen from them by Nazis during the Hitler era, agreed through government officials to administer a separate Holocaust compensation fund set up by three Swiss banks and contribute to it funds to be distributed to claimants.

## February 14

**DEMOCRATS' FUND-RAISING SCANDAL: Washington, D.C.** The National Security Council released documents that showed that it had advised Vice President Al Gore not to attend a 1996 fund-raising lunch at a Buddhist Temple in Los Angeles. Gore, did attend the lunch, said he did not know it was a fund-raiser, but later amended his remarks by saying that he knew it was "finance related."

## February 15

**SHOOTING: Bundang, South Korea** Lee Han Yong, a mid-level North Korean official who had defected, was shot outside of his home. He would die ten days later. South Korean officials believed Lee had been murdered by North Korean agents.

## February 18

**DRUGS: Mexico City, Mexico** Defense Minister Enrique Cervantes Aguirre announced that Gen. Jesús Gutiérrez Rebollo, had been compelled to resign as the chief of the country's top anti-drug agency and was under arrest, charged with taking enormous bribes from drug cartel boss Amado Carrillo Fuentes.

**MURDER: Newark, N.J.** Avi Kostner, on trial for killing his two children in June 1994, tearfully admitted that he had strangled his two children over a bitter custody battle and because he did not want the children raised outside the Jewish faith.

## February 19

**DRUGS: Washington, D.C.** U.S. officials reported that Gen. Jesús Gutiérrez Rebollo, one-time chief of Mexico's top anti-drug agency and who was then under arrest in Mexico for taking bribes from a drug cartel boss, had been briefed about everything the U.S. knew about Mexican drug trafficking, implying that this secret information had been passed along to the cartel chiefs.

**CRIME LEGISLATION: Washington, D.C.** In an attempt to head off what analysts thought would be escalating juvenile crime (because of heavy school enrollment), President Clinton proposed spending $495 million over two years to aid local and state governments in prosecuting juvenile offenders and combat gang violence. Funds would also be used to combat truancy and support after-school programs.

**MURDER: Tampa, Fla.** Lawrence Singleton, who had served eight years of a 14-year term for raping and chopping off the arms of a 15-year-old girl in 1978 in a notorious California case, was found covered with blood by police who found the body of Roxanne Hayes in his home.

## February 21

**BOMBINGS: Atlanta, Ga.** The Otherside Lounge, a gay and lesbian bar, was rocked by an explosion after a bomb placed on its patio exploded. When police arrived they found a second bomb inside a backpack and successfully detonated the device without injuries. This bombing attack was later attributed by the FBI to wanted fugitive Eric Robert Rudolph.

## February 23

**MURDER/TERRORISM: New York, N.Y.** Ali Abu Kamal, a 69-year-old Palestinian teacher and Islamic terrorist, shot and killed a tourist from Denmark on the observation deck of the Empire State Building, and wounded six others before he committed suicide. Found in a pouch hanging from his neck was a letter Kamal had written, one in which he vowed to kill as many "Zionists" as he could find in the city.

## February 25

**DEMOCRATS' FUND-RAISING SCANDAL: Washington, D.C.** The White House released documents to a House committee that confirmed that President Bill Clinton had rewarded campaign donors by allowing them to play golf with him or to stay overnight in the White House, some donors permitted to sleep in the hallowed Lincoln bedroom, listing 938 persons who had done so.

**DRUGS: Mexico City, Mexico** Government officials announced that 36 officers in the National Institute to Combat Drugs had been dismissed as being suspected of cooperating with drug cartel bosses and being heavily bribed to do so.

## February 27

**MURDER: Fayetteville, N.C.** James Burmeister II was found guilty of murdering Michael James and Jackie Burden, two blacks he had randomly killed as part of his initiation into a skinhead group.

**ROBBERY/SUICIDE: Aberdeen, Md.** Terrence Johnson, a former thief who had been rehabilitated and had earned several college degrees, was cornered by police after robbing a branch of the National Bank and, rather than surrender and return to prison, blew out his brains.

## February 28

**DEMOCRATS' FUND-RAISING SCANDAL: Washington, D.C.** The Democratic National Committee (DNC) stated that it would return about $1.5 million in contributions that may have been improper or illegal.

**DRUGS: Washington, D.C.** President Bill Clinton certified to Congress that Mexico was cooperating in the fight against drugs and hence was eligible for continued military and economic aid. On the other hand, Colombia, for the second straight year, was denied such certification. Madeleine Albright, U.S. Secretary of State, said that the influence of the Colombian drug cartels extended to the highest levels of the Colombian government, essentially branding Colombia what it truly was—a narco country.

**ESPIONAGE: Alexandria, Va.** Former FBI agent Earl Edwin Pitts, arrested in December 1996 and charged with selling classified data to Russia for more than $220,000, pleaded guilty to espionage in a federal court.

**MURDER: Toms River, N.J.** Michael LaSane, who had murdered a woman in a 1996 carjacking and who had been convicted after a jury heard the victim pleading for her life (she had turned on a pocket tape recorder during her abduction), was sentenced to life in prison.

**ROBBERY: North Hollywood, Calif.** Heavily armed masked gunmen robbed a branch of the Bank of America and in their flight, videotaped by overhead helicopters, shot and wounded many officers and passersby until two of the gunmen were killed.

### March 3

**ESPIONAGE: Alexandria, Va.** Harold Nicholson, former CIA official, pleaded guilty to spying for Russia, admitting that he had been paid more than $180,000 for delivering top-secret information between 1994 and 1996. Nicholson was sentenced to 23 years and seven months in prison.

### March 5

**MISAPPROPRIATED HOLOCAUST FUNDS: Switzerland** The government announced plans to establish a $4.7 billion government financed fund which would use interest from its vast gold reserves to compensate Holocaust victims, their descendants and aid victims of other human rights abuses throughout the world in response to worldwide criticism that Swiss banks during World War II allowed the misappropriation of Jewish funds.

### March 6

**MASS MURDER: Wheeling, W.Va.** Mark Storm, recently released from a psychiatric institution, killed his wife, two daughters, his mother and brother and then committed suicide.

**MURDER: Fayetteville, N.C.** James Burmeister II, who had been convicted of killing two persons, was given two life terms in prison.

**WHITEWATER: New York, N.Y.** The New York *Times* reported that former Associate Attorney General Webster Hubbell had been paid more than $400,000 from corporations that contributed to the Democrats or were controlled by friends of President Clinton, allegedly as legal fees, after Hubbell had resigned from office in March 1994 and before he pleaded guilty to two felony counts in December 1994. Many believed these payments were no more than hush money paid to Hubbell so he would not reveal what he knew about the involvement of Bill and Hillary Clinton in the Whitewater scandal.

### March 7

**BOMBING: Beijing, China** A bomb exploded on a bus moving along a busy Beijing street. Two persons were killed and many others wounded. Officials blamed unnamed "hooligans" for the bombing, although most Western authorities believed the explosion was set off by political foes of the repressive Communist regime.

### March 12

**MURDER/ROBBERY: Los Angeles, Calif.** Mikail Markhasev, an 18-year-old Russian immigrant, was arrested and charged with murdering and robbing Ennis Cosby, the son of entertainer Bill Cosby, on January 16, 1997.

### March 13

**MURDER: Naharayim Island, Jordan** Cpl. Ahmed Daqamseh began firing at a group of visiting Israeli school girls, killing seven and wounding many more before his fellow soldiers overpowered him. Jordan's King Hussein denounced Daqamseh's act as a "heinous crime," and said that the child killer should have been shot on the spot.

### March 16

**MURDER: Kobe, Japan** Ayaka Yamashita, a 10-year-old girl, was bludgeoned to death by a youthful attacker who, less than an hour later, so severely stabbed a 9-year-old girl that she almost bled to death.

### March 19-20

**CONSPIRACY: Phoenix, Ariz.** Ten members of the anti-government Viper Militia received varying prison sentences in federal court for conspiracy to make and possess unregistered destructive devices, for which they pleaded guilty in December 1996. On March 20, leader Gary Bauer was given a 9-year prison term for conspiracy, possessing machine guns and providing instructions in how to make bombs.

### March 20

**CRIMINAL SEXUAL MISCONDUCT: Aberdeen Proving Ground, Md.** Capt. Derrick Robertson was sentenced to four months in prison, dismissed from the Army and suffered the loss of his pension after pleading guilty to consensual sex with a private. Robertson was the only commissioned officer out of ten male servicemen at the base who stood accused of criminal sexual misconduct.

### March 21

**ASSAULT: Chicago, Ill.** Frank Caruso, 19, and two other youths cornered 13-year-old Lenard Clark, a black, in their predominately white neighborhood and beat him into unconsciousness—he would be in a coma for days—a racist assault that made national news and eventually sent Caruso to prison.

**BOMBING: Tel Aviv, Israel** A suicide bomber killed himself and four others and wounded dozens more when he exploded a bomb in a cafe. The bombing further delayed the Israeli-Palestinian peace negotiations.

**WEAPONS VIOLATIONS: Los Angeles, Calif.** Calvin Broadus, a rapper known as Snoop Doggy Dog, was convicted of gun violations and was given three years' probation and was ordered to anti-violence public service announcements.

*March 26*

**SUICIDE/MURDER?: Rancho Santa Fe, Calif.** Investigators found 39 bodies of members belonging to a doomsday cult called Heaven's Gate, along with the corpse of leader Marshall Applewhite, all apparent suicides, although murder was not ruled out in some instances. The cult, established in 1985, came to believe that only through self-destruction could its members spiritually board a spaceship following in the wake of the comet Hale-Bopp, then prominently seen in the night sky. The mass suicides had occurred March 22-23, 1997.

*March 29*

**ROBBERY: Jacksonville, Fla.** Philip Noel Johnson, a guard for Loomis, Fargo & Co., stole more than $20 million in cash from the security firm's warehouse, the largest heist in U.S. history to date.

*April 1*

**ATLANTA OLYMPIC PARK BOMBING REPORT: Washington, D.C.** The U.S. Department of Justice issued a report which severely criticized the FBI's handling of the July 27, 1996 bombing of Olympic Centennial Park in Atlanta, Ga., stating that agents had tried to trick suspect Richard Jewell into signing away his rights by saying that the interview was part of a "training video," knowing this would appeal to Jewell, a one-time sheriff's deputy and law enforcement groupie.

*April 3*

**MURDER: Pasadena, Texas** The body of 12-year-old Laura Smither was found in a pond; she had been decapitated. Her death was considered to be part of the 30 unsolved murders and disappearances occurring between Texas highways six and 146 and thought to be the work of a serial killer.

*April 11*

**FUGITIVE RECAPTURED: Yosemite, Calif.** A fugitive for 17 years, 75-year-old Annie Laurie Williams, who had been convicted of murdering her two young sons in 1955, was identified, arrested and returned to a Texas prison.

*April 14*

**WHITEWATER: Little Rock, Ark.** James McDougal, once a partner with Bill and Hillary Rodham Clinton in the scandal-wrapped Whitewater Development Corp., was sentenced to three years in prison for arranging fraudulent personal loans.

*April 15*

**FBI LABORATORY REPORT: Washington, D.C.** The U.S. Department of Justice issued a report in which it criticized FBI forensic experts and the sloppy procedures occurring at the Bureau's laboratories dealing with chemistry-toxicology, explosives and materials analysis. The report stated that reports by these units were often inconclusive and scien-

tifically unsound. The report specifically singled out 14 agents and one, explosives expert David Williams, was cited for slanting his testimony in the Oklahoma City and World Trade Center bombings.

*April 16*

**MURDER: River Oaks, Texas** Doris Angleton, wife of wealthy Robert Angleton, reportedly Houston's top gambler, was killed in her upscale home. Angleton and his brother Roger were suspected in the murder, but Roger committed suicide in his cell awaiting trial and Robert was acquitted for lack of evidence.

*April 19*

**MURDER; Franklin, N.J.** Two pizza delivery men were lured to a remote area so they could be fatally shot by thrill killers. Teenagers Thomas J. Koskovich and Jason Vreeland were later charged with the senseless slayings.

*April 22*

**HOSTAGE RESCUE: Lima, Peru** In a dramatic rescue, 170 Peruvian shock troops blew down doors and walls and dashed into the terrorist-held Japanese Embassy, liberating all the diplomats held hostage, while killing all 14 MRTA terrorists. Two soldiers were slain by the terrorists, along with one of the hostages.

*April 24*

**BOMBING: Denver, Colo.** Opening statements were made in the federal trial of Timothy McVeigh for the 1995 terrorist bombing of the Murrah Federal Building in Oklahoma City, Oklahoma. The federal trial had been moved from Oklahoma City to Denver because widespread animosity in Oklahoma had been displayed against the defendant. Terry Nicholas, accused of being McVeigh's accomplice, was scheduled to be tried separately at a later date. Judge Richard Matsch presided in U.S. District Court. Prosecutor Joseph Hartzler stated that McVeigh had carried out the bombing in revenge for the deaths of David Koresh and his Branch Davidian followers who perished in flames during the FBI siege of their Waco, Texas, compound in 1993. Defense attorney Stephen Jones said that he would establish the innocence of his client, Timothy McVeigh.

*April 25*

**SEXUAL MISCONDUCT: Fort Bliss, Texas** Three Army officers—Maj. Edward Brenham, Capt. Ivan Brown and 2nd Lt. Trevor Gordon—were found guilty of sexual misconduct with female enlisted personnel. All three were sentenced to prison terms ranging from three to 20 months and dismissed from the service. Nine other soldiers also found guilty of sexual misconduct received administrative punishment.

*April 26*

**MURDER: Crown Point, Ind.** Asterio Locquiao was given two 50-year prison terms for murdering his ex-wife and her lover in 1993.

*April 27*

**HOSTAGE-TAKING: Fort Davis, Texas** Several armed members of a separatist group calling itself the Republic of Texas seized a couple and held them hostage. The militia-type group, according to authorities, had passed millions of dollars in bogus checks and other financial instruments, and claimed that the U.S. had illegally annexed Texas in 1845 and that they represented the true government of Texas.

*April 28*

**HOSTAGE-TAKING: Fort Davis, Texas** The shack to which members of the Republic of Texas retreated and where they kept two hostages was surrounded by FBI agents and other federal and state officers. The separatists, wanted for passing bogus checks, released the hostages in exchange for a separatist who had been earlier arrested.

*April 29*

**MURDER: Louisville, Ky.** Deborah Bell, 46 and Patty Eitel, 43, two nursing home administrators, were shot down and killed as they walked into a parking lot. Arrested and charged with the murders was 23-year-old Kimberly Harris, a fired nursing assistant.

**MURDER: Minneapolis, Minn.** The body of Jeffrey Trail, a naval graduate, was found. He was the first known victim of homosexual spree killer Andrew Phillip Cunanan.

**RAPE: Aberdeen Proving Ground, Md.** Staff Sgt. Delmar Simpson was found guilty by an Army court-martial jury of raping six female trainees. Simpson, who had been a drill sergeant, claimed that the sexual liaisons were consensual.

*April 30*

**ARMED RESISTANCE: Fort Davis, Texas** Seven armed men who attempted to join the Republic of Texas members surrounded by police and federal agents were arrested and disarmed.

**MURDER: White Plains, N.Y.** Rita Gluzman was sentenced to life imprisonment for the ax murder of her husband, scientist Yakov Gluzman.

*May 2-3*

**ARMED RESISTANCE: Fort Davis, Texas** Of the nine members of the separatist group calling itself the Republic of Texas who were holed up in a shack and surrounded by lawmen, six, including leader Richard McLaren, surrendered to officers, while two escaped on foot and another was killed in a shootout with police. Richard McLaren, leader of the group, would be given a 99-year prison sentence on November 4, 1997, and his top lieutenant, Robert Otto, would be sent to prison for 50 years.

*May 3*

**MURDER: Minneapolis, Minn.** The body of architect David Madison was found in a lake near Minneapolis. Madison was the second known victim of homosexual spree killer Andrew Cunanan.

*May 4*

**MURDER: Chicago, Ill.** The savagely mutilated body of 74-year-old Lee Miglin, one of Chicago's wealthiest real estate developers, was found. Miglin was the third known victim of homosexual spree killer Andrew Cunanan, who stole Miglin's Lexus, driving it eastward.

*May 5*

**BOMBING: Denver, Colo.** In the bombing and murder trial of Timothy McVeigh (he had killed 168 persons, including one rescue worker, in his bombing of the federal building in Oklahoma City, Oklahoma, in 1995), his sister, Jennifer McVeigh, testified as a prosecution witness, saying her brother had twice told her shortly before the bombing that "something big is going to happen." She also stated that in 1994 her brother had long complained about the destruction of the Branch Davidians in Waco, Texas in 1993, directing his anger chiefly at agents of the Bureau of Alcohol, Tobacco and Firearms (ATF) which had besieged David Koresh and his Davidians. It was pointed out by prosecutors that an ATF office was housed in the bombed federal building in Oklahoma City and that this was McVeigh's target.

**MURDER: New York, N.Y.** Spree killer Andrew Cunanan, who had crossed the country from San Diego to Minneapolis (where he had killed two persons), to Chicago (where he killed another man), arrived in Manhattan, checking into a West 20th Street transient hotel frequented by homosexuals. According to receipts later found by police, Cunanan also went shopping for clothes on this day while a nation-wide police dragnet for him ensued.

*May 6*

**RAPE: Aberdeen Proving Ground, Md.** Staff Sgt. Delmar Simpson, found guilty of raping six female trainees on April 29, 1996, was sentenced to 25 years in prison.

*May 7*

**MURDER: New York, N.Y.** According to reports, Andrew Cunanan, who had already killed three persons, went to a movie theater on West 23rd Street where he viewed the film, *Liar, Liar*.

**SEXUAL MISCONDUCT: Washington, D.C.** Sgt. Maj. Gene McKinney, the Army's highest-ranking enlisted soldier, was accused of 18 offenses, including adultery, sexual assault, mistreatment of soldiers and obstruction of justice. McKinney denied the allegations.

**WAR CRIMES: The Hague, Netherlands** In the first war crimes trial dealing with civil strife in Bosnia, Dusan Tadic, a 41-year-old Bosnian Serb tried before a U.N. tribunal, was found guilty of killing two policemen and torturing and terrorizing scores of Muslim civilians.

*May 8*

**MURDER: New York, N.Y.** Hunted spree killer Andrew Cunanan, according to witnesses, went to a movie theater where he viewed the film, *The Devil's Own*. Later in the day, a cellular phone in the Lexus car stolen from Chicago real estate tycoon Lee Miglin was activated and traced to the Philadelphia area. Police were unable to pinpoint the car's location.

*May 9*

**BOMBING/MURDER: Denver, Colo.** Testimony continued in the trial of Oklahoma City bomber Timothy McVeigh, with Eldon Elliott, a prosecution witness, and the owner of a Ryder Truck rental agency in Junction City, Kansas, identifying McVeigh as the man who rented the truck believed to have been used in the bombing.

**MURDER: New Jersey** Andrew Cunanan, who had murdered three persons in the last two weeks, drove across the Delaware River into New Jersey where, in a remote federal cemetery, he killed William Reese, a graveworker, stealing his victim's red pickup truck and driving southward. Reese's body was found this same day.

*May 10*

**MURDER: Florence, S.C.** Spree killer Andrew Cunanan drove off Interstate Highway 95 where he stole a license plate which he affixed to the red pickup truck he had stolen from his latest victim, William Reese. He continued driving southward toward Florida.

*May 12*

**BOMBING/MURDER: Denver, Colo.** Testifying against Timothy McVeigh at his trial for the 1995 Oklahoma City bombing, former friend Michael Fortier stated that he accompanied McVeigh to Oklahoma City to inspect the Murrah Federal Building which he planned to bomb. Fortier said that McVeigh wanted the bombing to coincide with the anniversary of the Waco assault. Fortier had struck a plea-bargain with prosecutors, agreeing to testify in exchange for reduced charges.

**MURDER: Miami Beach, Fla.** The much-sought spree killer, Andrew Cunanan, having arrived in Florida the previous day and using an alias, checked into the Normandy Plaza Hotel at Normandy Drive and 71st Street.

*May 13*

**MURDER: Delaware County, Pa.** John E. du Pont, the eccentric multimillionaire who had been convicted of murdering wrestling coach David Schultz in February 1997, was sent to prison for between 13 and 30 years.

*May 16*

**MURDER: Rio Linda, Calif.** Michelle Montoya, 18, was found dying with her throat slit in the woodshop of Rio Linda High School. The girl died a short time later, three weeks before her graduation. Police arrested 34-year-old Alex Del Thomas, a substitute janitor who had been at work for only three days, after discovering that he had been a member of a notorious L.A. street gang (the Crips), and that he had served 12 years in prison for manslaughter. School board members explained to anxious students and parents that Thomas had gone to work before a background clearance check on him had been completed.

*May 19*

**BOMBING/MURDER: Denver, Colo.** Steven Burmeister, a chemist working for the FBI, testified at Timothy McVeigh's trial that the clothes McVeigh had worn when arrested contained a chemical used in the makeup of the bomb.

*May 20*

**BORDER SHOOTING: Redford, Texas** Esequiel Hernandez, Jr., an 18-year-old goat herder who was gathering his small herd of goats along the Rio Grande, 200 miles southeast of El Paso, was shot and killed by members of a U.S. Marine patrol which was aiding border guards in patrolling the U.S. border and under orders to prevent illegal aliens from entering the country. Cpl. Clemente Banuelos, who was in phone contact with his base superiors, shot and killed Hernandez with an M-16 rifle after the goat herder reportedly fired twice at the patrol and was about to fire a third time. Hernandez family members and friends later insisted that the teenager would never have fired at the Marines and used his rifle only to ward off wild dogs from his herd, or for occasional target practice. After investigating the shooting, retired Marine Maj. Gen. John Coyne criticized the patrol, stating that its mission "appears to have been viewed at every level of Marine Corps command as more of a training opportunity than a real world deployment." The Marine Corps took issue with Coyne and refused to bring charges against anyone involved in the shooting. The Hernandez family, however, later received a $1 million settlement.

*May 25*

**MURDER/CHILD MOLESTATION: Primadonna Resorts, Nev.** Jeremy Joseph Stroymeyer molested 7-year-old Sherrice Iverson in a washroom, then strangled her to death.

*May 27*

**MASS MURDER: Simi Valley, Calif.** Ahmad Salman, overwhelmed with debt, killed his wife and three children and then himself before police arrived at his upscale home.

*May 29*

**SEXUAL MISCONDUCT: Aberdeen Proving Ground, Md.** Staff Sgt. Vernell Robinson was convicted of 19 counts of adultery, sodomy, improper relations with female trainees, obstruction of justice and disobeying orders. A drill instructor, Robinson was sentenced the next day to six months in prison and was dishonorably discharged. On this date, 1st Lt. Kelly Flinn, the first female B-52 bomber pilot, was given a general discharge from the Air Force, following adultery charges in that she was having sex with Marc Zigo, a civilian and married man, as well as an enlisted man, which violated military regulations, along with making false statements. In addition, Army Brig. Gen. Stephen Xenakis was relieved of his command at Fort Gordon, Ga., because of a reported "improper relationship" with a civilian nurse who was then caring for his wife.

*May 30*

**MURDER: Vista, Calif.** Joshua Jenkins, convicted of murdering his parents and grandparents to death at age 15 in 1996, was sentenced to 116 years in prison.

*June 2*

**BOMBING/MURDER: Denver, Colo.** Timothy McVeigh was found guilty in the 1995 bombing of the federal building in Oklahoma City, Oklahoma, in which 168 persons were killed. The jury returned a unanimous verdict after deliberating for four days. Since no eye-witnesses to the crime came forward, McVeigh was convicted on circumstantial evidence.

**MURDER/KIDNAPPING: Jacksonville, Fla.** Jason Stephens and Horace Cummings burglarized a home and kidnapped 3-year-old Robert Sparrow III, later killing the child. Both would later be sentenced to death.

**SEXUAL MISCONDUCT: Washington, D.C.** A Pentagon spokesman announced the retirement of Army Maj.-Gen. John Longhouser, commander of the Aberdeen Proving Ground in Maryland. Longhouser had decided to retire after admitting that he had had an adulterous affair in the past.

### June 5
**MURDER: Santa Fe Springs, Calif.** Following an argument at work, Daniel S. Marsden, 38, entered the Omni Plastics Co., and shot six fellow employees, killing two and wounding four. He then ran outside and accosted two startled women, shouting: "This is my last day!" He shoved the barrel of a gun into his mouth and pulled the trigger, committing suicide before the horrified women.

### June 6
**EXECUTION: Atmore, Ala.** Henry Francis Hays became the first white man to be executed in Alabama for murdering a black person since 1913. Hays and another KKK member had randomly killed 19-year-old Michael Donald in Mobile in 1981.

### June 9
**SEXUAL MISCONDUCT: Washington, D.C.** Air Force Gen. Joseph Ralston, who was to be the next chief of the Joint Chiefs of Staff, withdrew from consideration after it was disclosed that he had had an adulterous affair.

### June 13
**BOMBING: Denver, Colo.** A federal jury which had earlier found Timothy McVeigh guilty of the 1995 bombing of the Murrah Federal Building in Oklahoma City, Oklahoma, unanimously voted to sentence the 29-year-old defendant to death.

### June 15-17
**MURDER/TERRORISM: Quetta, Pakistan** Pakistani officials and Afghan tribal leaders cooperating with a contingent of CIA and FBI agents, located and seized Mir Amal Kasi, who had shot and killed two CIA employees outside CIA headquarters at Langley, Virginia, on January 25, 1993. Kasi was rushed to Islamabad Airport and then flown to the U.S. to stand trial. He would be convicted and sentenced to death.

### June 16
**MURDER: Northern Ireland** IRA terrorists killed two policemen which prompted the British government to call off peace talks.

### June 20
**MURDER/CHILD MOLESTATION: Trenton, N.J.** Jesse Timmendequas, a convicted sex offender who had molested and murdered 7-year-old Megan Kankas in 1994, was sentenced to death. The case brought about "Megan's Law," which now requires convicted sex offenders to register with police in most states and to be identified to their communities.

### June 23
**ESPIONAGE: Alexandria, Va.** Earl Edwin Pitts, who had been convicted of espionage while serving as an FBI agent (only the second Bureau agent ever so convicted), was sentenced to 27 years in prison.

**JUDICIARY: Washington, D.C.** The U.S. Supreme Court ruled in a 5-4 vote to strengthen law enforcement officials against sexual predators in that states may confine convicted sex offenders in mental institutions, even after they have served their prison terms.

### July 1
**EXECUTION: Eddyville, Ky.** Harold McQueen, Jr. was executed by lethal injection for the 1980 robbery-murder of 22-year-old Rebecca O'Hearn.

### July 3
**DRUGS: Mexico City, Mexico** Boss of the Juarez drug cartel, Amado Carrillo Fuentes reportedly died while undergoing a plastic surgery operation to alter his features. His body was found the next day. The surgeons who botched the operation were reportedly executed.

### July 7
**MURDER: Miami Beach, Fla.** After having been in the Miami Beach area for almost two months, spree killer Andrew Cunanan, who had murdered four persons, sold a gold coin (reportedly stolen from Lee Miglin, killed by Cunanan in Chicago) for $190 at a pawnshop, Cash on the Beach, using his own name and providing a thumb print, information which was sent to Miami Beach police the next day.

### July 8
**ARSON/MURDER: San Bernadino, Calif.** Carey Thomas Meeks was arrested and charged with starting a fire in the San Bernadino National Forest by throwing illegal fireworks into brush, a towering blaze that took the life of firefighting helicopter pilot Floyd Dean Hiser, Sr., whose helicopter crashed into steep, rocky terrain while dumping water on flames below.

**ILLEGAL FUND-RAISING HEARINGS: Washington, D.C.** The Senate Governmental Affairs Committee began hearings into possible illegal fund-raising practices involving the 1994 and 1996 national elections. Senator Fred Thompson, committee chairman, stated that China had sought to influence the outcome of the 1996 presidential election through illegal contributions.

### July 9
**PRISON ESCAPE: Florence, Ariz.** In a failed attempt to free her husband from prison, Rebecca Thornton was killed by prison guards after she had reportedly shot and killed her husband, Floyd Thornton, Jr., who had been wounded as he tried to make his way to freedom.

*July 10*

**WAR CRIMINALS: Bosnia** British troops tracking down reported war criminals shot and killed one fleeing suspect, a Bosnian Serb who had been indicted by the war crimes tribunal in The Hague.

*July 11*

**MURDER: Miami Beach, Fla.** A worker at Miami Subs, a fast-food sandwich shop, called police to report that spree killer Andrew Cunanan was in his store. When police arrived they found the widely-sought Cunanan gone and a desperate search of the area turned up no clues.

*July 14-15*

**ILLEGAL FUND-RAISING HEARINGS: Washington, D.C.** FBI officials briefed the Senate Governmental Affairs Committee on evidence relating to attempts by China to influence U.S. policy. Evidence strongly indicated that the Chinese had attempted to influence the outcome of the 1996 election. The FBI disclosed that John Huang, a former Democratic National Committee official, had worked for the Lippo Group, an Indonesian firm that may have been underwritten by China, and that during 1993 and 1994, Huang had visited President Clinton at the White House 52 times.

**WAR CRIMES: The Hague, Netherlands** A U.N. tribunal sentenced Dusan Tadic, a Bosnian Serb, to 20 years in prison for terrorist murders and "crimes against humanity" in Bosnia which Serbs had euphemistically called "ethnic cleansing."

*July 15*

**MURDER: Kobe, Japan** An unidentified 15-year-old boy who had been under arrest for the murder and beheading of Jun Hase, an 11-year-old boy, was served with a second murder warrant, that of killing Ayaka Yamashita on March 16, 1997, and attacking another girl on that date. The boy had also confessed to attacking three other girls.

**MURDER: Miami Beach, Fla.** Spree killer Andrew Cunanan, shot and killed his fifth victim, the celebrated fashion designer Gianni Versace in front of Versace's trendy mansion. Police, who had conducted interviews that morning only a block from Versace's palatial home, later discovered a grainy film on a surveillance camera which showed the killer fleeing down an alley, but otherwise lost all track of the murderer. Police later that day located the red pickup truck Cunanan had stolen from a cemetery worker in New Jersey, a truck belonging to William Reese. The truck, parked only a few blocks from Versace's residence, had, according to receipts, been inside a parking garage since June 10.

*July 15-17*

**MURDER: Miami Beach, Fla.** Within forty-eight hours of the murder of Gianni Versace, spree killer Andrew Cunanan, according to a later FBI report, contacted a friend inside the homosexual network of Miami Beach, discussing how to use a false identification to get a passport in order to flee the country.

*July 16*

**MURDER: Miami Beach, Fla.** Police received a tip that the much-sought spree killer Andrew Cunanan was staying at the Normandy Plaza Hotel, but officers found not trace of him.

*July 17*

**MURDER: Miami Beach, Fla.** Police received a call from a MacDonald's restaurant—a cashier and a customer recognized killer Andrew Cunanan standing in line for service. By the time officers rushed to the site, the suspect had fled. Police then received a report that a man resembling Cunanan had broken into a sailboat. Again, officers found no trace of the suspect.

*July 18*

**MURDER: Miami Beach, Fla.** A clerk at the Normandy Plaza Hotel identified a name similar to Cunanan's which led detectives to inspect a room where they found hair clippings and fashion magazines.

**MURDER: San Diego, Calif.** Frederick Davidson, who had shot and killed three professors at San Diego State University in 1996, was given three life terms.

*July 23*

**EXECUTION: Jarratt, Va.** Joseph Roger O'Dell III was executed in spite of a massive campaign to grant him clemency. He had been convicted of the brutal 1985 rape-murder of a Virginia Beach woman.

**MURDER/SUICIDE: Miami Beach, Fla.** Spree killer Andrew Cunanan was located living in an unoccupied houseboat docked on the intracoastal waterway known as Indian Creek. The houseboat wa owned by Las Vegas club owner Torsten Reineck (who, ironically, was wanted in Germany for fraud and tax evasion). Fernando Careira, a 71-year-old caretaker, entered the houseboat and found the interior in disarray. As he went outside to call police, Careira heard a gunshot. Police arrived to find Andrew Cunanan, killer of five persons, sprawled on a bed wearing only shorts. He had committed suicide by firing a bullet into his head.

*July 24*

**RAPE: Stamford, Conn.** Alex Kelly, who had been a fugitive for years (living in European resorts with money supplied by his parents), and who had been convicted of rape, was sentenced to 16 years in prison.

**TERRORISM: Tipaza, Algeria** According to government reports, Anta Zouabri, the 26-year-old leader of the Armed Islamic Group, had been killed in a shootout with security forces.

*July 25*

**EXTORTION: New York, N.Y.** Autumn Jackson, 22, who claimed to be the out-of-wedlock daughter of Bill Cosby, was convicted of attempting to extort $40 million from the comedian. Jackson had told Cosby that if he did not pay her the money, she would sell her story to a tabloid newspaper. Cosby testified at the trial, stating that although he had had a one-night affair with Jackson's mother in 1974 and had sent her money over the years to keep her quiet about that incident, he was not the father of Autumn Jackson.

**MURDER: Elk Creek, Va.** Emmett Cressell, Jr. and Louis

Ceparano beat up and burned to death Garnett P. Johnson, Jr., a black handyman, in a drunken racist killing.

**ORGANIZED CRIME: New York, N.Y.** Vincent Gigante, head of the Gambino crime family, was convicted of racketeering and two murder conspiracies.

### July 26

**MURDER: Fort Wayne, Ind.** Joseph Corcoran reportedly admitted to police that he shot four men to death in his sister's home, including his sister's fiance, following an argument. Corcoran had been acquitted of killing his parents in Ball Lake, Indiana, four years earlier.

**SMUGGLING IMMIGRANTS, Chicago, Ill.** Francisco Duenas, Francisco Limon, and Norma Alacantara, Mexican nationals illegally in the U.S., were arrested and charged with smuggling undocumented immigrants who were deaf (as was Alacantara). Dozens of deaf Mexican immigrants, smuggled into the U.S. from Mexico, worked for the Paoletti family in New York and Chicago, compelled to sell key chains on the streets, turning over their meager profits to clan members to cover the cost of food and cheap housing.

### July 30

**BOMBING: Jerusalem, Israel** Two terrorists exploded a bomb in a crowded marketplace, killing themselves and 13 others, as well as wounding another 150 persons. Hamas, a Palestinian terrorist organization, took credit for the bombing.

### August 1

**MURDER: Hisperia, Calif.** Robert James, a 2-year-old boy, was shot in the head when his father tried to avoid a car whose driver was menacing them. The driver of the car in front of the father and his son kept speeding up and then jamming on the brakes. When the father tried to change lanes, a passenger in the car leaned out of the window and fired several shots, one of the bullets fatally striking the boy.

### August 3

**BURGLARY: Aurora, Ill.** Larry Harris, who had burglarized the same tavern three times earlier in one month, ignored warning signs and was electrocuted to death by a new 220-volt security system installed by the owner when he broke into the building for a fourth time.

### August 5

**KIDNAPPING/RAPE: Delaware, Ohio** Three women were indicted for kidnapping and raping a convicted child molester, holding 27-year-old Rodney Hosler captive, brutalizing and raping him and then scribbling "I am a child molester" on his body before dumping him wrapped only in a blanket behind a pizza parlor. The women were Hosler's 28-year-old wife, Jewel, her mother, Mary Franks, 44, and her aunt, Vickie Colter, 39.

### August 6

**KIDNAPPING/ATTEMPTED MURDER: Thibodaux, La.** John Bruce, 26, and Jeremy Billiot, 21, were arrested and charged with kidnapping and attempted murder after they abducted 17-year-old Adam Trahan, Jr., a teenager they suspected of raping a 4-year-old boy. Trahan was beaten, tortured and left hanging by the neck in a swamp. He survived but was hospitalized with two fractures of the spine.

### August 14

**BOMBING: Denver, Colo.** Timothy McVeigh, convicted bomber of the federal building in Oklahoma City, Oklahoma, was sentenced to death by a federal judge, following a jury recommendation.

### August 16

**RIOTS: Germany** Thousands of neo-Nazis and leftists clashed in several cities throughout Germany, the Nazis celebrating the 10th anniversary of Rudolf Hess' death. More than 400 persons were arrested for fighting and rioting in Frankfurt, Munich and other towns.

### August 19

**MURDER: Colebrook, N.H.** Enraged over taxes, Carl C. Drega shot and killed Judge Vickie Bunnell and three others before he was shot to death by officers.

### August 22

**SEXUAL HARASSMENT: Little Rock, Ark.** Federal Judge Susan Webber Wright scheduled a sexual harassment trial for President Bill Clinton for May 1998, based upon the complaint of Paula Corbin Jones, who said that Clinton had sexually harassed her when he was Governor of Arkansas and had used the power of his office to deny her constitutional rights.

### August 26

**DRUGS/POLITICAL CORRUPTION: Cali, Colombia** Mauricio Guzman, the mayor of Cali, was arrested and charged with taking money from the drug cartel that controlled the area. The 42-year-old Guzman was accused of taking $200,000 from a company fronting for the Cali cartel to finance his 1994 election campaign.

**POLITICAL CORRUPTION: Miami, Fla.** Cesar Odio, former city manager, was sentenced to one year in prison for taking bribes and kickbacks.

### August 28

**PRISON RIOT: El Dorado, Venezuela** A battle between rival gangs of prison inmates at a maximum security prison brought about the deaths of 29 prisoners and the wounding of another 13 inmates before guards could regain control of the cell block areas.

### September 3

**FRAUD: Phoenix, Ariz.** Governor Fife Symington of Arizona was convicted by a federal jury on seven felony counts of fraud involving his real estate deals before he became governor. He was found guilty of making false statements to a Japanese bank in order to avoid defaulting on a loan. As a result of the criminal conviction, Symington resigned on September 5.

*September 4*

**BOMBING: Jerusalem, Israel** Three terrorists suicidally exploded a bomb which killed themselves and wounded more than 200 Israelis and tourists at the Ben Yehuda outdoor mall. Hamas, a Palestinian terrorist group, was thought to be responsible. Israeli forensic experts, matching blood samples from relatives in Assira, West Bank to those taken from body parts found at the scene of the bombing were able to identify the suicide bombers as Moawiya Jarara, 22, Bashar Salawah, 23, and Tawfiq Yassin, 25.

*September 5*

**MASS MURDER: Algeria** Government forces shot and killed 68 Muslims in Chrea. In Djerba, four candidates for office were murdered this same date. More than 100 persons were killed in Beni Messous.

*September 6*

**PRISON RIOT: Mansfield, Ohio** Death Row inmates rioted for four hours until a tactical unit fired tear gas into their cell block. Five of the prisoners were injured.

*September 11*

**SEXUAL MISCONDUCT: Washington, D.C.** Following a nine-month investigation, the Army released a report stating that "sexual harassment exists throughout the Army, crossing gender, rank and racial lines." The Army, which blamed its own leadership for this condition, stated it would extend basic training by one week to include instructions on ethics and behavior and that prospective drill sergeants, the most common rank in which sexual offenses occurred, would be compelled to undergo psychological testing and criminal background checks.

*September 12*

**FAKE KIDNAPPING: Jerusalem, Israel** Yaacov Schwartz, a 63-year-old Israeli who had been missing for two days was found tied up in an abandoned building. Schwartz later admitted that he had faked his abduction during a state visit by U.S. Secretary of State Madeleine Albright in order to "unite the Israeli people."

*September 15*

**DEATH SENTENCE: Hanoi, Vietnam** Duong Van Khanh, described by prosecutors as a mob chief who had run an extortion racket, was sentenced to death. Sentenced to prison were 22 of Duong's accomplices.

*September 16*

**DRUGS/SUICIDE: Lake Zurich, Ill.** Robert Cook and his common-law wife Carol Johnson, discovered to be manufacturing a huge quantity of marijuana on their property, were surrounded by police, but rather than surrender and face prison terms, the couple committed suicide.

*September 18*

**EXECUTION: Grozny, Chechnya** Two men convicted of murdering two women and an 11-year-old girl were ex-

ecuted by firing squad as a crowd of thousands watched in the ironically-named Friendship Square. The firing squad was made up of six relatives of the victims, allowable under the law.

**ILLEGAL CAMPAIGN CONTRIBUTIONS: New York, N.Y.** The campaign manager and two consultants involved with the election of Ron Carey to the presidency of the Teamsters Union, pleaded guilty to having funneled illegal donations to Carey's campaign. It was stated that a representative of the Democratic National Committee had asked a foreign citizen to contribute $100,000 to Carey's campaign so that, in turn, the Teamsters would later donate large cash amounts to the Democrats.

**TERRORIST ATTACK: Cairo, Egypt** Two or more terrorists attacked a bus loaded with tourists outside the Egyptian Museum in Cairo, killing ten persons, nine being German tourists, and wounding at least a dozen others. The terrorists, two militant Muslim brothers (three or four terrorists were reported), Sabir Abu al-Ila and Mahmoud Abu al-Ila, attacked the tourist bus as it was disembarking its thirty-three tourists, throwing gasoline bombs, charring its interior, and then spraying the fleeing tourists with rapid-fire weapons. In October 1993, Sabir Ila had killed two American businessmen and a Frenchman and wounded an Italian visitor in a berserk gun attack as they ate in the restaurant of Cairo's posh Semiramis Hotel. He was judged insane and institutionalized but escaped three days before the bus attack. Both brothers were captured and held for trial. Attacks on tourists in Egypt had continued throughout the 1990s in an effort by Muslim extremists to force the government to meet its political demands, damaging one of the country's chief economies. Tourism in Egypt dropped to 2.51 million in 1993, but rose, however, to 4.2 million at the end of 1997, despite the lethal hazards of tourist travel in the country. Said one tourist following the September 18, 1997 bus attack in Cairo: "If you don't feel safe to travel in this country, then you cannot enjoy your holiday."

*September 21*

**MASSACRE: Beni-Slimane, Algeria** A group of heavily armed men shot and killed 53 civilians and then hacked up the bodies of the victims and burned them. The massacre was attributed to Islamic terrorists attempting to overthrow the government.

**MURDER/BURGLARY: Stanwood, Wash.** David Dodge, a 17-year-old who had escaped from a Seattle halfway house where he was confined for theft, was arrested and charged with beating to death 12-year-old Ashley Jones the previous day. Jones had been baby-sitting five children in a home Dodge entered to commit a burglary.

*September 22*

**FRAUD: Philadelphia, Pa.** John Bennett, Jr., convicted of defrauding $354 million from contributors to his phoney charities, was sentenced to 12 years in prison.

**TERRORIST ATTACK: Algiers, Algeria** Islamic terrorists seeking to overthrow the government swarmed into Baraki, the eastern suburb of the capital, and opened fire on civilians, killing more than 200 people, wounding another 100 persons. A bomb attack also occurred this date in Reghala, a town 19 miles east of Algiers, which killed two people and wounded another 25 persons.

**TERRORIST ATTACK: Amman, Jordan** Two Israeli security guards were wounded when terrorists drove past the Israeli Embassy and fired at the guards. Jordanian officials condemned the attack as "a cowardly terrorist" act.

*September 25*

**ATTEMPTED MURDER: Amman, Jordan** Two Israeli agents tried to kill Hamas leader Khalid Mashaal, but were foiled in the attempt.

*September 26*

**BOMBING: Salem, Va.** Frank Halvestine, 76, was sentenced to 12 years in prison for providing materials that blew up a car and killed a child in 1975.

**MURDER: Atlanta, Ga.** Jan Barry Sandlin was convicted of the 1971 beating death of his 4-month-old son, after his daughter, Tracy Rhame, originally blamed for the death, prodded police and forensic experts to re-examine the case.

**ROBBERY: Skokie, Ill.** William Hertzog Thompson, a 46-year-old commodities broker from upscale Winnetka who had turned to bank robbery because of financial problems, pleaded guilty to one bank robbery and an attempted bank robbery. Thompson had been arrested on June 24 after police chased him down following an abortive robbery of the Oakbrook Bank branch in Glenview, Ill.

*September 28*

**MURDER: Lowell, Mass.** Peter Contos, 31, was arrested and charged with the murder of his common-law wife Catherine Rice, 35, and his two sons, Benjamin, 4, and 2-month-old Ryan. It was then disclosed that Contos had been living a double life, one with his girlfriend and two sons, another with a second life who lived only fifteen miles away.

*September 29*

**RAPE: San Bernandino, Calif.** A 14-year-old girl chatting on the Internet made the mistake of giving her address to a stranger and within hours, a 6-foot-4-inch, 250-pound man burst through her door and raped her. Charged with the rape was Richard Robert Brooks of Redlands, Calif.

*September 30*

**MANSLAUGHTER: Sonora, Calif.** Vigilante slayer Ellie Nesler, who had shot and killed Daniel Mark Driver, the reported molester of her son, in 1993, pleaded guilty to manslaughter and was immediately paroled, half of her sentence already having been served.

**PRISONER RELEASE: Tel Aviv, Israel** The government announced that, as a gesture of peace, it was releasing 20 prisoners, including Hamas founder, Sheik Ahmed Yassin.

*October 1*

**MASS MURDER: Pearl, Miss.** Luke Woodham, 17, killed his mother and then shot nine classmates, killing two

and wounding seven at Pearl High School. He later claimed that he had been under the mental control of another youth who headed a Satanic cult.

**PRISON RELEASE: Ayalon Prison, Israel** Shiek Ahmed Yassin, the ailing founder of Hamas, the Palestinian terrorist group, was released after having served eight years for ordering the murders of Israeli soldiers and "turncoat" Palestinians.

**RAPE/CHILD MOLESTATION: Miami, Fla.** Stevie J. Stubbs, 42, was arrested and charged with raping and molesting his 14-year-old niece after the girl's teacher read her diary in which she had written: "Lord, I'm tired of being RAPED!!! I can't do nothing about it cause I'm too damn AFRAID!!! HELP ME, PLEASE!!!"

*October 2*

**MASS MURDER: Memphis, Tenn.** Timothy Prink reported shot and killed for of his family members after having an argument with his sister.

*October 3*

**CHILD MOLESTATION: Fairfax County, Va.** Using phone records to trace a missing 12-year-old boy from Palm Springs, Calif., police arrested Ronald L. Iliff, a 31-year-old part-time tutor and grocery store clerk. The boy was found in Iliff's home, hidden in a crawl space underneath a closet with a fake back where he had reportedly been held prisoner and repeatedly sodomized by Iliff.

*October 5*

**MASS MURDER/ROBBERY: Mangum, N.C.** Five Mexican migrant pumpkin pickers were shot to death and robbed. Police charged two brothers, Jose Luis Cruz Osorio, 28 and Alonso Cruz Osorio, 18, with the slayings, but both had fled.

*October 6*

**EMBEZZLEMENT: Los Angeles, Calif.** Yasuyoshi Kato, convicted of embezzling $67 million from his meat packing company, was sentenced to 63 months in a federal prison.

*October 7*

**MURDER: Middlesex County, Mass.** Louise Woodward, 19, a British au pair, was tried for murdering 8-month-old Matthew Eappen, prosecutors contending that Woodward had shaken the baby and then struck him against a hard surface, fatally injured him in February 1996.

*October 8*

**TERRORISM: Washington, D.C.** The U.S. government labelled 30 international groups as terrorist organizations and banned contributions to these foreign groups, and also made it illegal for any member of such terrorist groups to enter the U.S.

*October 9*

**ATTEMPTING TO SEDUCE A MINOR: Yucca Valley, Calif.** Anthony Delgado, a 20-year-old convicted sex offender, was arrested and charged with attempting to seduce a minor and mailing sexually explicit letters to a 12-year-old boy whom he had met on the Internet.

### October 10

**MURDER: Seoul, South Korea** Edward K. Lee, from New York City, was sentenced to life imprisonment for the 1997 stabbing murder of a South Korean college student.

### October 12

**MURDER: Moreno Valley, Calif.** John Gose reportedly entered a home in Hidden Springs and shot and killed a man, a woman and her 10-year-old son, before fleeing to his home where he shot and wounded himself.

### October 13

**MURDER: Las Vegas, Nev.** Sara Gruber, a 16-year-old high school drop-out and runaway from Palo Alto, Calif., who was working as a prostitute, was murdered in a room at the Luxor Hotel. Arrested for her murder was Michael Joseph Hathaway, 30, who reportedly told police that he gave Gruber $200 for sex, but when she upped her price to $1,500 he choked her. She fell to the floor and begged for her life, but Hathaway said he stood on her neck for 10 minutes until she was dead. He then raped her corpse and stole her money, including the cash he had given her.

### October 24

**MURDER: Bronx, N.Y.** Michael Vernon, who had shot and killed five persons and wounded another four people in a 1995 shooting rampage inside a shoe store, was convicted and given five life terms.

### October 30

**MURDER: Middlesex County, Mass.** Louise Woodward was convicted of killing 8-month-old Matthew Eappen, a child entrusted to her care. The next day, Judge Hiller B. Zobel sentenced Woodward to life in prison.

### October 31

**MURDER: Salem, Va.** A jury convicted Earl Bramblett of murdering his friends, Teresa and Blaine Hodges and their two daughters.

### November 4

**MURDER/RAPE: Chicago, Ill.** Cleshawn Hopes, 25, testified at the murder trial of Hubert Geralds, Jr., dubbed the "Englewood Strangler," by prosecutors, stating that Geralds had attacked and raped her on April 14, 1995, after the two had spent the night smoking crack cocaine, but that she had managed to escape and summon police. Geralds was on trial for murdering six women and attempting to murder Hopes.

### November 6

**ASSASSINATION: Kingston, Jamaica** Alfredo Enrique Vargas, Venezuelan ambassador, was shot dead in his apartments by an unknown assailant.

**BOMBING: San Juan, Puerto Rico** Jose Solis was arrested by federal agents and charged with the 1992 bombing of a U.S. military officer in Chicago. He was reportedly a member of the Boricua Revolutionary Front which sought through terrorist means the independence of Puerto Rico.

**ROBBERY: Sao Paulo, Brazil** A gang of heavily armed men overpowered guards at a regional airport, and held up an armored plane, taking $5 million in cash and then disappearing into city traffic.

### November 10

**MURDER: Middlesex County, Mass.** Judge Hiller B. Zobel reduced the sentence of Louise Woodward, convicted of killing 8-month-old Matthew Eappen, to the time she had already served, 279 days, saying that the child might have had a preexisting blood clot that was affected by rough handling and that Woodward's actions had not been prompted by malice. The decision caused worldwide debate.

### November 12

**BOMBING: New York, N.Y.** Ramzi Ahmed Yousef and Eyad Ismoil were both convicted of bombing the World Trade Center in 1993. Yousef was the alleged mastermind of the bombing, while Ismoil reportedly drove the truck bomb into the underground parking lot.

**MURDER/ROBBERY: Stockton, Calif.** Louis James Peoples was arrested and charged with a murder spree in this city, beginning on October 29 when police say Peoples shot and killed James Loper with whom Peoples had once worked. People reportedly robbed a liquor and tobacco store on November 4, killing its owner, Stephen Chacko. On November 11, Peoples allegedly robbed a grocery store and killed its owners, Besun Yu and Jun Gao.

### November 15

**PRISONER RELEASE: Beijing, China** Wei Jingsheng, one of China's most prominent dissidents who had been imprisoned for 18 years, was granted medical parole. Wei was put aboard a U.S.-bound flight. He arrived in Detroit the next day and was hospitalized.

### November 17

**CHILD ABUSE: Brillion, Wis.** Police arrested Michael and Angeline Rogers for beating and keeping their daughter in a dog cage in the basement of their home.

**KIDNAPPING: San Juan, Puerto Rico** Officials announced that Crystal Leann Anzaldi, who had been kidnapped in San Diego, Calif., on December 8, 1990, had been found in San Juan, and the woman falsely claiming to be her mother, Nilza Gierbolini Guzman, 35, had been arrested. Authorities first investigated Guzman on charges that she had been abusing the girl and, after checking more than 500 photos on the Internet site, the National Center for Missing and Exploited Children, found a match, identifying the girl from a photo and posted information describing the missing girl with a tiny birthmark to the left of her nose. The Anzaldi couple, who had earlier divorced, were overjoyed that their long-lost daughter had been found.

**TERRORIST ATTACK: Luxor, Egypt** Using explosives,

guns, hand grenades and knives, six Islamic terrorists seeking to overthrow the secular government, indiscriminately killed 58 foreign tourists and four Egyptians, striking at the most popular tourist site, the Temple of Queen Hatshepsut. The terrorists fled on a hijacked bus and one was killed at a police checkpoint. The other five were hunted down in the nearby hills and shot to death.

### November 18

**AIRCRAFT EXPLOSION: New York, N.Y.** The FBI announced that after an exhaustive investigation it ruled out criminal sabotage as a possible cause for the explosion that destroyed TWA Flight 800 off Long Island, N.Y. in July 1996. Bureau spokesmen stated that there was no evidence to support sabotage.

**JUDICIARY: Washington, D.C.** The U.S. Supreme Court ruled 8-1 to strengthen the powers of police in dealing with drivers and passengers during routine traffic stops.

### November 23

**DRUGS; Nogales, Mexico** Mexican customs agents became involved in a shootout with six to eight men after confiscating from their van $123,000 in what was thought to be drug money. The men opened fire on the Mexican agents, killing one agent and wounding several others before escaping back across the border from Arizona into Mexico.

### November 24

**MURDER/ROBBERY: Oakland, Calif.** Thomas Wheelock, a guard working for Armored Transport, reportedly shot and killed his fellow security guard, Rodrigo J. Cortez, and stole an armored car containing $300,000.

### November 27

**MURDER/ROBBERY: Centerville, Ut.** Security guard Thomas Wheelock, who had reportedly killed his partner and stole an armored car with $300,000, was arrested and held for extradition back to California.

### December 1

**MURDER: West Paducah, Ky.** Michael Carneal, 14, entered Heath High School and began firing into a group of students gathered in a hallway at a prayer meeting, killing three girls and injuring five others, until he was subdued by another student.

### December 3

**PRISONER RELEASE: Ciudad Juarez, Mexico** David Carmos, after spending five years in a Mexican jail on what he called trumped up drug charges, was released to U.S. authorities. The release was largely effected by U.S. Representative J. Joseph Moakley of Massachusetts—Carmos was originally from Boston—who brought pressure on Mexican officials.

### December 4

**MURDER/KIDNAPPING: Alma, Ga.** Jerry Scott Heidler was arrested and charged with killing Danny and Kim Daniels and two of their adopted children in Santa Claus, Ga. He was also charged with kidnapping three other children, but let them out of his car many miles distant from their home and then fled. Police stated that Heidler was burglarizing the Daniels home when the killings occurred.

### December 5

**SEX SLAVES: Taipei, Taiwan** The government paid $15,600 each to 30 women in their 70s who had been sex slaves of the Japanese Army during World War II, an established war crime for which Japan refused to apologize or make restitution.

### December 9

**BOMBINGS: Southern India** Bombs on three separate trains crossing southern India exploded, killing 10 people and injuring another 64 persons. No one took responsibility for the bombings.

**EXECUTIONS: Hunstsville, Texas/Jarrett, Va.** Serial killer Michael Lee Lockhart was executed in Texas. Michael Charles Satcher, who had killed a young woman in 1990, was put to death by lethal injection in Virginia.

**MURDER: Winter Park, Fla.** John E. Armstrong reportedly shot and killed a man he thought had been involved with his girlfriend.

**RIOTS: Athens, Greece** More than 200 anarchist youths damaged shops and cars in a running riot that was finally halted by heavily armed police squads. The anarchists hurled gasoline bombs and stones at officers before the riot was quelled.

### December 10

**ROBBERY: Bloomfield Township, Mich.** After a rash of bank robberies, police in Bloomfield Township assigned officers to stake out many banks. On this date, two officers watched as a man arrived before the Michigan National Bank in a white Oldsmobile Cutlass, the getaway car described in earlier robberies. He packed snow over the license plates to prevent their identification then, donning a camouflage mask and carrying a satchel, he entered the bank. He emerged a few minutes later, jumping into the Oldsmobile and racing off. Officers followed and, a short time later, arrested 46-year-old Mike Witoszysnki, who explained that he had lost his job as a medical supplies salesman and had been robbing banks to support his wife and children. He admitted to robbing seven banks at gunpoint

### December 11

**EXECUTION: Jarratt, Va.** Thomas H. Beavers was executed by lethal injection for the 1990 rape-murder of 61-year-old Margaret E. Lowery.

**MURDER/PROSTITUTION: New York, N.Y.** Lora Pitoscia, 34, who had been arrested 120 times for prostitution, was charged with murder in the death of her 2-month-old son. While serving a two-week jail term for prostitution on Riker's Island, she told no one that she had a baby in her apartment, fearing she said later, that she would be charged with neglect. When she was released, she returned to the apartment to find the child dead. (Neighbors who heard the child crying for several days did not nothing, called no one.) Pitoscia dumped the baby's body down a garbage chute, but it was discovered and traced back to her.

**TERRORISM: Tehran, Iran** The Organization of the Islamic Conference issued a declaration in which it condemned terrorism as incompatible with Islam and that Islam forbids the killing of innocent persons.

*December 12*
**EXTORTION: New York, N.Y.** Autumn Jackson, convicted of attempting to extort $40 million from comedian Bill Cosby, was sentenced to 26 months in prison.

*December 17*
**HOSTAGE-TAKING: Plano, Texas** James Monroe Lipscomb, Jr., 33, stormed into a day care center where his wife worked—he had recently received divorce papers—and he took her, four other adults and 63 children hostage, standing off police in a 30-hour siege, but eventually surrendered without injuring anyone.

**MURDER: Salem, Va.** Earl Bramblett, convicted of murdering a family of four, was sentenced to death by Judge Roy Willett.

*December 19*
**MURDER/SUICIDE: Milwaukee, Wis.** Anthony Deculit, a black postal worker, shot and wounded his supervisor and killed another postal employee—both his victims were white—before turning a gun on himself and committing suicide.

*December 22*
**MASS MURDER: San Cristobal de Las Casas, Mexico** Forty-five members of the Zapatista party were killed by gunmen. Of those ruthlessly slaughtered, 15 of those killed were children. Members of the ruling Institutional Revolutionary Party are blamed for the mass murder.

**MURDER/KIDNAPPING: Moreno Valley, Calif.** Donald Nichols, who had kidnapped and murdered his former girlfriend Angel Zingarelli, was shot to death by police officers when he apparently resisted arrest.

**UNABOMBER: Sacramento, Calif.** The trial began for Theodore Kaczynski, who had been charged with the bombing murders and crimes of the Unabomber.

*December 23*
**BOMBING: Denver, Colo.** Terry Nichols, Timothy McVeigh's co-defendant in the 1995 bombing of the federal building in Oklahoma City, Oklahoma, was found guilty of one count of conspiracy to use a weapon of mass destruction and eight counts of involuntary manslaughter of federal agents (but not of murder). He would later be sentenced to life imprisonment.

*December 24*
**TERRORISM/MURDER/KIDNAPPING: Paris, France** Illich Ramirez Sanchez, the notorious Carlos or The Jackal, who had been captured by French agents in Sudan in

1994, was convicted of kidnapping and murder and was sentenced to prison for life.

*December 29*
**MURDER: Clinton, Indiana** Orville Lynn Majors, a 31-year-old former male nurse, was arrested and charged with giving lethal injections to at least six patients at Vermillion County Hospital (now known as West Central Community Hospital) where he worked from 1993 to 1995. Majors, whose demeanor reportedly changed from tenderness and care to outright hatred for his patients—at the end he called the elderly patients "whiners" and "white trash"—was suspected in the deaths of as many as 147 people who died while Majors was employed at the hospital. Tried for the murder of Dorothea Hixon—her daughter witnessed Majors giving her an unauthorized injection—and five others, Majors would be convicted of all six killings in Brazil, Indiana, on October 18, 1999.

*December 30*
**BOMBING/MURDER: Oakwood, Ill.** The United Methodist Church was bombed and church caretaker Brian Plawer was killed.

*December 31*
**MASSACRE: Algeria** The government announced that in the last nine days of December more than 400 persons had been massacred by Muslim extremists attempting to control local elections.

# 1998

*January 3*
**HATE CRIMES: Stockholm, Sweden** Members of the rock band Max Resist were arrested for shouting "Sieg Heil," a banned Nazi slogan and charged with violating the country's hate crimes laws.

*January 7*
**ATTEMPTED MURDER: Santa Cruz de Tenerife** Heide Fittkau-Garthe, a 57-year-old German psychologist and leader of a doomsday cult, was arrested at her chalet on the Spanish resort island of Tenerife in the Canary Islands. She was held without bail and charged three days later with "inducement to suicide," involving her thirty-two cult followers, many of whom lived with Fittkau-Garthe at her chalet, while others dwelled in tents on a nearby farm. Police stated that they foiled a mass suicide plot by interrupting a "last supper" at Fittkau-Garthe's chalet and that they found poisonous chemicals at the chalet which were to be used by the cultists to commit suicide. According to reports, sect members were convinced that the world would end on January 8, 1998, and that a spaceship would rescue their souls and take them to a new world, a belief not unlike that held by the 39 Heaven's Gate cultists in California who committed suicide in March 1997.

**INVESTIGATING THE PRESIDENT: Washington, D.C.** White House intern Monica Lewinsky (on the payroll in the Office of Legislative Affairs since December 1995), a 21-

year-old woman, denied in an affidavit in the Paula Jones case that she had had an affair with President Clinton.

### January 10

**ILLEGAL WIRETAPPING: Cuba** A Vatican official in Rome reported that a surveillance bug was found in a room which was reserved for Pope John Paul II during his trip to Cuba of January 21-25, 1998. *El Pais*, the Madrid newspaper, first reported the discovery of the bug in December 1997, stating that a hidden microphone was unearthed by Cuban Catholic church officials when inspecting a room reserved for the Pope in a provincial city he was scheduled to visit. Officials for Fidel Castro's Communist regime denied planting the bug, claiming that the device dated back to the dictatorship of Fulgencio Batista, who was overthrown by Castro in 1959. Upon examination, the microphone was determined to be of newer origin.

**SPONSORING A FAILED GOVERNMENT COUP: Lusaka, Zambia** Kenneth Kaunda, 73, who led Zambia to independence from Great Britain and ruled that country almost unchallenged for twenty-seven years, was charged with backing a coup on October 28, 1998, that failed to oust ruling President Frederick Chiluba, who replaced Kaunda when elected to office in 1991. Kaunda had been under arrest for more than a month until the charges were brought against him and two others, Dean Mung'omba and Roger Chongwe.

### January 12

**INVESTIGATING THE PRESIDENT: Washington, D.C.** Linda Tripp, a former White House employee who had befriended intern Monica Lewinsky, turned over 20 hours of audio tape to independent counsel Kenneth Starr. The tapes reportedly held conversations between Lewinksky and Tripp in which Lewinsky admitted that she had had a sexual relationship with President Clinton since November 1995, when she was an unpaid intern at the White House. Starr began to focus on possible attempts by Clinton and his associates to cover up the affair which might lead to charges of obstruction of justice. Starr had FBI officials wire Tripp to obtain additional evidence. Tripp then met with Lewinsky at a hotel in Arlington, Va., the next day.

### January 13

**ROBBERY: New York, N.Y.** Three masked men accosted two Brink's guards as they went toward a foreign currency office of the Bank of America on the 11th floor of one of the twin towers of the World Trade Center. Brandishing a gun, the three bandits bound the guards and five other persons on an elevator, snatched three bags of money from a cart (leaving three other bags behind) and made off with $1.7 million, $300,000 in cash and the rest in foreign currency. For all their fine planning, police reported that the thieves then removed their ski masks before walking past hidden security cameras and all three were identified—their photos flashed on TV and published in newspapers—before they

returned to their Brooklyn residences. Arrested for the heist were Michael Reed 34, and William Desmond Folk, 44. An arrest warrant was issued for the third suspect, 39-year-old Richard Gillette.

### January 14

**MURDER: Richmond, Va.** Eric Christopher Payne, who had been convicted of murdering two women and attacking several other people in 1997, was sentenced to death. Said Payne at the time: "I agree with the jury. I deserve the death penalty."

### January 16

**PRISON MURDERS: Caracas, Venezuela** A shootout between rival gangs of prisoners in La Planta Prison resulted in five inmates murdered and another 14 prisoners seriously wounded. The shootout was over control of the drug trade inside the prison. No information on how the prisoners obtained their guns was forthcoming. Heavily armed National Guardsmen had to be rushed to the prison to restore order.

**INVESTIGATING THE PRESIDENT: Washington, D.C.** A 3-judge panel supervising special prosecutors approved of Kenneth Starr's expanded inquiry to include possible obstruction of justice in the Jones case. Starr's staff members questioned Monica Lewinsky for several hours.

### January 17

**INVESTIGATING THE PRESIDENT: Washington, D.C.** Deposed by lawyers representing Paula Jones, President Clinton reportedly denied having a sexual affair with Monica Lewinsky. Clinton, however, did reportedly admit having a sexual affair with Gennifer Flowers, even though in the 1992 presidential election he had denied her claim that she had had a long-term affair with him.

### January 21

**INVESTIGATING THE PRESIDENT: Washington, D.C.** The nation's press made public the Lewinsky story and President Clinton, carefully choosing his words, appeared to deny having a sexual relationship with Lewinsky, as well as asking her to lie about their relationship.

### January 22

**INVESTIGATING THE PRESIDENT: Washington, D.C.** President Clinton, in response to questions about his alleged affair with Monica Lewinsky and reports that he had asked her to lie in her affidavit in the Paula Jones case, stated that he would "never ask anybody to do anything other than tell the truth." Prominent Washington lawyer and Clinton crony Vernon Jordan admitted that he had attempted to find Lewinsky a job outside government. (Lewinsky had been transferred from her White House job in April 1996 to a position in the Department of Defense at the Pentagon, allegedly because White House aides thought Lewinsky was too near the President too often. It was later thought that Hillary

Rodham Clinton, the President's wife, had had a hand in the transfer. Lewinsky had resigned from the Pentagon post in December 1997.) Jordan made a point of telling the press that Lewinsky had told him she had not had an affair with the President.

### January 26

**INVESTIGATING THE PRESIDENT: Washington, D.C.** President Clinton appeared on national television to emphatically state (while wagging a finger at viewers): "I did not have sexual relationships with that woman, Ms. Lewinsky! I never told anybody to lie, not a single time, never!"

**RACKETEERING/GRAND THEFT/EXTORTION/ BANK FRAUD: Largo, Fla.** Rev. Henry Lyons, president of the National Baptist Convention USA, was brought to trial, along with accused accomplice Bernice Edwards, 42, on racketeering and other charges that included elaborate schemes to divert $4 million intended for the convention in order to buy expensive homes, cars and jewelry.

**WAR CRIMES: The Hague, Netherlands** Goran Jelisic, who had been seized in Bosnia by U.S.-NATO troops on January 22, appeared before the U.N. war crimes tribunal to plead not guilty to several charges.

### January 27

**FALSIFYING DOCUMENTS: Washington, D.C.** Federal officials indicted 20 persons on charges of falsifying the naturalization examinations of more than 13,000 immigrants in 22 states over the last two years.

**INVESTIGATING THE PRESIDENT: Washington, D.C.** Hillary Rodham Clinton appeared on the "Today Show," to label Kenneth Starr's investigation of President Clinton as part of "a vast right-wing conspiracy that has been conspiring against my husband since the day he announced for president." She provided no evidence to support what many believed was a preposterous claim and what some believed to be a smoke-screen designed to obscure the real facts. Kenneth Starr dismissed Mrs. Clinton's remarks, stating that he had initiated the investigation into the Clinton-Lewinsky affair after he had received "credible evidence of serious federal crimes."

### January 28

**ILLEGAL CAMPAIGN CONTRIBUTIONS: Washington, D.C.** Long-time friend of President Clinton Yah Lin "Charlie" Trie, along with Yuan Pei "Antonio" Pan, were indicted on charges of having influenced persons to act as conduits for cash contributions to the Democratic National Committee while the political donations really stemmed from foreign nationals who were prohibited by law from making such contributions. Trie had fled the country and was indicted in absentia.

### January 29

**BOMBING: Birmingham, Ala.** A bomb exploded outside the door of the New Woman All Women abortion clinic, shattering windows and creating a deep crater in the ground.

Robert Sanderson, an off-duty police officer was killed and Emily Lyons, a nurse, was severely injured. The FBI later attributed this terrorist attack to fugitive Eric Rudolph.

### January 30

**CHILD PORNOGRAPHY: St. Charles, Ill.** Randall Wilke, 46, was sentenced to five months in prison and eight months of home confinement, and fined $2,500, following his conviction of transporting child pornography. Wilke won a lenient sentence after convincing a judge that he was vulnerable to attack in prison because of the nature of his crime.

### February 3

**EXECUTION: Huntsville, Texas** Karla Faye Tucker, 38, despite widespread efforts to save her life, was executed by lethal injection, becoming the first female killer to be executed in Texas in 135 years. She had confessed to and had been convicted of committing two ax murders in 1983 and had become a born-again Christian while in prison, an action some dismissed as a ploy to save her life.

**ILLEGAL CAMPAIGN CONTRIBUTIONS: Washington, D.C.** Yah Lin "Charlie" Trie, who had been indicted for arranging illegal contributions to the Democratic National Committee, returned to the U.S., arrested at Dulles International Airport. His co-defendant, Yuan Pei Pan, could not be located.

**INVESTIGATING THE PRESIDENT: Washington, D.C.** The New York *Times* reported that Monica Lewinsky had visited the White House 37 times after she had left her position there in 1996.

**NEGLIGENT HOMICIDE: Italian Alps** A U.S. Air Force fighter plane reportedly violating regulations on speed and altitude, sliced the cable of a gondola carrying 20 skiers, sending all of them crashing to their deaths. Four U.S. airmen were later charged with negligent homicide.

### February 6

**CHILD PORNOGRAPHY: Montgomery, Ala.** A grand jury indicted Barnes & Noble, a national bookstore chain, for selling child pornography in the form of two books by photographers.

**INVESTIGATING THE PRESIDENT: Washington, D.C.** President Clinton stated that he would never consider resigning over his reported affair with White House intern Monica Lewinsky.

### February 8-9

**MASS MURDER: Noble, Ill.** Five persons were reportedly hammered to death by 16-year-old Christopher Churchill, a high school dropout.

### February 9

**ASSASSINATION ATTEMPT: Tbilisi, Georgia** Premier Eduard Shevardnadze, 70, escaped another assassination attempt when terrorists fired a rocket-propelled grenade at his passing car. Seven suspected terrorist would later be arrested and charged with the attack, these being supporters of Shevardnadze's predecessor, Zviad Gamsakhurdia, a former Soviet foreign minister who was overthrown in a 1992 coup and who had died under mysterious circumstances in 1993. The attack was reportedly led by Gocha Esebua, who then became the subject of a police dragnet.

### February 14

**BOMBING: Coimbatore, India** Thirteen bombs were exploded by Muslim terrorists in several crowded sections of the city prior to a speech by Hindu leader Lal Krishna Advani. Hindu-Muslim clashes had increased in this city since a Hindu policeman was killed by two Muslims in November 1997.

**BOMBING: Wuhan, China** At least sixteen persons were killed and dozens were injured in a bomb explosion that tore apart a bus, damaging three other buses and two taxis. Some estimates had as many as 30 people killed, although Chinese authorities refused to confirm the bombing. Unofficially, authorities stated that this explosion and several others in the recent past had been carried out by workers angry at being laid off or by Muslim separatists from the province of Xinjiang.

**MASS MURDER: Noble, Ill.** The bodies of five persons—Debra Smith, 35, Jonathan Lloyd, 17, and Smith's three children, Jennifer, 12, Korey, 10, and Kenneth, 8—were found in Smith's home, bludgeoned to death by a blunt instrument.Christopher Churchill, a 16-year-old high school dropout became a suspect.

**TERRORISM/CRIMES AGAINST HUMANITY: Bosanski Samac, Bosnia-Herzegovina** Two Bosnian Serbs, Milan Simic and Miroslav Tadic, surrendered themselves to U.S. officials to stand trial for creating a "campaign of terror designed to force most Bosnian Croat and Muslim residents to leave the area" of Bosanski Samac, according to a U.N. indictment of July 1995. Denying they had committed crimes against humanity and war crimes, Simic and Tadic were escorted under heavy guard to face trial in The Hague, Netherlands.

### February 15

**MASS MURDER: San Cristobal de Las Casas, Mexico** The bodies of seven men, reportedly Zapatista sympathizers, were found in a pit. All were victims, it was alleged, of murder squads of the ruling Institutional Revolutionary Party.

### February 16

**OUTLAWED COMPUTER GAME: Brasilia, Brazil** The Justice Department of the Brazilian government outlawed the computer game "Grand Theft Auto," and ordered all copies of the CD-ROM removed from store shelves. The game allowed players to gain points by stealing cars and killing police officers. Government officials considered the game irresponsible and dangerous in that it trivialized robbery and murder and might have inspired players to commit actual robberies and killings.

### February 17

**CHILD ABUSE: Blountville, Tenn.** Stephen Yeaney, 40, the pastor of Rock Springs United Methodist Church, and his 39-year-old wife Donna, a state psychologist, were both indicted for child abuse in that they reportedly forced their 13-

year-old son to go naked outside their home in freezing rain on January 17, 1998, to discipline him, a measure the couple had reportedly taken several times.

**FRAUD: Farmington, N.M.** Thomas Stanley Huntington, 51, was charged with fraud after he had allegedly sold what he called "California Red Superworms" which could eat nuclear waste.

**WAR CRIMES: The Hague, Netherlands** Milan Simic and Miroslav Tadic, accused of conducting a "campaign of terror" in Bosnia, pleaded innocent before a U.N. war crimes tribunal. Another accused terrorist leader, Simo Zaric, agreed to surrender to the court.

### February 18

**MURDER: Naples, Italy** Giovanni Gargiulo, 14, was shot to death by two pistol-wielding youths on a motorcycle. The boy's brother was a member of the Mazzarella Mafia gang which had been feuding with another Mafia gang.

### February 19

**EMBEZZLEMENT: New York, N.Y.** Ricardo Carassco, the 41-year-old chief executive of the international branch of BankBoston in New York, disappeared after superiors had questioned some of large loans he had made. Paid a $200,000-a-year salary, Carasco, who spoke many languages, was thought to have embezzled as much as $73 million before fleeing. He abandoned his posh home in East Hampton, Long Island, a swanky 2,500-square-foot Bleeker Street apartment, a Toyota Land Cruiser and a Jaguar.

### February 20

**IMPROPER JUDICIAL BEHAVIOR: Lakewood, Wash.** While a jury was deliberating a drunk driving case, Judge Ralph Baldwin left the courtroom and returned with a 12-pack of beer, offering drinks to a court administrator, an assistant state's attorney and the defense lawyer in the case. When the administrator declined, Baldwin reportedly called her a "wimp." A judicial watchdog board later filed charges against Baldwin who promptly resigned his $65,000-a-year position, one he had held for only three months. Baldwin admitted he had shown "poor judgment."

### February 27

**MURDER: Orlando, Fla.** Self-styled vampire killer Roderick Justin Ferrell, was sentenced to death in the electric chair for the 1996 murders of Richard and Naomi Wendorf.

### March 4

**ILLEGAL INTERNET GAMBLING: New York, N.Y.** Indictments of 15 betting companies headquartered in the Caribbean and operated by U.S. citizens were indicted for illegally operating sports betting businesses over the Internet.

**JUDICIARY: Washington, D.C.** The U.S. Supreme Court ruled unanimously that sexual harassment statutes apply even when the harasser and the victim are the same sex.

### March 6

**MASS MURDER: Newington, Ct.** Matthew Beck, a disgruntled employee, arrived at the offices of the Connecticut Lottery and shot and killed four executives before killing himself.

## March 8

**PRISON DEATH: Fort Worth, Texas** James B. McDougal, who was the center of the Whitewater investigation, died in his prison cell of a heart attack. McDougal was being held at the Federal Medical Center.

## March 9

**BOMBINGS: Lahore-Quetta, Punjab, india** A time-activated bomb exploded inside a compartment on the Chiltan Express train as it crossed a bridge over a canal, killing seven persons and wounding another 35 passengers. Another bomb exploded outside a court building in the province of Sind, injuring 13, including six policemen.

**WAR CRIMES: The Hague, Netherlands** Dragoljub Kunarac, 37, admitted before the U.N. war crimes tribunal that he had raped several Muslim women in 1992 during the Bosnian war. Human rights groups claimed that more than 30,000 Muslim women had been raped during 1992-1995 by Serbian forces, many of whom telling their victims that it was their purpose to impregnate them with Serbian babies and thus increase the Serbian population (and its voting power) in the area.

## March 13

**SEXUAL MISCONDUCT: Washington, D.C.** Sgt. Major Gene McKinney, accused of sexual misconduct, was acquitted on 17 out of 18 charges. He was reduced one rank and received a reprimand; McKinney had, prior to his court martial, lost his position as the Army's top soldier among non-commissioned officers.

## March 16

**ILLEGAL CAMPAIGN CONTRIBUTIONS: Washington, D.C.** Businessman Johnny Chung pleaded guilty to bank fraud, conspiracy and tax evasion. Chung had illegally contributed $20,000 to the Democratic Party by persuading 20 persons to contribute $1,000 each (the legal limit) and then reimbursing them.

**MURDER/RAPE: Struecklingen, Germany** Christina Nytsch, an 11-year-old girl, disappeared after her swimming class. She was found later in some woods, having been raped, stabbed and strangled to death. Authorities using bodily fluids left by the killer, ran DNA tests against that of 16,400 men, the largest such DNA testing ever, and reported in May 1998 that they had identified the killer as a 30-year-old mechanic who confessed to the crime.

## March 18

**FALSE STATEMENTS: Washington, D.C.** Ronald H. Blackley, a top aide to former Agriculture Secretary Mike Espy, was sentenced to two years and three months in prison. Blackley had been convicted in December 1997 of failing to disclose $22,000 he had received from associates in Mississippi and then later making false statements in trying to cover up the payoff.

## March 19

**BOMBING: Fairhaven, Vt.** Christopher Marquis, 17, died from a bomb explosion that seriously injured his mother, Sheila Rockwell.

**POLICE CORRUPTION: Cleveland, Ohio** Charles Xenakis, the former police chief of Campbell, Ohio, was charged with protecting illegal gambling while in office.

**POLICE BRUTALITY: Afyon, Turkey** Five police officers were sentenced to more than seven years each in prison for beating to death Metin Goktepe, a 27-year-old journalist, on January 9, 1996.

## March 23

**ARSON/MANSLAUGHTER: Seattle, Wash.** Martin Pang, who had been convicted of setting a fire that burned down his parents' frozen food business in 1995, a blaze in which four firefighters died, was sentenced to 35 years in prison.

## March 24

**MASS MURDER: Jonesboro, Ark.** Andrew Golden, 11 and Mitchell Johnson, 13, after stealing guns from Golden's grandfather, went to their West Side Middle School, and, after one of them set off a fire alarm to draw the children and teachers outside, took hidden positions in a nearby woods and shot students and teachers as they ran outside. They killed four school girls and a teacher, and wounded eight other girls, one boy and another teacher. Quickly apprehended and jailed, Golden and Johnson would be tried as juveniles, as mandated by state law.

## March 25

**LYNCHING: Huejutla, Mexico** Salvador Valdez and Jose Santos Vasquez, two men who were jailed for reportedly attempting to abduct small girls and were about to be released on bond, were seized by a crowd of more than 1,000 people and lynched in a town square. It had been reported that the two victims had been kidnapping small girls in order to kill them and sell their organs on the black market.

**MURDER: Daly City, Calif.** Megan Hogg was arraigned on three counts of murder, charged with suffocating her three young daughters. After wrapping her children's heads with duct tape and holding them down, police stated, the 29-year-old Hogg made a feeble attempt to commit suicide.

## March 26

**MANSLAUGHTER: Berlin, Germany** Five former East German officers were found guilty of manslaughter in several shooting deaths of persons attempting to scale the East Berlin wall and escape to West Berlin in the 1960s. Former Maj. Gen. Erich Woellner, 67, was found guilty on six counts of manslaughter for signing shoot-to-kill orders from 1979 to 1989.

**MASS MURDER: Redfield, Ark.** Two young women and three children were slain, all shot to death, in a trailer area. A suspect was taken into custody after being wounded by police.

**NEGLIGENT HOMICIDE: Washington, D.C.** The Marine Corps charged four jet crewmen with negligent homicide in the severing of a gondola cable in Italy in February that caused the deaths of 20 persons. The charged crewmen were Capt. Richard Ashby, Capt. Joseph Schweitzer, Capt. William Raney II and Capt. Chandler Seagraves.

### March 29

**TERRORISM: Ramallah, West Bank** Mohiyedine Sharif, chief bomb maker for Hamas, a Palestinian terrorist organization, was killed in a premature car bombing. Officials for the Palestinian Authority claimed that Sharif was murdered by gunfire before the bomb exploded, shot to death by Adel Awadallah, a rival member of his own terrorist group involved in an Islamic power struggle

### March 30

**EXECUTION: Starke, Fla.** Judy Buenoano, a convicted 54-year-old killer—she had murdered her husband and son for insurance money, and perhaps killed several more persons and had been dubbed the "Black Widow"—was executed in Florida's electric chair.

### March 31

**JUDICIARY: Washington, D.C.** The U.S. Supreme Court ruled 8-1 that a defendant does not have a right to present polygraph evidence at trial because of continuing doubts about the validity of lie- detector tests.

**TERRORISM: Georgia** Gocha Esebua, leader of a 20-man terrorist group opposed to the government of Eduard Shevardnadze, was shot and killed by police. Esebua and others had captured U.N. observers and had held them hostage for more than a week in February 1998, before releasing them and escaping. Esebua had been branded a public enemy.

### April 1-2

**MURDER SPREE: Indiana-Illinois** Steven A. Hale, a 21-year-old resident of Washington, Ind., and 19-year-old Chalk A. Wessell, reportedly went on a killing spree that began on April 1 and lasted for 15 hours, until the alleged killers were captured. Jeremiah Miller, 18, was the first victim, shot and killed in his red pickup truck. The shootings occurred randomly thereafter, with Marlin Knepp, 26, of Loogootee, Ind., shot and killed as he was driving down a country road near an Amish settlement, then 36-year-old Pam Cook shot and killed on her front porch outside of Odom, Ind. The next night, near Albion, Ill., David L. Chalcraft, 48 and 48-year-old Larry Sams went to investigate suspicious-looking headlights in a lonely lane when two men opened fire. Chalcraft, wounded in the neck, fell to the ground and pretended to be dead as the men raced forward to shoot Sams to death before fleeing. Police searched the area and a helicopter cornered Hale in a cornfield. He was taken into custody and charged with murder and attempted murder. Wessell was taken to the morgue; he was found in the cornfield dead, a bullet in his head, thought by police to either be a suicide or another victim of Hale's.

### April 2

**CRIMES AGAINST HUMANITY: Paris, France** Maurice Papon, 87, who had been a Vichy official and was accused of transporting hundreds of Jews to Nazi death camps in 1942-1944, was found guilty of crimes against humanity and sentenced to 10 years in prison.

### April 5

**BOMBINGS: Kampala, Uganda** Terrorists exploded two bombs—one on the terrace of the Speke Hotel, the other at the Nile Grill restaurant—killing five persons and injuring five other people.

**TAVERN RIOT: Athens, Ohio** About 2,000 rowdy, drunken university students began throwing bricks and bottles at riot police in protest against bars closing early in compliance with switching to daylight saving time. Police fired rubber and wooden bullets and used batons to break up the mobs. Several persons were injured. A similar riot occurred in 1997 in protest of the time change.

**TERRORIST ATTACK: Zugdidi, Georgia** Terrorists opened fire and threw a grenade at a funeral procession for terrorist Gocha Esebua, killing five persons and wounding another eight people

### April 6

**BOMBING: Riga, Latvia** An anti-personnel mine was detonated outside the Russian Embassy, reportedly causing no injuries but doing considerable damage. Officials stated that right-wing terrorists made up of S.S. veterans of World War II were behind the bombing, the same terrorists who had recently bombed a local synagogue.

**JUDICIARY: Washington, D.C.** The U.S. Supreme Court rejected a motion for a new trial presented by attorneys for Manuel Noriega, former dictator of Panama who was convicted of conspiracy and drug racketeering charges in 1992. Noriega had been sentenced to 40 years in prison.

### April 7

**CHILD ABUSE: Cheboygan, Mich.** Earl Richard Schleben, Jr., the 27-year-old live-in boyfriend of Sharica Irwin, was charged with three counts of first-degree child abuse for forcing Irwin's 3-year-old daughter into a three-by-two-foot box for periods of 30 minutes at time over two months to discipline her. Irwin, who reportedly did nothing to stop this brutal punishment, was charged with second-degree child abuse, while her daughter was placed in a foster home.

**PRISON RELEASE: Philippines** Robin Padilla, one of the country's most popular actors, was released from prison after serving three years of a 21-year-prison term for illegal possession of firearms. He was pardoned by President Fidel Ramos, a man he had helped to elect. Padilla stated that prison had helped him cure his addiction to drugs and that "my life in prison taught me ... that power and popularity do not serve you well when you do wrong."

### April 14

**ASSAULT: Dallas, Texas** Three boys, ages 7, 8 and 11 were arrested in the kidnapping, beating and sexual assault of a 3-year-old girl.

**EXECUTION: Jarrett, Va.** Angel Francisco Breard was executed by lethal injection for the 1992 rape-murder of Ruth Dickie.

**FRAUD: Dallas, Texas** Eight members of the so-called Republic of Texas were convicted on several counts of fraud. Richard McLaren, the group's leader, who was then serving time for kidnapping, was convicted on 26 counts of writing bad checks that totaled in the millions of dollars.

**ORGANIZED CRIME: Borgetto, Sicily** Much wanted Mafia fugitive Vito Vitale was captured in a remote farmhouse. The 39-year-old Vitale, who had been sought for three years and had been identified as head of the Corleone Mafia family, first denied being the fugitive, but police made a positive identification and jailed Vitale, holding him for trial on charges of murder and racketeering.

### April 15

**KIDNAPPING: Mogadishu, Somali** Ten aid workers were kidnapped at gunpoint by unidentified gunmen just after their plane landed.

**MURDER/SUICIDE: Florida Keys** Lawrence F. King III, 18, wanted for killing his 16-year-old girlfriend Janaya Roberson in Austin, Texas, was trapped by police on Highway 1, the road running through the Florida Keys, but before he could be captured, King put a gun to his head and killed himself.

### April 16

**DEATH OF A MASS MURDERER: Dangret Mountains, Cambodia** Pol Pot (Saloth Sar, b. 1925), one-time leader of the Communist Khmer Rouge, and the man responsible for murdering more than a million of his fellow Cambodians, died peacefully in his bed inside the two-room hut of a mountain retreat. Pot, who took power in Cambodia in April 1976, remained a largely faceless despot who directed a "cleansing" of Cambodia wherein all former government workers, teachers, scientists, anyone showing signs of education, wealth, culture or even those who wore eyeglasses (and thus thought to be physically unfit) were murdered *en masse* by Pot's fanatical, mostly teenage troops. Pot decreed all family life at an end and ordered everyone to live in barracks and dine in mess halls where Communist propaganda was constantly chanted into the ears of all. The capital of Phnom Penh was utterly destroyed— all hospitals, schools, banks (money was blown up and burned, abolished with all other forms of private property) were razed. After four years of slaughter, which saw more than a million Cambodians murdered, Pot was ousted by Vietnam in 1979, its occupying Communist troops remaining in Cambodia for ten years. Pot, who murdered most of his lieutenants over the years, as well as his wife and nine children, ordering a tractor to crush his family to death, was placed under "house arrest for life," in 1996 by his top aide, Ta Mok, whom Pot was planning to murder. The cause of Pot's death was undetermined but one report had it that Ta Mok poisoned his former master, then, three days later, on April 25, 1998, had Pot's body thrown onto a pile of brush and rubber tires drenched with gasoline and burned to ashes. Ta Mok, who had fought alongside Pot for decades, then conducted a brief television interview. His eulogy for Paul Pot was terse: "He was cow dung."

**GENOCIDE: Rwanda** Two Catholic priests were convicted in the genocidal murder of more than 2,000 Tutsi tribe members in a single village during the 1994 campaign by right-wing Hutus to wipe out the Tutsi tribe.

### April 19

**DRUGS: Detroit, Mich.** A small plane flown from Texas and followed by three Customs Service planes, crashed onto a school baseball field, flipping upside-down and killing the pilot. The plane spilled out large bundles of marijuana and wads of cash. Witnesses said that many persons rushed to the plane, ostensibly to help, but wound up running away with the bundles of drugs.

### April 23:

**ASSASSINATION:** James Earl Ray, convicted of killing black civil rights leader Martin Luther King, Jr., in 1968, died in prison of liver failure. Ray had convinced many that he either had not acted alone (Ray had often spoken of a mysterious "Raoul," claiming that he was the real shootist, a red herring Ray may have invented) and/or had nothing to do with the King killing. Even some of King's relatives came to believe the latter claim, although there is little evidence to suggest others were involved in the King murder.

### April 24

**GENOCIDE: Rwanda** The government executed 22 persons who had been convicted of genocide during the 1994 civil war in which an estimated 500,000 Tutsis and moderate Hutus had been killed.

**MASS MURDER: Norwalk, Conn.** Geoffrey Ferguson, 47, was found guilty of killing three of his tenants and two of their guests in 1995 and then setting his building on fire to cover the murders. Ferguson, according to police, grew enraged when the tenants bounced a rent check and then complained to police about his attempts to evict them.

**MURDER: Edinboro, Pa.** Andrew Wurst, 14, went to a graduation dance where he shot and killed teacher John Gillette, and wounded another teacher and two students.

### April 26

**ASSASSINATION: Guatemala City, Guatemala** Bishop Juan Gerardi Conedera, 75, was beaten to death with a concrete block, the murder coming only two days after the Catholic prelate released a shocking report on human rights violations during Guatemala's 36-year civil war.

**KIDNAPPING/ROBBERY: New Bedford, Mass.** Two gunmen robbed a McDonald's restaurant, then tied up 13 employees and customers, before exchanging shots with police. One of the gunmen was killed and the other fled with two hostages, driving to New York City where he bound and gagged his hostages in a Bronx motel. The women managed to escape and call police, but the gunman had fled.

### April 29

**AGGRAVATED BATTERY: Peoria, Ill.** Four teachers were rushed to a hospital after suffering serious pain from what was later discovered to be a prank by three 12-year-old girls who laced their teachers' coffee and soft drinks with powerful laxatives. The girls were arrested and pleaded guilty to aggravated battery. They were sentenced to 15 days in jail, 90 days' home detention and two years' probation.

**MURDER: Naples, Italy** The parents of Mario Ciotola, a Camorra gangster turned government informer, were shot dead by two killers riding a motorcycle. Maria Rosaria Abbate was shot in the head on a Naples street and Raffaele Ciotola, 54, was gunned down as he tried to run away. The killings were thought to be in retaliation for Ciotola's betrayal of the Camorra, a Mafia-type organization that controlled all rackets in Naples.

*April 30*

**CAUSING A CATASTROPHE: Hannibal, Mo.** James Scott of Fowler, Ill., was found guilty of causing a catastrophe when he removed sandbags along a Mississippi River levee which caused thousands of acres of farmland near Quincy, Ill. to flood. Scott reportedly broke the levee so that he could strand his wife on the other side of the river and party without her knowledge.

**MURDER/ATTEMPTED MURDER: Bartow, Fla.** Three teenagers—Sylathum Antwan Streeter, 16, Victor Lester, 17, and Curtis Shuler, 16—were charged with murder and attempted murder after a shooting spree, beginning on April 26, left two persons dead and seven people wounded, all victims randomly selected and shot by the teens in Dundee and Haines City, Fla., according to police

**MURDER: Carmel, Ind.** Antoine Whitehead, 19, shot and killed 32-year-old Penny Schmitt, an officer at the KeyBank branch in this upscale Indianapolis suburb, after she told him that she was denying his application for a loan. Whitehead walked out of the bank, Schmitt going after him to offer him an umbrella to ward off a heavy rain. Whitehead went to his car, retrieved a gun and re-entered the bank just as Schmitt approached him. He shot her dead, and opened fire on other bank employees, wounding three other persons before he grabbed a stack of $20 bills and fled. Police found Whitehead a block away from the bank, crouched in a pine tree and, after trading fire, shot and killed Whitehead.

*May 1*

**TERRORISM: Pomona, Calif.** Eldridge Cleaver died in the Pomona Valley (Calif.) Medical Center. The 62-year-old, one-time Black Panther leader, while serving a term for assault in 1968, wrote *Soul on Ice*, a black racist view of the world. When released from jail, Cleaver joined the Black Panther Party (founded in 1962) and was subsequently involved in a gunfight with police in Oakland, Calif. He fled to Algeria, Cuba and then Paris where he reportedly embraced anti-Communist groups and advocated evangelical Christianity. After his return to the U.S., Cleaver claimed to be reformed and ran for the Republican Senate nomination in 1986 in California but was beaten.

**UNLAWFUL IMPRISONMENT: Syracuse, N.Y.** John Dennee, his wife Kathleen and his daughter Janet were arrested and charged with unlawful imprisonment, charged with holding two disabled women captive, mother and daughter, in order to gain their disability checks. The women were reportedly

chained to a box spring for days without food and were severely beaten by family members.

*May 2*

**ASSAULT: Moscow, Russia** The Russian Foreign Ministry reported that a black U.S. Marine stationed at the U.S. Embassy, strolling through Fili Park in southwest Moscow with a female embassy translator, also black, was severely beaten by four right-wing skinheads. Although the U.S. Embassy admitted that the Marine had been beaten, it did not identify him. For some time Russian skinheads had been assaulting dark-skinned persons or foreigners throughout Russia. A month earlier, two young Asian women were brutally beaten by twenty skinheads, causing the U.S. Embassy to issue a warning to all Americans in Moscow of possible skinhead attacks against American blacks and minorities. The racist assaults were condemned by Russian officials who described by them as "repulsive."

*May 4*

**FRAUD/THEFT: New York, N.Y.** All in One Auto Parts and six persons were indicted and charged with selling stolen car air bags nationwide. The defendants were also charged in laundering $1.5 million in illegal proceeds.

**ROBBERY: Rochester Hills, Mich.** Derek Schroeder, a 16-year-old high school honor student, according to police, carefully planned the robbery of the NBD bank in Oxford Township, showing a gun and threatening to blow up the place with a fake bomb. He reportedly took $145,000 and fled on his bicycle, but was stopped by police who responded to a silent bank alarm. Schroeder was charged as an adult with armed robbery.

**WHITEWATER: Little Rock, Ark.** Susan McDougal, who had already served a jail term for civil contempt in refusing to testify before a grand jury in Little Rock and was imprisoned for bank fraud relating to Whitewater, was again indicted for criminal contempt and obstruction of justice after she again refused to testify in April.

*May 4*

**UNABOMBER: Sacramento, Calif.** Theodore Kaczynski, who had been convicted for the many bombings and murders committed by the ubiquitous Unabomber, was sentenced to four consecutive life terms.

*May 5*

**DRUGS/ORGANIZED CRIME: Boca Raton, Fla.** Joseph DiFronzo, a fugitive since he was charged in July 1993 with overseeing the largest indoor marijuana-growing operation in Illinois history, was located and arrested on drug charges. DiFronzo, the brother of reputed Mafia boss John DiFronzo, was identified as a member of the crime syndicate.

**INVESTIGATING THE PRESIDENT: Washington, D.C.** Kenneth Starr's grand jury continued to hear testimony from Vernon Jordan, President Clinton's friend, who had tried to find White House intern Monica Lewinsky a job and (on May 6-7) testimony from Betty Currie, the President's secretary. District Judge Norma Holloway Johnson had previously ruled that Clinton could not invoke executive privilege or attorney-client privilege to prevent aides from testifying about Lewinsky.

## May 6

**DRUGS/ORGANIZED CRIME: Italy** Pasquale Cuntrera, a Sicilian Mafia boss extradited from Venezuela who had been convicted of running an international drug trafficking ring between Italy, Canada and Venezuela, was released from prison pending a second appeals trial. The wheelchair-bound Cuntrera promptly disappeared with embarrassed police and court officials ordering a nation-wide manhunt for the fugitive.

## May 9:

**CRIMES AGAINST HUMANITY: Arusha, Tanzania** Jean Kambanda, 42, former Prime Minister of Rwanda, pleaded guilty before a U.N. tribunal to crimes against humanity and genocide. More than 500,000 persons were killed in 1994 during Kambanda's oppressive regime.

## May 11

**ASSAULT: Sofia, Bulgaria** Anna Zarkova, a journalist who had exposed widespread political corruption and who had been threatened with injury and death if she did not cease her political exposes, was attacked at a bus stop where an assailant hurled sulfuric acid into her face, burning away her left ear and damaging the sight of her left eye. The attacker was not caught.

**ESPIONAGE: Jerusalem, Israel** After years of insisting that Navy analyst Jonathan Pollard had acted alone, Israel admitted that it had employed Pollard, a U.S. citizen imprisoned for life at this writing in Butner, S.C., as a spy for its nation. The admission, according to Pollard's attorneys, was thought to help win Pollard a release.

## May 12

**ASSASSINATION: Bogata, Colombia** General Gernando Landazabal Reyes, 76, a conservative political activist, was shot dead in front of his residence, reportedly by drug cartel killers.

**RIOTS: Jakarta, Indonesia** In a brutal suppression of student demonstrations, dictator Suharto ordered his police to fire into crowds, killing six students and wounding another 16. This incident would force Suharto to resign his dictatorship on May 21, 1998 and be replaced by President B.J. Habibie.

**TERRORISM LEGISLATION: Washington, D.C.** President Bill Clinton announced that he would ask Congress to pass legislation providing $280 million more in combating terrorism and drug trafficking.

## May 12-15

**RIOTS: Jakarta, Indonesia** Thousands of protestors rioted against the 32-year-old dictatorship of President Suharto. More than 5,000 students formed into groups on the campus of the Trisatki University in West Jakarta (organized by terrorists, it was reported) and then stormed down streets, hurling rocks and other objects at police who first fired rubber bullets (which can be fatal at less than 150 feet) and then changed to real bullets after a police spy was severely beaten by students. On May 15, tens of thousands of protestors invaded the Chinese district, destroying entire blocks of Chinese businesses which represented the richest minority in Indonesia. This section caught fire and several hundred looters were trapped in the flames and killed. Suharto, away on a state visit, returned to call out more than 10,000 troops and police to quell the worst rioting in Indonesian history.

## May 13

**BOMBING: Moscow, Russia** A synagogue was bombed, injuring construction workers who were at labor next door. The synagogue was empty at the time, 70 children and their teacher just having left the structure.

## May 14

**INVOLUNTARY MANSLAUGHTER: Boise, Id.** U.S. District Judge Edward Lodge dismissed charges of involuntary manslaughter against former FBI agent Len Horiuchi. The charges had been brought against Horiuchi by a state prosecutor regarding the 1992 siege of separatist Randall Weaver and his family at Ruby Ridge, Idaho, in which Weaver's wife and son had been killed, ostensibly shot to death by sharpshooter Horiuchi. Judge Lodge found that Horiuchi, when firing at the Weavers (who reportedly initiated or returned fire), Horiuchi was acting within the scope of his assigned duties. This court action finally ended the Ruby Ridge matter.

## May 15

**BOMBING: New York, N.Y.** A federal judge sentenced Abdul Hakim Murad, 30, to life in prison for setting off a bomb on a Philippine Airlines jet in 1994 in which a Japanese passenger was killed, and for plotting to bomb U.S. airliners in the Far East in January 1995.

## May 17

**TERRORIST ATTACK: Barrancabermeja, Colombia** At least 10 persons were killed and 20 more injured when "death squads" swept through the town, apparently to disrupt the upcoming presidential election.

## May 20

**AGGRAVATED HARASSMENT: El Mira, N.Y.** Dale Sheehan, a 48-year-old postal employee, when told of a hearing that would terminate his 12-year-old service, shouted: "Do you guys want me to come down and show you my new rocket launcher?" He was arrested and charged with aggravated harassment.

## May 22

**BOMBING: Algiers, Algeria** A bomb exploded in an open-air market, killing 16 persons, including three children, and injuring another 61 people.

**MURDER: Springfield, Ore.** Kipland Phillip Kinkel, after shooting his parents to death, went to Thurston High School where he was a freshman, and entered the cafeteria, shooting and killing two students and wounding another 18 classmates.

*May 24*

**CHILD ENDANGERMENT: Cherry Hill, N.J.** Samantha Wann, 3, drowned in a shallow pool while her father reportedly got high on PCP at a neighbor's party. The girl had been sexually assaulted before her death, according to officials who charged 34-year-old Michael Wann with child endangerment.

**EXECUTION: Cairo, Egypt** Two brothers, Sabir Abu al-Ila and Mahmoud Abu al-Ila, were executed by hanging at Istinaf Prison for their 1997 terrorist attack which killed nine German tourists and their Egyptian bus driver. The brothers, both Islamic fundamentalists, claimed they were not part of any organized terrorist group and had acted out of revenge after a Jewish woman posted pictures of the Prophet Mohammad as pig in marketplaces on the West Bank last year.

**STALKING: New York, N.Y.** Michael Falkner, 28, who had sent more than 50 e-mails to 27-year-old singer-actress Deborah Gibson, many of them appearing to be threats, was arrested and charged with stalking.

*May 25*

**TERRORIST ATTACK: Tehran, Iran** A pro-democracy rally by 2,000 students protesting the rigid Islamic government, was broken up by 400 right-wing Islamic thugs, reportedly members of the terrorist group Hezbollah, who wielded pipes and chains, injuring several of the students.

*May 26*

**BOMB PLOT: Wheeling, W. Va.** William Jeremy Dotson and Jesse Shingleton, both 18, were arrested and charged with conspiracy to violate federal explosive laws. The two seniors at St. Mary's High School reportedly planned to bomb their graduation ceremonies. The charges were later dropped.

**JUDICIARY: Washington, D.C.** The U.S. Supreme Court ruled unanimously that police who take part in high-speed car chases are not liable for consequent injuries to the fleeing parties or to bystanders unless the police acted "with purpose to cause harm."

**SCHOOL THREAT: Little Egg Harbor, N.J.** A 15-year-old boy was arrested for threatening to shoot his 9th grade teacher (he showed her a picture of a human figure in the crosshairs of a rifle scope), and 20 pistols, rifles and shotguns were confiscated from his home, weapons all legally owned by the boy's father.

**TERRORISM: France, Belgium, Italy, Germany, Switzerland** More than 450 anti-terrorist police specialists conducted raids in five countries that rounded up scores of Islamic terrorists, confiscating cash and weapons. The chief terrorist group in France, the Armed Islamic Group, was all but broken up when dozens of its members were arrested in Lyon, Marseilles, Paris and on the island of Corsica.

*May 27*

**BOMBING: Denver, Colo.** Michael Fortier, close friend of Timothy McVeigh, who had been convicted and sentenced to death for his bombing of the federal building in Oklahoma City, Oklahoma, and who had testified against McVeigh and his accomplice Terry Nichols in two separate trials, was sen-

tenced to prison for 12 years and fined $200,000 in a plea-bargain deal with prosecutors. Fortier had withheld prior knowledge of the bombing.

*May 29*

**CHILD ABUSE: Morristown, N.J.** Siobhan Diaz, a 30-year-old nanny who was caught on videotape beating a 9-month-old baby girl and stuffing a towel into her mouth on May 2, 1996, was sentenced to four years in prison.

**MURDER/SUICIDE: Encino, Calif.** Brynn Hartman, the troubled wife of comedian Phil Hartman, shot and killed her husband and then committed suicide.

**MURDER/SUICIDE: Fort Lauderdale, Fla.** Michael Grammig, 30, waited for his former girlfriend, Nicole Weiser, to arrive at the parking lot of Stranahan High School, where the 26-year-old Weiser worked as a teacher. When she drove into the lot, Grammig fired four bullets through her car window, killing her. He then shot himself to death.

*June 1*

**AGGRAVATED BATTERY TO A CHILD: Chicago, Ill.** Gregory Johnson, 24, was sentenced to 26 years in prison for shaking his 14-month-old son, Terrell Johnson, so hard that he permanently disabled the child.

*June 3*

**CONSPIRACY/EMBEZZLEMENT/MONEY LAUNDERING: Miami, Fla.** Three men controlling the Port of Miami used the facility "as a personal bank," according to prosecutor Thomas Scott. Calvin Grigsby, owner of the firm that operated the port's container cargo cranes, Carmen Lunetta, a former port director, and Neal Harrington, a Port contractor, were charged with stealing $1.3 million from 1990 to 1998. The three men, charged with embezzlement, money laundering and theft, used the Port's funds to purchase Super Bowl tickets, lingerie, bar tabs and luxury items, as well as make an illegal $120,000 contribution to the Democratic National Committee in 1994, according to officials.

*June 4*

**BOMBING: Denver, Colo.** Convicted in 1997 of conspiracy in the 1995 bombing of the federal building in Oklahoma City, Oklahoma, Terry Nichols was sentenced by Judge Richard Matsch to life imprisonment without parole, plus eight consecutive 6-year terms for his conviction of manslaughter in the deaths of eight federal agents who died in the bombing.

**MURDER: Allentown, Pa.** William Muth, Jr., 41, who had been sent home for disciplinary reasons, returned to the U.S. Foodservice, Inc. warehouse where he had worked for 12 years and shot and killed warehouse manager Earl Moritz, 48, wounded two other supervisors and then shot himself.

*June 7*

**MURDER: Jasper, Texas** John William King, Shawn Allen Berry and Lawrence Russell Brewer picked up James Byrd, Jr., an unemployed black man, and, after torturing him, dragged him by the neck from a rope tied to their speeding pickup, decapitating him. All three brutal killers would be convicted.

*June 8*

**DICTATOR DIES: Nigeria** Gen. Sani Abacha, iron-fisted dictator of Nigeria, who had committed many human rights crimes and imprisoned his political foes, died of a liver ailment. He was replaced by Gen. Abdulsalem Abubakar, who released political prisoners and promised to establish a democracy.

*June 12*

**ASSAULT ON AIRLINE: Bahamas to Ft. Lauderdale, Fla.** David Christopher Kreyer, 28, a resident of Warwick, R.I. was arrested after a red-eye flight from Freeport, Bahamas landed at Ft. Lauderdale, Fla., charged with head-butting a flight attendant, fracturing her cheek and biting a passenger.

*June 14*

**MURDER: Chicago, Ill.** Joan Tribblet, 27 and her common-law husband, Everett Johnson, 29, were charged with murdering and dismembering their 16-month-old daughter Onowanique. Tribblet and Johnson reportedly beat the child with their hands and with a stick on the night of December 18-19, 1997, when she would not stop crying and go to sleep. She was then strangled or smothered to death and her body was dismembered, according to police who stated that the victim's hands, feet and one forearm were then fried and fed to dogs and other animals while the remains were soaked in a tub of battery acid for four to six weeks to destroy the evidence of the crime. Chicago Judge William Wise, who ordered the couple held without bond, stated that the murder was "the most despicable case I've ever been involved with."

*June 18*

**CHILDREN CARRYING GUNS: Washington, D.C.** PRIDE, a non-profit drug prevention program released a report stating that 973,000 students carried a gun to school during the 1997-1998 school year. The study also reported that 64 percent of these students also used an illegal drug on a monthly basis. Of the overall student numbers carrying guns 59 percent were white, 18 percent black, 12 percent Hispanic, 3 percent Asian and 3 percent American Indian. The study stated that 51 percent of those who carried guns had threatened to harm a teacher and 63 percent had threatened to harm another student.

**MURDER: Hastings-on-Hudson, N.Y.** Michael Laudor, 35, whose struggle with schizophrenia had been the subject of a New York *Times* profile and who had sold his story to the movies, was arrested and charged with stabbing to death Caroline Costello, his 37-year-old pregnant girlfriend.

*June 22*

**JUDICIARY: Washington, D.C.** The U.S. Supreme Court ruled 5-4 that a student who had been sexually harassed by a teacher could not sue the school district unless a district official actually knew about the harassment and did nothing to stop it.

*June 23*

**PRISONERS ESCAPE: Salerno, Italy** While other defendants in a courtroom cage covered their actions, Giuseppe Autorino and Ferdinando Cesarano, two bosses of the Camorra crime family, made an escape through a tunnel dug through the courtroom floor. Both had been serving life terms for various crimes and were seen fleeing to a waiting car in a field beyond the courthouse.

*June 24*

**MURDER: New York, N.Y.** Heriberto Seda was convicted of the 1990 Zodiac shootings, was sentenced to prison for life.

**RIOTS: Lome, Togo** Thousands of residents rioted in protest of what they believed was an election rigged by President Gngassigbe Eyadema, who had ruled the country for 31 years and who declared that he was again the winner in a presidential election. The head of Togo's election commission resigned after saying that she had been intimidated and harassed by Eyadema's thugs.

*June 25*

**WHITEWATER: Little Rock, Ark.** After serving 18 months in prison for contempt in refusing to testify before a grand jury probing Whitewater, and two months of her two-year sentence for bank fraud, Susan McDougal was released on an order from U.S. District Judge George Howard, Jr., who stated that the prisoner suffered from curvature of the spine which had been aggravated by her imprisonment. She was placed under home detention for three months.

*June 26*

**DEATH SENTENCE COMMUTED: Brownsville, Texas** Henry Lee Lucas, reputed serial killer who was scheduled to die by lethal injection, was reprieved and his sentence commuted to life in prison by Governor George Bush, after serious doubts arose about Lucas' guilt in the murder of an unidentified woman found wearing only orange socks in a ditch north of Austin on Halloween, 1979, a killing that brought Lucas' only death sentence, despite the fact that he had confessed to murdering more than 600 persons.

**JUDICIARY: Washington, D.C.** The U.S. Supreme Court ruled that private employers were liable for misconduct by their supervisory employees.

*June 30*

**RIOT: New York, N.Y.** More than 30,000 union construction workers blocked 5th Avenue in mid-town Manhattan in protest of a city contract worth $33 million being awarded to a non-union company. Rocks, bottles and other obstacles were thrown at police dressed in riot gear who closed on the dense crowd of protestors, arresting 33 persons, including one man who punched a police horse. Injured were 31 persons, including 18 officers.

*July 1*

**ARSON: Northern Ireland** Ten Roman Catholic churches in Northern Ireland were set on fire by arsonists said to be members of a Protestant dissident group.

**MASS MURDER: Santa Clarita, Calif.** Sandi Nieves, the 34-year-old mother of five children, was booked on suspicion of murdering her four pajama-clad daughters, ages 5, 7, 11, and 12. She called 911 to say her house was filled with smoke. When firefighters arrived, they found her daughters all dead from smoke inhalation, but she and her 14-year-old son were relatively unharmed.

### July 1-4

**RIOTS: Lagos, Nigeria** Following the sudden death of Moshood Abiola, a political foe of recently deceased dictator Sani Abacha, who died suddenly before being released from prison, Abiola's followers, suspecting foul play, rioted for several days, disturbances that took the lives of 45 people.

### July 2

**BOMBING: Budapest, Hungary** A car bomb exploded on a crowded downtown street, killing four persons and injuring more than 25 others. Restaurant owner Jozsef Tamas Boross, who had asked for police protection earlier after receiving numerous threats, was one of those killed. The bomb, police said, was set off by remote control apparently as Boross walked by. More than 140 bombings had occurred in the city since 1991, these explosions the work of the many Russian, Ukrainian, Romanian, Turkish and Arab gangs plaguing the city.

### July 3

**HOME INVASION: Chicago, Ill.** John Davis, 42, began pounding on doors inside his West Side apartment building and forced his way into an apartment of an 88-year-old man and a 92-year-old woman. When police arrived, Davis, completely naked, had barricaded himself in a bedroom with the woman. Police broke down the door and threw a blanket over Davis. As they led him outside in handcuffs, Davis dropped dead, ostensibly from a heart attack.

### July 4

**SHOOTING: Pleasanton, Calif.** A man arguing with a woman at a rock concert suddenly pulled a gun and shot her. He then began randomly shooting at others in the crowd of 1,500, his bullets wounding at least five other persons. The crowd stampeded and several others were injured in the crush.

### July 5

**MASS MURDER: Tacoma, Wash.** Five persons, a waitress and four patrons, were shot to death at the Trang Dai restaurant, a mass slaying that was attributed to one of the many Asian gangs in the area. Four teenage Asian gang members were arrested as suspects. Two others, Ri Ngoc Le, 22, and Khanh Van Trinh, 17, were trapped by police and shot themselves to death on July 21, 1998.

### July 7

**BRIBERY: Milan, Italy** Silvio Berlusconi, who had served as the country's premier for seven months in 1994, was convicted of bribing government inspectors so that he could obtain favorable tax audits for his businesses. Berlusconi received a prison sentence of two years and nine months.

**MURDER/ROBBERY: Los Angeles, Calif.** Mikail Markhasev, a 19-year-old Russian immigrant, was found guilty

of murdering Ennis Cosby, son of entertainer Bill Cosby, in January 1997, while Cosby was attempting to fix a flat tire on his mother's Mercedes-Benz on a L.A. freeway exit ramp.

### July 8

**FRAUD: Billings, Mt.** Four so-called Montana Freemen were convicted of conspiring to defraud four banks in issuing bogus bank instruments. Prosecutors stated that 12 Freemen had tried to cash 3,432 checks for $15.5 billion, as part of a conspiracy to disrupt the U.S. banking system.

### July 9

**MURDER: Tepexitla, Mexico** Eusebio Vazquez Juarez, the leader of the Organization of Peasants of the Sierra Sur was shot four times and killed as he rode his bicycle home. Vazquez had openly denounced police and the military for widespread abuses of peasants.

### July 12

**ARSON: Muncie, Ind.** The one-story storefront United Methodist Church was burned down by arsonists, according to police. There were 13 arson church fires in Indiana in 1997 and five to date in 1998. There were 72 church burnings in the U.S. to date in 1998.

**BOMBING/MURDER: Ballymoney, Northern Ireland** A firebomb thrown at a public house killed three Catholic brothers, ages 9 to 11, the killers thought to be members of the Protestant Orange Order which had been conducting parades and demonstrations for several days to celebrate 12th century Protestant victories over Catholic forces, these demonstrations leading to widespread violence. Three men were held as suspects in the firebombing.

### July 13

**BRIBERY: Milan, Italy** Silvio Berlusconi, who had been convicted of bribing government inspectors on July 7, 1998, was, in a separate case, convicted of illegally giving $12 million to then Premier Bettino Craxi in 1991. For this conviction, Berlusconi drew a prison term of two years and four months and a fine of $5.6 million. Craxi, then living out of the country, was convicted of bribery in absentia.

**COMPENSATION FOR WRONGFUL CONVICTION: Miami, Fla.** Freddie Pitts, 54 and Wilbert Lee, 62, two black men who had been wrongfully convicted and sentenced to death for the 1963 robbery murders of two white gas station attendants in Port St. Joe, a Florida panhandle fishing town, were each awarded $500,000. Both men had been freed in 1975 after having spent nine years on Death Row by then Governor Reubin Askew who cited substantial doubt about their guilt. The two men had since petitioned the state for compensation.

**MURDER: Edgartown, Mass.** Troy Toon, a 24-year-old Boston resident, was charged with fatally stabbing Gary Moreis on Martha's Vineyard, the first reported murder on the island in 20 years.

### July 14

**MASS MURDER: Ballwin, Mo.** Reginald Sublet, a former Texas police officer who had been fighting a custody battle with his ex-girlfriend of their son, was found dead with four other bodies inside of a garage. Sublet was found kneeling inside the garage holding a gun. In a car were the bodies of the ex-girlfriend, Rosalind Tramble, 33, her husband, Michael Tramble, Jr., 32, and, in another car, the bodies of Reginald Sublet, Jr., 12, and Michael Tramble III, almost 2. Police believed that Sublet had forced the couple and children into the garage and held them at bay while he turned on the car ignition and waited for car fumes to kill all of them.

### July 15

**LOOTING: West Palm Beach, Fla.** Trucker Hebert Gross reported to police that he left his truck loaded with shoes after pulling off Interstate Highway 95 and, while he was visiting a prostitute in a nearby house, someone broke the lock on his truck and hundreds of residents looted the truck of as many as 3,400 pairs of sneakers and shoes by Rockport, Nike, Tommy Hilfiger and Timberland. The frenzy of looting the shoes was such that two cars crashed as drivers rushed to take part in gathering the spoils. Police found hundreds of pairs of old shoes littering the area, all left by those who had put on the new footwear and ran off. No charges were made.

### July 16

**MASS MURDER: Canoncito Navajo Indian Reservation, N.M.** Stanley Secatero, a 25-year-old Navajo Indian, reportedly shot and killed his grandmother, two aunts and an uncle and wounded another person after becoming enraged over the fact that they had turned in his brother for a $1,000 reward. Secatero fled to a mountainous area, but was tracked down and arrested by police the following day.

### July 23

**EXECUTION: Jarratt, Va.** Joseph Roger O'Dell III, who had become a worldwide cause celebre through the efforts of many prominent persons attempting to have him pardoned, was executed by lethal injection for the 1985 rape-murder of 44-year-old Helen Schartner.

**MURDER: Sault Ste. Marie, Mich.** Anthony Gillespie, the 48-year-old circulation manager for the *Evening News* was killed at his desk by two shotgun blasts reportedly fired by news carrier Nathan Hanna, who fled in his pickup truck. Employees scrambled for cover, hiding in the dark room or under desks as Gillespie was shot, Ken Fazzari, the editor of the paper, calling 911 as he crouched under a desk.

**MURDER: Washington, D.C.** Russell E. Weston, Jr., who had a long history of mental disorders, arrived in Washington from his father's rural Illinois farm and entered the Capitol Building through a visitor's entrance where, in the hallways, he inexplicably shot and wounded a female visitor and shot and killed two security guards until he was wounded by one of the mortally-wounded guards.

### July 25

**PRISON ESCAPE: Youngstown, Ohio** Six prisoners cut their way to freedom through fences and razor wire, four of the escapees being convicted murderers. All six had fled the Northeast Ohio Correctional Center. They were recaptured, the

last being Ronald Holmes, who was found hiding in Buffalo house on August 27, 1998.

### July 27

**MURDER: Hodeida, Yemen** Three nuns, one from the Philippines and two from India, who were part of Mother Theresa's order, were shot and killed by gunman firing automatic weapons from a passing car. A suspect, Abdullah Nashri, 25, who had a history of mental illness, was arrested and charged with the senseless murders. The murders are not unusual in Yemen where tribal members routinely kidnap or murder foreigners.

**MURDER: Washington, D.C.** Russell E. Weston, Jr., who had been hospitalized with wounds received in a shootout with a Capitol Building security guard whom he had killed, along with another guard, was charged with murdering officer Jacob Chestnut and special agent John Gibson.

### July 30

**BURGLARY: Mt. Clemens, Mich.** A 10-year-old girl who had earlier been several times arrested on burglary charges, was again arrested and charged with burglarizing two homes. "You just look at her," said a police officer, "she seems like a cute, adorable little girl, but she's been a terror around here for the past couple of months."

**MURDER: Kenosha, Wis.** Silvester Donoe, a 16-year-old from Waukegan, Illinois, who, on February 20, 1998, had been convicted of kidnapping and murdering Sigmund Zagoren, a 77-year-old optometrist from Skokie, Illinois, was sentenced to life in prison. Donoe had stopped Zagoren's car and abducted him, robbing and then murdering him.

**CHILD PORNOGRAPHY: Tulsa, Okla.** While Donald C. Johnson, a dentist, was on vacation, 148 photos were reportedly found in his office which showed the dentist with 40 or more young girls (ages 4 to 16) performing oral sex on him. They appeared in the photos to be in a state of semi-consciousness. One report had it that Johnson had anesthetized his victims while their parents sat in a waiting room and then sexually abused them. Johnson was charged with child pornography.

### July 31

**GENOCIDE: Buheta and Raba, Rwanda** Hutu terrorists armed with machetes and clubs killed 110 villagers, according to Rwandan officials.

**ORGANIZED CRIME: Marbella, Spain** Francesco Martello, a top Mafia boss in Europe who was wanted in Italy for numerous crimes, was tracked down and arrested. Police questioned him concerning the whereabouts of Bernardo Provenzano, considered by authorities to be the Mafia supreme boss of bosses. Martello reportedly gave no information.

### August 1

**BOMBING: Banbridge, Northern Ireland** A car bomb exploded, injuring 35 people and creating widespread damage. Police stated that they had received a warning and had mostly cleared an area outside a shoe store when the bomb exploded. No one claimed responsibility for the explosion.

**WAR CRIMES: The Hague, Netherlands** Milan

Kovacevic, a 57-year-old Bosnian Serb, who stood accused of genocide—he had set up three notorious prison camps in Bosnia where many offenses took place—died in his prison cell of a heart attack.

### August 2

**MURDER: Uwharrie National Forest, N.C.** Two campers, Derek Andrew Marston, 24, and Tommi Danielle Bryd, 24, of Charlotte, N.C., were shot and slashed to death at their campsite, reportedly by James Andrew Finley, Jr., 21, who stole their car and abandoned the vehicle two days later.

### August 3

**MURDER: Port-au-Prince, Haiti** Rev. Jean Pierre-Louis, a Catholic priest, was gunned down on a busy street. The day earlier, businessman Jovnel Bruno, the owner of a rental car company, was shot and killed near the city's airport.

### August 7

**BOMBINGS: Nairobi, Kenya; Dar-es-Salaam, Tanzania** At about 10:35 a.m., a powerful bomb exploded outside the U.S. Embassy in Nairobi and, a few minutes later in what investigators would describe as a coordinated terrorist attack, another bomb exploded outside the U.S. Embassy in Dar es Salaam, killing altogether 224 persons (213, including 12 Americans in Nairobi, with more than 540 seriously injured and 11 persons dead in Dar es Salaam, with more than 70 injured).

### August 8

**BOMBING: Buenos Aires, Argentina** Kamal Kharrazi, Iran's foreign minister, denied the allegations appearing in a recently released FBI report that stated Iran had been behind the July 18, 1994 bombing of the Argentine Jewish Mutual Association in Buenos Aires which had killed 86 persons and wounded another 200.

**BOMBINGS: Washington, D.C.** Officials announced that Osama bin Laden, a multimillionaire Saudi who headed a terrorist organization in Afghanistan, was suspected of being behind the two deadly bombings of August 7, 1998 in Nairobi, Kenya and Dar es Salaam, Tanzania, and that bin Laden had most probably been behind the bombings of U.S. military facilities in Saudi Arabia in 1995 and 1996.

### August 8-9

**RIOT: Reno, Nev.** Thousands of unruly youths celebrating Hot August Nights had to be subdued by police wearing riot gear and using pepper spray and dogs. Police reported that more than 2,000 gang members from California augmented the rioting mobs. Police arrested 130 people.

### August 11

**MURDER: Jonesboro, Ark.** Andrew Golden and Mitchell Johnson were found guilty on charges of murder and capital battery in the fatal shootings of four classmates and one teacher, along with wounding ten others, in March 1998. The boys, who were ages 11 and 13 respectively at the time of the shootings, were ordered confined at a juvenile detention center, the length of their sentences to be determined by the state agency operating the center.

### August 12

**HOLOCAUST CLAIMS SETTLEMENT: Switzerland** Swiss banking officials and representatives of Holocaust survivors reached an agreement wherein Switzerland agreed to compensate Holocaust victims in the amount of $1.25 billion, that figure representing funds deposited in Swiss banks by Jews who were later killed or by Nazis who had seized their assets before and during World War II.

**MURDER: Sara, Philippines** Bandits lying in wait along a roadside, shot and killed 10 motorists, including Robert Bock, an American Peace Corps worker from Virginia, robbing them and fleeing into the jungle.

### August 14

**STATUTORY SEXUAL SEDUCTION: Las Vegas, Nev.** Teacher Joseph DeBaca, 33, was arrested and charged with statutory sexual seduction of a 12-year-old girl in his math class at Brinley Middle School in 1990. The girl, now 20, had recently come forward to tell her story to police.

### August 15

**BOMBINGS: Nairobi, Kenya** Officials announced that Pakistan had detained and returned to Nairobi a suspect in the embassy bombings of August 7, the man being Mohammed Saddiq Odeh, an engineer who confessed to having been part of the bombings. Odeh also stated that Osama bin Laden had organized the bombings and headed a Muslim force of 5,000 Islamic fanatics in a rocky retreat in Afghanistan where he was equipped with ground-to-air missiles and a sophisticated communications network.

**BOMBING: Omagh, Northern Ireland** After police received two phone warnings that a bomb would explode near the courthouse, police evacuated the building and moved scores of people hundreds of yards from the building. The bomb that exploded, however, was in the midst of the crowds (some later said this warnings intended to have victims herded next to the bomb instead of away from it). Killed outright were 28 men, women and children and more than 300 were seriously wounded (a wounded man later died, bringing the death toll to 29). It was the worst terrorist bombing in the last 29 years in Northern Ireland, and brought worldwide condemnation of the bombers. The Real IRA, a splinter group of the IRA took responsibility for the bombing.

### August 17

**INAPPROPRIATE RELATIONSHIP: Washington, D.C.** President Bill Clinton testified before a grand jury and then addressed the nation in a televised speech regarding accusations that he had had an affair with White House intern Monica Lewinsky, a sexual affair he had repeatedly denied in the past. At this time, however, Clinton admitted to having an "inappropriate relationship" with Lewinsky. His testimony before the grand jury was also televised, but not then made public. Clinton admitted that he had been "wrong" in maintaining the Lewinsky relationship and that he had "misled" the nation, including his wife, about the affair, but insisted that he had not tried to conceal evidence or asked anyone else to do so.

**KIDNAPPER CAPTURED: Naucalpan (Mexico City), Mexico** The most feared kidnapper in the country, Daniel Arizmendi Lopez, called "Ear Lopper," because he cut off the ears of his millionaire kidnap victims to prove he was holding them for ransom, was captured in a car with more than $1 million in cash. Officials said that Arizmendi's huge gang which stretched into four states and included police officers had been thoroughly dismantled by numerous arrests.

**PRISON RELEASE: Providence, R.I.** Maria Manuela Dickerson, 47, imprisoned in January 1996 without trial for failing to pay some of the $3,000 in child support she owed, was all but forgotten by the court system which routinely reviewed such civil contempt cases each month. Family Court Judge John O'Brien failed to conduct such reviews and Dickerson remained in prison for more than two-and-a-half years, until her release was ordered by the state Supreme Court on this date.

### August 18

**BATTERY: Santa Monica, Calif.** James Orr, the ex-boyfriend of actress Farrah Fawcett, was convicted of battery, when he had earlier slammed her head and choked her in the driveway of his home on January 28, 1998. Fawcett admitted that she had smashed the windows of Orr's house with a baseball bat and had attacked him with a bar stool.

**RESIGNATION OF PRESIDENT DEMANDED: Washington, D.C.** Representative Paul McHale, a Democrat from Pennsylvania, demanded that President Clinton resign. More than 100 daily newspapers also made the same demands. Clinton continued to indicate that he had no intention of leaving office and his wife, Hillary Rodham Clinton said, in the light of her husband's admission, that she was "committed to her marriage." The couple immediately went on vacation to Martha's Vineyard.

### August 20

**RECKLESS ENDANGERMENT/ATTEMPTED ASSAULT: New York, N.Y.** Nushawn Williams, 21, was charged with reckless endangerment and attempted assault by exposing numerous women in upstate New York to the AIDS virus he carried. Williams was charged with knowingly infecting a 15-year-old New York City girl and infecting nine of 28 sex partners in Chautauqua County.

**RETALIATION FOR TERRORIST BOMBINGS: Khartoum, Sudan/Afghanistan** U.S. military forces, including U.S. Navy vessels, fired missiles at sites in Khartoum, Sudan, where the missiles destroyed the Al Shifa Pharmaceutical Industries factory, a site reportedly financed by Osman bin Laden and where chemical weapons were being produced, and at bin Laden's terrorist compound in Afghanistan, where undetermined damage was done.

### August 24

**TREASON: Freetown, Sierra Leone** Sixteen persons, including five journalists, were found guilty of treason in that they had collaborated with the country's ousted military junta.

### August 25

**BOMBING: Cape Town, South Africa** A bomb exploded inside Planet Hollywood restaurant, killing one person (a woman), and seriously injuring another 19 people. Police were unable to fix responsibility.

**MURDER: Big Cypress Wilderness Institute, Fla.** Jermaine Jones, 16, and Mazer Jean, 17, two inmates at a juvenile camp, located 30 miles east of Naples, were disciplined for swearing by Mike Sierra, a 40-year-old counselor and ex-Marine. Ordered to chop wood, Jones and Jean instead picked up an ax and machete and reportedly hacked Sierra to death before fleeing. Both were later captured and charged with murder.

### August 26

**MURDER: Poughkeepsie, N.Y.** Catina Newmaster, 26, disappeared, the last of eight women who vanished in the area. Police would link her disappearance to 27-year-old Kendall Francois, a worker at Arlington Middle School. Francois was arrested and charged with killing Newmaster, after officers wearing white jump suits and surgical style face masks pulled her decomposing body from a small house he shared with his parents and sister on September 2, 1998. They also found several other bodies hidden in the home and believed Francois was responsible for abducting and killing all eight missing women.

### August 27

**ASSASSINATION PLOT: San Juan, Puerto Rico** Seven members of a Cuban exile group pleaded not guilty to charges that they plotted to kill Cuban Communist dictator Fidel Castro.

**BOMBING, Tel Aviv, Israel** A crudely-made bomb wrapped with nails and placed in a garbage can exploded in front of a row of shops at the corner of Allenby and Rothschild streets, close to the Great Synagogue, injuring more than twenty persons. Although no one claimed responsibility for the bombing, the explosion was attributed to Palestinian terrorists by Israeli officials.

**FRAUD: Miami Fla.** Humberto Hernandez, 35, one of the most powerful politicians in southern Florida, pleaded guilty to bank fraud, mail fraud, wire fraud and making a false statement to secure a loan. Hernandez had been sentenced to a 1-year prison sentence on August 19, 1998 in a separate conviction for vote fraud.

### August 27-28

**BOMBINGS: New York, N.Y.** Mohamed Rashed Daoud al-Owhali, arrested as a suspect in the Nairobi embassy bombing of August 7, was flown to the U.S. where he was arraigned on murder charges connected to the Nairobi bombing. Mohommed Saddiq Odeh was also flown to NYC the following day and arraigned on similar charges.

### August 30

**EXECUTIONS: Gaza Strip** Ten members of a Palestinian firing squad wearing black hoods (so as not to be identified by relatives of those being executed) shot and killed two former Palestinian policemen—Mohammed Abu Sultan, 25 and Raed

Abu Sultan, brothers—for murdering two other policemen who were also brothers. The executions sent a strong signal from Palestinian leader Yasir Arafat that police abuse of power would not be tolerated.

## September 1

**MASS POISONINGS: Nagano, Japan** A house painter died after drinking tea which had been contaminated with cyanide. The poison was found in other tins of tea in the area. In the past few weeks, four persons had been killed by poisons slipped into drinks and food and 67 others had been injured. Police seemed powerless to discover the culprits.

**RIOTS: Jakarta, Indonesia** Hundreds of ethnic Chinese merchants and their families fled their shops when stone-throwing mobs stormed through their business district, destroying homes and stores. Looters shouted separatist slogans as they rampaged through the business district, grabbing anything they could carry. Riot police shot two looters. Hundreds more were injured. A day earlier, rioters broke into a local prison and freed 90 inmates.

## September 3

**DEPORTATION OF DRUNK DRIVERS: Texas** More than 500 immigrants, most of them legal residents and most of them from Mexico, with three or more drunken driving convictions, were rounded up in several Texas cities and were scheduled for deportation back to Mexico.

**INAPPROPRIATE RELATIONSHIP: Washington, D.C.** With the Clinton-Lewinsky scandal capturing full media attention, U.S. Senator Joseph Lieberman (Dem., Conn.), a long-time supporter and close friend of President Clinton, stated publicly that Clinton's "behavior" with Monica Lewinsky was "not just inappropriate, it is immoral." Lieberman then added that Clinton's conduct was harmful, because it sent a message to Americans, especially children, that such conduct was acceptable. Such searing criticism from Lieberman prompted a jarred Clinton to say for the first time the next day that he was "sorry" for what he had done.

## September 4

**GENOCIDE: Arusha, Tanzania** Jean Kambanda, former prime minister of Rwanda, was sentenced to life in prison for genocidal crimes against humanity.

## September 8

**MASS MURDER: Aurora, Colo.** Two teenagers wearing bandannas over their heads, shot and killed five persons in two homes a few blocks apart and then one of them shot and killed the other, 18-year-old Michael Martinez. The 17-year-old survivor was charged with six counts of first-degree murder.

## September 9

**IMPEACHMENT PROCEEDINGS: Washington, D.C.** Independent counsel Kenneth Starr sent a 445-page report to the House of Representatives which he believed contained "substantial and credible information ... that may constitute grounds" for the impeachment of President Bill Clinton. The report centered its attention on the affair between President Clinton and White House intern Monica Lewinsky and Clinton's reported perjury and obstruction of justice in his attempt to cover up that affair. Starr delivered 36 boxes of materials to Congress.

## September 9-10

**IMPEACHMENT PROCEEDINGS: Washington, D.C.** Starr's report on President Clinton chiefly focused on Clinton's affair with Lewinsky and touched hardly at all on all other matters, including Whitewater, which Starr had been investigating for four years. Published in many daily newspapers, Starr's report cited 11 possible grounds for impeachment and alleged that Clinton had committed perjury, obstructed justice, tampered with a witness and abused his power. The report stated that Lewinsky, according to her grand jury testimony, had had sexual contact with Clinton on 10 occasions in the Oval Office, and she stated that she had performed oral sex on him nine times, twice while he was talking on the phone. The tawdry report went on to state that a dress Lewinsky had worn on one of these occasions had been turned over to FBI analysts who found a trace of Clinton's semen on it. The report stated that Betty Currie, the President's secretary had been asked by Clinton to retrieve gifts he had given to Lewinsky. It also pointed out that Clinton, once he knew that Lewinsky was on a list of potential witnesses in the Paula Jones suit, talked to several persons in the White House and outside friends, asking that they try to find a job for Lewinsky. Further, it stated that Clinton called Currie to the White House on January 18, 1998, a Sunday, and asked her such leading questions as "You were always there when she was there, right?"

## September 10

**TERRORISM/RIOTS: Hebron, West Bank** Two brothers, Adel and Imad Awadallah, both Palestinian terrorists, were shot and killed by Israeli soldiers. The Awadallahs, according to Israeli reports, were in the act of preparing another terrorist attack when they were confronted by the Israelis. Imad Awadallah had only a short time earlier escaped from a Palestinian jail by fleeing through an unguarded bathroom window, a purposeful lapse in security, according to Israeli officials who charged the Palestininan security forces with collusion. The mother of the slain terrorists, Kounu Awadallah, later delivered a fiery speech, shouting to a crowd of several hundred Palestinians in El-Birah, a suburb of Ramallah, that "God will punish the Jews." She also condemned Palestinian security officials whom she blamed for working with the Israelis in tracking down her errant sons. As a result of her speech, and at the urgings of Sheik Ahmed Yassin, the so-called spiritual leader of the terrorist group Hamas, hundreds of Palestinians rioted in Jerusalem and in the West Bank. Several rock-throwing Palestinians were injured by rubber bullets fired by Israeli soldiers who were under attack at Israeli checkpoints. The killing of the Awadallahs and resulting riots further delayed the ongoing peace talks between Israeli Prime Minister Benjamin Netanyahu and Palestinian leader Yasir Arafat, their talks mediated by U.S. envoy Dennis Ross. Israeli officials pointed to the fact that Arafat had failed to live up to the Oslo agreements to suppress the terrorist elements of his community. It was noted that during the rioting following the shootings of the

Awadallahs, Palestinian security forces stood by as spectators, doing nothing for some time, and, only after some hours, dispersed the rioting Palestinians.

### September 12

**MURDER/MUTINY: Murmansk, Russia** Russian troops swarmed aboard a nuclear-powered submarine to shoot and kill Alexander Kuzminykh, a 19-year-old sailor who had commandeered the sub the previous day, killing a sentry and using the man's gun to kill seven more sailors on board before barricading himself inside the torpedo room. Kuzminykh had threatened to blow up the 360-foot submarine, although Russian officials later claimed that he could not have done the job after the vessel's power had been shut off.

### September 16

**MURDER: Trotwood, Ohio** Rev. Andrew Lofton, pastor of Christ Temple Apostolic Faith Church, was urging Bible students to prepare for their afterlife when Kenneth Nance, a 58-year-old parishioner, reportedly got up from a pew, approached Lofton and fatally shot him several times. Nance, charged with murder, gave no reason for the killing.

**RAPE: Akron, Ohio** Four boys, ages 8 to 14 and a 12-year-old girl were charged in juvenile court with repeatedly raping a 6-year-old girl over a period of several weeks.

### September 17

**MANSLAUGHTER: Boston, Mass.** Prosecutors charged the Massachusetts Institute of Technology fraternity of Phi Gamma Delta with manslaughter and hazing in the drinking death of Scott Krueger, an 18-year-old student who had been found in the frat house's "harassment" room where he was confined until he drank a certain amount of alcohol.

### September 18

**ARSON/MURDER: Murray, Ky.** A blaze on the fourth story of the 8-story Hester Hall at Murray State University, caused the death of one student and injured several more. On October 29, 1998, seven people were charged with setting the fire. Fredrick McGrath, 23, was charged with murder, arson, falsely reporting an incident and three counts of wanton endangerment. The others were charged as being accomplices.

**CHILD MOLESTATION/MURDER: Miami, Fla.** Juan Carlos Chavez was convicted of child molestation and murder in the death of 9-year-old Jimmy Ryce. He would be sentenced to death.

### September 19

**ABDUCTION: Salt Lake City, Ut.** Christopher Fink, 23, abducted his malnourished 21-month-old son David from a hospital (video cameras recorded the abduction) and fled with him and his wife Kyndra to a remote Montana area where they were apprehended on October 5, 1998.

### September 22

**CONSPIRACY: Detroit, Mich.** Daniel Granger, 18, president of his Grosse Pointe Woods high school class, admitted that he had fed alcohol to three 14-year-old girls in order to have sex with them, along with three other boys. Granger, in a plea-bargain deal, had charges reduced from criminal sexual conduct to conspiracy to contribute to the delinquency of a minor. He would be given a 70-day jail term on October 26, 1998.

**CONSPIRACY TO MURDER: Las Vegas, Nev.** Christopher Moseley and two others were indicted on charges of conspiracy to murder in that they arranged to have Patricia Margello murdered—she was found strangled on August 5, 1998. Moseley's wife, Lisa Dean Moseley, a great-granddaughter of a former du Pont Co. president, did not approve of Margello as a girlfriend for her son, Dean MacGuigan.

### September 23

**MURDER: Akron, Ohio** Douglas Prade, former police captain, was found guilty of murdering his wife and was sentenced to life in prison. When the verdict was read, Prade shouted: "This is an egregious miscarriage of justice!"

### September 24

**DEATH SENTENCE REVOKED: New York, N.Y.** Iran's Foreign Minister Kamal Kharazzi announced at the United Nations that his country had dropped its call for the death of author Salmon Rushdie, author of *The Satanic Verses*, which criticized Islamic fundamentalism, and which many Muslims found blasphemous at the time of its publication in 1989. Ayatollah Rhuhollah Khomeini called on Muslims everywhere to seek out Rushdie and kill him and a large monetary reward was posted for anyone who would murder him.

### September 27

**WAR CRIMES: Bosanski Samac, Bosnia** Stevan Todorovic, a Bosnian Serb police chief who was reportedly responsible "for some of the worst heinous crimes" (according to President Bill Clinton) that took place during the civil war in Bosnia, was arrested without incident by NATO troops.

### September 28

**BURGLARY: Chicago, Ill.** Yehuda Mishali, a 46-year-old Israeli citizen, was charged with burglarizing a safe deposit box at a Michigan Avenue bank and taking more than $500,000 in diamonds. Mishali was already in custody in New York on an unrelated bank robbery charge.

### September 29

**DRUGS: Chicago, Ill.** Authorities seized 1,100 pounds of cocaine having a street value of $62 million, one of the largest drug seizures in the city's history. Five men were arrested during the confiscation of the drugs and charged with possession of cocaine and conspiracy.

**FRAUD: Washington, D.C.** Federal officials announced that they had expelled 80 mental health care units from Medicare after discovering that the program to provide psychiatric services to the elderly was riddled with fraud. A spokeswoman stated that 91 percent of the $349 million paid out for Medicare treatment was for "unallowable and highly questionable services."

**MASSACRE: Gornje Obrinje, Kosovo** Western observers discovered a gulley filled with 19 bodies, including women and infants, who had been massacred—their throats slit, shot in the back of the head—by invading Serbian troops. The atrocity shocked the world.

**MURDER: Austin, Texas** Nine persons—three owners and four employees of B&B Amusements of Yuma, Ariz., and two ride inspectors—were indicted on murder charges in the death of 15-year-old Leslie Lane, killed on March 19, 1998, when she fell out of the Himalaya, a circular thrill ride. The indictments stated that the defendants had intentionally caused the girl's death by operating the ride at an excessive speed and with an inadequate safety bar. The operators had been earlier warned about the ride's potential dangers.

*September 30*
**ILLEGAL CAMPAIGN CONTRIBUTIONS: Washington, D.C.** Mark B. Jimenez, a Miami businessman, was charged with using phony contributors to make $39,500 in illegal contributions to President Clinton's 1996 re-election campaign and to other Democrats.

*October 2*
**GENOCIDE: Arusha, Tanzania** Jean-Paul Akayesu, mayor of Taba, Rwanda, was sentenced to life in prison by a U.N. tribunal for encouraging genocidal murder of Tutsi tribe members in his area by gangs of invading Hutus.

*October 5*
**DRUGS: Philadelphia, Pa.** Two Amish men, Abner King, 23, and Abner Stoltzfus, 24, pleaded guilty to conspiring to sell cocaine to other Amish. The men had been purchasing cocaine from the Pagans, a motorcycle group, and selling it to Amish youth from 1992 to 1997. The plea shocked the 22,000 members of the Old Order Amish.

*October 7*
**MURDER/KIDNAPPING/ROBBERY: Laramie, Wyo.** Matthew Shepard, an openly gay student at the University of Wyoming, was found tied to a ranch fence outside of town after he had been robbed and severely beaten. He would die in a hospital on October 12, and his reported attackers, Russell Henderson and Aaron McKinney, were charged with kidnapping, robbery and murder.

*October 8*
**IMPEACHMENT PROCEEDINGS: Washington, D.C.** The House of Representatives voted 258-176, including 31 Democrats voting yes, to pass a resolution to hold hearings on the impeachment of President Bill Clinton.

**RIOTS: Hebron, West Bank** Palestinians rioted, hurling rocks and other objects at Israeli troops who fired on them with rubber bullets. One rioter was shot and killed and a dozen more were injured.

*October 9*
**MANSLAUGHTER: Cairns, Australia** Capt. Geoffrey Ian Nairn, who skippered a tour boat called the Outer Edge, was charged with manslaughter after he had left behind two American Scuba divers when returning to shore. The two

Americans, Thomas Lonergan, 33, and his 28-year-old wife, Eileen, were part of two dozen divers taken out to sea by Nairn, who was severely criticized for not checking his dive master's log and conducting a head count of passengers before taking his boat to shore. Diver equipment was later found which supposedly belonged to the Lonergans, including a writing board used by divers to communicate underwater. The board, which washed ashore at north Queensland, bore the message: "Please help us. Find us soon before we die."

*October 10*
**DEATH SENTENCE RENEWED: Tehran, Iran** The Association of Hezbollah University students renewed a death sentence for author Salmon Rushdie, author of *The Satanic Verses*, offering $335,000 to anyone who murdered the author. Ayatollah Ruhollah Khomeini had decreed Rushdie's death in 1989, saying that he had blasphemed against the Prophet Mohammed and placed a $2.5 million reward for anyone who killed the author. Foreign Minister Kamal Kharrazi had only weeks earlier said that the death sentence had been dropped.

*October 13*
**KIDNAPPING: Brooklyn, N.Y.** Theresa Goldberg, the 40-year-old babysitter for Chaim Weill, reportedly kidnapped the 6-year-old boy to ostensibly take him to South Carolina where his cerebral palsy could be treated by "holistic healing." FBI agents found the boy, who could not talk because of his condition, and Goldberg, in Richmond, Va. on October 15, returning the child to his parents in New York. Goldberg and her husband, who admitted he planned to send his wife money to support her and the boy, were charged with kidnapping.

*October 14*
**MURDER: St. Petersburg, Russia** Financier and political boss Dmitry Filipov was shot to death in the foyer of his apartment building.

*October 15*
**EXECUTIONS: Nassau, Bahamas** Two convicted murderers, Trevor Fisher, 28, and Richard Woods, 51, were executed by hanging. Dozens of Bahamians cheered when the death notices were posted. Both men had appealed to several human rights organizations who pressured Bahamian authorities to spare the men. The appeals were ignored.

**RIOTS: France** More than 500,000 high school students took to the streets of almost all major cities to protest against their crowded classrooms, lack of resources and course overloads. In Paris, rioting took place and several persons were injured when, according to police, hooligans who were not part of the student protestors, began battling police.

*October 16*
**TERRORISM BUREAU ESTABLISHED: Washington, D.C.** U.S. Attorney Janet Reno announced that the FBI had set up a new bureau to combat terrorism and the FBI would offer local police, fire and rescue workers one-stop shopping for federal training and equipment to respond to terrorist attacks.

*October 17*

**GENOCIDE: London, England** In response to and indictment by a Spanish judge, British police arrested General Augusto Pinochet Ugarte, 82, the former military dictator of Chile, charging him with "crimes of genocide and terrorism that include murder." The charges stated that Pinochet was responsible for human rights violations that caused the deaths of more than 3,000 persons during his 17-year-rule.

*October 18*

**MURDER: Urbana-Champaign, Ill.** Thomas McClain, reportedly opened fire on a fraternity party held by Omega Delta, killing Kevin Moore, a 22-year-old student from Jamaica, and wounding another persons. McClain, who was allegedly angry at not being invited to the party, was charged with murder and held on a $750,000 bond. It was claimed that McClain had not intended to shoot anyone, but merely fired at the large stone building.

**SABOTAGE: Warri, Nigeria** Several thousand villagers rushed to scavenge oil from a ruptured line, but they were soon surrounded by a searing wall of flames when the oil caught fire. More than 500 were killed in what some said was an act of sabotage and intentional murder.

*October 23*

**MURDER: Amherst, N.Y.** Wealthy abortion doctor Barnett Slepian was shot and killed by a sniper firing a fatal bullet into him through a kitchen window. Slepian had been the target of anti-abortion demonstrators for years. He was the third physician performing abortions who had been killed in the U.S. since 1993.

*October 26*

**MURDER: Santa Ana, Calif.** Serial killer Charles Ng (pronounced Ing), was put on trial for slaying at least 12 persons in the 1980s in Calaveras County, luring people to a remote cabin so that he and Leonard Lake, since dead, could torture and murder them. Ng, who had fled to Canada and had fought extradition to the U.S., would be convicted and sentenced to death in 1999.

*October 31*

**MASS MURDER: Memphis, Tenn.-Atlanta, Ga.** Harry Lee Johnson, a 31-year-old resident of Stone Mountain, Ga., was arrested while speeding through a construction zone near Memphis, Tenn., and inside his car police reportedly found credit cards taken from three men who were shot execution style on the 24th floor of the Atlanta Hilton & Towers in mid-October, along with credit cards from a woman robbed at a Cobb County hotel. A 45-caliber handgun was also found in Johnson's car that police said was used to kill the three men and another man killed three days earlier at a suburban Atlanta hotel.

*November 4*

**MURDER: Chicago, Ill.** Richard Fikejs, 31, was sentenced to life in prison without parole for fatally stabbing three dockworkers in October 1996. Co-defendant Kevin Aalders, 37, had earlier been sentenced to life imprisonment. Fikejs and Aalders had beaten and stabbed to death Donald Mikesh, 27, Kevin Carroll, 39, and Keith Chavez, 40. Each victim had been stabbed more than 30 times and all had their throats cut.

**MURDER: Los Angeles, Calif.** Ralonzo Phelectron Cochran, the 43-year-old brother of criminal defense lawyer Johnnie Cochran, Jr., was found shot to death on a sidewalk near his home. Police could find no suspects.

*November 5*

**MURDER: Ft. Wayne, Ind.** Courtney Dixie, 31, was found guilty in a bench trial of killing 34-year-old Vicky Gallespie by Judge Fran Gull, despite the fact that Dixie said he had acted in self-defense, saying that the victim grabbed a 10-inch butcher knife and tried to stab him. He admitted that the took the knife away from her and stabbed her ten times while she was breast-feeding her baby.

*November 6*

**BOMBING: Jerusalem, Israel** A car bomb exploded, killing two terrorist bombers and wounding 25 others in a busy marketplace. Hamas, the Palestinian terrorist group, claimed responsibility for the blast.

*November 8*

**RIOTS: Baku, Azerbaijan** More than 15,000 persons at a political rally rioted after gangs of thugs attacked demonstrators, injuring dozens, including Abulfaz Elchibey, Azerbaijan's first president after the breakup of the Soviet Union.

*November 13*

**NEGLECT OF A DISABLED ADULT: Clearwater, Fla.** Prosecutors charged the Church of Scientology with abuse or neglect of a disabled adult in the December 5, 1995 death of 36-year-old Lisa McPherson, after being in the 24-hour care of church members. McPherson reportedly went without fluids for possibly as long as 17 days before dying. The Church of Scientology pleaded not guilty on November 30, 1998.

*November 14*

**MURDER: Baltimore County, Md.** Michael Howard, 19, shot and killed a bicyclist for reportedly throwing eggs on is father's car.

**MURDER: Oceanside Harbor, Calif.** Wilson Brandon, by his own later admission, stabbed to death 9-year-old Matthew Louis Cecchi in a campground restroom.

**RIOTS: Jakarta, Indonesia** More than 20,000 demonstrators rioted, setting buildings on fire, looted shops and attacked police in their pro-democracy campaign.

*November 17*

**EXECUTION: Huntsville, Texas** Serial killer Kenneth Allen McDuff was executed by lethal injection.

**ROBBERY: Fanwood, N.J.** Michael Howard, who had shot and killed a bicyclist three days earlier in Baltimore County, Md., robbed the First Savings Bank.

*November 18*

**DRUGS: Evanston, Ill.** After a four-month investigation, Cook County Sheriff's deputies seized a huge amount of crack cocaine valued at $500,000 and arrested three men, charging them with distributing drugs.

*November 20*

**EXTORTION: Chicago, Ill.** Angela L. Jackson, a one-time law school student, was convicted of attempting to extort money from United Parcel Service by writing racial slurs on several packages she had delivered to her own home. She was also convicted of sending under the UPS logo racist hate mail to several prominent black politicians in order to support her own allegations against UPS. Jackson had earlier been convicted by a federal jury of nine counts of mail and wire fraud and one count of obstruction of justice.

**ESPIONAGE: Larnaca, Cyprus** Udi Hargov, 27, and Igal Damary, 47, were charged with spying for Israel, after being arrested in the coastal village of Ziya a month earlier. Officials reportedly found sophisticated wireless equipment for espionage use.

**SHOOTING: Plainfield, N.J.** Michael Howard, who had earlier killed a bicyclist and robbed a bank, shot and wounded a man with whom he had been arguing over a period of six months.

*November 21*

**MURDER: Tehran, Iran** Opposition leader Dariushi Foruhar and his wife were found stabbed to death in their home. Foruhar was the leader of the People's Party of Iran, a small opposition group tolerated by the Islamic fundamentalist government.

*November 22*

**RIOTS: Jakarta, Indonesia** Thousands of Muslim demonstrators rioted once again, burning four churches, ransacking seven others, and attacking Christians. Six persons were killed and one was mutilated and paraded through the streets by his slayers. More than 90 percent of Indonesia's population is Muslim. The current riots, stemming from Indonesia's worst economic crisis in 30 years, was agitated, demonstrators claimed, by Christians who had thrown rocks at a mosque. This tale was fabricated by demonstrators to excuse their oppression of Christians, claimed Christian victims.

**THEFT: New York, N.Y.** Jeffrey Forster, an attorney from San Jose, California, placed three bags on the sidewalk while hailing a cab. When he turned around, he discovered his briefcase had been stolen. The briefcase reportedly contained a rare 1869 stamp collection valued at $1 million.

*November 24*

**SHOOTING: Plainfield, N.J.** Michael Howard, who had killed one man, wounded another and robbed a bank, pulled his red minivan alongside a police car and shot and wounded officer Anthony Hoofatt in the right arm. When backup policeman Steven Francisco arrived, Howard shot and wounded him in the hip and leg before speeding off.

*November 25*

**MURDER/ROBBERY: Elizabeth, N.J.** Michael Howard, wanted for killing one man, wounding three others, including two police officers, and robbing a bank in a 10-day crime spree, was shot and killed by police officers in a wild gunfight where Howard, firing two handguns, went down with several bullets in him. He died a short time later at a hospital in Newark, N.J.

*November 26*

**LEWD AND LASCIVIOUS CONDUCT WITH MINORS: Pleasanton, Calif.** Steven Schmitt, a 29-year-old male stripper, was arrested and charged with lewd and lascivious conduct with minors after he reportedly fondled four underage girls at a party given by one of the girls' mother, who was also charged with exhibiting lewd materials to minors. The mother had distributed leaflets for the "Girls Night Out" party at Amador Valley High School, charging $3 to $5 for admission to her home.

**SEXUAL ASSAULT: Harare, Zimbabwe** Rev. Canaan Banana, Zimbabwe's former president, was convicted of 11 counts of sodomy, attempted sodomy and indecent assault on young male bodyguards, gardeners and cooks assigned to him when he was president from 1980 to 1987. Banana fled Zimbabwe just prior to his conviction and hid out in Botswana and South Africa before he turned himself into authorities who ordered him confined to his mansion.

*November 27*

**MURDER: Seattle, Wash.** Bus driver Mark McLaughlin, 44, was shot several times by a passenger, reportedly Steven Gary Coole, causing the bus, carrying 35 people, to crash 50 feet off a bridge. Dead were McLaughlin, Coole and 69-year-old passenger Herman Liebelt. All remaining 32 persons were injured, 17 of them hospitalized.

*November 28*

**ACQUITTAL FOR MASS MURDER: Rio de Janeiro, Brazil** In what was regarded by many as a shameful verdict, a judge announced the acquittal of 10 police officers who had been charged in the slayings of 21 people in the poverty-stricken Vigario Geral of Rio on August 19, 1993. On that date, the 10 police officers, joined by many other policemen, all wearing hoods so as not to be recognized, entered Vigario Geral to avenge the earlier ambush murders of four policemen by drug dealers. They sprayed gunfire into the home of an evangelical Christian family, killing eight of 10 adults, then threw a grenade into a bar, and shot seven patrons. In all 21 persons died in the mass murder, including two children. Upon hearing the verdict, the policemen fell to their knees and then rose cheering to lift their black-robed lawyer to their shoulders.

*December 3*

**PERJURY/GAMBLING: Chicago, Ill.** Four former Northwestern University football players, Dennis Lundy, 26, Christopher Gamble, 26, Michael Senters, 26 and Gregory Gill, 27, were charged with perjury for denying under oath that they bet against their own team with campus bookie Brian Ballarini.

*December 5*

**EXECUTION: Guangzhou, China** Cheung "Big Spender" Tze-keung, head of a Hong Kong kidnapping and smuggling ring, was executed by a gunshot to the back of the head.

*December 8*

**MURDER/KIDNAPPING: Dovydenko, Russia** The severed heads of four men, three British engineers and an engineer from New Zealand who had been installing a mobile phone system, were discovered in a sack on a deserted highway. The men, Darren Hickey, Rudolf Petschi, Peter Kennedy and Stanley Shaw, had been kidnapped on October 3, 1998 by Chechen gunmen. Officials later suggested that the four men were spies for Great Britain.

*December 9*

**CRIMINAL SOLICITATION: New York, N.Y.** Abe Hirschfeld, the parking lot tycoon who had offered Paula Jones $1 million to settle her sexual harassment lawsuit against President Bill Clinton (who gave Jones $850,000 to settle in November 1998), was arrested and charged with criminal solicitation. Prosecutors said that the 79-year-old Hirschfeld had given an intermediary $75,000 last year as a down payment for a hit man to kill Stanley Stahl, his real estate investment partner of 40 years. Hirschfeld denied the charges, pleading not guilty.

*December 10*

**EXECUTION DELAYED: Huntsville, Texas** The U.S. Supreme Court delayed the execution of Joseph Stanley Faulder, 61, who was scheduled to go into the death chamber for the 1975 murder of Inez Phillips, the 75-year-old matriarch of a Texas oil family. The Court held up the death sentence to consider the claim that Faulder, a Canadian, had not been told of his right under international law to contact the Canadian consulate where he had been arrested. Madeleine Albright, U.S. Secretary of State, had also pleaded for the stay of execution.

**MURDER: Clarkston, Mich.** Michael Barnhart was charged with beating four persons to death with a hammer.

**MURDER: Detroit, Mich.** Professor Andrzej Olbrot, 52, was reportedly shot and killed in his Wayne State University classroom by a 48-year-old resident of Hamtramck, Mich.

**SMUGGLING: Washington, D.C.** U.S. Attorney Janet Reno said that a widespread smuggling operation that brought in thousands of illegal Chinese to the U.S. had been smashed and that 35 members of the smuggling ring, including Indian accomplices that aided them in bringing the aliens through a remote Indian reservation from Canada, had been arrested.

*December 14*

**GENOCIDE: Tanzania** Omar Serushago, a former militia leader, wept as he pleaded guilty to genocide, murder and extermination and torture of Rwandan Tutsis.

*December 15*

**TAX EVASION: Chicago, Ill.** Henry D. Paschen, Jr., one of the city's leading building contractors, was indicted for tax evasion.

*December 16*

**FRAUD: Newark, N.J.** John A. Field III, the former U.S. Attorney in Charleston, W. Va. (1972-1977), pleaded guilty to telemarketing schemes that reportedly cheated investors out of an estimated $200 million. Field had previously pled guilty to racketeering and money laundering charges in New Hampshire.

*December 17*

**MURDER: Chicago, Ill.** José E. Vielma, 26, who had been feuding with his mother for years, was charged with killing her on November 12, 1998 in the Chicago apartment they shared. Police stated that Vielma struck 50-year-old Maria C. Navaten times on the head with a hammer, then strangled her and finally stabbed her in the chest. He then reportedly wrapped her body in a blanket and placed it in a West Side storage locker. When informed that the locker was about to be sealed because he had failed to pay locker fees, Vielma removed the body which police later recovered when they stopped Vielma for speeding in his mother's black 1988 Chevrolet Cavalier.

*December 19*

**IMPEACHMENT OF THE PRESIDENT: Washington, D.C.** In an historic vote, the U.S. House of Representatives impeached President William Jefferson Clinton on two counts of perjury and one count of obstruction of justice. On February 12, 1999, on a party line basis, the U.S. Senate voted to acquit Clinton of all charges, with enough Republicans joining with all Democratic Senators voting against conviction. The President, his administration forever stained by his immoral conduct in the Lewinsky affair, had narrowly survived political extermination and held onto the power of the White House by a thin political margin. Clinton's integrity and credibility was no longer viable and he was reportedly held in widespread contempt by Congress, including members of his own party.

*December 20*

**BOMBING SUSPECT: Munich, Germany** Mamdough Mahmud Salim, who was suspected as playing a central part in the bombings of U.S. embassies in Kenya and Tanzania in August 1998, was handed over to U.S. officials for extradition to the U.S. to stand trial on the bombing charges.

*December 23*

**KIDNAPPING/TORTURE: Jakarta, Indonesia** Military officials announced that court martial proceedings would ensue against 11 members of its elite Kopassus unit which reportedly kidnapped and tortured hundreds of anti-Suharto activists when dictator Suharto was in power. Lt. Gen. Prabowo Subianto, Suharto's son-in-law, who had headed the unit, was sacked from the army in August 1998 when an inquiry found that troops under his command were responsible.

*December 25*

**DRUGS: Off the coast of Netherlands/Buenaventura, Colombia** Dutch and British customs ships intercepted a vessel off the Netherlands coast and, boarding it, seizing 19 tons of marijuana, while Colombian police seized 17.9 tons of marijuana packed into shipping containers in the Colombian port of Buenaventura.

**TERRORISM: Gaza City, Gaza Strip** Released briefly from confinement by the Palestinian Authority, Hamas founder and leader Sheik Ahmed Yassin addressed a crowd of 10,000 Palestinians, urging them to continue their terrorist campaign against Israel and the West.

*December 27-28*

**PRISON ESCAPE: Nashville, Tenn.** Six inmates broke out of a maximum-security prison, but all were recaptured. The last to be apprehended was 24-year-old Aaron Tyrone James, who had been serving a 50-year sentence for murder, kidnapping and robbery. James reportedly met with some of his old drinking buddies after escaping. The drinking buddies, however, turned him in to police in order to obtain a $5,000 reward for his capture.

*December 27*

**HORSE SLAUGHTER: Devil's Flat, Nev.** Thirty-one wild horses were found shot to death at close range, the worst slaughter of free-roaming horses in a decade. The horses included dead colts and pregnant mares. A reward of more than $10,000 for the killers was posted.

*December 28*

**KIDNAPPING: Mawdiyah, Yemen** Tribesmen opened fire on a tourist caravan and kidnapped 16 tourists, including two Americans. They were driven to an unknown destination where they were reportedly held captive pending ransom payments.

**RIOTS: Medan (Sumatra), Indonesia** Police fired on hundreds of rioting farmers who had occupied a state plantation, demanding better wages and living conditions. Dozens of farmers were injured.

*December 29*

**FELONY HIT-AND-RUN: San Jose, Calif.** Scott Davis, 34, was arrested on a felony hit-and-run charge and causing the deaths of four teenagers after he drove his car at nearly 100 m.p.h. on foggy Highway 101 that brought about five car wrecks.

# EXECUTIONS IN THE U.S., JANUARY 1989-JUNE 1998

| NAME | DATE EXECUTED | STATE | RACE:DEF/VIC | GEN/VIC |
|------|---------------|-------|--------------|---------|
| Adams, Aubrey | 05-04-89 | FL | W/W | F |
| Adams, Sylvester | 08-18-95 | SC | B/B | M |
| Adanandus, Dwight D. | 10-01-97 | TX | B/W | M |
| Albanese, Charles | 09-20-95 | IL | W/W | F |
| Allridge, Ronald K. | 06-08-95 | TX | B/W | F |
| Amos, Bernard | 12-06-95 | TX | B/W | M |
| Anderson, Johnny Ray | 05-17-90 | TX | W/W | M |
| Anderson, Larry N. | 04-26-94 | TX | W/W | F |
| Andrews, William (+ 3)3. | 07-30-92 | UT | B/3W | 2F1M |
| Arnold, John | 03-06-98 | SC | W/B | F |
| Atkins, Phillip | 12-04-95 | FL | W/L | M |
| Aua Lauti | 11-04-97 | TX | A/A | F |
| Baal, Thomas | 06-30-90 | NV | W/W | F |
| Bailey, Billy | 01-25-96 | DE | W/W | M |
| Baldree, Ernest | 04-29-97 | TX | W/W | F |
| Banda, Esequel (*) | 12-11-95 | TX | L/W | M |
| Bannister, Alan J. "AJ" | 10-22-97 | MO | W/W | M |
| Barfield, John | 03-12-97 | TX | B/W | F |
| Barnard, Harold | 02-02-94 | TX | W/A | M |
| Barnes, Herman | 11-13-95 | VA | B/W | M |
| Battle, Thomas | 08-07-96 | MO | B/B | F |
| Beaver, Gregory | 10-03-96 | VA | W/W | M |
| Beaver, Thomas | 12-11-97 | VA | W/B | F |
| Beavers, Richard Lee (*) | 04-04-94 | TX | W/W | M |
| Behringer, Earl (2) | 06-11-97 | TX | W/2W | FM |
| Bell, Larry Gene | 10-04-96 | SC | W/W | F |
| Belyeu, Clifton | 05-16-97 | TX | W/W | F |
| Bennett, Ronald | 11-21-96 | VA | B/W | F |
| Bertolotti, Anthony | 07-27-90 | FL | B/W | F |
| Bird, Jerry Joe | 06-18-91 | TX | W/W | M |
| Black, Robert (+) | 05-22-92 | TX | W/W | F |
| Blair, Walter | 07-21-93 | MO | B/W | F |
| Boggess, Clifford Holt | 06-11-98 | TX | W/W | M |
| Boggs, Ricky | 07-19-90 | VA | W/W | F |
| Bolender, Bernard (4) | 07-18-95 | FL | W/3L1W | 4M |
| Bolton, Darren (*) | 06-19-96 | AZ | W/W | F |
| Bonham, Antonio | 09-28-93 | TX | B/W | F |
| Bonin, William (4) | 02-23-96 | CA | W/4W | 4M |
| Boulder, Martsay | 01-27-93 | MO | B/B | M |
| Boyle, Benjamin | 04-21-97 | TX | W/W | F |
| Breard, Angel Francisco | 04-14-98 | VA | L/W | F |
| Brecheen, Robert | 08-11-95 | OK | W/W | F |
| Brewer, Benjamin | 04-26-96 | OK | W/W | F |
| Brewer, John (*) | 03-03-93 | AZ | W/W | F |
| Briddle, James M. | 12-12-95 | TX | W/W | M |
| Bridge, Warren E. | 11-22-94 | TX | W/W | M |
| Brimage, Richard, Jr. | 02-10-97 | TX | W/W | F |
| Brown, John | 04-24-97 | LA | W/W | M |
| Buchanan, Douglas, Jr.(4) | 03-18-98 | VA | W/4W | F3M |
| Buenoano, Judy (fem.) | 03-30-98 | FL | W/W | M |
| Bunch, Timothy | 12-10-92 | VA | W/A | F |
| Bundy, Theodore "Ted" | 01-24-89 | FL | W/W | F |
| Burger, Christopher (J)5. | 12-07-93 | GA | W/W | M |
| Burris, Gary | 11-20-97 | IN | B/B | M |
| Bush, John Earl | 10-21-96 | FL | B/W | M |

| NAME | DATE EXECUTED | STATE | RACE:DEF/VIC | GEN/VIC |
|------|---------------|-------|--------------|---------|
| Butler, M. Jerome (*) | 04-21-90 | TX | B/B | M |
| Buxton, Lawrence L. | 02-26-91 | TX | B/W | M |
| Byrd, Maurice (4) | 08-23-91 | MO | B/4W | 3F1M |
| Callins, Bruce | 05-21-97 | TX | B/W | M |
| Campbell, Charles (3) | 05-27-94 | WA | W/3W | 3F |
| Cannon, Joseph (J) | 04-22-98 | TX | W/W | F |
| Cantu, Ruben (J) | 08-24-93 | TX | L/L | M |
| Cargill, David Loomis (2) | 06-09-98 | GA | W/2W | FM |
| Carpenter, Scott (*) | 05-07-97 | OK | N/W | M |
| Carter, Robert A. (J) | 05-18-98 | TX | B/L | F |
| Ceja, Jose Jesus (2) | 01-21-98 | AZ | L/WL | FM |
| Chabrol, Andrew (*) | 06-17-93 | VA | W/W | F |
| Clark, David (2) | 02-28-92 | TX | W/2W | FM |
| Clark, Herman R. | 12-06-94 | TX | B/W | M |
| Clark, James (* 2) | 04-19-96 | DE | W/2W | FM |
| Clark, James D. (4) | 04-14-93 | AZ | W/4W | 1F3M |
| Clark, Raymond R. | 11-19-90 | FL | W/W | M |
| Clines, Hoyt 6. | 08-03-94 | AR | W/W | M |
| Clisby, Willie | 04-28-95 | AL | B/B | M |
| Clozza, Albert | 07-24-91 | VA | W/W | F |
| Cockrum, John W. | 09-30-97 | TX | W/W | F |
| Coleman, Charles T. | 09-10-90 | OK | W/W | M |
| Coleman, Roger K. | 05-22-92 | VA | W/W | F |
| Cook, Anthony (*) | 11-10-93 | TX | W/W | M |
| Cordova, Joe Angel | 01-22-92 | TX | L/W | M |
| Correll, Walter | 01-04-96 | VA | W/W | M |
| Crank, Denton | 06-14-94 | TX | W/W | M |
| Cuevas, Ignacio (+ 2) | 05-23-91 | TX | L/2W | FM |
| Davidson, Mickey (* 3) | 10-19-95 | VA | W/3W | 3F |
| Davis, Gary Lee | 10-13-97 | CO | W/W | F |
| Davis, Girvies | 05-17-95 | IL | B/W | M |
| Davis, James Carl Lee | 09-09-97 | TX | B/B | F |
| Deluna, Carlos | 12-07-89 | TX | L/L | M |
| del Vecchio, George | 11-22-95 | IL | W/W | M |
| Demouchette, James (2) | 09-22-92 | TX | B/2W | 2M |
| Deputy, Andre (2) | 06-23-94 | DE | B/2B | FM |
| Derrick, Mikel | 07-18-90 | TX | W/W | M |
| DeShields, Kenneth | 08-31-93 | DE | B/W | F |
| Devier, Darrell | 05-17-95 | GA | W/W | F |
| Dodd, Westley A. (* 3) | 01-05-93 | WA | W/3W | 3M |
| Drew, Robert N., Sr. | 08-02-94 | TX | W/W | M |
| Drinkard, Richard (3) | 05-19-97 | TX | W/3W | 2FM |
| Duff-Smith, Markham (+) | 06-29-93 | TX | W/W | F |
| Dunkins, Horace F. | 07-14-89 | AL | B/W | F |
| Durocher, Michael (* 3) | 08-25-93 | FL | W/3W | 2F1M |
| Eaton, Dennis Wayne | 06-18-98 | VA | W/W | M |
| Eddmonds, Durlyn | 11-19-97 | IL | B/B | M |
| Edmonds, Dana Ray | 01-24-95 | VA | B/W | M |
| Edwards, Leo | 06-21-89 | MS | B/B | M |
| Elkins, Michael (*) | 06-12-97 | SC | W/W | F |
| Ellis, Edward | 03-03-92 | TX | W/W | F |
| Evans, Wilbert L. | 10-17-90 | VA | B/B | M |
| Fairchild, Barry Lee | 08-31-95 | AR | B/W | F |
| Fearance, John, Jr. | 06-20-95 | TX | B/W | M |
| Felker, Ellis Wayne | 11-15-96 | GA | W/W | F |
| Feltrop, Ralph C. | 08-06-97 | MO | W/W | F |
| Fitzgerald, Edward | 07-23-92 | VA | W/W | F |

| NAME | DATE EXECUTED | STATE | RACE:DEF/VIC | GEN/VIC |
|---|---|---|---|---|
| Flamer, William (2) | 01-30-96 | DE | B/2B | FM |
| Flannagan, Sean P. (*) | 06-23-89 | NV | W/W | M |
| Foster, Emmett | 05-03-95 | MO | B/B | M |
| Francis, Bobby M. | 06-25-91 | FL | B/B | M |
| Free, James | 03-22-95 | IL | W/W | F |
| Fuller, Aaron Lee | 11-06-97 | TX | W/W | M |
| Gacy, John Wayne (12) | 05-10-94 | IL | W/12W | 12M |
| Gardner, Billy | 02-16-95 | TX | W/W | F |
| Gardner, John (2) | 10-23-92 | NC | W/2W | FM |
| Garrett, Johnny (J) | 02-11-92 | TX | W/W | F |
| Gaskins, Donald | 09-06-91 | SC | W/B | M |
| Gentry, Kenneth | 04-26-97 | TX | W/W | M |
| George, Michael Carl | 02-06-97 | VA | W/W | M |
| Gilmore, George C. (2)1. | 08-31-90 | MO | W/2W | FM |
| Gonzales, Joe (*) | 09-18-96 | TX | L/L | M |
| Gosch, Lesley Lee | 04-24-98 | TX | W/W | F |
| Granviel, Kenneth | 02-27-96 | TX | B/B | F |
| Grasso, Thomas (*) | 03-20-95 | OK | W/B | F |
| Gray, Coleman Wayne | 02-26-97 | VA | B/W | M |
| Green, G. W. (+)2. | 11-12-91 | TX | W/W | M |
| Green, Ricky Lee | 10-02-97 | TX | W/W | M |
| Greenawalt, Randy (4) | 01-23-97 | AZ | W/4W | 2F2M |
| Gretzler, Douglas E. | 06-03-98 | AZ | W/2W | FM |
| Griffin, Jeffery L. | 11-19-92 | TX | B/B | M |
| Griffin, Larry | 06-21-95 | MO | B/B | M |
| Griffin-El, Milton | 03-25-98 | MO | B/B | M |
| Grubbs, Ricky Lee | 10-21-92 | MO | W/W | M |
| Guinan, Frank | 10-06-93 | MO | W/W | M |
| Gutierrez, Jesse | 09-16-94 | TX | L/W | F |
| Hai Hai Vuong (2) | 12-07-95 | TX | A/2A | 2M |
| Hamblen, James W. | 09-21-90 | FL | W/W | F |
| Hammond, Karl | 06-21-95 | TX | B/W | M |
| Hampton, Lloyd Wayne (*) | 01-21-98 | IL | W/W | M |
| Hance, William H. | 03-31-94 | GA | B/B | F |
| Harding, Donald E. (2) | 04-06-92 | AZ | W/2W | 2M |
| Harich, Roy A. | 04-24-91 | FL | W/W | F |
| Harris, Curtis Paul (J)4. | 07-01-93 | TX | B/W | M |
| Harris, Danny (J)4. | 07-30-93 | TX | B/W | M |
| Harris, Kenneth | 06-03-97 | TX | B/W | F |
| Harris, Robert Alton (2) | 04-21-92 | CA | W/2W | 2M |
| Hatch, Steven (2) | 08-09-96 | OK | W/2W | FM |
| Hawkins, Samuel | 02-21-95 | TX | B/W | F |
| Hays, Henry | 06-06-97 | AL | W/B | M |
| Heath, Larry (+) | 03-20-92 | AL | W/W | F |
| Henderson, Robert D. (3) | 04-21-93 | FL | W/3W | 1F2M |
| Herman, David | 04-02-97 | TX | W/W | F |
| Herrera, Leonel | 05-12-93 | TX | L/L | M |
| Hill, Steven D. (+) | 05-07-92 | AR | W/W | M |
| Hill, Walter (3) | 05-02-97 | AL | B/3B | 1F2B |
| Hogue, Jerry Lee | 03-11-98 | TX | W/W | F |
| Hoke, Ronald | 12-16-96 | VA | W/W | F |
| Holland, David | 08-12-93 | TX | W/W | F |
| Holmes, James 6. | 08-03-94 | AR | W/W | M |
| Hopkinson, Mark (+) | 01-22-92 | WY | W/W | M |
| Horsley, Edward, Jr. | 02-16-96 | AL | B/W | F |
| Hunt, Flint Gregory | 07-02-97 | MD | B/W | M |
| Ingle, Phillip (* 4) | 09-22-95 | NC | W/4W | 2F2M |

| NAME | DATE EXECUTED | STATE | RACE:DEF/VIC | GEN/VIC |
|------|---------------|-------|--------------|---------|
| Ingram, Nicholas | 04-07-95 | GA | W/W | M |
| Jacobs, Jesse D. (+) | 01-04-95 | TX | W/W | F |
| James, Antonio (+) | 03-01-96 | LA | B/B | M |
| James, Johnny | 09-03-93 | TX | W/W | F |
| Jeffers, Jimmie | 09-13-95 | AZ | W/W | F |
| Jenkins, Leo (*) | 02-09-96 | TX | W/W | F |
| Jernigan, Joseph P. | 08/05-93 | TX | W/W | M |
| Johnson, Carl, Jr. | 09-19-95 | TX | B/B | M |
| Johnson, Curtis L. | 08-11-92 | TX | B/W | M |
| Johnson, Dorsie | 06-04-97 | TX | B/W | M |
| Johnson, Eddie (3) | 06-17-97 | TX | B/3W | 2FM |
| Johnson, Larry Joe | 05-05-93 | FL | W/W | M |
| Jones, Andrew Lee | 07-22-91 | LA | B/B | F |
| Jones, Leo Alexander | 03-24-98 | FL | B/W | M |
| Jones, Willie L. (2) | 09-11-92 | VA | B/2B | FM |
| Joubert, John (2) | 07-17-96 | NE | W/2W | 2M |
| Julius, Arthur | 11-17-89 | AL | B/B | F |
| Justus, Buddy Earl | 12-13-90 | VA | W/W | F |
| Kelly, Carl | 08-20-93 | TX | B/W | M |
| Kennedy, Edward D. (2) | 07-21-92 | FL | B/2W | 2M |
| King, Leon Rutherford | 03-22-89 | TX | B/W | M |
| Kinnamon, Raymond | 12-12-94 | TX | W/W | M |
| Kornahrens, Fred (3) | 07-19-96 | SC | W/3W | 1F2M |
| Lackey, Clarence | 05-20-97 | TX | W/W | F |
| Lane, Harold J. | 10-04-95 | TX | W/W | F |
| Langford, Terry Allen (2) | 02-24-98 | MT | W/2W | 2M |
| Larette, Anthony | 11-29-95 | MO | W/W | F |
| Lashley, Frederick (J) | 07-28-93 | MO | B/B | F |
| Laws, Leonard (* 2)1. | 05-17-90 | MO | W/2W | FM |
| Lawson, David | 06-15-94 | NC | W/W | M |
| Lincecum, Kavin G. | 12-10-92 | TX | B/W | F |
| Lindsey, Michael | 05-26-89 | AL | B/W | F |
| Livingston, Charlie | 11-21-97 | TX | B/W | F |
| Lockhart, Michael L. | 12-09-97 | TX | W/W | M |
| Lonchar, Larry (3) | 11-14-96 | GA | W/3W | 1F2M |
| Long, Michael E. (* 2) | 02-20-98 | OK | W/2W | FM |
| Losada, Davis | 06-04-97 | TX | L/L | F |
| Lott, George (* 2) | 09-20-94 | TX | W/2W | 2M |
| Lucas, Doyle Cecil (* 2) | 11-15-96 | SC | W/2W | FM |
| McCleskey, Warren | 09-25-91 | GA | B/W | M |
| McCoy, Stephen | 05-24-89 | TX | W/W | F |
| McDonald, Samuel, Jr. | 09-24-97 | MO | B/B | M |
| McDougall, Michael | 10-18-91 | NC | B/W | F |
| McFarland, Frank Basil | 04-29-98 | TX | W/W | F |
| McKenzie, Duncan | 05-10-95 | MT | W/W | F |
| McQueen, Harold | 07-01-97 | KY | W/W | M |
| Mackall, Tony A. | 02-10-98 | VA | B/W | F |
| Madden, Robert | 05-28-97 | TX | W/W | M |
| Mann, Fletcher T. | 06-01-95 | TX | W/W | M |
| Marquez, Mario S. | 01-17-95 | TX | L/L | F |
| Martin, Nollie L. | 05-12-92 | FL | W/W | F |
| Mason, David (* 5) | 08/24/93 | CA | W/5W | 3F2M |
| Mata, Luis | 08-22-96 | AZ | L/W | F |
| Matthews, Earl, Jr. | 11-07-97 | SC | B/W | F |
| May, Justin Lee | 05-07-92 | TX | W/W | F |
| Mays, Noble D. | 04-06-95 | TX | W/W | M |
| Medina, Pedro | 03-25-97 | FL | L/B | F |

| NAME | DATE EXECUTED | STATE | RACE:DEF/VIC | GEN/VIC | |
|------|---------------|-------|--------------|---------|---|
| Mercer, George "Tiny" | 01-06-89 | MO | W/W | F | |
| Middleton, Frank (2) | 11-22-96 | SC | B/BW | 2F | |
| Mills, John, Jr. | 12-06-96 | FL | B/W | M | |
| Montoya, Ireneo | 06-18-97 | TX | L/W | M | |
| Montoya, Ramon | 03-25-93 | TX | L/W | M | |
| Moore, Harry C. (* 2) | 05-15-97 | OR | W/2W | FM | |
| Moran, Richard A. (2) | 03-30-96 | NV | W/2W | FM | |
| Moser, Leon (* 3) | 08-15-95 | PA | W/3W | 3F | |
| Motley, Jeffrey D. | 02-07-95 | TX | W/L | F | |
| Mu'min, Dawud Majid | 11-13-97 | VA | B/W | F | |
| Muniz, Pedro Cruz | 05-19-98 | TX | L/W | F | |
| Murphy, Mario Benjamin | 09-17-97 | VA | W/W | M | |
| Murray, Anthony R. (+ 2) | 07-26-95 | MO | B/2B | 2M | |
| Narvaiz, Leopoldo (4) | 06-26-98 | TX | L/4W | 3FM | |
| Nave, Emmett | 07-31-96 | MO | N/W | F | |
| Nethery, Stephen | 05-27-94 | TX | W/W | M | |
| O'Dell, Joseph | 07-23-97 | VA | W/W | F | |
| O'Neal, Robert | 12-06-95 | MO | W/B | M | |
| Otey, Harold Lamont | 09-02-94 | NE | B/W | F | |
| Oxford, Richard (2) | 08-21-96 | MO | W/2W | FM | |
| Parker, William Frank (2) | 08-08-96 | AR | W/2W | FM | |
| Parks, Robyn | 03-10-92 | OK | B/A | M | |
| Paster, James "Skip" | 09-20-89 | TX | W/W | M | |
| Pennell, Steven (* 2) | 03-14-92 | DE | W/2W | 2F | |
| Perry, Eugene Wallace (2) | 08-06-97 | AR | W/2W | FM | |
| Peterson, Derick | 08-22-91 | VA | B/W | M | |
| Phillips, Clifford | 12-14-93 | TX | B/W | F | |
| Pickens, Charles | 05-11-94 | AR | B/B | M | |
| Pope, Carleton Jerome | 08-19-97 | VA | B/W | F | |
| Poyner, Syvasky (5) | 03-18-93 | VA | B/4W1B | 5F | |
| Powell, Reginald (2) | 02-25-98 | MO | B/2B | 2M | |
| Prejean, Dalton (J) | 05-18-90 | LA | B/W | M | |
| Pruett, David | 12-16-93 | VA | W/W | F | |
| Pyles, Johnny | 06-15-98 | TX | W/W | M | |
| Ransom, Kenneth Ray | 10-28-97 | TX | B/L | M | |
| Rector, Ricky Ray | 01-24-92 | AR | B/W | M | |
| Red Dog, James Allen (*) | 03-03-93 | DE | N/W | M | |
| Reese, Donald Eugene (4) | 08-13-97 | MO | W/4W | 4M | |
| Remeta, Daniel | 03-31-98 | FL | N/W | M | |
| Renfro, Steven Ceon (* 3) | 02-09-98 | TX | W/3W | 2FM | |
| Resnover, Greg (+) | 12-07-94 | IN | B/W | M | |
| Richardson, Herbert | 08-18-89 | AL | B/B | F | |
| Richley, Darryl 6. | 08-03-94 | AR | W/W | M | |
| Robison, Olan (3) | 03-13-92 | OK | W/3W | | 2F1M |
| Rogers, Patrick | 06-02-97 | TX | B/W | M | |
| Romero, Jesus | 05-20-92 | TX | L/L | F | |
| Ross, Arthur Martin (*) | 04-29-98 | AZ | W/W | M | |
| Rougeau, Paul | 05-03-94 | TX | B/B | M | |
| Ruiz, Paul (2) | 01-08-97 | AR | L/2W | 2M | |
| Russell, Clifton C. | 01-31-95 | TX | W/W | M | |
| Russell, James | 09-19-91 | TX | B/W | M | |
| Sanderson, Ricky Lee (*) | 01-30-98 | NC | W/W | F | |
| Santana, Carlos (+) | 03-23-93 | TX | L/L | M | |
| Satcher, Michael C. | 12-09-97 | VA | B/W | F | |
| Sattiewhite, Vernon | 08-15-95 | TX | B/W | F | |
| Savino, Joseph | 07-17-96 | VA | W/W | M | |
| Sawyer, Robert | 03-05-93 | LA | W/W | F | |

| NAME | DATE EXECUTED | STATE | RACE:DEF/VIC | GEN/VIC |
|------|---------------|-------|--------------|---------|
| Sawyers, John | 05-18-93 | TX | W/W | F |
| Schneider, Eric (2) | 01-29-97 | MO | W/2W | 2M |
| Sharp, Michael E. | 11-19-97 | TX | W/W | F |
| Shelton, Nelson (*) | 03-17-95 | DE | W/W | M |
| Sidebottom, Robert | 11-15-95 | MO | W/W | F |
| Simmons, Ronald (* 16) | 06-25-90 | AR | W/16W | 9F7M |
| Singleton, Cornelius | 11-20-92 | AL | B/W | F |
| Six, Andrew | 08-20-97 | MO | W/W | F |
| Sloan, Jeffrey | 02-21-96 | MO | W/W | M |
| Smith, Gerald (*) | 01-18-90 | MO | W/W | F |
| Smith, James (*) | 06-26-90 | TX | B/W | M |
| Smith, Kermit, Jr. | 01-24-95 | NC | W/B | F |
| Smith, Robert A. (*) | 01-29-98 | IN | W/W | M |
| Smith, Roy | 07-17-97 | VA | W/W | M |
| Smith, Tommie | 07-18-96 | IN | B/W | M |
| Snell, Richard | 04-19-95 | AR | W/W | M |
| South, Robert (*) | 05-31-96 | SC | W/W | M |
| Spence, David | 04-03-97 | TX | W/W | F |
| Spencer, Timothy | 04-27-94 | VA | B/W | F |
| Stafford, Roger (6) | 07-01-95 | OK | W/6W | 6M |
| Stamper, Charles (3) | 01-19-93 | VA | B/3W | 1F2M |
| Stano, Gerald | 03-23-98 | FL | W/W | F |
| Stevens, Thomas Dean 5. | 06-29-93 | GA | W/W | M |
| Stewart, Darryl | 05-04-93 | TX | B/W | F |
| Stewart, Ray (3) | 09-18-96 | IL | B/2B1W | 3M |
| Stewart, Roy Lee | 04-22-94 | FL | W/W | F |
| Stewart, Walter (2) | 11-19-97 | IL | B/AW | 2M |
| Stockton, Dennis | 09-27-95 | VA | W/W | M |
| Stoker, David | 06-16-97 | TX | W/W | M |
| Stokes, Winford | 05-11-90 | MO | B/W | F |
| Stone, Benjamin (* 2) | 09-25-97 | TX | W/2W | 2F |
| Stout, Larry | 12-10-96 | VA | B/W | F |
| Sweet, Glennon | 04-22-98 | MO | W/W | F |
| Swindler, John E. | 06-18-90 | AR | W/W | M |
| Tafero, Jesse (2) | 05-04-90 | FL | W/2W | MM |
| Taylor, John Albert | 01-27-96 | UT | W/W | F |
| Thanos, John (*) | 05-16-94 | MD | W/W | M |
| Thomas, Wallace N. | 07-13-90 | AL | B/W | F |
| Thompson, Steven A. (*) | 05-08-98 | AL | W/W | F |
| Thompson, William | 06-19-89 | NV | W/W | M |
| Torrence, Michael (* 2) | 09-06-96 | SC | W/2W | 2M |
| Townes, Richard | 01-23-96 | VA | B/W | F |
| Tucker, Karla Faye (fem.) | 02-03-98 | TX | W/W | M |
| Tuggle, Lem | 12-12-96 | VA | W/W | F |
| Turner, Jessel | 09-22-97 | TX | B/B | M |
| Turner, Willie Lloyd | 05-26-95 | VA | B/W | M |
| Villafuerte, Jose | 04-22-98 | AZ | L/L | F |
| Von Denton, Earl (2) | 01-08-97 | AR | W/2W | 2M |
| Wainwright, Kirt | 01-08-97 | AR | B/W | F |
| Waldrop, Billy | 01-10-97 | AL | W/W | M |
| Walker, Charles (* 2) | 09-12-90 | IL | W/2W | FM |
| Ward, Thomas Lee | 05-16-95 | LA | B/B | M |
| Washington, Terry | 05-07-97 | TX | B/W | F |
| Watkins, Johnny | 03-03-94 | VA | B/W | F |
| Watkins, Ronald | 03-25-98 | VA | B/W | M |
| Waye, Alton | 08-30-89 | VA | B/W | F |
| Webb, Freddie, Sr. | 03-31-94 | TX | B/W | M |

| NAME | DATE EXECUTED | STATE | RACE:DEF/VIC | GEN/VIC |
|------|---------------|-------|--------------|---------|
| Weeks, Varnell | 05-12-95 | AL | B/B | M |
| Wells, Keith E. (* 2) | 01-06-94 | ID | W/2W | FM |
| West, Robert W., Jr. | 07-29-97 | TX | N/W | F |
| Westley, Anthony (+) | 05-13-97 | TX | B/W | M |
| White, Jerry | 12-05-95 | FL | B/W | M |
| White, Larry | 05-22-97 | TX | W/W | F |
| White, William W. | 04-23-92 | TX | B/W | F |
| Whitmore, Jonas | 05-11-94 | AR | W/W | F |
| Wilkerson, Richard | 08-31-93 | TX | B/W | M |
| Williams, Doyle | 04-10-96 | MO | W/W | M |
| Williams, Hernando | 03-22-95 | IL | B/W | F |
| Williams, Keith | 05-03-96 | CA | W/3L | 3M |
| Williams, Robert E. (2) | 12-02-97 | NE | B/2W | 2F |
| Williams, Walter | 10-05-94 | TX | B/W | M |
| Williams, Willie Ray | 01-31-95 | TX | B/W | M |
| Willis, Henry | 05-18-89 | GA | B/W | M |
| Wise, Joe Louis, Sr. | 09-13-93 | VA | B/W | M |
| Woods, Billy Joe | 04-14-97 | TX | W/W | M |
| Woomer, Ronald R. | 04-27-90 | SC | W/W | F |
| Woratzeck, William Lyle | 06-25-97 | AZ | W/W | F |
| Wright, Douglas (* 3) | 09-06-96 | OR | W/3W | 3M |
| Zeitvogel, Richard | 12-11-96 | MO | W/W | M |
| Zettlemoyer, Keith (*) | 05-02-95 | PA | W/W | M |

Indicates:

(*) Defendants who gave up their appeals

(J) Juvenile

(T) Defendants executed after tie votes at the U.S. Supreme Court on stays of execution.

(+) "Non-triggerman"

(2) Number of multiple victims for which defendant was convicted and executed.

A: Asian

B: Black

F: Female

L: Latino

M: Male

N: Native American (U.S. Indian)

W: White

**Notes:**

1. Leonard Laws and George C. Gilmore were convicted and executed for crimes they committed together.
2. G.W. Green was convicted and sentenced for the crime committed with Joseph Starvaggi, who was executed on 09-10-87. Starvaggi was reportedly the actual killer.
3. William Andrews was convicted and sentenced for the crime committed with Dale Pierre Selby who was executed on 08-28-87.
4. Danny Harris was convicted and sentenced for the crime committed with Curtis Paul Harris who was executed on 07-01-93.
5. Christopher Burger was convicted and sentenced for the crime committed with Thomas Dean Stevens who was executed on 06-29-93.
6. Darryl Richley was convicted and sentenced for the crime committed with Hoyt Clines and James Holmes; all three executed on the same day.

# ENTRIES BY COUNTRY/U.S. STATE INDEX

NOTE: Entries by country (main A-Z text; Vol. VII (A-Q): pages 1-428; Vol. VIII (R-Z): pages 429-575. Entries for the U.S. are shown A-Z by state.

# INDEX

Note: Proper names in **boldface** indicate main title entries; crime categories are also in **boldface**.

Peterson, Gregory 414–415
Peterson, Joyce 425
Peterson, Jr., Brian C. 731, 733
Peterson, Mikaeiner 8, 415
Peterson, Robert 237–238
Petit Palais 579
Petix, Steve 549
Petix, Vickie Linn 549
Petrie, Robert 129
Petro, Charles 599
Petrocelli, Daniel 486, 732, 735
Petrocelli, William "Butch" 12
Petrolini, James 703
Petrolini, James 187
Petrosky, Albert L. 710
Petrosky, Terry 710
Petrovich, Anna 415
Petrovich, Oliver 415
Petrovich, Svetozar 415
Petrus, Donada 599
Petschi, Rudolf 295, 768
Pettersson, Christer 402
Pettit, Samuel Andrew 415
Pfaelzer, Judge Mariana R. 373, 609, 733
Pfaff, Anthony 632
Pfannenstiel, Lisa Ann 635
Pfingsten, James 556–557, 681
PFLP 428
Pham, Hiep Duy 47
Pham Ngoc Minh Hung 591
Pharaon, Ghaith 668
Phillips, Patrick 587
Philadelphia Orchestra 59
Philippine Airlines 711, 728, 756
Phillips, Billie Marie Redmon 627
Phillips, Claire 615
Phillips, Claude 22
Phillips, Joshua Earl Patrick 415–416
Phillips, Julia 615
Phillips, Justice 237
Phillips, Karen 416
Phillips, Malcolm 33
Phillips, Maryanne 198
Phillips Petroleum 176
Phillips, Robert 615
Phillips, Ronald 480
Phimah, Amin Khalif 428
Phimmachack, Kinghamvong 709
Phineas Priesthood 35, 416
Phinney, Roland Douglas Jr. 605
Phoenix Cardinals 649
Phoenix, River 177
Piazza, Bruce A. 200
Picasso, Pablo 628, 709
Pick-up Artist 637
Pickens, Joe 590
Piedmont Cemetery 17
Pierce, Alexis 416
Pierce, Arthur 416
Pierce, Bruce 613
Pierce, Cecelia 490
Pierce, Denise 416
Pierce, Samuel 651
Pierce, Tabatha 416
Pierce, Tiffany 416
Pierre, Joseph 665
Pierre-Louis, Jean 761
Pierro, Janet 629
Pike, Lucien Elwood 416
Pikul, Diane 416–417
Pikul, Joseph 416–417

Pilon, Alan 417
Pimental, Dr. Henry 607
Pimental, Edward 254
Pincus, Judge S. Michael 18
Pineda, Luis 395
Ping Chen, William 724
Ping On 306
Pinochet, Augusto 418, 625, 766
Piper, Virginia 679
Pires, Joseph 616
Pitchford, Shadrach 691
Pitera, Thomas "Tommy Karate" 661
Pitoscia, Lora 747
Pittman, George 225, 686
Pitts, Earl Edwin 189–190, 737, 741
Pitts, Freddie 759
Pitts, Judge Donald 436
Pizarro Leongomez, Carlos 651
PKK 394, 395
Placek, Marcin 424
Planet Hollywood 418
Planned Parenthood clinic, Brookline, Mass. 462
Plant, Mack 512
Platt, Judge Thomas 366
Platt, Lois 252
Playboy 485, 642, 659
Plaza Health Laboratories 595
Plaza Hotel 215
Pleasants, Steven 641
Plumley-Walker, Peter 540
Plummer, Chauncey 596
Plummer, Ronald R. 588
Plunkett, Judge Paul 575Podde, Raphael 418
Poaching
    Bivens, James 66
Podkolzhin, Yevgeny 21
PoFolks Restaurant 477
Poindexter, John M. 263, 327, 649, 650, 655, 669
Poitier, Hartman Delano 435
Pol Pot 420, 516, 754
Polevoi, Jerry 371
Polhill, Robert 650
Police Officers Promotions 505
Polichemi, Joseph 730
Politan, Judge Nicholas H. 474
Polite Bandit, The 492
Political corruption
    Abrantes Fernández, José 3
    Belgium 56
    Brazil 80
    Chen Xitong 111
    Chicago, Illinois 112
    Chun Doo Hwan 121
    Churbanov, Yuri 121
    Colombia 131
    Craxi, Bettino 141
    Crowell, Gentry 145
    Cuba 147
    González, Roberto 3
    Iran-Contra Affair 263
    Japan 273
    Japan Stock Scandal 275
    Karbaschi, Gholamhossein 290
    Mafia 335
    Marcos, Ferdinand E. 340
    Martinez, Pascual 3
    McDermott, Jason 324
    McDonald, Kevin 324
    McDonnell, John J. 326

McFarlane, Robert 327
Mexico 359
Roh Tae Woo 121
Rostenkowski, Daniel 332
Salinas de Gortari, Raul 461
Shields, David J. 475
Wedtech Scandal 548
Yilmaz, Mesut 569
Pollard, Bernie 605
Pollard, Jonathan 269, 687, 692, 717, 723, 756
Pollard, Raymond D. 599
Polo 499
Polonia, Luis 418–419
Polreis, David 419
Polreis, Renee 419
Polson, David 419
Polyukhovich, Ivan Timofeyevich 645
Pomaro, Judge Nicholas 426, 571
Pomerantz, Sherwin 612
Pompelio, Tony 582
Pompilio, Marie 622
Ponce, Carlos Tapia 620
Ponce, René Emilio 682
Pontiac Correctional Center 182, 407, 612
Ponzi scheme 59, 131
Poole, Annette 604
Poole, Walter 601
Poole, Warren 419
Pope, Eddie 606
Pope Giulio II 525
Pope John Paul II 138, 165, 348, 393, 396, 525, 749
Pope Pius IX 525
Pope, Reginald Wayne 615
Popp, Christine 419–420
Popp, William 419
Popper, Ami 653
Popular Liberation Movement 19
Popular Revolutionary Army 360
Porter, Anthony 420
Porter, Billy Don "Pete" 322
Porter, Bobby 629
Porter, Christopher R. 633
Porter, Clifford 656
Porter, Earl 73
Porter, Gary 623
Porter, Jacqueline 225, 607
Porter, Katherine Ann 690, 691
Porter, William Maurice 627
Portlaoise Prison 267
Portofaix, Gaston 466
Porubcan, Richard 155
Posada, Deysi 613
Posada, John 613
Posadas Ocampo, Juan Jesus 685, 710
Post, Frank 578
Posten, Judge William 495
Potempa, Joseph 113
Potkin, Dr. Nathan 607
Potter, Gayle 93
Potter, Judge Robert 46, 174
Potter, Shanno 658
Potts, Donald 273
Potts, Frank 420, 709
Potts, Judge Humphrey 466
Potts, Larry 547, 713
Poughkeepsie High School 554
Pouncey, Leshea 413
Pouyandeh, Mohammad Jafa 263, 420
Pouyandeh, Nazanin 420
Povinelli, James 636

Santiago, Maria Victoria 464
Tan, Marilyn 710
**Tan, Tak Sun** 516
Tanenbaum, Robert 229
Taney, Emanuel 475
**Tang Mihong** 516
Tankleff, Arlene 592
Tankleff, Martin 592
Tankleff, Seymour 592
Tano, Nicolas C. 614
Tapia, Alphonso 579
Tapper, Alex 13
Tarango, Alberto 117
Target store (South Gate, Calif.) 17
Tarnower, Herman 679
Tarr, Glenn B. 628
Tarr, Wanda 628
Tarrant County Community College 153
Tarrant County Jail 573
**Tashjian, Ralph** 516, 636
Tate, Arthur 683
Tate-LoBianca killings 424, 486, 639
Tateoka Sejichi 276
**Tatum, Paul** 517, 730
Tau Kappa Epsilon 49
**Taufield, Arnold** 517
Taus, Richard 581
**Tax evasion**
    Bachman, Jack 42
    Bakker, Jim 44
    Dortch, Richard W. 44
    Helmsley, Leona 247
    Hoffman, Matthias 253
    Hunter, Nancy Hoover 257
    LaRouche, Lyndon H., Jr. 309
    **Licari, Joseph V.** 247–248
    Mitchelson, Marvin 372
    Profeta, Eugene 424
    Taggert, David 44
    Taggert, James 44
    Turco, Frank J. 247
**Tax fraud**
    Kim, John C. 297
    Paschen, Henry D., Jr. 405
Taylor, Ada Joann 645
Taylor, Billie 164
Taylor, Carol 630
Taylor, Charles 316
Taylor, Darrell 726
Taylor, Darryl 23
Taylor, Diane 348
Taylor, Gabriel 377
Taylor, Gary L. 71
Taylor, Harvey 420
Taylor, James 604
Taylor, Jeffrey 585
**Taylor, John Merlin** 517, 608
Taylor, Judge Wilford 490
Taylor, Judith 629
**Taylor, Kenneth** 517–518
Taylor, Kynara 348, 674
Taylor, Larry Anthony 590
Taylor, Lashawnte 619
**Taylor, Lonnie** 518
Taylor, Loren 368
Taylor, Matthew 627
Taylor, Meara Brooke 628
**Taylor, Michael Douglas** 518
Taylor, Paul 592
**Taylor, Renee** 518
Taylor, Robert 182, 623

Taylor, Rufus 541
Taylor, Shanna 630
Taylor, Susan 157, 689
Taylor, Valerie Susan 628
Tchaikovsky, Peter 199
Tchaikovsky Violin Competition 203
Tchakalian, Maureen J. 526
Teamster's Union 586
Teamsters 11
Teamsters Union 744
Teatro Massimo 336
Teeter, William 613
Teets, Shari 502
Tehran University 290
Teilh, Judge Paul R. 463
Tekle, Saba 566
Tel Aviv Strangler, 630
Telander, Judge Brian 59
Telecom, Granger 294–295
Teledyne Electronics 412
Tellez, Ronald 637
Tello, Alfredo Enrique, Jr. 474
Tembo, Christon 613
Temple of Queen Hatshepsut 747
Templeton, Pauline 219
*Ten Days That Shook the World (October)* 353
Tenebaum, Ehud 260
**Tenney, Edward L.** 518
Teresa, Winter 75–77
Teriipia, Tarita 78, 79
Tern Hill Army Barracks 265
TerreBlanche, Eugene 720
**Terrorism**, 518-519
    Abu Nidal 3–4
    Abu Talb, Mohammed 4
    Action-Directe 5
    Amtrak Derailment 23
    Awadallah, Adel 39
    Awadallah, Imad 39
    Berenson, Lori 60
    Cerpa Cartolini, Néstor 105
    de Lange, Damian 167
    Dladla, Simon 183
    Ebrahim, Ebrahim Ismail 183
    Ethiopian Airlines Flight 961 191
    Extraditables 192
    Guzmán, Abimael 231
    Hamas 234
    Hogefeld, Birgit 253
    Iran 262
    Iraq 267
    Irish Republican Army 265
    Islamic Jihad 268
    Kaczynski, Theodore 286
    Kelkal, Khaled 293
    Keshet 295
    Kikumura, Yu 296
    Kim Hyun Hui 296
    Lockerbie, Scotland 316
    Marks, Claude 342
    Maseko, Mandla 183
    Moeller, Irmgard 374
    Mokhtari, Nahrim 374
    Montana Freemen 374
    Ocalan, Abdullah 394
    Phineas Priesthood 416
    Pinochet, Augusto 418
    Qaddafi, Muammar, al- 428
    Ramirez Sanchez, Illich 310, 748
    Red Brigade, The 316
    Rezaq, Omar Mohammaed Ali 320

Salah, Mohammad 459
Sarsour, Salem Rajah al 465
Shining Path, The 476
Sikh Terrorists 477
Soldiers of Justice 494
Somali Executions 495
Sri Lanka Massacre 498
Stone, Michael 504
U.S. Embassies bombings 531
Ulla, Mahmoud 531
Ulla, Saber Abu el- 531
Wijeweera, Rohana 556
Willmott, Donna Jean 342
World Trade Center bombing 564
**Terrorism (victim)**
    Rogers, Sharon Lee 330
**Terrorist threats**
    Somerman, Andrew I. 495
Terry Helvey 686
**Terry, Narkey Keval** 519–520
Terry, Randall 588, 604
Teshman, Don 681
Testa, Joseph 601
Testa, Robert 602
Tetro, Anthony Gene 606
Texas A&M University 473
Texas Board of Pardons and Paroles 527
Texas Christian University 153
Texas Commerce Motor Bank 385, 671
Texas Instruments, Inc. 17
Texas Southmost College 135
Thakkar, Pravin D. 584
Tham, Michael Rudy 598
Thatcher, Amy Lynn 617
Thatcher, Margaret 228, 256, 265, 418, 656
Thayer County Hospital 396
**Theft**
    Baillie, Nissa 130
    Benson, Quinntella 59
    Buckley, Doreen G. 90
    Buckley, Gailene J. 90
    Burns, Brian 92
    Cole, Christopher 130
    Flowers, Stephen Douglas 202
    Heiss, Robert 59
    Irfan, Muhammed Usman 265
    Jackson, Renee 283
    Jordan, Yolanda 283
    Karbaschi, Gholamhossein 290
    Kivana, Milos 299
    Lowder, Ronald 320
    MacDonald, Matthew 325
    Miller, Thomas 130
    Mrozowski, Craig Allen 381
    National Gallery of Modern Art (Italy) 384
    Petersen, Justin Tanner 414
    Stramaglio, Ralph F., Jr. 505
    Taborsky, Petr 515
    Thomas, Robert 283
    Vitale, Francis, Jr. 536
*Thelma and Louise* 529
Theodore Kaczynski 705, 714
Thezan, Larry 27
Thigpen, David 592
Thin Blue Line 585
**Thipyaso, Chamoy** 520
Thistle, Charlotte 630
Thistle, Eleanor 630
Thistle, Elizabeth 630
Thomas, Arvella Louis 28
Thomas, Carol 607